SMITH AND THOMAS
A CASEBOOK ON
CONTRACT

THIRTEENTH EDITION

By

PROFESSOR ROGER BROWNSWORD

SWEET & MAXWELL

THOMSON REUTERS

First Edition 1957
Second Impression 1959
Second Edition 1961
Second Impression 1963
Third Edition 1966
Fourth Edition 1969
Fifth Edition 1973
Second Impression 1974
Third Impression 1976
Sixth Edition 1977
Second Impression 1980
Seventh Edition 1982
Eighth Edition 1987
Second Impression 1990
International Student Edition 1990
Third Impression 1991
Ninth Edition 1992
International Student Edition 1992
Second Impression 1994
Tenth Edition 1996
Eleventh Edition 2000
Second Impression 2001
Third Impression 2002
Fourth impression 2003 (twice)
Fifth impression 2004
Twelfth Edition 2009
Thirteenth Edition 2015

Published in 2015 by Thomson Reuters (Professional) UK Limited
trading as Sweet & Maxwell, Friars House, 160 Blackfriars Road,
London, SE1 8EZ
(Registered in England & Wales, Company No 1679046.
Registered Office and address for service: 2nd floor, 1 Mark Square,
Leonard Street, London EC2A 4EG

For further information on our products and services, visit
www.sweetandmaxwell.co.uk

ISBN 978-0-414-03532-4

Typeset by Servis Filmsetting Ltd, Stockport, Cheshire
Printed in Great Britain by Ashford Colour Press, Gosport, Hants

No natural forests were destroyed to make this product; only farmed timber was used and re-planted

A CIP catalogue for this book is available from the British Library.
Crown Copyright material is reproduced with the permission of the Controller
of HMSO and the Queen's Printer in Scotland.

SMITH AND THOMAS
A CASEBOOK ON CONTRACT

WITHDRAWN

ACKNOWLEDGEMENTS

Grateful acknowledgment is made to the following authors and publishers for their permission to quote from their works:

Atiyah, P.S.: *Consideration in Contracts* (1971). Reprinted by permission of the Australian National University Press.

Cheshire & Fifoot: *Law of Contract* (5th edn, 2006) p.46. Reprinted by permission of Oxford University Press.

Corbin, Arthur L.: "Does a Pre-existing Duty Defeat Consideration?—Recent Noteworthy Decisions" 27 Yale L.J. 362–381. Reprinted by permission of The Yale Law Journal Company, Inc., from *The Yale Law Journal*, Vol.27, pp.362.

Finnemore and James: *Benjamin on Sale* (8th edn, 1950) p.622. Reprinted by permission of Sweet & Maxwell.

Freeman, Professor Michael: "Contracting in the Haven: Balfour v Balfour Revisited" in *Exploring the Boundaries of Contract* Ed. R. Halson (1996), p.68. Reprinted by permission of Michael Freeman.

Goode, Prof. Roy: "International Restatements of Contract and English Contract Law" in *Contemporary Issues in Commercial Law* (1997) 63 at 69–71. Reprinted by permission of Sweet & Maxwell.

Hamson, C.J.: "The Reform of Consideration" (1938) 54 L.Q.R. 233, 234, 242; Pollock, Sir Frederick: 20 L.Q.R. 4; Steyn, Lord: "Contract Law: Fulfilling the Reasonable Expectations of Honest Men" (1997) 113 L.Q.R. 433 at 438–439; Wade, E.C.S.: "Mistaken Identity in the Law of Contract" 38 L.Q.R. 201, 204; Winfield: "Some Aspects of Offer and Acceptance" (1939) 55 L.Q.R. 499, 516–517; Reprinted by permission of Sweet & Maxwell.

McElroy and Williams: "The Coronation Cases" 4 M.L.R. 241, 247, 254. Reprinted by permission of Blackwell Publishing.

Merton L. Ferson: "The Formation of Simple Contracts" (1924) 9 Cornell Law Quarterly, 402 Selected Readings, 128, 137. Reprinted by permission of the Cornell Law Review

Pollock, Sir Frederick: *Principles of Contract* (13th edn, 1950) p.133. Reprinted by permission of Sweet & Maxwell.

Smith, J.C.: "The Law of Contract—Alive or Dead?" (1979) 13 The Law Teacher 73, 77. Reprinted by permission of Routledge.

Steyn, Lord: "Contract Law: Fulfilling the Reasonable Expectations of Honest Men" (1997) 113 L.Q.R. 433 at 438–439

Wade, E.C.S.: "Mistaken Identity in the Law of Contract" 38 L.Q.R. 201, 204.

Williams, Glanville: "Mistake and Rectification in Contract" 17 M.L.R. 154. Reprinted by permission of Blackwell Publishing.

Winfield: "Some Aspects of Offer and Acceptance" (1939) 55 L.Q.R. 499, 516–517

Wormser, Maurice I.: "The True Conception of Unilateral Contracts" 26 Yale L.J. 136 Selected Readings 136–142. Reprinted by permission of The Yale Law Journal Company, Inc., from *The Yale Law Journal*, Vol.26, pp.136.

While every care has been taken to establish and acknowledge copyright, and contact the copyright owners, the publishers tender their apologies for any accidental infringement. They would be pleased to come to a suitable arrangement with the rightful owners in each case.

PREFACE TO THE THIRTEENTH EDITION

In this new edition of the casebook, I have tried (as in the previous edition) to preserve the essential identity of *Smith and Thomas*—that is, as a valued resource that conveys the sense of challenge as well as the intellectual curiosity that is experienced at the cutting edges of the law of contract. However, I have also tried to give student readers a more explicit steer, highlighting the 'learning objectives' for each chapter, 'signposting' the structure of each chapter more clearly, and pulling together the cases in more obvious clusters. I have also added sections to the introductory chapter offering some guidance on how to read the cases, how to write essays and how to answer problem questions in contract law.

At the same time, although many of the cases to be included in this new edition are self selecting—notably, for example, *Rainy Sky* (on interpretation of terms), *Belize Telecom* (on implied terms), *RTS Flexible Systems* (on formation), and *Yam Seng* (on good faith)—the emphasis in my commentaries betrays my reading of the 'dual transformation' of the modern law of contract. On the one hand, the bifurcation between the consumer law of contract and the commercial law becomes ever more apparent. Indeed, as this new edition of the casebook was going to press, the Consumer Rights Act 2015, the latest example of bespoke consumer contract law, was completing its passage through Parliament. On the other hand, on the commercial wing of contract law, a new 'contextualism' (coupled with a pronounced commercial realism) promises not only to shape the interpretation and implication of terms in commercial contracts but also to insinuate itself into all doctrines that hinge on standards of reasonableness and fair dealing. If there is a unity in the modern law of contract it is now at a high level of generality, captured in the idea that it is the purpose of the law to protect, reflect, and promote the reasonable expectations of honest contractors.

While these modifications to the style and substance of the casebook should make it more accessible to student readers, it is not intended to be a textbook. In fact, the assumption is that, by the time that students engage more seriously with the cases in a particular area of the law of contract, they will already have had a textbook overview of the main doctrinal features of that area. The function of the casebook is not so much to duplicate such an introduction but to build on it by helping students to think for themselves, to understand how legal argumentation works, and to form a critical view of a body of law that has a venerable pedigree but that now strives to connect with the marketplace principles and practices of the present century.

Roger Brownsword
London, March 2015

CONTENTS

TABLE OF CASES

TABLE OF STATUTES

TABLE OF STATUTORY INSTRUMENTS

1

INTRODUCTION

LEARNING OBJECTIVES

By the end of this introductory chapter, you should understand:

- **that the law does not normally require contracts to be in writing;**
- **when and how the law of contract becomes relevant to a dispute;**
- **that there are not "right" answers in any straightforward sense to the kinds of cases that raise contested points of contract law;**
- **that the absence of a contract does not preclude the possibility of another kind of claim (e.g. in tort);**
- **that both EC law and human rights law are relevant to domestic contract law;**
- **that online transactions are subject to the law of contract;**
- **how to read cases;**
- **how to write essays and answer problem questions in contract law.**

For most readers of this casebook, there will already have been a textbook, a lecture, or a tutorial **1–001** introduction to the English law of contract. In all likelihood, readers will already be aware that the law of contract regulates transactions, typically transactions between suppliers of goods and services and their purchasers. Readers will be aware too that, on most days of the week, they are themselves parties (usually as purchasers) to transactions of this kind—that is, to transactions that are regulated by the law of contract. Yet, for the most part, the law of contract does not openly advertise its presence; to the extent that our daily transactions are regulated by the law of contract, the law is very much in the background—indeed, so much so that, for many students of the law of contract, it is not until they actually start their studies that they realise that the law has this kind of application. Why is it, then, that we can make our daily purchases without realising that the law of contract is in play and without having to consult the law books? Might it be because we assume, incorrectly as it turns out, that the law of contract is not engaged unless the terms of the transaction are in some legally prescribed documentary form with seals and signatures or, at the very least, in writing?

In this introductory chapter to the casebook, we will respond to a number of questions of this kind, questions that are frequently asked and that betray some initial confusion about the nature and the scope of the law of contract. We will also respond to a question that is a particularly appropriate one to be asked by student users of this casebook, namely: how should the cases be read? And, we close by offering some short comments in response to the questions: (i) how should contract essays be written; and (ii) how should contract problem questions be answered? The questions that structure this chapter and the order in which they will be posed and answered are as follows:

(i) Does a contract need to be in writing?

(ii) When does the law of contract become practically relevant?

(iii) Are there always "right" answers to questions of contract law?

(iv) If there is no contract, is there no case?

(v) Does EC law impact on contract law?

(vi) Does the Human Rights Act impact on contract law?

(vii) Does contract law apply to online transactions?

(viii) How should the cases be read?

(ix) How should the writing of essays and the answering of problems in contract law be approached?

Much of what follows addresses the third of these questions because it is vital, right at the outset, to understand why and how the law is contestable. Moreover, as we work through this list of questions, we can begin to grasp the distinctive window that the casebook offers on the world of consumer and commercial contracting, a view that pays close attention to the context of particular disputes, as well as observing the law in action in the context of the sharpening, settling and resolving of disputes.

1. Does a Contract Need to be in Writing?

1–002   Typically, the terms of our everyday purchasing transactions, at the supermarket or the cinema, are not reduced to writing. Goods or services are selected; payment is made; receipts are issued; but that is all. Lawyers are not called in to draft the covering agreements and yet these routine daily transactions are treated as legally binding contracts. Not only this, in principle, the law will recognise a high value, exceptional, transaction (for example, an agreement for the sale of a parcel of diamonds for a price of one million pounds) as a legally binding contract, the lack of writing notwithstanding—a shake of hands will suffice. Of course, where there is no writing to cover a transaction, this might invite disputes about what precisely was said or agreed; but, in principle, the general rule is that an agreement made by word of mouth is every bit as legally binding as the same agreement made in writing.

Having said this, there are some statutory exceptions to the general rule—notably, the statutory requirements that regulate the (written) form of consumer credit transactions and that apply to contracts for the sale or other disposition of an interest in land (such as domestic house sales).[1] Students and contractors alike also ignore at their peril the provisions of the Statute of Frauds 1677 which for several centuries required, inter alia, written evidence of contracts for the sale of goods of the value of £10 or upwards. Although this particular requirement was repealed in 1954, it has almost certainly cast a shadow over the lay perception of the need for contract formalities; and, although students can largely focus on correcting their untutored assumption that contracts need to be in writing, they should bear the statute in mind when reading some of the older cases, such as *Warlow v Harrison* (below, Ch.2) and *Felthouse v Bindley* (below, Ch.3). While most of the statute is long gone, one requirement survives: this, in the antique language of s.4 of the Act, is in relation to 'a special promise

---

[1]   We should be aware, too, that some provisions rooted in EU consumer contract law might require certain formalities to be observed: see, for example, arts 7 and 8 of the Directive on Consumer Rights, 2011/83/EU (OJEU L 304/64, 22.11.2011) implemented by the Consumer Contracts (Information, Cancellation and Additional Charges) Regulations 2013 (SI 2013/3134). For discussion of the increasing application of EU measures to English contract law, see below at para.1–011.

to answer for the debt, default or miscarriage of another person.' In plain terms, a contract of guarantee needs to be evidenced in writing.

A contract of guarantee applies in the following kind of three-party situation. A is, or may become, liable in contract (or tort[2]) to B. C (the guarantor, or surety) promises B (for consideration[3] supplied by B) that, if A does not discharge his liability, he, C, will do so. C, thus, guarantees the performance of A's obligation and, in practice, this is an important security to cover the risk that B is otherwise taking in relation to A. However, unless C's promise is evidenced in writing, it will not be enforceable. As if this were not a sufficient trap for the unwary, there is a fine distinction between a guarantee (which needs to be evidenced in writing) and an indemnity (which is enforceable without any written evidence), the latter being a promise by C to meet A's liability *in any event*, that is, irrespective of whether A performs.[4] On the face of it, this makes little sense; for, the risk and burden assumed by C as an indemnifier is greater than that assumed by C as a guarantor, and yet it is C's promise to act as a guarantor that attracts the need for written evidence. The seriousness of this trap is illustrated by *Actionstrength Ltd v International Glass Engineering In.Gl.EN.Spa* [2003] UKHL 17 (the material facts of which are summarised in para.5 of Lord Bingham's speech).

ACTIONSTRENGTH LIMITED v INTERNATIONAL GLASS ENGINEERING IN.GL.EN. SpA

House of Lords [2003] UKHL 17

LORD BINGHAM OF CORNHILL

5. [The assumed facts are as follows]. Actionstrength agreed with Inglen to supply labour to enable Inglen (the main contractor chosen by St-Gobain) to build a factory for St-Gobain. Inglen's deficiencies as a contractor led to Actionstrength being drawn, more closely than would be normal for a labour-only sub-contractor, into the oversight of Inglen's performance. From an early date Actionstrength had difficulty obtaining payment by Inglen and considerable arrears built up. Actionstrength was contractually entitled to terminate its contract with Inglen on 30 days' notice if duly approved invoices had not been paid within 30 days and remained unpaid. Such termination would have been seriously prejudicial to St-Gobain, whose interest was to take expeditious possession of a completed factory. Actionstrength threatened to withdraw its labour. St-Gobain induced it not to do so by promising that, if Inglen did not pay Actionstrength any sums which were or became owing, it (St-Gobain) would do so. On that undertaking Actionstrength forebore to withdraw its labour and continued to supply labour to Inglen, whose indebtedness to Actionstrength increased fivefold over the weeks that followed. St-Gobain received the benefit of the work done by the labour which Actionstrength supplied. When Actionstrength, unable to obtain payment by Inglen, sought to enforce the agreement against St-Gobain, that company relied on the absence of a written memorandum or note of the agreement to defeat Actionstrength's claim.

6. While section 4 of the Statute of Frauds has been repealed or replaced in its application to the other four

1–003

---

[2] Tort, like contract, is a branch of private law. However, whereas the focus of contract is on transactions, the focus of tort is on interactions (most importantly regulating liability for injury and damage occasioned by a failure to exercise reasonable care). See, further, para.1–010 below.

[3] Typically, in a contract for the supply of goods or services, the supplier provides "consideration" by supplying (or promising to supply) goods or services to the purchaser's order and the purchaser provides "consideration" by paying (or promising to pay) for the goods or services. Putting this more generically, we can say that, in a contractual exchange consideration is reciprocally provided, whether in the form of conferring benefits or incurring detriments. See further Ch.10.

[4] For the distinction between a contract of guarantee and a contract of indemnity, see *Halsbury's Laws of England 4th edn* (2004) Vol.20(1), para.109. Whereas, under a contract of guarantee, the guarantor "assumes a secondary liability to the creditor for the default of another who remains primarily liable to the creditor", under a contract of indemnity, "the indemnifier undertakes an independent obligation which does not depend upon the existence of any other obligation of any other obligor".

classes of contract originally specified, it has been retained in relation to guarantees. In 1937 the Law Revision Committee (in its Sixth Interim Report, *Statute of Frauds and the Doctrine of Consideration*, Cmd 5449, paragraph 16) recommended the repeal of so much as remained of section 4. But a minority headed by Goddard J. dissented in relation to guarantees, on the grounds

(1) that there was a real danger of inexperienced people being led into undertaking obligations which they did not fully understand, and that opportunities would be given to the unscrupulous to assert that credit was given on the faith of a guarantee which the alleged surety had had no intention of giving;

(2) that a guarantee was a special class of contract, being generally one-sided and disinterested as far as the surety was concerned, and the necessity of writing would give the proposed surety an opportunity for thought;

(3) that the requirement of writing would ensure that the terms of the guarantee were settled and recorded;

(4) that Parliament had imposed a requirement of writing in other contractual contexts;

(5) that judges and juries were not infallible on questions of fact, and in the vast majority of cases the surety was getting nothing out of the bargain;

(6) that it was desirable to protect the small man; and

(7) that the necessity for guarantees to be in writing was generally understood.

No action was taken on the 1937 report. In 1953 the Law Reform Committee (First Report, *Statute of Frauds and Section 4 of the Sale of Goods Act 1893*, Cmd 8809) endorsed the recommendation of its predecessor that section 4 of the Statute of Frauds should be largely repealed but, agreeing with those who had earlier dissented, unanimously recommended that the section should continue to apply to guarantees. Effect was given to this report by enactment of the 1954 Act. Whatever the strength of the reasons given by the dissenting minority for retaining the old rule in relation to conventional consumer guarantees, it will be apparent that those reasons have little bearing on cases where the facts are such as those to be assumed here. It was not a bargain struck between inexperienced people, liable to misunderstand what they were doing. St-Gobain, as surety, had a very clear incentive to keep the Actionstrength workforce on site and, on the assumed facts, had an opportunity to think again. There is assumed to be no issue about the terms of the guarantee. English contract law does not ordinarily require writing as a condition of enforceability. It is not obvious why judges are more fallible when ruling on guarantees than other forms of oral contract. These were not small men in need of paternalist protection. While the familiar form of bank guarantee is well understood, it must be at least doubtful whether those who made the assumed agreement in this case appreciated that it was in law a guarantee [i.e. they might have taken it to be an indemnity]. The judge at first instance was doubtful whether it was or not. The Court of Appeal reached the view that it was, but regarded the point as interesting and not entirely easy: [2002] 1 WLR 566, 568, [2001] EWCA Civ 1477, paragraph 2. Two members of the court discussed the question at a little length, with detailed reference to authority.

7. It may be questionable whether, in relation to contracts of guarantee, the mischief at which section 4 was originally aimed, is not now outweighed, at least in some classes of case, by the mischief to which it can give rise in a case such as the present, however unusual such cases may be. But that is not a question for the House in its judicial capacity. Sitting judicially, the House must of course give effect to the law of the land of which (in England and Wales) section 4 is part . . .

9. It is implicit in the assumed facts that Actionstrength believed itself to be the beneficiary of an effective guarantee. Its difficulty, in my view insuperable, [is that] . . . in seeking to show inducement or encouragement Actionstrength can rely on nothing beyond the oral agreement of St-Gobain which, in the absence of writing, is rendered unenforceable by section 4. There was no respresentation by St-Gobain that it would honour the agreement despite the absence of writing, or that it was not a contract of guarantee, or that it would confirm the agreement in writing. Nor did St-Gobain make any payment direct to Actionstrength which could arguably be relied on as affirming the oral agreement or inducing Actionstrength to go on supplying labour. If St-Gobain were held to be estopped [i.e., precluded from relying on the fact that this was a contract of guarantee needing to be evidenced in writing] in this case it is hard to see why any oral guarantor, where credit was extended to a debtor on the strength of a guarantee, would not be similarly estopped. The result would be to render nugatory a provision which, despite its age, Parliament has deliberately chosen to retain.

10. For these reasons, and those given by Lord Hoffmann, Lord Clyde and Lord Walker of Gestingthorpe, with which I agree, I am of the reluctant but clear opinion that the appeal must be dismissed . . .

In the light of the decision and discussion in *Actionstrength*, we might wonder (i) whether it is sound policy to require that a guarantee is evidenced in writing, (ii) whether, if it is, the same requirement should apply to a third-party indemnity, and (iii) whether the law of contract fulfils a useful function in supporting commercial transactions when its application can hinge on arcane exceptions and fine distinctions. Even if the general rule is that writing is not required, we might draw from *Actionstrength* the precautionary lesson that it is better to err on the side of formality and make sure that any transactional promises that really matter are put in writing.

2. WHEN DOES THE LAW OF CONTRACT BECOME PRACTICALLY RELEVANT?

In practice, parties (especially commercial parties) might need to check out the law of contract before **1-004** they enter into a transaction or they might turn to the law of contract where a dispute of some kind arises in connection with a transaction. Where a transaction is of a high value, or where a contractual relationship is planned to extend over a period of time, or where the parties to a transaction are located in different legal systems, a prior check on (or deliberate and explicit choice of) the applicable legal rules is no more than prudent business. However, for our introductory purposes, we can focus on the position where the turn to contract law is ex post rather than ex ante.

Characteristically, where a contractual dispute arises, the claimant (the plaintiff as it was) will contend that the defendant is in breach of contract and that some remedy (typically damages) should be made available. After all, the purpose of the law of contract is to support marketplace transactions; it is there to be engaged where one party to a transaction (the claimant) is let down by the other party (the defendant). If this were not the case, we might expect there to be difficulties in developing markets between strangers or in maintaining the confidence of those who deal in the market (whether as suppliers or as consumers).

If we extend the claimant's characteristic contention, we can see that, in the usual case, it comprises three key elements, namely: (i) that a contract exists between himself and the defendant; (ii) that the defendant is in breach of one of the terms of the contract; and (iii) that, in order to protect the claimant's legitimate marketplace expectations, a remedy should be granted.

In many cases, the defendant might simply acknowledge and accept the claim. However, where the defendant contests the claim, where the defendant denies liability, it might be as a matter of fact (for example, the defendant might respond that he has no idea who the claimant is, or that he has never dealt with him, or that (as in *Actionstrength* above para.1–003) the claimant's version of the facts associated with the transaction is incorrect, and so on) or it might be on a point of law. In principle, where the defendant contests the claim as a matter of law, the defence might rest on any one or more of the three key elements in the claimant's contention.

First, the defendant might argue that the transaction fails to qualify as an enforceable contract. The defendant's argument might be (a) that the transaction fails to meet one or more of the recognised formation requirements (including an exceptional requirement of the kind illustrated by *Actionstrength*), or (b) that the transaction is void or voidable because of a bargaining defect, such as duress, undue influence, or mistake, or (c) that the transaction is unenforceable because it is contrary to public policy or illegal.

Secondly, the defendant, conceding that the transaction qualifies as an enforceable transaction, nevertheless might deny that there has been a breach of any relevant term. The defendant might argue (a) that, on its correct interpretation, the particular express term relied on by the claimant does not bear the meaning advanced by the claimant, or (b) that no relevant term may be implied. Alternatively, the defendant might argue (a) that the claimant is precluded from alleging breach by virtue of a fair dealing principle such as waiver or equitable estoppel, or (b) that non-performance is excused by virtue of the background doctrine of frustration.

Thirdly, the defendant, conceding that the transaction qualifies as an enforceable transaction and that there has been a breach of a relevant term, might deny that the claimant is entitled to the remedy claimed. Here, the defendant might rely on express terms that purport to limit or exclude liability in the event of a breach. Or, the defendant might contest the availability of a particular remedy (such as specific performance or the right to withdraw) or the extent of exposure to damages in this light, the doctrines of mitigation, causation and remoteness can be viewed as a triple opportunity for the defendant to argue for damage limitation.

To be sure, there are other points that might be taken by the defendant. For example, the defendant might invoke the principle of privity to dispute the personal eligibility of the claimant (as a third-party to the transaction) or the law relating to capacity to assert a degree of immunity to the claim. There is also the possibility that the claimant might plead misrepresentation rather than, or as well as, a breach of contract, in which case the defendant will have a variety of openings that are offered by the common law and legislation in this particular area.

Accordingly, where a defendant contests liability as a matter of law, we can find that a number of aspects of contract law are in play (compare, for example, the catalogue of arguments raised by the defendants in *Carlill v Carbolic Smoke Ball Co* [1893] 1 Q.B. 256 (below, Ch.2)). In general, as a case moves into the appeal courts, the critical points of law become more precisely identified; there is some filtering and focusing of the issues. Nevertheless, students should realise that although the textbooks present the law in neat compartments (formation, terms, interpretation, remedies, and so on), this is simply for expository convenience. In practice, there is a unity about the law of contract that militates against discrete division of this kind.

3. ARE THERE ALWAYS "RIGHT" ANSWERS TO QUESTIONS OF CONTRACT LAW?

1–005   No matter how excellent one's tutors, no matter how excellent the books, as a novice student of the law of contract it is all too easy to find oneself deeply confused. On the one hand, the textbooks tend to offer a fairly tidy and clear account of the rules and principles of the English law of contract—offers are to be distinguished from mere invitations to treat; offers stay open until withdrawn; offerees have the option of accepting or rejecting an offer made to them; English law is slightly unusual in preferring a mailbox rather than a receipt rule for postal acceptances but this is the rule here, and so on. On the other hand, the casebooks, while confirming much of the learning to be drawn from the textbooks, seem to be looking for difficulties; things are much less clear—for example, how precisely is the distinction between offers and invitations to treat applied; does the mailbox (or postal) rule apply also to offers; what if an offeree, having posted a rejection of an offer, then telephones an acceptance to the offeror; and how do the rules of offer and acceptance apply to communications by email or to online transactions? If we stick to the textbooks, we think that we know the answers; but if we delve into the casebooks, we might start entertaining doubts.

In my own case, as an undergraduate law student, I found myself confused at a very early stage of the year, in fact, immediately after the first tutorial for which we had been instructed to read two cases—*Phillips v Brooks* (para.8–013) and *Ingram v Little* (para.8–016)—on so-called mistakes of identity. The essential scenario in both these cases is as follows: (i) a crook, C, pretending to be X, tricks an owner/seller of goods, O, into parting with the goods before payment has been cleared; (ii) the payment (a cheque in both cases) fails; (iii) C sells the goods to a purchaser, P, who has no reason to suspect that C has obtained the goods by deception; (iv) O, having realised that he has been deceived by C, is unable to trace C (and, thus, is not able to pursue the obvious claim for non-payment against

C); but (v) O, having traced the goods to P, claims that P must return the goods on the ground that O's contract with C is void for mistake of identity (in consequence of which O remains the owner of the goods). The puzzle is that, whereas in *Phillips v Brooks* the court rejects O's claim, in *Ingram v Little* the court allows it. According to the former decision, the legal position (assuming that O is not able to trace and sue C) is that O's only option is to try to avoid the contract with C (C's fraud rendering the contract voidable); but, this option is subject to the important restriction that appropriate steps of avoidance must be taken by O before C disposes of the goods to an innocent third-party purchaser, P. Yet, in the latter decision, it was held that, where O is the victim of a fraudulent deception of this kind (as a result of which O makes a fundamental mistake of identity, and not simply a mistake as to the creditworthiness of the crook's assumed identity), O is permitted to recover the goods from P even though O takes no steps to avoid the contract before C sells to P. On the face of It, the two decisions seem to be (as, indeed, they are) flatly contradictory. Doctrinally, whereas *Phillips* declines to recognise a role for mistake of identity, *Ingram* does just the opposite; and, whereas the policy of *Phillips* is to place the initial risk of C's deception on O, the policy of *Ingram* is to shield O against this risk. It was, thus, that my naïve assumption that the function of the law is to provide answers to disputes, not to introduce fresh doubts and difficulties, was seriously challenged. Despite this, I continued for a long time labouring under the fundamental misapprehension that there are always (in a very straightforward sense) unproblematic (or right) answers to legal questions.

Accordingly, one of the most important clusters of introductory lessons is to appreciate (i) that the law is not always clear and settled, (ii) that, even where the law is clear and settled, the cases might not be decided in the way that the precedents indicate, and (iii) that much of law school education (particularly much of the casebook-based education) is focused on those situations where the law is not clear or where the decision handed down by the court seems to be at odds with the settled law. We can say a bit more about the first two of these points and then we can look in some detail at *Shogun Finance v Hudson* [2003] UKHL 62, this being the latest addition to the jurisprudence of mistake of identity and a model of the sort of case that perplexes law students. Indeed, it was in this case that Lord Millett said:

> "56. A makes an offer to B. B accepts it, believing that he is dealing with C. A knows of B's mistake, and may even have deliberately caused it. What is the result of the transaction? Is there a contract at all? There is obviously no contract with C, who is not a party to the transaction and knows nothing of it. But is there a contract with A? And if so is it void or merely voidable?
>
> 57. Generations of law students have struggled with this problem. They may be forgiven for thinking that it is contrived by their tutors to test their mettle. After all, the situation seems artificial and is one which is seldom likely to arise in practice, at least in the absence of fraud."

Are law students entitled to think that cases of this kind are some kind of tutorial conspiracy? Is such confusion just one of the rites of passage for students of contract law? The answer is that there is no conspiracy here. The law is often less clear than we might think, and the sooner that we come to terms with this the sooner that we will be able to get fully engaged with legal argument.

A. The Law is Not Always Clear and Settled

Imagine a spectrum representing the extent to which the law is clear and settled. At one end of the spectrum, there are those cases in which the law is perfectly clear and settled; no one is in any doubt as to the legal position. At the other end of the spectrum, the law is not at all settled; the legal position is unclear; not only will lawyers disagree with one another, they will often characterise their

1–006

disagreement as perfectly reasonable. For example, in the important case of *Transfield Shipping Inc v Mercator Shipping Inc* [2008] UKHL 48 (see below, Ch.19), where the charterers of a vessel were in breach of contract by being some nine days late in redelivering it to the owners, the House of Lords faced a difficult choice between two plausible ways of calculating the owners' damages. According to Baroness Hale (at para.89):

> "There is no obviously right answer: two very experienced commercial judges have reached one answer, your lordships have reached another. There is no obviously just answer: the charterer's default undoubtedly caused the owner's loss, but a loss for which no-one has ever had to pay before. The examiners would surely have given first class marks to all the judges who have answered the question so far."

At this end of the spectrum, in other words, there are no black and white answers; the legal position is grey. This does not mean that 'any old answer' will do. It is not a licence to ignore what guidance there is in the existing law—getting a first class mark is not quite so simple. However, it does mean that, with a footing in existing law, more than one plausible account of the legal position is available.

To return to the example of mistake of identity, how might one advise a client in *Ingram v Little* on the assumption that *Phillips v Brooks* is the only relevant prior decision on mistake of identity? On the face of it, the legal advice would be that a plea of mistake of identity would fail. However, *Phillips* was a High Court decision and one might entertain the thought that an appeal court might take a different view—particularly so if there had been some hint of disquiet about the position taken in *Phillips*. In such circumstances, the legal position would still be towards the clear and settled end of the spectrum but one would not have quite such confidence in *Phillips*. By contrast, after the decision handed down in *Ingram*, the legal position was wholly unclear. *Ingram* did not convincingly distinguish *Phillips*; and the Court of Appeal was divided, 2 to 1, in ruling in favour of the owner sellers. Lawyers could reasonably disagree about the legal position and if a further case came through to test the point once again one would have little difficulty in writing an opinion with some legal support for either O (based on *Ingram*) or P (based on *Phillips*).

In thinking about the spectrum of legal (un)certainty, it is helpful to relate the position of the case to the so-called pyramid of dispute settlement. At the base of the pyramid, we have the vast majority of disputes; these are disputes that are settled out of court; and, in many instances, settlement will be facilitated precisely because the doctrinal position is itself reasonably clear. However, some disputes will not be settled and they will go to arbitration or to trial. Often, the unresolved differences between the parties will turn on questions of fact; and so, in some sectors (e.g. building and engineering) a great deal of the arbitrator's or trial judge's judgment will concern findings of fact. Sometimes, though, a dispute will highlight a point on which the law is uncertain and, where this is so, there might be enough in the point to make it fit for the attention of the appeal courts. Whether or not the dispute is of sufficient value to justify committing to the cost of an appeal court hearing is, of course, a critical matter. At all events, where disputes reach the appeal courts, there is almost always a seriously arguable (a moot) point of law at issue. Or, to put this another way, while one of the functions of appeal courts is to ensure that lower courts stay on the right legal track, they are also charged with clarifying the law where it is found to be unclear. Moreover, because it is the decisions of appeal courts that not only monopolise the attention of law reporters but also are the focus of much law school discussion, it is tempting to think that the law is pathologically uncertain.

So, here is a key point to hang on to. The casebook view of contract law, like law school mooting, tends to highlight those parts of the law that lie towards the uncertain end of the spectrum. At that end of the spectrum, even if there is in some deep philosophical sense a 'right answer', the law is contestable; there will be two sides to the argument; choices might have to be made between conflicting precedents, and between competing principles or policies; and, unsettling though this might be, this is where we get to the core activities of common law reasoning.

B. Another Kind of Hard Case

Even where the law is clear and settled, cases might not be decided in the way that the precedents indicate because, to follow the precedents, would be to decide 'against the merits'. In the *Actionstrength* case, for example, we can detect signs of a tension between the law and the merits (at any rate, on Actionstrength's version of the facts) and, where the tension is acute, some judges might be tempted to follow the merits. However, to justify a decision on the merits, the precedents notwithstanding, is far from straightforward and the reasons given can cloud the legal position—this inviting the accusation that "hard cases make bad law".   **1–007**

If we recall the spectrum (of legal certainty and uncertainty), therefore, we can identify two rather different types of hard case. One type of difficulty arises where the law is unsettled and where a choice between conflicting lines of precedent has to be made; and the other arises where the law is clear enough but where the precedents point to a result that is at odds with the perceived merits of the case.

During the middle years of the last century, this latter kind of hard case arose fairly regularly and in a common form. Essentially, the precedents at that time reflected the classical groundrules for business-to-business dealing, centring on the principles of freedom and sanctity of contract, and backed by an assumption that contractors of this kind were capable of looking after their own financial interests. However, as the consumer marketplace expanded, and as consumer claimants took their disputes into court, it soon became apparent that the principles of classical contract law stood in the way of what many would judge to be fair results. Confronted with a clash between the law and the (consumer) merits, many judges worked overtime to find reasons for deciding with the merits. Inevitably, unless the court had the authority to put the record straight by overruling precedents that no longer seemed fair and reasonable, the legacy of these hard cases (hard cases of the second type) was to generate hard cases of the first type. What the courts needed to say was that the law regulating business contracts was different and distinct from the law regulating consumer contracts; but, they could not say this and, thus, the precedents no longer gave clear guidance. Eventually, legislative intervention brought some clarity to the law but it also signalled that, in many respects, we no longer have a single body of contract law—rather, the legislation confirmed the embryonic pattern of the case-law in which, to a considerable extent, there were special rules for the protection of consumer contractors.

C. Shogun Finance

The *Shogun Finance* case, as we have said, is the latest chapter in the saga of mistake of identity. Stated shortly, the dispute in the case was between the claimant finance company and a Mr Norman Hudson, each of whom were the innocent victims of a fraud perpetrated by an unknown crook. The crook, having dishonestly acquired the driving licence of a Mr Patel, and assuming the identity of Mr Patel, purchased a car on hire purchase terms from motor dealers in Leicester. The finance for the transaction was arranged with the claimants (the claimants assuming that they were advancing credit to Mr Patel); and, Mr Patel's name, address, and his driving licence number were duly entered in the relevant part of the paperwork associated with the hire purchase transaction. The crook, having paid the dealer a 10 per cent deposit, partly in cash and partly by cheque, left with the vehicle which he duly sold to Mr Hudson for some £17,000. The crook having disappeared, the question was whether the   **1–008** title (or property) in the vehicle had passed to the crook, and then to Mr Hudson so as to preclude the finance company from recovering their losses against the defendant.

In *Shogun*, the trial judge at the Leicester County Court found that good title had not passed; the claimants might have parted with possession of the vehicle but no more than that. In the Court of Appeal, the majority (Brooke and Dyson LJJ) took the same view: if the finance company had a contract with anyone, it was with Mr Patel (and they plainly had no contract with Mr Patel who was wholly unaware of events at the motor dealers). Against this, Sedley LJ took the view that the finance company should be treated as contracting with the party physically present at the car dealers (even though this party was a crook), and that the finance company should bear the responsibility for the fraud. On final appeal, the House of Lords, like the Court of Appeal, was divided. Splitting three to two, the majority Law Lords (Lords Hobhouse, Phillips, and Walker) ruled in favour of the finance company, with the minority (Lord Nicholls and Lord Millett) ruling in favour of Mr Hudson. While each of these speeches repays careful study, in the extract that follows, we highlight just two, namely, Lord Nicholls' leading minority speech and Lord Hobhouse's majority speech (in Ch.8, we also extract Lord Phillips' ambivalent speech in which his Lordship eventually votes with the majority position).

SHOGUN FINANCE LIMITED v HUDSON

[2003] UKHL 62

LORD NICHOLLS OF BIRKENHEAD

1–009   1. This appeal raises a difficult problem about the effect of fraudulent misrepresentation on the formation of a contract. If a crook (C) fraudulently represents to the owner of goods (O) that he is another identifiable person (X) and on that basis O parts with goods to C by way of sale, is there in law a contract between O and C? Does the answer to this question differ according to whether O and C communicated face to face, or by correspondence, or over the telephone, or by e-mail? The law on cases involving this type of fraudulent conduct, euphemistically described as cases of "mistaken identity", is notoriously unsatisfactory. The reported decisions are few in number and they are not reconcilable. In the present case Sedley L.J. said the law has tied itself into a Gordian knot. Brooke L.J. said the law is in a "sorry condition" which only Parliament or your Lordships' House can remedy: see [2002] QB 834, 847, 855.

2. Two features are usually present when cases of this type come before the court. The first feature is that a seller of goods is concerned with the creditworthiness of the proposed buyer. The seller wants to be sure he will be paid for the goods he is handing over. Here the common law seems to have drawn a distinction between two kinds of fraudulent misrepresentation. The common law distinguished between a case (1) where a crook fraudulently asserts he is creditworthy and a case (2) where a crook fraudulently asserts he is someone else known to be creditworthy. One might suppose there is no difference of substance between these two cases. These are merely two ways a crook may assert a spurious creditworthiness. But, historically, the law seems to have been otherwise. In case (1), when the seller parts with his goods he does so pursuant to a *voidable* contract. This is said to be a case of mistake as to a person's attributes. In case (2), in some circumstances but not all, the seller has been held to part with his goods pursuant to a *void* contract, that is, no contract at all. This is said to be a case of mistake as to a person's identity.

3. The second feature usually present in cases of this type is that the crook then sells the goods to an innocent third party. This feature explains why the distinction between a voidable and a void contract matters. Having fraudulently acquired the goods from their owner, the crook then sells them to an unsuspecting third party. The rights of this innocent third party may depend upon the nice distinction between a voidable contract and a void contract. In case (1), where the crook fraudulently misrepresents his own financial standing, the loss falls on the unfortunate owner of the goods who was tricked into parting with them to the crook. *King's Norton Metal Co Ltd v Edridge, Merrett and Co Ltd* (1897) 14 TLR 98 is an instance of this. There the crook ordered some brass rivet wire from a metal manufacturer. On his writing paper he represented he was in business in a big way, running a large factory and having several depots and agencies. The manufacturer, King's Norton,

supplied the goods sought but was not paid. King's Norton was unable to recover the goods or their value from the third party to whom the crook subsequently sold them.

4. This outcome is to be contrasted with case (2), where the crook asserts he is someone else. In such a case the loss sometimes, but not always, falls upon the unfortunate third party who also was a victim of the crook's trickery. The third party paid for the goods in all honesty, but he must return them to their original owner or pay their value. Thus in *Cundy v Lindsay* (1878) 3 App Cas 459 Cundy had to pay the linen manufacturers Lindsay & Co for the 250 dozen cambric handkerchiefs the crook acquired from Lindsay by fraudulently representing he was the respectable business firm of Blenkiron.

5. The distinction in outcome thus drawn between these two kinds of fraudulent misrepresentation, one as to "attributes" and the other as to "identity", is unconvincing. It has been described as a reproach to the law. To a considerable extent the distinction has now been eroded. *Cundy v Lindsay* (1878) 3 App Cas 459 was decided over a century ago, and since then there have been significant developments in this area of case law. Unfortunately these developments have left the law in a state of disarray. The question before the House on this appeal is whether this distinction, so far as it remains, should still be regarded as good law.

Fraudulent Misrepresentation and Intention

6. The question before the House calls first for some analysis of the effect of fraudulent misrepresentation on a person's intention to enter into a contract. A contract of sale and purchase, like any other contract, requires agreement, a meeting of minds. The seller must intend, or appear to intend, to sell the goods, and the buyer must intend, or appear to intend, to buy the goods on the agreed terms. The presence of fraud does not negative the existence of such an intention on the part of either party. Fraud does not negative intention. A person's intention is a state of mind. Fraud does not negative a state of mind. The existence of a fraudulent misrepresentation means that a person's intention is formed on a false basis—a basis, moreover, known by the other party to be false. The effect of fraud is to negative legal rights or obligations otherwise flowing from an intention to enter into a contract. Fraud enables the victim of the fraud to decline to proceed with a contract into which, by reason of the fraudulent misrepresentation, he was induced to enter, and he has a claim for damages for any loss he may suffer. But fraud does not have the consequence of negativing the formation of a contract.

7. Similarly with consent: as noted by Robert Goff L.J. in *Whittaker v Campbell* [1984] QB 318, 327, in this context fraud does not "vitiate" consent. Professor Glanville Williams rightly said that the maxim "fraud vitiates consent" is thoroughly misleading: see 23 Canadian Bar Review (1945) 271, 291–292. Whether a person has consented to this or that is a question of fact. Fraud does not negative a fact. As with intention, so with consent, fraud negatives legal rights or obligations otherwise flowing from a person having given his consent to a particular happening. Fraud can destroy legal rights; it cannot destroy facts.

8. This distinction, between negativing intention or consent and negativing the rights otherwise flowing from intention or consent, is important. It explains why the law treats a contract induced by fraud as voidable, not void. The necessary coincidence of intention, or consensus ad idem, may exist even where the intention and consent of the victim were induced by fraud. An intention thus induced is regarded by the law as sufficient to found a contract, even though the victim may repudiate the contract as soon as he discovers the fraud.

9. Thus, if a person is induced to buy goods by a fraudulent misrepresentation that the goods are sound, in law a contract to buy the goods is created even though the goods are different from the goods the buyer intends to buy and even though the other party knows this. The fact that the goods are different in quality from the goods which, as the crook knows, the victim wishes to buy is not regarded by the law as meaning that no contract was made.

10. This approach is not confined to cases of differences of quality. The law adopts the same approach where the goods offered for sale are fraudulently misrepresented to be a unique item such as the original of a specific painting by a named artist or the football shirt worn by Bobby Moore in the 1966 World Cup final match. The buyer wishes ("intends") to buy the particular original painting or the particular shirt and nothing else. The seller knows this. But the effect of the misrepresentation is that the buyer, believing the proffered goods to be as represented, agrees to buy the proffered goods. He enters into a contract on the basis of what he believes is the position. In law he contracts to buy the proffered goods even though, looking more broadly at his state of mind, he had no intention of buying anything other than the original of the particular painting or the particular football shirt. If intention is considered in this broad sense, there is no "meeting of minds" whenever one party is persuaded by the other to enter into a contract by a material fraudulent misrepresentation made by the other. But for the purpose of deciding whether a person had the necessary intention to enter into a contract with the crook, a person's intention is considered more narrowly. It is assessed by reference to what he *believed* the position to be. The fact that his belief was induced by the other's fraudulent misrepresentation entitles him

to repudiate the contract. His belief means there was a contract, but the fraudulent inducement of his belief means the contract is voidable.

11. The position is similar if the owner of goods agrees to sell them to a prospective buyer on the basis of a fraudulent assertion of his financial reliability. The buyer's fraudulent statement about himself does not negative the seller's intention to sell the goods to the crook on the agreed terms. Nor does it negative the fact that, when the crook acquired the goods from the seller, he did so with the seller's consent. The fraud means only that the seller's contractual intention was formed, and his consent to hand over the goods obtained, on a fraud-induced basis. There is a contract, but it may be avoided on discovery of the fraud.

Fraudulent Misrepresentation and Identity

12. Fraudulent misrepresentations about a person's identity have to be considered against this background of legal principle. The factual postulate now under consideration, as mentioned at the outset, is that a crook (C) fraudulently misrepresents to the owner of goods (O) that he, C, is another identifiable person (X) whom O believes to be creditworthy. In reliance on this representation O agrees to sell the goods and he hands them over to C. Is this pursuant to a voidable contract between O and C? Or is there no contract between them at all? As between O and C the answer is of no moment. Either way O has ample remedies against C, assuming C has some money and can be traced. As already noted, however, the answer to these question may be of crucial importance to a third party who subsequently bought the goods in good faith from C.

13. In cases of this type there are two innocent parties, O and the third party purchaser. Striking the right balance when one of two innocent parties must sustain a loss is seldom easy. In 1960 Devlin L.J. suggested that in this type of case the loss should be divided between O and the third party in such proportion as is just in all the circumstances: see *Ingram v Little* [1961] 1 QB 31, 73–74. Lord Gardiner L.C. then referred this problem to the Law Reform Committee. In its 12th Report "Transfer of Title to Chattels" (1966, Cmnd 2958) the committee rejected Devlin L.J.'s apportionment suggestion as impracticable. The committee recommended that where goods are sold under a mistake as to the buyer's identity the contract should, so far as third parties are concerned, be voidable and not void: paragraphs 9–12 and 15.

14. Parliament did not implement this recommendation. Instead the Sale of Goods Act 1979 re-enacted the relevant law in much the same terms as the Sale of Goods Act 1893. In general, proprietary rights of an owner of goods endure against a third party who buys them in good faith from a thief. That is the effect of section 21(1). But there are statutory exceptions in some cases where the owner of goods parted with his goods consensually. The third party may acquire a good title if C, who purported to sell the goods to him, had a voidable title: section 23. Or if C had agreed to buy the goods from O and was in possession of the goods with O's consent: section 25. Additionally, section 27 of the Hire-Purchase Act 1964 made a limited exception for the protection of purchasers of motor vehicles. Section 27 of the Hire-Purchase Act 1964, as substituted by the Consumer Credit Act 1974, provides:

"(1)   This section applies where a motor vehicle has been bailed . . . under a hire-purchase agreement, or has been agreed to be sold under a conditional sale agreement, and, before the property in the vehicle has become vested in the debtor, he disposes of the vehicle to another person.

(2)   Where the disposition referred to in subsection (1) above is to a private purchaser, and he is a purchaser of the motor vehicle in good faith, without notice of the hire-purchase or conditional sale agreement . . . that disposition shall have effect as if the creditor's title to the vehicle has been vested in the debtor immediately before that disposition."

"Creditor" means the person by whom goods are bailed under a hire-purchase agreement, and "debtor" means the person to whom a motor vehicle is bailed under such an agreement: section 29(1), (4).

The Proceedings

15. The present case concerns this latter exception. The crucial issue is whether Norman Hudson, who bought a Mitsubishi Shogun S.W.B. motor car from a crook who promptly disappeared, can bring himself within section 27 of the Hire-Purchase Act 1964. Mr Hudson was a private purchaser who bought the vehicle in good faith. His right to retain this vehicle depends upon whether he can establish that the crook acquired possession of the vehicle under the written hire-purchase agreement which on its face was made between the finance company, Shogun Finance Ltd, and a Mr Durlabh Patel. When signing this agreement the crook pretended to be Mr Durlabh Patel, living at an address in Leicester. As proof of his identity the crook produced Mr Patel's driving licence which he had obtained improperly. The finance company checked Mr Patel's credit rating.

Finding this to be satisfactory the finance company instructed the motor dealer who had been dealing with the crook to let the crook have the car. Mr Patel knew nothing about any of these goings on.

16. If Mr Hudson is to bring himself within section 27 of the Hire-Purchase Act 1964 he must establish that possession of the car obtained by the crook in this way was under a hire-purchase agreement made between him, the crook, and Shogun Finance. There is of course no question of an agreement between Mr. Patel and Shogun Finance. At the trial the judge, assistant recorder D E B Grant sitting in the Leicester County Court, held that Mr Hudson failed to do so. He gave judgment for Shogun Finance in the amount of £18,374.

17. The majority of the Court of Appeal, Brooke and Dyson L.JJ., agreed with the judge's decision: see [2002] QB 834. Brooke L.J. said the hire-purchase agreement, if made between anyone, was made between the finance company and Mr Patel. The finance company did not make the agreement with anyone else. Dyson L.J. held that section 27 of the Hire Purchase Act 1964 did not avail Mr Hudson because the crook was not the hirer named in the written hire-purchase agreement and therefore he was not the debtor under the agreement. Sedley L.J. dissented. The finance company, using the dealer as its agent, had in law contracted face to face with a fraudsman in circumstances insufficient to rebut the presumption that it was with him, and not with the person he claimed to be, that the company was contracting.

Fraudulent Misrepresentation: Face to Face Dealings

18. I can now turn to the effect of a fraudulent misrepresentation made by a person about his identity. In cases of face to face dealings the law, as declared by the preponderance of authority, is tolerably clear. The owner of the goods believes the person in front of him is X, and in that belief he contracts with the person in front of him. The fraudulent misrepresentation by the crook C regarding his identity no more negatives O's intention to contract with C than, in my earlier example, the seller's misrepresentation about the identity of the proffered goods negatives the buyer's intention to buy the proffered goods. In each case the relevant intention is to be ascertained by looking at the position which, as a result of the misrepresentation, the other party believes to exist. On that footing there is consensus, in the relevant respect, between the parties. O believes C, the person in front of him, to be X *and he deals with C in that belief*. The fraud entitles O to avoid the contract, but it does not negative the formation of a contract with C.

19. Thus in *Phillips v Brooks Ltd* [1919] 2 KB 243 Horridge J. held that the jeweller contracted to sell the ring to the crook in the shop who represented he was Sir George Bullough. The jeweller had heard of Sir George Bullough and checked he lived at the address given. The jeweller gave evidence he had no intention of making any contract with any person other than Sir George Bullough. Horridge J. rightly analysed what that meant by adopting a passage from the judgment of Morton C. J. in the Massachusetts case of *Edmunds v Merchants' Despatch Transportation Co* 135 Mass 283, 283–284:

> "The fact that the seller was induced to sell by fraud of the buyer made the sale voidable, not void. He could not have supposed that he was selling to any other person; his intention was to sell to the person present, and identified by sight and hearing; *it does not defeat the sale because the buyer assumed a false name, or practised any other deceit to induce the vendor to sell*." (emphasis added)

20. In *Ingram v Little* [1961] 1 QB 31, another "face to face" case, the majority of the Court of Appeal reached the contrary conclusion. A crook responded to an advertisement for a car and fraudulently introduced himself as P.G.M. Hutchinson living at a stated address in Caterham. The owners of the car checked in the telephone directory there was a person of that name living at that address. The crook paid for the car with a cheque made out in his assumed name. Sellers and Pearce L.JJ. held that the owners did not enter into a contract with the crook. Sellers L.J. considered the offer made by the owners of the car was capable of acceptance only by the honest P.G.M. Hutchinson of Caterham. Pearce L.J. considered that whether a party was not contracting with the physical person to whom he uttered the offer but with another individual whom he believed to be the person physically present was a question of fact.

21. Devlin L.J. disagreed. He pointed out, at p 65:

> "If Miss Ingram had been asked whether she intended to contract with the man in the room or with P.G.M. Hutchinson, the question could have no meaning for her, since she believed them both to be one and the same. The reasonable man of the law—if he stood in Miss Ingram's shoes—could not give any better answer."

22. Devlin L.J. suggested, at p 66, that to deal with this difficulty the law should formulate a presumption that a person is intending to contract with the person to whom he is actually addressing the words of contract. That should be the starting point. Devlin L.J. stressed that the presumption could not be rebutted by piling up evidence that Miss Ingram would never have contracted with the person in front of her unless she had thought

him to be P.G.M. Hutchinson. There was everything to show that Miss Ingram would never have accepted the crook's offer if she had known the truth, but nothing to rebut "the ordinary presumption" that she was addressing her acceptance, "in law as well as in fact", to the person to whom she was speaking.

23. The majority decision in *Ingram v Little* [1961] 1 QB 31 was doubted when the same problem came before a differently constituted Court of Appeal ten years later, in *Lewis v Averay* [1972] 1 QB 198. The court comprised Lord Denning M. R., Phillimore and Megaw L.JJ. In the *Lewis* case a crook represented orally to the owner of a car that he was a well known actor, Richard Greene. Lord Denning M. R., characteristically, enunciated a broad proposition: mistake as to identity renders an apparent contract voidable, not void. In this type of case the third party knew nothing of what passed between the seller and the rogue and he acted with complete circumspection and in good faith. It was the seller who let the rogue have the goods and thus enabled him to commit the fraud on the third party. Phillimore L.J., at p 208, considered there was nothing to displace the prima facie presumption that the car owner was dealing with the person present in the flat, the rogue: "this case really is on all fours with *Phillips v Brooks* which has been good law for over 50 years". Megaw L.J., at p 209, based his decision on the ground that the mistake of the owner of the car went no further than a mistake as to the attributes of the rogue: it "was simply a mistake as to the creditworthiness of the man who was there present and who described himself as Mr Green".

24. Sometimes in these cases the transaction is evidenced in writing. This can make no difference to the outcome. Clearly there is no magic attaching to a misrepresentation made in writing rather than by word of mouth. The presence or absence of a written record of a transaction negotiated face to face, such as an invoice or receipt made out in favour of Sir George Bullough, with or without his address, or a cheque ostensibly signed by Sir George Bullough, is neither here nor there for present purposes. Writings such as these are no more than stark contemporary confirmation that the misrepresentation was made and that the seller believed it.

25. Similarly the contractual position between O and C must be the same if they meet face to face and the deal arranged by them is later embodied in a written agreement. This further step does not relevantly change the legal position. The written contract is expressed to be made between O and X. But C, the person with whom O was physically dealing, asserted he was X, and O believed him. So the description of C in the contract as X was a fraudulent misnomer. C used a false name and address, and the written contract is to be construed accordingly.

Fraudulent Misrepresentation: Dealing by Correspondence

26. But what of the case where a fraudulent misrepresentation is made in writing but O and C do not meet each other? C writes to O saying he is X and the deal proceeds on that basis. O parts with his goods to the person with whom he is in fact dealing, namely, C, in the belief he is X.

27. At first sight it seems counter-intuitive to speak of a contract between O and C in cases of this type. It seems counter-intuitive because on its face a contract in writing or in correspondence expressed to be made between O and X is inconsistent, agency apart, with its being a contract between O and C. But this intuitive response is not a sound guide if it leaves out of account, as all too easily it may, the vitally important underlying fraudulent misrepresentation. In his dealings with O the crook C represented he was X, and O proceeded to *deal with him (C)* in that belief.

28. When this feature is kept in mind it readily becomes apparent that in principle cases of this type are no different from cases of face to face dealings. The existence of physical immediacy in one case, and the absence of it in the other, is immaterial. The physical immediacy of C in face to face cases tends to emphasise O's intention to deal with the person in front of him. With other forms of communication such as the telephone or correspondence this physical immediacy is lacking. But in each case, whatever the mode of communication, what matters is *whether* O agreed to sell his goods to the person with whom he was dealing, not *why* he did so or under what name. The latter is relevant to remedy, not to formation of a contract.

29. In this regard mention must be made of reasoning sometimes advanced here, along the lines that the identity of the person to whom a written offer is made is a question solely of construction of the document. The offer, it is said, is made to the person identified in the document and no one else. A written offer made by O to X is not capable of acceptance by C. Hence, it is said that, whatever the position in face to face dealings, in cases of written contracts or contracts made by correspondence there can be no contract between O and C, contradicting as this would the terms of the document.

30. The flaw in this reasoning is that it begs the crucial question: to whom was the offer made? The reasoning assumes this is a straightforward case of an offer made to the person named. Indeed the person named is X. But that is only part of the picture. O believes that X, the person to whom he is writing and to whom he addressed the offer, is one and the same person as the person with whom he is dealing. In fact he is not dealing

with X. He is dealing with C. O's misapprehension in this regard, induced by C's fraud, is no different in principle from a case where C's misrepresentation is made orally in the course of the face to face meeting. The legal problem is the same in both cases. The presence or absence of writing does not constitute a principled ground of distinction.

31. Thus, when Lindsay & Co supplied linen handkerchiefs in response to a written order they were under a misapprehension regarding the identity of the person placing the order in the same way as the jeweller in the shop was under a misapprehension regarding the identity of his customer ("I am Sir George Bullough") in *Phillips v Brooks Ltd* [1919] 2 KB 243. If the approach adopted in *Phillips v Brooks* is correct, Lindsay's misapprehension no more negatived the formation of a contract with the person placing the written order for handkerchiefs than did the like misapprehension by the jeweller in the case of *Phillips v Brooks*. The jeweller parted with his ring to the customer in his shop. Lindsay parted with their linen by sending it to the address supplied by the crook. On what terms? The answer must be, on the terms agreed between Lindsay and the person with whom they were dealing. That was a contract Lindsay could enforce, should they have wished, or repudiate on the grounds of fraudulent misrepresentation.

32. In *Cundy v Lindsay* (1878) 3 App Cas 459 the House reached the contrary conclusion. The reasoning of all their Lordships was to the same effect. Lord Cairns L.C. encapsulated this reasoning, at p 465:

"Of [the crook Blenkarn] [Lindsay] knew nothing, and of him they never thought. With him they never intended to deal. Their minds never, even for an instant of time, rested upon him, and as between him and them there was no consensus of mind which could lead to any arrangement or any contract whatever."

Lord Hatherley and Lord Penzance left open what the position would be had the crook come into personal contact with Lindsay.

The Choice

33. In my view this decision is not reconcilable with *Phillips v Brooks Ltd* [1919] 2 KB 243 or with *Lewis v Averay* [1972] 1 QB 198 or with the starting point "presumption" formulated by Devlin L.J. in *Ingram v Little* [1961] 1 QB 31. The legal principle applicable in these cases cannot sensibly differ according to whether the transaction is negotiated face to face, or by letter, or by fax, or by e-mail, or over the telephone or by video link or video telephone. Typically today a purchaser pays for goods with a credit or debit card. He produces the card in person in a shop or provides details of the card over the telephone or by e-mail or by fax. When a credit or debit card is fraudulently misused in this way the essence of the transaction is the same in each case. It does not differ from one means of communication to the next. The essence of the transaction in each case is that the owner of the goods agrees to part with his goods on the basis of a fraudulent misrepresentation made by the other regarding his identity. Since the essence of the transaction is the same in each case, the law in its response should apply the same principle in each case, irrespective of the precise mode of communication of offer and acceptance.

34. Accordingly, if the law of contract is to be coherent and rescued from its present unsatisfactory and unprincipled state, the House has to make a choice: either to uphold the approach adopted in *Cundy v Lindsay* and overrule the decisions in *Phillips v Brooks Ltd* and *Lewis v Averay*, or to prefer these later decisions to *Cundy v Lindsay*.

35. I consider the latter course is the right one, for a combination of reasons. It is in line with the direction in which, under the more recent decisions, the law has now been moving for some time. It accords better with basic principle regarding the effect of fraud on the formation of a contract. It seems preferable as a matter of legal policy. As between two innocent persons the loss is more appropriately borne by the person who takes the risks inherent in parting with his goods without receiving payment. This approach fits comfortably with the intention of Parliament in enacting the limited statutory exceptions to the proprietary principle of *nemo dat non quod habet*. Thus, by section 23 of the Sale of Goods Act 1979 Parliament protected an innocent buyer from a seller with a voidable title. The classic instance of a person with a voidable title is a person who acquired the goods by fraud: see Bramwell L.J. in *Babcock v Lawson* (1880) 5 QBD 284, 286. Further, this course is supported by writers of the distinction of Sir Jack Beatson: see Anson's Law of Contract, 28th edition, p 332. It is consistent with the approach adopted elsewhere in the common law world, notably in the United States of America in the Uniform Commercial Code, 14th edition, section 2–403. And this course makes practical sense. In a case such as the present the owner of goods has no interest in the identity of the buyer. He is interested only in creditworthiness. It is little short of absurd that a subsequent purchaser's rights depend on the precise manner in which the crook seeks to persuade the owner of his creditworthiness and permit him to take the goods away with him. This ought not to be so. The purchaser's rights should not depend upon the precise form the crook's misrepresentation takes.

36. *Cundy v Lindsay* has stood for a long time. But I see no reason to fear that adopting this conclusion will unsettle the law of contract. In practice the problems surrounding *Cundy v Lindsay* arise only when third parties' rights are in issue. To bring the law here into line with the law already existing in "face to face" cases will rid the law of an anomaly. Devlin L.J.'s starting point presumption is a workable foundation which should apply in all cases. A person is presumed to intend to contract with the person with whom he is actually dealing, whatever be the mode of communication.

37. Although expressed by Devlin L.J. as a presumption, it is not easy to think of practical circumstances where, once in point, the presumption will be displaced. The factual postulate necessary to bring the presumption into operation is that a person (O) believes that the person with whom he is dealing is the person the latter has represented himself to be. Evidence that the other's identity was of importance to O, and evidence of the steps taken to check the other's identity, will lead nowhere if the transaction proceeds on the basis of the underlying factual postulate.

The Present Case

38. It follows that I would allow this appeal. The principles applicable to the formation of a contract of sale are equally applicable to the formation of a hire-purchase agreement. The document submitted to Shogun Finance, and signed by the crook in the name of Mr Patel, does of course refer unequivocally to Mr Patel. The document identifies him with some particularity: his full name and address, his date of birth, his driving licence number, and his employer's name and address. These details were of prime importance to Shogun Finance because they identified the person whose credit rating it had checked and approved. The company intended to contract with this person. But it is clear from the evidence that Shogun Finance, as much as the dealer in the car showroom, thought this was one and the same person as the individual in the showroom. Shogun Finance proceeded in this (fraud-induced) belief.

39. This is manifest because Shogun Finance authorised the dealer to hand over the car to the person in the showroom, he being (as the finance company knew) the person who had signed the agreement and he being (so the finance company believed) the person whose credit rating it had checked. Shogun Finance believed he was Mr Patel, in the same way as the jeweller in *Phillips v Brooks* believed the customer in his shop was Sir George Bullough. In the belief that the person in the dealer's showroom was Mr Patel, Shogun Finance intended to hire the car *to that person*. That is what the finance company intended to do by the written hire-purchase agreement, and that is what it thought it had done. Had this not been so it would not have released the car to him. Shogun Finance was mistaken in its belief about the identity of the person in the showroom, in the same way as the jeweller was mistaken in his belief about the identity of the person in his shop. But that mistaken belief, induced by the crook's fraudulent misrepresentation, did not negative the finance company's intention to let the car on hire to the person in the showroom on the terms set out in the hire-purchase agreement. Nor could the crook assert he had no contractual intention: he signed the hire-purchase agreement, albeit using a false name and address. The alternative conclusion involves the proposition that when the dealer released the car to the crook, the dealer was guilty of converting the car and was liable to the finance company accordingly. That would be a distorted appraisal of the facts.

40. The finance company sought to gain assistance from *Hector v Lyons* 58 P. & C.R. 156, a decision binding upon the Court of Appeal. Suffice to say, that decision should not be taken as authority for the proposition that if O intends to contract with C in the belief he is X, there can be a contract between O and C if the contract is oral but not if it is reduced into writing and expressed to be made between O and X. Evidence of the fraudulent misrepresentation and of O's belief is admissible to identify who are the parties to the written contract.

41. One further point may be noted. Some time was taken up in this case with arguments on whether the dealer was an agent for the finance company and for what purposes. This was in an endeavour to bring the case within the "face to face" principle. The need for such singularly sterile arguments underlines the practical absurdity of a principle bounded in this way. The practical reality is that in the instant case the presence or absence of a representative of the finance company in the dealer's showroom made no difference to the course of events. Had an authorised representative of the finance company been present no doubt he would have inspected the driving licence himself and himself obtained the information needed by his company. As it was, a copy of the licence, together with the necessary information, were faxed to the finance company. I can see no sensible basis on which these different modes of communication should affect the outcome of this case. I would set aside the orders of the assistant recorder and the Court of Appeal, and dismiss this action. Mr Hudson acquired a good title to the car under section 27 of the Hire-Purchase Act 1964.

LORD HOBHOUSE OF WOODBOROUGH

My Lords,

42. The question at issue on this appeal is: Did Mr Hudson acquire a good title to the car when he bought the car from the rogue ("R") who himself had no title? The basic principle is *nemo dat quod non habet*: see the Sale of Goods Act 1979 s.21(1) and *Helby v Matthews* [1895] AC 471 where it was held that the same rule applied to a sale by a hire-purchaser. The hire-purchaser has no title to the goods and no power to convey any title to a third party. The title to the goods and the power to transfer that title to any third party remains with the hire purchase company and with it alone. Clause 8 of the hire-purchase "agreement" and the printed words in the form immediately below the space for the customer's signature also expressly say the same. There are common law and statutory exceptions to this rule (*eg*, sales in market overt or by a mercantile agent in possession of the goods with the consent of the owner).

43. In the present case, the statutory exception relied on by Mr Hudson is that in Part III of the Hire-Purchase Act 1964 as re-enacted in the Consumer Credit Act 1974:

"where a motor vehicle has been bailed . . . under a hire-purchase agreement . . . and, before the property in the vehicle has become vested in the debtor, he disposes of the vehicle to another person . . . [who is] a private purchaser [who has purchased] the motor vehicle in good faith without notice of the hire-purchase . . . agreement . . . that disposition shall have effect as if the creditor's title to the vehicle has been vested in the debtor immediately before that disposition." (s.27(1) and (2),

Section 29(4) adds:

"the 'debtor' in relation to a motor vehicle which has been bailed . . . under a hire-purchase agreement . . . means the person who at the material time (whether the agreement has before that time been terminated or not) . . . is . . . the person to whom the vehicle is bailed . . . under that agreement."

44. The relevant question is therefore one of the application of this statutory provision to the facts of this case (no more, no less). Thus the question becomes:

"Was R a debtor under the hire-purchase agreement relating to the car?"

Mr Hudson contends that R was; the Finance Company contends that he was not. The judge and the majority of the Court of Appeal found that he was not; Sedley L.J. would have held that he was.

45. What was the "hire-purchase" "agreement" relied on? It was a written agreement on a standard hire-purchase printed form purporting to be signed as the "customer" by one Durlabh Patel, the person who lived at 45 Mayflower Rd, Leicester, to whom driving licence No."PATEL506018DJ9FM" had been issued and with a date of birth 01/06/58. This was an accurate identification of the real Mr Durlabh Patel, but in no respect of R who was not the person who lived at that address, not the person to whom the driving licence had been issued and (one suspects) not a twin in age of the real Mr Patel. R forged Mr Patel's signature so as to make the signature on the hire-purchase "agreement" appear to be the same as that on the driving licence. The parties to the written "agreement" are Mr Patel (the "customer"), and Shogun Finance Ltd (the creditor). There is also an offer and acceptance clause:

"You ['the customer named overleaf'] are offering to make a legal agreement by signing this document. We [the creditor] can reject your offer, or accept it by signing it ourselves."
  If we sign this document it will become legally binding at once (even before we send you a signed copy). . . ."

46. The effect of this is that—

(i) it re-emphasises that the customer/hirer is, and is only, the person *named* on the front of the document;

(ii) it makes it clear that the agreement is the written agreement contained in the written document;

(iii) the offer being accepted by the creditor is the offer contained in the document and that alone, that is to say, the offer of Mr Durlabh Patel of the address in Leicester and to whom the driving licence was issued;

(iv) for a valid offer to be made, the form must have been signed by Mr Durlabh Patel; and,

(v) most importantly of all, the question in issue becomes a question of the construction of this written document, not a question of factual investigation and evaluation.

I will take these points in turn but the second and fifth are fundamental to them all and to the giving of the correct answer to this case.

47. The first point is a matter of the construction of the written document. It admits of only one conclusion. There is no mention in the document of anyone other than Mr Durlabh Patel. The language used is clear and specific, both in the substance of the identification—name and address and driving licence number and age—and in the express words of the offer and acceptance clause—"the customer named overleaf". The "agreement" is a consumer credit agreement. It is unlike a mere retail sale where, although title may, indeed, will normally have already passed to the buyer, the seller is not obliged to part with the goods until he has been paid or is satisfied that he will be paid. Credit is only relevant to the release of the seller's lien and to his obligation to deliver, not to the basic transaction; the basic transaction is unaffected and will stand. Under a contract for the sale of goods, the contract has been made and, normally, the title to the goods has vested in the buyer before the time for payment has arrived. (Retention of title clauses are a modern development.) By contrast, in a consumer credit transaction, the identity of the customer is fundamental to the whole transaction because it is essential to the checking of the credit rating of the applicant borrower. All this *precedes* the making of any contract at all. No title to the goods is obtained by the hirer at any stage. If the finance company does not accept the proposer's offer, the proposer has acquired nothing. Unlike in the sale of goods, there is nothing—no status quo—which has to be undone. The observations of Devlin L.J. in *Ingram v Little* [1961] 1 QB at p.69 are not pertinent; the approach and dicta of Denning M. R. in *Lewis v Averay* [1972] 1 QB 198 are misplaced and wrong.

48. It has been suggested that the finance company was willing to do business with anyone, whatever their name. But this is not correct: it was only willing to do business with a person who had identified himself in the way required by the written document so as to enable it to check before it enters into any contractual or other relationship that he meets its credit requirements. Mr Durlabh Patel was such an identified person and met its credit requirements so it was willing to do business with him. If the applicant had been, say, Mr B. Patel of Ealing or Mr G. Patel of Edgbaston, it would not have been willing to deal with them if they could not be identified or did not meet with its credit requirements. Correctly identifying the customer making the offer is an essential precondition of the willingness of the finance company to deal with that person. The Rogue knew, or at least confidently expected, that the finance company would be prepared to deal with Mr Durlabh Patel but probably not with him, the Rogue; and he was, in any event, not willing himself to enter into any contract with the finance company. This is not a case such as that categorised by Sedley L.J. ([2002] QB at 846) as the use of a "simple alias" to disguise the purchaser rather than to deceive the vendor—the situation which resembles that in *King's Norton Metal v Edridge Merrett & Co* (14 TLR 98). But, even then, in a credit agreement it would be useless to use a pseudonym as no actual verifiable person against whom a credit check could be run would have been disclosed and the offer would never be accepted. Mr Durlabh Patel is the sole hirer under this written agreement. No one else acquires any rights under it; no one else can become the bailee of the motor car or the "debtor" "under the agreement". It is not in dispute that R was not Mr Durlabh Patel nor that R had no authority from Mr Patel to enter into the agreement or take possession of the motor car.

49. Mr Hudson seeks to escape from this conclusion by saying: "but the Rogue was the person who came into the dealer's office and negotiated a price with the dealer and signed the form in the presence of the dealer who then witnessed it." The third and fourth points address this argument. The gist of the argument is that oral evidence may be adduced to contradict the agreement contained in a written document which is the only contract to which the finance company was a party. The agreement is a written agreement with Mr Durlabh Patel. The argument seeks to contradict this and make it an agreement with the Rogue. It is argued that other evidence is always admissible to show who the parties to an agreement are. Thus, if the contents of the document are, without more, insufficient unequivocally to identify the actual individual referred to or if the identification of the party is non-specific, evidence can be given to fill any gap. Where the person signing is also acting as the agent of another, evidence can be adduced of that fact. None of this involves the contradiction of the document: *Young v Schuler* 11 QBD 651, which was a case of an equivocal agency signature and it was held that evidence was admissible that the signature was also a personal signature—"evidence that he intended to sign in both capacities . . . does not contradict the document and is admissible". (per Cotton L.J. at p.655) But it is different where the party is, as here, specifically identified in the document: oral or other extrinsic evidence is not admissible. Further, the Rogue was no one's agent (nor did he ever purport to be). The rule that other evidence may not be adduced to contradict the provisions of a contract contained in a written document is fundamental to the mercantile law of this country; the bargain is the document; the certainty of the contract depends on it. The relevant principle is well summarised in Phipson on Evidence, paragraphs 42–11 and 42–12: "When the parties have deliberately put their agreement into writing, it is conclusively presumed between

themselves and their privies that they intend the writing to form a full and final statement of their intentions, and one which should be placed beyond the reach of future controversy, bad faith or treacherous memory." (See also *Bank of Australasia v Palmer* [1897] AC 540, per Lord Morris at p.545.) This rule is one of the great strengths of English commercial law and is one of the main reasons for the international success of English law in preference to laxer systems which do not provide the same certainty. The case of *Hector v Lyons* 58 P&CR 156 is simply an application of this basic and long established principle. The father was claiming to be able to enforce a contract of sale of land. The father had conducted the negotiations. Woolf L.J. said, at pp. 160–161:

> "In this case there is no dispute as to who, according to the written contract, are the parties. The son was described in the contract as one of the parties. He does exist and, in so far as there was a contract at all, it was between him and the other party identified in the contract, Mrs Pamela Doris Lyons."

Browne-Wilkinson V.-C. delivered to a judgment to the same effect. On p.159 he referred to the cases "entirely concerned with transactions between two individuals face to face entering into oral agreement", saying.

> "In my judgment the principle there enunciated has no application to a case such as the present where there is a contract and wholly in writing. There the identity of the vendor and of the purchaser is established by the names of the parties included in the written contract."

Mr Hudson submitted, as he had to, that this decision was wrong and should be overruled. In my opinion the Court of Appeal's decision was clearly correct and correctly reasoned in accordance with well established principles.

50. The argument also fails on another ground. There was no *consensus ad idem* between the finance company and the Rogue. Leaving on one side the fact that the Rogue never had any intention himself to contract with the finance company, the hire-purchase "agreement" to which Mr Hudson pins his argument was one purportedly made by the acceptance by the finance company, by signing the creditor's box in the form, of a written offer by Mr Durlabh Patel to enter into the hire-purchase agreement. This faces Mr Hudson with a dilemma: either the contract created by that acceptance was a contract with Mr Durlabh Patel or there was no *consensus ad idem*, the Rogue having no honest belief or contractual intent whatsoever and the finance company believing that it was accepting an offer by Mr Durlabh Patel. On neither alternative was there a hire-purchase agreement with the Rogue.

51. It is as well to digress at this stage to consider the chain of contracts or alleged contracts relied upon by Mr Hudson. First, Mr Hudson relies upon a contract of sale he made with the Rogue when he agreed to buy the motor car from the Rogue. He says he got a good title to it from the Rogue under this contract notwithstanding that R had no title. In support of this statute-based contention he argues that there was another contract which he has to say was a contract of hire-purchase between the Rogue and the finance company, the supposed contract contained in the written hire-purchase agreement. There is no dispute that the finance company had bought the motor car from the dealer and was or had become the owner of the car at the time when the finance company signed the document and thereby accepted the offer (if any) in the written hire-purchase document. (That contract of purchase was never put in evidence.) The title to the car was in the finance company. The hirer/debtor under the "agreement" was Mr Durlabh Patel not the Rogue. The Rogue only comes into the picture because he was the unidentified individual who came into the dealer's office and caused the dealer to sell the motor car to the finance company and the dealer, thereafter, to deliver it to him although he was not in fact Mr Durlabh Patel. (He, of course, came into the story again later as the person who purported to sell the car to Mr Hudson.) The dealer (as his witness signature testifies) apparently believed the Rogue when the Rogue said his name was Mr Patel and negotiated with him, face to face, the price at which the dealer would be willing to sell the car. That negotiation enabled the dealer to fill in the appropriate finance details which the "customer" should ask for. But the Rogue never had any face to face dealings with the finance company; he dealt with it solely by submitting a written document containing an offer and acceptance clause. There is no room for the application of the "face to face" principle between the Rogue and the finance company. Nor was the dealer the agent of the finance company to enter into any contract on behalf of the finance company. The dealer is a mere facilitator serving primarily his own interests. If there could have been any doubt or room for argument about this point, it is put beyond argument or doubt by the terms of the offer and acceptance clause in the governing document. R and the dealer are not two individuals conducting negotiations in which all the terms necessary to constitute a binding contract are agreed.

52. As regards the delivery of the motor car by the dealer to the Rogue, it is not in dispute that, in making that delivery, the dealer was acting as the agent of the finance company. But he was acting without authority. The dealer's authority was to deliver the car to Mr Durlabh Patel, not to anyone else. That delivery did

not create any bailment of the car by the finance company to the Rogue. The Rogue was a thief. Albeit by an elaborate but effective course of action, he stole the car from the possession of the dealer just as surely as if he was a thief stealing it from the forecourt. The dealer may have acted under an innocent mistake induced by the fraud the Rogue had practised on him; but it will, nevertheless, have been a tortious disposal of the motor car by the dealer. But the matter does not stop there. It would not be a delivery "under a hire-purchase agreement". This follows from the fact that there was no hire-purchase agreement (or any agreement or contract) between the finance company and the Rogue. It further follows from the fact that the only "debtor" under the supposed agreement was Mr Durlabh Patel. It was never the Rogue and neither the finance company nor the Rogue ever intended that it should be.

53. The final point was the fact that the purported customer's signature was not in truth that of Mr Durlabh Patel. The supposed hire-purchase agreement therefore from the outset lacked an essential ingredient and within the terms of the document was never an offer eligible for acceptance. A forged signature is neither the signature of the purported signatory nor of the forger. There may be an exception where the "forger" had the authority of the actual party to sign on his behalf and in his name, in which case it probably would not be a forgery unless there was some dishonest intent to deceive. The same applies to using a "mere pseudonym" or a trading name. But that is not this case.

54. It follows that the appeal must be dismissed and the majority judgment of the Court of Appeal affirmed.

55. But, before I leave this case, I should shortly summarise why the argument of the appellant's counsel was so mistaken. The first reason was that they approached the question as if it was simply a matter of sorting out the common law authorities relating to the sale of goods. They did not treat it as a matter of applying a statutory exception to the basic common law rule, *nemo dat quod non habet*. Further, they did not analyse the structure of the overall transaction and the consumer credit agreement within it. Accordingly, they misrepresented the role of the dealer, wrongly treating him as the contracting agent of the finance company which he was not. They never analysed the terms of the written document and had no regard at all to the offer and acceptance clause it contained which, if there was any contract between a "debtor" and the finance company, governed their relationship and which expressly set out the *only* way in which such a contract could come into existence. They made submissions which contradicted the express written contract and were therefore contrary to principle and long established English mercantile law. They submitted that *Cundy v Lindsay* (1878) 3 App Cas 459 was wrongly decided and should be overruled, substituting for it a general rule which, in disregard of the document or documents which constitute the agreement (if any), makes everything depend upon a factual enquiry into extraneous facts not known to both of the parties thus depriving documentary contracts of their certainty. They sought to convert a direct documentary contract with the finance company into a face to face oral contract made through the dealer as the contracting agent of the finance company, notwithstanding that the dealer was never such an agent of the finance company. Finally they sought, having by-passed the written contract, to rely upon authorities on oral contracts for the sale of goods, made face to face and where the title to the goods had passed to the "buyer", notwithstanding that this was a documentary consumer credit transaction not a sale and, on any view, no title had ever passed to R. In the result they have invited a review of those authorities by reference to the particular facts of each of them. They have sought to draw your Lordships into a discussion of the evidential tools, *eg* rebuttable presumptions of fact and the so-called face-to-face "principle", used by judges in those cases to assist them in making factual decisions (see also the dictum of Gresson P. in *Fawcett v Star Car Sales* [1960] NZLR at 413), notwithstanding that the present case concerns the construction of a written contract. They forget that the, presently relevant, fundamental principles of law to be applied—*consensus ad idem*, the correspondence of the contractual offer and the contractual acceptance, the legal significance of the use of a written contract—are clear and are not in dispute. Inevitably over the course of time there have been decisions on the facts of individual "mistaken identity" cases which seem now to be inconsistent; the further learned, but ultimately unproductive, discussion of them will warm academic hearts. But what matters is the principles of law. They are clear and sound and need no revision. To cast doubt upon them can only be a disservice to English law. Similarly, to attempt to use this appeal to advocate, on the basis of continental legal systems which are open to cogent criticism, the abandonment of the soundly based *nemo dat quod non habet* rule (statutorily adopted) would be not only improper but even more damaging.

----

4. If There is No Contract, is There No Case?

In *Shogun Finance*, the finance company had no contract with Mr Hudson. How, then, in the absence of a contract, were they able to sue Mr Hudson? The short answer is that the finance company, in seeking to recover the vehicle, were not relying at all on a contract claim; their claim was in tort, for the conversion of their property. It was Mr Hudson who relied on the contract, and on the argument that the chain of contracts had passed a good title in the vehicle to him, in order to resist the finance company's claim. Another key point to bear in mind, therefore, is that the absence of a contract claim does not signal that there is no action—and this, we might reflect, is a jolly good thing too because we would otherwise lack legal resources to claim damages where we are injured through the careless actions of others (whom we might sue in the tort of negligence) or where we are troubled by excessively noisy neighbours (where we might rely on the tort of nuisance), or where we seek to vindicate our reputation (by relying on the tort of libel), and so on.

1–010

Nowadays, there is a fashion for talking about the common law of obligations. This body of law comprises three elements: the law of contract, the law of tort, and the law of restitution (which is essentially concerned with the reversal of unjust enrichment). Two points need to be noted. First, the point that has just been made, namely that the absence of a claim in contract does not necessarily signify that there is no claim available elsewhere in the law of obligations (in tort or restitution). For example, even in the absence of a contract, if A confers a benefit on B at the request of B but for which B subsequently refuses to pay, then A might be entitled to redress under the law of restitution. Secondly, where there are contracts with public authorities or with parties that are discharging public functions, there might well be a range of possible claims in private and/or public law (compare, e.g., *YL (by her litigation friend the Official Solicitor) (FC) v Birmingham City Council* [2007] UKHL 27).

The interfaces between different branches of the law are notoriously difficult and this is not a topic for an introduction. However, imagine that a contract provides that reasonable care is to be taken in the performance of the contract. If reasonable care is not taken, does it follow that the innocent party has the option of suing for breach of contract and/or for the tort of negligence? In principle, the law might regulate the claimant's remedy in one of three ways:

(i)   the claimant is permitted to cumulate, coordinate, or combine features of the contract and tort claims in the manner most advantageous to his case;

(ii) the claimant's remedy is exclusively in contract or exclusively in tort, the law prescribing whether the claim lies in contract or in tort; or

(iii) the claimant has the choice or election of pursuing a remedy in either contract or tort.

Legal systems have rarely adopted cumulation, although it has been supported in Germany; but both contractual exclusivity and the principle of claimant election have enjoyed support in a number of legal systems. In English law, there have been decisions in support of both the second and the third of these positions. However, following the decision of the House of Lords in *Henderson v Merrett Syndicates Ltd* [1995] 2 A.C. 145, it seems that the third position now represents English law.

The question in *Henderson* was whether Lloyd's "names" could sue their agent for negligence in failing to exercise reasonable care. This was important because the limitation period (the period within which an action must be brought) was more favourable to the names in tort than in contract. Responding to an argument that no term should be implied in a contract if it would be co-extensive with a duty in tort, Lord Goff said:

"It is however my understanding that by the law in this country contracts for services do contain an implied promise to exercise reasonable care (and skill) in the performance of the relevant services; indeed, as Mr Weir has pointed out (XI Int Enc Comp Law ch 12, para 67), in the nineteenth century the field of concurrent liabilities was expanded 'since it was impossible for the judges to deny that contracts contained an implied promise to take reasonable care, at the least, not to injure the other party'. My own belief is that, in the present context, the common law is not antipathetic to concurrent liability, and that there is no sound basis for a rule which automatically restricts the claimant to either a tortious or a contractual remedy. The result may be untidy; but, given that the tortious duty is imposed by the general law, and the contractual duty is attributable to the will of the parties, I do not find it objectionable that the claimant may be entitled to take advantage of the remedy which is most advantageous to him, subject only to ascertaining whether the tortious duty is so inconsistent with the applicable contract that, in accordance with ordinary principle, the parties must be taken to have agreed that the tortious remedy is to be limited or excluded. . .

. . .In the present case liability can, and in my opinion should, be founded squarely on the principle established in *Hedley Byrne* itself, (see below, Ch.14) from which it follows that an assumption of responsibility coupled with the concomitant reliance may give rise to a tortious duty of care irrespective of whether there is a contractual relationship between the parties, and in consequence, unless his contract precludes him from doing so, the plaintiff, who has available to him concurrent remedies in contract and tort, may choose that remedy which appears to him to be the most advantageous."

In the above case (and in *Barclays Bank Plc v Fairclough Building Ltd*, below, Ch.19) the contractual and tortious duties to take care were assumed to be co-extensive; but the duty in tort imposed by *Hedley Byrne* on a party to a contract may sometimes be wider than his contractual obligation: *Holt v Payne Skillington (a Firm), The Times*, December 22, 1995, CA. In such a case the other contracting party might succeed in tort when he would fail in contract.

For further discussion of the relationship between contract and tort (in the context of A negligently performing a contract with B and, in consequence, causing financial loss to C), see Ch.12.

5. Does EC Law Impact on Contract Law?

1–011   The short answer to the question of whether EC law impacts on the contract law of England and Wales is: "Yes, it is increasingly the case that EC law impacts on the domestic contract law of member states, and particularly so in relation to the regulation of consumer contracts". Thus, from the 1980s onwards, in an attempt to standardise the groundrules for consumer contracting in the single European marketplace, Directives have been issued dealing with such particular matters as doorstep selling,[5]

---

[5]   Directive 85/577/EEC, repealed and replaced by Directive 2011/83/EU. In *Robertson v Swift* [2014] UKSC 50, the dispute hinged on the interpretation of the Cancellation of Contracts made in a Consumer's Home, or Place of Work etc Regulations 2008 (SI 2008/1816), these Regulations giving effect to Council Directive 85/577/EEC. Briefly, Robertson contracted with Swift to undertake some furniture removal work, but then decided that he was paying too much and cancelled the contract. Even though it was Robertson who contacted Swift to ask for a quotation for the work, the fact that the contract was made away from Swift's business premises (i.e., at Robertson's home) meant that the Regulations applied. Swift, having failed to supply a written notice of Robertson's right to cancel as required by the Regulations, was unable to enforce the cancellation charges provided for by the contract; and, for his part, Robertson was entitled to cancel and recover his deposit. Reading the Regulations literally it was arguable that, because no notice of the right to cancel had been served, the clock had not started to run on the 7-day cancellation period given to consumers. However, the Supreme Court rejected this argument saying that to "hold that the consumer did not have the right to cancel because the trader had not served written notice of the right to cancel would run directly counter to the overall purpose of the Directive in ensuring that a consumer has the opportunity to withdraw from a contract without suffering significant adverse consequences. The circumstances in which

consumer credit,[6] product liability,[7] package holidays,[8] unfair terms,[9] distance selling,[10] the sale of consumer goods and associated guarantees,[11] and, most recently, unfair commercial practices.[12]

With the exception of the Directive on Unfair Commercial Practices, each of the above-mentioned Directives seeks to harmonise the law by targeting a particular segment of contracting. This has created concerns about two forms of regulatory fragmentation: first, vertical fragmentation (within Directives and their implementation) and, secondly, horizontal fragmentation (across Directives). The former arises because minimum harmonisation Directives permit Member States who so wish to "gold-plate" their implementation above the prescribed floor of consumer rights; and the latter arises because sector specific Directives have been enacted without the benefit of any schematic or overarching guidance. As a result, rather than a single European market, we have what some deride as "27 mini-markets". One way forward—exemplified by the Unfair Commercial Practices Directive as well as the more recent Consumer Rights Directive[13]—is to use maximum (rather than minimum) harmonisation measures. Such measures are designed to prevent member states from increasing the level of consumer protection above the ceiling set by the Directive; but, this is a very substantial and controversial interference with national law-making power.[14] An alternative way forward is to stick with minimum harmonisation measures but, at the same time, to offer a standard European regime for *cross-border* contracts—and, indeed, this is the strategy adopted by the proposed Regulation on a Common European Sales Law.[15]

In addition to its programme of harmonising consumer contract law, for some years, the Commission has orchestrated a major debate about the possible development of a European code of contract law.[16] A so-called Common Frame of Reference (CFR), setting out a framework of principles, definitions, and model rules was elaborated by a pan-European group of contract scholars[17]; but the use to which the framework should be put remained unclear and contested. Some critics did not like the way that the CFR was developed, others objected to the substance of the principles, and others

---

the particular contract in this appeal was made and in which Dr Robertson sought to cancel it may be out of the ordinary. There may even be reason to suppose that Mr Swift, the owner of a small business, fared rather badly out of this transaction. But if the right to cancel could be effectively nullified by a failure (or refusal) of a trader to give written notice of the right to the consumer, this would create a considerable gap in the level of protection that the Directive sought to provide" (Lord Kerr at para.25).

[6] Directive 87/102/EEC, amended by 90/88/EEC and 98/7/EEC.

[7] Directive 85/374/EEC, implemented by the Consumer Protection Act 1987.

[8] Directive 90/314/EEC, implemented by the Package Travel, Package Holidays and Package Tours Regulations 1992, SI 1992/3288.

[9] Directive 93/13/EEC, currently implemented by the Unfair Terms in Consumer Contracts Regulations 1999, SI 1999/2083. For amendment to the reporting requirements, see Directive 2011/83/EU.

[10] Directive 97/7/EC implemented by the Consumer Protection (Distance Selling) Regulations 2000, SI 2000/2334, repealed and replaced by Directive 2011/83/EU.

[11] Directive 99/44/EC implemented by the Sale and Supply of Goods to Consumers Regulations 2002, SI 2002/3045. For amendment to the reporting requirements, see Directive 2011/83/EU.

[12] Directive 2005/29/EC, implemented by the Consumer Protection from Unfair Trading Regulations 2008, SI 2008/1277, amended by SI 2013/3134, SI 2014/549, and SI 2014/870. See, too, the joint report by the Law Commission and the Scottish Law Commission on *Consumer Redress for Misleading and Aggressive Practices* (March 2012, Cm 8323) (LAW COM No 332 and SCOT LAW COM No 226).

[13] 2011/83/EU.

[14] Compare the critical voices in Geraint Howells and Reiner Schulze (eds), *Modernising and Harmonising Consumer Contract Law* (Munich: Sellier, 2009).

[15] Proposal for a Regulation of the European Parliament and Council on a Common European Sales Law, COM(2011) 635 final (Brussels 11.10.2011).

[16] The Commission initiated the debate in 2001: see 'Communication from the Commission to the Council and the European Parliament on European Contract Law' COM (2001) 398 final (11 July 2001).

[17] C von Bar, E Clive, H Schulte-Nölke et al (eds), *Principles, Definitions and Model Rules of European Private Law, Draft Common Frame of Reference (DCFR), Outline Edition* (Munich: Sellier, 2009).

strenuously resisted any move towards mandatory imposition of the code.[18] After many twists and turns, it seems likely that the CFR will serve as background guidance (or "toolbox") for the development of *optional* codes that relate to *cross-border* contracts (that is to say, codes such as the proposed Regulation on Sales); and whatever momentum that there once might have been towards a regional code of contract law seems to have been lost.

6. DOES THE HUMAN RIGHTS ACT IMPACT ON CONTRACT LAW?

1-012   The Human Rights Act 1998 (HRA) seems to reach far and wide in the law. But, does the HRA have any application to contracts? Certainly, the Act applies to contracts made by public authorities (and, in some circumstances, to contracts made by bodies that, although private, are carrying out public functions). Accordingly, if the terms of such a contract are incompatible with any of the rights (such as the right to private and family life, the right to freedom of expression, or the like) that are protected by the European Convention on Human Rights (via the HRA), then the Act is relevant.

Where public authorities are not involved as contracting parties—in other words, where the contract is purely private in nature—one view is that the Act simply has no application. However, one of the first cases that fell to be decided under the Act, *Wilson v First County Trust* [2001] EWCA Civ 633; [2003] UKHL 40, suggests that the HRA cannot be dismissed so swiftly. In *Wilson*, the dispute was between private contracting parties, their agreement being regulated by the Consumer Credit Act 1974. How could the HRA possibly apply to such a loan agreement? For the Court of Appeal, the answer was simple: according to s.6(1) of the HRA, the court, as a public authority, should not act in a way that is incompatible with Convention rights. However, the House of Lords held that the Court of Appeal had fundamentally misdirected itself by giving the Act a retrospective application to a transaction that was entered into before the HRA was in force. As a result, the Court of Appeal's view on the s.6(1) requirement is not addressed head-on; but, for what it is worth, their Lordships did not reject the application of the Act simply because the disputants were contracting in a private capacity.

Where it is accepted that the HRA applies to a contract (whether with a public authority or between private parties), the next question is which of the Convention rights might be engaged. In *Wilson*, for example, it was claimed that s.127(3) of the Consumer Credit Act—providing that a court has no discretion to enforce a loan agreement where the debtor has not signed a document containing all the prescribed terms of the agreement—was incompatible with the *creditor's* art.6 right to a fair trial as well as the right to peaceful enjoyment of one's possessions (as provided for by art.1 of the First Protocol to the Convention); and, in *Nisshin Shipping Co Ltd v Cleaves & Co Ltd* (below, Ch.12), it is faintly (and unsuccessfully) argued that restrictions in the Contracts (Rights of Third Parties) Act 1999 infringe a third-party claimant's art.6 rights. Similarly, in *Copsey v WWB Devon Clays Ltd* [2005] EWCA Civ 932, it was accepted that, where an employer seeks to change the working hours and terms of his contract of employment with his employee in such a way as to interfere materially with the employee's right to manifest his religion, then art.9(1) of the Convention is potentially engaged.

If a Convention right is engaged, and if there is some incompatibility between the right so engaged and either the background law of contract or the particular terms of the contract, how is the law

---

[18]   For stiff opposition to the idea, see Gert Brüggemeir et al (the Study Group on Social Justice in European Private Law), 'Social Justice in European Contract Law: a Manifesto' (2004) 10 *European Law Journal* 653, where it is argued that the completion of the market is not a simple technocratic challenge; and HL European Union Committee, *European Contract Law—the Way Forward?* HL Paper 95 (London: TSO, April 5, 2005) in which there is much evidence of a concern that a European code of contract would be an unwelcome competitor to English law as the law of choice for international commercial contracts. Generally, see R. Brownsword, H. Micklitz, L. Niglia, and S. Weatherill (eds), *The Foundations of European Private Law* (Oxford: Hart, 2011).

to respond? In a case such as *Wilson*, where it is a legislative provision that is claimed to be non-compliant, the court should seek to "read down" the provision to render it compatible or, failing that, issue a declaration of incompatibility (as the Court of Appeal did in *Wilson*). Where the incompatibility resides in the particular nature or provisions of the contract, the court might declare the contract unenforceable as contrary to public policy[19] or it might be possible to bring the contract into line (particularly in relation to the rights protected by arts 8–11 of the Convention) by processes of implication or interpretation (especially in relation to employment contracts such as that in *Copsey*).

Finally, there is an unresolved question about the effect of a waiver, or an agreed exclusion or restriction of the benefit of a Convention right. Some such provisions may be black-listed as contrary to public policy. Others, however, may be valid provided that they satisfy a procedural test (i.e., to the effect that they were freely agreed) or a substantive justificatory test (i.e., that they are reasonable restrictions), or both (i.e., that they were both freely agreed and reasonable). On this, as on a number of other large questions concerning the impact of the HRA, we await judicial guidance.[20]

7. DOES THE LAW OF CONTRACT APPLY TO ONLINE TRANSACTIONS?

With the development of platforms for e-commerce, and with the growth of online dealing, one might wonder how far a body of law that was designed for off-line markets applies to sales that take place via eBay and the like. Interestingly, in the case of eBay, the founding intention was to keep things very informal, relying on community trust and good faith rather than the law. However, with the rapid growth of the site, it simply was not practical to proceed without some legal back-up (especially the back-up of the criminal law to counteract fraud). Elsewhere, governments, anxious that they should not miss out on the new business opportunities (especially for small businesses) presented by e-commerce, rushed to regulate online transactions. The immediate imperative was to make it clear that, in principle, online transactions were recognised as valid by the law of contract. In the event, having so clarified the law, e-commerce regulations typically make little further provision for online transactions, leaving it to traditional contract law to regulate remedies, interpretation, and the like. So, for example, art.9 of the EC Directive on Electronic Commerce[21] places member states under a duty not only to "ensure that their legal system allows contracts to be concluded by electronic means" but also, and in particular, to "ensure that the legal requirements applicable to the contractual process neither create obstacles for the use of electronic contracts nor result in such contracts being deprived of legal effectiveness and validity on account of their having been made by electronic means." As it is commonly put in this context, there needs to be an equivalence between the rules for off-line contracts and those for online contracts.

A much-debated area of uncertainty concerns the rules for formation of online contracts. In particular, where the parties communicate by emails, is this to be treated like a telephone conversation (such that acceptance is effective only on transmission and receipt) or like a land mail exchange (such that acceptance is effective on posting)? And, where a purchase is made by clicking through an online retail site, at what stage precisely is the contract formed?[22] Generally, these questions are of

1–013

---

[19] Compare, e.g., *Horwood v Millar's Timber and Trading Co Ltd* [1917] 1 K.B. 305.
[20] For a comprehensive discussion, see Roger Brownsword, *Contract Law: Themes for the Twenty-First Century*, 2nd edn (Oxford: Oxford University Press, 2006) Ch.10.
[21] Directive 2000/31/EC.
[22] For contrasting views, see, e.g., L. Davies, 'Contract Formation on the Internet: Shattering a Few Myths' in Lilian Edwards and Charlotte Waelde (eds) *Law and the Internet*, 1st edn (1997), 97; and Andrew Murray 'Entering into Contracts Electronically: The Real WWW' in Edwards and Waelde (eds) *Law and the Internet*, 2nd edn (2000), 17. See, too, *Chwee Kin Keong v Digilandmall.com Pte Ltd* [2004] 2 S.L.R. 594 (and, for comment, Andrew Phang (2005) 21 J.C.L. 97).

no great practical importance but, where the parties are located in different countries, the time and place at which the transaction was formed might be relevant to determining which body of contract law applies to the deal and which country's courts will accept jurisdiction to settle a dispute arising under the transaction. In this light, the decision of the House of Lords in *OFT v Lloyds TSB Bank Plc* [2007] UKHL 48 is of some significance because this confirms that the protection given to credit card holders by s.75(1) of the Consumer Credit Act 1974 applies to transactions made with overseas suppliers. Given that the majority of consumer online purchases are paid for by credit cards, it follows that consumers who use their credit cards to finance an online transaction that is within the range of minimum and maximum values covered by the Act will be able to seek recourse against their card companies rather than having to chase an overseas supplier against whom they have a claim for misrepresentation or breach of contract.

Finally, it is worth emphasising that, whether one is dealing online or off-line, the paper remedies given by the law of contract do not necessarily translate into practical real remedies. Where a claimant's co-contractor is a crook (as in the *Shogun Finance* case, above), in serious financial difficulty or insolvent (as in *Actionstrength*, above) or inconveniently located in some distant land, recourse to contract law is of limited practical value.

8. How Should the Cases be Read?

1–014   Traditionally, the advice to undergraduate students of the law of contract has been "to read the case, the whole case (meaning that students should not limit their reading to the headnote), and nothing but the case (meaning that potted summaries or nutshells should be avoided)." But, *how* should cases be read? To some considerable extent, this depends on the prior knowledge of the reader and the reader's particular reasons for reading the case. In the case of student readers, there will be little prior knowledge of the law and the reasons for reading the case will be to get to grips with the law and to gain some understanding of the thinking underlying the decisions. How should this class of readers proceed?

Alongside the traditional advice, student readers often will be given a standard checklist of points to be noted. The purpose of this checklist—a checklist, it should be said, that might be specified for reading a case in any area of law, not just in the law of contract—is to ensure that, having read the case, the student will be able to answer the following questions:

- In which court was the case decided? Was it a trial court (for example, the High Court) or an appeal court (for example, the Court of Appeal or, nowadays, the Supreme Court)?

- If the case was in an appeal court, was the decision of the court unanimous or was the court divided?

- What were the facts that led to the dispute?

- What were the questions of law that arose on those facts?

- How did the court rule on those questions of law?

- What were the reasons that were given in support of the rulings and what is the ratio decidendi of the case?

- What was the outcome of the case? Did the claimant/appellant or defendant/respondent win?

Some of these questions, particularly the first two and the last, are relatively straightforward to answer. Moreover, if the case is in an appeal court, there will usually be an accessible summary of the facts as found by the trial court, of the questions of law raised by the appeal, and (at some point) of the rulings made by the court in relation to the questions raised. However, where the judgments are quite discursive, or where different judges give different reasons for their decisions, the answer to the sixth question is going to be more complex and it will require some interpretation. Similarly, formulating the ratio of the case—in the sense of formulating a principle that best supports the decision and that can be applied to cases with materially similar facts in the future—requires some interpretative care.

While this traditional approach to reading cases continues to reflect mainstream law school thinking, some would consider it misguided. For example, commentators who are influenced by US Legal Realism might say that, because adjudication is result-orientated, the critical parts of the case are the facts and the outcome (i.e. which party wins); on this view, the legal reasoning that links the facts and the questions of law raised to the concluding rulings is no more than a legal rationalisation of an outcome already decided.[23] Some judges, according to this view, are disposed to favour the interests of certain classes of litigants—for example, in contract cases, the interests of consumers or those of business people—or to prioritise considerations of certainty in the law over considerations of individual justice, or vice versa; and so it is very important to know which judges are sitting in the case and to know what their dispositions are. Following this line of thinking, these factors are the keys not only to understanding what is happening in a particular case but also to being able to predict how future cases will come out. For example, if the culture of a particular appeal court is to give more weight to the "merits" of a claim than to the precedents, a legal realist will predict that a meritorious claimant will win even if the law is stacked against the claim. Even if we disagree with this radical view, or think that it is over-stated, there is no doubt that, in the development of the modern English law of contract, the influence of a handful of judges—notably Lord Denning, Lord Wilberforce, Lord Bingham, Lord Steyn and Lord Hoffmann—has been absolutely crucial.

Given the potential significance of a particular judge sitting in the case, should there be a further question on the checklist asking which judges heard the case? Students who are taking their first steps will have no difficulty in answering the question because the report of the case will state very clearly which judge or judges sat in the case. However, until students have quite a sophisticated appreciation of both adjudication and the law of contract, the significance of this information will not be appreciated.

Taking a less radical view, we might still question whether the traditional advice is sound. If students try heroically to learn the law by reading cases, *and only cases*, their early experience will be one of great frustration. They will spend long hours in the law library, surrounded by law reports, getting more and more confused. Possibly, there was a time when this was the best way of getting to grips with the law, but it makes little sense today when students can choose from any number of user-friendly textbooks that aim to make the basic rules and principles of the law accessible. Today, reading cases—indeed, even reading the whole case—is as important as ever; but students need to be much smarter about when, why, and how they read the cases.

First, it goes without saying that cases should be read *carefully*. Unless students are really going to concentrate on what they are reading, there is no point; they might as well stick with their textbook understanding of the law. The point of reading the case is not simply to tick it off the reading list; the point is to read it for oneself, to give the case one's own reading.

Secondly, it helps enormously if students can come to a case with a relevant *context*. Cases do not

---

[23]   See, e.g., Karl N Llewellyn, *The Common Law Tradition: Deciding Appeals* (Boston: Little, Brown, 1960).

come out of nowhere. The questions of law to be decided relate to some area of the law of contract—possibly to do with some point of formation, or third-party claims, or the interpretation of terms, or the assessment of damages, and so on. If a student already has a sense of the general principles that are in play in the relevant area of law, they will be able to locate the case in its particular doctrinal context—they should already have a good sense of the lie of the land. This is a bit like viewing a map in quite large scale before zooming in to take a more detailed look at some of the geography. It helps to know roughly where you are before immersing yourself in the details of the arguments presented, and reasons given, in the particular case.

The context is important, too, in indicating where the case stands in the development of the juris-prudence. Many of the cases in the contract law casebooks were decided in the nineteenth century. This was an important time for the formulation of general principles of the law of contract and many of these cases are seminal in setting the law on a particular track. By the twenty-first century, the principles established by these cases have been rehearsed and applied so many times that the cases themselves are largely of historical interest. Nevertheless, there is a good pedagogic case for insisting that reading these cases is a necessary part of any law student's education. Other cases, by contrast, are located in areas where the law is much less settled—for example, the House of Lords' decision in *Shogun Finance Limited v Hudson* that we considered at some length earlier in this chapter is the latest addition to a deeply unsettled line of cases on the effect of fraudulently-induced mistakes of identity. Yet other cases are at the cutting-edge of the jurisprudence, pushing the law in a particular direction. This is, so to speak, where the action is; these are the cases that will agitate tutors; and these are cases that need to be given high priority by student readers.

Thirdly, the cases should be read *critically*. Following on from the previous point, where there is pressure to modify the law, the court might decline to make any adjustment (compare the reluctance of the House of Lords in the *Actionstrength* case (above, para.1–003) to interfere with a statutory rule that is arguably dysfunctional) or it might tweak the law, or develop it in some way, or create some limited exception, and the like. Different readers might have different opinions about how far the law has moved on, if at all; and, indeed, about whether any movement in the law is desirable or not. Put very simply, while some readers will be extremely concerned if a case leaves matters unclear so that contractors no longer know quite where they stand, others will accept some lack of clarity if it gives the law the flexibility that it needs to respond to the merits of particular disputes. Of course, critical engagement with the case does not mean that one must take a negative view of the outcome or the reasoning; however, it does mean that, having read the case, the student will have the basis for taking their own position on the law.

In these characteristics of smart reading, we see the difference between a student who relies on the standard textbook exposition and one who engages carefully, contextually, and critically with the cases: the former makes no independent judgment, the latter does; the former has no personal take on the law, the latter does; the former is on track to pass, the latter, other things being equal, is on track to excel.

In the spirit of *careful, contextual, and critical* reading, what should we make of the following two illustrative cases: *Pharmaceutical Society of Great Britain v Boots Cash Chemists (Southern) LD* [1953] 1 Q.B. 401; and *Jet2.Com Limited v Blackpool Airport Limited* [2012] EWCA Civ 417?

We can start with the *Boots* case, a case that students typically meet early on in their contract courses. Although the case is significant for the law of contract, the Court of Appeal (hearing an appeal from the decision of Lord Goddard CJ) is not actually faced with a contract claim as such. Rather, the decision by Boots to convert its then traditional across-the-counter chemists' stores to modern supermarket-style stores raised a question about Boots' compliance with s.18(1)(a) of the Pharmacy and Poisons Act 1933 which requires listed poisons (such as strychnine and codeine) to be sold "by, or under the supervision of, a registered pharmacist". Where pharmacists sold drugs of this kind across the counter to customers, this clearly complied with the statutory requirements. However, where customers placed such drugs in their shopping baskets some time before getting to the cashier at the checkout, it was unclear where the sale took place, and it was unclear whether the pharmacist was in the right place at the right time. In order to answer these questions, the court needed to determine (as a matter of contract law) when the sale of relevant drugs took place in the new supermarket-style chemists' shop. Framing the question in the language of contract law, the court had to decide which party (the customer or the shop) was making the offer (to buy or to sell) and by whom and at what point the offer was accepted. As those students who read the case after having read the textbook account will know, the Court of Appeal upheld the decision handed down by Lord Goddard CJ to the effect that Boots were compliant with the statutory requirement. The court reasoned that the goods on display in the new supermarket-style shops were an "invitation to treat" (inviting customers to make an offer to buy), that customers made an offer to buy the goods in their baskets when they reached the cashier, and that, in response to the customer's offer to buy, Boots were in a position to accept or decline. Accordingly, where Boots accepted the offer made by a customer, the sale took place at the cashier's desk, at which point it was under the supervision of the registered pharmacist.

PHARMACEUTICAL SOCIETY OF GREAT BRITAIN V BOOTS CASH CHEMISTS (SOUTHERN) LTD

[1953] 1 Q.B. 401

The defendants' branch shop, consisting of a single room, was adapted to the "self-service" system. **1–015** The room contained chemist's department, under the control of a registered pharmacist, in which various drugs and proprietary medicines included, or containing substances included, in Part I of the Poisons List compiled under s.17(1) of the Pharmacy and Poisons Act, 1933, (but not in Sch. I to the Poisons Rules, 1949), were displayed on shelves in packages or other containers, with the price marked on each. A customer, on entering the shop, was provided with a wire basket, and having selected from the shelves the articles which he wished to buy, he put them in the basket and took them to the cashier's desk at one or other of the two exits, where the cashier stated the total price and received payment. That latter stage of every transaction involving the sale of a drug was supervised by the pharmacist in control of the department, who was authorized to prevent the removal of any drug from the premises.

In an action brought by the plaintiffs alleging an infringement by the defendants of s.18(1)(a)(iii) of the Pharmacy and Poisons Act, 1933, which requires the sale of poisons included in Part I of the Poisons List to be effected by or under the supervision of a registered pharmacist:

Held, that the self-service system did not amount to an offer by the defendants to sell, but merely to an invitation to the customer to offer to buy; that such an offer was accepted at the cashier's desk under the supervision of the registered pharmacist; and that there was therefore no infringement of the section.

Decision of Lord Goddard CJ [1952] 2 Q.B. 795; [1952] 2 T.L.R. 340; [1952] 2 All E.R. 456 affirmed.

Appeal from Lord Goddard CJ.

Special case stated by the parties under R.S.C., Ord. 34, r.1.

The defendants carried on a business comprising the retail sale of drugs at premises at Edgware, which were entered in the register of premises kept pursuant to section 12 of the Pharmacy and Poisons Act, 1933, and from which they regularly sold drugs by retail. The premises comprised a single room, so adapted that customers might serve themselves, and the business there was described by a printed notice at the entrance as "Boot's Self-Service." On entry each customer passed a barrier where a wire basket was obtained. Beyond the barrier the principal part of the room, which contained accommodation for 60 customers, contained shelves around the walls and on an island fixture in the centre, on which articles were displayed. One part of the room was described by a printed notice as the "Toilet Dept." and another part as the "Chemists' Dept." On the shelves in the chemists' department drugs, including proprietary medicines, were severally displayed in individual packages or containers with a conspicuous indication of the retail price of each. The drugs and proprietary medicines covered a wide range, and one section of the shelves in the chemists' department was devoted exclusively to drugs which were included in, or which contained substances included in, Part I of the Poisons List referred to in section 17 (1) of the Pharmacy and Poisons Act, 1933; no such drugs were displayed on any shelves outside the section, to which a shutter was fitted so that at any time all the articles in that section could be securely enclosed and excluded from display. None of the drugs in that section came within Sch. I to the Poisons Rules, 1949 (S.I. 1949, No. 539).

The staff employed by the defendants at the premises comprised a manager, a registered pharmacist, three assistants and two cashiers, and during the time when the premises were open for the sale of drugs the manager, the registered pharmacist, and one or more of the assistants were present in the room. Each customer selected from the shelves the article which he wished to buy and placed it in the wire basket; in order to leave the premises the customer had to pass by one of two exits, at each of which was a cash desk where a cashier was stationed who scrutinized the articles selected by the customer, assessed the value and accepted payment. The chemists' department was under the personal control of the registered pharmacist, who carried out all his duties at the premises subject to the directions of a superintendent appointed by the defendants in accordance with the provisions of section 9 of the Act.

The pharmacist was stationed near the poisons section, where his certificate of registration was conspicuously displayed, and was in view of the cash desks. In every case involving the sale of a drug the pharmacist supervised that part of the transaction which took place at the cash desk and was authorized by the defendants to prevent at that stage of the transaction, if he thought fit, any customer from removing any drug from the premises. No steps were taken by the defendants to inform the customers, before they selected any article which they wished to purchase, of the pharmacist's authorization.

On April 13, 1951, at the defendants' premises, two customers, following the procedure outlined above, respectively purchased a bottle containing a medicine known as compound syrup of hypophosphites, containing 0.01% W/V strychnine, and a bottle containing medicine known as famel syrup, containing 0.23% W/V codeine, both of which substances are poisons included in Part I of the Poisons List, but, owing to the small percentages of strychnine and codeine respectively, hypophosphites and famel syrup do not come within Sch. I to the Poisons Rules, 1949.

The question for the opinion of the court was whether the sales instanced on April 13, 1951, were effected by or under the supervision of a registered pharmacist, in accordance with the provisions of section 18 (1) (a) (iii) of the Pharmacy and Poisons Act, 1933.[24]

The Lord Chief Justice answered the question in the affirmative.

The Pharmaceutical Society appealed.

H. V. Lloyd-Jones Q.C.and T. Dewar for the Pharmaceutical Society. The real question at issue in this appeal is whether under the self-service system of trading devised by the defendants the sale in fact takes place at the point where the customer removes from the shelves the article that he wishes to buy, and puts it in the basket, or whether it takes place at the cash desk, where the money is paid and the pharmacist is stationed. We contend that the self-service system invites the customer to purchase, the price of each article being fully displayed, and that the taking of an article by the customer is an acceptance of the trader's offer to sell. Even if it be the law that a customer cannot demand goods merely because they are displayed in a shop window, the position is different where goods are displayed inside a self-service shop. It is submitted that the contract is made and the property passes at the moment when the customer takes an article from the shelf and puts it in the receptacle. [*Cheshire and Fifoot's Law of Contract*, 3rd ed., p. 26, and *Timothy v. Simpson*,[25] referred to.] In *Wiles v. Maddison*[26] a butcher was charged with offences against the Rationing Order, 1939, and the Meat (Maximum Retail Prices) Order, 1940, by offering meat for sale to registered customers at a price exceeding the maximum, and in excess of the rationing quantity. He was acquitted, although he had put aside the

---

[24] Pharmacy and Poisons Act 1933 s.18: "(1) . . . it shall not be lawful—(a) for a person to sell any poison included in Part I of the Poisons List, unless—(i) he is an authorized seller of poisons; and (ii) the sale is effected on premises duly registered under Part I of this Act; and (iii) the sale is effected by, or under the supervision of, a registered pharmacist."

[25] (1834) 6 C. & P. 499.

[26] [1943] W.N. 40; [1943] 1 All E.R. 315, 317.

meat, with the price affixed, because the customers had given no specific orders for the meat and he had not intended to deliver it until the following day. In the words of Lord Caldecote C.J., "the facts were not such as to justify or permit a finding that there had been an offer." Tucker J., agreeing, said: "or myself, I think that the position might be different if the course of conduct between the butcher and the customer in this case had been different, that is to say, if the evidence had been that the custom was for the butcher to put . . . in his shop certain quantities of meat allocated to certain customers at certain prices and if the practice had been for the customers to call on a particular day and take away the meat." In the present case, by their deliberately devised self-service system the defendants are making an offer to sell, and the customer, when he takes an article from the shelf and puts It in the receptacle, is accepting the offer. By section 17 (2) of the Sale of Goods Act, 1893, the property in goods passes when it is intended to pass, and here there is clearly an intention that the sale shall take place at the spot where the customer takes the article from the shelf. The intention of the legislature under the Act of 1933 was to interpose the possibility of guidance or veto on the part of the pharmacist when a customer is selecting poisons, and even though at the time of payment the pharmacist is present, the sales In question, it is submitted, were not effected in accordance with the provisions of section 18.

[*Roberts v. Littlewood's Mail Order Stores*[27] also referred to.]

G. G. Baker Q.C. and G. D. Everington for the defendants were not called on to argue.

SOMERVELL LJ

This is an appeal from a decision of the Lord Chief Justice on an agreed statement of facts, raising a question under section 18 (1) (a) (iii) of the Pharmacy and Poisons Act, 1933. The plaintiffs are the Pharmaceutical Society, incorporated by Royal charter. One of their duties is to take all reasonable steps to enforce the provisions of the Act. The provision in question is contained in section 18.

[His Lordship read the section and stated the facts, and continued:] It is not disputed that in a chemist's shop where this self-service system does not prevail a customer may go in and ask a young woman assistant, who will not herself be a registered pharmacist, for one of these articles on the list, and the transaction may be completed and the article paid for, although the registered pharmacist, who will no doubt be on the premises, will not know anything himself of the transaction, unless the assistant serving the customer, or the customer, requires to put a question to him. It is right that I should emphasize, as did the Lord Chief Justice, that these are not dangerous drugs. They are substances which contain very small proportions of poison, and I imagine that many of them are the type of drug which has a warning as to what doses are to be taken. They are drugs which can be obtained, under the law, without a doctor's prescription.

The point taken by the plaintiffs is this: it is said that the purchase is complete if and when a customer going round the shelves takes an article and puts it in the receptacle which he or she is carrying, and that therefore, if that is right, when the customer comes to the pay desk, having completed the tour of the premises, the registered pharmacist, if so minded, has no power to say: "This drug ought not to be sold to this customer." Whether and in what circumstances he would have that power we need not inquire, but one can, of course, see that there is a difference if supervision can only be exercised at a time when the contract is completed.

I agree with the Lord Chief Justice in everything that he said, but I will put the matter shortly in my own words. Whether the view contended for by the plaintiffs is a right view depends on what are the legal implications of this layout—the invitation to the customer. Is a contract to be regarded as being completed when the article is put into the receptacle, or is this to be regarded as a more organized way of doing what is done already in many types of shops—and a bookseller is perhaps the best example—namely, enabling customers to have free access to what is in the shop, to look at the different articles, and then, ultimately, having got the ones which they wish to buy, to come up to the assistant saying "I want this"? The assistant in 999 times out of 1,000 says "That is all right," and the money passes and the transaction is completed. I agree with what the Lord Chief Justice has said, and with the reasons which he has given for his conclusion, that in the case of an ordinary shop, although goods are displayed and it is intended that customers should go and choose what they want, the contract is not completed until, the customer having indicated the articles which he needs, the shopkeeper, or someone on his behalf, accepts that offer. Then the contract is completed. I can see no reason at all, that being clearly the normal position, for drawing any different implication as a result of this layout.

The Lord Chief Justice, I think, expressed one of the most formidable difficulties in the way of the plaintiffs' contention when he pointed out that, if the plaintiffs are right, once an article has been placed in the receptacle

---

[27]   [1943] K.B. 269.

the customer himself is bound and would have no right, without paying for the first article, to substitute an article which he saw later of a similar kind and which he perhaps preferred. I can see no reason for implying from this self-service arrangement any implication other than that which the Lord Chief Justice found in it, namely, that it is a convenient method of enabling customers to see what there is and choose, and possibly put back and substitute, articles which they wish to have, and then to go up to the cashier and offer to buy what they have so far chosen. On that conclusion the case fails, because it is admitted that there was supervision in the sense required by the Act and at the appropriate moment of time. For these reasons, in my opinion, the appeal should be dismissed.

BIRKETT LJ

I am of the same opinion. The facts are clearly stated in the agreed statement of facts, and the argument on them has been very clearly stated by Mr. Lloyd-Jones. I think that clearest of all was the judgment of the Lord Chief Justice, with which I agree. In view of an observation which I made during the argument, I should like to add that under section 25 of the Pharmacy and Poisons Act, 1933, it is the duty of the Pharmaceutical Society of Great Britain, by means of inspection and otherwise, "to take all reasonable steps to enforce the provisions of Part I of this Act"—that really deals with the status of the registered pharmacist—"and to secure compliance by registered pharmacists and authorized sellers of poisons with the provisions of Part II of this Act." This action has been brought by the Pharmaceutical Society in pursuance of that duty which is laid upon them by statute, and the short point of the case is, at what point of time did the sale in this particular shop at Edgware take place? My Lord has explained the system which had been introduced into that shop in March of 1951. The two women customers in this case each took a particular package containing poison from the particular shelf, put it into her basket, came to the exit and there paid. It is said, on the one hand, that when the customer takes the package from the poison section and puts it into her basket the sale there and then takes place. On the other hand, it is said the sale does not take place until that customer, who has placed that package in the basket, comes to the exit.

The Lord Chief Justice dealt with the matter in this way, and I would like to adopt his words[28] : "It seems to me, therefore, that the transaction is in no way different from the normal transaction in a shop in which there is no self-service scheme. I am quite satisfied it would be wrong to say that the shopkeeper is making an offer to sell every article in the shop to any person who might come in and that that person can insist on buying any article by saying 'I accept your offer.'" Then he went on to deal with the illustration of the bookshop, and continued: "Therefore, in my opinion, the mere fact that a customer picks up a bottle of medicine from the shelves in this case does not amount to an acceptance of an offer to sell. It is an offer by the customer to buy and there is no sale effected until the buyer's offer to buy is accepted by the acceptance of the price. The offer, the acceptance of the price, and therefore the sale take place under the supervision of the pharmacist. That is sufficient to satisfy the requirements of the section, for by using the words 'the sale is effected by, or under the supervision of, a registered pharmacist' the Act envisages that the sale may be effected by someone not a pharmacist. I think, too, that the sale is effected under his supervision if he is in a position to say 'You must not have that: that contains poison', so that in any case, even if I were wrong in the view that I have taken on the question as to when the sale was completed, and it was completed when the customer took the article from the shelf, it would still be effected under the supervision of the pharmacist within the meaning of section 18."

I agree with that, and I agree that this appeal ought to be dismissed.

ROMER LJ

I also agree. The Lord Chief Justice observed that, on the footing of the plaintiff society's contention, if a person picked up an article, once having picked it up, he would never be able to put it back and say that he had changed his mind. The shopkeeper would say: "No, the property has passed and you will have to pay." If that were the position in this and similar shops, and that position was known to the general public, I should imagine that the popularity of those shops would wane a good deal. In fact, I am satisfied that that is not the position, and that the articles, even though they are priced and put in shops like this, do not represent an offer by the shopkeeper which can be accepted merely by the picking up of the article in question. I quite agree with the reasons on which the Lord Chief Justice arrived at that conclusion and which Birkett L.J. has just referred to, and to those observations I can add nothing of my own. I agree that the appeal fails.

Representation

Solicitors: A. C. Castle; Masons.

---

[28]   [1952] 2 Q.B. 795, 802.

Appeal dismissed. Leave to appeal to House of Lords refused.

Having read the case, there are several aspects of the court's reasoning that might engage a critical reader.

First, all the judges seem to be persuaded that, if the display of goods were to be treated as an offer, and if the act by the customer of putting a particular item in their basket were to be treated as an acceptance, then this would be exceedingly inconvenient for shoppers. Let us concede that, if this were the legal position, it would involve some inconvenience. Only recently, I was re-assured by a shop assistant who clearly knew the legal position that, if I used a basket (as the shop encouraged customers to do), it did not mean that I was bound to buy every item that I placed in the basket. Nevertheless, why should we treat the customer's act of putting an item in the basket as the relevant act of acceptance? Why not delay the act of acceptance until the customer presents the goods to the cashier at the checkout—or even to the point when payment is about to be made by the customer? On this alternative analysis, there would be no risk of inconvenience to the customer and the sale would take place under the supervision of the pharmacist.

Secondly, why does Somervell LJ think it relevant to start by highlighting that traditional across-the-counter sales routinely take place without the registered pharmacist being aware that a sale has taken place? The implication is that, in practice, the requirement that the sale should take place 'under the supervision of' a registered pharmacist is not interpreted strictly and that it will suffice if a registered pharmacist is on the premises. If this is Somervell LJ's point, then Boots' new layout would probably be compliant whether the sale occurred when a customer took the drugs off the shelf and put them in her basket or when the customer presented the goods at the checkout. On this view, the importance of determining the point of sale would not be whether or not Boots were compliant with the statutory requirements; it would simply be a matter of coming up with an analysis that would not cause inconvenience (which is, indeed, a key consideration for the court).

Thirdly, the case is argued on the basis that "the normal position", as Somervell LJ puts it, is that the customer makes the offer. This means that the burden is on the Pharmaceutical Society to show why there should be a departure from the normal position. They might have argued that most people think, contrary to the law, that the normal position is that goods displayed in shop windows or on supermarket shelves are on offer (at the stated prices) and that customers accept the offer made by the store. However, as we can see from the outline arguments of counsel (Lloyd-Jones and Dewar) for the Pharmaceutical Society, they suggested that there is a distinction between goods displayed in a shop window and goods displayed inside a self-service shop—presumably (although the report does not explicitly confirm this) because, in the latter case, the customer can usually take possession of the goods without the intervention of the seller, this further reinforcing the non-lawyer's impression that the goods are being offered for sale. The Court, however, shows no interest in aligning the analysis of offer and acceptance with ordinary expectations and relies on the argument about inconvenience to stick with the normal position.

Fourthly, giving the case a realist reading, we might say that it was obvious that Boots would win this case. Appeal Court judges of the time were sufficiently attuned to commerce to see that supermarket and self-service stores were clearly something for the future and to understand that their development should not be held up by 'nice' points of the kind tested in the case. To be sure, it was not obvious quite how the court would square the circle and say that the sale of listed drugs took place under the supervision of a registered pharmacist; but there were a number of ways of doing this and the particular option taken by the court is a relatively unimportant detail. In other words, the realist reading would treat the principle for which the *Boots* case stands as no more than a footnote—the headline story is about contract law functioning to facilitate commerce.

Finally, as supermarket stores further evolve, so that customers are encouraged to do their own checkout, we might wonder how the *Boots* analysis works where customers do not deal with a human cashier. Somervell LJ rightly says that, in practice, human cashiers process the sale without question in 999 cases out of a 1,000. When this happens 1,000 times out of a 1,000 at a self-serve checkout, does it still make sense to treat the customer as making an offer to buy? And, in practice, how often does this really matter?

Turning to the second illustrative case, *Jet2.Com Limited v Blackpool Airport Limited* [2012] EWCA Civ 417, it is apparent that this is not only a more modern case, it is in a more accessible format. At the top of the *Jet2.Com* case, readers are given the so-called neutral citation number of the case (viz [2012] EWCA Civ 417); they are told that the report is of an appeal to the Court of Appeal (Civil Division) from the High Court (the neutral citation number of the High Court decision is also given: viz, [2011] EWHC 1529 (Comm)); they are told that the case was argued before Lord Justice Longmore, Lord Justice Moore-Bick, and Lord Justice Lewison; that it was between Jet2.Com Limited, the claimant/respondent, and Blackpool Airport Limited, the defendant/appellant; and they are given the names of the lawyers who represented the parties as well as the hearing dates. We then have the three judgments given in the appeal, starting with the judgment handed down by Lord Justice Moore-Bick.

However, before we read the judgments, what might a student reader already know about the context of this case? Quite possibly, the textbooks will not have paid a great deal of attention to this case. The traditional story that is told about the law of contract will say that agreements will fail for uncertainty if the parties have not specified their respective obligations with sufficient precision, the implicit assumption being that the parties can always be clear and precise and that a failure to do so is simply due to a lack of care and attention. However, in many business relationships it is not possible to nail down the parties' obligations in this way; rather, the agreement expresses a requirement of the kind that we find in the *Jet2.Com* case, namely that the parties will cooperate and use "best endeavours" to promote Jet2.Com's low-cost airline operation at Blackpool Airport. Traditionalists can quickly condemn provisions of this kind as being too vague to be enforced; but, if contract law is to track the kinds of deals that businesspeople actually make, then it needs to respond more constructively to these declarations of cooperative intention. So, at one level, *Jet2.Com* is simply another case that decides whether and how a "best endeavours" clause should be enforced; but, at another level, the case is emblematic of several fault lines that run through the modern law. We can return to this deeper question after the judgments in the case have been read.

Jet2.Com Limited v Blackpool Airport Limited

[2012] EWCA Civ 417

LORD JUSTICE MOORE-BICK :

Background

1-016   1. The appellant, Blackpool Airport Ltd ("BAL"), owns and operates a commercial airport on the outskirts of Blackpool. The respondent, Jet2.com Ltd ("Jet2"), is a low-cost airline operating out of a number of domestic airports offering flights to various United Kingdom and European destinations. BAL is currently 95% owned by Balfour Beatty Plc, but until 2008 it was owned by City Hopper Airports Ltd ("City Hopper"), a company which owned a number of smaller airports from which low-cost airlines operated.

2. In September 2005 BAL, City Hopper and Jet2 signed a document described as a Letter Agreement setting out the terms on which Jet2 would operate from Blackpool over the course of the following 15 years. The agreement provided that Jet2 and BAL would co-operate to promote Jet2's low-cost services from Blackpool

and set out the terms on which BAL would provide ground services and marketing support for Jet2's business. Jet2 proposed to begin a service between Blackpool and Belfast as soon as practicable, to base an aircraft at Blackpool from March 2006 and to build its fleet at Blackpool in accordance with demand.

3. Under the legislation governing the licensing of airports the licence holder is required to notify the Civil Aviation Authority of the hours between which the airport is open for business to anyone who wishes to use it. In the case of Blackpool these were 7.00 a.m. to 9.00 p.m. local time throughout the year. For convenience I shall refer to these as the "normal opening hours". There is nothing to prevent an airport from opening outside those hours by agreement with airline operators, provided the Civil Aviation Authority is informed of any arrangements made for that purpose.

4. For over four years from March 2006 Jet2 operated flights out of Blackpool in accordance with schedules submitted to and accepted by BAL, under which there were regular arrivals and departures outside normal opening hours. Keeping an airport open outside normal opening hours inevitably causes the operator to incur additional costs in providing support services. Blackpool Airport has apparently never made a profit, at any rate during the years up to and including 2010, and in 2010 BAL became increasingly concerned at the costs that were being incurred as a result of aircraft movements taking place outside normal opening hours. Relations between the parties became increasingly strained until eventually, on 22nd October 2010, BAL told Jet2 that from midnight on 29th October it would not accept departures or arrivals scheduled outside normal opening hours. As a result, two of Jet2's flights were diverted from Blackpool to Manchester at short notice causing considerable inconvenience to passengers and expense to Jet2.

5. In response Jet2 brought proceedings against BAL seeking damages for breach of contract and a declaration that under the Letter Agreement it was obliged to accept aircraft movements outside normal opening hours. It also obtained an interim injunction against BAL, the effect of which was to require BAL to handle aircraft movements over the winter season 2010-2011 broadly in accordance with the flight schedules agreed for the winter season the previous year. At the conclusion of the trial the judge held that BAL was in breach of contract in refusing to handle flights outside normal opening hours, but he declined to grant Jet2 the declaration it sought. BAL now appeals against the judge's decision.

The Letter Agreement

6. The Letter Agreement takes the form of a letter dated 23rd September 2005 from Jet2 to BAL and City Hopper, which was counter-signed by representatives of both addressees to indicate their agreement. The opening paragraph and clauses 1 and 2 are of most relevance to the present appeal. They provide as follows:

"This Letter Agreement sets out the terms of the agreement between Blackpool Airport Limited . . . and City Hopper Airports Limited . . . and Channel Express (Air Services) Limited . . . trading as Jet2.com . . . in relation to low cost services from and to Blackpool Airport (BA).

1. Jet2.com and BAL will co-operate together and use their best endeavours to promote Jet2.com's low cost services from BA and BAL will use all reasonable endeavours to provide a cost base that will facilitate Jet2.com's low cost pricing.

Jet2.com proposes to commence a service between Belfast International Airport and BA as soon as practicable and to base one B737-300 aircraft, or its equivalent, at BA from the commencement of the Summer operating season, 26 March, 2006, and to operate and build its fleet at BA in accordance with demand for an initial period of 15 years from the date of the first service by Jet2.com from BA and the terms set out in this Letter Agreement will, except as otherwise stated, apply for the 15 year period.

Not later than three months prior to the expiry of such initial period of 15 years, senior representatives of the parties of this letter agreement will meet in good faith to review and agree a new Charging Scheme which will enable Jet2.com to continue to develop its base at BA and increase its low cost services from BA.

2. In consideration of the investment that Jet2.com is making in offering such services from BA, BAL will make available the following pricing and other benefits to Jet2.com in relation to BA:

(a) (i) BAL will levy airport charges on Jet2.com on the basis of the Charging Scheme as set out in Appendix A for the initial period of 15 years commencing on the date of Jet2.com's first flight from BA. These charges include all BAL's aircraft movement, handling and passenger charges to Jet2.com including landing, navigation, marshalling etc., parking, passenger facilities charges, passenger security charges, security, baggage x-ray and security screening, baggage handling, bussing, CUTE and check-in desk charges.

. . .

(b) BAL will provide a contribution towards Jet2.com's marketing expenditure to be calculated in accordance with Schedule B, such payment to be paid quarterly in arrears following Jet2.com's first flight of its BA based aircraft.

(c) BAL will arrange for prominent Airport advertising at BA of Jet2.com's low cost product and its destinations, together with frequent promotional facilities at such sites as BA controls and will facilitate editorial and news coverage of Jet2.com's activities in its magazines and with newspapers, all at no cost to Jet2.com.
(d) BAL and Jet2 will mount joint PR promotions with the aim of promoting and enhancing BAL and Jet2.com's operations to the general public."

Paragraphs (e) to (m) set out other obligations undertaken by BAL in the provision of airport services of various kinds.

7. Before the judge Jet2 argued that the obligation imposed on both parties by clause 1 to use their best endeavours to promote Jet2's low-cost services obliged BAL to handle its arrivals and departures between 6.00 a.m. and midnight and to do its best to accommodate occasional movements outside those hours. BAL argued that its obligation was limited to promoting Jet2's services in the sense of advertising and marketing them, that the agreement was silent about the hours during which it would accept aircraft movements and that it was under no obligation to accept movements outside normal opening hours. It also argued that it was entitled to take into account its own commercial interests when deciding what steps to take in the exercise of its best endeavours to promote Jet2's services. It was not obliged to handle aircraft movements outside normal opening hours if the additional revenue it obtained did not cover the cost of doing so.

8. The judge heard a good deal of evidence about the background to the agreement and about the economics of operating a low-cost airline. He made the following findings:

"23. Blackpool is a small regional airport with published opening hours which provide for other hours only by agreement. The cost of opening the airport to service a single flight greatly exceeds the revenue which the operation will generate. The low cost services described in the Agreement would have been seen by the parties in 2005 as requiring flexibility in scheduling early departures and late arrivals. This is so particularly during the peak summer season when maximum utilisation of aircraft is required on flying days. This requirement is obvious and is also supported, for example, by a document produced by the European Low Fares Airlines Association. The need for a low cost and flexible base for Jet2.com was also identified by BAL in presentations made to Jet2 in 2004 and 2005 before the Agreement was entered into. The need for flexibility increases where an airline has aircraft based at the airport because there are significant costs associated with diverting aircraft crews and support services from one airport to another. As both parties knew from, for example, the list of destinations used in BAL's presentations to Jet2 the services would be primarily to summer sun destinations.

24. At some time in 2005 BAL produced the "Master Plan Passenger Forecast 2005 to 2030" described as a "methodology and output for the long-term forecasts developed as part of the Blackpool International Airport master planning process". BAL witnesses sought to play down the significance of this document and argue that as it was a document which Jet2 did not see at the time it is not part of the matrix. Mr Orrell described the master plan as a "very aspirational document", Mr Spooner said it was simply a "statement of ambition". Although neither was around at the time that may well be right. But the document does contain indications that assumptions made by Jet2 were shared at the time within BAL. Thus "based aircraft need to depart between 0600 and 0730 in order to keep utilisation high but operate within a two crew roster; which in turn creates additional pressures on runway capacity on a morning peak." It is pointed out that "typically, low-cost airlines look to achieve around twelve hours airborne per unit per day, four rotations or sectors using two sets of crew".

25. Obtaining "slots" to visit high summer demand destinations is competitive and those available to Jet2 would often be outside peak hours. It would be known to both parties that allocation of slots is often 'grandfathered' in favour of those who have operated the longest. Furthermore because of the distance to some of those destinations and the commercial requirement to operate two or three rotations each day, early and late departures and arrivals might well be necessary. The direct first hand experience of Mr Ward of Jet2 was more convincing than the less detailed and more anecdotal evidence put forward by BAL.

26. At the time the Agreement was being negotiated both Ryanair and Monarch were operating scheduled services at Blackpool outside BAL's promulgated opening hours.

27. Unforeseen delays are a fact of life in air travel.

28. This picture would be of no surprise to any member of the public who has struggled to stay awake at an airport early in the morning or late in the evening when going to or returning from holiday."

9. In the light of that factual background the judge held that the word "promote" had been used in clause 1 of the Letter Agreement to mean "advance" in a general sense, rather than merely to advertise and market; that

the provision of "a cost base that [would] facilitate Jet 2's low-cost pricing" meant providing facilities and services that would enable low-cost pricing; that the absence of an express provision about opening hours suggested that it was too obvious to need mentioning that Jet2, like its competitors at Blackpool, would not be confined to normal opening hours; and that the object to which the parties were obliged to direct their best endeavours included securing flexible working hours extending beyond normal opening hours. As to best endeavours, he held that BAL did not have complete freedom to consult its own commercial interests, but he was acutely conscious that the obligation to provide a low cost base was not absolute and that the exercise of best endeavours had to be judged in the light of events as they occurred. For that reason he was unwilling to grant a declaration in the terms sought by Jet2, but he did hold that BAL was in breach of contract in October 2010 in refusing to handle Jet2's flights outside normal opening hours.

10. On behalf of BAL Mr. George Leggatt Q.C. submitted that clause 1 of the Letter Agreement was not intended to create legally enforceable obligations of any kind. He likened it to a preamble in which the parties described in general terms the intent and purpose of the detailed provisions contained in clause 2 and the two appendices. He emphasised that Jet2 had not entered into an enforceable obligation to build up its fleet at Blackpool and submitted that it would be surprising in those circumstances if BAL had entered into an obligation to keep the airport open for Jet2's operations between particular hours, or at all, for a period of 15 years. The absence of any reference to opening hours was, he submitted, a strong indication that it was not a matter within the scope of the agreement. He argued that the Letter Agreement was analogous to a tariff of charges which would remain available to Jet2 for a period of 15 years. The parties contemplated no more than that flights would be handled in accordance with schedules agreed between Jet2 and BAL from time to time, as indeed happened.

11. On behalf of Jet2 Mr. Philip Shepherd Q.C. relied heavily on the nature of the low-cost airline business in support of his submission that the parties had taken it for granted that Jet2 would need to schedule aircraft movements outside normal opening hours and that, in the performance of its obligation to use best endeavours to promote Jet2's business, BAL would ensure that it could so.

The nature and scope of the agreement

12. Perhaps the first point to note is that the Letter Agreement does not read like a mere tariff of charges, nor does clause 1 read like a mere preamble or statement of aspirations. On the contrary, in my view the language of the opening paragraph makes it quite clear that the intention of the parties was to enter into a binding agreement on the terms that follow. Insofar as the clauses of the agreement call for a preamble to set them in context, the opening paragraph provides it and does so in terms that are inconsistent with the suggestion that clause 1 was intended to be nothing more than a statement of the parties' aspirations. Each of the numbered clauses, apart from the second (unnumbered) paragraph of clause 1, is couched in language of a kind that indicates an intention to create binding obligations. Whether the language is apt in all cases to achieve that object, and, if so, with what effect, may be open to argument, but I do not myself doubt that the parties intended that each paragraph should give rise to one or more obligations in accordance with its terms. The fact that the agreement was expressed to continue in effect for 15 years is not in my view inconsistent with an intention to enter into binding obligations once one recognises the nature and scale of the investment involved in basing one or more aircraft at Blackpool and building up a business that was hoped and expected to be profitable to both parties. The more difficult question concerns the nature and content of whatever obligations are created by clause 1.

13. It is convenient first to consider what the parties meant by the use of the word "promote" and the expression "provide a cost base that will facilitate Jet2.com's low cost pricing" in that context. The word "promote" may carry various shades of meaning. Mr. Shepherd submitted that it is used here in the general sense of "advance" and is apt to cover any steps designed to lead to the growth of Jet2's business. Mr. Leggatt submitted that it has the narrower meaning of "market" and points to the use of the expressions "promotional facilities", "promotions" and "promoting" in clauses 2(c) and (d), both of which are concerned with advertising and marketing. He submitted that the parties are likely to have used the word in the same sense in clause 1.

14. I am not particularly impressed by the argument from consistency of use. This was a document apparently drafted by the parties themselves, probably without the benefit of legal advice. Clause 1 is worded in broad terms, as Mr. Leggatt often reminded us, and was intended to express the parties' intentions on a broad scale. In those circumstances I do not think that the narrower meaning of the word is to be preferred. The fact that the same or similar words are used in a narrower sense in the context of the more specific provisions of clauses 2(c) and (d) does not point strongly to an intention to adopt the same narrower meaning in the rather different context of clause 1. Although clause 1 no doubt looks forward to clause 2, its horizons are in my view much wider. I think the judge was right in his construction of the word "promote" and that in this instance it bears the broader meaning of "advance".

15. I find the expression "use all reasonable endeavours to provide a cost base that will facilitate Jet2.com's low cost pricing" rather more difficult to interpret. The natural meaning of the expression is that BAL would do its best to ensure that charges made for ground services would support Jet2's low-cost pricing model, but since the parties had agreed the charges payable by Jet2 in clause 2(a)(i) and Appendix A (and, insofar as they were not covered by Appendix A, by adopting BAL's standard conditions of use), it cannot have that meaning. The cost base of any business is linked to the use it can obtain from its assets. In the case of an airline the unit cost of tickets reflects, among other things, the number of seats filled and the number of round trips the aircraft can make each day. I think this (admittedly somewhat opaque) phrase was probably intended to impose on BAL an obligation to use all reasonable endeavours to enable Jet2 to keep its unit costs (and therefore ticket prices) down by using the aircraft in the most efficient manner. That is consistent in commercial terms with the earlier obligation to promote Jet2's services.

16. This brings me to the question at the heart of the appeal, namely, whether by virtue of clause 1 of the Letter Agreement BAL was under an obligation to accept arrivals and departure of Jet2's aircraft in October 2010 outside normal opening hours. It is necessary to consider the matter in those terms because it was not argued before the judge that the acceptance by BAL of the winter 2010 schedule was itself sufficient to give rise to an enforceable agreement to accept aircraft movements in accordance with it. Jet2 contended that the obligation arose under clause 1; BAL denied that the clause gave rise to any obligation, but argued that, if it did, the obligation was no more than to use best or all reasonable endeavours (which it was agreed meant the same thing), which did not oblige it to act contrary to its commercial interests.

17. There was a good deal of evidence before the judge to support his finding that low-cost airlines depend on being able to obtain maximum use of their aircraft and that that in turn means operating schedules under which aircraft movements occur early in the morning and late at night. In 2005 other low-cost airlines, notably Ryanair and Monarch, were operating out of Blackpool and it was common for planes to arrive and depart outside normal opening hours. In early 2005 BAL published a revised schedule of charges which included Out of Hours Surcharges for aircraft movements outside normal opening hours calculated by reference to the demands imposed by the aircraft involved. Those surcharges covered the periods between 9.00 p.m. and 10.00 p.m. and between 10.00 p.m. and 7.00 a.m. respectively in respect of which different rates applied. The very publication of the surcharges suggests that aircraft movements outside normal opening hours were commonplace, a conclusion borne out by the judge's findings. Indeed, the judge found that it was too obvious to need mentioning that the movements of Jet2's aircraft, like those of its competitors at Blackpool, would not be confined to normal opening hours.

18. Mr. Leggatt submitted that the first paragraph of clause 1 of the Letter Agreement was too uncertain in its content to give rise to any obligation enforceable in law. In general an obligation to use best endeavours, or all reasonable endeavours, is not in itself regarded as too uncertain to be enforceable, provided that the object of the endeavours can be ascertained with sufficient certainty: see, for example, *R. & D. Construction Ltd v Hallam Land Management Ltd* [2010] CSIH 96, to which I shall refer in more detail later. It is necessary, therefore, to concentrate on the two objects identified in that paragraph, namely, the promotion of Jet2's low cost services and the provision of a cost base that would facilitate Jet2's low cost pricing.

19. Mr. Leggatt submitted that neither object was defined with the degree of certainty that enabled the obligation to be enforced and he cautioned against proceeding on the basis that although the scope of the obligation was uncertain, it was possible to say that certain conduct did or did not involve a breach of it. He also submitted that even if the obligation was capable of enforcement, it did not require BAL to act contrary to its own commercial interests.

20. In support of his submissions he drew the court's attention to a number of cases in which the courts have considered the effect of an obligation to use reasonable or best endeavours. The first was *Sheffield District Railway Co. v Great Central Railway Co.* (1911) 27 T.L.R. 451, a decision of the Rail and Canal Commissioners chaired by A.T. Lawrence J. In that case the Sheffield District Railway ("the Sheffield") had entered into an arrangement with the Lancashire, Derbyshire and East Coast Railway ("the Derbyshire") for the operation of a short line with two stations by means of which traffic gained access to Sheffield. The Derbyshire was originally a competitor of the Great Central Railway which had many more stations and arranged for goods to be carted to and from its own stations rather than being left to use the stations of its competitors. The Derbyshire subsequently amalgamated with the Great Central Railway which took over the operation of the Sheffield on the terms in force between it and the Derbyshire. These included an obligation to use best endeavours to develop the Sheffield's traffic. Following the amalgamation the Great Central continued to act as it had before, with the result that goods which could have been taken to or from one of the Sheffield's stations were instead taken to or from one of the Great Central's stations. The Sheffield complained that the Great Central was in breach of the obligation to use its beast endeavours to develop its traffic. The Commissioners held that the words imposed

on the Great Central an obligation to leave no stone unturned, within the bounds of reason, to develop the Sheffield's traffic. The object of the endeavours was not considered too uncertain to be capable of enforcement.

21. The next case to which Mr. Leggatt referred was *Terrell v Mabie Todd and Co. Ltd* [1952] 2 T.L.R. 574, a case concerning an obligation to use best endeavours to promote the sales of fountain pens and ink bottles designed by the plaintiff. The court held that such an obligation did not require the directors to act in a way that would ruin the company or to act in complete disregard of the interests of the shareholders, but only to do what could reasonably be done in the circumstances. The standard of reasonableness was held to be that of a reasonable and prudent board of directors acting properly in the interests of the company and applying their minds to their contractual obligations to exploit the inventions. Again, it was not suggested that the object of the endeavours was too uncertain to enable the clause to be enforced.

22. *A.P. Stephens v Scottish Boatowners Mutual Insurance Association (The 'Talisman')* [1989] 1 Lloyd's Rep. 535 concerned a claim against insurers for the loss of a fishing vessel. The policy excluded liability for loss when the insured had not used all reasonable endeavours to save the vessel. The vessel was lost while working as a result of the entry of seawater through the seacocks which the master wrongly thought had to be left open when pumping out the bilges. The House of Lords held that the proper standard to apply when deciding whether the owner had failed to use all reasonable endeavours was that of an ordinary competent fishing boat skipper. In my opinion the circumstances of that case are too far removed from those of the present for the decision to afford much assistance.

23. In *P. & O. Property Holdings Ltd v Norwich Union Life Insurance Society* (1994) 68 P. & C.R. 261 a property developer undertook to use reasonable endeavours to obtain lettings of units in a new shopping centre, the construction of which was financed by the defendant insurer. A question arose whether the developer was obliged to agree to the payment of reverse premiums to induce potential tenants to enter into leases when under the terms of the development agreement it alone would have to bear the cost. The House of Lords rejected the submission that by agreeing to use reasonable endeavours the parties were to be taken as having adopted an objective standard for determining what terms it would be reasonable to agree, but the dispute turned on the construction of the particular clause in the development agreement and provides little assistance in deciding the present case.

24. In *Phillips Petroleum Co. UK Ltd v Enron Europe Ltd* [1997] C.L.C. 329 the question for decision was whether an obligation to use reasonable endeavours to agree the date on which deliveries of natural gas by the claimant to the defendant should commence, subject to an agreed fall-back date, gave rise to an enforceable obligation or constituted no more than an obligation to attempt to reach agreement and so was unenforceable. Kennedy L.J. found it impossible to construe the obligation in the context of its contractual setting as imposing on the buyer an obligation to disregard the financial effect of agreeing a commissioning date earlier than the fall-back date. Potter L.J. considered that an agreement to use reasonable endeavours to agree is unenforceable because its content is too uncertain. Apart from reinforcing the well established principles that the terms of the relevant clause must be construed in their contractual and factual context and that an agreement to use reasonable endeavours to agree is unenforceable, this case also does not in my view assist greatly.

25. Mr. Leggatt next referred us to *Baird Textiles Holdings Ltd v Marks & Spencer plc* [2002] 1 All E.R. (Comm) 737, a case in which the claimant attempted to derive from a series of individual orders for the manufacture and sale of clothing a long-term contract to purchase garments in reasonable quantities and at reasonable prices. The attempt failed, principally because the contract which the claimant sought to establish contained no objective criteria by which the court could establish what would be reasonable either as to quantity or price and was therefore too uncertain to be capable of enforcement. That very lack of certainty was held to confirm the absence of any intention to enter into contractual relations.

26. *Yewbelle Ltd v London Green Developments Ltd* [2006] EWHC 3166 (Ch) (unreported) concerned an undertaking to use all reasonable endeavours to obtain an agreement under section 106 of the Town and Country Planning Act 1990 for the construction of a library and other facilities. It was not suggested that the obligation was unenforceable; the issue was whether Yewbelle had done all that it should have done in performance of the obligation. Having considered both *P. & O. Property Holdings v Norwich Union* and *Phillips Petroleum v Enron*, Lewison J. (as he then was) expressed the view that Yewbelle was not required to sacrifice its own commercial interests in discharging its obligation to use reasonable endeavours. However, he agreed that the obligation to use reasonable endeavours continues until the point is reached at which all reasonable efforts have been exhausted.

27. In *EDI Central Ltd v National Car Parks Ltd* [2010] CSOH 141 the relevant obligation was to procure that a development of a project was pursued "with all reasonable endeavours and as would be expected of a normal prudent commercial developer". Lord Glennie, following *Yewbelle v London Green Developments*, expressed

the view that an obligation to use all reasonable endeavours does not require a person to act against his own commercial interests, but he did acknowledge that the reference to a normal prudent commercial developer was important in defining the scope of the obligation in that case.

28. Finally Mr. Leggatt referred to *R. & D. Construction Ltd v Hallam Land Management Ltd*, in which the defendant had agreed to sell to the claimant at an agreed price a parcel of land to be purchased from a third party. The sale was conditional upon the defendant's agreeing a price with the third party that was "wholly acceptable" to it as buyer, the defendant being under an obligation "to use all reasonable endeavours in this regard". Following the defendant's failure to agree a purchase price with the third party and withdrawal from the contract, the claimant brought proceedings for breach of contract, as a result of which the court had to consider the effect of the condition and the undertaking to use reasonable endeavours. The discussion in the judgments was directed primarily to whether the obligation was sufficiently certain to be enforceable, not because it was couched in terms of best endeavours, but because the object of those endeavours was to obtain an agreement on terms that were acceptable to the defendant himself. All three members of the court were satisfied that it was capable of enforcement, because the defendant's state of mind was capable of being ascertained objectively, however difficult that might prove to be. I have some reservations about the correctness of the decision in that case, because, in the absence of some objective criterion by reference to which the defendant's satisfaction was to be judged, the clause allowed him to decide for himself whether any particular terms were or were not acceptable. The contract therefore imposed on him no more than an obligation to agree terms if he so wished. Nonetheless, the decision is of assistance in as much as it emphasises the importance of concentrating on the object of the endeavours that are to be exercised.

29. As to Mr. Leggatt's submission that the first paragraph of clause 1 of the Letter Agreement is too uncertain to be capable of giving rise to any legal obligation, I think there is an important difference between a clause whose content is so uncertain that it is incapable of creating a binding obligation and a clause which gives rise to a binding obligation, the precise limits of which are difficult to define in advance, but which can nonetheless be given practical content. A famous example of the former is to be found in *G. Scammell and Nephew Ltd v H.C. and J.G. Ouston* [1941] A.C. 251, in which the court held that a contract to purchase a van on terms that part of the price should be paid "on hire-purchase terms over a period of two years" was too uncertain to be enforceable. An example of the latter is an obligation to promote the sale of the claimant's product, as in *Terrell v Mabie Todd and Co. Ltd*. The content of an obligation to use best endeavours to promote another person's business is not so uncertain as to be incapable of giving rise to a legally binding obligation, although it may be difficult to determine in any given case whether there has been a breach of it. In my view the obligation to use best endeavours to promote Jet2's business is no more uncertain than the obligation to use best endeavours to develop a railway's traffic (*Sheffield District Railway Co. v Great Central Railway Co.*), or to promote the sales of fountain pens and ink bottles (*Terrell v Mabie Todd and Co. Ltd*). There may be argument about what constitutes best endeavours in any particular circumstances (see, for example, *Terrell v Mabie Todd and Co. Ltd.*), but that is a different matter.

30. The judge held in paragraph [79] of his judgment that opening outside normal hours was taken to be part of the service BAL provided and part of the deal, by which I think he meant that both parties contemplated and intended that operations would be conducted in that way. He did not seek to define with any great precision the meaning of the word "promote" in that context and it was unnecessary for him to do so, since it followed from his findings about the nature of the low-cost airline business that the ability to operate aircraft early in the morning and late at night was necessary in order for it to prosper. Conversely, an inability to operate aircraft at such times would undermine its viability.

31. In my view the obligation to use best endeavours to promote Jet2's business obliged BAL to do all that it reasonably could to enable that business to succeed and grow and I do not think the object of the best endeavours is too uncertain to be capable of giving rise to a legally binding obligation. In my view the promotion of Jet2's business did extend to keeping the airport open to accommodate flights outside normal hours, subject to any right it might have to protect its own financial interests. Accordingly, I think the judge's decision on that aspect of the matter was correct. On the other hand, an obligation to use all reasonable endeavours to provide a cost base that will facilitate some essential element of another person's business seems to me to pose greater problems, because it is much more difficult to identify its content. The words are said to import an obligation to use all reasonable endeavours to enable Jet2 to keep its unit costs (and therefore ticket prices) down by enabling it to use its aircraft in the most efficient manner, but I find them too opaque to enable me to give them that meaning with any confidence. However, it is unnecessary to reach any final decision on that question in the present case.

32. It was a central plank of BAL's argument before the judge that the obligation to use best endeavours did not require it to act contrary to its own commercial interests, which, in the context of this case, amounts to saying that BAL was not obliged to accept aircraft movements outside normal hours if that would cause it

financial loss. Some support for that conclusion can be found in the cases, notably *Terrell v Mabie Todd and Co. Ltd* and *Yewbelle Ltd v London Green Developments Ltd*, but I think the judge was right in saying that whether, and if so to what extent, a person who has undertaken to use his best endeavours can have regard to his own financial interests will depend very much on the nature and terms of the contract in question. In *Terrell v Mabie Todd and Co. Ltd* the context in which the undertaking was given was sufficient in my view to make it clear that the company was not expected to do more than could reasonably be expected of a prudent board of directors acting in the interests of the shareholders. In neither *Yewbelle Ltd v London Green Developments Ltd* nor *EDI Central Ltd v National Car Parks Ltd* was there any extended discussion of what sacrificing its own interests might involve, either in the context of the case under consideration or more generally. I approach with some caution the submission that BAL was entitled to refuse to accept aircraft movements outside normal opening hours if that caused it to incur a loss, because on the judge's findings the ability to schedule aircraft movements outside those hours was essential to Jet2's business and was therefore fundamental to the agreement. In those circumstances one would not expect the parties to have contemplated that BAL should be able to restrict Jet2's aircraft movements to normal opening hours simply because it incurred a loss each time it was required to accept a movement outside those hours, or because keeping the airport open outside normal hours proved to be more expensive than it had expected. On the other hand, I can see force in the argument that if, for example, it were to become clear that Jet2 could never expect to operate low cost services from Blackpool profitably, BAL would not be obliged to incur further losses in seeking to promote a failing business.

33. Before the judge BAL relied solely on what it submitted was its right to refuse to act in a way that caused it to incur a loss in relation to individual aircraft movements outside normal opening hours. For the reasons I have given I am unable to accept that argument. I think the judge was right to hold that its refusal in October 2010 to accept further aircraft movements outside those hours involved a breach of contract and that is sufficient to uphold his decision. Whether under other circumstances BAL might be entitled to refuse to handle aircraft movements outside normal hours is a question that does not arise for consideration on this appeal. Given the uncertainty about the future course of events, I think the judge was right not to grant a declaration in terms that would rigidly define the scope of BAL's obligation for the ensuing ten years.

Estoppel by convention

34. As an alternative to its argument that the effect of the Letter Agreement was to give it a contractual right to require BAL to handle aircraft movements outside normal opening hours Jet2 submitted that, having regard to the way in which the parties had acted towards each other, BAL was estopped from denying that such a right existed. It relied on the established principle of estoppel by convention first recognised in *Amalgamated Investment Property Co. Ltd v Texas Commerce International Bank Ltd* [1982] Q.B. 84 and most recently approved by the House of Lords in *Republic of India v India Steamship Co. Ltd (The 'Indian Grace') (No. 2)* [1998] A.C. 878. In the latter case Lord Steyn expressed the principle as follows (page 913E-F):

> "It is settled that an estoppel by convention may arise where parties to a transaction act on an assumed state of facts or law, the assumption being either shared by them both or made by one and acquiesced in by the other. The effect of an estoppel by convention is to preclude a party from denying the assumed facts or law if it would be unjust to allow him to go back on the assumption: *K. Lokumal & Sons (London) Ltd. v. Lotte Shipping Co. Pte. Ltd.* [1985] 2 Lloyd's Rep. 28; *Norwegian American Cruises A/S v. Paul Mundy Ltd.* [1988] 2 Lloyd's Rep. 343; *Treitel, The Law of Contract*, 9th ed. (1995), pp. 112-113. It is not enough that each of the two parties acts on an assumption not communicated to the other. But it was rightly accepted by counsel for both parties that a concluded agreement is not a requirement for an estoppel by convention."

35. In the present case Mr. Shepherd submitted that an estoppel arose out of the practice adopted by the parties over the preceding four years under which Jet2 submitted, and BAL accepted, flight schedules which included regular aircraft movements outside normal opening hours. As a result BAL was estopped from denying Jet2's right to require aircraft movements outside those hours.

36. In my view this argument cannot succeed. It is unlikely, though not impossible, that each of the parties assumed that clause 1 of the agreement imposed an unqualified obligation on BAL in this respect, despite the fact that it was expressed in terms of an obligation to use best endeavours, but cogent evidence would be necessary to establish both that they had shared that assumption to the knowledge of each other and that they had conducted themselves on that basis. In my view there is no such evidence. All Mr. Shepherd could point to was a longstanding practice under which Jet2 (along with other airlines) submitted flight schedules for the ensuing six-month period which were accepted, with or without negotiation and modification, by BAL. That is sufficient to demonstrate that Jet2 did submit flight schedules and that they were in practice accepted by BAL,

but it falls far short of demonstrating that the parties shared a common assumption that Jet2 had a right to insist on aircraft movements taking place outside normal opening hours and that BAL had an obligation to accommodate them. The need for a shared common assumption, in the sense that each party must have acted in the knowledge that the other shared its understanding of the position, is reflected in the passage in Lord Steyn's speech in *The 'Indian Grace' (No. 2)*, to which I referred earlier. The evidence in the present case is more consistent with ordinary business co-operation than with the reliance on, and recognition of, a legal obligation.

Conclusion

37. For these reasons I would dismiss the appeal and uphold the order below.

LORD JUSTICE LEWISON:

38. It is, of course, possible for a commercial organisation to undertake a positive commitment to run a business for a period as long as fifteen years. It is even possible for such an organisation to undertake a positive commitment to run a loss-making business for that period. But it would, I think, be an unusual obligation; and a businessman would expect such an obligation to be spelled out in clear words. In other contexts, such as a clause regulating the use of leased property, even where the language of a clause appears to impose on the tenant a positive obligation to run a business, the courts have often treated the clause as no more than an emphatic negative: see, for example *Montross Associated Investments Ltd v Moussaief* [1989] 2 EGLR 62; *Chorley BC v Ribble Motor Services Ltd* (1996) 74 P & CR 182; *Blumenthal v Church Commissioners for England* [2005] 1 EGLR 78.

39. The contract in the present case is one between two commercial organisations, each with its own commercial interest. Although in some places the contract requires them to co-operate or to act jointly, the contract as a whole does not create a fiduciary relationship in which the fiduciary must subordinate his own interests to those of his principal. Even if to some extent the arrangement can be characterised as a joint venture, that does not necessarily import fiduciary obligations. As the High Court of Australia recently pointed out in *John Alexander's Clubs Pty Ltd v White City Tennis Club Ltd* [2010] HCA 19 (§ 44)

> Describing the arrangements as a "joint venture" does not however have any particular legal consequences. The rights and obligations of the parties remain to be determined by examination of the detail of what they have agreed and done."

40. What, then, have the parties agreed? Clause 2 of the contract sets out a large number of detailed obligations. It deals with charges for use of the airport, the provision of office accommodation, car parking, staff passes and so on. Mr Leggatt submits, and I agree, that if BAL had contractually committed itself to keeping the airport open at whatever hours Jet2.com required, clause 2 would surely have said something about opening hours.

41. I agree with the judge that the content of an obligation to use reasonable endeavours (or, for that matter, best endeavours) depends on the context in which that expression is used. But the most important part of the context is the objective towards which the endeavours are to be directed. If the endeavours are directed towards a result which can be identified with certainty, then whether the endeavours satisfy the obligation can also be decided, if necessary with the aid of expert evidence. At one end of the spectrum is a case like *The Talisman* [1989] 1 Lloyd's Rep 535 where the question was whether the skipper of a fishing boat had used reasonable endeavours to prevent the boat from sinking. The object of the endeavours was clearly defined. In that context, as Lord Keith explained, the test was :

> ". . . an objective one, directed to ascertaining what an ordinarily competent fishing boat skipper might reasonably be expected to do in the same circumstances."

42. In some cases the contract itself will lay down an objective test. Thus in *EDI Central Ltd v National Car Parks Ltd* [2010] CSOH 141 (on appeal [2012] CSIH 6) the contract in question was one directed towards the redevelopment of a car park in Edinburgh owned by NCP. EDI was the developer. The contract contained an obligation on the part of the developer to procure that the redevelopment was "procured with all reasonable endeavours as would be expected of a normal prudent commercial developer experienced in developments of that nature". The issue in the case was whether the developer had complied with that obligation. Lord Glennie (and on appeal the Inner House) held that it had. There was no issue about the objective towards which the endeavours were to be directed; nor was there any conceptual difficulty about applying the contractual test. *Linder v Pryor* (1838) 8 C & P. 518, 173 ER 600, to which Longmore LJ refers, was a case in which the primary obligation was to keep the house open as a "public licensed" house. It is not surprising that a failure to take any step to renew the licence was held to amount to a breach of that clause. I would not regard that as a case which turned on the more general aspiration to increase trade; but rather on the specific goal of renewing the licence.

43. At the other end of the spectrum are cases like *P & O Property Holdings Ltd v Norwich Union Life Insurance Society* (1994) 68 P & CR 261. That case concerned a development agreement between a developer and a funder for the development of the St Nicholas shopping centre in Sutton. The basic structure of the agreement was that in return for agreeing to fund the development up to a stated maximum the funder was to acquire a long lease of the completed centre. The developer was to receive a profit share calculated by reference to a multiple of the net income generated by letting the individual units. The funder had in fact advanced the maximum sum it was obliged to advance; and consequently could not be made to pay any more. The funding agreement required the funder and the developer to "use their reasonable endeavours to obtain a letting of each lettable part of the Development". The issue between the parties was whether, as the funder argued, this obligation required the developer to pay reverse premiums to incoming tenants in order to maximise the passing or headline rent. One reason why the argument was rejected by the House of Lords was because as Lord Browne-Wilkinson explained:

"I am quite unable to extract from the words of the clause any such objective test of the reasonableness of the terms which have to be agreed if the reasonable endeavours obligation is to be discharged. . ."

44. Another was that the parties should not be taken to have intended an unworkable scheme which would have given an arbitrator an impossible question to decide. As Lord Browne-Wilkinson put it:

"The desirability of paying a reverse premium depends upon the circumstances and wishes of the landlord. For a landlord whose cash flow is sufficient to pay the reverse premium, it will be a possible, though not necessarily desirable, course: for a landlord without liquid resources, it would be impossible. Since, under the judge's declaration, the incidence of the cost of a reverse premium is to be ignored, is the arbitrator to assume a reasonable landlord with sufficient funds looking for long term high rent tenants or a reasonable landlord without sufficient funds seeking a quick let at the best annual rent for the time being available? The former would be prepared to pay a reverse premium, the latter quite reasonably would not. The fact is that an arbitrator would be unable to reach a conclusion as to the reasonableness of the hypothetical landlord's attitude without being given a series of assumptions as to the nature, means and management aims of the hypothetical landlord."

45. This was a case in which the House concentrated on the uncertainty inherent in the concept of "reasonable endeavours" rather than the objective towards which the endeavours were directed. In *Little v Courage Ltd* (1995) 70 P & CR 469 it was the objective itself that was uncertain. The lease in that case contained an option to renew which was conditional on (among other things) the parties having agreed a business plan. No business plan had in fact been agreed. The tenant argued that the parties had an obligation to use their best endeavours to reach an agreement. This court rejected that argument. Millett LJ said:

"An undertaking to use one's best endeavours to obtain planning permission or an export licence is sufficiently certain and is capable of being enforced: an undertaking to use one's best endeavours to agree, however, is no different from an undertaking to agree, to try to agree, or to negotiate with a view to reaching agreement; all are equally uncertain and incapable of giving rise to an enforceable legal obligation."

46. This, then, was a case in which the objective towards which the endeavours were to be directed was too uncertain to enforce. In *R & D Construction Ltd v Hallam Land Management* [2010] CSIH 96 [2011] SC 286 the parties entered into a contract for the sale of land. However, the seller did not own the land at the date of the contract, but had the benefit of an option to acquire it as part of a larger parcel. The option was conditional on the seller using best endeavours to agree a price for the larger parcel with the proprietor of it in terms wholly acceptable to itself. The Court of Session Inner House held that the clause was legally effective, but that the seller was not in breach. In the course of their judgments the judges considered a number of the English cases. Lord President Hamilton said (§ 37):

"Accordingly whether a provision to use best endeavours is or is not sufficiently definite to be enforceable turns, on this approach, on the object of the endeavour. It may, as with the obtaining of a specific planning permission or a particular export licence, involve persuading an authority or other third party to adopt a particular position. The same is true, in my view, of a provision to use all reasonable endeavours."

47. As I read his judgment it was an approach with which he agreed. Dealing with the particular agreement in that case he said (§ 39) omitting references to authority:

"In the present case the object of the endeavours is not, in my view, uncertain. It is an agreement (presumably legally binding) between the respondent and a third party (the current proprietor) on a purchase price for the subjects 'in terms wholly acceptable to [the respondent]'. It may be difficult to prove, as at any particular point of time, what terms are (or were) wholly acceptable to the respondent; but, if that subjective state of mind can be proved, then the object of the reasonable endeavours is clear. It is to secure an agreement on such terms with the proprietor. That is not an aspirational provision which parties adopt 'to make clear a future co-operative intention without providing for an enforceable legal obligation which in negotiations one or other may have refused to agree' . . . Nor is it a purported obligation to procure co-operation with a view to negotiation of terms yet to be. . . . Rather it is, in my view, an obligatory provision which requires one party in certain defined circumstances to take certain definite steps in relation to a third party. The circumstance that the obligation is in relation to dealings with a third party rather than between the parties themselves may not be immaterial. . . .. While the purchase price wholly acceptable to the respondent may not have been known at the time when the missives were entered into, if it was ascertainable at the material time that, in my view, is sufficient . . ."

48. The key to this reasoning is that the object of the endeavours was clear; and that it required the party in question to take defined steps in defined circumstances. Lord Reed said (§ 57) again omitting reference to authority:

"An obligation to use reasonable endeavours (or all reasonable endeavours) is generally enforceable, provided that the object of the endeavours is sufficiently definite . . . That is because, granted a definite objective, it is possible for a court to determine whether the endeavours, if any, made by a party to achieve that objective were reasonable in the circumstances (or, in an 'all reasonable endeavours' case, whether the party made all the endeavours to achieve the objective which were reasonable in the circumstances). In the present case, the object of the endeavours is that the seller should agree a purchase price for the subjects with the current proprietor in terms wholly acceptable to the seller. For the reasons I have explained, that object is not lacking in certainty but has a definite meaning. It follows that an obligation to use all reasonable endeavours in that regard also has a sufficiently definite meaning to be enforceable."

49. Finally Lord Drummond Young said (§§ 63, 64):

". . . there must in my opinion be minimum requirements before it is possible for a court to hold that a binding contract has been concluded. The critical minimum is in my view that there should exist a contractual obligation that can be measured against objective criteria. It is only in that way that an obligation can attain the certainty that is necessary for it to exist as an obligation . . .
The question of whether an obligation can be given objective content goes to whether an obligation can truly be said to exist at all. It is, however, closely related to the enforcement of the obligation. If an obligation has objective content the court can readily enforce it; by contrast, if a party is entitled to do as he chooses, it is difficult to see how effective enforcement is possible. In a number of cases courts have referred to the problems of enforcing or policing an obligation, and I think that this may reasonably be construed as recognition of the fact that objective content is required for an obligation to exist."

50. Although I share Moore-Bick LJ's reservations whether there truly was an objective criterion in that case, the principles it espouses are correct. In my judgment the object of the endeavours and the range of possible endeavours must be considered together in order to decide whether there is a justiciable obligation. Moreover it is wrong in principle to focus on the particular factual situation which has given rise to the dispute without considering to what other factual situations the clause might extend if one side or the other is correct. As Potter LJ put it in *Phillips Petroleum Co UK Ltd v Enron Europe Ltd* [1997] CLC 329, 343:

"Finally, the unwillingness of the courts to give binding force to an obligation to use 'reasonable endeavours' to agree seems to me to be sensibly based on the difficulty of policing such an obligation, in the sense of drawing the line between what is to be regarded as reasonable or unreasonable in an area where the parties may legitimately have differing views or interests, but have not provided for any criteria on the basis of which a third party can assess or adjudicate the matter in the event of dispute. In the face of such difficulty, the court does not give a remedy to a party who may with justification assert, 'well, whatever the criteria are, there must have been a breach in this case'. It denies the remedy altogether on the basis of the unenforceability in principle of an obligation which may fall to be applied across a wide spectrum of arguable circumstances. This case seems to me to afford a good example of the wisdom of that approach."

51. Although these observations were directed to an apparent obligation to use reasonable endeavours to agree, in my judgment they apply more generally. The principle that a clause must be considered across the

whole potential range of its application is also made clear in Lord Diplock's speech in *The Miramar* [1984] AC 676, 682.

52. Mr Shepherd QC submitted that the obligation in clause 1 of the letter agreement was "open textured". But that, to my mind, is precisely the problem. How is a court to define or recognise the limits of the obligation? Mr Shepherd argued that the obligation required BAL to accept a flight schedule promulgated by Jet2.com operating between 0600 and 2400. But why those hours? If Jet2.com wanted to operate between 0500 and 0200 on the following day would they be entitled to insist that the airport remained open during the whole of that period? If not, why not? The difficulties to my mind do not stop there. Naturally the focus of debate has been the issue of opening times, because that was the *casus belli*. But the obligation is so open textured that it could potentially have repercussions elsewhere. The letter agreement excluded check-in charges from the agreed tariff and entitled Jet2.com to use its own check in staff. But it did not *require* Jet2.com to use its own check-in staff. If Jet2.com decided not to use its own staff for that purpose was it entitled to require BAL to provide the staff? After all, a low cost airline cannot operate without checking in its passengers. So why is the provision of check in staff not part of a general obligation to "promote" Jet2.com's business at the airport? Mr Shepherd replied that in fact Jet2.com and BAL had entered into a separate ground handling agreement. That, with all respect, is no answer. The question is not what the parties *did* but what they were *obliged* to do. Moreover, if the obligation in clause 1 of the letter agreement envisaged that the parties would (or might) enter into a separate agreement dealing with ground handling, why does the same not apply equally to the details of the flight schedule? Then there is the question of potential conflict between Jet2.com and other carriers using the airport. Does the obligation to "promote" Jet2.com's business at the airport entitle it to first pick of take off or landing slots in preference to other carriers? Mr Shepherd recognised that some operational adjustment might be necessary to a flight schedule proffered by Jet2.com. But I cannot get that out of the clause. Leaving aside the question of flight times, to what else does the obligation extend? Would it, for example, require BAL to provide enhanced passenger lounges for Jet2.com's departing passengers; or to offer them complimentary refreshments while they wait?

53. An additional problem lies in the fact that clause 1 (whatever it means) was expressed to endure for fifteen years. Mr Shepherd did not suggest that there might come a time during those fifteen years when BAL ceased to be obliged to keep the airport open outside its promulgated hours. And even if such a time were to come, how would the parties recognise it? On the other hand he said that Jet2.com were free to withdraw aircraft during that period if they were not flying profitably for Jet2.com. This uneven effect of clause 1 is unlikely to have been the meaning that a reasonable reader of the contract would have understood.

54. Rather less attention was paid to BAL's obligation in the second part of clause 1 "to use all reasonable endeavours to provide a cost base that will facilitate Jet2.com's low cost pricing". That was understandable. This part of the clause is concerned with costs; that is to say what payments Jet2.com is obliged to make (presumably to BAL). It is not concerned with the provision of additional services. The judge said "The provision of a cost base means, as I see it, providing in a broad sense facilities and services that will bring about the low cost pricing." But to my mind this interpretation concentrates too much on "Jet2.com's low cost pricing" and not enough on "provide a cost base"; and gives little, if any, weight to the word "cost" in the phrase "cost base".

55. Mr Shepherd relied heavily on the factual background to the agreement. The background did show that low cost airlines require flexibility in scheduling early departures and (more importantly) late arrivals, especially during the summer months. The background also showed that both parties knew that. At the date of the contract both Ryanair and Monarch were operating scheduled services at Blackpool outside BAL's promulgated opening hours. Mr Shepherd also placed heavy reliance on the fact that Jet2.com intended to acquire an aircraft to operate from the airport. He emphasised that this required considerable capital investment on the part of Jet2.com whereas BAL had all its fixed infrastructure in place, and, on his interpretation of the agreement, was required merely to incur additional marginal costs. I did not find this part of the background (to which the judge did not refer) persuasive. Granted that passenger aircraft are very expensive, the fact is that they can be based anywhere. If Jet2.com did not like Blackpool airport they could move their very expensive aircraft elsewhere. So the capital investment would not go to waste.

56. Moreover as the judge rightly said:

"First the factual matrix does not dictate what the terms of the contract are. It provides the background against which the words of an agreement are interpreted."

57. So the question is always: what do the words mean? As the judge pointed out:

"The Agreement says nothing about operations outside Blackpool's normal opening hours."

58. If a contract says nothing about a particular topic, then even if that topic is demonstrated by the admissible background to be an important one, the default position must surely be that the topic in question is simply not covered by the contract.

59. I recognise, of course, how reluctant a court is to reach a conclusion that an apparent obligation intended to have legal content in fact has no enforceable content at all. But if the concept embodied in the clause in question is too vague, and there are no objective criteria that the court can apply in deciding whether or not the clause has been honoured, then there may be no alternative conclusion. In some cases a clause that appears to be too uncertain to enforce can be saved by a provision referring disputes to an expert or arbitrator. But that is not the case here. There is a way in which the clause can be given some content, albeit not as a free-standing and independent obligation. That is by treating clause 1 as setting out the general principle which is then implemented by the more detailed provisions of clause 2.

60. In my judgment the judge's conclusion was not "construction of the contract" in the sense of "interpreting the contract". It was "construction of the contract" in the sense of "making the contract" which the parties had not themselves made.

61. If, as I think, flight scheduling was to be the subject of separate agreement then a precipitate decision by BAL not to accommodate a previously agreed schedule might well amount to a breach of *that* agreement; but it would not be a breach of clause 1 of the letter agreement. But that is not the way that the case was run at trial. I would not, myself, rely on the fact that the parties had in fact operated without trouble for a number of years in order to decide what the contract meant. That seems to me to come close to using the parties' subsequent conduct in order to interpret the contract.

62. For these reasons I regret that I do not agree with Longmore and Moore-Bick LJJ on the question of interpretation. I do, however, agree with Moore-Bick LJ that the plea of estoppel fails. I would allow the appeal.

LORD JUSTICE LONGMORE:

63. The only question before the judge (and the only question before us) was and is whether BAL was in breach of contract in declaring with minimal notice that they would no longer accommodate Jet 2's wish to operate outside the formal opening hours of the airport, although BAL had done so for some years previously without question. The judge concluded that BAL was in breach of clause 1 of the letter agreement. Moore-Bick LJ agrees with the judge; Lewison LJ has decided that clause 1 of the letter agreement is too vague to have any legal content and that BAL was not therefore in breach of contract. He says that flight scheduling was to be the subject of a separate agreement and, if such agreement was reached, there might be a breach of that agreement. Since no allegation of any such agreement was made at trial, it is impossible to know whether there was any such agreement. We can only ask ourselves whether clause 1 of the letter agreement constituted a binding agreement and, if so, whether there was a breach of it.

64. If the parties call a document in letter form, which sets out terms of business, a "letter agreement" and if the first clause of that letter agreement uses words such as "will", it is evident that the parties must, at least, think they have made an arrangement intended to be contractually binding between them. Of course that is not conclusive but courts should not, in my view, be too astute to decide that such an agreement is too vague to be legally enforceable. The putative obligation in question is that the parties will co-operate together

"and use their best endeavours to promote Jet2.com's low cost services"

from Blackpool Airport.

65. As both Moore-Bick and Lewison LJJ agree, the object of the best endeavours will always be important in deciding whether the commitment is to be legally enforceable. An agreement to use best endeavours to reach an agreement may be unenforceable as an agreement to agree as effectively held in *Little v Courage Ltd* (1995) 70 P & CR469, but even in such a case the matter may not be completely beyond argument since a best endeavours obligation might at least be held to import an agreement to negotiate in good faith, as to which see *Petromec Inc v Petroleo Brasiliero* [2006] 1 Lloyd's Rep 121 paras 125-121. No doubt, damages for breach of such an obligation could be problematical.

66. The phrase "best endeavours" has, however, a respectable legal history behind it. It has been used in leases of public houses since Napoleonic times in the context of keeping the house open and increasing its trade, a context perhaps not wholly dissimilar to promoting the services of an airline.

67. On 23rd January 1815 the brewers Thomas and Robert Pryor became the lessees of a public house for 21 years and covenanted to use

> "their best and utmost endeavours to continue the house open as a public licences victualling house and to increase the trade and custom thereof"

for a rent of £30 per year and a premium of £300. They sub-let to a series of tenants but business fell off because many of the customers from "the several ship-builders' yards in the neighbourhood . . . did not pay their bills" and the 1824 tenant only paid £20 per year without any premium. In 1829 the house fell into the hands of a Mr Davison during whose occupation there were frequent complaints of disorderly conduct and the magistrates took the licence away. After the lease expired in 1836 the landlord's heirs complained that the Pryor brothers, in breach of contract, had not used their "best and utmost endeavours" to continue to keep the house open but allowed the house to be discontinued and the licence to be removed or not renewed. Tindal CJ directed the jury that there had been a breach and that they would have to assess the damages saying:-

> "It is my opinion . . . as the affirmative of the issue is on the defendant, that it is incumbent on him to show that he did some act after the refusal to renew the licence – that he applied for a re-hearing of the case, or did some act to endeavour to obtain, the continuance of it, and get the house open again. Therefore the question is, what damages are to be given."

68. That was *Linder v Pryor* (1838) 8 C & P. 518, 173 ER 600. It is, of course, redolent of another age in one sense but it is not an isolated example, see e.g. *Moore v Robinson* (1878) 48 LJQB 176 where it was held that non-residence at the public house would not, of itself, be a breach of an obligation to "use . . . best endeavours to extend the custom and business" of the public-house.

69. The combination of these cases and the twentieth century cases referred to in my Lords' judgments, to my mind, justify the conclusion that an obligation to use best endeavours should usually be held to be an enforceable obligation unless

    i)   the object intended to be procured by the endeavours is too vague or elusive to be itself a matter of legal obligation; or

    ii) the parties have, in the words of Potter LJ in *Phillips Petroleum v Enron Europe Ltd* [1997] CLC 329 at 343, provided no criteria on the basis of which it is possible to assess whether best endeavours have been, or can be used.

70. It is in the context of (ii) above that it may be relevant to consider the extent to which a party can be obliged to act against his own interests. The fact that he has agreed to use his best endeavours pre-supposes that he may well be put to some financial cost, so financial cost cannot be a trump card to enable him to extricate himself from what would otherwise be his obligation. As A.T. Lawrence J said in the *Sheffield District Railway Co* case, best endeavours does not mean second best endeavours. But I would agree with Moore-Bick LJ (para 32) that, if it became clear that Jet2 could never expect to operate low cost services profitably from Blackpool, BAL could not be expected themselves to incur losses after that time in seeking to promote (or effectively propping up) a failing business.

71. For my part, I do not consider the promotion of a low cost airline to be so vague or elusive an object that the best endeavours obligation assumed by BAL should be regarded an unenforceable in law. Nor do I consider that the parties have not provided criteria by which it is possible to assess whether best endeavours can be, or have been, used.

72. I say that because the status quo will always be an essential matter to be considered. Any question of best endeavours was most unlikely to arise before the agreement started to be performed. Once performance had begun, the party who proposed to change the status quo should have to justify that change of stance. The "out of normal hours" use of the airport caused no problems for four years; reasonable endeavours had been used to promote Jet2's low cost services. BAL's sudden change of stance needed a justifiable explanation. The judge did not think there was one and neither do I.

73. I therefore agree with Moore-Bick LJ rather than Lewison LJ. The judge was, moreover, right to refuse a declaration that BAL were obliged for the whole 15 years duration of the contract to continue to keep the airport open otherwise than during normal hours. There might indeed be circumstances in which BAL, after proper notice, might be entitled to refuse to continue handling aircraft movements outside normal hours but that is not a question raised on this appeal which I would accordingly dismiss.

The first thing to say about the *Jet2.Com* case is that it is a far more challenging read than the *Boots* case. There is a dissenting judgment, by Lewison LJ, to set against the majority judgments given by Moore-Bick and Longmore LJJ; there are a number of somewhat similar cases to which the question in *Jet2.Com* is related; and, one of the key cases, *R & D Construction Ltd v Hallam Land Management Ltd*,[29] is thought to be helpful in establishing the right question even if the way that the question is answered seems unconvincing. Nevertheless, a *careful* student reader should at least be able to report that the case supports the view that a 'reasonable endeavours' or a 'best endeavours' clause will not always fail for uncertainty. Rather, such a clause will fail for uncertainty unless (i) the 'object' or 'objective' towards which best endeavours are to be directed is sufficiently clear and (ii) there are some criteria for determining whether the endeavours applied are 'reasonable' or 'best'. That said, as *Jet2.Com* itself amply illustrates, there is no guarantee that even very experienced judges will agree in a particular case on whether the two limbs of this test are satisfied; and, as the jurisprudence shows, each case depends very much on its own particular facts. On this basis, a student reader might fairly conclude that, while the legal principle is relatively clear, its application is difficult to predict.

What the student reader is unlikely to appreciate is that the commercial law of contract is undergoing a fundamental transformation. To strengthen one's critical and contextual appreciation of the *Jet2.Com* case, it needs to be understood that, for the last 20 years or so, where disputes are between business contractors, adjudication has been progressively driven by the following considerations:

- that the courts should be sensitive to the 'factual matrix' or the 'context' in which the parties dealt with one another (initially, this concerned only questions of the interpretation of a contractual document[30] but it now applies more broadly[31]);

- that the law of contract and its adjudicated outcomes should reflect the reasonable expectations of the parties[32] and, indeed, align with the custom and practice of particular markets as well as, more generally, commercial common sense[33]; and

- that, in practice, a huge amount of commercial dealing takes place on the basis of informal norms that encourage cooperation and compromise; and that the law should reflect this.[34]

This represents a considerable change in the direction of the law and departs very radically from the assumptions on which the traditional law (and traditional contract law textbooks) are predicated (favouring, among other things, a "literal" approach to interpretation, a focus on the "paper deal" [to the exclusion of the "real deal"], a tough line on uncertainty, a reluctance to imply terms unless absolutely necessary, a rejection of good faith in contracts, and the assumption that contractors deal in an adversarial and entirely self-interested way). Of course, this shift in direction is highly contro-

---

[29] [2010] CSIH 96.

[30] See Ch.15.

[31] See *Attorney General of Belize v Belize Telecom Limited* [2009] UKPC 10; and Ch.16.

[32] The seminal paper is Johan Steyn, 'Contract Law: Fulfilling the Reasonable Expectations of Honest Men' (1997) 113 *Law Quarterly Review* 433.

[33] For a good example, see *Rainy Sky v Kookmin Bank* [2011] UKSC 50 (below, Ch.17). Compare, too, *RTS Flexible Systems Limited v Molkerei Alois Müller Gmbh and Co (UK Production)* [2010] UKSC 14, where (at paras 58, 62, and 86-87) Lord Clarke rejects the Court of Appeal's view that there was "no contract" between the parties as making no commercial sense; and, *Kudos Catering (UK) Limited v Manchester Central Convention Complex Limited* [2013] EWCA Civ 38, where Tomlinson LJ counters the objection that his interpretation of the contract deviates too much from the text by insisting that this is "a legitimate exercise in construing a contract consistently with business common sense and not in a manner which defeats its commercial object" (para.28).

[34] For an account of these major developments, see Roger Brownsword, 'The Law of Contract: Doctrinal Impulses, External Pressures, Future Directions' (2014) 31 *Journal of Contract Law* 73; and *Contract Law: Themes for the Twenty-First Century* (Oxford: Oxford University Press, 2006); and John Wightman, 'Contract in a Pre-Realist World: Professor Macaulay, Lord Hoffmann and the Rise of Context in the English Law of Contract' in Jean Braucher, John Kidwell, and William C. Whitford (eds), *Revisiting the Contracts Scholarship of Stewart Macaulay* (Oxford: Hart, 2013) p.377.

versial and the leading edge of contracts scholarship is now devoted to re-assessing the purpose of contract law (what is its intended function?) and how well it is served by, respectively, the traditional and the more recent contextualist rules.[35] Against this backcloth, the *Jet2.Com* case is an indication that the contextualist approach (taken here by the majority) has the edge over waning support for a traditional approach (taken here by Lewison LJ, especially in paras 57-58) that demands that any supposed contractual obligations (keeping the airport open outside normal hours) that cut against a party's economic interests must be clearly and explicitly specified in the agreement (otherwise, they are not part of the deal).

9. How Should the Writing of Essays and the Answering of Problems in Contract Law be Approached?

Many students enter law school having had a great deal of practice in writing essays and little or no experience of answering the kind of problem questions that dominate assessment in case-law subjects such as Contract and Tort. What advice might be given to students who are unclear about what is expected in legal essay writing and about the conventions of writing answers to problem questions in the law of contract?   **1–017**

Essay writing

The general advice about essay writing is familiar and rather obvious: essays should have beginnings, middles and ends (preferably in that order); they should be "responsive" to the question or title that is set; and they should be clearly structured. It follows that, even under the pressure of examination conditions, every effort should be made to avoid passing off an unstructured stream of consciousness as an essay or simply rehearsing a block of notes that might well be in the right ball-park but that is not responsive.   **1–018**

As a model of essay writing, articles published in US law reviews are worth reading. To be sure, such articles are sometimes caricatured as being rather long and formulaic in the sense that they comprise: an introduction; a section outlining what will be argued for; a section emphasising what will *not* be covered; the body of the article; a section reminding readers what has *not* been covered or claimed; a section summarising the main points; and a conclusion. Nevertheless, if all essays, even short essays, could be as clearly "signposted" as this, there would be no complaint.

Turning specifically to essay writing in Contracts, the general advice holds good; but, is there anything more to say? Typically, essay titles set for Contracts invite students to argue in a critical and independent way for a particular position—for example, the question might ask whether students believe that it would be desirable for English law to adopt a general principle of good faith and fair dealing, or whether it would be desirable to introduce a bespoke legal regime for transactions between large commercial contractors and SMEs, or whether the adoption of a regional Contract code for Europe would be a good thing, or whether the move towards "contextualism" in the law should be reversed, and so on. Where should a student start with tough questions of this kind? In many instances, the key materials for questions of this kind will be in law review articles, monographs, and debates between legal scholars. Some cases might be emblematic of particular aspects of these debates but, commonly, students are being taken back to much more general ideas about the coherence of the law or its purpose and so on. Students who are familiar with the debates and who can rehearse the salient points made

---

[35]   Compare, e.g., Catherine Mitchell, *Contract Law and Contract Practice* (Oxford: Hart, 2013) (which, broadly speaking, is in favour of contextualism) with Jonathan Morgan, *Contract Law Minimalism* (Cambridge: Cambridge University Press, 2013) (against contextualism).

by the protagonists will have plenty of content for their essays. However, ultimately, these questions push back into economic or philosophical theories of law; where, as with conflicting indications in the case-law, there are no easy answers; where finding some terra firma is a challenge for experienced law review writers; and, where this is all an exceedingly tough call for a first-year law student.

Even seemingly undemanding essay questions can be challenging. For example, I sometimes asked my students, in their end-of-year examination, to pick out the three Contract cases that they thought were the most significant and to explain why. Clearly, the first question to be addressed is what we might mean by "significant". A legitimate response to this question is that a case is significant if it is "leading" in the sense that it anchors a particular line of the jurisprudence. Applying this understanding of "significant", there would be many candidate cases but it would be difficult, without more, to explain why one "leading" case is more significant than another. Alternatively, a student might attempt a much higher tariff response treating cases as significant to the extent that they reflect a more general policy, principle, or priority for the development of the law. At the time that I liked to set this question, the cases were showing signs of recognising that consumer contractors should be shielded against the full-blooded application of the principles of "freedom of contract" and "sanctity of contract"—and, in due course, the law was to bifurcate so that, while commercial (business-to-business) transactions continued to be subject to the general law, consumer transactions became regulated in their own distinctive way. Nowadays, it would be natural to look for significant developments in the rapidly changing scenery of commercial contracting as the classical values of "market-individualism" are qualified by more cooperative ideals, as "contextualism" replaces "literalism", and as many of the rules of the law are increasingly recognised as no more than defaults which the parties are free to switch (see above, section 8).

Pulling these threads together, we can say that students might approach an essay question with different degrees of understanding of the law of contract. At minimum, a student will have, as it were, a textbook expository understanding; they will know the doctrinal landmarks. Such a student will be able to rehearse the main rules and principles of the law of contract; and, if this is what an essay question invites the student to do, then that level of understanding will be adequate. The snag is that university law school essay questions will normally want more than that. What they will require is either a deeper familiarity with the cases (or, at least, some cases); or—and this is the more likely requirement—a familiarity with the more critical and more theoretical literature (in monographs, edited collections of essays, and law review articles). The moral is that, in researching their essays, students of contract law need to make full use of the resources available to them—that is to say, their textbooks, their casebooks, and the critical literature.

Answering problem questions

1–019   Although many students will think that they know how to write an essay, they will be less clear about the expectations in answering a problem question. Students can learn a lot about how to engage with doctrinal questions of law by reading the cases; and the conventions of modern judgment writing are designed not only to identify the issues clearly but also to help readers to follow the arguments advanced and the decisions made. On occasion, some judges do offer a mini-essay during the course of their judgment—and this might well be very helpful; but it is clear that, generally speaking, responding to a problem question is a less discursive kind of exercise.

Problem questions can be pitched at more than one level and, as ever, it is essential to respond to the question that is actually asked. For example, the problem might comprise only a bare statement of facts, leaving a good deal of preliminary work to be undertaken before the legal issues are identified, let alone answered (this is akin to a problem in the form that a client might first present it to a solicitor); or, with the legal issues having been identified, the problem might be to develop arguments in relation to those issues, whether for the claimant or the defendant (rather in the way that one might seek an opinion from counsel); or, the problem might take up the story in the courts, with the legal issues identified, the arguments laid out, and a decision to be made.

To illustrate, consider the following problem, pitched in several ways, and with each pitch we have a different question to be answered. In the first version, the problem comprises only a bare statement of facts:

"In 2005, a new shopping mall, Eastways, opened in Oldtown. The mall, which is managed by Eastways Development and Management (EDM) comprises some 50 retail units. At the centre of the mall, there is a very large unit which is occupied by a major department store, Bigshop (the 'anchor' store in the mall).

From 2005 until 2010, most of the shops at Eastways stayed open until 22.00 and it was commonly said in Oldtown that you could shop at Eastways from 10.00 in the morning until 10.00 at night. However, year by year, the number of shoppers visiting Eastways between 18.00 and 22.00 steadily declined. Reflecting this fall in trade after 18.00, in Spring 2011, Bigshop informed EDM that it no longer made business sense to stay open until 22.00 and that, in future, it would be closing at 18.00.

EDM is concerned that, if Bigshop closes at 18.00, this will have a significant negative impact on trade at Eastways and that this will make the mall less attractive to both retailers and shoppers.

EDM seeks advice on whether Bigshop would be in breach of contract by closing at 18.00 and, if so, what remedies it might have.

In order to advise EDM, identify what further information you would require and outline, as best you can, the advice you would give."

Clearly, the first thing to establish is whether EDM has a contract with Bigshop and, then, if there is a contract, what the express terms of the contract are. If the contract explicitly requires Bigshop to stay open until after 18.00, there is prima facie a breach. Consideration might then be given to any further provisions in the contract that might be relevant in establishing the limits of Bigshop's obligations, or any excusing circumstances, and the like.

If there is a contract between EDM and Bigshop but it is silent on the point at issue, what then? Might there be an implied term that requires Bigshop to stay open after 18.00? In order to make any headway with this question, there will need to be further inquiries about the context in which the parties contracted, custom and practice in the sector, and so on.

Inquiries might also be made about the facts surrounding the practice of staying open until 22.00. Was there any commitment to do this? Had Bigshop made any promises to do this or encouraged others to believe that it would stay open in this way? Might there be the basis for a contractual relationship in this practice? Or, moving into a murkier area of law, might there be some kind of "estoppel" to be pleaded against Bigshop, or would this be over-extending the idea (see Chapter 11)?

With a blank page on which to work, this initial sweep through the case is designed to bring the legal issues more clearly into focus; and the first priority is to gather up all potentially relevant information about a contractual relationship between EDM and Bigshop.

EDM also wishes to know about its remedies if there is a contract. Until the existence and terms of the contract have been established, this is a secondary matter. However, it is possible to outline the reluctance of the courts to make an order for specific performance of a contract (i.e. ordering Bigshop to stay open after 18.00) where damages would be an adequate remedy for EDM (see *Co-operative Insurance Society Ltd v Argyll Stores (Holdings) Ltd* [1998] A.C. 1, below, Ch.18).

In a second version, the problem supplies at least some of the "missing facts" and instructs the student to advise EDM:

"Each retailer at the mall enters into a contract with EDM that contains an identical set of terms and conditions. So far as is material, these terms and conditions provide:
Clause 1: retailers are required 'to open for business each weekday at 10.00 and to remain open until at least 10.00';
Clause 8: retailers should 'cooperate with EDM and use their best endeavours to promote the success of the Eastways shopping mall'.
Advise EDM whether Bigshop would be in breach of contract by closing at 18.00 and, if so, what remedies it might have."

This changes the focus of the response required. Now, the answer should consider whether Bigshop would be in breach of clause 1 (which turns on how we interpret "until at least 18.00") and/or clause 8 (which hinges on what we make of the requirement to cooperate and use best endeavours). With regard to the reading of clause 1, there is now a high-level jurisprudence on the 'contextual' interpretation of commercial contracts (see below Ch.17); and, as we have seen in section 8 of this introductory chapter, the applicability of "best endeavours" clauses is far from straightforward. As in the first version of the problem, something can be said about the remedies that might be available to EDM, but this still presupposes that Bigshop is in breach; and, whether or not Bigshop is in breach is still unclear—not because we need to establish whether there is a contract between the parties but because we cannot be entirely confident about the best interpretation of the two key provisions of the contract. It is always worth remembering that many points of law are contestable and that, where the relevant law is not settled or straightforwardly applicable to the facts, there is no obvious "right answer" (see section 3 above).

In a third version of the problem, matters are made more complex by the introduction of a third-party claim. This is a claim by Smallshop, a retailer at Eastways, also concerned about Bigshop's plan to close at 18.00. This version of the question runs as follows:

"In 2005, a new shopping mall, Eastways, opened in Oldtown. The mall comprises some 50 retail units. At the centre of the mall, there is a very large unit which is occupied by a major department store, Bigshop (the 'anchor' store in the mall).
The mall is managed by Eastways Development and Management (EDM). Each retailer at the mall enters into a contract with EDM that contains an identical set of terms and conditions. So far as is material, these terms and conditions provide:
Clause 1: retailers are required 'to open for business each weekday at 10.00 and to remain open until at least 18.00';
Clause 8: retailers should 'cooperate with EDM and use their best endeavours to promote the success of the Eastways shopping mall'; and,
Clause 25: with reference to the Contracts (Rights of Third Parties) Act 1999, the parties do not intend that any term should be enforceable by a third party.
From 2005 until 2010, most of the shops at Eastways stayed open until 22.00 and it was commonly said in Oldtown that you could shop at Eastways from 10.00 in the morning until 10.00 at night. However, year by year, the number of shoppers visiting Eastways between 18.00 and 22.00 steadily declined. Reflecting this fall in trade after 18.00, in Spring 2011, Bigshop informed EDM that it no longer made business sense to stay open until 22.00 and that, in future, it would be closing at 18.00.

EDM, together with one of the smaller retailers, Smallshop, commenced proceedings against Bigshop claiming that, by closing at 18.00, Bigshop would damage the trading prospects of other retailers and be in breach of contract.

You are instructed by Bigshop to draft a defence to these claims. [Or simply 'Advise Bigshop']"

In this version, the student is being asked to view the problem through the eyes of Bigshop, and to extract from the case-law those points that lend support to the argument that there is no breach of contract. So, for example, in relation to any part of the claim that rests on a supposed breach of clause 8 of the contract, Bigshop would be assisted by the dissenting judgment in *Jet2.Com Limited v Blackpool Airport Limited* [2012] EWCA Civ 417 (above) rather than by the majority judgments; and the inherent uncertainty of 'best endeavours' provisions would be talked up rather than talked down. As for the claim made by Smallshop, insofar as this rests on a breach of the contract between EDM and Bigshop, clause 25 seems to close off the possibility of a claim (by Smallshop) on that contract (see further Ch.12). If Smallshop could "construct" an implied contract between itself and Bigshop, the possibility of a claim might remain open; however, the student will need to venture into some greyer areas of the law to see whether this is an argument that might fly.

In a fourth and final version of the problem, the legal issues have already been identified, narrowed down, and decided by a trial judge. The problem picks up the story as the case is heading for the Court of Appeal. This is how it now reads:

"In 2005, a new shopping mall, Eastways, opened in Oldtown. The mall comprises some 50 retail units. At the centre of the mall, there is a very large unit which is occupied by a major department store, Bigshop (the 'anchor' store in the mall).

The mall is managed by Eastways Development and Management (EDM). Each retailer at the mall enters into a contract with EDM that contains an identical set of terms and conditions. So far as is material, these terms and conditions provide:

Clause 1: retailers are required 'to open for business each weekday at 10.00 and to remain open until at least 18.00';

Clause 8: retailers should 'cooperate with EDM and use their best endeavours to promote the success of the Eastways shopping mall'; and,

Clause 25: with reference to the Contracts (Rights of Third Parties) Act 1999, the parties do not intend that any term should be enforceable by a third party.

From 2005 until 2010, most of the shops at Eastways stayed open until 22.00 and it was commonly said in Oldtown that you could shop at Eastways from 10.00 in the morning until 10.00 at night. However, year by year, the number of shoppers visiting Eastways between 18.00 and 22.00 steadily declined. Reflecting this fall in trade after 18.00, in Spring 2011, Bigshop informed EDM that it no longer made business sense to stay open until 22.00 and that, in future, it would be closing at 18.00.

EDM, together with one of the smaller retailers, Smallshop, commenced proceedings against Bigshop claiming that, by closing at 18.00, Bigshop would damage the trading prospects of other retailers and be in breach of contract.

EDM, relying on *Jet2.Com Limited v Blackpool Airport Limited* [2012] EWCA Civ 417, claimed that Bigshop were in breach of Clause 8 (the 'best endeavours' clause).

Smallshop, citing by analogy *Clarke v Earl of Dunraven* [1897] AC 59, claimed: (i) that in a networked scheme such as the shopping mall, each retailer's contract with EDM was actionable by other retailers at Eastways (and, indeed, was actionable as a direct contract between each of the retailers); and (ii) that Bigshop were in breach of Clause 8.

At the trial, Mr Justice Safehands dismissed the claims made by both EDM and Smallshop.

Ruling against EDM, Safehands J rested his decision on the fact that Bigshop were compliant with the explicit, clear, and specific requirements of Clause 1 (the opening hours' clause). Given that Bigshop were so compliant, the vague and arguably uncertain requirements of the 'best endeavours' clause could not convert their new policy of closing at 18.00 into a breach of contract.

Ruling against Smallshop, Safehands J (distinguishing *Clarke v Earl of Dunraven*) rested his decision on Clause 25 where the parties expressly excluded third-party claims. Given such an express provision, Safehands J rejected the argument that, *by implication*, the network of contracts at Eastways gave rise to third-party claims or to contractual rights and obligations arising directly as between the retailers. Although Safehands J did not decide the point, he also indicated that, even if Smallshop had a contractual claim against Bigshop, he doubted that the latter were in breach of the best endeavours clause.

EDM and Smallshop now appeal, against these rulings by Safehands J, to the Court of Appeal."

The instruction (or rubric) for this problem might be simply "Discuss" (which is not particularly helpful) or more specifically "Draft the terms of the appeals by EDM and Smallshop" or "Outline how you would decide this appeal".

Although the problem does not get any easier as it unfolds, at least we now see how Smallshop is developing its "grey area" claim against Bigshop (which is not to say, of course, that this is the best way for Smallshop to support its claim; but this is the particular argument that is raised by the appeal).

At whatever stage the student meets this problem, it is imperative that the instruction given is followed. Unless there is an instruction to include practical advice (such as "try to settle the claim" or "do not contemplate taking legal proceedings for such a small amount of money", or the like) students should assume that their advice is required on questions of law. Moreover, where there is more than one question involved, it is important to take the points one at a time. Coming back to have several bites at the same cherry is usually none too impressive.

Finally, there is one other important bit of advice. Often, a model answer will involve something like a "decision tree", and particularly so where the instruction is to adjudicate the legal issues. Viewing the dispute from the perspective of the claimant, the adjudicator will identify a number of contested points on each of which the claimant must prevail if the claim is to be successful. If we treat each of these contested points as hurdles standing in the way of the claim, then the case may fall at one or more of these hurdles or, of course, it may succeed. If you judge that the claimant falls at the first hurdle, you know that you must conclude that the claim fails; but, is this all that you need to say? For example, if the first question is whether the parties intended to create legal relations, and if your view is that they did not, then your view is that there is no contract between them and any further questions about breach or remedies or whatever are merely "academic": the claim for breach of contract must fail. Nevertheless, if the problem is intended to raise discussion of these further questions—and the safe assumption is to assume that it is so intended—then they should be addressed. To do this, it is only necessary to say that if a different view had been taken on the question of intention to create legal relations, then the further questions would arise and they can then be addressed. If this seems odd, as you are reading the cases, keep an eye open for judges who say that, while a decision on a particular point is no longer strictly necessary, they will nevertheless express a view—which is precisely what they then proceed to do.[36] As always, in handling contract issues, we

---

[36]   See, e.g., Lord Hoffmann's speech in *Chartbrook Limited v Persimmon Homes Limited* [2009] UKHL 38 where, although the House holds that Persimmon win the appeal on the construction of the contract, two other major questions of law raised by the appeal are reviewed at some length.

can learn from the way that judges reason, reflect and resolve issues; we can learn from the cases and from the practices of adjudicators.

Further reading

John N Adams and Roger Brownsword, *Understanding Contract Law*, 5th edn (London: Sweet and Maxwell, 2007)

Roger Brownsword, *Contract Law: Themes for the Twenty-First Century*, 2nd edn (Oxford: Oxford University Press, 2006)

Roger Brownsword, 'The Law of Contract: Doctrinal Impulses, External Pressures, Future Directions' (2014) 31 *Journal of Contract Law* 73

Duncan Kennedy, 'Form and Substance in Private Law Adjudication' (1976) 89 HLR 1685

Johan Steyn, 'Contract Law: Fulfilling the Reasonable Expectations of Honest Men' (1997) 113 *Law Quarterly Review* 433

PART I

THE FORMATION OF A CONTRACT

2

CONTRACT: FORM, FLEXIBILITY AND FAIR DEALING

LEARNING OBJECTIVES

By the end of this chapter, you should understand that:

- according to the traditional view, the first necessary step towards forming a contract is that an "offer" is made; and that the contract is formed when the offer is "accepted";
- an offer is to be distinguished from invitations to treat (invitations to tender) or other indications that fall short of an offer;
- there is considerable flexibility in the way that the "offer and acceptance" model is applied to different factual situations;
- the modern courts, recognising that commercial deals are not always put together in quite the way that the traditional view suggests, tend to hold, nevertheless, that there is a contract;
- the modern law pays increasing attention to the parties' reasonable expectations, one of the corollaries of which is that the law will enforce at least a minimum standard of good faith and fair dealing in the formation of contracts.

INTRODUCTION

The law of contract is one segment of the common law of obligations (see Ch.1, above). As such, it is generally characterised as that branch of the law which determines whether a promise is binding and, if it is, what are the consequences of breaking it. A contract is, in Sir Frederick Pollock's words, "a promise or a set of promises which the law will enforce." So, the first essential of a contract is that there should be an identifiable promise (or set of promises) representing the contractual offer that is then open for acceptance. However, as Lord Wilberforce famously remarked in *New Zealand Shipping Co Ltd v Satterthwaite (AM) & Co Ltd: The Eurymedon* [1975] A.C. 154 (below, Ch.13) at 167, "English law, having committed itself to a rather technical and schematic doctrine of contract, in application takes a practical approach, often at the cost of forcing the facts to fit uneasily into the marked slots of offer, acceptance and consideration."

Sometimes, as the cases in this chapter highlight, English law sticks rigidly to its orthodox understanding of the process that leads to the formation of a contract (see, e.g., the House of Lords' approach in *Gibson v Manchester City Council*, below); but, at other times, a degree of flexibility is found, whether to reflect the actualities of business practice (see, e.g., the *RTS Flexible Systems* case, below), the connected or linked nature of agreements (see, e.g., *Clarke v Dunraven*, below), or

2–001

compelling considerations of fair dealing (see, e.g., *Blackpool v Fylde Aeroclub Ltd v Blackpool Borough Council*, below). Where the law favours flexibility or gives priority to considerations of fair dealing, we might say that the law moves into line with what it judges to be the (practice-based) reasonable expectations of contractors (see, e.g., *Barry v Davies*, below).

The cases in this chapter are presented in three principal sections. In the first section, the cases are largely concerned with differentiating between those market signals that are to be treated as "offers" and those that fall short of an offer; in the second section, the focus is on, so to speak, the "chronology" of contracting—that is, on the classical model of contract as a process in which the first step is for a promisor to make an offer and then, and only then, may the promisee (with full knowledge of the offer) respond by accepting; and, in the third section, the cases give a first glimpse of how the courts view a party's complaint that there has been an element of unfair dealing.

1. Promises, Offers and Contract Form

2–002   In this section of the chapter, the cases are clustered around the following three issues: (i) whether indications of price and whether (and which) indications of a willingness to sell will be recognised as constituting an offer; (ii) how far the explicit and implicit groundrules for bids, tenders, and auctions are treated as contractually binding; and (iii) how the law of contract treats promotional gifts and "offers".

A. Indications of Price and Willingness to Sell

2–003   How clearly must a party signal a definite intention to sell before the law of contract will recognise that an offer has been made? For example, is it enough to say that one might be prepared to sell or to give an indication of the price that one hopes to get, and so on?

In the famous case of *Harvey v Facey* [1893] A.C. 552, Harvey sent a telegram to Facey: "Will you sell us Bumper Hall Pen (a property in Jamaica)? Telegraph lowest cash price—answer paid". Facey replied: "Lowest price for Bumper Hall Pen £900" whereupon Harvey telegraphed "We agree to buy Bumper Hall Pen for the sum of £900 asked by you. . .". Facey declined to sell and the Privy Council held that he was not bound. Harvey's first telegram asked two questions and Facey answered only the second. He had made no promise, express or implied, to sell. The decision may be criticised on the ground that, truly, a promise was implicit in Facey's reply—if he was not willing to sell why did he answer the second question and not the first? "Bumper Hall Pen not for sale" would have been the natural reply. Why state a price unless he was willing to sell? It is a question of the interpretation of the telegrams, on which opinions differ.

Harvey v Facey concerned a contract for the sale of land. In 1893 the telegrams (if they had been interpreted to imply a promise to sell) would have been a sufficient memorandum to satisfy the Statute of Frauds. But, if the facts recurred in England today, a written contract would be required. A valid contract for the sale of land can no longer be made by an exchange of letters, telex or faxed messages. But the great majority of contracts may be so made and *Harvey v Facey* remains a good (though controversial) authority on the general principles of the formation of contracts.

GIBSON v MANCHESTER CITY COUNCIL

House of Lords [1979] 1 W.L.R. 294; [1979] 1 All E.R. 972; (1979) 77 L.G.R. 405; [1979] J.P.L. 532

2–004   In November 1970 the council sent to council tenants details of a scheme for the sale of council houses, giving favourable terms as to prices and mortgages. G immediately replied. He paid a £3 administration fee and forwarded his application on the printed form. The city treasurer replied saying: "The corporation may be prepared to sell the house to you at the purchase price of £2,725 less 20 per cent. £2,180 (freehold)". The letter gave details about a mortgage and went on, "This letter should not be regarded as a firm offer of a mortgage. If you would like to make a formal application to buy your council house, please complete the enclosed application form and return it to me as soon as possible".

G filled in and returned the form but left the purchase price blank, saying in a covering letter that repairs needed to be done and asking the corporation to lower the price or repair the premises. The corporation replied that they had taken into account the state of the property in fixing the price and they could not undertake to do the repairs. On March 18 G replied: "In view of your remarks I would be obliged if you will carry on with the purchase as per my application already in your possession".

In May Labour took control of the council from the Conservatives and instructed their officers not to sell council houses unless they were legally bound to do so. The council declined to sell to G and 350 other tenants in a similar situation.

The Court of Appeal (Denning MR and Ormrod LJ, Geoffrey Lane LJ dissenting) affirmed the judgment of Judge Bailey ordering the council specifically to perform (see below, Ch.18) the contract. The council appealed.

LORD DIPLOCK

Lord Denning M.R. rejected what I have described as the conventional approach of looking to see whether on the true construction of the documents relied on there can be discerned an offer and acceptance. One ought, he said, to "look at the correspondence as a whole and at the conduct of the parties and see therefrom whether the parties have come to an agreement on everything that was material." . . .

My Lords, there may be certain types of contract, though I think they are exceptional, which do not fit easily into the normal analysis of a contract as being constituted by offer and acceptance, but a contract alleged to have been made by an exchange of correspondence between the parties in which the successive communications other than the first are in reply to one another is not one of these. I can see no reason in the instant case for departing from the conventional approach of looking at the handful of documents relied on as constituting the contract sued on and seeing whether on their true construction there is to be found in them a contractual offer by the council to sell the house to Mr Gibson and an acceptance of that offer by Mr Gibson. I venture to think that it was by departing from this conventional approach that the majority of the Court of Appeal was led into error . . .

My Lords, the words I have italicised, (see italicised words in statement of facts, above, p. 7) seem to me, as they seemed to Geoffrey Lane L.J., to make it quite impossible to construe this letter as a contractual offer capable of being converted into a legally enforceable open contract for the sale of land by Mr Gibson's written acceptance of it. The words "may be prepared to sell" are fatal to this; so is the invitation, not, it is to be noted, to accept the offer, but "to make formal application to buy" on the enclosed application form. It is, to quote Geoffrey Lane L.J., a letter setting out the financial terms on which it may be the council would be prepared to consider a sale and purchase in due course.

My Lords, the application form and letter of March 18, 1971 were relied on by Mr Gibson as an unconditional acceptance of the council's offer to sell the house; but this cannot be so unless there was a contractual offer by the council available for acceptance, and, for the reason already given I am of opinion that there was none. It is unnecessary to consider whether the application form and Mr Gibson's letters of March 5 and 18, 1971 are capable of amounting to a contractual offer by him to purchase the freehold interest in the house at a price of £2,180 on the terms of an open contract, for there is no suggestion that, even if it were, it was ever accepted by the council. Nor would it ever have been even if there had been no change in the political control of the council, as the policy of the council before the change required the incorporation in all agreements for sale of council houses to tenants of the conditions referred by Lord Denning M.R. in his judgment and other conditions inconsistent with an open contract . . .

Lord Edmund-Davies and Lord Russell made speeches allowing the Appeal and Lords Fraser and Keith agreed with Lord Diplock.

Appeal Allowed.

Questions

2–005   1. Might the result have been different if the city treasurer had written: "The corporation is prepared to sell the house to you. . ."?

2. Lord Denning said that the parties had agreed on everything that was material. But is agreeing
on the terms necessarily the same as agreeing to be bound by them? Was the Council saying, "If
we agree to sell you the house, these are the terms on which we will do so"? Cf. *Attorney General
of Hong Kong v Humphreys Estate*, below, Ch.4.

SPENCER v HARDING

Common Pleas (1870) L.R. 5 C.P. 561; 39 L.J.C.P. 332; 23 L.T. 237; 19 W.R. 48

2–006   The defendants sent out a circular as follows:

"We are instructed to offer to the wholesale trade for sale by tender the stock-in-trade of Messrs. G. Eilbeck &
Co amounting as per stock-book to £2,503 13s. 1d. and which will be sold at a discount in one lot. Payment to
be made in cash. The stock may be viewed on the premises . . . up to Thursday, the 20th instant, on which day,
at 12 o'clock, noon precisely, the tenders will be received and opened at our offices . . ."

The plaintiffs alleged that the circular amounted to an offer and undertaking to sell the stock to the highest
bidder for cash; and that they, the plaintiffs, had submitted the highest tender; and the defendants refused to
accept it and sell the goods to them.

Demurrer on the ground that the declaration showed no promise to accept the plaintiffs' tender or sell them
the goods.

Holl in support of the demurrer: Although the declaration is somewhat ambiguous, it is evidently intended
to raise the question whether one who advertises for tenders for the purchase of goods thereby engages to sell
them to the highest bidder. The nearest analogous case is that of an advertisement for tenders for building. It has
never been held or suggested that the advertiser is bound to accept the lowest tender. Suppose here there had
been only one tender, would the defendants have been bound to accept that? The advertisement clearly does not
amount to a contract; it only invites offers.

Morgan Lloyd, contra: The words of the circular and the averments in the declaration taken together, disclose
a contract on the part of the defendants to sell the goods to whoever should make the highest tender. This
is not like the case of tenders for a building. There, the acceptance of the lowest tender is always subject to
the architect's judgment as to the character and capacity of the builder. Here, the offer is to sell for cash. The
allegation in the count may be sustained either by evidence of a direct promise, or by evidence of the custom
of the trade.

The nearest analogy is that of advertisements offering rewards for the discovery and conviction of an offender,
of which one of the leading instances is the case of *Williams v Carwardine* (below) where Littledale J says: "The
advertisement amounts to a general promise to give a sum of money to any person who shall give information
which might lead to the discovery of the offender."

WILLES J

I am of opinion that the defendants are entitled to judgment. The action is brought against persons who issued a
circular offering a stock for sale by tender, to be sold at a discount in one lot. The plaintiffs sent in a tender which
turned out to be the highest, but was not accepted. They now insist that the circular amounts to a contract or
promise to sell the goods to the highest bidder, that is, in this case, to the person who should tender for them
at the smallest rate of discount; and reliance is placed on the cases as to rewards offered for the discovery of an
offender. In those cases, however, there never was any doubt that the advertisement amounted to a promise to
pay the money to the person who first gave information. The difficulty suggested was that it was a contract with

all the world. But that, of course, was soon overruled. It was an offer to become liable to any person who before the offer should be retracted should happen to be the person to fulfil the contract of which the advertisement was an offer or tender. That is not the sort of difficulty which presents itself here. If the circular had gone on, "and we undertake to sell to the highest bidder," the reward cases would have applied, and there would have been a good contract in respect of the persons. But the question is, whether there is here any offer to enter into a contract at all, or whether the circular amounts to anything more than a mere proclamation that the defendants are ready to chaffer for the sale of the goods, and to receive offers for the purchase of them. In advertisements for tenders for buildings, it is not usual to say that the contract will be given to the lowest bidder, and it is not always that the contract is made with the lowest bidder. Here there is a total absence of any words to intimate that the highest bidder is to be the purchaser. It is a mere attempt to ascertain whether an offer can be obtained within such a margin as the sellers are willing to adopt.

Keating and Montague Smith J. J. concurred.

Judgment for the Defendants.

Questions

1. Would a reasonable reader of the circular have supposed that the defendants intended to make any binding promise? Was it reasonable to suppose that the defendants intended to bind themselves to sell to the highest bidder, however low the bid might be? **2–007**

2. In *Rooke v Dawson* [1895] 1 Ch. 480 trustees announced an examination for an endowed scholarship. The plaintiff and one other candidate presented themselves for the examination. The plaintiff obtained 570 marks and the other candidate 496 marks.

   Chitty J, following *Spencer v Harding*, dismissed the plaintiff's action for a declaration that he was entitled to the scholarship: the announcement did not state that the scholarship would be awarded to the candidate who obtained the highest marks.

   Was the plaintiff reasonably entitled to believe that the defendants were promising to give the scholarship to that candidate, however low his marks might be?

3. Would the plaintiffs in *Spencer v Harding* and *Rooke v Dawson* have had any redress if the goods had been sold to the second highest bidder, or the scholarship given to the second candidate? Would that have been a breach of any promise, express or implied, by the defendants in either case? For example, "If we sell [award the scholarship] it will be to the highest bidder [candidate with the highest marks]".

PHARMACEUTICAL SOCIETY OF GREAT BRITAIN v BOOTS

Court of Appeal [1953] 1 Q.B. 401; [1953] 2 W.L.R. 427; 117 J.P. 132; 97 S.J. 149; [1953] 1 All E.R. 482

According to the *Boots* decision (see Ch.1), even though the price of goods in a supermarket is clearly indicated and even though the goods are accessible to customers, the general rule is that their display constitutes no more than an invitation to treat; it is the customers who make the offers which are then open for acceptance or rejection by the supermarket. **2–008**

Points for reflection

2–009
1. The *Boots* case decides who makes the offer in a supermarket. It does not decide what constitutes acceptance. Is the contract concluded (i) when the seller records the price, via a bar code or an old-fashioned till, thereby accepting the offer to buy? or (ii) when the buyer pays the price, thereby accepting a counter-offer from the seller? See Bernard S. Jackson, 'Offer and Acceptance in the Supermarket' (1979) 129 New L.J. 775.

2. In *Lasky v Economy Grocery Stores* (1946) 65 N.E. (2d) 305; 163 A.L.R. 235, the plaintiff picked up a bottle of "tonic" in a self-service grocery shop owned by the defendant. As she was about to place it in the carrier basket provided the bottle exploded and severely injured her. She brought an action for breach of an implied warranty under a contract of sale. The Massachusetts Supreme Judicial Court held that the action failed as there was neither a sale nor an agreement to sell at the time the bottle exploded. The Court said that the display of goods constituted an offer which could not be accepted before the goods reached the cashier. Until then the customer was free to return an article to the shelf even though she had put it in the basket.

   In *Sancho-Lopez v Fedor Food Corp* (1961) 211 N.Y.S. (2d) 953 the plaintiff succeeded in the City Court of New York in circumstances similar to those in *Lasky's* case except that he was removing the bottle from the carrier basket and handing it to the cashier when it exploded. Cf. 108 S.J. 207.

   In cases of this kind the shopkeeper may have been in no way negligent. It may have been impossible to detect that there was anything wrong with the bottle. So he could not be made liable in the tort of negligence. But contractual liability is strict. If the seller has promised that the bottle is fit for its purpose and it is not, his promise is broken and he is liable in damages. Of course the manufacturer may have been negligent and, if so, he is liable to the injured customer in tort. But it may be impracticable to sue the manufacturer—perhaps the goods are imported—and, anyway, negligence may be difficult to prove. So the simplest and most convenient course is to sue the shopkeeper in contract; and this is possible only if a contract has been concluded before the explosion. Since 1985, a person injured by a defective product is likely to have an alternative remedy under the wide-ranging provisions of the Consumer Protection Act 1987.

3. In *Fisher v Bell* [1961] 1 Q.B. 394 a shopkeeper was charged with "offering for sale" a flick knife contrary to the Restriction of Offensive Weapons Act 1959. The flick knife was not actually sold to a customer but it was on display in the shop window with a price tag attached. Applying the general rule that goods on display in shops are merely invitations to treat, it was held that the shopkeeper had not "offered" the knife for sale and accordingly no offence had been committed. This was somewhat inconvenient for the criminal justice system. Did the logic of the *Boots* case lead inexorably to the decision in *Fisher v Bell*?

Problem

2–010
Ada picks up a chicken marked '£1.50' in a self-service shop and tenders it to the cashier who says that the price tag is erroneous and the true price is £2.50. Advise Ada. What would be the position under the Massachusetts or New York rule?

Winfield, "Some Aspects of Offer and Acceptance" (1939) 55 L.Q.R. 499, 517

. . . surely a more natural interpretation of the display of goods in a shop with a marked price on them would be that the shopkeeper impliedly reserves to himself a right of selecting his customer. A shop is a place for bargaining, not for compulsory sales. Presumptively, the importance of the personality of the customer cannot be eliminated. If the display of such goods were an offer, then the shopkeeper might be forced to contract with his worst enemy, his greatest trade rival, a reeling drunkard, or a raggard and verminous tramp. That would be a result scarcely likely to be countenanced by the law. Even in a business like that of the innkeeper or the common carrier, where there is by law a duty to render services to such persons as may apply for them, the personal element is never entirely excluded. An innkeeper is not bound to accommodate a common prostitute, a railway company is not bound to find transport for one who is not in a fit condition to travel. Of course, a tradesman may frame his proposal in such way as to abrogate any choice in his selection of a customer. But it is not easy to imagine a case in which he would be likely to do so, and some instances, which might at first sight appear to amount to such abrogation, are more likely to be construed as retaining it. Thus even if the ticket on a clock in a jeweller's window were "For sale for £1, cash down, to first comer," we still think that it is only an invitation to do business and that the first comer must be one of whom the jeweller approves.

B. Bids, Tenders and Auctions

Much of the modern law is guided by the importance of protecting the reasonable expectations of contractors, an idea that extends to the protection of the reasonable expectations of those who submit tenders in accordance with the advertised rules. The opening case in this section, *Blackpool and Fylde Aeroclub Ltd v Blackpool Borough Council*, is one of the best illustrations of this modern philosophy.   2–011

BLACKPOOL AND FYLDE AEROCLUB LTD v BLACKPOOL BOROUGH COUNCIL

Court of Appeal [1990] 1 W.L.R. 1195; [1990] 3 All E.R. 25

From time to time the council granted a concession to an operator to provide pleasure flights from the airport which the council owned. The plaintiff obtained the concession in 1975, 1978 and 1980. As the last concession was reaching its end, the council invited the club and six other parties to tender. The invitations stated that tenders were to be submitted in the envelope provided, which was not to bear any name or mark to identify the sender and that tenders received after the time specified, 12 noon on March 17, 1983 would not be considered. The club and two other invitees responded. The club's tender was delivered by hand and put in the Town Hall letter box at 11 am on March 17, but the letter box was not cleared by council staff at 12 noon as it should have been. The club's tender was recorded as having been received late and was not considered. The club sued for breach of an alleged warranty that a tender received by the deadline would be considered. The judge awarded damages for breach of contract and negligence. The council appealed.   2–012

BINGHAM LJ

. . . having considered the arguments of both sides, continued: A tendering procedure of this kind is, in many respects, heavily weighted in favour of the invitor. He can invite tenders from as many or as few parties as he chooses. He need not tell any of them who else, or how many others, he has invited. The invitee may often, although not here, be put to considerable labour and expense in preparing a tender, ordinarily without recompense if he is unsuccessful. The invitation to tender may itself, in a complex case, although again not here, involve time and expense to prepare, but the invitor does not commit himself to proceed with the project, whatever it is; he need not accept the highest tender; he need to accept any tender; he need not give reasons to justify his acceptance or rejection of any tender received. The risk to which the tenderer is exposed does not end with the risk that his tender may not be the highest (or, as the case may be, lowest). But where, as here, tenders are solicited from selected parties all of them known to the invitor, and where a local authority's invitation prescribes a clear, orderly and familiar procedure (draft contract conditions available for inspection and plainly not open to negotiation, a prescribed common form of tender, the supply of envelopes designed to preserve the absolute anonymity of tenderers and clearly to identify the tender in question and an absolute deadline) the invitee is in my judgment protected at least to this extent: if he submits a conforming tender before the deadline he is entitled, not as a matter of mere expectation but of contractual right, to be sure that his tender will after the deadline be opened and considered in conjunction with all other conforming tenders or at least that his tender will be considered if others are. Had the club, before tendering, inquired of the council whether it could rely on any timely and conforming tender being considered along with others, I feel quite sure that the answer would have been "of course." The law would, I think, be defective if it did not give effect to that.

It is of course true that the invitation to tender does not explicitly state that the council will consider timely and conforming tenders. That is why one is concerned with implication. But the council does not either say that it does not bind itself to do so, and in the context of a reasonable invitee would understand the invitation to be saying, quite clearly, that if he submitted a timely and conforming tender it would be considered, at least if any other such tender were considered.

I readily accept that contracts are not to be lightly implied. Having examined what the parties said and did, the court must be able to conclude with confidence both that the parties intended to create contractual relations and that the agreement was to the effect contended for. It must also, in most cases, be able to answer the question posed by Mustill L.J. in *Hispanica de Petroleos SA v Vencedora Oceanica Navegacion SA, The Kapetan Markos N. L. (No. 2)* [1987] 2 Lloyd's Rep. 321 at 331: "What was the mechanism for offer and acceptance?" In all the circumstances of this case (and I say nothing about any other) I have no doubt that the parties did intend to create contractual relations to the limited extent contended for. Since it has never been the law that a person is only entitled to enforce his contractual rights in a reasonable way (*White & Carter (Councils) Ltd v McGregor* [1962] A.C. 413 at 430 per Lord Reid, below, p.454), counsel for the club was in my view right to contend for no more than a contractual duty to consider. I think it plain that the council's invitation to tender was, to this limited extent, an offer, and the club's submission of a timely and conforming tender an acceptance . . .

I accordingly agree with the judge's conclusion on the contractual issue, essentially for the reasons which he more briefly gave.

Stocker L.J. delivered judgment dismissing the appeal and Farquharson L.J. agreed.

Appeal Dismissed.

Questions

2-013   1. Was the club reasonably entitled to suppose that the council was promising: "If you submit a timely tender, we will consider it?" See Adams and Brownsword, (1991) 54 *Modern Law Review* 301.

2. How can damages be assessed for loss of an opportunity to be considered? (The court did not have to discuss that question.) Cf. *Chaplin v Hicks* [1911] 2 K.B. 786, below, Ch.19 (plaintiff, in breach of contract, denied opportunity of taking part in a beauty contest). What of the case where the tenderer has been put to considerable trouble and expense?

3. Could the timely tenderers have had any redress (a) if the concession had not been awarded at all? (b) if it had been awarded to one who submitted a late tender?

HARVELA INVESTMENTS LTD v ROYAL TRUST CO OF CANADA LTD

House of Lords [1986] A.C. 207; [1985] 3 W.L.R. 276; [1985] 2 All E.R. 966

2-014   The Royal Trust Co, by telex, invited Harvela and the second defendant, Sir Leonard Outerbridge, to make offers by sealed tender for shares in a company and undertook to accept the highest offer. Harvela's offer was $2,175,000 and Sir Leonard's was "$2,100,000 or $101,000 in excess of any other offer . . . expressed as a fixed monetary amount, whichever is higher". The vendors thought they were bound to accept, and so did accept, Sir Leonard's bid.

Harvela obtained an injunction preventing Royal Trust from accepting Sir Leonard's "referential bid" of $2,276,000 and claimed a right to enforce a contract for the sale of the shares to it for $2,175,000. Peter Gibson J, following *Liverpool City Council v Irwin* (below, para.16–009), held that there was an implied term in Royal Trust's invitation excluding referential bids and gave judgment for Harvela. The Court of Appeal allowed Sir Leonard's appeal. Harvela appealed to the House of Lords.

Lord Diplock made a speech allowing the appeal.

Lords Fraser and Edmund-Davies said they agreed with Lords Diplock and Templeman.

LORD BRIDGE OF HARWICH

My Lords, on the main issue I agree that, for all the reasons given in the speeches of my noble and learned friends Lord Diplock and Lord Templeman, Sir Leonard's referential bid was not, on the true construction of the invitation, a valid offer. Without intending to derogate in any way from the cogency of the other grounds for reaching that conclusion, there seems to me to be one that is decisive. The invitation embodied an undertaking not to disclose the details of any offer to any party before the deadline of 3 p.m. on Wednesday, September 16, 1981. Sir Leonard's referential bid could not be quantified without reading into it the amount of Harvela's fixed bid. To do this before the deadline would have been, in my opinion, a breach of the undertaking. To do it after the deadline would have been too late.

LORD TEMPLEMAN

A fixed bidding sale met all the requirements of the vendors deducible from the terms of the invitation. A fixed bidding sale was bound to result in a sale of shares save in the unlikely event of both Harvela and Sir Leonard failing to respond to the invitation. A fixed bidding sale gave an equal opportunity to Harvela and Sir Leonard to acquire the shares. A fixed bidding sale provoked the best price, or at any rate something approximate to the best price, which the purchaser was prepared to pay to secure the shares and to ensure that the rival bidder did not acquire the shares. On the other hand, if the invitation is construed so as to create an auction sale by means of referential bids, the requirements of the vendors deducible from the terms of the invitation could not be met.

First, if referential bids were permissible, there was a danger, far from negligible, that the sale might be abortive and the shares remain unsold. The shares would only be sold if at least one bidder submitted a fixed bid and the other bidder based his referential offer on that fixed bid. In the events which happened, Harvela put forward a fixed bid of $2,175,000 and Sir Leonard made a referential bid of $101,000 more than Harvela's fixed bid, thus enabling Sir Leonard's referential bid to be quantified at $2,276,000. But if Sir Leonard's referential bid had not been expressed to be based on Harvela's fixed bid, or if Harvela had not not made a fixed bid but only a referential bid, then Sir Leonard's bid could not have been quantified. Similarly, if Harvela had made a referential bid not expressed to be tied to Sir Leonard's fixed bid, or if Sir Leonard had not made a fixed bid but only a referential bid, then Harvela's bid could not have been quantified. The sale would have been abortive although both bidders were anxious to purchase and submitted offers.

Secondly, if referential bids were permissible, there was also a possibility, which in fact occurred, that one bidder would never have an opportunity to buy. In the present case Harvela, by putting forward a fixed bid, could never succeed in buying the shares although the invitation had been extended to them. Harvela's only part in the sale was unwittingly to determine the price at which Sir Leonard was entitled and bound to purchase the shares. Harvela could not win and Sir Leonard could not lose. There was nothing in the invitation to warn Harvela that they must submit a referential bid if they wished to make sure of being able to compete with Sir Leonard. There was nothing in the invitation which indicated to Sir Leonard that he was entitled to submit a referential bid. But no one has argued that the invitation did not invite fixed bids; indeed, Sir Leonard submitted a fixed bid, albeit as an unsuccessful alternative to his referential bid.

Thirdly, if referential bids were permissible, the vendors' object of provoking the best price that Harvela and Sir Leonard were each prepared to offer in ignorance of the rival bid was frustrated. Harvela put forward the fixed bid of $2,175,000 which represented the amount which Harvela hoped would exceed Sir Leonard's bid and which, because Harvela were bidding in ignorance of Sir Leonard's bid, must be or approximate to the best price which Harvela were prepared to pay to secure the shares and to ensure that Sir Leonard did not acquire the shares. Sir Leonard did not put forward his best price; Sir Leonard put forward his worst price,

$2,100,000, but declared that he would pay $101,000 more than Harvela. Sir Leonard could have achieved the same purpose by offering five dollars or one dollar more than Harvela. If Sir Leonard had appreciated that he was taking part in a fixed bidding sale, then, judging by his minimum fixed bid of $2,100,000 and his unlimited referential bid, he might have been prepared to offer as his best price more than the sum of $2,276,000 which he now claims to be the purchase price of the shares. We shall never know because Sir Leonard did not reveal his best price.

Finally, if referential bids were permissible by implication, without express provision in the invitation for that purpose, and without any indication in the invitation of the nature of the referential bids which would be acceptable, the results could have been bizarre. In the present case, Sir Leonard bid $2,100,000 or $101,000 in excess of Harvela's fixed bid. If Harvela had bid $2,000,000 or one dollar more than Sir Leonard's fixed bid, then Sir Leonard would have become the purchaser with his referential bid of $2,101,000 as against Harvela's referential bid of $2,100,001. But if Harvela had offered $1,900,000 or one dollar more than Sir Leonard's fixed bid, then Harvela would have been the purchaser at their referential bid of $2,100,001 as against Sir Leonard's referential bid of $2,001,000. Sir Leonard's bid in the second example is the same as his bid in the first example but he loses. Harvela's bid in the second example is lower than Harvela's bid in the first example but Harvela wins. The vendors are worse off by $999 in the second example.

It would have been possible for the vendors to conduct an auction sale through the medium of confidential referential bids but only by making express provision in the invitation for the purpose. It would not have been sufficient for the invitation expressly to authorise "referential bids" without more. For such an authorisation would have rendered the result of the sale uncertain and random in view of the illustrations and examples I have already given. It would have been necessary for the invitation to require each bidder who made a referential bid to specify a maximum sum he was prepared to bid. That requirement would ensure that the sale was not abortive and that both bidders had a genuine chance of winning. A maximum bid requirement would ensure a sale at a price in excess of the maximum bid of the unsuccessful bidder, but it would not necessarily procure a sale at the maximum price of the successful bidder. The sale would in effect be an auction sale and produce the consequences of an auction sale because the vendors would have made express provision for bids to be adjusted and finalised by reference to the maximum bid of the unsuccessful bidder. But without such express provisions the invitation is not consistent with an auction sale.

To constitute a fixed bidding sale all that was necessary was that the vendors should invite confidential offers and should undertake to accept the highest offer. Such was the form of the invitation. It follows that the invitation upon its true construction created a fixed bidding sale and that Sir Leonard was not entitled to submit and the vendors were not entitled to accept a referential bid.

Appeal Allowed.

It is instructive to analyse the *Harvela* case apart from the complexity caused by the submission of a referential bid. The Royal Trust's telex to Harvela and Sir Leonard was an offer to each of them which could be accepted only by one—the one who made the higher valid bid. The telex was an offer of a unilateral contract, like an offer to give a prize to the one of two entrants for a race who comes first. The 'prize' was a contract for the sale of the shares—the Trust was bound to accept the higher bidder's offer to buy them.

Until that bid was made, no one was under any obligation. The Trust could have withdrawn its offer and the two offerees were under no obligation to bid. While the offer stood, the Trust was, of course, liable to become bound to one of the offerees through the acceptance of its offer, but that is the position of all offerors, so long as their offer remains open to acceptance. When the higher bid was ascertained, the Trust was bound to accept it. At that moment there was just one contract—a contract by the Trust to accept the higher bidder's offer—a unilateral contract. The bidder was free to withdraw his bid until the Trust accepted it, but when they did he became bound to buy the shares. This was the construction favoured by Peter Gibson J [1984] 2 All E.R. at 78, e–c.

The point is made here because the diligent student who reads Lord Diplock's speech in the full report of the case will find that his Lordship considered that the telex messages, when received by Harvela and Sir Leonard, amounted not merely to offers but to unilateral contracts with each of them; and that, on receipt of the bids, that of the higher bidder would be converted into a bilateral contract to buy and to sell whereas that of the unsuccessful bidder would be terminated. This analysis seems not only unnecessarily complex but also inaccurate in two respects.

(i) The telexes were not contracts but offers. It might be argued that the telexes were 'conditional contracts' because the Trust would be bound if the condition (that is, making the higher bid) were satisfied; but the answer is that this is true of all offers; the offeror will become bound if the condition (the act of acceptance) is fulfilled. If the argument were right, all offers would be contracts which is absurd.

(ii) A bilateral contract did not come into existence on receipt of the higher bid. The Trust had invited offers and it had received offers. Offers are revocable until accepted. The Trust was bound to accept the offer but, until it did so, the bidder could have revoked his offer.

Harvela made the only valid bid so the Trust was bound to accept that. However the Trust thought (excusably, because the Court of Appeal were of the same opinion) that Sir Leonard's was a higher and valid bid so they accepted that. So they had contracted (i) to accept Harvela's offer to buy the shares and (ii) to sell the shares to Sir Leonard. Peter Gibson J ([1984] 2 All E.R. at 78–79) held that the second contract was not invalid but Harvela's prior contract prevailed and Harvela was entitled to specific performance of it. He awarded Sir Leonard nominal damages of £2. Lord Templeman, however, held that the contract with Sir Leonard was a nullity because both parties were under the mistaken impression that the Trust was bound to make it. On this, see below, para.23–014.

SALE OF GOODS ACT 1979

Auction sales

57.—(1) Where goods are put up for sale by auction in lots, each lot is prima facie deemed to be the subject of a separate contract of sale.   **2–015**

(2) A sale by auction is complete when the auctioneer announces its completion by the fall of the hammer, or in other customary manner; and until the announcement is made any bidder may retract his bid.

(3) A sale by auction may be notified to be subject to a reserve or upset price, and a right to bid may also be reserved expressly by or on behalf of the seller.

(4) Where a sale by auction is not notified to be subject to a right to bid by or on behalf of the seller, it is not lawful for the seller to bid himself or to employ any person to bid at the sale, or for the auctioneer knowingly to take any bid from the seller or any such person.

(5) A sale contravening subsection (4) above may be treated as fraudulent by the buyer.

(6) Where, in respect of a sale by auction, a right to bid is expressly reserved (but not otherwise) the seller or any one person on his behalf may bid at the auction.

It should be noted that s.57(2) codifies the common law rule laid down in *Payne v Cave* (1789) 3 Term. Rep. 148; 100 E.R. 502. There, the plaintiff alleged that the defendant had bought the plaintiff's goods at an auction sale. The defendant had made the highest bid but had withdrawn it before the hammer fell. Lord Kenyon nonsuited the plaintiff and it was held that the nonsuit was very proper. The court said: 'The auctioneer is the agent of the vendor, and the assent of both parties is necessary to make the contract binding; that is signified on the part of the seller by knocking down the hammer, which was not done here till the defendant had retracted. An auction is not unaptly called locus poenitentiae. Every bidding is nothing more than an offer on one side, which is not binding on either side till it is assented to. But according to what is now contended for, one party would be bound by the offer, and the other not, which can never be allowed'.

That said, the conditions under which a sale takes place may allow it to be reopened after the fall of the hammer, as where The National Conditions of Sale provided that if any dispute arose respecting a bid, 'the auctioneer may determine the dispute, or the property may, at the vendor's option, either be put up again at the last undisputed bid or be withdrawn': *Richards v Phillips* [1969] 1 Ch.39.

Questions

2–016

1. The conditions of sale at an auction sometimes provide "No person shall retract his bidding". What is the effect of this? Cf. *Routledge v Grant,* below, Ch.3.

2. Who makes the offer in a Dutch auction? (". . . the offer of articles to be bid for at successively decreasing prices . . .", Mock Auctions Act 1961 s.3).

WARLOW v HARRISON

Exchequer Chamber (1859) 1 E. & E. 309; 29 L.J.Q.B. 14; 1 L.T. 211; 6 Jur.(n.s.) 66; 8 W.R. 95; 120 E.R. 925

2–017   The defendant was an auctioneer in Birmingham, where he had a repository for the sale of horses. In June 1858, he advertised a sale by auction at the repository. The items for sale included: "the three following horses, the property of a gentleman, without reserve." One of these was a mare called Janet Pride. The plaintiff attended the sale and bid 60 guineas for her. Mr Henderson, the owner of the mare, then bid 61 guineas. The plaintiff was informed that the last bidder was the owner and declined to bid further. The defendant knocked the mare down to Mr Henderson and entered his name in the sale book as purchaser. The plaintiff went at once to the auctioneer's office and claimed the mare as the highest bona fide bidder. Mr Henderson said "I bought her in; and you shall not have her; I gave £130 for the mare; and it is not likely I am going to sell her for £63." On the same day the plaintiff tendered to the defendant £63 in sovereigns as the price of the mare and demanded her. The defendant refused to receive the money or to deliver the mare.

The plaintiff alleged in his declaration that the defendant became and was the agent of the plaintiff to complete the contract on behalf of the plaintiff for the purchase of the said mare, but wholly omitted and refused to do so; whereby the plaintiff was deprived of the benefit of the said contract, and unable to obtain the said mare, as he otherwise would have done, and was put to and incurred divers expenses.

The defendant pleaded: (1) Not guilty. (2) That the plaintiff was not the highest bidder at the sale as alleged. (3) That the defendant did not become the plaintiff's agent as alleged.

The Court of Queen's Bench entered a nonsuit on the ground that the relationship of principal and agent between the plaintiff and the defendant had never come in to existence.

The plaintiff appealed.

MARTIN B.

In the Exchequer Chamber, Martin B. delivered the judgment of the court.

After stating the facts, he went on:

Upon the pleadings as they stand, we think the judgment of the Court of Queen's Bench is right, and that the defendant is entitled to the verdict upon the issue on the third plea: but there is power given to the court to amend; and it has been held that this power extends to the Court of Appeal; and we think we ought to exercise it largely in order to carry out the object of the Common Law Procedure Acts, 1852 and 1854, viz., to determine the real question in controversy between the parties in the existing suit. Upon the facts of the case, it seems to us that the plaintiff is entitled to recover. In a sale by auction there are three parties, viz., the owner of the property to be sold, the auctioneer, and the portion of the public who attend to bid, which of course includes the highest bidder: In this, as in most cases of sales by auction, the owner's name was not disclosed: he was a concealed principal. The name of the auctioneers, of whom the defendant was one, alone was published; and the sale was announced by them to be "without reserve." This, according to all the cases both at law and equity, means that neither the vendor nor any person in his behalf shall bid at the auction, and that the property shall be sold to the highest bidder, whether the sum bid be equivalent to the real value or not: *Thornett v Haines* (15M. & W. 367). We cannot distinguish the case of an auctioneer putting up property for sale upon such a condition from the case of the loser of property offering a reward, or that of a railway company publishing a time-table stating the times when, and the places to which, the trains run. It has been decided that the person giving the information advertised for, or a passenger taking a ticket, may sue as upon a contract with him: *Denton v Great Northern Rly.* (5E. & B. 860).[1] Upon the same principle, it seems to us that the highest bona fide bidder at an auction may sue the auctioneer as upon a contract that the sale shall be without reserve. We think the auctioneer who puts the property up for sale upon such a condition pledges himself that the sale shall be without reserve; or in other words, contracts that it shall be so; and that this contract is made with the highest bona fide bidder; and, in case of a breach of it, that he has a right of action against the auctioneer. The case is not at all affected by the 17th section of the Statute of Frauds,[2] which relates only to direct sales, and not to contracts relating to or connected with them. Neither does it seem to us material whether the owner, or person on his behalf, bid with the knowledge or privity of the auctioneer. We think the auctioneer has contracted that the sale shall be without reserve; and that the contract is broken upon a bid being made by or on behalf of the owner, whether it be during the time when the property is under the hammer, or it be the last bid upon which the article is knocked down; in either case, the sale is not "without reserve," and the contract of the auctioneer is broken. We entertain no doubt that the owner may, at any time before the contract is legally complete, interfere and revoke the auctioneer's authority: but he does so at his peril; and, if the auctioneer has contracted any liability in consequence of his employment and the subsequent revocation or conduct of the owner, he is entitled to be indemnified.

We do not think the conditions of sale stated in the case (assuming the plaintiff to be taken to have had notice of them) affect it. As to the first, Mr Henderson could not be the buyer: he was the owner; and, if it were material, there is ample evidence that the defendant knew him to be so: indeed, we think he ought not to have taken his bid, but to have refused it; stating, as his reason, that the sale was "without reserve." We feel inclined to differ with the view of the Court of Queen's Bench in this, that we rather think the bid of Mr Henderson was not a revocation of the defendant's authority as auctioneer. The third condition has nothing to do with the case; and the eighth only provides that, if, upon a sale without reserve, the owner act contrary to the conditions, he must pay the usual commission to the auctioneer. For these reasons, if the plaintiff think fit to amend his declaration, he, in our opinion, is entitled to the judgment of the court.

WILLES J

My brother Bramwell and myself do not dissent from the judgment which has been pronounced. But we prefer to rest our decision, as to the amendment, upon the ground that the defendant undertook to have, and yet there was evidence that he had not, authority to sell without reserve.[3] The result is the same.

Judgment of the Court of Queen's Bench to be affirmed; unless the parties elect to enter a stet processus, or the plaintiff amend his declaration, in which latter case, a new trial to be had.

---

[1]   Railway companies have since taken care to exclude any such liability.
[2]   See above, para.1–002.
[3]   Under a doctrine of the law of agency. A, who purports to make a contract as agent for P with T, is taken to promise T that if T will enter into the contract with P, he, (A) has P's authority to contract. If A does not have P's authority he has committed a breach of warranty of authority.

Questions

2–018   1. What was the significance of the reference to the Statute of Frauds? Was the contract, in the opinion of the majority or the minority, one of sale?

Was it a contract by the auctioneer that, after the highest bona fide bid, he would not withdraw the horse? Is that different in substance from a contract to sell it? The auctioneer may, after the highest bid, have been bound to sell but the "buyer" was not bound to buy until the auctioneer brought down the hammer. Is that a contract for the sale of goods—defined by the Sale of Goods Act 1979 s.2(1) as "a contract by which the seller transfers or agrees to transfer the property in goods to the buyer for a money consideration called the price?" Does 'buyer' mean a person who is bound to buy? Cf. *Spiro's* case, below, Ch.4.

2. What is the difference between the view expressed by Willes J and Bramwell B on the one hand, and the rest of the Court on the other?

3. Can you reconcile the law as stated by Martin B with *Payne v Cave*?

4. How can a contract with the highest bidder be broken by the owner's bidding during the auction since the highest bidder is not yet known? Is the answer that there is a contract with every bidder in turn? For example, "If you will come to the sale and bid, I promise that I will not bid (or withdraw the property); provided that, if someone makes a higher bid, this promise is to lapse"? Cf. the *Harvela* case, above.

Point for reflection

2–019   Although conduct such as that of the seller in *Warlow v Harrison* is now made unlawful by s.57(4) of the Sale of Goods Act (above), the case is still relevant on the question whether the auctioneer can withdraw the property. (See, further, *Barry v Davies*, below).

HARRIS v NICKERSON

Queen's Bench (1873) L.R. 8 Q.B. 286; 42 L.J.Q.B. 171; 28 L.T. 410; 37 J.P. 536; 21 W.R. 635

2–020   The defendant, an auctioneer, advertised in the London papers and distributed catalogues to the effect that certain brewing materials, plant and office furniture would be sold to him at Bury St. Edmunds on a certain day. The conditions were the usual conditions, the first being: "The highest bidder to be the buyer". The plaintiff, a commission broker in London, had a commission to purchase at the sale the "office furniture" advertised to be sold. He went to Bury St. Edmunds, attended the sale, and purchased certain lots. Those described as "office furniture" were not put up for sale, but were withdrawn.

The plaintiff brought an action to recover £2 12s. 6d. for two days loss of time, and, on these facts, the judge gave judgement for the plaintiff, but, at the request of the defendant, gave him leave to appeal.

BLACKBURN J

I am of the opinion that the judge was wrong.

The facts were that the defendant advertised bona fide that certain things would be sold by auction on the days named, and on the third day a certain class of things, viz., office furniture, without any previous notice of their withdrawal, were not put up. The plaintiff says, inasmuch as I confided in the defendant's advertisement, and came down to the auction to buy furniture (which it is found as a fact he was commissioned to buy) and have had no opportunity of buying, I am entitled to recover damages from the defendant, on the ground that the advertisement amounted to a contract by the defendant with anybody that should act upon it, that all the things advertised would be actually put up for sale, and that he would have an opportunity of bidding for them and buying. This is certainly a startling proposition, and would be excessively inconvenient if carried out. It amounts to saying that anyone who advertises a sale by publishing an advertisement becomes responsible to everybody who attends the sale for his cab hire or travelling expenses. As to the cases cited: in the case of *Warlow v Harrison* [above], the opinion of the majority of the judges in the Exchequer Chamber appears to have been that an action would lie for not knocking down the lot to the highest bona fide bidder when the sale was advertised as without reserve; in such a case it may be that there is a contract to sell to the highest bidder, and that if the owner bids there is a breach of the contract; there is very plausible ground at all events for saying, as the minority of the court thought, that the auctioneer warrants that he has power to sell without reserve. In the present case, unless every declaration of intention to do a thing creates a binding contract with those who act upon it, and in all cases after advertising a sale the auctioneer must give notice of any articles that are withdrawn, or be liable to an action, we cannot hold the defendant liable.

QUAIN J

I am of the same opinion. To uphold the judge's decision it is necessary to go to the extent of saying that when an auctioneer issues an advertisement of the sale of goods, if he withdraws any part of them without notice, the persons attending may all maintain actions against him. In the present case, it is to be observed that the plaintiff bought some other lots; but it is said that he had a commission to buy the furniture, either in whole or in part, and that therefore he has a right of action against the defendant. Such a proposition seems to be destitute of all authority; and it would be introducing an extremely inconvenient rule of law to say that an auctioneer is bound to give notice of withdrawal or to be held liable to everybody attending the sale. The case is certainly of the first impression. When a sale is advertised as without reserve, and a lot is put up and bid for, there is ground for saying, as was said in *Warlow v Harrison* [above], that a contract is entered into between the auctioneer and the highest bona fide bidder, but that has no application to the present case; here the lots were never put up and no offer was made by the plaintiff nor promise made by the defendant, except by his advertisement that certain goods would be sold. It is impossible to say that that is a contract with everybody attending the sale, and that the auctioneer is to be liable for their expenses if any single article is withdrawn. *Spencer v Harding* [above], which was cited by the plaintiff's counsel, as far as it goes, is a direct authority against his proposition.

ARCHIBALD J

I am of the same opinion. This is an attempt on the part of the plaintiff to make a mere declaration of intention a binding contract. He has utterly failed to show authority or reason for his proposition. If a false and fraudulent representation had been made out, it would have been quite another matter. But to say that a mere advertisement that certain articles will be sold by auction amounts to a contract to indemnify all who attend, if the sale of any part of the articles does not take place, is a proposition without authority or ground for supporting it.

Judgment for the Defendant.

BARRY v DAVIES (TRADING AS HEATHCOTE BALL & CO)

Court of Appeal [2000] 1 W.L.R. 1962

The claimant was interested in bidding for two machines (each with a new value of £14,521) that he saw were to be disposed of (on behalf of Customs and Excise) at an auction advertised as being without reserve. On the viewing day, prior to the auction, the claimant double-checked with the auctioneer who confirmed that the machines were to be offered without a reserve price. At the auction, the auctioneer failed to attract an opening bid of £5,000 for the machines; there was no interest either at £3,000; whereupon the claimant bid £200 for each of the machines. The auctioneer refused to accept the claimant's bid (as being too low); and so the claimant sued for breach of contract. The trial judge took the view that those who bid at an auction without reserve reasonably expect that the

2–021

highest bidder is entitled to the lot to which the bid applies. Accordingly, following the approach of the majority in *Warlow v Harrison* (above, para.2–017), the judge held that the auctioneer was in breach of a collateral contract with the highest bidder.

SIR MURRAY STUART SMITH

Mr Moran on behalf of the Appellant criticises this conclusion [in favour of the claimant] on a number of grounds. First he submits that the holding of an auction without reserve does not amount to a promise on the part of the auctioneer to sell the lots to the highest bidder. There are no express words to the effect, merely a statement of fact that the vendor has not placed a reserve on the lot. Such an intention, he submits is inconsistent with two principles of law, namely that the auctioneer's request for bids is not an offer which can be accepted by the highest bidder (*Payne v Cave* (1789) 3 TR 148) and that there is no completed contract of sale until the auctioneer's hammer falls and the bidder may withdraw his bid up until that time (Sale of Goods Act 1979 S57(2) which reflects the common law). There should be no need to imply such a promise into a statement that the sale is without reserve, because there may be other valid reasons why the auction-eer should be entitled to withdraw the lot, for example if he suspected an illegal ring or that the vendor had no title to sell.

Secondly Mr Moran submits that there is no consideration for the auctioneer's promise. He submits that the bid itself cannot amount to consideration because the bidder has not promised to do anything, he can with-draw the bid until it is accepted and the sale completed by the fall of the hammer. At most the bid represents a discretionary promise, which amounts to illusory consideration, for example promising to do something "if I feel like it". The bid only had real benefit to the auctioneer at the moment the sale is completed by the fall of the hammer. Furthermore the suggestion that consideration is provided because the auctioneer has the opportunity to accept the bid or to obtain a higher bid as the bidding is driven up depends upon the bid not being withdrawn.

Finally Mr Moran submits that where an agent is acting for a disclosed principal he is not liable on the contract (Bowstead and Reynolds on Agency 16th Ed para 9–001 and *Mainprice v Westley* (1865) 6 B&S 421). If therefore there is any collateral contract it is with the principal and not the agent.

These submissions were forcefully and attractively argued by Mr Moran. The authorities, such as they were, do not speak with one voice. The starting point is S57 of the Sale of Goods Act 1979, which re-enacted the 1893 Act, itself in this section a codification of the common law. I have already referred to the effect of subsection (2). Subsections (3) and (4) are also important. They provide:

> "(3) A sale by auction may be notified to be subject to a reserve or upset price, and a right to bid may also be reserved expressly by or on behalf of the seller.
> (4) Where a sale by auction is not notified to be subject to the right to bid by or on behalf of the seller, it is not lawful for the seller to bid himself or to employ any person to bid at the sale, or for the auctioneer knowingly to take any bid from the seller or any such person."

Although the Act does not expressly deal with sales by auction without reserve, the auctioneer is the agent of the vendor and unless subsection (4) has been complied with, it is not lawful for him to make a bid. Yet withdrawing the lot from the sale because it has not reached the level which the auctioneer considers appropriate is tanta-mount to bidding on behalf of the seller. The highest bid cannot be rejected simply because it is not high enough.

The judge based his decision on the reasoning of the majority of the Court of Exchequer Chamber in *Warlow v Harrison* . . .

So far as text-book writers are concerned both Chitty (28th Edition para 2–010) and Benjamin of Sale of Goods (5th Ed para 2–005) adopt the view expressed by the majority of the Court in *Warlow's* case.

As to consideration, in my judgment there is consideration both in the form of detriment to the bidder, since his bid can be accepted unless and until it is withdrawn, and benefit to the auctioneer as the bidding is driven up. Moreover attendance at the sale is likely to be increased if it is known that there is no reserve.

As to the agency point, there is no doubt that when the sale is concluded, the contract is between the pur-chaser and vendor and not the auctioneer. Even if the identity of the vendor is not disclosed, it is clear that the auctioneer is selling as agent. It is true that there was no such contract between vendor and purchaser. But that does not prevent a collateral agreement existing between the auctioneer and bidder. A common example of this is an action for breach of warranty of authority, which arises on a collateral contract.

For these reasons I would uphold the judge's decision on liability.

Point for reflection

Tenders, auctions, cash sales in shops and many other types of contractual transactions have been   **2–022**
with us for centuries and the principles are well established. But business methods change and, when
disputes about some new method of dealing arise, the courts must provide an answer. If the precedents
do not provide one, the court must invent it. Payment by credit card is one such innovation. *In Re Charge
Card Services Ltd* [1989] Ch.497; [1988] 3 All E.R. 762 CA, the credit card company had gone into
liquidation and the question arose whether the acceptance of the card (the 'Fuel Card') by a garage in
payment for petrol bought by the cardholder amounted to an absolute or a conditional payment. If it
was conditional, the cardholder remained liable to pay the garage when the company defaulted.

BROWNE-WILKINSON VC [IN THE CHARGE CARD SERVICES CASE]

The answer to this question must depend on the terms of the forecourt agreement since this is the only contract made between the garage and the cardholder. The terms on which the garage accepted payment from
the cardholder must be determined by the only contract to which they are parties. To determine the terms of
the forecourt agreement is not an easy task. Such agreement is at best oral and, in the majority of cases, not
even that. The sale contract is made by putting the fuel in the tank before the parties have met; tender of the
card and the making out of the signature of the voucher for the sale is often conducted in complete silence.
Moreover, although both garage and cardholder are in general aware that some underlying contract exists
between the garage and the company and between the cardholder and the company, neither the garage nor
the cardholder is aware of the exact terms of the contract to which they are not a party. Therefore the terms of
the forecourt agreement have to be inferred from the surrounding circumstances known to the parties.

At the time of the sale, it is almost inconceivable that either party addressed its mind to the question: what
will be the position if the company does not pay the garage? At one stage in the argument, both parties were
contending that The Moorcock test [see below] should be applied to determine what term should be implied
in the agreement. If such test were to be applied, one would be looking for a term that any reasonable garage
proprietor and cardholder would have agreed should be the result. On such a test, it is most unlikely that any
term could properly be implied. But, in my judgment, this is not the right test since in a case such as the present
there has to be some term regulating the legal effect of the acceptance of the card. The law has to give an
answer to the problem. In my judgment, the correct approach in such a case is that the court should seek to
infer from the parties' conduct and the surrounding circumstances what is the fair term to imply; this approach
became common ground between the parties.

A sale using the Fuel Card for payment did not, in my judgment, differ in any material respect from an
ordinary credit card sale. The one peculiarity of the transaction (viz. that the contract for sale of the petrol took
place when the tank was filled and not, as in a supermarket at the till) does not make any relevant difference.
The question remains: on what terms did the supplier accept the card in payment?

Although neither party to the forecourt agreement knew the exact terms of the other party's contract with
the company, both parties were aware of the underlying contractual structure. The customer/cardholder knew
that, if he signed the voucher, the supplier/garage would be entitled to receive a payment for the petrol which
would fully discharge the customer's liability for the price; depending on his sophistication, the customer/
cardholder might or might not have known that the company would deduct commission in paying the garage.
On the other side, the garage knew that on signing the voucher the cardholder rendered himself liable to the
company to pay to the company the price of the petrol. Before entering into the forecourt agreement, both
parties had entered into their respective contracts with the company and their underlying assumption must
have been that on completion of the sale of the petrol by use of the Fuel Card, the parties' future rights and
obligations would be regulated by those underlying contracts. In the majority of cases, the garage had no
record of the address of the customer and no ready means of tracing him.

To my mind, all these factors point clearly to the conclusion that, quite apart from any special features of the
Fuel Card Scheme, the transaction was one in which the garage was accepting payment by card in substitution
for payment in cash, i.e. as an unconditional discharge of the price. The garage was accepting the company's
obligation to pay instead of cash from a purchaser of whose address he was totally unaware. One way of looking

at the matter is to say that there was a quasi-novation of the purchaser's liability. By the underlying scheme, the company had bound the garage to accept the card and had authorised the cardholder to pledge the company's credit. By the signature of the voucher all parties became bound: the garage was bound to accept the card in payment; the company was bound to pay the garage; and the cardholder was bound to pay the company. The garage, knowing that the cardholder was bound to pay the company and knowing that it was entitled to payment from the company which the garage itself had elected to do business with, must in my judgment be taken to have accepted the company's obligation to pay in place of any liability on the customer to pay the garage direct.

The Moorcock test applies only where it is necessary to invoke a particular term to give the contract "business efficacy", i.e. to make it work: any reasonable person would agree that that term was necessary. That was not so in this case. But it was necessary to imply some term—the payment has to be either absolute or conditional; so the court implies the term which it considers to be fair. Is that the right solution? What other is possible?

Another modern problem is contracting via the internet. See Brownsword and Howells, 'When Surfers Start to Shop: Internet Commerce and Contract Law' (1999) 19 L.S. 287: "Whilst we contend that a revolution in the technology of contracting does not imply a revolution in contractual principles, we accept that it will not always be straightforward for the law to implement or respond to the reasonable expectations of Internet contractors (particularly so where, as is increasingly the case, contractors from radically different cultures are connected by the Internet)." See, also, the discussion of online transactions in Ch.1.

C. Promotional Gifts and Offers

ESSO PETROLEUM LTD v COMMISSIONERS OF CUSTOMS AND EXCISE

House of Lords [1976] 1 W.L.R. 1; [1976] 1 All E.R. 117

2–023   Under a sales promotion scheme devised by Esso, petrol station proprietors displayed posters supplied by Esso stating: 'The World Cup Coins', "One coin given with every four gallons of petrol". Millions of coins were distributed. The Commissioners claimed that the coins were chargeable to purchase tax under s.2(1) of the Purchase Tax Act 1963 on the ground that they had been "produced in quantity for general sale." Esso argued that the coins were the subject of a gift not a sale. Pennycuick VC held that the transaction constituted a sale. The poster was an invitation to treat which became a contract. The Court of Appeal allowed Esso's appeal, holding ("as a matter of common sense," per Lord Denning MR) that the coins were not sold but were distributed as free gifts. The Commissioners' appeal to the House of Lords was dismissed, Lord Fraser dissenting. Lord Simon, with whom Lord Wilberforce agreed, held that there was a contract to supply the coins but it was not a contract of sale. The poster was an offer to supply a coin which the motorist accepted by offering to buy four gallons of petrol. The consideration for the promise to supply a coin was not money (and therefore it was not a sale) but the offer to buy petrol. Viscount Dilhorne and Lord Russell held that Esso did not intend to enter into legal relations (see below, p.208); it was like an advertisement offering "free air"; and the coins were free gifts; but, if there was a contract, they agreed that it was not a contract of sale. Lord Fraser agreed with Pennycuick VC that the motorist contracted to buy four gallons of petrol and a coin: it was like the case of a baker offering an extra bun "free of charge" to anyone who bought a dozen buns. But is not that a contract to sell 13 buns?

Questions

1. Lord Simon: "The law happily matches the reality. The garage proprietor is saying, 'If you will buy four gallons of my petrol, I will give you one of these coins'." Professor Atiyah (39 M.L.R., 335) writes, "Contrary to Lord Simon's assertion, the reality of the matter surely was that the buyer, having paid for the four gallons of petrol, was entitled by virtue of that payment to a coin." Who is right?

2. Bobby, whose petrol tank is low, keeps going under pressure from his children until he comes to an Esso station owned by Nobby. He orders 12 gallons. When one gallon has been delivered, the pump runs dry. Is Nobby in breach of contract (i) to supply petrol (ii) to supply coins?

2–024

Problem

The following news item appeared in *The Times*, December 7, 1973: 'The Crisis and the Law'—A motorist queued up for half an hour at a Harpenden, Hertfordshire, garage yesterday, then filled up his tank with 2p worth of petrol. But the driver got an unpleasant shock when he was charged £1 for the few drops.

The garage owner said: "We have put up a notice saying '£1 worth. No more, no less.' We checked with the police and we are perfectly within our rights to keep his money".

Were the police right? Was it a contract to pay £1 for £1 worth of petrol or such lesser amount as the tank would hold? Or was it a contract for the sale of £1 worth of petrol? If the latter, was the motorist in breach because of his inability to take delivery? If he was in breach, was the garage owner entitled to the price (see s.49(1) and (2) of the Sale of Goods Act, 1979) or only to damages? If he was entitled only to damages, what damage had he suffered? See below, para.19–043).

2–025

CARLILL v CARBOLIC SMOKE BALL CO

Court of Appeal [1893] 1 Q.B. 256; 62 L.J.Q.B. 257; 67 L.T. 837; 41 W.R. 210; 57 J.P. 325; 4 R. 176

Appeal from a decision of Hawkins J [1892] 2 Q.B. 484.

The defendants, who were the proprietors and vendors of a medical preparation called "The Carbolic Smoke Ball," inserted in the Pall Mall Gazette of November 13, 1891, and in other newspapers, the following advertisement:

2–026

> "£100 reward will be paid by the Carbolic Smoke Ball Company to any person who contracts the increasing epidemic of influenza, colds, or any disease caused by taking cold, after having used the ball three times daily for two weeks according to the printed directions supplied with each ball. £1,000 is deposited with the Alliance Bank, Regent Street, showing our sincerity in the matter.
>
> During the last epidemic of influenza many thousand carbolic smoke balls were sold as preventatives against this disease, and in no ascertained case was the disease contracted by those using the carbolic smoke ball.
>
> One carbolic smoke ball will last a family several months, making it the cheapest remedy in the world at the price 10s., post free. The ball can be refilled at a cost of 5s. Address, Carbolic Smoke Ball Company, 27 Princes Street, Hanover Square, London."

The plaintiff, a lady, on the faith of this advertisement, bought one of the balls at a chemist's and used it as directed, three times a day from November 20, 1891 to January 17, 1892, when she was attacked by influenza. Hawkins J held that she was entitled to recover the £100. The defendants appealed.

BOWEN LJ

We were asked to say that this document was a contract too vague to be enforced.

The first observation which arises is that the document itself is not a contract at all, it is only an offer made to the public. The defendants contend next, that it is an offer the terms of which are too vague to be treated as a definite offer, inasmuch as there is no limit of time fixed for the catching of the influenza, and it cannot be supposed that the advertisers seriously meant to promise to pay money to every person who catches the influenza at any time after the inhaling of the smoke ball. It was urged also, that if you look at this document you will find much vagueness as to the persons with whom the contract was intended to be made—that, in the first place, its terms are wide enough to include persons who may have used the smoke ball before the advertisement was issued; at all events, that it is an offer to the world in general, and, also, that it is unreasonable to suppose it to be a definite offer, because nobody in their senses would contract themselves out of the opportunity of checking the experiment which was going to be made at their own expense. It is also contended that the advertisement is rather in the nature of a puff or a proclamation than a promise or offer intended to mature into a contract when accepted. But the main point seems to be that the vagueness of the document shows that no contract whatever was intended. It seems to me that in order to arrive at a right conclusion we must read this advertisement in its plain meaning, as the public would understand it. It was intended to be issued to the public and to be read by the public. How would an ordinary person reading this document construe it? It was intended unquestionably to have some effect, and I think the effect which it was intended to have, was to make people use the smoke ball, because the suggestions and allegations which it contains are directed immediately to the use of the smoke ball as distinct from the purchase of it. It did not follow that the smoke ball was to be purchased from the defendants directly, or even from agents of theirs directly. The intention was that the circulation of the smoke ball should be promoted, and that the use of it should be increased. The advertisement begins by saying that a reward will be paid by the Carbolic Smoke Ball Company to any person who contracts the increasing epidemic after using the ball. It has been said that the words do not apply only to persons who contract the epidemic after the publication of this advertisement, but include persons who had previously contracted the influenza. I cannot so read the advertisement. It is written in colloquial and popular language, and I think that it is equivalent to this: "£100 will be paid to any person who shall contract the increasing epidemic after having used the carbolic smoke ball three times daily for two weeks." And it seems to me that the way in which the public would read it would be this, that if anybody, after the advertisement was published, used three times daily for two weeks the carbolic smoke ball, and then caught cold, he would be entitled to the reward. Then again it was said: "How long is this protection to endure? Is it to go on forever, or for what limit of time?" I think that there are two constructions of this document, each of which is good sense, and each of which seems to me to satisfy the exigencies of the present action. It may mean that the protection is warranted to last during the epidemic, and it was during the epidemic that the plaintiff contracted the disease. I think, more probably, it means that the smoke ball will be a protection while it is in use. That seems to me the way in which an ordinary person would understand an advertisement about medicine and about a specific against influenza. It could not be supposed that after you have left off using it, you are still to be protected for ever, as if there was to be a stamp set upon your forehead that you were never to catch influenza because you had once used the carbolic smoke ball. I think the immunity is to last during the use of the ball. That is the way in which I should naturally read it, and it seems to me that the subsequent language of the advertisement supports that construction. It says: "During the last epidemic of influenza many thousand carbolic smoke balls were sold, and in no ascertained case was the disease contracted by those using" (not "who had used") "the carbolic smoke ball," and it concludes with saying that one smoke ball will last a family several months (which imports that it is to be efficacious while it is being used), and that the ball can be refilled at a cost of 5s. I, therefore, have myself no hesitation in saying that I think, on the construction of this advertisement, the protection was to enure during the time that the carbolic smoke ball was being used. My brother, the Lord Justice who preceded me, thinks that the contract would be sufficiently definite if you were to read it in the sense that the protection was to be warranted during a reasonable period after use. I have some difficulty myself on that point; but it is not necessary for me to consider it further, because the disease here was contracted during the use of the carbolic smoke ball.

Was it intended that the £100 should, if the conditions were fulfilled, be paid? The advertisement says that

£1,000 is lodged at the bank for the purpose. Therefore, it cannot be said that the statement that £100 would be paid was intended to be a mere puff. I think it was intended to be understood by the public as an offer which was to be acted upon.

But it was said there was no check on the part of the persons who issued the advertisement, and that it would be an insensate thing to promise £100 to a person who used the smoke ball unless you could check or superintend his manner of using it. The answer to that argument seems to me to be that if a person chooses to make extravagant promises of this kind he probably does so because it pays him to make them, and, if he has made them, the extravagance of the promises is no reason in law why he should not be bound by them.

It was also said that the contract is made with all the world—that is, with everybody; and that you cannot contract with everybody. It is not a contract made with all the world. There is the fallacy of the argument. It is an offer made to all the world; and why should not an offer be made to all the world which is to ripen into a contract with anybody who comes forward and performs the condition? It is an offer to become liable to anyone who, before it is retracted, performs the condition, and, although the offer is made to the world, the contract is made with that limited portion of the public who come forward and perform the condition on the faith of the advertisement. It is not like cases in which you offer to negotiate, or you issue advertisements that you have got a stock of books to sell, or houses to let, in which case there is no offer to be bound by any contract. Such advertisements are offers to negotiate—offers to receive offers—offers to chaffer, as, I think, some learned judge in one of the cases has said. If this is an offer to be bound, then it is a contract the moment the person fulfils the condition. That seems to me to be sense, and it is also the ground on which all these advertisement cases have been decided during the century; and it cannot be put better than in Willes J's judgment in *Spencer v Harding* [see above, para.2–006]. "In the advertisement cases," he says, "there never was any doubt that the advertisement amounted to a promise to pay the money to the person who first gave information. The difficulty suggested was that it was a contract with all the world. But that, of course, was soon overruled. It was an offer to become liable to any person who before the offer should be retracted should happen to be the person to fulfil the contract, of which the advertisement was an offer or tender. That is not the sort of difficulty which presents itself here. If the circular had gone on, 'and we undertake to sell to the highest bidder,' the reward cases would have applied, and there would have been a good contract in respect of the persons." As soon as the highest bidder presented himself, says Willes J, the person who was to hold the vinculum juris on the other side of the contract was ascertained, and it became settled.

Then it was said that there was no notification of the acceptance of the contract. One cannot doubt that, as an ordinary rule of law, an acceptance of an offer made ought to be notified to the person who makes the offer, in order that the two minds may come together. Unless this is done, the two minds may be apart, and there is not that consensus which is necessary according to the English law—I say nothing about the laws of other countries—to make a contract. But there is this clear gloss to be made upon that doctrine, that as notification of acceptance is required for the benefit of the person who makes the offer, the person who makes the offer may dispense with notice to himself if he thinks it desirable to do so, and I suppose there can be no doubt that where a person in an offer made by him to another person, expressly or impliedly intimates a particular mode of acceptance as sufficient to make the bargain binding, it is only necessary for the other person to whom such offer is made to follow the indicated method of acceptance; and if the person making the offer, expressly or impliedly intimates in his offer that it will be sufficient to act on the proposal without communicating acceptance of it to himself, performance of the condition is a sufficient acceptance without notification.

That seems to me to be the principle which lies at the bottom of the acceptance cases, of which two instances are the well-known judgment of Mellish LJ in *Harris's* case (L.R. 7 Ch. 587), and the very instructive judgment of Lord Blackburn in *Brogden v Metropolitan Ry.* ((1876) 2 App. Cas. 666), in which he appears to me to take exactly the line I have indicated.

Now, if that is the law, how are we to find out whether the person who makes the offer does intimate that notification of acceptance will not be necessary in order to constitute a binding bargain? In many cases you look to the offer itself. In many cases you extract from the character of the transaction that notification is not required, and in the advertisement cases it seems to me to follow as an inference to be drawn from the transaction itself that a person is not to notify his acceptance of the offer before he performs the condition, but that if he performs the condition notification is dispensed with. It seems to me that from the point of view of common sense no other idea could be entertained. If I advertise to the world that my dog is lost, and that anybody who brings the dog to a particular place will be paid some money, are all the police or other persons whose business it is to find lost dogs to be expected to sit down and write me a note saying that they have accepted my proposal? Why, of course, they at once look after the dog and as soon as they find the dog they have performed the condition. The essence of the transaction is that the dog should be found, and it is not necessary under such circumstances, as it seems to me, that in order to make the contract binding there should be any notification of acceptance. It follows from the nature of the thing that the performance of the condition is sufficient acceptance without the notification of it, and a person who makes an offer in an advertisement of that kind makes an offer which must be read by the light of that common-sense reflection. He does, therefore, in his offer impliedly indicate that he does not require notification of the acceptance of the offer.

A further argument for the defendants was that this was a nudum pactum—that there was no consideration for the promise—that taking the influenza was only a condition, and that the using the smoke ball was only a condition, and that there was no consideration at all; in fact, that there was no request, express or implied, to use the smoke ball. Now, I will not enter into an elaborate discussion upon the law as to requests in this kind of contracts. I will simply refer to *Victors v Davies* (12 M. & W. 758) and Sergeant Manning's note to *Fisher v Pyne* (1 M. & G. 265), which everybody ought to read who wishes to embark in this controversy. The short answer, to abstain from academical discussion, is, it seems to me, that there is here a request to use involved in the offer. Then as to the alleged want of consideration. The definition of "consideration" given in Selwyn's *Nisi Prius* (8th ed.), p. 47, which is cited and adopted by Tindal CJ in the case of *Laythoarp v Bryant* (3 Scott 238, 250), is this: "Any act of the plaintiff from which the defendant derives a benefit or advantage, or any labour, detriment, or inconvenience sustained by the plaintiff, provided such act is performed or such inconvenience suffered by the plaintiff, with the consent, either express or implied, of the defendant." Can it be said here that if the person who reads this advertisement applies thrice daily, for such time as may seem to him tolerable, the carbolic smoke ball to his nostrils for a whole fortnight, he is doing nothing at all—that it is a mere act which is not to count towards consideration to support a promise (for the law does not require us to measure the adequacy of the consideration). Inconvenience sustained by one party at the request of the other is enough to create a consideration. I think therefore, that it is consideration enough that the plaintiff took the trouble of using the smoke ball. But I think also that the defendants received a benefit from this user, for the use of the smoke ball was contemplated by the defendants as being indirectly a benefit to them, because the use of the smoke balls would promote their sale . . . if you once make up your mind that there was a promise made to this lady who is the plaintiff, as one of the public—a promise made to her that if she used the smoke ball three times daily for a fortnight and got the influenza, she should have £100, it seems to me that her using the smoke ball was sufficient consideration. I cannot picture to myself the view of the law on which the contrary could be held when you have once found who are the contracting parties. If I say to a person, "If you use such and such a medicine for a week I will give you £5," and he uses it, there is ample consideration for the promise.
Lindley and A.L. Smith LJJ delivered concurring judgments.

Questions

2–027

1. At what moment was the contract made?

2. The Principles of European Contract Law,[4] 1998 art. 2:205(3): "If by virtue of the offer . . . the offeree may accept the offer by performing an act without notice to the offeror, the contract is concluded when the performance of the act begins."

   If this represents English law, when was the contract made with Mrs Carlill? When she acquired the ball? Or when she began to use it? What would be the obligation of the company in a contract made then? To pay her £100 if she completed the course and caught flu? Would that be different in substance from a contract not to revoke the offer? Does it properly distinguish between the consideration (using the smoke ball three times daily for two weeks) and the condition (catching flu)? No obligation to pay £100, not even a conditional one, arises until the consideration has been supplied. So how can the express contract be held to have been concluded until that time?

---

[4]   Formulated by the Commission on European Contract Law (a private organisation consisting of scholars from all the Member States of what is now the European Union).

3. Suppose the company had published an advertisement on December 8, 1892, in all the newspapers in which the original advertisement appeared, withdrawing the offer. X, Y and Z had been using the ball regularly since November 20. X completed the course and promptly caught flu. Y completed the course and never caught flu. Z, on seeing the withdrawal, immediately put his ball in the dustbin and caught flu a week after he would have completed the course. What redress, if any, do they have against the company?

4. If Carlill had used the smoke ball three times daily for two weeks without knowing anything about the advertisement offering the reward, and had then caught influenza and learned of the advertisement through her doctor, could she have recovered the £100?

5. If Carlill, knowing of the advertisement, used the smoke ball hoping to avoid influenza and, therefore, hoping not to be eligible for the reward, ought she to have recovered the £100? (See the next case.)

6. Did the company promise that Carlill would not catch influenza? Were they in breach of contract when she did? (See below, para.20–003.)

7. The following year, the company repeated its promotion of the smoke ball. What do you think that the advert said? See A.W.B. Simpson, 'Quackery and Contract Law: the Case of the Carbolic Smoke Ball' (1985) 14 *Journal of Legal Studies* 345.

Points for reflection

1. Consider Lord Simon's examples in *The Eurymedon* of A inviting B to dig his garden below, Ch.13; and the question below, para.13–007. **2–028**

2. In *Bowerman v Association of British Travel Agents Ltd* [1996] C.L.C. 451; [1995] 145 N.L.J. 1815 a school skiing trip was booked with a tour operator, a member of Association of British Travel Agents (ABTA), in whose offices a notice was prominently displayed, stating that, where holiday arrangements failed, ABTA arranged the reimbursement of money paid. The tour operator became insolvent before the trip began and it was cancelled. The Court of Appeal, Hirst LJ dissenting, held that ABTA was bound to reimburse the full cost of the holiday. There was a contract between ABTA and those members of the public who booked a holiday with ABTA members in reliance on the scheme. ABTA had said, in effect, "If you book a holiday with one of our members, we undertake . . .". Waite LJ said "Whenever a customer is induced to deal with one of its members by ABTA's promises of protection, there is a gain to the commercial purposes for which it was founded, providing a clear consideration for those promises." The majority construed the notice objectively from the standpoint of an ordinary person in all the relevant circumstances—the well-known risks of tour operators becoming insolvent, etc. Hirst LJ concentrated on the actual wording of the notice and failed to find a contractual intention. Cf. *Shanklin Pier Ltd v Detel Products Ltd,* and *Wells v Buckland,* below, Ch.15.

----

2. THE "CHRONOLOGY" OF CONTRACTING

A promise, other than one which is in a deed, is potentially binding on the promisor only if he has asked   **2–029**
for something in return. Virtually all offers to contract can be reduced to the form, "I promise this if (in return for my promise) you will do, or promise, that." Contract then is a bargain between the parties

and the natural way to make a bargain is for one side to propose the terms and the other to agree to them. So, in practice, contracts are almost invariably made by a process of offer and acceptance, the chronology being that the offer is made first and then the acceptance follows. The law looks for an offer and acceptance, not for some technical reason but because this is the way in which contracts are in fact made. However, it should not be thought that the standard chronology of offer and acceptance is an essential process; a contract might be made without it if the necessary bargain can be discerned from the facts in some other way (for example, as in the *RTS Flexible Systems* case below).

Questions

2–030   Is there (i) an offer and acceptance, (ii) a contract, in the following cases?:

1. A and B, wishing to enter into a partnership, instruct C to draw up a contract. C does so and the document is signed, first by A and then by B.

2. A and B are unable to reach agreement as to the terms of a sale. C, a bystander, proposes the terms of a compromise. A and B say, simultaneously, "I agree."

3. A writes to B offering to sell certain property at a stated price. B writes to A offering to buy the same property at the same price. The letters cross in the post.

The third case, it should be noted, was discussed, obiter, by the Court of Exchequer Chamber in *Tinn v Hoffman* (1873) 29 L.T. 271. Blackburn, Keating, Brett, Grove and Archibald JJ said that cross-offers do not make a binding contract. Honyman J said they do.

HONYMAN J: "I cannot see why the fact of the letters crossing each other should not make a good contract. If I say I am willing to buy a man's house on certain terms and he at the same moment says he is willing to sell it, and these two letters are posted so that they are irrevocable with respect to the writers, why should that not constitute a good contract? The parties are ad idem at one and the same moment."

GROVE J: "Numberless inconveniences might result from our holding that [cross-offers may amount to a contract]. A letter may be put into the post or may be sent out by private messenger, and then the writer may repent of what he has written, and may dispatch a telegram or send a special messenger on horseback, saying, 'I have posted or sent to you a letter making you a certain offer, I cannot fulfil it, consider it cancelled.' This second message or telegram may arrive before the letter itself, which may have been miscarried, and yet in a few days or a week, the parties having meanwhile considered there was no contract, the letter might come to hand. Is it then to become a contract? . . . there must be an offer which the person accepting has had an opportunity of considering, and which when he accepts he knows will form a binding contract. Unless that is done, where each of them is, so to speak, making an offer or a cross-offer, they are, so to speak, in fieri, and do not constitute a contract."

BRETT J: ". . . cross-offers are not an acceptance of each other, therefore there will be no offer of either party accepted by the other . . . where the contract is to be made by the letters themselves, you cannot make it by cross-offers, and say that the contract was made by one party accepting the offer which was made to him."

BLACKBURN J: "When a contract is made between two parties there is a promise by one in consideration of the promise made by the other; there are two assenting minds, the parties agreeing in opinion, and one having promised in consideration of the promise of the other—there is an exchange of promises; but I do not think exchanging offers would, upon principle, be at all the same thing . . . The promise or offer being made on each side in ignorance of the promise or offer made on the other side neither of them can be construed as an acceptance of the other. Either of the parties may write and say 'I accept your offer, and, as you perceive, I have already made a similar offer to you,' and then people would know what they were about, I think either side might revoke. Such grave inconvenience would arise in mercantile business if people could doubt whether there was an acceptance or not, that it is desirable to keep to the rule that an offer that has been made should be accepted by an acceptance such as would leave no doubt on the matter."

CLARKE v DUNRAVEN

House of Lords [1897] A.C. 59; 66 L.J.Adm. 1; 75 L.T. 337; 8 Asp.M.C. 190

The Mudhook Yacht Club having advertised a regatta to be held on the Clyde in July 1894, the appellant entered his yacht the Satanita and the respondent entered his yacht the Valkyrie, for a first class race in the regatta, each owner signing a letter to the secretary of the club undertaking that while sailing under the entry he would obey and be bound by the sailing rules of the Yacht Club Association. Those rules contained a number of regulations to be observed in races, and among them rule 18, which corresponded to article 14 of the Regulations for Preventing Collisions at Sea. By rule 24: ". . . If a yacht, in consequence of her neglect of any of these rules, shall foul another yacht, or compel other yachts to foul, she shall forfeit all claim to the prize, and shall pay all damages." By rule 32: "Any yacht disobeying or infringing any of these rules, which shall apply to all yachts whether sailing in the same or different races, shall be disqualified from receiving any prize she would otherwise have won, and her owner shall be liable for all damages arising therefrom."

2–031

While sailing under the entry the Satanita, without the actual fault or privity of the owner, broke the 18th rule and ran into and sank the Valkyrie. The respondent and the master and crew of the latter vessel brought an action in the Admiralty Division against the appellant claiming damages.

The appellant paid into court the limited sum for which he was liable[5] in the absence of a contract between him and the respondent (£8 per ton on the registered tonnage of the Satanita). The respondent alleged that by the terms of the entry and in consideration that the owner of the Valkyrie would race with the appellant under these rules, the appellant had agreed to be liable for all damages arising from a breach of the rules. Bruce J held that even if there was a contract it was not so express as to override the statutory limitation. The Court of Appeal reversed this decision, holding that there was a contract under which the defendant was liable for all damages. Lord Esher M.R. said, [1895] P. 248 at 255, that it was clear that the defendant had entered into a contractual obligation with the plaintiff "and the way that he has undertaken that obligation is this. A certain number of gentlemen formed themselves into a committee and proposed to give prizes for matches sailed between yachts at a certain place on a certain day, and they promulgated certain rules, and said: 'If you want to sail in any of our matches for our prize, you cannot do so unless you submit yourselves to the conditions which we have thus laid down. And one of the conditions is, that if you do sail for one of such prizes you must enter into an obligation with the owners of the yachts who are competing, which they at the same time enter into similarly with you, that if by a breach of any of our rules you do damage or injury

---

5   Under the Merchant Shipping Act Amendment Act 1862 s.54(1).

to the owner of a competing yacht, you shall be liable to make good the damage you have so done.' If that is so, then when they do sail, and not till then, that relation is immediately formed between the yacht owners. There are other conditions with regard to these matches which constitute a relation between each of the yacht owners who enters his yacht and sails it and the committee; but that does not in the least do away with what the yacht owner has undertaken, namely, to enter into a relation with the other yacht owners, that relation containing an obligation."

The defendant appealed to the House of Lords.

LORD HERSCHELL

I cannot entertain any doubt that there was a contractual relation between the parties to this litigation. The effect of their entering for the race, and undertaking to be bound by these rules to the knowledge of each other, is sufficient, I think, where those rules indicate a liability on the part of the one to the other, to create a contractual obligation to discharge that liability. That being so, the parties must be taken to have contracted that a breach of any of these rules would render the party guilty of that breach liable, in the language of rule 24, to "pay all damages," in the language of rule 32, to be "liable for all damages arising therefrom." The language is somewhat different in the two rules; but I do not think they were intended to have, with regard to payment or liability to damages, any different effect. It is admitted that the appellant broke one of those rules, and, having broken or disobeyed that rule, it is quite clear, on the assumption of a contract such as I have described, that there arose the liability to "pay all damages," or "to be liable for all damages arising therefrom."

Point for reflection

2–032   While the implication of a contract between the competitors in *Clarke v Dunraven* makes sense (i.e. it accords with reasonable expectations), it is unclear how this is best explained in terms of offer and acceptance. A standard explanation runs along the lines that A, the first party to enter the competition, made an offer to all subsequent entrants, B, C, and D, and so on, undertaking to observe the competition rules, if they gave a reciprocal undertaking. When B, the second competitor, entered B, by so doing, accepted A's offer, and himself made a similar offer to all subsequent entrants. When C, the third competitor entered, C accepted the offers made by A and by B, and made a similar offer to all subsequent entrants. And so on. However, this account seems to ignore the fact that none of the competitors appreciated that they were making the relevant offers or, indeed, that by entering the competition they were accepting offers made by other competitors. However, unless contract law recognises competitions of this kind as a special case of connection, the standard explanation seems to be the best that is available. (It should be noted that where A takes shares in a company, the memorandum and articles of association of the company constitute a contract between A and the company. Do they also constitute a contract between A and B, another shareholder of the company? It was held by Vaisey J that they do in *Rayfield v Hands* [1960] Ch. 1, relying, inter alia, on *Clarke v Dunraven*. See Gower, 21 M.L.R. 401 and 657. See also Jeremy Phillips discussing *Moorgate Mercantile Co Ltd v Twitchings* [1977] A.C. 890; (1976) 92 L.Q.R. 499.)

RTS FLEXIBLE SYSTEMS LIMITED (RESPONDENTS) V MOLKEREI ALOIS MÜLLER GMBH AND COMPANY KG (UK PRODUCTION) (APPELLANTS)

[2010] UKSC 14

2–033   The facts of this case are messy and complex. Stated shortly, RTS had done work and supplied equipment for two production lines at Müller's plant; and, in fact, they had been paid quite substantial sums as the work was ongoing. However, at a relatively late stage of the installation, a dispute arose between the parties. Normally, we would expect such a dispute to be settled by reference to the agreed terms of the contract; but, instead, the parties found themselves disputing the prior question of whether there was any contract at all and, if so, what the terms of the contract were.

How could such an extraordinary situation arise? Why was there such a disconnect between the on-the-ground performance of the project and the finalisation of the terms of the contract? Quite simply, the pressure to get the work underway meant that RTS commenced their performance before the formal contract was agreed and the contract signed off. This "back to front" way of proceeding threw up two particular issues: one was whether the paper indication that the parties were interacting "subject to contract" precluded a finding that the parties had a contract; and the other was whether, from the totality of the terms being negotiated by the parties (while the work was underway), those terms that had been agreed could be treated as constituting the contract.

In relation to the first of these issues, the Court of Appeal takes a rather traditional approach: if the parties deal on the basis that they are not legally bound until they have signed the agreed terms and conditions, then in the absence of such signature there is no contract. The Supreme Court, agreeing with the trial judge, adopts a far more pragmatic approach: the "subject to contract" clause notwithstanding, no reasonable businessman would view the dealings between the parties and conclude that there was no contract. On the second issue, the Supreme Court interprets the content of the contract more broadly than the trial judge.

LORD CLARKE (GIVING THE JUDGMENT OF THE COURT)

44. Discussion

The principles

45. The general principles are not in doubt. Whether there is a binding contract between the parties and, if so, upon what terms depends upon what they have agreed. It depends not upon their subjective state of mind, but upon a consideration of what was communicated between them by words or conduct, and whether that leads objectively to a conclusion that they intended to create legal relations and had agreed upon all the terms which they regarded or the law requires as essential for the formation of legally binding relations. Even if certain terms of economic or other significance to the parties have not been finalised, an objective appraisal of their words and conduct may lead to the conclusion that they did not intend agreement of such terms to be a pre-condition to a concluded and legally binding agreement.

46. The problems that have arisen in this case are not uncommon, and fall under two heads. Both heads arise out of the parties agreeing that the work should proceed before the formal written contract was executed in accordance with the parties' common understanding. The first concerns the effect of the parties' understanding (here reflected in clause 48 of the draft written contract) that the contract would "not become effective until each party has executed a counterpart and exchanged it with the other"—which never occurred. Is that fatal to a conclusion that the work done was covered by a contract? The second frequently arises in such circumstances and is this. Leaving aside the implications of the parties' failure to execute and exchange any agreement in written form, were the parties agreed upon all the terms which they objectively regarded or the law required as essential for the formation of legally binding relations? Here, in particular, this relates to the terms on which the work was being carried out. What, if any, price or remuneration was agreed and what were the rights and obligations of the contractor or supplier?

47. We agree with Mr Catchpole's submission that, in a case where a contract is being negotiated subject to contract and work begins before the formal contract is executed, it cannot be said that there will always or even usually be a contract on the terms that were agreed subject to contract. That would be too simplistic and dogmatic an approach. The court should not impose binding contracts on the parties which they have not reached. All will depend upon the circumstances. This can be seen from a contrast between the approach of Steyn LJ in the *Percy Trentham* case, which was relied upon by the judge, and that of Robert Goff J in *British Steel Corporation v Cleveland Bridge and Engineering Co Ltd* [1984] 1 All ER 504, to which the judge was not referred but which was relied upon in and by the Court of Appeal.

48. These principles apply to all contracts, including both sales contracts and construction contracts, and are clearly stated in *Pagnan SPA v Feed Products Ltd* [1987] 2 Lloyd's Rep 601, both by Bingham J at first instance and by the Court of Appeal. In *Pagnan* it was held that, although certain terms of economic significance to the

parties were not agreed, neither party intended agreement of those terms to be a precondition to a concluded agreement. The parties regarded them as relatively minor details which could be sorted out without difficulty once a bargain was struck. The parties agreed to bind themselves to agreed terms, leaving certain subsidiary and legally inessential terms to be decided later.

49. In his judgment in the Court of Appeal in *Pagnan* Lloyd LJ (with whom O'Connor and Stocker LJJ agreed) summarised the relevant principles in this way at page 619:

"(1) In order to determine whether a contract has been concluded in the course of correspondence, one must first look to the correspondence as a whole. . .

(2) Even if the parties have reached agreement on all the terms of the proposed contract, nevertheless they may intend that the contract shall not become binding until some further condition has been fulfilled. That is the ordinary 'subject to contract' case.

(3) Alternatively, they may intend that the contract shall not become binding until some further term or terms have been agreed. . .

(4) Conversely, the parties may intend to be bound forthwith even though there are further terms still to be agreed or some further formality to be fulfilled. . .

(5) If the parties fail to reach agreement on such further terms, the existing contract is not invalidated unless the failure to reach agreement on such further terms renders the contract as a whole unworkable or void for uncertainty

(6) It is sometimes said that the parties must agree on the essential terms and it is only matters of detail which can be left over. This may be misleading, since the word 'essential' in that context is ambiguous. If by 'essential' one means a term without which the contract cannot be enforced then the statement is true: the law cannot enforce an incomplete contract. If by 'essential' one means a term which the parties have agreed to be essential for the formation of a binding contract, then the statement is tautologous. If by 'essential' one means only a term which the Court regards as important as opposed to a term which the Court regards as less important or a matter of detail, the statement is untrue. It is for the parties to decide whether they wish to be bound and if so, by what terms, whether important or unimportant. It is the parties who are, in the memorable phrase coined by the Judge [at page 611] 'the masters of their contractual fate'. Of course the more important the term is the less likely it is that the parties will have left it for future decision. But there is no legal obstacle which stands in the way of the parties agreeing to be bound now while deferring important matters to be agreed later. It happens every day when parties enter into so-called 'heads of agreement'.

The same principles apply where, as here, one is considering whether a contract was concluded in correspondence as well as by oral communications and conduct.

50. Before the judge much attention was paid to the *Percy Trentham* case, where, as Steyn LJ put it at page 26, the case for Trentham (the main contractor) was that the sub-contracts came into existence, not simply from an exchange of contracts, but partly by reason of written exchanges, partly by oral discussions and partly by performance of the transactions. In the passage from the judgment of Steyn LJ at page 27 quoted by the judge at para 66 he identified these four particular matters which he regarded as of importance. (1) English law generally adopts an objective theory of contract formation, ignoring the subjective expectations and the unexpressed mental reservations of the parties. Instead the governing criterion is the reasonable expectations of honest sensible businessmen. (2) Contracts may come into existence, not as a result of offer and acceptance, but during and as a result of performance. (3) The fact that the transaction is executed rather than executory can be very relevant. The fact that the transaction was performed on both sides will often make it unrealistic to argue that there was no intention to enter into legal relations and difficult to submit that the contract is void for vagueness or uncertainty. Specifically, the fact that the transaction is executed makes it easier to imply a term resolving any uncertainty, or, alternatively, it may make it possible to treat a matter not finalised in negotiations as inessential. This may be so in both fully executed and partly executed transactions. (4) If a contract only comes into existence during and as a result of performance it will frequently be possible to hold that the contract impliedly and retrospectively covers pre-contractual performance.

51. By contrast, in the Court of Appeal much attention was paid to the decision of Robert Goff J in the *British Steel* case, which had not been cited to the judge. At para 51 Waller LJ said that the factors which influenced Robert Goff J to conclude in that case that there was no binding contract apply with equal force to the factual matrix here. He thought (para 59) that, if the judge had had Robert Goff J's judgment cited to him (and/or if the no contract point had been fully developed before him) the judge would not have reached the conclusion he did.

52. The particular passage in Robert Goff J's judgment (starting at page 510G) on which Waller LJ relied reads as follows:

"The real difficulty is to be found in the factual matrix of the transaction, and in particular the fact that the work was being done *pending* a formal sub-contract the terms of which were still in a state of negotiation. It is, of course, a notorious fact that, when a contract is made for the supply of goods on a scale and in circumstances such as the present, it will in all probability be subject to standard terms, usually the standard terms of the supplier. Such standard terms will frequently legislate, not only for the liability of the seller for defects, but also for the damages (if any) for which the seller will be liable in the event not only of defects in the goods but also of late delivery. It is a commonplace that a seller of goods may exclude liability for consequential loss, and may agree liquidated damages for delay. In the present case, an unresolved dispute broke out between the parties on the question whether CBE's or BSC's standard terms were to apply, the former providing no limit to the seller's liability for delay and the latter excluding such liability altogether. Accordingly, when, in a case such as the present, the parties are still in a state of negotiation, it is impossible to predicate what liability (if any) will be assumed by the seller for, eg defective goods or late delivery, if a formal contract should be entered into. In these circumstances, if the buyer asks the seller to commence work 'pending' the parties entering into a formal contract, it is difficult to infer from the [seller] acting on that request that he is assuming any responsibility for his performance, except such responsibility as will rest on him under the terms of the contract which both parties confidently anticipate they will shortly enter into. It would be an extraordinary result if, by acting on such a request in such circumstances, the [seller] were to assume an unlimited liability for his contractual performance, when he would never assume such liability under any contract which he entered into."

(Waller LJ rightly put 'seller' in parenthesis since, although the report reads 'buyer', Robert Goff J must have meant 'seller'.)

53. In that passage Robert Goff J recognised that contracts for the supply of goods on a significant scale will in all probability be subject to standard terms, which will frequently legislate, not only for the liability of the seller for defects, but also for the damages (if any) for which the seller will be liable in the event not only of defects in the goods but also of late delivery. Thus a seller may exclude liability for consequential loss, and may agree liquidated damages for delay. In the *British Steel* case itself there was an unresolved dispute as to whose standard terms were to apply. One set of terms provided no limit to the seller's liability for delay and the other excluded such liability altogether. We can understand why, in such a case, if the buyer asks the seller to commence work 'pending' the parties entering into a formal contract, it is difficult to infer from the seller acting on that request that he is assuming any responsibility for his performance, "except such responsibility as will rest on him under the terms of the contract which both parties confidently anticipate they will shortly enter into". By the last words, Robert Goff J was not suggesting that there was, in the case before him, any contract governing the performance rendered, merely that the parties had anticipated (wrongly in the event) that there would be.

54. There is said to be a conflict between the approach of Steyn LJ in the *Percy Trentham* case and that of Robert Goff J in the *British Steel* case. We do not agree. Each case depends upon its own facts. We do not understand Steyn LJ to be saying that it follows from the fact that the work was performed that the parties must have entered into a contract. On the other hand, it is plainly a very relevant factor pointing in that direction. Whether the court will hold that a binding contract was made depends upon all the circumstances of the case, of which that is but one. The decision in the *British Steel* case was simply one on the other side of the line. Robert Goff J was struck by the likelihood that parties would agree detailed provisions for matters such as liability for defects and concluded on the facts that no binding agreement had been reached. By contrast, in *Pagnan* Bingham J and the Court of Appeal reached a different conclusion, albeit in a case of sale not construction.

55. We note in passing that the *Percy Trentham* case was not a 'subject to contract' or 'subject to written contract' type of case. Nor was *Pagnan*, whereas part of the reasoning in the *British Steel* case in the passage quoted above was that the negotiations were throughout conducted on the basis that, when reached, the agreement would be incorporated in a formal contract. So too was the reasoning of the Court of Appeal in *Galliard Homes Ltd v J Jarvis & Sons Ltd* (1999) 71 Con LR 219. In our judgment, in such a case, the question is whether the parties have nevertheless agreed to enter into contractual relations on particular terms notwithstanding their earlier understanding or agreement. Thus, in the *Galliard Homes* case Lindsay J, giving the only substantive judgment in the Court of Appeal, which also comprised Evans and Schiemann LJJ, at page 236 quoted with approval the statement in *Megarry & Wade, The Law of Real Property*, 5th ed (1984) at pages

568-9 that it is possible for an agreement 'subject to contract' or 'subject to written contract' to become legally binding if the parties later agree to waive that condition, for they are in effect making a firm contract by reference to the terms of the earlier agreement. Put another way, they are waiving the 'subject to [written] contract' term or understanding.

56. Whether in such a case the parties agreed to enter into a binding contract, waiving reliance on the 'subject to [written] contract' term or understanding will again depend upon all the circumstances of the case, although the cases show that the court will not lightly so hold. We turn to consider the facts.

Application of the principles to the facts

57. There are three possible conclusions which could be reached. They are (1) that, as the Court of Appeal held, there was no contract between the parties; (2) that, as the judge held, there was a contract between the parties on the limited terms found by the judge; and (3) that there was an agreement between the parties on wider terms. In the third case there is some scope for argument as to the precise terms. As appears below, it is our view that, if the third solution is adopted, the most compelling conclusion is that the terms were those agreed on and before 5 July as subsequently varied on 25 August. We consider each possible conclusion in turn.

(1) No contract

58. We agree with the judge that it is unrealistic to suppose that the parties did not intend to create legal relations. This can be tested by asking whether the price of £1,682,000 was agreed. Both parties accept that it was. If it was, as we see it, it must have formed a part of a contract between the parties. Moreover, once it is accepted (as both parties now accept) that the LOI Contract expired and was not revived, the contract containing the price must be contained in some agreement other than the LOI Contract. If the price is to be a term binding on the parties, it cannot, at any rate on conventional principles, be a case of no contract. Although it did not address this question, the Court of Appeal's solution involves holding that there was no binding agreement as to price or anything else and that evidence of the agreed price is no more than some evidence of what a reasonable price would have been for quantum meruit purposes. The difficulty with that analysis seems to us to be threefold. First, neither party suggested in the course of the project that the price was not agreed and RTS invoiced for percentages of the price and Müller paid sums so calculated as described above. Second, the price of £1,682,000 was agreed and included in the LOI Contract on the footing that there would be a detailed contract containing many different provisions including, as expressly recognised in the LOI Contract, the MF/1 terms. Third, there was an agreed variation on 25 August which nobody suggested was not a contractual variation.

59. In these circumstances the no contract solution is unconvincing. Moreover, it involves RTS agreeing to proceed with detailed work and to complete the whole contract on a non-contractual basis subject to no terms at all.

(2) Contract on the terms found by the judge

60. We entirely agree with the judge that the parties initially intended that there should be a written contract between them which was executed by each and exchanged between them. We further accept that, if the matter were tested on, say, 5 July, the correct conclusion may well have been that that remained the position and that there was no binding agreement between them. However, that is not on the basis that the parties had not reached agreement (or sufficient agreement) but because the agreement they had reached remained (in the traditional language) 'subject to contract'. Thus, as correctly submitted in Müller's skeleton argument before the judge, the agreement was ready for execution at that stage but was subject to contract. In the same skeleton argument Müller correctly submitted that the question was, objectively speaking, whether the parties' intentions took a new turn at some stage such that they intended to be bound by the 'final draft contract' without the need for its formal execution. As we read it, the skeleton defined the 'final draft contract' as the draft sent by Mr Morris on 16 May, subject to subsequent e-mail agreement as stated above.

61. The striking feature of this case which makes it very different from many of the cases which the courts have considered is that essentially all the terms were agreed between the parties and that substantial works were then carried out and the agreement was subsequently varied in important respects. The parties treated the agreement of 25 August as a variation of the agreement that they had reached by 5 July. Nobody suggested in August that there was no contract and thus nothing to vary. It was not until November, by which time the parties were in dispute, that points were taken as to whether there was a contract.

62. We have reached the firm conclusion that by 25 August at the latest the parties' communications and actions lead to the conclusion that they had agreed that RTS would perform the work and supply the materials on

the terms agreed between them up to and including 5 July as varied by the agreement of 25 August. Thereafter the work continued on a somewhat different basis because of the provision of Line 1 before Line 2. As stated above, it does not seem to us to make commercial sense to hold that the parties were agreeing to the works being carried out without any relevant contract terms. In this regard we agree with the judge.

63. On the other hand it does not seem to us to make commercial sense to hold that the work was carried out on some but not all the terms agreed by 5 July. The terms were negotiated on the basis that the Schedules would form part of the Contract, which also contained the detailed Conditions in Schedule 1, which had themselves been subject to much discussion and comprised clauses 8 to 48. We accept Mr Catchpole's submission that the Conditions, based as they were on the MF/1 terms which were put forward by Müller and expressly referred to in the LOI Contract and which (among many other things) defined RTS' performance obligations, set out the warranties provided by RTS and identified the limit of its potential liability. It is, in our judgment, inconceivable that the parties would have agreed only some of the terms, namely those in the specific documents identified by Müller, and not those in clauses 8 to 48. It seems to us that this was one of the considerations which the Court of Appeal had in mind in reaching the extreme conclusion which it did, namely that there was no contract at all.

. . .

(3) Contract on terms wider than found by the judge

69. The first question under this head is whether the parties departed from the understanding or agreement that it was to be subject to contract, as had been the original understanding of the parties and as expressly provided in clause 48. The second is whether the parties intended to be bound by what was agreed or whether there were further terms which they regarded as essential or which the law regards as essential in order for the contract to be legally enforceable. It is convenient to consider the second point first.

All essential terms agreed?

70. [Lord Clarke reviewed the evidence. . .

. . .

85. In all these circumstances we agree with Waller LJ's conclusion at para 58 of his judgment that the MF/1 conditions had to all intents and purposes been agreed and the limit of RTS' liability had been agreed. In short, by 25 August there was in our judgment unequivocal conduct on the part of both parties which leads to the conclusion that it was agreed that the project would be carried out by RTS for the agreed price on the terms agreed by 5 July as varied on 25 August.

Clause 48 and subject to contract

86. The first point remains. Had the parties agreed to be bound by the agreed terms without the necessity of a formal written contract or, put another way, had they agreed to waive that requirement and thus clause 48? We have reached the conclusion that they had. The circumstances point to the fact that there was a binding agreement and that it was not on the limited terms held by the judge. The Price had been agreed, a significant amount of work had been carried out, agreement had been reached on 5 July and the subsequent agreement to vary the Contract so that RTS agreed to provide Line 1 before Line 2 was reached without any suggestion that the variation was agreed subject to contract. The clear inference is that the parties had agreed to waive the subject to contract clause, viz clause 48. Any other conclusion makes no commercial sense. RTS could surely not have refused to perform the contract as varied pending a formal contract being signed and exchanged. Nobody suggested that it could and, of course, it did not. If one applies the standard of the reasonable, honest businessman suggested by Steyn LJ, we conclude that, whether he was an RTS man or a Müller man, he would have concluded that the parties intended that the work should be carried out for the agreed price on the agreed terms, including the terms as varied by the agreement of 25 August, without the necessity for a formal written agreement, which had been overtaken by events.

87. By contrast we do not think that the reasonable honest businessman in the position of either RTS or Müller would have concluded as at 25 August that there was no contract between them or that there was a contract on some but not all of the terms that had been agreed on or before 5 July as varied by the agreement of 25 August. Although this is not a case quite like the *Percy Trentham* case because that was not a subject to contract case, it was equally not a case like the *British Steel* case because here all the terms which the parties treated as essential were agreed and the parties were performing the contract without a formal contract being signed or exchanged, whereas there parties were still negotiating terms which they regarded as essential. As Mr Brown said, instead of signing the contract the parties here simply let sleeping dogs lie or, as Mr Manzoni put it in his

skeleton argument at first instance, neither party wanted the negotiations to get in the way of the project. The project was the only important thing. The only reasonable inference to draw is that by or on 25 August, the parties had in effect agreed to waive the 'subject to contract' provision encapsulated by clause 48. We have considered whether it would be appropriate to take a later date than 25 August, perhaps 5 September when most of RTS' equipment for Line 1 was delivered, or even 8 September when a second 30 per cent instalment of the Price was paid. However, on balance we prefer 25 August because by then the die was cast and all the parties' efforts were directed to preparations for Line 1.

88. By the time the contract was concluded, there had been some delay for reasons which were already contentious (see para 24 above and paras 53-57 of the judge's judgment). The contract, once concluded on 25 August, must, as we presently see it (though the point was not fully explored before us), be treated as applicable to the whole period of contractual performance. Any issues arising in respect of such delay would, on that basis, fall to be determined under the terms of the contract (subject to any waiver which there may have been of particular terms), as if these had already been in force during the period of such delay.

CONCLUSION

89. For the reasons we have given, we have a reached a different conclusion from both the judge and the Court of Appeal. It was agreed in the course of the argument that the court would reach its conclusions on the issues of principle before it and that the parties would subsequently have an opportunity to make submissions on the form of the order. However, subject to submissions on the precise form of order, including the precise formulation of the declarations to be made, our conclusion is that the appeal should be allowed, the order of the Court of Appeal set aside and declarations made (1) that the parties reached a binding agreement on or about 25 August on the terms agreed on or before 5 July as subsequently varied on 25 August and (2) that that binding agreement was not subject to contract or to the terms of clause 48.

----

3. First Thoughts about Fairness in the Law of Contract

2–034   Nowadays, commentators distinguish between the classical law and the modern law of contract. For some, the difference is one of degree: whereas the classical law prioritised the principles of freedom and sanctity of contract and assumed a relatively thin view of fairness, the modern law takes a more qualified approach to freedom and sanctity of contract and, in so doing, assumes a much thicker view of fairness (particularly in its protection of consumers and more vulnerable contracting parties) (see Ch.1 above). For others, the difference is one of kind: on this more radical view, the modern law that regulates consumer transactions is of a fundamentally different order to that which (still with a classical legacy) regulates business-to-business dealing. On either view, however, it is the classical law that sets the benchmark for where we are in the modern law of contract.

According to the classical view, the courts should regard it as their function to enforce whatever contract the parties have made, however bad a bargain it might be for one of them. The courts might refuse to enforce the contract where there had been fraud or misrepresentation, or where duress or undue influence had been exercised. Where none of these factors was present, the court was not concerned with the question whether there had been unfairness in the formation of the contract, or in its terms. The principle of freedom of contract required that it be left to the parties to make whatever bargain they chose. Having made the contract, they must perform it or face the prospect of being ordered to pay damages for not doing so. In the modern law, at any rate on the less radical reading, this is still the general principle though it is now much qualified by legislation relating to particular types of contract. For example, certain promises by the seller are implied in contracts for the sale of goods whether he likes it or not; and, an employer who exercises his contractual right to dismiss an employee must do so "fairly" or the employee can claim damages for unfair dismissal.

In addition to provisions relating to particular contracts there are a number of more general legislative controls, notably, the Unfair Contract Terms Act 1977 and the Unfair Terms in Consumer Contracts Regulations 1999 (and note, too, the Consumer Rights Act 2015). But these enactments are not as wide-ranging as they sound. The 1977 Act is not concerned with all contract terms which might be thought "unfair" but only with exclusion, limitation, and indemnity clauses; and the 1999 Regulations, though not restricted to these types of term, apply only to "a term in a contract concluded between a seller or supplier and a consumer where the said term has not been individually negotiated." Even in respect of these contracts the Regulations provide (reg.6(2)) that:

"In so far as it is in plain intelligible language, the assessment of fairness of a term shall not relate—

(a) to the definition of the main subject-matter of the contract, or
(b) to the adequacy of the price or remuneration, as against the goods or services supplied in exchange."[6]

On the other hand, although these provisions announce themselves as targeting unfair terms, it is characteristic of the modern law that it applies a much greater control over both the processes leading up to the formation of a contract and the terms that are included in contracts—as it is commonly put, the modern law applies a greater control over matters of both procedural and substantive fairness (see Ch.22 below).

A. Unfairness in the Formation of Contracts

Broadly speaking, unfairness in the process of negotiating or forming a contract might arise from two sources. First, one of the parties might be in a position to apply unfair pressure to the other, this militating against the ideal that a contract should be the result of an unforced choice, or that agreements should be freely made. Secondly, there might be an informational asymmetry such that one party fails to disclose material facts or alert the other to the small print of the agreement, this militating against the ideal that contract should be the product of an informed choice and leading to complaints of unfair surprise.

2–035

Following the classical view, in commercial transactions, one party may take advantage of his greatly superior bargaining power to drive a very hard bargain: *CTN Cash and Carry v Gallagher*, below, Ch.26. A party may also take advantage of his superior knowledge. In *Turner v Green* [1895] 2 Ch. 205 the plaintiff, having heard the result of a case, concluded a contract settling a dispute with the defendant, knowing that the defendant had not heard the result of that case and would not have agreed to the settlement if he had known of it. The court thought that this was not the sort of conduct to be expected of solicitors, it was 'a shabby trick', but it did not invalidate the contract. Similarly in *Smith v Hughes* (below, Ch.5) Cockburn CJ put the case of a person who buys an estate knowing that, unknown to the seller, there is a valuable mine under the surface. He thought the case "one in which a man of tender conscience or high honour would be unwilling to take advantage of the ignorance of the seller, but there can be no doubt that the contract for the sale of the estate would be binding . . .". The buyer's conduct might certainly be regarded as "unfair"; but the enactments do not affect it. The general principle of the common law was re-stated by Slade LJ in the *Banque Financiere* case, below, Ch.14. Whether it may be affected by certain developments in case-law is a matter for further consideration.

Professor Roy Goode, "International Restatements of Contract and English Contract Law" in Contemporary Issues in Commercial Law, (1997) 63 at 69–71 (footnotes omitted).

---

[6]   This particular provision has been revised by s.64(1) of the Consumer Rights Act 2015.

Good Faith and Fair Dealing

2–036   English contract law is increasingly isolated in its refusal to recognise a general duty of good faith. In the civil law subjective good faith, together with its objective counterpart, fair dealing, is a fundamental tenet of the law of contract, affecting every phase, from negotiation to performance and enforcement.

> "The principle of good faith and fair dealing is recognised or at least appears to be acted on as a guideline for contractual behaviour in all EC countries. There is, however, a considerable difference between the legal systems as to how extensive and how powerful the penetration of the principle has been. At the one end of the spectrum figures a system where the principle has revolutionized the contract law (and other parts of the law as well) and added a special feature to the style of that system (GERMANY). At the other end we find systems which do not recognize a general obligation of the parties to conform to good faith in the performance of a contract, but which in many cases by specific rules reach the results which the other systems have reached by the principle of good faith (ENGLAND and IRELAND)." [Principles of European Contract Law formulated by the Commission on European Contract Law]

American contract law has also embraced a general duty of good faith, though it begins only on conclusion of the contract and does not extend to pre-contractual negotiations: "Every contract imposes upon each party a duty of good faith and fair dealing in its performance and its enforcement."

The PECL are even more succinct: "Each party must act in accordance with good faith and fair dealing." Further, the parties may not exclude or limit this duty, which also finds expression in specific provisions in the definition of reasonableness and in the rules relating to co-operation, the conduct of negotiations, fraud, adaptation of the contract on the ground of excessive benefit or unfair advantage, contract terms not individually negotiated, change of circumstances, and clauses excluding or limiting liability.

There are several reasons why English law has been reluctant to embrace a generalised concept of good faith. In the first place, we do not quite know what the concept means. Is it, for example, contrary to good faith to negotiate concurrently with several parties in relation to the same contract without disclosing the fact to each of them? Or to exercise a contractual right to terminate a contract when this would cause hardship to the other party? Or to sell a house without disclosing structural defects? The concern engendered by open-textured rules such as duty of good faith is, perhaps, not entirely unjustified when one considers the huge volume of litigation generated by section 242 of the German Civil Code, the principal source of the duty of good faith in German contract law which has provided the foundation for the creation or elaboration of a whole network of contractual theories, including culpa in contrahendo, clausula rebus sic stantibus, contracts for the benefit of third parties, and the duty to provide information needed to invoke rights. Secondly, judges adjudicating in one of the world's leading financial centres rightly sense that for the commercial enterprise the predictability of the legal outcome is more important than absolute justice. Thirdly, English law takes the view that in general it is for the parties themselves to allocate risk through the terms of their contract, and it is not the role of the courts to do it for them.

But with the advent of the Directive on Unfair Terms in Consumer Contracts, and its implementation in the Unfair Terms in Consumer Contracts Regulations 1994, English courts will for the first time be faced with the problem of deciding whether a term which has not been individually negotiated and which is contained in a contract for the supply of goods or services to a customer is unfair, and therefore of no effect, because, contrary to the requirement of good faith, it causes a significant imbalance in the parties' rights and obligations arising under the contract, to the detriment of the consumer. It is true that the Directive and regulations apply only to consumer contracts. But once the courts have become accustomed to applying this open-textured concept of good faith, they may well find that to utilise it on a broader basis is not as difficult or unsatisfactory as might have been supposed. The fact that two separate groups of scholars working largely independently of each other, and including lawyers from the United Kingdom, United States and Ireland, produced restatements embodying in almost identical terms a general requirement of good faith should give a powerful spur to reconsideration of the traditional perspective of English law at least in international transactions.

Lord Steyn, "Contract Law: Fulfilling the Reasonable Expectations of Honest Men,"
(1997) 113 L.Q.R. 433 at 438–439 (footnotes omitted).

2–037   Next I turn to the approach of English law to the concept of good faith. In the new jus commune of Europe there is a general principle that parties must negotiate in good faith, conclude contracts in good faith and carry out contracts in good faith. The important point to note is that in exercising his rights and performing his duties each party must act in accordance with good faith and fair dealing. And the parties may not exclude this duty. The Principles of International Commercial Contracts published by Unidroit also provide that in international trade parties must act in accordance with good faith and fair dealing, and that they may not exclude or limit this duty. In the United States the influential Uniform Commercial Code is explicitly and squarely based on the concept of good faith. Elsewhere in the common law world, outside the United Kingdom, the principle of good faith in contract law is gradually gaining ground. It is the explicit basis of many international contracts. Since English law serves the international market place it cannot remain impervious to ideas of good faith, or of fair dealing. For my part I am quite confident that businessmen and indeed people on the Underground have no problem with the concept of good faith, or fair dealing. They understand very well what bad faith means. But English lawyers remain resolutely hostile to any incorporation of good faith principles into English law. The hostility is not usually bred from any great familiarity with the way in which the principle works in other systems. But it is intense. My impression is that the basis of the hostility is suspicion about what good faith means. If it were a wholly subjective notion, one could understand the scepticism. If it were an impractical and open-ended way of fastening contractual liability onto parties, it would deserve no place in international trade. But it is none of these things. While I accept that good faith is sometimes used in different senses I have in mind what I regard as the core meaning. Undoubtedly, good faith has a subjective requirement: the threshold requirement is that the party must act honestly. That is an unsurprising requirement and poses no difficulty for the English legal system. But good faith additionally sets an objective standard, viz., the observance of reasonable commercial standards of fair dealing in the conclusion and performance of the transaction concerned. For our purposes that is the important requirement. Used in this sense judges in the greater part of the industrialised world usually have no great difficulty in identifying a case of bad faith. It is not clear why it should perplex judges brought up in the English tradition.

Point for reflection

In *R. v Hinks* [2000] 1 Cr. App. R. 1; [1998] Crim. L.R. 908, CA (Crim. Div.) H befriended a 53 year old man, who was naive, gullible and of limited intelligence. She successfully encouraged him to give her £60,000 and a television set. She was convicted of theft of this property and her conviction was upheld even though it was not proved that the gifts were voidable for misrepresentation, or undue influence, i.e. under the civil law as presently understood, these were valid, indefeasible, gifts which H was entitled to retain. The jury had found that she was "dishonest", i.e. that ordinary decent people would regard what she did as dishonest and she knew that. That was sufficient. *Hinks* concerned a gift, but there seems to be no difference in principle here between a gift and a sale. The possible implications are considered by Beatson and Simester, (1999) 115 L.Q.R. 372, 374–375.

2–038

It may be thought that *Hinks*, a criminal case, need have no implications for the civil law. This possibility must be taken seriously, since criminal and civil laws frequently are driven by different rationalia. The issue turns on what is to happen when, after *Hinks*, D is convicted of stealing property to which he has an indefeasible title. There are two ways in which that apparent conflict between criminal and civil laws may be resolved. First, the civil law may yield, in which case title obtained by theft will become voidable notwithstanding the normal operation of civil law rules. This option surely cannot be taken seriously. Property offences are designed to protect property rights. Unlike crimes such as assault, the rights being protected are necessarily rooted in the civil law. Remove dependence on the law of property, and property offences have no rationale. To hold otherwise is not merely to put the cart before the horse, but to motorise it.

The implications of this move would be, to say the least, radical. In contract law, for example, the effect of the distinction between fundamental mistake and mistake going to motive would matter only if the other party were not dishonest (and therefore a thief). Dishonesty, itself a judgment call by the jury, would become a reason for undoing property transfers—regardless whether there be any observable difference in the behaviour of the parties, or any act of wrongdoing. In turn, it would become impossible for innocent third parties to determine the legal effect of a transaction by looking at the overt conduct of the parties. No one could be sure where he stood. The law on non-disclosure would have to be fundamentally rethought.

The alternative is to leave the civil law unaffected by findings of theft. That, too, is unsatisfactory. Sometimes a thief would be able to assert, and pass, good title; sometimes he would not. It may be hard to tell when. Bona fide purchasers would still be subject to the nemo dat rule. On the other hand, a third-party transferee from Hinks herself, even one with notice, would get good title. Stopping this sort of mess was why Parliament abolished market overt. By its decision, the Court of Appeal has under-mined that reform.

Moreover, severing the link between civil and criminal law would mean the principle that no-one may benefit by his wrong would have immediately to be abandoned. In case such as *Hinks*, there is no civil wrong but there is a criminal wrong. These cases occur, from time to time, throughout the law (e.g. when murderers are named as beneficiaries by the will of the deceased). The principle that one may not benefit by one's wrong is the vehicle by which such tensions are reconciled. Its application means that a person is not entitled to retain civil entitlements garnered by her criminal wrong; thus, in *Hinks*, D's elderly benefactor could recover the £60,000. To abrogate the no-benefit principle, for the sake of maintaining a conviction in *Hinks* without affecting the civil law, would entail losing the ability to control wrongdoers elsewhere in the law. There is no principled ground upon which an application of the principle in *Hinks* can be distinguished from the case of a murdering beneficiary.

S. Gardiner, 'Property and Theft' [1998] Crim. L.R. 35, 40, 41, argues that 'it would not be startling' for the civil law to hold that a person committing theft should not acquire an indefeasible title. If the law of theft was correctly applied in *Hinks*, this would be to enforce "good faith and fair dealing" in property transactions with a vengeance! Would it be a desirable development?

B. Good Faith and Fair Dealing in the Performance of Contracts

2-039   While English contract law has been notoriously reluctant to embrace an expansive general principle that requires good faith, it is recognised that, in the performance of contracts, there are some minimal requirements of good faith and fair dealing without which contract simply could not function as a useful institution. As Richard Hooley has put it:

"There is a growing body of case law which shows that the courts are willing to control the way a party may exercise discretionary powers conferred under the terms of a contract. These authorities provide that a decision-maker's discretion will be limited, as a matter of necessary implication, by concepts of honesty, good faith and genuineness, and that it must not be exercised in an arbitrary, capricious or, perhaps, unreasonable manner."[7]

---

[7]   Richard Hooley, 'Controlling Contractual Discretion' (2013) 72 CLJ 65. For support in the case-law, see e.g., *Paragon v Nash* [2001] EWCA Civ 1466. There, at para.26, Dyson LJ (quoting Mr Recorder Havelock-Allen QC) said that 'a contract where one party truly found himself subject to the whim of the other would be a commercial and practical absurdity.' As in public law decision-making, we might argue that in private law decision-making too there are some minimal (and relatively undemanding) requirements of good faith. Compare T. Daintith, 'Contractual Discretion and Administrative Discretion: A Unified Analysis' (2005) 68 MLR 554.

Moreover, once the idea takes hold, first, that it is the mission of the law of contract to do justice to the reasonable expectations of honest people and, secondly, that the reasonableness of expectations might vary from one transactional context to another, the ground has been prepared for recognising a variable (but above minimum) requirement of good faith in the performance of contracts. It is against this background that the decision and reasoning of Leggatt J in *Yam Seng Pte Limited v International Trade Corporation Limited*[8] is regarded as particularly striking and significant.

The dispute in *Yam Seng* centred on a contract, entitled 'Manchester United Distribution Agreement', made in May 2009. Under the agreement, ITC granted Yam Seng the exclusive right to distribute a range of 'Manchester United' fragrances (Eau de Toilette, Deodorant Body Spray, hair gel, and so on) in various parts of the world; but, for the purposes of the dispute, it was mainly to duty-free outlets in Singapore and Dubai that Yam Seng intended to supply the brand. However, ITC proved to be unreliable and, in July 2010, Yam Seng purported to terminate the contract, citing various breaches by ITC. ITC contested this and the question for Leggatt J was whether Yam Seng had grounds for termination. Leggatt J had little difficulty in confirming Yam Seng's view that ITC had committed several breaches of contract (for example, by making late deliveries in response to Yam Seng's orders) and it was clear that such breaches had put Yam Seng in a difficult position in relation to its own retailer customers. However, for the most part, these breaches either were not so serious as to justify termination or, faced with the breach, Yam Seng had decided to continue with the contract. It followed that, where this was the case, Yam Seng's remedy was limited to the recovery of damages (see Ch.20). This left Yam Seng with a small set of alleged breaches on which to rest their termination; and it is in one of these claims that the interest in the case lies.

The claim in question concerns (i) the actions taken by ITC to ensure that retail outlets in Singapore were not undercutting the price of 'Manchester United' fragrances in the duty-free outlets at Singapore's international airport and (ii) what ITC told Yam Seng about the local retail prices. For Yam Seng, it was essential that the duty-free outlets had the edge in pricing the brand and that ITC kept them properly informed. In fact, as Leggatt J found, ITC had not directly sanctioned a domestic retail price that would undercut the duty-free price of the product; but they had been selective in what they told Yam Seng about the situation—in particular, ITC led Yam Seng to believe that domestic retail prices were under control when retailers had told ITC that it would actually take a month or two to get the prices adjusted. In other words, ITC painted a rosier picture (on which Yam Seng relied) than the facts justified. This Leggatt J held was a repudiatory breach of an implied term that required a high level of honesty which, in turn, rested on an implied term that the parties would deal with one another in good faith.

YAM SENG PTE LIMITED v INTERNATIONAL TRADE CORPORATION

[2013] EWHC 111 (QB)

LEGGATT J

An Implied Duty of Good Faith?

119. As pleaded in the Particulars of Claim, it is Yam Seng's case that there was an implied term of the Agreement that the parties would deal with each other in good faith.   **2–040**

120. The subject of whether English law does or should recognise a general duty to perform contracts in good faith is one on which a large body of academic literature exists. However, I not am aware of any decision of an English court, and none was cited to me, in which the question has been considered in any depth.

---

[8]   [2013] EWHC 111 (QB).

121. The general view among commentators appears to be that in English contract law there is no legal principle of good faith of general application: see *Chitty on Contract Law* (31st Ed), Vol 1, para 1-039. In this regard the following observations of Bingham LJ (as he then was) in *Interfoto Picture Library Ltd v Stiletto Visual Programmes Ltd* [1989] 1 QB 433 at 439 are often quoted:

> "In many civil law systems, and perhaps in most legal systems outside the common law world, the law of obligations recognises and enforces an overriding principle that in making and carrying out contracts parties should act in good faith. This does not simply mean that they should not deceive each other, a principle which any legal system must recognise; its effect is perhaps most aptly conveyed by such metaphorical colloquialisms as 'playing fair', 'coming clean' or 'putting one's cards face upwards on the table.' It is in essence a principle of fair open dealing... English law has, characteristically, committed itself to no such overriding principle but has developed piecemeal solutions in response to demonstrated problems of unfairness."

122 Another case sometimes cited for the proposition that English contract law does not recognise a duty of good faith is *Walford v Miles* [1992] 2 AC 128, where the House of Lords considered that a duty to negotiate in good faith is "inherently repugnant to the adversarial position of the parties when involved in negotiations" and "unworkable in practice" (per Lord Ackner at p.138). That case was concerned, however, with the position of negotiating parties and not with the duties of parties who have entered into a contract and thereby undertaken obligations to each other.

123. Three main reasons have been given for what Professor McKendrick has called the "traditional English hostility" towards a doctrine of good faith: see McKendrick, *Contract Law* (9th Ed) pp.221-2. The first is the one referred to by Bingham LJ in the passage quoted above: that the preferred method of English law is to proceed incrementally by fashioning particular solutions in response to particular problems rather than by enforcing broad overarching principles. A second reason is that English law is said to embody an ethos of individualism, whereby the parties are free to pursue their own self-interest not only in negotiating but also in performing contracts provided they do not act in breach of a term of the contract. The third main reason given is a fear that recognising a general requirement of good faith in the performance of contracts would create too much uncertainty. There is concern that the content of the obligation would be vague and subjective and that its adoption would undermine the goal of contractual certainty to which English law has always attached great weight.

124. In refusing, however, if indeed it does refuse, to recognise any such general obligation of good faith, this jurisdiction would appear to be swimming against the tide. As noted by Bingham LJ in the *Interfoto* case, a general principle of good faith (derived from Roman law) is recognised by most civil law systems—including those of Germany, France and Italy. From that source references to good faith have already entered into English law via EU legislation. For example, the Unfair Terms in Consumer Contracts Regulations 1999, which give effect to a European directive, contain a requirement of good faith. Several other examples of legislation implementing EU directives which use this concept are mentioned in *Chitty on Contract Law* (31st Ed), Vol 1 at para 1-043. Attempts to harmonise the contract law of EU member states, such as the Principles of European Contract Law proposed by the Lando Commission and the European Commission's proposed Regulation for a Common European Sales Law on which consultation is currently taking place, also embody a general duty to act in accordance with good faith and fair dealing. There can be little doubt that the penetration of this principle into English law and the pressures towards a more unified European law of contract in which the principle plays a significant role will continue to increase.

125. It would be a mistake, moreover, to suppose that willingness to recognise a doctrine of good faith in the performance of contracts reflects a divide between civil law and common law systems or between continental paternalism and Anglo-Saxon individualism. Any such notion is gainsaid by that fact that such a doctrine has long been recognised in the United States. The New York Court of Appeals said in 1918: "Every contract implies good faith and fair dealing between the parties to it": *Wigand v Bachmann-Bechtel Brewing Co*, 222 NY 272 at 277. The Uniform Commercial Code, first promulgated in 1951 and which has been adopted by many States, provides in section 1-203 that "every contract or duty within this Act imposes an obligation of good faith in its performance or enforcement." Similarly, the Restatement (Second) of Contracts states in section 205 that "every contract imposes upon each party a duty of good faith and fair dealing in its performance and enforcement."

126. In recent years the concept has been gaining ground in other common law jurisdictions. Canadian courts have proceeded cautiously in recognising duties of good faith in the performance of commercial contracts but have, at least in some situations, been willing to imply such duties with a view to securing the performance and enforcement of the contract or, as it is sometimes put, to ensure that parties do not act in a way

that eviscerates or defeats the objectives of the agreement that they have entered into: see e.g. *Transamerica Life Inc v ING Canada Inc* (2003) 68 OR (3d) 457, 468.

127. In Australia the existence of a contractual duty of good faith is now well established, although the limits and precise juridical basis of the doctrine remain unsettled. The springboard for this development has been the decision of the New South Wales Court of Appeal in *Renard Constructions (ME) Pty v Minister for Public Works* (1992) 44 NSWLR 349, where Priestley JA said (at 95) that:

> ". . . people generally, including judges and other lawyers, from all strands of the community, have grown used to the courts applying standards of fairness to contract which are wholly consistent with the existence in all contracts of a duty upon the parties of good faith and fair dealing in its performance. In my view this is in these days the expected standard, and anything less is contrary to prevailing community expectations."

128. Although the High Court has not yet considered the question (and declined to do so in *Royal Botanic Gardens and Domain Trust v Sydney City Council* (2002) 186 ALR 289) there has been clear recognition of the duty of good faith in a substantial body of Australian case law, including further significant decisions of the New South Wales Court of Appeal in *Alcatel Australia Ltd v Scarcella* (1998) 44 NSWLR 349, *Burger King Corp v Hungry Jack's Pty Ltd* [2001] NWSCA 187 and *Vodafone Pacific Ltd v Mobile Innovations Ltd* [2004] NSWCA 15.

129. In New Zealand a doctrine of good faith is not yet established law but it has its advocates: see in particular the dissenting judgment of Thomas J in *Bobux Marketing Ltd v Raynor Marketing Ltd* [2002] 1 NZLR 506 at 517.

130. Closer to home, there is strong authority for the view that Scottish law recognises a broad principle of good faith and fair dealing: see the decision of the House of Lords in *Smith v Bank of Scotland*, 1997 SC (HL) 111 esp. at p.121 (per Lord Clyde).

131. Under English law a duty of good faith is implied by law as an incident of certain categories of contract, for example contracts of employment and contracts between partners or others whose relationship is characterised as a fiduciary one. I doubt that English law has reached the stage, however, where it is ready to recognise a requirement of good faith as a duty implied by law, even as a default rule, into all commercial contracts. Nevertheless, there seems to me to be no difficulty, following the established methodology of English law for the implication of terms in fact, in implying such a duty in any ordinary commercial contract based on the presumed intention of the parties.

132. Traditionally, the two principal criteria used to identify terms implied in fact are that the term is so obvious that it goes without saying and that the term is necessary to give business efficacy to the contract. More recently, in *Attorney General for Belize v Belize Telecom Ltd* [2009] 1 WLR 1988 at 1993-5, the process of implication has been analysed as an exercise in the construction of the contract as a whole. In giving the judgment of the Privy Council in that case, Lord Hoffmann characterised the traditional criteria, not as a series of independent tests, but rather as different ways of approaching what is ultimately always a question of construction: what would the contract, read as a whole against the relevant background, reasonably be understood to mean?

133. The modern case law on the construction of contracts has emphasised that contracts, like all human communications, are made against a background of unstated shared understandings which inform their meaning. The breadth of the relevant background and the fact that it has no conceptual limits have also been stressed, particularly in the famous speech of Lord Hoffmann in *Investors Compensation Scheme Ltd v West Bromwich Building* Society [1998] 1 WLR 896 at pp.912–3, as further explained in *BCCI v Ali* [2002] 1 AC 251 at p.269.

134. Importantly for present purposes, the relevant background against which contracts are made includes not only matters of fact known to the parties but also shared values and norms of behaviour. Some of these are norms that command general social acceptance; others may be specific to a particular trade or commercial activity; others may be more specific still, arising from features of the particular contractual relationship. Many such norms are naturally taken for granted by the parties when making any contract without being spelt out in the document recording their agreement.

135. A paradigm example of a general norm which underlies almost all contractual relationships is an expectation of honesty. That expectation is essential to commerce, which depends critically on trust. Yet it is seldom, if ever, made the subject of an express contractual obligation. Indeed if a party in negotiating the terms of a contract were to seek to include a provision which expressly required the other party to act honestly, the very fact of doing so might well damage the parties' relationship by the lack of trust which this would signify.

136. The fact that commerce takes place against a background expectation of honesty has been recognised by the House of Lords in *HIH Casualty v Chase Manhattan Bank* [2003] 2 Lloyd's Rep 61. In that case a contract of insurance contained a clause which stated that the insured should have "no liability of any nature to the

insurers for any information provided". A question arose as to whether these words meant that the insured had no liability even for deceit where the insured's agent had dishonestly provided information known to be false. The House of Lords affirmed the decision of the courts below that, even though the clause read literally would cover liability for deceit, it was not reasonably to be understood as having that meaning. As Lord Bingham put it at [15]:

> "Parties entering into a commercial contract . . . will assume the honesty and good faith of the other; absent such an assumption they would not deal."

To similar effect Lord Hoffmann observed at [68] that parties "contract with one another in the expectation of honest dealing", and that:

> ". . . in the absence of words which expressly refer to dishonesty, it goes without saying that underlying the contractual arrangements of the parties there will be a common assumption that the persons involved will behave honestly."

137. As a matter of construction, it is hard to envisage any contract which would not reasonably be understood as requiring honesty in its performance. The same conclusion is reached if the traditional tests for the implication of a term are used. In particular the requirement that parties will behave honestly is so obvious that it goes without saying. Such a requirement is also necessary to give business efficacy to commercial transactions.

138. In addition to honesty, there are other standards of commercial dealing which are so generally accepted that the contracting parties would reasonably be understood to take them as read without explicitly stating them in their contractual document. A key aspect of good faith, as I see it, is the observance of such standards. Put the other way round, not all bad faith conduct would necessarily be described as dishonest. Other epithets which might be used to describe such conduct include "improper", "commercially unacceptable" or "unconscionable".

139. Another aspect of good faith which overlaps with the first is what may be described as fidelity to the parties' bargain. The central idea here is that contracts can never be complete in the sense of expressly providing for every event that may happen. To apply a contract to circumstances not specifically provided for, the language must accordingly be given a reasonable construction which promotes the values and purposes expressed or implicit in the contract. That principle is well established in the modern English case law on the interpretation of contracts: see e.g. *Rainy Sky SA v Kookmin Bank* [2011] 1 WLR 2900; Lloyds TSB Foundation for *Scotland v Lloyds Banking Group Plc* [2013] UKSC 3 at [23], [45] and [54]. It also underlies and explains, for example, the body of cases in which terms requiring cooperation in the performance of the contract have been implied: see *Mackay v Dick* (1881) 6 App Cas 251, 263; and the cases referred to in *Chitty on Contracts* (31st Ed), Vol 1 at paras 13-012–13-014.

140. The two aspects of good faith which I have identified are consistent with the way in which express contractual duties of good faith have been interpreted in several recent cases: see *Berkeley Community Villages Ltd v Pullen* [2007] EWHC 1330 (Ch) at [95]-[97]; *CPC Group Ltd v Qatari Diar Real Estate Investment Co* [2010] EWHC 1535 (Ch) at [246].

141. What good faith requires is sensitive to context. That includes the core value of honesty. In any situation it is dishonest to deceive another person by making a statement of fact intending that other person to rely on it while knowing the statement to be untrue. Frequently, however, the requirements of honesty go further. For example, if A gives information to B knowing that B is likely to rely on the information and A believes the information to be true at the time it is given but afterwards discovers that the information was, or has since become, false, it may be dishonest for A to keep silent and not to disclose the true position to B. Another example of conduct falling short of a lie which may, depending on the context, be dishonest is deliberately avoiding giving an answer, or giving an answer which is evasive, in response to a request for information.

142. In some contractual contexts the relevant background expectations may extend further to an expectation that the parties will share information relevant to the performance of the contract such that a deliberate omission to disclose such information may amount to bad faith. English law has traditionally drawn a sharp distinction between certain relationships—such as partnership, trusteeship and other fiduciary relationships—on the one hand, in which the parties owe onerous obligations of disclosure to each other, and other contractual relationships in which no duty of disclosure is supposed to operate. Arguably at least, that dichotomy is too simplistic. While it seems unlikely that any duty to disclose information in performance of the contract would be implied where the contract involves a simple exchange, many contracts do not fit this model and involve a longer term relationship between the parties which they make a substantial commitment. Such "relational"

contracts, as they are sometimes called, may require a high degree of communication, cooperation and predictable performance based on mutual trust and confidence and involve expectations of loyalty which are not legislated for in the express terms of the contract but are implicit in the parties' understanding and necessary to give business efficacy to the arrangements. Examples of such relational contracts might include some joint venture agreements, franchise agreements and long term distributorship agreements.

143. The Agreement in this case was a distributorship agreement which required the parties to communicate effectively and cooperate with each other in its performance. In particular, ITC needed to plan production and take account of the expected future demand from Yam Seng for Manchester United products. For its part Yam Seng, which was incurring expense in marketing the products and was trying to obtain orders, was arguably entitled to expect that it would be kept informed of ITC's best estimates of when products would be available to sell and would be told of any material change in this information without having to ask. Yam Seng's case was not advanced in this way, however, and it is therefore unnecessary for me to decide whether the requirements of good faith in this case extended to any such positive obligations of disclosure.

144. Although its requirements are sensitive to context, the test of good faith is objective in the sense that it depends not on either party's perception of whether particular conduct is improper but on whether in the particular context the conduct would be regarded as commercially unacceptable by reasonable and honest people. The standard is thus similar to that described by Lord Nicholls in a different context in his seminal speech in *Royal Brunei Airlines v Tan* [1995] 2 AC 378 at pp.389-390. This follows from the fact that the content of the duty of good faith is established by a process of construction which in English law is based on an objective principle. The court is concerned not with the subjective intentions of the parties but with their presumed intention, which is ascertained by attributing to them the purposes and values which reasonable people in their situation would have had.

145. Understood in the way I have described, there is in my view nothing novel or foreign to English law in recognising an implied duty of good faith in the performance of contracts. It is consonant with the theme identified by Lord Steyn as running through our law of contract that reasonable expectations must be protected: see *First Energy (UK) Ltd v Hungarian International Bank Ltd* [1993] 2 Lloyd's Rep 194, 196; and (1997) 113 LQR 433. Moreover such a concept is, I believe, already reflected in several lines of authority that are well established. One example is the body of cases already mentioned in which duties of cooperation in the performance of the contract have been implied. Another consists of the authorities which show that a power conferred by a contract on one party to make decisions which affect them both must be exercised honestly and in good faith for the purpose for which it was conferred, and must not be exercised arbitrarily, capriciously or unreasonably (in the sense of irrationally): see e.g. *Abu Dhabi National Tanker Co v. Product Star Shipping Ltd (The "Product Star")* [1993] 1 Lloyd's Rep 397, 404; *Socimer International Bank Ltd v Standard Bank London Ltd* [2008] 1 Lloyd's Rep 558, 575-7. A further example concerns the situation where the consent of one party is needed to an action of the other and a term is implied that such consent is not to be withheld unreasonably (in a similar sense): see e.g. *Gan v Tai Ping (Nos 2 & 3)* [2001] Lloyd's Rep IR 667; *Eastleigh BC v Town Quay Developments Ltd* [2010] 2 P&CR 2. Yet another example, I would suggest, is the line of authorities of which the *Interfoto* case is one which hold that an onerous or unusual contract term on which a party seeks to rely must be fairly brought to the notice of the other party if it is to be enforced.

146. There are some further observations that I would make about the reasons I mentioned earlier for the reluctance of English law to recognise an implied duty on contracting parties to deal with each other in good faith.

147. First, because the content of the duty is heavily dependent on context and is established through a process of construction of the contract, its recognition is entirely consistent with the case by case approach favoured by the common law. There is therefore no need for common lawyers to abandon their characteristic methods and adopt those of civil law systems in order to accommodate the principle.

148. Second, as the basis of the duty of good faith is the presumed intention of the parties and meaning of their contract, its recognition is not an illegitimate restriction on the freedom of the parties to pursue their own interests. The essence of contracting is that the parties bind themselves in order to co-operate to their mutual benefit. The obligations which they undertake include those which are implicit in their agreement as well as those which they have made explicit.

149. Third, a further consequence of the fact that the duty is based on the parties' presumed intention is that it is open to the parties to modify the scope of the duty by the express terms of their contract and, in principle at least, to exclude it altogether. I say "in principle at least" because in practice it is hardly conceivable that contracting parties would attempt expressly to exclude the core requirement to act honestly.

150. Fourth, I see no objection, and some advantage, in describing the duty as one of good faith "and fair dealing". I see no objection, as the duty does not involve the court in imposing its view of what is substantively

fair on the parties. What constitutes fair dealing is defined by the contract and by those standards of conduct to which, objectively, the parties must reasonably have assumed compliance without the need to state them. The advantage of including reference to fair dealing is that it draws attention to the fact that the standard is objective and distinguishes the relevant concept of good faith from other senses in which the expression "good faith" is used.

151. Fifth, in so far as English law may be less willing than some other legal systems to interpret the duty of good faith as requiring openness of the kind described by Bingham LJ in the Interfoto case as "playing fair" "coming clean" or "putting one's cards face upwards on the table", this should be seen as a difference of opinion, which may reflect different cultural norms, about what constitutes good faith and fair dealing in some contractual contexts rather than a refusal to recognise that good faith and fair dealing are required.

152. Sixth, the fear that recognising a duty of good faith would generate excessive uncertainty is unjustified. There is nothing unduly vague or unworkable about the concept. Its application involves no more uncertainty than is inherent in the process of contractual interpretation.

153. In the light of these points, I respectfully suggest that the traditional English hostility towards a doctrine of good faith in the performance of contracts, to the extent that it still persists, is misplaced.

154. I have emphasised in this discussion the extent to which the content of the duty to perform a contract in good faith is dependent on context. It was Mr Salter's submission that the relevant content of the duty in this case was captured by two more specific terms which Yam Seng contends are to be implied into the Agreement. I therefore turn to consider these.

A Duty Not to Give False Information?

155. The first more specific term said by Yam Seng to be implied in the Agreement is a term that "insofar as [ITC] instructed or encouraged [Yam Seng] to incur marketing expenses it would not do so for products which it was unable or unwilling to supply, nor offer false information on which [Yam Seng] was likely to rely to its detriment."

156. As I see it, the essential difficulty with this formulation is that it does not distinguish between encouraging expenditure in the expectation that products would be supplied, or providing false information, dishonestly and doing so innocently. In my view, such a distinction is critical. To take the first limb of the alleged implied term, in so far as ITC led Yam Seng to expect that products were going be supplied believing that it would be able to supply them and intending to do so, there would be no lack of good faith on the part of ITC. The position would be different if ITC wilfully led Yam Seng to expect that products would be supplied in circumstances where ITC did not in fact intend to supply them or knew that it would be unable to do so. Conduct of the latter kind would be clearly contrary to standards of commercial dealing which the parties would reasonably have taken for granted; but I can see no basis for implying any more onerous obligation. The same distinction needs to be drawn in relation to the second limb of the alleged implied term. I can see no justification for implying an unqualified obligation not to provide false information—equivalent to a warranty that any information given by ITC on which Yam Seng was likely to rely would be true. By contrast, it was clearly implied that ITC would not knowingly provide false information on which Yam Seng was likely to rely. Such conduct would plainly infringe the core expectation of honesty discussed earlier.

A Duty Not to Undercut Duty Free Prices?

157. The second more specific term which Yam Seng contends was implied in the Agreement is a term that "[ITC] would not prejudice [Yam Seng]'s sales by offering the same products for sale within the same territories at a lower price than [Yam Seng] was permitted to offer."

158. As pointed out by Mr Eaton Turner, this alleged term as formulated does not accord with the facts, as ITC did not itself make any direct sales in any territory. In particular, in Singapore—which was the focus of Yam Seng's complaint—ITC sold the Manchester United 100ml EDT to a distributor, Kay Ess, which in turn sold the product to retailers for sale to consumers. There is no evidence of the price at which ITC sold the product to Kay Ess. In any case, the price about which Yam Seng complained was not the price paid or charged by Kay Ess but was the retail price in stores. ITC could not directly dictate the retail price. What ITC could do is agree with its distributor, Kay Ess, a recommended retail price for the Singapore domestic market and ask Kay Ess to seek to ensure so far as it could that retailers offered the product for sale at that price.

159. The highest that the putative implied term could therefore be put is as an obligation not to approve a retail price for any product for any domestic market which was lower than the duty free retail price for the product agreed with Yam Seng.

160. In ordinary circumstances I would see no justification for implying such a term. The reasonable com-

mercial expectation would be that ITC was free to sell its products to others on such terms as it chose unless it had expressly agreed otherwise with Yam Seng. Three particular contextual features of this case, however, lead me to conclude that there was in fact such an implied term of the Agreement.

161. The first is that the Agreement is a skeletal document which does not attempt to specify the parties' obligations in any detail. In relation to such a document it is easier than in the case of a detailed and professionally drafted contract to suppose that a part of the bargain has not been expressly stated.

162. Second, I think it significant that the Agreement (at Clause E) specified the "duty free retail price" for each product. Yam Seng was thus constrained by the Agreement from selling or authorising the sale of any product in duty free outlets at any lower price than the specified duty free retail price. It would be surprising in these circumstances if the parties had intended that ITC should be free to authorise the sale of a product in the domestic market of any territory at a lower price than Yam Seng was permitted by its contract with ITC to sell the same product in duty free.

163. The third and in my view decisive contextual feature is that, as was common ground, the background to the Agreement included an industry assumption that retail prices in domestic markets will be higher than the corresponding duty free retail prices at airports or on board aeroplanes. The parties would reasonably have understood and expected that their obligations would reflect this assumption without needing to spell this out.

164. In my view these matters, taken together, lead to the necessary implication that ITC would not authorise the sale of any product in the domestic market of any territory covered by the Agreement at a lower retail price than the duty free retail price for the product which had been specified in the Agreement with Yam Seng.

Was there a Breach by ITC?

165. The next question is therefore whether there was a breach by ITC of either of the particular terms which I have held was implied in the Agreement: namely, the implied duty of honesty in the provision of information and the implied duty not to approve a domestic retail price for a product which undercut the duty free retail price.

166. It is convenient to take the latter first. I find that Yam Seng has not established that ITC was in breach of this implied term.

167. The retail price agreed by ITC with Kay Ess for sales of the 100ml EDT in the Singapore domestic market was S$59, equivalent to just over US$42. The duty free retail price for the 100ml EDT specified in the Agreement was US$42. Therefore, ITC did not agree a lower price for the domestic market than the retail price agreed with Yam Seng for duty free sales.

168. The problem seems to have arisen because the duty free retail price which Yam Seng communicated to Nuance Watson, the duty free operator at Changi Airport in Singapore, and to the airlines, was US$44. There is no evidence, however, that before setting this price Mr Tuli obtained Mr Presswell's agreement to vary the duty free retail price for the 100ml EDT specified in the Agreement.

169. Where I consider that Yam Seng has legitimate cause for complaint in relation to domestic pricing in Singapore is that Mr Presswell misled Mr Tuli about what ITC had done. For the reasons indicated, Yam Seng was not entitled to insist that ITC instruct Kay Ess to set the Singapore domestic retail price for the 100ml EDT above US$44. However, Mr Presswell agreed to do so and in his email to Mr Tuli dated 26 January 2010 said that he had informed Kay Ess that they must increase the Singapore domestic retail price to S$65 being the equivalent of US$46.40. I have found that at the time when he sent this email Mr Presswell had not yet sent such an instruction to Kay Ess, and that when he did so on 29 January 2010 he was told in reply that the product had already gone on sale at a price of S$59 and that Kay Ess was not willing go back to its customers and inform them that the retail price had increased within a matter of days. Mr Presswell nevertheless left the matter there and did not inform Mr Tuli that the domestic retail price had not, after all, been increased. Instead he left Mr Tuli with the understanding, for which he was responsible and on which he knew that Yam Seng would be relying, that the domestic retail price was being increased when he knew that this information was false.

170. Mr Presswell showed no sign either in the emails exchanged when the facts came to light in July 2010 or in his evidence in court that he saw anything dishonest about his conduct. When Mr Tuli accused him in their correspondence of having lied about the Singapore domestic price, Mr Presswell took great offence and (in an email dated 9 July 2010) demanded "by return email your retraction and sincere apology". Despite numerous requests, however, Mr Presswell never gave any answer in correspondence to the accusation that he had knowingly misled Mr Tuli. He simply ignored the requests for an explanation.

171. There can, however, be no doubt that objectively, whether Mr Presswell recognised it or not, his conduct in leaving Mr Tuli with the belief that the domestic retail price had been increased to S$65 when Mr Presswell knew that to be untrue was dishonest. Furthermore, the nature of the dishonesty, on a matter of commercial importance in Yam Seng's dealings with its customers, was in my view such as to strike at the heart of the trust

which is vital to any long term commercial relationship, particularly one which is dependent as this relation-ship was on the mutual trust of two individuals. I do not think that a businessman in Mr Tuli's position could reasonably be expected to continue to do business with ITC after Mr Presswell's dishonest behaviour regarding the Singapore pricing had come to light—all the more so given Mr Presswell's refusal to explain his conduct. I therefore have no hesitation in holding that this was a repudiatory breach of contract.

172. There was a further matter about which Mr Presswell appears to have misled Mr Tuli, although it is not one of which Mr Tuli was aware at the time of his decision to terminate the Agreement. This concerned the steps taken to register the products in China. I have found that both before the Agreement was made and afterwards Mr Presswell gave information to Mr Tuli about the time frame within which registration would take place which was wholly unrealistic. That in itself did not amount to breach of the duty of honesty in the provi-sion of information which I have held was implied. However, when, as I have found that he did, Mr Presswell told Mr Tuli in early May 2010 that an application for registration had been made some two weeks earlier, it is hard to suppose that he did not appreciate that this information was false and that, as ITC has admitted in these proceedings, an application had still not in fact been made. Yam Seng did not allege, however, that the information given in early May 2010 was a further instance of bad faith, and in these circumstances it is not right that I should make any finding to that effect.

Point for reflection

2-041   It should not be assumed that, after *Yam Seng*, there will be an overnight conversion to a general requirement of good faith and fair dealing in English contract law. In *TSG Building Services Plc v South Anglia Housing Ltd* [2013] EWHC 1151 (TCC), where the context—underlined by the express terms of the contract—required the parties (who were "partnering team members") to "work together and individually in the spirit of trust, fairness and mutual co-operation", Akenhead J held that South Anglia's unexplained termination of TSG's appointment was in no way constrained by either the express provision for co-operation or by a term for good faith that TSG argued should be implied. The scope of the express provision was limited by a somewhat literal reading of the contract; and a general term for good faith was not to be implied where the express terms already set limits to the level of co-operation that was required. Moreover, in the not dissimilar case of *Mid Essex Hospital Services NHS Trust v Compass Group UK and Ireland Ltd (Trading as Medirest)* [2013] EWCA Civ 200, the Court of Appeal held unanimously that an express provision requiring the parties to "co-operate with each other in good faith" did not signal a general duty to act in good faith; rather, the obligation to co-operate in good faith was limited by both the provisions of the contract and the overall context. Cautioning against an extended reading of the provision, Beatson LJ said (at para.154):

> "The contract in the present case is a detailed one which makes specific provision for a number of particular eventualities . . . In a situation where a contract makes such specific provision . . . care must be taken not to construe a general and potentially open-ended obligation such as an obliga-tion to 'co-operate' or 'to act in good faith' as covering the same ground as other, more specific, provisions, lest it cut across those more specific provisions and any limitations in them."

Given this approach, where terms for co-operation or good faith are already expressed within the contract, the relevance of context is to identify the precise scope of the obligations that the parties have assumed.

C.   *Baird Textiles: A Test Case for the Limits of Good Faith and Cooperation?*

BAIRD TEXTILE HOLDINGS LTD v MARKS & SPENCER PLC

Court of Appeal [2001] EWCA Civ 274

Baird Textile Holdings Ltd ('Baird') had been one of the principal suppliers of garments to Marks   **2–042**
and Spencer Plc ('M&S') for 30 years when, on October 19, 1999 M&S, without warning, determined
all supply arrangements between them with effect from the end of the then current production
season. On January 10, 2000 Baird commenced proceedings against M&S contending that M&S was
precluded by both contract and estoppel from determining such arrangements without reasonable
notice. M&S applied under CPR Rule 24.2 for summary judgment against Baird on the ground that
it had no reasonable prospect of succeeding on either claim. On June 29, 2000 Morison J dismissed
the claim in so far as it was based on contract but directed that it proceed to trial in so far as it was
based on estoppel. Each party appealed against that part of Morison J's order that was against it.
Accordingly the issues which arise were whether Baird had a real prospect of succeeding on its claim
based on (1) contract, and (2) estoppel, or, if not, whether there was some other compelling reason
why that claim or issue should be disposed of at a trial.

[In the following extract, it is only the question of contract that is considered].

SIR ANDREW MORRITT VC

Contract

13. In paragraph 11 of the Particulars of Claim Baird alleged that the summary determination of the relationship
between it and M&S was in breach of the contract pleaded in paragraph 9. The judge did not agree. He summarised the arguments of counsel and described the principles to be applied as

> "(1) A court will only imply a contract by reason of the conduct of the parties if it is necessary to do so. It
> will be fatal to the implication of a contract that the parties would or might have acted as they did without
> any such contract. In other words, it must be possible to infer a common intention to be bound by a contract
> which has legal effect. If there were no such intent the claim would fail.
>
> (2) All contracts, to be enforceable must be sufficiently certain to enable the courts to give effect to the
> parties' intentions rather than to give effect to a contract which the court has had to write for them. On the
> other hand it can be said that the Courts do not incline to adopt a 'nit-picking' attitude to such matters and
> will endeavour, where possible, to construe the obligations in a way which gives effect to the parties' bargain.
> There is a line to be drawn between a generous attitude to making contracts work and striking them down
> on grounds of uncertainty."

14. In his application of those principles to this case the judge said:

> "13. On this head of the claim I am satisfied that Baird's case in favour of an implied contract cannot succeed.
> In the first place, it would be unlikely that one could properly imply a contract when it is the pleaded case of
> Baird that M & S deliberately refrained from concluding any express contract because it could achieve greater
> flexibility without one. To imply a contract against such a party would seem to me to offend against the prin-
> ciple that the parties' conduct must show an implied common intention to create legal relations by contract.
>
> In any event, the alleged terms are far too imprecise to be capable of being enforced. [After referring
> by way of analogy to *Blue Metal Ltd v Robert Frank Hughes & Others* (1963) A.C. 74. Morison J continued]
> Mr. Field [counsel for Baird] could not say that so long as the implied contract continued with Baird, M & S
> were prevented from appointing principal suppliers. And I cannot understand how the various factors listed
> by him would work in practice. If M & S's future requirements were for fewer and more expensive garments
> of a type which Baird was unable or unwilling to produce at an acceptable cost, what then? There is, in my
> judgment, no firm base upon which one could ascertain either a particular quantity or a particular share
> which should be attributed to Baird in the future. Were the alleged contract to have legal effect then the
> court would, to all intents and purposes, be making a bargain for the parties rather than seeking to enforce
> a bargain which they themselves had made."

15. For Baird counsel submits that where, as alleged in paragraph 9, one party intentionally induces a particular belief in another, on which the other relies, such conduct attracts legal responsibility. The responsibility relied on is (1) to give reasonable notice to terminate the relationship and (2) during the subsistence of the relationship, to acquire garments from Baird in such quantities and at such prices as were in all the circumstances reasonable. More specifically he contends that the judge was wrong in three respects, namely (a) necessity is not the test for the implication of a contract from conduct, (b) there is a sufficient prospect of success in establishing an intention to create the legal relations relied on, and (c) the obligations are sufficiently certain to be enforceable as part of the alleged contract.

16. In connection with the wide proposition counsel referred to academic discussion with regard to "relational contracts" and the legal implications to which they may give rise. But the articles which he produced did not suggest that the normal rules as to the implication and formation of contracts or the usual requirements of certainty did not apply to "relational contracts". Accordingly it is to those rules that I turn.

17. Counsel suggested that the requirement of necessity to which the judge referred was derived from the judgment of Bingham L.J. in *The Aramis* [1989] 1 Ll.L.R 213. He submitted that it was either confined to the cases exemplified in that case or, at least, inapplicable to cases in which there had been a long continuing relationship or an intentional inducement such as Baird relies on in this case.

18. *The Aramis* [1989] 1 Ll.L.R 213 concerned the question whether a contract could be implied between the transferee of a bill of lading to whom the goods had been delivered and the carrier. Prior to the Carriage of Goods By Sea Act 1992 the implication of such a contract was necessary if the transferee and the carrier were to have rights enforceable between themselves in respect of, for example, damage to the goods or the payment of freight. Bingham L.J. considered the authorities at some length to see how the implication of contracts in this field had grown and developed. He cited with approval from the judgment of May L.J. in *The Elli* [1985] 1 Ll.R. 107, 115 that

". . . no such contract should be implied on the facts of any given case unless it is necessary to do so: necessary, that is to say, to give business reality to a transaction and to create enforceable obligations between parties who are dealing with one another in circumstances in which one would expect that business reality and those enforceable obligations to exist."

Bingham L.J. accepted that the authorities showed that "a contract will only be implied if it is necessary to do so". In expressing his own view Bingham L.J. said (page 224):

". . . it would, in my view, be contrary to principle to countenance the implication of a contract from conduct if the conduct relied upon is no more consistent with an intention to contract than with an intention not to contract. It must, surely, be necessary to identify conduct referable to the contract contended for or, at the very least, conduct inconsistent with there being no contract made between the parties. Put another way, I think it must be fatal to the implication of a contract if the parties would or might have acted exactly as they did in the absence of a contract."

19. Counsel for Baird relied on the fact that in *Blackpool and Fylde Aero Club Ltd v Blackpool Borough Council* [1990] 1 WLR 1195, a case concerning the implication of a contract from a request for tenders and a submission in response, Bingham L.J. put the matter somewhat differently. In that case he referred (pp.1201 and 1202) to the "confident assumptions of commercial men" and the need to "be able to conclude with confidence both that the parties intended to create contractual relations and that the agreement was to the effect contended for".

20. For M&S it was submitted that it would be odd if the principle for the implication of a contract at all should be different or less onerous than the principle for the implication of a term in a contract. Reliance was placed on *Wilson v Partenreederei Hannah Blumenthal* [1983] AC 854 and *The Gudermes* [1993] 1 Ll.R.311. The former concerned the question whether a contract to abandon an arbitration might be implied from conduct, or more precisely lack of conduct. Lord Brandon of Oakbrook considered (p.914) that an actual abandonment, as opposed to an estoppel precluding an assertion of continuance, required proof of conduct of each party, as evinced to the other party and acted on by him, as "leads necessarily to the inference of an implied agreement" between them to abandon the contract. Lord Roskill referred (p.923) to "the only possible inference [being] that the agreement to arbitrate has been rescinded by mutual consent". Though Lord Diplock made no similar observation both Lords Keith of Kinkel and Brightman agreed with Lords Brandon and Roskill. In *The Gudermes* the cargo owner sought to establish a further contract with the ship-owners arising out of arrangements made to cope with the situation arising from an unauthorised diversion to Malta rather than Ravenna. The judge, Hirst J., held that the appropriate test was that described by May L.J. in *The Elli*

[1985] 1 Ll.R. 107, 115. The Court of Appeal upheld that direction. Staughton L.J. giving the judgment of the court considered (p.320) that

". . . it is not enough to show that the parties have done something more than, or something different from, what they were already bound to do under obligations owed to others. What they do must be consistent only with there being a new contract implied, and inconsistent with there being no such contract."

21. In my view the judge did not adopt the wrong test for the implication of a contract from conduct. It is apparent that the statements in *The Aramis* are not confined to the limited circumstances with which that case was concerned and are reflected in one form or another in *Blackpool and Fylde Aero Club Ltd v Blackpool Borough Council, Wilson v Partenreederei Hannah Blumenthal* and *The Gudermes*.

22. The second issue arises not only from the terms of paragraph 12(1) of the judgment of Morison J. but also from the terms of paragraph 9.28 of the particulars of claim. Baird contends that the judge placed undue weight on that allegation and overlooked the references to "detailed contract or contracts". It submitted that the wish to maintain flexibility and so to abstain from detailed contracts was not inconsistent with an intention to have a contractual umbrella to regulate the commercial relationship, more particularly given the belief M&S had intentionally induced in Baird as alleged in paragraph 9 of the Particulars of Claim. In this connection counsel relied on the speech of Lord Hoffmann in *Carmichael v National Power Plc* [1999] 1 WLR 2042, 2050/1 to the effect that the subjective views of one party is some evidence as to what, objectively, the court should conclude to have been agreed.

23. Counsel for M&S pointed out that the allegation is that M&S "abstained from concluding any express contract . . . to regulate the parties on-going relationship . . .". Nevertheless Counsel for M&S did not suggest that the allegation in paragraph 9.28 was conclusive, merely a serious impediment to the implication for which Baird contends. In my view it would be inappropriate at this stage to take too literal a view of the pleading. I am prepared to assume that in the passage I have quoted some reference to "detail" should be implied so as to reflect the later reference to the need to maintain flexibility by abstaining from detailed contracts. On that reading there is some force in this point. But it cannot be conclusive either way.

24. The crucial point, in my view, arises from the third issue, namely whether the obligations arising from the alleged implied contract would be sufficiently certain to be contractually enforceable. Counsel for Baird submitted that on questions of certainty the court takes a benevolent view and seeks to uphold the contract by so construing its terms as to produce certainty rather than the converse. He relied on the dictum of Steyn L.J. in *First Energy (UK) Ltd v Hungarian International Bank* [1993] 2 Ll.R. 194, 196 on the need for the law to protect the reasonable expectations of honest men. He cited as examples *Abrahams v Reiach Ltd* [1922] 1 KB 477 and *Paula Lee v Robert Zehil & Co Ltd* [1983] 2 AER 390 in which problems of certainty were overcome by the implication of a requirement of reasonableness.

25. In relation to the facts Counsel for Baird suggested that there were a number of links in the relevant chain. He relied on a representation to Baird of a long term relationship to induce it to participate in the M&S supply base. He asserted that given that intentional representation M&S must have intended that Baird would get a reasonable level of M&S business year on year. He contended that not only did Baird so understand the representation but that was the way the relationship was in fact operated. Although, as I have already pointed out in paragraph 5, the proportion of business given by M&S to Baird remained relatively constant in percentage terms Counsel did not contend that M&S allocated its business amongst the four principal suppliers in accordance with any predetermined formula. He contended that the past could, with the assistance of experts, indicate what would be a reasonable allocation for the future.

26. Any debate about certainty of contractual terms and implications of reasonableness to avoid uncertainty must start with the decision of the House of Lords in *Hillas v Arcos* (1932) 147 LT 503. In that case the question was whether an option to buy "100,000 Standards for delivery in 1931" was sufficiently certain against the background of a contract concluded and performed the previous year for the purchase of "22,000 standards softwood goods of fair specification over the season 1930". The House of Lords concluded that the contract was sufficiently certain. Lord Tomlin interpolated into the option the requirement of "fair specification" expressly required by the previous year's contract. He considered that (p.512) in that context the words

"mean that the 22,000 standards are to be satisfied in goods distributed over kinds, qualities and sizes in the fair proportions having regard to the output of the season 1930, and the classifications of that output in respect of kinds, qualities and sizes. That is something which if the parties fail to agree can be ascertained just as much as the fair value of a property."

Lord Wright (p.517) referred to the legal implication of reasonableness running through modern English commercial law and supplying the requisite degree of certainty in appropriate cases. The distinction between those cases in which the implication of reasonableness provides for certainty and those in which it does not appears most clearly from the speech of Lord Thankerton. He distinguished (p.513) between cases where the contract provides for an objective standard which the court applies by ascertaining what is reasonable and those where, there being no such standard, the test of reasonableness is being used to make an agreement for the parties which they have not made for themselves. He was impressed by the consideration that a commercial matter was involved and the parties themselves thought that they had made a contract.

27. The same principle is apparent from *Australian Blue Metal Ltd v Hughes* [1963] AC 74. That case concerned a mining lease containing a grant of the right to mine for magnesite in a specific area for an agreed royalty. The lease was silent as to the period for which it was to run, the means of its termination, the quantity of magnesite which might be mined and whether or not the right was exclusive. The issue was whether it was terminable at will or only on notice. The Privy Council considered that it was terminable at will. Lord Devlin giving the advice of the Board said (p.94/5)

"The second feature is that no express obligation was imposed on the appellants to do any mining at all, and in their Lordships' opinion none can be implied. The only practical way of framing such an obligation with sufficient precision to make it enforceable is to do what was done in the 1942 agreement and specify a minimum quantity of material that has to be won in a given period. Their Lordships were referred to *Hillas & Co Ltd v Arcos Ltd* a case in which the House of Lords was able to use the implication of reasonableness to fill the gaps left by the parties. But in the present case there are no criteria which would enable a court of law to determine what would be a reasonable quantity. There would be too many uncertain factors to be taken into account, such as the profitability of mining in the future and the possibility of mining being done by other licensees . . ."

28. In both the cases relied on by Baird, namely *Abrahams v Reiach Ltd* [1922] 1 KB 477 and *Paula Lee v Robert Zehil & Co Ltd* [1983] 2 AER 390, the existence of a contract was not in doubt. The court was concerned with the assessment of damages for the breach of an undoubted obligation. The issue was how it was to be performed. I do not consider that either of them is of relevance to this case.

29. The issue of certainty arises, not with regard to the alleged obligation to give reasonable notice of termination, but with the allegation that

". . . during the subsistence of the relationship Marks & Spencer would acquire garments from BHT in quantities and at prices which in all the circumstances were reasonable . . ."

Counsel for Baird accepted that this involved an obligation on Baird to supply such garments irrespective of whether it had accepted the order. It is not alleged that there was some objective criteria by which to assess what was a reasonable quantity or price. Counsel disclaimed any contention that M&S in fact allocated business from year to year in accordance with some formula of its own. The annual allocation was separately determined in each year in the light of the circumstances then prevailing.

30. I agree with the conclusion of the judge. The alleged obligation on M&S to acquire garments from Baird is insufficiently certain to found any contractual obligation because there are no objective criteria by which the court could assess what would be reasonable either as to quantity or price. This is not a case in which, the parties having evidently sought to make a contract, the court seeks to uphold its validity by construing the terms to produce certainty. Rather it is a case in which the lack of certainty confirms the absence of any clear evidence of an intention to create legal relations. The allegation in paragraph 9.28 also confirms the lack of intention to create legal relations for if there had been the requisite certainty of the objective criteria then to that extent there would have been a detailed contract and a loss of flexibility. It cannot be said, let alone with confidence, that the conduct of the parties is more consistent with the existence of the contract sought to be implied than with its absence. The implication of the alleged contract is not necessary to give business reality to the commercial relationship between M&S and Baird. In agreement with the judge, I do not think that Baird has a real prospect of success on its claim in contract.

31. Whether there is some other compelling reason for requiring the contractual claim to be disposed of at a trial depends on the view one takes of the estoppel claim. If, as the judge thought, the estoppel claim has a real prospect of success then it may be inconvenient to preclude any consideration of a contractual claim. I turn, then, to consider the estoppel claim.

What should we make of *Baird Textiles*? In the case, there was no dispute about the conspicuously co-operative relationship between the parties. Baird had been a principal supplier to Marks and Spencer for 30 years and, in practice, there was a considerable degree of horizontal integration between the businesses. Even Marks and Spencer's director for procurement attested that the relationship with suppliers, such as Baird, was symbiotic—if not a partnership in the strict legal sense, business was most definitely conducted in a spirit of co-operation. If there had been an express framework contract governing the relationship between the parties and including a termination clause, Baird might have argued that, in the light of the prevailing co-operative culture, the notice period should be extended to reflect the duration of the dealings between the parties. However, in the absence of such an express contract, Baird relied on the co-operative culture to argue for an implied contract. The Court of Appeal took their bearings from individualistic thinking in order to reject this argument. As Mance LJ put it:

> "It is evident that Baird felt, quite rightly, that it had achieved a long and very close relationship, an informal business 'partnership', with M & S, and that it could, as a practical matter, rely on this and M & S's management's general goodwill and good intentions. But managements, economic conditions and intentions may all change, and businessmen must be taken to be aware that, without specific contractual protection, their business may suffer in consequence. I do not think that the law should be ready to seek to fetter business relationships, even—and perhaps especially—those as long and as close as the present, with its own view of what might represent appropriate business conduct, when the parties have not chosen, or have not been willing or able, to do so in any identifiable legal fashion or terms themselves." (para.76)

So, even in a strongly co-operative context, classical individualistic doctrinal thinking can assert itself—here, by seizing on the absence of an explicit contractual commitment or by declining to imply a contract (or a term) articulating a co-operative obligation to give extended notice. Sometimes, as Stewart Macaulay would put it, the courts seize on the "paper deal" (or, in *Baird*, the absence of a paper deal) to trump what one party at least has taken to be the "real (co-operative) deal".[1]

Drawing together these threads, it is clear that the contrast between the ethic of individualism and that of co-operativism is one of the keys to contract doctrine; that it is also a key to understanding contract practice; and that, insofar as contract doctrine takes its lead from contract practice (via doctrines of reasonableness, reasonable expectation, good faith, and the like), it is a distinction that is central to the moulding of doctrine.

Further Reading

Rex Ahdar, 'Contract Doctrine, Predictability and the Nebulous Exception' (2014) 73 CLJ 39

Roger Brownsword, 'Individualism, Co-operativism and an Ethic for European Contract Law' (2001) 64 MLR 628

David Campbell, 'Good Faith and the Ubiquity of the "Relational" Contract' (2014) 77 MLR 475

E.A. Farnsworth, 'Pre-Contractual Liability and Preliminary Agreements: Fair Dealing and Failed Negotiations' (1987) 87 *Columbia Law Review* 217

---

[1]   Stewart Macaulay, 'The Real and the Paper Deal: Empirical Pictures of Relationships, Complexity and the Urge for Transparent Simple Rules' (2003) 66 M.L.R. 44.

Stewart Macaulay, 'Elegant Models, Empirical Patterns, and the Complexities of Contract' (1977) 11 *Law and Society Review* 507

Stewart Macaulay, 'The Real and the Paper Deal: Empirical Pictures of Relationships, Complexity and the Urge for Transparent Simple Rules' (2003) 66 M.L.R. 44

Jonathan Morgan, 'In Defence of *Baird Textiles*: A Sceptical View of Relational Contract Law' in David Campbell, Linda Mulcahy and Sally Wheeler (eds), *Changing Concepts of Contract* (Basingstoke: Palgrave Macmillan, 2013) p.166

A.W.B. Simpson, 'Quackery and Contract Law: the Case of the Carbolic Smoke Ball' (1985) 14 *Journal of Legal Studies* 345

3

OFFER AND ACCEPTANCE

LEARNING OBJECTIVES

By the end of this chapter, you should understand that:

- contracts are typically in a bilateral form, constituted by an exchange of promises—such as a promise to supply goods or services in return for a promise to pay an agreed price;
- contracts may also be in a unilateral form, constituted by a promise in return for a specified act—such as a promise to pay a sum of money for the actual provision of (not the promise of provision of) some service;
- in relation to unilateral contracts, there are difficult questions where the offeree performs the specified act without knowing about or relying on the offer, and where the offeror purports to withdraw the offer before completion of the specified act;
- in relation to bilateral contracts, there are difficult questions where the offeror stipulates that the offeree's silence or inaction shall be treated as acceptance, or where the offeree deviates from the prescribed mode of acceptance;
- in relation to bilateral contracts, acceptance usually takes place when it is received by the offeror but, when the postal service is used, the default rule in English law is that acceptance takes place at the time of posting the letter of acceptance;
- even if an offer that is made "subject to contract" is accepted, this does not usually amount to a binding contract;
- in relation to both unilateral and bilateral offers, there are a number of ways in which the offer may be withdrawn;
- where each party agrees to contract on their own standard terms and conditions, and where in some material respect those terms and conditions do not coincide, then the resulting "battle of the forms" presents English law with one of its most challenging formation puzzles.

INTRODUCTION

Schematically, English law distinguishes between two classes of contracts: those contracts that are **3-001** unilateral and those that are bilateral. Whereas a unilateral contract takes the form of a promise (typically of payment) in return for the performance of a requested act, a bilateral contract takes the form of an exchange of promises. Whereas, in the former (unilateral) case, the offeree has no obligation to perform the requested act, in the latter (bilateral case), the offeree has accepted a commitment to perform the requested act by promising to do so.

Sometimes the promisor wants a promise (and then performance as per the promise) from the other party. For example, A offers B a job at a salary of £30,000 a year to commence on January 1 next year. When B accepts, there is a binding exchange of promises. A has received consideration in the shape of B's promise to do the work specified in the job description. B has received consideration in the shape of A's promise to pay her salary and fulfil the other obligations of an employer. This is called a "bilateral" contract because there are two (reciprocal) promisors and two (reciprocal) promisees.

On other occasions, the promisor asks not for a promise but for an act in return for his promise. The standard example is that of an offer of a reward—for example, the offer of a reward of £50 to anyone who returns my lost dog. A, the offeror, is not asking for promises but for action. If B finds the dog and returns it, other things being equal, the promise is binding. B has supplied the consideration by returning the dog—that act was the price of the promise. This is called a "unilateral" contract because, though there are two parties, only one (the promising offeror) has actually made a promise.

In the case of the bilateral contract we say that the consideration on both sides is "executory" because it is to be performed in the future. In the case of the unilateral contract we say that the consideration supplied by B is "executed"—it is already performed at the moment the contract to pay the reward is made—that is, when the dog is returned (this being the time, on the orthodox analysis, at which A's offer is accepted by B).

For the most part, contracts are bilateral in form (as is the case with standard contracts for the sale of goods or the supply of services) and it is only exceptionally that the distinction between unilateral and bilateral contracts causes any problems (but see *United Dominion Trust (Commercial) Ltd v Eagle Aircraft Services Ltd* [1968] 1 W.L.R. 74).

In this chapter, the first group of cases concerns issues arising in relation to unilateral contracts and the second group concerns bilateral contracts. In the third part of the chapter, the cases deal with the duration of the offer and the offeror's right to withdraw an offer; and, in the final part, we deal with the vexed question of the so-called "Battle of the Forms".

1. UNILATERAL CONTRACTS

3–002   A unilateral contract is offered when O promises A that he will do something if A will do a certain act, other than make a promise. A accepts O's offer by doing that act. O's promise is binding when the act is completed and not before. To use a stock example, where O promises A £100 if A will walk to York, then if A falls in a faint five yards from the city boundary and completes the journey in an ambulance, he is entitled to nothing. Similarly, the logic of the traditional analysis is that, since offers are revocable until accepted, O may revoke his offer when A is only five yards from York and going strong, which would seem to be very unjust. If the English law of contract embraced a general requirement of "good faith and fair dealing" (above Ch.2), or a limiting principle such as "abuse of right", there would be a direct way of addressing the unfairness of O's last-minute revocation of his offer. In the absence of such a principle, as we will see below, English law has to resort to some "creative accounting", implying terms or secondary contracts that give A some protection. However, as the cases immediately following illustrate, unfair revocation by the offeror is not the only puzzle to which unilateral offers can give rise. What is the legal position, for example, if the offeree does the requested act but without knowing about the offer, or without relying on the offer, or without being motivated by the offer, and so on?

WILLIAMS v CARWARDINE

King's Bench (1833) 5 C. & P. 566; 4 B. & Ad. 621; 1 Nev. & M.(K.B.) 418; 2 L.J.K.B. 101; 172 E.R. 1104

3–003

The defendant offered a reward to any person giving information leading to the discovery of a particular murderer. Subsequently, the plaintiff was severely beaten and bruised by one Williams. Believing she had not long to live and to ease her conscience, she gave information which led to Williams' conviction of the murder. The jury found that she was not induced by the offer of the reward but by other motives. Parke J directed a verdict for the plaintiff.

Curwood moved for a rule to show cause why a nonsuit should not be entered on the ground that the plaintiff was not a meritorious informer; and that she sued on a contract which had in effect been negatived by the finding of the jury.

DENMAN CJ

Was any doubt suggested as to whether the plaintiff knew of the handbill at the time of her making the disclosure?
  Curwood: She must have known of it, as it was placarded all over Hereford, the place at which she lived.

PARKE J

I take this to have been a contract with anyone who did the thing.

LITTLEDALE J

If the person knows of the handbill and does the thing, that is quite enough. It does not say, whoever will come forward in consequence of this handbill.

DENMAN CJ

As the plaintiff is within the terms of the handbill, she is entitled to the reward.

PATTESON J

The plaintiff being within the terms, her motive is not material.

Rule Refused.

R. v CLARKE

High Court of Australia (1927) 40 C.L.R. 227

3–004

A proclamation by the Government of Western Australia offered a reward for information leading to the arrest of certain murderers and a pardon to an accomplice who gave the information. Clarke saw the proclamation in May. On June 6 he gave false information to protect the murderers. On June 10 he gave information which led to their conviction. He admitted that his only object in doing so was to clear himself of a charge of murder and that he had no intention of claiming the reward at that time. He sued the Crown for the reward by petition of right. The High Court (Isaacs ACJ, Higgins and Starke JJ), reversing the Full Court of Western Australia, dismissed his claim.

ISAACS ACJ

Instances easily suggest themselves where precisely the same act done with reference to an offer would be performance of the condition, but done with reference to a totally distinct object would not be such a performance. An offer of £100 to any person who should swim a hundred yards in the harbour on the first day of the year, would be met by voluntarily performing the feat with reference to the offer, but would not in my opinion be satisfied by a person who was accidentally or maliciously thrown overboard on that date and swam the distance simply to save his life, without any thought of the offer. The offeror might or might not feel morally impelled to give the sum in such a case, but would be under no contractual obligation to do so.

HIGGINS J

If the case so much relied on for Clarke, the case of *Williams v Carwardine* [above], can be taken as deciding that mutual consent to the terms is not necessary, as well as communication of assent by the offeree, I can only point to higher and more recent authority, such as that of Lord Westbury L.C. in *Chinnock v Marchioness of Ely* (1865) 4 De G. J. & S. 638 at p. 643: "An agreement is the result of the mutual assent of two parties to certain terms, and if it be clear that there is no consensus, what may have been written or said becomes immaterial." This pronouncement is cited by *Leake on Contracts* (7th ed.), p. 2; and the author adds: "A consensus ad idem is a prime essential to the validity of a contract." The distinction should be clear between the essential mental assent, and the essential communication of that assent; as in *Re National Savings Bank Association; Hebb's Case* (1867) L.R. 4 Eq. 12; "I am of opinion that an offer does not bind the person who makes it until it has been accepted, and its acceptance has been communicated to him or his agent."

But I do not regard *Williams v Carwardine* as deciding anything to the contrary of this doctrine. That case seems to me not to deal with the essential elements for a contract at all: it shows merely that the motive of the informer in accepting the contract offered (and the performing the conditions is usually sufficient evidence of acceptance) has nothing to do with his right to recover under the contract. The reports show (as it was assumed by the judges after the verdict of the jury in favour of the informer), that the informer knew of the offer when giving the information, and meant to accept the offer though she had also a motive in her guilty conscience. The distinguished jurist, Sir Frederick Pollock, in his Preface to Vol. 38 of the *Revised Reports*, makes comments adverse to the case; but I concur with Burnside J. in his view that we cannot treat such comments as equivalent to an overruling of a clear decision. The case of *Gibbons v Proctor* (1891) 64 L.T. 594 is much more difficult to explain. There a policeman was held entitled to recover a reward offered by handbills, for information given to the superintendent of police which led to arrest and conviction, although the policeman did not know of the handbills before he sent the information by his agents, or before the handbills reached the superintendent. This would seem to mean that a man can accept an offered contract before he knows that there is an offer—that knowledge of the offer before the informer supplies the information is immaterial to the existence of the contract.[2] *Anson on Contracts* (16th ed.), p. 55, thinks that this decision must be wrong. I venture to think so too, and, though we cannot well overrule it, we ought not to follow it for the purposes of this court. It should be noted in this connection that the great judgment of Lord Blackburn in *Brogden v Metropolitan Ry.* (1876) 2 App.Cas. 666 is addressed to the other condition of contract, that acceptance must be communicated; but the whole judgment assumes that consensus of mind pre-existed—"simple acceptance in your own mind, without any intimation to the other party, and expressed by a mere private act, such as putting a letter into a drawer," does not complete a contract (and see per Lord Cairns L.C.). The reasoning of Woodruff J. in *Fitch v Snedaker* (1868) 38 N.Y. 248 seems to me to be faultless; and the decision is spoken of in Anson (p. 24) as being undoubtedly correct in principle: "The motive inducing consent may be immaterial, but the consent is vital. Without that there is no contract. How then can there be consent or assent to that of which the party has never heard?" Clarke had seen the offer, indeed; but it was not present to his mind—he had forgotten it, and gave no consideration to it, in his intense excitement as to his own danger. There cannot be assent without knowledge of the offer; and ignorance of the offer is the same thing whether it is due to never hearing of it or forgetting it after hearing. But for this candid confession of Clarke's it might fairly be presumed that Clarke, having once seen the offer, acted on the faith of it, in reliance on it; but he has himself rebutted that presumption.

---

[2]   *Gibbons v Proctor* has generally been considered to be—and condemned as—a case where the court held that a contract had been formed though the plaintiff did not know of the offer when he gave the information requested. The plaintiff certainly did not know of the offer when he gave the information to a fellow policeman, Coppin. But Coppin gave the information to Inspector Lennan who then wrote to Superintendent Penn. The giving of the information to Penn was the acceptance and, according to the report in (1891) 55 J.P. 616 at 617, "The information ultimately reached Penn at a time when the plaintiff knew that the reward had been offered." See Treitel, *Law of Contract* (10th edn), p.34, and A. H. Hudson, '*Gibbons v Proctor* Revisited' (1968) 84 L.Q.R. 503.

Questions

1. It is not clear that Clarke had in mind the offer of the pardon. Suppose he had. If two rewards are **3–005** promised in a single offer and A accepts with only one in view is he entitled (1) only to the reward he has in view; or (2) to both rewards; or (3) to no reward?

2. O offers a reward for information. A, not knowing of the offer, posts the information. Before the information reaches O, A learns of the offer and resolves to claim the reward. Is he entitled to it? If Isaacs ACJ's New Year's Day swimmer happened to know of the reward, should he be entitled to it?

3. Should a person be able to recover a reward offered to any member of the public who does a certain act, when he has done that act in ignorance of the offer? See *Hudson* (1968) 84 L.Q.R. 503. A and B both give information leading to the conviction of bank robbers. A, who is unaware that the Bank has offered a reward, gives the information because he is a public-spirited citizen. B does so only because he knows the Bank has offered a reward. Can A not recover? What about C, who (unlike A) is aware that the Bank has offered a reward, and who (unlike B) gives the information purely as a matter of what C views as a citizen's public duty?

Law Revision Committee, 6th Interim Report (Statute of Frauds and the Doctrine of Consideration)
(Cmd. 5449) 1937, para. 39 (p. 23)

English law traditionally divides parol contracts into two classes, the bilateral contract of a promise for a **3–006** promise, and the unilateral contract of a promise for an act. In the case of bilateral contracts one promise is held to be consideration for the other, the agreement therefore becoming effective at the moment when the promises are exchanged. In the case of a unilateral contract, however, the promise does not become binding until the act has been completely performed. A promisor may therefore withdraw his promise at any time before completion of the act, even though he knows that the promisee has already entered upon the performance and nearly completed it. Where performance of the requested act requires considerable time and effort, it is obvious that grave injustice may be done if the offeror is permitted to revoke his offer because he has not as yet received the whole consideration for it. A simple illustration will make this clear: A promises B £50 if he walks from London to York in three days. A can withdraw his promise at any time before B has reached York. It is suggested in some of the books that in these circumstances A is estopped from withdrawing his offer, but this is clearly incorrect, as estoppel is only a rule of evidence and cannot create a cause of action where none exists. It is true that in some cases B can recover on a quantum meruit for the services he has rendered, but this may be an unsatisfactory remedy, as the damages in quantum meruit are measured by the value of the services to A and not by the loss suffered by B. To avoid this undesirable result the courts have in certain cases implied a second promise on the part of the promisor that he will not do anything to interfere with the promisee's performance of the required act, the consideration for this implied promise being the promisee's beginning of the requested act. This, however, is not satisfactory, for there is considerable doubt at the present time as to when this second promise can be implied and what are its terms. We therefore recommend that a promise made in consideration of the promisee performing an act shall be enforceable as soon as the promisee has entered upon performance of the act, unless the promise includes expressly or by implication a term that it can be revoked before the act has been completed. It is desirable to emphasise that this provision will in no way affect the rule in *Cutter v Powell* [6 T.R. 320, below, para.20–026] that if the promisee fails fully to perform the requested act, he is not entitled to recover anything under the contract.
[The Committee's recommendation has never been implemented.]

Point for reflection

Although estoppel is not a cause of action (see para.11–009, below), we might question whether the **3–007** Committee's argument is sound. If B, having reached York, sues for £50, his cause of action is for breach of contract. He then relies on estoppel which would be invoked (as it usually is) to support an independent cause of action. Is the objection rather that the estoppel would be as to a promise and not a statement of fact? (Cf. *Jorden v Money* (1854) 5 HL Cas. 185, below, Ch.11.)

The implication of a second promise referred to by the Committee is a solution which has often been proposed (see, e.g. McGovney, 'Irrevocable Offers' (1914) 27 Harv.L.Rev. 644, at 659) and sometimes applied by the English courts (for example, by Denning LJ in *Errington v Errington* (below)). The theory is that when A says to B, "I will pay you £100 if you walk from London to York", he is making two promises, (i) the express promise to pay the £100 when the walk is completed and (ii) a "collateral" promise not to revoke his offer to pay £100 if B sets out on the walk. There are two unilateral contracts. The consideration requested for the first is the complete walk to York. The consideration requested for the second is setting out on the walk. If A "revokes" his offer when B is on his way, B can treat the "revocation" as inoperative (*Mountford v Scott* below) or at least recover damages for the loss of his chance to earn £100.

The Committee questions this solution because of doubts as to when the second promise can be implied. But is it any more uncertain than the implication generally of terms to give "business efficacy" to a contract? Perhaps the solution gives the court a necessary degree of flexibility, because it may not always be right that the offeror should be precluded from revoking his offer. Cf. *Luxor v Cooper*, below.

Wormser, 'The True Conception of Unilateral Contracts,' 26 Yale Law Journal, 136 Selected Readings 307, 308.

3–008   The writer discusses the case where A says to B, "I will give you $100 if you will walk across Brooklyn Bridge". He points out that until the act is done A is not bound since no contract arises until the completion of the act called for. He goes on:

> The objection is made, however, that it is very "hard" upon B that he should have walked half-way across the Brooklyn Bridge and should get no compensation. This suggestion, invariably advanced, might be dismissed with the remark that "hard" cases should not make bad law. But going a step further, by way of reply, the pertinent inquiry at once suggests itself, "Was B bound to walk across the Brooklyn Bridge?" The answer to this is obvious. By hypothesis, B was not bound to walk across the Brooklyn Bridge . . . If B is not bound to continue to cross the bridge, if B is will-free, why should not A also be will-free? Suppose that after B has crossed half the bridge he gets tired and tells A that he refuses to continue crossing. B, concededly, would be perfectly within his rights in so speaking and acting. A would have no cause of action against B for damages. If B has a locus poenitentiae, so has A. . . .

It should be noted that, in *Offord v Davies* (below), Williams J asked, during the course of the argument, "suppose I guarantee the price of a carriage to be built for a third party, who, before the carriage is finished, and consequently before I am bound to pay for it, becomes insolvent—may I recall my guarantee?" Counsel (E. James, QC) replied, "Not after the coach-builder has commenced the carriage." Erle CJ said, "Before it ripens into a contract, either party may withdraw, and so put an end to the matter. But the moment the coach-builder has prepared the materials, he would probably be found by the jury to have contracted."

ERRINGTON v ERRINGTON AND WOODS

Court of Appeal [1952] 1 K.B. 290; [1952] 1 T.L.R. 231; 96 S.J. 119; [1952] 1 All E.R. 149

3–009   Appeal by the plaintiff from the dismissal of her action against her daughter-in-law for the possession of a dwelling house.

DENNING LJ

The facts are reasonably clear. In 1936 the father bought the house for his son and daughter-in-law to live in. The father put down £250 in cash and borrowed £500 from a building society on the security of the house, repayable with interest by instalments of 15s. a week. He took the house in his own name and made himself responsible for the instalments. The father told the daughter-in-law that the £250 was a present for them, but he left them to pay the building society instalments of 15s. a week themselves. He handed the building society book to the daughter-in-law and said to her: "Don't part with this book. The house will be your property when the mortgage is paid." He said that when he retired he would transfer it into their names. She has in fact paid the building society instalments regularly from that day to this with the result that much of the mortgage has been repaid, but there is a good deal yet to be paid. The rates on the house came to 10s. a week. The couple found that they could not pay those as well as the building society instalments, so the father said he would pay them and did so.

It is to be noted that the couple never bound themselves to pay the instalments to the building society; and I see no reason why any such obligation should be implied. It is clear law that the court is not to imply a term unless it is necessary; and I do not see that it is necessary here. Ample content is given to the whole arrangement by holding that the father promised that the house should belong to the couple as soon as they paid off the mortgage. The parties did not discuss what was to happen if the couple failed to pay the instalments to the building society, but I should have thought it clear that, if they did fail to pay the instalments, the father would not be bound to transfer the house to them. The father's promise was a unilateral contract—a promise of the house in return for their act of paying the instalments. It could not be revoked by him once the couple entered on performance of the act, but it would cease to bind him if they left it incomplete and unperformed, which they have not done. If that was the position during the father's lifetime, so it must be after his death. If the daughter-in-law continues to pay all the building society instalments, the couple will be entitled to have the property transferred to them as soon as the mortgage is paid off; but if she does not do so, then the building society will claim the instalments from the father's estate and the estate will have to pay them. I cannot think that in those circumstances the estate would be bound to transfer the house to them, any more than the father himself would have been . . . the couple were licensees, having a permissive occupation short of a tenancy, but with a contractual right, or at any rate, an equitable right to remain so long as they paid the instalments, which would grow into a good equitable title to the house itself as soon as the mortgage was paid. This is, I think, the right view of the relationship of the parties . . . They were not tenants at will but licensees . . . They were licensees with a contractual right to remain. As such they have no right at law to remain, but only in equity, and equitable rights now prevail . . .

In the present case it is clear that the father expressly promised the couple that the property should belong to them as soon as the mortgage was paid, and impliedly promised that so long as they paid the instalments to the building society they should be allowed to remain in possession. They were not purchasers because they never bound themselves to pay the instalments, but nevertheless they were in a position analogous to purchasers. They have acted on the promise, and neither the father nor his widow, his successor in title, can eject them in disregard of it. The result is that in my opinion the appeal should be dismissed and no order for possession should be made.

Somervell and Hodson L.JJ. delivered judgments dismissing the appeal.

Appeal Dismissed.

Questions

1. Lord Denning says, "The father's promise was a unilateral contract". Was it a contract? Or was it an offer which, when they "entered on performance", became a contract not to revoke his promise to give them the house when they paid off the mortgage?   **3–010**

2. What was the contract which created a "contractual right . . . to remain so long as they paid the instalments"?

3. What does the case decide, or assume, about the effect of death on (i) an offer, (ii) a contract? See below, para.3–058, and Ch.24.

LUXOR (EASTBOURNE) LTD AND OTHERS v COOPER

House of Lords [1941] A.C. 108; [1941] 1 All E.R. 33; 110 L.J.K.B. 131; 164 L.T. 313; 57 T.L.R. 213

3–011   On September 23, 1935, the two appellant companies orally agreed that if the respondent introduced a party who should buy the two cinemas owned by the appellants, each of the appellants would pay the respondent £5,000. The respondent introduced a prospective purchaser who agreed, subject to contract, to buy the cinemas for £185,000 and remained throughout ready and willing to buy at that figure. The appellants did not proceed with the sale and the cinemas were ultimately disposed of by way of a sale of shares in the appellant companies to another party. The respondent brought an action claiming £10,000 commission or, alternatively, £10,000 damages for breach of an implied term that the appellants would "do nothing to prevent the satisfactory completion of the transaction so as to deprive the respondent of the agreed commission". The House of Lords, reversing the decision of the Court of Appeal, held (i) that commission was only payable on completion of the sale and (ii) that there was no room for any such implied term as was alleged.

LORD RUSSELL OF KILLOWEN

A few preliminary observations occur to me. (1) Commission contracts are subject to no peculiar rules or principles of their own; the law which governs them is the law which governs all contracts and all questions of agency. (2) No general rule can be laid down by which the rights of the agent or the liability of the principal under commission contracts are to be determined. In each case these must depend upon the exact terms of the contract in question, and upon the true construction of those terms. And (3) contracts by which owners of property, desiring to dispose of it, put it in the hands of agents on commission terms, are not (in default of specific provisions) contracts of employment in the ordinary meaning of those words. No obligation is imposed on the agent to do anything. The contracts are merely promises binding on the principal to pay a sum of money upon the happening of a specified event, which involves the rendering of some service by the agent. There is no real analogy between such contracts, and contracts of employment by which one party binds himself to do certain work, and the other binds himself to pay remuneration for the doing of it.

I do not assent to the view, which I think was the view of the majority in the first *Trollope Case* [1934] 2 K.B. 436, that a mere promise by a property owner to an agent to pay him a commission if he introduces a purchaser for the property at a specified price, or at a minimum price, ties the owner's hands, and compels him (as between himself and the agent) to bind himself contractually to sell to the agent's client who offers that price, with the result that if he refuses the offer he is liable to pay the agent a sum equal to or less than the amount of the commission either (a) on a quantum meruit or (b) as damages for breach of a term to be implied in the commission contract. As to the claim on a quantum meruit, I do not see how this can be justified in the face of the express provision for remuneration which the contract contains. This must necessarily exclude such a claim, unless it can (upon the facts of a particular case) be based upon a contract subsequent to the original contract, and arising from some conduct on the part of the principal.

As to the claim for damages, this rests upon the implication of some provision in the commission contract, the exact terms of which were variously stated in the course of the argument, the object always being to bind the principal not to refuse to complete the sale to the client whom the agent has introduced.

I can find no safe ground on which to base the introduction of any such implied term. Implied terms, as we all know, can only be justified under the compulsion of some necessity. No such compulsion or necessity exists in the case under consideration. The agent is promised a commission if he introduces a purchaser at a specified or minimum price. The owner is desirous of selling. The chances are largely in favour of the deal going through, if a purchaser is introduced. The agent takes the risk in the hope of a substantial remuneration for comparatively small exertion. In the case of the plaintiff his contract was made on September 23, 1935; his client's offer was made on October 2, 1935. A sum of £10,000 (the equivalent of the remuneration of a year's work by a Lord Chancellor) for work done within a period of eight or nine days is no mean reward, and is one well worth a risk. There is no lack of business efficacy in such a contract, even though the principal is free to refuse to sell to the agent's client.

The position will no doubt be different if the matter has proceeded to the stage of a binding contract having been made between the principal and the agent's client. In that case it can be said with truth that a "purchaser" has been introduced by the agent; in other words the event has happened upon the occurrence of which a right to the promised commission has become vested in the agent. From that moment no act or omission by the principal can deprive the agent of that vested right.

My Lords, for myself, I do not favour the view that an agent who has not earned his commission according to the express terms of the contract is entitled to damages for breach of some term to be implied. I see no necessity which compels the implication.

(Viscount Simon L.C. and Lords Thankerton, Wright and Romer also made speeches allowing the appeal.)

Questions

1. Was Lord Russell accurate (or consistent) in saying that the plaintiff made a contract on September 23, 1935? What consideration did the plaintiff give on that day? Was not an offer to make a unilateral contract all that happened that day? **3–012**

2. It was evidently a breach of contract to revoke the offer in *Errington v Errington*, not so in *Luxor v Cooper*. Consider what factors might justify such a difference in result in the two cases.

----

2. BILATERAL CONTRACTS

It is worth restating that contracts typically assume a bilateral form. On the one side, a supplier promises to supply goods or services; and, on the other side, a purchaser promises to pay the agreed price for those goods or services. Even where the purchaser (as in some consumer transactions) is given a "cooling off" period during which it is possible to withdraw from the contract, the contract as formed is bilateral: both parties, supplier and purchaser alike, are committed to the transaction; both parties have a contractual obligation to perform in accordance with their respective promises. **3–013**

However, as the cases below illustrate, there is many a slip twixt cup and lip and some nice points of law can arise. For example, what is the position if the offeror says that he will treat the offeree's silence or inaction as a sign of acceptance? When precisely does a letter of acceptance take effect (on posting or on receipt), and what if the offeree retracts the "acceptance" by a method that ensures that the retraction arrives before the letter? And, how does the law view an "acceptance" that is given "subject to contract"?

A. Has There Been an Acceptance?

POWELL v LEE

King's Bench Division (1908) 99 L.T. 284

The six defendants were the managers of a school. They were minded to appoint a headmaster. The plaintiff applied for the post and with two other candidates was selected for the final choice of the managers. By three votes to two the managers passed a resolution on March 26 that the plaintiff should be appointed. No directions were given by the meeting as to communicating the results of the voting to the plaintiff, but one of the managers, Dismore, was requested by Lee to send a telegram to one of the other candidates, Parker, telling him that he had not been elected. Two of the managers subsequently sought to reopen the question and Lee supported them. **3–014**

On April 1, without any instruction to do so from the managers as a body, Dismore sent the following telegram to the plaintiff: "The Cranford School managers selected you as headmaster on Tuesday last.—Dismore, Hon. Sec".

On April 2 the managers held a meeting at which all except Dismore were present and passed unanimously a resolution rescinding the resolution of the previous meeting, and appointing Parker headmaster. On April 5 the plaintiff was informed by Lee that Parker had been appointed, and he brought this action, alleging that by breach of a contract to employ him he had suffered damages in loss of salary to the extent of £11 5s.

The county court judge held that there was no contract as there had been no authorised communication of intention to contract on the part of the body, that is, the managers, alleged to be a party to the contract.

The plaintiff appealed.

CHANNELL J

I think the decision of the learned county court judge was right. In my opinion the case depends on this, that where, as in this case, a body of six people, acting not as a corporation or as a board of directors, but as six persons having the power to appoint to a post, vote on the question and resolve to appoint someone, they do not make a concluded contract then and there. There must be something more. There must be a communication made by the body of persons to the selected candidate. In this case the managers authorised a communication to Mr Parker to the effect that he had not been elected; but they did not authorise a communication to Mr Powell to the effect that he had been elected. To my mind, that implies that they reserved the power to consider the matter. Then one of the parties desired to reopen the matter, and he told the plaintiff that there was a difficulty. Later, another party, Mr Dismore, told the plaintiff that he had been elected on March 26. I think Mr Dismore made that communication to the plaintiff acting as an individual, and not for the body of the managers. If the mere knowledge of what happened at the meeting was sufficient to complete the contract, as, for instance, if the result of the voting was overheard at the door, the matter would rest upon a different footing. But I do not think that is sufficient to complete the contract. There must be notice of acceptance from the contracting party in some way, and the mere fact that the managers did not authorise such a communication, which is the usual course adopted, implies that they meant to reserve the power to reconsider the decision at which they had arrived. On these grounds, and on the grounds stated by the learned county court judge, I think his decision was right, and the appeal must be dismissed.

SUTTON J

I am of the same opinion.

Appeal Dismissed.

Questions

3–015

1. Cf. *Dickinson v Dodds*, below. Is it true to say that unintended communication of the revocation of an offer is effective when unintended communication of an acceptance is not? If so, why? May the cases be distinguished on the ground that there was no more than a decision to accept in *Powell v Lee* whereas in *Dickinson v Dodds* the offeror had done an act inconsistent with the continuance of the offer?

2. Ed applies for a post at the X University. The application states that it is a firm offer to take the post if appointed. The day after the interview Ed receives a letter from R. V. Winkle, the Registrar of the University, informing him that he has been appointed. In fact, the interviewing committee decided to appoint Ted but Winkle had dozed off and misheard the name. Advise Ed.

3. In *Robophone Facilities Ltd v Blank* [1966] 1 W.L.R. 1428 Lord Denning held that, where a written offer provided that it should become binding only upon its being signed by the offeree, no contract arose until the offeree signed the document and notified the offeror that he had done so. Otherwise, "[The offeree] would be able to keep the form in the office unsigned, and then play fast and loose as they pleased. The [offeror] would not know whether or not there was a contract

binding them to supply or him to take . . .". Diplock LJ explicitly refrained from, and Harman LJ did not express, any opinion on this point. Is it arguable that the offeror had waived his right to communication?

FELTHOUSE v BINDLEY

Common Pleas (1862) 11 C.B. (n.s.) 869; 31 L.J.C.P. 204; 142 E.R. 1037; Exchequer Chamber (1863) 1 New Rep. 401; 7 L.T. 835; 11 W.R. 429

The plaintiff discussed with his nephew, John, the purchase of a horse belonging to John. A few days later John wrote to the plaintiff, saying that he had learned that there was a misunderstanding as to the price; the plaintiff apparently believed that he had bought the horse for £30, John that he had sold it for 30 guineas. The plaintiff, on January 2, wrote to John proposing to split the difference and adding, "If I hear no more about him, I consider the horse is mine at £30 15s". No reply was sent to this last letter, nor was any money paid, and the horse remained in John's possession. Six weeks later (on February 25) the defendant, an auctioneer, who was employed by John to sell his farming stock, and who had been directed by John to reserve the horse in question, as it had already been sold, by mistake put it up with the rest and sold it.

3–016

On February 26 the defendant wrote to the plaintiff admitting that he had been told by John to reserve the horse, but that he had forgotten to do so. On the 27th John wrote to the plaintiff saying that he had told the defendant that "that horse (meaning the one I sold to you) is sold," but that the defendant had, in error, sold it.

In an action for conversion, a verdict was found for the plaintiff, damages £33, leave being reserved to the defendant to enter a nonsuit, if the court should be of the opinion that the objection was well founded.

A rule nisi was obtained on the grounds that "sufficient title or possession of the horse, to maintain the action, was not vested in the plaintiff at the time of the wrong; that the letter of John Felthouse of February 27, 1861, was not admissible in evidence against the defendant; that, if it was admissible, being after the sale of the horse by the defendant, it did not confer title on the plaintiff; and that there was, at the time of the wrong, no sufficient memorandum in writing, or possession of the horse, or payment, to satisfy the Statute of Frauds". (For the Statute of Frauds, see above, para.1–002).

WILLES J

I am of opinion that the rule to enter a nonsuit should be made absolute. [The learned judge stated the facts and continued:] It is clear that there was no complete bargain on January 2: and it is also clear that the uncle had no right to impose upon the nephew a sale of his horse for £30 15s. unless he chose to comply with the condition of writing to repudiate the offer. The nephew might, no doubt, have bound his uncle to the bargain by writing to him; the uncle might also have retracted his offer at any time before acceptance. It stood an open offer; and so things remained until February 25, when the nephew was about to sell his farming stock by auction. The horse in question being catalogued with the rest of the stock, the auctioneer (the defendant) was told that it was already sold. It is clear, therefore, that the nephew in his own mind intended his uncle to have the horse at the price which he (the uncle) had named, £30 15s.: but he had not communicated such his intention to his uncle, or done anything to bind himself. Nothing, therefore, had been done to vest the property in the horse in the plaintiff down to February 25, when the horse was sold by the defendant. It appears to me that, independently of the subsequent letters, there had been no bargain to pass the property in the horse to the plaintiff, and therefore that he had no right to complain of the sale. Then, what is the effect of the subsequent correspondence? The letter of the auctioneer amounts to nothing. The more important letter is that of the nephew, of February 27, which is relied on as showing that he intended to accept and did accept the terms offered by his uncle's letter of January 2. That letter, however, may be treated either as an acceptance then for the first time made by him, or as a memorandum of a bargain complete before February 25, sufficient within the Statute of Frauds. It seems to me that the former is the more likely construction: and, if so, it is clear that the plaintiff cannot recover. But, assuming that there had been a complete parol bargain before February 25, and that the letter of the 27th was a mere expression of the terms of that prior bargain, and not a bargain then for the first time concluded, it would be directly contrary to the decision of the Court of Exchequer in *Stockdale v Dunlop* (6 M. & W. 224) to hold that that acceptance had relation back to the previous offer so as to bind third persons in respect of a dealing with the property by them in the interim. Byles and Keating J. J. concurred.

In the Court of Exchequer Chamber (Pollock C. B., Mellor and Blackburn J. J., Martin and Wilde B. B.), Pollock C. B. said the judgment of the Common Pleas must be affirmed. The Statute of Frauds had not been complied with. There had been no delivery, part payment or memorandum in writing, to vest the property in the plaintiff.

Questions

3–017
1. If using the smoke ball three times daily for two weeks was a sufficient acceptance in *Carlill's* case (above, Ch.2), why was not the nephew's directing the auctioneer to keep the horse out of the sale a sufficient acceptance in *Felthouse v Bindley*? Cf. C.J. Miller (1972) 35 M.L.R. 489; *Fairline Shipping Corp v Adamson* [1975] Q.B. 180 at 188–189 (Kerr J).

2. If the horse had died after the nephew had directed the auctioneer to keep it out of the sale, and before the day of the sale, could the nephew have recovered the price from his uncle? (Assuming that the Statute of Frauds was satisfied.)

TAYLOR v ALLON

Divisional Court [1966] 1 Q.B. 304; [1965] 2 W.L.R. 598; [1965] 1 All E.R. 557

3–018   T was convicted of using a motor-car on a road on April 15, 1964, without insurance against third-party risks, contrary to s.201 of the Road Traffic Act, 1960. His insurance had expired on April 5, 1964. The insurance company, in accordance with normal practice, sent him a temporary cover-note for 15 days from April 6. T did not intend, however, to renew that insurance and had obtained a temporary cover-note from a new insurer for 30 days from April 16.

LORD PARKER CJ

Bearing in mind that a valid insurance for the purposes of the section must arise from an enforceable contract, it seems to me that the contract, if any, contained in the temporary covering note must arise by offer and acceptance. It is conceded that the policy that expired had no provisions for extended cover, and accordingly this document sending this temporary covering note must in my judgment be treated as an offer to insure for the future. It may be, although I find it unnecessary to decide in this case, that there can be an acceptance of such an offer by conduct and without communication with the insurance company. It may well be, as it seems to me, that if a man took his motor-car out on the road in reliance on this temporary cover, albeit that there had been no communication of that fact to the insurance company, there would be an acceptance, and that the contract so created would contain an implied promise by the insured to pay, either in the renewal premium when that was paid, or if it was not paid, for the period for which the temporary cover note had, as it were, been accepted.

I find it unnecessary in the present case to decide that matter, and for this reason, that it seems to me that the defendant must at any rate go to the length of saying that he knew of the temporary cover and that he took out his motor-car in reliance on it. In fact, as I have already said, the defendant never gave any evidence at all. Further, from the justices' clerk's notes, which again we have been allowed to refer to, it appears that when he was stopped by the police and asked to produce his insurance certificate, he produced the old certificate of insurance which expired on April 5, and he also produced the cover note from the new insurance company which commenced on April 16. When the police pointed out that therefore on April 15 he was not covered, he not only did not refer to this temporary cover note, but he said then that he had been negotiating a change of insurance companies, and did not realise that it, presumably the original certificate, had run out. It was only at the hearing, and I think at the second hearing, that this temporary cover note, this extended cover, was produced by the defendant's solicitor.

In those circumstances it seems to me that the defendant has never gone to the length of showing that he knew of the temporary cover, that he acted in reliance on it, and thereby had accepted their offer contained in it. I think the justices came to a correct decision in law and I would dismiss this appeal.

Marshall and Widgery J. J. agreed.

Problem

Alonzo, who had had discussions with Bertram concerning the sale of Bertram's car, wrote to Bertram on January 1, saying: "I offer you £500 for the car. I am going abroad on January 8 and if I do not hear from you before then I shall consider the car mine at that price and will collect it from you on my return on February 1".

Bertram decided to accept Alonzo's offer, but did not reply. On January 15 Charlie offered Bertram £600 for the car. Bertram replied that he must reluctantly refuse the offer as the car was already sold to Alonzo. Alonzo now refuses to take the car. The market price of cars has fallen considerably. Advise Bertram.

3–019

Notes

1. In *Re Selectmove Ltd* [1995] 1 W.L.R. 474; [1995] 2 All E.R. 531 CA, below, Ch.10, Peter Gibson LJ said that the authorities for the general rule that acceptance cannot be inferred from silence are cases where an offeror sought to impose on the offeree a term that silence would amount to acceptance. He went on: 'Where the offeree himself indicates that an offer is to be taken as accepted if he does not indicate to the contrary by an ascertainable time, he is undertaking to speak if he does not want the agreement to be concluded. I see no reason why that should not be an exceptional circumstance such that the offer can be accepted by silence. But it is unnecessary to express a concluded opinion on the point.' Has not the offeree, in the case envisaged, accepted the offer conditionally so as to become bound when the condition is fulfilled?

3–020

2. Aggressive sellers have sometimes sent unsolicited goods offering to sell them and advising the offeree that he will be taken to have accepted the goods if he does not reply or return the goods within a certain period. It has always been clear that a contract could not be forced on an unwilling offeree by an ultimatum of this kind. However, "inertia selling" is now regulated by the Unsolicited Goods and Services Act 1971 and the Consumer Protection (Distance Selling) Regulations 2000. Broadly speaking, the legal position is that the recipient of unsolicited goods may treat the goods as if they were an unconditional gift to him and the sender's rights will be extinguished provided that (i) the recipient has no reason to believe that the goods were sent to him with a view to their being acquired for the purposes of a business and (ii) the recipient has not agreed to acquire or return the goods.

The legislation apart, if a recipient of unsolicited goods were to exercise the rights of an owner over them, it is possible that he might be held to have accepted the offer by his conduct and to be bound to pay for the goods. See *Weatherby v Banham* (1832) 5 C. & P. 228, and *Trinder and Partners v Haggis* [1951] W.N. 416.

On the inference of contracts from silence and inaction, see Robert Goff LJ in *Allied Marine Transport v Vale do Rio Doce* [1985] 2 All E.R. 796 at 805.

MANCHESTER DIOCESAN COUNCIL FOR EDUCATION v COMMERCIAL AND GENERAL INVESTMENTS LTD

Chancery Division [1970] 1 W.L.R. 241; [1969] 3 All E.R. 1593; P. & C.R. 38

3-021   The plaintiff owned property which could be sold only subject "to the approval of the Secretary of State for Education and Science". The plaintiff decided to sell the property by tender and prepared a form of tender. Clause 4 provided: "The person whose tender is accepted shall be the purchaser and shall be informed of the acceptance of his tender by letter sent to him by post addressed to the address given in the tender". The defendant completed the form of tender and sent it (from 15 Berkeley St.) to the plaintiff's surveyor who, on September 1, informed the defendant's surveyor that he would recommend acceptance and, on September 15, wrote to the defendant's surveyor that the plaintiff had approved the sale and that the approval of the Secretary of State was being sought. That approval was given on November 18. On December 23 the plaintiff's solicitors wrote to the defendant's solicitors that the consent had been given and that the contract was binding. The defendant's solicitors replied that they did not agree. On January 7 the plaintiff's solicitors wrote to the defendant company at the address given by it in the form of tender giving formal notification of acceptance. The plaintiff sued for a declaration that either the letter dated September 15 or that dated January 7 constituted a binding contract.

BUCKLEY J

The offer contained in the tender was to the effect that in the event of its being accepted in accordance with the conditions of sale on or before the day named therein for that purpose—and none was so named—the defendant would pay the price and complete the purchase. An offeror may by the terms of his offer indicate that it may be accepted in a particular manner. In the present case the conditions included condition 4 which I have read. It is said, on the defendant's behalf, that that condition was not complied with until January 7, 1965; that until that date the offer was never accepted in accordance with its terms; and that consequently nothing earlier than that date can be relied on as an acceptance resulting in a binding contract. If an offeror stipulates by the terms of his offer that it may, or that it shall, be accepted in a particular manner a contract results as soon as the offeree does the stipulated act, whether it has come to the notice of the offeror or not. In such a case the offeror conditionally waives either expressly or by implication the normal requirement that acceptance must be communicated to the offeror to conclude a contract. There can be no doubt that in the present case, if the plaintiff or its authorised agent had posted a letter addressed to the defendant at 15 Berkeley Street on or about September 15 informing the defendant of the acceptance of its tender, the contract would have been complete at the moment when such a letter was posted, but that course was not taken. Condition 4, however, does not say that that shall be the sole permitted method of communicating an acceptance. It may be that an offeror, who by the terms of his offer insists upon acceptance in a particular manner, is entitled to insist that he is not bound unless acceptance is effected or communicated in that precise way, although it seems probable that, even so, if the other party communicates his acceptance in some other way, the offeror may by conduct or otherwise waive his right to insist upon the prescribed method of acceptance. Where, however, the offeror has prescribed a particular method of acceptance, but not in terms insisting that only acceptance in that mode shall be binding, I am of opinion that acceptance communicated to the offeror by any other mode which is no less advantageous to him will conclude the contract. Thus in *Tinn v Hoffman & Co* [above], where acceptance was requested by return of post, Honeyman J. said at p. 274:

> "That does not mean exclusively a reply by letter or return of post, but you may reply by telegram or by verbal message or by any other means not later than a letter written by return of post."

If an offeror intends that he shall be bound only if his offer is accepted in some particular manner, it must be for him to make this clear. Condition 4 in the present case has not, in my judgment, this effect.

Moreover, the inclusion of condition 4 in the defendant's offer was at the instance of the plaintiff, who framed the conditions and the form of tender. It should not, I think, be regarded as a condition or stipulation imposed by the defendant as offeror upon the plaintiff as offeree, but as a term introduced into the bargain by the plaintiff and presumably considered by the plaintiff as being in some way for the protection or benefit of the plaintiff. It would consequently be a term strict compliance with which the plaintiff could waive, provided the defendant was not adversely affected. The plaintiff did not take advantage of the condition which would have resulted in a contract being formed as soon as a letter of acceptance complying with the condition was posted, but adopted another course, which could only result in a contract when the plaintiff's acceptance was actually communicated to the defendant.

For these reasons, I have reached the conclusion that in accordance with the terms of the tender it was open to the plaintiff to conclude a contract by acceptance actually communicated to the defendant in any way; and, in my judgment, the letter of September 15 constituted such an acceptance. It follows that, in my judgment, and subject to a point relating to the need to obtain ministerial consent to which I will refer in a moment, the parties thereupon became contractually bound . . .

Buckley J. then held that while the power to complete a sale was conditional upon ministerial approval, the power to contract was not. For the second part of his judgment, in which he considered whether, if no contract was made on September 15, one was concluded on January 7 (see below, para.3–057).

The more general question of whether a contractual provision that specifies that certain methods of notification may be used is exclusionary (in the sense that no other methods may be used) was considered again in *Ener-G Holdings Plc v Hormell* (below). By an agreement dated April 2, 2008, Hormell sold certain shares to Ener-G. Clause 6.3.3(b) of the agreement provided that Ener-G should give to Hormell written notice of any claim for breach of warranty by April 2, 2010; and clause 6.3.7(a) provided that claims should be deemed to have been "irrevocably withdrawn and lapsed unless. . .proceedings in respect of that claim have been issued and served on the seller not later than the expiry of the period of twelve months after the date of that notice." Clause 13 provided for "notice" and "service" in the following terms:

"13.1 Notice in writing
Any notice or other communication under this Agreement shall be in writing [which included faxes but not emails] and signed by or on behalf of the party giving it.

13.2 Service
Any such notice may be served by delivering it personally or by sending it by pre-paid recorded delivery post to each party (in the case of the Buyer, marked 'for the attention of directors') at or to the address referred in the Agreement or any other address in England and Wales which he or it may from time to time notify in writing to the other party.

13.3. Deemed service
Any notice delivered personally shall be deemed to be received when delivered (or if delivered otherwise than between 9.00 a.m. and 5.00 p.m. on a Business Day, at 9.00am on the next Business Day), any notice sent by pre-paid recorded delivery post shall be deemed to be received two Business Days after posting and in proving the time of despatch it shall be sufficient to show that the envelope containing such notice was properly addressed, stamped and posted.

Clause 14(2) further provided:

"The parties agree that the documents which start any legal proceedings relating to a dispute ("Proceedings") and any other documents required to be served in relation to those Proceedings may be served on any party in accordance with this Agreement. These documents may, however, be served in any other manner allowed by law. This clause applies to all Proceedings wherever started."

On March 30, 2010, Ener-G made two attempts to serve notice on Hormell of a claim for breach of warranty. Acting on Ener-G's instructions, a process server called with the 'first' notice at Hormell's address. Having failed to obtain a reply when he rang the doorbell, the process server left an envelope with the notice inside the front porch. Hormell received and read this (first) notice that afternoon. On the same day, Ener-G sent an identical 'second' notice by recorded delivery to Hormell's home address. The following year, on March 29, 2011, Ener-G served a claim form on Hormell, using a process server as with the first notice. Again, Hormell was not at home and the process server placed the claim form in the letter box. The question was whether and when Ener-G had served an effective notice of claim and then whether the claim form served a year later was in time.

Seeking to rely on the first notice, Ener-G argued that it had been effectively served by personal delivery on March 30, 2010 and that the claim form, served in the same way a year later, was just in time on March 29, 2011. However, the Court of Appeal unanimously agreed with the trial judge (Burton J) that, when clause 13 referred to notices delivered 'personally' this meant delivered to the recipient (Hormell) in person not delivered personally by the sender. This left Ener-G to seek reliance on the second notice. It was agreed that, under clause 13.3, this notice was deemed received two business days after posting, that is, on April 1, 2010; and it was also common ground that, in this scenario, Ener-G's service of the claim form took effect on March 31, 2011. Accordingly, on the face of it, Ener-G had served both a notice of claim and their claim form in time. However, in response to this line of argument, Hormell contended that, although Ener-G's first notice was not effective as personal delivery, it was nevertheless effective when Hormell read it later that particular afternoon; and, so Hormell argued, this was the operative notice that set the date for calculating the 12 months within which Ener-G must serve their claim form. In other words, time started running on March 30, 2010; and, by March 31, 2011, when the claim form took effect, Ener-G were out of time. But, to succeed with this argument, clause 13 had to be read as permitting service of notice by means other than personal delivery or recorded delivery; clause 13 should not be read as exclusive. The trial judge ruled in Hormell's favour on this point and, with some hesitation, the majority in the Court of Appeal (Lord Dyson MR and Gross LJ) also held that clause 13 was not exclusive—even though this meant that Ener-G, having tried to use the two methods of service explicitly given in the agreement were deemed to be out of time by reference to a method of service not mentioned in the contract.

ENER-G HOLDINGS PLC v HORMELL

[2012] EWCA Civ 1059

LORD DYSON MR

3-022   25. The second issue is whether it was open to ENER-G to serve the Notice in a manner different from that described in clause 13.2. In other words: are the methods of service in clause 13.2 exclusive or permissive? Unusually, it is ENER-G, the server of the document in question, who is contending that the contractually prescribed methods of service are exclusive, and it is the intended recipient of the document, Mr Hormell, who is contending that they are permissive.

26. The Judge held that the methods of service set out in clause 13.2 were no more than permissive, and, although I have not found the point easy, I have reached the same conclusion.

27. The notion that clause 13.2 was intended to be permissive rather than exclusive, receives obvious support from the fourth word of the clause, 'may' , particularly when it is contrasted with the mandatory word 'shall' in the immediately preceding clause 13.1. The force of the point is only slightly diluted by the fact that clause 13.2 envisages two alternative means of delivery: the word 'shall' would have been quite appropriate if it had been intended to be exhaustive.

28. I consider that some support for this conclusion is to be found in clause 1.5.7, with its statement that '[u]nless expressly stated to the contrary . . . "in writing" or "written" includes faxes . . .'. There is nothing in clause 13.2 which appears to exclude clause 1.5.7, and, if delivery by fax is permitted, it would seem to be inconsistent with the notion that the two prescribed methods of delivery in clause 13.2 were exclusive. I accept that it can be said that, if clause 13.2 does permit delivery only by the two specified methods, then delivery by fax is 'expressly' precluded, but it seems to me that, if one is looking to find the intention of the parties, clause 1.5.7 does provide mild assistance to Mr Hormell's case.

29. The argument that it would have been pointless to spell out two methods of service in clause 13.2, unless they were intended to be exclusive, has some initial attraction. However, in my view, on closer analysis, the argument has no force. The purpose of a provision such as clause 13.2, if it is not exclusive, is to shift any risk from the server to the intended recipient—see per Robert Walker LJ in *Blunden* [2003] 2 P&CR 84, paras 27–8. Thus, if a document is served in accordance with clause 13.2, it is treated as served, or delivered, even if it does not come to the attention of, or even if it is not received by, the intended recipient (see the cases cited at para 23 above). But if a document is served or delivered in any other way (e.g. by ordinary post or by being left at the intended recipient's premises rather than being handed personally to him), there is no such presumption.

30. That argument works perfectly well for the provision for sending by recorded delivery. However, at least at first sight, it is unnecessary for personal service: there would appear to have been no need for any presumption in such a case, as personal service, once established as a matter of fact, will always be effective. I consider that the answer to that point lies in the fact that personal delivery of a document on ENER-G might involve the document not coming to the attention of the directors, as it would encompass delivery on a non-director who had actual or ostensible authority to accept service (see per Peter Gibson LJ in *Bottin* [2004] EWCA Civ 1386, para 46, cited in para 21 above). If a document was personally delivered to such a person, who then failed to pass on the document to a director, clause 13.2 would make it clear that service had been effected.

31. In my judgment, commercial common sense also assists Mr Hormell's argument. If ENER-G had not sent the second Notice by recorded delivery, it would have been very unattractive for Mr Hormell to argue that ENER-G's right to claim on the warranties was lost by virtue of no Notice having been delivered within the two year period prescribed by clause 6.6.3(b). The purpose of providing for the Notice was to ensure that Mr Hormell was notified within the two year period of a warranty claim, so that he would know that he was free of any such claim if he received no such Notice within the two year period. As he saw the first Notice within the two year period, that aim would have been achieved even without the second Notice.

32. In my view, clear words would normally be required before one could ascribe to the parties an intention that a recipient who actually receives a notice in time should nonetheless be treated as not having received the notice at all. In this case, the point is rather reinforced by the point mentioned in para 23 above, namely that, if a notice is sent by recorded delivery to the prescribed address, it is deemed to have been served, even if it is not actually received. If that is right, it would seem a little curious to ascribe to the parties an intention that a notice sent or delivered in another way was, in the absence of clear words, deemed not to have been served, even though it was clear that, as a matter of fact, it had been received and read by the intended recipient.

33. Accordingly, there is a strong commercial argument, as well as a strong argument based on the language of the Agreement, for saying that the first Notice was delivered when Mr Hormell saw it. If that is right, then the fact that ENER-G delivered the second Notice, cannot, as it were, retrospectively cause the first Notice not to have been validly delivered.

34. Further, while reliance on previous judicial decisions on this sort of point has obvious dangers, I consider that this conclusion derives some support from the reasoning of the Court of Appeal in *Yates Building Company v RJ Pulleyn & Sons (York) Ltd* [1976] 1 EGLR 157. In that case, it was unanimously held that a notice exercising an option, sent by ordinary post, was valid, even though the contractual provision, after requiring the option to be exercised by notice in writing', continued 'such notice to be sent by registered or recorded delivery post'. Lord Denning MR, with whom Orr LJ agreed, described the latter provision as 'directory' rather than 'mandatory'. I have no doubt that Scarman LJ's characterisation of the provision as 'permissive' rather than 'obligatory' (see at [1976] 1 EGLR 157, 158) is to be preferred. In a sense, the present case is *a fortiori*, because that case concerned an option, and the contractual requirements of an option are gENERally more strictly construed than those of other contractual rights (see *United Scientific Instruments Ltd v Burnley Borough Council* [1978] AC 904).

35. However, there are arguments the other way, and it is necessary to address them. First, there is the fact that clause 13.3 would result in a document served in accordance with clause 13.2 being, at least potentially, served later than a document served other than in accordance with clause 13.2. Thus, at first sight at any rate, it would seem to be a little odd that a document sent by ordinary post might be delivered the day after it was sent, but one sent by recorded delivery would be treated as delivered two days after it was sent. In my view, the answer to that point is that, if the server of a document wishes to take advantage of the risk transfer, or the irrebuttable presumption of service, conferred on him by clause 13.2 (as discussed in paras 29-30 above and by Scarman LJ in *Yates* [1976] 1 EGLR 157, 158), part of the price is the consequence of the presumed date of delivery as set out in clause 13.3.

36. If the server wants to take advantage of the deemed delivery by serving in accordance with clause 13.2, he takes the consequences as to deemed date of delivery in clause 13.3; whereas if the server chooses to deliver in some other way, he has to prove service (rather than relying on deeming) and has to prove the date of service

(again, rather than relying on deeming). I see nothing surprising about this, although it is fair to say that it may produce somewhat oddly contrasting results on comparing particular hypothetical sets of facts. Further, clause 13.3 can produce somewhat odd results on any view: it appears that, if a document is personally delivered before 9.00 a.m. on a particular day, it is deemed to be received the next day, whereas if it is personally delivered between 9.00 a.m. and 5.00 p.m. on a particular day, it is deemed to be received on that day.

37. It can also be said that the word 'however' in the second sentence of clause 14.2 implies that the methods of service described in clause 13.2 (as impliedly referred to in the preceding sentence) were envisaged as being exclusive, as, otherwise, the word would not have been included. In my view, that is not a strong point, as the word 'however' is not inconsistent with the notion that clause 13.2 is permissive.

38. There is also something in the point that it accords with commercial common sense to make it clear that service of documents can only be served in certain specified ways. The point has added force in a case such as this when the date of service of a Notice acts not merely to give rise to a right, but also to start time running against the server in relation to another step (namely service of a Claim Form). However, I find the commercial common sense argument the other way rather more telling—see paras 29–32 above. In any event, clause 13 does not only apply to a Notice under clause 6.6.3(b). Further, even in the case of such a Notice, it is up to the person who delivers the Notice to make sure (i) that he knows when the notice was delivered, and (ii) that the Claim Form is served properly and in time, both being matters which are wholly or largely within his control. If, as in this case, he leaves service of the Claim Form to the last minute, he only has himself to blame.

Conclusion

39. Accordingly, I agree with Burton J that (i) the first Notice was not 'deliver[ed] . . . personally' within the meaning of clause 13.2 on 30 March 2010, and neither was the Claim Form 'deliver[ed] . . . personally' on 29 March 2011, but that (ii) the first Notice was nonetheless validly served on 30 March 2010 and the Claim Form was deemed to have been served on 1 April 2011.

40. I have considered whether it might be argued that, even though the first Notice was validly served by it having been left at Ringerlane and received and read by Mr Hormell on 30 March 2011, it was nonetheless open to ENER-G to contend that, having served the second Notice strictly in accordance with clause 13.2 on 1 April 2011, it was entitled to treat the second Notice rather than the first Notice as the effective notice under clause 6.6.3(b). That was not a point argued by Mr Bompas, although it was raised during the hearing by Longmore LJ. I have concluded that it cannot be sustained: if the first Notice was validly served, then there was no room for a second Notice, not least because a second notice cannot retrospectively invalidate, or cancel, an earlier notice, valid when it was served.

41. For these reasons, I would dismiss ENER-G's appeal.

LONGMORE LJ

42. I agree with the Master of the Rolls that the words "delivering it personally" mean that the notice must be served on the person of the recipient and not that it must be served by a personal deliverer.

43. I have not found the question of exclusivity (as it has been called) easy to decide but I have concluded that the judge was wrong not to have construed clause 13.2 of the contract regarding the methods of service of any notice (such as that required by clause 6.3.3 of the share sale contract) as exclusive.

44. My main reason is that it is counter-intuitive to conclude, when the parties have taken the trouble to spell out (a) that a notice given under the agreement can be served either "by delivering it personally" or "by sending it by pre-paid recorded delivery post" and (b) that, in a case where a notice is to be served on the Buyer (a company) it is to be marked "for the attention of Directors", that a notice can be served in any other way the deliverer of the notices chooses. The contract could have made the matter clearer by inserting the word "only" before the words "be served" in the expression "may be served"; equally the parties could have added the words "or in any other way" at the end of clause 13.2. But they did neither and it can therefore be said that the clause has either of those meanings. But the common sense of the matter is that by spelling out two methods by which a notice could be served, they did not intend that it be served in any other way. This conclusion is, to my mind, strongly supported by the fact that clause 14.2 provides that any legal proceedings may be served in accordance with the agreement and then says

"These documents may, however, be served in any other manner allowed by law."

45. Mr Lavender for the defendant relied heavily on the use of the word "may" in clause 13.2 in contradistinction to the word "must" or "shall" as used in other clauses of the contract, notably in clause 13.1 which provides that "any notice shall be in writing". That argument has some, but by no means conclusive, force; it is clear that a notice has

to be in writing but if one is then providing for service of such a notice in two possible ways, it is a natural use of language to say that the parties "may" use one method of service or a second method of service. Such expression does not mean that it is not compulsory to use one method or the other.

46. Burton J made the powerful point that if the claimant had just left the notice on the table in the porch (without also sending it by recorded delivery) and if the notice had actually come to the attention of the defendant (as it did in this case) shortly after being so left and the defendant claimed that he had not been properly served with the notice so that no claim could be brought against him, "he would have a hard time of it in court". But I respectfully wonder about that; one can always propose hard cases where, on different facts, a harsh result apparently ensues. The defendant could always say that a claimant who has two years within which to serve a contractual notice and always has the fall-back of sending it by recorded delivery has only himself to blame if he chooses to try to serve by some other method which (for whatever reason) does not contractually work out.

47. It seems to me that the judgment, with respect, produces the rather more perverse consequence that the actual method of service which was not contractual (because not served on the defendant personally) effectively becomes a contractual method once it has come to the notice of the defendant and therefore operates as a trigger for the second period (within which proceedings have to be served pursuant to clause 6.3.7) at a time of which the claimant cannot be aware, with the result that his claim is unexpectedly barred because the year allowed has begun before the year allowed by the second (contractual) method of service.

48. For myself I am not influenced by decided cases about contractually prescribed methods of making offers or communicating acceptances or exercising options because they relate to the making (or otherwise) of contracts. I do not see why the law in that area should be transposed to notices given pursuant to contracts already made. Traditionally and understandably the law is stricter about the service of documents (or at any rate proceedings) than it is about the transmission of offers and acceptances. I would therefore distinguish *Yates Building Co. v R J Pulleyn & Sons (York) Ltd* [1976] 1 EGLR 157 on which the Master of the Rolls places some reliance. Indeed I did not understand Mr Lavender to argue that the matter was concluded by authority which (after all) businessmen are unlikely to know much about, see *BCCI v Ali* [2002] 1 A.C. 251 para 51 per Lord Hoffman.

49. Left to myself therefore, while acknowledging the force of my Lord's conclusion and that of the judge, I would have allowed this appeal.

GROSS LJ

Introduction

50. I gratefully adopt the summary of the provisions of the Agreement and the facts contained in the judgment of the Master of the Rolls.

51. On the question of the meaning of the words "delivering it personally" in cl. 13.2 of the Agreement, I agree with both the Master of the Rolls and Longmore LJ and there is nothing I can usefully add. It follows that the appeal must be dismissed unless the Appellant is entitled to succeed on the "exclusivity" question.

52. With regard to that question, I find myself in an invidious position, given that the Master of the Rolls and Longmore LJ disagree as to the answer. Like them, I have not found the point easy.

The Rival Cases

53. The rival cases were, if I may say so, clearly and attractively articulated by Mr. Bompas QC for ENER-G (the Appellant) and Mr. Lavender QC for Mr. Hormell (the Respondent).

54. Mr. Bompas submitted that the methods of service set out in clause 3.2 were exclusive. The consequence was that the 12 month period provided for in clause 6.3.7 started later, on the 1st April, 2010, so that the Claim Form was served in time, on the 31st March, 2011. In essence, Mr. Bompas submitted that in clause 13.2 of the Agreement, the parties had carefully stipulated for two modes of service, reinforced by the provisions of cl. 13.3. It was implausible that the parties would have constructed this detailed scheme if the modes of service were no more than permissive. Further, the wording of clause 14.2 lent support to the Appellant's case. The additional flexibility provided for the service of documents starting or relating to legal proceedings (e.g., the Claim Form) and the service of notices or other communications (e.g., the 2010 First and Second Notices) was stark. The former, not the latter, could be served "in any other manner allowed by law" rather than "in accordance with this Agreement". It is common ground that if Mr. Bompas is right on the exclusivity question, then the appeal must be allowed.

55. Mr. Lavender submitted that the Judge was right; the methods of service set out in clause 13.2 were no more than permissive. Accordingly, time started running on the 30th March 2010 and the purported service of the Claim Form, on the 31st March, 2011, was out of time. The word "may" in clause 13.2 told

decisively against the argument for exclusivity. "May" did not mean "must"; contrast, for instance, the word "shall" in clause 13.1. It did not follow that clauses 13.2 and 13.3 were deprived of meaning. To the contrary, a party, following either mode of service for which express provision was made, obtained "copper bottomed" protection (or a "safe harbour") against the risk of the document in question not actually coming to the attention of or being received by the intended recipient. Even if, which Mr. Lavender sought to resist, clause 14.2 furnished a pointer in favour of exclusivity, it could not outweigh the impact of the permissive word "may". Mr. Lavender further submitted that the Respondent's construction enabled meaning to be given to the provision contained in clause 1.5.7 as to delivery by fax. Still further, although on the facts of the present dispute, the conclusion that clause 13.2 provided for exclusive modes of service would mean that the proposed claim was not time barred, there would be other situations when it would lead to a very different and unattractive outcome: for instance, it would mean that service of a notice could be out of time, simply because of the use of some other mode of service and even though the intended recipient had, as a matter of fact read the notice and was aware of its contents. Indeed, it was on that very footing that the Appellant's argument for a later start to the clause 6.3.7 period depended.

Discussion

56. *(1) Preliminary matters:* I begin with a number of preliminary matters which inform my consideration of the exclusivity issue.

57. First, as was common ground, the approach to the construction of the Agreement was that set out in *Rainy Sky v Kookmin Bank* [2011] UKSC 50; [2011] 1 WLR 2900. It suffices to refer to two passages in the judgment of Lord Clarke of Stone-cum-Ebony:

> " 14. . . . the ultimate aim of interpreting a provision in a contract, especially a commercial contract, is to determine what the parties meant by the language used, which involves ascertaining what a reasonable person would have understood the parties to have meant. . . .
>
> 21. The language used by the parties will often have more than one potential meaning. I would accept the submission . . . that the exercise of construction is essentially one unitary exercise in which the court must consider the language used and ascertain what a reasonable person, that is a person who has all the background knowledge which would reasonably have been available to the parties in the situation in which they were at the time of the contract, would have understood the parties to have meant. In doing so, the court must have regard to all the surrounding circumstances. If there are two possible constructions, the court is entitled to prefer the construction which is consistent with business common sense and to reject the other. "

Elaboration is unnecessary, save to observe that one of the difficulties in the present case is that considerations of business common sense can properly be relied upon for each of the rival constructions.

58. Secondly, as observed by the Judge (judgment, at [9 ii)]), certainty is important in commercial transactions, so that parties can know where they stand and act accordingly. Strict time bars are an aspect of certainty; there is certainly nothing uncommercial about them and they are not infrequently encountered in commercial contracts. When there is a time bar, then, as Lord Nicholls observed in *Valentines Properties Limited v Huntco Corporation Limited* [2001] UKPC 14, at [20]

> " Inherent in a time limit is the notion that the parties are drawing a line. Once the line is crossed, a miss is as good as a mile."

Mr. Bompas, rightly, disclaimed any suggestion of seeking sympathy as to the operation of clause 6.3.7(a); his submissions were instead exclusively focused on the proposition that service of the proceedings was just in time, not just too late.

59. Thirdly, despite the desirability and importance of certainty, a good many commercial contracts are less tidy than might be desirable as a matter of strict theory. In this respect, commercial contracts reflect the realities of commercial life. It is thus no surprise to find in a commercial contract surplus language, for instance that which merely states the obvious. Likewise, it is by no means uncommon to find that whichever of two rival constructions is preferred, anomalies or apparent anomalies will remain. The present case is no exception, as the judgments of the Master of the Rolls and Longmore LJ readily allow. The task, accordingly, is to ascertain which construction best, if imperfectly, fits the language used by the parties in the context in which the Agreement is located.

60. Fourthly, if I may be permitted to put it this way, the purpose of a notice provision is to give notice—i.e., to require the intended recipient to be made aware of the facts and matters in question. However, it by no means necessarily follows from the intended recipient having actual knowledge of such facts and matters that he has been properly served; thus, to take an example removed from the facts of this case:

" If a claimant is required to serve X and, mistakenly purports to serve Y, the mere fact that Y informs X of the purported service so that X knows of it, cannot convert Y's receipt of the documents into good service upon X."

See *Lantic Sugar Ltd v Baffin Investments* [2009] EWHC 3325 (Comm); [2010] 2 Lloyd's Rep. 141, at [40]. The example of course serves to illustrate why pleas of hardship in this area are untenable. Conversely, however, there is much to be said for reducing the risk of a person, who has actually received a notice and become aware of its contents, asserting that he has nonetheless not been properly served. A construction which serves to reduce this risk may be thought to have obvious attraction as giving effect to the underlying commercial purpose of any typical notice provision.

61. *(2) Decision:* Very much on balance, respectfully parting company with Longmore LJ but in agreement with the Judge and the Master of the Rolls, I have concluded that clause 13.2 is permissive rather than exclusive as to the modes of service there specified. My reasons follow.

62. First, I begin with the language of clause 13.2. Here, I do regard the use of the word "may" as striking. As clause 13.1 so clearly illustrates, the parties knew how to say "shall" when they intended to do so. While it is true that "may" foreshadows two specified modes of service and thus there is nothing unnatural about its usage, it is also true that "shall" or "must" would have served equally well. Moreover, either "shall" or "must" would have conveyed the exclusivity of the modes of service in question, had that been the parties' intention. For my part, I am unable to read "may" as meaning "must", at least unless persuaded by other language in the Agreement or its commercial context that I should do so. At all events, I regard the use of the word "may" as a most powerful pointer to the permissive rather than exclusive nature of clause 13.2.

63. Secondly, I seek to test my provisional view of clause 13.2 as permissive having regard to the Agreement as a whole.

i)   On the hypothesis that clause 13.2 is permissive, the scheme of clauses 13.2 and 13.3 has the important and sensible commercial purpose of risk allocation. If one of the specified modes of service is used, risk is transferred from the server to the recipient, as explained by the Master of the Rolls at [29] *et seq* above. The certainty involved in this transfer of risk may be seen as a price worth paying for curiosities such as the possibility that service by one of the specified modes of service might be achieved later than by some other method of service permitted by law: see, [35] and [36] above. Accordingly, although I appreciate the attraction of the argument that the careful nature of the scheme of clauses 13.2 and 13.3 suggests that it was intended to be exclusive rather than permissive in nature, I am not persuaded by it.

ii) Clause 14.2 must next be addressed. At first blush, its wording does lend support to the Appellant's case. The point is an important one but, ultimately for me, not decisive. To begin with, there is some force in Mr. Lavender's submission that the provision "Proceedings may be served . . . in accordance with this Agreement" should be read as "neutral" on the question of whether clause 13.2 is permissive or exclusive. The next sentence, dealing with the service of documents commencing or relating to legal proceedings "in any other manner allowed by law" can be seen as no more than an example of "bootstraps" or a statement of the obvious, of the kind that (as already indicated) features in commercial contracts. Let it be assumed, however and contrary to Mr. Lavender's argument, that clause 14.2 tends to favour the Appellant's construction of the Agreement. On this footing, the question which arises is whether the pointer furnished by clause 14.2 serves to outweigh the importance to be attached to the use of the word "may" in clause 13.2. The better view, in my judgment, is that it does not do so; the best fit is to accord "may" the priority it warrants. To my mind—and a matter to which I return—clear words would be needed to treat clause 13.2 as exclusive rather than permissive. The use of the word "may" at once undermines any such suggestion of exclusivity; the suggestion conveyed by clause 14.2 (even assuming that it does favour the Appellant's case) falls well short of the clear wording needed to make good a case of exclusivity.

iii) Though of distinctly limited significance, treating clause 13.2 as permissive enables full effect to be given to clause 1.5.7 and service by fax.

64. Thirdly, I turn to questions of context and business common sense. On the one hand, I acknowledge the attraction of the Appellant's argument as promoting certainty. If clause 13.2 is exclusive as to modes of service, there would be greater certainty as to the start and, hence, the finish of the 12 month period provided by clauses 6.3.3 (b) and 6.3.7 (a). As already foreshadowed, that is a point of significance. It remains so— even though it can also fairly be said that it is not asking too much of the Appellant to issue and serve proceedings within a hardly ungenerous period of 12 months and to err on the side of caution having regard to the very limited range of possible dates when time could realistically start to count.

65. On the other hand, there is, for my part, the yet more persuasive argument that exclusivity requires clear wording because of the consequences which can follow. Exclusivity entails that, regardless of the actual knowledge of the intended recipient, any mode of service other than those specified in clause 13.2 will not suffice. The Court will of course give effect to exclusivity—notwithstanding the consequences—if indeed that is the bargain the parties have made; however, as already foreshadowed, there is no such clear wording here. Turning to the consequences, it is to be acknowledged that, on the facts of the present case, if clause 13.2 provided for exclusive modes of service, the Appellant would not be time barred from proceeding with its proposed claims. But, in other, readily conceivable, factual situations, the consequences could be much less attractive. As illustrated by the Judge (judgment, at [16]), treating clause 13.2 as exclusive would facilitate a party asserting that the initial clause 6.3.3 (b) notice was out of time despite actual receipt of the document and full knowledge of its contents. For reasons I have already sought to adumbrate, a construction which reduces the risk of such an outcome has much to be said for it. In my view, absent clear wording providing for exclusivity, this consideration strongly favours a permissive construction of clause 13.2—and, especially when considered together with the very considerable significance of the use of the word "may" in clause 13.2, it serves to tilt the balance in favour of the Respondent's case on the appeal.

66. Accordingly, treating the task of construction as a "unitary exercise" (*Rainy Sky, supra*, at [21]) and broadly for the same reasons as the Judge and the Master of the Rolls, the better view is that clause 13.2 of the Agreement is permissive rather than exclusive with regard to modes of service. It follows that I would dismiss the appeal. I am conscious that the consequence of doing so is that the Appellant's proposed claims against the Respondent are time barred but I fear that by leaving service until so late in the day, the Appellant has been the author of its own misfortune.

67. For completeness:

i) While, with respect, I am wary of relying on authority to aid in the construction of the Agreement, the judgment of Scarman LJ (as he then was) in *Yates Building Company v RJ Pulleyn,(supra)* at p.158 (cited by the Master of the Rolls at [34] above), helpfully highlights the distinction between "obligatory" and "permissive" wording—and, in my view, reinforces the need for clear wording before concluding that clause 13.2 was exclusive in nature.

ii) Again with respect, I express no view on the point canvassed by the Master of the Rolls, at [40], *supra*.

B.   At What Point Does an Acceptance Take Effect?

3-023   Where an offeree signals, through his or her words or conduct, that he or she wishes to accept an offer, when is that signal treated as effective in forming a contract? In principle, the law might treat the signal as effective at the moment it is given or at some later time such as at the moment that it is received by the offeror. In practice, this is likely to be an issue for the law of contract only where there is a significant lapse of time between the signal being given and the signal being received. Accordingly, where the parties are dealing face-to-face, the question is largely academic. However, where the parties are dealing at a distance, depending upon the means of communication used (and, in particular, whether transmission is instantaneous or not), there might be a practical question to be resolved. Famously, in the nineteenth century, when the postal service was developed, and when offerees used the post to transmit their acceptances, the courts had to decide whether letters of acceptance were binding on posting or on receipt.

HOUSEHOLD FIRE INSURANCE CO v GRANT

Court of Appeal (1879) 4 Ex.D. 216; 48 L.J.Ex. 577; 41 L.T. 298; 27 W.R. 858

3-024   One Kendrick was the agent of the company in Glamorgan. The defendant handed to Kendrick an application in writing for shares in the company, which stated the defendant had paid to the bankers of the company £5, being a deposit of 1s. per share, and requesting an allotment of 100 shares, and agreeing to pay a further sum of 19s. per share within 12 months of the date of the allotment. Kendrick forwarded the application to the plaintiffs in London and the secretary of the company made out a letter of allotment in favour of the defendant and posted it addressed to the defendant in Swansea. The letter never arrived. The defendant's name was entered on the register of shareholders and he was credited with two dividends amounting to 5s. The company then went into liquidation and the liquidator sued for £94 15s. being the balance due upon the 100 shares.

Lopes J found for the plaintiff and the defendant appealed.

THESIGER LJ

In this case the defendant made an application for shares in the plaintiffs' company under circumstances from which we must imply that he authorised the company, in the event of their allotting to him the shares applied for, to send the notice of allotment by post . . .

Now, whatever in abstract discussion may be said as to the legal notion of its being necessary, in order to the effecting of a valid and binding contract, that the minds of the parties should be brought together at one and the same moment, that notion is practically the foundation of English law upon the subject of the formation of contracts. Unless, therefore, a contract constituted by correspondence is absolutely concluded at the moment that the continuing offer is accepted by the person to whom the offer is addressed, it is difficult to see how the two minds are ever to be brought together at one and the same moment. This was pointed out by Lord Ellenborough in the case of *Adams v Lindsell* ((1818) 1 B. & A. 681), which is recognised authority upon this branch of the law. But on the other hand it is a principle of law, as well established as the legal notion to which I have referred, that the minds of the two parties must be brought together by mutual communication. An acceptance, which only remains in the breast of the acceptor without being actually and by legal implication communicated to the offerer, is no binding acceptance. How then are these elements of law to be harmonised in the case of contracts formed by correspondence through the post? I see no better mode than that of treating the post office as the agent of both parties, and it was so considered by Lord Romilly in *Hebb's Case* (L.R. 4 Eq. at p. 12) when in the course of his judgment he said: "*Dunlop v Higgins* (1 H.L.C. 381) decides that the posting of a letter accepting an offer constitutes a binding contract, but the reason of that is, that the post office is the common agent of both parties." Alderson B., also, in *Stocken v Collin* (7 M. & W. at p. 516), a case of notice of dishonour, and the case referred to by Lord Cottenham, says: "If the doctrine that the post office is only the agent for the delivery of the notice were correct no one could safely avail himself of that mode of transmission." But if the post office be such common agent, then it seems to me to follow that, as soon as the letter of acceptance is delivered to the post office, the contract is made as complete and final and absolutely binding as if the acceptor had put his letter into the hands of a messenger sent by the offerer himself as his agent to deliver the offer and receive the acceptance. What other principle can be adopted short of holding that the contract is not complete by acceptance until and except from the time that the letter containing the acceptance is delivered to the offerer, a principle which has been distinctly negatived? . . . The contract . . . is actually made when the letter is posted. The acceptor, in posting the letter, has, to use the language of Lord Blackburn, in *Brogden v Directors of Metropolitan Ry.* ((1876) 2 App. Cas. 666) "put it out of his control and done an extraneous act which clenches the matter, and shows beyond all doubt that each side is bound." How then can a casualty in the post, whether resulting in delay, which in commercial transactions is often as bad as no delivery, or in non-delivery, unbind the parties or unmake the contract? To me it appears that in practice a contract complete upon the acceptance of an offer being posted, but liable to be put an end to by an accident in the post, would be more mischievous than a contract only binding upon the parties to it upon the acceptance actually reaching the offerer, and I can see no principle of law from which such an anomalous contract can be deduced.

There is no doubt that the implication of a complete, final, and absolutely binding contract being formed, as soon as the acceptance of an offer is posted, may in some cases lead to inconvenience and hardship. But such there must be at times in every view of the law. It is impossible in transactions which pass between parties at a distance, and have to be carried on through the medium of correspondence, to adjust conflicting rights between innocent parties, so as to make the consequences of mistake on the part of a mutual agent fall equally upon the shoulders of both. At the same time I am not prepared to admit that the implication in question will lead to any great or general inconvenience or hardship. An offerer, if he chooses, may always make the formation of the contract which he proposes dependent upon the actual communication to himself of the acceptance. If he trusts to the post he trusts to a means of communication which, as a rule, does not fail, and if no answer to his offer is received by him, and the matter is of importance to him, he can make inquiries of the person to whom his offer was addressed. On the other hand, if the contract is not finally concluded, except in the event of the acceptance actually reaching the offerer, the door would be opened to the perpetration of much fraud, and, putting aside this consideration, considerable delay in commercial transactions, in which dispatch is, as a rule, of the greatest consequence, would be occasioned; for the acceptor would never be entirely safe in acting upon his acceptance until he had received notice that his letter of acceptance had reached its destination.

Upon balance of conveniences and inconveniences it seems to me, applying with slight alterations the language of the Supreme Court of the United States in *Tayloe v Merchants Fire Insurance Co* (9 Howard S. Ct. Rep. 390), more consistent with the acts and declarations of the parties in this case to consider the contract complete and absolutely binding on the transmission of the notice of allotment through the post, as the medium of communication that the parties themselves contemplated, instead of postponing its completion until the notice had been received by the defendant.

Baggallay LJ delivered a concurring judgment.

BRAMWELL LJ

If . . . posting a letter which does not reach is a sufficient communication of acceptance of an offer, it is equally a communication of everything else which may be communicated by post, for example, notice to quit. It is impossible to hold, if I offer my landlord to sell him some hay and he writes accepting my offer, and in the same letter gives me notice to quit, and posts his letter which, however, does not reach me, that he has communicated to me his acceptance of my offer, but not his notice to quit. Suppose a man has paid his tailor by cheque or banknote, and posts a letter containing a cheque or banknote to his tailor, which never reaches, is the tailor paid? If he is, would he be if he had never been paid before in that way? Suppose a man is in the habit of sending cheques and banknotes to his banker by post, and posts a letter containing cheques and banknotes, which never reaches. Is the banker liable? Would he be if this was the first instance of a remittance of the sort? In the cases I have supposed, the tailor and banker may have recognised this mode of remittance by sending back receipts and putting the money to the credit of the remitter. Are they liable with that? Are they liable without it? The question then is, is posting a letter which is never received a communication to the person addressed, or an equivalent, or something which dispenses with it? It is for those who say it is to make good their contention. I ask why is it? My answer beforehand to any argument that may be urged is that it is not a communication, and that there is no agreement to take it as an equivalent for or to dispense with a communication. That those who affirm the contrary say the thing which is not. That if Brian C. J. had had to adjudicate on the case, he would deliver the same judgment as that reported. That because a man, who may send a communication by post or otherwise, sends it by post, he should bind the person addressed, although the communication never reaches him, while he would not so bind him if he had sent it by hand, is impossible. There is no reason in it; it is simply arbitrary. I ask whether anyone who thinks so is prepared to follow that opinion to its consequence; suppose the offer is to sell a particular chattel, and the letter accepting it never arrives, is the property in the chattel transferred? Suppose it is to sell an estate or grant a lease, is the bargain completed? The lease might be such as not to require a deed, could be subsequent lessee be ejected by the would-be acceptor of the offer because he had posted a letter? Suppose an article is advertised at so much, and that it would be sent on receipt of a post office order. Is it enough to post the letter? If the word "receipt" is relied on, is it really meant that that makes a difference? If it should be said let the offerer wait, the answer is, maybe he may lose his market meanwhile. Besides, his offer may be by advertisement to all mankind. Suppose a reward for information, information posted does not reach, someone else gives it and is paid, is the offerer liable to the first man?

It is said that a contrary rule would be hard on the would-be acceptor, who may have made his arrangements on the footing that the bargain was concluded. But to hold as contended would be equally hard on the offerer, who may have made his arrangements on the footing that his offer was not accepted; his non-receipt of any communication may be attributable to the person to whom it was made being absent. What is he to do but act on the negative, that no communication has been made to him? Further, the use of the post office is no more authorised by the offerer than the sending an answer by hand, and all these hardships would befall the person posting the letter if he sent it by hand. Doubtless in that case he would be the person to suffer if the letter did not reach its destination. Why should his sending it by post relieve him of the loss and cast it on the other party? It was said, if he sends it by hand it is revocable, but not if he sends it by post, which makes the difference. But it is revocable when sent by post, not that the letter can be got back, but its arrival might be anticipated by a letter by hand or telegram, and there is no case to show that such anticipation would not prevent the letter from binding. It would be a most alarming thing to say that it would. That a letter honestly but mistakenly written and posted must bind the writer if hours before its arrival he informed the person addressed that it was coming, but was wrong and recalled; suppose a false but honest character given, and the mistake found out after the letter posted, and notice that it was wrong given to the person addressed . . .

I am of opinion that there was no bargain between these parties to allot and take shares, that to make such bargain there should have been an acceptance of the defendant's offer and a communication to him of that acceptance. That there was no such communication. That posting a letter does not differ from other attempts at communication in any of its consequences, save that it is irrevocable as between the poster and post office. The difficulty has arisen from a mistake as to what was decided in *Dunlop v Higgins* (1 H.L.C. 381), and from supposing that because there is a right to have recourse to the post as a means of communication, that right is attended with some peculiar consequences, and also from supposing that because if the letter reaches it binds from the time of posting, it also binds though it never reaches. Mischief may arise if my opinion prevails. It probably will not, as so much has been said on the matter that principle is lost sight of. I believe equal if not greater, will, if it does not prevail. I believe the latter will be obviated only by the rule being made nugatory by every prudent man saying, "your answer by post is only to bind if it reaches me." But the question is not to be decided on these considerations. What is the law? What is the principle? If Brian C. J. had had to decide this, a public post being instituted in his time, he would have said the law is the same, now there is a post, as it was before, viz., a communication to affect a man must be a communication, that is, must reach him.

Judgment Affirmed.

Even after the decision in *Household Fire Insurance Co v Grant*, some of the details of the postal rule remained unclear. For example, what would be the position where a letter of acceptance was handed to a postman? In *Re London and Northern Bank Ex p. Jones* [1900] 1 Ch. 220 at about 7.30 am on October 27 a servant of the Bank took to the GPO in London a letter addressed to Dr Jones in Sheffield accepting his offer to buy shares in the Bank. In the outer precincts of the GPO a postman came by and offered to take the letters. They were handed to him, he took them into the post office and came back and said it was all right. A letter from J withdrawing his offer was delivered at the Bank at 8.30 am on October 27 and opened by the secretary at 9.30 am. The letter of acceptance was not delivered to J until 7.30 pm that day, having been posted not at the GPO but at a district office. Cozens-Hardy J held that handing the letter to the postman outside the GPO was not a posting of the letter so as to amount to an acceptance; the Postal Guide expressly stated that town postmen were not allowed to take charge of letters for the post. As the Bank was unable to prove that the letter of acceptance was properly posted before 9.30 am it was held that J's offer was effectively withdrawn.

Questions

1. What would be the position if a letter of acceptance were handed to a postman in a country district where it was customary for the postman to collect the mail? **3–025**

2. Was the withdrawal complete at 8.30 am or at 9.30 am? Cf. *Byrne v Van Tienhoven* (below).

3. A makes an offer by letter to B. B posts an acceptance which is wrongly addressed and never arrives. Is there a contract?

4. A makes an offer by letter to B. All post office workers then go on strike. B posts an acceptance. Is there a contract? Would the answer be different if the strike began immediately after the posting of the acceptance?

5. What are the answers to the rhetorical questions put by Bramwell LJ in *Household Fire Insurance Co v Grant* (above).

6. If an offer is sent by telex or fax, is posting a letter an acceptance? Cf. *Quenerduaine v Cole* (1883) 32 W.R. 185.

HOLWELL SECURITIES LTD v HUGHES

Court of Appeal [1974] 1 W.L.R. 155; [1974] 1 All E.R. 161; (1973) 26 P. & C.R. 544

3-026   On October 19, 1971, the defendant granted the plaintiffs an option to purchase certain freehold property. The agreement provided: "The said option shall be exercisable by notice in writing to [the defendant] at any time within six months from the date hereof". On April 14, 1972, the plaintiffs wrote to the defendant's solicitor purporting to exercise the option. They posted a copy of that letter, with a covering letter properly addressed, to the defendant but these never arrived. The plaintiffs admitted that the letter to the defendant's solicitor was not a sufficient notice. The plaintiffs' action for specific performance of the option agreement, or damages, was dismissed by Templeman J The plaintiffs appealed.

RUSSELL LJ

The plaintiffs' main contention below and before this court has been that the option was exercised and the contract for sale and purchase was constituted at the moment that the letter addressed to the defendant with its enclosure was committed by the plaintiffs' solicitors to the proper representative of the postal service, so that its failure to reach its destination is irrelevant.

It is the law in the first place that prima facie acceptance of an offer must be communicated to the offeror. On this principle the law has engrafted a doctrine that, if in any given case the true view is that the parties contemplated that the postal service might be used for the purpose of forwarding an acceptance of the offer, committal of the acceptance in a regular manner to the postal service will be acceptance of the offer so as to constitute a contract, even if the letter goes astray and is lost. Nor, as was once suggested, are such cases limited to cases in which the offer has been made by post. It suffices I think at this stage to refer to *Henthorn v Fraser*.[3] In the present case, as I read a passage in the judgment below, Templeman J. concluded that the parties here contemplated that the postal service might be used to communicate acceptance of the offer (by exercise of the option); and I agree with that.

But that is not and cannot be the end of the matter. In any case, before one can find that the basic principle of the need for communication of acceptance to the offeror is displaced by this artificial concept of communication by the act of posting, it is necessary that the offer is in its terms consistent with such displacement and not one which by its terms points rather in the direction of actual communication. We were referred to *Henthorn v Fraser* and to the obiter dicta of Farwell J. in *Bruner v Moore* [1904] 1 Ch. 305, which latter was a case of an option to purchase patent rights. But in neither of those cases was there apparently any language in the offer directed to the manner of acceptance of the offer or exercise of the option.

The relevant language here is, "the said option shall be exercisable by notice in writing to the Intending Vendor . . .," a very common phrase in an option agreement. There is, of course, nothing in that phrase to suggest that the notification to the defendant could not be made by post. But the requirement of "notice . . . to," in my judgment is language which should be taken expressly to assert the ordinary situation in law that acceptance requires to be communicated or notified to the offeror, and is inconsistent with the theory that acceptance can be constituted by the act of posting, referred to by Anson,[4] as "acceptance without notification."

It is of course true that the instrument could have been differently worded. An option to purchase within a period given for value has the characteristic of an offer that cannot be withdrawn. The instrument might have

---

[3]   [1892] 2 Ch. 27. The plaintiff who lived in Birkenhead was handed a note at the defendant's office in Liverpool giving him an option to purchase certain property within 14 days. The next day the defendant posted a letter withdrawing the offer. That letter did not reach Birkenhead until after 5 pm. In the meantime, the plaintiff had posted a letter at 3.50 pm accepting the offer. That letter was delivered after the defendant's office was closed and was opened the following morning. The Court of Appeal held that the plaintiff was entitled to specific performance. Lord Herschell said that it was somewhat artificial to speak of the offeree having the implied authority of the offeror to send his acceptance by post: "Where the circumstances are such that it must have been within the contemplation of the parties that, according to the ordinary usages of mankind, the post might be used as a means of communicating the acceptance of an offer, the acceptance is complete as soon as it is posted".

[4]   *Law of Contract* (23rd edn, 1969), p.47.

said "The offer constituted by this option may be accepted in writing within six months": in which case no doubt the posting would have sufficed to form the contract. But that language was not used, and, as indicated, in my judgment the language used prevents that legal outcome. Under this head of the case hypothetical problems were canvassed to suggest difficulties in the way of that conclusion. What if the letter had been delivered through the letterbox of the house in due time, but the defendant had either deliberately or fortuitously not been there to receive it before the option period expired? This does not persuade me that the artificial posting rule is here applicable. The answer might well be that in the circumstances the defendant had impliedly invited communication by use of an orifice in his front door designed to receive communications . . . [His Lordship held that the rule in *Henthorn v Fraser* was also excluded by s.196 of the Law of Property Act 1925.]

This leaves an alternative contention for the plaintiffs which Templeman J.[5] dismissed with brevity. When the defendant's solicitors received the plaintiffs' solicitors' letter dated April 14[6] they communicated by telephone with the defendant. They did not read the letter to the defendant. . . . [His Lordship quoted the conversation.]

Counsel for the plaintiffs argued that since the defendant knew that the plaintiffs were anxious to exercise the option, and there was in existence a written notice exercising it, therefore there was a "notice in writing to the defendant." I consider this argument to be fallacious. A person does not give notice in writing to another person by sitting down and writing it out and then telephoning to that other saying, "Listen to what I have just written." Moreover, the defendant did not have knowledge of the existence of the combination of two letters which alone could be said to be an exercise of the option. *Dickinson v Dodds*,[7] which was referred to, does not assist on this point: all it does is to show that an offeree cannot accept a withdrawable offer after he has learnt, by whatever means, that it has been withdrawn.

Accordingly, I would dismiss the appeal . . . (Buckley LJ agreed).

LAWTON LJ

Does the rule [in *Henthorn v Fraser*, above] apply in all cases where one party makes an offer which both he and the person with whom he was dealing must have expected the post to be used as a means of accepting it? In my judgment, it does not. First, it does not apply when the express terms of the offer specify that the acceptance must reach the offeror. The public nowadays are familiar with this exception to the general rule through their handling of football pool coupons. Secondly, it probably does not operate if its application would produce manifest inconvenience and absurdity. This is the opinion set out in Cheshire and Fifoot's *Law of Contract* (8th ed., 1972), p. 43. It was the opinion of Bramwell B. as is seen by his judgment in *British & American Telegraph Co v Colson* ((1871) L.R. 6 Exch. 108), and his opinion is worthy of consideration even though the decision in that case was overruled by this court in *Household Fire and Carriage Accident Insurance Co Ltd v Grant* [above, para.3–024]. The illustrations of inconvenience and absurdity which Bramwell B. gave are as apt today as they were then. Is a stockbroker who is holding shares to the orders of his client liable in damages because he did not sell in a falling market in accordance with the instructions in a letter which was posted but never received? Before the passing of the Law Reform (Miscellaneous Provisions) Act 1970 (which abolished actions for breach of promise of marriage), would a young soldier ordered overseas have been bound in contract to marry a girl to whom he had proposed by letter, asking her to let him have an answer before he left and she had replied affirmatively in good time but the letter had never reached him? In my judgment, the factors of inconvenience and absurdity are but illustrations of a wider principle, namely, that the rule does not apply if, having regard to all the circumstances, including the nature of the subject-matter under consideration, the negotiating parties cannot have intended that there should be a binding agreement until the party accepting an offer or exercising an option had in fact communicated the acceptance or exercise to the other. In my judgment, when this principle is applied to the facts of this case it becomes clear that the parties cannot have intended that the posting of a letter should constitute the exercise of the option.

The option agreement was one to which section 196 of the Law of Property Act 1925 applied: see subsection (5) which is in these terms:

> "The provisions of this section shall extend to notices required to be served by any instrument affecting property executed or coming into operation after the commencement of this Act unless a contrary intention appears."

---

[5]   [1973] 2 All E.R. at 484; [1973] 1 W.L.R. at 765.
[6]   [1973] 2 All E.R. at 478; [1973] 1 W.L.R. at 758.
[7]   (1876) 2 Ch. 463, below, para.3–054.

The option agreement was an instrument affecting property. A notice in writing had to be given to exercise the option. Giving a notice means the same as serving a notice: see *Re 88 Berkeley Road* [1971] Ch. 648. The object of this subsection was to enable conveyancers to omit from instruments affecting property stipulations as to the giving of notices if they were prepared to accept the statutory ones. As there was nothing in the option agreement to a contrary effect, the statutory stipulations applied in this case. Subsection (4) is in these terms:

> "Any notice required or authorised by this Act to be served shall also be sufficiently served, if it is sent by post in a registered letter addressed to the lessee, lessor, mortgagee, mortgagor, or other person to be served, by name, at the aforesaid place of abode or business, office, or counting-house, and if that letter is not returned through the post-office undelivered; and that service shall be deemed to be made at the time at which the registered letter would in the ordinary course be delivered."

The object of this subsection, as also of subsection (3), is to specify circumstances in which proof of actual knowledge may be dispensed with. This follows from the use of the phrase "any notice . . . shall also be sufficiently served . . ." If the submissions of counsel for the plaintiffs are well-founded, a letter sent by ordinary post the evening before the option expired would have amounted to an exercise of it; but a registered letter posted at the same time and arriving in the ordinary course of post, which would be after the expiration of the option, would not have been an exercise. The parties to the option agreement cannot have intended any such absurd result to follow. When the provisions of section 196(4) are read into the agreement, as they have to be, the only reasonable inference is that the parties intended that the vendor should [sic ?not] be fixed with actual knowledge of the exercise of the option save in the circumstances envisaged in the subsection. This, in my judgment, was enough to exclude the rule.

I would dismiss the appeal.

Appeal Dismissed. Leave to Appeal to the House of Lords Refused.

Question

3-027   The posting of a letter has been held to be equivalent to communication to the addressee in respect of only one legal transaction—the acceptance of an offer. How many of Bramwell B's illustrations (above) were "apt" when that is borne in mind? Is Lawton LJ's illustration of the stockbroker apt?

Point for reflection

3-028   A famous puzzle arises where O makes an offer to A by post, A posts an acceptance and then, before the letter arrives, A communicates to O (by express letter, telephone or fax—or, nowadays, by a phone text or email) a withdrawal of the acceptance? Logically, if the contract was complete on the posting of the acceptance, A cannot withdraw from it without O's consent. Yet the first that O knows about A's response to his offer is that A does not wish to accept it. The question is whether A should be held to have made a contract.

In a Scottish case, *Countess of Dunmore v Alexander* (1830) 9 S. 190, the Court of Session, Lord Craigie dissenting, decided that there was no contract where the acceptance and the withdrawal of it reached the offeror together—so, a fortiori, the acceptance would have been invalid if the withdrawal had arrived first. But the decision is far from conclusive because of the implications of agency and some rather dubious reasoning.

Alexander, through X, made an offer to Dunmore to enter her service. On November 5 Dunmore posted a letter to X accepting the offer. X forwarded the letter to Alexander. On November 6 Dunmore posted a second letter to X cancelling the first. X forwarded this letter by express and Alexander received both letters together. If X was Alexander's agent to receive the acceptance (cf. *Financings Ltd v Stimson*, below), the contract was complete when X received Dunmore's first letter and her second letter was ineffective. This was the view of Lord Craigie, dissenting. But if X was Alexander's agent only to transmit the acceptance, then the acceptance and the withdrawal were received by the offeror simultaneously. The majority seem to have regarded X as an agent only to transmit and reasoned that the case was the same as if—

"a man put an order into the Post Office, desiring his agent to buy stock for him. He afterwards changes his mind but cannot recover his letter from the Post Office. He therefore writes a second letter countermanding the first. They both arrive together, and the result is, that no purchase can be made to bind the principal."

The example is undoubtedly correct—the agent's authority has been revoked before he has done any act to bind his principal—but is it apposite? Did X do anything on behalf of Dunmore that was not authorised by her?

Merton L. Ferson, The Formation of Simple Contracts (1924) 9 Cornell Law Quarterly, 402; Selected Readings, 128, 137

The court squares its decision with the utterance by deeming the post office the common agent of both parties. There is communication, on this assumption, when the letter of acceptance is turned over to the agent post office. It should require no argument, however, to show that the post office is not an agent of both or either party. It may properly be called an "agency" in the sense that it is a means employed, but it is not an "agent" in the technical sense, with everyone who uses it a correlative principal. An acceptance deposited in a hollow tree, if that were by the understanding of the parties a proper receptacle, would, no doubt, give rise instantly to a contract; yet it would be awkward to deem the hollow tree an agent.

3–029

Addressing this puzzle in the context of the modern law, however, the relevant question is whether holding A to the posted acceptance would defeat anyone's reasonable expectations. No doubt, we would want to know more about the parties, their transaction, and the reasons for A's change of mind. In other words, the questions would be whether O has a legitimate interest in holding A to the contract, whether A is dealing fairly in trying to withdraw, and whether there are any accepted business norms about this kind of scenario. Whatever the answer to these questions, in 2015, few would think that the right question is whether the 'logic' of offer and acceptance dictates that A is bound.

BYRNE & CO v VAN TIENHOVEN & CO

Common Pleas (1880) 5 C.P.D. 344; 49 L.J.C.P. 316; 42 L.T. 371

October 1. The defendants, in Cardiff, posted a letter to the plaintiffs, in New York, offering to sell them 1,000 boxes of tinplates.
October 8. The defendants posted a letter revoking their offer.
October 11. The plaintiffs telegraphed acceptance.
October 15. The plaintiffs confirmed their acceptance by letter.
October 20. The defendants' letter of revocation reached the plaintiffs.

3–030

LINDLEY J

. . . having stated the facts and held that a revocation, to be effective, must be communicated, continued: I pass, therefore, to the next question, viz., whether posting the letter of revocation was a sufficient communication of it to the plaintiff. The offer was posted on October 1, the withdrawal was posted on the 8th, and did not reach the plaintiff until after he had posted his letter [sic] of the 11th accepting the offer. It may be taken as now settled that where an offer is made and accepted by letter sent through the post, the contract is completed the moment the letter accepting the offer is posted: *Harris' Case* (L.R. 7 Ch. 587); *Dunlop v Higgins* (1 HL 381), even although it never reaches its destination. When, however, these authorities are looked at, it will be seen that they are based upon the principle that the writer of the offer has expressly or impliedly assented to treat an answer to him by a letter duly posted as a sufficient acceptance and notification to himself, or, in other words, he has made the Post Office his agent to receive the acceptance and notification of it. But this principle appears to me to be inapplicable to the case of the withdrawal of an offer. In this particular case I can find no evidence of any authority in fact given by the plaintiffs to the defendants to notify a withdrawal of their offer by merely posting a letter; and there is no legal principle or decision which compels me to hold, contrary to the fact, that the letter of October 8 is to be treated as communicated to the plaintiff on that day or on any day before the 20th, when the letter reached them. But before that letter had reached the plaintiffs they had accepted the offer, both by telegram and by post; and they had themselves resold the tinplates at a profit. In my opinion, the withdrawal by the defendants on October 8 of their offer of the 1st was inoperative; and a complete contract binding on both parties was entered into on October 11, when the plaintiffs accepted the offer of the 1st, which they had no reason to suppose had been withdrawn. Before leaving this part of the case it may be as well to point out the extreme injustice and inconvenience which any other conclusion would produce. If the defendants' contention were to prevail no person who had received an offer by post and had accepted it would know his position until he had waited such a time as to be quite sure that a letter withdrawing the offer had not been posted before his acceptance of it. It appears to me that both legal principles, and practical convenience require that a person who has accepted an offer not known to him to have been revoked, shall be in a position safely to act upon the footing that the offer and acceptance constitute a contract binding on both parties . . .

Judgment for the Plaintiffs.

Questions

3–031
1. Why is an acceptance complete on posting, while a revocation is incomplete until communicated? It has been suggested that 'the actual reason for the distinction is that the former rule was settled in the early part of the nineteenth century, and the latter rule not until the latter half of the century.' (Williston, 'Mutual Assent in the Formation of Contracts' (1919) 14 *Illinois Law Review*, 85; *Selected Readings*, 119.) The basis for this theory is that the subjective notions of consensus which prevailed in the early part of the nineteenth century were replaced in the latter half of the century by the modern, objective, approach. Can the distinction between the rules of acceptance and revocation be justified otherwise than on historical grounds?

2. Is a revocation complete when it arrives or when it is opened? Cf. *Re London and Northern Bank* (above, para.3–024).

Problem

3–032   On February 1 Rupert wrote to Samuel offering to sell him a house for £30,000, the offer to remain open for a week. On February 2 Samuel posted a letter saying, '£30,000 is too much; but I offer you £25,000.' Later the same day, Samuel posted a second letter saying, 'I have reconsidered the matter; £30,000 is reasonable and I accept your offer.' Rupert received Samuel's first letter on February 3 and at once entered into a contract to sell the house to Thomas. Samuel's second letter arrived on February 4. Advise Rupert.

ENTORES LTD v MILES FAR EAST CORPORATION

Court of Appeal [1955] 2 Q.B. 327; [1955] 3 W.L.R. 48; 99 S.J. 384; [1955] 2 All E.R. 493; [1955] 1 Lloyd's Rep. 511

3–033   The plaintiffs in London made an offer by Telex to the agents in Holland of the defendant corporation in New York. The offer was accepted by a communication received on the plaintiffs' Telex machine in

London. The plaintiffs sought leave to serve notice of a writ on the defendants in New York claiming damages for breach of the contract so made. By R.S.C., Ord.11, r.1, service out of the jurisdiction is allowed (inter alia) to enforce a contract "made within the jurisdiction." The defendants argued that the contract was made in Holland.

The Telex service enable a message to be dispatched by a teleprinter operated like a typewriter in one country and almost instantaneously received and typed in another.

DENNING LJ

When a contract is made by post it is clear law throughout the common law countries that the acceptance is complete as soon as the letter is put into the post box, and that is the place where the contract is made. But there is no clear rule about contracts made by telephone or by Telex. Communications by these means are virtually instantaneous and stand on a different footing.

The problem can only be solved by going in stages. Let me first consider a case where two people make a contract by word of mouth in the presence of one another. Suppose, for instance, that I shout an offer to a man across a river or a courtyard but I do not hear his reply because it is drowned by an aircraft flying overhead. There is no contract at that moment. If he wishes to make a contract, he must wait till the aircraft is gone and then shout back his acceptance so that I can hear what he says. Not until I have his answer am I bound. I do not agree with the observations of Hill J. in *Newcomb v De Roos*.[8]

Now take a case where two people make a contract by telephone. Suppose, for instance, that I make an offer to a man by telephone and, in the middle of his reply, the line goes "dead" so that I do not hear his words of acceptance. There is no contract at that moment. The other man may not know the precise moment when the line failed. But he will know that the telephone conversation was abruptly broken off: because people usually say something to signify the end of the conversation. If he wishes to make a contract, he must therefore get through again so as to make sure that I heard. Suppose next, that the line does not go dead, but it is nevertheless so indistinct that I do not catch what he says and I ask him to repeat it. He then repeats it and I hear his acceptance. The contract is made, not on the first time when I do not hear, but only the second time when I do hear. If he does not repeat it, there is no contract. The contract is only complete when I have his answer accepting the offer.

Lastly, take the Telex. Suppose a clerk in a London office taps out on the teleprinter an offer which is immediately recorded on a teleprinter in a Manchester office, and a clerk at that end taps out an acceptance. If the line goes dead in the middle of the sentence of acceptance, the teleprinter motor will stop. There is then obviously no contract. The clerk at Manchester must get through again and send his complete sentence. But it may happen that the line does not go dead, yet the message does not get through to London. Thus the clerk at Manchester may tap out his message of acceptance and it will not be recorded in London because the ink at the London end fails, or something of that kind. In that case, the Manchester clerk will not know of the failure but the London clerk will know of it and will immediately send back a message "not receiving." Then, when the fault is rectified, the Manchester clerk will repeat his message. Only then is there a contract. If he does not repeat it, there is no contract. It is not until his message is received that the contract is complete.

In all the instances I have taken so far, the man who sends the message of acceptance knows that it has not been received or he has reason to know it. So he must repeat it. But, suppose that he does not know that his message did not get home. He thinks it has. This may happen if the listener on the telephone does not catch the words of acceptance, but nevertheless does not trouble to ask for them to be repeated: or the ink on the teleprinter fails at the receiving end, but the clerk does not ask for the message to be repeated: so that the man who sends an acceptance reasonably believes that his message has been received. The offeror in such circumstances is clearly bound, because he will be estopped from saying that he did not receive the message of acceptance. It is his own fault that he did not get it. But if there should be a case where the offeror without any fault on his part does not receive the message of acceptance—yet the sender of it reasonably believes it has got home when it has not—then I think there is no contract.

My conclusion is, that the rule about instantaneous communications between the parties is different from

---

8   (1859) 2 E. & E. 271. Hill J said that if the parties were on different sides of a district boundary line and an order was verbally given and accepted, the contract would be made in the district in which the order was accepted. The defendant in London wrote to the plaintiff in Stamford instructing him to place advertisements in certain newspapers. The plaintiff did so in Stamford. The court held that the contract was made in Stamford. Was this right? Is it reconcilable with *Entores*?

the rule about the post. The contract is only complete when the acceptance is received by the offeror: and the contract is made at the place where the acceptance is received.

In a matter of this kind, however, it is very important that the countries of the world should have the same rule. I find that most of the European countries have substantially the same rule as that I have stated. Indeed, they apply it to contracts by post as well as instantaneous communications. But in the United States of America it appears as if instantaneous communications are treated in the same way as postal communications. In view of this divergence, I think that we must consider the matter on principle: and so considered, I have come to the view I have stated, and I am glad to see that Professor Winfield in this country (55 *Law Quarterly Review* 514), and Professor Williston in the United States of America (*Contracts* § 82, p. 239), take the same view.

Applying the principles which I have stated, I think that the contract in this case made in London where the acceptance was received. It was, therefore, a proper case for service out of the jurisdiction.

Birkett and Parker L.JJ. delivered concurring judgements.

Appeal Dismissed.

Questions

3–034
1. Is there any difference in principle between telex and fax or email and mobile phone "texting" used in the formation of contracts?

2. In some cultures, email exchanges are treated as akin to a phone conversation, in others more like the writing of letters. Should this be relevant to setting the default rule for the moment of acceptance where an email is used by the offeree? Compare Andrew Murray, "Entering into Contracts Electronically: The Real WWW" in Lilian Edwards and Charlotte Waelde (eds), *Law and the Internet* 2nd edn (2000), p.17.

Although it is not a case on formation, but rather on notice of termination, *The Brimnes* [1975] Q.B. 929; [1974] 3 All E.R. 88 CA offers guidance on the time at which communications by Telex take effect. In *The Brimnes*, the defendants hired a ship from the plaintiff shipowners. The contract provided that, if the hire was not paid punctually and regularly, the shipowner was to be at liberty to withdraw the ship. The defendants failed to pay the hire punctually and regularly. The shipowners complained. On April 1 the hire for the following month had not been paid as required by the contract. The shipowners sent a message by Telex, withdrawing the ship from the service, between 17.30 and 18.00 on April 2. It was not until the following morning that the defendants saw the message of withdrawal on the machine. Edmund Davies LJ said:

"The learned judge held here that the notice of withdrawal was sent during ordinary business hours, and that he was driven to the conclusion either that the charterers' staff had left the office on April 2 'well before the end of ordinary business hours' or that if they were indeed there, they 'neglected to pay attention to the Telex machine in the way they claimed it was their ordinary practice to do.' He therefore concluded that the withdrawal Telex must be regarded as having been 'received' as required by *The Georgios C* ([1971] 1 All E.R. 193; [1971] 1 Q.B. 488), at 17.45 hours on April 2 and that the withdrawal was effected at that time. I propose to say no more than that I respectfully agree with that conclusion . . ."

The question was whether the withdrawal was complete before the hire was paid because the majority of the Court of Appeal thought that the acceptance of the hire for April in advance would have amounted to waiver of the right to withdraw. It was held that withdrawal was effected some time between 17.30 and 18.00 and that the hire was paid at some time between 17.37 and 18.27. It followed that, on a balance of probabilities, withdrawal had been made before payment.

Problem

A in London, by Telex, makes an offer to B in Holland at 5 pm. B replies that he will make a decision in about two hours. At 7 pm B sends an acceptance by Telex. There is no acknowledgement but B is not surprised because he knows that A closes his office at 6 pm. If the message is read by A at 9.30 am the next day, when is the contract made? If the message is not recorded in A's office because the ink fails, is there a contract? Would it make any difference that the failure was due to A's neglect of his Telex machine? Cf. note, 72 L.Q.R. 10.

3-035

BRINKIBON LTD v STAHAG STAHL, ETC.

House of Lords [1983] 2 A.C. 34; [1982] 1 All E.R. 293; [1982] 2 W.L.R. 164

The buyers, an English company, by a telex sent from London to Vienna, accepted the terms of sale offered by the sellers, an Austrian company. The buyers issued a writ claiming damages for breach of the contract. The Court of Appeal held that the service of the writ should be set aside because the contract had not been made within the court's jurisdiction. The buyers' appeal to the House of Lords was dismissed, approving and following *Entores v Miles Far East Corporation* (above, p.85).

3-036

LORD WILBERFORCE

Since 1955 the use of telex communication has been greatly expanded, and there are many variants on it. The senders and recipients may not be the principals to the contemplated contract. They may be servants or agents with limited authority. The message may not reach, or be intended to reach, the designated recipient immediately: messages may be sent out of office hours, or at night, with the intention, or on the assumption, that they will be read at a later time. There may be some error or default at the recipient's end which prevents receipt at the time contemplated and believed in by the sender. The message may have been sent and/or received through machines operated by third persons. And many other variations may occur. No universal rule can cover all such cases; they must be resolved by reference to the intentions of the parties, by sound business practice and in some cases by a judgment where the risks should lie: see *Household Fire and Carriage Accident Insurance Co Ltd v Grant* [above, para.3-024] per Baggallay L.J. and *Henthorn v Fraser* [above] per Lord Herschell.

The present case is, as *Entores Ltd v Miles Far East Corp* itself, the simple case of instantaneous communication between principals, and, in accordance with the general rule, involves that the contract (if any) was made when and where the acceptance was received. This was on May 3, 1979 in Vienna.

Lord Fraser, having observed that there was little difference in the mechanics of transmission between a telex and a telegram, continued: Nevertheless I have reached the opinion that, on balance, an acceptance sent by telex directly from the acceptor's office to the offeror's office should be treated as if it were an instantaneous communication between principals, like a telephone conversation. One reason is that the decision to that effect in *Entores Ltd v Miles Far East Corp* seems to have worked without leading to serious difficulty or complaint from the business community. Secondly, once the message has been received on the offeror's telex machine, it is not unreasonable to treat it as delivered to the principal offeror, because it is his responsibility to arrange for prompt handling of messages within his own office. Thirdly, a party (the acceptor) who tries to send a message by telex can generally tell if his message has not been received on the other party's (the offeror's) machine, whereas the offeror, of course, will not know if an unsuccessful attempt has been made to send an acceptance to him. It is therefore convenient that the acceptor, being in the better position, should have the responsibility of ensuring that his message is received. For these reasons I think it is right that in the ordinary simple case, such as I take this to be, the general rule and not the postal rule should apply. But I agree with both my noble and learned friends that the general rule will not cover all the many variations that may occur with telex messages.

Point for reflection

3–037   In a famous early case in the United States Supreme Court, *Eliason v Henshaw* (1819) Wheat. 225; 4 L.Ed. 556, the defendant offered to purchase flour from the plaintiff. The offer was contained in a letter sent by the defendant with a wagoner employed by the plaintiff to haul flour from the plaintiff's mill at Mill Creek to Harper's Ferry where the defendant was. A postscript to the letter read: 'Please write by return of wagon whether you accept our offer.' Instead of sending a reply by wagon, the plaintiff sent a letter by mail addressed to the defendant at Georgetown, purporting to accept the offer. The mail took considerably longer than the wagon and, when the defendant received the 'acceptance', he had already bought all the flour he needed. The plaintiff's action for damages for failure to accept the flour failed. The court said that the purpose of requiring a reply by return of wagon was obviously to enable the defendant to calculate the time at which he would receive an answer—"and therefore it was entirely unimportant, whether it was sent by that, or another wagon, or in any other manner, provided it was sent to Harper's Ferry, and was not delayed beyond the time which was ordinarily employed by wagons engaged in hauling flour from the [plaintiff's] mill to Harper's Ferry. Whatever uncertainty there might have been as to the time when the answer would be received, there was none as to the place to which it was to be sent . . . The place . . . to which, the answer was to be sent constituted an essential part of the [defendant's] offer." Commenting on this case, Winfield [(1939) 55 L.Q.R. 516] asks,

> "[suppose] that H's postal acceptance had arrived earlier than, or as soon as, a reply by wagon would have done, could E have said, 'There is no contract. I told you to accept by wagon, but you have not done so'? H's retort would be, 'What of that? You are in exactly the same position as if I had replied by wagon; indeed, if my posted letter reached you earlier than a reply by wagon would have done, you are actually in a better position.' . . .
>
> But every case must be construed on its own facts. In *Eliason v Henshaw* it did not appear that E had an exclusive preference for reply by wagon. If, however, he had said, 'Reply by wagon only,' then a reply in any other way would have been useless. If it be argued that so long as he got his reply in time it was immaterial how he got it, the answer is that if an offeror clearly insists on a particular mode of acceptance, the law ought to respect his wishes. To do anything else would be to dictate to him how he should make his offer, and it is for the parties to make their own contract and not for the judges to make it for them. E might have had good reason for distrusting the post or he might have thought that there was a greater possibility of forgery of an acceptance if it were posted than if it were delivered by wagon. But whether his motives were reasonable or capricious, they are not relevant. The law is concerned with the mode of acceptance laid down by him; it is not concerned with the reason why he selected it."

From a modern perspective, what should we make of this? Are there limits on the application of a 'reasonable expectations' test where the offeror insists on a particular mode of acceptance? Or is respecting the offeror's insistence itself an application of a 'reasonable expectations' test?

Problem

3–038   Smith in Nottingham sends an offer by lorry driver to Thomas in London and requests a reply by the same means. Is there a contract (a) when Thomas hands his acceptance to the driver or (b) when it is given to Smith? Would it make any difference that the driver was (i) Smith's employee (ii) Thomas's employee (iii) an independent contractor?

C.   Qualified Acceptance

In the straightforward case of a bilateral contract, the offer is met with an unqualified acceptance—for **3–039** example, the buyer agrees to pay the price on the terms specified by the seller (or the seller agrees to the buyer's terms). If the offeree qualifies the ostensible "acceptance" in a material way, it will fail to be recognised as an acceptance (and, of course, where the response is in the form of a counter-proposal as to price and/or terms, it might amount to a counter-offer). However, what is the position where the dealings (or some elements thereof) are covered by a "subject to contract" proviso? How is the qualification "subject to contract" to be understood?

In some contexts—domestic house sales being the best known—it is standard practice for the parties to agree on a price "subject to contract" and, at that point, for estate agents to mark up properties as "SOLD subject to contract". In principle, once the parties have agreed on the price, they could be legally tied in to the sale. However, in English law, custom and practice has treated the sale of a property "subject to contract" as no more than binding in honour (see further Ch.4); until the contracts are formally exchanged (which might be some weeks after the parties have agreed the sale) the deal is not legally binding. Where market prices are rising or falling, the period between agreeing the price and exchanging contracts is one in which either the vendor or the purchaser might be tempted to defect for the sake of a better deal elsewhere. This invites many nice points of both law and common decency to be debated, one of which (considered in *Eccles v Bryant* below) concerns the significance of contracts being exchanged by post rather than face-to-face by the parties' lawyers.

ECCLES v BRYANT

Court of Appeal [1948] Ch. 93; [1948] L.J.R. 418; 177 L.T. 247; [1947] 2 All E.R. 865

LORD GREENE MR

The parties were minded to enter into a contract for the sale and purchase of a house. The matter was put **3–040** into the hands of their respective solicitors in the ordinary way. The basis on which the negotiations were being conducted was that the terms set out in the preliminary correspondence were stated to be subject to contract and survey. We are not troubled with the survey. The important words are "subject to contract"[9] This is one of those cases where quite clearly and admittedly no contract came into existence in the earlier correspondence. It is common ground that the parties contemplated a definitive binding contract which was to come into existence in the future. One thing is quite clear on the facts of this case to my mind, that both firms of solicitors, one of whom—that is the vendor's solicitors—practised in East Grinstead and the other of whom, the purchaser's solicitors, practised in London, when they were instructed to carry this matter through by their respective clients, contemplated and intended from beginning to end to do so in the customary way which is familiar to every firm of solicitors in the country, namely, by preparing the engrossment of the draft contract when agreed in duplicate, the intention being to do what I have no doubt at this very moment is happening in dozens of solicitors' offices all over the country, namely, to exchange the two parts when signed by their respective clients. That indeed, is what anyone would have understood, I think, from the language of the earlier correspondence and the words "subject to contract"—that the contract would be brought about in the way I have mentioned, by an exchange of the two parts signed by the respective parties.

Vaisey J. pointed out that what he called the ceremonial form of exchange, namely, the meeting of solicitors in the office of one of them—the vendors' solicitors office as a rule—and the passing of the two signed engrossments over the table may be taken to have fallen—and indeed, no doubt it has—into disuse to a certain extent, particularly when there are firms of solicitors in different parts of the country. He recognised that an exchange by post would, in many cases, take the place of the old more ceremonial exchange, but that an exchange was contemplated by both firms of solicitors from beginning to end appears to me to be clear from what took place

---

[9]   See below, para.4–017.

and from the correspondence. I am prepared to assume—and I think I should probably be right in assuming—that their intention was that the exchange should take place by post. When an exchange takes place by post and a contract comes into exist[e]nce through the act of exchange, the earliest date at which such a contract can come into existence, it appears to me, would be the date when the later of the two documents to be put in the post is actually put in the post. Another view might be that the exchange takes place and the contract thereby comes into existence when, and not before, the respective parties or their solicitors receive from their "opposite numbers" their parts of the contract. It is not necessary here to choose between those two views. I mention them particularly because Mr Hopkins, for the purchaser, here tried to suggest an intermediate stage, that where the parties contemplate an exchange by post the contract is completed not when an exchange takes place, but when one of the parties puts his part into the post. I am afraid I cannot accept that. It seems to me to be a contradiction in terms to speak of that as an exchange . . .

It was argued that exchange is a mere matter of machinery, having in itself no particular importance and no particular significance. So far as significance is concerned, it appears to me that not only is it not right to say of exchange that it has no significance, but it is the crucial and vital fact which brings the contract into existence. As for importance, it is of the greatest importance, and that is why in past ages this procedure came to be recognised by everybody to be the proper procedure and was adopted. When you are dealing with contracts for the sale of land, it is of the greatest importance to the vendor that he should have a document signed by the purchaser, and to the purchaser that he should have a document signed by the vendor. It is of the greatest importance that there should be no dispute whether a contract had or had not been made and that there should be no dispute as to the terms of it. This particular procedure of exchange ensures that none of those difficulties will arise. Each party has got what is a document of title, because directly a contract in writing relating to land is entered into, it is a document of title. That can be illustrated, of course, by remembering the simple case where a purchaser makes a sub-sale. The contract is a vital document for the purpose of the sub-sale. If he had not got the vendor's part, signed by the vendor, to show to the sub-purchaser, he would not be able to make a good title.

If the argument for the purchaser is right and the contract comes into existence before exchange takes place, it would mean that neither party could call upon the other to hand over his part. The non-exchanged part would remain the property of the party who signed it, because exchange would be no element in the contract at all and therefore you could get this position, that the purchaser might wish to resell and would have no right to obtain from the vendor the vendor's signed part . . .

What took place was this: Both parties did in fact sign their respective parts of the contract. The purchaser put his part in the post and it duly arrived. The vendor did not put his part in the post, but instead of doing so he wrote to repudiate the proposed bargain and declined to go on. There was no exchange. The vendor was doing exactly what he would have been entitled to do if the exchange was going to take place over a table. If one assumes that that had taken place and the purchaser had handed over his document to the vendor across the table, no contract would have come into existence if the vendor had said, "I change my mind" and refused to hand his part over. That, in my opinion, is elementary and in this case that is exactly what happened, except that the post was used to hand over the purchaser's part of the contract and not a manual delivery over the table . . .

It is of the greatest importance, it appears to me, that these principles should be upheld. The inconvenience and chaos into which these matters would be thrown by the adoption of any other rules appear to me to be very great; but ultimately the matter comes down to this: parties become bound by contract when, and in the manner in which, they intend and contemplate becoming bound. That is a question of the facts of each case, but in this case the manner of becoming bound which the parties and their solicitors must have contemplated from the very beginning was the ordinary, customary, convenient method of exchange. From that contemplation neither side and the solicitors to neither side ever resiled, and there is no justification for taking the view that some new method of making the contract was ever contemplated by anybody.

Points for reflection

3-041   1. Lord Greene's proposition that 'parties become bound by contract when, and in the manner in which, they intend and contemplate becoming bound' is now subject to an exception created by the Law of Property (Miscellaneous Provisions) Act 1989 s.2, below, para.4–018. Parties may intend to become bound by a contract for the disposition of an interest in land by offer and acceptance made orally or by correspondence but their intention is ineffective:

Commission for New Towns v Cooper (GB) Ltd [1995] 2 All E.R. 929. There is no binding contract until the terms are incorporated into one document and signed or, where contracts are exchanged, in each. The requirement of exchange still depends on the actual or presumed intention of the parties. If they want to dispense with it, they can; but the requirement of a written signed document incorporating all the terms is statutory and overrides the intention of the parties.

2. The formation of a contract to sell a house is frequently complicated by the fact that it is part of a chain of such transactions. X wants to buy Y's house, Y wants to sell the house to X and they have agreed, subject to contract, on the price. X, however, cannot afford to bind himself to buy until he has secured a binding contract to sell his own house to W, who has agreed, subject to contract, to buy it. Y cannot bind himself to sell until he has secured a binding contract to buy Z's house. The formation of the contract between W and X is dependent on the formation of that between X and Y which is dependent on the formation of that between Y and Z. The chain of contracts contemplated may be represented as follows:

W ◄——► X ◄——► Y ◄——► Z

If the procedure envisaged in *Eccles v Bryant* is followed and each contract is concluded only when an exchange through the post is complete, there is a grave risk that X may find that he has committed himself to buy but that W has changed his mind so that X has two houses on his hands. And Y may find that he has committed himself to sell to X, but Z has changed his mind, so Y is left without a house at all. The risks are inevitable because of the delay involved in the process of exchange. If the solicitors of all four parties could meet together and exchange the signed parts of the contracts virtually simultaneously, all risk could be eliminated; but it will usually be impracticable for them to meet. A solution has been found in a system of "exchange" by telephone. If all the contracts have been signed and all the parties are ready to proceed, W's solicitor may agree to hold the contract signed by W to the order of X's solicitor who in turn will agree to hold X's signed contract to sell to W to the order of W's solicitor. X's solicitor will also agree to hold X's signed contract to buy from Y to the order of Y's solicitor—and so on down the chain. Some of the contracts may have been physically delivered in advance and held to the order of the delivering solicitor until the time agreed for the 'constructive' (or notional) transfer. But it seems that there need be no physical delivery at all. In the leading case of *Domb v Isoz* [1980] Ch. 548 CA, Buckley LJ said: 'Exchange of a written contract for sale is in my judgment effected so soon as each part of the contract signed by the vendor or the purchaser as the case may be, is in the actual or constructive possession of the other party or of his solicitor.' When W's solicitor agreed to hold the contract signed by W to the order of X's solicitor, that document, though physically held by W's solicitor, was in the 'constructive' possession of X's solicitor. This, in Buckley LJ's words, satisfies 'the essential characteristic of exchange of contracts'—that 'each party shall have a document signed by the other party in his possession or control so that, at his own need, he can have the document available for his own use.' The assumption is that a client is no worse off when a document is held on his behalf by someone else's solicitor than when it is held by his own solicitor. The system assumes the integrity of solicitors. When a solicitor is instructed by a vendor or purchaser, he has, in the absence of instructions to the contrary, authority to carry the transaction through in accordance with the custom and practice of the profession, including the procedure of exchange and now the procedure of exchange by telephone. The Law Society's Conditions of Sale, 2.1.2 (1995), provide:

"If the parties' solicitors agree to treat exchange as taking place before duplicate copies are actually exchanged, the contract is made as so agreed."

3. In *Attorney General of Hong Kong v Humphreys Estate (Queen's Gardens) Ltd* [1987] 2 All E.R. 387 the Hong Kong government agreed with HKL Ltd, subject to contract, on an exchange of properties. In pursuance of an agreement in principle, the government took possession of HKL's flats, fitted them out, moved in civil servants and disposed of their former residences. HKL entered the Crown property and demolished the buildings with a view to redevelopment. All material terms had been agreed and the necessary documents drafted and agreed. Before the agreement was executed HKL withdrew and terminated the government's licence to occupy the flats. It was common ground that the agreement was still subject to contract but the government argued that HKL were estopped from withdrawing from it. The Privy Council held that they were not estopped. Lord Templeman said (p.395):

> "In the present case the government acted in the hope that a voluntary agreement in principle expressly made 'subject to contract' and therefore not binding would eventually be followed by the achievement of legal relationships in the form of grants and transfers of property. It is possible but unlikely that in circumstances at present unforeseeable a party to negotiations set out in a document expressed to be 'subject to contract' would be able to satisfy the court that the parties had subsequently agreed to convert the document into a contract or that some form of estoppel had arisen to prevent both parties from refusing to proceed with the transactions envisaged by the document. But in the present case the government chose to begin and elected to continue on terms that either party might suffer a change of mind and withdraw."

He distinguished *Salvation Army Ltd v W Yorks Metropolitan CC* (1980) 41 P. & C.R. 179 where the Bradford City Council told the Army that they intended to acquire the Army's meeting hall for road widening purposes and it was agreed, "subject to contract", that the Army would acquire a new site and build a new hall, receiving £29,097 as compensation. The contract was never executed but the Army acquired the site and built the new hall. The Metropolitan Council, which had taken over the functions of City Council, abandoned the road widening scheme and refused to pay. Woolf J held that they were bound to do so. The Army "were under a mistaken belief that they were under an obligation to vacate the old site and had a right to purchase the new site . . ."; and the defendant either knew or ought to have known that the plaintiffs were continuing to incur expenditure under that mistaken belief and allowed them to continue to do so. The defendant was estopped from denying that the supposed right and obligation existed. In the *Hong Kong* case neither party was under any mistake. (On estoppel, see below, Ch.11).

In the next chapter, we will revisit "subject to" (including "subject to contract") cases in the context of the requirement that agreements should be reasonably certain and complete. However, before we leave the need for unqualified offer and acceptance in the present chapter, we can consider the case of *Air Studios (Lyndhurst) Limited v Lombard North Central Plc* [2012] EWHC 3162 (QB), where the parties were negotiating for the sale of equipment used in the film, television and audio post-production business. There was a string of emails between the parties at one point in which Air Studios were invited to make "a FINAL offer by 12 noon tomorrow [August 19, 2011]". They duly made an offer on the morning of August 19 but it was expressed to be "subject to contract". Lombard, wanting a clean offer, sought clarification as to what Air Studios meant by "subject to contract". To which, Air Studios sent the following one line response: "Our offer is not conditional but there will have to be a sale contract." Later that day, Lombard confirmed to Air Studios that its offer had been successful. However, Lombard subsequently denied that this exchange constituted a binding contract between the parties, arguing (i) that Air Studios had not made a clean offer and (ii) that Lombard's own confirmation of Air Studios' offer having been successful was not an acceptance.

AIR STUDIOS (LYNDHURST) LIMITED v LOMBARD NORTH CENTRAL

[2012] EWHC 3162 (QB)

MALES J

Liability—the law

3–042

5. In deciding whether the parties have reached agreement, the whole course of the parties' negotiations must be considered and an objective test must be applied: *Chitty on Contracts*, 31st edition (2012), Vol 1, paras 2-028 and 2-029. Once the parties have to all outward appearances agreed in the same terms on the same subject matter, usually by a process of offer and acceptance, a contract will have been formed. The subjective reservations of one party do not prevent the formation of a binding contract. Further, it is perfectly possible for the parties to conclude a binding contract, even though it is understood between them that a formal document recording or even adding to the terms agreed will need to be executed subsequently. Whether they do intend to be bound in such circumstances, or only as and when the formal document is executed, depends on an objective appraisal of their words and conduct.

6. These principles are well established. They were summarised, for example, by Lord Clarke giving the judgment of the Supreme Court in *RTS Flexible Systems Ltd v. Molkerei Alois Muller GmbH* [2010] UKSC 14, [2010] 1 WLR 753 at [45]:

> "The general principles are not in doubt. Whether there was a binding contract between the parties and if so, upon what terms depends upon what they have agreed. It depends not upon their subjective state of mind, but upon a consideration of what was communicated between them by words or conduct, and whether that leads objectively to a conclusion that they intended to create legal relations and had agreed upon all the terms which they regarded or the law requires as essential for the formation of legally binding relations. Even if certain terms of economic or other significance have not been finalised, an objective appraisal of their words and conduct may lead to the conclusion that they did not intend agreement of such terms to be a precondition to a concluded and legally binding agreement."

7. Lord Clarke went on at [49] to set out the well known summary of the relevant principles by Lloyd LJ in *Pagnan SpA v. Feed Products Ltd* [1987] 2 Lloyd's Rep 601 at 619, adding that the same principles apply where the question is whether a contract was concluded in correspondence as well as by oral communications and conduct:

> "(1) In order to determine whether a contract has been concluded in the course of correspondence, one must first look to the correspondence as a whole. . .
> (2) Even if the parties have reached agreement on all the terms of the proposed contract, nevertheless they may intend that the contract shall not become binding until some further condition has been fulfilled. That is the ordinary 'subject to contract' case.
> (3) Alternatively, they may intend that the contract shall not become binding until some further term or terms have been agreed. . .
> (4) Conversely, the parties may intend to be bound forthwith even though there are further terms still to be agreed or some further formality to be fulfilled. . .
> (5) If the parties fail to reach agreement on such further terms, the existing contract is not invalidated unless the failure to reach agreement on such further terms renders the contract as a whole unworkable or void for uncertainty.
> (6) It is sometimes said that the parties must agree on the essential terms and it is only matters of detail

which can be left over. This may be misleading, since the word 'essential' in that context is ambiguous. If by 'essential' one means a term without which the contract cannot be enforced then the statement is true: the law cannot enforce an incomplete contract. If by 'essential' one means a term which the parties have agreed to be essential for the formation of a binding contract, then the statement is tautologous. If by 'essential' one means only a term which the Court regards as important as opposed to a term which the Court regards as less important or a matter of detail, the statement is untrue. It is for the parties to decide whether they wish to be bound and if so, by what terms, whether important or unimportant. It is the parties who are, in the memorable phrase coined by the Judge [at page 611] 'the masters of their contractual fate'. Of course the more important the term is the less likely it is that the parties will have left it for future decision. But there is no legal obstacle which stands in the way of the parties agreeing to be bound now while deferring important matters to be agreed later. It happens every day when parties enter into so-called 'heads of agreement'."

8. The fourth of these principles was already well established by the time of Parker J's judgment in *Von Hatzfeld-Wildenburg v. Alexander* [1912] 1 Ch 288. Parker J said at 288:

"It appears to be well settled by the authorities that if the documents or letters relied on as constituting a contract contemplate the execution of a further contract between the parties, it is a question of construction whether the execution of the further contract is a condition or term of the bargain or whether it is a mere expression of the desire of the parties as to the manner in which the transaction already agreed to will in fact go through. In the former case, there is no enforceable contract either because the condition is unfulfilled or because the law does not recognise a contract to enter into a contract. In the latter case, there is a binding contract and the reference to the more formal document may be ignored."

9. I refer also to the helpful summary by Andrew Smith J in *Bear Stearns Bank plc v. Forum Global Equity Ltd* [2007] EWHC 1576 (Comm) at [171]:

"The proper approach is, I think, to ask how a reasonable man, versed in the business, would have understood the exchanges between the parties. Nor is there any legal reason that the parties should not conclude a contract while intending later to reduce their contract to writing and expecting that the written document should contain more detailed definition of the parties' commitment than had previously been agreed."

10. More recently, this principle was applied by the Court of Appeal in *Immingham Storage Company Ltd v. Clear Plc* [2011] EWCA Civ 89, 135 Con LR 224. The facts there were particularly compelling in favour of a conclusion that the parties intended to be bound notwithstanding the contemplation that a formal contract would be signed in due course. The parties had reached express agreement in writing as to the application of one party's standard terms and conditions; certain subjects (board approval and tank availability) which had previously been stipulated had been lifted; the defendant had been expressly assured of the availability of the tank space in question and that it could now proceed to source its product; and the reference to a formal contract to be sent was stated to be in confirmation of what had been agreed. Giving the judgment of the court, David Richards J at [19] and [25] contrasted these factors with a case where agreement was stated to be subject to contract or subject to execution of a formal agreement and observed that they pointed overwhelmingly to an intention to create a contract. He added:

"Set against those factors, the provision that a 'formal contract will then follow in due course' does not indicate that the claimant's acceptance of the signed quotation will be no more than an agreement subject to contract."

11. Of course, these facts were merely an example, albeit a particularly strong one, of a case falling on one side of the line. Each case will depend on its own facts.

12. Because the existence of a binding agreement needs to be determined objectively and does not depend on the parties' subjective state of mind, evidence from the parties about what they intended by or understood from their written communications is of little or no relevance. There was a certain amount of such evidence from the witnesses on both sides in this case, despite the fact that the objective nature of the question was common ground, but such evidence was of no real assistance when all of the parties' relevant exchanges were in writing. The evidence was, however, relevant in informing me of the background against which the parties' negotiations took place.

The facts

35. [On 18 August 2011, Mr Howard for Lombard e-mailed Mr Boote for Air Studios in the following terms]:

"Please submit your final offer that, in your view, would reflect the value of the assets to you by 12 noon tomorrow (Friday 19 August). Please note that the assets will be sold as is where is (ex site) will be the customers responsibility to provide the landlord with suitable method statements of extraction where required."

36. Although something seems to have gone wrong with the wording of the last sentence, it is clear that the offer being sought was on the basis that it would be the buyer's responsibility to collect the equipment from the site at its own expense. Once again, a final offer capable of acceptance was requested, in the context of a competitive bidding process.

37. Mr Woolf tried again to obtain some further information, asking whether the competing bidder was taking over the premises as well as the equipment or just the equipment, but Mr Howard maintained his determination not to divulge any information about what other parties were offering. He repeated his request for Air Studios to confirm its "final offer by the due date", that is to say, noon on 19 August 2011.

38. On 19 August 2011 at 10.20 hours Mr Boote made an offer on behalf of Air Studios as follows:

"Air would subject to contract be prepared to increase our offer for the items on the lease summary, from the settlement figure we spoke about to £100,000. I trust this will be acceptable to you . . ."

39. I would make two comments regarding this offer. First, as was common ground, it was expressed to be "subject to contract" and therefore was not an offer capable of being accepted so as to give rise to a binding contract. Therefore it was not what Lombard had been asking for. Second, and leaving the "subject to contract" point on one side, it increased the price which Air Studios was willing to offer, but did not otherwise change the basis of the offer. Miss Windle submits that the "lease summary" referred to either was or might reasonably have been understood as a document prepared by Mr Howard which had listed the equipment identified at the Noel Street premises. However, I do not accept this. So far it had been clear that the "lease summary" referred to in earlier messages had set out the sums outstanding under the Agreements and that the parties were negotiating with a view to the sale of all of the equipment covered by those Agreements. If this e-mail had been intended, not merely to increase the price which Air Studios was willing to pay, but also to change the basis on which the parties were negotiating, much clearer language would have been expected.

40. The qualification that Air Studios' offer was "subject to contract" was immediately questioned by Mr Howard, who responded 20 minutes later, at 10.40 hours:

"Please can you clarify what you mean by subject to contract as any offers we receive need to be unconditional."

41. This reiterated, as was already clear, that Lombard was seeking an offer capable of being accepted immediately.

42. Air Studios replied, this time by Mr Woolf as Mr Boote was in the course of boarding a plane, at 10.50 hours on 19 August 2011:

"Our offer is not conditional but there will have to be a sale contract."

43. There is an issue between the parties as to the true meaning of this one sentence e-mail. Miss Smith [for Air Studios] submits that the first part of the sentence ("Our offer is not conditional") in effect withdrew the previous reference to "subject to contract" and made clear that the offer was indeed unconditional (and therefore capable of being accepted) as had been requested, while the second part ("but there will have to be a sale contract") explained that Air Studios was contemplating the execution of a formal contract after agreement had been reached, which would no doubt have been necessary or useful for both parties for record-keeping purposes, but which would not affect the binding nature of the agreement which would be reached in the event of acceptance of the offer. Miss Windle [for Lombard], however, submits that the sentence meant that no binding contract would be concluded until the sale contract referred to was executed. This would mean, however, that the two parts of the sentence contradicted each other, the clarification in the first part that the offer was not conditional being immediately superseded by the imposition of a condition to the same effect as the words "subject to contract" which had prompted the request for clarification in the first place.

44. In my judgment the natural meaning of this e-mail is as submitted by Miss Smith. That is the only meaning which gives proper effect to the sentence as a whole. For Air Studios to have sent a message to the effect submitted by Miss Windle would have made no commercial sense.

45. At 11.08 on 19 August 2011 Mr Howard sent a further e-mail as follows:

"Just to clarify, the assets will be sold as is where is (ex site) and it will be the purchasers responsibility to provide the landlord with suitable method statements of extraction where required and agree acceptable timescales for removal with the landlord/tenants.

If you are successful in your bid, which we will convey to you after 12 noon today, the selling process will be conducted by the issuing of an invoice with our standard terms and conditions as attached, with the additional comments outlined above.

The goods will pass title to the successful bidder once we have received the agreed funds in full "

A link to a web address containing Lombard's terms of sale was included at the foot of the e-mail.

46. Once again there is an issue as to the effect of this e-mail. The first paragraph merely repeated what was already clear. Miss Smith submits that the second paragraph ("If you are successful in your bid . . .") contemplated two steps. First, it contemplated that Air Studios would be notified (if that was the case) that it had been successful in its bid, which could only mean that its offer had been accepted, in preference to that of the competing bidder, so as to give rise to a binding contract upon such notification occurring. Second, it went on to explain the process which Lombard contemplated would then take place in order to draw up the formal contract which both parties would need and which Air Studios had already indicated would be necessary. Miss Windle, however, submits that this e-mail demonstrates an intention to be bound only at the conclusion of this process, so that there could be no binding contract until (at least) acceptance by Air Studios of the Lombard terms and conditions.

47. I consider that Miss Smith's submission makes better sense of this e-mail. On Lombard's approach, what was described as a notification that Air Studios had been successful in its bid would in reality be no such thing. It would amount to no more than an expression of willingness to negotiate further (in effect, "if you are successful, we will negotiate with you further", an interpretation which Miss Smith rightly described as unrealistic). Moreover, those further negotiations would take place in circumstances where (if notification of success was to mean anything) Lombard would be letting the rival bidder go before it had secured a binding commitment from Air Studios. That would not make much commercial sense.

48. At 15.08 hours on 19 August 2011 came the e-mail which Air Studios contends resulted in a binding contract and which is therefore the critical document in the case. Mr Howard wrote in the following terms (with paragraph numbering added by me for ease of reference):

"(1) Please accept this email as confirmation that you have been successful with your offer of £100,000 plus VAT for the assets covered by the three agreements AO11000394, AG37001367, AR530000316. Please see attached Excel sheet of the items positively identified by our agent.

(2) Please provide an order confirming your agreement to progress with the sale based on the Terms and Conditions provided to you within the previous email below, please confirm the invoice address and I will raise a VAT invoice and email a copy to you today.

(3) Please could you confirm on your order how quickly you will be able to provide us with cleared funds. Once we have obtained cleared funds we will provide consent for you to collect the assets.

(4) I have been made aware that the new tenants have moved into the premises yesterday, I would therefore like to complete this as quickly as possible to minimise any recourse or delaying tactics that the landlord tenant may try and level against you."

49. Miss Smith submits that this e-mail, in particular paragraph (1), constituted a clean acceptance of Air Studios' offer, so that a contract was concluded at that point, and that the remaining paragraphs of the e-mail do not detract from this conclusion. Miss Windle, however, submits that:

"(a) any acceptance of Air Studios' offer (if such there was) did not correspond with the terms of that offer, but introduced new and different terms, in particular as to the price to be paid and the terms and conditions which would apply;

(b) there was no agreement as to the items which were to be the subject of any sale contract;

(c) there was no agreement as to the terms and conditions which would apply to any contract; and

(d) it was clear that Lombard did not intend a binding contract to be concluded until further matters were agreed, including acceptance by Air Studios of Lombard's terms and conditions.

50. I take these points in turn. As to whether there was correspondence between offer and acceptance so far as the price was concerned, Miss Windle drew attention to the fact that whereas Air Studios' offer had been to buy the equipment for a price of £100,000, with no mention of VAT, this e-mail from Lombard referred to "your offer of £100,000 plus VAT". She suggested that there was as a result no correspondence even as to the basic question of price between the offer and its purported acceptance. However, this was clearly not a point which

occurred to anyone at the time. It is apparent that Lombard's reference to "your offer of £100,000 plus VAT" was not intended as a counter offer, but was merely a statement that it had understood Air Studios' offer to be an offer to purchase the equipment for a price of £100,000 plus VAT and not for a gross price of £100,000 inclusive of VAT. In my judgment that was a correct understanding of the effect of Air Studios' offer in its context, which context included the fact that, as would have been obvious, Air Studios would have been able to reclaim any VAT which it had paid as part of the purchase price. (I have no doubt, moreover, that if this understanding had not been correct, Air Studios would immediately have said so). Accordingly there is nothing in this VAT point.

51. As for the items which were to be the subject of any contract, I accept that in order for a binding contract of sale to be concluded there must be sufficient certainty as to what is to be sold. However, as I have already explained, the basis of the parties' negotiations thus far was that Lombard had invited Air Studios to bid for the entirety of the assets covered by the three leases. The issue, therefore, is whether the reference in paragraph (1) of the e-mail to "the attached Excel sheet of the items positively identified by our agent" either made clear that any contract was to be limited to the items thus identified or at any rate introduced sufficient uncertainty about the matter to mean that the parties were no longer operating on the same understanding. In my judgment it did neither of these things. It was merely a statement of fact identifying the items which Lombard's agent had positively identified. It did not say that any remaining items were not present, or were not intended to be the subject of any sale contract, or that the basis on which the parties had so far been negotiating no longer applied.

52. As for the fact that there was no agreement as to the terms and conditions which would apply to any contract, that is true but, as indicated at [5] to [11] above, this does not necessarily mean that the parties did not intend to conclude a binding contract at this stage leaving further matters to be agreed subsequently. The real question is whether, viewing the matter objectively, that is what they did intend.

53. Lombard's case is that this e-mail made clear that it did not intend to conclude a contract at this stage, that it was merely indicating a wish to pursue a possible contract with Air Studios further, and that no contract could be concluded until, at the least, three things had happened, namely (a) Air Studios submitted a formal written order, (b) that order confirmed its acceptance of Lombard's terms and conditions, and (c) Air Studios identified the address which should be stated on Lombard's invoice.

54. In order to determine whether this e-mail constituted an acceptance of Air Studios' offer or (in effect) a counter offer stating the terms on which Lombard would be prepared to contract, it is necessary to read the message as a whole against the background which I have set out, and to give it a meaning which makes commercial sense in preference to one which does not. Adopting that approach, I consider that the e-mail was a clean acceptance of Air Studios' offer to purchase the equipment which gave rise to a binding contract.

55. That conclusion gives proper effect to the opening paragraph which refers unequivocally to confirmation that Air Studios had been successful with its offer. If in fact the message is read as going on to say that further steps would be necessary before any contract would be concluded, that opening statement would be highly misleading. In my judgment the better reading of the message, which gives effect to it as a whole and also makes commercial sense, is that Air Studios' offer was accepted with immediate binding effect, and that Lombard went on in the remainder of the e-mail to indicate the further terms which it hoped to agree and the process which it wished to follow in order to implement what had been agreed, but that these matters were not intended to constitute conditions precedent to the conclusion of a binding contract. The fact that some of these matters, such as the provision of an invoice address, were purely administrative and cannot sensibly have been understood as essential to the formation of a contract supports this reading of the e-mail. This conclusion is confirmed also by the context in which the e-mail was sent, which was that Air Studios was known to be participating in a competitive bidding process, in which Lombard had repeatedly requested the submission of a final bid by a stated deadline, after which a firm decision whether to contract with Air Studios would be promptly notified without more ado. In those circumstances Air Studios was entitled to expect a firm decision one way or the other, and reasonably understood the message which it got to be precisely that.

Was an Agreement concluded by the parties on 19 August 2011?

70. A binding contract was concluded on 19 August 2011. Air Studios' e-mail at 10.20 hours on that day (see [38] above) was not an offer capable of being accepted because it was expressed to be "subject to contract", but this qualification was removed by the clarification sent at 10.50 hours ([42] above), whereupon the offer was an offer capable of being accepted notwithstanding that it contemplated the execution of a further more formal document. Lombard's own clarification sent at 11.08 hours ([45] above) referring to its standard terms and conditions was not a counter offer and did not change the basis on which the parties were negotiating, namely that Lombard would make a firm decision one way or the other whether to accept Air Studios' offer and would notify its decision after midday, albeit that in the event of an acceptance, further formalities (not such

as to prevent the conclusion of a binding contract) were contemplated. Lombard did then accept Air Studios' offer by its e-mail of 15.08 hours ([48] above).

3. The Duration of an Offer

HYDE v WRENCH

Rolls Court (1840) 3 Beav. 334; 4 Jur. 1106; 49 E.R. 132

3–043   June 6. The defendant wrote to the plaintiff offering to sell his farm for £1,000. The plaintiff's agent immediately called on the defendant, and made an offer of £950, which the defendant wished to have a few days to consider.

June 27. The defendant wrote to say that he could not accept this offer.

June 29. The plaintiff wrote "accepting" the offer of June 6. The plaintiff brought an action for specific performance. The defendant filed a general demurrer.

THE MASTER OF THE ROLLS (LORD LANGDALE)

> Under the circumstances stated in this bill, I think there exists no valid binding contract between the parties for the purchase of the property. The defendant offered to sell it for £1,000, and if that had been at once unconditionally accepted, there would undoubtedly have been a perfect binding contract; instead of that, the plaintiff made an offer of his own, to purchase the property for £950, and he thereby rejected the offer previously made by the defendant. I think that it was not afterwards competent for him to revive the proposal of the defendant, by tendering an acceptance of it; and that, therefore, there exists no obligation of any sort between the parties; the demurrer must be allowed.

STEVENSON v McLEAN

Queen's Bench Division (1880) 5 QBD 346; 49 L.J.Q.B. 701; 42 L.T. 897; 28 W.R. 916

3–044   The plaintiffs and the defendant were negotiating about the sale of a quantity of iron for which the defendant held warrants.

Saturday: The defendant wrote: ". . . I would now sell for 40s. net cash, open till Monday".

Monday: The plaintiffs telegraphed: "Please wire whether you would accept forty for delivery over two months, or if not, longest limit you would give".

The defendant received the telegram at 10.01 a.m. and subsequently sold the iron to a third party.

1.25 pm: the defendant telegraphed that he had sold the iron.

1.34 pm: the plaintiffs having had no reply to their telegram, telegraphed again, accepting the offer to sell at 40s. cash.

1.46 pm: the defendant's telegram arrived.

The plaintiff sued for breach of contract, and the defendant objected that the telegram sent by the plaintiffs on the Monday morning was a rejection of the defendant's offer and a new proposal on the plaintiffs' part, and therefore that the defendant had a right to regard it as putting an end to the original negotiation.

LUSH J

> Looking at the form of the telegram, the time when it was sent, and the state of the iron market, I cannot think this is its fair meaning. The plaintiff Stevenson said he meant it only as an inquiry, expecting an answer for his guidance, and this, I think, is the sense in which the defendant ought to have regarded it.
> It is apparent throughout the correspondence, that the plaintiffs did not contemplate buying the iron on

speculation, but that their acceptance of the defendant's offer depended on their finding someone to take the warrants off their hands. All parties knew that the market was in an unsettled state, and that no one could predict at the early hour when the telegram was sent how the prices would range during the day. It was reasonable that, under these circumstances, they should desire to know before business began whether they were to be at liberty in case of need to make any and what concession as to the time or times of delivery, which would be the time or times of payment, or whether the defendant was determined to adhere to the terms of his letter; and it was highly unreasonable that the plaintiffs should have intended to close the negotiation while it was uncertain whether they could find a buyer or not, having the whole of the business hours of the day to look for one. Then, again, the form of the telegram is one of inquiry. It is not "I offer forty for delivery over two months," which would have likened the case to *Hyde v Wrench* [above] . . . Here there is no counter proposal. The words are, "Please wire whether you would accept forty for delivery over two months, or, if not, the longest limit you would give." There is nothing specific by way of offer or rejection, but a mere inquiry, which should have been answered and not treated as a rejection of the offer. This ground of objection therefore fails.

(The defendant's second objection was that the offer was revoked before it was accepted: see *Byrne v Van Tienhoven*, above. Following that case, Lush J held that a "revocation is nothing till it has been communicated.")

Questions

1. Was the plaintiffs' telegram an offer capable of acceptance by the defendant?   **3–045**

2. Henry writes to George offering to sell him a farm, and adding, 'I expect you to reject this offer upon first consideration, but I want you to consider it further, because I think you will accept when you have thought about it a while.' George immediately writes a rejection which Henry ignores. A fortnight later, having thought the matter over, George sends an acceptance. Is Henry bound?

   (See Oliphant, 'The Duration and Termination of an Offer' 18 Mich.L.R. 201; *Selected Readings on the Law of Contracts*, 251.)

3. V wrote to P offering to sell a house for £30,000. P telegraphed: 'Send lowest cash price. Will give £25,000.' V telegraphed in reply: 'Cannot reduce price.' After receiving this telegram, P purported to accept the original offer. Discuss.

Cf. *Livingstone v Evans* (Alberta Supreme Court) (1925) 4 D.L.R. 762.

Points for reflection

In *Northland Airliners, Ltd v Dennis Ferranti Meters, Ltd* (1970) 114 S.J. 845; *The Times*, October 23, 1970,   **3–046**
the defendants sent a telegram offering to sell aircraft to the plaintiffs for £27,000. The plaintiffs replied by telegram purporting to accept. The Court of Appeal held that there was no contract because the offer required a deposit of £5,000 to be paid in advance but the acceptance stated that £5,000 had been forwarded to the defendants' bank payable to the defendants on delivery; and the offer, being silent as to delivery, required it within a reasonable time, whereas the "acceptance" required delivery within 30 days. (The plaintiffs evidently intended only to inquire if delivery would be made within 30 days but the omission of the word, 'if' through an error in transmission caused the intended inquiry to appear to be a stipulation; and the judge held that the plaintiffs were bound by the telegram as sent.) It was immaterial that the defendants at first thought that they were bound. The second telegram was a counter-offer.

ROUTLEDGE v GRANT

Common Pleas (1828) 4 Bing. 653; 1 M. & P. 717; 3 C. & P. 267; 6 L.J.C.P. 166; 29 R.R. 672; 130 E.R. 920

3-047   The defendant offered to take a lease of the plaintiff's premises, "a definitive answer to be given within six weeks from March 18, 1825." On April 9 the defendant withdrew his offer, and on April 29 the plaintiff purported to accept it. The Court of Common Pleas held that there was no contract.

BEST CJ

Here is a proposal by the defendant to take property on certain terms; namely, that he should be let into possession in July. In that proposal he gives the plaintiff six weeks to consider; but if six weeks are given on one side to accept an offer, the other has six weeks to put an end to it. One party cannot be bound without the other. This was expressly decided in *Cooke v Oxley*, where the defendant proposed to sell, at a certain price, tobacco to the plaintiff, who desired to have till four in the afternoon of that day to agree to or dissent from the proposal; with which terms the defendant complied; and the plaintiff having afterwards sued him for non-delivery of the tobacco, Lord Kenyon put it on the true ground by saying, "At the time of entering into this contract the engagement was all one side; the other party was not bound." Buller J. said, "It has been argued that this must be taken to be a complete sale from the time the condition was complied with: but it was not complied with; for it is not stated that the defendant did agree at four o'clock to the terms of the sale; or even that the goods were kept till that time." I put the present case on the same ground. At the time of entering into this contract the engagement was all on one side. [The Chief Justice then considered *Payne v Cave* (above) and *Adams v Lindsell* (above).] . . . As the defendant repudiated the contract on April 9, before the expiration of the six weeks, he had a right to say that the plaintiff should not enforce it afterwards.

Points for reflection

3-048   1. In *Mountford v Scott* [1975] 1 All E.R. 198 CA, V, in consideration of the payment of £1, granted in writing an option to P to purchase V's house for £10,000, exercisable within six months. Before the option was exercised, V purported to withdraw his offer. P exercised the option and it was held that he was entitled to specific performance of the contract to sell the house. The offer was irrevocable even though the consideration for it might be described as a token payment; and it was the contract for sale which was specifically enforced. The trial judge had wrongly concentrated on the question whether the option agreement was specifically enforceable.

   Was not the decision that the option was irrevocable (as distinct from affording a remedy only in damages) specific enforcement of it? The option was a promise to keep the offer open, and the court held that it must remain open.

   2. In *Watson v Canada Permanent Trust Co* (1972) 27 D.L.R (3d) 735 (British Columbia Supreme Court, Anderson J) it was held, applying the *High Trees* principle (below, Ch.11) that the grantor of an option to buy certain shares was estopped from withdrawing his offer to sell when he knew that the purchaser intended to act on his promise to keep the offer open. The grant of the option was not under seal and the court held that there was no consideration for it; but the grantor knew that the grantee intended to embark on a "salvage operation" of the company which it would not attempt unless it had the right to buy the shares in the company. He made a promise "which any reasonable optionee would believe was not to be withdrawn." He knew the grantee intended to act on the promise, the grantee did so, he would have suffered great prejudice if the grantor could withdraw his promise, so the grantor would not be allowed to do so.

OFFORD v DAVIES

Common Bench (1862) 12 C.B.(n.s.) 748; 31 L.J.C.P. 319; 6 L.T. 579; 10 W.R. 578; 9 Jur. 22 133 R.R. 491; 142 E.R. 1336

The plaintiff alleged that the defendants had promised that, in consideration that the plaintiff would, **3–049** at the request of the defendants, discount bills of exchange to the extent of £600 for Messrs. Davies & Co of Newtown, the defendants would guarantee "for the space of twelve calendar months" the due payment of all such bills. The plaintiff alleged that he had discounted various bills which were dishonoured and that the defendants had broken their promise and had not paid the sums of money payable by the bills of exchange.

The defendants' plea was that, after the making of the guarantee but before the plaintiff had discounted any bills, the defendants had countermanded the guarantee and had requested the plaintiff not to discount the bills.

To this plea the plaintiff demurred: "for that a party having given a guarantee (for a definite period) has no power to countermand it without the assent of the person to whom it is given".

ERLE CJ

The declaration alleged a contract by the defendants, in consideration that the plaintiff would at the request of the defendants discount bills for Davies & Co, not exceeding £600, the defendants promised to guarantee the repayment of such discounts for 12 months, and the discount, and no repayment. The plea was a revocation of the promise before the discount in question; and the demurrer raises the question whether the defendants had a right to revoke the promise. We are of opinion that they had, and that consequently the plea is good.

This promise by itself creates no obligation. It is in effect conditioned to be binding if the plaintiff acts upon it, either to the benefit of the defendants, or to the detriment of himself. But, until the condition has been at least in part fulfilled, the defendants have the power of revoking it. In the case of a simple guarantee for a proposed loan, the right of revocation before the proposal has been acted on did not appear to be disputed. Then, are the rights of the parties affected either by the promise being expressed to be for 12 months, or by the fact that some discounts had been made before that now in question, and repaid? We think not.

The promise to repay for 12 months creates no additional liability on the guarantor, but, on the contrary, fixes a limit in time beyond which his liability cannot extend. And, with respect to other discounts, which had been repaid, we consider each discount as a separate transaction, creating a liability on the defendant till it is repaid, and, after repayment, leaving the promise to have the same operation that it had before any discount was made, and no more.

Judgment for the Defendants.

Point for reflection

In its *6th Interim Report (Statute of Frauds and the Doctrine of Consideration)* (Cmd. 5449, 1937, **3–050** para.38) the Law Revision Committee expressed the following opinion on firm offers:

It appears to us to be undesirable and contrary to business practice that a man who has been promised a period, either expressly defined or until the happening of a certain event, in which to decide whether to accept or to decline an offer cannot rely upon being able to accept it at any time within that period. If the offeror wants a consideration for keeping it open, he can stipulate for it and his offer is then usually called an "option." Merely because he does not so stipulate, he ought not to be allowed to revoke his offer with impunity. We consider that the fixing of a definite period should be regarded as evidence of his intention to make a binding promise to keep his offer open, and that his promise should be enforceable. If no period of time is fixed, we think it may be assumed that no contractual obligation was intended.

It may be noted here that according to the law of most foreign countries a promisor is bound by such a promise. It is particularly undesirable that on such a point the English law should accept a lower moral standard.

Similarly, the Law Commission, in Working Paper No.60, "Firm Offers", provisionally recommended that "An offeror who has promised that he will not revoke his offer for a definite time should be bound by the terms of that promise for a period not exceeding six years, provided that the promise has been made 'in the course of a business' . . ."; and that an offeror who breaks such a promise should be liable to damages. And, in line with much thinking elsewhere, Article 16 of the United Nationas Convention on Contracts for the International Sale of Goods (New York, 2010 version) provides:

(1) Until a contract is concluded an offer may be revoked if the revocation reaches the offeree before he has dispatched an acceptance.

(2) However, an offer cannot be revoked:

(a) if it indicates, whether by stating a fixed time for acceptance or otherwise, that it is irrevocable; or

(b) if it was reasonable for the offeree to rely on the offer as being irrevocable and the offeree has acted in reliance on the offer.

SHUEY v UNITED STATES

Supreme Court of the United States (1875) 92 U.S. 73; 23 L.Ed. 697

3–051 On April 20, 1865, the Secretary of War caused to be published in the public newspapers and otherwise a proclamation, announcing that "liberal rewards will be paid for any information that shall conduce to the arrest of either of the above-named criminals or their accomplices." The proclamation was not limited in terms to any specific period. On November 24, 1865, the President caused to be issued an order revoking the offer of the reward.

In 1866 the claimant discovered and identified Surratt, one of the named persons, and informed the United States authorities. He was, at all times, unaware that the offer of the reward had been revoked.

The claimant's petition was dismissed by the Court of Claims, and he appealed to the Supreme Court of the United States.

STRONG J

> The offer of a reward for the apprehension of Surratt was revoked on November 24, 1865; and notice of the revocation was published. It is not to be doubted that the offer was revocable at any time before it was accepted, and before anything had been done in reliance upon it. There was no contract until its terms were complied with. Like any other offer of a contract, it might, therefore, be withdrawn before rights had accrued under it; and it was withdrawn through the same channel in which it was made. The same notoriety was given to the revocation that was given to the offer; and the findings of fact do not show that any information was given by the claimant, or that he did anything to entitle him to the reward offered, until five months after the offer had been withdrawn. True, it is found that then, and at all times until the arrest was actually made, he was ignorant of the withdrawal; but that is an immaterial fact. The offer of the reward not having been made to him directly, but by means of a published proclamation, he should have known that it could be revoked in the manner in which it was made.

Judgment Affirmed.

Point for reflection

3–052 In *Financings Ltd v Stimson* [1962] 1 W.L.R. 1184; [1962] 3 All E.R. 386, the defendant, on March 16, 1961, at the premises of a dealer signed a form by which he offered to take a car on hire-purchase terms from the plaintiffs. On March 18 he paid a deposit of £70 and was allowed to take the car away from the dealer's premises. He was dissatisfied with it and on March 20 returned it to the dealer, saying he did not want it and (believing himself to be bound by a contract) offered to forfeit his deposit. In the night of March 24 the car was stolen from the dealer's premises and badly damaged. On March 25 the plaintiffs, not having been told that the defendant had returned the car, signed the hire-purchase agreement. It was held by the Court of Appeal:

(i) that the defendant had revoked his offer by returning the car to the dealer. Though he thought he was seeking rescission of a contract, not revoking an offer, it was enough that he had made it clear that he did not want to go on with the transaction. Pearson LJ, dissenting, held that the dealer was an agent only to transmit the revocation which, not having been transmitted, was ineffective. Cf. *Dunmore v Alexander* (above).

(ii) In view of an express provision in the form of contract that the defendant had examined the car and satisfied himself that it was in good order and condition, the offer was conditional on the car remaining in substantially the same condition until the moment of acceptance. That condition not being fulfilled, the acceptance was invalid. Lord Denning M.R. said: ". . . suppose an offer is made to buy a Rolls Royce car at a high price on one day and before it is accepted, it suffers the next day severe damage. Can it be accepted and the offeror bound? My answer to that is: no, because the offer is conditional on the goods at the moment of acceptance remaining in substantially the same condition as at the time of the offer." On this case, see Atiyah, 'Judicial Techniques and the English Law of Contract' 2 *Ottawa Law Rev.* 337, 339.

Problems

1. P offered to buy V's garage business for £10,000, the offer to remain open for seven days. Two days later, plans were announced for a by-pass which would divert the bulk of the traffic from the garage. V posted an acceptance of P's offer before P had an opportunity to revoke it. Is there a contract? (Cf. Lord Atkin in *Bell v Lever Bros*, below, Ch.11).   **3–053**

2. S offered to ship goods from Port Sudan to Belfast on c.i.f. terms. The Suez Canal was then unexpectedly closed for an indefinite period. B accepted before S could revoke his offer. (Cf. Ch.24 below.)

DICKINSON v DODDS

Court of Appeal (1876) 2 Ch.D. 463; 45 L.J.Ch. 777; 34 L.T. 607

On Wednesday, June 10, the defendant delivered to the plaintiff a written offer to sell certain houses, "This offer to be left over until Friday, 9 o'clock a.m., June 12, 1874." In the afternoon of Thursday the plaintiff was informed by a Mr Berry that Dodds had been offering or agreeing to sell the property to one Allan. At about 7.30 that evening the plaintiff left a formal letter of acceptance at the house where Dodds was staying, but it appeared that this letter was overlooked and never delivered to Dodds. On Friday morning at about 7, Berry, who was acting as agent for the plaintiff, handed Dodds a duplicate of the letter of acceptance and explained its purport to him. It appeared that the day before Dodds had signed a formal contract for the sale of property to Allan. Bacon VC made a decree of specific performance against Dodds, who appealed.   **3–054**

JAMES LJ

It must, to constitute a contract, appear that the two minds were at one, at the same moment of time, that is, that there was an offer continuing up to the time of the acceptance. If there was not such a continuing offer, then the acceptance comes to nothing. Of course it may well be that the one man is bound in some way or other to let the other man know that his mind with regard to the offer has been changed; but in this case, beyond all question, the plaintiff knew that Dodds was no longer minded to sell the property to him as plainly and clearly as if Dodds had told him in so many words, "I withdraw the offer." This is evident from the plaintiff's own statements in the bill . . . It is to my mind quite clear that before there was any attempt at acceptance by the plaintiff, he was perfectly well aware that Dodds had changed his mind, and that he had in fact agreed to sell the property to Allan. It is impossible, therefore, to say there was ever that existence of the same mind between the two parties which is essential in point of law to the making of an agreement. I am of opinion, therefore, that the plaintiff has failed to prove that there was any binding contract between Dodds and himself.

MELLISH LJ

If an offer has been made for the sale of property, and before that offer is accepted, the person who has made the offer enters into a binding agreement to sell the property to someone else, and the person to whom the offer was first made receives notice in some way that the property has been sold to another person, can he after that make a binding contract by the acceptance of the offer? I am of the opinion that he cannot. The law may be right or wrong in saying that a person who has given to another a certain time within which to accept an offer is not bound by his promise to give that time; but, if he is not bound by that promise, and may still sell the property to someone else, and if it be the law that, in order to make a contract, the two minds must be in agreement at some one time, that is, at the time of the acceptance, how is it possible that when the person to whom the offer has been made knows that the person who has made the offer has sold the property to someone else, and that, in fact, he has not remained in the same mind to sell it to him, he can be at liberty to accept the offer and thereby make a binding contract? It seems to me that would be simply absurd. If a man makes an offer to sell a particular horse in his stable, and says, "I will give you until the day after tomorrow to accept the offer," and the next day goes and sells the horse to somebody else, and receives the purchase-money from him, can the person to whom the offer was originally made then come and say, "I accept," so as to make a binding contract, and so as to be entitled to recover damages for the non-delivery of the horse? If the rule of law is that a mere offer to sell property, which can be withdrawn at any time, and which is made dependent on the acceptance of the person to whom it is made, is a mere nudum pactum, how is it possible that the person to whom the offer has been made can by acceptance make a binding contract after he knows that the person who has made the offer has sold the property to someone else? It is admitted law that, if a man who makes an offer dies the offer cannot be accepted after he is dead, and parting with the property has very much the same effect as the death of the owner, for it makes the performance of the offer impossible. I am clearly of the opinion that, just as when a man who has made an offer dies before it is accepted it is impossible that it can be accepted, so when once the person to whom the offer was made knows that the property has been sold to someone else, it is too late for him to accept the offer, and on that ground I am clearly of opinion that there was no binding contract for the sale of the property by Dodds to Dickinson, and even if there had been, it seems to me that the sale of the property to Allan was first in point of time. However, it is not necessary to consider, if there had been two binding contracts, which of them would be entitled to priority in equity, because there is no binding contract between Dodds and Dickinson.

Baggallay J. A. concurred.

Decision of Bacon VC Reversed.

Question

3-055 In the headnote to *Dickinson v Dodds* in the Law Reports the following statement appears: "Semble, that the sale of the property to a third person would itself amount to a withdrawal of the offer even although the person to whom the offer was first made had no knowledge of the sale."

Do you consider that this is an accurate statement of the law?

Problems

1. On Monday Charles offers to sell Derek his house for £12,000, the offer to remain open for **3–056** seven days, "unless I sell the property in the meantime." On Tuesday Charles sells the house to Edward for £12,500. On Wednesday Derek, who has heard nothing of the transaction with Edward, communicates his acceptance of the original offer. Advise Charles.

2. On June 1 Angus wrote to Bruce offering to sell his Tudor house for £200,000, the offer to remain open for a week. On June 4 Angus reads in *The Times*: "Mr Bruce has informed the National Trust that he has bought Mr Angus's well-known Tudor Mansion . . .". Later the same day, Claymore offered Angus £210,000 for the house. Angus accepted, and 'phoned Bruce to say that the offer was no longer available. When the call came through Bruce was just about to leave his office to post a letter of acceptance, written the day before, but overlooked by the office boy. Advise Bruce

----

MANCHESTER DIOCESAN COUNCIL FOR EDUCATION v COMMERCIAL AND GENERAL INVESTMENTS LTD

For the facts, see above, para.3–021.

BUCKLEY J

If I am right in thinking that there was a contract on September 15, 1964, that disposes of the case but, in **3–057** case I should be held to be wrong in that view, I will now consider the other point in the case and will for this purpose assume that no contract was made at that date. On this basis no contract can have been concluded before January 7, 1965. The defendant contends that, as the tender stipulated no time within which it must be accepted, it was an implied term of the offer that it must be accepted, if at all, within a reasonable time. It is said that acceptance on January 7 was not within a reasonable time.

It has long been recognised as being the law that, where an offer is made in terms which fix no time limit for acceptance, the offer must be accepted within a reasonable time to make a contract. (*Chitty on Contracts*, (22nd edn, 1961), p. 90, para. 89; *Williams on Vendor and Purchaser*, (4th edn, 1936), p. 16; *Halsbury's Laws of England*, (3rd edn, 1954), Vol. 8, p. 71, para. 124). There seems, however, to be no reported case in which the reason for this is explained. There appear to me to be two possible views on methods of approaching the problem. First it may be said that by implication the offer is made upon terms that, if it is not accepted within a reasonable time, it must be treated as withdrawn. Alternatively, it may be said that, if the offeree does not accept the offer within a reasonable time, he must be treated as having refused it. On either view the offer would cease to be a live one upon the expiration of what, in the circumstances of the particular case, should be regarded as a reasonable time for acceptance. The first of these alternatives involves implying a term that if the offer is not accepted within a reasonable time, it shall be treated as withdrawn or lapsing at the end of that period, if it has not then been accepted: the second is based upon an inference to be drawn from the conduct of the offeree, that is, that having failed to accept the offer within a reasonable time he has manifested an intention to refuse it. If in the first alternative the time which the offeror is to be treated as having set for acceptance is to be such a time as is reasonable at the date of the offer, what is reasonable must depend on circumstances then existing and reasonably likely to arise during the continuance of the offer; but it would not be unlikely that the offeror and offeree would make different assessments of what would be reasonable, even if, as might quite possibly not be the case, they based those judgments on identical known and anticipated circumstances. No doubt a court could resolve any dispute about this, but this approach clearly involves a certain degree of uncertainty about the precise terms of the offer. If, on the other hand, the time which the offeror is to be treated as having set for acceptance is to be such a time as turns out to be reasonable in the light of circumstances then existing and of circumstances arising thereafter during the continuance of the offer, whether foreseeable or not, an additional element of uncertainty is introduced. The second alternative, on the other hand, involves simply an objective assessment of facts and the determination of the question whether on the facts the offeree should, in fairness to both parties, be regarded as having refused the offer.

It does not seem to me that either party is in greater need of protection by the law in this respect than the other. Until his offer has been accepted it is open to the offeror at any time to withdraw it or put a limit on the time for acceptance. On the other hand, the offeree can at any time refuse the offer or, unless he has been guilty of unreasonable delay, accept it. Neither party is at a disadvantage. Unless authority constrains me to do otherwise, I am strongly disposed to prefer the second alternative to the first.

I have dealt with this part of the case at some length because, if the first alternative were the correct view of the law and if what is reasonable had to be ascertained as at the time of the offer, the subsequent conduct of the parties would be irrelevant to the question how long the offer should be treated as remaining open. In my opinion, however, the subsequent conduct of the parties is relevant to the question, which I think is the right test, whether the offeree should be held to have refused the offer by his conduct.

In my judgment, the letter of September 15, 1964, excludes the possibility of imputing to the plaintiff a refusal of the offer. If that letter does not itself constitute an effective acceptance, it clearly discloses an intention to accept from which there is nothing to suggest a departure before January 7, 1965. Accordingly, if no contract was formed earlier, I am of the opinion that it was open to the plaintiff to accept it on January 7 and that the plaintiff's letter of that date was effectual to bind the defendant contractually.

Order for Specific Performance and Costs.

BRADBURY v MORGAN

Exchequer (1862) 1 H. & C. 249; 158 E.R. 877; 31 L.J.Ex. 462; 7 L.T. 104; 8 Jur.(n.s.) 918; 10 W.R. 776; 26 Digest 208, 1625

3-058 The defendants were the executors of J. M. Leigh who had written the following letter to the plaintiffs:

3 George Yard, Lombard St.,

London, May 3, 1858

Messrs. Bradbury, Greatorex and Co

Gentlemen,

I request that you will give credit in the usual way of your business to Henry Jones Leigh, of Leather Lane, Holborn; and in consideration of your doing so, I hereby engage to guarantee the regular payment of the running balance of his account with you, until I give you notice to the contrary, to the extent of one hundred pounds sterling.

I remain, etc.

J. M. Leigh.

Limit £100

The plaintiffs thereafter credited H.J. Leigh in the usual way of their business. J.M. Leigh died and the plaintiffs, having no notice or knowledge of his death, continued to supply H.J. Leigh with goods on credit. £100 was owing by H.J. Leigh to the plaintiffs and the defendants declined to pay, arguing that they were not liable as the debts were contracted and incurred after the death of J.M. Leigh and not in his lifetime.

POLLOCK CB

We are all of opinion that the plaintiff is entitled to judgment. No doubt, if this were merely an implied contract which arose from a request, it would be revoked by the death of either party. *Blades v Free* (9 B. & C. 167)[1] is an authority that a request is revoked, but a contract is not put an end to, by death. The language here used, "I request you will give credit," is a mere mode of civil expression, and the party using it never meant to request in that sense which Mr Brown has suggested. Instead of saying, "I will thank you to give credit"; or "you will oblige me by giving credit," he says, "I request you will give credit." Whether his death was contemplated, I do not know. The probability is, that if it had been suggested the plaintiffs would have required some notice before the guarantee was determined; but this is a contract, and the question is whether it is put an end to by the death of the guarantor. There is no direct authority to that effect; and I think that all reason and authority, such as there is, are against that proposition, and that the plaintiffs are therefore entitled to judgment.

BRAMWELL B

I am of the same opinion. The general rule is thus stated in *Williams on Executors* (5th edn), p. 1559: "The executors or administrators so completely represent their testator or intestate, with respect to the liabilities above mentioned, that every bond, or covenant, or contract of the deceased includes them, although they are not named in the terms of it; for the executors or administrators of every person are implied in himself."

The only exception is where the contract is in respect of the personal qualification of the testator or intestate, and that does not apply to the present case. If the guarantee had been in these terms: "I request you to deliver to A tomorrow morning goods to the value of £50, and in consideration of your so doing I will pay you," and before the morning the guarantor died, but the goods were duly delivered; I can see no reason why the personal representative of the guarantor should not be liable; and whether a guarantor says, "deliver some goods on a given day," or "deliver a quantity of goods upon any day or days," can make no difference. Very likely a tradesman, who would not trust in the first instance without a guarantee, would not deliver any goods after the death of the guarantor, but, however that may be, the executor must give some timely notice in order to put an end to the contract. Mr Brown relied on the words, "I request you will give credit," but they are of no importance; for this is not a case of authority given by the deceased.

Judgment for the Plaintiffs.

Question

When J. M. Leigh died, had he made a contract guaranteeing payment of debts incurred thereafter by H. J. Leigh? Or a standing offer to do so? (Cf. *Offord v Davies*, above). What was the court's view? Is the case an authority on the termination of offers?

3-059

It should be noted that, in *Coulthart v Clementson* (1879) 5 QBD 42 it was held by Bowen J that a continuing guarantee was revoked where the creditor (a bank) had notice of the guarantor's death and the fact that he had made a will. This amounted to notice of trusts which might be incompatible with the continuance of the guarantee. In *Re Whelan* [1897] 1 I.R. 575 Chatterton VC held that the same principle applied a fortiori where the guarantor died intestate; for, while an option to continue the guarantee might exist in the case of a will, it could not do so in the case of intestacy.

In both of these cases the guarantee was an ordinary standing offer and was revocable by the guarantor in his lifetime. The position is different where the guarantee is given for consideration and is therefore irrevocable. So *Coulthart v Clementson* was distinguished by the Court of Appeal in *Lloyd's v Harper* (1880) 16 Ch.D. 290 (and see below, Ch.13, section 4) where the deceased guarantor undertook responsibility for his son's engagements as a Lloyd's underwriter, in consideration of the son's being

---

[1]   T's mistress had authority to bind T by her contracts for necessaries as if she had been his wife. The plaintiff supplied goods to the mistress, not knowing that T had died. It was held that T's executor was not bound to pay for the goods. The authority of an agent is automatically terminated by the death of his principal.

admitted as such by Lloyd's. It was held that the guarantee, being given for a once for all consideration, was irrevocable in the testator's lifetime and was not revoked by his death.

----

4. THE BATTLE OF THE FORMS

3–060   In many business sectors, standard forms of contract and standard sets of terms and conditions are
regularly used. Where a particular standard form has been negotiated by the key stakeholders in the
sector, and where the expectation is that that form will be used, there is unlikely to be serious argument
about which terms apply to the transaction (although cf. *British Crane Hire Corp Ltd v Ipswich Plant Hire
Ltd*, below Ch.7). However, where each contractor seeks to introduce and then rely on its own standard
terms and conditions, this makes for a more complex process of negotiation; and, if those terms and
conditions are fundamentally inconsistent with one another, we have the makings of a "Battle of the
Forms" dispute. *Butler Machine Tool* (below) is the leading case in English law on this kind of problem.

BUTLER MACHINE TOOL CO LTD v EX-CELL-O CORPORATION (ENGLAND) LTD

Court of Appeal [1979] 1 W.L.R. 401; [1979] 1 All E.R. 965

3–061   On May 23, 1969 the plaintiffs offered to sell a machine to the defendants for £75,535. The terms
of the offer included a condition that all orders were accepted only on the sellers' terms which were
to prevail over any terms and conditions in the buyers' order. There was also a condition that any
increase in the cost of manufacture by the date of delivery should be added to the price. On May 27,
1969 the defendants replied ordering the machine but on different terms and conditions, not including a price variation clause. At the foot of the order was a tear-off slip reading, "We accept your order
on the Terms and Conditions stated thereon." On June 5, 1969 the plaintiffs signed and returned it,
writing, ". . . your official order . . . is being entered in accordance with our revised quotation of 23rd
May . . .". The plaintiffs recovered an additional £2,892 under the price variation clause. The defendants appealed.

LORD DENNING MR

> I have much sympathy with the judge's approach to this case. In many of these cases our traditional analysis
> of offer, counter-offer, rejection, acceptance and so forth is out-of-date. This was observed by Lord Wilberforce
> in *New Zealand Shipping Co Ltd v AM Satterthwaite* [below, para.13–006]. The better way is to look at all the
> documents passing between the parties and glean from them, or from the conduct of the parties, whether they
> have reached agreement on all material points, even though there may be differences between the forms and
> conditions printed on the back of them. As Lord Cairns L.C. said in *Brogden v Metropolitan Railway Co* (1877) 2
> App. Cas. 666 at 672:
>
>> ". . . there may be a consensus between the parties far short of a complete mode of expressing it, and
>> that consensus may be discovered from letters or from other documents of an imperfect and incomplete
>> description."
>
> Applying this guide, it will be found that in most cases when there is a "battle of forms" there is a contract as
> soon as the last of the forms is sent and received without objection being taken to it. That is well observed in
> *Benjamin on Sale* (9th ed.), pp. 84–85. The difficulty is to decide which form, or which part of which form, is a
> term or condition of the contract. In some cases the battle is won by the man who fires the last shot. He is the
> man who puts forward the latest term and conditions: and, if they are not objected to by the other party, he
> may be taken to have agreed to them. Such was *British Road Services Ltd v Arthur V. Crutchley & Co Ltd* [1968]
> 1 All E.R. at 816–817 per Lord Pearson; and the illustration given by Professor Guest in *Anson's Law of Contract*
> (24th ed.), pp. 37–38 [See 27th edn, p.40] where he says that "the terms of contract consist of the terms of the

offer subject to the modifications contained in the acceptance." That may however go too far. In some cases, however, the battle is won by the man who gets the blow in first. If he offers to sell at a named price on the terms and conditions stated on the back and the buyer orders the goods purporting to accept the offer on an order form with his own different terms and conditions on the back, then, if the difference is so material that it would affect the price, the buyer ought not to be allowed to take advantage of the difference unless he draws it specifically to the attention of the seller. There are yet other cases where the battle depends on the shots fired on both sides. There is a concluded contract but the forms vary. The terms and conditions of both parties are to be construed together. If they can be reconciled so as to give a harmonious result, all well and good. If differences are irreconcilable, so that they are mutually contradictory, then the conflicting terms may have to be scrapped and replaced by a reasonable implication.

In the present case the judge thought that the sellers in their original quotation got their blow in first; especially by the provision that "These terms and conditions shall prevail over any terms and conditions in the Buyer's order." It was so emphatic that the price variation clause continued through all the subsequent dealings and that the buyer must be taken to have agreed to it. I can understand that point of view. But I think that the documents have to be considered as a whole. And, as a matter of construction, I think the acknowledgement of June 5, 1969 is the decisive document. It makes clear that the contract was on the buyers' terms and not on the sellers' terms: and the buyers' terms did not include a price variation clause.

I would therefore allow the appeal and enter judgment for the buyers.

LAWTON LJ

The modern commercial practice of making quotations and placing orders with conditions attached usually in small print, is indeed likely, as in this case, to produce a battle of forms. The problem is how should that battle be conducted? The view taken by the judge was that the battle should extend over a wide area and the court should do its best to look into the minds of the parties and make certain assumptions. In my judgment, the battle has to be conducted in accordance with set rules. It is a battle more on classical 18th century lines when convention decided who had the right to open fire first rather than in accordance with the modern concept of attrition.

The rules relating to a battle of this kind have been known for the past 130-odd years. They were set out by the then Master of the Rolls, Lord Langdale, in *Hyde v Wrench* (above, para.3–043) and Lord Denning M.R. has already referred to them; and, if anyone should have thought they were obsolescent, Megaw J. in *Trollope & Colls Ltd v Atomic Power Constructions Ltd* [1962] 3 All E.R. 1035 at 1038, called attention to the fact that those rules are still in force.

When those rules are applied to this case, in my judgment, the answer is obvious . . .

As I pointed out in the course of argument to counsel for the sellers, if the letter of June 5 which accompanied the form acknowledging the terms which the buyers had specified had amounted to a counter-offer, then in my judgment the parties never were ad idem. It cannot be said that the buyers accepted the counter-offer by reason of the fact that ultimately they took physical delivery of the machine. By the time they took physical delivery of the machine, they had made it clear by correspondence that they were not accepting that there was any price escalation clause in any contract which they had made with the plaintiffs.

I agree with Lord Denning M.R. that this appeal should be allowed.

Bridge L.J. delivered judgment allowing the appeal.

Appeal Allowed.

Points for reflection

In *Butler Machine Tool*, reference was made to paras 1 and 2 of 'The Uniform Law on the Formation of Contracts for the International Sale of Goods' in Sch.2 to the Uniform Laws on International Sales Act 1967. These paragraphs provide: **3–062**

> "1. An acceptance containing additions, limitations, or other modifications shall be a rejection of the offer and shall constitute a counter-offer.
>
> 2. However, a reply to an offer which purports to be an acceptance but which contains additional or different terms which do not materially alter the terms of the offer shall constitute

an acceptance unless the offeror promptly objects to the discrepancy; if he does not so object, the terms of the contract shall be the terms of the offer with the modifications contained in the acceptance."

Rather obviously, any attempt to resolve the battle of the forms by considering whether the alteration is or is not "material" invites debate, not least as to which party's view of materiality is decisive. Moreover, we might question whether it is reasonable to treat the offeror as accepting the modification unless he "promptly objects to the discrepancy". How promptly must the offeror act? Why should he bear this burden? In the event, the court in *Butler Machine Tool* did not express any opinion on whether para.2 represented the common law of England. Lord Denning MR and Bridge LJ did, however, say that *Anson's Law of Contract* (24th edn), pp.37–38 (p.40 in the 27th edn) went too far in saying: "the terms of the contract consist of the terms of the offer subject to the modifications contained in the acceptance".

Questions

3–063   1. What if the plaintiffs reply of June 3 had said ". . . entered on the terms stated in our offer of May 23"? Would it have been possible to say there was a contract? What if the plaintiffs had delivered the machine and defendants had taken delivery?

2. The Principles of European Contract Law, 1998 art.2: 209:

"(1) If the parties have reached agreement except that offer and acceptance refer to conflicting general conditions of contract, a contract is nonetheless formed. The general conditions form part of the contract to the extent that they are common in substance.
(2) However, no contract is formed if one party:

(a) has indicated in advance, explicitly and not by way of general conditions, that it does not intend to be bound by a contract on the basis of paragraph (1); or
(b) without delay informs the other party that it does not intend to be bound by such contract.

(3) General conditions of contract are terms which have been formulated in advance for an indefinite number of contracts of a certain nature, and which have not been individually negotiated between the parties."

How can parties be said to have reached agreement if A intends his general conditions to apply and B intends his, quite different, conditions to apply? How could a court determine whether the price variation clause in Butler should apply if the parties had not agreed?

3. Compare the Court of Appeal's decision in *Tekdata Interconnections Ltd v Amphenol Ltd* [2009] EWCA Civ 1209 (below Chapter 13). Introducing the appeal, in para.1, Longmore LJ says:

This appeal raises the question whether in what is sometimes called "the battle of forms", there can be circumstances in which a traditional offer and acceptance analysis can be displaced by reference to the conduct of the parties over a long-term relationship. An offer to buy containing the purchaser's terms which is followed by an acknowledgement of purchase containing the seller's terms which is followed by delivery will (other things being equal) result in a contract on the seller's terms. If, however, it is clear that the neither party ever intended the seller's terms to apply and always intended the purchaser's terms to apply, it is conceptually possible to arrive at the conclusion that the purchaser's terms are to apply.

How does this sit alongside *Butler*?

Further reading

John N. Adams, 'The Battle of the Forms' (1983) *Journal of Business Law* 297
Brian Coote, 'The Instantaneous Transmission of Acceptances' [1971] 4 NZULR. 331
Paul Mitchell and John Phillips, 'The Contractual Nexus: Is Reliance Essential?' (2002) 22 OJLS 115

4

CONTRACT AS AN AGREEMENT: FINALITY AND CERTAINTY

LEARNING OBJECTIVES

By the end of this chapter, you should understand that:

■ it is a requirement for the formation of a contract that the essential terms have been agreed and, concomitantly, that the terms as agreed are sufficiently certain to be enforceable;

■ the requirement of certainty is sometimes applied very strictly but, at other times, particularly in commercial contracting, it is applied more flexibly and with much greater sensitivity to business practice—in other words, you should understand that courts do not always approach this requirement in quite the same way;

■ while "agreements to agree" and "agreements to negotiate" are likely to fail for uncertainty, the law recognises that "lock out" agreements and agreements to give a party "first refusal" may be sufficiently certain to be enforceable;

■ agreements "subject to contract" (which are made every day in the domestic property market) are not final and binding.

INTRODUCTION

According to the standard presentation of the requirements for the formation of a contract, we need to be able to tick the boxes for offer and acceptance, for consideration, and for intention to create legal relations (see Chs 9 and 10 for these latter two requirements). Often, it is also said that a further formation requirement is sufficient certainty of terms. In other words, when a contract is characterised as an agreement, it is implicit that the agreement satisfies a threshold test of certainty. So, for example, in *Carlill v Carbolic Smoke Ball Co* (above Ch.2), the company's omnibus defence that the advertisement was too vague to be treated as an offer included the argument that the terms of the promotion left it unclear whether, to qualify for the £100, the user of the smokeball must contract influenza during the current epidemic, or while the smokeball was being used, or during some other period. This argument, like the other defences pleaded by the company, failed. However, as the cases in this chapter suggest, the courts are sometimes more vigilant in checking for the finality and certainty of the agreement.

The first case extracted, *May and Butcher v R.*, represents something of a high-water mark in the demand for certainty of terms. For example, in *Fletcher Challenge Energy Ltd v Electricity Corporation of New Zealand Ltd* [2002] 2 N.Z.L.R. 433, at 446–447, the Court of Appeal of New Zealand

4–001

distanced itself from the decision remarking that the case "is no longer to be regarded as authority for any wider proposition than that an 'agreement' which omits an essential term . . . or a means of determining such a term does not amount to a contract." In contrast to *May and Butcher v R.*, it is the more relaxed approach of the House of Lords in *Hillas and Co Ltd v Arcos Ltd* (1932) 147 L.T. 503 that is thought to represent the spirit of the modern law. In *Hillas*, the appellants agreed to buy 22,000 standards of softwood goods over the season 1930, subject to certain conditions. A clause in the agreement gave them an option to buy a further 100,000 standards during the season 1931. The question was whether this agreement was enforceable. The Court of Appeal held, in the words of Scrutton LJ, that ". . . considering the number of things left undetermined, kinds, sizes and quantities of goods, times and ports and manner of shipment . . . the option clause was not an agreement, but . . . 'an agreement to make an agreement,' which is not an enforceable agreement." However, the House of Lords, taking a different view of business practice and need, allowed the appeal. The view of the Court of Appeal would have excluded the possibility of business men making forward contracts because of the impossibility of specifying in advance all the details of a complicated performance. As Lord Wright famously put it: "Business men often record the most important agreements in crude and summary fashion; modes of expression sufficient and clear to them in the course of their business may appear to those unfamiliar with the business far from complete or precise. It is accordingly the duty of the Court to construe such documents fairly and broadly, without being too astute or subtle in finding defects . . ." To do otherwise, as the House emphasised, would be to ignore ". . . the legal implication in contracts of what is reasonable, which runs through the whole of modern English law in relation to business contracts . . . After all, the parties, being business men, ought to be left to decide what degree of precision it is essential to express in their contracts, if no legal principle is violated."

The cases that follow in this chapter highlight the contrast between the traditionally strict approach to the requirement of certainty of terms and the more relaxed approach that tends to be taken by modern courts, including the way that this contrast shows up in relation to so-called "lock out" and "lock in" agreements.

1. HAVE THE PARTIES AGREED WITH SUFFICIENT CERTAINTY ON THE ESSENTIAL TERMS?

MAY AND BUTCHER v R.

House of Lords (1929) [1934] 2 K.B. 17n.; 103 L.J.K.B. 556n.; 151 L.T. 246n.

4-002   Petition of Right. The suppliants, May and Butcher, alleged that it was mutually agreed between them and the Controller of the Disposals Board for the purchase by the suppliants of the whole of the tentage which might become available for disposal in the United Kingdom up to March 31, 1923.

The relevant terms of the alleged agreement were as follows:

"(3)   The price or prices to be paid, and the date or dates on which payment is to be made by the purchasers to the Commission for such old tentage shall be agreed upon from time to time between the Commission and the purchasers as the quantities of the said old tentage become available for disposal, and are offered to the purchasers by the Commission.

(10)   It is understood that all disputes with reference to or arising out of this agreement will be submitted to arbitration in accordance with the provisions of the Arbitration Act, 1889."

By demurrer, answer and plea the Attorney General said that the petition of right disclosed no sufficient and binding contract of sale.

Rowlatt J held that the arrangement constituted no contract, but merely a series of clauses for adoption if and when contracts were made, because the price, date of payment and period of delivery had still to be agreed; and that the arbitration clause did not apply to differences of opinion on these questions. The Court of Appeal (Scrutton LJ dissenting) affirmed Rowlatt J's decision. The suppliants appealed.

LORD BUCKMASTER

In my opinion there never was a concluded contract between the parties. It has long been a well-recognised principle of contract law that an agreement between two parties to enter into an agreement in which some critical part of the contract matter is left undetermined is no contract at all. It is, of course, perfectly possible for two people to contract that they will sign a document which contains all the relevant terms, but it is not open to them to agree that they will in the future agree upon a matter which is vital to the arrangement between them and has not yet been determined. It has been argued that as the fixing of the price has broken down, a reasonable price must be assumed. That depends in part upon the terms of the Sale of Goods Act, which no doubt reproduces, and is known to have reproduced, the old law upon the matter. That provides in section 8 that "the price in a contract of sale may be fixed by the contract, or may be left to be fixed in manner thereby agreed, or may be determined by the course of dealing between the parties. Where the price is not determined in accordance with the foregoing provisions the buyer must pay a reasonable price"[2]; while, if the agreement is to sell goods on the terms that the price is to be fixed by the valuation of a third party, and such third party cannot or does not make such valuation, section 9 says that the agreement is avoided. I find myself quite unable to understand the distinction between an agreement to permit the price to be fixed by a third party and an agreement to permit the price to be fixed in the future by the two parties to the contract themselves. In principle it appears to me that they are one and the same thing . . .

The next question is about the arbitration clause, and there I entirely agree with the majority of the Court of Appeal and also with Rowlatt J. The clause refers "disputes with reference to or arising out of this agreement" to arbitration, but until the price has been fixed, the agreement is not there. The arbitration clause relates to the settlement of whatever may happen when the agreement has been completed and the parties are regularly bound. There is nothing in the arbitration clause to enable a contract to be made which in fact the original bargain has left quite open.

VISCOUNT DUNEDIN

I am of the same opinion. This case arises upon a question of sale, but in my view the principles which we are applying are not confined to sale, but are the general principles of the law of contract. To be a good contract there must be a concluded bargain, and a concluded contract is one which settles everything that is necessary to be settled and leaves nothing to be settled by agreement between the parties. Of course it may leave something which still has to be determined, but then that determination must be a determination which does not depend upon the agreement between the parties. In the system of law in which I was brought up, that was expressed by one of those brocards of which perhaps we have been too fond, but which often express very neatly what is wanted: "Certum est quod certum reddi potest." Therefore, you may very well agree that a certain part of the contract of sale, such as price, may be settled by someone else. As a matter of the general law of contract all the essentials have to be settled. What are the essentials may vary according to the particular contract under consideration. We are here dealing with sale, and undoubtedly price is one of the essentials of sale, and if it is left still to be agreed between the parties, then there is no contract. It may be left to the determination of a certain person, and if it was so left and that person either would not or could not act, there would be no contract because the price was to be settled in a certain way and it has become impossible to settle it in that way, and therefore there is no settlement. No doubt as to goods, the Sale of Goods Act, 1893, says that if the price is not mentioned and settled in the contract it is to be a reasonable price. The simple answer in this case is that the Sale of Goods Act provides for silence on the point and here there is no silence, because there is a provision that the two parties are to agree. As long as you have something certain it does

---

[2]   s.15 of the Supply of Goods and Services Act 1982 now makes similar provision for the payment of a reasonable charge for a service.

not matter. For instance, with regard to price it is a perfectly good contract to say that the price is to be settled by the buyer. I have not had time, or perhaps I have not been industrious enough, to look through all the books in England to see if there is such a case; but there was such a case in Scotland in 1760, where it was decided that a sale of a landed estate was perfectly good, the price being left to be settled by the buyer himself. I have only expressed in other words what has already been said by my noble friend on the Woolsack. Here there was clearly no contract. There would have been a perfectly good settlement of price if the contract had said that it was to be settled by arbitration by a certain man, or it might have been quite good if it was said that it was to be settled by arbitration under the Arbitration Act so as to bring in a material plan by which a certain person could be put in action. The question then arises, has anything of that sort been done? I think clearly not. The general arbitration clause is one in very common form as to disputes arising out of the arrangements. In no proper meaning of the word can this be described as a dispute arising between the parties; it is a failure to agree, which is a very different thing from a dispute.

As regards the option point, I do not think it can be more neatly put than it was by Rowlatt J. when he said: "It is an option to offer terms on terms that are not agreed. An option to offer a contract which is not a contract seems to me not to carry the case any further than the first way of putting it." For these reasons I agree in the motion.

Appeal Dismissed.

Points for reflection

4–003

1. In *Foley v Classique Coaches* [1934] 2 K.B. 1 the plaintiff agreed to sell some land to the defendants for a coach station in consideration of the defendants agreeing to buy all their petrol from him. The agreement concerning the sale of the land and that concerning the sale of the petrol were put into separate documents, the former agreement stating that it was conditional on the defendants' entering into the latter and the latter stating that it was supplemental to the former. The agreement about the petrol provided that it was to be supplied "at a price to be agreed by the parties in writing and from time to time." The land was conveyed and the petrol agreement was acted on for three years. The defendants then repudiated the petrol agreement. The plaintiff succeeded in an action for damages, a declaration that the agreement was binding and an injunction to restrain the defendants from buying petrol from elsewhere. The defendants' appeal was dismissed.
Scrutton LJ said: "In the present case the parties obviously believed they had a contract and they acted for three years as if they had; they had an arbitration clause which relates to the subject-matter of the agreement as to the supply of petrol, and it seems to me that this arbitration clause applies to any failure to agree as to the price. By analogy to the case of a tied house there is to be implied in this contract a term that the petrol shall be supplied at a reasonable price and shall be of reasonable quality." (See also *Sykes (F & G) Wessex v Fine Fare* [1967] 1 Lloyd's Rep. 53 CA).

2. In the modern jurisprudence, the contrast between *May and Butcher* and *Foley v Classique Coaches* surfaced again in the Court of Appeal's decision *in MRI Trading AG v Erdenet Mining Corporation Ltd* [2013] EWCA Civ 156. The parties in *MRI Trading* settled a dispute, the terms of the Settlement Agreement providing inter alia that EMC should supply specified quantities of Copper Concentrates to MRI Trading under three separate contracts (two contracts in 2009, one in 2010). The 2009 contracts were performed but a question arose as to the enforceability of the 2010 contract. EMC argued that it was unenforceable because clauses 6.1, 9.1, and 9.2 provided that, respectively, the shipping schedule, the treatment charge, and the refining charge "shall be agreed during the negotiations of terms for 2010." At arbitration, EMC's argument prevailed; as in *May and Butcher*, the 2010 contract was held to constitute no more than an agreement

to agree. Yet, was it commercially realistic to treat these parties as not yet intending to commit themselves contractually? On appeal, Eder J in the Commercial Court thought not; and, relying on the principles summarised by Rix LJ in *Mamidoil-Jetoil Greek Petroleum Company SA v Okta Crude Oil Refinery AD* [2001] 2 Lloyd's Rep 76 (at para.69) and by Chadwick LJ in *BJ Aviation Ltd v Pool Aviation Ltd* [2002] 2 P & CR 25 (at paras 19-24), the Court of Appeal agreed, holding that the context in *MRI Trading* was analogous to that in *Foley* and that the contract should not fail for uncertainty. According to Tomlinson LJ:

> 17.   The arbitrators then set out their conclusions as follows:

> "17. Clauses 6.1 and 9.1 and 9.2 constitute an agreement to agree. In *Foley v Classique Coaches* the court found that it could imply a term into the contract; however, in this case there had already been some lengthy period when the contract had been performed. In the case before the Tribunal, as noted above, the contract in question is to be construed in the light of its own wording, and it is clear that there had been no part performance. Relevantly, in *May and Butcher Ltd v the King* (1934), Viscount Dunedin observed

> > "*The simple answer in this case is that the Sale of Goods Act provides for silence on the point and here there is no silence, because there is a provision that the two parties are to agree.*"

> 18. In the light of the above, the Tribunal finds that the answer to the question "*Was there an enforceable obligation on Erdenet to deliver the copper concentrates?*" is no. The contract had left material terms as 'agreements to agree', and the Tribunal has no option but to conclude that the delivery obligation was therefore non-existent.
> 19. As the Tribunal finds there is no enforceable obligation to deliver, the second and third questions addressed, "*What is the reasonable price at which the concentrates should have been delivered*" and "*When should the concentrates have been delivered*" therefore fall away.'"

18.   The tribunal's approach to "part performance" was in my view flawed, as it was bound to be once the arbitrators had decided to leave the Settlement Agreement out of consideration. In his principle (vii) in *Mamidoil* Rix LJ stressed the importance of one or other party having already had the advantage of some performance reflecting the parties' agreement on a long-term relationship. The present situation is analogous. The overall transaction here comprised the settlement of the original dispute. MRI's claim against EMC was compromised in terms that three new contracts were entered into. EMC had derived the full benefit of the abandonment of MRI's claim. Moreover, rather as in *Foley v Classique Coaches* [1934] 2 KB 1, the 2010 contract is part of a wider arrangement between the parties, which wider arrangement the parties had for some time, here for over one year, been acting upon. In *Foley* the sellers sold to the buyers a piece of land for use by the buyers in their coach business, and also contracted with them as part and parcel of the same transaction but by separate contract to supply petrol required for that business "at a price to be agreed by the parties in writing and from time to time". There was an arbitration clause. The land was conveyed and for three years petrol was supplied at agreed prices lower than those paid by the public. In the third year the buyers thought that they could obtain cheaper petrol elsewhere and repudiated the petrol sale agreement, claiming that it was unenforceable as an agreement to agree. A strong Court of Appeal, Scrutton, Greer and Maugham LJJ, was in no doubt that the petrol sale agreement was enforceable. A term was to be implied into the agreement that the petrol should be sold at a reasonable price and if any dispute arose as to that it was to be determined by arbitration for which the parties had made provision. It weighed heavily with the court that the buyers had received the full benefit of the sale of the land and that both parties had conducted themselves for some time on the footing that there was between them a binding contract concerning the sale of petrol. The situation here is not of course exactly the same as the 2010 contract was not performed in any part. But the 2010 contract was, in turn, an integral part of an overall deal pursuant to which both parties had derived benefits, a deal which they had worked through together for over a year without any suggestion that the final part thereof fell into a different and unenforceable category of obligation.

3. In *Durham Tees Valley Airport Limited v Bmibaby Limited* [2010] EWCA Civ 485, the parties agreed that, for a period of 10 years, the carriers would establish a two aircraft operation at the airport. But, what did such operation entail? Was the requirement sufficiently certain? Taking a distinctly modern view, the Court of Appeal held that the provision, although giving the carriers a broad operating discretion, was sufficiently certain. According to Toulson LJ:

89. In a forceful argument, Mr Crane submitted that "a x2 aircraft based operation" lacks the necessary content to be capable of being the subject of an obligation by the airline. The contract did not specify a minimum number of hours or rotations for which each aircraft was to be flown over any particular period in order to constitute the aircraft being operated, nor did it contain any mechanism by which the court could determine as at the date of the contract what the minimum requirement would be. I accept that the uncertainties of what might happen during a 10 year period were such that nobody could have determined at the outset what would be the minimum number of flights or rotations during the lifetime of the contract in order for an aircraft to continue to be operated under it. Wars, strikes, pandemics, terrorism, bad weather conditions and many other factors might affect what would be practicable.

90. Therefore, argued Mr Crane, the obligation was void for uncertainty, because the obligee (the airline) could not know in advance how many flights it had to operate per aircraft in order to comply with its contractual obligation. At this point I part company with him. To my mind the proper test is not whether a court would have been able to determine on, say, an application for specific performance what would be the minimum number of flights required in order to constitute a x2 aircraft based operation during all vicissitudes which *might* occur during the period of the contract, but whether the court would be able to determine on a set of facts which had occurred (including any unusual vicissitudes) whether the airline had, or had not, maintained a x2 based aircraft operation at the airport. In reaching that decision it would have to take into account the factual circumstances. Facts might arise where the question whether the airline had continued to maintain such an operation might be borderline, but that may be said of many contractual obligations. In this case, the airline had a wide measure of discretion in fixing any programme. As Mummery LJ observed during the argument, an agreement allowing wide scope to one party to determine its manner of performance, which may be subject to future imponderables, may not be capable of enforcement by an order for specific performance without it necessarily following that the agreement is too uncertain to have legal effect at all.

91. It is not uncommon in commercial life for parties to enter into a contract by which one party is to conduct an operation over which it has a large degree of discretion; but it will usually be possible for a court to determine without too much difficulty whether that party has ceased to perform the operation at all. The present contract may be unusual in its length and the degree of discretion given to the airline, but I do not see that the court would have an insuperable difficulty in deciding whether the airline had altogether ceased to conduct the operation.

Questions

4-004

1. Is there a valid distinction between an agreement to permit the price to be fixed in the future by the two parties to the agreement and:

   (a) an agreement to permit the price to be fixed by a third party? (See *Campbell v Edwards* [1976] 1 W.L.R. 403.)

   (b) an agreement to permit the price to be fixed by one of the "agreeing" parties? (Viscount Dunedin's dictum that there may be a good contract where the price is to be settled by the buyer was followed in *Lombard Tricity Finance Ltd v Paton* [1989] 1 All E.R. 918 at 923 CA, holding that a provision in a contract of loan allowing the lender to vary the rate of interest at in its absolute discretion was not unlawful: ". . . we do not see that it can be different in a contract of loan, where the borrower has (in theory at any rate) the opportunity to repay the whole outstanding balance." Cf. UTCC Regulations 1999 Sch.2, sub-paras 1(j) and

2(b). "Solus" agreements (below, Ch.27) are not treated as invalid on the ground that the price of petrol is to be fixed by the seller.

2. Can *May and Butcher v R.* be properly distinguished from *Foley v Classique Coaches*?

3. What would have been the position if the defendant in *Foley* had repudiated both agreements immediately after they were signed?

4. What if, after the land had been conveyed, he had repudiated the petrol agreement only?

5. In *British Steel Corp v Cleveland Bridge and Engineering Co Ltd* [1984] 1 All E.R. 504 at 511, Robert Goff L.J. said of the facts of that case:

> "In my judgment, the true analysis of the situation is simply this. Both parties confidently expected a formal contract to eventuate. In these circumstances, to expedite performance under that anticipated contract, one requested the other to commence the contract work, and the other complied with that request. If thereafter, as anticipated, a contract was entered into, the work done as requested will be treated as having been performed under that contract; if, contrary to their expectation, no contract was entered into, then the performance of the work is not referable to any contract the terms of which can be ascertained, and the law simply imposes an obligation on the party who made the request to pay a reasonable sum for such work as has been done pursuant to that request, such an obligation sounding in quasi contract or, as we now say, in restitution. Consistently with that solution, the party making the request may find himself liable to pay for work which he would not have had to pay for as such if the anticipated contract had come into existence, for example, preparatory work which will, if the contract is made, be allowed for in the price of the finished work."

What is the difference between the situation found to exist by Robert Goff LJ and that in *Foley*?

6. Which is the better view in *MRI Trading*, that of the arbitrators or that of the Court of Appeal?

7. In the Australian case of *Coal Cliff Collieries Property Limited v Sijehama Property Limited* (1991) 24 NSWLR 1, at 21, Kirby P said:

> "Courts and lawyers may expect the agreements of business people to be clear and complete. Unfortunately, in the marketplace, agreements often fall short of these lawyerly desires. Yet the law of contracts serves the marketplace. It does not exist to satisfy lawyers' desires for neat rules."

What do you think follows for the requirement of certainty of terms from this realistic assessment of business practice?

SUDBROOK TRADING ESTATE LTD v EGGLETON

House of Lords [1983] 1 A.C. 444; [1982] 3 W.L.R. 315; [1982] 3 All E.R. 1

A lease gave the lessee an option to purchase the reversion "at such price, not being less than twelve thousand pounds as may be agreed upon by two Valuers one to be nominated by the Lessor and the other by the Lessees or in default of such agreement by an Umpire appointed by the said Valuers . . .". When the lessee sought to exercise the option the lessor refused to appoint a valuer, claiming that   **4–005** the option clause was void for uncertainty. The House of Lords (Lord Russell dissenting), reversing the Court of Appeal, held that the option was valid and had been effectively exercised and that it should be specifically performed, the price being fixed by a valuation ordered by the court.

LORD DIPLOCK

The option clause cannot be classified as a mere "agreement to make an agreement." There are not any terms left to be agreed between the parties. In modern terminology, it is to be classified as a unilateral or "if" contract. Although it creates from the outset a right on the part of the lessees, which they will be entitled, but not bound, to exercise against the lessors at a future date, it does not give rise to any legal obligations on the part of either party unless and until the lessees give notice in writing to the lessors, within the stipulated period, of their desire to purchase the freehold reversion to the lease. The giving of such notice, however, converts the "if" contract into a synallagmatic or bilateral contract, which creates mutual legal rights and obligations on the part of both lessors and lessees.

The first obligation on each of them, once the contract has become synallagmatic, is to appoint their respective valuers to fix what is the fair and reasonable price for the reversion. That this is a primary obligation under the contract follows from the use of the words "to be nominated," but it would, in my view, also be a necessary implication to give business efficacy to the option clause. The requirement that the price to be so fixed is one that will be fair and reasonable as between lessors and lessees appears to me to be a necessary implication from the description "valuers" applied to the persons by whom the price is to be fixed by agreement between them, if possible, and from the description "umpire" applied to the person by whom the price is to be fixed if the valuers cannot agree. The term "valuer" (with a capital "V" at any rate) is used nowadays to denote a member of a recognised profession comprised of persons possessed of skill and experience in assessing the market price of property, particularly real property.

The obligation of both lessors and lessees on appointing their respective valuers is to instruct them to carry out the functions for which the option clause requires that they should be appointed, viz. to try to reach agreement with one another on a price for the reversion that is fair and reasonable as between the lessors and the lessees and, failing such agreement, to agree on and appoint a suitably qualified impartial person to fix such price.

The option clause, to which the lessors and lessees alone are parties, cannot of itself impose on the valuers any legal duty to endeavour to reach agreement with one another as to a fair and reasonable price for the reversion or, if they fail to do so, to agree on what person is to be appointed by them jointly as umpire to fix the price. But that this, which is stressed in several of the cases cited by Templeman LJ, presents an obstacle to compelling performance of the contract contained in the option clause is a proposition that on examination proves, in my opinion, to be illusory. If a valuer appointed by the lessors or lessees does not carry out the instructions given him by his appointor, but in default of agreement with his fellow valuer on the price, fails to agree with him on the person to be appointed as umpire, the valuer will be in breach of his own contract with his appointor; his appointment can be revoked and a fresh valuer, who will comply with his instructions, appointed in his stead. In the (improbable) event contemplated, in my view it would by necessary implication be a contractual duty owed by the lessors and lessees to one another under the option clause to adopt this course.

So if both lessors and lessees carry out their primary contractual obligations to one another, under the option clause, the result will be a conveyance by the lessors to the lessees of the reversion in fee simple to the demised premises on the completion date fixed for completion by para. (b) of the clause at a price agreed on between valuers appointed by each party or failing such agreement determined by an umpire appointed jointly by the valuers. Until such conveyance and payment the contract remains executory; but so does any other contract for the sale of land. What Templeman LJ refers to in his summary of the effect of the authorities as the one central proposition from which the three principles that he states all stem, viz. until the price has been fixed by the method provided for in the contract "there is no complete agreement to enforce" (see [1981] 3 All E.R. 105 at 115, [1981] 3 W.L.R. 361 at 373), involves a fundamental fallacy. A contract is complete as a contract as soon as the parties have reached agreement as to what each of its essential terms is or can with certainty be ascertained, for it is an elementary principle of the English law of contract id certum est quod certum reddi potest. True it is that the agreement for the sale of land remains executory until transfer of title to the land and payment of the purchase price; but if this is the sense in which the agreement is said not to be complete it is only executory contracts that do require enforcement by the courts; and such enforcement may either take the form of requiring a party to perform his primary obligation to the other party under it (specific performance) or, if he has failed to perform a primary obligation, of requiring him to perform the secondary obligation, that arises only on such failure, to pay monetary compensation (damages) to the other party for the resulting loss that he has sustained.

Lord Fraser made a speech allowing the appeal.

Lord Russell, dissenting, asked: Why should it be thought that potential vendor and purchaser intended the price to be "fair"? The former would intend the price to be high, even though "unfairly" so. And the latter vice versa. Vendors and purchasers are normally greedy.

LORD SCARMAN

The question for decision is as to the true construction to be placed on an option granted to a lessee to buy the freehold reversion. The terms of the option have been set out in full by my noble and learned friend Lord Diplock. Were the parties agreeing to a sale "at a fair valuation," that is, "at a reasonable price"? Or were they treating their chosen mode of ascertaining the price as being of the essence of their contract? What was the object of their contract? A fair and reasonable price? Or a price reached only by the means specified?

Unembarrassed by authority, I would unhesitatingly conclude that the parties intended that the lessee should pay a fair and reasonable price to be determined as at the date when he exercised the option. The valuation formula was introduced into the contract merely as a convenient way of ascertaining the price at that future time. Should we be deterred from so construing the provision by the existence of a line of authority stretching back over 150 years in which provisions remitting to a valuer or arbitrator the ascertainment of a price have been construed as making the machinery of ascertainment an essential term of the contract?

I think not.

Lord Bridge made a speech allowing the appeal.

Questions

1. Is an agreement to buy and sell at a price to be fixed by the parties different in kind from an agreement to buy and sell at a price to be fixed by valuers appointed by the parties?   **4–006**

2. Is an agreement to buy and sell at a price to be fixed by the valuers to be appointed by the parties the same as an agreement to buy and sell at a reasonable price?

3. Would a valuer who failed to agree on a person to be appointed umpire be (as Lord Diplock says) in breach of contract? What if he had no confidence in any of the persons his fellow-valuer would agree to?

4. How does the modern law distinguish between a valuation machinery that is essential and one that is not? Cf. *Gillatt v Sky Television Ltd* [2000] 1 All E.R. (Comm) 461.

BRITISH BANK FOR FOREIGN TRADE v NOVINEX LTD

Court of Appeal [1949] 1 K.B. 623; [1949] L.J.R. 658; 93 S.J. 146; [1949]1 All E.R. 155

The defendants, by letter to the plaintiffs, agreed to buy from clients of the plaintiffs (Messrs. Pritchard and Gee Trading Co) 20,000 oilskin suits. In that letter the defendants wrote: "We confirm that we have agreed to cover you on this transaction with a commission of 4d. per oilskin suit . . . We also undertake to cover you with an agreed commission on any other business transacted with your friends. In return for this you are to put us in direct contact with your friends." The plaintiffs did put the defendants in direct contact with their friends and, in August 1947, the defendants bought from the friends by two transactions 1,000 and 20,000 oilskin suits. The second transaction did not arise directly from the introduction of the plaintiffs, but from the defendants having seen an advertisement in The Times.

The defendants denied liability to pay commission on these two transactions on the grounds (1) that no legally enforceable bargain arose under the letter quoted above; and (2) if the arrangement   **4–007** was an enforceable contract, it applied only to business arising directly from the introduction, which the transaction as to the 20,000 skins, at least, did not. Denning J appears to have accepted both submissions. The plaintiffs appealed.

COHEN LJ

Cohen L.J. dealt first with the second point, and held that there was nothing in the agreement to limit it to orders directly attributable to the introduction. He then went on: Is this an enforceable agreement? A number of authorities have been cited to us, to which I do not propose to refer in detail, because, in my view, the effect of the authorities is stated correctly in the learned judge's judgment where he said: "The principle to be deduced from the cases is that if there is an essential term which has yet to be agreed and there is no express or implied provision for its solution, the result in point of law is that there is no binding contract. In seeing whether there is an implied provision for its solution, however, there is a difference between an arrangement which is wholly executory on both sides and one which has been executed on one side or the other. In the ordinary way, if there is an arrangement to supply goods at a price "to be agreed" or to perform services on terms "to be agreed," then although, while the matter is still executory, there may be no binding contract, nevertheless, if it is executed on one side, that is, if the one does his part without having come to an agreement as to the price or the terms, then the law will say that there is necessarily implied, from the conduct of the parties, a contract that, in default of agreement, a reasonable sum is to be paid." With that statement of the principle of law, I respectfully agree. My difference with the learned judge is only on the question whether he has correctly applied that statement of principle to the facts of this case.

The learned judge continued: "The difficulty is to apply the distinction in this case. This is not a case of services to be rendered for wages or goods to be supplied for a price. It is an arrangement in regard to repeat transactions or follow-up transactions, in respect of which the person effecting the original introduction has performed no fresh service whatever apart from his original introduction. He has, however, done his part. He has effected the original introduction." Pausing there for a moment, I can see no difference in principle between a case where the service which is rendered is labour and a case where the service is an introduction. Whatever the value of the service may be, the plaintiffs have rendered to the defendants the service which was intended to be the consideration for the agreement to pay commission on future orders. I cannot think that there is a difference in principle between such a service and an agreement to serve an employer as a clerk or in any other capacity. The judge then said that, in his view, it was impossible to apply the principle as regards ordinary service contracts to the present case, because he said that there was so much left in the air. He said: "Is it to be implied that he is to receive a reasonable commission on all follow-up transactions?" I have already dealt with that point. It seems to me on that point the agreement is plain and unambiguous and is so expressed. Then he said: "Is commission to be payable until the crack of doom?" I think the observation applies that if the defendants go on dealing with Pritchard and Gee Trading Co Ltd, until the crack of doom, they will have to go on paying commission to the plaintiffs, if they are in existence, until that doom occurs. As was pointed out in *Levy v Goldhill* ([1917] 2 Ch. 297, 300) by Peterson J., parties having entered into a bargain may have it in their power to put an end to it. The defendants in this case need not continue to deal with Messrs. Pritchard and Gee Trading Co, Ltd I feel no difficulty on either of these points. Then the learned judge said: "Is it confined to oilskins or does it apply to business of an entirely different kind, in different commodities, by different departments, and so forth?" Here again I can find no ambiguity in the agreement, and I do not therefore feel any difficulty in answering this question in favour of the second alternative.

Then the judge continued on what, I think, is the principal issue: "And what is the amount of commission to be? If there is no usual or customary commission, how can anyone say what is a reasonable commission for a follow-up transaction or a repeat transaction? That appeared quite clearly from the evidence which showed when parties are negotiating for the price they are going to pay, they take account of any commission they have to pay to agents." Denning J went on to say that this showed that the agreement was too vague to be enforced. But the agreement had said in terms, instead of by implication: "we also undertake to cover you with a reasonable commission on any other business transacted with your friends." Denning J seems to have regarded that condition as being too vague to be enforceable. I cannot agree with this view. I think that a court should take the view that a jury properly directed would be able to arrive at a proper conclusion as to what in the circumstances of this case is a reasonable commission.

Cohen L.J. then considered what was a reasonable commission, and held it to be 1/4d. per skin.

The court should, I think, make a declaration that the defendants are liable to pay a reasonable commission on the value of any transaction between the defendants and Messrs. Pritchard and Gee Trading Co Ltd after

December 9, 1946, and order the payment of commission at the figure I have mentioned in respect of the two transactions in August 1947.

Bucknill and Singleton L.JJ. agreed.

Recently, in *Barbudev v Eurocom Cable Management Bulgari EOOD* [2012] EWCA Civ 548, the question concerned the enforceability of a so-called "Side Letter" agreed between the parties to the dispute. The context in which the Side Letter was drafted and signed was one in which Barbudev, who was selling his interest in a cable television and internet business, was becoming anxious that the purchasers might be able to prevent his planned investment in the new business (Barbudev was proceeding on the basis that he would be able to invest 1,650,000 euros for 10% of the registered share capital in the new business). To allay Barbudev's concerns, the idea of a Side Letter crystallised and it was duly drafted by a senior lawyer at Freshfields. However, when Barbudev sought to hold Eurocom to the Side Letter, they declined, arguing (i) there was no intention to create legal relations (at best, the Side Letter was a non-binding Letter of Comfort); (ii) the Side Letter was no more than an unenforceable agreement to agree; and (iii) the Side Letter failed for uncertainty because it left essential terms still to be settled. The Court of Appeal, treating *RTS Flexible Systems* (above, Ch.2) as the leading case now, found for Barbudev on the first point—which was perhaps no surprise given that City lawyers were brought in to draft the document. However, even though *RTS Flexible Systems* and much of the modern case-law insists that, where commercial parties believe that they have a deal, then the law should work hard to uphold the deal, the court found against Barbudev on the second point (also on the third point although it was not strictly necessary to decide it). According to Aikens LJ (at para.44): "[The] Side Letter is, without doubt, no more than an 'agreement to agree'. It is an agreement to offer Mr Barbudev *'the opportunity to invest in the Purchaser on the terms to be agreed between us'*. That is not the language of a binding commitment and no amount of taking account of the commercial context and Mr Barbudev's concerns and aims can make it so. Moreover, the next phrase makes it clear that the terms of the Investment Agreement are not agreed; they are to be negotiated '. . . *in good faith with you'*."

---

2. "LOCK OUT" AGREEMENTS AND GOOD FAITH NEGOTIATION

WALFORD AND OTHERS v MILES AND ANOTHER

House of Lords [1992] 2 A.C. 128; [1992] 1 All E.R. 453

M owned a company carrying on a photographic processing business. He decided to sell it. P made an offer of £1.9m. W heard the business was for sale. He thought it was "dramatically undervalued" and was enthusiastic to buy it for £2m. W and M reached an agreement by correspondence and telephone, "subject to contract", for the sale. M asked W for a "comfort letter" (see below, p.206) from W's bankers confirming that they would provide the finance. M agreed that if W provided that letter by a certain day he would terminate negotiations with any third party and consideration of any alternative with a view to concluding an agreement with W. W provided the comfort letter as agreed and M confirmed that he agreed, "subject to contract", to sell the property for £2m. W sent preliminary inquiries and a draft agreement to M's solicitors but M sold the property to P.

W sued for breach of an alleged oral agreement, collateral to the negotiations for the sale that, in consideration of W (i) agreeing to continue the negotiations and not withdraw and (ii) providing the comfort letter, M had agreed to terminate negotiations with, and not deal with, any third party or give

4–008

further consideration to any alternative. [A "lockout agreement."] By an amendment to his statement of claim, W also alleged that there was a term, necessarily implied to give business efficacy to the contract, that M would continue to negotiate in good faith with W. W claimed that the true value of the property was £3m and that he had lost £1m. (A further point relating to misrepresentation is omitted.)

The Court of Appeal by a majority held that the agreement was nothing more than an agreement to negotiate and was unenforceable. Bingham L.J, dissenting, held that the agreement was enforceable as a contract not to deal with any third party. W appealed.

Lord Keith of Kinkel agreed with Lord Ackner.

LORD ACKNER

Mr Naughton (counsel for the appellants) accepted that as the law now stands and has stood for approaching 20 years an agreement to negotiate is not recognised as an enforceable contract. This was first decided in terms in *Courtney & Fairbairn Ltd v Tolaini Bros. (Hotels) Ltd* [1975] 1 All E.R. 716 at 720, where Lord Denning M.R. said:

> "If the law does not recognise a contract to enter into a contract (when there is a fundamental term yet to be agreed) it seems to me it cannot recognise a contract to negotiate. The reason is because it is too uncertain to have any binding force . . . It seems to me that a contract to negotiate, like a contract to enter into a contract, is not a contract known to the law . . . I think we must apply the general principle that when there is a fundamental matter left undecided and to be the subject of negotiation, there is no contract."

In that case Lord Denning M.R. rejected as not well founded (and Lord Diplock expressly concurred with this rejection) the dictum of Lord Wright in *Hillas & Co Ltd v Arcos Ltd* [1932] All E.R. Rep. 494 at 505:

> "There is then no bargain except to negotiate, and negotiation may be fruitless and end without any contract ensuing; yet even then, in strict theory, there is a contract (if there is good consideration) to negotiate, though in the event of repudiation by one party the damages may be nominal, unless a jury think that the opportunity to negotiate was of some appreciable value to the injured party."

Before your Lordships it was sought to argue that the decision in the *Courtney & Fairbairn Ltd* case was wrong. Although the cases in the United States did not speak with one voice your Lordships' attention was drawn to the decision of the United States Court of Appeals, Third Circuit in *Channel Home Centers Division of Grace Retail Corp v Grossman* (1986) 795 F. 2d 291 as being "the clearest example" of the American cases in the appellants' favour. That case raised the issue whether an agreement to negotiate in good faith, if supported by consideration, is an enforceable contract. I do not find the decision of any assistance. While accepting that an agreement to agree is not an enforceable contract, the United States Court of Appeals appears to have proceeded on the basis that an agreement to negotiate in good faith is synonymous with an agreement to use best endeavours and, as the latter is enforceable, so is the former. This appears to me, with respect, to be an unsustainable proposition. The reason why an agreement to negotiate, like an agreement to agree, is unenforceable is simply because it lacks the necessary certainty. The same does not apply to an agreement to use best endeavours. This uncertainty is demonstrated in the instant case by the provision which it is said has to be implied in the agreement for the determination of the negotiations. How can a court be expected to decide whether, subjectively, a proper reason existed for the termination of negotiations? The answer suggested depends upon whether the negotiations have been determined "in good faith." However, the concept of a duty to carry on negotiations in good faith is inherently repugnant to the adversarial position of the parties when involved in negotiations. Each party to the negotiations is entitled to pursue his (or her) own interest, so long as he avoids making misrepresentations. To advance that interest he must be entitled, if he thinks it appropriate, to threaten to withdraw from further negotiations or to withdraw in fact in the hope that the opposite party may seek to reopen the negotiations by offering him improved terms. Mr Naughton, of course, accepts that the agreement upon which he relies does not contain a duty to complete the negotiations. But that still leaves the vital question: how is a vendor ever to know that he is entitled to withdraw from further negotiations? How is the court to police such an "agreement?" A duty to negotiate in good faith is as unworkable in practice as it is inherently inconsistent with the position of a negotiating party. It is here that the uncertainty lies. In my judgment, while negotiations are in existence either party is entitled to withdraw from these negotiations, at any time and for any reason. There can be thus no obligation to continue to negotiate until there is a "proper reason" to withdraw. Accordingly, a bare agreement to negotiate has no legal content.

Lord Goff of Chieveley, Lord Jauncey of Tulichettle and Lord Browne-Wilkinson agreed.

Appeal Dismissed.

Point for reflection

Lord Steyn, in the article cited above, para.2–037, continued: **4–009**

"It is therefore surprising that the House of Lords in *Walford v Miles* held that an express agreement that parties must negotiate in good faith is unenforceable. Lord Ackner observed that the concept of a duty to carry on negotiations in good faith is inherently repugnant to the adversarial position of the parties when involved in negotiations. As the Unidroit principles make clear it is obvious that a party is free to negotiate and is not liable for a failure to reach an agreement. On the other hand, where a party negotiates in bad faith not intending to reach an agreement with the other party he is liable for losses caused to the other party. That is a line of reasoning not considered in *Walford v Miles*. The result of the decision is even more curious when one takes into account that the House of Lords regarded a best endeavours undertaking as enforceable. If the issue were to arise again, with the benefit of fuller argument, I would hope that the concept of good faith would not be rejected out of hand. There is no need for hostility to the concept: it is entirely practical and workable. Indeed from July 1995 the E.C. Directive on Unfair Terms in Consumer Contracts has been in operation in England. The Directive treats consumer transactions within its scope as unfair when they are contrary to good faith. It is likely to influence domestic English law. Given the needs of the international market place, and the primacy of European Union law, English lawyers cannot avoid grappling with the concept of good faith. But I have no heroic suggestion for the introduction of a general duty of good faith in our contract law. It is not necessary. As long as our courts always respect the reasonable expectations of parties our contract law can satisfactorily be left to develop in accordance with its own pragmatic traditions. And where in specific contexts duties of good faith are imposed on parties our legal system can readily accommodate such a well tried notion. After all, there is not a world of difference between the objective requirement of good faith and the reasonable expectations of parties."

Questions

1. Was Lord Ackner inconsistent in regarding a "best endeavours undertaking" as enforceable? Cf.   **4–010**
   Little v Courage (1994) 70 P. & C.R. 469 CA, at 476 per Millett L.J.: "An undertaking to use one's best endeavours to obtain planning permission or an export licence is sufficiently certain and is capable of being enforced: an undertaking to use one's best endeavours to agree, however, is no different from an agreement to agree, or to try to agree, or to negotiate with a view to reaching an agreement; all are equally uncertain and incapable of giving rise to a legally enforceable obligation."

2. Is a lock-out agreement of any value if it does not imply an agreement to negotiate? What is the use of A's exclusive right to bombard B with offers if B has no obligation to respond in any way?

3. Must a valid lock-out agreement always include a term specifying its duration? Why should it not be valid for the time reasonably necessary to make the necessary investigations and to prepare an offer?

PITT v PHH ASSET MANAGEMENT LTD

Court of Appeal [1994] 1 W.L.R. 327; [1993] 4 All E.R. 961

4–011   The defendant placed a property on the market at the asking price of £205,000. Buckle offered £185,000. The plaintiff made an offer of £190,000 which the defendant accepted, subject to contract. Buckle increased her offer to £195,000. The defendant withdrew his acceptance of the plaintiff's offer. The plaintiff and Buckle then each offered £200,000. The defendant accepted the plaintiff's offer, subject to contract. Buckle increased her offer to £210,000. The defendant again withdrew his acceptance of the plaintiff's offer.

The plaintiff, annoyed, told the defendant (i) he would seek an injunction to prevent the sale to Buckle; (ii) he would tell Buckle he was withdrawing, leaving her alone in the field, and advise her to lower her offer; and (iii) he was in a position to exchange as soon as the defendant wanted. On October 3, 1991 the plaintiff and defendant entered into an oral agreement reflected in a letter, as follows, from the plaintiff to the defendant's agent, Mr Roberts:

"Following our telephone conversation of today, I write to confirm the main points discussed. 1. Your client has decided it is in his best interest to stay with my offer of £200,000 (Two hundred thousand pounds), subject to contract for the above property. 2. The Vendor will not consider any further offers for the property on the basis that I will exchange contracts within a period of two weeks of the receipt of that contract. 3. The Vendor will be writing to me to confirm the above."

After some delay a draft contract was sent to the plaintiff's solicitor on November 7. On November 12 the defendant announced their intention to sell to Buckle for £210,000 and subsequently the draft contract with the plaintiff was withdrawn and the property sold to Buckle. The plaintiff's action for breach of the agreement of October 3 succeeded. The defendant appealed.

PETER GIBSON LJ

In my opinion the crucial paragraph is para (2) of the letter from the plaintiff to Mr Roberts:

"The Vendor will not consider any further offers for the property on the basis that I will exchange contracts within a period of two weeks of the receipt of that contract."

As the learned judge put it in his judgment, there was a clear acceptance that Mr Pitt, the plaintiff, should have a clear run of achieving an exchange of contracts which was to be within two weeks after receipt of the draft. The defendant was agreeing that it would not consider further offers. That was its plain understanding and that is reflected in the letters from the defendant to Mr Roberts and from Mr Roberts to Miss Buckle's agents to the effect that only if the exchange of contracts did not take place within the required time would the defendant reconsider the second offer from Miss Buckle. I can see no reason why that agreement, whereby the defendant was locking itself out from negotiating with other prospective purchasers for a limited period, should be considered to be subject to contract, there being nothing further to agree. Accordingly I would reject Mr Payne's argument on the first point.

SIR THOMAS BINGHAM MR

I agree that this appeal should be dismissed for the reasons given by Peter Gibson L.J.

For very many people their first and closest contact with the law is when they come to buy or sell a house. They frequently find it a profoundly depressing and frustrating experience. The vendor puts his house on the market. He receives an offer which is probably less than his asking price. He agonises over whether to accept or hold out for more. He decides to accept, perhaps after negotiating some increase. A deal is struck. Hands are shaken. The vendor celebrates, relaxes, makes plans for his own move and takes his house off the market. Then he hears that the purchaser who was formerly pleading with him to accept his offer has decided not to proceed. No explanation is given, no apology made. The vendor has to embark on the whole dreary process of putting his house on the market all over again.

For the purchaser the process is, if anything, worse. After a series of futile visits to unsuitable houses he eventually finds the house of his dreams. He makes an offer, perhaps at the asking price, perhaps at what the agent tells him the vendor is likely to accept. The offer is accepted. A deal is done. The purchaser instructs soli[ci]tors to act. He perhaps commissions an architect to plan alterations. He makes arrangements to borrow money. He puts his own house on the market. He makes arrangements to move. He then learns that the vendor has decided to sell to someone else, perhaps for the price already offered and accepted, perhaps for an increased price achieved by a covert, unofficial auction. Again, no explanation, no apology. The vendor is able to indulge his self-interest, even his whims, without exposing himself to any legal penalty.

The reasons why purchaser and vendor can act in this apparently unprincipled manner are to be found in two legal rules of long standing: first, the rule that contracts for the sale and purchase of land must be evidenced (or now made) in writing; secondly, the rule that terms agreed subject to contract do not give rise to a binding contract. These rules are deeply imbedded in statute and authority. They make possible the behaviour I have described, but the validity and merits of those rules are not, and could not be, the subject of challenge in this appeal.

For the purchaser there is, however, one means of protection: to make an independent agreement by which the vendor agrees for a clear specified period not to deal with anyone other than that purchaser. The effect is to give that purchaser a clear run for the period in question. The vendor does not agree to sell to that purchaser—such an agreement would be covered by s.2 of the 1989 Act—but he does give a negative undertaking that he will not (for the given period deal with anyone else. That, I am quite satisfied, is what happened here, as the judge rightly held. The vendor and the prospective purchaser made what has come to be called a "lock-out agreement". That was a contract binding on them both. The vendor broke it. He is liable to the prospective purchaser for damages which remain to be assessed. I would dismiss the appeal.

Mann L.J. agreed.

Appeal Dismissed.

Questions

1. Should the two rules discussed by Bingham MR be abolished?   **4–012**

2. According to Article 2: 301 of the Principles of European Contract Law, 1998:

   "(1) A party is free to negotiate and is not liable for failure to reach an agreement.
   (2) However, a party who has negotiated or broken off negotiations contrary to good faith and fair dealing is liable for losses caused to the other party.
   (3) It is contrary to good faith and fair dealing, in particular, for a party to enter into or continue negotiations with no real intention of reaching an agreement with the other party."

   If this were the law of England, would a party's liability under paragraph (2) lie in contract, or tort, or be sui generis?

Problem

Adam makes a hobby of viewing properties which are advertised for sale. Should he be liable for   **4–013**
wasting the time of vendors and estate agents who show him round?

----

3. Clauses with Determinate and Indeterminate Meaning

4–014   In *AstraZeneca UK Ltd v Albemarle International Corporation* [2011] EWHC 1574 (Comm), clause H of a contract between the parties provided as follows:

"H-Switch to Propofol

> In the event that at any time BUYER reformulates or otherwise changes its Diprivan brand to substitute propofol for the PRODUCT, BUYER will so notify SELLER and will give SELLER the first opportunity and right of first refusal to supply propofol to BUYER under mutually acceptable terms and conditions."

Albemarle claimed that the effect of this clause was that, if AstraZeneca (AZ) decided to change the way in which it sourced propofol (the active ingredient of an anaesthetic), then Albemarle would have the "first opportunity and right of first refusal" to supply propofol to AZ. However, AZ argued, inter alia, that the clause lacked sufficient certainty to be enforceable.

ASTRAZENECA UK LIMITED v ALBEMARLE INTERNATIONAL CORPORATION

[2011] EWHC 1574 (Comm)

FLAUX J

4–015   28. At its most extreme, AZ's case is that clause H is too uncertain as regards both content and duration to be given any contractual effect. It is contended that, if the words "first opportunity" stood alone, they would have no meaning, like the words "first option" in Ryan v Thomas (1911) SJ 55, 364 per Warrington J. The short answer to that contention is that the words do not stand alone, but are accompanied by the words "and right of first refusal". Mr Odgers' [for AZ] argument that these words add nothing to "first option" and have an indeterminate meaning is misconceived and, in my judgment, contrary to authority, for reasons I will come on to shortly.

29. So far as uncertainty of duration is concerned, Mr Odgers submits that it is not clear whether the "first opportunity and right of first refusal" is intended to continue indefinitely after termination of the supply agreement, so that it is too uncertain. He relies upon the decision of the House of Lords in Walford v Miles [1992] 2 AC 128, where it was held that an essential requirement for a valid "lock-out" agreement is that it should state for how long it is to last. It seems to me that the short answer to this point is that, whatever rights clause H confers only last for the duration of the supply agreement and cease upon termination. There is nothing in the terms of the agreement to suggest that the rights it confers somehow survive the agreement.

30. Mr Odgers also submitted that the fact that the closing words of the clause recognised that the precise terms of any supply contract would require to be agreed between the parties meant that the provision as a whole was too uncertain to have any effect. I agree with Miss Carr [for Albemarle] that the fact that the precise terms of the contract would still be open for negotiation, once an offer was accepted or matched by Albemarle pursuant to its right of first refusal, does not deprive the right of first refusal of contractual effect: see Smith v Morgan [1971] 1 WLR 803 at 807 per Brightman J, where a similar argument that, because the provision containing the "first option" in that case stated that it was an option to purchase "at a figure to be agreed upon", it was void for uncertainty, was rejected by the learned judge.

31. In any event, the submission that the clause is too uncertain to have contractual effect is an unattractive one. Where parties have troubled to put a specific clause in their contract, then so far as possible the court should strive to give it some meaning commercially. For present purposes, it is not necessary to decide whether, as Albemarle sought to contend, the quid pro quo for the rights conferred by the clause was a competitive DIP price. It is enough that, once the clause is in the supply agreement, it should, so far as possible, be given some sensible meaning.

32. AZ's alternative construction of clause H is that, at most, it required AZ to give Albemarle an opportunity to negotiate with AZ a contract on mutually acceptable terms for the supply of propofol. Mr Odgers relies upon the fact that this construction is consistent with one of the three categories of right of first refusal recognised by Park J in Speciality Shops Ltd v Yorkshire & Metropolitan Estates Ltd [2002] EWHC 2969 (Ch), that is the third category mentioned at paragraph 28 of the judgment:

". . .the landowner is not obliged positively to offer to sell the land to the pre-emption holder, but rather he is obliged to notify the pre-emption holder of the situation, leaving it for the pre-emption holder to make his own offer to purchase the land if he chooses."

33. It seems to me that there are a number of problems with this construction. To begin with, since, as the current supplier of DIP, Albemarle would almost certainly always have been included as one of the potential suppliers of propofol in any request for proposal (RFP) process, in practice this limited construction of clause H adds nothing to what would have happened in any event. To the extent that AZ can argue that clause H gives Albemarle a contractual right to have an opportunity to participate in the RFP, (where otherwise there would have been no contractual right to do so even if in practice Albemarle would have been given the opportunity), it seems to me that, if it had been the intention of the parties that clause H should have such a limited effect, it would have been easy to say so in terms. Words such as "[AZ] will notify [Albemarle] and will give [Albemarle] the opportunity to participate in any request for proposal and to negotiate a contract on mutually acceptable terms" would have been sufficient to achieve that effect.

34. However, those were not the words used. Not only does clause H talk about "first" opportunity, suggesting that this is an opportunity before anyone else, but, against the commercial background to which I have referred, the right of "first refusal" seems to me most naturally to be referring to Albemarle being offered an opportunity to accept or refuse an offer on terms which AZ is minded to accept from a third party. It follows that, in my judgment, the analogy which AZ seeks to draw with **Speciality Shops** is not an apt one, as that case is not concerned with competing offers or bids for a supply contract. In any event, in so far as the three categories which Park J identifies are relevant at all in the present context, it seems to me the first category is closest to this case, namely that, where the triggering event occurs, the owner is obliged to offer to sell the property to the pre-emption holder and leave the offer open and capable of acceptance for a specified period.

35. I agree with Miss Carr that, as an irreducible minimum, a right of "first refusal" by its nature confers a right to obtain the subject matter of the right, whether it is land or another asset or a service or a business opportunity to enter a contract. In other words, it confers a right to be given an opportunity to match any third party offer which the grantor of the right might be otherwise minded to accept, and, in the event that the grantee matches the offer, to be awarded the business to which the offer relates. That construction of the right of first refusal is supported by a number of authorities, which, albeit all at first instance, seem to me to support Miss Carr's submission about this irreducible minimum.

52. . . . [One] of the further issues of construction which arises is whether the grantor is obliged to act in good faith and to provide the grantee with full disclosure of the terms of any third party "deal" which it is minded to accept. Albemarle pleads its case as to good faith and full disclosure in the alternative as express terms of clause H or as implied terms necessary to give clause H business efficacy. Both in its opening and in its written closing submissions, AZ expended much energy in arguing that there was no basis for any implication of terms because Albemarle was seeking to imply wide ranging and overwrought contractual obligations into clause H which could not and should not be implied.

53. I accept Miss Carr's submissions that this approach is misconceived because, on analysis, all that Albemarle is relying upon are obligations which are inherent in or incidents of the right of first refusal. Thus, if there is a third party deal with which the grantor is minded to proceed, in order to enable the grantee to exercise its right of first refusal and match that offer, full and fair disclosure of that deal by the grantor is required. That seems to me to be an incident of the obligation on the grantor to act in good faith recognised by both Brightman J and Park J. Furthermore, the passage from the judgment of Hirst J which I cited in paragraph 45 above recognises the importance of providing full details of whatever contractual "deal" is contemplated, so as to enable the right of first refusal to be properly exercised.

54. So far as the obligation to act in good faith is concerned, that is not some vague generalised obligation in the current context, but, as the cases I have cited recognise, what is required (consonant with the obligation to provide full and fair disclosure of any deal the grantor is minded to accept) is good faith in setting out the precise terms of the offer the grantee has to match and which the grantor is minded to accept. I agree with Miss Carr that, without good faith in that sense, the grantee will not have the opportunity to which the right of first refusal entitles it contractually, to understand and have the opportunity of matching the third party proposal.

55. A further aspect of the obligation on the grantor to act in good faith concerns the effect of the closing words of clause H: "under mutually acceptable terms and conditions". As already discussed, what those words recognise is that, even after the grantee has accepted the "contractual offer" or, in the present case, matched the third party offer the grantor is minded to accept, it may still be the case that no binding contract is entered, because for example, there is some insuperable difficulty between the parties as regards the detailed specification of the

Contract as an Agreement: Finality and Certainty

propofol to be supplied. However, in my judgment what the grantor is not entitled to do is to act in bad faith in relation to such detailed negotiations, declining ultimately to enter a contract with the grantee and then enter into a contract on essentially the same terms with a third party.

56. Equally, because clause H does not impose a binding obligation on AZ to enter a contract for the supply of propofol, if during the detailed negotiations, in all good faith it decided not to enter such a contract at all because, for example, it decided to continue distilling DIP at Macclesfield and not source propofol direct after all, it could not be criticised. What it could not do is break off negotiations with Albemarle on the basis it did not want to enter a contract after all and then, weeks or months later, enter a propofol supply contract with Sochinaz or someone else after all.

NICOLENE LTD v SIMMONDS

Court of Appeal [1953] 1 Q.B. 543; [1953] 2 W.L.R. 717; 97 S.J. 247; [1953] 1 All E.R. 882; [1953] 1 Lloyd's Rep. 189

Appeal from Sellers J

Singleton L.J. delivered judgment in favour of the respondent (plaintiff).

DENNING LJ

4–016   This case raises a short, but important, point which can be stated quite simply: the plaintiffs allege that there was a contract for the sale to them of 3,000 tons of steel reinforcing bars, and the seller broke his contract. When the buyers claimed damages the seller set up the defence that, owing to one of the sentences in the letters which constituted the contract, there was no contract at all. The material words are: "We are in agreement that the usual conditions of acceptance apply." There were no usual conditions of acceptance at all, so the words are meaningless. There is nothing to which they can apply. On that account it is said that there was never a contract at all between the parties. In my opinion a distinction must be drawn between a clause which is meaningless and a clause which is yet to be agreed. A clause which is meaningless can often be ignored, whilst still leaving the contract good; whereas a clause which has yet to be agreed may mean that there is no contract at all, because the parties have not agreed on all the essential terms . . .

I would just say a word about the recent decision of McNair J. in *British Electrical and Associated Industries (Cardiff) Ltd v Patley Pressings Ltd* [1953] 1 W.L.R. 280, 283, where the contract note contained the clause "subject to force majeure conditions." If the true construction of the documents in that case was that an essential term had yet to be agreed, it would fall within the cases to which I have referred, but if the true view was that the exempting clause was agreed but was "so vague and uncertain as to be incapable of any precise meaning" (which was how McNair J. described it) I should have thought that it could be ignored without impairing the validity of the contract. It was clearly severable from the rest of the contract, whereas the term in *G. Scammell & Nephew, Ltd v Ouston*[3] was not.

In the present case there was nothing yet to be agreed. There was nothing left to further negotiation. All that happened was that the parties agreed that "the usual conditions of acceptance apply." That clause was so vague and uncertain as to be incapable of any precise meaning. It is clearly severable from the rest of the contract. It can be rejected without impairing the sense or reasonableness of the contract as a whole, and it should be so rejected. The contract should be held good and the clause ignored. The parties themselves treated the contract as subsisting. They regarded it as creating binding obligations between them; and it would be most unfortunate if the law should say otherwise. You would find defaulters all scanning their contracts to find some meaningless clause on which to ride free.

---

[3] In *Scammell v Ouston* [1941] A.C. 251; [1941] 1 All E.R. 14, the respondents agreed to purchase from the appellants a new motor-van but stipulated that "this order is given on the understanding that the balance of the purchase price can be had on hire-purchase terms over a period of two years". The House of Lords held that this sentence was "so vaguely expressed that it cannot, standing by itself, be given a definite meaning—that is to say, it requires further agreement to be reached between the parties before there would be a complete consensus ad idem". It might have been different if there had been any well-known "usual terms" in such a contract, but there were not.

Hodson L.J. delivered judgment in favour of the respondent.

Appeal Dismissed.

4. AGREEMENTS "SUBJECT TO CONTRACT"

WINN v BULL

Chancery Division (1877) 7 Ch.D. 29; 47 L.J.Ch. 139; 26 W.R. 230

The defendant agreed in writing with the plaintiff to take a lease of a house for a certain term at a   **4–017**
certain rent, "subject to the preparation and approval of a formal contract". No other contract was
ever entered into between the parties. The plaintiff brought an action for specific performance.

JESSEL M.R.

I am of the opinion there is no contract. I take it the principle is clear. If in the case of a proposed sale or lease
of an estate two persons agree to all the terms and say, "We will have the terms put into form," then all
the terms being put into writing and agreed to, there is a contract. [See now the Law of Property Act (M.P.)
1989 s.2].

If two persons agree in writing that up to a certain point the terms shall be the terms of the contract, but that
the minor terms shall be submitted to a solicitor, and shall be such as are approved of by him, then there is no
contract, because all the terms have not been settled.

Now with regard to the construction of letters which are relied upon as constituting a contract, I have
always thought that the authorities are too favourable to specific performance. When a man agrees to buy an
estate, there are a great many more stipulations wanted than a mere agreement to buy the estate and the
amount of purchase-money that is to be paid. What is called an open contract is clearly a most perilous thing,
and even now, notwithstanding the provisions of a recent Act of Parliament—the Vendor and Purchaser Act
1874—no prudent man who has an estate to sell would sign a contract of that kind, but would stipulate that
certain conditions should be inserted for his protection. When, therefore, you see a stipulation as to a formal
agreement put into a contract, you may say it was not put in for nothing, but to protect the vendor against
that very thing. Indeed, notwithstanding protective conditions, the vendor has not unfrequently to allow a
deduction from the purchase-money to induce the purchaser not to press requisitions which the law allows
him to make.

All this shows that contracts for purchase of lands should contain something more than can be found in the
short and meagre form of an ordinary letter.

When we come to a contract for a lease the case is still stronger. When you bargain for a lease simply, it is
for an ordinary lease and nothing more; that is, a lease containing the usual covenants and nothing more; but
when the bargain is for a lease which is to be formally prepared, in general no solicitor would, unless actually
bound by the contract, prepare a lease not containing other covenants besides, that is, covenants which are
not comprised in or understood by the term "usual covenants." It is then only rational to suppose that when a
man says there shall be a formal contract approved for a lease he means that more shall be put into the lease
than the law generally allows. Now, in the present case, the plaintiff says in effect, "I agree to grant you a lease
on certain terms, but subject to something else being approved." He does not say, "Nothing more shall be
required beyond what I have already mentioned," but "something else is required" which is not expressed. That
being so, the agreement is uncertain in its terms and consequently cannot be sustained.

The distinction between an agreement which is final in its terms, and therefore binding, and an agreement
which is dependent upon a stipulation for a formal contract, is pointed out in the authorities . . .

[The Master of the Rolls then considered certain cases.]

It comes, therefore, to this, that where you have a proposal or agreement made in writing expressed to be
subject to a formal contract being prepared, it means what it says; it is subject to and is dependent upon a
formal contract being prepared. When it is not expressly stated to be subject to a formal contract it becomes
a question of construction, whether the parties intended that the terms agreed on should merely be put into
form, or whether they should be subject to a new agreement the terms of which are not expressed in detail. The

result is, that I must hold that there is no binding contract in this case, and there must therefore be judgment for the defendant.

Points for reflection

4-018

1. Section 2 of the Law of Property (Miscellaneous Provisions) Act 1989 provides:

> **2.**—(1) A contract for the sale or other disposition of an interest in land can only be made in writing and only by incorporating all the terms which the parties have expressly agreed in one document or, where contracts are exchanged, in each.
>
> (2) The terms may be incorporated in a document either by being set out in it or by reference to some other document.
>
> (3) The document incorporating the terms or, where contracts are exchanged, one of the documents incorporating them (but not necessarily the same one) must be signed by or on behalf of each party to the contract.

The section does not apply to contracts made before September 29, 1989. They are still governed by s.40 of the Law of Property Act 1925 and are valid though made orally but can be enforced only if there is written evidence as required by that section (s.2(7)). Section 2 does not apply to three classes of contract referred to in s. 2(5), the most important of which for the purposes of this book is "(b) a contract made in the course of public auction". A contract for the sale of land at a public auction need not be in writing and there is no longer even any need for written evidence, as there was until September 27, 1989. A binding contract is concluded as soon as the auctioneer's hammer falls if that is what the parties intend. Section 2(5) also provides that "nothing in this section affects the creation or operation of resulting, implied or constructive trusts". See *Yaxley v Gotts* [2000] 1 All E.R. 711 CA, below, Ch.11.

2. An "open contract" for the sale of land is one which specifies merely the names of the parties, the property to be sold and the price. There may be a valid contract even though the parties have agreed on nothing more than these fundamental matters, provided only that the parties have reached the end of their negotiations, and have agreed on everything which they consider requires agreement and, since September 27, 1989, the agreement is in writing and signed in accordance with the Law of Property (M.P.) Act 1989 s.2, above. "Open contracts" are unusual because of the difficulties and importance of the issues involved in the sale of land; and, in deciding whether the parties intended to contract, the court may bear in mind the improbability of their intending to bind themselves in such an informal way: *Clifton v Palumbo* [1944] 2 All E.R. 497.

Questions

4-019

1. Why is it essential that the price be fixed in a contract for the sale of land, when it need not be fixed in a sale of goods? (Cf. *May and Butcher v R.*, above).

2. If the parties agree that "the minor terms shall be submitted to a solicitor, and shall be such as are approved of by him . . ." why should there not be a contract? (Cf. ss.8 and 9 of the Sale of Goods Act, 1979, discussed above, and *Marten v Whale*, below, Ch.20). Is a contract now precluded by s.2 of the Law of Property (Miscellaneous Provisions) Act 1989, above?

CHILLINGWORTH v ESCHE

Court of Appeal [1924] 1 Ch. 97, 113; 93 L.J.Ch. 129;129 L.T. 808; 40 T.L.R. 23

SARGANT LJ

I desire to say one or two words as to the phrase "contract to enter into a contract." This phrase is used by **4-020** Parker J. in his classic judgment in *Hatzfeldt-Wildenburg v Alexander* [1912] 1 Ch. 284, but only, I think, as a secondary or less accurate method of stating the alternative. In the strictest sense of the words the court will often enforce a contract to make a contract. The specific performance of a formal agreement of purchase is the enforcement of a contract to make a contract; the ultimate conveyance being often in itself in many respects a contract. The same remarks apply to the specific performance of a clause in a lease giving the lessee an option to purchase the superior interest of the lessor, freehold or leasehold as the case may be. The true meaning of the phrase is that the court will not enforce a contract to make a second contract part of the terms of which are indeterminate and have yet to be agreed, so that there is not any definite contract at all which can be enforced, but only an agreement for a contract some of the terms of which are not yet agreed . . .

To my mind the words "subject to contract" or "subject to formal contract" have by this time acquired a definite ascertained legal meaning—not quite so definite a meaning perhaps as such expressions as f.o.b. or c.i.f. in mercantile transactions, but approaching that degree of definiteness. The phrase is a perfectly familiar one in the mouths of estate agents and other persons accustomed to deal with land; and I can quite understand a solicitor saying to a client about to negotiate for the sale of his land: "Be sure that to protect yourself you introduce into any preliminary contract you may think of making the words 'subject to contract'." I do not say that the phrase makes the contract containing it necessarily and whatever the context a conditional contract. But they are words appropriate for introducing a condition, and it would require a very strong and exceptional case for this clear prima facie meaning to be displaced.

There are many conditions that may be specified by a "subject to" agreement. As is well-known, where an agreement is made "subject to contract" it is not a concluded contract where that phrase signifies (as it usually does) that there is further negotiation to be conducted. The parties have agreed on certain terms but there is further agreement to be reached before they are willing to bind themselves. The principle is that applied in *May & Butcher v R.* (above).

It is common for an agreement to buy land to be made "subject to satisfactory survey", "subject to the purchaser obtaining a satisfactory mortgage" or "subject to planning permission being given". These all present a different problem from the "subject to contract" case because they do not contemplate further agreement between the parties. There will be a binding contract provided that, on its true construction, the clause—

(i)   is sufficiently precise and definite for a court to be able to say when it is satisfied; and

(ii)   it does not leave either of the parties with a discretion whether to go on with the transaction.

If the meaning of the clause is that one party has a complete discretion whether to proceed or not, there cannot be a contract because the essence of a bilateral contract is that both parties bind themselves (but see *Spiro v Glencrown Properties*, below, para.4–021).

In *Marks v Board* (1930) 46 T.L.R. 424, Rowlatt J held that a person who agreed to buy land, subject to surveyor's report, "reserved to himself the absolute and undisputed right to say whether he liked the surveyor's report." In *Graham and Scott (Southgate) Ltd v Oxlade* [1950] 2 K.B. 257 Roxburgh J and the Court of Appeal said that the buyer was the arbiter of whether the survey was satisfactory or not and Megaw J made a decision to that effect in relation to the sale of a yacht "subject to satisfactory survey": *Astra Trust Ltd v Williams* [1969] 1 Lloyds Rep. 81. If this is correct, there is clearly no contract because the buyer has an absolute discretion and, if he is not bound, the seller is not bound either.

But it does not follow that the legal position of the parties is the same as where they have agreed, "subject to contract".

In a "subject to contract" case, neither party can make the "agreement" binding without the consent of the other. In a "subject to survey" case, the buyer can bind the seller by having the property surveyed and informing the seller that the survey is satisfactory. "Subject to survey" (as interpreted in the cases cited above) leaves the seller in the position of an offeror. He can revoke his offer to sell at any time before the buyer finds the survey to be satisfactory and, probably until the buyer has so informed him. Once he is so informed, the agreement has become unconditional.

If the clause is, as it appears usually to be, for the exclusive benefit of the buyer, he could also bind the seller by simply informing him that he has waived the condition—he is not going to bother with a survey—whereupon the contract is concluded.

If the arbiter of the satisfactoriness of the survey is a third party, then in principle, there is a contract. A building society may have agreed to give the buyer a mortgage, subject to satisfactory survey. If the buyer were to agree to buy, "subject to the survey being satisfactory to the building society", then the agreement:

(i)   is sufficiently precise and definite because the building society either says that it is satisfied, in which case the contract is on, or it says that it is not satisfied, in which case it is off; and

(ii)   neither of the parties has a discretion, though the building society does. Cf. *Pym v Campbell* and *Marten v Whale*, (below, paras 20–004 and 20–006).

In *Ee v Kakar* (1979) 40 P. & C.R. 223, Walton J held that an agreement subject to survey was binding on the seller. The buyer was under an obligation to have the property surveyed and to consider bona fide whether the survey was satisfactory or not. If the survey would satisfy a reasonable person, it might be difficult for the buyer to satisfy the court that his dissatisfaction was bona fide. Though the same words may bear different meanings in different contexts, the decision on this point seems irreconcilable with *Marks v Board* and the *Astra Trust* case; but Walton J also held that the condition was for the exclusive benefit of the buyer and so he could waive and had waived it.

The words "subject to the purchaser obtaining a satisfactory mortgage" raise exactly the same issues of principle and have also caused a difference of judicial opinion. In *Lee Parker v Izzet* [1971] 1 W.L.R. 1688; [1971] 3 All E.R. 1099 Goff J held that there was a contract, "a satisfactory mortgage" meaning a mortgage to the satisfaction of the purchaser acting reasonably. But in *Lee Parker v Izzet (No.2)* [1972] 2 W.L.R. 775; [1972] 2 All E.R. 800, Goulding J held that a similar phrase was void for uncertainty.

In *Graham v Pitkin* [1992] 2 All E.R. 235, PC, Lord Templeman said of that case: "But since the purchaser, if he had the money, could always have declared that a mortgage of £10 from his brother-in-law was 'satisfactory' their Lordships doubt the finding that there was no contract." But if this means, as it seems to, that the purchaser had an absolute discretion as to what was "satisfactory", did not this confirm Goulding J.'s view that there was no contract?

"Subject to planning permission to develop" was held by Russell J to be sufficiently certain in the context of *Batten v White* (1960) 12 P. & C.R. 66. The buyer was bound to proceed with due diligence and bona fide to seek the relevant permission.

In *Bishop & Baxter, Ltd v Anglo-Eastern Trading and Industrial Co Ltd* [1943] 2 All E.R. 598, B made a counter-offer to buy 20,000 cardigans from S subject to various conditions including a "war clause". S accepted. 3,000 cardigans were delivered and accepted by B. S then repudiated the agreement. It was held by the Court of Appeal that while there had been a sale of the 3,000 cardigans, there was no contract for the sale of 20,000. There were many forms of "war clause" and the joint selection of one form was a necessary preliminary to the contract coming into existence. Scott LJ said: "The parties may, both of them . . . have erroneously supposed that a contract in writing was already in existence; but, if they did, it was because they did not realise that the appellants' counter-offer required a further consensual step, before the law could recognise the formation of a completed contract; and their bad law could not make a contract."

SPIRO v GLENCROWN PROPERTIES LTD AND ANOTHER

Chancery Division [1991] Ch. 537; [1991] 2 W.L.R. 931; [1991] 1 All E.R. 600

By an agreement in two parts, each signed by both parties and exchanged, containing all the agreed terms, the plaintiff granted the first defendant an option to buy a property for £745,000. The option was exercisable by notice in writing to the vendor on the same day and was duly exercised. The purchaser failed to complete. The vendor sued him and his guarantor, the second defendant, for damages for breach of contract.

4–021

HOFFMANN J

. . . having quoted s.2(1) of the Law of Property (Miscellaneous Provisions) Act 1989 [above, para.4–018]: If the "contract for the sale . . . of an interest in land" was for the purposes of s.2(1) the agreement by which the option was granted, there is no difficulty. The agreement was executed in two exchanged parts, each of which incorporated all the terms which had been agreed and had been signed by or on behalf of the vendor and purchaser respectively. But the letter which exercised the option was of course signed only on behalf of the purchaser. If the contract was made by this document, it did not comply with s.2.

Apart from authority, it seems to me plain enough that section 2 was intended to apply to the agreement which created the option and not to the notice by which it was exercised. Section 2, which replaced section 40 of the Law of Property Act 1925, was intended to prevent disputes over whether the parties had entered into a binding agreement or over what terms they had agreed. It prescribes the formalities for recording their mutual consent. But only the grant of the option depends upon consent. The exercise of the option is a unilateral act. It would destroy the very purpose of the option if the purchaser had to obtain the vendor's counter-signature to the notice by which it was exercised. The only way in which the concept of an option to buy land could survive section 2 would be if the purchaser ensured that the vendor not only signed the agreement by which the option was granted but also at the same time provided him with a counter-signed form to use if he decided to exercise it. There seems to be no conceivable reason why the legislature should have required this additional formality.

The language of section 2 places no obstacle in the way of construing the grant of the option as the relevant contract. An option to buy land can properly be described as a contract for the sale of that land conditional upon the exercise of the option . . .

[Hoffmann J discussed *Helby v Matthews* [1895] A.C. 471 a case of a contract for the hire purchase of piano. Hire purchase is a contract of hiring with an option to purchase. Before the hirer had paid all the instalments and exercised the option he pledged the piano with the defendant. The question was whether the pledgee got a good title. If the hirer had "agreed to buy" the piano within the meaning of the Factors Act 1889, by virtue of that Act, he gave a good title to the pledgee. (Cf. the provision to the same effect in the Sale of Goods Act 1979 s.25(1) discussed in *Marten v Whale*, below, para.20–006.) It was held that the hirer had not "agreed to buy", and therefore the pledgee had no title, because those words implied an obligation to buy and the hirer was under no such obligation; he was entitled to return the piano and terminate the agreement at any time Hoffmann J quoted, on the one hand, Lord Macnaghten who described the contract "on the part of the dealer" as "a contract of hiring with a conditional contract or undertaking to sell"; and, on the other hand, Lord Herschell LC who said that this was not an agreement to sell but "in truth merely an offer which cannot be withdrawn"; and Lord Watson who said that the dealer "was in exactly the same position as if he had made an offer to sell on certain terms, and had undertaken to keep it open for a definite period."]

Referring to the Factors Act 1889, Hoffmann J. continued: The language and purpose of the statute requires one to look at the arrangement from the buyer's point of view. And the essence of an option is that while the seller may be said to be conditionally bound, the buyer is free. In the *Helby v Matthews* context it was therefore true to say that pending exercise of the option, the position of the buyer was as if he had been made an offer which the seller could not withdraw.

But the concept of an offer is of course normally used as part of the technique for ascertaining whether the parties have reached that mutual consent which is a necessary element in the formation of a contract. In this primary sense, it is of the essence of an offer that by itself it gives rise to no legal obligations. It was for this reason that Diplock L.J. said in *Varty (Inspector of Taxes) v British South Africa Co* [1965] Ch. 508 at 523:

> "To speak of an enforceable option as an 'irrevocable offer' is juristically a contradiction in terms, for the adjective 'irrevocable' connotes the existence of an obligation on the part of the offeror, while the noun 'offer' connotes the absence of any obligation until the offer has been accepted."

This does not mean that in Diplock L.J.'s opinion, Lord Herschell L.C. and Lord Watson were speaking nonsense. They were not using "offer" in its primary sense but, as often happens in legal reasoning, by way of metaphor or analogy. Such metaphors can be vivid and illuminating but prove a trap for the unwary if pressed beyond their original context. As I said recently in another connection, ". . . there are dangers in reasoning from the metaphor as if it expressed a literal truth rather than from the underlying principle which the metaphor encapsulates" (see *Re K, Re F* [1988] Ch. 310 at 314).

Here the underlying principles are clear enough. The granting of the option imposes no obligation upon the purchaser and an obligation upon the vendor which is contingent upon the exercise of the option. When the option is exercised, vendor and purchaser come under obligations to perform as if they had concluded an ordinary contract of sale. And the analogy of an irrevocable offer is, as I have said, a useful way of describing the position of the purchaser between the grant and exercise of the option. Thus in *J. Sainsbury Plc v O'Connor (Inspector of Taxes)* [1990] S.T.C. 516 at 532 Millett J. used it to explain why the grantee of an option to buy shares did not become the beneficial owner until he had exercised the option.

But the irrevocable offer metaphor has much less explanatory power in relation to the position of the vendor. The effect of the "offer" which the vendor has made is, from his point of view, so different from that of an offer in its primary sense that the metaphor is of little assistance. Thus in the famous passage in *London and South Western Rly. Co v Gomm* (1882) 20 Ch.D. 562 at 581 Jessel M.R. had no use for it in explaining why the grant of an option to buy land confers an interest in the land upon the grantee:

> "The right to call for a conveyance of the land is an equitable interest or equitable estate. In the ordinary case of a contract for purchase there is no doubt about this, and an option for repurchase is not different in its nature. A person exercising the option has to do two things, he has to give notice of his intention to purchase, and to pay the purchase-money; but as far as the man who is liable to convey is concerned, his estate or interest is taken away from him without his consent, and the right to take it away being vested in another, the covenant giving the option must give that other an interest in the land."

The fact that the option binds the vendor contingently to convey was the reason why an option agreement was held to fall within section 40 of the Law of Property Act 1925: see *Richards v Creighton Griffiths (Investments) Ltd* (1972) 225 E.G. 2104, where Plowman J. rejected a submission that it was merely a contract not to withdraw an offer. Similarly in *Weeding v Weeding* (1861) 1 John & H. 424 at 430–431, 70 E.R. 812 at 815 Page Wood V.-C. held that the grant of an option to buy land was sufficient to deem that land converted into personality for the purposes of the grantor's will, even though the option had not yet been exercised when he died. Page Wood V.-C. said:

> "I cannot agree with the argument that there is no contract. It is as much a conditional contract as if it depended on any other contingency than the exercise of an option by a third person, such as, for example, the failure of issue of a particular person."

Thus in explaining the vendor's position, the analogy to which the courts usually appeal is that of a conditional contract. This analogy might also be said to be imperfect, because one generally thinks of a conditional contract as one in which the contingency does not lie within the sole power of one of the parties to the contract. But this difference from the standard case of a conditional contract does not destroy the value of the analogy in explaining the vendor's position. So far as he is concerned, it makes no difference whether or not the contingency is within the sole power of the purchaser. The important point is that his estate or interest is taken away from him without his consent . . .

. . . The purchaser's argument requires me to say that "irrevocable offer" and "conditional contract" are mutually inconsistent concepts and that I must range myself under one or other banner and declare the other to be heretical. I hope that I have demonstrated this to be a misconception about the nature of legal reasoning. An option is not strictly speaking either an offer or a conditional contract. It does not have all the incidents of the standard form of either of these concepts. To that extent it is a relationship sui generis. But there are ways in which it resembles each of them. Each analogy is in the proper context a valid way of characterising the situation created by an option. The question in this case is not whether one analogy is true and the other false, but which is appropriate to be used in the construction of section 2 of the Law of Property (Miscellaneous Provisions) Act 1989 . . .

In my judgment there is nothing in the authorities which prevents me from giving section 2 the meaning which I consider to have been the clear intention of the legislature. On the contrary, the purposive approach taken in cases like *Mulholland* encourages me to adopt a similar approach to section 2. And the plain purpose of section 2 was, as I have said, to prescribe the formalities for recording the consent of the parties. It follows that in my view the grant of the option was the only "contract for the sale or other disposition of an interest in land" within the meaning of the section and the contract duly complied with the statutory requirements. There must be judgment for the plaintiff against both defendants with costs.

Questions

1. What is "an irrevocable offer" if an option is not one, but only analogous to one? Does it exist? If not, how can there be an analogy to it?   **4–022**

2. It may be fair to say that there was a conditional contract to sell; but the question was whether the buyer was bound. Was there a conditional contract to buy?

3. Does the word "offer" imply revocability?

4. If the grant of the option was the only contract for the sale of land, what was the effect of the exercise of the option by the buyer if it was not to make a contract? By what process did he become bound to buy?

5. Was Hoffmann J coming to the rescue of Parliament (and the Law Commission whose recommendations Parliament had implemented) who had failed to realise that they were invalidating the exercise of options to buy land?

6. Is a written agreement for the sale of land, "subject to satisfactory survey" and signed by both parties, "a contract for the sale . . . of an interest in land" (i) before, (ii) after, the buyer declares the survey to be satisfactory?

Further reading

J.W. Carter and M.P. Furmston, 'Good Faith and Fairness in the Negotiation of Contracts' (1994) 8 *Journal of Contract Law* 1 (part one) and 93 (part two)

Ian R. Macneil, 'The Many Futures of Contract' (1974) 47 *Southern California Law Review* 691

Leon E. Trakman and Kunal Sharma, 'The Binding Force of Agreements to Negotiate in Good Faith' (2014) 73 CLJ 598

5

CONTRACT AS A MEETING OF MINDS

LEARNING OBJECTIVES

By the end of this chapter you should understand that:

- for the purposes of holding that a contract has been formed, it is not a requirement that there has been a subjective meeting of minds;
- generally speaking, the test of whether the parties have agreed, and on what terms they have agreed, is one of objective intention (of what a reasonable person would infer in the circumstances);
- where one party contracts on the basis of some mistake or misunderstanding, the courts will not readily treat this as a reason for avoidance of the contract;
- where a written contract fails to record accurately the agreement reached between the parties, it may be rectified; but, where one party has misunderstood the terms of the agreement, the courts will not readily treat this as a reason for rectification;
- in cases where one party pleads that the agreement is out of line with their subjective intentions or understanding, a general way of posing the relevant question is to ask whether it would be "unconscionable" to hold that party to the agreement (or to allow the other party to enforce the agreement).

INTRODUCTION

The courts used frequently to speak as if an actual agreement, a consensus ad idem, or a "meeting of minds", is essential for the formation of a contract. If this was ever the case, it is clear that it is not so today. If you behave in such a manner as to lead me reasonably to believe that you are making an offer to enter into a certain contract and I accept, there is a contract, even though, in fact, you did not intend to make an offer at all. Recall, for example, the Carbolic Smoke Ball Company's argument that it never intended the "offer" in the advertisement to be taken seriously (above, Ch.2). What mattered, the court said, was not the private or subjective intention of the company but how the advert would be read and understood by a reasonable reader of the Pall Mall Gazette. Similarly, if you make an offer which can reasonably bear only one meaning and I, understanding that offer in its one reasonable sense, accept, you cannot escape liability by saying, however truthfully, that you intended it to mean something else. This is a general, if not universal, principle of our law of contract because otherwise no one could ever safely act on a contract which he reasonably believed he had made. In order to protect reasonable reliance, the risk of subjective mistake or misunderstanding simply has to be accepted.

This approach, which attaches importance to what the party said or did instead (where there is a difference) of what he intended to say or do, is known as the "objective" approach, distinguishing it from the "subjective", which attempts to ascertain the actual state of the party's mind at the relevant time.

This is not to say that the actual state of mind of the parties is always ignored in the law of contract. Where, for example, the offer, looked at objectively, is so ambiguous that it is impossible to say what is its true meaning but both the parties in fact understood it in the same sense, it would be absurd not to give effect to the contract in the sense which they both actually intended. Even where the contract, looked at objectively, has only one reasonable meaning but both parties actually intended a different meaning, it would seem to be right to admit evidence as to their subjective intention.

Problems commonly arise because the parties have different notions as to the meaning of the promise given by one or other of them. The promisor intends to give X; the promisee expects to receive Y. If a reasonable man in the position of the promisee would have understood that he was being promised Y, then the contract is to give Y. But if he would have understood that he was being promised X, then the contract is to give X. If the promise is so framed that it may reasonably be understood to mean either X or Y, it seems likely that there is no contract; though it is arguable that the promisee should be able to enforce the promise in the sense that he in good faith gave to it—consider, for example, *Falck v Williams* (below).

It is conceivable that a reasonable person in the position of the promisee would have understood the promise in a third sense, Z, which does not represent the actual intention of either party. Arguably, in such a case, the promise should be enforced in sense Z at the suit of either party. "In seeing whether there is a contract or not, the law can only look to outward appearances. If an intelligent bystander would reasonably infer that a warranty was intended, that will suffice even though neither party in fact had it in mind": *Hornal v Neuberger Products Ltd* [1957] 1 Q.B. 247 at 257, per Denning LJ; [1956] 3 All E.R. 970.

The discussion and cases in this chapter are divided into three sections: in the first section, there is a short discussion of whether the doctrine of estoppel (which is the subject of Ch.11) is the underlying basis of the objective test—in other words, whether a party is precluded from asserting their subjective intention against the objective reading of their words and acts because this is what estoppel so requires; in the second section, a group of cases highlighting various kinds of mistakes and misunderstandings (one-sided mispprehensions, the parties being at cross-purposes, and so on) is presented; and, in the third section, the leading cases on rectification (where a party pleads that a formal document does not accurately represent the parties' agreement and, thus, should be rectified) are set out.

1. Estoppel and the Objective Test

5–002   It has sometimes been said that the basis of the objective test is the doctrine of estoppel. Estoppel takes a variety of different forms but the basic notion is that where one person (the representor) has led another (the representee) to believe that a certain fact or state of affairs exists, intending the representee to act on that belief, and the representee does so act to his detriment, then in any future litigation between them the representor will not be allowed to deny (that is, he will be estopped or precluded from denying) that the representation was true. The case will be decided as if the fact or state of affairs existed even if in truth this was not so.

Although the language of estoppel is used in some of the cases on the objective interpretation of contracts, this is not a satisfactory explanation. For one thing, the objective approach is itself employed to decide whether a person's act or representation is such as to found a potential estoppel, which implies that the objective approach is prior to and independent of estoppel. Furthermore, the essence of estoppel lies in the act done in detrimental reliance (or, at any rate, reliance—even if not detrimental—that reflects a change of position) on the relevant statement; but the objective interpretation of promises does not seem to require detrimental reliance, either in entering into the contract or on it after it has been made. In *Hasham v Zenab* [1960] A.C. 316 a person who had signed a contract to sell a two acre plot of land under the belief, not induced by fraud or misrepresentation, that the contract related to only half an acre of the plot was held bound although he tore up the agreement within minutes of signing it. Indeed, one of the criticisms (below) of the objective approach is that, under it, a person may acquire rights without any act of reliance other than that of entering into the contract.

Estoppel does, however, have a part to play in displacing the objective meaning of the contract. As noticed above, if both parties believe that the contract means X and each is aware of the other's belief, then it seems probable that it will be enforced in sense X even though the objective observer would have thought it meant Z (see Glanville Williams 17 M.L.R. 154 and the discussion below in section 3). This is certainly so where both parties have acted on the common assumption that the contract means X, for then there will be an 'estoppel by convention' precluding either of them from setting up the objective meaning (even though that be the 'true' meaning) of the agreement against the other. See *Amalgamated Investment etc v Texas Commerce*, below, Ch.11; and *Salvation Army Ltd v W Yorks Metropolitan CC*, above, Ch.4.

Estoppel may also, in effect, change the meaning of a contract after it has been entered into. If the true meaning of the contract at the time it is made is Z but A leads B to believe that the contract means X and B acts on that belief, A will not be allowed to deny that the contract means X. In effect, the meaning of the contract has changed from Z to X.

2. A MEETING OF MINDS: MISTAKES AND MISUNDERSTANDINGS

TAMPLIN v JAMES

Chancery Division (1880) 15 Ch.D. 215; 43 L.T. 520; 29 W.R. 311

Property was put up for sale under the description "Lot 1. All that Inn known as 'The Ship,' together with premises adjoining thereto, situate at Newerne, No. 454 and 455 on the tithe map, and containing 20 perches, more or less, now in the occupation of Mrs Knowles and Mr S. Merrick."

5–003

At the back of Lot 1 were two plots of ground in the occupation of the tenant of the inn. These plots did not belong to the vendor. At the auction plans of Lot 1 were lying on the table, and the auctioneer called the attention of the persons present to them. These plans showed clearly the extent of Lot 1, and that it excluded the two plots at the back.

Lot 1 was not sold at the auction but the defendant, who had been present, immediately afterwards made an offer for it which was accepted, and signed a contract for the purchase according to the conditions of sale for £750.

The defendant bought in the belief that he was buying all the land in the occupation of the tenant and declined to complete unless the two plots were conveyed to him. He deposed that he had not seen the plans and was not aware that there were any plans in the room; that he had known the property from a boy, and knew that the two plots all along had been occupied with "The Ship Inn."

The vendors brought an action for specific performance.

BAGGALLAY LJ

The defendant insists in his statement of defence that he signed the memorandum in the reasonable belief that the property comprised therein included the whole of the premises in the occupation of Mrs Knowles and of Mr Samuel Merrick, and not merely the messuages and hereditaments which the plaintiffs allege to be the only property comprised therein, and that such his belief was induced and confirmed by the acts and words of the auctioneer at the sale. The defendant has sworn positively that he had such a belief at the time he signed the memorandum, and I see no reason to doubt the statement so made by him; but was such a belief a reasonable belief?

It is doubtless well established that a court of equity will refuse specific performance of an agreement when the defendant has entered into it under a mistake, and where injustice would be done to him were performance to be enforced. The most common instances of such refusal on the ground of mistake are cases in which there has been some unintentional misrepresentation on the part of the plaintiff (I am not now referring to cases of intentional misrepresentation which would fall rather under the category of fraud), or where from the ambiguity of the agreement different meanings have been given to it by the different parties. The case of *Manser v Back* (6 Hare 443) is a well-known illustration of this. It is true also that specific performance has been refused in cases not coming under either of these heads, as in *Malins v Freeman* (2 Keen 25). But where there has been no misrepresentation, and where there is no ambiguity in the terms of the contract, the defendant cannot be allowed to evade the performance of it by the simple statement that he has made a mistake. Were such to be the law the performance of a contract could rarely be enforced upon an unwilling party who was also unscrupulous. I think that the law is correctly stated by Lord Romilly in *Swaisland v Dearsley* (29 Beav. 430, 433): "The principle on which the court proceeds in cases of mistake is this—if it appears upon the evidence that there was in the description of the property a matter on which a person might bona fide make a mistake, and he swears positively that he did make such mistake, and his evidence is not disproved, this court cannot enforce the specific performance against him. If there appears on the particulars no ground for the mistake, if no man with his senses about him could have misapprehended the character of the parcels, then I do not think it is sufficient for the purchaser to swear that he made a mistake, or that he did not understand what he was about." The observations of Wigram V.-C. in *Manser v Back* (6 Hare 443, 448) seem to me to tend in the same direction.

Now does it appear, or can it safely be held in this case that the defendant reasonably entertained a belief that the gardens were included in the property purchased by him? I will consider first the terms of the contract itself, and then the allegations as to the acts and words of the auctioneer and other agents of the plaintiffs, for it is possible that although the terms of the agreement taken per se may have been free from doubt, enough may have been said or done by the plaintiffs' agents to lead the defendant to attribute a different meaning to its terms.

Mr Pearson admitted, and I think he could not well have avoided admitting, that if the vendors had merely referred to the property as being in the occupation of Mrs Knowles and Mr Merrick without more, there would have been at any rate such an amount of ambiguity that the defendant might reasonably have understood that he was purchasing the whole of the property in their occupation. But the particulars go on to state that the property sold is Nos. 454 and 455 on the tithe map and contains 20 perches. The additional land which the defendant claims to have included is about 20 perches more. Therefore, if he is right in his contention, he would be entitled to double the amount which the printed particulars state the lot to contain. There, no doubt, is force in the argument that a person unaccustomed to measuring would not know whether a property contained 20 perches or 40 perches, but that does not get rid of the effect of the reference to the tithe map. The defendant appears to have purchased in reliance upon his knowledge of the occupation of the premises without looking at the plans, and probably without paying attention to the details of the particulars of Lot 1, but is a person justified in relying upon knowledge of that kind when he has the means of ascertaining what he buys? I think not. I think he is not entitled to say to any effectual purpose that he was under a mistake, when he did not think it worth while to read the particulars and look at the plans. If that were to be allowed, a person might always escape from completing a contract by swearing that he was mistaken as to what he bought, and great temptation to perjury would be offered. Here the description of the property is accurate and free from ambiguity, and the case is wholly unaffected by *Manser v Back* (6 Hare 443) and the other cases in which the defendant has escaped from performance of a contract on the ground of its ambiguity.

The decision of Baggallay L.J. was affirmed by the Court of Appeal, 15 Ch.D. 219.

It should be noted that the standard remedy for breach of contract provided by the common law is an award of monetary compensation (damages) for the loss which the plaintiff has suffered as a result of the breach. Where, however, damages are not an adequate remedy equity will compel the defendant actually to perform his contract by a decree of specific performance. Such orders are most commonly made in the case of contracts for the sale of land. No two pieces of land are exactly alike and courts of equity therefore consider that damages are not an adequate remedy for a failure to convey the land agreed upon. In the case of a sale of goods, on the other hand, it will usually be possible for the buyer to obtain exactly similar goods elsewhere; and, if the seller fails to deliver, the buyer will usually be deemed adequately compensated by damages for any extra expense to which he has been put. Specific performance of a sale of goods will be granted only where the goods are of a unique or very unusual character (see further Ch.18).

DENNY v HANCOCK

Court of Appeal in Chancery (1870) L.R. 6 Ch.App.1; 23 L.T. 686; 19 W.R. 54

On a sale of a small residential property the plan exhibited showed the western side as bounded by a strip of ground covered with a mass of shrubs or trees. The defendant went with the plan in his hand, inspected the property and found on the western side a belt of shrubs bounded on the west by an iron fence, and including three magnificent trees. He then bid for the property, believing that he was buying everything up to the fence. He afterwards discovered that the three trees and the iron fence stood on the adjoining property, the real boundary being denoted by stumps which were so shrouded by shrubs as not easily to be seen. The plan represented in a conspicuous way all the detached trees standing on the property, none of which was nearly so large as the trees in question, but did not show these trees. It was admitted that the existence of these trees was a material element in the value of the property as a residence.

5–004

The defendant declined to complete and Malins VC made a decree of specific performance against him.

SIR W. M. JAMES LJ

Now when we come to examine the evidence, I am bound to say, with all deference to the Vice-Chancellor's judgment in this matter, that the case is clear in favour of the defendant. The defendant tells just the sort of story that I myself should have told if I had been the intending purchaser, and had gone to inspect the property with the plan in my hand: [His Lordship read passages of the defendant's answer.] He has not been cross-examined, and I must say I have no doubt whatever that if I had done exactly what this gentleman did, and taken that plan in my hand, and gone through the property, and found a shrubbery, or ground covered partly with shrubs and partly with thorns, with an iron fence outside, I should have arrived at exactly the same conclusion as this gentleman did, and I should have gone to the sale and bid in the belief that I was buying the belt up to the iron fence with those trees upon it. Then the defendant's surveyor, who says he has been for 20 years in the profession, says: [His Lordship read an extract from the surveyor's evidence]. This gentleman, again, has not been cross-examined, and there really is not, in my judgment, a shadow of evidence in reply to his evidence that the plan was so made as to lead not only the general public, but persons who, like himself, had practical experience in mapping and planning, to the conclusion that the whole of the belt of shrubs up to the iron fence was included in the sale: [His Lordship then stated the effect of the plaintiff's evidence and continued:] There is no denial in evidence of this fact, that the plan produced was calculated to induce anybody to believe that the whole of the belt, or shrubbery, or whatever you may call it, was included in the property sold. It is urged, however, that the defendant was negligent. The substance of the argument seems to be this: that if he had looked at the plan very minutely he would have seen that the trees in the meadows and in the garden were marked, but these three fine trees, which added so much to the value of the property, were not marked; and it is urged that the absence of these remarkable trees from the plan is a thing calculated to put a man so completely on his guard that he ought not to have been misled, and is not to be believed when he says he was misled. But it seems to me that it never would occur to a person who entertained no doubt whatever about what the thing was that had been sold to him, to make any inquiry about the omission of two or three trees in that which appeared on the plan to be a mass of wood. If this gentleman did as he says, buy it under a mistake as to the property, such mistake was caused by the plan which was presented to him, drawn by the vendors' agent, and also caused by this fact, which alone might have been enough to mislead him, that there was on the ground an apparent visible boundary, quite distinct from the almost invisible real boundary. I think that, independently of the plan, and on this latter ground alone, it would have required great consideration before a court of equity would have fixed the purchaser with this contract, which he swears he entered into in the belief that the property extended to its apparent boundary; but coupling the state of the property with the representation made by the plan, I am of the opinion that it would not be according to the established principles of this court to compel the purchaser to complete his contract. I am also of opinion that the mistake was occasioned by at least *crassa negligentia* on the part of the vendors in respect to what they sent out to the public. I am, therefore, unable to agree with the Vice-Chancellor, and am of opinion that he ought to have dismissed this bill with costs.

The judgment of Sir G. Mellish L.J. is omitted.

It should be noted that the fact that a court of equity dismisses an action for specific performance does not necessarily mean that there was no contract enforceable at law. Equitable remedies are said to be "discretionary". This means that the court may take into account all the circumstances of the case, including, for example, the conduct of the plaintiff and the hardship which the order might cause the defendant, in deciding whether to grant the remedy. Thus where an action for specific performance fails the plaintiff might, nevertheless, recover damages, for breach of contract.

In *Malins v Freeman* (1837) 2 Keen 25; 48 E.R. 537 the defendant went to an auction intending to bid for property A. He arrived late but in time to hear the auctioneer describe Lot 3 in terms wholly inapplicable to Property A. He began to bid for Lot 3, supposing it to be Property A, and in due course Lot 3 was knocked down to him for an extravagant price. Lot 3 was a quite different property. The defendant's mistake could not be ascribed in any way to the conduct of the plaintiff or his agents, but Lord Langdale MR refused to decree specific performance, saying:

"I am of opinion that the defendant never intended to bid for this estate. He was hurried and inconsiderate, and, when his error was pointed out to him, he was not so prompt as he ought to have been in declaring it. It is probable that by his conduct he occasioned some loss to the plaintiff; for that he is answerable, if the contract was valid, and will be left so, notwithstanding the decision to be now made. But I think that he never meant to enter into this contract, and that it would not be equitable to compel him to perform it, whatever may be the responsibility to which he is left liable at law."

Questions

1. The legal position in *Denny v Hancock* admits of three possibilities:
   (1) There was no contract
   (2) There was a contract, not specifically enforceable by the vendor, for the sale of the land bounded by the stumps.
   (3) There was a contract for the sale of the land bounded by the iron fence. In such a case equity has jurisdiction to decree specific performance against the vendor and to order compensation to be paid to the purchaser for the discrepancy between what was agreed to be conveyed and what can be conveyed: *Rutherford v Acton-Adams* [1915] A.C. 866, PC. See Harpum, [1981] C.L.J. 47.

   Is it possible to say which was the actual legal position?

2. Can you formulate a general principle of law from *Tamplin v James* and *Denny v Hancock*?

Problem

Athelstan is the owner of an inn. To the north of the inn is a yard which does not belong to Athelstan, but which has always been occupied with the inn. To the east of the inn is a field which does belong to Athelstan. Athelstan intends to offer for sale the inn and the field. Unfortunately the auctioneer employed to carry out the sale misunderstands his instructions and prepares plans and a description of the property which include neither the yard nor the field. The property is put up for sale as Lot 2 and attention is drawn to the plan. Beowulf, who has known the property from a boy, is under the impression that Lot 2 includes the yard but excludes the field. Without examining the plan he bids £5,000 for Lot 2, but it is withdrawn. Later Beowulf meets Athelstan in the saleroom and says: "I offer you £6,000 for Lot 2". Athelstan believing that Lot 2 includes the field, says: "I accept". They sign a note: "Lot 2, the Ship Inn, sold for £6,000."

Is there a contract and, if so, what are its terms?

Point for reflection

In *Scriven Bros & Co v Hindley and Co* [1913] 3 K.B. 564, the defendants bid at an auction for two lots, believing both to be hemp. In fact Lot A was hemp but Lot B was tow, a different commodity in commerce (as the jury found) and of very little value. The defendants declined to pay for Lot B and the sellers sued for the price. The defendants' mistake arose from the fact that both lots contained the same shipping mark, 'SL', and witnesses stated that in their experience hemp and tow were never landed from the same ship under the same shipping mark. The defendants' manager had been shown bales of hemp as 'samples of the "SL" goods'. The auctioneer believed that the bid was made under a mistake but he had reasonable ground for believing that the mistake was merely one as to the value of tow.

5-007

A.T. Lawrence J said that as the parties were not ad idem the plaintiffs could recover only if the defendants were estopped from relying upon what was now admittedly the truth. He held that the defendants were not estopped since their mistake had been caused by or contributed to by the negligence of the plaintiffs.

In this case, the sellers' offer was at least ambiguous, as in *Denny v Hancock*. The decision was that there was no contract for the sale of the bales of tow. Where there is a valid contract for the sale of goods, the judge has no discretion to dismiss the seller's claim for the price (as he has a discretion to dismiss the vendor of land's action for specific performance).

In deciding whether there has been an unequivocal offer and acceptance, the court may consider not merely the words of the alleged offer and acceptance and the relevant surrounding circumstances, but also the history of the negotiations. In *Webster v Cecil* (1861) 30 Beav. 62; 54 E.R. 812 the defendant, having refused to sell some property to the plaintiff for £2,000, wrote a letter in which, as the result of a mistaken calculation, he offered to sell it for £1,250. The plaintiff accepted. Romilly MR refused a decree of specific performance, saying that the plaintiff "might bring such action at law as he might be advised." In *Hartog v Colin and Shields* [1939] 3 All E.R. 566 the defendants offered to sell 30,000 skins to the plaintiff at prices per pound. The previous negotiations had been carried on (as was customary in the trade) by reference to the price per piece. The value of a piece was about one-third that of a pound. The price stated was absurdly low and the defendants said they had written "pound" in error for "piece". Singleton J. dismissed an action for damages for breach of contract, saying, "The plaintiff could not reasonably have supposed that the offer contained the offerors' real intention."

On the other hand, it has been decided that the history of the negotiations is not admissible in order to interpret the contract: *Prenn v Simmonds* [1971] 1 W.L.R. 1381; [1971] 3 All E.R. 237 HL, below, and *City and Westminster Properties v Mudd* (below, Ch.15). Is this consistent with the cases cited above? The evidence was there admitted, not to interpret the words used, but to show that the words used did not, and could not reasonably be supposed by the other party to, represent the true intention of the parties. Is this a valid distinction? See also, *Roberts v Leicestershire CC* (below).

Questions

5-008   1. Suppose the buyers in *Scriven v Hindley* had sued the seller for breach of a contract to sell hemp. What would they have had to prove in order to succeed?

2. The defendants alleged that the auctioneer knew that they were bidding for hemp, not tow. What would have been the effect if they had been able to prove the truth of that allegation? See *Smith v Hughes*, below, and *Roberts v Leicestershire County Council*, below.

3. What would have been the result if the buyers had (as the auctioneer believed) been merely making a mistake as to the value of tow? If the buyers would have been bound, is that reconcilable with *Hartog v Colin & Shields*.

4. In Autumn 1999, the well-known retailer Argos mistakenly advertised a particular line of television sets as being for sale at £3 each rather than the intended price of £300 each. Would prospective purchasers who saw the advertisement have a legally enforceable claim if they purported to purchase a set for £3? Would it make any difference if the advertisement was (as, in fact, it was) on the Argos online shopping site? Would it make any difference if the purchaser purported to purchase 100 sets?

CENTROVINCIAL ESTATES PLC v MERCHANT INVESTORS ASSURANCE COMPANY LTD

Court of Appeal [1983] Com.L.R. 158; The Times, March 8, 1983; 1982 C. 6380 (Lexis transcript)

5-009   The defendants were tenants from December 1, 1978 to December 24, 1989 of premises at a yearly rent of £68,320, subject to review from December 25, 1982. Clause 1 of the lease required the lessor and lessee to endeavour, at least six months before December 25, 1982, to reach agreement on the then current market value of the premises and, if able to agree, to certify the amount of the current market rental value. In the event of failure to agree, the matter was to be referred to an independent valuer. The plaintiffs were about to become the landlords. On June 22, 1982, their solicitors wrote to the defendants proposing £65,000 per annum as the appropriate rental value and inviting them to agree this figure. The defendants replied on June 23 agreeing the figure, stating that they had attached the two letters to the lease and asking the plaintiffs to do the same with their copy. The plaintiffs received this letter on June 28 and on that day telephoned the defendants to say that the figure of £65,000 was a mistake and inviting them to treat the letter of June 22 as if it had quoted the figure they had intended to propose, £126,000. The defendants declined to do so. The plaintiffs issued a writ claiming a declaration that there was no binding agreement as to the rental value. They issued a summons for judgment under Ord.14 of the Rules of the Supreme Court (see Smith & Bailey, *The Modern English Legal System*, p.421). They claimed that the defendants were taking advantage of what they knew, or ought reasonably to have known, was an error on the part of the plaintiffs' solicitors; but they conceded that the issue as to the state of the defendant's knowledge could only be resolved at the trial. They nevertheless obtained summary judgment. The defendants appealed.

SLADE LJ

... giving the judgment of the Court (Slade and Robert Goff L.JJ.): This concession having been made, in our opinion correctly, the plaintiffs were confronted with at least formidable difficulties on their application for summary judgment. On the face of it, the letter of June 22, 1982 constituted a formal, unequivocal and unambiguous offer made to the defendants on behalf of the plaintiffs, with an intent to create legal relations, to agree that the "current market rental value" of the demised premises, for the purpose of sub-paragraph A of the rent review provision, was £65,000 per annum. On the face of it, the letter of June 23, 1982 constituted a formal, unequivocal and unambiguous acceptance of that offer by the defendants. The plaintiffs' solicitors indeed assert that they erroneously inserted the figure of £65,000 in the letter of June 22, 1982 in substitution for the figure of £126,000, which they had intended to insert; and like the learned Judge we are prepared to accept the truth of this assertion for the purpose of dealing with the present application. But in the absence of any proof, as yet, that the defendants either knew or ought reasonably to have known of the plaintiffs' error at the time when they purported to accept the plaintiffs' offer, why should the plaintiffs now be allowed to resile from that offer? It is a well-established principle of the English law of contract that an offer falls to be interpreted not subjectively by reference to what has actually passed through the mind of the offeror, but objectively, by reference to the interpretation which a reasonable man in the shoes of the offeree would place on the offer. It is an equally well-established principle that ordinarily an offer, when unequivocally accepted according to its precise terms, will give rise to a legally binding agreement as soon as acceptance is communicated to the offeror in the manner contemplated by the offer, and cannot thereafter be revoked without the consent of the other party. Accepting, as they do, that they have not yet proved that the defendants knew, or ought reasonably to have known, of their error at the relevant time, how can the plaintiffs assert that the defendants have no realistic hope of establishing an agreement of the relevant nature by virtue of the two letters of June 22 and 23, 1982?

Mr Richard Scott in answer has submitted an argument to the following effect. The "agreement" envisaged by sub-paragraphs A and B of the rent review provision is a genuine agreement, a real meeting of the minds. In the present case there was no real meeting of the parties' minds because of the plaintiffs' error. True it is that their intentions would have fallen to be judged objectively, according to their external manifestation, if the defendants had not only purported to accept the offer but had further altered their position as a result. However, so the argument runs, the general rule that the intentions of an offeror must be judged objectively is based on estoppel. Accordingly, if the person who has accepted the offer has not altered his position in reliance on the offer, no such estoppel arises. In the present case, it is submitted, the critical fact is that the figure of £65,000 was lower than the rent currently payable under the Lease immediately before December 25, 1982. In these circumstances, it is said, the defendants in agreeing that figure, did not alter their position in any way. Because of sub-paragraph E of the rent review provision, the current rent of £68,320 would have continued to be pay[a]ble after December 25, 1982, notwithstanding the agreement. In all the circumstances, it is submitted, the plaintiffs, having proved their error at the relevant time, were at liberty to withdraw the offer contained in the letter of June 22, 1982, even after it had been accepted, and they duly did so at the end of June 1982.

We understand from the learned Judge's judgment that an argument on much the same lines was submitted to him on behalf of the plaintiffs and that, though he regarded it as novel and surprising, he was in the end convinced by it.

As will have appeared, Mr Scott's submissions based on mistake involve the implicit proposition (among other propositions) that the defendants have given no consideration for the agreement on which they now rely; we understood him to accept that if the defendants had altered their position in any material respect in agreeing the figure of £65,000, the argument based on mistake could not avail the plaintiffs. Since, for reasons which we will explain later in this judgment, we have come to the clear conclusion that the defendants did give consideration, the argument based on mistake must in our opinion fail for this reason, if no other, and any further reference to the issue of mistake is not strictly necessary. Furthermore, it is right to record that Mr Scott, in an argument which brevity rendered no less forceful, did not burden (and indeed was not pressed to burden) the Court with citations of authority on this issue. In all the circumstances this judgment on an Order XIV summons is not an appropriate occasion to embark on a lengthy discussion on the law relating to mistake in contract. Nevertheless, we should perhaps attempt to explain briefly (albeit obiter) why, quite apart from questions of consideration, we respectfully differ from the learned Judge on the question of mistake, as a matter of broad principle.

The nature of the apparent contract concluded by the two letters of June 22 and 23, 1982 is what is sometimes called a "bilateral contract." It was concluded by

(a) an offer by the plaintiffs to treat £65,000 as the "current market rental value" of the premises for the purpose of the Lease if the defendants would promise to accept that figure as that value, followed by
(b) the giving of a promise by the defendants in those terms. Where the nature of an offer is to enter into a

bilateral contract, the contract becomes binding when the offeree gives the requested promise to the promisor in the manner contemplated by the offer; the mutual promises alone will suffice to conclude the contract. In our opinion, subject to what is said below relating to consideration, it is contrary to the well established principles of contract law to suggest that the offeror under a bilateral contract can withdraw an unambiguous offer, after it has been accepted in the manner contemplated by the offer, merely because he has made a mistake which the offeree neither knew nor could reasonably have known at the time when he accepted it. And in this context, provided only that the offeree has given sufficient consideration for the offeror's promise, it is nothing to the point that the offeree may not have changed his position beyond giving the promise requested of him.

For these reasons we think that the plaintiff's submissions based on mistake cannot, as matters stand, suffice to negative the existence of the apparent agreement of the parties to treat £65,000 as the current market rental value for the purpose of the Lease and to deprive the defendants of the right to defend this action on the basis of such agreement, though we are not, of course, saying that the plea of mistake as formulated in the statement of claim will not succeed at the trial.

We did, however, allow Mr Scott to submit another ground in support of the plaintiff's application, even though it appears that it did not emerge clearly in argument in the Court below and is not reflected in any respondents' notice. While the Court will not generally concern itself with the adequacy of consideration, by examining a bargain to see whether it is fair and beneficial to both sides, it will generally require some consideration to support a promise. A party to a contract can only enforce a promise not given under seal if in return for it he has given something of value in the eyes of the law: (see for example *Halsbury's Laws of England* (4th ed.), Vol. 9, paras. 316 and 317 in the cases there cited). Though one promise will by itself generally be sufficient consideration for another promise, in the present case Mr Scott forcefully submitted that, in entering into the agreement alleged by them, the defendants gave nothing whatever of value. In his submission they conferred no benefit on the plaintiffs, because the effect of the agreement would not have enabled them to claim any more rent than that to which they would have been entitled in its absence. For the same reason, he contended, the agreement subjected the defendants to no detriment; on any footing the agreement had no practical operative effect because of sub-paragraph F of the rent review provision Mr Scott submitted that this argument based on lack of consideration was perfectly capable of being decided on the affidavit and other documentary evidence before the Court and by itself sufficed to negative the existence of an agreement such as alleged by the defendants . . .

In our opinion, on the assumption that consideration is necessary to support the agreement alleged by them, they have plainly given it, if only because, by their letter of June 23, 1983, they have deprived themselves of the right to put forward any figure other than £65,000 as the relevant "current market rental value" or to have this rental value referred to an independent surveyor or valuer. We appreciate that these rights may be said to be of little value to the defendants, but we are not concerned with the adequacy of the consideration given by them for the plaintiffs' promise; and we are not prepared to say that these rights are of no value. It has to be remembered that, if the defendants had refused to agree any figure at all, considerable inconvenience to the plaintiffs might have resulted; an agreement should at least have had the merit of producing certainty and avoiding future disputes. Furthermore, if in the end the plaintiffs had been driven to have the matter referred to an independent valuer, they would have had to pay one half of the costs of the assessment: (see sub-paragraph F of the rent review provision). In all the circumstances in our judgment the surrender by the defendants of the rights to which we have referred clearly constituted sufficient consideration in law for the alleged agreement so that this last weapon in the plaintiffs' armoury on this present summons does not avail them.

Appeal Allowed with Unconditional Leave to Defend.

Questions

1. Professor Atiyah asks:

5–010

"Why should an offeree be entitled to create legal rights for himself by the bare act of acceptance when he has in no way relied upon the offer before being informed that it was made as a result of a mistake and did not in reality reflect the intention of the offeror? Now that liability for misleading statements is an accepted part of tort law, it becomes increasingly anomalous if in a contractual context a party is able to sue upon an unrelied-upon statement, whereas in any other context he is not. A misleading offer is a commercial or perhaps social nuisance which should be discouraged, and for which compensation may be due, if loss is thereby caused, but surely the principles governing such misleading communications ought not to depend upon whether the communication can be classified as an offer or not."

Do you agree? (Atiyah is discussing *The Hannah Blumenthal* [1983] 1 A.C. 854 which, he believes, throws doubt on the *Centrovincial* case and *The Leonidas D* [1985] 2 All E.R. 796 CA which he criticises: (1986) 102 L.Q.R. 363 at 368.)

2. How should the trial court have decided the above case if it had been proved (i) that the defendants knew or ought to have known that the plaintiffs were making a gross mistake about the current market value of the premises; or (ii) that the defendants knew or ought to have known that the figure of £65,000 did not represent the real intention of the plaintiffs?

3. The defendants were contracting to pay a sum less than they were already bound to pay under the lease. Why was not the rule in Pinnel's case (below, Ch.10) applicable?

Point for reflection

In *Watkin v Watson-Smith, The Times*, July 3, 1986, the plaintiff, a frail old man of 80, agreed on a   **5–011** purchase price for his bungalow of £2,950 rather than £29,500 by mistake. M. Wheeler QC, sitting as a deputy judge of the Chancery Division, held that there was no contract as the defendant knew or ought to have known of the mistake as in *Hartog v Colin*, above, or because the parties were never ad idem: *Scriven v Hindley*, above. In any event, he would have set the contract aside as an unconscionable bargain, taking into account the plaintiff's old age with accompanying diminution of capacity and judgment, his desire for a quick sale, the undervalue and the lack of independent advice. Cf. below, Ch.26.

Problem

Al wrote to several contractors, inviting them to tender for the supply and installation of windows in   **5–012** a building which Al was erecting. Ben put in a tender of £200. The prices submitted by the four other contractors who tendered ranged from £1,200 to £1,800. Al posted a letter accepting Ben's tender. Ben has now replied explaining that his clerk had put a decimal point in the wrong place when calculating the square footage of glass required and that the price quoted should be £2,000.

Is there a contract and, if so, what are its terms?

Cf. *Imperial Glass Ltd v Consolidated Supplies Ltd* (1960) 22 D.L.R. (2d) 759 and comment in (1961) 39 Can. Bar Rev. 625; *McMaster University v Wilchar Construction Ltd* (1971) 22 D.L.R. (3d) 9; *Belle River Community Arena v Kaufmann* (1978) 87 D.L.R. (3d) 761.

FALCK v WILLIAMS

Privy Council [1900] A.C. 176; 69 L.J.P.C. 17

The plaintiff and the defendant used a code for business purposes. The plaintiff through his agent,   **5–013** Buch, sent an offer in code by telegraph. The offer was ambiguous owing to the absence of punctuation. It was not clear whether an important word of the code ("escorte") went with one sentence or with the sentence following. The defendant accepted the offer. But the plaintiff understood the offer in one sense, the defendant in the other. The effect was that Williams thought the contract was for the carriage of a cargo of shale from Sydney to Barcelona and Falck thought it was a contract for the carriage of a cargo of copra from Fiji to the UK. The plaintiff's action for breach of contract in the Supreme Court of New South Wales failed. He appealed to the Privy Council. The appeal was dismissed. The judgment of their Lordships was delivered by Lord Macnaghten.

LORD MACNAGHTEN

> . . . the whole controversy when the matter is threshed out seems to be narrowed down to this question—"Is the word 'escorte' to be read with what has gone before or with what follows?" In their Lordships' opinion there is no conclusive reason pointing one way or the other. The fault lay with the appellant's agent. If he had spent a few more shillings on his message, if he had even arranged the words he used more carefully, if he had only put the word "escorte" before the word "begloom" instead of after it, there would have been no difficulty. It is not for their Lordships to determine what is the true construction of Buch's telegram. It was the duty of the appellant as plaintiff to make out that the construction which he put upon it was the true one. In that he must fail if the message was ambiguous, as their Lordships hold it to be. If the respondent had been maintaining his construction as plaintiff he would have equally failed.

Question

5-014   Do you agree with Lord Macnaghten's dictum that if the respondent had been suing as plaintiff he would equally have failed?

RAFFLES v WICHELHAUS

Exchequer (1864) 2 H. & C. 906; 159 E.R. 375; 33 L.J.Ex. 160

5-015   The declaration contained a count upon an agreement for the purchase, by the defendants, of "125 bales of Surat cotton, guaranteed middling fair merchants Dhollerah to arrive ex Peerless from Bombay, to be taken from the quay at the price of 171/4 per lb., to be paid within a certain time then agreed upon after the arrival of the goods in England." Averment—That the goods did arrive by the said ship from Bombay in England, and that the plaintiff was ready and offered to deliver, etc. Breach—That the defendants did not nor would, but wholly refused to accept the said goods, or pay the plaintiff for them, and have not paid him for them, by means whereof, etc.

Second plea—That the said ship mentioned in the agreement was meant and intended by the defendants to be the ship called the Peerless, which sailed from Bombay, to wit, in October, and that the plaintiff was not ready and willing and did not offer to deliver to the defendants, any bales of cotton which arrived by the last-mentioned ship, but instead thereof was only ready and willing to deliver, and offered to deliver to the defendants, 125 bales of Surat cotton, which arrived by another and different ship, which was also called the Peerless, and which sailed from Bombay to wit, in December.

Demurrer, and joinder in demurrer.

Milward, in support of the demurrer: The contract was for the sale of so much cotton of a particular nature, well described, which the plaintiff was ready to deliver. By which ship it should come was immaterial. The words "to arrive," etc., merely mean that, if the ship be lost, the contract is to go off.

[POLLOCK CB

> You may as well say that a description of goods as those "in a particular warehouse" is no part of the contract. Whether the same Peerless was meant by the plaintiff and the defendants is a matter of evidence for the jury.]
> It does not appear that the plaintiff had any goods in the other Peerless. If the defendants had said their speculation had fallen through in consequence, it might have been different.

[POLLOCK CB

If the plea fairly raises the question, it is as good a plea as ever was framed.]

The defendants are not justified in introducing parol evidence into a written contract, which has been performed by the plaintiff. They do not say that he misled them, but only that they fancied the ship was different. Intention is of no use, unless stated at the time of the contract.

The time of the sailing of the ship was no part of the contract; and, for the purposes of the plea, we must take it that both ships sailed on the same day.

Mellish (Cohen with him), in support of the plea: The contract was for cotton, "ex Peerless from Bombay." There is nothing on the face of the contract to show which Peerless was meant; so that this is a plain case of latent ambiguity, as soon as it is shown that there were two Peerlesses from Bombay; and parol evidence may be given when it will be found that the plaintiff meant one and the defendants the other. If this was the case, there was no consensus ad idem, and therefore no binding contract.

Per curiam (Pollock C. B., Martin B. and Pigott B.).

Judgment for the Defendants.

It should be noted that, where the parties have reduced their contract to writing it is not permissible, as a general rule, to adduce parol (oral) evidence to add to, vary or contradict the written instrument. This rule, known as "the parol evidence rule", is subject to many qualifications or exceptions (see Ch.11), one of which, established by *Raffles v Wichelhaus*, is that parol evidence is admissible to reveal a latent ambiguity. A latent ambiguity is one which does not appear on the face of the instrument, a patent ambiguity one which does so appear: see *Falck v Williams* (above). The Law Commission has recommended that no legislation is required to reform or clarify the parol evidence rule: (1986) Law Com. No.154 (Cmnd. 9700).

Questions

1. If the buyer had been thinking of the December Peerless would there have been a contract? If   **5–016**
   so, is this not a type of case in which the court is concerned with the actual state of mind of the parties?

2. Suppose the buyer had discovered his mistake but decided he would like the cargo of the December Peerless after all; the seller, having also discovered the mistake, declines to deliver. Has the buyer any rights?

3. The offer in the present case, (by whichever party it was made) was ambiguous. Does it, then, follow that Lord Macnaghten's dictum in *Falck v Williams* (above) is correct? Or is there a difference in the responsibility for the ambiguity which might affect the result?

4. See Gilmore, *The Death of Contract*, pp.35–44: ". . . the judges, no doubt mistakenly, believed that the identity of the carrying ship was important. . .." Were the judges mistaken? Does the case show, as Gilmore argues, that the courts "were approaching the problem of formation of contract from a purely subjectivist point of view. . ." ? Cf. J. C. Smith, (1979) 13 *The Law Teacher*, p.73.

SMITH v HUGHES

Queen's Bench (1871) L.R. 6 Q.B. 597; 40 L.J.Q.B. 221; 25 L.T. 329; 19 W.R. 1059

The plaintiff, a farmer, asked the manager of the defendant, who was a trainer of racehorses, if he   **5–017**
would like to buy 40 or 50 quarters of oats, and showed him a sample. The manager wrote to say

that he would take the whole quantity at 34s. a quarter. The plaintiff delivered a portion of them. The defendant complained that the oats were new oats, whereas he thought he was buying old oats, new oats being useless to him. The plaintiff, who knew that the oats were new—he had no old oats—refused to take them back and sued for the price. There was a conflict of evidence as to what took place between the plaintiff and the manager. According to the plaintiff the manager had said: "I am always a buyer of good oats," to which the plaintiff replied: "I have some good oats for sale." But according to the manager he said to the plaintiff: "I am always a buyer of good old oats," to which the plaintiff responded: "I have some good old oats for sale."

The judge left two questions to the jury:

1. Was the word "old" used? If so, verdict for the defendant.

2. If the word "old" was not used, did the plaintiff believe the defendant to believe or to be under the impression that he was contracting for old oats? If so, verdict for the defendant.

The jury found a verdict for the defendant. The plaintiff appealed.

COCKBURN CJ

It is to be regretted that the jury were not required to give specific answers to the questions so left to them. For, it is quite possible that their verdict may have been given for the defendant on the first ground; in which case there could, I think, be no doubt as to the propriety of the judge's direction; whereas now, as it is possible that the verdict of the jury—or at all events of some of them—may have proceeded on the second ground, we are called upon to consider and decide whether the ruling of the learned judge with reference to the second question was right.

For this purpose we must assume that nothing was said on the subject of the defendant's manager desiring to buy old oats, nor of the oats having been said to be old; while on the other hand, we must assume that the defendant's manager believed the oats to be old oats, and that the plaintiff was conscious of the existence of such belief, but did nothing, directly or indirectly, to bring it about, simply offering his oats and exhibiting his sample, remaining perfectly passive as to what was passing in the mind of the other party. The question is whether, under such circumstances, the passive acquiescence of the seller in the self-deception of the buyer will entitle the latter to avoid the contract. I am of opinion that it will not.

The oats offered to the defendant's manager were a specific parcel, of which the sample submitted to him formed a part. He kept the sample for 24 hours, and had, therefore, full opportunity of inspecting it and forming his judgment upon it. Acting on his own judgment, he wrote to the plaintiff, offering him a price. Having this opportunity of inspecting and judging of the sample, he is practically in the same position as if he had inspected the oats in bulk. It cannot be said that, if he had gone and personally inspected the oats in bulk, and then, believing—but without anything being said or done by the seller to bring about such a belief—that the oats were old, had offered a price for them, he would have been justified in repudiating the contract, because the seller, from the known habits of the buyer, or other circumstances, had reason to infer that the buyer was ascribing to the oats a quality they did not possess, and did not undeceive him.

I take the true rule to be, that where a specific article is offered for sale, without express warranty, or without circumstances from which the law will imply a warranty—as where, for instance, an article is ordered for a specific purpose—and the buyer has full opportunity of inspecting and forming his own judgment, if he chooses to act on his own judgment, the rule caveat emptor applies. If he gets the article he contracted to buy, and that article corresponds with what it was sold as, he gets all he is entitled to, and is bound by the contract. Here the defendant agreed to buy a specific parcel of oats. The oats were what they were sold as, namely, good oats according to the sample. The buyer persuaded himself they were old oats, when they were not so; but the seller neither said nor did anything to contribute to his deception. He has himself to blame. The question is not what a man of scrupulous morality or nice honour would do under such circumstances. The case put of the purchase of an estate, in which there is a mine under the surface, but the fact is unknown to the seller, is one in which a man of tender conscience or high honour would be unwilling to take advantage of the ignorance of the seller, but there can be no doubt that the contract for the sale of the estate would be binding . . .

Now, in this case, there was clearly no legal obligation in the plaintiff in the first instance to state whether the oats were new or old. He offered them for sale according to the sample, as he had a perfect right to do, and gave the buyer the fullest opportunity of inspecting the sample, which, practically, was equivalent to an inspection of the oats themselves. What, then, was there to create any trust or confidence between the parties, so as to make it incumbent on the plaintiff to communicate the fact that the oats were not, as the defendant assumed them to be, old oats? If, indeed, the buyer, instead of acting on his own opinion, had asked the question whether the oats were old or new, or had said anything which intimated his understanding that the seller was selling the oats as old oats, the case would have been wholly different; or even if he had said anything which showed that he was not acting on his own inspection and judgment, but assumed as the foundation of the contract that the oats were old, the silence of the seller, as a means of misleading him, might have amounted to a fraudulent concealment, such as would have entitled the buyer to avoid the contract. Here, however, nothing of the sort occurs. The buyer in no way refers to the seller, but acts entirely on his own judgment . . .

It only remains to deal with an argument which was pressed upon us, that the defendant in the present case intended to buy old oats, and the plaintiff to sell new, so the two minds were not ad idem; and that consequently there was no contract. This argument proceeds on the fallacy of confounding what was merely a motive operating on the buyer to induce him to buy with one of the essential conditions of the contract. Both parties were agreed as to the sale and purchase of this particular parcel of oats. The defendant believed the oats to be old, and was thus induced to agree to buy them, but he omitted to make their age a condition of the contract. All that can be said is, that the two minds were not ad idem as to the age of the oats; they were certainly ad idem as to the sale and purchase of them. Suppose a person to buy a horse without a warranty, believing him to be sound, and the horse turns out unsound, could it be contended that it would be open to him to say that, as he had intended to buy a sound horse, and the seller to sell an unsound one, the contract was void, because the seller must have known from the price the buyer was willing to give, or from his general habits as a buyer of horses that he thought the horse was sound? The cases are exactly parallel.

BLACKBURN J

The rule of law is that stated in *Freeman v Cooke* (1848) 2 Exch. 654. If, whatever a man's real intention may be, he so conducts himself that a reasonable man would believe that he was assenting to the terms proposed by the other party, and that other party upon that belief enters into the contract with him, the man thus conducting himself would be equally bound as if he had intended to agree to the other party's terms.

The jury were directed that, if they believed the word "old" was used, they should find for the defendant—and this was right; for if that was the case, it is obvious that neither did the defendant intend to enter into a contract on the plaintiff's terms, that is, to buy this parcel of oats without any stipulation as to their quality; nor could the plaintiff have been led to believe he was intending to do so.

But the second direction raises the difficulty. I think that, if from that direction the jury would understand that they were first to consider whether they were satisfied that the defendant intended to buy this parcel of oats on the terms that it was part of his contract with the plaintiff that they were old oats, so as to have the warranty of the plaintiff to that effect, they were properly told that, if that was so, the defendant could not be bound to a contract without any such warranty unless the plaintiff was misled. But I doubt whether the direction would bring to the minds of the jury the distinction between agreeing to take the oats under the belief that they were old, and agreeing to take the oats under the belief that the plaintiff contracted that they were old.

The difference is the same as that between buying a horse believed to be sound, and buying one believed to be warranted sound; but I doubt if it was made obvious to the jury, and I doubt this the more, because I do not see much evidence to justify a finding for the defendant on this latter ground if the word "old" was not used. There may have been more evidence than is stated in the case; and the demeanour of the witnesses may have strengthened the impression produced by the evidence there was; but it does not seem a very satisfactory verdict if it proceeded on this latter ground. I agree, therefore, in the result that there should be a new trial.

HANNEN J

The rule of law applicable to such a case is a corollary from the rule of morality which Mr Pollock cited from Paley (*Moral and Political Philosophy, Book III*, Chap. 5), that a promise is to be performed "in that sense in which the promiser apprehended at the time the promisee received it," and may be thus expressed: "The promiser is not bound to fulfil a promise in a sense in which the promisee knew at the time the promiser did not intend it." And in considering the question, in what sense a promisee is entitled to enforce a promise, it matters not in what way the knowledge of the meaning in which the promiser made it is brought to the mind of the promisee, whether by express words, or by conduct, or previous dealings, or other circumstances. If by any means he knows that there was no real agreement between him and the promiser, he is not entitled to insist that the promise shall be fulfilled in a sense to which the mind of the promiser did not assent.

If, therefore, in the present case, the plaintiff knew that the defendant, in dealing with him for oats, did so on the assumption that the plaintiff was contracting to sell him old oats, he was aware that the defendant apprehended the contract in a different sense to that in which he meant it, and he is thereby deprived of the right to insist that the defendant shall be bound by that which was only the apparent, and not the real bargain.

This was the question which the learned judge intended to leave to the jury, and, as I have already said, I do not think it was incorrect in its terms, but I think that it was likely to be misunderstood by the jury. The jury were asked, "whether they were of opinion, on the whole of the evidence, that the plaintiff believed the defendant to believe, or to be under the impression that he was contracting for the purchase of old oats? If so, there would be a verdict for the defendant." The jury may have understood this to mean that, if the plaintiff believed the defendant to believe that he was buying old oats, the defendant would be entitled to the verdict; but a belief on the part of the plaintiff that the defendant was making a contract to buy the oats, of which he offered him a sample, under a mistaken belief that they were old, would not relieve the defendant from liability unless his mistaken belief were induced by some misrepresentation of the plaintiff, or concealment by him of a fact which it became his duty to communicate. In order to relieve the defendant it was necessary that the jury should find not merely that the plaintiff believed the defendant to believe that he was buying old oats, but that he believed the defendant to believe that he, the plaintiff, was contracting to sell old oats . . .

New Trial Ordered.

Questions and Notes

5–018

1. If the word "old" was used, the plaintiff loses. Does he lose because:

    (a) there was no contract; or
    (b) there was a contract to sell oats which the plaintiff promised were old—that is, a contract which was not performed? Cf. *Roberts v Leicestershire County Council* (below).

2. Suppose the defendant's horses had suffered injury through eating new oats. Could the defendant (if the word "old" was used) have recovered damages from the plaintiff? (Cf. Lord Atkin in *Bell v Lever Bros*, below, Ch.23).

3. If the word "old" was not used, but the plaintiff knew that the defendant believed that the plaintiff was contracting to sell old oats, the plaintiff loses. Does he lose because:

    (a) there was no contract; or
    (b) there was a contract to sell oats which the plaintiff promised were old—that is, a contract which was not performed?

4. The plaintiff wins even though he knew the defendant was making a mistake of fact. Should he not, a fortiori, have won if he had been making the same mistake, i.e. he too thought the oats were old? But see *Solle v Butcher*, below, Ch.23 and *William Sindall Plc v Cambridgeshire CC*, below, Ch.14.

5. For more on what men of tender conscience or high honour would do, see Lord Rodger in *Hamilton v Allied Domecq Plc* [2007] UKHL 33 at para.20: "Doubtless, if [the defendant's representative] knew that this was [the claimant's] position, a failure on the part of [the former] to speak might be regarded as morally questionable. But that is different from saying that he was under a legal duty to speak."

The Principles of European Contract Law, 1998, Art. 4:103: Mistake as to facts or law

(1)   A party may avoid a contract for mistake of fact or law existing when the contract was concluded if:

    (i)   the mistake was caused by information given by the other party; or
    (ii)   the other party knew or ought to have known of the mistake and it was contrary to good faith and fair dealing to leave the mistaken party in error; or
    (iii)   the other party made the same mistake, and

    (b)   the other party knew or ought to have known that the mistaken party, had it known the truth, would not have entered the contract or would have done so only on fundamentally different terms.

(2)   However a party may not avoid the contract if:
    (a)   in the circumstances its mistake was inexcusable, or
    (b)   the risk of the mistake was assumed, or in the circumstances should be borne, by it.

Question

How would *Smith v Hughes* be decided under Article 4:103 PECL? See (1)(a)(ii) and (b). What about the art expert who recognises a painting offered for sale in a junk shop for £20 as a Constable worth £100,000 and buys it for £20? Would the article destroy the principle, caveat emptor? Would that be an improvement in the law?

5–019

----

3. RECTIFICATION

FREDERICK E ROSE (LONDON) LTD v WILLIAM H. PIM JNR & CO, LTD

Court of Appeal [1953] 2 Q.B. 450; [1953] 3 W.L.R. 497; 97 S.J. 556; [1953] 2 All E.R. 739; 70 R.P.C. 238

The plaintiffs, London merchants, were asked by their Eygptian house for "Moroccan horsebeans described here as feveroles." Their representative did not know what feveroles were, and asked the defendants' representative who, after making inquiries, told him that feveroles were just horsebeans and that his firm could procure them. After negotiations on that basis, written contracts were concluded (1) between North African suppliers and the defendant, (2) between the defendant and the plaintiffs, and (3) between the plaintiffs and Egyptian buyers, for the sale and purchase of "horse-beans," payment to be in London by confirmed irrevocable letters of credit against shipping documents. When the horsebeans, shipped from Tunis, were received by the Egyptian buyers, the latter found that the commodity supplied was not feveroles, but another type of bean; but as they had paid for the goods, they accepted them and claimed damages.

5–020

The plaintiffs now sought rectification of their contract with the defendants. The Court of Appeal (Singleton, Denning and Morris LJJ) held, reversing Pilcher J, that, as the concluded oral agreement was for horsebeans, and the written contracts were in the same terms, the remedy of rectification was not available.

DENNING LJ

I am clearly of opinion that the contract was not a nullity. It is true that both parties were under a mistake, and that the mistake was of a fundamental character with regard to the subject-matter. The goods contracted for—horsebeans—were essentially different from what they were believed to be—"feveroles." Nevertheless, the parties to all outward appearances were agreed. They had agreed with quite sufficient certainty on a contract for the sale of goods by description, namely, horsebeans. Once they had done that, nothing in their minds could make the contract a nullity from the beginning, though it might, to be sure, be a ground in some circumstances for setting the contract aside in equity. In *Ryder v Woodley* (1862) 10 W.R. 294, where a buyer contracted to buy a commodity described "St. Giles Marais wheat," believing that it was wheat when it was not, the contract was held to be binding on him and not a nullity. In *Harrison & Jones Ltd v Bunten & Lancaster Ltd* [1953]1 Q.B. 646, where parties contracted for the supply of "Calcutta kapok, 'Sree' brand," both believing it to be pure kapok containing no cotton whereas it in fact contained 10 to 12 per cent of cotton, Pilcher J. held that their mistake, although fundamental, did not make the contract a nullity. In *McRae v Commonwealth Disposals Commission* [below, para.23–010], where sellers contracted to sell a stranded oil tanker, described as lying at a specified point off Samarai, believing that there was a tanker at such a place when there was in fact no such tanker there, nor anywhere in the locality, the High Court of Australia held that the mistake, although fundamental, did not make the contract a nullity, and that the buyers were entitled to damages. The court showed convincingly that *Couturier v Hastie* [below, para.23–005] was a case of construction only. It was not a case where the contract was void for mistake. The other old cases at common law can likewise be explained. At the present day, since the fusion of law and equity, the position appears to be that when the parties to a contract are to all outward appearances in full and certain agreement, neither of them can set up his own mistake, or the mistake of both of them, so as to make the contract a nullity from the beginning. Even a common mistake as to the subject-matter does not make it a nullity. Once the contract is outwardly complete, the contract is good unless and until it is set aside for failure of some condition on which the existence of the contract depends, or for fraud, or on some equitable ground: see *Solle v Butcher* [below, para.23–019]. Could this contract, then, have been set aside? I think it could, if the parties had acted in time. This contract was made under a common mistake as to the meaning of "feveroles" and "horsebeans." This mistake was induced by the innocent misrepresentation of the defendants made to the buyers and passed on to the sub-buyers. As soon as the buyers and sub-buyers discovered the mistake, they could, I think, have rejected the goods and asked for their money back. The fact that the contract was executed would not be a bar to rescission. But once the buyers and sub-buyers accepted the goods, and treated themselves as the owners of them, they could no longer claim rescission: see *Leaf v International Galleries*, [below, para.14–015].

The buyers now, after accepting the goods, seek to rectify the contract. Instead of it being a contract for "horsebeans" simpliciter, they seek to make it a contract for "horsebeans described in Egypt as feveroles." The judge has granted their request. He has found that there was "a mutual and fundamental mistake" and that the defendants and the plaintiffs, through their respective market clerks, "intended to deal in horsebeans of the feverole type"; and he has held that, because that was their intention—their "continuing common intention"—the court could rectify their contract to give effect to it. In this I think he was wrong. Rectification is concerned with contracts and documents, not with intentions. In order to get rectification it is necessary to show that the parties were in complete agreement on the terms of their contract, but by an error wrote them down wrongly; and in this regard, in order to ascertain the terms of their contract, you do not look into the inner minds of the parties—into their intentions—any more than you do in the formation of any other contract. You look at their outward acts, that is, at what they said or wrote to one another in coming to their agreement, and then compare it with the document which they have signed. If you can predicate with certainty what their contract was, and that it is, by a common mistake, wrongly expressed in the document, then you rectify the document; but nothing less will suffice. It is not necessary that all the formalities of the contract should have been executed so as to make it enforceable at law (see *Shipley Urban District Council v Bradford Corporation* [1936] Ch. 375); but formalities apart, there must have been a concluded contract. There is a passage in *Crane v Hegeman-Harris Co Inc* [1939] 1 All E.R. 662, 664 which suggests that a continuing common intention alone will suffice; but I am clearly of opinion that a continuing common intention is not sufficient unless it has found expression in outward agreement. There could be no certainty at all in business transactions if a party who had entered into a firm contract could afterwards turn round and claim to have it rectified on the ground that the parties intended something different. He is allowed to prove, if he can, that they agreed something different: see *Lovell & Christmas v Wall*, per Lord Cozens-Hardy M.R. and per Buckley L.J. ([1911]) 104 L.T. 85, 88, 93) but not that they intended something different.

The present case is a good illustration of the distinction. The parties no doubt intended that the goods should satisfy the inquiry of the Egyptian buyers, namely, "horsebeans described in Egypt as feveroles." They assumed that they would do so, but they made no contract to that effect. Their agreement, as outwardly expressed, both orally and in writing, was for "horsebeans." That is all the defendants ever committed themselves to supply; and all that they should be bound to. There was, no doubt, an erroneous assumption underlying the contract—

an assumption for which it might have been set aside on the grounds of misrepresentation or mistake—but that is very different from an erroneous expression of the contract, such as to give rise to rectification.

The matter can best be tested by asking what would have been the position if the contract between the defendants and the plaintiffs had been for "feveroles." Surely, then, the defendants on their side would have stipulated with their Algerian suppliers for the delivery of "feveroles," and the plaintiffs on their side would have agreed with their sub-buyers to deliver "feveroles." It would not be fair to rectify one of the contracts without rectifying all three, which is obviously impossible.

Glanville Williams, "Mistake and Rectification in Contract", 17 M.L.R. 154

[The writer says with reference to the above case:]

Let it be supposed that with the contract as it was in the instant case, both parties had gone into the witness-box and testified that they realised the distinction between the ordinary horsebeans and "feveroles," but that they used the term "horsebeans" to mean "feveroles" and not to mean ordinary horsebeans. In that event, it is clear, the contract would be valid for the sale of feveroles and there would be no contract for the sale of ordinary horsebeans. A contract is not enforced according to its "outward appearance" if both parties concur in intending something else. It is not invariably true, therefore, to say, as Denning L.J. does, that in the formation of a contract "one does not look into the inner minds of the parties."

Points for reflection

1. In *London Weekend Television Ltd v Paris & Griffith* (1969) 113 S.J. 222, Megaw J is reported as **5–021** saying, "Where two persons agreed expressly with one another what was the meaning of a particular phrase but did not record their definition in the contract itself, if one of the parties sought to enforce the agreement on the basis of some other meaning, he could be prevented by an action for rectification."

2. In *Rose v Pim*, Denning LJ said that, if rectification is to be ordered, "formalities apart, there must have been a concluded contract" before the document to be rectified was signed. This would appear to be too wide a statement. There need not be an antecedent concluded contract, so long as the parties were in agreement up to the moment when they executed the formal contract and there had been some "outward expression of accord". In *Joscelyne v Nissen* [1970] 2 Q.B. 86; [1970] 1 All E.R. 1213, a father and daughter were agreed and intended, among other things, that the father should live in the ground floor of the daughter's house, she to pay the gas, electricity and coal bills and the cost of a home help to tend her afflicted mother. The agreement in fact signed by the father and daughter stated that the father should have the ground floor "free of all rent and outgoings of every kind in any event"; and, on ordinary construction, would not require the daughter to pay the gas bills, etc. The Court of Appeal held that the contract should be rectified to provide expressly that the daughter pay the gas bills, etc., Russell LJ said (p.99): "We wish to stress that this is a case of rectification based on antecedent expressed accord on a point adhered to in intention by the parties to the subsequent written contract . . ."

3. In construing a written contract, the court is entitled to take account of the circumstances with reference to which the words were used and the object, appearing from those circumstances, which the person using the words had in view (and, more generally, the factual matrix, see Ch.17); but it may not look at the prior negotiations of the parties as an aid to construction of the written contract resulting from those negotiations. According to Lord Wilberforce in *Prenn v Simmonds* [1971] 1 W.L.R. 1381, at 1384, the reason for excluding evidence of the negotiations is "simply that such evidence is unhelpful. By the nature of things, where negotiations are difficult, the parties' positions, with each passing letter, are changing and until the final agreement,

although converging, still divergent. It is only the final document which records a consensus. If the previous documents use different expressions, how does the construction of those expressions, itself a doubtful process, help on the construction of the contractual words? If the same expressions are used, nothing is gained by looking back; indeed something may be lost since the relevant surrounding circumstances may be different." Given the modern contextual approach to the interpretation of contracts, this exclusionary rule was reconsidered in *Chartbrook Limited v Persimmon Homes Limited* [2009] UKHL 38. However, on balance the court decided that the exclusion should remain. As Lord Hoffmann summarised it (at para 41):

> "The conclusion I would reach is that there is no clearly established case for departing from the exclusionary rule. The rule may well mean, as Lord Nicholls has argued, that parties are sometimes held bound by a contract in terms which, upon a full investigation of the course of negotiations, a reasonable observer would not have taken them to have intended. But a system which sometimes allows this to happen may be justified in the more general interest of economy and predictability in obtaining advice and adjudicating disputes. It is, after all, usually possible to avoid surprises by carefully reading the documents before signing them and there are the safety nets of rectification and estoppel by convention. Your Lordships do not have the material on which to form a view. It is possible that empirical study (for example, by the Law Commission) may show that the alleged disadvantages of admissibility are not in practice very significant or that they are outweighed by the advantages of doing more precise justice in exceptional cases or falling into line with international conventions. But the determination of where the balance of advantage lies is not in my opinion suitable for judicial decision. Your Lordships are being asked to depart from a rule which has been in existence for many years and several times affirmed by the House. There is power to do so under the *Practice Statement (Judicial Precedent)* [1966] 1 WLR 1234. But that power was intended, as Lord Reid said in *R v National Insurance Comrs, Ex p Hudson* [1972] AC 944, 966, to be applied only in a small number of cases in which previous decisions of the House were "thought to be impeding the proper development of the law or to have led to results which were unjust or contrary to public policy". I do not think that anyone can be confident that this is true of the exclusionary rule."

For an illustration, see *City and Westminster Properties v Mudd* (below, Ch.15) and compare *Roberts v Leics CC* (below). However, what if the history of the negotiations would show that the parties intended to use a word in a special sense—that they had, so to speak, a private dictionary (as in the example given by Glanville Williams above)? On the admissibility of such evidence, see further *Chartbrook* at paras 42-47, where Lord Hoffmann recognises that, where the exclusionary rule threatens to cause an injustice, it might be possible to avoid this by pleading rectification or estoppel by convention (in both cases allowing evidence of the negotiations to be introduced)?

4. It is well settled that "it is not legitimate to use as an aid to the construction of the contract anything which the parties said or did after it was made. Otherwise one might have the result that a contract meant one thing the day it was signed, but by reason of subsequent events meant something different a month or a year later": *James Miller v Whitworth Estates* [1970] 2 W.L.R. 728; [1970] 1 All E.R. 796 at 798, per Lord Reid. The House of Lords held that Denning MR and Widgery LJ in the Court of Appeal had been wrong to have regard to the conduct of the parties after the contract was made in order to decide whether they intended the contract to be governed by English or Scottish law. But where both parties have acted on a common assumption as to the meaning of the contract, they will be 'estopped by convention' from denying that the meaning on which they have acted is the true meaning

----

ROBERTS AND CO LTD v LEICESTERSHIRE COUNTY COUNCIL

[1961] Ch. 555; [1961] 2 W.L.R. 1000; [1961] 2 All E.R. 545

The plaintiffs, building contractors, submitted to the defendants a tender for the erection of a school, in which they offered to undertake to complete the work in 18 months. The defendants replied "accepting" the tender and forwarded contract documents. In these documents they specified, for their own benefit and not that of the company, a period of 30 months, instead of the 18 months referred to in the tender. The officers of the company executed the contract without noticing this change in the contract period. The officers of the county council realised that the plaintiffs were in error as to the contract period but did not draw their attention to the period actually stated and, subsequently, the county council executed the contract. There is a direct relationship between the price and the contract period, and if the company had made its tender on the basis of a 30-month period, the price would have been higher. A dispute having arisen, Pennycuick J. held that the contract must be rectified by the substitution of a period of 18 months for that of 30 months. Having held that the plaintiffs were not entitled to rectification on the ground of a common mistake because the parties did not have a common intention as to what period should be inserted in the contract, he went on:

5-022

PENNYCUICK J

The second ground rests on the principle that a party is entitled to rectification of a contract on proof that he believed a particular term to be included in the contract and that the other party concluded the contract with the omission or a variation of that term in the knowledge that the first party believed the term to be included. Counsel appearing for the council formulated the principle in slightly different terms, as follows, viz, the plaintiff must show that his intention was that the term sought to be introduced by rectification should be included in the contract and, so far as now relevant, that the omission of the term was occasioned by the dishonest conduct of the defendant in acceptance of the formation of the contract without the term, in the knowledge that the plaintiff thought the term was included. Counsel thus introduces into his formulation of the principle the word "dishonest," but he accepts that such conduct by the defendant in his formulation is of its nature dishonest, so that the word "dishonest" appears to carry the matter no further. I do not think that there is any substantial disagreement as to the scope of the principle.

The principle is stated in *Snell's Principles of Equity* (26th ed.), p.684, as follows: "By what appears to be a species of equitable estoppel, if one party to a transaction knows that the instrument contains a mistake in his favour but does nothing to correct it, he (and those claiming under him) will be precluded from resisting rectification on the ground that the mistake is unilateral and not common."

The exact basis of the principle appears to be in some doubt. If the principle is correctly rested on estoppel it seems to me that it is not an essential ingredient of the right of action to establish any particular degree of obliquity to be attributed to the defendant in such circumstances. If, on the other hand, the principle is rested on fraud, obviously dishonesty must be established. It is well established that a party claiming rectification must prove his facts beyond reasonable doubt, and I think that this high standard of proof must equally apply where the claim is based on the principle indicated above.

Questions

1. The court orders rectification where the contract as recorded differs from the contract which was in fact made. See Treitel (10th edn), pp.296–301. Thus Pennycuick J must have held that the true contract in the above case was for performance in 18 months. What light, then, does the decision cast on the answer to question 3(b) in para.5–018 above?

5-023

2. In *London Holeproof Hosiery Co Ltd v Padmore* (1928) 44 T.L.R. 499 a lessee of a factory which had been destroyed by fire exercised an option to renew the lease, believing that the lessor was promising to rebuild the premises. The lessor knew that the lessee so believed. The Court of Appeal dismissed both the lessee's action for failure to rebuild the premises and the lessor's

counterclaim for specific performance of a contract to take the premises in the condition in which they were. Following *Smith v Hughes*, the court held that the parties were not ad idem and that there was no contract. See P. S. Atiyah, (1968) 2 Ottawa L. R. 337.

Is this consistent with the decision in *Roberts v Leicestershire County Council*? Is it a correct application of *Smith v Hughes*? And is it right in principle?

3. Would the Misrepresentation Act 1967 be of relevance to the situation in *Rose v Pim* or *Roberts v Leicestershire County Council*?

Point for reflection

5–024   In *Thomas Bates & Son Ltd v Wyndham's (Lingerie) Ltd* [1981] 1 All E.R. 1077 CA, a rent review clause in a lease of a factory by B Ltd to W Ltd stated that the lessee had an option to renew the lease for a specific period at a rent to be agreed between the parties, and, in default of such agreement, at a rent to be fixed by a single arbitrator appointed by the President of the Royal Institution of Chartered Surveyors. When the lease came up for renewal, the provision concerning the reference to arbitration was omitted due to a mistake on the part of B Ltd's managing director. W Ltd knew that he did not realise his mistake, but they signed the lease without the clause concerned. B Ltd applied for rectification of the document.

It was held (Buckley, Eveleigh and Brightman LJJ) that rectification would be ordered. For the doctrine of rectification to apply, where there was a mistake on the part of one of the parties only, it had to shown that (1) one party erroneously believed that the document sought to be rectified contained a particular term or provision; (2) the other party was aware of the omission and that it was due to a mistake; (3) the other party had failed to draw the mistake to his attention; and (4) the mistake must be one calculated to benefit the other person. If those requirements were satisfied, the court might regard it as inequitable to allow the other party to resist rectification to give effect to the mistaken party's intention on the ground that the mistake was not, at the time of the execution of the document, a mutual mistake. In the present case the requirements had all been established. (*Roberts v Leicestershire County Council*, applied).

RIVERLATE PROPERTIES LTD v PAUL

Court of Appeal [1975] Ch. 133; [1974] 3 W.L.R. 564; [1974] 2 All E.R. 656; 28 P. & C.R. 220

5–025   The plaintiff granted a lease of a maisonette for 99 years to the defendant at a price of £6,500 with a ground rent of £25 per annum. The plaintiff intended that the lessee should pay half of the cost of exterior and structural repairs but the lease put the entire burden on the plaintiff. The defendant's understanding was that she was not responsible for these repairs. The plaintiff's claim for rectification or alternatively rescission of the lease was dismissed by Templeman J and the Court of Appeal.

RUSSELL LJ

. . . delivering the judgment of the court: What is there in principle, or in authority binding on this court, which requires a person who has acquired a leasehold interest on terms on which he intended to obtain it, and who thought when he obtained it that the lessor intended him to obtain it on those terms, either to lose the leasehold interest, or, if he wish to keep it, to submit to keep it only on the terms which the lessor meant to impose but did not? In point of principle, we cannot find that this should be so. If reference be made to principles of equity, it operates on conscience. If conscience is clear at the time of the transaction, why should equity disrupt the transaction? If a man may be said to have been fortunate in obtaining a property at a bargain price, or on terms that make it a good bargain, because the other party unknown to him has made a miscalculation or other mistake, some high-minded men might consider it appropriate that he should agree to a fresh bargain to cure the miscalculation or mistake, abandoning his good fortune. But if equity were to enforce the views of those high-minded men, we have no doubt that it would run counter to the attitudes of much the greater part of ordinary mankind (not least the world of commerce), and would be venturing on the field of moral philosophy in which it would soon be in difficulties.

Question

What if the defendant had been aware of the plaintiff's misunderstanding when the lease was signed?   5–026

COMMISSION FOR NEW TOWNS v COOPER (GB) LTD

Court of Appeal [1995] Ch. 529; [1995] 2 W.L.R. 677; [1995] 2 All E.R. 929

The question for the court was whether a contract entered into by correspondence between the plaintiff   5–027
and the defendant (then called CoopInd) granted to the defendant a put option (an option to require the plaintiff to take an assignment of an underlease). Differing from the trial judge, the court held that, on its true construction, the contract did not grant that option. In case they were wrong about that, the court went on to consider whether the contract should be rectified, so as to exclude the option, on the ground that the plaintiff entered into the contract believing that it contained no such option and that CoopInd knew, or at least suspected, that the plaintiff so believed.

STUART-SMITH LJ

Stuart-Smith L.J. referred to the judgment of Slade L.J. in *Agip SpA v Navigazione Alta SpA, The Nai Genova* [1984] 1 Lloyd's Rep. 353 stating that in all the cases, including *Roberts, Riverlate* and *Bates*, where rectification had been granted on the ground of a unilateral mistake, the defendant had actual knowledge of the plaintiff's mistake at the time the contract was signed and that he inclined to the view that rectification could only be granted where the defendant had actual knowledge. Stuart-Smith L.J. continued: It is only with great diffidence that I venture to think that this may not be an exhaustive statement of the law, although it undoubtedly covers the majority of situations. But were it necessary to do so in this case, I would hold that where A intends B to be mistaken as to the construction of the agreement, so conducts himself that he diverts B's attention from discovering the mistake by making false and misleading statements, and B in fact makes the very mistake that A intends, then notwithstanding that A does not actually know, but merely suspects that B is mistaken, and it cannot be shown that the mistake was induced by any misrepresentation, rectification may be granted. A's conduct is unconscionable and he cannot insist on performance in accordance with the strict letter of the contract; that is sufficient for rescission. But it may also not be unjust or inequitable to insist that the contract be performed according to B's understanding, where that was the meaning that A intended that B should put upon it. That is so here because, although on the assumption that CoopInd's construction is correct and the put option was included, the contract appeared to be a whole package, in truth CoopInd thought they were getting something for nothing.

[His Lordship referred to the analysis of mental states by Peter Gibson J. in *Baden's* case [1992] 4 All E.R. 161 at 235 as comprising: "(i) actual knowledge; (ii) wilfully shutting one's eyes to the obvious; (iii) wilfully and recklessly failing to make such inquiries as an honest and reasonable man would make; (iv) knowledge of circumstances which would indicate the facts to an honest and reasonable man; (v) knowledge of circumstances which would put an honest and reasonable man on inquiry." Having cited passages from the trial judge, he continued.]

The judge appears therefore to be holding that only Peter Gibson J.'s category (i) is sufficient. But with all respect to him, this is not so; categories (ii) and (iii) also constitute actual knowledge in law. In my judgment, it must have been plain that neither Mr Hill nor Mr Barton [representatives of the plaintiff] had any idea that they were dealing with the put option, far less agreeing to grant it to CoopInd. It did not suit CoopInd's plan, as the judge found, to draw attention to this or ask any questions about it. Their (CoopInd's representatives') conduct in raising the smokescreen in relation to the side land was dishonest and intended to deceive. If the question is posed as a jury question, I find it impossible to reach any other conclusion but that an honest and reasonable man would have mentioned the point expressly.

Evans L.J. agreed, saying that " 'knowledge' in this context includes 'shut-eye' knowledge."

Farquharson L.J. agreed.

Question

5-028   Should Peter Gibson J's category (iv) or (v) be a ground for rectification of a written contract?

CHARTBROOK LIMITED v PERSIMMON HOMES LIMITED

[2009] UKHL 38

LORD HOFFMANN

5-029   59. Until the decision of the Court of Appeal in *Joscelyne v Nissen* [1970] 2 QB 86 there was a view, based upon dicta in nineteenth and early twentieth century cases, that rectification was available only if there had been a concluded antecedent contract with which the instrument did not conform. In *Lovell and Christmas Ltd v Wall* (1911) 104 LT 85, 88 Sir Herbert Cozens-Hardy MR said that rectification "may be regarded as a branch of the doctrine of specific performance". It presupposed a prior contract and required proof that, by a common mistake, the final completed agreement as executed failed to give proper effect to the prior contract. In *Joscelyne*'s case the Court of Appeal declared itself puzzled by the reference to specific performance, but I think it is clear enough that the Master of the Rolls had in mind a contractual obligation to execute a lease, conveyance, settlement or similar instrument, giving rise to a specifically enforceable obligation to do so. A failure to execute a document giving effect to the terms of the agreement would be a breach of that obligation and the court, in rectifying the instrument, would be specifically performing the agreement. Since the decision in *Joscelyne*'s case extended the availability of rectification to cases in which there had been no enforceable prior agreement, specific performance is plainly an inadequate explanation of the doctrine. But for present purposes the significance of cases like *Lovell and Christmas Ltd v Wall* (1911) 104 LT 85 is that the terms of the contract to which the subsequent instrument must conform must be objectively determined in the same way as any other contract. Thus the common mistake must necessarily be as to whether the instrument conformed to those terms and not to what one or other of the parties believed those terms to have been.

60. Now that it has been established that rectification is also available when there was no binding antecedent agreement but the parties had a common continuing intention in respect of a particular matter in the instrument to be rectified, it would be anomalous if the "common continuing intention" were to be an objective fact if it amounted to an enforceable contract but a subjective belief if it did not. On the contrary, the authorities suggest that in both cases the question is what an objective observer would have thought the intentions of the parties to be. Perhaps the clearest statement is by Denning LJ in *Frederick E Rose (London) Ltd v William H Pim Jnr & Co Ld* [1953] 2 QB 450, 461:

> "Rectification is concerned with contracts and documents, not with intentions. In order to get rectification it is necessary to show that the parties were in complete agreement on the terms of their contract, but by an error wrote them down wrongly; and in this regard, in order to ascertain the terms of their contract, you do not look into the inner minds of the parties—into their intentions—any more than you do in the formation of any other contract. You look at their outward acts, that is, at what they said or wrote to one another in coming to their agreement, and then compare it with the document which they have signed. If you can predicate with certainty what their contract was, and that it is, by a common mistake, wrongly expressed in the document, then you rectify the document; but nothing less will suffice."

61. Likewise in the *Olympic Pride (Etablissements Georges et Paul Levy v Adderley Navigation Co Panama SA* [1980] 2 Lloyd's Rep 67, 72, Mustill J said:

"The prior transaction may consist either of a concluded agreement or of a continuing common intention. In the latter event, the intention must have been objectively manifested. It is the words and acts of the parties demonstrating their intention, not the inward thoughts of the parties, which matter."

62. An example of the application of this objective ascertainment of the terms of the prior transaction is *George Cohen Sons & Co Ltd v Docks and Inland Waterways Executive* (1950) 84 Lloyd's Rep 97 in which a landlord negotiating a new lease proposed to the tenant that "the terms and conditions contained in the present lease to be embodied in the new lease where applicable." The tenant accepted this offer, but the new lease as executed made the tenant liable for repairs which under the old lease had been the responsibility of the landlord. In answer to a claim for rectification, the landlord said that the new lease was in accordance with what he had understood to be the effect of his offer. The Court of Appeal said that this was irrelevant. What mattered was the objective meaning of what the landlord had written. Sir Raymond Evershed MR said, at p 107:

"If the defendants . . . did misconstrue [the letter] that is unfortunate for them, but at least they cannot be heard to say that their letter was intended to mean anything other than that which the words convey to the reader as a piece of ordinary English."

Points for reflection

In *Chartbrook*, Lord Hoffmann emphasises that, in order to determine what the parties have agreed, an objective approach must be taken. Nevertheless, the law (and its application) in relation to rectification remains problematic. It is not always clear whether the mistake should be characterised as common or as unilateral; and, fitting the facts into the legal matrix can be far from mechanical. Following the guidance in *Chartbrook*, some of the continuing difficulties were highlighted by the differences of opinion in the Court of Appeal in *Daventry District Council v Daventry & District Housing Limited* [2011] EWCA Civ 1153. There, Daventry District Council (DDC) had made arrangements to transfer its stock of council housing and garages to a registered social landlord, Daventry and District Housing Limited (DDH). Under this arrangement, DDC also agreed to transfer its housing department staff to DDH. The point at issue was which party, DDC or DDH, was to cover an estimated £2.4m deficit in the pension fund for these staff. In the formal contract—particularly reading clauses 14.10.2 and 14.10.3—it appeared that the responsibility lay with DDC; but DDC maintained that this was never the parties' intention, that the agreement was that there was to be a splitting of the responsibility, and that the contract should be rectified accordingly. While Vos J (in the High Court) and Etherton LJ (in the Court of Appeal) declined to order rectification, Lord Neuberger MR and Toulson LJ (in the Court of Appeal) held that DCC were entitled to have the contract rectified. The key facts are summarised by Lord Neuberger MR (at para 190) as follows:

5–030

190   DDC's claim for rectification of the Transfer Contract is to be assessed against the following basic history:

a) The negotiations between DDC and DDH for the transfer of DDC's housing stock and staff ("the staff") to DDH started in June, and were conducted by very senior personnel (primarily Mr Bruno for DDC and Mr Roebuck for DDH) and their respective external solicitors and financial advisers;
b) The negotiations had to address the question of the £2.4 million deficit ("the deficit") in respect of the staff pension scheme;
c) From 20 September, the negotiations were based on a document proffered by DDC to DDH, known as "Version 1";
d) The negotiations resulted in a formal signed agreement in principle ("the prior accord") on 11 October, and this reflected Version 1, and was contained in a signed "Valuation";
e) It could just about be argued that the prior accord required DDC to pay the deficit, but the interpretation which involved it being met by DDH "requires far less violence . . . and is the more natural construction", and made much better commercial sense, as the Judge said– [2010] EWHC 1935 (Ch), para 124;
f) Mr Roebuck, DDH's principal negotiator, knew DDC believed this was the effect of the prior accord, and

he knew that DDH's financial adviser had made it clear to DDC's consultants that that was the effect of the prior accord; but Mr Roebuck did not suggest to DDC that its understanding might be wrong;

g) However, the board of DDH believed that DDC would be paying off the deficit, and Mr Roebuck never disabused the board of this belief;

h) The parties' respective solicitors had been drafting the contract from June, and continued to do so after the prior accord;

i) The draft contract had always included clause 14.10.2, which suggested that DDC was to fund the deficit, and it remained in the contract;

j) On 1 November, RBS, who were DDH's funders, suggested to the solicitors including a new clause 14.10.3 in the contract, which clearly provided that DDC would pay the deficit;

k) DDC and DDH, through their respective solicitors, agreed to the inclusion of clause 14.10.3, and the Transfer Contract was executed on 5 November with clauses 14.10.2 and 14.10.3.

One way of framing the issue was to ask whether the agreement represented by the "prior accord" reached through to the terms of the Transfer Contract and how this related to an objective reading of the agreement as well as to the parties' subjective intentions. Helpfully, Etherton LJ suggested the following four scenarios (at paras 85-89):

85.   By way of reinforcement of those points, it may be helpful to consider the policy considerations justifying the intervention of equity by rectification for mutual mistake of a contract binding on the parties at common law. There are primarily four factual situations to consider. The first one is where the parties subjectively and objectively (that is to say in their communications passing between them— or "crossing the line") are in agreement but the formal documentation as executed fails to give effect to that prior agreement. The documentation should be rectified to bring it into line (retrospectively) with their prior accord. Subject to such matters as delay and prejudice to any third party interests, there is no good reason not to do so.

86.   The second scenario is where the parties never subjectively had the same intention, but the communications crossing the line show that objectively there was a common continuing intention at all relevant times prior to the execution of the final documentation, and the formal documentation reflected those prior communications. In that situation, whether or not rectified, one or other of the parties will be bound by a contract which they did not subjectively intend to enter into. It is right that the claimant should not be entitled to rectification to bring the documentation into line with a subjective intention and belief that was never communicated to the defendant and to which the defendant never agreed.

87.   The third scenario is where there was objectively a prior accord, but one of the parties then subjectively changed their mind, but objectively did not bring that change of mind to the attention of the other party. It is right that, if the documentation gives effect to the objective prior accord, the formal documentation should not be rectified to reflect the changed but uncommunicated subjective intention; and if the documentation as executed reflects the changed but uncommunicated subjective intention, it should be rectified to give effect to the objective prior accord. To do otherwise would be to force on one of the parties a contract which they never intended to make on the basis of an uncommunicated intention and belief.

88.   The fourth scenario is where there was objectively a prior accord (whether or not a subjective common intention), and one of the parties then objectively changed their mind, that is to say objectively made apparent to the other party that they intended to enter into the transaction on different terms. Leaving aside rectification for unilateral mistake (the requirements for which are quite different), it is right that, if the documentation as executed gives effect to the objectively indicated change of mind, a claim for rectification to give effect to the earlier prior accord should be refused. Once again, to do otherwise would force on the defendant a contract which they never intended to make on the basis of the claimant's uncommunicated subjective intention to enter into a contract on the basis of the original accord notwithstanding the defendant's objectively communicated change of mind.

89.   That analysis shows why it is good policy to favour objective accord or objective change of accord over subjective belief and intention in cases of rectification for mutual mistake.

Put this way, the question was whether the dealings between DDC and DDH fitted better with the third or the fourth scenario. For the majority in the Court of Appeal, it was the third scenario (essentially the prior accord, favouring DCC, followed by a mistake made by DDH); by contrast, for Etherton LJ, this was a fourth scenario case (with the prior accord objectively varied by the Transfer Contract). But, how did the majority arrive at their characterisation of the dealings between the parties? The short answer, certainly in the case of Lord Neuberger MR, is by a modern application of "contextualism". According to Lord Neuberger (at para.194 and again at 212-213):

194. . . . Rectification is an equitable remedy, which means that its origins lie in conscience and fair dealing, but those origins cannot be invoked to justify an unprincipled approach: far from it. Particularly as rectification is normally invoked in a contractual context, it seems to me that its principles should reflect the approach of the law to contracts, in particular to the formation and interpretation of contracts. Similarly, as rectification most commonly arises in a commercial context, it is plainly right that the applicable principles should be as clear and predictable in their application as possible . . .

212. Inevitably, the question whether the proposal of such a provision should be treated as a resiling from the prior accord will depend on all the circumstances of the particular case. As with virtually any issue involving the effect of the contents of a document, the question has to be assessed not merely by reference to the words of the document, but also to the factual and commercial context in which the document is produced. Having said that, I would accept that the more clear the terms of the provision the easier it is to contend that it signals such a resiling.

213. Despite the clear terms of the proffered clause 14.10.3 on 1 November, I am of the view that the hypothetical observer would not have concluded that DDH was signalling a departure from the prior accord: the observer would have believed that DDH was making a mistake. The contractual terms had been fully negotiated between the parties themselves and their respective advisers on about 11 October, when they reached the prior accord. The financial implications of those terms were well known to Mr Roebuck to have been agreed by DDC on the basis that DDH, not DDC, was to meet the deficit— and that was recorded in at least one email passing between the parties' representatives, as Mr Roebuck knew.

Neither option facing the court was attractive. If DDC were denied rectification, there was a heavy price to be paid. As Toulson LJ explained (at para.169):

169. A further striking factor is the commercial unreality of Mr Bruno consciously agreeing to a renegotiation of the agreement on 1 November 2007 so that DDC would pay the pension deficit to NCC. The net effect of the commercial agreement previously reached between the parties was that they would share the pension deficit. This would happen by a combination of three steps—the amount of the deficit would be deducted from the purchase price; the deficit would be paid by DDH to NCC; and DDC would receive back one half of the amount of the deficit payment which it had funded by receiving the top sliced £2.4 million from the VAT shelter (which would otherwise have been shared between the parties). As executed, the effect of the contract was very different. It meant that DDC would be paying the amount of the deficit twice—first by deducting it from the purchase price and then by paying it to NCC. DDC would therefore be worse off by £4.8 million (by deducting £2.4 million from the price and also paying £2.4 million to NCC), of which it would recoup £1.2 million net, leaving a shortfall much greater than if it had paid off the entire pension deficit and made no deduction from the purchase price. Nobody who understood the finances of the transaction could possibly have imagined that Mr Bruno would knowingly agree to such a change on the eve of the execution of the contract. There would have been no conceivable reason for him to do so. It would have been pure windfall for DDH amounting to £2.4 million. The only rational explanation for his conduct was that he failed to appreciate the significance of the clause.

On the other hand, by acceding to the claim for rectification, the majority foisted a contract on DDH in terms that they would never have signed up to. Lord Neuberger explained how this could, nevertheless, be justified (at paras 223-224):

223. In some cases, it would be right to hold that discretionary considerations justify refusing rectification, even where, on the basis of Lord Hoffmann's analysis of the law in *Chartbrook* [2009] 1 AC 1101, a claimant establishes a right in principle to rectification on the ground of common mistake. In this case, the fact that the DDH believed in good faith that the Transfer Contract was intended to mean what it stated in

clause 14.10.3 and implied in clause 14.10.2, and that the inclusion of those clauses in their actual terms was ineptly approved by DDC and/or their advisers, undoubtedly represents a promising basis for refusing rectification.

224. However, in my view that is more than outweighed by the fact that Mr Roebuck's knowledge and actions must be attributed to DDH, as they have always accepted, and his disreputable conduct throughout October, as found by the Judge, was responsible for the problem arising. So far as funding the deficit is concerned, he should have told DDH what he knew DDC intended and what the prior accord meant, and he should have told DDC what DDH intended. Effectively, as the only person with the necessary knowledge and information, he wrongly permitted both parties to be misled, and to enter into a contract, where they were at cross-purposes, and which was different from what at least one of them intended. It is true that, on the Judge's finding (not challenged on this appeal), he was, in a sense, saved by the *deus ex machina* of the acceptance of RBS's proposed clause 14.10.3. However, the RBS proposal was prompted by his telling them of the effect of the contract, at a time when he knew that DDC believed and intended that it should have a different effect, and that they had been told by DDH's financial advisers that DDH intended it to have that different effect. In effect, I do not consider that the events of 1 and 2 November discharge Mr Roebuck's, and therefore DDH's, culpability for the misunderstanding about the deficit persisting.

While there is no easy answer to a complex case of this kind, there are strong indications in the judicial divisions that the law needs to be clarified and put in a more coherent state.

Further reading

Roger Brownsword, 'Some New Notes on the Old Oats' (1987) 131 *Solicitors' Journal* 384
David McLaughlan, 'The "Drastic" Remedy of Rectification for Unilateral Mistake' (2008) 124 LQR 608
David McLaughlan, 'Commonsense Principles of Interpretation and Rectification?'(2010) 126 LQR 8.
John Phillips, "*Smith v Hughes*" in Paul Mitchell and Charles Mitchell (eds), *Landmark Cases in the Law of Contract* (Oxford: Hart, 2008), p.205

6

THE AUTHENTICITY OF AGREEMENT

LEARNING OBJECTIVES

By the end of this chapter, you should understand that:

- **in the absence of some general excusing condition (such as fraud or coercion), signing a contractual document is generally taken to signal consent;**
- **in the modern context of strong protection of consumers and other vulnerable contractors, it is open to question whether this signature rule would apply across the board to all transactions;**
- **the threshold for declaring a contract to be void on the grounds that it was mistakenly signed ("non est factum") is extremely high.**

INTRODUCTION

In this chapter, the question is whether a signal of apparent concurrence, classically the signal given by a signature at the foot of a contractual document, is to be taken as conclusive. What if the party who signs the document does not understand the nature or significance of the agreement? What if, in this sense, the agreement is not authentic? In the twenty-first century, if the contract contains terms that seem to have an unfair application, the party who has signed without appreciating the force of these terms might now have some protection under those various legislative provisions that regulate unfair or unreasonable terms (see Ch.22); but, in the days before this level of control was in place, the only option (in the absence of fraud or coercion) was to plead that the agreement, signature notwithstanding, was not authentic.

6–001

1. THE SIGNATURE RULE

L'ESTRANGE v GRAUCOB LTD

Divisional Court [1934] 2 K.B. 394; 103 L.J.K.B. 730; 152 L.T. 164

The plaintiff signed a "Sales Agreement" for the purchase of an automatic machine. The agreement was printed on brown paper and included a number of clauses "in regrettably small print but quite legible." The plaintiff did not read the document, it was not read over to her, nor did the defendants call her attention to the words in small type, and she said in evidence that she had no clear idea of

6–002

what she was signing. The machine failed to work properly. In an action for breach of warranty the defendants were held to be protected by one of the clauses in small print which exempted them from liability.

SCRUTTON LJ

> When a document containing contractual terms is signed, then, in the absence of fraud, or, I will add, misrepresentation, the party signing it is bound, and it is wholly immaterial whether he has read the document or not.

In cases like *L'Estrange v Graucob* the defendant is held liable although he does not really, in his mind, assent to the particular terms in the document because he does not know what they are. He has, however, signified his assent to them by his signature. In *Harris v Great Western Railway* (1876) 1 QBD 515 at 530 Blackburn J. explained this on the grounds of estoppel. The party who has signed without reading is bound—"on the ground that, by assenting to the contract thus reduced to writing, he represents to the other side that he has made himself acquainted with the contents of that writing and assents to them, and so induces the other side to act upon that representation by entering into the contract with him, and is consequently precluded from denying that he did make himself acquainted with those terms." If this were the basis of the rule, it would seem to follow that the signer should be able to repudiate the contract when the other party knew very well that he had not read the document before signing. There would then be no ground for implying a representation that the signer had read the document and, anyway, the other party would know any such representation to be untrue and so could not be said to act on it. In *McCutcheon v David MacBrayne Ltd* [1964] 1 W.L.R. 125 (below, para.7–010) Lord Devlin thought that Blackburn J's dictum might some day have to be examined more closely by their Lordships and went on: "It seems to me that when a party assents to a document forming the whole or part of his contract, he is bound by the terms of the document, read or unread, signed or unsigned, simply because they are in the contract; and it is unnecessary and possibly misleading to say that he is bound by them because he represents to the other party that he has made himself acquainted with them." Cf. *The Polyduke* (1978) 1 Lloyds Rep. 211.

J. R. Spencer in [1973] C.L.J. 104 criticises the rule stated in *L'Estrange v Graucob* as the product of an excessively objective theory of agreement under which the test is not what the other party would have thought—as in *Smith v Hughes* and *Hartog v Colin & Shields* (above, Ch.5)—but 'how things would have appeared to a reasonable fly on the wall', a theory which the author considers to have been applied in *Rose v Pim* (above, Ch.5). Spencer argues that an application of the rule in *Smith v Hughes* would have enabled L'Estrange to succeed in her action. *Smith v Hughes* shows that where, at the time of contracting, A knows that B is mistaken as to the terms of the contract, A cannot enforce it in the sense in which he, A, understood it: and *Roberts v Leicestershire CC* (above, Ch.5) shows that B may enforce the contract in the sense in which A knew that B understood it. But was L'Estrange under any mistake as to the terms of the contract? She knew that the paper contained contractual terms. As a classical individualist might ask: Did it not appear to Graucob (who was not guilty of fraud or misrepresentation), as well as to the reasonable fly on the wall that she was expressing her assent to those terms, whatever they might be?

TILDEN RENT-A-CAR CO v CLENDENNING

Ontario Court of Appeal (1978) 83 D.L.R. (3d) 400

6–003   The defendant rented a car from the plaintiff at Vancouver airport. The plaintiff's clerk asked him if he wanted "additional cover" and he said he did. He then signed the front of the contract under the words "I, the undersigned, have read and received a copy of above and reverse side of this contract." He did not read it in fact, as was apparent to the clerk. On the front of the contract it was stated that, in consideration of the payment of $2.00 per day, the customer's liability for damage to the car was limited to nil, but that the customer should be fully liable for collision damage if the vehicle was driven in violation of any provision of the rental agreement. On the reverse, conditions in small, faint type provided that the customer agreed that the vehicle would not be driven in violation of any law and would not be operated by any person who had consumed any intoxicating liquor, whatever the quantity. Subsequently the defendant drove the car into a pole and pleaded guilty to driving while intoxicated. The plaintiff's action in respect of damage to the vehicle was dismissed. He appealed.

DUBIN JA

[Having referred to *L'Estrange v Graucob*:] Consensus ad idem is as much a part of the law of written contracts as it is of oral contracts. The signature to a contract is only one way of manifesting assent to contractual terms. However, in the case of *L'Estrange v F. Graucob, Ltd*, there was in fact no consensus ad idem . . .

Although the subject of critical analysis by learned authors (see, for example, J. R. Spencer, "Signature, Consent, and the Rule in *L'Estrange v Graucob*" [1973] C.L.J. 104), the case has survived, and it is now said that it applies to all contracts irrespective of the circumstances under which they are entered into, if they are signed by the party who seeks to escape their provisions.

Thus, it was submitted that the ticket cases, which in the circumstances of this case would afford a ready defence for the hirer of the automobile, are not applicable.

As is pointed out in Waddams, *The Law of Contracts*, at p. 191: From the 19th century until recent times an extraordinary status has been accorded to the signed document that will be seen in retrospect, it is suggested, to have been excessive.

The justification for the rule in *L'Estrange v Graucob, Ltd*, appears to have been founded upon the objective theory of contracts, by which means parties are bound to a contract in writing by measuring their conduct by outward appearance rather than what the parties inwardly meant to decide. This, in turn, stems from the classic statement of Blackburn J. in *Smith v Hughes* (1871) L.R. 6 Q.B. 597 at p. 607: . . .

Even accepting the objective theory to determine whether Mr Clendenning had entered into a contract which included all the terms of the written instrument, it is to be observed that an essential part of that test is whether the other party entered into the contract in the belief that Mr Clendenning was assenting to all such terms. In the instant case, it was apparent to the employee of Tilden Rent-A-Car that Mr Clendenning had not in fact read the document in its entirety before he signed it. It follows under such circumstances that Tilden Rent-A-Car cannot rely on provisions of the contract which it had no reason to believe were being assented to by the other contracting party.

As stated in Waddams, *The Law of Contracts*, p. 191: One who signs a written document cannot complain if the other party reasonably relies on the signature as a manifestation of assent to the contents, or ascribes to words he uses their reasonable meaning. But the other side of the same coin is that only a reasonable expectation will be protected. If the party seeking to enforce the document knew or had reason to know of the other's mistake the document should not be enforced.

In ordinary commercial practice where there is frequently a sense of formality in the transaction, and where there is a full opportunity for the parties to consider the terms of the proposed contract submitted for signature, it might well be safe to assume that the party who attaches his signature to the contract intends by so doing to acknowledge his acquiescence to its terms, and that the other party entered into the contract upon that belief. This can hardly be said, however, where the contract is entered into in circumstances such as were present in this case.

A transaction, such as this one, is invariably carried out in a hurried, informal manner. The speed with which the transaction is completed is said to be one of the attractive features of the services provided.

The clauses relied on in this case, as I have already stated, are inconsistent with the over-all purpose for which the contract is entered into by the hirer. Under such circumstances, something more should be done by the party submitting the contract for signature than merely handing it over to be signed. [The judge quoted from Lord Devlin in *McCutcheon v MacBrayne*, below, para.7–010.]

An analysis of the Canadian cases, however, indicates that the approach in this country has not been so rigid. In the case of *Colonial Investment Co of Winnipeg, Man. v Borland* [1911] 1 W.W.R. 171 at p. 189, [affirmed 6 D.L.R. 21], Beck J. set forth the following propositions:

Consensus ad idem is essential to the creation of a contract, whether oral, in writing or under seal, subject to this, that as between the immediate parties (and merely voluntary assigns) apparent—as distinguished from real—consent will on the ground of estoppel effect a binding obligation unless the party denying the obligation proves:

(1) That the other party knew at the time of the making of the alleged contract that the mind of the denying party did not accompany the expression of his consent; or

(2) Such facts and circumstances as show that it was not reasonable and natural for the other party to suppose that the denying party was giving his real consent and he did not in fact give it;

In commenting on the *Colonial Investment Co of Winnipeg v Borland* case, Spencer, in the article above cited, observes at p. 121: It is instructive to compare a Canadian approach to the problem of confusing documents which are signed but not fully understood.

And at p. 122 the author concludes his article with the following analysis:

"Policy considerations, but of different kinds, no doubt lay behind both the Canadian and the English approaches to this problem. The Canadian court was impressed by the abuses which would result—and, in England, have resulted—from enabling companies to hold ignorant signatories to the letter of sweeping exemption clauses contained in contracts in standard form. The English courts, however, were much more impressed with the danger of furnishing an easy line of defence by which liars could evade contractual liabilities freely assumed. It would be very dangerous to allow a man over the age of legal infancy to escape from the legal effect of a document he has, after reading it, signed, in the absence of any express misrepresentation by the other party of that legal effect. Forty years later, most lawyers would admit that the English courts made a bad choice between two evils."

The significance of the circumstances under which a contract is entered into is noted by Taschereau J. in *Provident Savings Life Ass'ce Society of New York v Mowat et al.* (1902) 32 S.C.R. 147, as follows at p. 162:

As remarked by Mr Justice Maclennan [27 O.A.R. 675]:

"The case of a formal instrument like the present, prepared and executed, after a long negotiation, and correspondence delivered and accepted, and acted upon for years, is wholly different from the cases relating to railways and steamship and cloakroom tickets, in which it has been held that conditions qualifying the principal contract of carriage or bailment, not sufficiently brought to the attention of the passenger or bailor are not binding upon him. Such contracts are usually made in moments of more or less haste and confusion and stand by themselves."

I see no real distinction in contracts such as these, where the signature by itself does not truly represent an acquiescence of unusual and onerous terms which are inconsistent with the true object of the contract, and the ticket cases.

. . . In modern commercial practice, many standard form printed documents are signed without being read or understood. In many cases the parties seeking to rely on the terms of the contract know or ought to know that the signature of a party to the contract does not represent the true intention of the signer, and that the party signing is unaware of the stringent and onerous provisions which the standard form contains. Under such circumstances, I am of the opinion that the party seeking to rely on such terms should not be able to do so in the absence of first having taken reasonable measures to draw such terms to the attention of the other party, and, in the absence of such reasonable measures, it is not necessary for the party denying knowledge of such terms to prove either fraud, misrepresentation or non est factum.

In the case at bar, Tilden Rent-A-Car took no steps to alert Mr Clendenning to the onerous provisions in the standard form of contract presented by it. The clerk could not help but have known that Mr Clendenning had not in fact read the contract before signing it. Indeed the form of the contract itself with the important provisions on the reverse side and in very small type would discourage even the most cautious customer from endeavouring to read and understand it. Mr Clendenning was in fact unaware of the exempting provisions. Under such circumstances, it was not open to Tilden Rent-A-Car to rely on those clauses, and it was not incumbent on Mr Clendenning to establish fraud, misrepresentation or non est factum. Having paid the premium, he was not liable for any damage to the vehicle while being driven by him.

LACOURCIERE JA (DISSENTING)

Having read the conditions in the contract: These clauses are certainly not irrelevant or foreign to the contract . . . They do not, for example, purport to exempt Tilden from any implied undertaking as to the road worthy fitness of the vehicle. They are not exemptions from common law liability or statutory liability . . .

The clause is undoubtedly a strict one. It is not for a Court to nullify its effect by branding it unfair, unreasonable and oppressive. It may be perfectly sound and reasonable from an insurance risk viewpoint, and may indeed be necessary in the competitive business of car rentals, where rates are calculated on the basis of the whole contract. On this point, see the majority judgment delivered by Lord Wilberforce in *New Zealand Shipping Co Ltd v A.M. Satterthwaite & Co Ltd* [1975] A.C. 154 at p. 169, where it was held that the Court must give effect to the clear intent of a commercial document.

I am of the view that, even if the respondent's signature is not conclusive, the terms of the contract are not unusual, oppressive or unreasonable and are binding on the respondent. I would, therefore, allow the appeal with costs, set aside the judgment below and in lieu thereof substitute a judgment for the amount of the agreed damages and costs.

Zuber J. A. concurs with Dubin J. A.

Appeal Dismissed.

Questions

1. Does the case decide that, in a written but unread contract, clauses which are "stringent" or "onerous" are not binding but the other clauses are? **6–004**

2. Would the result have been different if the defendant had signed the contract without reading it in the absence of the clerk who did not know whether it had been read or not?

3. Dubin JA refers to the "exempting provisions". Were they "exempting provisions"? Did it—or should it—matter? (In England today an exempting provision would have to satisfy the requirement of reasonableness under the Unfair Contract Terms Act 1977, but the Act makes no such requirement in respect of other provisions).

4. Was there "in fact no consensus ad idem" in *L'Estrange v Graucob*? Would Dubin JA have held the contract to be void?

5. Did the case decide that the offending clause was not part of the contract? (". . . an essential part of [the objective theory] is whether the other party entered into the contract in the belief that Mr Clendenning was assenting to all such terms"). A ruling that the clause was not part of the contract would settle the matter; but if it were part of the contract, the question in England would now be whether the term, contrary to the requirement of good faith, "causes a significant imbalance in the parties' rights and obligations arising under the contract to the detriment of the consumer": Unfair Terms in Consumer Contracts Regulations reg.5(1) (and see now the Consumer Rights Act 2015).

----

2. NON EST FACTUM

Where A induces B to enter into a contract with him by fraud or misrepresentation, the contract is voidable at B's option . If, however, before the contract is avoided, a third person, C, acquires rights under it for value and in good faith, B cannot then avoid the contract against C, merely on the grounds of A's fraud or misrepresentation. B will be bound to C unless he can show that the contract with A was **6–005** not merely voidable but void. If the contract was void, C could acquire no rights under it. Under the doctrine known as Non est Factum, "it is not my deed,' a signed document may, in the circumstances considered in the following cases, be held to be void.

Non est factum is a doctrine of the common law originating in cases where illiterate or blind persons were induced to make deeds by fraud as to the nature of the document. The signer could, of course, repudiate the contract as against the person who deceived him on the ground of fraud but he could also plead non est factum against an innocent third party who had, or rather believed he had, acquired rights under the document for value. In the leading case of *Foster v MacKinnon* (1869) L.R. 4 C.P. 704 the plaintiff, as indorsee of a bill of exchange for £3,000, sued the defendant (M) as indorser. There was a question whether the endorsement was the defendant's signature but a witness, Callow, stated that he had produced the bill to M, an elderly man, telling him that the document was a guarantee and that M signed the bill in that belief. Bovill LCJ told the jury that if M signed, not knowing that it was a bill and believing it to be a guarantee, and if he was not guilty of any negligence in so signing, he was entitled to the verdict. The jury found for M. The Court of Common Pleas held that this was a correct direction.

This doctrine was subsequently held to apply only where the person signing was misled, not merely as to the contents of the document he signed, but as to its class or character. It was possibly applicable in *Foster v Mackinnon*, because a guarantee is plainly a document of a different character from a bill of exchange. But a person who signed a promissory note for £1,000, having been told it was a promissory note for £10, would not have been able to rely on the doctrine, because his mistake was merely to the contents—he knew the class of document he was signing.

If a person's mistake as to the character of the document he signed was due to his own negligence, then he might be precluded from relying on the defence of non est factum—but only, according to *Carlisle and Cumberland Banking Co v Bragg* [1911] 1 K.B. 489, if the document signed was in fact a negotiable instrument. In Bragg's case the Court of Appeal put a restrictive interpretation upon *Foster v Mackinnon* (where the document signed was in fact a negotiable instrument) and held that the principle of that case did not apply where the defendant carelessly signed a guarantee of an overdraft, having been deceived into believing that he was witnessing an insurance document. Notwithstanding his negligence, Bragg successfully pleaded non est factum against the bank which had advanced money in reliance on his signature.

The doctrine, as summarised above, was reconsidered by the House of Lords in *Gallie v Lee* (below).

GALLIE v LEE AND ANOTHER

House of Lords [1971] A.C. 1004; [1970] 3 W.L.R. 1078; [1970] 3 All E.R. 961

6–006   Mrs Gallie, a widow aged 78, had made a will leaving her house to her nephew, Parkin. Lee, a friend of Parkin, was heavily in debt and discussed with Parkin how money might be raised on the house. In Parkin's presence, Lee put before Mrs Gallie a document which he told her was a deed of gift of the house to Parkin. Mrs Gallie did not read it because she had broken her spectacles. The deed was in fact a deed of sale of the house to Lee for £3,000, the receipt of which Mrs Gallie acknowledged in the deed but did not in fact receive.

Using this deed, Lee purported to mortgage the house to the second defendant, the Anglia Building Society, and borrowed £2,000. Lee defaulted in instalments on the mortgage and the building society sought to recover possession of the house. Mrs Gallie sued for a declaration that the deed was void— non est factum—and for the recovery of the title deeds.

Stamp J found for the plaintiff: [1968] 2 All E.R. 322. He held that a deed of gift to X is a document of a totally different character or class from a deed of sale to Y. Mrs Gallie could plead non est factum and was not precluded from doing so by any carelessness on her part since the document signed was not a negotiable instrument.

The Court of Appeal unanimously allowed the appeal: [1969] 2 Ch. 17. Denning MR rejected (i) the distinction between the class of the document and the contents of the document; (ii) the view that mistake as to the person renders the contract void and (iii) the rule in *Bragg's case* that a party may be precluded by his negligence from setting up non est factum only where the document signed is a negotiable instrument. He applied the broad principle discussed below. Russell and Salmon LJJ while disliking it, felt bound to apply the law as laid down in the earlier authorities (the Master of the Rolls "has sought to wield a broom labelled 'For the use of the House of Lords only' "—per Russell LJ). Applying existing principles, Russell LJ held (i) that Mrs Gallie had not satisfied the heavy onus of proving that she believed that the conveyance was a deed of gift when she signed it; and (ii) even if she did believe this, it was not a mistake as to the character of the document. In determining whether a mistake is as to character, regard must be had to "the object of the exercise." Mrs Gallie knew that the transaction was intended to divest her of her interest in the property, in pursuance of a joint project of Lee and Parkin to raise money on the security of it. The document in fact carried out the object which she intended it to carry out. Salmon LJ held that the document was binding on Mrs Gallie because she would have executed it even if its true character and class had been explained to her. She was not concerned with the character of the document but was happy to sign anything which P advised her to sign.

Mrs Gallie appealed to the House of Lords.

LORD REID

Lord Reid said that he was in general agreement with Lord Pearson. He concluded: I think that in the older authorities difference in practical result was more important than difference in legal character. If a man thinks that he is signing a document which will cost him £10 and the actual document would cost him £1,000 it could not be right to deny him this remedy simply because the legal character of the two was the same. It is true that we must then deal with questions of degree but that is a familiar task for the courts and I would not expect it to give rise to a flood of litigation.

There must I think be a radical difference between what he signed and what he thought he was signing—or one could use the words "fundamental" or "serious" or "very substantial." But what amounts to a radical difference will depend on all the circumstances. If he thinks he is giving property to A whereas the document gives it to B the difference may often be of vital importance, but in the circumstances of the present case I do not think that it is. I think that it must be left to the courts to determine in each case in light of all the facts whether there was or was not a sufficiently great difference. The plea non est factum is in sense illogical when applied to a case where the man in fact signed the deed. But it is none the worse for that if applied in a reasonable way.

I would dismiss this appeal.

Lord Hodson and Viscount Dilhorne made speeches dismissing the appeal.

LORD WILBERFORCE

How, then, ought the principle, on which a plea of non est factum is admissible, to be stated? In my opinion, a document should be held to be void (as opposed to voidable) only when the element of consent to it is totally lacking, that is, more concretely, when the transaction which the document purports to effect is essentially different in substance or in kind from the transaction intended. Many other expressions, or adjectives, could be used—"basically" or "radically" or "fundamentally." In substance, the test does not differ from that which was applied in the leading cases of *Thoroughgood's Case* and *Foster v Mackinnon*, except in moving from the character/contents distinction to an area better understood in modern practice.

To this general test it is necessary to add certain amplifications. First, there is the case of fraud. The law as to this is best stated in the words of the judgment in *Foster v Mackinnon* where it is said that a signature obtained by fraud:

"... is invalid not merely on the ground of fraud, where fraud exists, but on the ground that the mind of the signer did not accompany the signature; in other words, that he never intended to sign, and therefore in contemplation of law never did sign, the contract to which his name is appended."

In other words, it is the lack of consent that matters, not the means by which this result was brought about. Fraud by itself may do no more than make the contract voidable.

Secondly, a man cannot escape from the consequences, as regards innocent third parties, of signing a document if, being a man of ordinary education and competence, he chooses to sign it without informing himself of its purport and effect. This principle is sometimes found expressed in the language that "he is doing something with his estate" (*Hunter v Walters* (1871) 7 Ch.App. 75, *Howatson v Webb*) but it really reflects a rule of common sense on the exigency of busy lives.

Thirdly, there is the case where the signer has been careless, in not taking ordinary precautions against being deceived. This is a difficult area. Until 1911 the law was reasonably clear; it had been stated plainly in *Foster v Mackinnon* that negligence—that is, carelessness—might deny the signer the benefit of the plea. Since *Bragg's* case was decided in 1911 (*Carlisle and Cumberland Banking Co v Bragg*) the law has been that, except in relation to negotiable instruments, mere carelessness is not disabling; there must be negligence arising from a duty of care to the third person who ultimately relies on the document. It does not need much force to demolish this battered precedent. It is sufficient to point to two major defects in it. First, it confuses the kind of careless conduct which disentitles a man from denying the effect of his signature with such legal negligence as entitles a person injured to bring an action in tort. The two are quite different things in standard and scope. Secondly, the judgment proceeds on a palpable misunderstanding of the judgment in *Foster v Mackinnon*; for Byles J., so far from confining the relevance of negligence to negotiable instruments (as Bragg's case suggests), clearly thought that the signer of a negotiable instrument would be liable, negligence or no negligence, and that negligence was relevant in relation to documents other than negotiable instruments; for example, (as in the actual case before him) to a guarantee.

In my opinion, the correct rule, and that which in fact prevailed until *Bragg's* case, is that, leaving aside negotiable instruments to which special rules may apply, a person who signs a document, and parts with it so that it may come into other hands, has a responsibility, that of the normal man of prudence, to take care what he signs, which, if neglected, prevents him from denying his liability under the document according to its tenor. I would add that the onus of proof in this matter rests on him, that is, to prove that he acted carefully and not on the third party to prove the contrary. I consider therefore that *Carlisle and Cumberland Banking Co v Bragg* was wrong, both in the principle it states and in its decision, and that it should no longer be cited as an authority for any purpose.

The preceding paragraphs contemplate persons who are adult and literate: the conclusion as to such persons is that, while there are cases in which they may successfully plead non est factum, these cases will, in modern times, be rare. As to persons who are illiterate, or blind, or lacking in understanding, the law is in a dilemma. On the one hand, the law is traditionally, and rightly, ready to relieve them against hardship and imposition. On the other hand, regard has to be paid to the position of innocent third parties who cannot be expected, and often would have no means, to know the condition or status of the signer. I do not think that a defined solution can be provided for all cases. The law ought, in my opinion, to give relief if satisfied that consent was truly lacking but will require of signers even in this class that they act responsibly and carefully according to their circumstances in putting their signature to legal documents.

This brings me to the present case. The plaintiff was a lady of advanced age, but, as her evidence shows, by no means incapable physically or mentally. It certainly cannot be said that she did not receive sympathetic consideration or the benefit of much doubt from the judge as to the circumstances in which the assignment was executed. But accepting all of this, I am satisfied, with Russell L.J., that she fell short, very far short, of making the clear and satisfactory case which is required of those who seek to have a legal act declared void and of establishing a sufficient discrepancy between her intentions and her act. I am satisfied to adopt, without repetition, the analysis of the facts which appears in the judgment of Russell L.J. as well as that of my noble and learned friend, Lord Pearson.

I would dismiss the appeal.

LORD PEARSON

In my opinion, the plea of non est factum ought to be available in a proper case for the relief of a person who for permanent or temporary reasons (not limited to blindness or illiteracy) is not capable of both reading and sufficiently understanding the deed or other document to be signed. By "sufficiently understanding" I mean understanding at least to the point of detecting a fundamental difference between the actual document and the document as the signer had believed it to be. There must be a proper case for such relief. There would not be a proper case if (a) the signature of the document was brought about by negligence of the signer in failing to take precautions which he ought to have taken, or (b) the actual document was not fundamentally different from the document as the signer believed it to be. I will say something later about negligence and fundamental difference.

In the present case the plaintiff was not at the material time a person who could read, because on the facts found she had broken her spectacles and could not effectively read without them. In any case her evidence (unless it was deliberately false, which has not been argued) shows that she had very little capacity for understanding legal documents and property transactions, and I do not think a reasonable jury would have found she was negligent. In my opinion, it would not be right to dismiss the plaintiffs appeal on the ground that the principle stated by the Master of the Rolls is applicable to her case. I do not think it is.

The principle as stated is limited to a case in which it is apparent on the face of the document that it is intended to have legal consequences. That allows for possible success of the plea in a case such as *Lewis v Clay* (1897) 67 L.J. Q.B. 224, where Clay had been induced to sign promissory notes by the cunning deception of a false friend, who caused him to believe that he was merely witnessing the friend's signature on several private and highly confidential documents, the material parts of which had been covered up . . .

Suppose that the very busy managing director of a large company has a pile of documents to be signed in a few minutes before his next meeting, and his secretary has arranged them for maximum speed with only the spaces for signature exposed, and he "signs them blind," as the saying is, not reading them or even looking at them. He may be exercising a wise economy of his time and energy. There is the possibility of some extraneous document, involving him in unexpected personal liability, having been fraudulently inserted in the pile, but this possibility is so improbable that a reasonable man would disregard it: *Bolton v Stone* [1951] A.C. 850, 858. Such conduct is not negligence in any ordinary sense of the word. But the person who signs documents in this way ought to be held bound by them, and ought not to be entitled to avoid liability so as to shift the burden of loss on to an innocent third party. The whole object of having documents signed by him is that he makes them his documents and takes responsibility for them. He takes the chance of a fraudulent substitution. I think the right view of such a case is that the person who signs intends to sign the documents placed before him, whatever they may be, and so there is no basis on which he could successfully plead non est factum . . .

Salmon L.J. has said in his judgment in this case [1969] 2 Ch. 17, 48: "If, . . . a person signs a document because he negligently failed to read it, I think he is precluded from relying on his own negligent act for the purpose of escaping from the ordinary consequences of his signature. In such circumstances he cannot succeed on a plea of non est factum. This is not in my view a true estoppel, but an illustration of the principle that no man may take advantage of his own wrong." I agree.

The degree of difference required: The judgments in the older cases used a variety of expressions to signify the degree or kind of difference that, for the purposes of the plea of non est factum, must be shown to exist between the document as it was and the document as it was believed to be. More recently there has been a tendency to draw a firm distinction between (a) a difference in character or class, which is sufficient for the purposes of the plea, and (b) a difference only in contents, which is not sufficient. This distinction has been helpful in some cases, but, as the judgments of the Court of Appeal have shown, it would produce wrong results if it were applied as a rigid rule for all cases. In my opinion, one has to use a more general phrase, such as "fundamentally different" or "radically different" or "totally different."

I would dismiss the appeal.

Appeal Dismissed.

Questions

1. What test replaces the distinction between "contents" and "class or character"?

2. Would the following mistakes pass the new test so as to found the plea? (a) D, believing he is witnessing a proposal of insurance, signs a guarantee of X's overdraft with the P Bank. (b) D signs a contract to hire a car, believing that he is signing a contract for the hire-purchase of the car. (c) D signs a contract to sell a two-acre plot of land, believing that the contract relates to

6–007

only half an acre of the plot. (Cf. *Hasham v Zenab* [1960] A.C. 316, PC, where it was held that the defence was not available because the mistake was not induced by fraud.)

3. Are estoppel and negligence separate grounds on which a person who has made a fundamental mistake may be precluded from relying on the defence? May estoppel be effective against a signer who has not been negligent?

NORWICH AND PETERBOROUGH BUILDING SOCIETY v STEED (NO.2)

Court of Appeal [1993] Ch. 116; [1992] 3 W.L.R. 669; [1993] 1 All E.R. 330

6-008 The appellant, Mr Steed, allowed his mother, his sister and her husband to live in his house while he was living in the United States. The sister and her husband persuaded him to execute a power of attorney in favour of his mother. They then tricked Mrs Steed into executing a transfer of the house to them and, on the same day, borrowed £15,000 from the building society on the security of the property. When they defaulted, the society brought an action for possession of the house. The appellant, who was joined as a party, claimed, inter alia, that he was entitled to rely on non est factum. The Judge and the Court of Appeal did not agree.

SCOTT LJ

Mr Lloyd Q.C. for the appellant has attacked this part of the judgment by relying heavily on the proposition that Mrs Steed did not know anything about the power of attorney and her status thereunder. In that state of ignorance she could not, when she signed the transfer, have known she was dealing with her son's property. She must have supposed she was dealing, in some way, with her own affairs. So, it was argued, she was mistaken as to the essential character of the document she signed and of the transaction which it effected.

Submissions on these lines, as Butler-Sloss L.J. pointed out during argument, placed Mr Steed on a species of Morton's fork. Let it be supposed that Mrs Steed was a lady of sufficient general understanding and capability to be a suitable donee of the power of appointment. Why then did she not inform herself of the purport and effect of the transfer before signing it? Her failure to do so brings the case within the second of Lord Wilberforce's amplifications. [See para.6–006 above.] On the other hand, let it be supposed that she lacked ordinary competence and capacity. Lord Wilberforce referred to persons "illiterate, or blind, or lacking in understanding". If Mrs Steed falls into this category, what was Mr Steed about when he appointed her his attorney? The donor of a power of attorney who appoints as his attorney a person incapable of understanding the import of a simple transfer can hardly be allowed, if the donee signs a transfer without any understanding of what he or she is doing, to repudiate the transfer on the ground of a lack of understanding on the part of the donee.

As to Mrs Steed's ignorance of the power of attorney, if she was ignorant of it, the ignorance was attributable to Mr Steed's incomprehensible failure to tell her either that he was about to or that he had made the appointment. It is known that he and she spoke on the telephone at about the time the power of attorney was executed. If it was really the case that he did not mention the power of attorney when speaking to her on that occasion and left her in ignorance of her responsibilities and status, his failure shows, in my opinion, such a want of care as to preclude him from relying, in support of his non est factum plea, on her ignorance of the power. As between an innocent third party purchaser such as the building society on the one hand and Mr Steed on the other hand, his failure to take the ordinary precautionary and prudent step of informing his mother of her appointment as his attorney requires, in my judgment, that the building society be preferred. In my judgment, and for substantially the same reasons as those given by the learned judge, the non est factum plea fails.

Further reading

E. Peden and J. Carter, 'Incorporation of Terms by Signature: *L'Estrange* Rules' (2006) 21 *Journal of Contract Law* 1

J. R. Spencer, 'Signature, Consent, and the Rule in *L'Estrange v Graucob*' [1973] CLJ 104

Julius Stone, 'The Limits of Non Est Factum after *Gallie v Lee*' (1972) 88 L.Q.R. 190

7

THE SCOPE OF THE AGREEMENT

LEARNING OBJECTIVES

By the end of this chapter, you should understand that:

- *Parker v South Eastern Ry* is a landmark case, adopting a fair and reasonable notice test for the incorporation of terms, rather than a test based on the actual knowledge and understanding of the recipient of the notice;
- *Thornton v Shoe Lane Parking Ltd* "ratchets up" the test for incorporation at a time when statutory controls over unfair terms in consumer contracts did not exist;
- the test of incorporation of terms by reference to previous dealings between the parties is applied with some flexibility, favouring incorporation in commercial contracts but setting a tougher standard for incorporation in consumer contracts.

INTRODUCTION

During the nineteenth century, it became commonplace for business contractors, especially carriers, 7–001 to display their terms and conditions at their business premises or to give customers notice of their terms less directly (for example, by referring to the terms on tickets that were issued to customers). Given that some customers might not be aware that their co-contractors intended to rely on such terms—and particularly so on terms that limited their liability to customers—the first priority for the courts was to establish clear principles for the effective incorporation of such terms and conditions. Having decided in *Parker v South Eastern Ry* (below) that incorporation would be effective provided that the customer had been given reasonable notice of the terms, for the next hundred years or so, the courts applied the principle (more or less strictly) on a case-by-case basis. However, in the 1960s and 1970s, it became clear that a reasonable notice test gave the courts some much-needed leverage over fair dealing in the consumer marketplace and the law became more demanding about the specificity of the warning to be given to consumer customers (see *Thornton* and *Interfoto*, below).

In this light, the case-law on incorporation of terms might be seen as having a dual significance. First, the case-law is important in its own right, determining the scope of the agreement for the purposes of contractual formation. Secondly, prior to the enactment of legislative controls over unfair contract terms, the law on incorporation played a key part in regulating unfair dealing; and, even after the enactment of the legislation, this branch of the law retains some relevance in this respect (see, e.g., the *Interfoto* case, below).

The cases in this chapter are divided into two sections: in the first section, the question is whether notice given of the terms is effective to incorporate them (and, after the decision in *Parker*, whether reasonable notice has been given); and, in the second section, the question is whether, where the parties have had previous dealings, those dealings might suffice (for the purposes of incorporation) to give notice of terms on the instant occasion. It bears repetition that, even if the terms are incorporated (whether by notice or by reference to a course of previous dealings), this means only that the party seeking to rely on the terms has succeeded in showing that the terms are part of the contract. How precisely the terms in question should be interpreted and whether they can survive the modern legislative tests of fairness and reasonableness are quite another matter (see Chs 15, 21, and 22)

1. INCORPORATION OF TERMS BY NOTICE

PARKER v SOUTH EASTERN RY

Court of Appeal (1877) 2 C.P.D. 416; 46 L.J.Q.B. 768; 36 L.T. 540; 41 J.P. 644; 25 W.R. 564

7-002   The plaintiff deposited a bag in a cloak-room at the defendants' railway station, paid the clerk 2d. and received a paper ticket on which were printed a number and a date and notices as to when the office would be open, and the words "See back." On the other side were printed several clauses including "The company will not be responsible for any package exceeding the value of £10." The plaintiff presented his ticket on the same day, but his bag could not be found. He claimed £24 10s. as the value of his bag, and the company pleaded that they had accepted the goods on the condition that they would not be responsible if the value exceeded £10. The questions left by Pollock B. to the jury were: (1) Did the plaintiff read or was he aware of the special condition upon which the articles were deposited? (2) Was the plaintiff, under the circumstances, under any obligation, in the exercise of reasonable and proper caution, to read or make himself aware of the condition? The jury answered both questions in the negative and the judge directed judgment to be entered for the plaintiff. The defendants moved to enter judgment and obtained an order nisi for a new trial on the ground of misdirection. The order was discharged and the motion refused by the Common Pleas Division. The defendants appealed.

MELLISH LJ

In this case we have to consider whether a person who deposits in the cloak-room of a railway company, articles which are lost through the carelessness of the company's servants, is prevented from recovering, by a condition on the back of the ticket, that the company would not be liable for the loss of goods exceeding the value of £10. It was argued on behalf of the railway company that the company's servants were only authorised to receive goods on behalf of the company upon the terms contained in the ticket; and a passage from Blackburn J.'s judgment in *Harris v Great Western Ry.*, 1 QBD 515 at p. 533, was relied on in support of their contention: "I doubt much—inasmuch as the railway company did not authorise their servants to receive goods for deposit on any other terms, and as they had done nothing to lead the plaintiff to believe that they had given such authority to their servants so as to preclude them from asserting, as against her, that the authority was so limited—whether the true rule of law is not that the plaintiff must assent to the contract intended by the defendants to be authorised, or treat the case as one in which there was no contract at all, and consequently no liability for safe custody." I am of opinion that this objection cannot prevail. It is clear that the company's servants did not exceed the authority given them by the company. They did the exact thing they were authorised to do. They were authorised to receive articles on deposit as bailees on behalf of the company, charging 2d. for each article, and delivering a ticket properly filled up to the person leaving the article. This is exactly what they did in the present case, and whatever may be the legal effect of what was done, the company must, in my opinion, be bound by it. The directors may have thought, and no doubt did think, that delivering the ticket to the person depositing the article would be sufficient to make him bound by the conditions contained in the ticket, and if they were mistaken in that, the company must bear the consequence.

The question then is, whether the plaintiff was bound by the conditions contained in the ticket. In an ordinary case, where an action is brought on a written agreement which is signed by the defendant, the agreement is proved by proving his signature, and, in the absence of fraud, it is wholly immaterial that he has not read the agreement and does not know its contents. The parties may, however, reduce their agreement into writing, so that the writing constitutes the sole evidence of the agreement, without signing it; but in that case there must be evidence independently of the agreement itself to prove that the defendant has assented to it. In that case, also, if it is proved that the defendant has assented to the writing constituting the agreement between the parties, it is, in the absence of fraud, immaterial that the defendant had not read the agreement and did not know its contents. Now if in the course of making a contract one party delivers to another a paper containing writing, and the party receiving the paper knows that the paper contains conditions which the party delivering it intends to constitute the contract, I have no doubt that the party receiving the paper does, by receiving and keeping it, assent to the conditions contained in it, although he does not read them, and does not know what they are. I hold, therefore, that the case of *Harris v Great Western Rly.* was rightly decided, because in that case the plaintiff admitted, on cross-examination, that she believed there were some conditions on the ticket. On the other hand, the case of *Henderson v Stevenson, L.R. 2 Sc. & Div 470*, is a conclusive authority that if the person receiving the ticket does not know that there is any writing upon the back of the ticket, he is not bound by a condition printed on the back. The facts in the cases before us differ from those in both *Henderson v Stevenson* and *Harris v Great Western Rly.*, because in both the cases which have been argued before us, though the plaintiffs admitted that they knew there was writing on the back of the ticket, they swore not only that they did not read it, but that they did not know or believe that the writing contained conditions, and we are to consider whether, under those circumstances, we can lay down as a matter of law either that the plaintiff is bound or that he is not bound by the conditions contained in the ticket, or whether his being bound depends on some question of fact to be determined by the jury, and if so, whether, in the present case, the right question was left to the jury.

Now, I am of the opinion that we cannot lay down, as a matter of law, either that the plaintiff was bound or that he was not bound by the conditions printed on the ticket, from the mere fact that he knew there was writing on the ticket, but did not know that the writing contained conditions. I think there may be cases in which a paper containing writing is delivered by one party to another in the course of a business transaction, where it would be quite reasonable that the party receiving it should assume that the writing contained in it no condition, and should put it in his pocket unread. For instance, if a person driving through a turnpike-gate received a ticket upon paying the toll, he might reasonably assume that the object of the ticket was that by producing it he might be free from paying toll at some other turnpike-gate, and might put it in his pocket unread. On the other hand, if a person who ships goods to be carried on a voyage by sea receives a bill of lading signed by the master, he would plainly be bound by it, although afterwards, in an action against the shipowner for the loss of the goods, he might swear that he had never read the bill of lading, and that he did not know that it contained the terms of the contract of carriage, and that the shipowner was protected by the exceptions contained in it. Now the reason why the person receiving the bill of lading would be bound seems to me to be that in the great majority of cases persons shipping goods do know that the bill of lading contains the terms of the contract of carriage; and the shipowner, or the master delivering the bill of lading, is entitled to assume that the person shipping goods has that knowledge. It is, however, quite possible to suppose that a person who is neither a man of business nor a lawyer might on some particular occasion ship goods without the least knowledge of what a bill of lading was, but in my opinion such a person must bear the consequences of his own exceptional ignorance, it being plainly impossible that business could be carried on if every person who delivers a bill of lading had to stop to explain what a bill of lading was.

Now the question we have to consider is whether the railway company were entitled to assume that a person depositing luggage, and receiving a ticket in such a way that he could see that some writing was printed on it, would understand that the writing contained the conditions of contract, and this seems to me to depend upon whether people in general would in fact, and naturally, draw that inference. The railway company, as it seems to me, must be entitled to make some assumptions respecting the person who deposits luggage with them: I think they are entitled to assume that he can read, and that he understands the English language, and that he pays such attention to what he is about as may be reasonably expected from a person in such a transaction as that of depositing luggage in a cloak-room. The railway company must, however, take mankind as they find them, and if what they do is sufficient to inform people in general that the ticket contains conditions, I think that a particular plaintiff ought not to be in a better position than other persons on account of his exceptional ignorance or stupidity or carelessness. But if what the railway company do is not sufficient to convey to the minds of people in general that the ticket contains conditions, then they have received goods on deposit without obtaining the consent of the persons depositing them to the conditions limiting their liability. I am of opinion, therefore, that the proper direction to leave to the jury in these cases is, that if the person receiving the ticket did not see or know that there was any writing on the ticket, he is not bound by the conditions; that if he knew there was writing, and knew or believed that the writing contained conditions, then he is bound by the conditions; that if he knew there was writing on the ticket, but did not know or believe that the writing contained conditions, nevertheless he would be bound, if the delivering of the ticket to him in such a manner that he could see there was writing upon it, was, in the opinion of the jury, reasonable notice that the writing contained conditions.

I have lastly to consider whether the direction of the learned judge was correct, namely, "Was the plaintiff, under the circumstances, under any obligation, in the exercise of reasonable and proper caution, to read or to make himself aware of the condition?" I think that this direction was not strictly accurate, and was calculated to mislead the jury. The plaintiff was certainly under no obligation to read the ticket, but was entitled to leave it unread if he pleased, and the question does not appear to me to direct the attention of the jury to the real question, namely, whether the railway company did what was reasonably sufficient to give the plaintiff notice of the condition.

On the whole, I am of opinion that there ought to be a new trial.

Baggallay L.J. delivered a concurring judgment, while Bramwell L.J. held that the question was one of law and judgment ought to be entered for the defendants.

Order Absolute for a New Trial.

Points for reflection

7–003

1. For the historical importance of the *Parker* case, see Stephen Waddams, *Principle and Policy in Contract Law* (Cambridge University Press, 2011) at 36-39. Remarking on the differences of opinion within the court, Waddams notes (at 39) that the emphasis of Bramwell LJ's judgment is "entirely on the reasonableness of the railway's conduct of its business and on the unreasonableness of the customers' claims; there is no concession whatever to the notion that they could only be bound by their actual consent." This, however, was "a step too far for the majority, who, by ordering a new trial, sought to maintain the principle that individual assent (albeit on an objective test) was theoretically necessary."

2. The dictum of Mellish LJ regarding the turnpike ticket was followed in *Chapelton v Barry Urban District Council* [1940] 1 K.B. 532 CA, where the plaintiff received two tickets on taking two deck chairs for which he paid 4d. On the back of the ticket were printed words purporting to exempt the council from liability. They were held ineffective. The ticket was a mere receipt; its object was that the hirer might produce it to prove that he had paid and to show him how long he might use the chair. Slesser LJ pointed out that a person might sit in one of these chairs for an hour or two before an attendant came round to take his money and give him a receipt.

   In *Olley v Marlborough Court* [1949] 1 K.B. 532 a similar point formed the ratio decidendi of the case. It was held that a notice in an hotel bedroom purporting to exempt the proprietors of the defendant hotel from liability for the loss of guests' luggage was not incorporated in the contract between the proprietors and a guest. The contract was made in the hall of the hotel before the plaintiff entered her bedroom and before she had an opportunity to see the notice.

   In *Mendelssohn v Normand Ltd* [1970] 1 Q.B. 177 CA, the plaintiff had frequently garaged his car at the defendants' garage and always received a ticket which stated that the defendants "will not accept responsibility for any loss or damage sustained by the vehicle, its accessories or contents, however caused." "He may not have read it. But that does not matter. It was plainly a contractual document; and, as he accepted it without objection, he must be taken to have agreed to it"—per Lord Denning. (Contrast *Thornton v Shoe Lane Parking*, below, para.7–005). The plaintiff on previous occasions had locked his car but on this occasion was prevented by the attendant from doing so; he pointed out that the car contained valuable property. The attendant said it was the rule that the car be left unlocked but if the plaintiff would leave the key he would lock the car as soon as he had moved it. The car was unlocked when the plaintiff returned and property had been stolen. Held: notwithstanding the condition in the contract, the defendants were liable because—

(i) The promise to lock up the car was within the ostensible authority of the attendant, was binding on the defendants and took priority over the written condition. (Cf. *Curtis v Chemical, etc. Co*, below, Ch.21).

(ii) the defendants had agreed to keep the car locked up; instead they left it unlocked.

"This was so entirely different a way of carrying out the contract that the exemption clause cannot be construed as extending to it."—per Lord Denning.

3. In the notorious case of *Thompson v London Midland & Scottish Rly Co* [1930] 1 K.B. 41 the plaintiff who could not read gave her niece, A, the money to buy a ticket for an excursion from Manchester to Darwen. A did so. On the face of the ticket was printed "Excursion, For Conditions see back"; and on the back, "Issued subject to the conditions and regulations in the company's time-tables and notices and excursion and other bills." The excursion bills referred to the conditions in the company's timetables, which provided that excursion ticket holders should have no right of action against the company in respect of any injury, however caused. There was only one copy of the time-tables in the booking office and it cost 6d. to buy one. The plaintiff sustained an injury on Darwen station. At the trial the judge left to the jury the question whether the defendants had taken reasonable steps to bring the conditions to the notice of the plaintiff. The jury found that they had not and assessed damages at £176. The judge nevertheless entered judgment for the defendants.

The Court of Appeal held that the judge was right. The Court thought that the verdict of the jury was probably based on the fact that the passenger had to make a considerable search to find the conditions; but that was no answer. There was no evidence on which the jury could find that the company did not take reasonable steps to bring the conditions to the notice of the plaintiff. Lord Hanworth MR said that the company had made an offer to intending passengers to carry them on terms which could be ascertained and that offer had been accepted. Anyone who took the ticket was conscious that there were some conditions and it was obvious that the company did not provide for 2s. 7d. (the price of an excursion ticket) what it provided for the usual fare of 5s. 4d. Having regard to the condition of education in this country, it was irrelevant that the plaintiff could not read. Lawrence and Sankey LJJ both said that it would have been different if the condition had been unreasonable to the knowledge of the company; but this condition was not unreasonable.

If the condition had applied to regular, as well as excursion services, might the notice have been held to be insufficient?

Consider the effect of the UTCC Regulations 5(1) and Sch.2 (below Ch.22).

Questions

1. "*Henderson v Stevenson*, 2 Sc. & Div. 470, is a conclusive authority that if the person receiving the ticket does not know that there is any writing upon the back of the ticket, he is not bound by a condition printed on the back" (per Mellish LJ, above). The ticket in that case was "complete upon the face of it" and did not refer to the conditions printed on the back. Could a plaintiff rely on his ignorance of the writing on the back of a ticket if any person who "pays

7–004

such attention to what he is about as may reasonably be expected" would necessarily have known of it?

2. Is a blind man bound by the conditions printed on a ticket in such a way that a person with normal sight could not fail to know of them?

3. "I ask for a ticket to Aberdeen: the clerk in error gives me a ticket for Aberdovey: the inspector points out the error. I cannot get my money back because I have contracted for conveyance to Aberdovey: the ticket constitutes the offer and Aberdovey is printed on it. I must buy another ticket for Aberdeen." (J.D.I. Hughes, 'The Constructive Acceptance of Uncommunicated Offers' 47 L.Q.R. 459, 463.) Do you agree?

THORNTON v SHOE LANE PARKING LTD

Court of Appeal [1971] 2 Q.B. 163; [1971] 2 W.L.R. 585; [1971] 1 All E.R. 686; [1971] R.T.R. 79; [1971] 1 Lloyd's Rep. 289

7–005   The plaintiff drove into the entrance to the defendants' car park where a notice stated. "All cars parked at owner's risk." A light changed from red to green as he drove in. He took a ticket from a machine and drove into the garage. He looked at the ticket to see the time printed on it and saw other printed wording which he did not read. When the plaintiff collected the car, there was an accident in which he suffered personal injuries, partly through the negligence of the defendants. The defendants relied on the ticket which stated that it was "issued subject to the conditions of issue as displayed on the premises." Conditions displayed inside the garage stated that, "The customer is deemed to be fully insured . . ." and that the defendants should not be liable for any loss, mis-delivery of or damage to the vehicle or injury to the customer. Mocatta J held that the defendants were liable. They appealed.

DENNING MR

Lord Denning M.R., having referred, inter alia, to *Parker v South Eastern Railway* (above, para.7–002), *McCutcheon v MacBrayne* (below) and *Thompson v LMS* (above, para.7–003) continued:

None of those cases has any application to a ticket which is issued by an automatic machine. The customer pays his money and gets a ticket. He cannot refuse it. He cannot get his money back. He may protest to the machine, even swear at it. But it will remain unmoved. He is committed beyond recall. He was committed at the very moment when he put his money into the machine. The contract was concluded at that time. It can be translated into offer and acceptance in this way: the offer is made when the proprietor of the machine holds it out as being ready to receive the money. The acceptance takes place when the customer puts his money into the slot. The terms of the offer are contained in the notice placed on or near the machine stating what is offered for the money. The customer is bound by those terms as long as they are sufficiently brought to his notice before-hand but not otherwise. He is not bound by the terms printed on the ticket if they differ from the notice, because the ticket comes too late. The contract has already been made: see *Olley v Marlborough Court, Ltd* [above, para.7–003]. The ticket is no more than a voucher or receipt for the money that has been paid (as in the deckchair case, *Chapelton v Barry Urban District Council* [above, para.7–003], on terms which have been offered and accepted before the ticket is issued.

In the present case the offer was contained in the notice at the entrance giving the charges for garaging and saying "at owner's risk," that is, at the risk of the owner so far as damage to the car was concerned. The offer was accepted when Mr Thornton drove up to the entrance and, by the movement of his car, turned the light from red to green, and the ticket was thrust at him. The contract was then concluded, and it could not be altered by any words printed on the ticket itself. In particular, it could not be altered so as to exempt the company from liability for personal injury due to their negligence.

Assuming, however, that an automatic machine is a booking clerk in disguise—so that the old-fashioned ticket cases still apply to it. We then have to go back to the three questions[1] put by Mellish L.J. in *Parker v South Eastern Railway Co*, subject to this qualification: Mellish L.J. used the word "conditions" in the plural, whereas it would be more apt to use the word "condition" in the singular, as indeed the lord justice himself did on the next page. After all, the only condition that matters for this purpose is the exempting condition. It is no use telling the customer that the ticket is issued subject to some "conditions" or other, without more: for he may reasonably regard "conditions" in general as merely regulatory, and not as taking away his rights, unless the exempting condition is drawn specifically to his attention. (Alternatively, if the plural "conditions" is used, it would be better prefaced with the word "exempting," because the exempting conditions are the only conditions that matter for this purpose.) Telescoping the three questions, they come to this: the customer is bound by the exempting condition if he knows that the ticket is issued subject to it; or, if the company did what was reasonably sufficient to give him notice of it.

Mr Machin admitted here that the company did not do what was reasonably sufficient to give Mr Thornton notice of the exempting condition. That admission was properly made. I do not pause to inquire whether the exempting condition is void for unreasonableness. All say is that it is so wide and so destructive of rights that the court should not hold any man bound by it unless it is drawn to his attention in the most explicit way. It is an instance of what I had in mind in *J. Spurling, Ltd v Bradshaw* [1956] 1 W.L.R. 461, 466. In order to give sufficient notice, it would need to be printed in red ink with a red hand pointing to it—or something equally startling. (Lord Denning rejected an argument that the plaintiff knew that the writing contained conditions—the burden of proof was on the defendants and there was no finding to that effect—and said that he would dismiss the appeal.)

MEGAW LJ

For myself, I would reserve a final view on the question at what precise moment of time the contract was concluded . . .

The essence of the decision in *Parker v South Eastern Railway Co* was analysed by Lord Hodson in *McCutcheon v David MacBrayne, Ltd* as follows: "That case, affirmed in *Hood v Anchor Line (Henderson Brothers) Ltd* [1918] A.C. 837, established that the appropriate questions for the jury in a ticket case were: (1) Did the passenger know that there was printing on the railway ticket? (2) Did he know that the ticket contained or referred to conditions? and (3) Did the railway company do what was reasonable in the way of notifying prospective passengers of the existence of conditions and where their terms might be considered?"

[The judge held that the first and second questions must be answered in the negative.]

So I come to the third of the three questions. That question, if I may return to the speech of Lord Dunedin in *Hood v Anchor Line (Henderson Brothers) Ltd* was posed by him in this way: "Accordingly it is in each case a question of circumstance whether the sort of restriction that is expressed in any writing (which, of course, includes printed matter) is a thing that is usual, and whether, being usual, it has been fairly brought before the notice of the accepting party."

That, though it is more fully stated by Lord Dunedin, is essentially the same question, I think, as was formulated by Mellish L.J. in *Parker's* case, at the very end of his judgment, where he said that the question which ought to have been left to the jury was: whether the railway company did what was reasonably sufficient to give the plaintiff notice of the condition. (I emphasise the use by Mellish L.J. of the definite article and of the word "condition" in the singular.) I agree with Lord Denning M.R. that the question here is of the particular condition on which the defendants seek to rely, and not of the conditions in general.

When the conditions sought to be attached all constitute, in Lord Dunedin's words, "the sort of restriction . . . that is usual," it may not be necessary for a defendant to prove more than that the intention to attach some conditions has been fairly brought to the notice of the other party. But at least where the particular condition relied on involves a sort of restriction that is not shown to be usual in that class of contract, a defendant must show that his intention to attach an unusual condition of that particular nature was fairly brought to the notice of the other party. How much is required as being, in the words of Mellish L.J., "reasonably sufficient to give the plaintiff notice of the condition," depends upon the nature of the restrictive condition.

In the present case what has to be sought in answer to the third question is whether the defendant company did what was reasonable fairly to bring to the notice of the plaintiff, at or before the time when the contract

---

[1]   See Lord Hodson's analysis of *Parker's* case, quoted by Megaw LJ, below.

was made, the existence of this particular condition. This condition is that part of the clause—a few words embedded in a lengthy clause—which Lord Denning M.R. has read, by which, in the midst of provisions as to damage to property, the defendants sought to exempt themselves from liability for any personal injury suffered by the customer while he was on their premises. Be it noted that such a condition is one which involves the abrogation of the right given to a person such as the plaintiff by statute, the Occupiers' Liability Act, 1957. True, it is open under that statute for the occupier of property by a contractual term to exclude that liability. In my view, however, before it can be said that a condition of that sort, restrictive of statutory rights, has been fairly brought to the notice of a party to a contract there must be some clear indication which would lead an ordinary sensible person to realise, at or before the time of making the contract, that a term of that sort, relating to personal injury, was sought to be included. I certainly would not accept that the position has been reached today in which it is to be assumed as a matter of general knowledge, custom, practice, or whatever is the phrase that is chosen to describe it, that when one is invited to go upon the property of another for such purposes as garaging a car, a contractual term is normally included that if one suffers any injury on those premises as a result of negligence on the part of the occupiers of the premises they shall not be liable.

Even if I were wrong in the view which I take that the third question has to be posed in relation to this particular term, it would still not avail the defendants here. In my view the judge was wholly right on the evidence in the conclusion which he reached that the defendants have not taken proper or adequate steps fairly to bring to the notice of the plaintiff at or before the time when the contract was made that any special conditions were sought to be imposed.

I think it is a highly relevant factor in considering whether proper steps were taken fairly to bring that matter to the notice of the plaintiff that the first attempt to bring to his notice the intended inclusion of those conditions was at a time when as a matter of hard reality it would have been practically impossible for him to withdraw from his intended entry upon the premises for the purpose of leaving his car there. It does not take much imagination to picture the indignation of the defendants if their potential customers, having taken their tickets and observed the reference therein to contractual conditions which, they said, could be seen in notices on the premises, were one after the other to get out of their cars, leaving the cars blocking the entrances to the garage, in order to search for, find and peruse the notices! Yet unless the defendants genuinely intended that potential customers should do just that, it would be fiction, if not farce, to treat those customers as persons who have been given a fair opportunity, before the contracts are made, of discovering the conditions by which they are to be bound.

I agree that this appeal should be dismissed.

SIR GORDON WILLMER

It seems to me that the really distinguishing feature of this case is the fact that the ticket on which reliance is placed was issued out of an automatic machine. I think it is right to say—at any rate, it is the fact so far as the cases that have been called to our attention are concerned—that in all the previous so-called "ticket cases" the ticket has been proffered by a human hand, and there has always been at least the notional opportunity for the customer to say—if he did not like the conditions—"I do not like your conditions: I will not have this ticket." But in the case of a ticket which is proffered by an automatic machine there is something quite irrevocable about the process. There can be no locus poenitentiae. I do not propose to say any more upon the difficult question which has been raised as to the precise moment when a contract was concluded in this case; but at least it seems to me that any attempt to introduce conditions after the irrevocable step has been taken of causing the machine to operate must be doomed to failure. It may be that those who operate garages of this nature, as well as those who insta[l]l other types of automatic machines, should give their attention to this problem. But it seems to me that the judge below was on the right track when he said, towards the end of his judgment, that in this sort of case, if you do desire to impose upon your customers stringent conditions such as these, the least you can do is to post a prominent notice at the entrance to the premises, warning your customers that there are conditions which will apply.

Appeal Dismissed with Costs.

Questions

7-006   1. "Does the law applicable to the purchase of a ticket from a machine in the Underground differ from the law applicable to the purchase of a similar ticket from the clerk in the booth?" (A. L. G. in a note in 87 L.Q.R. 296, 298.)

2. A ticket contains a number of conditions, ranging in nature from the very unusual and far-reaching to the commonplace. Is it possible that the ticket constitutes notice of some but not all of the conditions?

INTERFOTO PICTURE LIBRARY LTD v STILETTO VISUAL PROGRAMMES LTD

Court of Appeal [1989] Q.B. 433; [1988] 2 W.L.R. 615; [1988] 1 All E.R. 348

The plaintiffs ran a library of photographic transparencies. The defendants required photographs of the 1950's for a client. In response to a telephone inquiry by the defendants (with whom they had not dealt previously) the plaintiffs, on March 5, delivered a bag of 47 transparencies with a delivery note. This clearly stated that the transparencies were to be returned by March 19. Under the prominently printed heading, "Conditions," Condition 2 stated that all transparencies were to be returned within 14 days from the date of delivery and that "A holding fee of £5.00 plus VAT per day will be charged for each transparency which is retained by you longer than the said period of 14 days." It is unlikely that the defendants read any of the conditions but a director, Mr Beeching, telephoned that one or two of the transparencies could be of interest and that he would get back to them within a few days. He did not do so. The defendants did not use any of the transparencies but put them aside and forgot about them until April 2 when they were returned. The plaintiffs claimed £3,783.50, being the holding charge at £5 per transparency per day from March 19 to April 2. The defendants refused to pay. The judge gave judgment for the plaintiffs. The defendants appealed.

7–007

DILLON LJ

Dillon L.J., having held that a contract was made when Mr Beeching telephoned and having discussed *Parker v South Eastern Railway Co*, above and *Thornton v Shoe Lane Parking Ltd*, above, continued:

Counsel for the plaintiffs submits that *Thornton v Shoe Lane Parking Ltd* was a case of an exemption clause and that what their Lordships said must be read as limited to exemption clauses and in particular exemption clauses which would deprive the party on whom they are imposed of statutory rights. But what their Lordships said was said by way of interpretation and application of the general statement of the law by Mellish L.J. in *Parker v South Eastern Rly. Co* and the logic of it is applicable to any particularly onerous clause in a printed set of conditions of the one contracting party which would not be generally known to the other party.

Condition 2 of these plaintiffs' conditions is in my judgment a very onerous clause. The defendants could not conceivably have known, if their attention was not drawn to the clause, that the plaintiffs were proposing to charge a "holding fee" for the retention of the transparencies at such a very high and exorbitant rate.

At the time of the ticket cases in the last century it was notorious that people hardly ever troubled to read printed conditions on a ticket or delivery note or similar document. That remains the case now. In the intervening years the printed conditions have tended to become more and more complicated and more and more one-sided in favour of the party who is imposing them, but the other parties, if they notice that there are printed conditions at all, generally still tend to assume that such conditions are only concerned with ancillary matters of form and are not of importance. In the ticket cases the courts held that the common law required that reasonable steps be taken to draw the other parties' attention to the printed conditions or they would not be part of the contract. It is in my judgment a logical development of the common law into modern conditions that it should be held, as it was in *Thornton v Shoe Lane Parking Ltd*, that, if one condition in a set of printed conditions is particularly onerous or unusual, the party seeking to enforce it must show that that particular condition was fairly brought to the attention of the other party.

In the present case, nothing whatever was done by the plaintiffs to draw the defendants' attention particularly to condition 2; it was merely one of four columns' width of conditions printed across the foot of the delivery note. Consequently condition 2 never, in my judgment, became part of the contract between the parties.

I would therefore allow this appeal and reduce the amount of the judgment which the judge awarded against the defendants to the amount which he would have awarded on a quantum meruit on his alternative findings, that is, the reasonable charge of £3.50 per transparency per week for the retention of the transparencies beyond a reasonable period, which he fixed at 14 days from the date of their receipt by the defendants.

BINGHAM LJ

In many civil law systems, and perhaps in most legal systems outside the common law world, the law of obligations recognises and enforces an overriding principle that in making and carrying out contracts parties should act in good faith. This does not simply mean that they should not deceive each other, a principle which any legal system must recognise; its effect is perhaps most aptly conveyed by such metaphorical colloquialisms as "playing fair," "coming clean" or "putting one's cards face upwards on the table." It is in essence a principle of fair and open dealing. In such a forum it might, I think, be held on the facts of this case that the plaintiffs were under a duty in all fairness to draw the defendants' attention specifically to the high price payable if the transparencies were not returned in time and, when the 14 days had expired, to point out to the defendants the high cost of continued failure to return them.

English law has, characteristically, committed itself to no such overriding principle but has developed piecemeal solutions in response to demonstrated problems of unfairness. Many examples could be given. Thus equity has intervened to strike down unconscionable bargains. Parliament has stepped in to regulate the imposition of exemption clauses and the form of certain hire-purchase agreements. The common law also has made its contribution, by holding that certain classes of contract require the utmost good faith, by treating as irrecoverable what purport to be agreed estimates of damage but are in truth a disguised penalty for breach, and in many other ways.

The well-known cases on sufficiency of notice are in my view properly to be read in this context. At one level they are concerned with a question of pure contractual analysis, whether one party has done enough to give the other notice of the incorporation of a term in the contract. At another level they are concerned with a somewhat different question, whether it would in all the circumstances be fair (or reasonable) to hold a party bound by any conditions or by a particular condition of an unusual and stringent nature . . .

[Having examined the authorities Bingham LJ continued:] Turning to the present case, I am satisfied for reasons which Dillon L.J. has given that no contract was made on the telephone when the defendants made their initial request. I am equally satisfied that no contract was made on delivery of the transparencies to the defendants before the opening of the Jiffy bag in which they were contained. Once the Jiffy bag was opened and the transparencies taken out with the delivery note, it is in my judgment an inescapable inference that the defendants would have recognised the delivery note as a document of a kind likely to contain contractual terms and would have seen that there were conditions printed in small but visible lettering on the face of the document. To the extent that the conditions so displayed were common form or usual terms regularly encountered in this business, I do not think the defendants could successfully contend that they were not incorporated into the contract.

The crucial question in the case is whether the plaintiffs can be said fairly and reasonably to have brought condition 2 to the notice of the defendants. The judge made no finding on the point, but I think that it is open to this court to draw an inference from the primary findings which he did make. In my opinion the plaintiffs did not do so. They delivered 47 transparencies, which was a number the defendants had not specifically asked for. Condition 2 contained a daily rate per transparency after the initial period of 14 days many times greater than was usual or (so far as the evidence shows) heard of. For these 47 transparencies there was to be a charge for each day of delay of £235 plus value added tax. The result would be that a venial period of delay, as here, would lead to an inordinate liability. The defendants are not to be relieved of that liability because they did not read the condition, although doubtless they did not; but in my judgment they are to be relieved because the plaintiffs did not do what was necessary to draw this unreasonable and extortionate clause fairly to their attention. I would accordingly allow the defendants' appeal and substitute for the judge's award the sum which he assessed on the alternative basis of quantum meruit.

In reaching the conclusion I have expressed I would not wish to be taken as deciding that condition 2 was not challengeable as a disguised penalty clause. [See below, paras 19–052–19–058.] This point was not argued before the judge nor raised in the notice of appeal. It was accordingly not argued before us. I have accordingly felt bound to assume, somewhat reluctantly, that condition 2 would be enforceable if fully and fairly brought to the defendants' attention.

Appeal Allowed.

Questions

7–008

1. If the contract was made when the defendants' telephoned the picture library, and if no reference was made at that time to the library's standard terms and conditions, how were they incorporated by the delivery note?

2. What if condition 2 had been printed in red, with a red hand pointing to it and had still not been read?

3. What if the defendants had signed the delivery note without reading it?

4. Is it realistic to say, for example, that sufficient notice has been given of conditions 1 and 3 to 9 and that they are part of the contract but that no sufficient notice has been given of condition 2? If the reasonable man would have been aware of any of them, would he not have been aware of all of them?

It is important to note that neither the Unfair Contract Terms 1977 nor the UTCC Regulations 1999 would be applicable in this case. The Act did not apply because, though the contract was made on Interfoto's 'written standard terms of business' (s.3(1)), the relevant condition was not an exclusion clause. The Regulations would not apply as the contract was not a 'consumer contract' both because (i) Stiletto was not a 'natural person' but a limited company and (ii) it was acting for the purposes of its business. So the matter would still be governed by the common law.

O'BRIEN v MGN

Court of Appeal [2001] EWCA Civ 1279

LADY JUSTICE HALE

7–009

1. The claimant suffered a cruel disappointment on Monday 3 July 1995. He thought that he had won £50,000 in the scratchcard game played in the Daily Mirror that day. Mirror Group Newspapers thought otherwise. The issue is whether the contract between them incorporated the Mirror Group's rules. It would make an excellent question in an undergraduate contract law seminar or examination. Like all good questions, it is easy to ask and difficult to answer. On 29 June 2000, in the Queen's Bench Division of the High Court sitting in Liverpool, H. H. J. Hegarty Q.C. answered it in the affirmative and dismissed the claimant's claim. He gave permission to appeal to this court.

10. . . . The first announcement of the game, in the Daily Mirror on 29 April 1995, had a heading in capital letters with white text in a black box INSTANT SCRATCH RULES. Under this were printed eight numbered paragraphs ("the Rules"). Rules 2 and 5 read as follows:

"2. The prizes for each game will be awarded to the player or players who make a successful claim . . .
5. Should more prizes be claimed than are available in any prize category for any reason, a simple draw will take place for the prize."

The judge concluded that

"only one £50,000 prize was 'available' on 3 July 1995 in the sense that MGN Ltd and Europrint Ltd had previously determined that there should be only a single prize in that category. I have also concluded that the terms should not be construed in a sense which required the precise number of prizes to be published or drawn to the attention of participants at or before the time when the telephone game was announced."

Hence more prizes were claimed than were available. If the Rules formed part of the contract, MGN were entitled to insist upon holding a draw . . .

Conclusion

19. In my view the judge was right to hold that the contract was made on 3 July. The offer was contained in the paper that day. In my view it was accepted when the claimant telephoned to claim his prize. The offer and therefore the contract clearly incorporated the term "Normal Mirror Group rules apply". The words were there to be read and it makes no difference whether or not the claimant actually read or paid attention to them.

20. The question, therefore, is whether those words, in the circumstances, were enough to incorporate the Rules, including Rule 5, into the contract. In the words of Bingham L.J. in *Interfoto Library Ltd v Stiletto Ltd* [1989] 1 QB 433, at p 445E, can the defendant "be said fairly and reasonably to have brought [those rules] to the notice of" the claimant? This is a question of fact. It is clear from the passage in the same judgment quoted earlier (at para 13) that one has to look at the particular contract made on the particular day between the particular parties. But what is fair and reasonable notice will depend upon the nature of the transaction and upon the nature of the term. As Dillon L.J. summed it up in *Interfoto*, at pp 438H to 439A:

> "In the ticket cases the courts held that the common law required that reasonable steps be taken to draw the other parties' attention to the printed conditions or they would not be part of the contract. It is, in my judgment, a logical development of the common law into modern conditions that it should be held, as it was in *Thornton v Shoe Lane Parking Ltd* [1971] 2 QB 163, that if one condition in a set of printed conditions is particularly onerous or unusual, the party seeking to enforce it must show that that particular condition was fairly brought to the attention of the other party."

Bingham L.J. put the same point in this way at p 443C:

> ". . . what would be good notice of one condition would not be good notice of another. The reason is that the more outlandish the clause the greater the notice which the other party, if he is to be bound, must in all fairness be given."

21. In my view, although Rule 5 does turn an apparent winner into a loser, it cannot by any normal use of language be called "onerous" or "outlandish". It does not impose any extra burden upon the claimant, unlike the clause in *Interfoto*. It does not seek to absolve the defendant from liability for personal injuries negligently caused, unlike the clause in *Thornton v Shoe Lane Parking*. It merely deprives the claimant of a windfall for which he has done very little in return. He bought two newspapers, although in fact he could have acquired a card and discovered the hotline number without doing either. He made a call to a premium rate number, which will have cost him some money and gained the newspaper some, but only a matter of pennies, not pounds.

22. The more difficult question is whether the rule is "unusual" in this context. The judge found that the claimant knew that there was a limit on the number of prizes and that there were relevant rules. Miss Platell's evidence was that these games and competitions always have rules. Indeed I would accept that this is common knowledge. This is not a situation in which players of the game would assume that the newspaper bore the risk of any mistake of any kind which might lead to more people making a claim than had been intended. Some people might assume that the "get out" rule would provide for the prize to be shared amongst the claimants. Some might assume that it would provide for the drawing of lots. In the case of a single prize some might think drawing lots more appropriate; but it seems to me impossible to say that either solution would be "unusual". There is simply no evidence to that effect. Such evidence as there is was to the effect that such rules are not unusual.

23. In any event, the words "onerous or unusual" are not terms of art. They are simply one way of putting the general proposition that reasonable steps must be taken to draw the particular term in question to the notice of those who are to be bound by it and that more is required in relation to certain terms than to others depending on their effect. In the particular context of this particular game, I consider that the defendants did just enough to bring the Rules to the claimant's attention. There was a clear reference to rules on the face of the card he used. There was a clear reference to rules in the paper containing the offer of a telephone prize. There was evidence that those rules could be discovered either from the newspaper offices or from back issues of the paper. The claimant had been able to discover them when the problem arose.

24. The judge had "great sympathy for Mr O'Brien who struck me as a thoroughly decent young man who must have suffered a cruel disappointment when his hopes were raised only to be dashed." There can be little sympathy for a newspaper which introduces such a game to attract publicity and readers, and then devotes space which could have been devoted to printing the Rules to hyperbole about the prizes to be won and the

people who have won them. But the fact of the matter is that there was nothing at all outlandish about the rules of this game and indeed it would have been surprising if there had been no protection on the lines of Rule 5. I would dismiss this appeal.

Sir Anthony Evans and Potter L.J. agreed that the appeal should be dismissed.

2. INCORPORATION OF TERMS BY A COURSE OF DEALING

McCUTCHEON v DAVID MacBRAYNE LTD

House of Lords (Scotland) [1964] 1 W.L.R. 125; [1964] 1 All E.R. 430;
[1964] 1 Lloyd's Rep. 16; 1964 S.L.T. 66

McCutcheon's brother-in-law, McSporran, shipped McCutcheon's car on MacBrayne's ship. The ship was negligently sailed into a rock and sank. McCutcheon sued for the value of the car. MacBrayne relied on condition 19 of their elaborate contract of carriage which purported to exempt them from liability for negligence. It was their practice to require consignors to sign "risk notes" containing these conditions; but on the occasion in question the purser forgot to ask McSporran to sign. McSporran had consigned goods on a number of previous occasions. Sometimes he was asked to sign a risk note, sometimes not. He had never read the risk note. He knew it contained conditions but did not know what they were. MacBrayne contended that, because of the knowledge gained by his agent, McSporran, on these previous occasions, McCutcheon was bound by the terms. The House of Lords held that the printed conditions were not part of the contract and MacBrayne was liable.

7–010

Lord Reid took the view that there had been no consistent course of dealing. Sometimes McSporran was asked to sign and sometimes he was not. He did not know what the conditions were. This time he was offered an oral contract without reference to any conditions, and he accepted the offer in good faith.

Lord Hodson thought it would be scarcely tolerable to treat a contracting party as if he had signed and so bound himself by the terms of a document with conditions embodied in it when, as here, he had done no such thing but may be supposed having regard to his previous experience to have been willing to sign what was put before him if he had been asked.

LORD GUEST

All that the previous dealings in the present case can show is that the appellant and his agent knew that the previous practice of the respondents was to impose special conditions. But knowledge on their part did not and could not by itself import acceptance by them of these conditions, the exact terms of which they were unaware, into a contract which was different in character from those in the previous course of dealing.

LORD DEVLIN

If a man is given a blank ticket without conditions or any reference to them, even if he knows in detail what the conditions usually exacted are, he is not, in the absence of any allegation of fraud or of that sort of mistake for which the law gives relief, bound by such conditions. It may seem a narrow and artificial line that divides a ticket that is blank on the back from one that says "For conditions see time-tables," or something of that sort, that has been held to be enough notice. I agree that it is an artificial line and one that has little relevance to every-day conditions. It may be beyond your Lordships' power to make the artificial line more natural: but at least you can see that it is drawn fairly for both sides and that there is not one law for individuals and another for organi-sations that can issue printed documents. If the respondents had remembered to issue a risk note in this case, they would have invited your Lordships to give a curt answer to any complaint by the appellant. He might say that the terms were unfair and unreasonable, that he had never voluntarily agreed to them, that it was impossi-ble to read or understand them and that anyway if he had tried to negotiate any change the respondents would not have listened to him. The respondents would expect him to be told that he had made his contract and must abide by it. Now the boot is on the other foot. It is just as legitimate, but also just as vain, for the respondents to say that it was only a slip on their part, that it is unfair and unreasonable of the appellant to take advantage of it and that he knew perfectly well that they never carried goods except on conditions. The law must give the same answer they must abide by the contract they made. What is sauce for the goose is sauce for the gander. It will remain unpalatable sauce for both animals until the legislature, if the courts cannot do it, intervenes to secure that when contracts are made in circumstances in which there is no scope for free negotiation of the terms, they are made upon terms that are clear, fair and reasonable and settled independently as such. That is what Parliament has done in the case of carriage of goods by rail and on the high seas.

LORD PEARCE

It is the consistency of a course of conduct which gives rise to the implication that in similar circumstances a similar contractual result will follow. When the conduct is not consistent, there is no reason why it should still produce an invariable contractual result. The respondents having previously offered a written contract, on this occasion offered an oral one.

BRITISH CRANE HIRE CORPORATION LTD v IPSWICH PLANT HIRE LTD

Court of Appeal [1975] Q.B. 303; [1974] 2 W.L.R. 856; [1974] 1 All E.R. 1059

7–011   Plaintiffs and defendants were both in the business of hiring out heavy earth-moving equipment. Defendants, carrying out drainage work themselves, urgently needed a dragline crane. By telephone they agreed to hire one from plaintiffs. Charges were agreed but nothing was said about conditions of hire. Plaintiffs, in accordance with usual practice, sent a printed form to be signed by defendants. Before it was signed, the crane, without anyone's fault, sank in marshy ground. Under the conditions in the printed form, which were similar to those used by all firms in the plant-hiring business, including defendants, defendants were liable to indemnify plaintiffs. Defendants appealed from a finding that the printed conditions were incorporated into the contract.

LORD DENNING MR

[Having referred to *Hollier v Rambler Motors*, (below), where Salmon LJ held that three or four transactions over a period of five years could not be described as "a course of dealing":] That was a case of a private individual who had had his car repaired by the defendants and had signed forms with conditions on three or four occasions. The plaintiff there was not of equal bargaining power with the garage company which repaired the car. The conditions were not incorporated.

But here the parties were both in the trade and were of equal bargaining power. Each was a firm of plant hirers who hired out plant. The defendants themselves knew that firms in the plant-hiring trade always imposed conditions in regard to the hiring of plant; and that their conditions were on much the same lines. The defendants' manager, Mr Turner (who knew the crane), was asked about it. He agreed that he had seen these conditions or similar ones in regard to the hiring of plant. He said that most of them were, to one extent or another, variations of a form which he called "the Contractors' Plant Association form." The defendants themselves (when they let out cranes) used the conditions of that form. The conditions on the plaintiffs' form were in rather different words, but nevertheless to much the same effect . . . it is clear that both parties knew quite well that conditions were habitually imposed by the supplier of these machines: and both parties knew the substance of those conditions. In particular that, if the crane sank in soft ground, it was the hirer's job to recover it; and that there was an indemnity clause. In these circumstances, I think the conditions on the form should be regarded as incorporated into the contract. I would not put it so much on the course of dealing, but rather on the common understanding which is to be derived from the conduct of the parties, namely, that the hiring was to be on the terms of the plaintiffs' usual conditions.

As Lord Reid said in *McCutcheon v David MacBrayne Ltd* [above], quoting from the Scottish textbook *Gloag on Contract* (2nd ed., 1929), p. 7: "the judicial task is not to discover the actual intentions of each party: it is to decide what each was reasonably entitled to conclude from the attitude of the other." It seems to me that, in view of the relationship of the parties, when the defendants requested this crane urgently and it was supplied at once—before the usual form was received—the plaintiffs were entitled to conclude that the defendants were accepting it on the terms of the plaintiffs' own printed conditions . . .

Megaw L.J. agreed.

Sachs L.J. said that the case was wholly different from that where the owner and the user are in wholly different walks of life as in *Hollier's* case. He held that the plaintiffs were entitled to conclude that the defendants accepted the plaintiffs' conditions, at any rate if they were reasonable: and he had no doubt but that both parties contracted on the basis of those conditions.

Questions

1. The All England headnote states: "Since the bargaining power of the defendants was equal to that of the plaintiffs and the defendants knew that printed conditions in similar terms to those of the plaintiffs were in common use in the business, the plaintiffs were entitled to conclude that the defendants were accepting the crane on the terms of their conditions." Would the plaintiffs not have been entitled so to conclude if the bargaining power had been unequal? Is equality of bargaining power relevant to this issue?   **7–012**

2. Suppose the plaintiffs were a large, powerful and prosperous firm and the defendants were a small, weak firm on the verge of bankruptcy. Should the answer have been different? (Cf. *Lloyds Bank v Bundy*, below, Ch.26).

3. Were the plaintiffs dealing "on [the defendants'] written standard terms of business"? See Unfair Contract Terms Act 1977 s.3(1).

HOLLIER v RAMBLER MOTORS (AMC) LTD

Court of Appeal [1972] 2 W.L.R. 401; [1972] 1 All E.R. 399; [1972] R.T.R. 190

The plaintiff made an oral contract with the defendants, garage proprietors, for repairs to his car. A fire   **7–013** broke out in the garage through the defendants' negligence and the car was damaged. The plaintiff had had his car repaired or serviced by the defendants three or four times during the previous five years. On two at least of these occasions the plaintiff signed an "invoice" which it was the defendants' practice to require customers to sign, which contained the clause: "The company is not responsible for damage caused by fire to customers' cars on the premises. Customers' cars are driven by staff at owner's risk." The County Court Judge held that the defendants were protected from liability by this clause. The plaintiff appealed, arguing that the clause ought not to be imported into the oral contract; and that if it were, it did not protect the defendants.

SALMON LJ

I am bound to say that, for my part, I do not know of any other case in which it has been decided or even argued that a term could be implied into an oral contract on the strength of a course of dealing (if it can be so called) which consisted at the most of three or four transactions over a period of five years.

We have been referred to *Hardwick Game Farm v Suffolk Agricultural Poultry Producers Association* [1969] 2 A.C. 31. That was a case in which some feeding-stuff was sold by some merchants to a farmer. The feeding-stuff was found to be defective. The farmer sued the merchants. The merchants brought in as third party the persons from whom they had purchased the feeding-stuff; they in their turn brought in their suppliers, and there was a long list of many parties brought in right down the chain. As between two of these suppliers a point arose as to whether a term that the buyer under the contract took the responsibility for any latent defects was a term which had been imported into the contract in question by reason of the course of dealing between those parties. It is to be observed that in that case there had been three or four dealings each month between the parties during the previous three years. The course of dealing had been that the feeding-stuff was ordered orally by the buyer and the order was accepted orally by the suppliers. Then on the day of the oral contract, or perhaps the next day, the suppliers sent on to the buyer a sold note. One of the terms appearing on the sold note was that the buyer under the contract took the responsibility for any latent defects. Three or four times each month, year in and year out for three years, sold notes had been sent on to the buyer, and the buyer had never raised any protest or said anything which would have led the sellers to assume that the buyers were doing anything other than accepting the terms of the contract which appeared on the sold note. In that case, although this practice had been going on all that time, and the buyers had received well over 100 sold notes containing the condition to which I have referred, they had not actually read the condition and knew nothing about it. It was argued that, therefore, the condition could not be implied into the contract in question, although it had been made in exactly the same way as all the other contracts, namely, orally, with a sold note in the usual form sent on after the contract had been made. The House of Lords decided that the fact that the buyer had not read the condition on the sold notes, having had every opportunity of doing so, did not avail him, because any reasonable seller in circumstances such as those, having had no intimation from the buyer that he took any objection to the condition, would have had good cause to assume that the buyer was agreeing to the condition.

That case is obviously very different from the present case. The *Hardwick Game Farm* case seems to be a typical case where a consistent course of dealing between the parties makes it imperative for the court to read into the contract the condition for which the sellers were contending. Everything that the buyer had done, or failed to do, would have convinced any ordinary seller that the buyer was agreeing to the terms in question. The fact that the buyer had not read the term is beside the point. The seller could not be expected to know that the buyer had not troubled to acquaint himself with what was written in the form that had been sent to him so often, year in and year out during the previous three years, in transactions exactly the same as the transaction then in question . . . [The judge then discussed *McCutcheon v MacBrayne Ltd*, above]

It seems to me that if it was impossible to rely on a course of dealing in *McCutcheon v David MacBrayne Ltd*, still less would it be possible to do so in this case, when the so-called course of dealing consisted only of three or four transactions in the course of five years.[2] As I read the speeches of Lord Reid, Lord Guest and Lord Pearce, one, but only one amongst many, of the facts to be taken into account in considering whether there had been a course of dealing from which a term was to be implied into the contract was whether the consignor actually knew what were the terms written on the back of the risk note. Lord Devlin said that this was a critical factor. Even on the assumption that Lord Devlin's dictum went further than was necessary for the decision in that case, and was wrong—which I think is the effect of the *Hardwick Game Farm* case [1969] 2 A.C. 31—I do not see how that can help the defendants here. The speeches of the other members of the House and the decision itself in *McCutcheon's* case [1964] 1 W.L.R. 125 make it plain that the clause upon which the defendants seek to rely cannot in law be imported into the oral contract they made in March 1970 . . . [In case he was wrong on this point, the judge went on to consider what effect the clause would have, had it been incorporated into the contract.]

Point for reflection

7–014   The plaintiff in the *Hardwick Game Farm* case was not a consumer but he might now argue that the contract was made on the seller's "written standard terms of business" and was therefore subject to the test of reasonableness. The UTCC regulations, could not apply because Hardwick was not a 'consumer'. In the light of this, we might ask whether the way that the courts apply the test of a regular and consistent course of dealing should be affected by (i) whether the dispute is between a business and a consumer or between two businesses, and (ii) whether any terms that are in dispute can be challenged directly under the UCTA or the UTCC regulations. Whatever we make of the question of whether the courts *should* be so affected, we need to take account of this in understanding why cases are pleaded in the way that they are and, possibly, why judges (at different times) have decided the cases in the way that they have done.

Further reading

John N. Adams and Roger Brownsword, 'The Ideologies of Contract' (1987) 7 *Legal Studies* 205

---

[2]   Cf. *British Crane Hire v Ipswich Plant*, above.

8

THE IDENTITY OF THE OFFEROR AND THE OFFEREE

LEARNING OBJECTIVES

By the end of this chapter, you should:

■ be familiar with the leading cases on so-called "mistakes of identity";
■ understand that there is no easy choice to be made between the interests of two innocent parties (the original seller and the downstream good faith buyer);
■ have reflected on the attempts made in the case-law to draw distinctions between one kind of case and another (particularly between face-to-face dealing and dealing at a distance) and between one kind of mistake and another (particularly a mistake as to identity and a mistake as to creditworthiness);
■ have thought about how far the problem can be addressed by drawing on simple concepts of offer and acceptance.

INTRODUCTION

Suppose that A makes an offer which A intends to be directed at and open only to B, then other things being equal that offer will not be open to acceptance by C—or, to take the clearest case, a purported acceptance by C will not be effective where (i) A has made it absolutely clear that the offer is open only to B and (ii) C is aware that A's offer is open only to B. Where C has actively misled A by fraudulently pretending to be B (in consequence of which A believes that the offer, intended only to be open to B, is actually directed at and addressed to B), the plot thickens; for, in addition to an arguable failure of the acceptance to engage with the offer, we have to contend with elements of fraudulent misrepresentation and mistake. As we saw in Ch.1, the leading modern case on such a scenario is *Shogun Finance Ltd v Hudson* [2003] UKHL 62; and it follows that the historic canon of cases on these matters must now be read in the light of *Shogun Finance*. In this chapter, after setting out the canon (in section 1), we extract the speech given by Lord Phillips, in the course of which his Lordship reviews the standard precedents before casting his vote in favour of the majority view (in section 2).

8–001

1. The Classic Case-Law

BOULTON v JONES

Passage Court of Liverpool (1857) 27 L.J. Ex. 117; 2 H. & N. 564; 157 E.R. 232; 3 Jur. 1156; 6 W.R. 107

8-002 Action (in the Passage Court of Liverpool) for goods sold.

Plea, never indebted.

The evidence was, that on January 13 the defendant sent to the shop of one Brocklehurst, who had that day, unknown to the defendant, sold his stock-in-trade and assigned his business to his foreman, the plaintiff, an order in writing, addressed to Brocklehurst, for certain goods. The goods were sent by the plaintiff, and at the trial the written order appeared with Brocklehurst's name struck out, but there was no evidence when that was done. There was contradictory evidence on a collateral point, but none as to whether the defendant had notice of the change of business before the plaintiff sent in an invoice, which was not until after the goods were consumed. The defendant had a running account with, and a set-off against Brocklehurst. The objection was taken that the contract was with him and not the plaintiff, and the learned Assessor reserved the point.

The jury found for the plaintiff, and Mellish had obtained a rule to enter a verdict for the defendant, or to enter a nonsuit . . .

POLLOCK CB

The point raised was this, whether the order in writing did not import, on the part of the buyer, the defendant, an intention to deal exclusively with Brocklehurst; the person who had succeeded him, the plaintiff, having executed the order without any notice to the defendant of the change, until he received the invoice, subsequently to his consumption of the goods. The decision of the jury did not dispose of that point, and it was the point reserved. Now the rule of law is clear, that if you propose to make a contract with A, then B cannot substitute himself for A without your consent and to your disadvantage, securing to himself all the benefit of the contract. The case being, that if B sued, the defendant would have the benefit of a set-off, of which he is deprived by A's suing. If B sued, the defendant could plead his set-off; as B does not sue, but another party, with whom the defendant did not contract, all that he can do is deny that he ever was indebted to the plaintiff.

MARTIN B

That being the point, there can be no doubt upon the matter. This was not a case of principal and agent at all, because the plaintiff was not Brocklehurst's agent, but his successor in the business, and made the contract on his own account, not for the plaintiff [sic]. Where the facts prove that the defendant never [sic] meant to contract with A alone, B can never force a contract upon him; he has dealt with A, and a contract with no one else can be set up against him.

BRAMWELL B

It is an admitted fact, that the defendant supposed he was dealing with Brocklehurst; and the plaintiff misled him by executing the order unknown to him. It is clear also, that if the plaintiff were at liberty to sue, it would be a prejudice to the defendant, because it would deprive him of a set-off, which he would have had if the action had been brought by the party with whom he supposed he was dealing. And upon that my judgment proceeds. I do not lay it down that because a contract was made in one person's name another person cannot sue upon it, except in cases of agency. But when any one makes a contract in which the personality, so to speak, of the particular party contracted with is important for any reason, whether because it is to write a book or paint a picture, or do any work of personal skill, or whether because there is a set-off due from that party, no one else is at liberty to step in and maintain that he is the party contracted with, that he has written the book or painted the picture, or supplied the goods; and that he is entitled to sue, although, had the party really contracted with sued, the defendant would have had the benefit of his personal skill, or of a set-off due from him. As to the difficulty suggested, that if the plaintiff cannot sue for the price of the goods, no one else can, I do not feel pressed by it any more than I did in such a case as I may suppose, of work being done to my house, for instance, by a party different from the one with whom I had contracted to do it. The defendant has, it is true, had the goods; but it is also true that he has consumed them and cannot return them. And that is no reason why he should pay money to the plaintiff which he never contracted to pay, but upon some contract which he never made, and the substitution of which for that which he did make would be to his prejudice, and involve a pecuniary loss by depriving him of a set-off.

CHANNELL B

The plaintiff is clearly not in a situation to sustain this action, for there was no contract between himself and the defendant. The case is not one of principal and agent; it was a contract made with B, who had transactions with the defendant and owed him money, and upon which A seeks to sue. Without saying that the plaintiff might not have had a right of action on an implied contract, if the goods had been in existence, here the defendant had no notice of the plaintiff's claim, until the invoice was sent to him, which was not until after he had consumed the goods, and when he could not, of course, have returned them. Without saying what might have been the effect of the receipt of the invoice before the consumption of the goods, it is sufficient to say that in this case the plaintiff clearly is not entitled to sue and deprive the defendant of his set-off.

Rule Absolute for a Nonsuit.

The above is taken from the Law Journal report.

Questions

1. Was not Boulton reasonably entitled to suppose that the offer was made to the owner of the business for the time being? If so, was he not entitled to accept? Was the existence of the set-off material if it was not known to Boulton?   **8–003**

2. If there was no contract, did not the goods remain Boulton's property? Might he not have succeeded in an action for conversion?

Problem

Belfridge, the owner of a chain of department stores (trading under the name 'Belfridge's'), at 12 noon on February 1 sold his entire business to Ramage. At 1 pm on February 1 Clarence agreed to buy an expensive carpet in one of 'Belfridge's' shops. He knew nothing of the sale to Ramage. He now wishes to avoid the contract. Advise him.   **8–004**

See Stoljar, *Mistake and Misrepresentation*, Ch.4.

LINDSAY v CUNDY

Queen's Bench Division (1876) 1 QBD 348; 45 L.J.Q.B. 381; 34 L.T. 314; 24 W.R. 730; 13 Cox C.C. 162

The action was brought by Messrs. Roberts, Lindsay & Co, who are linen manufacturers at Belfast, against Messrs. Cundy for the conversion of 250 dozen handkerchiefs. At the trial before Blackburn J it appeared that one Alfred Blenkarn, in 1873, hired a third floor at No. 37, Wood Street, and 5, Little Love Lane, Cheapside. There was a well-known firm of William Blenkiron & Sons, which had for many years carried on business at No. 123, Wood Street. Blenkarn wrote letters at the end of 1873 to the plaintiffs; by the first proposing to order, and by the others ordering, a large quantity of handkerchiefs from the plaintiffs. Those letters had a printed heading, "37, Wood Street, Cheapside, London; entrance, second door in Little Love Lane," and were signed "A. Blenkarn & Co" written in such a way   **8–005** that it was evidently intended to be read "A. Blenkiron & Co" One of the plaintiffs had known the firm of Blenkiron & Sons several years before, and knew they were respectable. The plaintiffs wrote several letters addressed to "Messrs. Blenkiron & Co, 37, Wood Street," and they forwarded several lots of handkerchiefs to the same address, heading the invoices, "Messrs. Blenkiron and Co, London."

The fraud was afterwards discovered, and Blenkarn was, in April 1874, convicted of obtaining the goods by the false pretence of being Blenkiron & Sons.

In the meantime the defendants had bought of Blenkarn 250 dozen cambric handkerchiefs, and had resold them all to different persons before the fraud of Blenkarn was discovered. The jury found that the defendants were bona fide purchasers of the handkerchiefs, and that they were part of the handkerchiefs sold by the plaintiffs to Blenkarn. The learned judge reserved the question for the court, whether on the facts and findings the action was maintainable.

(The above statement of facts is taken from the judgment of Mellish LJ in the Court of Appeal (1877) 2 QBD 98.)

BLACKBURN J

(in the QBD): I think that judgment should be entered for the defendants. The first question that arises is one of fact, were these goods, which were originally the property of the plaintiffs, Messrs. Lindsay & Co, obtained from them by fraud, so that the property passed from them under a contract, though a contract liable under certain circumstances to be avoided; or did the property never pass from the plaintiffs at all? Upon that question reliance was placed on the case of *Hardman v Booth* (1 H. & C. 803), and that case unquestionably lays down very good law. The question for us is whether the facts are the same, and whether we ought to draw the same inference from the facts that the Court of Exchequer did in *Hardman v Booth*. That case lays down this law, that where a person has sold goods to A. B., or has been led to believe he has sold them to A. B., and delivered them as he supposes to A. B., and the person who led him into that belief receives and carries off the goods, and disposes of them to another—there has not been a selling to the person who fraudulently represented himself to be a servant or agent of the supposed purchaser, A. B., and he cannot confer a good title upon anyone else, the property never having vested in him. The facts in *Hardman v Booth* seem to have been these: The plaintiffs, meaning to deal with Thomas Gandell & Sons, went to their office and took an order from a person who, as they believed, and in point of fact was, the son of Thomas Gandell, and whom they believed to be acting for the firm of Thomas Gandell & Sons; and they took away a card of the firm of Thomas Gandell & Sons, to show to whom they were to send them, and they sent them to Thomas Gandell & Sons' place of business. Edward Gandell, who was the son of Thomas Gandell, had a private business of his own, and he it was who in that office had given the order for Thomas Gandell & Sons without any authority, and he it was, as it was proved upon the trial, who intercepted the goods when they arrived at Messrs. Gandell's, and carried them away, and sold them to the defendant. Upon these facts, the Court of Exchequer drew the inference that there never was any property vested in Edward Gandell as purchaser under a contract voidable through fraud; for there never was intended to be a contract with anybody but Thomas Gandell & Sons, and in point of fact that contract did not exist, because Thomas Gandell and Sons had not meddled in the matter in any way; and what had been done by the plaintiffs did not in the slightest degree constitute a contract with Edward Gandell vesting the property in him. I think that is good law, and the inference would seem upon the evidence to have been correctly drawn.

The same law was applied in the case of *Hollins v Fowler* (L.R. 7 Q.B. 616; L.R. 7 HL 757), which was subsequently affirmed in the House of Lords, the facts there being clear.

When we look at the facts of the present case they are not the same at all. The plaintiffs having received a letter from a person who signed himself with the name of "Blenkarn," looking like "Blenkiron" & Co, of 37, Wood Street, they address all their letters to him, and send the goods to him at 37, Wood Street, and deliver them there, and everything is done with him at 37, Wood Street. The fact was, that there was a highly respectable firm in the name of William Blenkiron & Co, at 123, Wood Street, and this man set up a pretended business at 37, Wood Street, in the hope that people would confuse him with his namesake, and he would get the advantage of his namesake's character. In this particular case he did get the advantage of his namesake's character, and it being found that he did so intentionally, and that it was a fraudulent intention, he was guilty of obtaining the goods under false pretences; but nonetheless was the contract by the plaintiffs made with him . . . upon the facts of this case, the intention of the plaintiffs was to contract with the person who was carrying on the business at 37, Wood Street, and there was therefore a contract with him, although it was obtained by fraud.

The Court of Appeal (Mellish L.J. and Brett and Amphlett J. J. A.) reversed the judgment of the Queen's Bench Division, holding that the plaintiffs intended to deal with Blenkiron & Sons and therefore there was no contract with Blenkarn; that the property in the goods never passed from the plaintiffs; and that they were accordingly entitled to recover in the action: (1877) 2 QBD 96. The defendant appealed to the House of Lords.

CUNDY v LINDSAY

House of Lords (1878) 3 App.Cas. 459; 38 L.T. 573; 42 J.P. 483; 26 W.R. 406; 14 Cox C.C. 93

THE LORD CHANCELLOR (LORD CAIRNS)

My Lords, you have in this case to discharge a duty which is always a disagreeable one for any court, namely, to determine as between two parties, both of whom are perfectly innocent, upon which of the two the consequences of a fraud practised upon both of them must fall. My Lords, in discharging that duty your Lordships can do no more than apply, rigorously, the settled and well-known rules of law. Now, with regard to the title to personal property, the settled and well-known rules of law may, I take it, be thus expressed: by the law of our country the purchaser of a chattel takes the chattel as a general rule subject to what may turn out to be a certain infirmities in the title. If he purchases the chattel in market overt, he obtains a title which is good against all the world; but if he does not purchase the chattel in market overt, and if it turns out that the chattel has been found by the person who professed to sell it, the purchaser will not obtain a title good as against the real owner. If it turns out that the chattel has been stolen by the person who has professed to sell it, the purchaser will not obtain a title. If it turns out that the chattel has come into the hands of the person who professed to sell it, by a de facto contract, that is to say, a contract which has purported to pass the property to him from the owner of the property, there the purchaser will obtain a good title, even although afterwards it should appear that there were circumstances connected with that contract, which would enable the original owner of the goods to reduce it, and to set it aside, because these circumstances so enabling the original owner of the goods, or of the chattel, to reduce the contract and to set it aside, will not be allowed to interfere with a title for valuable consideration obtained by some third party during the interval while the contract remained unreduced.

My Lords, the question, therefore, in the present case, as your Lordships will observe, really becomes the very short and simple one which I am about to state. Was there any contract which, with regard to the goods in question in this case, had passed the property in the goods from the Messrs. Lindsay to Alfred Blenkarn? If there was any contract passing that property, even although, as I have said, that contract might afterwards be open to a process of reduction, upon the ground of fraud, still, in the meantime, Blenkarn might have conveyed a good title for valuable consideration to the present appellants.

Now, my Lords, there are two observations bearing upon the solution of that question which I desire to make. In the first place, if the property in the goods in question passed, it could only pass by way of contract; there is nothing else which could have passed the property. The second observation is this, your Lordships are not here embarrassed by any conflict of evidence, or any evidence whatever as to conversations or as to acts done, the whole history of the whole transaction lies upon paper. The principal parties concerned, the respondents and Blenkarn, never came into contact personally—everything that was done was done by writing. What has to be judged of, and what the jury in the present case had to judge of, was merely the conclusion to be derived from that writing, as applied to the admitted facts of the case.

Now, my Lords, discharging that duty and answering that inquiry, what the jurors have found is in substance this: it is not necessary to spell out the words, because the substance of it is beyond all doubt. They have found that by the form of signatures to the letters which were written by Blenkarn, by the mode in which his letters and his applications to the respondents were made out, and by the way in which he left uncorrected the mode and form in which, in turn, he was addressed by the respondents; that by all those means he led, and intended to lead, the respondents to believe, and they did believe, that the person with whom they were communicating was not Blenkarn, the dishonest and irresponsible man, but was a well-known and solvent house of Blenkiron & Co, doing business in the same street. My Lords, those things are found as matters of fact, and they are placed beyond the range of dispute and controversy in the case.

8–006

If that is so, what is the consequence? It is that Blenkarn—the dishonest man, as I call him—was acting here just in the same way as if he had forged the signature of Blenkiron & Co, the respectable firm, to the applications for goods, and as if, when, in return, the goods were forwarded and letters were sent, accompanying them, he had intercepted the goods and intercepted the letters, and had taken possession of the goods, and of the letters which were addressed to, and intended for, not himself but, the firm of Blenkiron & Co. Now, my Lords, stating the matter shortly in that way, I ask the question, how is it possible to imagine that in that state of things any contract could have arisen between the respondents and Blenkarn, the dishonest man? Of him they know nothing, and of him they never thought. With him they never intended to deal. Their minds never, even for an instant of time rested upon him, and as between him and them there was no consensus of mind which could lead to any agreement or any contract whatever. As between him and them there was merely the one side to a contract, where, in order to produce a contract, two sides would be required. With the firm of Blenkiron & Co of course there was no contract, for as to them the matter was entirely unknown, and therefore the pretence of a contract was a failure.

The result, therefore, my Lords, is this, that your Lordships have not here to deal with one of those cases in which there is de facto a contract made which may afterwards be impeached and set aside, on the ground of fraud; but you have to deal with a case which ranges itself under a completely different chapter of law, the case namely in which the contract never comes into existence. My Lords, that being so, it is idle to talk of the property passing. The property remained, as it originally had been, the property of the respondents, and the title which was attempted to be given to the appellants was a title which could not be given to them.

Lords Hatherley and Penzance delivered concurring speeches and Lord Gordon concurred.

Appeal Dismissed.

Questions

8–007
1. Which of the following statements is true? Or are they both true?
   (i) The plaintiffs intended to contract with Blenkiron & Sons.
   (ii) The plaintiffs intended to contract with the person who was carrying on business at 37, Wood Street.

If both statements are true is it possible to decide between the views of the Queen's Bench Division and the House of Lords?

2. Would it have made any difference if Blenkarn had not been fraudulent, but had innocently misled Lindsay into thinking he was Blenkiron & Sons?

KING'S NORTON METAL CO LTD v EDRIDGE, MERRETT & CO LTD

Court of Appeal (1897) 14 T.L.R. 98; 39 Digest 534, 1455

8–008
The plaintiffs were metal manufacturers at King's Norton, Worcestershire, and the defendants were metal merchants at Birmingham. It appeared that in 1896 the plaintiffs received a letter purporting to come from Hallam & Co, Soho Hackle Pin and Wire Works, Sheffield, at the head of which was a representation of a large factory with a number of chimneys, and in one corner was a printed statement that Hallam & Co had depots and agencies at Belfast, Lille and Ghent. The letter contained a request by Hallam & Co for a quotation of prices for brass rivet wire. In reply, the plaintiffs quoted prices, and Hallam & Co then by letter ordered some goods, which were sent off to them. These goods were never paid for. It turned out that a man named Wallis had adopted the name of Hallam & Co, and fraudulently obtained goods by the above means, and that Wallis sold the goods to the defendants, who bought them bona fide, and that with no notice of any defect of title in Wallis. The

plaintiffs brought this action to recover damages for the conversion of these goods. It appeared that the plaintiffs had been paid for some goods previously ordered by Hallam & Co, by a cheque drawn by "Hallam & Co." At the trial, the learned judge nonsuited the plaintiffs upon the ground that the property in the goods had passed to Wallis, who sold them to the defendants before the plaintiffs had disaffirmed the contract.

A. L. SMITH LJ

A. L. Smith L.J. said that the case was a plain one. The question was whether the plaintiffs, who had been cheated out of their goods by a rogue called Wallis, or the defendants were to bear the loss. The law seemed to him to be well settled. If a person, induced by false pretences, contracted with a rogue to sell goods to him and the goods were delivered the rogue could until the contract was disaffirmed give a good title to a bona fide purchaser for value. The facts here were that Wallis, for the purpose of cheating, set up in business as Hallam & Co, and got notepaper prepared for the purpose, and wrote to the plaintiffs representing that he was carrying on business as Hallam & Co. He got the goods in question and sold them to the defendants, who bought them bona fide for value. The question was, With whom, upon this evidence, which was all one way, did the plaintiffs contract to sell the goods? Clearly with the writer of the letters. If it could have been shown that there was a separate entity called Hallam & Co and another entity called Wallis then the case might have come within the decision in *Cundy v Lindsay*. In his opinion there was a contract by the plaintiffs with the person who wrote the letters, by which the property passed to him. There was only one entity, trading it might be under an alias, and there was a contract by which the property passed to him. Cave J. said that this was nothing more than a long firm fraud. Did anyone ever hear of an attempt being made by a person who had delivered his goods to a long firm to get his goods back on the ground that he had made no contract with the long firm? The indictment against a long firm was always obtaining the goods by false pretences, which presupposed the passing of the property. For these reasons there was no question to go to the jury, and the nonsuit was right.

Rigby and Collins L.JJ. delivered judgment to the same effect.

Questions

1. Would it have made any difference if there had in fact been a firm of the name of Hallam & Co with all the various attributes stated on Wallis's letterhead (a) if that firm was not known to the plaintiffs? (b) if it was known to them?

2. Would it have made any difference if Wallis had described his fictitious business as Hallam & Co Ltd? See *Newborne v Sensolid Ltd*, below.

3. What would have been the result if Lindsay had sued Blenkarn in contract for the price of the goods? (Cf. Atiyah, *Introduction to the Law of Contract* (4th edn), p.69.)

8–009

Problem

Twister induces Sparkler, a jeweller, to sell him a ring by representing falsely that his father is Lord X. Is there a contract between Twister and Sparkler (a) if, as Sparkler knows, Lord X has one son? (b) if, as Sparkler knows, Lord X has two sons?

8–010

NEWBORNE v SENSOLID LTD

Court of Appeal [1954] 1 Q.B. 45; [1952] 2 T.L.R. 763; 97 S.J. 209; [1953] 1 All E.R. 708

The plaintiff formed a limited company called Leopold Newborne, Ltd Before the company was registered a contract form, bearing the name and address of Newborne, Ltd, and signed "Yours faithfully,

8–011

Leopold Newborne (London), Ltd," with the name of Leopold Newborne underneath, was sent to the defendant. The defendant signed it, and thereby agreed to buy certain goods from Leopold Newborne, Ltd Leopold Newborne, Ltd, issued a writ claiming damages for failure to accept the goods. The plaintiffs' solicitors then discovered that the company had not been registered at the time of the contract, and they took steps to substitute the name of Leopold Newborne for that of the company. The defendants then contended that Newborne was trying to sue on a contract which he had not made, but which purported to have been made by a limited liability company which had not been registered. Parker J found for the defendant and was affirmed by the Court of Appeal.

LORD GODDARD CJ

> This contract purports to be a contract by the company; it does not purport to be a contract by Mr Newborne. He does not purport to be selling his goods but to be selling the company's goods. The only person who had any contract here was the company, and Mr Newborne's signature merely confirmed the company's signature . . .
>
> In my opinion, unfortunate though it may be, as the company was not in existence when the contract was signed there never was a contract, and Mr Newborne cannot come forward and say: "Well, it was my contract." The fact is, he made a contract for a company which did not exist.

Questions

8–012

1. If there was a contract between Wallis and the King's Norton Metal Co Ltd, why was there no contract between Newborne and Sensolid, Ltd? (Cf. (1957) 20 M.L.R. 38.)

2. The Companies Act 1985 s.36C (1) (replacing the former s.36(4)) provides: "A contract which purports to be made by or on behalf of a company at a time when the company has not been formed has effect, subject to any agreement to the contrary, as one made with the person purporting to act for the company or as agent for it, and he is personally liable on the contract accordingly."

   Does this subsection overrule *Newborne v Sensolid*? It appears to make Newborne liable on the contract. Does it enable him to enforce it? Cf. *Phonogram Ltd v Lane* [1982] Q.B. 938.

PHILLIPS v BROOKS LTD

King's Bench Division [1919] 2 K.B. 243; 88 L.J.K.B. 953; 121 L.T. 249

Action tried by Horridge J.

8–013

The plaintiff, who was a jeweller, sued the defendants, who were pawn-brokers, for the return of a ring or, alternatively, its value, and damages for its detention.

On April 15, 1918, a man entered the plaintiff's shop and asked to see some pearls and some rings. He selected pearls at the price of £2,550 and a ring at the price of £450. He produced a cheque-book and wrote out a cheque for £3,000. In signing it, he said: "You see who I am, I am Sir George Bullough," and he gave an address in St. James's Square. The plaintiff knew that there was such a person as Sir George Bullough, and finding on reference to a directory that Sir George lived at the address mentioned, he said: "Would you like to take the articles with you?" to which the man replied: "You had better have the cheque cleared first, but I should like to take the ring as it is my wife's birthday tomorrow," whereupon the plaintiff let him have the ring. The cheque was dishonoured, the person who gave it being in fact a fraudulent person named North who was subsequently convicted of obtaining the ring by false pretences. In the meantime, namely on April 16, 1918, North, in the name of Firth, had pledged the ring with the defendants who, bona fide and without notice, advanced £350 upon it.

HORRIDGE J

I have carefully considered the evidence of the plaintiff, and have come to the conclusion that, although he believed the person to whom he was handing the ring was Sir George Bullough, he in fact contracted to sell and deliver it to the person who came into his shop, and who was not Sir George Bullough, but a man in the name of North, who obtained the sale and delivery by means of the false pretence that he was Sir George Bullough. It is quite true the plaintiff in re-examination said he had no intention of making any contract with any other person than Sir George Bullough; but I think I have myself to decide what is the proper inference to draw where a verbal contract is made and an article delivered to an individual describing himself as somebody else . . .

It was argued before me that the principle quoted from Pothier (Traitè des Obligations, § 19), in *Smith v Wheatcroft* (9 Ch.D. 223, 230), namely, "Whenever the consideration of the person with whom I am willing to contract enters as an element into the contract which I am willing to make, error with regard to the person destroys my consent and consequently annuls the contract" applies. I do not think, however, that that passage governs this case, because I think the seller intended to contract with the person present, and there was no error as to the person with whom he contracted, although the plaintiff would not have made the contract if there had not been a fraudulent misrepresentation. Moreover, the case of *Smith v Wheatcroft* was an action for specific performance, and was between the parties to the contract, and had no relation to rights acquired by third parties innocently under the contract, and misrepresentation would have been an answer to the enforcement of the contract. In this case, I think, there was a passing of the property and the purchaser had a good title, and there must be judgment for the defendants with costs.

Judgment for Defendants.

Points for reflection

A learned correspondent, discussing *Phillips v Brooks*, in 35 L.Q.R. 289, asks:

8–014

"What if A, wearing a false nose and beard, had represented to B that he was Lord Rothschild or Mr Bernard Shaw? It could hardly be said that in such a case B would not be in 'error with regard to the person' with whom he was contracting. And it is difficult to believe that the element of a false nose and beard makes the difference between a good title and no title."

Having contrasted *Phillips v Brooks* and *Cundy v Lindsay*, E.C.S Wade (in 38 LQR 201, at 204) continues:

"The solution, it seems, of the vexed question as to which of two innocent parties is to suffer for the fraud of a third party is to turn upon the mode by which the parties to the original transaction came into contact. If it be through the medium of written communications, the original owner does not suffer, but can recover his goods, even though in the hands of bona fide purchasers for value. It is otherwise if he had an opportunity of meeting his customer face to face; for he is enabled to rely on his own judgment, as well as the customer's assertion, and not merely upon a written representation. But this distinction is specious; for the seller who relies on a written representation has the opportunity of verifying it at his leisure. And why should he be protected—as he undoubtedly is by *Cundy v Lindsay*—in the event of his being mistaken? For the shopkeeper, who has in the interests of his business often to decide on the spur of the moment, runs the risk of being unable to have the contract set aside after the pretender has parted with his acquisitions to a purchaser or pawnbroker; this, of course, he invariably hastens to do. It is to be noted, moreover, that the Scottish courts have decided (*Morrison v Robertson*, 1908 S.C. 332) that such a transaction as took place in *Phillips v Brooks* is void ab initio."

The writer then suggests an alternative view of the facts:

"A collation of the various reports of this case shows the following sequence of facts:

(1) A sale of pearls for £2,550 and a ring for £450 by B to A, whereupon (2) by virtue of section 18 of the Sale of Goods Act, 1893, the property passed from B to A; (3) a fraudulent misrepresentation by A as to his identity which (4) successfully induced voluntary delivery of the ring on the part of B to A.

This alternative view of the facts is a possible one, and will support the decision of Horridge J. that the swindler obtained a voidable title to the ring and was able to pass a good title to the pawnbrokers . . . it can be taken that the fraud was practised to induce the plaintiff to deliver the ring, after the contract of sale had been completed."

Whether Professor Wade's explanation of *Phillips v Brooks* is acceptable may be debated (cf. Pearce L.J., in *Ingram v Little*, below). However, cases have certainly occurred in which the course of events was similar to that posed in Professor Wade's analysis. In *Dennant v Skinner* [1948] 2 K.B. 164, for example, a man bid for a car at an auction sale and it was knocked down to him. The auctioneer did not know the bidder. He asked him his name so as to complete the memorandum of sale and the bidder said he was King of King's Motors Oxford. Other cars were knocked down to the bidder and subsequently, by repeating the statement that he represented King's of Oxford (which was false) and other statements, he induced the auctioneer to accept a cheque and allow him to take the cars away. Hallett J. held that the property in the cars passed to the bidder. "At an auction sale, apart from any question of the reserve price, the lot is knocked down to the highest bidder, whoever he might be."

Question

8–015   "Did the shopkeeper believe that he was entering into a contract with Sir George Bullough and did North know this? If both answers are in the affirmative then it is submitted that there was no contract. If a blind man makes an offer to A, who is present, in the mistaken belief that he is B, can A, who is aware of the mistake, accept the offer?" (Goodhart, 'Mistake as to Identity in Contract' 57 L.Q.R. 228, 240.)

INGRAM AND OTHERS v LITTLE

Court of Appeal [1961] 1 Q.B. 31; [1960] 3 W.L.R. 504; [1960] 3 All E.R. 332; 104 S.J. 704

8–016   Three plaintiffs, Elsie Ingram, Hilda Ingram and Mrs Badger, who were the joint owners of a car, advertised it for sale. A rogue, introducing himself as Hutchinson, offered to buy it. He was taken for a run in the car in the course of which he talked about his family and said that they were in Cornwall but that his home was in Caterham. Later, "Hutchinson" offered Elsie Ingram, who conducted the negotiations for the plaintiffs, £700 and she refused. He then offered £717 which she was prepared to accept. When the rogue pulled out a cheque book, she said that she would not under any circumstances accept a cheque and that the proposed deal was finished. The rogue then said that he was a P. G. M. Hutchinson with business interests in Guildford and living at Stanstead House, Stanstead Road, Caterham. Hilda Ingram checked in the telephone directory that there was such a person as P. G. M. Hutchinson, living at that address. The plaintiffs then let the rogue have the car in exchange for the cheque.

The rogue was not P. G. M. Hutchinson who had nothing to do with the transaction. The cheque was dishonoured. The rogue sold the car to the defendant and then disappeared and remained untraced. The plaintiffs sued the defendant for the return of the car or damages for its conversion. Slade J gave judgment for the plaintiffs. The defendant appealed.

Sellers LJ delivered judgment dismissing the appeal.

PEARCE LJ

I agree. The question here is whether there was any contract, whether offer and acceptance met. For, as Gresson P. said in *Fawcett v Star Car Sales Ltd* [1960] N.Z.L.R. 406: "a void contract is a paradox; in truth there is no contract at all." . . .

When an offeror seeks to avoid an apparent contract on the ground of mistaken identity the investigation must start with his actual state of mind. For it would be absurd if he could avoid the contract when he was not really mistaken in his own mind as to the offeree's identity or when the apparent contract was not induced by mistake, when he was equally prepared to make the contract had he not been mistaken. That, as it seems to me, is a preliminary essential. But the courts, in deciding the question whether the apparent contract is non-existent owing to mistake in identity, apply the usual objective test (see Holmes on the Common Law (1881), p. 308, Lecture 9), rather than a subjective test which would gravely impair the certainty and stability of contracts. The judge approached the matter on an objective basis. He pointed out, however, that he would have reached the same result by approaching the matter on the subjective test suggested by Pothier. In cases such as this the cheat is fully aware of the offeror's actual state of mind. Moreover, he could not be heard to say that he was not aware of the offeror's state of mind when he has himself deliberately and fraudulently induced it. Thus the objective and subjective tests produce the same result in such a case, and it is the offeror's intention which provides the answer. It is for that reason, I think, that in such cases as this so many observations have been made that are equally referable to the subjective and objective test . . .

An apparent contract made orally inter praesentes raises particular difficulties. The offer is apparently addressed to the physical person present. Prima facie, he, by whatever name he is called, is the person to whom the offer is made. His physical presence identified by sight and hearing preponderates over vagaries of nomenclature. Praesentia corporis tollit errorem nominis, said Lord Bacon (Law Tracts (1737), p. 102). Yet clearly, though difficult, it is not impossible to rebut the prima facie presumption that the offer can be accepted by the person to whom it is physically addressed. To take two other extreme instances. If a man orally commissions a portrait from some unknown artist who had deliberately passed himself off whether by disguise or merely by verbal cosmetics, as a famous painter, the imposter could not accept the offer. For though the offer is made to him physically, it is obviously, as he knows, addressed to the famous painter. The mistake in identity on such facts is clear and the nature of the contract makes it obvious that identity was of vital importance to the offeror. At the other end of the scale, if a shopkeeper sells goods in a normal cash transaction to a man who misrepresents himself as being some well-known figure, the transaction will normally be valid. For the shopkeeper was ready to sell goods for cash to the world at large and the particular identity of the purchaser in such a contract was not of sufficient importance to override the physical presence identified by sight and hearing. Thus the nature of the proposed contract must have a strong bearing on the question of whether the intention of the offeror (as understood by his offeree) was to make his offer to some other particular identity rather than to the physical person to whom it was orally offered.

In our case, the facts lie in the debatable area between the two extremes. At the beginning of the negotiations, always an important consideration, the name or personality of the false Hutchinson were of no importance and there was no other identity competing with his physical presence. The plaintiffs were content to sell the car for cash to any purchaser. The contractual conversation was orally addressed to the physical identity of the false Hutchinson. The identity was the man present, and his name was merely one of his attributes. Had matters continued thus, there would have clearly been a valid but voidable contract.

I accept the judge's view that there was no contract at the stage when the man pulled out his cheque book. From a practical point of view negotiations reached an impasse at that stage. For the vendor refused to discuss the question of selling on credit. It is argued that there was a contract as soon as the price was agreed at £717 and that from that moment either party could have sued on the contract with implied terms as to payment and delivery. That may be theoretically arguable, but in my view, the judge's more realistic approach was right. Payment and delivery still needed to be discussed and the parties would be expecting to discuss them. Immediately they did discuss them it became plain that they were not ad idem and that no contract had yet been created. But, even if there had been a concluded agreement before discussion of a cheque, it was rescinded. The man tried to make Mrs Ingram take a cheque. She declined it and said that the deal was off. He did not demur but set himself to reconstruct the negotiations. For the moment had come, which he must all along have anticipated, as the crux of the negotiations, the vital crisis of the swindle. He wanted to take away the car on credit against his worthless cheque, but she refused. Thereafter, the negotiations were of a different kind from what the vendor had mistakenly believed them to be hitherto. The parties were no longer concerned with a cash sale of goods where the identity of the purchaser was prima facie unimportant. They were concerned with a credit sale in which both parties knew that the identity of the purchaser was one of the utmost importance. She now realised that she was being asked to give him possession of the car on the faith of his cheque.

This was an important stage of the transaction because it demonstrated quite clearly that she was not prepared to sell on credit to the mere physical man in her drawing-room though he represented himself as a man of substance. He proceeded to "give to airy nothing a local habitation and a name." He tried to persuade her to sell to him as P. G. M. Hutchinson of Stanstead House, a personality which no doubt he had selected for the purpose of inspiring confidence into his victim. This was unsuccessful. Only when she had ascertained (through her sister's short excursion to the local post office and investigation of the telephone directory) that there was a P. G. M. Hutchinson of Stanstead House in the directory did she agree to sell on credit. The fact that the man wrote the name and address on the back of the cheque is an additional indication of the importance attached by the parties to the individuality of P. G. M. Hutchinson of Stanstead House.

It is not easy to decide whether the vendor was selling to the man in her drawing-room (fraudulently misrepresented as being a man of substance with the attributes of the real Hutchinson) or to P. G. M. Hutchinson of Stanstead House (fraudulently misrepresented as being the man in her drawing room). Did the individuality of P. G. M. Hutchinson of Stanstead House or the physical presence of the man in her drawing room preponderate? Can it be said that the prima facie predominance of the physical presence of the false Hutchinson identified by sight and hearing was overborne by the identity of the real Hutchinson on the particular facts of the present case?

The judge said: "I have not the slightest hesitation in reaching the conclusion that the offer which the plaintiffs made to accept the cheque for £717 was one made solely to, and one which was capable of being accepted only by, the honest Hutchinson—that is to say Philip Gerald Morpath Hutchinson of Stanstead House, Stanstead Road, Caterham, Surrey, and that it was capable of being accepted only by the honest Hutchinson." In view of the experience of the judge and the care which he devoted to the present case, I should hesitate long before interfering with that finding of fact, and I would only do so if compelled by the evidence or by the view that the judge drew some erroneous inference. Where, as here, a borderline case is concerned with ascertaining the intention of the parties, the views of the trial judge who hears the witnesses should not lightly be discarded. I am not persuaded that on the evidence he should have found otherwise.

[His Lordship then considered *Phillips v Brooks Ltd* and concluded:] In my view, it was a borderline case decided on its own particular facts, and is in no wise decisive of the case before us. [His Lordship then considered *Hardman v Booth* (see above, para.8–005) and concluded:] That case, however, was a clearer case of there being no contract than is the present one, since there the plaintiffs had gone to the premises of Gandell & Co to deal with that firm, and on those premises they had dealt with someone who duped them into believing that he was a member of the firm. Had the plaintiffs in the present case gone to Stanstead House especially to deal with the real Hutchinson and been duped on the premises by the false Hutchinson, their case would have been very clear. [His Lordship then considered *Lake v Simmons* [1927] A.C. 487.]

Each case must be decided on its own facts. The question in such cases is this. Has it been sufficiently shown in the particular circumstances that, contrary to the prima facie presumption, a party was not contracting with the physical person to whom he uttered the offer, but with another individual whom (to the other party's knowledge) he believed to be the physical person present. The answer to that question is a finding of fact.

It is argued that although such a finding might properly have been reached if the cheat had pretended to be some great man or someone known already to the vendor by dealing or by reputation, it could not be so in this case, since the vendor had no knowledge of P. G. M. Hutchinson of Stanstead House. Had it not been for investigation of the telephone directory, that might well be so; but here the entry represented an individual of apparent standing and stability, a person whom the vendor was ready to trust with her car against his cheque. His individuality was less dominating than that of a famous man would be, but that is a question of degree. It does not, I think, preclude the judge from finding that it was with him that the vendor was intending to deal.

Devlin L.J. said that the question was: with whom did Miss Ingram intend to contract?—the person to whom she was speaking or the person whom he represented himself to be?—and that this was a mixed question of fact and law which the trial judge, who had seen the witnesses, was no better equipped to answer than the Court of Appeal, who had not. He continued:

In my judgment, the court cannot arrive at a satisfactory solution in the present case except by formulating a presumption and taking it at least as a starting point. The presumption that a person is intending to contract with the person to whom he is actually addressing the words of contract seems to me to be a simple and sensible one and supported by some good authority. It is adopted in *Benjamin on Sale* (8th ed., 1950), p. 102, where two decisions in the United States are referred to, *Edmunds v Merchants Despatch Co* and *Phelps v McQuade*.

The reasoning in the former was adopted by Horridge J. in *Phillips v Brooks Ltd* and the latter case is a decision of the New York Court of Appeals. All these three cases still stand as the law in their respective jurisdictions. *Corbin on Contract* (1951), Vol. 3, s.602, p. 385, cites them and a number of others, and states the general principle in the United States as follows: "The courts hold that if A appeared in person before B, impersonating C, an innocent purchaser from A gets the property in the goods against B."

I do not think that it can be said that the presumption is conclusive, since there is at least one class of case in which it can be rebutted. If the person addressed is posing only as an agent, it is plain that the party deceived has no thought of contracting with him but only with his supposed principal; if then there is no actual or ostensible authority, there can be no contract. *Hardman v Booth* [above] is, I think, an example of this. Are there any other circumstances in which the presumption can be rebutted? It is not necessary to strain to find them, for we are here dealing only with offer and acceptance; contracts in which identity really matters may still be avoided on the ground of mistake. I am content to leave the question open, and do not propose to speculate on what other exceptions there may be to the general rule. What seems plain to me is that the presumption cannot in the present case be rebutted by piling up the evidence to show that Miss Ingram would never have contracted with H. unless she had thought him to be P. G. M. Hutchinson. That fact is conceded and, whether it is proved simpliciter or proved to the hilt, it does not go any further than to show that she was the victim of fraud. With great respect to the judge, the question that he propounded as the test is not calculated to show any more than that. He said: "Is it to be seriously suggested that they were willing to accept the cheque of the rogue other than in the belief, created by the rogue himself, that he, the rogue, was in fact the honest P. G. M. Hutchinson of the address in Caterham with the telephone number which they had verified?" In my judgment, there is everything to show that Miss Ingram would never have accepted H's offer if she had known the truth, but nothing to rebute the ordinary presumption that she was addressing her acceptance, in law as well as in fact, to the person to whom she was speaking. I think, therefore, that there was offer and acceptance in form . . .

There can be no doubt, as all this difference of opinion shows, that the dividing line between voidness and voidability, between fundamental mistake and incidental deceit, is a very fine one. That a fine and difficult distinction has to be drawn is not necessarily any reproach to the law. But need the rights of the parties in a case like this depend on such a distinction? The great virtue of the common law is that it sets out to solve legal problems by the application to them of principles which the ordinary man is expected to recognise as sensible and just; their application in any particular case may produce what seems to him a hard result, but as principles they should be within his understanding and merit his approval. But here, contrary to its habit, the common law, instead of looking for a principle that is simple and just, rests on theoretical distinctions. Why should the question whether the defendant should or should not pay the plaintiff damages for conversion depend upon voidness or voidability, and upon inferences to be drawn from a conversation in which the defendant took no part? The true spirit of the common law is to override theoretical distinctions when they stand in the way of doing practical justice. For the doing of justice, the relevant question in this sort of case is not whether the contract was void or voidable, but which of two innocent parties shall suffer for the fraud of a third. The plain answer is that the loss should be divided between them in such proportion as is just in all the circumstances. If it be pure misfortune, the loss should be borne equally; if the fault or imprudence of either party has caused or contributed to the loss, it should be borne by that party in the whole or in the greater part. In saying this, I am suggesting nothing novel, for this sort of observation has often been made. But it is only in comparatively recent times that the idea of giving to a court power to apportion loss has found a place in our law. I have in mind particularly the Law Reform Acts of 1935, 1943 and 1945, that dealt respectively with joint tortfeasors, frustrated contracts and contributory negligence. These statutes, which I believe to have worked satisfactory, show a modern inclination towards a decision based on a just apportionment rather than one given in black or in white according to the logic of the law. I believe it would be useful if Parliament were now to consider whether or not it is practicable by means of a similar act of law reform to provide for the victims of a fraud a better way of adjusting their mutual loss than that which has grown out of the common law.

Appeal Dismissed with Costs.

Law Reform Committee, Twelfth Report (Transfer of Title to Chattels) (Cmnd. 2958 of 1966)

The Report, having referred to the above judgment of Devlin LJ, continues:

9. A power of apportionment is plainly attractive at first sight, and we ourselves would have been in favour of a solution on these lines had we not come to the conclusion that there were overriding objections to it. We think that if the courts were given power to apportion loss in the type of case with which we are concerned it

8–017

would introduce into a field of law where certainty and clarity are particularly important that uncertainty which inevitably follows the grant of a wide and virtually unrestrained judical discretion. Such a discretion is not appropriate in the case of transactions involving the transfer of property, and we do not regard any change in the law as desirable which is likely to increase litigation and make it more difficult for businessmen and others to obtain reliable legal advice or to assess the likely financial outcome of their dealings and insure against the risks involved.

10. The practical and procedural difficulties to which any system of apportionment would give rise would, in our view, be considerable. Let us suppose that goods belonging to O have been wrongfully obtained by a rogue, R, who sells them to an innocent purchaser, A, from whom they pass in succession to B and C. The title to the goods remains in O. But by virtue of section 12 of the Sale of Goods Act, 1893, each of the sales from R to A, from A to B, and from B to C contains an implied condition that the seller has a right to sell the goods. Under the present law, if O has not recovered the goods he will have an action in conversion or detinue against C; C will have an action against B for breach of the condition as to title implied by the Sale of Goods Act, and B will have the same against A, who will (in theory) have the same against R. If O, C and B succeed in their actions and if, as usually happens, R cannot be found or is a man of straw, all the damages and costs fall on A. This, of course, is essentially the situation which a power to apportion is designed to remedy, but how would it operate in practice? C, when sued by O, would, presumably, have to establish the fact and extent of O's "negligence"—we put this in inverted commas because it seems clear that O would not be in breach of any common law duty to C—in failing to take adequate care of his goods. (It is true that in *Ingram v Little* Lord Justice Devlin suggested that where the loss was "pure misfortune" it should be borne equally, but we see no reason why the owner of a chattel, if he is to retain the title to it—a matter with which we deal later in this Report—should be penalised when he has been in no way at fault.) It would, however, be difficult for C to establish negligence against O. He would not be able to give particulars of negligence in his pleading and discovery would be unlikely to assist as there would be no relevant documents in most cases, although interrogatories might sometimes establish a prima facie case. The extent to which C in his turn had acted reasonably would, of course, be relevant in ascertaining the extent of his right to any contribution, and the same difficulties of proof would arise.

11. The situation becomes much more complex when A and B are brought in, as they would have to be if the apportionment were to do justice between all parties. Any contribution which C was able to obtain from O would reduce the amount of damages in his action against B and those in B's action against A. This would be a very fortuitous benefit to A because it would depend on what C could prove about O's lack of care: indeed C would usually have little interest in obtaining contribution from O since the benefit of it would accrue not to him (unless B were insolvent) but to B, and through him to A. Thus the real issue would be between O and A, however many subsequent purchasers there might have been, but this issue could not be settled until all the other purchasers had been brought in. The need to take account of the extent to which any of them had been "negligent" would require the court to disregard any special provisions in the contracts between A and B, B and C, and so on down the chain of purchasers. These difficulties would add greatly to the complications about onus of proof, evidence, and procedure which we have mentioned above and thus to the length and cost of the proceedings. Consideration would have to be given to the case in which any of the parties was insolvent, as well as to the case in which R (the rogue) was found and was worth suing before, or, alternatively, after, an apportionment had taken place. We need not pause to consider the further complications which would arise if any of the contracts had a foreign element.

12. It may be suggested that these difficulties could be avoided if, instead of attempting to apportion the loss among all parties concerned, provision were to be made merely for contribution as between the two parties directly affected, namely, the owner of the goods and the purchaser in whose hands they are found. This would enable the person having possession of the goods to recover a contribution from the true owner based on the extent to which the latter had failed to take the care which might reasonably have been expected of him. But it would hardly be satisfactory to ignore any negligence on the part of earlier purchasers in the chain as res inter alios acta and to do so would certainly be unjust to the owner of the goods. This is underlined by the fact that the good faith of the first purchaser in a chain is often suspect even though it may be difficult to prove anything against him. Moreover, the last purchaser would have little inducement to attempt to establish negligence against the owner when he could recover the whole of his loss from his immediate vendor in an action based on the implied condition as to title. Yet if this right were to be made subject to the right of recovery from the owner the last purchaser might well find himself in a worse position than he is today. We therefore think that any procedure for contribution would inevitably involve bringing in all the earlier purchasers in the chain, a solution which we have already given reasons for rejecting.

[The Committee's second and third recommendations are as follows:

(2) Where goods are stolen the owner should retain his title except where the goods are subsequently bought by a purchaser in good faith by retail at trade premises or at a public auction.
(3) Where goods are sold under a mistake as to the buyer's identity, the contract should, so far as third parties are concerned, be voidable and not void.]

LEWIS v AVERAY

Court of Appeal [1972] 1 Q.B. 198; [1971] 3 W.L.R. 603; [1971] 3 All E.R. 907

Lewis advertised his car for sale. A man who gave no name rang up and arranged to see the car. He tested it and said he liked it. They went to the flat of Lewis's fiancée. The man told them he was Richard Greene, the well-known actor who played Robin Hood in the "Robin Hood" series. They agreed a price of £450 and he wrote a cheque for £450 signed "R. A. Green." He said he would like the car now and told Lewis not to bother about one or two small jobs he intended to do to the car. Lewis asked if he had anything to prove he was Richard Greene and the man produced an admission pass to Pinewood Studios, bearing an official stamp, the name of "Richard A. Green" and a photograph of the man. They exchanged receipts and Lewis allowed the man to take the car and log book. The cheque was worthless, being taken from a stolen cheque book. The man was not Richard Greene, the well-known actor. He sold the car, in the name of Lewis, for £200 to a bona fide purchaser, Averay, to whom he produced the log book. In the County Court Averay was held liable to Lewis for conversion of the car. Averay appealed.

8–018

LORD DENNING MR

[Having stated the facts and discussed *Phillips v Brooks* and *Ingram v Little*, continued:] Who is entitled to the goods? original seller? Or the ultimate buyer? The courts have given different answers. In *Phillips v Brooks*, the ultimate buyer was held to be entitled to the ring. In *Ingram v Little* the original seller was held to be entitled to the car. In the present case the deputy county court judge has held the original seller entitled.

It seems to me that the material facts in each case are quite indistinguishable the one from the other. In each case there was, to all outward appearance, a contract: but there was a mistake by the seller as to the identity of the buyer. This mistake was fundamental. In each case it led to the handing over of the goods. Without it the seller would not have parted with them.

This case therefore raises the question: What is the effect of a mistake by one party as to the identity of the other? It has sometimes been said that if a party makes a mistake as to the identity of the person with whom he is contracting there is no contract, or, if there is a contract, it is a nullity and void, so that no property can pass under it. This has been supported by a reference to the French jurist Pothier; but I have said before, and I repeat now, his statement is no part of English law. I know that it was quoted by Lord Haldane in *Lake v Simmons* [1927] A.C. 487, 501, and, as such, misled Tucker J. in *Sowler v Potter* [1940] 1 K.B. 271, into holding that a lease was void whereas it was really voidable.[3] But Pothier's statement has given rise to such refinements that it is time it was dead and buried altogether.

For instance, in *Ingram v Little* the majority of the court suggested that the difference between *Phillips v*

---

[3] In May 1938 the defendant, then known as Ann Robinson, was convicted of permitting disorderly conduct in a café. In June 1938 she applied for a lease of Sowler's premises for use as a café, under the name of Potter. Shortly afterwards she changed her name by deed poll to Potter. The lease was then entered into in August 1938. Sowler's agent, when letting the premises, remembered the conviction of Robinson and would not have let the flat to the defendant had he known she was Robinson. He believed that, whoever he was contracting with, it was not Robinson. Tucker J held the lease to be void. Since the defendant had submitted a fraudulent reference, he might have avoided the lease on the grounds of fraud. See the criticism of the case by Goodhart, 57 L.Q.R. 228; Cheshire Fifoot & Furmston (12th edn), p.251; and Denning LJ in *Solle v Butcher*, below, Ch.23.

Brooks and *Ingram v Little* was that in *Phillips v Brooks* the contract of sale was concluded (so as to pass the property to the rogue) before the rogue made the fraudulent misrepresentation: see [1961] 1 Q.B. 31, 51, 60: whereas in *Ingram v Little* the rogue made the fraudulent misrepresentation before the contract was concluded. My own view is that in each case the property in the goods did not pass until the seller let the rogue have the goods.

Again it has been suggested that a mistake as to the identity of a person is one thing: and a mistake as to his attributes is another. A mistake as to identity, it is said, avoids a contract: whereas a mistake as to attributes does not. But this is a distinction without a difference. A man's very name is one of his attributes. It is also a key to his identity. If then, he gives a false name, is it a mistake as to his identity? or a mistake as to his attributes? These fine distinctions do no good to the law.

As I listened to the argument in this case, I felt it wrong that an innocent purchaser (who knew nothing of what had passed between the seller and the rogue) should have title depend on such refinements. After all, he has acted with complete circumspection and in entire good faith: whereas it was the seller who let the rogue have the goods and thus enabled him to commit the fraud. I do not, therefore, accept the theory that a mistake as to identity renders a contract void. I think the true principle is that which underlies the decision of this court in *King's Norton Metal Co Ltd v Edridge Merret & Co Ltd* and of Horridge J. in *Phillips v Brooks*, which has stood for these last 50 years. It is this: When two parties have come to a contract—or rather what appears, on the face of it, to be a contract—the fact that one party is mistaken as to the identity of the other does not mean that there is no contract, or that the contract is a nullity and void from the beginning. It only means that the contract is voidable, that is, liable to be set aside at the instance of the mistaken person, so long as he does so before third parties have in good faith acquired rights under it.

Applied to the cases such as the present, this principle is in full accord with the presumption stated by Pearce L.J. and also Devlin L.J. in *Ingram v Little*. When a dealing is had between a seller like Mr Lewis and a person who is actually there present before him, then the presumption in law is that there is a contract, even though there is a fraudulent impersonation by the buyer representing himself as a different man than he is. There is a contract made with the very person there, who is present in person. It is liable no doubt to be avoided for fraud, but it is still a good contract under which title will pass unless and until it is avoided. In support of that presumption, Devlin L.J. quoted, at p. 66, not only the English case of *Phillips v Brooks*, but other cases in the United States where "the courts hold that if A appeared in person before B, impersonating C, an innocent purchaser from A gets the property in the goods against B." That seems to me to be right in principle in this country also.

In this case Mr Lewis made a contract of sale with the very man, the rogue, who came to the flat. I say that he "made a contract" because in this regard we do not look into his intentions, or into his mind to know what he was thinking or into the mind of the rogue. We look to the outward appearances. On the face of the dealing, Mr Lewis made a contract under which he sold the car to the rogue, delivered the car and the logbook to him, and took a cheque in return. The contract is evidenced by the receipts which were signed. It was, of course, induced by fraud. The rogue made false representations as to his identity. But it was still a contract, though voidable for fraud. It was a contract under which this property passed to the rogue, and in due course passed from the rogue to Mr Averay, before the contract was avoided.

Though I very much regret that either of these good and reliable gentlemen should suffer, in my judgment it is Mr Lewis who should do so. I think the appeal should be allowed and judgment entered for the defendant. Phillimore L.J. allowed the appeal.

MEGAW LJ

For myself, with very great respect, I find it difficult to understand the basis, either in logic or in practical considerations, of the test laid down by the majority of the court in *Ingram v Little* [1961] 1 Q.B. 31. That test is, I think, accurately recorded in the headnote, as follows:

> "—where a person physically present and negotiating to buy a chattel fraudulently assumed the identity of an existing third person, the test to determine to whom the offer was addressed was how ought the promisee to have interpreted the promise."

The promisee, be it noted, is the rogue. The question of the existence of a contract and therefore the passing of property, and therefore the right of third parties, if this test is correct, is made to depend upon the view which some rogue should have formed, presumably knowing that he is a rogue, as to the state of mind of the opposite party to the negotiation, who does not know that he is dealing with a rogue.

However that may be, and assuming that the test so stated is indeed valid, in my view, this appeal can be decided on a short and simple point . . . When one looks at the evidence of the plaintiff, Mr Lewis himself, it is, I think, clear . . . that there was not any evidence that would justify the finding that he, Mr Lewis, regarded the identity of the man who called himself Mr Green as a matter of vital importance.

I agree that the appeal should be allowed.

Questions

1. Can *Lewis v Averay* be reconciled with *Ingram v Little*? If not, which is right? Or, is that not a sensible question (see Ch.1)?   **8–019**

2. In *Gallie v Lee* (above, Ch.6) Lord Denning MR said in the Court of Appeal [1969] 2 Ch. at 116: "I have long had doubts about the theory that, in the law of contract, mistake as to the identity of the person renders the contract a nullity and void. *Cundy v Lindsay* (above) can be explained on the ground that the offer was made to one person (Blenkiron & Co) and accepted by another person (Alfred Blenkarn) and for that reason there was no contract at all." (See also Lord Denning's dictum in *Solle v Butcher* below, Ch.23.) Is there any difference between Lord Denning's explanation of *Cundy v Lindsay* and the theory that mistake as to identity renders the contract void? Are Lord Denning's remarks in *Lewis v Averay* reconcilable with *Cundy v Lindsay*?

----

2. THE LAW AFTER SHOGUN FINANCE

The materials facts of *Shogun Finance* are set out in Ch.1 above.

SHOGUN FINANCE LIMITED v HUDSON

House of Lords [2003] UKHL 62

LORD PHILLIPS OF WORTH MATRAVERS

My Lords,   **8–020**

111. This appeal is a variation on a theme that has bemused courts and commentators alike for over 150 years. Two individuals conduct negotiations in which all the terms necessary to constitute a binding contract are agreed. One of those individuals has, however, been masquerading as a third party. Does a binding contract result? Grappling with this problem in *Fawcett v Star Car Sales Ltd* [1960] NZLR 406 at 413, Gresson P remarked that "the difficulty in deciding whether a mistake of identity prevents the formation of a concluded contract is a proper assessment of the facts rather than the ascertainment of the law". The issues that arise in this case require the facts to be set out with some particularity.

[His Lordship then set out the facts and the relevant provisions of the Hire Purchase Act 1964.]

119. The critical issue in this case is whether a hire-purchase agreement was ever concluded between Shogun and the rogue. If an agreement was concluded, then the rogue was the "debtor" under section 27 of the 1964 Act and passed good title in the vehicle to Mr Hudson. If no agreement was concluded, then the rogue stole the vehicle by deception and passed no title to Mr Hudson.

"What's in a Name?"

120. This area of the law has developed because of confusion about names and it may be helpful at the outset to reflect on the nature of a name. Words in a language have one or more ordinary meaning, which will be known to anyone who speaks that language. Names are not those kind of words. A name is a word, or a series of words, that is used to identify a specific individual. It can be described as a label. Whenever a name is used, extrinsic evidence, or additional information, will be required in order to identify the specific individual that the user of the name intends to identify by the name—the person to whom he intends to attach the label. Almost

all individuals have two or more names which they use to identify themselves and where a name is mentioned in a particular context, or a particular milieu, those who hear it may have the additional information that they need to identify to whom the speaker is referring.

121. Where a name appears in a written document, the document itself may contain additional information which will enable the reader to identify the individual to whom the writer intended to refer when he wrote the name.

122. Where a person introduces himself by name to someone, his intention will normally be to tell that person the name that he uses to identify himself. This may also assist that other person to identify him in the future. If a person introduces himself by a false name, that may be because he does not wish to be identified in the future. If a person introduces himself by the name of somebody else, that may be because he wishes the person to whom he introduces himself to believe that he is that other person.

Formation of contract

123. A contract is normally concluded when an offer made by one party ("the offeror") is accepted by the party to whom the offer has been made ("the offeree"). Normally the contract is only concluded when the acceptance is communicated by the offeree to the offeror. A contract will not be concluded unless the parties are agreed as to its material terms. There must be *"consensus ad idem"*. Whether the parties have reached agreement on the terms is not determined by evidence of the subjective intention of each party. It is, in large measure, determined by making an objective appraisal of the exchanges between the parties. If an offeree understands an offer in accordance with its natural meaning and accepts it, the offeror cannot be heard to say that he intended the words of his offer to have a different meaning. The contract stands according to the natural meaning of the words used. There is one important exception to this principle. If the offeree knows that the offeror does not intend the terms of the offer to be those that the natural meaning of the words would suggest, he cannot, by purporting to accept the offer, bind the offeror to a contract—*Hartog v Colin and Shields* [1939] 3 All ER 566; *Smith v Hughes* (1871) LR 6 QB 597. Thus the task of ascertaining whether the parties have reached agreement as to the terms of a contract can involve quite a complex amalgam of the objective and the subjective and involve the application of a principle that bears close comparison with the doctrine of estoppel. Normally, however, the task involves no more than an objective analysis of the words used by the parties. The object of the exercise is to determine what each party *intended*, or must be deemed to have *intended*.

124. The task of ascertaining whether the parties have reached agreement as to the terms of a contract largely overlaps with the task of ascertaining what it is that the parties have agreed. The approach is the same. It requires the construction of the words used by the parties in order to deduce the *intention* of the parties—see *Chitty on Contracts, 28th Ed Volume 1, paragraphs 12–042,3* and the cases there cited. This is true, whether the contract is oral or in writing. The words used fall to be construed having regard to the relevant background facts and extrinsic evidence may be admitted to explain or interpret the words used. Equally, extrinsic evidence may be necessary to identify the subject matter of the contract to which the words refer.

125. Just as the parties must be shown to have agreed on the terms of the contract, so they must also be shown to have agreed the one with the other. If A makes an offer to B, but C purports to accept it, there will be no contract. Equally, if A makes an offer to B and B addresses his acceptance to C there will be no contract. Where there is an issue as to whether two persons have reached an agreement, the one with the other, the courts have tended to adopt the same approach to resolving that issue as they adopt when considering whether there has been agreement as to the terms of the contract. The court asks the question whether each *intended*, or must be deemed to have *intended*, to contract with the other. That approach gives rise to a problem where one person is mistaken as to the identity of the person with whom he is dealing, as the cases demonstrate. I propose at this point to consider those cases.

The decided cases

[His Lordship, having considered *Boulton v Jones* (1857) 27 L.J. Ex. 117, above para.8–002, *Hardman v Booth* (1863) 1 H. & C. 803, above para.8–005, *Cundy v Lindsay* (1878) 3 App. Cas. 459, above para.8–006, *King's Norton Metal Company Ltd v Edridge, Merrett & Company Ltd* (1897) 14 T.L.R. 98, above para.8–008, and *Phillips v Brooks Ltd* [1919] 2 K.B. 243, above para.8–013, turned to consider *Lake v Simmons*]

140. *Lake v Simmons* [1927] AC 487 involved a claim by a jeweller on a policy of insurance. A fraudulent woman named Ellison induced him, in face-to-face dealings, to part with possession of two necklaces by false pretences. She pretended that she was the wife of a local gentleman called Van der Borgh, with whom she was living, and that he wanted a necklace on approval as he was contemplating giving it to her. She further pretended that a Commander Digby, who was engaged to her sister, wanted the other necklace on approval.

There was no such man. Miss Ellison disposed of the necklaces. The issue was whether the underwriters were exempted from liability under an exclusion in respect of "loss by theft or dishonesty committed by . . . any customer in respect of goods entrusted to" the customer. The House held that they were not. Viscount Haldane, when considering whether the goods were "entrusted" to Miss Ellison, applied the test of whether the face-to-face dealings between her and the jeweller were capable of giving rise to a contract. He held that they were not because of the mistake as to her identity:

> "The latter was entirely deceived as to the identity of the person with whom he was transacting. It was only on the footing and in the belief that she was Mrs. Van der Borgh that he was willing to deal with her at all. In circumstances such as these, I think that there was no such consensus ad idem as, for example, Lord Cairns, in his judgment in *Cundy v Lindsay* (1878) 3 App. Cas. 459, declared to be requisite for the constitution of a contract. No doubt physically the woman entered the shop and pretended to bargain in a particular capacity, but only on the footing of being a different person from what she really was. There was never any contract which could afterwards become voidable by reason of a false representation made in obtaining it, because there was no contract at all, nothing excepting the result of a trick practised on the jeweller."

141. Viscount Haldane was applying a test of intention, but in a manner which differs from that adopted by Horridge J. Although he purported to distinguish rather than overrule *Phillips v Brooks*, I find his approach to be inconsistent with that decision. Devlin L.J., in *Ingram v Little* [1961] 1 QB 31, carefully analysed the speeches in *Lake v Simmons*, and concluded that no other member of the House adopted Viscount Haldane's approach. I agree with that conclusion. The speeches of the other members of the House do not bear on the issue before us.

142. [His Lordship moved on then to consider in *Ingram v Little* [1961] 1 Q.B. 3, above para.8–016, and *Lewis v Averay* [1972] 1 Q.B. 198, above para.8–018, before continuing:]

153. The difficulty in applying a test of *intention* to the identification of the parties to a contract arises, so it seems to me, only where the parties conduct their dealings in some form of inter-personal contact, and where one purports to have the identity of a third party. There the innocent party will have in mind, when considering with whom he is contracting, both the person with whom he is in contact and the third party whom he imagines that person to be.

154. The same problem will not normally arise where the dealings are carried out exclusively in writing. The process of construction of the written instruments, making appropriate use of extrinsic evidence, will normally enable the court to reach a firm conclusion as to the person with whom a party intends to contract. This was the position in *Boulton v Jones, Cundy v Lindsay* and *King's Norton Metal Company v Edridge, Merrett & Company Ltd*. There is a substantial body of authority that demonstrates that the identity of a party to a contract in writing falls to be determined by a process of construction of the putative contract itself. I shall refer to some examples.

155. In *Young v Schuler* (1883) 11 QBD 651 the issue was whether Schuler had signed an agreement simply under a power of attorney on behalf of one of the named parties or, additionally, on his own behalf as a guarantor. As to this, Sir William Brett M.R. observed at pp.654–655:

> "But the questions whether a person has signed his name at the foot of a document, and if so, for what purpose, are questions of evidence, and any evidence on the subject *which does not contradict the document* is admissible . . . This evidence *does not contradict anything on the face of the document*, and is, in my opinion, plainly admissible." (The emphasis is mine.)

Cotton L.J. gave a judgment to like effect and Bowen L.J. agreed.

156. [His Lordship, having considered *Newborne v Sensolid (Great Britain) Ltd* [1954] 1 Q.B. 45, above para. 8–011, continued]

158. Where contracts were subject to the Statute of Frauds the required memorandum in writing had to identify the parties to the contract and a person could not intervene to claim that he was the true party to the contract when this was not consistent with the terms of the memorandum: *Lovesy v Palmer* [1916] 2 Ch 233; *Basma v Weekes* [1950] AC 441.

159. In the field of agency, an undisclosed principal will not be permitted to claim to be party to a contract if this is contrary to the terms of the contract itself. Thus the provision in the standard form B contract of the London Metal Exchange "this contract is made between ourselves and yourselves as principals, we alone being liable to you for its performance" is effective to preclude any contention that the parties named in the contract are contracting as agents for others—*JH Rayner Ltd v Dept of Trade* [1990] 2 AC 418 at p. 516.

160. In the field of shipping law a question sometimes arises as to who is the party to a contract of carriage and this is determined as a question of construction—see *Homburg Houtimport BV v Agrosin Ltd* [2003] UKHL 12; [2003] 2 WLR 711 and *Internaut Shipping GMBH v Fercometal SARL* [2003] EWCA Civ 812 for recent examples.

161. The effect of these authorities is that a person carrying on negotiations in writing can, by describing as one of the parties to the putative agreement an individual who is unequivocally identifiable from that description, preclude any finding that the party to the putative agreement is other than the person so described. The process of construction will lead inexorably to the conclusion that the person with whom the other party intended to contract was the person thus described.

162. That the identification of the parties to a written contract involves construing the contract was the basis of the decision in *Hector v Lyons* (1988) 58 P & CR 156. The majority of the Court of Appeal in the present case considered that this decision weighed conclusively in favour of Shogun. *Hector v Lyons* involved a claim for specific performance of a contract to buy a house. The appellant rejoiced in the name Martin Aloysius Handel Hector. He had a son, aged less than 18, more modestly christened Martin Aloysius Hector. The father negotiated the purchase of the house face-to-face with the Respondent, who at all times understood that she was contracting with the father. The father instructed solicitors to draw up the formal contract for exchange. For reasons not apparent he led them to understand that the purchaser was to be his son, and they described the purchaser in the contract as "Martin Aloysius Hector", understanding that they were thereby identifying the son. The father signed the purchaser's copy of the contract with a signature that differed from his normal signature. What was behind all of this is not clear to me nor was it, I suspect, to the trial judge, who found that the father gave a lot of false evidence.

163. The father sought to enforce the contract on the footing that he was the purchaser. The respondent argued that he was not a party to the written contract; the purchaser under that contract was the son. The trial judge found in her favour. The basis upon which he did so was that the solicitors handed over the purchaser's part of the contract as being the document of the son and the signature that it bore purported to be that of the son.

164. In the Court of Appeal counsel for the appellant argued that the contract had been concluded between the appellant and the respondent, relying on the line of cases ending with *Lewis v Averay*. The Vice-Chancellor dismissed this argument at pp.158–9:

"In the case of a face to face sale, where the sale is over a counter or between two individuals, the law is well established that the mere fact that the vendor V is under the misapprehension as to the identity of the person in front of him does not operate so as to render the contract void for mistake, it being a mere unilateral mistake as to a quality of the purchaser; only in cases where the identity of the purchaser is of direct and important materiality in inducing the vendor to enter into the contract is a mistake of the kind capable of avoiding the contract.

With one exception those cases are entirely concerned with transactions between two individuals face to face entering into oral agreement. In my judgement the principle there enunciated has no application to a case such as the present where there is a contract wholly in writing. There the identity of the vendor and the purchaser is established by the names of the parties included in the written contract. Once those names are there in the contract, the only question for the court is to identify who they are.

In the present case the deputy judge has found as a fact that the party named in the written contract was Mr Hector junior. It follows, in my judgement, that in the absence of rectification, which has not been claimed, or Mr Cogley's alternative argument based on agency the only person who can enforce that contract is the party to it, namely Mr Hector junior. He has never at any stage sought to do so. It is for these purposes in my judgement irrelevant whom Mrs Lyons thought she was contracting with: she is entitled to say 'I entered into a contract with the person named in the contract, and nobody else.' As the learned deputy judge pointed out, if Mrs Lyons had sought to enforce the contract against Mr Hector senior, the position might have been different, in that Mr Hector senior might have estopped himself by his conduct from denying that he was the person named in the contract. But that is quite a different case."

165. In concurring with the Vice-Chancellor, Woolf L.J. said this:

"Parties to the contract are normally to be ascertained from the document or documents containing the contract. There can be limited circumstances where it is possible to allow oral evidence to be given in relation to a written contract, but those circumstances are recognised as being exceptional and should, in my view, be strictly confined.

        . . .

In this case there is no dispute as to who, according to the written contract, are the parties. The son was described in the contract as one of the parties. He does exist and, insofar as there was a contract at all, it was between him and the other party identified in the contract, Mrs Pamela Doris Lyons."

166. Given the premise that, as a matter of construction, the purchaser described in the contract was the son, the conclusion of the Court of Appeal is readily understandable. I do, however, have difficulty in understanding the basis on which the trial judge concluded that the purchaser described in the contract was the son rather than the father. The father had carried out the negotiations, he had signed the agreement, albeit not with his customary signature, and he bore the forenames and the surname of the purchaser, as described in the contract. The trial judge's finding does not, however, appear to have been challenged in the Court of Appeal. While the facts of this decision are not easy to follow, it supports the proposition that the identity of the parties to a contract in writing fall to be determined by a process of construction of the contract.

The result in the present case
167. I have had the advantage of reading in draft the opinions of my noble and learned friends who have sat with me on this appeal. Lord Hobhouse of Woodborough and Lord Walker of Gestingthorpe have concluded that, as the contract was a written document, the identity of the hirer falls to be ascertained by construing that document. Adopting that approach, the hirer was, or more accurately purported to be, Mr Patel. As he had not authorised the conclusion of the contract, it was void.

168. Lord Nicholls of Birkenhead and Lord Millett have adopted a different approach. They point out the illogicality of applying a special approach to face-to-face dealings. What of dealings on the telephone, or by videolink? There also it could be said that each of the parties to the dealings is seeking to make a contract with the other party to the dealings. And this can even be said when the dealings are conducted by correspondence. If A writes to B making an offer and B writes back responding to that offer, B is intending to contract with the person who made that offer. If a contract is concluded in face-to-face dealings, notwithstanding that one party is masquerading as a third party, why should the result be different when the dealings are by letter?

169. Lord Nicholls of Birkenhead and Lord Millett propose an elegant solution to this illogicality. Where two individuals *deal with each other*, by whatever medium, and agree terms of a contract, then a contract will be concluded between them, notwithstanding that one has deceived the other into thinking that he has the identity of a third party. In such a situation the contract will be voidable but not void. While they accept that this approach cannot be reconciled with *Cundy v Lindsay*, they conclude that *Cundy v Lindsay* was wrongly decided and should no longer be followed.

170. While I was strongly attracted to this solution, I have found myself unable to adopt it. *Cundy v Lindsay* exemplifies the application by English law of the same approach to identifying the parties as is applied to identifying the terms of the contract. In essence this focuses on deducing the intention of the parties from their words and conduct. Where there is some form of personal contact between individuals who are conducting negotiations, this approach gives rise to problems. In such a situation I would favour the application of a strong presumption that each intends to contract with the other, with whom he is dealing. Where, however, the dealings are exclusively conducted in writing, there is no scope or need for such a presumption. This can be illustrated by a slight adaption of the facts of the present case. Assume that the rogue had himself filled in the application form and sent it and a photocopy of Mr Patel's driving licence to Shogun. Assume further that he had been authorised to do so by Mr Patel. There can be no doubt that a contract would have been concluded between Shogun and Mr Patel. Mr Patel would have intended to contract with Shogun; Shogun would have intended to contract with Mr Patel; and this would have been demonstrated by the application form.

171. Assume now that the rogue had wrongly understood that he had been requested by Mr Patel to fill in and submit the application form on his behalf, but in fact had no authority to do so. In this situation, according to established principles of the law of agency, an apparent contract would have been concluded between Shogun and Mr Patel but, being concluded without the latter's authority, it would be a nullity. Shogun might have a claim against the rogue for breach of warranty of authority, but could not have demonstrated that a contract had been concluded with the rogue.

172. Turning to the true position—that the rogue knew he had no authority to conclude a contract in the name of Mr Patel, but fraudulently wished to induce Shogun to believe that they were entering into such a contract—I do not see by what legal principle this change in the mental attitude of the rogue could result in a binding contract being concluded with him.

173. The position is not, of course, as simple as that. Negotiations between the rogue and Shogun were not conducted exclusively by written correspondence. They were conducted with the aid of the dealer and the use of fax and telephone communications. Acceptance of the offer was conveyed by telephone via the dealer—and this might have been capable of concluding a contract, notwithstanding that Clause 1 of the standard terms provided for acceptance by signature—see the discussion in Chitty on Contracts 28th Ed. Vol 1 at paragraph 2–062. Sedley L.J. considered that the dealings were analogous to face-to-face dealings and that the dealer was, in effect, the face of Shogun Finance Ltd. He considered that the face-to-face presumption should be applied.

174. The majority of the Court of Appeal considered that *Hector v Lyons* required them to determine the identity of the parties to the putative contract as a simple question of construction. On that basis they concluded that the putative hirer was Mr Patel and that, as the apparent contract was concluded without his authority, it was a nullity.

175. Dyson L.J. considered what the result would have been had the negotiations been treated as face-to-face. He concluded that the presumption would have been displaced by the importance that Shogun attached to the identity of the person with whom they were contracting.

176. My Lords, I started this opinion by quoting Gresson P's remark that the difficulty in a case such as this is a proper assessment of the facts rather than an assessment of the law. I have not found the assessment of the law easy, but nor is the application of the law to the facts. Shogun's representatives were aware of the presence of the prospective hirer in the dealer's showrooms in Leicester. To an extent the dealings were inter-personal through the medium of the dealer. Should one treat them as comparable to face-to-face dealings and conclude that there was a presumption that Shogun intended to contract with the man with whom they were dealing? Should one treat the written agreement as no more than peripheral to the dealings and conclude that it does not override that presumption? I have concluded that the answer to these questions is "no".

177. Shogun had, on the evidence, set up a formal system under which contracts would be concluded in writing on a standard form. This form was designed to cater for both regulated and non-regulated hire purchase agreements. In order to be suitable for the former it had to comply with the requirements of the Consumer Credit (Agreements) Regulations 1983. Schedule 1 to these regulations, under the heading "*Parties to the agreement*", requires the agreement to set out "The name and a postal address of the creditor" and "The name and a postal address of the debtor". The agreement with which this appeal is concerned was not a regulated agreement, for the purchase price of the vehicle exceeded what was, at the time, the maximum to which the relevant provisions of the Consumer Credit Act 1974 applied. I do not see, however, that the approach to the identification of the parties to the putative agreement can turn on whether or not the agreement was subject to the regulations. Shogun put in place a system for concluding contracts that required both regulated and unregulated agreements to be entered into in writing in a form which provided essential information, including the identity of the parties to the agreement.

178. These considerations lead me to conclude that the correct approach in the present case is to treat the agreement as one concluded in writing and to approach the identification of the parties to that agreement as turning upon its construction. The particulars given in the agreement are only capable of applying to Mr Patel. It was the intention of the rogue that they should identify Mr Patel as the hirer. The hirer was so identified by Shogun. Before deciding to enter into the agreement they checked that Mr Patel existed and that he was worthy of credit. On that basis they decided to contract with him and with no-one else. Mr Patel was the hirer under the agreement. As the agreement was concluded without his authority, it was a nullity. The rogue took no title under it and was in no position to convey any title to Mr Hudson.

179. For these reasons I would dismiss this appeal.

Further reading

Glanville Williams, 'Mistake as to Party in the Law of Contract' (1945) 23 *Canadian Bar Review* 271
J.F. Wilson, 'Identity in Contract and the Pothier Fallacy' (1954) 17 MLR 515

9

INTENTION TO CREATE LEGAL RELATIONS

LEARNING OBJECTIVES

By the end of this chapter, you should understand:

- **that the law will not treat a transaction as an enforceable contract unless it is supported by an intention to create legal relations;**
- **that there is a presumption that domestic and social agreements are not usually intended to create legal relations and that, conversely, there is a presumption that business agreements are intended to create legal relations;**
- **that there are "borderline" cases where it is arguable that the relevant presumption should be rebutted;**
- **that such borderline cases tend to turn on their own particular facts and have relatively little value as precedents.**

INTRODUCTION

If, within the broad field of transactions, the distinctive function of the law of contract is to identify and support those promises that are legally enforceable (as a matter of contractual obligation), then the law needs a test (or tests) to differentiate between those promises which are enforceable and those which are not. A number of possibilities present themselves. For example, the mark of a contractually enforceable promise might be:

9–001

(i) that it is expressed in a certain form (such as in a deed, or in writing); or

(ii) that it is made with a sufficient seriousness of intention; or

(iii) that it is seriously intended by the promisor and actually relied on by the promisee; or

(iv) that it is reciprocated by a requested return promise or act; or

(v) that it satisfies some combination of the above requirements.

Until the historic case of *Balfour v Balfour* (below), the English law of contract largely relied upon the first and especially the fourth of these tests, the latter being represented by the requirement of consideration (or exchange) (see Ch.10). So long as English law relied on formality and consideration rather than intention, it stood in contrast to many other regimes of contract law.

When the Court of Appeal, in *Balfour*, highlighted the significance of intention, it did not do so as an alternative to consideration. In other words, after *Balfour*, unless a promise was in a deed, English law treated a promise as contractually binding only if (i) it was made with an intention to create legal relations with the promisee and (ii) it was supported by consideration moving from the promisee. By retaining the requirement of consideration, on paper at least, English law remains at some distance from both civilian and common law regimes that recognise either intention alone or intention coupled with reliance as sufficient for the creation of contractually enforceable promissory obligation.

The cases in this chapter are in two sections: first, there is the leading (and root) authority, *Balfour v Balfour*, which establishes the requirement that there should be an intention to create legal (contractual) relations; and, secondly, there are a number of cases illustrating how the courts determine whether, in the particular context, the parties intended their agreement to have legal effect.

1. Establishing the Basic Requirement

BALFOUR v BALFOUR

Court of Appeal [1919] 2 K.B. 571; 88 L.J.K.B. 1054; 121 L.T. 346

9–002   The defendant, who was a civil servant stationed in Ceylon, in November 1915, came to England with the plaintiff, his wife. They remained in England until August 1916, when the husband's leave was up and he had to return. The plaintiff, on the doctor's advice, remained in England, and the husband, before sailing, promised to give her £30 a month until she returned. He did so after assessing the sum she would require for maintenance in consultation with her. Later the husband wrote saying that it would be better if they remained apart, and in 1918 the wife obtained a decree nisi. The plaintiff sued on the promise to pay her £30 per month. Sargant J gave judgment for the plaintiff, holding that the husband was under an obligation to support his wife and the parties had contracted that the extent of that obligation should be defined in terms of so much a month. The consent of the wife to that arrangement was a sufficient consideration to constitute a contract which could be sued upon. The husband appealed.

Warrington and Duke LJJ gave judgment allowing the appeal.

ATKIN LJ

> . . . it is necessary to remember that there are agreements between parties which do not result in contracts within the meaning of that term in our law. The ordinary example is where two parties agree to take a walk together, or where there is an offer and an acceptance of hospitality. Nobody would suggest in ordinary circumstances that those agreements result in what we know as a contract, and one of the most usual forms of agreement which does not constitute a contract appears to me to be the arrangements which are made between husband and wife. It is quite common, and it is the natural and inevitable result of the relationship of husband and wife, that the two spouses should make arrangements between themselves—agreements such as are in dispute in this action—agreements for allowances, by which the husband agrees that he will pay to his wife a certain sum of money, per week, or per month, or per year, to cover either her own expenses or the necessary expenses of the household and of the children of the marriage, and in which the wife promises either expressly or impliedly to apply the allowance for the purpose for which it is given. To my mind those agreements, or many of them, do not result in contracts at all, and they do not result in contracts even though there may be what as between other parties would constitute consideration for the agreement. The consideration, as we know, may consist either in some right, interest, profit or benefit accruing to one party or some forbearance, detriment, loss or responsibility given, suffered or undertaken by the other. That is a well-known definition, and it constantly happens, I think, that such arrangements made between husband and wife are arrangements in which there are mutual promises, or in which there is consideration in form within the definition that I have mentioned. Nevertheless, they are not contracts, and they are not contracts because the parties did not intend that they should be attended by legal consequences. To my mind it would be of the worst possible example to

hold that agreements such as this resulted in legal obligations which could be enforced in the courts. It would mean this, that when the husband makes his wife a promise to give her an allowance of 30s. or £2 a week, whatever he can afford to give her, for the maintenance of the household and children, and she promises so to apply it, not only could she sue him for his failure in any week to supply the allowance, but he could sue her for non-performance of the obligation, express or implied, which she had undertaken upon her part. All I can say is that the small courts of this country would have to be multiplied one hundredfold if these arrangements were held to result in legal obligations. They are not sued upon, not because the parties are reluctant to enforce their legal rights when the agreement is broken, but because the parties, in the inception of the arrangement, never intended that they should be sued upon. Agreements such as these are outside the realm of contracts altogether. The common law does not regulate the form of agreements between spouses. Their promises are not sealed with seals and sealing wax. The consideration that really obtains for them is that natural love and affection which counts for so little in these cold courts. The terms may be repudiated, varied or renewed as performance proceeds or as disagreements develop, and the principles of the common law as to exoneration and discharge and accord and satisfaction are such as find no place in the domestic code.

Professor Michael Freeman, 'Contracting in the Haven: Balfour v Balfour Revisited', in Exploring the Boundaries of Contract (ed. R. Halson, 1996), p.68 (footnotes omitted):

Balfour v Balfour is one of those wise decisions in which the courts allow the realities of life to determine the legal norm which they formulate (Otto Kahn-Freund, 'Inconsistencies and Injustices in the Law of Husband and Wife' (1952) 15 M.L.R. 133, 138).   **9–003**

   Balfour v Balfour, three quarters of a century after it was decided, remains a leading case. It features prominently in all contract textbooks and, as Treitel observes, it has not been judicially questioned. It has had one in-depth critical article devoted to it but this, by Stephen Hedley (1985) 5 O.J.L.S. 391, concentrates mainly on the place of the case in the law of contract.

   My starting point is somewhat different. As a family lawyer I am struck by a paradox. The ruling orthodoxy remains *Balfour v Balfour* but increasingly English law extends to those in family relationships the power to regulate their own lives. Nor is English law alone in exemplifying this trend. Oddly, as commercial law has come to learn the perils of an uncritical embrace of freedom of contract as its governing principle, so family law, for so long its paradigmatic antithesis, has welcomed the ideological framework of contract. As contract law has shifted its direction towards status, as it has come to reflect ongoing relationships with reliance rather than choice its key, so modern family law has steadily embraced contract as its governing principle and in the process has cast off many of its status associations. Once no clearer antimony was drawn than that which separated the family and the market. The family was quintessentially 'private': commerce, by contrast, belonged to the 'public' world. But the family, that 'haven from the heartless world' of the market has now adopted many of the same concepts and principles that (once) commerce embraced.

   And yet *Balfour v Balfour* remains ruling orthodoxy . . .

[Professor Freeman's article concludes:]

Marriage has become 'a personal rather than a social institution' fit for private ordering rather than state regulation. And yet the official version of the truth is that husbands and wives do not subject their arrangements to the law of contract. If *Balfour v Balfour* was a 'wise' decision based on the 'realities' of life, then wisdom dictates that we rethink the doctrine it embodies. It no longer reflects realities nor is it in line with developments taking place in family law. Once the fiction is rejected we will be in a position to assess the role of contract in intimate relationships and to examine the relevance of the modern law of contract on the family.

2. DID THE PARTIES HAVE AN INTENTION TO CREATE LEGAL RELATIONS?

COWARD v MOTOR INSURERS' BUREAU

Court of Appeal [1963] 1 Q.B. 259; [1962] 2 W.L.R. 663; [1962] 1 All E.R. 531; [1962] 1 Lloyd's Rep 583

Coward was a pillion passenger on a motor-cycle owned and driven by Cole when, by an accident due to Cole's negligence, both were killed. In an action by Coward's widow the court thought it necessary   **9–004** to decide whether there was a contract between Coward and Cole. [In *Albert v Motor Insurers' Bureau* [1971] 3 W.L.R. 291, the majority of the House of Lords held that it was not necessary to decide this question in cases of this kind and Coward's case was disapproved; but it is not necessarily wrong on the question whether there was a contract.]

UPJOHN LJ

The practice whereby workmen go to their place of business in the motor car or on the motor cycle of a fellow workman upon the terms of making a contribution to the costs of transport is well known and widespread. In the absence of evidence that the parties intended to be bound contractually, we should be reluctant to conclude that the daily carriage by one of another to work upon payment of some weekly (or it may be daily) sum involved them in a legal contractual relationship. The hazards of everyday life, such as temporary indisposition, the incidence of holidays, the possibility of a change of shift or different hours of overtime, or incompatibility arising, make it most unlikely that either contemplated that the one was legally bound to carry and the other to be carried to work. It is made all the more improbable in this case by reason of the fact that alternative means of transport seem to have been available to Coward.

On the probabilities of the case, therefore, we reach the conclusion that, while admitting the evidence rejected by the judge, which in our judgment clearly proved an arrangement whereby Coward paid a weekly sum to Cole for transporting him to and from his work, neither party intended to enter into a legal contract.

Points for reflection

9–005   In *Simpkins v Pays* [1955] 1 W.L.R. 975, Sellers J held binding an arrangement between A, a paying boarder at B's house, B and B's grand-daughter, C. They entered a fashion competition in a Sunday newspaper each week, each filling in one line, but the entry being sent in B's name. Sellers J found that there was an agreement that, whichever line won, all should share equally, and that A was entitled to recover one-third of the prize from B.

In *Parker v Clark* [1960] 1 W.L.R. 286, Devlin J held that an arrangement between relatives to share a house was binding in view particularly of the fact that it was necessary for Parker to take the drastic and irrevocable step of disposing of his own residence in order to adopt the arrangement. The judge could not believe that Clark really believed that the law would allow him, if he chose, "to tell the Parkers when they arrived that he had changed his mind, that they could take their furniture away, and that he was indifferent whether they found anywhere else to live or not."

In *Gage v King* [1961] 1 Q.B. 188, Diplock J held that when a husband and wife open a joint banking account, prima facie, there is no intention to enter into legal relations inter se. And where a husband promised his wife to buy her a car in an effort to improve their strained matrimonial relationship and entered into a hire-purchase agreement in respect of a car which was delivered at their home, it was held that this was a purely domestic arrangement, not intended to create legal relationships and that, accordingly, the wife acquired no rights in the car or under the hire-purchase agreement: *Spellman v Spellman* [1961] 1 W.L.R. 921.

In *Merritt v Merritt* [1970] 1 W.L.R. 1211; [1970] 2 All E.R. 760, the Court of Appeal held that the presumption that agreements between husband and wife are not intended to create legal relations does not apply when they are not living in amity but are separated or about to separate. H had left W and was living with another woman. He agreed to pay W £40 a month, and signed a written agreement that, in consideration of W's paying off the mortgage on their jointly owned house, he would then transfer it to her sole ownership. W paid off the mortgage. Stamp J made a declaration that W was the sole beneficial owner. H's appeal was dismissed. Lord Denning said: "In all these cases the court does not try to discover the intention by looking into the minds of the parties. It looks at the situation in which they were placed and asks itself: would reasonable people regard this agreement as intended to be binding?"

In *Gould v Gould* [1970] 1 Q.B. 275, in deciding whether there was an intent to create legal relations, the court had regard to the uncertainty of the words. H on leaving W promised orally to pay her £15 per week "as long as he had it" or "as long as business was O.K." (according to W) or (according to H) "as long as I can manage it." The uncertainty of the words used led Edmund Davies and Megaw LJJ to conclude that there was no intent to create legal relations. Lord Denning, dissenting, thought an oral separation agreement, by which H agrees to pay W so much a week, is legally enforceable; terms should not be held void for uncertainty "unless it is utterly impossible to put a meaning on them"; and meaning could be given by implying a term that, if H could not keep up payments, he could determine the agreement by reasonable notice.

In *Jones v Padavatton* [1969] 1 W.L.R. 328; [1969] 2 All E.R. 616, a mother (M) promised her daughter (D), aged 34, that if D would give up her well-paid job in Washington, DC, and come to England to study for the bar, M would pay her $200 a month until she had completed her studies. D came to England in 1962 and studied for the bar. Danckwerts and Fenton Atkinson LJJ held that M and D did not intend to create legal relations. Salmon LJ held that there was a binding unilateral contract requiring M to pay D $200 a month for a reasonable time; but a reasonable time could not possibly exceed five years, so she could not rely on the contract in 1968. Fenton Atkinson LJ relied heavily on the conduct of the parties subsequent to the agreement (but see *Jas. Miller & Partners Ltd v Whitworth St. Estates* [1970] 2 W.L.R. 728; [1970] 1 All E.R. 796 [above, Ch.6]).

In *Buckpitt v Oates* [1968] 1 All E.R. 1145 the plaintiff and defendant, both aged seventeen, were in the habit of riding in each other's cars. The plaintiff sustained injury while riding in the defendant's car through the defendant's negligence. He had paid the defendant 10s. towards the cost of the petrol. John Stephenson J found that "there was a friendly arrangement, or (I can hardly avoid using the phrase) a 'gentleman's agreement' to go on this trip, which gave rise to no legal obligations or rights, except those which the general law of the land imposes or implies."

In *Edwards v Skyways Ltd* [1964] 1 W.L.R. 349 the defendant airline company agreed with the British Airline Pilots Association to pay certain 'ex gratia' payments 'approximating to' a readily ascertainable figure to pilots declared redundant. An action was brought by the plaintiff, a redundant pilot, for his payment under this agreement. It was admitted that consideration had moved from the plaintiff but the defendant company sought to escape liability by showing that the agreement was not intended to create legal relations and was too vague. Megaw J considered that the subject of the present agreement related to business matters, so that the onus of establishing that there was no intention to create legal relations lay on the defendant company as the party seeking to use it as a defence. The company had not, he thought, discharged that onus. In so far as the term 'ex gratia' had been used, he decided that its use had been simply in order to indicate that the company did not admit any pre-existing liability on its part. The words did not mean, to put it another way, that the promise, when accepted, should have no binding effect at law.

The use of the words 'approximating to' by the defendant company did not in his Lordship's view make the terms of the agreement too vague. On the evidence he took this to mean at most a 'rounding off' of a few pounds downwards so as to achieve a round figure. The plaintiff accordingly succeeded.

ROSE AND FRANK CO v CROMPTON BROS

Kings Bench Division [1923] 2 K.B. 261, 276; House of Lords [1925] A.C. 445; 94 L.J.K.B. 120; 132 L.T. 641; 30 Com. Cas. 163

The defendants were an English firm which manufactured paper tissues. In 1913 the defendants   **9–006** entered into an arrangement with the plaintiffs, an American firm, whereby the plaintiffs were constituted sole agents for the sale in the United States of the tissues supplied by the English firm, for three years with an option to extend that time. The document contained the following clause, described as the "Honourable Pledge Clause":

"This arrangement is not entered into, nor is this memorandum written, as a formal or legal agreement, and shall not be subject to legal jurisdiction in the law courts either of the United States or England, but it is only a definite expression and record of the purpose and intention of the three parties concerned to which they each honourably pledge themselves with the fullest confidence, based on past business with each other, that it will be carried through by each of the three parties with mutual loyalty and friendly co-operation."

The agreement was subsequently extended to March 1920, but in 1919 the defendants terminated it without notice. The defendants had received and accepted a number of specific orders for tissues before the termination, and these they refused to execute. The plaintiffs sued for breach of contract and for non-delivery of the goods.

Bailhache J held that the 1913 arrangement and the orders and acceptances were legally binding contracts. The Court of Appeal (Bankes, Scrutton and Atkin LJJ) were unanimous in holding that the 1913 arrangement was not legally binding and they also held by a majority (Atkin LJ dissenting) that the orders and acceptances did not constitute legally binding contracts.

SCRUTTON LJ

Now it is quite possible for parties to come to an agreement by accepting a proposal with the result that the agreement concluded does not give rise to legal relations. The reason of this is that the parties do not intend that their agreement shall give rise to legal relations. This intention may be implied from the subject-matter of the agreement, but it may also be expressed by the parties. In social and family relations such an intention is readily implied, while in business matters the opposite result would ordinarily follow. But I can see no reason why, even in business matters, the parties should not intend to rely on each other's good faith and honour, and to exclude all idea of settling disputes by any outside intervention, with the accompanying necessity of expressing themselves so precisely that outsiders may have no difficulty in understanding what they mean. If they clearly express such an intention I can see no reason in public policy why effect should not be given to their intention.

Both legal decisions and the opinions of standard text writers support this view . . . Mr Leake says (7th ed., 1921), p. 3, that "an agreement as the source of a legal contract imports that the one party shall be bound to some performance, which the latter [sic] shall have a legal right to enforce." In Sir Frederick Pollock's language (9th ed., 1921), p. 3, an agreement to become enforceable at law must "be concerned with duties and rights which can be dealt with by a court of justice. And it must be the intention of the parties that the matter in hand shall, if necessary, be so dealt with, or at least they must not have the contrary intention." Sir William Anson requires in contract "a common intention to affect" the legal relations of the parties.

Judged by this test, I come to the same conclusion as the learned judge, that the particular clause in question shows a clear intention by the parties that the rest of their arrangement or agreement shall not affect their legal relations, or be enforceable in a court of law, but in the words of the clause, shall be "only a definite expression and record of the purpose and intention of the three parties concerned to which they each honourably pledge themselves," "and shall not be subject to legal jurisdiction." If the clause stood first in the document, the intention of the parties would be exceedingly plain.

ATKIN LJ

In this case the defendants by the honourable understanding entered into the vague engagement contained in the document which had as a basis the average turnover for the last three years before the agreement. But whatever the terms of the agreement or understanding, it contemplated, as nearly all such agreements do, that the actual business done under it should be done by particular contracts of purchase and sale upon the terms of the general agreement so far as applicable. The actual business was done in this case, as in countless others, by orders for specific goods given by the "agent" and accepted by the manufacturer or merchant . . . [His Lordship then examined the correspondence between the parties.] Pausing there, this is the common formula of acceptance in the business world which has been treated as acceptance in countless cases since merchants first wrote to one another. It would be understood as an acceptance passing between two merchants where there was no obligation at all on the part of the vendor to accept. Why it should bear a different meaning in a case where there is an honourable understanding by the merchant to accept up to some vague limit, I am unable to understand.

The House of Lords held (1) that the arrangement of 1913 was not a binding contract, but, (2) the orders given and accepted constituted enforceable contracts of sale.

A letter of comfort, it should be explained, usually takes the form of encouragement by A of B to advance money to C, falling short of a guarantee by A. It appears that it originated in the United States in the 1960s. Parent companies were reluctant to guarantee the debts of their subsidiaries because guarantees had to be disclosed in their accounts as contingent liabilities. Letters of comfort, not amounting to legal obligations, need not be shown. They appear now to be widely used in international business transactions.

KLEINWORT BENSON LTD v MALAYSIA MINING CORP Bhd

Court of Appeal [1989] 1 W.L.R. 379, [1989] 1 All E.R. 785

9–007

The plaintiff bank agreed to make a loan of up to £10 million to MMC Metals Ltd ("Metals"), a wholly owned subsidiary of the defendants. The plaintiffs had tried to secure the joint and several liability of the defendants and Metals, or a guarantee by the defendants of the liability of Metals to the plaintiffs, but the defendants had refused to assume either form of obligation. Instead the plaintiffs accepted (but with a higher rate of interest) a "letter of comfort" drafted by them and signed by the defendants stating:

"[2] We confirm that we will not reduce our current financial interest in MMC Metals Ltd until the above facilities have been repaid or until you have confirmed that you are prepared to continue the facilities with new shareholders.
[3] It is our policy to ensure that the business of MMC Metals Ltd is at all times in a position to meet its liabilities to you under the above arrangements."

It was accepted that [2] created a legal obligation. The issue was whether [3] did so. Hirst J held that it did. The defendants appealed.

RALPH GIBSON LJ

The submission in this court for the plaintiffs can be more shortly stated because counsel adopted and relied on the reasoning of the judge. As to the effect and meaning to be given to para. 3, his main submissions were that: (i) the statement in para. 3 was made in a commercial contractual document and it is to be treated as a contractual promise if it appears on the evidence to have been so intended: see *Esso Petroleum Co Ltd v Mardon* [below para.15–024]; (ii) it is shown to have been so intended because the statement was made for the purpose of inducing the plaintiffs to enter into the acceptance credit transaction with Metals under the credit facility and it was plainly of decisive commercial importance to the transaction; (iii) the statement as to present policy must be taken as including a promise that that policy will remain in force. This proposition can be tested, it was said, by taking an example remote from banking: suppose a shop, by notice, announced that "it is our policy to take back all goods purchased and to refund the price, without any questions, on return of the goods in good condition within 14 days of purchase", if a customer should return goods, having bought them in reliance on the notice, the shop could not (said counsel for the plaintiffs) refuse to refund the price on the ground that the notice only stated the shop's policy on the day of purchase so that the shop was free to change its policy within the 14-day period. So in this case it is absurd in commercial terms for the defendants to claim to be free to change their announced policy after money has been advanced in reliance on it. To treat the words of para. 3 as no more than a representation of fact is to give no force to the words "at all times".

For my part, I am persuaded that the main criticisms of the judgment of Hirst J. advanced by counsel for the defendants are well founded and I would, for the reasons which follow, allow this appeal. In my judgment the defendants made a statement as to what their policy was, and did not in para. 3 of the comfort letter expressly promise that such policy would be continued in future. It is impossible to make up for the lack of express promise by implying such a promise, and indeed, no such implied promise was pleaded. My conclusion rests on what, in my judgment, is the proper effect and meaning which, on the evidence, is to be given to para. 3 of the comfort letters . . .

The central question in this case, in my judgment, is that considered in *Esso Petroleum Co Ltd v Mardon*, on which counsel for the plaintiffs relied in this court but which was not cited to Hirst J. That question is whether the words of para. 3, considered in their context, are to be treated as a warranty or contractual promise. Paragraph 3 contains no express words of promise. Paragraph 3 is in its terms a statement of present fact and not a promise as to future conduct. I agree with the submission of counsel for the defendants that, in this regard, the words of para. 3 are in sharp contrast with the words of para. 2 of the letter: "We confirm that we will not" etc. The force of this point is not limited, as Hirst J. stated it, to the absence from para. 3 of the words "We confirm". The real contrast is between the words of promise, namely "We will not" in para. 2, and the words of statement of fact, "It is our policy" in para. 3. Hirst J. held that, by the words of para. 3, the defendants gave an undertaking that now and at all times in the future, so long as Metals should be under any liability to the plaintiffs under the facility arrangements, it is and will be the defendants' policy to ensure that Metals is in a position to meet their liabilities. To derive that meaning from the words it is necessary to add the words emphasised, namely "and will be", which do not appear in para. 3. In short, the words of promise as to the future conduct of the defendants were held by Hirst J. to be part of the necessary meaning of the words used in para. 3. The question is whether that view of the words can be upheld . . .
[Ralph Gibson LJ held that that meaning could not be upheld.]

If my view of this case is correct, the plaintiffs have suffered grave financial loss as a result of the collapse of the tin market and the following decision by the defendant company not to honour a moral responsibility which it assumed in order to gain for its subsidiary the finance necessary for the trading operations which the defendants wished that subsidiary to pursue. The defendants have demonstrated, in my judgment, that they made no relevant contractual promise to the plaintiffs which could support the judgment in favour of the plaintiffs. The consequences of the decision of the defendants to repudiate their moral responsibility are not matters for this court.

I would allow this appeal.

Nicholls and O'Connor L.JJ. agreed.

Appeal Allowed.

Point for reflection

9–008   In *Banque Brussels Lambert v Australian National Industries Ltd* (1989) 21 N.S.W.L.R. 502 Rogers CJ said of the *Kleinwort Benson* case that the judgment of Hirst J reflected "the bias of experienced commercial judges to pay high regard to the fact that the comfort letters before them came into existence as part and parcel of a commercial banking transaction and that the promises were an important feature of the letters." He said: "The Court of Appeal subjected the letters to minute textual analysis. Courts will become irrelevant in the resolution of commercial disputes if they allow this approach to dominate their consideration of commercial documents . . . [Ralph Gibson LJ's] construction of the letter renders the document a scrap of paper. If the Lord Justice is correct, the writer has not expressed itself on anything relevant as a matter of honour."

Question

9–009   If A says to B; "I would like you to advance money to C. It is my intention to indemnify you if C defaults but I am not prepared to enter into any legal obligation to do so. You can rely on my word"; and B, relying on A's "words of comfort", then agrees to make the advance but at a higher rate of interest than if he had received a guarantee, should A be liable to B if C defaults and A declines to pay?

ESSO PETROLEUM LTD v COMMISSIONERS OF CUSTOMS AND EXCISE

House of Lords [1976] 1 W.L.R. 1; [1976] 1 All E.R. 117

The facts are given above, para.2-023.   9-010

VISCOUNT DILHORNE

[Having referred to statements in *Rose and Frank v Crompton* and *Edwards v Skyways* that in business matters there is a heavy onus on a party who asserts that legal relations were not intended:] I do not wish in any way to criticise or qualify these statements, but I do not feel that they provide a sound foundation for the decision of this appeal.

True it is that Esso are engaged in business. True it is that they hope to promote the sale of their petrol, but it does not seem to me necessarily to follow or to be inferred that there was any intention on their part that their dealers should enter into legally binding contracts with regard to the coins; or any intention on the part of the dealers to enter into any such contract or any intention on the part of the purchaser of four gallons of petrol to do so.

If on the facts of this case the conclusion is reached that there was any such intention on the part of the customer, of the dealer and of Esso, it would seem to exclude the possibility of any dealer ever making a free gift to any of his customers, however negligible its value, to promote his sales.

If what was described as being a gift would be given if something was purchased was something of value to the purchaser, then it could readily be inferred that there was a common intention to enter into legal relations. But here, whatever the cost of production, it is clear that the coins were of little intrinsic value.

I do not consider that the offer of a gift of a free coin is properly to be regarded as a business matter in the sense in which that word was used by Scrutton L.J. in the passage cited above. Nor do I think that such an offer can be comprehended within the "business relations" which were in the *Skyways* case, as Megaw L.J. said, "the subject-matter of the agreement." I see no reason to imply any intention to enter into contractual relations from the statements on the posters that a coin would be given if four gallons of petrol were bought.

Nor do I see any reason to impute to every motorist who went to a garage where the posters were displayed to buy four gallons of petrol any intention to enter into a legally binding contract for the supply to him of a coin. On the acceptance of his offer to purchase four gallons there was no doubt a legally binding contract for the supply to him of that quantity of petrol, but I see again no reason to conclude that because such an offer was made by him, it must be held that, as the posters were displayed, his offer included an offer to take a coin. The gift of a coin might lead to a motorist returning to the garage to obtain another one, but I think the facts in this case negative any contractual intention on his part and on the part of the dealer as to the coin and suffice to rebut any presumption there may be to the contrary . . .

LORD SIMON OF GLAISDALE

My Lords, I have had the advantage of reading in draft the speech prepared by my noble and learned friend Lord Russell of Killowen. I beg to take advantage of his explanation of the facts that have led to the appeal and the statutory provisions by which they are to be judged.

I am, however, my Lords, not prepared to accept that the promotion material put out by Esso was not envisaged by them as creating legal relations between the garage proprietors who adopted it and the motorists who yielded to its blandishments. In the first place, Esso and the garage proprietors put the material out for their commercial advantage, and designed it to attract the custom of motorists. The whole transaction took place in a setting of business relations. In the second place, it seems to me in general undesirable to allow a commercial promoter to claim that what he has done is a mere puff, not intended to create legal relations (cf. *Carlill v Carbolic Smoke Ball Co*. above, para.2-026). The coins may have been themselves of little intrinsic value; but all the evidence suggests that Esso contemplated that they would be attractive to motorists and that there would be a large commercial advantage to themselves from the scheme, an advantage in which the garage proprietors also would share. Thirdly, I think that authority supports the view that legal relations were envisaged.

Points for reflection

9–011 It has often been laid down that "An agreement purporting to oust the jurisdiction of the courts is illegal and void on grounds of public policy" (Halsbury, *Laws of England*, Vol.9, p.352). The rule may be illustrated by *Baker v Jones* [1954] 1 W.L.R. 1005. The rules of the British Amateur Weightlifters' Association provided that the council of the Association should be the sole interpreter of its rules (r.40(vii)) and that the council's decision in all cases should be final (r.40(viii)). When a member of the Association claimed a declaration that the use of the Association's funds for a certain purpose was unlawful under the Association's rules, Lynskey J held that he had jurisdiction to entertain the action. The contract between the plaintiff and the Association could not exclude the jurisdiction of the courts and r.40(vii) and r.40(viii), in so far as they purported to do so, were contrary to public policy and void. Cf. also *Lee v Showmen's Guild* [1952] 2 Q.B. 329 at 342.

Thus it appears that the parties are at liberty to declare that their arrangement is not a contract at all, but only a gentleman's agreement: *Rose and Frank v Crompton* [1925] A.C. 445; but they may not make a contract which provides that the courts shall not have jurisdiction over it: *Baker v Jones*. In effect this seems to mean that the parties are at liberty to provide that their agreement shall not be enforced by any authority whatsoever; but they may not set up some other contract-enforcing authority to the exclusion of the court. If the Weightlifters' Association had included an 'Honourable Pledge Clause' in the contract with its members this might have prevented the rules being enforced at all—but that was certainly not what the Association wanted. They wanted the rules to be enforceable by their council; but if the contract is to be enforceable at all, the jurisdiction of the courts cannot be excluded.

Agreements not to enforce particular legal rights stand on a different footing and are generally binding: *Cook v Wright*, below, Ch.10. In some cases it is contrary to public policy to allow a person to give up his right and, in such a case, a contract to do so is void. Thus a wife's promise not to apply to the Divorce Court for maintenance is not binding on her; "The wife's right to future maintenance is a matter of public concern—which she cannot barter away." (Lord Atkin in *Hyman v Hyman* [1929] A.C. 601; discussed in *Combe v Combe* [1951] 2 K.B. 215, below, Ch.11).

Further reading

James Gordley (ed), *The Enforceability of Promises in European Contract Law* (Cambridge: Cambridge University Press, 2009)

Stephen Hedley, 'Keeping Contract in its Place—*Balfour v Balfour* and the Enforceability of Informal Agreements' (1985) 5 OJLS 391

10

CONSIDERATION

LEARNING OBJECTIVES

By the end of this chapter, you should:

- be familiar with the leading cases that elaborate the requirement that, for a promise to be contractually enforceable, it must be supported by consideration;
- understand the concept of "past consideration" and know how the courts might respond to cases where promises are given in response to past acts or services;
- understand the sense in which consideration must be "sufficient";
- be familiar with the case-law that determines whether the performance of an existing obligation (or a promise to perform an existing obligation) constitutes "consideration";
- have reflected on the significance of *Williams v Roffey Bros and Nicholls (Contractors) Ltd*, not only for the requirement of consideration but more generally for the modern idea that contract law should align with the reasonable expectations of business people;
- have a view about whether the law is coherent in enforcing a promise to pay more for the performance of an existing contractual obligation but not a promise by a creditor (to a debtor) to accept a lesser payment of a debt.

INTRODUCTION

As we saw in the previous chapter, prior to *Balfour v Balfour* [1919] 2 K.B. 571, a promise would be treated as contractually enforceable if either (a) it was made in a deed or (b) it was supported by consideration. After *Balfour*, the position became that a promise would be treated as contractually enforceable if either (a) it was made in a deed or (b) it was backed by an intention to create legal relations *and* it was supported by consideration. In *Balfour* itself, of course, the promise was neither supported by consideration nor backed by an intention to create legal relations (the former deficiency probably reinforcing the latter). At all events, since the vast majority of contracts are not made by deed, the requirement of consideration assumes great significance—indeed, to say that the requirement of consideration is one of the cornerstones of the traditional English law of contract is no over-statement.

The terminology of "consideration" is apt to confuse; but the idea is simple enough. Essentially, to say that a promise must be supported by consideration, or to say that a promise is binding only if it is given for consideration, is to say that the promisor must have asked for and received something (a reciprocal promise or an act) in return for his promise. Hence, a purely gratuitous promise (unless it is made in a deed) is not contractually binding, such a promise being the perfect example of a promise made without consideration. A promise that is not in a deed is binding only if the promisee has "bought" it by paying the "price"—the consideration—requested by the promisor. The consideration may be the payment of money or (with a few exceptions) it may be any other lawful act—whatever the promisor has required as the price for his promise. If the promisor has asked for nothing in return, then he is promising to make a gift which is not binding, and the promisee cannot make it binding merely by promising or (without the promisor's request) giving something in return.

Where, exceptionally, a contract is made by deed, the formalities are governed by the Law of Property (Miscellaneous Provisions) Act 1989 s.1. Following this enactment, the execution of a deed by an individual, as distinct from a corporation, no longer requires a seal. It is sufficient that—

   (i)   it makes it clear on its face that it is intended to be a deed (by describing itself as a deed or expressing itself to be executed and signed as a deed or otherwise);

   (ii) it is signed (and "signed" includes making one's mark) either (a) by the maker in the presence of a witness who attests the signature or (b) at the maker's direction and in his presence and the presence of two witnesses who each attest the signature; and

   (iii) it is 'delivered' as a deed by him or his agent. ("Delivery" includes any act done by the maker which indicates that he considers the deed to be binding).

Where a regime of contract law expands and refines its doctrines so that it has an array of means to regulate transactional unfairness or inappropriate contractualisation of a relationship, it will become less reliant on a broad sweep doctrine of consideration. Accordingly, the general trajectory of the English law of contract is to become more relaxed about the requirement of consideration. Formally, without consideration there will be no contract (unless a deed has been used); but, in practice, if commercial contractors believe that they have a deal, their expectations will rarely be defeated purely on the technical ground of a lack of consideration.

The chapter is divided into four sections. In the first section, there is some food for thought about the purpose and function of the consideration requirement, about whether the underlying model of an exchange can be reduced to mutual benefit and detriment, and so on. In the second section, the focus is mainly on the question of whether acts or services that have been provided in the past can be recognised as valid consideration for a promise that is made today. One way of expressing this question is to ask whether so-called "past consideration" is "sufficient"; and, in the third section of the chapter, having dealt with whether consideration need be "adequate" (for example, whether the price paid need be fair and reasonable or the bargain "balanced"), the case-law concerning the "sufficiency'" of particular promises or acts is reviewed. It is in this third section that we meet the question of whether a promise to perform an existing obligation is sufficient to qualify as valid consideration. This question can arise in a number of different contexts, one of which is that in which A promises to pay B an additional sum, over and above the agreed contract price, for the work as specified by the contract to be done. On the face of it, A is gifting B the additional sum; and, even if B promises to do the work in return for the additional sum, it seems to lack the traditional features of sufficient consideration because B gets something for nothing. On the other hand, if A freely agrees to pay the additional sum and sees some practical advantage in the arrangement, why should a strict requirement of consideration stand in the way of treating the transaction as a contract (or as a binding variation of the original contract)? These were the kind of issues debated in the landmark case of *Williams v Roffey Bros and Nicholls (Contractors) Ltd*—a case that, in many ways, marks a watershed between the traditional law of contract and the modern law. Finally, in the fourth section, the cases engage with the vexed question of whether a creditor's promise to accept a lesser sum in settlement of a debt can ever be more than a non-binding gratuitous promise—or, viewing this from the debtor's side, whether the debtor's payment of the lesser sum can be treated as sufficient consideration for the creditor's promise.

1. SOME BASIC QUESTIONS CONCERNING CONSIDERATION

Corbin, Does a Pre-existing Duty Defeat Consideration?—Recent Noteworthy Decisions, 27 Yale L.J. 362, 376

In all contract law our problem is to determine what facts will operate to create legal duties and other legal relations. We find at the outset that bare words of promise do not so operate. Our problem then becomes one of determining what facts must accompany promissory words in order to create a legal duty (and other legal relations). We must know what these facts are in order that we can properly predict the enforcement of reparation, either specific or compensatory, in case of non-performance. We are looking for a sufficient cause or reason for the legal enforcement of a promise. This problem was also before the Roman lawyers and it must exist in all systems of law. With us it is called the problem of consideration.

10–002

C. J. Hamson, The Reform of Consideration (1938) 54 L.Q.R. 233, 234, 242

What is today the significance of consideration in the law of simple contract? So far from being an additional and unnecessary mystery, an accidental tom-tit in an otherwise rational theory of contract, consideration in its essential nature is an aspect merely of the fundamental notion of bargain, other aspects of which, no less but no more important, are offer and acceptance. Consideration, offer and acceptance are an indivisible trinity, facets of one identical notion which is that of bargain. Indeed, consideration may conveniently be explained as merely the acceptance viewed from the offeror's side. Acceptance is defined to be the doing of that act (which may be the giving of a promise or the rendering of a performance) which is requested by the offeror in exchange for his promise; it is the response to the offer. An act done at the request of the offeror in response to his promise is consideration; and consideration in its essence is nothing else but response to such a request. To a gratuitous promise the common law notion of offer and acceptance does not apply. We can no doubt separate offer, acceptance and consideration for our convenience in treating of them: but they are logical and interdependent entities abstracted from the one entire reality which is bargain. We can no more abolish one without destroying the others than we can think of a circle without a circumference . . . .

10–003

If it were clear when a party has formed an intention to incur legal obligation, if a person did commonly define the obligation he desired to assume in terms which left little doubt as to its nature, it would be unnecessary, and indeed merely foolish, to require an additional test of that intention. It is because persons commonly do not so define their intention, and because the common law recognises that fact, that the common law requires a test. To dismiss the doctrine of consideration as not worth serious attention because "it came into being not as an essential part of a theory of the law of contract but more or less fortuitously as an expedient adopted in order to determine when persons injured by the breach of a promise ought to be allowed to bring an action" (paragraph 18 of the 6th interim report of the Law Revision Committee 1937 Cmd. 5449) is, to my mind, to misunderstand what is an essential part of a practical law of contract.

P. S. Atiyah, Consideration in Contracts (1971)

. . . to talk of abolition of the doctrine of consideration is nonsensical. Consideration means a reason for the enforcement of a promise. Nobody can seriously propose that all promises should become enforceable; to abolish the doctrine of consideration, therefore, is simply to require the Courts to begin all over again the task of deciding what promises are to be enforceable. They will, of course, have to set new technical justifications for this task, and the obvious one that lies to hand is the "intent to create legal relations." No doubt there is something to be said for beginning this task all over again, and for using a new technique for the purpose. Changes in social and commercial conditions, and changes in the moral values of the community, mean that the Courts will not always find the same reasons for the enforcement of promises to be good today as their forbears did; equally it is likely that they will often find good reasons for the enforcement of promises where their predecessors did not. Moreover, I think there is less likelihood of the "intent to create legal relations" formula ossifying into a "doctrine"; though there is the converse danger that its application may create uncertainty as to what promises will be enforceable. But I question whether the "intent to create legal relations" formula will in the long run work any better than the rules of consideration.

10–004

The Principles of European Contract Law, 1998 art.2:101: Conditions for the Conclusion of a Contract

10–005
(1) A contract is concluded if:
    (a) the parties intend to be legally bound, and
    (b) they reach a sufficient agreement

without any further requirement.

(2) A contract need not be concluded or evidenced in writing nor is it subject to any other requirement as to form. The contact may be proved by any means, including witnesses.

Pollock, Principles of Contract (13th ed.), p.133

The following description of Consideration was given by the Exchequer Chamber in 1875: "A valuable consideration, in the sense of the law, may consist either in some right, interest, profit, or benefit accruing to the one party, or some forbearance, detriment, loss, or responsibility, given, suffered, or undertaken by the other": *Currie v Misa* (1875) L.R. 10 Ex. at 162.

The second branch of this judicial description is really the more important one. Consideration means not so much that one party is profited as that the other abandons some legal right in the present, or limits his legal freedom of action in the future, as an inducement for the promise of the first. It does not matter whether the party accepting the consideration has any apparent benefit thereby or not: it is enough that he accepts it, and that the party giving it does thereby undertake some burden, or lose something which in contemplation of law may be of value.

An act or forbearance of the one party, or the promise thereof, is the price for which the promise of the other is bought, and the promise thus given for value is enforceable. [Words adopted by Lord Dunedin in *Dunlop v Selfridge*, below, para.12–004.]

J. C. Smith, The Law of Contract—Alive or Dead? 13, The Law Teacher (1979), 73, 77

10–006
The language of benefit and detriment is, and I believe long has been, out of date. So is the idea that consideration must be an economic benefit of some kind. All that is necessary is that the defendant should, expressly or impliedly, ask for something in return for his promise, an act or a promise by the offeree. If he gets what he has asked for, then the promise is given for consideration unless there is some vitiating factor. Though lip-service has been paid to the notions of benefit and detriment, they have no substantial meaning, in the light of the principle that the court will not inquire into the adequacy of the consideration. If I make a promise to you in return for your supplying me with three, quite useless, chocolate wrappers, which I will instantly throw away, there is a perfectly good contract provided that the promise was seriously intended [below, para.10–026.] I have got what I asked for and that is a sufficient "benefit". You have parted with something that you might have kept and that is a sufficient "detriment." But the wrappers are of no value to me, and you are perhaps glad to be rid of them. As for economic value, the judges have recognised, for over a century, the validity of the contract to pay £100 if the promisee will walk to York (a famous example given by Brett J. in *Great Northern Rly. v Witham* (1873) L.R.9C.P 16); and no one has ever demonstrated what economic value there is in walking to York. Similarly with promises of reward for not smoking; (*Hamer v Sidway* 27 N.E. 256; 124 N.Y. 538, 1891) or by the father of an illegitimate child to pay the mother an allowance if she proves to him that the child is well looked after and happy [below, para.10–047].

The Principles of European Contract Law, 1998, Art. 2:107: Promises binding without acceptance

10–007
A promise which is intended to be legally binding without acceptance is binding.

Problem

10–008
Uncle, hearing of nephew's success in the GCSE, writes: "I know that you intend to go to the University and I promise that I will pay all your fees. No reply required." Two years later when nephew gets the required grades at A level, Uncle writes: "Sorry, times are hard. I have changed my mind about paying your fees." How would we decide whether Uncle intended his promise to be legally binding? Should such a promise be legally binding?

Points for reflection

A number of authorities suggest that a promise to pay money, or to do any other act, in a certain event **10–009** but without any express or implied request to the promisee to bring about, or to promise to bring about, that event, is made without consideration. In *Dickinson v Abel* [1969] 1 W.L.R. 295; [1969] 1 All E.R. 484, W told A that he was willing to pay £100,000 for a certain farm. A had no proprietary interest in the farm but had transmitted earlier offers for it to the bank who were trustees of it. A asked 'What's in it for me?' and was told that he would receive £10,000 if W bought it for £100,000 or less. W did not specify any service to be rendered by A and A did not know what was in W's mind. The sale took place and A received £10,000. It was held that it was not taxable because it was not paid under an enforceable contract. Pennycuick J found that there was no implied request for any service or promise of service (for example, to use his best endeavours to persuade the bank to sell at £100,000 or to act as a go-between—cf. the putting in touch with X in *British Bank for Foreign Trade v Novinex* (above, Ch.4)). The judge obviously thought that A had told a tall story, but he had to accept the facts in the Case Stated by the Crown.

A similar problem provoked a difference of judicial opinion in *Wyatt v Kreglinger and Fernau* [1933] 1 K.B. 793. The defendant firm lawfully terminated the employment of the plaintiff who had worked for them for many years. The plaintiff had no right to any pension. The defendants wrote to him and told him that they had decided to pay him a pension of £200 a year and that he was at liberty to enter into any other employment or enter any business, "except in the wool trade." The plaintiff did not enter the wool trade but after nine years the defendants stopped the pension. The plaintiff claimed that they were bound by contract to continue the pension. All the judges in the Court of Appeal were agreed that, if there was a contract, it was illegal as being in restraint of trade. Scrutton L.J., agreeing with the trial judge, Macnaghten J, thought there was no contract. The pension was a voluntary gratuitous payment and the words "except in the wool trade" were merely an intimation to Mr Wyatt that if he did enter the wool trade he must not expect them to continue the pension. Slesser and Greer LJJ thought that there was a contract but that it was illegal as being in restraint of trade.

If a gratuitous unconditional promise is revocable should it become irrevocable because a condition is added? Suppose that D promises his widowed or divorced daughter-in-law, P, to pay her £5,000 a year. Could he not withdraw the promise on finding himself in straitened circumstances, or on falling out with P, or because she had married a wealthy man? Suppose then that D's promise is to pay the money 'so long as you remain unmarried.' Is this merely a definition of the limits of a gratuitous promise (as in *Thomas v Thomas*, infra) or is it an offer to contract, the consideration being P's forbearance from marriage? Might it be different if D, on hearing of P's intention to remarry, were to say, "Please do not remarry. I will pay you £5,000 a year so long as you remain unmarried." In this case D is clearly asking a price for his promise but is he in the former case?

Is there a difference between requesting an act and specifying an act to be done in return for the promise? Or are these two ways of describing the same thing? See Atiyah, *Consideration in Contracts*, pp.33–34.

Problems

1. William is very worried as to whether he will pass his solicitor's final examination which he has **10–010** already failed twice. In order to allay his anxiety his father says, "If you fail again I will take you into my book-binding business as a partner." William fails again. His father now refuses to give him the partnership. Advise William.

Would your answer be different if William's father had said, "If you pass the examination I will take you, etc.?"

(See Smith, 'Unilateral Contracts and Consideration' (1953) 69 L.Q.R. 102; and cf. F. H. Lawson, 'Analogues of the Stipulatio in English Law' *XXth Century Comparative and Conflicts Law*, p.117 and following).

2. In what circumstances, if any, would a contract arise in either of the following situations:
    (a) A, who has a new Rolls-Royce car, says to B, "I will give you my car if you fetch it from the garage."
    (b) A, who has an ancient and dilapidated Rolls-Royce immobilised in his garage says to B, "I will give you my car if you fetch it from the garage"?

----

2. CONSIDERATION—EXECUTED, EXECUTORY AND PAST

THOMAS v THOMAS

Queen's Bench (1842) 2 Q.B. 851; 2 G & D. 226; 11 L.J.Q.B. 104; 6 Jur. 645; 114 E.R. 330

10–011 The plaintiff, the widow of John Thomas, sued the defendants, his executors, for breach of a written agreement to convey to her a cottage. The agreement recited that John had left all his estate to his executors by his will but that, shortly before his death, he had declared in the presence of several witnesses that he wished his widow to have the cottage for her life or so long as she continued a widow; and that, though this wish was never put into writing, the executors were convinced that it was his desire and were willing and desirous that it should be put into effect. The agreement stated that "in consideration of such desire" the executors would convey the cottage to the widow for her life or so long as she should continue a widow. It was provided and further agreed that the widow would pay to the executors "the sum of £1 yearly, towards the ground-rent, payable in respect of the said dwelling house," and would keep it in good repair.

   The executors refused to convey the cottage. A jury awarded the widow £100 damages and the Queen's Bench discharged a rule to enter a non-suit.

PATTESON J

The cause for the gift was unquestionably respect for the memory of the testator. But we must not confound motive with consideration. A consideration, such as is recognised and known to our law, means a consideration of some value, moving from the plaintiff. Mere respect for the memory and wishes of a testator cannot be in any way construed as such. It is then argued, that, this being so, there is no consideration for the agreement at all, and that it is an agreement for a voluntary gift on certain conditions; but, looking at the agreement, we find, not a mere proviso, but an express agreement by the plaintiff to pay £1 towards a certain ground-rent, which apparently has been for the first time apportioned, and to pay it to the defendant, who is, I presume, liable to the whole ground-rent. It is not, therefore, a burden incident to the taking of the lease; if it were, it would be to pay to the superior landlord. Then again, as to the repairs: it may be that the original lease from the ground landlord contained covenants compelling repairs to be made by the lessee; but we know nothing of such a lease or such covenants. For anything we know, it is an agreement entered into for the first time, in consequence of this instrument . . .

Questions

1. What was the consideration to support the defendant's promise: (a) expressed in the agreement? (b) found by the court?

2. What promise, express or implied, was made by the plaintiff?

3. Both Lord Denman CJ and Patteson J emphasise the need to distinguish between consideration and the motive which induces entry into a contract. Is not the price which one party is to receive for his undertaking a motive for his entry into the contract with the other party?

10–012

Point for reflection

The court assumes that, if the ground-rent was "a burden incident to the taking of the lease" or (Lord Denman CJ) "a necessary burden on the premises", the plaintiff's promise to pay it would not have been a sufficient consideration: a promise to make a gift of onerous property is still a mere promise to make a gift, though the promisee agrees to assume the burden. However, this is questionable. In *Price v Jenkins* (1877) 5 Ch.D. 619 CA, which was followed in *Johnsey Estates Ltd v Lewis & Manley (Engineering) Ltd* (1987) 54 P. & C.R. 296, it was held that a settlement of leasehold property was a conveyance for valuable consideration because the donee would have to undertake payment of the rent and performance of the covenants. James LJ asked, "Can an assignment of leasehold property ever be strictly speaking voluntary?" In *Cheale v Kenward* (1858) 27 L.J. Ch. 784 it was held that a promise to transfer shares in a company on which no deposit or other sum had been paid was made for consideration when the transferee agreed to do all acts necessary to relieve the transferor of liability in respect of the shares. And cf. *Merritt v Merritt*, above, Ch.9.

10–013

Question

Uncle says to nephew: "I intend to give you my shares in the Super Company on your twenty-first birthday. They are worth about a million. You will have to pay calls of about £500. Will you accept them?" Nephew replies with alacrity that he will. Has Uncle contracted to transfer the shares? If he does transfer them, has he made a gift or performed a contract?

10–014

LAMPLEIGH v BRATHWAIT

Common Bench (1615) Hob. 105; Moore K. B. 866; 1 Sm. L.C. (13th edn) 148; 80 E.R. 255

In assumpsit in the Common Bench, it was alleged that Brathwait, having killed a man, asked the plaintiff to use his endeavours to obtain him a pardon, wherefore the plaintiff did go to Royston to the King to get the pardon and, in consideration of this service, the defendant promised the plaintiff £100. To this declaration, it was demurred that the consideration was executed before the promise was made . . . Nicols, Winch and Hobart held that the action was well laid because it was alleged that there was a request before the endeavour was made and where there is such a precedent request, a subsequent assumpsit after the execution of the consideration is binding.

10–015

First it was agreed, that a mere voluntary curtesy will not have a consideration to uphold an assumpsit. But if that curtesy were moved by a suit or request of the party that gives the assumpsit, it will bind, for the promise, though it follows, yet it is not naked, but couples itself with the suit before, and the merits of the party procured by that suit, which is the difference.

(A second point, upon which Warburton J. based a dissenting judgment is omitted.)

Question

10–016   In *Kennedy v Broun* (1863) 13 C.B. 677 (Common Pleas) Erle CJ said that in *Lampleigh v Brathwait* "it was assumed that the journeys which the plaintiff performed at the request of the defendant, and the other services he rendered, would have been sufficient to make any promise binding if it had been connected therewith in one contract; the peculiarity of the decision lies in connecting a subsequent promise with a prior consideration after it had been executed. Probably, at the present day [i.e. in the mid nineteenth century], such service on such request would have raised a promise by implication to pay what it was worth; and the subsequent promise of a sum certain would have been evidence for the jury to fix the amount." What would be the implication in the twenty-first century? Or, does this question need a particular context before it can be answered?

Re CASEY'S PATENTS, STEWART v CASEY

Court of Appeal [1892] 1 Ch. 104; 61 L.J. Ch. 61; 66 L.T. 93; 40 W.R. 180

10–017   J Stewart and T Charlton wrote to the defendant, Casey, the following letter:

"Stewart and Charlton's Patents

Dear Sir,

We now have pleasure in stating that in consideration of your services as the practical manager in working both our patents as above for transit by steamer or for any land purposes, we hereby agree to give you one third share of the patents above-mentioned, the same to take effect from this date. This is in addition to and in combination with our agreement of the 29th November last."

They later transferred the letters patent to Casey during some negotiations which eventually came to nothing. After the death of Stewart, the present plaintiffs—his executor and Charlton—asked Casey to return the letters patent: Casey refused, claiming to be entitled to possession as owner of a third share, and registered the letter set out above.

In the present action, the plaintiffs claimed delivery up of the letters patent and damages for their detention. Romer J dismissed the action and his judgment was affirmed by the Court of Appeal (Lindley, Bowen and Fry LJJ).

Inter alia, it was argued before the Court of Appeal that there was no assignment of a share to Casey because there was no consideration for the agreement contained in the letter.

BOWEN LJ

. . . But then it was said by Mr Daniel, "But there is no consideration, and this document is not under seal." We will see if there is consideration. The consideration is stated, such as it is. It is, "in consideration of your services as the practical manager in working our patents as above for transit by steamer." Then says Mr Daniel, "Yes, but that is a future consideration and a future consideration, if nothing were done under it or nothing was proved to be done, would fail." The answer to that is that the consideration is not the rendering of the services, as is plain from the fact that the document is to take effect in Equity from the date. The consideration must be something other than rendering services in the future. It is the promise to render them which those words imply, that constitutes the consideration; and the promise to render future services, if an effectual promise, is certainly good consideration. Then, driven from that, Mr Daniel said, "Oh! but it is past services that it means, and past services are not a consideration for anything." Well, that raises the old question—or might raise it, if there was not an answer to it—of *Lampleigh v Brathwait* [above], a subject of great interest to every scientific lawyer, as to whether a past service will support a promise. I do not propose to discuss that question, or, perhaps, I should not have finished this week. I should have to examine the whole state of the law as to, and the history of the subject of, consideration, which, I need hardly say, I do not propose to do. But the answer to Mr Daniel's point is clear. Even if it were true, as some scientific students of law believe, that a past service cannot support a future promise, you must look at the document and see if the promise cannot receive a proper effect in some other way. Now, the fact of a past service raises an implication that at the time it was rendered it was to be paid for, and, if it was a service which was to be paid for, when you get in the subsequent document a promise to pay, that promise may be treated either as an admission which evidences or as a positive bargain which fixes the amount of that reasonable remuneration on the faith of which the service was originally rendered. So that here for past services there is ample justification for the promise to give the third share. Therefore, this is an equitable assignment which cannot be impeached.

Questions

1. Would every "past service" raise an implication that it was to be paid for, so as to allow action on a subsequent promise of payment?   **10–018**

2. (a) What is the difference between
   (i) a promise which evidences the amount of payment and
   (ii) a positive bargain which fixes the amount of reasonable remuneration?

   (b) A does services for B for which a reasonable remuneration would be £100.
   (i) Without discussion, B promises to give A £500 for his services;
   (ii) A demands £500, B offers £100. A says he will accept £250. B agrees to pay £250.

Consider the consequences in each case, if B should subsequently refuse to give A the money.

Point for reflection

The principles of *Lampleigh v Brathwait* as interpreted in *Re Casey's Patents* were applied by the Privy Council in *Pao On v Lau Yiu Long* [1980] A.C. 614, below. Lord Scarman said: **10–019**

"An act done before the giving of a promise to make a payment or to confer some other benefit can sometimes be consideration for the promise. The act must have been done at the promisors' request: the parties must have understood that the act was to be remunerated either by a payment or the conferment of some other benefit: and payment, or the conferment of a benefit, must have been legally enforceable had it been promised in advance. All three features are present in this case . . .

Their Lordships agree that the mere existence or recital of a prior request is not sufficient in itself to convert what is prima facie past consideration into sufficient consideration in law to support a promise, as they have indicated, it is only the first of three necessary preconditions. As for the second of those preconditions, whether the act done at the request of the promisor raises an implication of promised remuneration or other return is simply one of the construction of the words of the contract in the circumstances of its making."

The Board held that, on the somewhat complex facts of the particular case, it mattered not whether the subsequent promise was regarded as the best evidence of the benefit intended to be conferred or as the positive bargain, the benefit on the faith of which the promise was given.

ROSCORLA v THOMAS

Queen's Bench (1842) 3 Q.B. 234; 2 G. & D. 508; 11 L.J.Q.B. 214; 6 Jur. 929; 61 R.R. 216; 114 E.R. 496

10–020 The relevant facts appear in the judgment of the court delivered by Lord Denman CJ:

LORD DENMAN CJ

This was an action of assumpsit for breach of warranty of the soundness of a horse. The first count of the declaration, upon which alone the question arises, stated that, in consideration that the plaintiff, at the request of the defendant, had bought of the defendant a horse for the sum of £30, the defendant promised that it was sound and free from vice. And it was objected, in arrest of judgment, that the precedent executed consideration was insufficient to support the subsequent promise. And we are of opinion that the objection must prevail.

It may be taken as a general rule, subject to exceptions, not applicable to this case, that the promise must be co-extensive with the consideration. In the present case, the only promise that would result from the consideration, as stated, and be co-extensive with it, would be to deliver the horse upon request. The precedent sale, without a warranty, though at the request of the defendant, imposes no other duty or obligation upon him. It is clear, therefore, that the consideration stated would not raise an implied promise by the defendant that the horse was sound or free from vice.

But the promise in the present case must be taken to be, as in fact it was, express: and the question is, whether that fact will warrant the extension of the promise beyond that which would be implied by law; and whether the consideration, though insufficient to raise an implied promise, will nevertheless support an express one. And we think that it will not.

The cases in which it has been held that, under certain circumstances, a consideration insufficient to raise an implied promise will nevertheless support an express one, will be found collected and reviewed in the note (a) to *Wennall v Adney* (3 Bos. & Pul. 249), and in the case of *Eastwood v Kenyon* (1840) 11 Ad. & E. 438). There are cases of voidable contracts subsequently ratified, of debts barred by operation of law, subsequently revived, and of equitable and moral obligations, which, but for some rule of law, would of themselves have been sufficient to raise an implied promise. All these cases are distinguishable from, and indeed, inapplicable to, the present, which appears to us to fall within the general rule, that a consideration past and executed will support no other promise than such as would be implied by law.

The rule for arresting the judgment upon the first count must therefore be made absolute.

Rule Absolute.

Question

10–021 If the precedent sale was at the request of the defendant, who later made the express promise of the guarantee, why should not the guarantee have been enforceable under *Lampleigh v Brathwait*?

Law Reform Committee, 6th Interim Report, para.32

The inconvenience of this rule (sc. that past consideration is no consideration) is frequently evaded by means of the fiction that the promise made subsequent to the consideration merely fixes the amount due under an earlier promise deemed to exist contemporaneously with the consideration. In a very important class of case, namely, actions upon cheques and other bills of exchange, the rule does not apply and we can see no reason why it should apply at all. The fact that the promisor has already received consideration for his promise before he makes it, so far from enabling him to break his promise seems to us to form an additional reason for making him keep it. We therefore recommend the abolition of this rule.

Question

10–022 What is meant here by "past consideration"? (See Hamson, 54 L.Q.R. 233, 251–253.)

BILLS OF EXCHANGE ACT 1882

27—(1).   Valuable consideration for a bill may be constituted by:

    (a) Any consideration sufficient to support a simple contract;

    (b) An antecedent debt or liability. Such a debt or liability is deemed valuable consideration whether the bill is payable on demand or at a future time.

  (2) Where value has at any time been given for a bill the holder is deemed to be a holder for value as regards the acceptor and all parties to the bill who became parties prior to such time.

  (3) Where the holder of a bill has a lien on it arising either from contract or by implication of law, he is deemed to be a holder for value to the extent of the sum for which he has a lien.

30—(1).   Every party whose signature appears on a bill is prima facie deemed to have become a party thereto for value.

10–023

(The limited nature of the exception created by s.27(1)(b) should be noted. In *Thoni Gesellschaft v RTP Eqpt* [1979] 2 Lloyd's Rep. 282 CA, a bill for one million Austrian schillings was given by a debtor to his creditor. Only 400,000 schillings were actually due. It was held that the creditor could recover only 400,000.)

----

3. ADEQUACY AND SUFFICIENCY OF CONSIDERATION

If the promisor gets what he asks for in return for his promise, he has received consideration and is bound. It is immaterial that his promise is far more valuable than the price he has asked for it. The courts are generally concerned only with the question whether the promisor has made a bargain, not with whether he has made a good or a bad bargain. They will not inquire into the adequacy of the consideration he has asked for and received. See *Mountford v Scott*, above, Ch.3, *Centrovincial Estates Plc v Merchant Investors*, above, Ch.5, and *Thomas v Thomas* above.

10–024

There are, however, certain promises and acts which, for various reasons of policy, are deemed to be of no value in law and which are therefore an insufficient consideration. Hence the curious but traditional terminology of the law—the consideration need not be adequate but must be sufficient (or real). If the law deems a promise to be void, it is not sufficient consideration. A wife's promise not to go to court to seek maintenance from her estranged husband was deemed to be void as being contrary to public policy and, consequently, the husband's promise to pay her money in consideration of her agreeing not to go to court was made without consideration and also void: *Gaisberg v Storr* [1950] 1 K.B. 107, but see, now, Matrimonial Causes Act 1973 s.34, below. The doing of an act which there is a public duty to do—for example, attendance as a witness in response to a subpoena has similarly been held to have no value in the law and to be insufficient consideration for a promise made in return for the doing of it. A New Zealand court held that an undertaking by the government not to introduce legislation regarding the advertising of cigarettes was incapable of being consideration for a promise by a tobacco company because the government's promise was of no value: it could not fetter the legislature: *Rothmans of Pall Mall (NZ) Ltd v Attorney General* [1991] N.Z.L.R. 323.

There are exceptions to the rule that the court will not inquire into the adequacy of the consideration. These apply in some contracts made by minors and generally where because of a special relationship, one party is able to take unfair advantage of another. Cf. *Thorne v Motor Trade Association*, below.

A. Adequacy of Consideration

BAINBRIDGE v FIRMSTONE

Queen's Bench (1838) 1 P. & D. 2; 8 Ad. & El. 743; 1 W.W. & H. 600; 53 R.R. 234; 112 E.R. 1019

10-025   Assumpsit. The declaration stated that, whereas heretofore, to wit, etc., in consideration that the plaintiff, at the request of the defendant, had then consented to allow the defendant to weigh divers, to wit two, boilers of the plaintiff, of great value, etc., defendant promised that he would, within a reasonable time after the said weighing was effected, leave and give up the boilers in as perfect and complete a condition, and as fit for use by plaintiff, as the same were in at the time of the consent so given by plaintiff; and that, although in pursuance of the consent so given, defendant to wit, on, etc., did weigh the same boilers, yet defendant did not nor would, within a reasonable time after the said weighing was effected, leave and give up boilers in as perfect, etc., but wholly neglected and refused so to do, although a reasonable time for that purpose had elapsed before the commencement of this suit; and, on the contrary thereof, defendant afterwards, to wit on, etc., took the said boilers to pieces and did not put the same together again, but left the same in a detached and divided condition, and in many different pieces, whereby plaintiff hath been put to great trouble, etc. Plea, non assumpsit.

On the trial before Lord Denman CJ at the London sittings after last Trinity term, a verdict was found for the plaintiff.

John Bayley now moved in arrest of judgment. The declaration shows no consideration. There should have been either detriment to the plaintiff, or benefit to the defendant: 1 Selwyn's N. P. 45 (9th edn). It does not appear that the defendant was to receive any remuneration. Besides, the word "weigh" is ambiguous.

LORD DENMAN CJ

It seems to me that the declaration is well enough. The defendant had some reason for wishing to weigh the boilers; and he could do so only by obtaining permission from the plaintiff, which he did obtain by promising to return them in good condition. We need not inquire what benefit he expected to derive. The plaintiff might have given or refused leave.

PATTESON J

The consideration is, that the plaintiff, at the defendant's request, had consented to allow the defendant to weigh the boilers. I suppose the defendant thought he had some benefit; at any rate, there is a detriment to the plaintiff from his parting with the possession for even so short a time.

Williams and Coleridge JJ. concurred.

Rule Refused.

CHAPPELL & CO LTD v NESTLé CO LTD

House of Lords [1960] A.C. 87; [1959] 3 W.L.R. 168; [1959] 2 All E.R. 701; 103 S.J. 561

10-026   Nestlé Co entered into a contract with the Hardy Co, manufacturers of gramophone records, to purchase a number of recordings of a piece of music, "Rockin' Shoes," the copyright of which was vested in Chappell & Co The Hardy Co supplied the records to Nestlé Co for 4d. each. Nestlé Co advertised to the public that the records could be obtained from Nestlé Co for 1s. 6d. each together with three wrappers from Nestlé's 6d. milk chocolate bars. The wrappers when received were thrown away.

Section 8(1) of the Copyright Act 1956 permits a person to make a record of a musical work for the purpose of its being sold retail, if he gives notice to the owner of the copyright and pays him a royalty of 61/4 per cent of "the ordinary retail selling price." The Hardy Co gave notice of their intention to manufacture stating 1s. 6d. to be the ordinary retail selling price and offered to pay Chappell & Co royalties thereon, which Chappell and Co refused.

Chappell & Co sought an injunction restraining Nestlé & Co and the Hardy Co from manufacturing the records on the ground that the transaction involved breaches of copyright. Upjohn J granted an order restraining the defendants from infringing Chappell & Co's copyright. This decision was reversed by the Court of Appeal (Jenkins and Ormerod LJJ, Romer LJ dissenting). Chappell & Co now appealed to the House of Lords.

VISCOUNT SIMONDS (DISSENTING)

It appears to me that, in order to comply with the provisions of section 8 and thus obtain its protection, there are three relevant conditions to be satisfied by the manufacturer of an article which would otherwise be an infringement of copyright. By "relevant conditions" I mean those conditions about which an issue arises in this case. First, there must be a "sale" of the article in question: secondly, the sale must be a "retail sale": thirdly, it must be possible to predicate of it that there is an "ordinary retailing selling price" of it, for if there is not, an essential part of the prescribed notice cannot be given.

Upon the first point I cannot feel any doubt. It had not been contended in the course of the case that there was not a sale, until during the debate in your Lordships' House that suggestion was made, and I think that, beyond doubt, anyone, who in answer to the advertisement acquired a record, would say that he had bought it and would be surprised that any doubt should be cast upon what he regarded as an obvious fact. Whether the consideration or the price that he paid was 1s. 6d. only or 1s. 6d. and three wrappers is a matter not for him but for your Lordships to determine . . .

[His Lordship held that the sale was a "retail" sale.]

In my opinion, my Lords, the wrappers are not part of the selling price. They are admittedly themselves value-less and are thrown away and it was for that reason, no doubt, that Upjohn J. was constrained to say that their value lay in the evidence they afforded of success in an advertising campaign. That is what they are. But what, after all, does that mean? Nothing more than that someone, by no means necessarily the purchaser of the record, has in the past bought not from Nestlé's but from a retail shop three bars of chocolate and that the purchaser has thus directly or indirectly acquired the wrappers. How often he acquires them for himself, how often through another, is pure speculation. The only thing that is certain is that, if he buys bars of chocolate from a retail shop or acquires the wrappers from another who has bought them, that purchase is not, or at the lowest is not necessarily, part of the same transaction as his subsequent purchase of a record from the manu-facturers . . . What can be easier than for a manufacturer to limit his sales to those members of the public who fulfil the qualification of being this or doing that? It may be assumed that the manufacturer's motive is his own advantage. It is possible that he achieves his object. But that does not mean that the sale is not a retail sale to which the section applies or that the ordinary retail selling price is not the price at which the record is ordinarily sold, in this case 1s. 6d. I would dismiss the appeal.

Lord Keith of Avonholme delivered a speech to similar effect.

LORD REID

The manufacturer pays royalty on records which he intends to be sold by retail. Apart from the last purpose set out in condition (c) he is not entitled to make them for any other purpose. And if later someone disposes of a record in some other way no part of the royalty can be recovered.

I can now turn to what appears to me to be the crucial question in this case: was the 1s. 6d. an "ordinary retail selling price" within the meaning of section 8? That involves two questions, what was the nature of the contract between the Nestlé Co and a person who sent 1s. 6d. plus three wrappers in acceptance of their offer, and what is meant by "ordinary retail selling price" in this context.

To determine the nature of the contract one must find the intention of the parties as shown by what they said and did. The Nestlé Co's intention can hardly be in doubt. They were not setting out to trade in gramo-phone records. They were using these records to increase their sales of chocolate. Their offer was addressed to everyone.

It seems to me clear that the main intention of the offer was to induce people interested in this kind of music to buy (or perhaps get others to buy), chocolate which otherwise would not have been bought. It is, of course, true that some wrappers might come from the chocolate which had already been bought or from chocolate which would have been bought without the offer, but that does not seem to me to alter the case. Where there is a large number of transactions—the notice mentions 30,000 records—I do not think we should simply consider an isolated case where it would be impossible to say whether there had been a direct benefit from the acquisition of the wrappers or not. The requirement that wrappers should be sent was of great importance to the Nestlé Co; there would have been no point in their simply offering records for 1s. 6d. each. It seems to me quite unrealistic to divorce the buying of the chocolate from the supplying of the records. It is a perfectly good contract if a person accepts an offer to supply goods if he (a) does something of value to the supplier and (b) pays money: the consideration is both (a) and (b). There may have been cases where the acquisition of the wrappers conferred no direct benefit on the Nestlé Co, but there must have been many cases where it did. I do not see why the possibility that in some cases the acquisition of the wrappers did not directly benefit the Nestlé Co should require us to exclude from consideration the cases where it did. And even where there was no direct benefit from the acquisition of the wrappers there may have been an indirect benefit by way of advertisement.

I do not think that it matters greatly whether this kind of contract is called a sale or not. The appellants did not take the point that this transaction was not a sale. But I am bound to say that I have some doubts. If a contract under which a person is bound to do something as well as pay money is a sale, then either the price includes the obligation as well as the money, or the consideration is the price plus the obligation. And I do not see why it should be different if he has to show that he has done something of value to the seller. It is to my mind illegitimate to argue—this is a sale, the consideration for a sale is the price, price can only include money or something which can be readily converted into an ascertainable sum of money, therefore anything like wrappers which have no money value when delivered cannot be part of the consideration.

The respondents avoid this difficulty by submitting that requiring and delivering the wrappers was merely a condition which gave a qualification to buy and was not part of the consideration for sale. Of course, a person may limit his offer to persons qualified in a particular way, for example, members of a club. But where the qualification is the doing of something of value to the seller, and where the qualification only suffices for one sale and must be reacquired before another sale, I find it hard to regard the repeated acquisitions of the qualification as anything other than parts of the consideration for the sales. The purchaser of records had to send three wrappers for each record, so he had first to acquire them. The acquisition of wrappers by him was, at least in many cases, of direct benefit to the Nestlé Co, and required expenditure by the acquirer which he might not otherwise have incurred. To my mind the acquiring and delivering of the wrappers was certainly part of the consideration in these cases, and I see no good reason for drawing a distinction between these and other cases.

LORD SOMERVELL OF HARROW

My Lords, section 8 of the Copyright Act 1956, provides for a royalty of an amount, subject to a minimum, equal to 61/4 per cent of the ordinary retail selling price of the record. This necessarily implies, in my opinion, that a sale to be within the section must not only be retail, but one in which there is no other consideration for the transfer of property in the record but the money price . . .

The question, then, is whether the three wrappers were part of the consideration or, as Jenkins L.J. held, a condition of making the purchase, like a ticket entitling a member to buy at a co-operative store.

I think they are part of the consideration. They are so described in the offer. "They," the wrappers, "will help you to get smash hit recordings." They are so described in the record itself—all you have to do to get such new record is to send three wrappers from Nestlé's 6d. milk chocolate bars, together with postal order for 1s. 6d." This is not conclusive but, however described, they are, in my view, in law part of the consideration. It is said that when received the wrappers are of no value to Nestlé's. This I would have thought irrelevant. A contracting party can stipulate for what consideration he chooses. A peppercorn does not cease to be good consideration if it is established that the promisee does not like pepper and will throw away the corn. As the whole object of selling the record, if it was a sale, was to increase the sales of chocolate, it seems to me wrong not to treat the stipulated evidence of such sales as part of the consideration. For these reasons I would allow the appeal.

Lord Tucker delivered a speech allowing the appeal.

Appeal Allowed.

Questions

1. Suppose that the advertisement had run, "Yours for 1s. 6d.—'Rockin' Shoes'. Offer open only to 'members', that is, people who have bought three Nestlé bars. To prove you qualify, send three wrappers with your money." Would this be a condition or would the wrappers still constitute part of the consideration? (Cf. Wedderburn, 1959 CLJ 160.)   **10–027**

2. Would there have been a contract to supply a record if the advertisement had asked only for three wrappers and no money?

In *De La Bere v Pearson, Ltd* [1908] 1 K.B. 280, the defendants, owners of a newspaper, carried an advertisement in each issue informing readers who wanted financial advice to write to a given address. The plaintiff wrote for such advice and also for the name of a 'good stockbroker.' The editor passed the letter to a person whom he knew to be an 'outside broker' (one who does Stock Exchange business but is not a member of the Exchange) but whose honesty he had no reason to suspect. This person was in fact an undischarged bankrupt who wrote to the plaintiff as being recommended by the editor and who misappropriated the funds sent to him by the plaintiff for investment. The plaintiff sued the defendants for breach of contract to exercise due care in giving him financial advice. The Court of Appeal (Vaughan Williams LJ, Gorell Barnes P, and Bigham J) affirmed the decision of Lord Alverstone CJ in favour of the plaintiff. In *Hedley Byrne & Co v Heller & Partners* Lord Devlin said of this case: "I think that today the result can and should be achieved by the application of the law of negligence . . . I agree with Sir Frederick Pollock's note on the case of *De La Bere v Pearson, Ltd* when he wrote in Pollock on Contracts (13th edn), 140 (n.31) that 'the cause of action is better regarded as arising from default in the performance of a voluntary undertaking independent of contract.'" See further below, Ch.14.

Problem

Suppose that a newspaper advertises: "We want letters (which we may publish) from readers seeking advice; and we undertake that, if we give advice, we will exercise all proper care." Is it in any way artificial or unrealistic to regard that as an offer of a contract? But should such an undertaking be implied from a mere invitation to the reader to seek advice?   **10–028**

B. Forbearance as Consideration

WHITE v BLUETT

Exchequer (1853) 23 L.J.Ex. 36; 2 C.L.R. 301; 2 W.R. 75

John Bluett had received a promissory note from his son, William, the present defendant, in respect of money lent by him to William. The present action was brought by John's executor, the declaration containing a count on the promissory note and a count for money lent.   **10–029**

Plea that the note was given to secure the loan; that, subsequent to the loan and the giving of the note, the defendant had complained to John Bluett that he had not received equal favourable treatment with John Bluett's other children; that John Bluett had conceded the truth of these complaints and agreed with the defendant that, in consideration that the defendant should cease his complaints and also out of his natural love and affection for the defendant, he would discharge the defendant from all liability in respect of the loan and the note.

The plaintiff demurred that there was no consideration for the agreement between the deceased and the defendant.

T. J. Clark for the defendant argued that the adequacy of consideration is not to be investigated; that the defendant had a right to complain and that promising to forgo that right constituted good consideration.

POLLOCK CB

The plea is clearly bad. By the argument a principle is pressed to an absurdity, as a bubble is blown until it bursts. Looking at the words merely, there is some foundation for the argument, and, following the words only, the conclusion may be arrived at. It is said, the son had a right to an equal distribution of his father's property, and did complain to his father because he had not had an equal share, and said to him, I will cease to complain if you will not sue upon this note. Whereupon the father said, if you will promise me not to complain I will give up the note. If such a plea as this could be supported, the following would be a binding promise: A man might complain that another person used the public highway more than he ought to do, and that other might say, do not complain, and I will give you five pounds. It is ridiculous to suppose that such promises could be binding. So, if the holder of a bill of exchange were suing the acceptor, and the acceptor were to complain that the holder had treated him hardly, or that the bill ought never to have been circulated, and the holder were to say, Now, if you will not make any more complaints, I will not sue you. Such a promise would be like that now set up. In reality, there was no consideration whatever. The son had no right to complain for the father might make what distribution of his property he liked; and the son's abstaining from doing what he had no right to do can be no consideration.

ALDERSON B

If this agreement were good, there could be no such thing as a nudum pactum. There is a consideration on one side, and it is said the consideration on the other is the agreement itself: if that were so there could never be a nudum pactum.

Judgment for Plaintiff.

(The judgment of Parke B. is omitted; Platt B. concurred.)

Questions

10–030
1. Was it true to say that the son "had no right to complain"? Did he commit any legal wrong by complaining? Why should not his giving up his liberty to complain be consideration? Is it any different from giving up a liberty to smoke? Cf. *Hamer v Sidway*, above. But could refraining, or a promise to refrain, from smoking cannabis be sufficient consideration? (It is an offence under s.5 of the Misuse of Drugs Act 1971 to be in possession of cannabis.) Cf. *Hohfeld, Some Fundamental Legal Conceptions*; Salmond, *Jurisprudence* (12th edn), p.217.

2. Is an agreement by a father, made in consideration that his son will not bore him, a binding contract? (Parke B in the course of argument.)

3. Is an agreement by a husband separately to maintain his wife, if she will not "molest" him, a binding contract?

In *Dunton v Dunton* (1892) 18 V.L.R. 114 (Supreme Court of Victoria), the Court (Higinbotham and Williams JJ, Hood J dissenting) held that an agreement between ex-spouses whereby the former husband undertook to pay the former wife £6 per month, "so long as she . . . shall conduct herself with sobriety, and in a respectable, orderly, and virtuous manner" was a valid contract made for a consideration. Williams J. said, "In effect, (the former husband) says to (the former wife): 'If you, who now owe me no duty as a wife, will agree to my stipulation, I will, so long as you observe that stipulation, pay you £6 per month.' Thereupon she signifies her agreement and her assent to the stipulation by signing the agreement . . . there is sufficient consideration to support the agreement sued upon."

Williston, Selections from Williston on Contracts, §133

. . . courts have not been so strict in denying the validity of consideration where a moral duty was performed, as they have in holding agreements invalid as against public policy where they contemplated a violation of the same duty. In other words, there are differences of degree in immoral conduct; some acts within this category may be classed as immoral liberties, since not specifically punishable by law. Thus, an agreement to get drunk would doubtless be against public policy, but an agreement to refrain from doing so would be sufficient consideration for a return promise. And the same may be said of most other merely moral duties.

THORNE v MOTOR TRADE ASSOCIATION

House of Lords [1937] A.C. 797; 106 L.J.K.B. 495; 157 L.T. 399; 53 T.L.R. 810; [1937] 3 All E.R. 157

The MTA by its constitution had a power to put on a stop list the name of a member or person who infringed its rule forbidding the sale of articles at other than the list prices relevant thereto unless such person should pay to the Association a fine within limits to be laid down by the Council of the Association. This was an action by Thorne, a member of the MTA, against the Association to determine whether a demand of a sum of money in lieu of placing a person's name on the stop list would constitute a demand of money with menaces and without reasonable or probable cause within s.29(1)(i) of the Larceny Act 1916. MacKinnon J found for the defendant and his decision was affirmed by the Court of Appeal (Greer and Greene LJJ, Talbot J). On appeal by the plaintiff to the House of Lords.

10–031

LORD ATKIN

The ordinary blackmailer normally threatens to do what he has a perfect right to do—namely, communicate some compromising conduct to a person whose knowledge is likely to affect the person threatened. Often, indeed, he has not only the right but also the duty to make the disclosure, as of a felony, to the competent authorities. What he has to justify is not the threat, but the demand of money. The gravamen of the charge is the demand without reasonable or probable cause: and I cannot think that the mere fact that the threat is to do something a person is entitled to do either causes the threat not to be a "menace" within the Act or in itself provides a reasonable or probable cause for the demand . . .

It appears to me that if a man may lawfully, in the furtherance of business interests, do acts which will seriously injure another in his business he may also lawfully, if he is still acting in the furtherance of his business interests, offer that other to accept a sum of money as an alternative to doing the injurious acts. He must no doubt be acting not for the mere purpose of putting money in his pocket, but for some legitimate purpose other than the mere acquisition of money . . .

I think that the absence of reasonable or probable cause is in a criminal charge under this subsection a question of fact for the jury. But if the cause is reasonably capable of being associated with the promotion of lawful business interests the judge should not allow the case to go to the jury if there is no evidence of the accused's intention going beyond such lawful business interests . . . I think this appeal should be dismissed with costs.

LORD WRIGHT

I think the jury should be directed by the judge that the respondent Association had a legal right to put the person's name on the stop list, so long as they did so in order to promote the trade interests of the Association and its members and not with intent to injure, and so long as the money, fine or penalty demanded was reasonable and not extortionate.

. . . (T)here are many cases where a man who has a "right," in the sense of a liberty or capacity of doing an act which is not unlawful, but which is calculated seriously to injure another, will be liable to a charge of blackmail if he demands money from that other as the price of abstaining . . . Thus a man may be possessed of knowledge of discreditable incidents in the victim's life and may seek to extort money by threatening, if he is not paid, to disclose the knowledge to a wife or husband or employer, though the disclosure may not be libellous. Such is a common type of blackmail. Cases where the non-disclosure to the proper authority is illegal, as amounting to compounding a felony or a misdemeanour of public import, or where the publication would constitute a public libel, are a fortiori. Again a legal liberty (that is something that a man may do with legal justification) may form the basis of blackmail. Thus a husband who has proof of his wife's adultery, may threaten the paramour that he will petition in the Divorce Court unless he is bought off. Though it is possible that the facts of such a case might show merely the legitimate compromise of a claim to damages, on the other hand, the facts might be such as to constitute extortion and blackmail of a serious type.

Lords Thankerton, Russell of Killowen and Roche also made speeches dismissing the appeal.

Appeal Dismissed.

(It should be noted that this decision followed a conflict of authority between the Court of Appeal and the Court of Criminal Appeal. In the civil case of *Hardie & Lane v Chilton* [1928] 2 K.B. 306, the Court of Appeal had held that a trade association which by its constitution had power to put the name of a person infringing its rules on a stop list, could instead lawfully ask the person concerned to make a money payment by way of compromise. In the Court of Criminal Appeal in *R. v Denyer* [1926] 2 K.B. 258 it had been held that a request for money in such circumstances did constitute an offence under the Larceny Act 1916 s.29(1)(i). In the present case the House of Lords found that *Hardie & Lane v Chilton* was correctly decided but not that a demand for money in lieu of placing on the stop list would be lawful in all circumstances.

The practice, in issue in this case, 'collective resale price maintenance', was invalidated by the Resale Prices Act 1964. See now the Enterprise Act 2002.)

Questions

10–032

1. Where A demands money from B in return for not disclosing B's wrongdoing, A will usually be guilty of blackmail contrary to s.21 of the Theft Act 1968 and, if "the offer" constitutes a crime, it clearly cannot lead to a contract; but what if B, without any demand, express or implied by A, offers A money not to disclose B's wrongdoing, and A accepts? That is not blackmail, or any offence. Is it a contract?

See, generally, Goodhart, 'Blackmail and Consideration in Contracts' 44 L.Q.R. 436.

2. A, a notoriously loose-living man, offers to refrain from publishing his memoirs in a Sunday newspaper, if B will give him £1,000 in recompense for the loss of the fee of £1,000 that he would receive from the newspaper. Consider the validity of the agreement between A and B. Would your answer be different if A asked for £3,000 instead of £1,000?

(Cf. Lord Denning's Report, Cmnd. 2152 of 1963, p.35.)

3. D. Co, who own a chain of multiple stores, agree with E, a private trader, that they will not open a branch in his locality if E will give them £2,500. Consider the validity of the agreement.

4. Does not the court indicate that it is necessary to inquire into the adequacy of the consideration in cases of this type? What principle determines whether a case falls within the category where adequacy of consideration is relevant?

WADE v SIMEON

Common Pleas (1846) 2 C.B. 548; 135 E.R. 1061

Assumpsit. The first count of the declaration stated that the plaintiff had commenced action against the defendant in the Court of Exchequer to recover two sums of £700 and £1,300, respectively, issue had been joined and the hearing was to take place on December 7, 1844; that the defendant, on December 6, 1844, promised the plaintiff that, if he (plaintiff) would forbear prosecuting the proceedings until December 14, the defendant would on that day pay the money with interest and costs; that the plaintiff, relying on this promise, forbore prosecuting the action until the day named but that the defendant did not pay the money or costs. By his fourth plea, the defendant pleaded that the plaintiff never had any cause of action against the defendant in respect of the £2,000, the subject of the Exchequer proceedings, which the plaintiff, at the commencement of that action and thence until and at the time of the making of the alleged promise, well knew. The plaintiff demurred.

10-033

TINDAL CJ

The only question now remaining is upon the demurrer to the fourth plea. The fourth plea states that the plaintiff never had any cause of action against the defendant in respect of the subject-matter of the action in the Court of Exchequer, which he, the plaintiff, at the time of the commencement of the said action, and thence until the time of the making the promise in the first count mentioned, well knew. By demurring to that plea, the plaintiff admits that he had no cause of action against the defendant in the action therein mentioned, and that he knew it. It appears to me, therefore, that he is estopped from saying that there was any valid consideration for the defendant's promise. It is almost contra bonos mores, and certainly contrary to all the principles of natural justice, that a man should institute proceedings against another, when he is conscious that he has no good cause of action. In order to constitute a binding promise, the plaintiff must show a good consideration, something beneficial to the defendant, or detrimental to the plaintiff. Detrimental to the plaintiff it cannot be, if he has no cause of action; and beneficial to the defendant it cannot be; for, in contemplation of law, the defence upon such an admitted state of facts must be successful, and the defendant will recover costs, which must be assumed to be a full compensation for all the legal damage he may sustain. The consideration, therefore, altogether fails. On the part of the plaintiff, it has been urged that the cases cited for the defendant were not cases where actions had already been brought, but only cases of promises to forbear commencing proceedings. I must, however, confess, that, if that were so, I do not see that it would make any substantial difference. The older cases, and some of the modern ones, too, do not afford any countenance to that distinction . . .

. . . the defendant asserts, and the plaintiff admits, that there never was any cause of action in the original suit, and that the plaintiff knew it. I therefore think the fourth plea affords a very good answer, and that the defendant is entitled to judgment thereon

CRESSWELL J

It has been surmised, in the course of the argument, that there is a distinction between abstaining from commencing an action, and forbearing to prosecute one already commenced. In the older cases I find no such distinction. Lord Coke lays it down broadly that the staying of an action that has been unjustly brought is no consideration for a promise to pay money. I cannot help thinking, on broad principles, that the staying proceedings in an action brought without any cause is no good consideration for a promise such as is relied on here. The plea, in plain terms, avers that the plaintiff never had any cause of action, and he well knew it. Are we to assume that the defendant might by some slip in pleading, have failed in his defence to that action, if it had proceeded? I think not.

(The judgments of Maule and Erle J. J. are omitted.)

Judgment for the Defendant on the Fourth Plea.

COOK v WRIGHT

Queen's Bench (1861) 1 B. & S. 559; 30 L.J.Q.B. 321; 4 L.T. 704; 7 Jur. 1121; 124 R.R. 649; 121 E.R. 822

BLACKBURN J

10–034   Before the Queen's Bench, after a verdict for the defendant, on a motion that the evidence did not prove want of consideration and that, upon the evidence, the plaintiffs were entitled to a verdict. The relevant facts are stated in the judgment of the court (Cockburn C. J., Wightman and Blackburn J. J.), delivered by Blackburn J.: In this case it appeared on the trial that the defendant was agent for a Mrs Bennett, who was non-resident owner of houses in a district subject to a local Act. Works had been done in the adjoining street by the Commissioners for executing the Act, the expenses of which, under the provisions of their Act, they charged on the owners of the adjoining houses. Notice had been given to the defendant, as if he had himself been the owner of the houses, calling on him to pay the proportion chargeable in respect of them. He attended at a board meeting of the Commissioners, and objected both to the amount and nature of the charge, and also stated that he was not the owner of the houses, and that Mrs Bennett was. He was told that, if he did not pay, he would be treated as one Goble had been. It appeared that Goble had refused to pay a sum charged against him as owner of some houses, and the Commissioners had taken legal proceedings against him, and he had then submitted and paid, with costs. In the result, it was agreed between the Commissioners and the defendant that the amount charged upon him should be reduced, and that time should be given to pay it in three instalments; he gave three promissory notes for the three instalments; the first was duly honoured; the others were not, and were the subject of the present action. At the trial it appeared that the defendant was not in fact owner of the houses. As agent for the owner he was not personally liable under the Act. In point of law, therefore, the Commissioners were not entitled to claim the money from him; but no case of deceit was alleged against them. It must be taken that the Commissioners honestly believed that the defendant was personally liable, and really intended to take legal proceedings against him, as they had done against Goble. The defendant, according to his own evidence, never believed that he was liable in law, but signed the notes in order to avoid being sued as Goble was. Under these circumstances the substantial question reserved (irrespective of the form of the plea) was whether there was any consideration for the notes. We are of the opinion that there was.

There is no doubt that a bill or note given in consideration of what is supposed to be a debt is without consideration if it appears that there was a mistake in fact as to the existence of the debt; Bell v Gardiner (4 M. & Gr. 11); and, according to the cases of *Southall v Rigg* and *Forman v Wright* (11 C.B. 481), the law is the same if the bill or note is given in consequence of a mistake of law as to the existence of a debt. But here there was no mistake on the part of the defendant either of law or fact. What he did was not merely the making an erroneous account stated, or promising to pay a debt for which he mistakenly believed himself liable. It appeared on the evidence that he believed himself not to be liable; but he knew that the plaintiffs thought him liable, and would sue him if he did not pay, and in order to avoid the expense and trouble of legal proceedings against himself he agreed to a compromise; and the question is, whether a person who has given a note as a compromise of a claim honestly made on him, and which but for that compromise would have been at once brought to a legal decision, can resist the payment of the note on the ground that the original claim thus compromised might have been successfully resisted . . .

In the present case we think that there was sufficient consideration for the notes in the compromise made as it was.

The rule to enter a verdict for the plaintiff must be made absolute.

Points for reflection

10–035   1.   The court suggests that if the defendant (D) had (wrongly) believed himself to be liable to pay the charges, he would not have been liable on the notes; but, because he (rightly) believed himself not to be liable to pay the charges, he is liable on the notes. Cf. Bills of Exchange Act 1882 s.27(1), above (which applies to promissory notes). In neither case is there an "antecedent debt or liability" because D is not in fact liable to pay the charges. In the latter case, however, the commissioners give consideration because they refrain from pursuing the threatened proceedings. In the former case there is no express threat of proceedings to be withdrawn if the defendant pays up promptly because he believes himself to be liable. But suppose that, though believing himself to be liable, he gives a note or cheque only in response to a demand threatening legal proceedings? Is he liable on the note or cheque? If he is, does it really make a difference that he gives the note or cheque promptly on receiving the first demand for payment? Is there not an implicit threat of legal proceedings in even the first demand for payment of a debt? Cf. *Alliance Bank v Broom*.

It seems very unjust that D should have been required to pay Mrs Bennett's debt; but note that he could probably have recovered the money from her as money paid to her use. See generally, Cheshire, Fifoot and Furmston (12th edn), pp.667–669. The modern doctrine of economic duress would have been of no help to D. See *CTN Cash and Carry Ltd v Gallagher Ltd*, below, Ch.26.

2. If D has admitted that a particular sum (say £50 out of a larger claim—say £150) claimed by P is due, P has a legal right to payment of the admitted debt; if D then sends a cheque for £50 to P 'in full satisfaction' of P's claim and P cashes the cheque, P may claim the outstanding £100. The payment of £50 which is admittedly due, is no consideration for any promise which P may have appeared objectively to have made to forgo the balance he claimed; *Ferguson v Davies* [1997]1 All E.R. 315 CA, Henry LJ, applying *Foakes v Beer*, below and *D & C Builders v Rees*, below, Ch.11. Evans LJ held that, taking the particular circumstances into account, P was not to be taken to have agreed for forgo his claim and there was no need to decide the consideration point. Aldous LJ agreed with both judgments.

3. In *Callisher v Bischoffsheim* (1870) L.R 5 Q.B. 449 at 451, Cockburn CJ said: "The authorities clearly establish that if an agreement is made to compromise a disputed claim, forbearance to sue in respect of that claim is good consideration; and whether proceedings to enforce the disputed claim have or have not been instituted makes no difference. If the defendant's contention were adopted, it would result that in no case of a doubtful claim could a compromise be enforced. Every day a compromise is effected on the ground that the party making it has a fair chance of succeeding in it, and if he bona fide believes he has a fair chance of success he has a reasonable ground for suing, and his forbearance to sue will constitute a good consideration."

See also *Miles v New Zealand Alford Estate Co* (1886) 32 Ch. D. 266 CA, and compare the views of Denning L.J. in *Williams v Williams* (below).

C. Compliance with Legal Obligations

One of the classic puzzles in the law of contract is whether a promise to perform an exisiting obligation, or (assuming a unilateral contract) the actual performance of the obligation, can constitute
consideration. If the obligation exists as a matter of the general law, there are likely to be public policy
questions about paying for its performance. If the obligation exists as a matter of an existing contract,
it might not seem to matter whether the obligation is owed (a) to the party who now promises to pay   **10–036**

extra for the performance of the obligation or (b) to a third party. Either way, the promisee seems to be getting something for nothing. However, while the courts decided in the nineteenth century that consideration could be recognised in the latter kind of case, the former case has remained much more problematic. One of the obvious concerns is that the law should not offer any encouragement to the practice of putting in a low and attractive bid in order to win a contract and then, when the time is right, presenting the client with an ultimatum to the effect that unless the agreed price is increased the contract will not be performed. If a promise to perform an existing contractual obligation that is already owed to the client is not recognised as sufficient consideration, then this is one way of easing the concern; but, as the modern law has developed a doctrine of economic duress, another way of responding to the concern is to treat the pressure applied by the contractor as illegitimate and as a basis for the client to avoid the promise to pay more. In the context of the renegotiation of a commercial contract, the case of *Williams v Roffey Bros and Nicholls* (below) marks an important stage in the maturing relationship between the requirement of consideration and the doctrine of economic duress.

Law Revision Committee, 6th Interim Report, para.36, p.21

10–037   Three cases must be discussed:

(a) Where A makes a promise to B in consideration of B doing or promising to do something which he is already bound to do by reason of a duty imposed upon him by law, whether by a Statute or otherwise: for instance, the duty of a local polic authority to afford adequate protection to A and his property;

(b) Where A makes a promise to B in consideration of B doing or promising to do something which he is already bound to do under a contract with A;

(c) Where A makes a promise to B in consideration of B doing or promising to do something which he is already bound to do under a contract with C.

In cases (a) and (b) where the thing promised or performed is precisely the thing which the promisor is already bound to do and no more, and there is no dispute that he is bound to do it, there is said to be no consideration or only illusory consideration for the new promise, and it is not enforceable. In case (c) the law is not so clear and frequently other factors are present out of which a consideration for the promise can be manufactured.

In our opinion, in all three cases, a promise made by A to B in consideration of B doing or promising to do something which he is already bound to do should be enforced by the law, provided that in other respects such as legality and compat[i]bility with public policy it is free from objection; thus a promise in return for an agreement by a police authority to give precisely the amount of protection it was by law bound to give and no more should be unenforceable as being against public policy.

The dominant factor is that A thought it worth his while to make the promise to B in order that he should feel more certain that B would do the thing bargained for, and we can see no reason in general why A, having got what he wanted, should be allowed to evade his promise. Moreover, why did the promisor make the promise if it was to have no legal effect?

i. Performance of a Duty Imposed by Law

COLLINS v GODEFROY

King's Bench (1831) 1 B. & Ad. 950; 109 E.R. 1040; 1 Dowl. 326; 9 L.J.(o.s.) K.B. 158

10–038   Assumpsit to recover a remuneration for the plaintiff's loss of time during his attendance upon subpoena as a witness in an action. At the trial before Lord Tenterden CJ it appeared that Godefroy brought an action against one Dalton, and caused Collins to be subpoenaed to attend. Collins, who attended for six days but was not called, on November 2, 1829, demanded of Godefroy six guineas as his fee for attendance and commenced his action on the following day. Lord Tenterden was of opinion that the plaintiff was not entitled to recover because, in point of law, he was bound to give evidence pursuant upon a subpoena. The plaintiff was nonsuited but with leave reserved to enter a verdict for six guineas.

A rule nisi having been obtained.

LORD TENTERDEN CJ

Assuming that the offer to pay the six guineas without costs was evidence of an express promise by the defendant to pay that sum to the plaintiff as a compensation to him for his loss of time, still, if the defendant was not bound by law to pay that sum, the offer to do so not having been accepted will not avail the plaintiff. If it be a duty imposed by law upon a party regularly subpoenaed to attend from time to time to give his evidence then a promise to give him any remuneration for loss of time incurred in such attendance is a promise without consideration. We think that such a duty is imposed by law; and on consideration of the Statute of Elizabeth,[1] and of the cases which have been decided on this subject, we are all of the opinion that a party cannot maintain an action for compensation for loss of time in attending a trial as a witness. We are aware of the practice which has prevailed in certain cases, of allowing, as costs between party and party, so much per day for the attendance of professional men, but that practice cannot alter the law. What the effect of our decision may be, is not for our consideration. We think, on principle, that an action does not lie for a compensation to a witness for loss of time in attendance under a subpoena. The rule, therefore, must be discharged.

Rule Discharged.

Point for reflection

In *Arrale v Costain* [1976] 1 Lloyds Rep. 98 the plaintiff who had been injured in the course of his employment in Dubai was paid by his employer, the defendants, the amount of compensation required by the law of Dubai. He signed a document stating that he received the money in full satisfaction of all claims in respect of personal injury. Subsequently he brought an action for negligence in England. The Court of Appeal held that the action was not barred by the agreement. Lord Denning, applying *D & C Builders v Rees*, below, held that there was no true accord and satisfaction—there was inequality of bargaining power and the plaintiff was unaware of his rights at common law. Geoffrey Lane LJ said that if the defendants were doing no more than performing an obligation already cast upon them by law there was no consideration for the plaintiff's agreement not to sue. He rejected the argument that the defendants had done something more by refraining from setting up certain answers to the claim permitted by the Dubai law; as a matter of policy it was never their intention to do so and "It is no consideration to refrain from a course of action which it was never intended to pursue; see *Cook v Wright* (1861) 1 B. & S. 559, 589 [above]." Stephenson LJ agreed that there was no consideration.

10–039

WILLIAMS v WILLIAMS

Court of Appeal [1957] 1 W.L.R. 148; 121 J.P. 93; [1957] 1 All E.R. 305; 101 S.J. 108

The relevant facts appear in the judgment of Denning LJ

10–040

DENNING LJ

In this case a wife claims sums due to her under a maintenance agreement. No evidence was called in the court below because the facts are agreed. The parties were married on April 25, 1945; they have no children. On January 24, 1952, the wife deserted the husband. On March 26, 1952, they signed the agreement now sued upon which has three clauses: "(1) the husband will pay to the wife for her support and maintenance a weekly sum of One Pound Ten Shillings to be paid every four weeks during the joint lives of the parties so long as the wife shall lead a chaste life the first payment hereunder to be made on the Fifteenth day of April 1952. (2) The

---

[1]   5 Eliz. 1, c.9 (Perjury Act).

wife will out of the said weekly sum or otherwise support and maintain herself and will indemnify the husband against all debts to be incurred by her and will not in any way at any time hereafter pledge the husband's credit. (3) The wife shall not so long as the husband shall punctually make the payments hereby agreed to be made commence or prosecute against the husband any matrimonial proceedings other than proceedings for dissolution of marriage but upon failure of the husband to make the said weekly payments as and when the same become due the wife shall be at full liberty on her election to pursue all and every remedy in this regard either by enforcement of the provisions hereof or as if this agreement had not been made." So far as we know, the parties have remained apart ever since. On June 1, 1955, the husband petitioned for divorce, on the grounds of his wife's desertion, and on October 12, 1955, a decree nisi was made against her. On December 2, 1955, the decree was made absolute. In this action the wife claims maintenance at the rate of £1 10s. a week under the agreement for a period from October 1954 to October 1955. The sum claimed is £30 5s. 9d., which is the appropriate sum after deduction of tax.

The husband disputes the claim, on the ground that there was no consideration for his promise. Let me first deal with clause 3. It is settled law that a wife, despite such a clause as clause 3, can make application to the magistrates or to the High Court for maintenance. If this wife made such an application the husband could set up the fact of desertion as an answer to the claim, but he could not set up clause 3 as a bar to the proceedings. The clause is void and as such no consideration to support the agreement: see *Bennett v Bennett* [below, para.27–038].[2] Now let me deal with clause 2.

Now I agree that in promising to maintain herself whilst she was in desertion, the wife was only promising to do that which she was already bound to do. Nevertheless, a promise to perform an existing duty is, I think, sufficient consideration to support a promise, so long as there is nothing in the transaction which is contrary to the public interest. Suppose that this agreement had never been made, and the wife had made no promise to maintain herself and did not do so. She might then have sought and received public assistance or have pledged her husband's credit with tradesmen: in which case the National Assistance Board might have summoned him before the magistrates, or the tradesmen might have sued him in the county court. It is true that he would have an answer to those claims because she was in desertion, but nevertheless he would be put to all the trouble, worry and expense of defending himself against them. By paying her 30s. a week and taking this promise from her that she will maintain herself and will not pledge his credit, he has an added safeguard to protect himself from all this worry, trouble and expense. That is a benefit to him which is good consideration for his promise to pay maintenance. That was the view which appealed to the county court judge: and I must say it appeals to me also.

There is another ground on which good consideration can be found. Although the wife was in desertion, nevertheless it must be remembered that desertion is never irrevocable. It was open to her to come back at any time. Her right to maintenance was not lost by desertion. It was only suspended. If she made a genuine offer to return which he rejected, she would have been entitled to maintenance from him. She could apply to the magistrates or the High Court for an order in her favour. If she did so, however, whilst this agreement was in force the 30s. would be regarded as prima facie the correct figure. It is a benefit to the husband for it to be so regarded, and that is sufficient consideration to support his promise.

I construe this agreement as a promise by the husband to pay his wife 30s. a week in consideration of her promise to maintain herself during the time she is living separate from him, whether due to her own fault or not.

I would dismiss the appeal accordingly.

HODSON LJ

Mr Priestley has argued that [as the wife was in desertion when the agreement was made] she had forfeited all right to be maintained by her husband and so she was giving no consideration at all when she said she would maintain herself, because that is what she would have to do anyway. The short answer to that is I think that she had not forfeited her right to be maintained by her husband by being in desertion: she had only suspended her right and not destroyed it. Authority for that proposition is contained in the judgment of Lord Reading C. J. in *Jones v Newtown and Llanidloes Guardians* [1920] 3 K.B. 381, 384[3]: "There is no doubt that at common law if a wife chooses wilfully and without justification to live away from her husband she cannot, so long as she

---

2   The actual decision of *Bennett v Bennett* was overruled by the provisions of the Maintenance Agreements Act 1957 s.1(2), now represented by the Matrimonial Causes Act 1973 s.34.

3   Cf. also *Pinnick v Pinnick* [1957] 1 W.L.R. 644, esp. 653.

continues absent, render him liable for the necessaries supplied to her, or for her maintenance by the union, for the reason that she has of her own free will deprived herself of the opportunity which the husband was affording her of being maintained in the home. But the relief of the husband from the obligation of maintenance continues only so long as she voluntarily remains absent. Her absence, although wrongful, does not affect the relationship of husband and wife." That passage applies to this case, looking at it, as we must do, as at the time when the agreement was entered into. The wife had then deserted the husband and was temporarily wrongfully away from home; but she might at any time return. In those circumstances, if she returned or offered to return, her husband's liability to maintain her would revive. So that there was good consideration there to meet that contingency, which was a real contingency and not a fanciful one at that time . . .

MORRIS LJ

. . . I consider that we must proceed on the basis that at the date this agreement was entered into, March 26, 1952, the wife was then in desertion. But it seems to me that the wife might thereafter have offered to return and might have ceased to be in desertion, and that clause 2 would at that stage and in that event have been in operation: therefore it does not seem to me that it can be said that clause 2 was not of value to the husband. The probability of the happening of such events need not be measured, for the court does not inquire as to the adequacy of consideration.

I think that for that reason the county court judge came to a correct conclusion. Like my Lord, Hodson L.J., I prefer to base my judgment on that ground rather than on the alternative ground—that apart from any question of an offer by the wife to return, while she was still in desertion, there might have been trouble, expense or embarrassment if the wife had incurred debts.

I, therefore, agree that the appeal fails.

Appeal Dismissed.

Questions

1. If the wife were to pledge her husband's credit in these circumstances, she would be guilty of obtaining by false pretences or obtaining credit by fraud under the then law (now obtaining by deception—Theft Act 1968). Should her promise to refrain from so doing constitute good consideration?   **10–041**

2. Is the wife's duty to support herself when in desertion (cf. Denning LJ) a legal duty? Is not the wife while in desertion, bound in law to refrain from pledging her husband's credit? Is her promise not to do so good consideration for the husband's agreement to pay the 30s. per week? Does the case, from this standpoint, require reconciling with *Collins v Godefroy* (above) and *Stilk v Myrick* (below)?

3. If the wife were to return to her husband, would the contract, as found by the court, still be binding upon the parties?

Points for reflection

1. The Matrimonial Causes Act 1973 s.34, provides: **10–042**

   (1) If a maintenance agreement includes a provision purporting to restrict any right to apply to a court for an order containing financial arrangements, then—

   (a) that provision shall be void; but

   (b) any other financial arrangements contained in the agreement shall not thereby be rendered void or unenforceable and shall, unless they are void or unenforceable for any other reason (and subject to sections 35 and 36, below) be binding on the parties to the agreement.

(2) In this and in section 35 below—

"maintenance agreement" means any agreement in writing made, whether before or after the commencement of this Act, between the parties to a marriage, being—

(a) an agreement containing financial arrangements, whether made during the continuance or after the dissolution or annulment of the marriage; or

(b) a separation agreement which contains no financial arrangements in a case where no other agreement in writing between the same parties contains such arrangements.

2. In *Pitt v PHH Asset Management Ltd*, above, p.117, Peter Gibson LJ said: "On the second point, the consideration moving from the plaintiff, Mr Payne submitted that in reality there was no consideration provided by the plaintiff. The plaintiff was expressing himself to be ready, willing and able to proceed to exchange contracts, which was, he submitted, simply what he would have to do in any case. Further, he said that the learned judge rightly described the threat by the plaintiff to issue an injunction as vapid, that is to say of no substance. He accordingly submitted that there was nothing by way of valuable consideration which the defendant received. I cannot accept these submissions either. I accept that the threat of an injunction only had a nuisance value in that I cannot see how the plaintiff could have succeeded in any claim. Nevertheless, that nuisance was something which the defendant was freed from by the plaintiff agreeing to the lock-out agreement. Further, the threat of causing trouble with Miss Buckle was again a matter which could have been a nuisance to the defendant and again removal of that threat provided some consideration. But I also believe that the promise by the plaintiff to get on by limiting himself to just two weeks if he was to exchange contracts was of some value to the defendant. The defendant had the benefit of knowing that if it chose to give the plaintiff a draft contract to agree, there would be no delay on the plaintiff's part beyond a maximum of two weeks thereafter. The learned judge held that these three items constituted valuable consideration sufficient to support the lock-out agreement and I respectfully agree with him."

Question

10–043   Were all or any of the following capable of being consideration?

(i) The withdrawal of the "vapid" threat to issue an injunction? Cf. *Wade v Simeon*, above, and *Williams v Williams*, above.

(ii) Refraining from advising Buckle that she could lower her offer.

(iii) A promise to return contracts within 14 days—faster than usual in such circumstances.

GLASBROOK BROS LTD v GLAMORGAN COUNTY COUNCIL

House of Lords [1925] A.C. 270; 94 L.J.K.B. 272; 132 L.T. 611; 89 J.P. 29; 41 T.L.R. 213; 69 S.J. 212; 23 L.G.R. 61

10–044   Appeal from an order of the Court of Appeal affirming a judgment of Bailhache J.
The action was brought by the respondents against the appellants to recover the sum of £2,200 11s.

10d. for the services of police specially supplied by the respondents at the request of and by agreement with the appellants.

The appellants owned a colliery near Swansea, employing about 1,000 men. A general colliery strike in South Wales ended early in July 1921, but work was not resumed at their colliery. After a hostile demonstration by some 500 or 600 of the men, the appellants' colliery manager, James, was informed by the men's committee that the strikers were going to get the "safety men" out. Without the safety men, the mine would have become flooded. James went to the local police superintendent, one Smith, and asked for 100 police to be billeted on the colliery premises, as, otherwise, the safety men, who were frightened, would not come to work. Smith was of opinion that adequate protection could be given by keeping a mobile force ready, who, on warning of danger, could be swiftly moved to the danger area; but, if police were to be billeted in the colliery, 70 would be sufficient. James finally agreed to 70, and signed a requisition form, agreeing on behalf of the appellants to pay for the services of the men provided at certain specified rates per diem and also for their travelling expenses and to provide them with food and sleeping accommodation. When the police were billeted in the colliery, the safety men came to work, which they would not have done but for the presence of the police. The police remained on the premises until the end of the strike.

The defence to the action was that there was no consideration for the promise of payment, it being the duty of the county council to supply police protection; there was also a counterclaim for £1,330 4s., the cost of feeding and housing the police supplied. Bailhache J. gave judgment for the respondents on the claim and dismissed the counterclaim. The Court of Appeal by a majority (Bankes and Scrutton LJJ, Atkin LJ dissenting) affirmed the judgment.

VISCOUNT CAVE LC

No doubt there is an absolute unconditional obligation binding the police authorities to take all steps which appear to them to be necessary for keeping the peace, for preventing crime, or for protecting property from criminal injury; and the public, who pay for this protection through the rates and taxes, cannot lawfully be called upon to make a further payment for that which is their right . . . But it has always been recognised that, where individuals desire that services of a special kind which, though not within the obligations of a police authority, can most effectively be rendered by them, should be performed by members of the police force, the police authorities may (to use an expression which is found in the Police Pensions Act 1890) "lend" the services of constables for that purpose in consideration of payment. Instances are the lending of constables on the occasions of large gatherings in and outside private premises, as on the occasions of weddings, athletic or boxing contests or race meetings, and the provision of constables at large railway stations. Of course no such lending could possibly take place if the constables were required elsewhere for the preservation of order; but (as Bankes L.J. pointed out) an effective police force requires a margin of reserve strength in order to deal with emergencies, and to employ that margin of reserve, when not otherwise required, on special police service for payment is to the advantage both of the persons utilising their services and of the public who are thereby relieved from some part of the police charges. Atkin L.J. put the contrary view in the form of a dilemma when he said: "Either they were performing this public duty in giving the protection asked for, in which case I think they cannot charge, or, which no one suggests, they were at the request of an individual doing something which it was not their duty to do, in which case it seems to me both public policy and section 10 of the County Police Act 1839, make the contract illegal and void." With great respect to the learned Lord Justice I am disposed to think that this reasoning rests on an ambiguous use of the word "duty." There may be services rendered by the police which, although not within the scope of their absolute obligations to the public may yet fall within their powers, and in such cases public policy does not forbid their performance. I do not understand the reference in the above passage to section 10 of the Act of 1839.

[His Lordship then proceeded to consider whether in this case the billeting of the police was a special duty for which a charge might be made.]

. . . In this connection I think it important to bear in mind exactly what it was that the learned trial judge had to decide. It was no part of his duty to say—nor did he purport to say—whether in his judgment the billeting of the 70 men at the colliery was necessary for the prevention of violence or the protection of the mines from criminal injury. The duty of determining such questions is cast by law, not upon the courts after the event, but upon the police authorities at the time when the decision has to be taken; and a court which attempted to review such a decision from the point of view of its wisdom or prudence would (I think) be exceeding its proper functions. The question for the court was whether on July 9, 1921, the police authorities acting, reasonably and in good faith, considered a police garrison at the colliery necessary for the protection of life and property from violence, or, in other words, whether the decision of the chief constable in refusing special protection unless paid for was such a decision as a man in his position and with his duties could reasonably take. If in the judgment of the police authorities, formed reasonably and in good faith, the garrison was necessary for the protection of life and property, then they were not entitled to make a charge for it, for that would be to exact a payment for the performance of a duty which they clearly owed to the appellants and their servants; but if they thought the garrison a superfluity and only acceded to Mr James's request with a view to meeting his wishes, then in my opinion they were entitled to treat the garrison duty as special duty and to charge for it . . .

. . . In my opinion, therefore, this appeal fails and should be dismissed with costs.

Viscount Finlay and Lord Shaw of Dunfermline made speeches to similar effect.

Lord Carson and Lord Blanesburgh dissented, holding that, in the circumstances of the case, the billeting of the police was not a special service.

Point for reflection

10–045   In *Harris v Sheffield United Football Club* [1987] 2 All E.R. 838 the police authority claimed from the club £51,699 for providing special police services at the club's ground between August 1982 and November 1983. The club contended that in attending the matches the police were merely fulfilling their duty to enforce the law and their attendance did not constitute the provision of "special police services" within s.15(1) of the Police Act 1964. That section provided statutory authority for the long established practice of charging a person who requested "special police services". The judge upheld the authority's claim and the Court of Appeal, considering *Glasbrook v Glamorgan*, dismissed the appeal. In deciding whether police services are "special" the court will take into account: (1) whether the officers are required to attend on private premises or in a public place; (2) whether violence has already occurred or is imminent—if so, the services cannot be "special"; (3) the nature of the event—public events like elections lie at one end of the spectrum, private events like weddings at the other, and events like football matches somewhere in the middle; (4) whether protection can be provided without using officers who would otherwise be on other duties or off duty.

Questions

10–046   1. The Rovers' FC secretary telephones the Chief Constable—"The crowd is fighting—police are overwhelmed—send help." The Chief Constable replies, "Only if you agree to pay." The secretary agrees. Does the Club have to pay the bill? If not, why not?—is it a question of consideration? What if, a month before the game, the Chief Constable had advised that 50 officers would be required in the ground but the Club was willing to pay for only 25?

2. In *Sykes v DPP* [1962] A.C. 528; [1961] 3 All E.R. 33, it was held that the crime of misprision of felony consisted in concealment of or failure to reveal a felony known to have been committed, regardless whether the accused kept silent for profit. Citizens thus had a legal duty to reveal felonies known to them. Does that mean that, in the "'reward cases" (above, Ch.3), a promise

was enforceable, the consideration for which was the performance of an existing legal duty? (Misprision of felony has ceased to be a crime since the Criminal Law Act 1967.)

WARD v BYHAM

Court of Appeal [1956] 1 W.L.R. 496; 100 S.J. 341; [1956] 2 All E.R. 318

When the parents of an illegitimate child separated, the father paid a neighbour £1 per week to look after the child. Later the mother, having taken a housekeeping job where she could have the child with her, wrote to the father to let her have the child and the £1 per week. The father replied, "I am prepared to let you have (the child) and pay you up to £1 a week allowance for her providing you can prove that she will be well looked after and happy and also that she is allowed to decide for herself whether or not she wishes to come and live with you." It was agreed that the child should go to the mother and the father paid the £1 per week until the mother married her employer, when the father stopped payments. The county court judge gave judgment for the mother in an action brought by her for the £1 per week based upon the father's undertaking. The father appealed.

10–047

DENNING LJ

I look on the father's letter as dealing with two things. One is the handing over of the child to the mother. The father agrees to let the mother have the child, provided the child herself wishes to come and provided also that the mother satisfies the father that she will be well looked after and happy. The other thing is the future maintenance of the child. The father promises to pay the mother up to £1 per week so long as the mother looks after the child. [His Lordship then referred to the fact that the mother of an illegitimate child was bound to maintain it, whereas the father was not under such obligation. (See s.42 of the National Assistance Act 1948).].

I approach the case, therefore, on the footing that, in looking after the child, the mother is only doing what she is legally bound to do. Even so, I think there was sufficient consideration to support the promise. I have always thought that a promise to perform an existing duty, or the performance of it, should be regarded as good consideration, because it is a benefit to the person to whom it is given. Take this very case. It is as much a benefit for the father to have the child looked after by the mother as by a neighbour. If he gets the benefit for which he stipulated, he ought to honour his promise, and he ought not to avoid it by saying that the mother was herself under a duty to maintain the child.

I regard the father's promise in this case as what is sometimes called a unilateral contract, a promise in return for an act, a promise by the father to pay £1 per week in return for the mother's looking after the child. Once the mother embarked on the task of looking after the child, there was a binding contract. So long as she looked after the child, she would be entitled to £1 a week . . .

MORRIS LJ

It seems to me, therefore, that the father was saying, in effect: Irrespective of what may be the strict legal position, what I am asking is that you shall prove that the child will be well looked after and happy, and also that you must agree that the child is to be allowed to decide for herself whether or not she wishes to come and live with you. If those conditions were fulfilled, the father was agreeable to pay. On those terms, which in fact became operative, the father agreed to pay £1 a week. In my judgment, there was ample consideration there to be bound for his promise, which I think was binding.

Parker L.J. concurred.

Appeal Dismissed.

Questions

1. What was the consideration for the father's promise as found by:
   (a) Denning LJ;
   (b) Morris LJ?

2. Though not under a legal liability to maintain his illegitimate child, the father is under a moral duty to do so. Would the promise of a complete stranger to pay a mother to maintain her illegitimate child be binding on the promisor? Cf. *Williams v Williams* (above).

3. Treitel (10th edn), p.88 says of *Ward v Byham*: "One basis of the decision is that the mother had provided consideration by showing that she had made the child happy, etc.: in this way she can be said to have conferred a factual benefit on the father, even though she may not have suffered any detriment." Why is it not a detriment to the mother to have to prove a fact to the father—something she has no prior obligation to do? Treitel adds "But if a son's promise not to bore his father is not good consideration (*White v Bluett* above), it is hard to see why a mother's promise to make her child happy should stand on a different footing . . .". Can the two cases be reconciled?

----

ii. Duty Owed by Contract with a Third Party

SHADWELL v SHADWELL

Common Bench (1860) 9 C.B.(n.s.) 159; 30 L.J.C.P. 145; 7 Jur. 311; 3 L.T. 628; 9 W.R. 163; 127 R.R. 604; 142 E.R. 62

The declaration stated that the testator in his lifetime (in consideration that the plaintiff would marry Ellen Nicholl) agreed with and promised the plaintiff, then unmarried, in the terms of and contained in the following letter:

"August 11, 1838,

Gray's Inn

My Dear Lancey,
   I am glad to hear of your intended marriage with Ellen Nicholl, and, as I promised to assist you at starting, I am happy to tell you that I will pay to you one hundred and fifty pounds yearly during my life, and until your annual income derived from your profession of a Chancery barrister shall amount to six hundred guineas, of which your own admission will be the only evidence that I shall receive or require.

Your ever affectionate uncle,

Charles Shadwell.

Averment that everything necessary happened to entitle the plaintiff to have the said testator pay to him eighteen of the yearly sums of £150 and that the time therefore elapsed after he had married

Ellen Nicholl and during the testator's lifetime and that plaintiff's annual income from his profession as a Chancery barrister never amounted to 600 guineas; that the testator paid 12 of the 18 annual sums and part of the 13th but that the residue of that and the five subsequent instalments were due and unpaid.

Fourth plea, that the plaintiff's marriage with Ellen Nicholl had been arranged before the alleged agreement without any request from the testator and that there was no consideration for the alleged agreement.

Second replication to the fourth plea, that the agreement was in the terms of and contained in the letter set out above. Averment that the plaintiff married Ellen Nicholl, relying on the said promise and so married while his income as a Chancery barrister did not amount to 600 guineas per annum. Demurrer to the replication to the fourth plea. Joinder in demurrer.

ERLE CJ

The question raised by the demurrer to the replication to the fourth plea is, whether there was a consideration to support the action on the promise to pay an annuity of £150 per annum . . . The circumstances are, that the plaintiff had made an engagement to marry Ellen Nicholl, his uncle promising him to assist him at starting, by which, as I understand the words, he meant on commencing his married life. Then the letter containing the promise declared on is said to specify what the assistance would be, namely, £150 per annum during the uncle's life, and until the plaintiff's professional income should be acknowledged by him to exceed 600 guineas; and a further averment, that the plaintiff, relying upon his promise, without any revocation on the part of the uncle, did marry Ellen Nicholl. Then, do these facts show that the promise was in consideration, either of the loss to be sustained by the plaintiff, or the benefit to be derived from the plaintiff to the uncle, at his, the uncle's request? My answer is in the affirmative. First, do these facts show a loss sustained by the plaintiff at the uncle's request? When I answer this in the affirmative, I am aware that a man's marriage with the woman of his choice is in one sense a boon, and in that sense the reverse of a loss; yet, as between the plaintiff and the party promising an income to support the marriage, it may be a loss. The plaintiff may have made the most material changes in his position, and have induced the object of his affections to do the same, and have incurred pecuniary liabilities resulting in embarrassments, which would be in every sense a loss, if the income which had been promised should be withheld; and if the promise was made in order to induce the parties to marry, the promise so made would be, in legal effect, a request to marry. Secondly, do these facts show a benefit derived from the plaintiff to the uncle at his request? In answering again in the affirmative, I am at liberty to consider the relation in which the parties stood, and the interest in the status of the nephew which the uncle declares. The marriage primarily affects the parties thereto; but in the second degree it may be an object of interest with a near relative, and in that sense a benefit to him. This benefit is also derived from the plaintiff at the uncle's request, if the promise of the annuity was intended as an inducement to the marriage; and the averment that the plaintiff, relying on the promise, married, is an averment that the promise was one inducement to the marriage. This is a consideration averred in the declaration, and it appears to me to be expressed in the letter, construed with the surrounding circumstances. No case bearing a strong analogy to the present was cited; but the importance of enforcing promises which have been made to induce parties to marry has been often recognised, and the cases of *Montefiori v Montefiori* ((1762) 1 W.Bl. 363) and *Bold v Hutchinson* (1855) 20 Beavan 250) are examples. I do not feel it necessary to add anything about the numerous authorities referred to in the learned arguments addressed to us, because the decision turns on a question of fact, whether the consideration for the promise is proved as pleaded. I think it is, and therefore my judgment on the first demurrer is for the plaintiff.

Keating J. concurred.

BYLES J (DISSENTING)

I am of opinion that the defendant is entitled to the judgment of the court on the demurrer to the second replication to the fourth plea. It is alleged by the fourth plea, that the defendant's testator never requested the plaintiff to enter into the engagement to marry, or to marry, and that there never was any consideration for the testator's promise, except what may be collected from the letter itself set out in the declaration. The inquiry, therefore, narrows itself to this question: Does the letter itself disclose any consideration for the promise? The consideration relied on by the plaintiff's counsel being the subsequent marriage of the plaintiff, I think the letter discloses no consideration. It is in these words: [his Lordship read it]. It is by no means clear that the words "at starting" mean "on marriage with Ellen Nicholl," or with anyone else. The more natural meaning seems to me to be, "at starting in the profession," for it will be observed that these words are used by the testator in reciting a prior promise made when the testator had not heard of the proposed marriage with Ellen Nicholl, or, so far as appears, heard of any proposed marriage. This construction is fortified by the consideration that the annuity is not, in terms, made to begin from the marriage, but, as it should seem, from the date of the letter. Neither is it in terms made defeasible if Ellen Nicholl should die before marriage. But even on the assumption that the words "at starting" mean "on marriage," I still think that no consideration appears sufficient to sustain the promise. The promise is one which, by law, must be in writing; and the fourth plea shows that no consideration or request, dehors the letter, existed, and, therefore, that no such consideration, or request, can be alluded to by the letter. Marriage of the plaintiff at the testator's express request would be, no doubt, an ample consideration; but marriage of the plaintiff without the testator's request is no consideration to the testator. It is true that marriage is, or may be, a detriment to the plaintiff; but detriment to the plaintiff is not enough, unless it either be a benefit to the testator, or be treated by the testator as such, by having been suffered at his request. Suppose a defendant to promise a plaintiff, "I will give you £500 if you break your leg," would that detriment to the plaintiff, should it happen, be any consideration? If it be said that such an accident is an involuntary mischief, would it have been a binding promise if the testator had said, "I will give you £100 a year while you continue in your present chambers"? I conceive that the promise would not be binding for want of a previous request by the testator. Now, the testator in the case before the court derived, so far as appears, no personal benefit from the marriage. The question, therefore, is still further narrowed to this point: Was the marriage at the testator's request? Express request there was none. Can any request be implied? The only words from which it can be contended that it is to be implied are the words, "I am glad to hear of your intended marriage with Ellen Nicholl." But it appears from the fourth plea that that marriage had already been agreed on, and that the testator knew it. These words, therefore, seem to me to import no more than the satisfaction of the testator at the engagement as an accomplished fact. No request can, as it seems to me, be inferred from them. And, further, how does it appear that the testator's implied request, if it could be implied, or his promise, if that promise alone would suffice, or both together, were intended to cause the marriage, or did cause it, so that the marriage can be said to have taken place at the testator's request, or, in other words, in consequence of that request? It seems to me, not only that this does not appear, but that the contrary appears; for the plaintiff before the letter had already bound himself to marry, by placing himself not only under a moral, but under a legal, obligation to marry, and the testator knew it. The well-known cases which have been cited at the Bar in support of the position, that a promise, based on the consideration of doing that which a man is already bound to do, is invalid, apply to this case; and it is not necessary, in order to invalidate the consideration, that the plaintiff's prior obligation to afford that consideration should have been an obligation to the defendant. It may have been an obligation to a third person: see *Herring v Dorell* ((1840) 8 Dowl. P.C. 604); *Atkinson v Settree* ((1744) Willes 482). The reason why the doing what a man is already bound to do is no consideration, is not only because such a consideration is in judgment of law of no value, but because a man can hardly be allowed to say that the prior legal obligation was not his determining motive. But, whether he can be allowed to say so or not, the plaintiff does not say so here. He does, indeed, make an attempt to meet this difficulty, by alleging, in the replication to the fourth plea, that he married relying on the testator's promise; but he shrinks from alleging, that though he had promised to marry before the testator's promise to him, nevertheless, he would have broken his engagement, and would not have married without the testator's promise. A man may rely on encouragements to the performance of his duty, who yet is prepared to do his duty without those encouragements. At the utmost, the allegation that he relied on the testator's promise seems to me to import no more than that he believed the testator would be as good as his word. It appears to me, for these reasons, that this letter is no more than a letter of kindness, creating no legal obligation.

Judgment for The Plaintiff.

(A second point arising on the fifth plea and replication thereto is omitted.)

Questions

10–050   1. Although this case is always cited on the issue of whether the performance of a contractual obligation owed to a third party can be good consideration, the principal point at issue was whether the testator made an offer of contract at all. Erle CJ thought he had because he had requested the plaintiff to marry Ellen. Byles J thought that he had not because he had made no such request. He had no doubt that "Marriage of the plaintiff at the testator's express request would be. .. an ample consideration." In *Jones v Padavatton* [1969] 1 W.L.R. 328 at 333, above, Ch.9, Salmon LJ said of *Shadwell v Shadwell*: "I confess that I should have decided it without hesitation in accordance with the views of Byles J, but this is of no consequence." Who was right? Was there a request (express or implied) in the letter or not? (Because writing was required by the Statute of Frauds (above, Ch.1), it had to be found there, or not at all.)

2. Suppose that nephew had told uncle that he intended to break off the engagement and uncle had written: "I am disappointed to hear you are thinking of breaking off your engagement. Ellen Is a splendid girl. If you marry her, I will pay you . . ." How would Byles J (and, presumably, Salmon LJ) then have decided the case?

3. Is a promise to give a wedding present binding when the marriage takes place? Does it matter that the present is so substantial that it is a powerful inducement to marry?

PAO ON v LAU YIU LONG

Privy Council [1980] A.C. 614; [1979] 3 W.L.R. 435; [1979] 3 All E.R. 65

One of the questions raised was whether the plaintiffs had given consideration to the defendants by promising to perform an existing contract between the plaintiffs and a third party, Fu Chip, in the performance of which the defendants had an interest. The plaintiffs had said that they were not going to perform that contract unless the defendants entered into the contract with them which was in issue.

10–051

LORD SCARMAN

Their Lordships do not doubt that a promise to perform, or the performance of, a pre-existing contractual obligation to a third party can be valid consideration. In *New Zealand Shipping Co Ltd v A M Satterthwaite & Co Ltd (The Eurymedon)*, below, para.13–006 the rule and the reason for the rule were stated:

> "An agreement to do an act which the promisor is under an existing obligation to a third party to do, may quite well amount to valid consideration . . . the promisee obtains the benefit of a direct obligation . . . This proposition is illustrated and supported by *Scotson v Pegg* (supra) which their Lordships consider to be good law."

Unless, therefore the guarantee was void as having been made for an illegal consideration or voidable on the ground of economic duress, the extrinsic evidence establishes that it was supported by valid consideration. [Having referred to *Harris v Watson* and *Stilk v Myrick*, below, paras 10–054–10–055 his Lordship proceeded:]
When one turns to consider cases where a pre-existing duty imposed by law is alleged to be valid consideration for a promise, one finds cases in which public policy has been held to invalidate the consideration. A promise to pay a sheriff in consideration of his performing his legal duty, a promise to pay for discharge from illegal arrest, are to be found in the books as promises which the law will not enforce: see the cases cited in paragraph 326, footnote 2 of Halsbury's Laws of England (4th ed., 1974), Vol. 9. Yet such cases are also explicable upon the ground that a person who promises to perform, or performs, a duty imposed by law provides no consideration. In cases where the discharge of a duty imposed by law has been treated as valid consideration, the courts have usually (but not invariably) found an act over and above, but consistent with, the duty imposed by law: see *Williams v Williams*, (above). It must be conceded that different judges have adopted differing approaches to such cases: contrast, for example, Denning L.J. with the view of the majority in *Williams'* case. But where the pre-existing obligation is a contractual duty owed to a third party, some other ground of public policy must be relied on to invalidate the consideration (if otherwise legal) . . .
[The Board went on to hold that the contract was not voidable for economic duress—see below, Ch 26, and Atiyah (1982) 98 L.Q.R. 197 and (1983) 99 L.Q.R. 353 and Tiplady (1983) 99 L.Q.R. 188.]

Points for reflection

10–052   1. In *Scotson v Pegg* (1861) 30 L.J.Ex. 225 the plaintiffs had contracted with a third party, A, to deliver a cargo of coal to A or to the order of A. A sold the cargo to the defendant and directed the plaintiffs to deliver it to the defendant as per contract. The defendant then made an agreement with the plaintiffs in which "in consideration that the plaintiffs, at the request of the defendant, would deliver to the defendant" the cargo of coal, the defendant promised to unload it at a stated rate. The plaintiffs sued for the defendant's failure to honour this promise and the defendant pleaded lack of consideration, the plaintiffs being already under a duty of delivery by the contract with A. The Court of Exchequer (Martin and Wilde BB) found for the plaintiffs: Wilde B thought that the plaintiffs might have found it advantageous not to comply with their contract with A so that their agreement with the defendant was a detriment to them; in any event, they agreed to part with the cargo to the defendant which was a benefit to him.

2. It will be noted that in the passage cited from *The Eurymedon*, above, the Privy Council regarded the promise to perform the existing agreement as consideration and that Lord Scarman made no distinction between the performance of, and the promise to perform, the existing obligation.

3. In *Jones v Waite* (1839) 5 Bing. N.C. 341; 132 E.R. 1136 (affirmed on a different ground, 9 Cl. & Fin. 101; 8 E.R. 353) the Court of Exchequer Chamber held that a promise by A to pay existing debts that he owed B was no consideration for a promise by C. Lord Abinger C.B. said: "Now a consideration to support a promise must either operate to the advantage of the party making the promise, or to the detriment of the party who is to perform the consideration. But a man is under a moral and legal obligation to pay his just debts. It cannot therefore be stated, as an abstract proposition, that he suffers any detriment from the discharge of that duty; and the declaration does not show in what way the defendant could have derived any advantage from the plaintiff paying his own debts. The plea therefore shows the insufficiency of that part of the consideration."

Questions

10–053   1. Does the duty to pay a debt differ from other legal duties in nature?

2. Might not a debtor legitimately seek release from his creditor? Could not a promise in effect to forgo this liberty constitute consideration?

3. Do you think that the decision in *Jones v Waite* would be the same today?

----

iii. Duty in Contract with the Promisor

STILK v MYRICK

King's Bench (1809) 2 Camp. 317; 11 R.R. 717; 6 Esp. 129, 170 E.R. 1168

10–054   This was an action for seaman's wages, on a voyage from London to the Baltic and back.
         By the ship's articles, executed before the commencement of the voyage, the plaintiff was to be

paid at the rate of £5 a month; and the principal question in the cause was, whether he was entitled to a higher rate of wages. In the course of the voyage two of the seamen deserted; and the captain, having in vain attempted to supply their places at Cronstadt, there entered into an agreement with the rest of the crew, that they should have the wages of the two who had deserted equally divided among them, if he could not procure two other hands at Gottenborg. This was found impossible, and the ship was worked back to London by the plaintiff and eight more of the original crew, with whom the agreement had been made at Cronstadt.

LORD ELLENBOROUGH

> I think *Harris v Watson* was rightly decided; but I doubt whether the ground of public policy, upon which Lord Kenyon is stated to have proceeded, be the true principle on which the decision is to be supported. Here, I say, the agreement is void for want of consideration. There was no consideration for the ulterior pay promised to the mariners who remained with the ship. Before they sailed from London they had undertaken to do all that they could under all the emergencies of the voyage. They had sold all their services till the voyage should be completed. If they had been at liberty to quit the vessel at Cronstadt, the case would have been quite different; or if the captain had capriciously discharged the two men who were wanting, the others might not have been compellable to take the whole duty upon themselves, and their agreeing to do so might have been a sufficient consideration for the promise of an advance of wages. But the desertion of a part of the crew is to be considered an emergency of the voyage as much as their death; and those who remain are bound by the terms of their original contract to exert themselves to the utmost to bring the ship in safety to her destined port. Therefore, without looking to the policy of this agreement, I think it is void for want of consideration, and that the plaintiff can only recover at the rate of £5 a month.

Verdict Accordingly.

Points for reflection

1. In *Harris v Watson* (1791) Peake 102; 170 E.R. 94, the plaintiff, a seaman, claimed that the defendant, the captain of his ship, had promised him five guineas over and above his ordinary wages if he would perform some extra work in navigating the ship, the promise having been made, when the ship was in danger, to induce the seamen to exert themselves. Nonsuiting the plaintiff, Lord Kenyon CJ said, "If this action was to be supported, it would materially affect the navigation of this kingdom. It has been long since determined, that when the freight is lost, the wages are also lost. This rule was founded on a principle of policy, for if sailors were in all events to have their wages, and in times of danger entitled to insist on an extra charge on such a promise as this, they would in many cases suffer a ship to sink, unless the captain would pay an extravagant demand they might think proper to make." **10–055**

   According to the report of *Stilk v Myrick* in Espinasse (see P. Luther, 'Campbell, Espinasse and the Sailors' (1999) 19 L.S. 526), Lord Ellenborough said that "he recognised the principle of the case of *Harris v Watson* as founded on just and proper policy." See Gilmore, *The Death of Contract*, pp.22–28. Note that there is no evidence of a demand by the seamen in either *Harris v Watson* or *Stilk v Myrick*. Of course, a demand may be implied as well as express; but, if there was no demand, could either case be explained on the ground of duress? Should there be a difference between the case where the demand comes from the seamen and that where the master takes the initiative with a generous offer?

2. In *Hartley v Ponsonby* (1857) 7 El. & Bl. 872 an able seaman successfully sued the master of the Mobile on a promise to pay him £40 if he would assist in taking the ship from Port Philip to Bombay with a crew of 19 hands. The defence was that there was no consideration for the promise because the plaintiff was bound by his existing contract to assist in sailing the ship. The

ship had left England with a crew of 36 but, as a result of desertions, only 19 remained and only four or five of them were able seamen. The Queen's Bench held that the crew was so reduced that it was dangerous to life to sail and unreasonable for the master to require his crew to do so. Their contract had come to an end (see Ch.24, where the doctrine of frustration is discussed) and they were in the same position as any other free seamen in Port Philip: "they might stipulate for any amount of remuneration; and, considering the circumstances, £40 might not have been an exorbitant sum"—per Erle J.

Suppose £40 had been an 'exorbitant' sum. Should it have made any difference? Could not a free seaman in Port Philip properly have taken full advantage of a seller's market? Would it now be regarded as economic duress?

WILLIAMS v ROFFEY BROS & NICHOLLS (CONTRACTORS) LTD

Court of Appeal [1990] 2 W.L.R. 1153; [1990] 1 All E.R. 512

10–056   The defendants who had contracted to refurbish a block of flats sub-contracted the carpentry work to the plaintiff for a price of £20,000 to be paid in instalments related to the work completed. The plaintiff got into financial difficulties because the price was too low and he did not supervise the work properly. He had received over 80 per cent of the price but still had far more than 20 per cent. of the work to do. The defendants were liable to a penalty clause in the main contract if the work was not completed on time. They were aware of the plaintiff's difficulties and that the price was too low. They met him and agreed to pay him an extra £10,300 at £575 per flat to ensure that he continued with the work and completed on time. The plaintiff completed eight further flats and received a payment of £1,500. He stopped work and sued for the money he alleged to be owing. The defendants denied liability and, in particular, that they were liable to pay any part of the additional £10,300 because their agreement to pay it was not supported by any consideration. The judge held that the plaintiff was entitled to eight payments of £575, less certain deductions. The defendants appealed.

GLIDEWELL LJ

[Having reviewed the authorities, concluding with *Pao On v Lau Yiu*, continued:] It is true that *Pao On v Lau Yiu* is a case of a tripartite relationship, that is, a promise by A to perform a pre-existing contractual obligation owed to B, in return for a promise of payment by C. But Lord Scarman's words seem to me to be of general application, equally applicable to a promise made by one of the original two parties to a contract. Accordingly, following the view of the majority in *Ward v Byham* and of the whole court in *Williams v Williams* and that of the Privy Council in *Pao On v Lau Yiu* the present state of the law on this subject can be expressed in the following proposition: (i) if A has entered into a contract with B to do work for, or to supply goods or services to, B in return for payment by B and (ii) at some stage before A has completely performed his obligations under the contract B has reason to doubt whether A will, or will be able to, complete his side of the bargain and (iii) B thereupon promises A an additional payment in return for A's promise to perform his contractual obligations on time and (iv) as a result of giving his promise B obtains in practice a benefit, or obviates a disbenefit, and (v) B's promise is not given as a result of economic duress or fraud on the part of A, then (vi) the benefit to B is capable of being consideration for B's promise, so that the promise will be legally binding.

As I have said, counsel for the defendants accepts that in the present case by promising to pay the extra £10,300 the defendants secured benefits. There is no finding, and no suggestion, that in this case the promise was given as a result of fraud or duress.

If it be objected that the propositions above contravene the principle in *Stilk v Myrick*, I answer that in my view they do not: they refine and limit the application of that principle, but they leave the principle unscathed, for example, where B secures no benefit by his promise. It is not in my view surprising that a principle enunciated in relation to the rigours of seafaring life during the Napoleonic wars should be subjected during the succeeding 180 years to a process of refinement and limitation in its application in the present day.

It is therefore my opinion that on his findings of fact in the present case, the judge was entitled to hold, as he did, that the defendants' promise to pay the extra £10,300 was supported by valuable consideration, and thus constituted an enforceable agreement.

As a subsidiary argument, counsel for the defendants submits that on the facts of the present case the consideration, even if otherwise good, did not "move from the promisee." This submission is based on the principle illustrated in the decision in *Tweddle v Atkinson* [below, 12–004].

My understanding of the meaning of the requirement that "consideration must move from the promisee" is that such consideration must be provided by the promisee, or arise out of his contractual relationship with the promisor. It is consideration provided by somebody else, not a party to the contract, which does not "move from the promisee." This was the situation in *Tweddle v Atkinson*, but it is, of course, not the situation in the present case. Here the benefits to the defendants arose out of their agreement of April 9, 1986 with the plaintiff, the promisee. In this respect I would adopt the following passage from *Chitty on Contracts* (25th ed., 1983), para. 173, and refer to the authorities there cited:

"The requirement that consideration must move from the promisee is most generally satisfied where some detriment is suffered by him: for example, where he parts with money or goods, or renders services, in exchange for the promise. But the requirement may equally well be satisfied where the promisee confers a benefit on the promisor without in fact suffering any detriment."

That is the situation in this case.

I repeat, therefore, my opinion that the judge was, as a matter of law, entitled to hold that there was valid consideration to support the agreement under which the defendants promised to pay an additional £10,300 at the rate of £575 per flat.

For these reasons I would dismiss this appeal.

RUSSELL LJ

[Having cited the judgments in *Amalgamated Investment and Property Co Ltd v Texas Commerce International Bank Ltd* (below, para.11–014), continued:] These citations demonstrate that while consideration remains a fundamental requirement before a contract not under seal can be enforced, the policy of the law in its search to do justice between the parties has developed considerably since the early nineteenth century when *Stilk v Myrick* was decided by Lord Ellenborough C. J. In the late twentieth century I do not believe that the rigid approach to the concept of consideration to be found in *Stilk v Myrick* is either necessary or desirable. Consideration there must still be but in my judgment the courts nowadays should be more ready to find its existence so as to reflect the intention of the parties to the contract where the bargaining powers are not unequal and where the finding of consideration reflects the true intention of the parties.

What was the true intention of the parties when they arrived at the agreement pleaded by the defendants in para. 5 of the amended defence? The plaintiff had got into financial difficulties. The defendants, through their employee Mr Cottrell, recognised that the price that had been agreed originally with the plaintiff was less than what Mr Cottrell himself regarded as a reasonable price. There was a desire on Mr Cottrell's part to retain the services of the plaintiff so that the work could be completed without the need to employ another sub-contractor. There was further a need to replace what had hitherto been a haphazard method of payment by a more formalised scheme involving the payment of a specified sum on the completion of each flat. These were all advantages accruing to the defendants which can fairly be said to have been in consideration of their undertaking to pay the additional £10,300. True it was that the plaintiff did not undertake to do any work additional to that which he had originally undertaken to do but the terms on which he was to carry out the work were varied and, in my judgment, that variation was supported by consideration which a pragmatic approach to the true relationship between the parties readily demonstrates.

For my part I wish to make it plain that I do not base my judgment on any reservation as to the correctness of the law long ago enunciated in *Stilk v Myrick*. A gratuitous promise, pure and simple, remains unenforceable unless given under seal. But where, as in this case, a party undertakes to make a payment because by so doing it will gain an advantage arising out of the continuing relationship with the promisee the new bargain will not fail for want of consideration. As I read the judgment of the assistant recorder this was his true ratio on that part of the case wherein the absence of consideration was raised in argument. For the reasons that I have endeavoured to outline, I think that the assistant recorder came to a correct conclusion and I too would dismiss this appeal.

PURCHAS LJ

The question must be posed: what consideration has moved from the plaintiff to support the promise to pay the extra £10,300 added to the lump sum provision? In the particular circumstances which I have outlined above, there was clearly a commercial advantage to both sides from a pragmatic point of view in reaching the agreement of April 9. The defendants were on risk that as a result of the bargain they had struck the plaintiff would not or indeed possibly could not comply with his existing obligations without further finance. As a result of the agreement the defendants secured their position commercially. There was, however, no obligation added to the contractual duties imposed on the plaintiff under the original contract. Prima facie this would appear to be a classic *Stilk v Myrick* case. It was, however, open to the plaintiff to be in deliberate breach of the contract in order to "cut his losses" commercially. In normal circumstances the suggestion that a contracting party can rely on his own breach to establish consideration is distinctly unattractive. In many cases it obviously would be and if there was any element of duress brought on the other contracting party under the modern development of this branch of the law the proposed breaker of the contract would not benefit. With some hesitation and comforted by the passage from the speech of Lord Hailsham L.C. [in [1972] A.C. 741 at 757–758], to which I have referred, I consider that the modern approach to the question of consideration would be that where there were benefits derived by each party to a contract of variation even though one party did not suffer a detriment this would not be fatal to the establishing of sufficient consideration to support the agreement. If both parties benefit from an agreement it is not necessary that each also suffers a detriment. In my judgment, on the facts as found by the judge, he was entitled to reach the conclusion that consideration existed and in those circumstances I would not disturb that finding. This is sufficient to determine the appeal. The judge found as a fact that the flats were "substantially completed" and that payment was due to the plaintiff in respect of the number of flats substantially completed, which left an outstanding amount due from the defendants to the plaintiff in the absence of the payment of which the plaintiff was entitled to remove from the site. For these reasons and for the reasons which have already been given by Glidewell L.J., I would dismiss this appeal.

Appeal Dismissed. (Leave to Appeal to the House of Lords was Granted but not Pursued.)

Questions

10–057

1. Do the cases cited by Glidewell LJ support the conclusion (vi) in his proposition?

2. Was *Stilk v Myrick* distinguishable as a case where the master secured no benefit by his promise? Was it not a benefit to him to have the crew sail the ship home rather than abandon him and it in a foreign port? Did not the master "gain an advantage out of the continuing relationship" with the sailors? And cf. *Atlas Express Ltd v Kafko Ltd*, below, Ch.26.

3. Is it not always a "benefit" to a contracting party to have the other party perform rather than default? Did the defendants receive any benefit other than (i) the performance of the contract by the plaintiff and (ii) avoidance of the penalty? How if at all did the existence of the penalty clause affect the consideration given by the plaintiff? Did the plaintiff give anything other than the performance of his contract? Is this what counsel had in mind when he argued that consideration (for example, relief from the penalty) did not "move from the promisee"?

4. Does the case suggest that the worse the plight of the promisor (for example, the bigger the penalty clause) the greater the benefit to him and the more likely it is that performance of the contract will be held to be consideration?

5. Would the result have been the same if the original agreed price for the carpentry had been a fair price? Or a generous price?

6. If competent contracting parties *freely* agree to a modification, what policy reasons (if any) could there be for denying the binding effect of the variation? Compare *Antons Trawling Co Ltd v Smith* [2003] 2 N.Z.L.R. 23.

7. Is the decision reconcilable with *Foakes v Beer*, below? Note that Lord Blackburn was convinced that prompt part payment of a debt is in fact a benefit to the creditor but he abandoned the opinion that it is for that reason consideration for the creditor's promise not to claim the balance. See Adams and Brownsword (1990) 53 *Modern Law Review* 536 (cited in *Re Selectmove* below).

8. In *Anangel Atlas Compania Naviera SA v Ishikawajima Harima Heavy Industries Co Ltd (No.2)* [1990] 2 Lloyds Rep. 526 Hirst J held that it was a clear benefit or an avoidance of a disbenefit to the defendants that the plaintiffs agreed to take delivery of a ship on the contract date since "Their own evidence conclusively demonstrated that their main object was to make sure that the plaintiffs, whom they described as their 'core' customers, did indeed take delivery on July 25, in order to encourage their other reluctant customers to follow suit." It was the "very substantial practical avoidance of disbenefit" arising from the anticipated behaviour of the other customers which supplied the consideration. This was apparently the distinction discerned by Hirst J between the case before him and *Stilk v Myrick* which, he said, still applies where "there is a wholly gratuitous promise." A promise is gratuitous unless the promisee is paying a price for it by giving something in return. Was the existence of the penalty clause in *Williams v Roffey* or the potential default of the other buyers in *Anangel* an element in the price paid by the respective promisees? Suppose there had been no other likely defaulters in *Anangel*. Would the promise have then been gratuitous? Was the promise in *Atlas Express Ltd v Kafko Ltd*, below, Ch.26, rightly held to be gratuitous?

NORTH OCEAN SHIPPING CO v HYUNDAI CONSTRUCTION CO

Queen's Bench Division [1979] Q.B. 705; [1979] 3 W.L.R. 419; [1978] 3 All E.R. 1170; sub nom. The Atlantic Baron, [1979] 1 Lloyd's Rep. 89

Shipbuilders ("the yard") on April 10, 1972, entered into a contract to build a tanker for shipowners ("the owners") for the fixed price of US $30,950,000, payable in five instalments as the work progressed. The contract required the yard to open a letter of credit to provide security for repayment of instalments in the event of their default in performance of the contract. The owners paid the first instalment on April 28, 1972. On February 12, 1973, the US dollar was devalued by 10 per cent. The yard claimed an increase of 10 per cent on the four remaining instalments. The owners did not agree and offered to submit the dispute to arbitration. The yard declined and by telex on June 26, 1973, said that, if the owners did not agree to pay the extra 10 per cent they would terminate the contract and refund the first instalment. The owners in May, 1973, had entered into a very advantageous agreement to charter the tanker on completion to Shell for three years, and they would have lost this advantage if the yard carried out its threat. Accordingly, the owners replied by telex on June 28:

10-058

"We are in receipt of your telex dated 26th June, 1973. Although we are convinced we are under no obligation to make additional payments which you ask, we are prepared as you demand in your telex of the 26th June, 1973, and in order to maintain an amicable relationship and without prejudice to our rights, to make an increase of 10 per cent in instalments payable subsequent to the 12th February, 1973. No doubt you will arrange for corresponding increases in the letter of credit provided for in article XI(2)(iii)."

The yard replied acknowledging that the difference of opinion had been settled and promising to increase the letter of credit. The yard did not appreciate the significance of the words, "without prejudice to our rights," the owners realised that this was so and deliberately did not draw the yard's attention to the significance of the reservation. The letter of credit was increased, the instalments were paid with the additional 10 per cent without protest, the final instalment being expressed to be "in full and final settlement"; and the tanker was delivered on November 27, 1974.

On July 30, 1975 the owners claimed the return of the excess 10 per cent. They refrained from claiming until that date because they had a contract with the yard for another tanker and it was suggested that they feared that, if they initiated the claim before the tanker was delivered, the yard might have refused to deliver. The arbitrators found that there was no ground for such an inference.

The arbitrators held that the owners' claim failed and, at the request of the parties, stated their award in the form of a special case.

MOCATTA J

[Having stated the facts:]

Counsel's argument for the owners that the agreement to pay the extra 10 per cent. was void for lack of consideration was based on the well-known principle that a promise by one party to fulfil his existing contractual duty towards his other contracting party is not good consideration: he relied on the well-known case of *Stilk v Myrick* for this submission. Accordingly there was no consideration for the owner's agreement to pay the further 10 per cent, since the yard were already contractually bound to build the ship and it is common ground that the devaluation of the dollar had in no way lessened the yard's legal obligation to do this. There has of course been some criticism in the books of the decision in *Stilk v Myrick* which is somewhat differently reported in the two sets of reports, but Campbell's reports have the better reputation and what I have referred to as being the law on this point is referred to as "the present" rule in *Chitty on Contracts*: see, also, Cheshire and Fifoot. The law seems still to be the same in Australia: see *T. A. Sundell & Sons Pty Ltd v Emm Yannoulatos (Overseas) Pty Ltd* [1956] S.R. (N.S.W.) 323.

Counsel for the yard relied on what Denning L.J. said in two cases dealing with very different subject matters. [His Lordship discussed *Ward v Byham* and *Williams v Williams*, and pointed out that the other judges in those cases found that there was ample consideration.]

I do not therefore think either of these cases successfully enables counsel for the yard to avoid the rule in *Stilk v Myrick* . . .

[His Lordship then considered whether the increase of 10 per cent in the letter of credit amounted to consideration.]

I remain unconvinced, however, that by merely securing an increase in the instalments to be paid of 10 per cent the yard automatically became obliged to increase the return letter of credit pro tanto and were therefore doing no more than undertaking in this respect to fulfil their existing contractual duty. I think that here they were undertaking an additional obligation or rendering themselves liable to an increased detriment. I therefore conclude, though not without some doubt, that there was consideration for the new agreement . . .

Having reached the conclusion that there was consideration for the agreement made on June 28 and June 29, 1973, I must next consider whether even if that agreement, varying the terms of the original ship-building contract of April 10, 1972, was made under a threat to break that original contract and that the various increased instalments were made consequentially under the varied agreement, the increased sums can be recovered as money had and received. Counsel for the owners submitted that they could be, provided they were involuntary payments and not made, albeit perhaps with some grumbling, to close the transaction. Certainly this is the well-established position if payments are made, for example, to avoid the wrongful seizure of goods where there is no prior agreement to make such payments.

[His Lordship considered the authorities, including *Smith v William Charlick Ltd* [1924] 34 C.L.R. 38 at 56 where Isaacs J. said: "It is conceded that the only ground on which the promise to repay could be implied is 'compulsion.' The payment is said by the respondent not to have been 'voluntary' but 'forced' from it within the contemplation of the law . . . 'compulsion' in relation to a payment of which refund is sort, and whether it is also variously called 'coercion,' 'extortion,' 'exaction' or 'force,' includes every species of duress or conduct analogous to duress actual or threatened, exacted by or on behalf of the payee and applied to the person or the property or any right of the person who pays. . . Such compulsion is a legal wrong, and the law provides a remedy by raising a fictional promise to repay."]

Before proceeding further it may be useful to summarise the conclusions I have so far reached. First, I do not take the view that the recovery of money paid under duress other than to the person is necessarily limited to duress to goods falling within one of the categories hitherto established by the English cases. I would respectfully follow and adopt the broad statement of principle laid down by Isaacs J. cited earlier and frequently quoted and applied in the Australian cases. Secondly, from this it follows that the compulsion may take the form of "economic duress" if the necessary facts are proved. A threat to break a contract may amount to such "economic duress." Thirdly, if there has been such a form of duress leading to a contract for consideration, I think that contract is a voidable one which can be avoided and the excess money paid under it recovered.

I think the facts found in this case do establish that the agreement to increase the price by 10 per cent reached at the end of June, 1973, was caused by what may be called "economic duress." The yard were adamant in insisting on the increased price without having any legal justification for so doing and the owners realised that the yard would not accept anything other than an unqualified agreement to the increase. The owners might have claimed damages in arbitration against the yard with all the inherent unavoidable uncertainties of litigation, but in view of the position of the owners vis-à-vis their relations with Shell it would be unreasonable to hold that this is the course they should have taken: see *Astley v Reynolds* (1731) 2 Str. 915. The owners made a very reasonable offer of arbitration coupled with security for any award in the yard's favour that might be made, but this was refused. They then made their agreement, which can truly I think be said to have been made under compulsion, by the telex of June 28, without prejudice to their rights. I do not consider the yard's ignorance of the Shell charter material. It may well be that had they known of it they would have been even more exigent.

If I am right in the conclusion reached with some doubt earlier that there was consideration for the 10 per cent increase agreement reached at the end of June, 1973, and if it be right to regard this as having been reached under a kind of duress in the form of economic pressure, then what is said in *Chitty on Contracts* (24th ed.), para. 442, to which both counsel referred me, is relevant, namely that a contract entered into under duress is voidable and not void—

"that a person who has entered into the contract may either affirm or avoid such contract after the duress has ceased; and if he has so voluntarily acted under it with a full knowledge of all the circumstances he may be held bound on the ground of ratification, or if, after escaping from the duress, he takes no steps to set aside the transaction he may be found to have affirmed it."

[His Lordship reviewed the facts.]

I have come to the conclusion that the important points here are that (i) since there was no danger at this time in registering a protest, (ii) the final payments were made without any qualification, and (iii) were followed by a delay until July 31, 1975, before the owners put forward their claim, the correct inference to draw, taking an objective view of the facts, is that the action and inaction of the owners can only be regarded as an affirmation of the variation in June, 1973, of the terms of the original contract by the agreement to pay the additional 10 per cent In reaching this conclusion I have not, of course, overlooked the findings in the special case [that the owners never intended to affirm the agreement for extra payments] but I do not think that an intention on the part of the owners not to affirm the agreement for the extra payments, not indicated to the yard, can avail them in view of their overt acts. As was said in *Deacon v Transport Regulation Board* (1958) V.R. 458, 460, in considering whether a payment was made voluntarily or not: "No secret mental reservation of the doer is material. The question is—what would his conduct indicate to a reasonable man as his mental state." I think this test is equally applicable to the decision this court has to make whether a voidable contract has been affirmed or not and I have applied this test in reaching the conclusion I have just expressed.

I think I should add very shortly that having considered the many authorities cited, even if I had come to a different conclusion on the issue about consideration, I would have come to the same decision adverse to the owners on the question whether the payments were made voluntarily in the sense of being made to close the transaction.

Judgment for the Yard.

Questions

10–059   1. In the light of *Williams v Roffey*, should Mocatta J have held that the performance of their contract by the yard was a benefit, and therefore consideration, to the owners because it enabled them to perform their very advantageous charter agreement with Shell (corresponding to the avoidance of the penalty in *Williams* and the encouragement of the potential defaulters in *Anangel*)?

2. Was Mocatta J right to hold that the automatic obligation to increase the return letter of credit was consideration? If the extra 10 per cent was a gift, was it perhaps an onerous gift like that in *Johnsey Estates Ltd v Lewis & Manley*?

----

4. The Effect of a Creditor's Promise to Reduce the Debt

Re SELECTMOVE LTD

Court of Appeal [1995] 1 W.L.R. 474; [1995] 2 All E.R. 531

10–060   S Ltd owed the Revenue large sums of income tax (PAYE) and national insurance (NIC). For the purposes of the decision, it was accepted that, at a meeting on July 15, 1991 with Mr Polland (P), a collector of taxes, S's managing director, Mr ffooks (ff), suggested that it would not be in anyone's interest for the company to be put into compulsory liquidation and proposed that the company should pay future PAYE and NIC as it fell due and the arrears at £1,000 per month from February 1, 1992. P said that he would have to seek approval and would come back to ff if the proposal was unacceptable. S made two payments under the alleged agreement. S heard no more from the Revenue until October 9, 1991 when they demanded payment of arrears of PAYE and NIC amounting to £24,650 and threatened a winding-up petition. The question was whether the proposal for payment by instalments on July 15, 1991 had become a binding agreement. On the issue of acceptance, see above, para.3–020. On the issue of consideration—

PETER GIBSON LJ

There are two elements to the consideration which the company claims was provided by it to the Crown. One is the promise to pay off its existing liability by instalments from 1 February 1992. The other is the promise to pay future PAYE and NIC as they fell due. Mr Nugee [Counsel for S Ltd] suggested that implicit in the latter was the promise to continue trading. But that cannot be spelt out of Mr ffooks' evidence as to what he agreed with Mr Polland. Accordingly, the second element is no more than a promise to pay that which it was bound to pay under the fiscal legislation at the date at which it was bound to make such payment. If the first element is not good consideration, I do not see why the second element should be either.

[Peter Gibson L.J. considered *Foakes v Beer, Vanbergen v St. Edmunds Properties* and *D & C Builders Ltd v Rees* (below) and continued:] Mr Nugee, however, submitted that an additional benefit to the Crown was conferred by the agreement in that the Crown stood to derive practical benefits therefrom: it was likely to recover more from not enforcing its debt against the company, which was known to be in financial difficulties, than from putting the company into liquidation. He pointed to the fact that the company did in fact pay its further PAYE and NIC liabilities and £7,000 of its arrears. He relied on the decision of this court in *Williams v Roffey Bros.* (above) for the proposition that a promise to perform an existing obligation can amount to good consideration provided that there are practical benefits to the promisee.

[Having discussed *Williams'* case and cited Glidewell L.J.'s six propositions (above) Peter Gibson L.J. continued:] Mr Nugee submitted that although Glidewell L.J. in terms confined his remarks to a case where B is to do the work for or supply goods or services to A, the same principle must apply where B's obligation is to pay

A, and he referred to an article by Adams and Brownsword "Contract, Consideration and the Critical Path" (1990) 53 MLR 536 at 539–540 which suggests that *Foakes v Beer* might need reconsideration. I see the force of the argument, but the difficulty that I feel with it is that if the principle of *Williams'* case is to be extended to an obligation to make payment, it would in effect leave the principle in *Foakes v Beer* without any application. When a creditor and a debtor who are at arm's length reach agreement on the payment of the debt by instalments to accommodate the debtor, the creditor will no doubt always see a practical benefit to himself in so doing. In the absence of authority there would be much to be said for the enforceability of such a contract. But that was a matter expressly considered in *Foakes v Beer* yet held not to constitute good consideration in law. *Foakes v Beer* was not even referred to in *Williams'* case, and it is in my judgment impossible, consistently with the doctrine of precedent, for this court to extend the principle of *Williams'* case to any circumstances governed by the principle of *Foakes v Beer*. If that extension is to be made, it must be by the House of Lords or, perhaps even more appropriately, by Parliament after consideration by the Law Commission.

In my judgment, the judge was right to hold that if there was an agreement between the company and the Crown it was unenforceable for want of consideration.

[Peter Gibson L.J. held promissory estoppel was inapplicable because (i) P had no actual or ostensible authority to make the alleged promise and (ii) S Ltd had failed to honour its promises to pay. Stuart-Smith and Balcombe L.JJ. agreed.]

Questions

1. Is there a valid distinction, in the context of consideration, between an obligation to pay money and an obligation to render services? Cf. *Ruxley Electronics*, below, Ch.19.

10–061

2. Might the court have taken a different view if the offer had come from the Revenue—e.g., "If you will promise to pay by instalments, we will not apply for a winding up order"? Or are *Foakes v Beer* and *Vanbergen* still an insuperable obstacle?

FOAKES v BEER

House of Lords (1984) 9 App.Cas. 605; 54 L.J.Q.B. 130; 51 L.T. 833; 33 W.R. 233

Appeal from an order of the Court of Appeal.

10–062

On August 11, 1875, the respondent recovered judgment against the appellant for £2,077 17s. 2d. for debt and £13 1s. 10d. for costs. On December 21, 1876, a memorandum of agreement was made and signed by the appellant and respondent in the following terms:

"Whereas the said John Weston Foakes is indebted to the said Julia Beer and she has obtained a judgment in Her Majesty's High Court of Justice, Exchequer Division, for the sum of £2,090 19s. And whereas the said John Weston Foakes has requested the said Julia Beer to give him time in which to pay such judgment, which she has agreed to do on the following conditions. Now this agreement witnesseth that in consideration of the said John Weston Foakes paying to the said Julia Beer on the signing of this agreement the sum of £500, the receipt whereof she doth hereby acknowledge in part satisfaction of the said judgment debt of £2,090 19s., and on condition of his paying her or her executors, administrators, assigns or nominee the sum of £150 on the 1st day of July and the 1st day of January or within one calendar month after each of the said days respectively in every year until the whole of the said sum of £2,090 19s. shall have been fully paid and satisfied, the first of such payments to be made on the 1st day of July next, then she the said Julia Beer hereby undertakes and agrees that she, her executors, administrators or assigns, will not take any proceedings whatever on the said judgment."

The respondent having in June, 1882, taken out a summons for leave to proceed on the judgment, an issue was directed to be tried between the respondent as plaintiff and the appellant as defendant whether any and what amount was on July 1, 1882, due upon the judgment.

At the trial of the issue before Cave J it was proved that the whole sum of £2,090 19s. had been paid by instalments, but the respondent claimed interest. The jury under his Lordship's direction found that the appellant had paid all the sums which by the agreement of December 21, 1876, he undertook to pay and within the times therein specified. Cave J was of the opinion that whether the judgment was satisfied or not, the respondent was, by reason of the agreement, not entitled to issue execution for any sum on the judgment.

The Queen's Bench Division (Watkin Williams and Mathew JJ) discharged an order for a new trial on the ground of misdirection.

The Court of Appeal (Brett MR, Lindley and Fry LJJ) reversed that decision and entered judgment for the respondent for the interest due with costs: (1883) 11 QBD 221.

EARL OF SELBORNE LC

My Lords, upon the construction of the agreement of December 21, 1876, I cannot differ from the conclusion in which both the courts below were agreed. If the operative part could properly be controlled by the recitals, I think there would be much reason to say that the only thing contemplated by the recitals was giving time for payment, without any relinquishment, on the part of the judgment creditor, of any portion of the amount recoverable (whether for principal or for interest) under the judgment. But the agreement of the judgment creditor, which follows the recitals, is that she "will not take any proceedings whatever on the judgment," if a certain condition is fulfilled. What is that condition? Payment of the sum of £150 in every half year, "until the whole of said sum of £2,090 19s." (the aggregate amount of the principal debt and costs, for which judgment had been entered) "shall have been fully paid and satisfied." A particular "sum" is here mentioned, which does not include the interest then due, or future interest. Whatever was meant to be payable at all, under this agreement, was clearly to be payable by half-yearly instalments of £150 each; any other construction must necessarily make the conditional promise nugatory. But to say that the half-yearly payments were to continue till the whole sum of £2,090 19s., "and interest thereon," should have been fully paid and satisfied, would be to introduce very important words into the agreement which are not there, and of which I cannot say that they are necessarily implied. Although, therefore, I may (as indeed I do) very much doubt whether the effect of the agreement, as a conditional waiver of the interest to which she was by law entitled under the judgment, was really present to the mind of the judgment creditor, still I cannot deny that it might have that effect, if capable of being legally enforced.

The question, therefore, is nakedly raised by this appeal, whether your Lordships are now prepared, not only to overrule, as contrary to law, the doctrine stated by Sir Edward Coke to have been laid down by all the judges of the Common Pleas in *Pinnel's Case* (1602) 5 Co.Rep. 117a, in 1602, and repeated in his note to Littleton, § 344, Co.Litt. 212b, but to treat a prospective agreement, not under seal, for satisfaction of a debt by a series of payments on account to a total amount less than the whole debt, as binding in law, provided these payments are regularly made; the case not being one of a composition with a common debtor, agreed to, inter se, by several creditors . . . The doctrine itself, as laid down by Sir Edward Coke, may have been criticised as questionable in principle by some persons whose opinions are entitled to respect, but it has never been judicially overruled; on the contrary I think it has always, since the sixteenth century, been accepted as law. If so, I cannot think that your Lordships would do right, if you were now to reverse, as erroneous, a judgment of the Court of Appeal, proceeding upon a doctrine which has been accepted as part of the law of England for 280 years . . .

The distinction between the effect of a deed under seal, and that of an agreement by parol, or by writing not under seal, may seem arbitrary, but it is established in our law; nor is it really unreasonable or practically inconvenient that the law should require particular solemnities to give a gratuitous contract the force of a binding obligation. If the question be (as, in the actual state of the law, I think it is), whether consideration is, or is not, given in a case of this kind, by the debtor who pays down part of the debt presently due from him, for a promise by the creditor to relinquish, after certain further payments on account, the residue of the debt, I cannot say that I think consideration is given, in the sense which I have always understood that word as used in our law. It might be (and indeed I think it would be) an improvement in our law, if a release or acquittance of the whole debt, on payment of any sum which the creditor might be content to receive by way of accord and satisfaction (though less than the whole), were held to be, generally, binding, though not under seal; nor should I be unwilling to see equal force given to a prospective agreement, like the present, in writing though not under seal; but I think it impossible, without refinements which practically alter the sense of the word, to treat such a release or acquittance as supported by any new consideration proceeding from the debtor. All the authorities subsequent to *Cumber v Wane* (1721) 1 Stra. 426 which were relied upon by the appellant at your Lordships' Bar (such as *Sibree v Tripp* (1846) 15 M. & W. 23; *Curlewis v Clark* (1849) 3 Exch. 375 and *Goddard v O'Brien* (1882) 9 QBD 37) have proceeded upon the distinction that, by giving negotiable paper or otherwise, there has been some new consideration for a new agreement, distinct from mere money payments in or towards discharge of the original liability.[4] I think it unnecessary to go through those cases, or to examine the particular grounds on which each of them was decided. There are no such facts in the case now before your Lordships. What is called "any benefit, or even any legal possibility of benefit," in Mr Smith's notes to *Cumber v Wane*, is not (as I conceive) that sort of benefit which a creditor may derive from getting payment of part of the money due to him from a debtor who might otherwise keep him at arm's length, or possibly become insolvent, but is some independent benefit, actual or contingent, of a kind which might in law be a good and valuable consideration for any other sort of agreement not under seal.

My conclusion is, that the order appealed from should be affirmed, and the appeal dismissed, with costs, and I so move your Lordships.

LORD BLACKBURN

[Having held that the agreement was one to take £500 in satisfaction of the whole sum of £2,090 19s., subject to the condition that, unless the balance of the principal debt was paid by instalments, the whole might be enforced with interest, turned to the question whether payment of a lesser sum is good satisfaction:]

This is a question, I think, of difficulty.

In Coke, Littleton 212b., Lord Coke says: "where the condition is for payment of £20, the obligor or feoffor cannot at the time appointed pay a lesser sum in satisfaction of the whole, because it is apparent that a lesser sum of money cannot be a satisfaction of a greater . . . If the obligor or feoffor pay a lesser sum either before the day or at another place than is limited by the condition, and the obligee or feoffee receiveth it, this is a good satisfaction." For this he cites *Pinnel's Case*. That was an action on a bond for £16, conditioned for the payment of £8 10s. on November 11, 1600.[5] Plea that defendant, at plaintiff's request, before the said day, to wit, on October 1, paid to the plaintiff £5 2s. 2d., which the plaintiff accepted in full satisfaction of the £8 10s. The plaintiff had judgment for the insufficient pleading.[6] But though this was so, Lord Coke reports that it was resolved by the whole Court of Common Pleas "that payment of a lesser sum on the day in satisfaction of a greater cannot be any satisfaction for the whole, because it appears to the judges that by no possibility a lesser sum can be satisfaction to the plaintiff for a greater sum: but the gift of a horse, hawk, or robe, etc., in satisfaction is good for it shall be intended that a horse, hawk, or robe, etc., might be more beneficial to the plaintiff than the money, in respect of some circumstance, or otherwise the plaintiff would not have accepted it in satisfaction. But when the whole sum is due, by no intendment the acceptance of parcel can be a satisfaction to the plaintiff; but in the case at bar it was resolved that the payment and acceptance of parcel before the day in satisfaction of the whole would be a good satisfaction in regard of circumstance of time; for peradventure parcel of it before the day would be more beneficial to him than the whole at the day, and the value of the satisfaction is not material; so if I am bound in £20 to pay you £10 at Westminster, and you request me to pay you £5 at the day at York, and you will accept it in full satisfaction for the whole £10, it is a good satisfaction for the whole, for the expenses to pay it at York is sufficient satisfaction."

There are two things here resolved. First, that where a matter paid and accepted in satisfaction of a debt

---

[4]   *D & C Builders v Rees* (below, Ch.11) decides that there is no material distinction between giving a small sum in cash and giving the same amount by a negotiable instrument.

[5]   The bond was a common form of agreement whereby, e.g. C loaned D £8 10s. and D executed a bond (under seal) promising to pay a larger sum, say £16, on a certain day, say, November 11, 1600, subject to a condition that, if he paid £8 10s. before that day, the bond was to be void. See A. W. B. Simpson, "The Penal Bond with Conditional Defeasance" (1966) 82 L.Q.R. 392.

[6]   The defendant omitted to plead that he tendered the money in full satisfaction: "And always the manner of the tender and of the payment shall be directed by him who made the tender or payment, and not by him who accepts it."

certain might by any possibility be more beneficial to the creditor than his debt, the court will not inquire into the adequacy of the consideration. If the creditor, without any fraud, accepted it in satisfaction when it was not a sufficient satisfaction it was his own fault. And that payment before the day might be more beneficial, and consequently that the plea was in substance good, and this must have been decided in the case.

There is a second point stated to have been resolved, viz.: "That payment of a lesser sum on the day cannot be any satisfaction of the whole, because it appears to the judges that by no possibility a lesser sum can be a satisfaction to the plaintiff for a greater sum." This was certainly not necessary for the decision of the case; but though the resolution of the Court of Common Pleas was only a dictum, it seems to me clear that Lord Coke deliberately adopted the dictum, and the great weight of his authority makes it necessary to be cautious before saying that what he deliberately adopted as law was a mistake, and though I cannot find that in any subsequent case this dictum has been made the ground of the decision, except in *Fitch v Sutton* (1804) 5 East 230, as to which I shall make some remarks later, and in *Down v Hatcher* (1839) 10 Ad. & El. 121, as to which Parke B., in *Cooper v Parker* (1855) 15 C.B. 828, said, "Whenever the question may arise as to whether *Down v Hatcher* is good law, I should have a great deal to say against it," yet there certainly are cases in which great judges have treated the dictum in *Pinnel's Case* as good law.

For instance, in *Sibree v Tripp*, Parke B. says, "It is clear if the claim be a liquidated and ascertained sum, payment of part cannot be satisfaction of the whole, although it may, under certain circumstances, be evidence of a gift of the remainder." And Alderson B., in the same case, says, "It is undoubtedly true that payment of a portion of a liquidated demand, in the same manner as the whole liquidated demand which ought to be paid, is payment only in part, because it is not one bargain, but two: viz., payment of part, and an agreement without consideration to give up the residue. The courts might very well have held the contrary, and have left the matter to the agreement of the parties, but undoubtedly the law is so settled." After such strong expressions of opinion, I doubt much whether any judge sitting in a court of the first instance would be justified in treating the question as open. But as this has very seldom, if at all, been the ground of the decision even in a court of the first instance, and certainly never been the ground of a decision in the Court of Exchequer Chamber, still less in this House, I did think it open in your Lordships' House to reconsider this question. And, notwithstanding the very high authority of Lord Coke, I think it is not the fact that to accept prompt payment of a part only of a liquidated demand can never be more beneficial than to insist on payment of the whole. And if it be not the fact, it cannot be apparent to the judges . . .

[Having considered the earlier authorities his Lordship continued:]

What principally weighs with me in thinking that Lord Coke made a mistake of fact is my conviction that all men of business, whether merchants or tradesmen, do every day recognise and act on the ground that prompt payment of a part of their demand may be more beneficial to them than it would be to insist on their rights and enforce payment of the whole. Even where the debtor is perfectly solvent, and sure to pay at last, this is often so. Where the credit of the debtor is doubtful it must be more so. I had persuaded myself that there was no such long-continued action on this dictum as to render it improper in this House to reconsider the question. I had written my reasons for so thinking; but as they were not satisfactory to the other noble and learned Lords who heard the case, I do not now repeat them nor persist in them.

I assent to the judgment proposed, though it is not that which I had originally thought proper.

Lords Watson and Fitzgerald held that, on the true construction of the agreement, Beer was entitled to recover the interest. The only effect of the agreement was to give Foakes time to pay and not to forgive him anything. If they were wrong about that, they agreed that there was no consideration for a promise to forgo the interest.

Order Appealed from Affirmed; and Appeal Dismissed with Costs.

Questions

10–063   1. What was the meaning of the agreement (a) according to Beer, (b) according to Foakes? Which view was accepted by the majority of the House?

2. What was the expressed "consideration"? Was it (a) the promise of £500, or (b) the payment of £500, or (c) the payment of £500 and the promise of the remainder by instalments?

3. What was the ratio decidendi of *Pinnel's Case*? Was the rule in *Pinnel's Case* binding on the House of Lords?

4. Did the judges think the rule they applied was a good one?

5. Cheshire and Fifoot (8th edn), p.90, wrote: ". . . Doctor Foakes was not seeking 'legally to enforce the agreement' against Mrs Beer. He was setting it up by way of defence to her application for leave to proceed on the judgment. He was therefore under no necessity to establish a contract and the question of consideration was irrelevant. The learned Lords concentrated on the wrong issue." Do you agree? Was not the question whether Beer's promise not to take proceedings was binding?

6. Cheshire, Fifoot and Furmston (12th edn), p.93, say "It will be observed that the plaintiff sued in Pinnel's Case not in assumpsit but in debt, so that no question of consideration arose." But it was not the promise to pay the debt which was in issue but the promise not to enforce the debt. Did not that raise an issue of consideration?

See also below, Ch.11 and Kelly, (1964) 27 M.L.R. 540.

7. If the parties did not intend the interest to be forgiven, might not the contract have been rectified (if the argument based on consideration had failed)? How would Lord Denning have decided the case? See *D & C Builders v Rees*, below, Ch.11.

VANBERGEN v ST EDMUNDS PROPERTIES LTD

Court of Appeal [1933] 2 K.B. 223; 102 L.J.K.B. 369; 149 L.T. 182

Appeal from a decision of Macnaghten J on the further consideration of an action tried by him with a special jury.   **10–064**

In July 1932 the plaintiff was indebted to the defendants in the sum of £208 odd for costs under a judgment and order.

By his statement of claim, the plaintiff alleged that on July 6, 1932, the defendants by their solicitor, a Mr Kennard, verbally agreed with him that, if he would on July 7, 1932, pay the £208 in cash into a bank at Eastbourne for the credit of the solicitor's firm at the Law Courts branch of the Bank of England, that payment would satisfy all sums that he owed them and a bankruptcy notice which they had issued in respect of part of the debt would not be served on him. On July 7, the plaintiff did pay the £208 to the Eastbourne bank with instructions to remit it as agreed. He alleged that, the same day, he advised the solicitors of the payment and, on July 8, the defendants' clerk; but that, in breach of the agreement, the bankruptcy notice was served on him. He claimed damages for the breach of contract.

The defendants denied the agreement and pleaded that, if it were made, there was no consideration for making it.

The jury found that the agreement was made and returned a verdict for the plaintiff, awarding damages of £500.

On the further consideration of the action, Macnaghten J held that, as the plaintiff, under the agreement, was to pay not to the creditors but to the credit of their solicitors there was a sufficient consideration.

The defendants appealed.

LORD HANWORTH MR

[After stating the facts and accepting the principle that a creditor is not bound by an agreement to accept a smaller sum in satisfaction of a larger ascertained amount, unless there be a benefit or even any legal possibility of benefit to the creditor thrown in:] We have, therefore, to consider whether the agreement that was made here on July 6 was an agreement to do anything else than simply to pay on Friday, July 8, into the hand of the creditors the sum which was already ascertained and in respect of which there was not only the legal liability, but a duty enforceable by any mode of execution against the debtor. Was there any sort of advantage, any sort of independent benefit, actual or contingent, of a kind which might be a good and valuable consideration moving towards the creditors?

Macnaghten J. dealt with the question whether the action is maintainable on the ground of the principle of *Foakes v Beer* [above], to which I have referred, and he says: "In the present case the jury, by their verdict, have found that on July 6 Mr Kennard made an offer that if, on the following day, the plaintiff obtained the money and paid it into a bank at Eastbourne with instructions to remit it to the account of Stanley Evans & Co at the Law Courts branch of the Bank of England, he would not serve the bankruptcy notice. That offer became a contract when the plaintiff accepted it. The plaintiff, by going to Eastbourne, obtaining the money, and remitting it in the manner suggested, made it a binding contract on the part of Mr Kennard that he would not serve the bankruptcy notice." I cannot find out of the evidence any facts which support the view or which justify the inference. The words which I have read are plain: it was Mr Vanbergen who said he was going down to Eastbourne, that he was going down as part of his business, and that he did not think he would be getting back after his business on Thursday in time to pay it on Thursday, and the concession arose out of the question whether or not the debtor could be back in town in time to bring it himself, because he frankly said he was trying to get a little more time. When the creditors found that the debtor had to go down to Eastbourne in any event, then the concession was given by the creditors. But they reaped no advantage; there was nothing moving towards them which could be deemed to be a consideration, with the result that the case is one in which the contract is made, but remains unenforceable in law . . .

The appeal must be allowed and judgment entered for the defendants with costs.

Lawrence and Romer L.JJ. delivered concurring judgments.

Appeal Allowed.

Question

10–065   Because the variation in mode of payment is exclusively for the benefit of the debtor it is no consideration to the creditor. But suppose that the creditor accepts the debtor's old car in satisfaction of a debt of £2,000, protesting that he would much rather have the cash and eventually taking the car only because there seems to be no hope of anything better. Can he resile from this agreement when the debtor subsequently comes into money?

Points for reflection

10–066   In *Couldery v Bartrum* (1881) 19 Ch.D. 394 at 400, Jessel MR, discussing the rule in *Pinnel's Case* and compositions with creditors, said ". . . as every debtor had not a stock of canary birds, or tomtits, or rubbish of that kind, to add to his dividend, it was felt desirable to bind the creditors in a sensible way by saying that, if they all agreed, there should be a consideration imported from the agreement constituting an addition to the dividend, so as to make the agreement no longer nudum pactum, but an agreement made for valuable consideration, then there would be satisfaction." But in 1937 the Law Revision Committee, 6th Interim Report, para.22, p.16, referred to "the problem, still unsolved, of discovering the consideration for a debtor's composition with his creditors."

There is no difficulty in finding consideration between the creditors. Each agrees to accept the dividend in full satisfaction in consideration of every other creditor who is a party to the agreement doing so. If one creditor then sues for the balance of his debt he commits a breach of contract with each of those creditors. But the debtor is not a party to the contract. However in *West Yorkshire Darracq Agency Ltd (in liquidation) v Coleridge* [1911] 2 K.B. 326, where the debtor (the liquidator) was a party to the agreement between the creditors (the directors of the company), Horridge J held that "by becoming a party he obtained the benefit of the consideration which each of the directors gave to his co-director by waiving his right to his fees." The basis of the debtor's defence seems to be that the action is a fraud on the other parties to the contract to forbear from suing. Cf. *Gore v Van der Lann* [1967] 2 Q.B. 31 CA and *Snelling v John Snelling Ltd* [1972] 2 W.L.R. 588. If that is so, should it make any difference whether the debtor is a party to the agreement (he is not a party to the contract) or not? Are not the forbearing creditors equally defrauded in either case?

If the creditors decide to rescind their agreement and sue for the full amount of their debts, can the creditor rely on the agreement as a defence, whether or not he was a party to it?

In *Comr of Stamp Duties v Bone* [1976] 2 All E.R. 354 at 360, PC Lord Russell, speaking for five Lords of Appeal, said: "A debt can only be truly released and extinguished by agreement for valuable consideration or under seal. By 'giving' or 'forgiving' or 'releasing' by will a debt to the debtor, a testator, in their Lordships' opinion, is but leaving a legacy of the amount of the debt . . . The debt remains outstanding as an asset of the estate . . ."

HIRACHAND PUNAMCHAND v TEMPLE

Court of Appeal [1911] 2 K.B. 330; 80 L.J.K.B. 1155; 105 L.T. 277; 27 T.L.R. 430

Appeal from the judgment of Scrutton J.

10–067

Sir Richard Temple, father of Lt. Temple who was indebted to the plaintiffs as the maker of a promissory note, wrote to the plaintiffs offering an amount less than that of the debt in full settlement of the debt and enclosed a draft for the smaller amount. The plaintiffs, having cashed and retained the proceeds of the draft, brought the present action against Lt. Temple for the balance.

Scrutton J gave judgment for the plaintiffs for the amount claimed. The defendant appealed.

VAUGHAN WILLIAMS LJ

. . . In my judgment, this draft having been sent to the plaintiffs by Sir Richard Temple, and retained and cashed by them, we ought to draw the conclusion that the plaintiffs, who kept and cashed the draft, agreed to accept it on the terms upon which it was sent . . . Under these circumstances, assuming that there was no accord and satisfaction, what form of defence, if any, could be pleaded by the defendant? In my judgment it would be that the plaintiffs had ceased really to be holders of the negotiable instrument on which they sued. They had ceased to be such holders, because, in effect, in their hands the document had ceased to be a negotiable instrument quite as much as if there had been on the acceptance of the draft by the plaintiffs an erasure of the writing of the signature to the note. But, alternatively, assuming that this was not so, and that the instrument did not cease to be a negotiable instrument, then, in my judgment, from the moment when the draft sent by Sir Richard Temple was cashed by the plaintiffs a trust was created as between Sir Richard Temple and the moneylenders in favour of the former, so that any money which the latter might receive upon the promissory note, if they did receive any, would be held by them in trust for him

. . . then, without any question of resort to a court of equity, there might have been a defence in a court of law on the ground that any money recoverable on the note by the plaintiffs was recoverable by them merely as trustees for Sir Richard Temple, and that, under the circumstances disclosed by the correspondence, the relations between the father and son were such that it was impossible to suppose that the father wished to insist on payment of the note by the son.

Having said thus much, I desire to add a word or two with regard to the case of *Cook v Lister* (13 C.B.(n.s.) 543) in the Common Pleas. If the judgments in that case are looked at, it will be found that

Willes J. said, in explaining the grounds of his judgment that under circumstances like those of the present case, the debt is gone, because it would be a fraud upon the stranger who pays part of a debt in discharge of the whole, that an action should be brought for the debt. I have founded my judgment upon the grounds which I have already expressed, but I do not wish to be understood as thereby negativing the proposition that a defence might be set up on the alternative basis mentioned by Willes J. In my opinion this appeal should be allowed.

FLETCHER MOULTON LJ

I am of the opinion that by that transaction between the plaintiffs and Sir Richard Temple the debt on the promissory note became extinct. I agree with the view expressed by Willes J. in *Cook v Lister*. The effect of such an agreement between a creditor and a third party with regard to the debt is to render it impossible for the creditor afterwards to sue the debtor for it. The way in which this is worked out in law may be that it would be an abuse of the process of the court to allow the creditor under such circumstances to sue, or it may be, and I prefer that view, that there is an extinction of the debt; but, whichever way it is put, it comes to the same thing, namely that, after acceptance by the creditor of a sum offered by a third party in settlement of the claim against the debtor, the creditor cannot maintain an action for the balance . . . [His Lordship then distinguished *Foakes v Beer* as applying between debtor and creditor.] If a third person steps in and gives a consideration for the discharge of the debtor, it does not matter whether he does it in meal or in malt, or what proportion the amount given bears to the amount of the debt. Here the money was paid by a third person, and I have no doubt that, upon the acceptance of that money by the plaintiffs with full knowledge of the terms on which it was offered, the debt was absolutely extinguished.

FARWELL LJ

The plaintiffs could only accept the money on the terms upon which it was offered. We were pressed with *Day v McLea* ((1889) 22 QBD 610), where the debtor himself sent a cheque for an amount smaller than that of the debt to the creditor on the terms that it should be in satisfaction of the debt. In that case, there being no consideration for the discharge of the balance of the debt, it was held that the creditor could retain the money, and sue for the balance. The same reasoning does not apply where the money is sent by a stranger, in which case it can only be accepted on the terms upon which it is sent. In the former case the creditor can reply to the debtor, "you owe me more than this, and if you sue for a return of this, I shall set off my larger claim against it." In the latter case, the creditor has no excuse or justification for retaining the stranger's money, unless he complies with the conditions on which it was paid. I agree with Fletcher Moulton L.J. that the plaintiffs cannot be heard to say that they have acted dishonestly when an honest construction can be put upon their conduct by treating their acceptance and retention of the money as being upon the terms on which it was offered.

Appeal Allowed.

Question

10-068 Do you agree with Fletcher Moulton LJ that refusal of the creditor's claim comes to the same thing as the extinction of the debt? Suppose that the father had later authorised the creditor to sue for the balance of the debt—or required him to do so as trustee (see Vaughan Williams LJ)? Would the son be liable? Suppose, father being impoverished and son having come into money, the father had required the creditor to sue for the whole sum?

Further reading

J. Carter, A. Phang, and J. Poole, 'Reactions to *Williams v Roffey*' (1995) 8 *Journal of Contract Law* 248

M. Chen-Wishart, 'Consideration: Practical Benefit and the Emperor's New Clothes' in J. Beatson and D. Friedmann (eds), *Good Faith and Fault in Contract Law* (Oxford: Oxford University Press, 1995) p.123

Grant Gilmore, *The Death of Contract* (Columbus: Ohio State University Press, 1974)

James Gordley (ed), *The Enforceability of Promises in European Contract Law* (Cambridge: Cambridge University Press, 2009)

11

EQUITABLE ESTOPPEL

LEARNING OBJECTIVES

By the end of this chapter, you should:

- understand that the principle of equitable estoppel may operate to preclude a party from asserting (and enforcing) their original rights under a contract;
- understand that the principle operates within quite strict limits and that it is particularly problematic where it is relied on as the basis of a claim (as a cause of action);
- have reflected on the relationship between the requirement of consideration and the scope for equitable estoppel to operate;
- understand that the equity in play here reflects a basic principle of good faith and fair dealing;
- be aware that the estoppel may arise in various ways—for example, by acts or promises that encourage non-performance, or by acquiescence;
- have considered how far equitable estoppel qualifies the rule that a creditor is not bound by a promise to accept part payment of a debt as settling the debt;
- have a view about whether this development in the law is in line with the modern approach that insists that the reasonable expectations of contractors should be respected

Introduction

So long as the English law of contract treats a promise as contractually enforceable only if either (a) it is made in a deed or (b) it is supported by consideration (together with an intention to create legal relations), it follows that a promise made neither in a deed nor with consideration will lack contractual effect notwithstanding that such a promise is made seriously, with an intention to be relied on and is actually relied on by the promisee. Yet, this could seem to be contrary to the spirit of fair dealing.

11–001

Suppose, for example, that S has contracted to deliver goods to B on August 1, 2015. A few days before the goods are due to be delivered, S requests B to allow him an additional 24 hours to make the delivery. Faced with this request, B may respond by:

(i) simply agreeing to S's request (implicitly promising that delivery on August 2, rather than on August 1, will not be treated as a breach of contract by S); or

(ii) agreeing to S's request provided that S gives B a discount on the price; or

(iii) refusing to give S extra time for the delivery.

B is entitled to respond in any of these ways. If B responds as in (iii), he is simply insisting on his contractual rights. If B responds as in (ii), there is an agreed variation to the original contract fully supported by fresh consideration (the extension of time for delivery in return for a reduction in the price). And, if B responds as in (i), as he might well do if later delivery happens to suit him or if he has a long-term trading relationship with S that implies some give and take, then so far so good. However, what does the law say if B's promise is put to the test? What if, when S duly arrives with the goods on August 2, B refuses to accept delivery or signals an intention to claim compensation from S for alleged breach of contract (failing to deliver on August 1)? Would we not think that this was wholly unreasonable? Surely, no court would permit B to mislead S in this way. But, if a promise is contractually binding only where it is supported by consideration (as in response (ii)), how is the law to avoid an unconscionable result?

One way to avoid this result is to "invent" consideration, for example, by saying that, even in (i), there is some benefit to B (such as maintaining a good working relationship with S). However, if the result cannot be avoided by such creative accounting, a new doctrine needs to come to the rescue. The doctrine might be a rather limited one that recognises in exceptional circumstances that a promise will be contractually binding where, even though it is not supported by consideration, it is seriously intended to be acted on and the promisee actually relies on the promise (as when S delivers the goods on August 2). Alternatively, a legal regime that is restricted by its requirement of consideration might try to override such unfair results by introducing a general doctrine of good faith and fair dealing or a doctrine that regulates for unconscionability. In this chapter, we will see how English law has responded—principally by developing a doctrine of equitable estoppel that precludes contractors such as B from reneging on their promises where they have explicitly authorised what would otherwise be a breach of contract and where the promisee has relied on the promise.

With the requirement of consideration set to present this challenge to principles of fair dealing (or vice versa), it needs only a trigger—the right kind of case with the right kind of judge—to crystallise this tension. In English law, that case was *High Trees* (para.11–002) and Lord Denning who tried the action was exactly the right kind of judge. Ever since *High Trees*, English law has been endeavouring to stabilise and clarify the relationship between the exchange basis of contract (expressed through the requirement of consideration) and the demand for fair dealing (articulated, in this case, through the principle of equitable estoppel).

The cases in this chapter are presented in five sections. First, there is the *High Trees* decision itself in which the idea of equitable estoppel is revived in the modern law; and this is followed in the second section by the key cases prior to *High Trees* being decided. This is followed by three sections in which the scope, details, and limits of the doctrine of equitable estoppel are put to the test. In section three, it is the possibility of pleading equitable estoppel as the basis of a claim (rather than merely as a defence to a claim) that is at issue; in section four, it is the question of whether the effect of equitable estoppel is to suspend a claim or to extinguish it; and, in the final section, we revisit the question (broached in Ch.10) of whether a creditor might be bound by a promise to accept a lesser sum in full settlement of a debt—even though such a promise might lack consideration, is it arguable that the creditor is in some way restricted from recovering the balance of the debt by virtue of equitable estoppel?

1. HIGH TREES AND FAIR DEALING

CENTRAL LONDON PROPERTY TRUST LTD v HIGH TREES HOUSE LTD

King's Bench Division [1947] 1 K.B. 130; [1947] L.J.R. 77; 175 L.T. 333; 62 T.L.R. 557; [1956] 1 All E.R. 256

11–002   Action tried by Denning J.

By a lease under seal made on September 24, 1937, the plaintiffs, Central London Property Trust Ltd, granted to the defendants High Trees House Ltd, a subsidiary of the plaintiff company, a tenancy of a block of flats for the term of 99 years from September 29, 1937, at a ground rent of £2,500 a year. The block of flats was a new one and had not been fully occupied at the beginning of the war owing to the absence of people from London. With war conditions prevailing, it was apparent to those responsible that the rent reserved under the lease could not be paid out of the profits of the flats and, accordingly, discussions took place between the directors of the two companies concerned, which were closely associated, and an arrangement was made between them which was put into writing. On January 3, 1940, the plaintiffs wrote to the defendants in these terms, "we confirm the arrangement made between us by which the ground rent should be reduced as from the commencement of the lease to £1,250 per annum," and on April 2, 1940, a confirmatory resolution to the same effect was passed by the plaintiff company. On March 20, 1941, a receiver was appointed by the debenture holders of the plaintiffs and on his death on February 28, 1944, his place was taken by his partner. The defendants paid the reduced rent from 1941 down to the beginning of 1945, by which time all the flats in the block were fully let, and continued to pay it thereafter. In September, 1945, the then receiver of the plaintiff company looked into the matter of the lease and ascertained that the rent actually reserved by it was £2,500. On September 21, 1945, he wrote to the defendants saying that rent must be paid at the full rate and claiming that arrears amounting to £7,916 were due. Subsequently, he instituted the present friendly proceedings to test the legal position in regard to the rate at which the rent was payable. In the action the plaintiffs sought to recover £625, being the amount represented by the difference between rent at the rate of £2,500 and £1,250 per annum for the quarters ending September 29 and December 25, 1945. By their defence the defendants pleaded (1) that the letter of January 3, 1940, constituted an agreement that the rent reserved should be £1,250 only, and that such agreement related to the whole term of the lease, (2) in the alternative, that the plaintiff company were estopped from alleging that the rent exceeded £1,250 per annum, and (3) as a further alternative, that by failing to demand rent in excess of £1,250 before their letter of September 21, 1945 (received by the defendants on September 24), they had waived their rights in respect of any rent, in excess of that at the rate of £1,250, which had accrued up to September 24, 1945.

DENNING J

[Stated the facts and continued:] If I were to consider this matter without regard to recent developments in the law, there is no doubt that, had the plaintiffs claimed it, they would have been entitled to recover ground rent at the rate of £2,500 a year from the beginning of the term, since the lease under which it was payable was a lease under seal which, according to the old common law, could not be varied by an agreement by parol (whether in writing or not), but only by deed. Equity, however, stepped in, and said that if there had been a variation of a deed by a simple contract (which in the case of a lease required to be in writing would have to be evidenced by writing), the courts may give effect to it as is shown in *Berry v Berry* [1929] 2 K.B. 316. That equitable doctrine, however, could hardly apply in the present case because the variation here might be said to have been made without consideration. With regard to estoppel, the representation made in relation to reducing the rent was not a representation of an existing fact. It was a representation, in effect, as to the future, namely, that payment of the rent would not be enforced at the full rate but only at the reduced rate. Such a representation would not give rise to an estoppel, because, as was said in *Jorden v Money* (1854) 5 H.L.C. 185 [below, para.11–004], a representation as to the future must be embodied as a contract or be nothing.

But what is the position in view of developments in the law in recent years? The law has not been standing still since *Jorden v Money*. There has been a series of decisions over the past 50 years which, although they are said to be cases of estoppel are not really such. They are cases in which a promise was made which was intended to create legal relations and which, to the knowledge of the person making the promise, was going to be acted on by the person to whom it was made, and which was in fact so acted on. In such cases the courts have said that the promise must be honoured. The cases to which I particularly desire to refer are: *Fenner v Blake* [1900] 1 Q.B. 426; *Re Wickham* (1917) 34 T.L.R. 158; *Re William Porter & Co Ltd* [1937] 2 All E.R. 361 and *Buttery v Pickard* [1946] W.N. 25. As I have said they are not cases of estoppel in the strict sense. They are really promises promises intended to be binding, intended to be acted on, and in fact acted on. *Jorden v Money* can be distinguished, because there the promisor made it clear that she did not intend to be legally bound, whereas in the cases to which I refer the proper inference was that the promisor did intend to be bound. In each case the court held the promise to be binding on the party making it, even though under the old common law it might be difficult to find any consideration for it. The courts have not gone so far as to give a cause of action in damages for the breach of such a promise, but they have refused to allow the party making it to act inconsistently with it. It is in that sense, and that sense only, that such a promise gives rise to an estoppel. The decisions are a natural result of the fusion of law and equity: for the cases of *Hughes v Metropolitan Railway* [below, para.11–007]; *Birmingham and District Land Co v London & North Western Rly.* [below, para.11–008]; and *Salisbury (Marquess) v Gilmore* [1942] 2 K.B. 38, 51, afford a sufficient basis for saying that a party would not be allowed in equity to go back on such a promise. In my opinion, the time has now come for the validity of such a promise to be recognised. The logical consequence, no doubt, is that a promise to accept a smaller sum in discharge of a larger sum, if acted upon, is binding notwithstanding the absence of consideration: and if the fusion of law and equity leads to this result, so much the better. That aspect was not considered in *Foakes v Beer* [above, para.10–062]. At this time of day, however, when law and equity have been joined together for over 70 years, principles must be reconsidered in the light of their combined effect. It is to be noticed that in the Sixth Interim Report of the Law Revision Committee, paras. 35, 40, it is recommended that such a promise as that to which I have referred, should be enforceable in law even though no consideration for it has been given by the promisee. It seems to me that, to the extent I have mentioned, that result has now been achieved by the decisions of the courts.

I am satisfied that a promise such as that to which I have referred is binding and the only question remaining for my consideration is the scope of the promise in the present case. I am satisfied on all the evidence that the promise here was that the ground rent should be reduced to £1,250 a year as a temporary expedient while the block of flats was not fully, or substantially fully let, owing to the conditions prevailing. That means that the reduction in the rent applied throughout the years down to the end of 1944, but early in 1945 it is plain that the flats were fully let, and, indeed the rents received from them (many of them not being affected by the Rent Restrictions Acts), were increased beyond the figure at which it was originally contemplated that they would be let. At all events the rent from them must have been very considerable. I find that the conditions prevailing at the time when the reduction in rent was made, had completely passed away by the early months of 1945. I am satisfied that the promise was understood by all parties only to apply under the conditions prevailing at the time when it was made, namely, when the flats were only partially let, and that it did not extend any further than that. When the flats became fully let, early in 1945, the reduction ceased to apply.

In those circumstances, under the law as I hold it, it seems to me that rent is payable at the full rate for the quarters ending September 29 and December 25, 1945.

If the case had been one of estoppel, it might be said that in any event the estoppel would cease when the conditions to which the representation applied came to an end, or it also might be said that it would only come to an end on notice. In either case it is only a way of ascertaining what is the scope of the representation. I prefer to apply the principle that a promise intended to be binding, intended to be acted on and in fact acted on, is binding so far as its terms properly apply. Here it was binding as covering the period down to the early part of 1945, and as from that time full rent is payable.

I therefore give judgment for the plaintiff company for the amount claimed.

Judgment for the Plaintiff.

Points for reflection

11–003   Denning J hints that *Foakes v Beer* (1884) might have been decided differently if the fusion of law and equity by the Judicature Acts 1873–1875 had been considered. He says that the decisions on which he relies, the most important of which is *Hughes v Metropolitan Railway* (1877), below, were a natural result of that fusion.

Why, then, was the principle in *Hughes* not applied in *Foakes v Beer*? Lords Selborne and Blackburn sat in both cases. Is the answer that the principle applied in *Hughes* was entirely inapplicable to both *Foakes v Beer* and *High Trees*? That principle might be formulated as follows: if A tells B (by words or conduct) that B need not perform a contractual (or other) obligation owed by B to A and B takes A at his word and does not perform that obligation, A cannot treat that non-performance as a breach of contract entitling him to damages or to terminate the contract. It would be entirely wrong that A should be allowed to treat as a legal wrong that to which he has consented. It was this principle which applied in *Hughes*. A, the landlord, having (by conduct) told B, his tenant, "You need not fulfil your contractual duty to repair the premises within six months of the notice I have given you," could not forfeit the lease (that is, terminate the contract) on the ground that B had broken his contract.

Foakes v Beer appears to be an application of a second, quite different, principle: if A tells B that B need not perform a contractual (or other) obligation owed by B to A, A can change his mind and require B to perform that obligation in so far as it is still possible to do so. A is not alleging that B has broken his contract—he is simply saying "Now you must perform—and if you fail to do so, that will be a breach of contract."

If *Hughes* was relevant to the decision in *Foakes* it must follow that *Pinnel's Case* was equally relevant to the decision in *Hughes* but it was not cited in the latter case and it would surely have been very surprising it if had been.

Many of the cases which have from time to time been relied on in support of the *High Trees* doctrine are clearly examples of only the first principle. For example, *Panoutsos v Raymond Hadley* [1917] 2 K.B. 473 CA, a case frequently cited by Lord Denning: under a contract of sale by A to B, B has a duty to open a confirmed credit. A, by words or conduct, tells B that the unconfirmed credit which B has opened will do. A may not terminate the contract on the ground that B has committed a breach by not opening a confirmed credit—but he may insist that B opens a confirmed credit within a reasonable time and, if B does not do so, he will then be in breach of contract.

In *High Trees*, the landlord, having accepted half rent for, say, one year, would clearly have been precluded from asserting, "You have broken your contract and I forfeit the lease." That would have been exactly analogous to *Hughes*. It does not follow that he could not say, "You must now pay me the arrears of rent for the past year." *Foakes v Beer* says he could do that. Denning J denies it. It is the doctrine that the promise has this wider effect which is known as 'equitable estoppel' or, more commonly, 'promissory estoppel.' See *Maharaj v Chand* [1986] 3 All E.R. 107, PC.

----

2. THE LAW BEFORE HIGH TREES

JORDEN v MONEY

House of Lords (1854) 5 H.L.C. 185; 10 E.R. 868

M had borrowed £1,200 from J's brother, C, for an unsuccessful financial speculation with other persons. Judgment for the sum had been entered against M but not executed. M gave C a bond and warrant of attorney to secure repayment of the money. On C's death, J as his executrix became entitled to the bond and warrant. J often stated that she never intended to enforce the claim secured, saying that she believed M to have been unfairly treated in being obliged to enter into the securities. Such statements were made by J, among other occasions, in circumstances which were calculated to lead and did lead to their being communicated to relatives of the intended wife of M at the time when his marriage was in course of preparation. His prospective parents in law wanted assurance that he was free from all liability in respect of the debt of £1,200 and the bond and warrant. In consequence of J's assurances, the marriage of M and his wife took place. M now brought an action, by Bill in Chancery praying that the debt secured by the bond and warrant be declared to have been abandoned, that J be decreed to have released M from the bond, that the warrant of attorney be delivered up to be cancelled and that satisfaction be entered upon the judgment which had been obtained against M by C. Romilly MR granted an injunction restraining J from enforcing the judgment on the warrant

11-004

of attorney. On appeal, the Court of the Lords Justices was divided, Knight-Bruce LJ supporting the order of the Master of the Rolls and Lord Cranworth LJ thinking that it should be reversed, and accordingly the order of the Master of the Rolls stood. J then appealed to the House of Lords. Their Lordships (Lord Cranworth LC and Lord Brougham, Lord St. Leonards dissenting) allowed the appeal and ordered that the case go back to the Court of Chancery with a declaration that the Bill should be dismissed without costs.

LORD CRANWORTH LC

There are two grounds upon which it is said that the parties have lost their right to enforce the bond. The one is, that previously to William Money's marriage, Mrs Jorden, then Miss Marnell, represented that the bond had been abandoned, that she had given up her legal right upon it, and upon the faith of that representation the marriage was contracted. And then it is said that upon a principle well known in the law, founded upon good faith and equity, a principle equally of law and of equity, if a person makes any false representation to another, and that other acts upon that false representation, the person who has made it shall not afterwards be allowed to set up that what he said was false, and to assert the real truth in place of the falsehood which has so misled the other. That is a principle of universal application, and has been particularly applied to cases where representations have been made as to the state of the property of persons about to contract marriage, and where, upon the faith of such representations, marriage has been contracted. There the person who has made the false representations has in a great many cases been held bound to make his representations good.

[Having considered various authorities, his Lordship proceeded:] I am bound to state my view of the case: I think that the doctrine does not apply to a case where the representation is not a representation of fact but a statement of something which the party intends or does not intend to do. In the former case it is a contract, in the latter it is not; what is here contended for is this, that Mrs Jorden, then Miss Marnell, over and over again represented that she abandoned the debt. Clothe that in any words you please, it means no more than this, that she would never enforce the debt: she does not mean, in saying that she had abandoned it, to say that she had executed a release of the debt so as to preclude her legal right to sue. All that she could mean, was that she positively promised that she would never enforce it. My opinion is, that if all the evidence had come up to the mark, which, for reasons I shall presently state, I do not think it did, that if upon the very eve of the marriage she had said, "William Money, I never will enforce the bond against you," that would not bring it within these cases.[7]

LORD BROUGHAM

In my opinion, there was a misrepresentation by Louisa Marnell of an intention as to her will, and a promise was made by her; but of misrepresentation of fact there was none. She simply stated what was her intention; she did not misrepresent her intention; and I have no manner of doubt that at the time she made that statement, she had the intention which it is stated she professed, of never putting William Bailey Money in trouble, by proceeding upon the bond . . . I certainly have, after very considerable doubt upon some parts of the case, but after fully viewing the whole particulars, and examining those depositions, come to the conclusion by which my noble and learned friend abides, the conclusion to which he arrived in the court below, that there was not an abandonment of the debt, by Mrs Jorden; not only that there was not an abandonment of it, but that there was rather a refusal of abandonment, when you come to examine in what sense, and with what intent the word "abandonment" has been used.

Lord St Leonards made a dissenting speech.

Appeal Allowed.

Point for reflection

11–005   Atiyah, *Consideration in Contracts*, pp.53–58, argues that the facts in *Jorden v Money* really reveal a contract with good consideration which would have been enforceable at law, had it not lacked

---

[7]   The second ground, concerning the Statute of Frauds, is omitted.

the evidence in writing then necessary, for a promise given in consideration of marriage, under the Statute of Frauds, above. The plaintiff was thus attempting to evade the Statute by calling his cause of action estoppel instead of contract. Atiyah is able to reach this conclusion because he believes the promisee's action in reliance on the promise constitutes consideration even though it is not requested. Jorden did not request Money to marry, but he acted on her promise. But cf. the insistence upon the need for a request by all judges in *Shadwell v Shadwell* (above, Ch.10) only six years later—though, admittedly, the majority were able to discern a request in rather unpromising material. See also *Argy Trading Development Co Ltd v Lapid Developments Ltd* [1977] 3 All E.R. 785 at 796 per Croom-Johnson J.

Question

Suppose that Mrs Jorden had said to Money, "I have executed a release of the debt under seal," whereafter Money got married. If she had subsequently sued him for the sum, what would be the effect of her previous statement?   11–006

HUGHES v METROPOLITAN RLY CO

House of Lords (1877) 2 App. Cas. 439; 46 L.J.C.P. 583; 36 L.T. 932; 25 W.R. 680

A landlord had, in October 1874, given his tenant six months' notice to repair the prermises, the lease being forfeitable if the tenant failed to comply with the notice. The tenant replied, agreeing to do the necessary repairs but also suggesting that the landlord who owned the freehold might like to purchase the lease and indicating that repairs would not be effected while negotiations on this suggestion were in progress. In November the landlord began negotiations with the tenant for the surrender of the lease but these were broken off on December 31. Meanwhile the tenant had done no repairs on the premises. When six months from the original notice had expired, the landlord claimed to treat the lease as forfeit.   11–007

The House of Lords (Lord Cairns LC, Lords O'Hagan, Selborne, Blackburn and Gordon) held that the tenant was entitled to relief in equity against the forfeiture, the landlord's opening of negotiations having been the reason for the tenant's failure to do any repairs, the six months allowed therefor should run from the failure of the negotiations.

LORD CAIRNS LC

It is the first principle upon which all courts of equity proceed, that if parties who have entered into definite and distinct terms involving certain legal results—certain penalties or legal forfeiture—afterwards by their own act or with their own consent enter upon a course of negotiation which as the effect of leading one of the parties to suppose that the strict rights arising under the contract will not be enforced, or will be kept in suspense, or held in abeyance, the person who otherwise might have enforced those rights will not be allowed to enforce them where it would be inequitable having regard to the dealings which have thus taken place between the parties.

Point for reflection

In *Birmingham and District Land Co v L & North Western Rly* (1888) 40 Ch.D. 268; 60 L.T. 527 CA, Bowen LJ (referring to the principle expressed by Lord Cairns in *Hughes'* case above) said: 11–008

"Now, it was suggested by (counsel) that that proposition only applied to cases where penal rights in the nature of forfeiture, or analogous to those of forfeiture, were sought to be enforced. I entirely fail to see any such possible distinction. The principle has nothing to do with forefeiture . . . It was applied in *Hughes v Metropolitan Rly* in a case in which equity could not relieve against forfeiture upon the mere ground that it was a forfeiture, but could interfere only because there had been something in the nature of acquiescence, or negotiations between the parties, which made it inequitable to allow the forfeiture to be enforced. The truth is that the proposition is wider than cases of forfeiture. It seems to me to amount to this, that if persons who have contractual rights against others induce by their conduct those against whom they have such rights to believe that such rights will either not be enforced or will be kept in suspense or abeyance for some particular time, those persons will not be allowed by a court of equity to enforce the rights until such time has elapsed, without at all events placing the parties in the same position as they were before. That is the principle to be applied. I will not say it is not a principle that was recognised by courts of law as well as of equity. It is not necessary to consider how far it was always a principle of common law."

----

3. Estoppel as a Cause of Action?

COMBE v COMBE

Court of Appeal [1951] 2 K.B. 215; [1951] 1 T.L.R. 811; 95 S.J. 317; [1951] 1 All E.R. 767

11–009   Appeal from Byrne J.

The parties, a husband and wife, were married in 1915, but separated in 1939. On February 1, 1943, on the wife's petition, a decree nisi of divorce was pronounced. On February 9, 1943, the wife's solicitor wrote to the husband's solicitor. "With regard to permanent maintenance, we understand that your client is prepared to make her an allowance of £100 per year, free of income tax." On February 19, 1943, the husband's solicitor replied that the husband had "agreed to allow your client £100 per annum, free of tax." On August 11, 1943, the decree was made absolute. The wife's solicitor wrote for the first instalment of £25 on August 26, and asking that future instalments should be paid on November 11, February 11, May 11, and August 11. The husband, himself, replied that he could not be expected to pay in advance. In fact, he never made any payment. The wife pressed for payment but made no application to the Divorce Court for maintenance. She had an income of between £700 and £800 a year. Her husband had only £650 a year.

On July 28, 1950, the wife brought an action in the King's Bench Division claiming from her husband £675, being arrears of payments at the rate of £100 per year for six and three-quarter years. Byrne J. held that the first three quarterly instalments of £25 were barred by the Limitation Act 1939, but gave judgment for the wife for £600. He held on the authority of *Gaisberg v Storr* [1950] 1 K.B. 107 that there was no consideration for the husband's promise to pay his wife £100, but nevertheless he held that the promise was enforceable on the principle stated in *Central London Property Trust, Ltd v High Trees House, Ltd* (above) and *Robertson v Minister of Pensions* [1949] 1 K.B. 227, because it was an unequivocal acceptance of liability, intended to be binding, intended to be acted on and, in fact, acted on.

The husband appealed.

DENNING LJ

[After stating the facts]: Much as I am inclined to favour the principle stated in the High Trees case, it is important that it should not be stretched too far, lest it be endangered. That principle does not create new causes of action where none existed before. It only prevents a party from insisting upon his strict legal rights, when it would be unjust to allow him to enforce them, having regard to the dealings which have taken place between the parties. That is the way it was put in *Hughes v Metropolitan Rly.* [above], the case in the House of Lords in which the principle was first stated, and in *Birmingham etc., Land Company v London and North Western Rly.* [above], the case in the Court of Appeal where the principle was enlarged . . . It is also implicit in all the modern cases in which the principle has been developed. That is, I think, its true function. It may be part of a cause of action, but not a cause of action in itself.

[Having reviewed the authorities his Lordship proceeded:] The principle, as I understand it, is that, where one party has, by his words or conduct, made to the other a promise or assurance which was intended to affect the legal relations between them and to be acted on accordingly, then, once the other party has taken him at his word and acted on it, the one who gave the promise or assurance cannot afterwards be allowed to revert to the previous legal relations as if no such promise or assurance had been made by him, but he must accept their legal relations subject to the qualification which he himself has so introduced, even though it is not supported in point of law by any consideration but only by his word.

Seeing that the principle never stands alone as giving a cause of action in itself, it can never do away with the necessity of consideration when that is an essential part of the cause of action. The doctrine of consideration is too firmly fixed to be overthrown by a side-wind. Its ill-effects have been largely mitigated of late, but it still remains a cardinal necessity of the formation of a contract, though not of its modification or discharge. I fear that it was my failure to make this clear which misled Byrne J. in the present case. He held that the wife could sue on the husband's promise as a separate and independent cause of action by itself, although as he held there was no consideration for it. That is not correct. The wife can only enforce it if there was consideration for it. That is, therefore, the real question in the case: was there sufficient consideration to support the promise?

If it were suggested that, in return for the husband's promise, the wife expressly or impliedly promised to forbear from applying to the court for maintenance—that is, a promise in return for a promise—there would clearly be no consideration, because the wife's promise was not binding on her and was therefore worth nothing. Notwithstanding her promise, she could always apply to the Divorce Court for maintenance—maybe only with leave—and no agreement by her could take away that right: *Hyman v Hyman* [1929] A.C. 601, as interpreted by this court in *Gaisberg v Storr*.

There was, however, clearly no promise by the wife, express or implied, to forbear from applying to the court. All that happened was that she did in fact forbear—that is, she did an act in return for a promise. Is that sufficient consideration? Unilateral promises of this kind have long been enforced, so long as the act or forbearance is done on the faith of the promise and at the request of the promisor, express or implied. The act done is then in itself sufficient consideration for the promise even though it arises ex post facto, as Parker J. pointed out in *Wigan v English and Scottish Law Life Assurance Association* [1909] 1 Ch. 291, 298. If the findings of Byrne J. were accepted, they would be sufficient to bring this principle into play. His finding that the husband's promise was intended to be binding, intended to be acted upon, and was, in fact, acted on—although expressed to be a finding on the *High Trees* principle—is equivalent to a finding that there was consideration within this long settled rule, because it comes to the same thing expressed in different words: see *Oliver v Davis* [1949] 2 K.B. 727. But my difficulty is to accept the finding of Byrne J. that the promise was "intended to be acted upon." I cannot find any evidence of any intention by the husband that the wife should forbear from applying to the court for maintenance, or, in other words, any request by the husband, express or implied, that the wife should so forbear. He left her to apply if she wished to do so. She did not do so and I am not surprised, because it is very unlikely that the Divorce Court would have then made any order in her favour, seeing that she had a bigger income than her husband. Her forbearance was not intended by him, nor was it done at his request. It was, therefore, no consideration . . .

ASQUITH LJ

The judge has decided that, while the husband's promise was unsupported by any valid consideration, yet the principle in *Central London Property Trust, Ltd v High Trees House, Ltd* entitles the wife to succeed. It is unnecessary to express any view as to the correctness of that decision, though I certainly must not be taken to be questioning it; and I would remark, in passing, that it seems to me a complete misconception to suppose that it struck at the roots of the doctrine of consideration. But assuming, without deciding, that it is good law, I do not think, however, that it helps the plaintiff at all. What that case decides is that when a promise is given which (1) is intended to create legal relations, (2) is intended to be acted upon by the promisee, and (3) is in fact so acted upon, the promisor cannot bring an action against the promisee which involves the repudiation of his promise or is inconsistent with it. It does not, as I read it, decide that a promisee can sue on the promise. On the contrary, Denning J. expressly stated the contrary. Neither in the *High Trees* case nor in *Minister of Pensions v Robertson* (another decision of my Lord which is relied upon by the plaintiff) was an action brought by the promisee on the promise. In the first of those two cases the plaintiff was in effect the promisor or a person standing in the shoes of the promisor, while in the second the claim, though brought by the promisee, was brought upon a cause of action which was not the promise but was an alleged statutory right . . .

(The concurring judgment of Birkett L.J. is omitted.)

Appeal Allowed.

Points for reflection

11–010   In *Robertson v Minister of Pensions* the War Office wrote to the plaintiff stating, "Your disability has been accepted as attributable to military service." On the faith of that assurance the plaintiff took no steps to obtain an independent medical opinion as otherwise he would have done. Subsequently, a pensions appeal tribunal decided that his injury was not due to war service. Denning J, following, inter alia, the *High Trees* case, held that the assurance by the War Office was binding on the Minister of Pensions, both being agents of the Crown. An award must issue that the injury was attributable to war service. Arguably, this was an ordinary estoppel, being a representation of fact. Whatever its nature, it enabled the plaintiff to make out his cause of action on his legal right to a pension. The oft-cited dictum of Birkett LJ (quoting counsel for the husband) in *Combe v Combe*, that the *High Trees* doctrine can be used as a shield but not a sword, is misleading. Like estoppel generally, it may be part of the armoury of the attacker just as readily as that of the defender. Estoppel (with the possible exception of "proprietary estoppel") is never a cause of action in the sense of breach of contract, tort, or breach of trust, because it is not a recognised legal injury: but it may assist to establish the conditions necessary for the success of any cause of action, no less than it may establish the conditions necessary for a defence. See Brandon LJ in *Amalgamated Investment v Texas Commerce*, below.

The so-called 'proprietary estoppel' has been held to arise where A purports to give, but does not effectively convey, or promises to give, land or an interest in land to B, knowing that B will expend money or otherwise act to his detriment in reliance on the supposed or promised gift. When B does so act, this gives him an 'equity' to require A to complete the gift. In *Dillwyn v Llewellyn* (1862) 4 De G.F. & J. 517 CA in Chancery, a father, wishing his son to reside near him, signed a memorandum "presenting [a freehold estate] to my son for the purpose of furnishing him with a dwelling-house." The son took possession and expended a large sum in building a house and generally improving the property. The father never conveyed the estate and, after his death, the son, claiming to be the equitable owner in fee simple, sued for and obtained an order that the trustees convey the estate to him. Lord Westbury LC said that "the subsequent expenditure by the son with the approbation of the father supplied a valuable consideration, originally wanting." The case might therefore be explained simply as one of unilateral contract (above, p.61), the element of request being implicit in the father's wish that his son live near him; but later cases are not readily explicable on this ground. See, for example, *Inwards v Baker* [1965] 2 Q.B. 29 CA. Perhaps the explanation is that the action in reliance on the promise creates the "equity" in the nature of a constructive trust and the plaintiff sues on that. Cf. *Re Basham* [1987] 1 All E.R. 405 (Nugee QC).

CRABB V ARUN DISTRICT COUNCIL

Court of Appeal [1976] Ch. 179; [1975] 3 W.L.R. 847; [1975] 3 All E.R. 865

11–011   The plaintiff owned a plot of land, the adjacent portion to which had been sold by his predecessor in title to the defendant for the erection of houses. It was the intention of the parties that the council should build a new road between the two pieces of land and, in the conveyance, the plaintiff was granted access (at point A) and a right of way over the road. Before the development was started, the plaintiff decided that it would be to his advantage to divide his land into two portions in such a way that he would need access to the road at a second point. He informed the council of his plan and at a meeting with council representatives, received a clear impression that he would be given the second access point (point B), but no formal grant of a right of way was ever made. The council built the road and fenced it off from the plaintiff's land, leaving a gap at point B. Subsequently, the plaintiff sold the part of his land with access at point A so that he was dependent for access to the land that he retained at point B. However, the council fenced off this access point and refused either to reopen it or to grant the plaintiff an easement save on payment. The plaintiff claimed a declaration that he was entitled to a right of way and an injunction. Brightman J dismissed the claim. The plaintiff appealed.

LORD DENNING MR

When counsel for Mr Crabb said that he put his case on an estoppel, it shook me a little, because it is commonly supposed that estoppel is not itself a cause of action. But that is because there are estoppels and estoppels. Some do give rise to a cause of action. Some do not. In the species of estoppel called proprietary estoppel, it does give rise to a cause of action. We had occasion to consider it a month ago in *Moorgate Mercantile Co Ltd v Twitchings* [1975] 3 All E.R. 314 where I said that the effect of estoppel on the true owner may be that—

"his own title to the property, be it land or goods, has been held to be limited or extinguished, and new rights and interests have been created therein. And this operates by reason of his conduct—what he has led the other to believe—even though he never intended it."

. . . The question then is: were the circumstances here such as to raise an equity in favour of Mr Crabb? True the council on the deeds had the title to their land, free of any access at point B. But they led Mr Crabb to believe that he had or would be granted a right of access at point B. At the meeting of July 26, 1967, Mr Alford and Mr Crabb told the council's representative that Mr Crabb intended to split the two acres into two portions and wanted to have an access at point B for the back portion, and the council's representative agreed that he should have this access . . .

The judge found that there was "no definite assurance" by the council's representative, and "no firm commitment," but only an "agreement in principle," meaning I suppose that, as Mr Alford said, there were "some further processes" to be gone through before it would become binding. But if there were any such processes in the minds of the parties, the subsequent conduct of the council was such as to dispense with them. The council actually put up the gates at point B at considerable expense. That certainly led Mr Crabb to believe that they had agreed that he should have the right of access through point B without more ado.

The judge also said that, to establish this equity or estoppel, the council must have known that Mr Crabb was selling the front portion without reserving a right of access for the back portion. I do not think this was necessary. The council knew that Mr Crabb intended to sell the two portions separately and that he would need an access at point B as well as point A. Seeing that they knew of his intention—and they did nothing to disabuse him, but rather confirmed it by erecting gates at point B—it was their conduct which led him to act as he did; and this raises an equity in favour against them . . .

I would, therefore, hold that Mr Crabb, as the owner of the back portion, has a right of access at point B over the verge on to Mill Park Road and a right of way along that road to Hook Lane without paying compensation. I would allow the appeal and declare that he has an easement, accordingly.

LAWTON LJ

I ask myself whether any principle of equity applies. I am grateful to counsel for the defendants for having drawn our attention this morning to *Ramsden v Dyson* (1866) L.R. 1 H.L. 129. If there had been any doubt in my mind about the application of principles of equity to the facts as I have recounted them, that case would have dissipated it. As was pointed out to counsel for the defendants in the course of the argument, if one changes the parties in a passage in the speech of Lord Cranworth L.C. L.R. 1 H.L. at 142 into the names of the parties in this case, one has a case for the intervention of equity which Lord Cranworth regarded with favour. The passage to which I refer is in these terms:

. . . if I had come to the conclusion that Thornton, when he erected his building in 1837, did so in the belief that he had against Sir John an absolute right to the lease he claims, and that Sir John knew that he was proceeding on that mistaken notion, and did not interfere to set him right, I should have been much disposed to say that he was entitled to the relief he sought."

The answer of counsel for the defendants was that the plaintiff had not got an absolute right to have the gates put up. For the reasons I have stated, I am of the opinion that he had in the sense that he had been given a firm undertaking. The defendants, knowing that the plaintiff intended to sell part of his land, stood by when he did so and, without a word of warning, allowed him to surround himself with a useless piece of land from which there was no exit. I would allow this appeal and grant relief in the terms indicated by Lord Denning M.R.

SCARMAN LJ

[Having stated that the enquiry must be whether an equity was established and, if so, what was its extent and appropriate remedy:] In pursuit of that enquiry I do not find helpful the distinction between promissory and proprietary estoppel. This distinction may indeed be valuable to those who have to teach or expound the law, but I do not think that, in solving the particular problem raised by a particular case, putting the law into categories is of the slightest assistance . . .

What is needed to establish an equity? In the course of an interesting addition to his submissions this morning, counsel for the defendants cited *Ramsden v Dyson*[1] to support his proposition that in order to establish an equity by estoppel, there must be a belief by the plaintiff in the existence of a right created or encouraged by the words or actions of the defendant. With respect, I do not think that that is today a correct statement of the law. I think the law has developed so that today it is to be considered as correctly stated by Lord Kingsdown in his dissenting speech in *Ramsden v Dyson*. Like Lord Denning M.R., I think that the point of dissent in *Ramsden v Dyson* was not on the law but on the facts. Lord Kingsdown's speech, insofar as it dealt with propositions of law, has been often considered, and recently followed, by this court in *Inwards v Baker* [1965] 2 Q.B. 29. Lord Kingsdown said:[2]

"The rule of law applicable to the case appears to me to be this: If a man, under a verbal agreement with a landlord for a certain interest in land, or what amounts to the same thing, under an expectation, created or encouraged by the landlord [my italics], that he shall have a certain interest, takes possession of such land, with the consent of the landlord, and upon the faith of such promise or expectation, with the knowledge of the landlord, and without objection by him, lays out money upon the land, a Court of equity will compel the landlord to give effect to such promise or expectation."

Counsel for the defendants, in the course of an interesting and vigorous submission, drew the attention of the court to the necessity of finding something akin to fraud before the equity sought by the plaintiff could be established. "Fraud" was a word often in the mouths of those robust judges who adorned the bench in the 19th century. It is less often in the mouths of the more wary judicial spirits who sit today on the Bench. But it is clear that whether one uses the word "fraud" or not, the plaintiff has to establish as a fact that the defendant, by setting up his right, is taking advantage of him in a way which is unconscionable, inequitable or unjust. It is to be observed . . . that the fraud or injustice alleged does not take place during the course of negotiation, but only when the defendant decides to refuse to allow the plaintiff to set up his claim against the defendant's undoubted right. The fraud, if it be such, arises after the event, when the defendant seeks by relying on his right to defeat the expectation which he by his conduct encouraged the plaintiff to have. There need not be anything fraudulent or unjust in the conduct of the actual negotiations—the conduct of the transaction by the defendant.

Appeal Allowed.

Points for reflection

11–012   In *Yaxley v Gotts and another* [2000] 1 All E.R. 711 CA, BG decided to purchase a property to convert into flats and made an arrangement with Y that, in return for doing work on the flats on the two upper floors and managing the whole property, Y would acquire the ground floor flats. When Y had done work on the flats costing over £9,000, AG, BG's son who had become a party to the arrangement with

[1]   (1866) L.R. 1 H.L. 129 at 142.
[2]   (1866) L.R. 1 H.L. 129 at 170.

Y, excluded Y from the property. Because the arrangement was not in writing, as required by s.2(1) of Law of Property (Miscellaneous Provisions) Act 1989, above, Ch.4, it was void. The court was not persuaded by the opinion in Goff & Jones, *The Law of Restitution* (5th edn, 1998) p.580, which states that—"even if the purchaser can demonstrate that the vendor's conduct was so unconscionable that it would be inequitable for him to rely on the absence of writing, to order the conveyance of, or to declare him trustee of, the property is an inappropriate remedy in that it frustrates the policy underlying section 2(1) of the 1989 Act."

It held that the Y's reliance on the arrangement created a constructive trust, closely akin to, if not indistinguishable from, a proprietary estoppel which was saved by s.2(5) of the 1989 Act—"nothing in this section affects the creation or operation of resulting, implied or constructive trusts . . ." Y's equitable interest in the ground floor would be satisfied by the grant of a 99-year lease.

Was the court, in effect, enforcing a contract which Parliament had declared to be void? Robert Walker LJ said that s.2 of the 1989 Act "can be seen as embodying Parliament's conclusion, in the general public interest, that the need for certainty as to the formation of contracts of this type must in general outweigh the disappointment of those who make informal bargains in ignorance of the statutory requirement." Has Parliament's purpose been subverted?

Questions

1. It has been suggested (Atiyah, 91 L.Q.R. 174) that the decision could have been based on contract in that the plaintiff's acting to his detriment would constitute consideration. The council did not ask him to sell the plot dependent on point B. Can unrequested detriment to a promisee constitute consideration? See Millett, 92 L.Q.R. 342.

2. If there had been a contract to grant an easement it would have been a contract for the sale or disposition of an interest in land and so unenforceable in the absence of a memorandum in writing: Law of Property Act 1925 s.40, above, and now void under the Law of Property (Miscellaneous Provisions) Act 1989. So the "equity" is better than a contract?

3. The Council led Mr Crabb to believe that "he had or would be granted a right of access". Is there a significant difference between "had" and "would be granted"? Does not the one indicate a statement of fact and the other a promise? Is there a similar distinction between the passages from Lord Cranworth and Lord Kingsdown quoted from *Ramsden v Dyson* by Lawton and Scarman LJJ respectively?

4. Lord Denning and Scarman LJ appear to differ as to the practical significance of categorising an estoppel as "proprietary". Who is right? Cf. *Jorden v Money*, above.

See also *Pascoe v Turner* [1979] 2 All E.R. 945; *Greasley v Cooke* [1980] 3 All E.R. 710; *Taylor Fashions Ltd v Liverpool Victoria Trustees Co Ltd* [1981] 1 All E.R. 897; and the next case.

AMALGAMATED INVESTMENT & PROPERTY CO LTD (IN LIQUIDATION) v TEXAS COMMERCE INTERNATIONAL BANK LTD

Court of Appeal [1982] Q.B. 84; [1981] 3 W.L.R. 565; [1981] 3 All E.R. 577

The plaintiff (AIP) requested the defendant (the bank) to make advances to AIP's subsidiary (ANPP) in the Bahamas and covenanted to pay on demand money owed by ANPP to the bank (the guarantee).

11–013

11–014

To circumvent Bahamian restrictions, money was advanced by the bank to a Bahamian company (Portsoken) which advanced the same sum to ANPP (the NASSAU loan). The guarantee was a standing offer to repay any money advanced by the bank to ANPP. No such money was ever advanced. Both parties, however, believed the guarantee to be binding and effective. The mistake originated with the bank but AIP represented to the bank and encouraged it to believe that the guarantee was binding and effective. Robert Goff J dismissed a claim by AIP that it was under no liability to the bank under the guarantee. AIP appealed.

Lord Denning MR and Eveleigh LJ delivered judgments dismissing the appeal.

BRANDON LJ

The judge . . . based his decision on the question of estoppel on three matters. The first matter was that, from 1974 to 1976, both the bank and AIP conducted the transactions which took place between them in what must for present purposes be regarded as the mistaken belief that the guarantee relating to the Nassau loan effectively bound AIP to discharge any indebtedness of ANPP to Portsoken in respect of that loan. The second matter was that, although it had originally been due to the bank's own error that it came to hold its mistaken belief, AIP, being under the same mistaken belief itself, by its conduct encouraged and reinforced the mistaken belief held by the bank. The third matter was that the bank, in reliance on the mistaken belief concerned, accorded various indulgences to, and refrained from exercising various rights against, AIP in a way which, but for the bank's mistaken belief, it would never have done . . .

Two main arguments against the existence of an estoppel were advanced on behalf of AIP both before Robert Goff J. and before us. The first argument was that, since the bank came to hold its mistaken belief in the first as a result of its own error alone, and AIP had at most innocently acquiesced in that belief which it also held, there was no representation by AIP to the bank on which an estoppel could be founded. The second argument was that, in the present case, the bank was seeking to use estoppel not as a shield, but as a sword, and that that was something which the law of estoppel did not permit.

I consider first the argument based on the origin of the bank's mistaken belief. In my opinion this argument is founded on an erroneous view of the kind of estoppel which is relevant in this case. The kind of estoppel which is relevant in this case is not the usual kind of estoppel in pais based on a representation made by A to B and acted on by B to his detriment. It is rather the kind of estoppel which is described in *Spencer Bower and Turner on Estoppel by Representation* (3rd ed., 1977), pp. 157–160 as estoppel by convention:

"This form of estoppel is founded, not on a representation of fact made by a representor and believed by a representee, but on an agreed statement of facts the truth of which has been assumed, by the convention of the parties, as the basis of a transaction into which they are about to enter. When the parties have acted in their transaction upon the agreed assumption that a given state of facts is to be accepted between them as true, then as regards that transaction each will be estopped as against the other from questioning the truth of the statement of facts so assumed."

Applying that description of estoppel by convention to the present case, the situation as I see it is this. First, the relevant transactions entered into by AIP and the bank were the making of new arrangements with regard to the overall security held by the bank in relation to both the U.K. and Nassau loans. Second, for the purposes of those transactions, both the bank and AIP assumed the truth of a certain state of affairs, namely that the guarantee given in relation to the Nassau loan effectively bound AIP to discharge any indebtedness of ANPP to Portsoken. The transactions took place on the basis of that assumption, and their course was influenced by it in the sense that, if the assumption had not been made, the course of the transactions would without doubt have been different.

Those facts produce, in my opinion, a classic example of the kind of estoppel called estoppel by convention as described in the passage from Spencer Bower and Turner on Estoppel by Representation and so deprive the first argument advanced on behalf of AIP of any validity which, if the case were an ordinary one of estoppel by representation, it might otherwise have.

I turn to the second argument advanced on behalf of AIP, that the bank is here seeking to use estoppel as a sword rather than a shield, and that that is something which the law of estoppel does not permit. Another way in which the argument is put is that a party cannot found a cause of action on an estoppel.

In my view much of the language used in connection with these concepts is no more than a matter of semantics. Let me consider the present case and suppose that the bank had brought an action against AIP before it went into liquidation to recover moneys owed by ANPP to Portsoken. In the statement of claim in such an action the bank would have pleaded the contract of loan incorporating the guarantee, and averred that, on the true construction of the guarantee, AIP was bound to discharge the debts owed by ANPP to Portsoken. By their defence AIP would have pleaded that, on the true construction of the guarantee, AIP was only bound to discharge debts owed by ANPP to the bank, and not debts owed by ANPP to Portsoken. Then in their reply the bank would have pleaded that, by reason of an estoppel arising from the matters discussed above, AIP were precluded from questioning the interpretation of the guarantee which both parties had, for the purpose of the transactions between them, assumed to be true.

In this way the bank, while still in form using the estoppel as a shield, would in substance be founding a cause of action on it. This illustrates what I would regard as the true proposition of law, that, while a party cannot in terms found a cause of action on an estoppel, he may, as a result of being able to rely on an estoppel, succeed on a cause of action on which, without being able to rely on that estoppel, he would necessarily have failed. That, in my view, is, in substance, the situation of the bank in the present case.

It follows from what I have said above that I would reject the second argument against the existence of an estoppel put forward on behalf of AIP as well as the first. It further follows, from my rejection of both arguments against the existence of an estoppel, that I would answer the second of the two questions which I formulated earlier by holding that, if AIP did not, by the contract relating to the Nassau loan, undertake to the bank to discharge any indebtedness of ANPP to Portsoken, it is nevertheless estopped from denying that it did so by reason of the basis, accepted by both the bank and AIP, on which the transactions between them were later conducted during the period from 1974 to 1976.

Appeal Dismissed.

Question

It appears that, if the parties to a contract misconstrue their agreement and act upon that misconstruction, there will be an estoppel by convention; and, if a dispute arises, the contract will be enforced, not according to its real meaning but according to the "false" meaning put upon it by the parties. What if the parties enter into the contract under a common misapprehension as to the effect of their agreement? Is the contract to be enforced in its true or false meaning? What if, in performing the contract, the parties act on the assumption that the false meaning is the true one? Has not the formerly false meaning now become the "true" meaning? How does the law on rectification of a formal contract bear on questions of this kind?

11–015

----

4. Estoppel having a Suspensory or an Extinctive Effect?

TOOL METAL MANUFACTURING CO LTD v TUNGSTEN ELECTRIC CO LTD

House of Lords [1955] 1 W.L.R. 761; 99 S.J. 470; [1955] 2 All E.R. 657; 72 R.P.C. 209

In 1938 the Tool Metal Manufacturing Co Ltd (TMMC) who owned certain patents entered into a formal agreement with the Tungsten Electric Co Ltd (TECO), whereby TMMC gave TECO a licence to deal in the products protected by the patents (styled "contract materials") until 1947, terminable by six months' notice in writing on either side, in consideration of TECO's paying a royalty of 10 per cent on the net value of all contract material used by TECO other than material supplied by TMMC. Clause 5 of the agreement provided that, if in any month the contract material used by TECO exceeded a quota of 50 kilograms, TECO should pay to TMMC "compensation" equal to 30 per cent of the net value of the excess contract material. After the outbreak of war in 1939 the payment of compensation was suspended but royalties were paid down to March 1942. In 1942 TMMC orally intimated to TECO that they would prepare a new agreement and would not, meantime, claim compensation and would

11–016

be satisfied with a flat royalty of 10 per cent, as the national interest required the maximum output of contract material: no compensation was claimed during the war and TECO regulated their production accordingly. In September 1944 TMMC submitted to TECO the draft of a proposed new agreement which contained a provision for the revival of compensation and which was rejected by TECO In 1945, TECO brought an action against TMMC for fraudulent misrepresentation or breach of contract in the 1938 agreement and alleged in their claim for damages that it had been agreed that no compensation should be payable after December 31, 1939. TMMC denied the alleged agreement and maintained that if there were such agreement there was no consideration for it: and they counterclaimed, alleging that since 1942, TECO, in breach of their contract, had not paid royalties or compensation on the contract material they had used. They did not seek compensation for the period December 31, 1939–May 31, 1945, but sought compensation in respect of material used since June 1, 1945.

The Court of Appeal (Somervell, Singleton and Cohen LJJ), affirming in part the decision of Devlin J, held ((1952) 69 R.P.C. 108, 112) that there had been no contract for the final termination of the payment of compensation, only a temporary arrangement pending a new agreement; but, on the principle of *Hughes v Metropolitan Rly* and *Birmingham and District Land Co v L & North Western Rly* this arrangement to suspend the payment of compensation was binding in equity upon TMMC until terminated by proper notice and the presentation of the draft new agreement in 1944 did not constitute such notice.

In 1950, TMMC commenced an action claiming compensation as from January 1, 1947, treating their delivery of the counterclaim in the first action as a sufficient notice to determine the agreement to suspend payment of compensation. TECO pleaded inter alia, that the counterclaim was not sufficient notice because no time was specified in it for the termination of the arrangement. The House of Lords (Viscount Simonds, Lords Oaksey, Tucker, and Cohen), reversing the decision of the Court of Appeal ([1954] 1 W.L.R. 862), restored the decision of Pearson J ((1954) 71 R.P.C. 1) in favour of TMMC.

LORD TUCKER

My Lords, the parties to the present action are estopped from disputing the correctness of the decision of the Court of Appeal in the first action to the effect that circumstances existed which gave rise to the application of the equitable principle in *Hughes v Metropolitan Rly*, and that no sufficient intimation to terminate the period of suspension of payment had been given prior to the counterclaim in that action, but it would be wrong, in my opinion, if the view were to prevail that your Lordships in the present case are tacitly accepting the correctness of that decision . . .

The sole question . . . before the courts on this issue in the present action has been throughout: Was the counterclaim in the first action a sufficient intimation to determine the period of suspension which has been found to exist?

LORD COHEN

[The findings of the Court of Appeal in the first case] necessarily involve that, in the present case, equity required TMMC to give some form of notice to TECO before compensation would become payable. But it has never been decided that in every case notice should be given before a temporary concession ceases to operate. It might, for instance, cease automatically on the occurrence of a particular event. Still less has any case decided that, where notice is necessary, it must take a particular form.

Romer L.J. seems to have taken the view that the counterclaim could not be a notice, because you cannot terminate an agreement by repudiating it. With all respect, the fallacy of this argument consists in treating the arrangement found to exist by the Court of Appeal in the first action as an agreement binding in law. It was not an agreement, it was a voluntary concession by TMMC which, for reasons of equity, the court held TMMC could not cease to allow without plain intimation to TECO of their intention to do so. The counterclaim seems to me a plain intimation of such change of intention operating as from June 1, 1945, and for the future. Nonetheless, the intimation would fall short of what was required if it was the duty of TMMC to specify in the intimation the reasonable time which they would allow after receipt of the intimation to enable TECO to readjust their business to the altered conditions. I see no reason why equity should impose this burden on TMMC.

Points for reflection

There has been much discussion as to whether promissory estoppel extinguishes or merely sus-   **11–017**
pends the estopped party's rights. The answer seems reasonably clear: as regards existing obligations it is extinctive, as regards future obligations it is suspensory. Both these points emerge in the
Tool Metal case. TMMC's right to the 20 per cent balance of 'compensation' during the period of
operation of the estoppel was gone for ever. They sued for it and Devlin J and the Court of Appeal
in the first action held that they failed. This is obviously what Denning J intended in the *High Trees*
case. If, during the war years, the landlord could have required payment of the whole of the back
rent, the doctrine would have achieved precisely nothing; that would have been no more than an
application of *Foakes v Beer*. It, on the other hand, during the war years, the landlord had told the
tenant that, from a reasonable period, say three months, hence, he must again begin to pay the
full rent, that according to *Tool Metal* (but perhaps not Denning J) would have been effective. This
would have been the same as TMMC resuming its right to the full amount of compensation for the
future. The suspensory aspect can apply only when there is a continuing series of obligations some
of which are in the future—to pay rent, royalties, interest, or whatever.

The problem of reconciling the dictum in *High Trees* and the decision of the Court of Appeal in
Tool Metal with *Foakes v Beer* remains. Denning J apparently took the view that they were irreconcilable, *Foakes v Beer* having been decided per incuriam through overlooking a principle of equity.
The irreconcilability may be accepted—what is the difference between agreeing to forgo interest
which would otherwise accrue from day to day and agreeing to forgo rent or royalties which would
otherwise accrue from time to time? The opinion that the Law Lords forgot about equity is harder to
swallow. It will be noted that in *Tool Metal* their Lordships were concerned to make it clear that they
were not deciding that promissory estoppel applied to the facts of the case. As between the parties,
it had been finally decided by the Court of Appeal in the first action that it did apply—the parties
were estopped by the record (a different kind of estoppel) from denying it—but the House was not
saying that that decision was right or wrong. Given that a promissory estoppel was in operation,
the only question for them was whether a sufficient notice had been given to bring it to an end. The
House may be taken to have decided only that, if there is a doctrine of promissory estoppel which
operates in these circumstances, its operation may be terminated by reasonable notice; and, in the
circumstances, reasonable notice had been given.

Notwithstanding the enormous amount of discussion of the *High Trees* case, the occasions for its
application seem to have been very few. Most of the cases in which it has been cited were decided,
or could have been decided, on the basis of previously recognised principles of estoppel or the principle of *Hughes v Metropolitan Railway*. Indeed, the only two cases which directly raise the apparent
conflict with *Foakes v Beer* seem to be *D & C Builders v Rees* and the *Tool Metal* case. In the former
case, below, *Foakes v Beer* was applied. In the *Tool Metal* case, the Court of Appeal, though purporting to apply *Hughes*, went beyond that case, at least as interpreted above, and applied the extension of it favoured by Denning J in *High Trees*—though without mentioning that case.

In *F A Ajayi v R T Briscoe (Nigeria) Ltd* [1964] 1 W.L.R. 1326; [1964] 3 All E.R. 556, Lord Hodson,
delivering the judgment of the JCPC said:

> "Their Lordships are of opinion that the principle of law as defined by Bowen L.J. has been con-
> firmed by the House of Lords in the case of *Tool Metal Manufacturing Co Ltd v Tungsten Electric
> Co Ltd* where the authorities were reviewed and no encouragement was given to the view that
> the principle was capable of extension so as to create rights in the promisee for which he had
> given no consideration. The principle, which has been described as quasi-estoppel and perhaps
> more aptly as promissory estoppel, is that when one party to a contract in the absence of fresh

consideration agrees not to enforce his rights an equity will be raised in favour of the other party. This equity is, however, subject to the qualifications (1) that the other party has altered his position, (2) that the promissor can resile from his promise on giving reasonable notice, which need not be a formal notice, giving the promisee reasonable opportunity of resuming his position, (3) the promise only becomes final and irrevocable if the promisee cannot resume his positon."

5. EQUITABLE ESTOPPEL AND PART PAYMENT OF DEBTS

D & C BUILDERS LTD v REES

Court of Appeal [1966] 2 Q.B. 617; [1966] 2 W.L.R. 288; [1965] 3 All E.R. 837

LORD DENNING MR

11–018   D & C Builders Ltd ("the plaintiffs") are a little company. "D" stands for Mr Donaldson, a decorator, "C" for Mr Casey, a plumber. They are jobbing builders. The defendant, Mr Rees, has a shop where he sells builders' materials.

In the spring of 1964 the defendant employed the plaintiffs to do work at his premises, 218 Brick Lane. The plaintiffs did the work and rendered accounts in May and June, which came to £746 13s. 1d. altogether. The defendant paid £250 on account. In addition the plaintiffs made an allowance of £14 off the bill. So in July 1964 there was owing to the plaintiffs the sum of £482 13s. 1d. At this stage there was no dispute as to the work done. But the defendant did not pay.

On August 31, 1964, the plaintiffs wrote asking the defendant to pay the remainder of the bill. He did not reply. On October 19, 1964, they wrote again, pointing out that the "outstanding account of £480 is well overdue." Still the defendant did not reply. He did not write or telephone for more than three weeks. Then on Friday, November 13, 1964, the defendant was ill with influenza. His wife telephoned the plaintiffs. She spoke to Mr Casey. She began to make complaints about the work: and then said: "My husband will offer you £300 in settlement. That is all you'll get. It is to be in satisfaction." Mr Casey said he would have to discuss it with Mr Donaldson. The two of them talked it over. Their company was in desperate financial straits. If they did not have the £300, they would be in a state of bankruptcy. So they decided to accept the £300 and see what they could do about the rest afterwards. Thereupon Mr Donaldson telephoned the defendant's wife. He said to her: "£300 will not even clear our commitments on the job. We will accept £300 and give you a year to find the balance." She said: "No, we will never have enough money to pay the balance. £300 is better than nothing." He said: "We have no choice but to accept." She said: "Would you like the money by cash or by cheque. If it is cash you can have it on Monday. If by cheque, you can have it tomorrow (Saturday)." On Saturday, November 14, 1964, Mr Casey went to collect the money. He took with him a receipt prepared on the company's paper with the simple words: "Received the sum of £300 from Mr Rees." She gave him a cheque for £300 and asked for a receipt. She insisted that the words "in completion of the account" be added. Mr Casey did as she asked. He added the words to the receipt. So she had the clean receipt: "Received the sum of £300 from Mr Rees in completion of the account. Paid, M. Casey." Mr Casey gave in evidence his reason for giving it: "If I did not have the £300 the company would have gone bankrupt. The only reason we took it was to save the company. She knew the position we were in."

The plaintiffs were so worried about their position that they went to their solicitors. Within a few days, on November 23, 1964, the solicitors wrote complaining that the defendant had "extricated a receipt of some sort or other" from them. They said that they were treating the £300 as a payment on account. On November 28, 1964, the defendant replied alleging bad workmanship. He also set up the receipt which Mr Casey gave to his wife, adding: "I assure you she had no gun on her." The plaintiffs brought this action for the balance. The defendant set up a defence of bad workmanship and also that there was a binding settlement. The question of settlement was tried as a preliminary issue. The judge made these findings:

"I concluded that by the middle of August the sum due to the plaintiffs was ascertained and not then in dispute. I also concluded that there was no consideration to support the agreement of November 13 and 14. It was a case of agreeing to take a lesser sum, when a larger sum was already due to the plaintiffs. It was not a case of agreeing to take a cheque for a smaller amount instead of receiving cash for a larger amount. The payment by cheque was an incidental arrangement."

The judge decided, therefore, the preliminary issue in favour of the plaintiffs. The defendant appeals to this court. He says there was here an accord and satisfaction—an accord when the plaintiffs agreed, however reluctantly, to accept £300 in settlement of the account—and satisfaction when they accepted the cheque for £300 and it was duly honoured. The defendant relies on the cases of *Sibree v Tripp* (1846) 15 M. & W. 23) and *Goddard v O'Brien* ((1882) 9 QBD 37) as authorities in his favour.

This case is of some consequence: for it is a daily occurrence that a merchant or tradesman, who is owed a sum of money, is asked to take less. The debtor says he is in difficulties. He offers a lesser sum in settlement, cash down. He says he cannot pay more. The creditor is considerate. He accepts the proffered sum and forgives him the rest of the debt. The question arises: is the settlement binding on the creditor? The answer is that, in point of law, the creditor is not bound by the settlement. He can the next day sue the debtor for the balance, and get judgment. The law was so stated in 1602 by Lord Coke in *Pinnel's Case* ((1602) 5 Co.Rep. 117a)—and accepted in 1884 by the House of Lords in *Foakes v Beer* [above, Ch.10].

Now, suppose that the debtor, instead of paying the lesser sum in cash, pays it by cheque. He makes out a cheque for the amount. The creditor accepts the cheque and cashes it. Is the position any different? I think not. No sensible distinction can be taken between payment of a lesser sum by cash and payment of it by cheque. The cheque, when given, is conditional payment. When honoured, it is actual payment. It is then just the same as cash. If a creditor is not bound when he receives payment by cash, he should not be bound when he receives payment by cheque. This view is supported by the leading case of *Cumber v Wane* ((1721) 1 Stra. 426), which has suffered many vicissitudes but was, I think, rightly decided in point of law.

The case of *Sibree v Tripp* ((1846) 15 M. & W. 23) is easily distinguishable. There the plaintiffs brought an action for £500. It was settled by the defendant giving three promissory notes amounting in all to £250. Those promissory notes were given on a new contract, in substitution for the debt sued for, and not as conditional payment. The plaintiff's only remedy thenceforward was on the notes and not on the debt. The case of *Goddard v O'Brien* ((1882) 9 QBD 37) is not so easily distinguishable. There a creditor was owed £125 for some slates. He met the debtor and agreed to accept £100 in discharge of it. The debtor gave a cheque for £100. The creditor gave a written receipt "in settlement on the said cheque being honoured." The cheque was clearly given by way of conditional payment. It was honoured. The creditor sued the debtor for the balance of £25. He lost, because the £100 was paid by cheque and not by cash. The decision was criticised by Fletcher Moulton L.J. in *Hirachand Punamchand v Temple* [above, Ch.10], and by the editors of *Smith's Leading Cases* (13th ed.), Vol. 1, p. 380. It was, I think, wrongly decided. In point of law payment of a lesser sum, whether by cash or by cheque, is no discharge of a greater sum.

This doctrine of the common law has come under heavy fire. It was ridiculed by Sir George Jessel M.R. in *Couldery v Bartrum* ((1881) 19 Ch.D. 394 at p. 399). It was held to be mistaken by Lord Blackburn in *Foakes v Beer*. It was condemned by the Law Revision Committee in their Sixth Interim Report (Cmnd. 5449), para. 20 and para. 22. But a remedy has been found. The harshness of the common law has been relieved. Equity has stretched out a merciful hand to help the debtor. The courts have invoked the broad principle stated by Lord Cairns L.C. in *Hughes v Metropolitan Rly* [above]:

". . . it is the first principle upon which all courts of equity proceed, that if parties, who have entered into definite and distinct terms involving certain legal results . . . afterwards by their own act, or with their own consent, enter upon a course of negotiation which has the effect of leading one of the parties to suppose that the strict rights arising under the contract will not be enforced, or will be kept in suspense, or held in abeyance, the person who otherwise might have enforced those rights will not be allowed to enforce them where it would be inequitable, having regard to the dealings which have taken place between the parties."

It is worth noting that the principle may be applied, not only so as to suspend strict legal rights, but also so as to preclude the enforcement of them.

This principle has been applied to cases where a creditor agrees to accept a lesser sum in discharge of a greater. So much so that we can now say that, when a creditor and a debtor enter on a course of negotiation, which leads the debtor to suppose that, on payment of the lesser sum, the creditor will not enforce payment of the balance, and on the faith thereof the debtor pays the lesser sum and the creditor accepts it as satisfaction: then the creditor will not be allowed to enforce payment of the balance when it would be inequitable to do so. This was well illustrated during the last war. Tenants went away to escape the bombs and left their houses unoccupied. The landlords accepted a reduced rent for the time they were empty. It was held that the landlords could not afterwards turn round and sue for the balance: see *Central London Property Trust Ltd v High Trees House Ltd* [above]. This caused at the time some eyebrows to be raised in high places. But they have been lowered since. The solution was so obviously just that no one could well gainsay it.

In applying this principle, however, we must note the qualification. The creditor is barred from his legal rights only when it would be inequitable for him to insist on them. Where there has been a true accord, under which the creditor voluntarily agrees to accept a lesser sum in satisfaction, and the debtor acts on that accord by paying the lesser sum and the creditor accepts it, then it is inequitable for the creditor afterwards to insist on the balance. But he is not bound unless there has been truly an accord between them.

In the present case, on the facts as found by the judge, it seems to me that there was no true accord. The debtor's wife held the creditor to ransom. The creditor was in need of money to meet his own commitments, and she knew it. When the creditor asked for payment of the £480 due to him, she said to him in effect: "We cannot pay you the £480. But we will pay you £300 if you will accept it in settlement. If you do not accept it on those terms, you will get nothing. £300 is better than nothing." She had no right to say any such thing. She could properly have said: "We cannot pay you more than £300. Please accept it on account." But she had no right to insist on his taking it in settlement. When she said: "We will pay you nothing unless you accept £300 in settlement," she was putting undue pressure on the creditor. She was making a threat to break the contract (by paying nothing) and she was doing it so as to compel the creditor to do what he was unwilling to do (to accept £300 in settlement): and she succeeded. He complied with her demand. That was on recent authority a case of intimidation (see *Rookes v Barnard* [1964] A.C. 1129, and *J. T. Stratford & Son Ltd v Lindley* [1965] A.C. 269 at pp. 283, 284). In these circumstances there was no true accord so as to found a defence of accord and satisfaction (see *Day v McLea* (1889) 22 QBD 610). There is also no equity in the defendant to warrant any departure from the due course of law. No person can insist on a settlement procured by intimidation.

In my opinion there is no reason in law or equity why the creditor should not enforce the full amount of the debt due to him. I would, therefore, dismiss this appeal.

Danckwerts L.J. gave a judgment concurring with Lord Denning M.R.

WINN LJ

. . . The question to be decided may be stated thus. Did the defendant's agreement to give his own cheque for £300 in full settlement of his existing debt to the plaintiffs of £482 13s. 1d. and the plaintiffs' agreement to accept it in full payment of that debt, followed by delivery and due payment of such a cheque, constitute a valid accord and satisfaction discharging the debt in law?

Apart altogether from any decided cases bearing on the matter, there might be a good deal to be said, as a matter of policy, in favour of holding any creditor bound by his promise to discharge a debtor on his paying some amount less than the debt due: some judges no doubt so thought when they held readily that acceptance by the creditor of something of a different nature from that to which he was entitled was a satisfaction of the liability (cf. *Pinnel's Case* (1602) 5 Co Rep. 117a, *Smith v Trowsdale* (1854) 3 E. & B. 83, *Cooper v Parker* (1855) 15 C.B. 882). A like approach might at some time in the past have been adopted by the courts to all serious assurances of agreement, but as English law developed, it does not now permit in general of such treatment of mere promises. In the more specific field of discharge of monetary debt there has been some conflict of judicial opinion.

Where a cheque for a smaller sum than the amount due is drawn by a person other than the debtor and delivered in satisfaction of his debt, it is clear that the debt is discharged if the cheque be accepted on that basis and duly paid [cf. *Hirachand Punamchand v Temple*, above, Ch.10].

In the instant case the debtor's own cheque was accepted, though not stipulated for by the creditor, as the equivalent of cash, conditionally of course on its being duly paid on presentation: such is the modern usage in respect of payments of money due, common, though not yet universal, in domestic no less than commercial transactions. This court must now decide the effect of that transaction.

[Having discussed *Goddard v O'Brien*, his Lordship continued:] I interpose the comment that I find it impossible in the instant case to visualise any benefit or legal possibility of benefit to the builders which might derive from the receipt of the defendant's cheque for £300 instead of the same amount of cash.

Only two years after the decision in *Goddard's* case the House of Lords, in the case of *Foakes v Beer* [above, Ch.10], had to consider the effect of an agreement between a judgment debtor and a judgment creditor that in consideration of the debtor paying down part of the judgment debt and costs and paying the residue by instalments, the creditor would not take any proceedings on the judgment. The House held this to be a nudum pactum, being without consideration, and that it did not prevent the creditor after payment of the whole debt and costs from proceeding to enforce payment of interest on the judgment. *Pinnel's Case* and *Cumber v Wane* were expressly followed.

[Having discussed *Foakes v Beer* and *Hirachand Punamchand v Temple*, his Lordship proceeded:] In my judgment it is an essential element of a valid accord and satisfaction that the agreement which constitutes the accord should itself be binding in law, and I do not think that any such agreement can be so binding unless it is either made under seal or supported by consideration. Satisfaction, viz., performance, of an agreement of accord does not provide retroactive validity to the accord, but depends for its effect on the legal validity of the accord as a binding contract at the time when it is made: this I think is apparent when it is remembered that, albeit rarely, existing obligations of debt may be replaced effectively by a contractually binding substitution of a new obligation.

In my judgment this court should now decline to follow the decision in *Goddard v O'Brien* and should hold that where a debtor's own cheque for a lesser amount than he indisputably owes to his creditor is accepted by the creditor in full satisfaction of the debt, the creditor is to be regarded, in any case where he has not required the payment to be made by cheque rather than in cash, as having received the cheque merely as conditional payment of part of what he was entitled to receive: he is free in law, if not in good commercial conscience, to insist on payment of the balance of the amount due to him from the debtor.

I would dismiss this appeal.

Appeal Dismissed.

Questions

1. Lord Denning recognises that *Foakes v Beer* continues to represent the common law and, apparently, is glad to follow it. But he considers that the *High Trees* principle will prevail where this is equitable. Is this a satisfactory principle or does it leave too much discretion to the judge in deciding whether it is "equitable" to apply the principle? **11–019**

2. In the absence of the element of intimidation, would the decision have been unanimous?

3. "Accord and satisfaction is the purchase of a release from an obligation, whether arising under contract or tort, by means of any valuable consideration, not being the actual performance of the obligation itself." *Salmond and Williams on Contracts,* 328, adopted in *British Russian Gazette v Associated Newspapers Ltd* [1933] 2 K.B. 616 at 643–644. The accord is the agreement, the satisfaction is the consideration; so this is merely the name for a particular type of contract. Is agreement generally precluded by the fact that one party takes advantage of another's weak position? Suppose that X, knowing that D. & C. Builders are desperate for work, beats them down until they agree to do work at very low cost. Are they bound by the agreement? Was there any less of an "accord" in the actual case than in that example? Is the difference that Rees was threatening to break his contract by not paying at all?

4. If a threat to break a contract is intimidation, why was there no intimidation in *High Trees* when the tenant said, "We cannot pay the full rent?" Is there a difference between "we can't" and "we won't?" Cf. *Williams v Roffey Bros*, above, Ch.10 and *Atlas Express Ltd v Kafko Ltd*, below, Ch.26.

5. Lord Denning says that *Sibree v Tripp* was easily distinguishable because there was a "new contract." There was no dispute as to the amount due in that case. How can promissory notes for £250 be consideration for £500—except by regarding the notes as something different from cash?

6. In *Woodhouse A.C. Israel Cocoa Ltd SA v Nigerian Produce Marketing Co Ltd* [1972] A.C. 741, Lord Hailsham of St. Marylebone LC said (at 758): "I desire to add that the time may soon come when the whole sequence of cases based on promissory estoppel since the war beginning with *Central London Property Trust Ltd v High Trees House Ltd*, may need to be reviewed and reduced to a

coherent body of doctrine by the courts. I do not mean to say that any are to be regarded with suspicion. But as is common with an expanding doctrine they do raise problems of coherent exposition which have never been systematically explored." Do you agree that this area of the law of contract lacks coherence?

In *Collier v P & MJ Wright (Holdings) Ltd* (below), Collier sought to set aside a statutory demand served by Wright for the sum of £58,814.32, this being the balance of a judgment debt (dating back to April 1999) entered against Collier and his (then) business partners Broadfoot and Flute. When the partnership came to an end in 2000, Collier continued to pay monthly instalments of £200 as his share of the joint debt. Evidently, Broadfoot and Flute had difficulty in making their payments; they were declared bankrupt in 2004 and 2002 respectively; and Wright duly sought to recover the whole balance of the debt from Collier. Resisting the demand, Collier relied on a meeting that he had with Wright at the end of 2000. At this meeting, which took place at the office of Collier's employer, Mr Redfern, it was alleged by Collier that Wright promised that, provided that Collier continued to pay his share of the judgment debt, he would look only to Broadfoot and Flute for the balance. In other words, it was alleged that Wright had agreed that Collier would not be asked to pay any more than his share. The trial judge dismissed Collier's application but his appeal succeeded before the Court of Appeal.

COLLIER v P & MJ WRIGHT (HOLDINGS) LIMITED

Court of Appeal [2007] EWCA Civ 1329

LADY JUSTICE ARDEN

(1) The agreement issue

11–020
22. The judge found that there was a triable dispute on the facts but held that, even if the facts alleged were established, there was in law no substantial dispute. The triable issue identified by the judge on the facts was whether Mr Wright entered into a binding agreement with Mr Collier that, if Mr Collier paid one-third share of the joint judgment debt, he would not be liable for the balance. The judge found that this was a triable issue because of Mr Collier's evidence. The judge did not consider that the triable issue emerged from Mr Wright's evidence (Judgment, [24]). In my judgment, this is not correct because Mr Collier in his witness statement indicated that Mr Wright had given him an assurance that if he continued paying his share in monthly instalments he would look to Messrs Broadfoot and Flute for the balance. Mr Redfern's evidence confirms that this was the alleged agreement.

23. What then was the effect of the alleged agreement? It was an alleged agreement that, if Mr Collier paid a one-third share or (which is not the same thing but which is not materially different for the purpose of this case) agreed to pay the balance of his one-third share, Wrights would not pursue him for any part of the balance of the judgment debt. Wrights' promise on this basis is easy to see. But on the face of it Mr Collier's promise is only a promise to pay part of what he already owed. This is not good consideration: see the rule in *Pinnel's case* as explained in *Foakes v Beer*.

24. Mr Uff seeks to avoid the problem posed by the rule in *Pinnel's* case pointing out that, under the judgment debt, Mr Collier was a joint debtor for 100% of the judgment debt whereas under his agreement with Mr Wright he was solely and severally liable for one-third of it. He submits that in consequence Mr Collier forwent the advantages of being a joint debtor. He gave up the possibility that Mr Wright would release Mr Broadfoot or Mr Flute (without reserving Wrights' position against Mr Collier), which would by law discharge Mr Collier automatically. He also gave up the possibility that he would predecease his partners and that his liability would then pass to them.

25. Mr Siward Atkins, for Wrights, relies on the following passage from *Chitty on Contracts*, vol 1 at 17–018:

"The courts generally construe a release as a covenant not to sue if it contains an indication of intention that the other debtors are not to be discharged. Moreover, even an accord and satisfaction with one joint or joint and several debtor will not discharge the others if the agreement, expressly or impliedly, provides that the creditor's rights against them shall be preserved."

26. In this case, submits Mr Atkins, taking the alleged agreement at its highest, there was simply a promise not to sue Mr Collier on his joint liability. The parties clearly intended that Wrights should be free to pursue Messrs. Broadfoot and Flute. Accordingly, Mr Collier did not assume any fresh several liability. An agreement to pay part of a debt is not valid consideration and there is no evidence to support any other consideration. He also submits that the judge correctly held at the end of [26] of his judgment that no consideration had moved from Mr Collier.

27. I do not consider that there is a genuine triable issue that the alleged agreement was a binding one. To be binding, Mr Collier had to provide consideration for Wrights' promise. I reach this conclusion for four reasons:

(i)   It is common ground that neither Mr Wright nor Mr Collier intended to affect the position of the other partners, and indeed Mr Wright proceeded to take steps against them. Accordingly, as Mr Atkins submits, the most to which the agreement could amount is a promise by Wrights not to sue Mr Collier if he paid one-third of the joint debt. That was a new collateral agreement added to the existing arrangements. His joint liability was unaffected. An agreement to pay part of an existing debt is not on the authorities sufficient to constitute consideration in law.

(ii)   Mr Atkins accepts that, if a promise had been given, for example that Mr Collier would not petition for his own bankruptcy, there would have been consideration. However, there is no evidence to this effect.

(iii) It would make no difference if it were subsequently established that Mr Wright did agree to release Mr Collier from liability for the judgment debt, other than a one-third share (so far as not already discharged). (In the light of the evidence, this release would have to have been on the basis that Wrights effectively reserved their rights against the other joint debtors.) It is correct, as Mr Uff submits, that there would be legal consequences resulting automatically from that agreement. For instance, Mr Collier, as well as benefiting by ceasing to be liable to claims to contribution for further amounts from his former partners or being entitled to be indemnified by Wrights against them, would lose certain other benefits he would have had because he was a joint debtor. In particular, he would have had the benefit of discharge in the event of his predeceasing them. He would also lose the benefit of a discharge from his liability to Wrights if Wrights released them without reserving its position against Mr Collier. On this scenario, Wrights makes an offer to Mr Collier that he should be liable for a third-share of the judgment debt only. But there was no evidence of any communication from Mr Collier which could be construed as an offer on his part to release any right and thus no meeting of the minds can be established on any of these matters. In any event, they were legal consequences which attached to the offer by Wrights and which flowed from it and thus could not constitute consideration moving from Mr Collier at all. Further, there is no evidence that these matters were of any benefit to Wrights.

(iv)   Mr Collier says in his witness statement that he "might well" have been able to reach some accommodation with his former partners if he had not had the assurance from Wrights. The judge refers to this point in [28]. I do not consider that Mr Collier's failure to take steps against the former partners can provide consideration for Wrights' alleged promise to look to Mr Collier for a one-third share only, because it is not alleged that Mr Collier agreed with Wrights not to pursue his former partners.

28. It follows that the mere fact that a creditor agrees with a joint debtor to accept payment from him alone of his proportionate share does not result in a binding agreement. Accordingly, this factual paradigm does not constitute yet another situation when the rule in *Pinnel's* case is avoided. Mr Collier can therefore succeed in his application to set aside the statutory demand only if he can show a triable issue bringing him within some existing exception to that rule as described above. For that reason he relies on promissory estoppel, to which I now turn.

(2) The promissory estoppel point

29. Mr Uff also relies on the doctrine of promissory estoppel, which the common law and in particular Lord Denning, both at first instance and in this court, developed to meet the hardship created by the rule in *Pinnel's* case. The principal authority is *Central London Property Trust v High Trees House Ltd* [1947] 1 KB 130. This case concerns a rent reduction given by concession during the Second World War. After that war, the landlord

sought to recover the difference between the reserved rent and the concessionary rent for the period following the war. Denning J. held that the agreement to reduce the rent was intended to apply only while the war lasted. It was not intended to run for the full term of the lease. Accordingly the landlord could recover the full rent for the post-war period.

30. Denning J. went on to hold (obiter) that the landlord was bound by the earlier agreement as a result of what we now call promissory estoppel: the landlord had made a representation on which the tenants relied and it would be inequitable for the landlord to be allowed to resile from his promise. Denning J. relied on *Hughes v Metropolitan Railway* (1887) 2 App Cas 439. In that case, a landlord gave his tenant six months' notice to repair the premises. The lease could be forfeited if the tenant failed to comply. During the six months following service of the notice, the parties entered into negotiations for the landlord to buy the lease and with his concurrence no repairs were done during that period. When the negotiations failed, the landlord claimed to treat the lease for forfeit on the expiry of six months from the original notice. The House of Lords held that the tenant was entitled to relief in equity against forfeiture, and that the six months allowed for repair should run from the date of the failure of the negotiations. The landlord had waived his right to strict performance. Denning J. observed that the principle in *Hughes* had not been considered in *Foakes v Beer*. In that case, the parties' agreement for the giving of time was contained in a written agreement and there was no suggestion as to any representation by the creditor. The crucial element in the *Hughes* case was that the tenant had been induced to act on the basis of a representation by the landlord.

31. The doctrine of promissory estoppel has been approved and developed in later cases. In *Tool Metal Manufacturing Co Ltd v Tungsten Electric Co Ltd* [1955] 1 WLR 761 the House of Lords (per Viscount Simmonds, Lord Tucker and Lord Cohen) accepted in principle that *Hughes v Metropolitan Railway* could apply to a reduction by concession in payments due to a creditor and held that the concession could be terminated by giving reasonable notice. The doctrine of promissory estoppel only applies when it is inequitable for the creditor (or other representor) to insist on his full rights: see *D & C Builders v Rees* [1966] 2 QB 617.

32. Mr Uff accepts that there must be reliance on the promise but submits that there does not have to be detriment. In this regard he relies on the following passage from *Chitty* at 3–136:

> "Inequitable. By making the part payment, the debtor acts in reliance on the creditor's promise, and so makes it *prima facie* 'inequitable' for the creditor peremptorily to go back on his promise. But other circumstances may lead to the conclusion that it would not be 'inequitable' for the creditor to reassert his claim for the full amount: this would, for example, be in the position where the debtor had failed to perform his promise to pay the smaller amount."

33. He also relies on the following passage from the judgment of Lord Denning M.R. in *D & C Builders v Rees*, with which Dankwerts L.J. agreed:

> "This principle [the principle of promissory estoppel] has been applied to cases where a creditor agrees to accept a lesser sum in discharge of a greater. So much so that we can now say that, when a creditor and a debtor enter upon a course of negotiation, which leads the debtor to suppose that, on payment of the lesser sum, the creditor will not enforce payment of the balance, and on the faith thereof the debtor pays the lesser sum and the creditor accepts it as satisfaction: then the creditor will not be allowed to enforce payment of the balance when it would be inequitable to do so. This was well illustrated during the last war. Tenants went away to escape the bombs and left their houses unoccupied. The landlords accepted a reduced rent for the time they were empty. It was held that the landlords could not afterwards turn round and sue for the balance, see *Central London Property Trust Ltd v High Trees House Ltd*. This caused at the time some eyebrows to be raised in high places. But they have been lowered since. The solution was so obviously just that no one could well gainsay it.
> In applying this principle, however, we must note the qualification: The creditor is only barred from his legal rights when it would be *inequitable* for him to insist upon them. Where there has been a *true* accord, under which the creditor voluntarily agrees to accept a lesser sum in satisfaction, and the debtor *acts* upon that accord by paying the lesser sum and the creditor accepts it, then it is inequitable for the creditor afterwards to insist on the balance. But he is not bound unless there has been truly an accord between them."

34. Mr Uff accepts that the doctrine is generally suspensory because the courts do the minimum necessary to satisfy the equity. However, he submits that the requirement of detriment, and perhaps other requirements of the doctrine, have to be approached as part of a broader enquiry as to whether repudiation of an assurance

is or is not unconscionable in all the circumstances (see generally per Robert Walker L.J. (as he then was) in *Gillett v Holt* [2001] Ch 210 at 232D). Here, he submits, there is a triable issue as to the basic question of unfairness. There had been part payments over a number of years and the lapse of 5 1/2 years between promise and repudiation. The part payments were maintained over a number of years. By inference, Mr Collier conducted his affairs on the premise that his obligation was a several obligation and undertook new commitments based on the belief that he had so conducted his finances as to enable those payments and no more. Mr Uff further submits that Mr Collier did not take steps he would otherwise have taken, including on the evidence considering bankruptcy or composition with his creditors or pursuing or pressing the joint debtors to contribute. In addition, by each payment he would have been misled into acknowledging the joint debt for the purposes of limitation.

35. Mr Atkins submits that the requirements for promissory estoppel are set out in the following passage from *Chitty* at 3–086:

> "Requirements. For the equitable doctrine to operate there must be a legal relationship giving rise to rights and duties between the parties; a promise or a representation by one party that he will not enforce against the other his strict legal rights arising out of that relationship; an intention on the part of the former party that the latter will rely on the representation; and such reliance by the latter party. Even if these requirements are satisfied, the operation of the doctrine may be excluded if it is, nevertheless, not 'inequitable' for the first party to go back on his promise. The doctrine most commonly applies to promises not to enforce contractual rights, but it also extends to certain other relationships. These points will be discussed in the following paragraphs."

36. He further submits that Mr Collier must raise some factor which would make it inequitable for Mr Wright now to resile from the alleged assurance in the agreement. On his submissions, the matters relied upon by Mr Collier are misconceived or totally unsupported by evidence. He submits that the mere lapse of time cannot be enough. He further submits that it is not enough that Mr Collier conducted his affairs on the premise that his obligation was a several obligation. In any event there is no agreement as to that. He has to show detrimental reliance. The assumption of a several debt in place of a joint one cannot be a detriment but only a benefit. He further submits that it is not enough for Mr Collier to say that he maintained the agreed payments because that of itself does not suggest any prejudice. He further submits that there is no evidence that Mr Collier would have entered bankruptcy or proposed a compromise with his creditors or an individual voluntary arrangement. The evidence of Mr Redfern was that Mr Collier did not want to go into bankruptcy. Likewise, submits Mr Atkins, there is no evidence that Mr Collier would have been able to recover anything from his partners. In 2000 Mr Collier could not have been misled into making instalment payments. He was always liable to make those payments. I note that there is no evidence that Mr Collier's position now is in any material respect different from that immediately before the agreement was made. For instance, there is no evidence that he entered into any business venture or made any substantial investment on the strength of the agreement. Nor is there any evidence that he could not raise the money now to meet Wrights' claim. Mr Collier has had plenty of time to produce this evidence, since service of the statutory demand on 31 May 2007.

37. I now turn to my conclusions. Mr Collier has to show that it is inequitable for Wrights to resile from its alleged promise: see the *Tool Metal* case. The effect of promissory estoppel is usually suspensory only, but, if the effect of resiling is sufficiently inequitable, a debtor may be able to show that the right to recover the debt is not merely postponed but extinguished: see the *High Trees* case and the *Tool Metal* case with respect to the wartime payments.

38. In this case, the burden was on Mr Collier to show that there was a genuine triable issue that it would be inequitable for Wrights now to insist on payment. He does not have to prove his case at this stage. On the other hand, as I have said, it is not enough for a debtor merely to assert that he thinks that he has a defence. He has to produce some tangible evidence in support, though it need not be all his evidence that he would adduce if there were a trial, nor even need he raise all the possible defences open to him. What matters therefore is whether Mr Collier has adduced enough to support his case.

39. The mere fact that the time had elapsed would not be enough of itself to give rise to promissory estoppel. Mr Atkins submits that the payment by Mr Collier of his instalments would not be enough because he was already bound to make those payments. Mr Collier's case, however, is that he made the payments on the faith of the agreement he had made with Mr Wright. He contends that there is a triable issue as to whether there has been an accord and satisfaction since he has now paid his share of the judgment and (if he can prove that the alleged agreement was made) that Wrights voluntarily agreed to accept that sum. It follows from the

judgment of Lord Denning M.R. in *D & C Builders* which I have already set out that that is enough to make it inequitable for Wrights in those circumstances to pursue him for the balance because Lord Denning held:

> "Where there has been a *true* accord, under which the creditor voluntarily agrees to accept a lesser sum in satisfaction, and the debtor *acts* upon that accord by paying the lesser sum and the creditor accepts it, then it is inequitable for the creditor afterwards to insist on the balance."

40. The passage from *Chitty* quoted at [32] above reflects this part of Lord Denning's judgment. In all the circumstances, Mr Collier has in my judgment raised a triable issue as to promissory estoppel.

Some concluding observations on the rule in Pinnel's case

41. In *Couldery v Bartrum* (1881) 19 Ch D 394 at 399, Sir George Jessel M.R. observed:

> "According to English common law a creditor might accept anything in satisfaction of his debt except a less amount of money. He might take a horse, or a canary, or tomtit if he chose, and that was accord and satisfaction; but, by a most extraordinary peculiarity of the English common law he could not take 19 shillings and sixpence in the pound; that was *nudum pactum*."

42. The facts of this case demonstrate that, if (1) a debtor offers to pay part only of the amount he owes; (2) the creditor voluntarily accepts that offer, and (3) in reliance on the creditor's acceptance the debtor pays that part of the amount he owes in full, the creditor will, by virtue of the doctrine of promissory estoppel, be bound to accept that sum in full and final satisfaction of the whole debt. For him to resile will of itself be inequitable. In addition, in these circumstances, the promissory estoppel has the effect of extinguishing the creditor's right to the balance of the debt. This part of our law originated in the brilliant obiter dictum of Denning J., as he was, in the *High Trees* case. To a significant degree it achieves in practical terms the recommendation of the Law Revision Committee chaired by Lord Wright M.R. in 1937.

Disposition

43. For the above reasons, I allow this appeal.

Further reading

A.T. Denning, 'Recent Developments in the Doctrine of Consideration' (1952) 15 MLR 1

Tony Dugdale and David Yates, 'Variation, Waiver and Estoppel—A Re-Appraisal' (1976) 39 MLR 680

David Jackson, 'Estoppel as a Sword' (1965) 81 LQR 84 (Part One) and 223 (Part Two)

Michael Lobban, '*Foakes v Beer* (1884)' in Charles Mitchell and Paul Mitchell (eds) *Landmark Cases in the Law of Contract* (Oxford: Hart, 2008) p.223

PART II

THIRD PARTY CLAIMS AND LIABILITIES

12

PRIVITY OF CONTRACT I

LEARNING OBJECTIVES

By the end of this chapter, you should:

- **understand the significance and restrictive effect of the doctrine of privity of contract;**
- **have reflected on the relationship between the requirement of consideration and the privity doctrine;**
- **understand the scope and nature of the relaxation of the privity restrictions introduced by the Contracts (Rights of Third Parties) Act 1999;**
- **be familiar with the post-Act jurisprudence.**

INTRODUCTION

In this chapter we are concerned with the question whether a person who is not a party to a contract can acquire rights under it. The short answer at common law—and this was an answer of considerable practical significance—was that, subject to certain exceptions, he could not. The Contracts (Rights of Third Parties) Act 1999 now creates a major exception to that rule. However, the Act does not apply to some classes of contract; the parties can (and, in standard forms of contract, quite commonly do) exclude its operation if they so wish; and where the Act either does not apply or is disapplied by the parties, then the old law will continue to apply.

    This chapter is divided into three sections. In the first section, the focus is on the relationship between the requirement of consideration and the supposedly distinct matter of privity (and third-party rights); in the second, the provisions and scheme of the 1999 Act are set out; and, in the third section, the case-law on the interpretation and application of the Act is considered.

12–001

1. CONSIDERATION AND PRIVITY

Privity, which regulates who is able to enforce a contractual promise (or invoke a contractual defence), is said to encompass two principles. The first ('Case 1') is that only a promisee can enforce the promise. Here, A promises B, for consideration supplied by B, that he will do something for the benefit of C. C acquires no rights.

12–002

$$A \longleftrightarrow B$$
$$C$$

The second principle ('Case 2') is that 'consideration must move from the promisee.' Here, A promises B and C, for consideration supplied by B, that he will do something for the benefit of C.

C is no better off in Case 2 than in Case 1. In the former, C acquires no rights because he is not a party to the agreement. In the latter, C acquires no rights because, though he is a 'promisee,' the consideration does not move from him. Since it is immaterial whether C is a promisee or not, it is clear that the crucial principle is the second one. The question is not whether C is a promisee or not but whether he is a contracting party or not; and, while he may be a party to the agreement, he is not a contracting party unless he gives consideration.

The 'doctrine of privity' (Case 1) thus appears to be no more than the application of the rule that the consideration must move from the promisee (Case 2). If C gave consideration to the promisor, he is a party to the contract and can enforce the promise. If he did not, he cannot enforce it. There is nothing for a separate privity rule to do. It is because the original authors of this book (in 1956) considered privity to be merely an aspect of the doctrine of consideration that the whole question has always been considered at this point instead of, as is common in law books, much later. But, if a separate doctrine of privity is a myth, it is an extraordinarily pervasive and persistent one, being found in many of the leading authorities and innumerable dicta. Consider the following example (given by Treitel (10th edn) at p.545:

"A father might promise his daughter to pay £1000 to anyone who married her. A man [C] who married the daughter with knowledge of and in reliance on such a promise might provide consideration for it, but could not enforce it, as it was not addressed to him."

The argument is that consideration moves from C but he cannot sue because he is not a party. But a promise to pay money if a certain event occurs is not a contract at all: no one is giving consideration. Only an offeree can give consideration to the offeror so as to make a contract and C is not an offeree. No question of privity arises because there is no contract for anyone to be, or not be, privy to. If, however, the father is saying to his daughter, "Marry someone, anyone, and I will pay him £1000," then that is a contract with the daughter when she marries C; but C cannot sue at common law because the consideration moves from her, not him. Alternatively—and more plausibly—if the father intends his daughter (perhaps, like Oscar Wilde's Miss Prism, she is "a female of repellant aspect") to hold out his promise to any man she fancies as an inducement, then the promise and the request to marry is made to that man and he can enforce the promise at common law: he is a promisee and he supplies consideration.

A similar example is given in Anson (p.95):

"If . . . A and B enter into an agreement under which A promises B that if C will dig A's garden A will pay £10 to B, B cannot enforce the promise. B is the promisee under the agreement but has provided no consideration."

So there is no contract between A and B for C to be privy, or not to be privy to; and there is certainly no contract between A and C. The question does not arise. If, as Anson speculates, "B impliedly undertook to procure that C would dig the garden" then there would be a contract between A and B when B had procured C to do so; but C could not enforce it at common law, because the consideration (procuring C to dig the garden) did not move from him but from B.

Do these examples provide a convincing argument that there is a separate doctrine of privity? What is needed in order to prove the existence of such a separate doctrine, is an example of a person supplying consideration to the promisor whose action fails because he is not privy to some contract or other. Do not the examples signally fail to do so? And why? Is it not that such a person does not exist?

The rule that consideration must move from the promisee, and any separate doctrine of privity that may exist, has been abolished for most contracts by the Contracts (Rights of Third Parties) Act 1999. The Act came into force on November 11, 1999, and applies to contracts made on or after May 11, 2000, and any contracts made between those dates which expressly provide that it should. Persons who were previously barred from suing by either of these rules (if there are two) will now have a right of action. It may be worth considering whether the Act will give a cause of action to C in either of the examples given by Treitel and Anson. If not, is not that because they are not examples of the operation of these rules?

The argument above is that all the work is done by just the one rule, namely that C will succeed only where C has provided consideration for the promise. If the rule that consideration must move from the promisee were abolished, as has occurred in Malaysia, then there could be something for a privity rule to do; and there it has been held that it does operate to preclude a third party who is not a promisee from suing: *Kepong Prospecting Ltd v Schmidt* [1968] A.C. 810, PC. In view of the many assertions of the existence of the privity rule, this was not a surprising result; but did it not amount in substance to the creation of a new rule, with a real function, to fill a vacuum left by the abolition of the old?

This analysis is based on the traditional view of the second principle. It should be noted, however, that it has been strenuously argued in recent years that one joint promisee may sue even though the consideration was supplied exclusively by the other. If this were right, however, would it not follow that it is the rule that consideration must move from the promisee which is a myth? In Case 2, above, C is a promisee but the argument is that he can sue although he gave no consideration. In Case 1 above, C is not a promisee. But the rule that consideration must move from the promisee has been reiterated so many times in relation to both Case 1 (see *Tweddle v Atkinson* below) and Case 2 (*Dunlop v Selfridge*, as explained below) that this is difficult to believe. Nevertheless, this theory has the support of the dicta of four out of five judges of the High Court of Australia in *Coulls v Bagot's Executor and Trustee Co Ltd* (1967) 119 C.L.R. 460 and of Professors Atiyah (*Consideration in Contracts: A Fundamental Restatement*, pp.41–42), Treitel (*Law of Contract* (10th edn), p.536) and Waddams (*The Law of Contracts* (2nd edn), p.200). The contrary has been cogently argued by Professor Coote, 'Consideration and the Joint Promisee' [1978] C.L.J. 300. Most important is the fact that the traditional view has the support of the leading case, the decision of the House of Lords in *Dunlop v Selfridge*, below.

A. Consideration Moving from B and C

Even according to the traditional view, C acquires rights in the following two special cases. **12–003**

(i) B gives consideration on behalf of himself and C. B deposits money in a bank in the names of B and C. Whether the money belongs to B alone (or indeed to C alone) is simply not the bank's business. The consideration has been supplied on behalf of both and that is the end of the matter. The question was discussed, obiter, by Lord Atkin in *McEvoy v Belfast Banking Corporation* [1935] A.C. 24. C's claim against the bank failed on other grounds but, rejecting the argument that C could in no circumstances succeed, he said:

"My Lords, to say this is to ignore the vital difference between a contract purporting to be made by B with the bank to pay B or C and a contract purporting to be made by B and C with the bank to pay B or C. In both cases of course payment to C would discharge the bank whether the bank contracted with B alone or with B and C. But the question is whether in the case put C has any rights against the bank if payment to him is refused. I have myself no doubt that in such a case C can sue the bank. The contract on the face of it purports to be made with B and C, and I think with them jointly and severally. B purports to make the contract on behalf of C as well as himself and the consideration supports such a contract. If B has actual authority from C to make such a contract, C is a party to the contract ab initio. If he has not actual authority then subject to the ordinary principles of ratification C can ratify the contract purporting to have been made on his behalf and his ratification relates back to the original formation of the contract. If no events had happened to preclude C from ratifying, then on compliance with the contract conditions, including notice and production of the deposit receipt, C would have the right to demand from the bank so much of the money as was due on the deposit account.

In my view, therefore, if nothing had happened to prevent the son [C] from ratifying the contract, he could sue the bank on the original deposit account . . . I think the case is rightly put on ratification, for I can find no sufficient evidence that the father had the actual authority of the son to enter into this contract on the son's behalf."[1]

(ii) Where, though it is expected that B will supply the consideration, C will be bound to supply it if he does not. C is a contracting party because he is (usually impliedly) promising that he will supply the consideration, at least if B does not. So in *Lockett v Charles* [1938] 4 All E.R. 170 a wife successfully sued a restaurateur in contract for supplying unfit food although her husband had paid the bill. In *Olley v Marlborough Court*, the wife's action against the hotel in contract as well as tort, succeeded although the husband booked the accommodation and paid the bill.

Coulls v Bagot's Executor presents a more difficult problem. In consideration of a payment of £5, B gave A the right to quarry on B's land and A promised to pay a royalty. B authorised A to pay the royalty to B and C (A's wife) as joint tenants. The agreement was signed by A, B and C. On B's death, the question was whether the royalties were payable to B's estate or to C. The majority held that the contract was between A and B with a revocable mandate from B to pay moneys to C. The mandate was revoked by B's death so the money was payable to B's executor. Four of the judges thought that, if it had been a contract by A to pay B and C jointly, C would have been entitled to sue, although she personally gave no consideration. Barwick CJ and Windeyer J, dissenting, thought C was a party to the contract. Barwick CJ treated the case as if it fell within case (i), above:

"... as I construe this writing, we have here not a promise by A with B for consideration supplied by B to pay C. It was, in my opinion, a promise by A made to B and C for consideration to pay B and C. In such a case it cannot lie in the mouth of A, in my opinion, to question whether the consideration which he received for his promise moved from both B and C or, as between themselves, only from one of them. His promise is not a gratuitous promise as between himself and the promisees as on the view I take of the agreement it was a promise in respect of which there was privity between A on the one hand and B and C on the other . . . I find nothing in *Dunlop Pneumatic Tyre Co Ltd v Selfridge & Co Ltd* to suggest that [A could successfully deny either privity or consideration]."

The difficulty about this approach is that the reality, known to all the parties, was that only B, the owner of the land, was doing anything for A. Windeyer J. said:

---

[1]   The identification of the parties in Lord Atkin's dictum has been altered to conform with that used above and throughout this chapter.

"Still, it was said, no consideration moved from [C]. But that, I consider, mistakes the nature of a contract made with two or more persons jointly. The promise is made to them collectively. It must, of course, be supported by consideration, but that does not mean by considerations furnished by them separately. It means a consideration given on behalf of them all, and therefore moving from all of them. In such a case the promise of the promisor is not gratuitous; and, as between him and the joint promisees, it matters not how they were able to provide the price of his promise to them."

If C was joining in the promise by B to provide A with the price of his promise, there was consideration. As Coote points out ([1978] CLJ at 311), "the benefit to the quarrying company . . . would have been, not her provision of the quarry but her accountability in law should her husband have defaulted." The difficulty is to see that she did join in the promise. Accepted principles support Coote's conclusion:

"To sum up, then it is submitted that the joint promisee doctrine enunciated in *Coulls v Bagot's Executor and Trustee Co Ltd* was based on a misapprehension of what constitutes the provision of consideration and of what constitutes a 'party' to a contract. The requirement of the common law remains that consideration move from the promisee. To that requirement joint promisees are no exception."

B. The Leading Cases

The two leading cases on the "doctrine of privity" before the 1999 Act were *Tweddle v Atkinson* (1861) 1 **12–004** B. & S. 393, QB (Wightman, Crompton and Blackburn JJ) and *Dunlop Pneumatic Tyre Co Ltd v Selfridge & Co Ltd* [1919] A.C. 847 HL. In both cases the ratio decidendi was that the plaintiff failed because he had given no consideration for the alleged promise. In *Tweddle v Atkinson*, after the marriage of the plaintiff, C, his father, B, made a written contract with the bride's father, A, by which A undertook to pay £200 to C, and B undertook to pay £100 to C. The last sentence of the agreement provided that C should have "full power to sue the said parties in any court of law or equity for the aforesaid sums." C was not a party to the agreement but he and his wife "ratified" it. It was admitted that all things necessary to entitle the plaintiff, C, to be paid by A had happened but A had not paid when he died. C's action against A's executor failed. Wightman J said that it was established that "no stranger to the consideration can take advantage of the contract though made for his benefit." Reliance had been placed on old cases holding that natural love and affection can be a sufficient consideration. Crompton J said, "The modern cases have, in effect, overruled the old decisions; they show that the consideration must move from the party entitled to sue on the contract. It would be a monstrous proposition to say that a person was a party to the contract for the purpose of suing upon it for his own advantage and not a party to it for the purpose of being sued." Blackburn J said that "Mr Mellish [for the plaintiff] admits that in general no action can be maintained upon a promise unless the consideration moves from the party to whom it is made" and went on to reject the argument that, exceptionally, natural love and affection was a sufficient consideration.

   In *Dunlop v Selfridge* Dunlop sold their tyres to a wholesaler, Dew. In order to maintain the prices of their tyres, they included a term in their contract of sale requiring Dew to obtain from any trade customers to whom he re-sold the tyres an undertaking in writing that, in consideration of being allowed a discount off the list prices of the tyres, they would observe the list prices on any further re-sale to a consumer and would pay Dunlop £5 for every tyre sold in breach of that agreement. Dew sold a tyre to Selfridge and duly obtained the undertaking in favour of Dunlop from Selfridge. Selfridge sold the tyre in breach of this agreement and Dunlop sued for the £5. Thus—

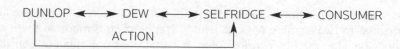

The action failed because Dunlop gave no consideration to Selfridge for the latter's promises to observe the list price and to pay Dunlop £5 if they failed to do so. It seems clear that Dew were acting as agents for Dunlop in exacting from Selfridge the undertaking in Dunlop's favour. A promise made to, and received by, one's agent to receive it is as good as a promise made to oneself—but no better. So this might be regarded fairly as a case where the promise was made to C (Dunlop), as well as to B (Dew); but that did not avail C. Five of the six judges in the House of Lords were prepared to accept that Dew might have been acting as Dunlop's agents in obtaining Selfridge's promise; but Dunlop gave Selfridge no consideration for that promise—and that was fatal.

It was argued that Dunlop gave consideration to Selfridge by allowing them to buy the tyres at a discount—below list price; but their Lordships had no difficulty in exposing the fallacy in that argument. The tyres belonged to Dew and any reduction in the price charged to Selfridge came out of Dew's pocket, not Dunlop's.

The question in *Dunlop v Selfridge* could not arise in that form today because resale price maintenance agreements of that kind have been outlawed since the Resale Prices Act 1956, now replaced by the Competition Act 1998, but this in no way impairs the authority of the case on the principles of the common law involved. Now, however, it has been overtaken by the 1999 Act and, provided that Dunlop were identified as an intended third party beneficiary of the contract between Dew and Selfridge, they should succeed against Selfridge.

2. THE CONTRACTS (RIGHTS OF THIRD PARTIES) ACT 1999

12–005   Broadly speaking, the Contracts (Rights of Third Parties) Act 1999 proceeds on the basis that the intentions of contracting parties should be respected. Hence, where it is the clear intention of the contractors that an identified third party should benefit under the contract, the law should seek to give effect to that intention; and, conversely, where it is not the clear intention of the contractors that a third party should benefit (or, at any rate, it is not the contractors' intention to grant a third party a right to enforce the contract), the law should not support a claim made by a third party to enforce the contract. The legislative scheme, in other words, is premised on the sovereignty of the contractors' intentions, not on some free-standing third-party rights. The Act makes provision for third-party claims (and defences) in the following terms.

Right of third party to enforce contractual term

12–006   **1.**—(1) Subject to the provisions of this Act, a person who is not a party to a contract (a "third party") may in his own right enforce a term of the contract if—

> (a) the contract expressly provides that he may, or
> (b) subject to subsection (2), the term purports to confer a benefit on him.

> (2) Subsection (1)(b) does not apply if on a proper construction of the contract it appears that the parties did not intend the term to be enforceable by the third party.

> (3) The third party must be expressly identified in the contract by name, as a member of a class or as answering a particular description but need not be in existence when the contract is entered into.

> (4) This section does not confer a right on a third party to enforce a term of a contract otherwise than subject to and in accordance with any other relevant terms of the contract.

(5) For the purpose of exercising his right to enforce a term of the contract, there shall be available to the third party any remedy that would have been available to him in an action for breach of contract if he had been a party to the contract (and the rules relating to damages, injunctions, specific performance and other relief shall apply accordingly).

(6) Where a term of a contract excludes or limits liability in relation to any matter references in this Act to the third party enforcing the term shall be construed as references to his availing himself of the exclusion or limitation.

(7) In this Act, in relation to a term of a contract which is enforceable by a third party—

"the promisor" means the party to the contract against whom the term is enforceable by the third party, and
"the promisee" means the party to the contract by whom the term is enforceable against the promisor.

Variation and rescission of contract

2.—(1) Subject to the provisions of this section, where a third party has a right under section 1 to enforce a term of the contract, the parties to the contract may not, by agreement, rescind the contract, or vary it in such a way as to extinguish or alter his entitlement under that right, without his consent if—

(a) the third party has communicated his assent to the term to the promisor,
(b) the promisor is aware that the third party has relied on the term, or
(c) the promisor can reasonably be expected to have foreseen that the third party would rely on the term and the third party has in fact relied on it.

(2) The assent referred to in subsection (1)(a)—

(a) may be by words or conduct, and
(b) if sent to the promisor by post or other means, shall not be regarded as communicated to the promisor until received by him.

(3) Subsection (1) is subject to any express term of the contract under which—

(a) the parties to the contract may by agreement rescind or vary the contract without the consent of the third party, or
(b) the consent of the third party is required in circumstances specified in the contract instead of those set out in subsection (1)(a) to (c).

(4) Where the consent of a third party is required under subsection (1) or (3), the court or arbitral tribunal may, on the application of the parties to the contract, dispense with his consent if satisfied—

(a) that his consent cannot be obtained because his whereabouts cannot reasonably be ascertained, or
(b) that he is mentally incapable of giving his consent.

(5) The court or arbitral tribunal may, on the application of the parties to a contract, dispense with any consent that may be required under subsection (1)(c) if satisfied that it cannot reasonably be ascertained whether or not the third party has in fact relied on the term.

(6) If the court or arbitral tribunal dispenses with a third party's consent, it may impose such conditions as it thinks fit, including a condition requiring the payment of compensation to the third party.

(7) The jurisdiction conferred on the court by subsections (4) to (6) is exercisable by both the High Court and a county court.

Defences etc. available to promisor

3.—(1) Subsections (2) to (5) apply where, in reliance on section 1, proceedings for the enforcement of a term of a contract are brought by a third party.

(2) The promisor shall have available to him by way of defence or set-off any matter that—

(a) arises from or in connection with the contract and is relevant to the term, and
(b) would have been available to him by way of defence or set-off if the proceedings had been brought by the promisee.

(3) The promisor shall also have available to him by way of defence or set-off any matter if—

   (a) an express term of the contract provides for it to be available to him in proceedings brought by the third party, and
   (b) it would have been available to him by way of defence or set-off if the proceedings had been brought by the promisee.

(4) The promisor shall also have available to him—

   (a) by way of defence or set-off any matter, and
   (b) by way of counterclaim any matter not arising from the contract,

that would have been available to him by way of defence or set-off or, as the case may be, by way of counterclaim against the third party if the third party had been a party to the contract.

(5) Subsections (2) and (4) are subject to any express term of the contract as to the matters that are not to be available to the promisor by way of defence, set-off or counterclaim.

(6) Where in any proceedings brought against him a third party seeks in reliance on section 1 to enforce a term of a contract (including, in particular, a term purporting to exclude or limit liability), he may not do so if he could not have done so (whether by reason of any particular circumstances relating to him or otherwise) had he been a party to the contract.

Enforcement of contract by promisee

   4. Section 1 does not affect any right of the promisee to enforce any term of the contract.

Protection of promisor from double liability

   5. Where under section 1 a term of a contract is enforceable by a third party, and the promisee has recovered from the promisor a sum in respect of—

   (a) the third party's loss in respect of the term, or
   (b) the expense to the promisee of making good to the third party the default of the promisor,

then, in any proceedings brought in reliance on that section by the third party, the court or arbitral tribunal shall reduce any award to the third party to such extent as it thinks appropriate to take account of the sum recovered by the promisee.

Exceptions

6.—(1) Section 1 confers no rights on a third party in the case of a contract on a bill of exchange, promissory note or other negotiable instrument.

(2) Section 1 confers no rights on a third party in the case of any contract binding on a company and its members under section 14 of the Companies Act 1985.

(3) Section 1 confers no right on a third party to enforce—

   (a) any term of a contract of employment against an employee,
   (b) any term of a worker's contract against a worker (including a home worker), or
   (c) any term of a relevant contract against an agency worker.

(4) In subsection (3)—

   (a) "contract of employment", "employee", "worker's contract", and "worker" have the meaning given by section 54 of the National Minimum Wage Act 1998,
   (b) "home worker" has the meaning given by section 35(2) of that Act,
   (c) "agency worker" has the same meaning as in section 34(1) of that Act, and
   (d) "relevant contract" means a contract entered into, in a case where section 34 of that Act applies, by the agency worker as respects work falling within subsection (1)(a) of that section.

(5) Section 1 confers no rights on a third party in the case of—

   (a) a contract for the carriage of goods by sea, or

(b) a contract for the carriage of goods by rail or road, or for the carriage of cargo by air, which is subject to the rules of the appropriate international transport convention,

except that a third party may in reliance on that section avail himself of an exclusion or limitation of liability in a contract.

(6) In subsection (5) "contract for the carriage of goods by sea" means a contract of carriage—

(a) contained in or evidenced by a bill of lading, sea waybill or a corresponding electronic transaction, or
(b) under or for the purposes of which there is given an undertaking which is contained in a ship's delivery order or a corresponding electronic transaction.

(7) For the purposes of subsection (6)—

(a) "bill of lading", "sea waybill" and "ship's delivery order" have the same meaning as in the Carriage of Goods by Sea Act 1992, and
(b) a corresponding electronic transaction is a transaction within section 1(5) of that Act which corresponds to the issue, indorsement, delivery or transfer of a bill of lading, sea waybill or ship's delivery order.

(8) In subsection (5) "the appropriate international transport convention" means—

(a) in relation to a contract for the carriage of goods by rail, the Convention which has the force of law in the United Kingdom under section 1 of the International Transport Conventions Act 1983,
(b) in relation to a contract for the carriage of goods by road, the Convention which has the force of law in the United Kingdom under section 1 of the Carriage of Goods by Road Act 1965, and
(c) in relation to a contract for the carriage of cargo by air—
    (i) the Convention which has the force of law in the United Kingdom under section 1 of the Carriage by Air Act 1961, or
    (ii) the Convention which has the force of law under section 1 of the Carriage by Air (Supplementary Provisions) Act 1962, or
    (iii) either of the amended Conventions set out in Part B of Schedule 2 or 3 to the Carriage by Air Acts (Application of Provisions) Order 1967.

Supplementary provisions relating to third party

7.—(1) Section 1 does not affect any right or remedy of a third party that exists or is available apart from this Act.

(2) Section 2(2) of the Unfair Contract Terms Act 1977 (restriction on exclusion etc. of liability for negligence) shall not apply where the negligence consists of the breach of an obligation arising from a term of a contract and the person seeking to enforce it is a third party acting in reliance on section 1.

(3) In sections 5 and 8 of the Limitation Act 1980 the references to an action founded on a simple contract and an action upon a specialty shall respectively include references to an action brought in reliance on section 1 relating to a simple contract and an action brought in reliance on that section relating to a specialty.

(4) A third party shall not, by virtue of section 1(5) or 3(4) or (6), be treated as a party to the contract for the purposes of any other Act (or any instrument made under any other Act).

[Sections 8 (Arbitration Provisions), 9 (Northern Ireland) and 10 (Short title commencement and extent) are omitted.]

Points for reflection

The Contracts (Rights of Third Parties) Act 1999 is introduced as "An Act to make provision for the **12–007** enforcement of contractual terms by third parties." That might be thought ambiguous. Does it mean third parties to the contract? Or third parties to the promise? If the former, C, in both Case 1 and Case 2 (above) is a third party. If the latter, C is a third party in Case 1, but not in Case 2.

The Law Commission, in their Report 'Privity of Contract: Contracts for the Benefit of Third Parties' (Law Com. No. 242, 1996) intended the Act to apply only to Case 1. Clause 8 of their draft Bill made this clear:

"(1) Where the persons to whom a contractual promise is made include a person who does not provide consideration for the promise, that person shall not be treated as a third party for the purposes of this Act.
(2) Subsection (1) above is without prejudice to any right or remedy of such a person in relation to the contract which exists or is available apart from this Act."

This clause was not included in the Bill introduced in Parliament nor does the provision appear in the Act. It is now a question of the construction of the Act. According to s.1(1), a third party is "a person who is not a party to a contract." However, this begs the question: is C in Case 2 "a party to a contract"?

The Law Commission acknowledged that it would be absurd if C were better off if he was not a promisee than if he was: Law Com. No.242, para.6.10; but they proposed to exclude the promisee because (i) they assumed he would have a more secure right at common law (he would not have to satisfy the test of enforceability under the Act) of which he should not be deprived and (ii) the rules of joint creditors, which are different from the new rules regarding third parties, should continue to apply: para.6.11.

Are these problems perhaps illusory? If a promisee, C, acquires enforceable rights under the contract made by A and B (as in *McEvoy v Banking Belfast Corporation*, above) he is a party to the contract, not a third party; and he is a joint creditor of the Bank. But if C acquires no enforceable rights he is not a party to the contract, or a joint creditor, and his only rights are those given to him by the Act. Should not the Act then be construed to apply to both Case 1 and Case 2? It is true that C may then have to plead his case in the alternative. If he has acquired enforceable rights, e.g. *Coulls v Bagot's Executors* is applied—he cannot rely on the Act because he is a party to the contract, not a third party; but if has acquired no such rights, he may be able to rely on the Act.

Questions

12–008   1. In *Tweddle v Atkinson*:

(a) Would the plaintiff have any problem today in the light of s.1(1) of the 1999 Act?

(b) Suppose the agreement had recited that it was made between A, B and C and provided that it was agreed between them that A and B should each pay C £100. Would C, at that date, have been any better off? If the Law Commission's draft cl.8 had been passed, would he now be worse off? Would the opinions in *Coulls v Bagot's Executor* have helped him?—could it possibly be said that a consideration to be paid to him (as both sums were) was in any sense consideration moving from him? But does the Act as passed exclude C in this case?

(c) Would it now be any different, if the last sentence of the agreement had been omitted?

(d) What if, before any money had been paid, A and B had fallen out with the married couple, or the stock market had crashed, leaving A and B in financial difficulties, and they had agreed to release each other from the obligation to pay? See s.2(1) of the 1999 Act.

2. In *Beswick v Beswick*, below, Ch.13, Lord Denning MR said in the Court of Appeal [1966] 3 All E.R. 1 at 6:

"The case of *Tweddle v Atkinson* is readily distinguishable . . . The action failed for the very good reason that the [C's] father [B] had not done his part. He had not paid his promised £100. [C] could not himself be sued for his father's [B's] failure to pay the £100. So he could not be allowed to sue his wife's father [A] for the £200."

These do not seem to have been the real facts. There is nothing in the reports to suggest that C's father, B, had not paid as he promised. As noted above, it was agreed that "all things necessary to entitle [C] to have the £200 paid by [A] had happened"—those things presumably include payment by B, or at least B's being ready and willing to pay. If B had in fact repudiated the contract, A would have been discharged from his liability. But, suppose Lord Denning's version was true. What would be the position today? Could C succeed in an action against A? Or against B? Or against A and B? Consider s. 3(2) of the 1999 Act.

3. Suppose that B has not paid and has died insolvent and with no assets. Does A remain liable? What if it can be proved that B never had the slightest intention of paying? See s.3(2).

4. B makes a contract with A Ltd to deliver flowers to B's mother, C, with a card saying "Happy –Birthday". If the flowers are dead on arrival, can C recover damages from A Ltd? Does the implied term in the contract between A Ltd and B that the flowers will be of satisfactory quality "purport to confer a benefit" on C?

5. Do the parties "intend the term to be enforceable by the third party" if one of them (A) intends to retain the freedom to agree with the other (B) to cancel or vary the term in favour of the third party, C? Is the test wholly objective?

6. The Commission wrote of the second limb of the test of enforceability (s.1(1)(b)): "In general terms it establishes a rebuttable presumption in favour of there being a third party right where a contractual provision purports to confer a benefit on an expressly designated third party. But that presumption is rebutted where on a proper construction of the contract the parties did not intend to confer a right of enforceability on the third party" (Law Com. 242, para.7.17). In some—perhaps most—cases A and B may not have given any thought to the question of enforceability by C. If the matter is brought to their attention after the contract has been concluded and C has assented, is the presumption rebutted by their assertion that they would never have agreed to its being enforceable, had they considered the matter?

7. Why give C a right anyway? (i) A promises C to give him £100. C acquires no rights. (ii) A promises B to give C £100. C now has, prima facie, an enforceable right. Is C any more deserving of a remedy in case (ii) than in case (i)? If not, what is the justification for giving him one? Is it to do justice to B? But would not that be done by ensuring that B has an effective right to enforce A's promise? Atiyah asks "why should an offeree be entitled to create legal rights for himself by the bare act of acceptance when he has in no way relied on the offer . . ." (above, Ch.5). Could he consistently argue that C should be able to create rights for himself by the bare act of accepting a gift-promise? The offeree is undertaking an obligation by his acceptance of the offer. C is not.

Is the 1999 Act consistent in principle with the doctrine of consideration? Is the logical next step the abolition of that doctrine?

---

3. THE POST-ACT JURISPRUDENCE

NISSHIN SHIPPING CO LTD V CLEAVES & CO LTD

High Court [2003] EWHC 2602

MR JUSTICE COLMAN

Introduction

12-009   1. In 1999, following an admirable report by the Law Commission, Parliament dealt a long overdue body blow to the doctrine of privity of contract. It enacted the Contracts (Rights of Third Parties) Act 1999. That broadly had the purpose of enabling a third party to a contract under which one party had promised to confer a benefit on that third party to enforce that promise direct against the promisor. That facility is of particular importance to chartering brokers, like the Respondents to this application, and to others who create contracts under which one party promises to pay them commission.

2. This case is, I understand, the first time that the 1999 Act has been before the courts. It raises questions highly relevant to the shipping industry as to how a third party may enforce a promise of a benefit for him where there is an arbitration clause in the underlying contract.

3. This is an application under section 67 of the Arbitration Act 1996 for the court to declare that arbitrators have no jurisdiction to determine claims for commission said to be due to the Respondent chartering brokers ("Cleaves"), payment of such commission having been sought from the Applicant owners/guarantors.

4. There were nine relevant time charters negotiated by Cleaves on behalf of the Applicant, Nisshin. Each charterparty contained an arbitration clause. The Applicant challenges the entitlement of Cleaves to commission on the principal ground that Cleaves were in repudiatory breach of the agency relationship because their principal and controlling interest became a shareholder and member of the senior management team of a competitor of the Applicant. It is said that this breach was accepted by Nisshin as terminating the agency relationship.

5. Each charterparty provided for the payment of commission to Cleaves. Each arbitration clause contained wording referring to disputes between the "parties" to the charterparty or between Owners and Charterers. However, the wording was in each case in terms wide enough to cover a claim by the charterers against the owners for failure by the owners to perform their promise to pay commission to Cleaves.

6. The issue of entitlement to commission was referred by Cleaves to arbitration notwithstanding it was not a party to any of the nine arbitration agreements.

7. The issue as to the arbitrators' jurisdiction was raised and argued on paper before a tribunal consisting of Mr Timothy Young Q.C. and Mr Timothy Rayment. Both are extremely experienced in the field of maritime law and arbitration. In an interim final arbitration award dated 24 January 2003 they concluded that the effect of sections 1 and 8 of the 1999 Act was that they did have jurisdiction.

8. There are four other charterparties involved which are not covered by the 1999 Act. The Respondents, Cleaves, have commenced proceedings in this court claiming commission in relation to all 13 charterparties. The Applicant wishes all the claims to proceed in one set of proceedings before the court.

9. The relevant sections of the 1999 Act are as follows [the judge then set out ss.1 and 8 of the Act]

Do Cleaves fall within Section 1 of the 1999 Act?

10. It is accepted on behalf of Cleaves that in none of the charters did the commission clauses expressly provide that Cleaves could enforce such clauses directly against the owners. However the real issues are (i) whether those clauses purported to confer a benefit on Cleaves within sub-section (1)(b) of section 1 and (ii) whether sub- section 1(b) is disapplied by sub-section (2) because "on a proper construction of the contact it appears that the parties did not intend the term to be enforceable by the third party".

11. It is argued by Mr Michael Ashcroft, on behalf of Nisshin, that under four of the charterparties—those numbered (ii), (iii), (iv) and (v) in the arbitration award—the commission clauses did not purport to confer a benefit on Cleaves alone. Although there was an issue before the arbitrators as to whether certain words had been deleted from numbers (iv) and (v) before or after the contract was entered into, it is common ground that, for the purposes of this application only, I should disregard deletions of part of these clauses which were made at some stage. The relevant wording for all four charterparties is thus as follows:

"A commission of 2 per cent for equal division is payable by the vessel and owners to Messrs Ifchor S. A. Lausanne and Messrs Cleaves and Company Ltd, London on hire earned and paid under this Charter, and also upon any continuation or extension of this charter".

12. It is argued that the phraseology is such that the benefit conferred by the clause is to be subsequently divided between the two firms as distinct from a provision which specifies that a particular percentage should be paid to a particular broker.

13. I cannot accept this argument. These provisions leave no doubt as to the identity of the broker to whom payment is to be made and as to the amount to be paid. It is in substance exactly the same as if the clause had provided that there was to be a commission of 2 per cent of which 1 per cent was to be paid to Ifchor and 1 per cent to Cleaves. There is nothing in this clause to suggest that the total 2 per cent commission is to be paid to Ifchor and that Ifchor will then pay half of that to Cleaves. The words "for division" do not, in my judgment, bear that connotation in the absence of any indication as to the broker to whom payment is first to be made. Nor do the words support the submission that the obligation to pay commission can only be enforced jointly by both the firms of brokers. There is no conceivable commercial purpose in a construction which creates a joint and indivisible right of enforcement. Absent of much clearer wording than this, I do not consider that the clause should be thus construed.

14. Accordingly, I hold that the effect of the clause was to confer a benefit to the extent of 1 per cent commission on Cleaves alone.

15. It is then further argued by Mr Ashcroft, on behalf of Nisshin, that on the proper construction of the charterparties the parties to them did not intend the commission clause to be enforceable by Cleaves and accordingly section 1(1)(b) of the 1999 Act is disapplied by section 1(2).

16. In support of this argument Nisshin relies on three distinct points.

17. First, it is argued that the arbitration clauses in all of the charterparties do not make express provision for enforcement by a broker of a claim for commission. All except those numbered (viii) and (ix) include substantially the standard New York Produce Exchange arbitration clause:

"Should any dispute arise between Owners and the Charterers, the matter in dispute shall be referred to three persons at London, one to be appointed by each of the parties hereto, and the third by the two so chosen."

18. Those charterparties numbered (viii) and (ix) which substantially incorporated the Shelltime 4 standard claims provided as follows:

"41(a) This charter shall be construed and the relations between the parties determined in accordance with the laws of England. (b) Any dispute arising under this charter shall be decided by the English Courts to whose jurisdiction the parties hereby agree. See also LMAA Arbitration Clause. See additional Clause 48. (c) Notwithstanding the foregoing, but without prejudice to any party's right to arrest or maintain the arrest of any maritime property, either party may, by giving written notice of election to the other party, elect to have any such dispute referred to the arbitration of a single arbitrator in London in accordance with the provisions of the Arbitration Act 1950, or any statutory modification or re-enactment thereof for the time being in force."

19. The relevant part of the LMAA arbitration clause provided:

"48. LMAA Arbitration Clause. All disputes or differences arising out of this contract which cannot be amicably resolved shall be referred to arbitration in London. Unless the parties agree upon a sole arbitrator, one arbitrator to be appointed by each party . . . This contract is governed and construed by English law both in regards to substance and procedure, and there shall apply to all proceedings under this Clause the terms of the London [Maritime] Arbitrators Association current at the time when the arbitration proceedings were commenced . . ."

20. The references to "Owners and Charterers" and to two arbitrators to be appointed by "the parties hereto" in the NYPE form are thus expressly inconsistent with the brokers being obliged to utilise that arbitration agreement in order to enforce their rights to commission: the only parties being obliged or entitled to arbitrate are the Owners and Charterers similarly the reference in the Shelltime 4 clause to "either party" is a reasonably clear indication that its application is confined to disputes between Owners and Charterers.

21. It is accepted by Miss Philippa Hopkins, on behalf of Cleaves, that the brokers were not parties to the arbitration agreements as a matter of construction of those clauses. Her case is that the effect of section 8 of

the 1999 Act is to impose the arbitration clauses on the Owners and the brokers as the means of enforcement of the commission benefit conferred by the commission clause. I shall have to consider this submission more fully when I come to discuss the effect of section 8. However, for the purposes of the submission in relation to absence of intention to confer a benefit, the wording of the arbitration clauses is, in my judgment, of little or no materiality. Firstly, although the parties to the charterparties clearly expressed their mutual intention that *their* disputes should be arbitrated, that mutual intention is entirely consistent with a mutual intention that the brokers should be obliged to recover their commission by court action rather than by arbitration. Secondly, if, on the proper construction of the 1999 Act, the third party is obliged to enforce the commission benefit by arbitration, even where the agreement does not on its proper construction provide for any participants in an arbitration other than the parties to the main contract, identification of the intention to be imputed to the parties as to enforceability of the third party commission benefit clearly has to take this into account. That is to say, if, as a matter of law, it makes no difference to the broker's ability to enforce his right to commission benefit that no express provision is made for this in the arbitration agreement, the strength of any inference derived from the absence of such express provision could be little more than negligible.

22. Secondly, it is argued by Mr Ashcroft on behalf of Nisshin that there is no positive indication in the charterparties that the parties did intend the brokers to have enforceable rights. There is no suggestion in those contracts that the Owners and Charterers were mutually in agreement that the brokers should be entitled to claim against the Owners as if they were parties to the contract.

23. It is to be noted that section 1(2) of the 1999 Act does not provide that subsection 1(b) is disapplied unless on a proper construction of the contract it appears that the parties intended that the benefit term should be enforceable by the third party. Rather it provides that sub-section 1(b) is disapplied if, on a proper construction, it appears that the parties did not intend third party enforcement. In other words, if the contract is neutral on this question, sub-section (2) does not disapply sub-section 1(b). Whether the contract does express a mutual intention that the third party should not be entitled to enforce the benefit conferred on him or is merely neutral is a matter of construction having regard to all relevant circumstances. The purpose and background of the Law Commission's recommendations in relation to sub-section (2) are explained in a paper by Professor Andrew Burrows who, as a member of the Law Commission, made a major contribution to the drafting of the bill as enacted. He wrote at [2000] LMCLQ 540 at 544:

> "The second test therefore uses a rebuttable presumption of intention. In doing so, it copies the New Zealand Contracts (Privity) Act 1982, s.4, which has used the same approach. It is this rebuttable presumption that provides the essential balance between sufficient certainty for contracting parties and the flexibility required for the reform to deal fairly with a huge range of different situations. The presumption is based on the idea that, if you ask yourself, 'When is it that parties are likely to have intended to confer rights on a third party to enforce a term, albeit that they have not expressly conferred that right', the answer will be: 'Where the term purports to confer a benefit on an expressly identified third party'. That then sets up the presumption. But the presumption can be rebutted if, as a matter of ordinary contractual interpretation, there is something else indicating that the parties did not intend such a right to be given."

24. In the present case, apart from Mr Ashcroft's third point, the charterparties are indeed neutral in the sense that they do not express any intention contrary to the entitlement of the brokers to enforce the commission term.

25. Thirdly, Mr Ashcroft submits that the parties' mutual intention on the proper construction of the contracts was to create a trust of a promise in favour of the brokers—a trust enforceable against the Owners at the suit of the Charterers as trustees. That being the proper construction of the contracts by reference to the state of the law at the time when the 1999 Act came into force, the very same contract wording did not, subsequently to that, evidence a different mutual intention. Accordingly, the mutual intention evidenced by the contracts was that the enforcement of the promise to pay commission would be at the suit of the Charterers who must be joined by the brokers as co-claimants.

26. The starting point for consideration of this point is *Les Affreteurs Reunis SA v Leopold Walford (London) Ltd* [1919] AC 801. The House of Lords in that case confirmed the decision in *Robertson v Wait* (1853) 8 Ex 299. In relation to that authority Lord Birkenhead L.C. said this at pages 806–807:

> "My Lords, so far as I am aware, that case has not before engaged the attention of this House, and I think it right to say plainly that I agree with that decision and I agree with the reasoning, shortly as it is expressed, upon which the decision was founded. In this connection I would refer to the well-known case of *In re Empress Engineering Company*. In the judgment of Sir George Jessel M.R. the principle is examined which, in my view, underlies and is the explanation of the decision in *Robertson v Wait*. The Master of the Rolls uses

this language: 'So, again, it is quite possible that one of the parties to the agreement may be the nominee or trustee of the third person. As Lord Justice James suggested to me in the course of the argument, a married woman may nominate somebody to contract on her behalf, but then the person makes the contract really as trustee for somebody else, and it is because he contracts in that character that the cestui que trust can take the benefit of the contract.'

It appears to me plain that for convenience, and under long established practice, the broker in such cases, in effect, nominates the charterer to contract on his behalf, influenced probably by the circumstance that there is always a contract between charterer and owner in which this stipulation, which is to enure to the benefit of the broker, may very conveniently be inserted. In these cases the broker, on ultimate analysis, appoints the charterer to contract on his behalf. I agree therefore with the conclusion arrived at by all the learned judges in *Robertson v Wait*, that in such cases charterers can sue as trustees on behalf of the broker."

27. Viscount Finlay and Lords Atkinson and Wrenbury adopted identical reasoning.

28. Accordingly, the position in 1853 and 1919 was that when a charterparty was entered into and incorporated a term that the owners could pay commission to the brokers the only means of enforcement of that promise was an action by the charterers and the brokers as co-plaintiff because, the charterer having contracted for commission on behalf of the broker, once the contract had been signed, the charterer became trustee of the broker's right to recover that commission, the broker being unable to enforce the promise direct and without the charterer's intervention because he was not a party to the contract and therefore had no cause of action available to him against the owner. With regard to this trustee relationship it could then be said that when the charterparty was entered into neither Owners nor Charterers contemplated that the brokers could sue the owners direct.

29. What is the position arising from the contract itself following the coming into force of the 1999 Act? As a matter of analysis of the underlying relationship between the parties, it must be precisely the same. Thus, the charterer is no less the trustee of the Owners' promise to pay the commission, having regard to the fact that the charterer contracts for payment of the commission on behalf of a non-contracting party. Indeed, the only thing that has changed is the coming into force of the 1999 Act and the introduction of the statutory facility of a direct right of action for a non-contracting party on whom a contract purports to confer a benefit.

30. Accordingly, the argument advanced by the Owners can only succeed if it is to be inferred from the existence of the underlying trustee relationship that it was the mutual intention of Owners and Charterers that the broker beneficiary should not be entitled to avail himself of the facility of direct action by the 1999 Act.

31. This proposition is, in my judgment, entirely unsustainable. The fact that prior to the 1999 Act it would be the mutual intention that the only available facility for enforcement would be deployed by the broker does not lead to the conclusion that, once an additional statutory facility for enforcement had been introduced, the broker would not be entitled to use it, but would instead be confined to the use of the pre-existing procedure. Indeed, quite apart from the complete lack of any logical basis for such an inference, the very cumbersome and inconvenient nature of the procedure based on the trustee relationship (described by Lord Wright as a "cumbrous fiction") would point naturally to the preferred use by the broker of the right to sue directly provided by the 1999 Act. Not only would that original procedure be inconvenient, but it might involve risk that the broker would be prevented from recovering his commission, for example, in a case where the charterer had been dissolved in its place of incorporation or where, in the absence of co-operation by the charterer, proceedings had to be served on it outside the jurisdiction and service could not be effected. There are therefore very strong grounds pointing against any mutual intention to confine the brokers to the old procedure and to deny them the right to rely on the Act.

32. I therefore reject the third ground relied upon by Nisshin. In so doing I reach the same conclusion as the arbitrators. [The judge dealt then with the s.8 issue] . . .

52. The effect of sections 1 and 8 of the 1999 Act as analysed in this judgment is to provide to a third party a remedy which would otherwise have been denied to him. Where a contract included an agreement to arbitrate, a provision whereby a benefit was to be conferred on a third party could neither be directly enforced by the third party nor, if the third party were a broker claiming his commission, could it be enforced by means of the enforcement of a trust because the third party was not a party to the underlying contract or the arbitration agreement. This was a grave defect in the law which could give rise to considerable injustice. The enactment of the 1999 Act has removed that injustice by putting the third party in the position of the promisee to the extent of enforcement of the promise for his benefit and has thereby enabled him to bring proceedings direct against the promisor either by a direct claim in court or by commencing proceedings by arbitration where

the arbitration agreement covered the claim. He no longer has to rely on the co-operation of the promisee to proceed as co-claimant where there can be a claim by means of court action and he is not deprived of all remedy because he was not a party to the arbitration agreement or the underlying contract. It is against this change in the law that one is bound to ask whether by requiring him to arbitrate a claim to enforce a promise which, had the promisee wished to pursue it, he would have had to refer to arbitration, the Act has infringed the third party's right under Article 6(1) of the European Convention on Human Rights.

53. The question has only to be postulated to demonstrate the absurdity of the underlying proposition. That proposition involves the third party's right to access to the courts being infringed unless the law provides him with an enforcement facility which neither he nor the promisee party to the contract ever previously had. Thus stated the argument fails in limine. If it were correct every provision for statutory arbitration would be unlawful . . .

AVRAAMIDES v COLWILL

Court of Appeal [2006] EWCA Civ 1533

LORD JUSTICE WALLER

12–010   1. Mr Avraamides and his wife (the respondents) brought an action against two individuals, Mark Colwill and Stephen Martin (the appellants), seeking to hold them personally liable for failures in the refurbishment of two bathrooms. His Honour Judge Levy Q.C. ordered to be tried a preliminary issue in the following terms:

"Did the Claimants contract with the Defendants for the installation of their bathrooms and/or did the Defendants owe a concurrent duty of care in tort to the Claimants in respect of the installation of their bathrooms?"

2. That preliminary issue came on for trial before His Honour Judge Dean Q.C. The respondents were represented by counsel (not Mr Mills who represented them on this appeal), and the appellants were in person. Judge Dean decided that the respondents' contract for refurbishment of the bathrooms was with a company Bathroom Trading Company (Putney) Limited. He further decided that all the work of refurbishment including that carried out by an individual Phil Durham was the responsibility of that company. That, on his findings, would have been determinative of the preliminary issue as ordered.

3. However in the pleadings, albeit only in their reply, the respondents had referred to the existence of an agreement in these terms:

"In view of the defendant's assertion that BTC purchased the assets and the goodwill of the business from BTC Ltd on 1 April 2003 it will be averred that in the alternative that as a matter of fact the defendants as partners of BTC also assumed the liabilities of BTC Ltd on 1 April 2003. These liabilities included any liability of BTC Ltd to the claimants which was pre-existing at 1 April."

4. The full terms of the agreement (the transfer agreement) were short and provided as follows:

"(1) The Purchasers agree to buy the assets, and to settle the current liabilities of the company at the value of Net Assets as determined in the final accounts for the year ended 31 March 2003.
(2) Any tax liability on the company arising from the transaction to be settled by the purchaser.
(3) The purchasers (sic) undertakes to complete outstanding customer orders taking into account any deposits paid by customers as at 31 March 2003, and to pay in the normal course of time any liabilities properly incurred by the company as at 31 March 2003. The Colwill loan account after adjustment to be transferred on by the partnership." [I have inserted numbers for convenience.]

5. During the course of counsel's opening before Judge Dean counsel also referred to this agreement, and it was the judge that posed the question whether counsel was relying on the Contracts (Rights of Third Parties) Act 1999. At that stage the suggestion was not apparently taken up by counsel. However in the course of his closing submissions, counsel did take up the suggestion that in the alternative to the case they had been running, if the company was the appropriate contracting party by virtue of the transfer agreement, the respondents were entitled to succeed under the 1999 Act.

6. [His Lordship then set out the terms of s.1 of the Act as relied on by the respondents]

7. The judge, albeit he took the view that there was no adequate pleading of the point, allowed the point to be taken, and decided that the respondents were third parties on whom the transfer agreement, by its third

paragraph, had purported to confer a benefit. He found the Act applied and gave judgment on the preliminary issue in favour of the respondents. He also granted permission to appeal.

8. The question whether the 1999 Act applies is the critical issue on this appeal . . .

12. Against the above background, I turn to the real point on the appeal—the question whether the respondents are third parties who are entitled to enforce the transfer agreement under the 1999 Act. It will be noted that the transfer agreement is between the shareholders of the company and the appellants. Mr Mills submitted that the agreement clearly evidenced an agreement between the company and the appellants and that it should be on that basis that the court should proceed. Mr Hartman was prepared to approach the matter on that basis.

13. Both counsel recognised that the third paragraph was the critical paragraph, as did the judge. It is only that paragraph which could be said to confer a benefit on third parties. The issues are accordingly one of construction of that paragraph and the relevant provisions of the 1999 Act. Mr Mills in his skeleton puts the issues in this way in my view accurately:

"(1) whether any term in Agreement "purports to confer a benefit" on the Claimants with s.1(1)(b) of the 1999 Act; and if so

(2) whether s.1(1)(b) is disapplied by section 1(2) because on a proper construction of the Agreement it appears that the parties did not intend the term to be enforceable by the Claimants;

(3) whether the Claimants are expressly identified in the contract as a member of a class or as answering a particular description within the meaning of s.1(3);

(4) whether the Claimants failed to plead, properly or at all, any claim in reliance of the 1999 Act."

14. Both parties recognised that the liabilities under paragraph 1 of the Agreement and the liabilities under paragraph 3 had to be different. But since the liability which the judge had found to exist had at all times been denied by the company they also recognised at least during the course of argument, the force of the point that what the appellants would have paid for under paragraph 1 would be unlikely to have taken account of the liability to the appellants. Further, Mr Hartman for the appellants recognised the strength of the argument that the words in the third paragraph "and to pay in the normal course of trade any liabilities properly incurred by the company as at 31st March 2003" could be said to benefit those to whom the liabilities had been "properly" incurred, and would include any liabilities "properly" incurred but not taken into account under paragraph 1. He attempted to argue that there was a distinction between liabilities incurred and liabilities "properly" incurred and that the liability to the respondents was a liability improperly incurred.

15. I would accept that there may be a distinction between liabilities incurred and those "properly" incurred, but I did not follow the argument that there was anything "improper" in the incurring of the liabilities to the respondents.

16. Mr Mills, possibly with an eye on the provision which requires "express" identification of the third party to which I will come, in his written submissions argued that the liabilities properly incurred as at 31st March 2003 were simply liabilities to customers. His argument was that the third paragraph must be read as one, and that thus the obligation was to complete orders outstanding for "customers", and to pay liabilities properly incurred to "customers". He suggested that the order of the appellants had not been completed as at 31st March 2003 and that thus the obligation was to complete the order and pay the liabilities properly incurred. Whether factually he was right as to whether the order had been completed as to which there would seem to be considerable doubt, in my view there is nothing in the third paragraph which limits "liabilities properly incurred" to liabilities to customers. On any natural reading liabilities to suppliers or for telephone bills or whatever would seem to come within the compass of liabilities properly incurred.

17. That brings me to the provision and the main plank of Mr Hartman's argument. It is a provision which creates most difficulty for Mr Mills, and one which I am not sure the judge fully faced up to. By section 1(3) of the 1999 Act "The third party must be expressly identified in the contract by name, as a member of a class or as answering a particular description . . .". The second part of the third paragraph simply does not identify any third party or class of third parties.

18. The temptation in the circumstances of a case such as this, to find a route which renders the appellants liable, is great. They have taken over the assets of the company and agreed with the company to meet liabilities. The remedy of the respondents if the 1999 Act does not apply seems to be to pursue the company which, according to the evidence, now has no assets, with the possibility of persuading the liquidator of the company to then pursue the appellants for failing to discharge the liabilities which under the transfer agreement they have agreed to do. Why not save the appellants that exercise by use of the 1999 Act?

19. The answer I am afraid is that section 1(3), by use of the word "express", simply does not allow a process of construction or implication. I considered whether it would be possible for Mr Mills to rely on the fact that

"customers" are identified in the contract as beneficiaries of the first part of paragraph 3, even if liabilities in the second part includes persons other than customers. Could he submit that even though others are included within the liabilities under the second part, "customers" as a class are identified and that is sufficient. The difficulty is that the section is concerned with the benefit conferred on a third party, and with the identification of that person. The benefit from the obligation to pay liabilities properly incurred would benefit third parties but of a large number of unidentified classes.

20. I should add that, although both parties have fought the appeal on the basis that the written agreement evidences an agreement between the company and the appellants, the fact is that the written contract is between the appellants and the shareholders, and when one adds that point to the failure to identify, I am actually doubtful whether it can be said that this agreement, on its true construction, was one under which it was intended that any persons with rights against the company were to be able to enforce them directly against the appellants.

21. With some reluctance therefore I would allow the appeal.

Points for reflection

12–011   What should we make of these two cases? The indications in *Nisshin* (and, similarly, in *Laemthong International Lines Co Ltd v Artis (The Laemthong Glory) (No.2)* [2005] EWCA Civ 519) are that the courts will not interpret and apply the enforceability test in s.1(1)(b) in a way that makes it difficult for third parties to be eligible. Nor, in relation to s.1(2), will the courts seize on any argument that hints at the contractors intending to deprive a third party of the right to enforce. By contrast, in *Avraamides*, even though the court has considerable sympathy for the position of the third parties, the requirement of express identification in s.1(3) is given its natural interpretation and strictly applied. If we suppose that the third parties in *Avraamides* could not have been assisted under the pre-Act common law, even with its considerable flexibility, the fact that they fail under the Act is not a great cause for concern. However, if the Act constrains courts in ways that they were not constrained under the common law, and if meritorious third-party claims fail as a result, the legislative attempt to put the protection of legitimate third-party interests on a more secure footing would have proved something of a mixed blessing.

More recently, in *Far East Chartering Limited and Binani Cement Limited v Great Eastern Shipping Company Limited* [2012] EWCA Civ 180, Tomlinson LJ referred to *The Laemthong Glory* (above) as:

"the first reported occasion upon which shipowners sought to rely upon a letter of indemnity which was addressed not to themselves but to the charterers. It is important to note that in that case the letter of indemnity was addressed by the receivers to the charterers by name. Cooke J, with whom the Court of Appeal agreed, held that the shipowners were entitled to enforce against the receivers the letter of indemnity which the receivers had given to the charterers. They were entitled so to do by reliance upon the Contracts (Rights of Third Parties) Act 1999. The letter of indemnity by clause 1 offered to indemnify 'you', i.e. the charterers, your servants and agents. Delivery of the cargo could in practice be effected only by the shipowners who were in possession of it. The charterers could not themselves deliver the cargo except by making use of the shipowners to do so. Thus the charterers could only procure the delivery of the cargo to the receivers through the agency of the owners. The owners were accordingly the agents of the charterers for the purpose of complying with the receivers' request in the receivers' letter of indemnity addressed to the charterers, namely to deliver the cargo to them under the receivers' letter of indemnity and were thus properly to be regarded as falling within the category of 'agents' whom the receivers promised to indemnify in clause 1 of the letter of indemnity. The letter of indemnity therefore, in the statutory language, purported to confer a benefit upon the shipowners."

In the *Great Eastern Shipping Company* case itself, in response to a similar claim by the shipowners, the receivers of the cargo argued that the letter of indemnity that they had issued was addressed to the shipowners rather than to the charterers. If this were correct, it followed that there was no indemnity between the receivers and the charterers to be enforced indirectly by the shipowners as third parties—the 1999 Act simply would not be engaged. Indeed, if this were correct, and other things being equal, the shipowners would have a direct claim against the receivers on the letter of indemnity. To counter this latter point, the receivers, relying on the principle that an offeree must know of an offer in order to accept it, argued that at the relevant time the shipowners were ignorant of the existence of the letter of indemnity. The Court of Appeal held that, in the context, "the natural and proper meaning of the letter of indemnity is that it is addressed to both the owners and the charterers" (para.42). It followed that, irrespective of whether the shipowners had a direct claim, it was open to them (as in *The Laemthong Glory*) to take the benefit of the indemnity as third parties. While the *Great Eastern Shipping Company* case is in line with *The Laemthong Glory*, because it turns very much on its own facts (and the way that the court interprets the factual matrix), it does not significantly add to the jurisprudence.

Further reading

John N. Adams, Deryck Beyleveld, and Roger Brownsword, 'Privity of Contract—the Benefits and the Burdens of Law Reform' (1997) 60 MLR 238

Roger Brownsword and and Dale Hutchison 'Privity of Contract: Beyond Promissory Principle and Protective Pragmatism' in Peter Kincaid (ed), *Privity: Private Justice or Public Regulation* (Aldershot: Ashgate, 2001) p.126

Andrew Burrows, 'The Contracts (Rights of Third Parties) Act 1999 and its Implications for Commercial Contracts' [2000] LMCLQ 540

Peter Kincaid, 'Privity Reform in England' (2000) 116 LQR 43

S.A. Smith, 'Contracts for the Benefit of Third Parties: In Defence of the Third-Party Rule' (1997) 7 OJLS 643

13

PRIVITY OF CONTRACT II

LEARNING OBJECTIVES

By the end of this chapter, you should:

- **have an appreciation of the many ways in which, prior to the 1999 Act, the courts sought to qualify the restrictive effects of the privity doctrine;**
- **understand that the principal reasons for so qualifying the doctrine were fairness to third-party beneficiaries and commercial convenience;**
- **appreciate that ad hoc steps taken to respond to the perceived unfairness or inconvenience of the privity restrictions can have disruptive effects on other areas of law;**
- **have a view about the need for, and desirability of, a more relaxed regime of third-party effects where the context is one of connected contracts or networks.**

INTRODUCTION

The pressure to reform the common law privity rule arose from two principal sources: one was simple third-party beneficiary cases of the kind represented by Beswick v Beswick (below); the other was the kind of case generated by complex chains or networks of commercial contracts, where one party (whether the client, main contractor, or downstream sub-contractor) sought to rely on provisions in a contract in the chain or network to which it was not directly a party. Although the Law Commission focused on the former kind of case, much of the momentum for reform, particularly in the two decades before the legislative intervention, derived from concerns about the latter kind of case.

13–001

Stated formally, one puzzle arises where A is in contract with B, B is in contract with C, and A now seeks to recover financial losses by suing C (who is the cause of A's financial losses). If A's claim is barred in contract (because of lack of privity), there is a tension if the same claim is recognised as a matter of tort law (as happened in the notorious *Junior Books* case, see below). Another puzzle arises where A sues C in negligence (for example, because C has negligently damaged A's property), the principal questions now being whether C may respond to A's claim by relying on terms in the contract between A and B, or in the contract between B and C. Section 1(6) of the 1999 Act provides for this kind of case in a somewhat cryptic and oblique fashion:

> "Where a term of a contract excludes or limits liability in relation to any matter references in this Act to the third party enforcing the term shall be construed as references to his availing himself of the exclusion or limitation."

However, it will be apparent already that there might be different arguments depending upon whether C is seeking to rely on the contract between A and B (to which A, but not C, is a party) or the contract between B and C (to which C, but not A, is a party). Moreover, because these disputes are set at a difficult interface between contract and tort, we cannot understand the issues at stake without giving some consideration to this doctrinal setting.

The discussion and cases in this chapter are divided into seven sections. In the first section, the relationship between claims for breach of contract and claims for a failure to take reasonable care as required by the tort of negligence is considered. The point, here, is that, where the law of contract is so restrictive that meritorious (third-party) claims are barred, there is real pressure on the law of tort to find a way round the restrictions. However, any adjustments made by tort law cannot be entirely ad hoc without compromising the coherence and calculability of negligence liability. The second section deals with the availability of contractual defences and limitations of liability where a downstream contractor (such as a sub-contractor) is sued by an upstream contractor (such as the client). If privity restricts the availability of such defences, this might well defeat the reasonable expectations of the defendant contractor and, given the ethos of the modern law, this would be problematic (Lord Wilberforce's remarks in *The Eurymedon* should be read carefully in this light). The third section considers those cases in which B sues A for breach of the A/B contract but where, in effect, B is seeking to recover damages that represent the loss of the intended beneficiary C (C being barred by the doctrine of privity from making a claim against A). If B is not able to recover substantial damages (because, strictly, B has no loss) and C has no claim, this (to say the least) seems unsatisfactory. But, how is this circle to be squared? The question in the fourth section is whether the concept of a trust (with enhanced third-party protection) can be 'imposed' on some three-party contract situations. In section five, the focus is the principle that the contractors should not be permitted to 'burden' a third-party. Certainly, if C is not permitted to take the benefit of a contract between A and B, there is no reason why C should be burdened by such a contract; and, even if the former (benefit) principle seems to be unduly restrictive, there is no rush to change the latter principle. Section six reviews a number of so-called exceptions to the privity principle (quite apart the 1999 Act). And, finally, in section seven, consideration is given to the live question of whether the sets of contracts that are commonly found in various kinds of business networks should be given special doctrinal recognition, so that (inter alia) the usual third-party restrictions are revised.

1. Contract and Tort

13–002   Where A negligently performs his contract with B and causes damage to a third party, C, C may sometimes have a remedy in the tort of negligence. It depends on whether the law imposes a duty on A to take reasonable care not to cause the injury in question to C. Such duties have long been recognised in the case of physical injury to person or property. The leading case is *Donoghue v Stevenson* [1932] A.C. 562 where the injured consumer of defective ginger beer successfully sued the manufacturer although there was no contract between them. Modern cases have extended the principle to purely economic loss. For example, in *Ross v Caunters* [1980] Ch. 297 solicitors (A) negligently allowed the husband of the plaintiff (C) to attest a will drawn up on the instructions of the testator (B) with the result that a gift made by B to C in the will was invalidated. Megarry VC held that C was entitled to damages from A. A owed a duty of care to C when carrying out his contract with B. (Would the Contracts (Rights of Third Parties) Act 1999 have helped C in any way? The Law Commission thought not: Law Com. No.242, para.1.9.)

The same result was reached, Lords Keith and Mustill dissenting, in *White v Jones* [1995] 1 All E.R. 691 HL. Solicitors (A) negligently delayed in carrying out B's instructions to prepare a new will. Consequently, it remained unexecuted when B died. C recovered damages for the loss of the legacy which she would have received if the will had been prepared within a reasonable time and executed by B. Lord Goff said that "an ordinary action in tortious negligence on the lines proposed by Megarry VC in *Ross v Caunters* must . . . be regarded as inappropriate, because it does not meet any of the conceptual problems which have been raised"; but it was open to the House "to fashion a remedy to fill a lacuna in the law and so prevent the injustice which would otherwise occur . . ." So, Lord Goff proposed that they should extend to C a remedy under the *Hedley Byrne* principle (below, para.14–014) "by holding that the assumption of responsibility by the solicitor towards his client should be held in law to extend to the intended beneficiary who (as the solicitor can reasonably foresee) may, as a result of the solicitor's negligence, be deprived of his intended legacy in circumstances in which neither the testator nor his estate will have a remedy against the solicitor."

Lord Mustill, dissenting, said that "it does not conduce to the orderly development of the law, or to the certainty which practical convenience demands, if duties are simply conjured up as a matter of positive law, to answer the injustice of an individual case." He could see nothing special about the calling of a solicitor to distinguish him from others in a much broader category. "If the claim in the present case is sound . . . it must be sound in every instance of the general situation which I have already identified, namely: where A promises B for reward to perform a service for B, in circumstances where it is foreseeable that performance of the service with care will cause C a benefit and that failure to perform it may cause C not to benefit. To hold that a duty exists, even prima facie, in such a situation would be to go far beyond anything so far contemplated by the law of negligence."

Arguably, by extending the doctrine of *Hedley Byrne*, Lord Goff was doing precisely the thing, namely allowing the "ordinary action in tortious negligence", which he had just characterised as inappropriate. Were not the 'conceptual problems' left unmet? If the decision establishes the broad principle stated (and deplored) by Lord Mustill, does it not make a substantial inroad into the privity rule? An earlier decision of the House which seemed to do so was *Junior Books v Veitchi* [1983] A.C. 520. Though probably wrongly decided, it still provides interesting material for discussion.

Junior Books (C) engaged a building contractor (B) to build a factory for them. C's architects nominated Veitchi (A) as specialist sub-contractors to lay a concrete floor with a special surface. A then entered into a contract with B, the main contractor, to carry out that work. There was no contractual relationship between A and C. Two years after it had been laid the floor developed cracks, requiring constant maintenance to keep it usable. C brought an action in negligence against A, claiming the cost of replacing the floor and consequential economic loss. No explanation was offered why C did not sue B on what would seem to have been a straightforward action for breach of contract. It has subsequently emerged that C had already settled a contractual claim against B. Presumably the damage had turned out to be worse than they had realised so they were coming back for more. This may reduce their claim to sympathy but it has no effect on the law—it is the same as if they had never sued B because, for example, B was insolvent. A claimed that C's pleading did not disclose a good cause of action because there was no contractual relationship between A and C and because C did not claim that the floor was a danger to health or safety of any person or to any other property belonging to A. The House of Lords, Lord Brandon dissenting, held that A was liable to C for the economic loss caused.

A's duty to lay the floor arose out of their contract with B. If they had never lifted a finger, only B could have sued. The same applies to their duty to lay a good floor—one which was reasonably fit for the purpose envisaged in the contract. Contractual duties are usually strict and, even if there had been no evidence of negligence, C would probably have been liable to B (who might in turn have been liable to A) for failure to provide a floor which was fit for its purpose. But if all that could be proved was a breach of that strict duty there would have been no question of C's liability in tort to A. It was only because there was a negligent failure to make the floor fit that the case got off the ground. But to say that (i) A owed no duty to C to provide a fit floor but (ii) A owed a duty to C to take reasonable care to provide a fit floor looks very odd. The decision seems to be, in substance, that an action would lie for damages for a negligent breach of a contract to lay a proper floor; and the plaintiff, C, was not a party to that contract. Lord Roskill in his speech set out no fewer than eight facts which he regarded as crucial to the decision; but there is nothing to avoid the conclusion that the defendant was liable because he had negligently performed a contract to which the plaintiff was not a party. The decision was heavily criticised. The courts noted its possible wide-ranging effects and sprang to the defence of privity as a doctrine which it was necessary to preserve. In *Balsamo v Medici* [1984] 2 All E.R. 304 Walton J said:

"If the principle [in Junior Books] does not have some certain limits, it will come perilously close to abrogating completely the concept of privity of contract. A sub-bailee will be liable directly to the bailor, and the sub-agent will be directly liable to the principal for all negligent breaches of whatever agreement he makes with the bailor or agent as the case may be, at any rate over a wide field. I do not think the law has yet got to this point, if it ever will."

In *Simaan v Pilkington Glass (No.2)* [1988] 1 All E.R. 791 at 805, Dillon LJ went so far as to say that he found it difficult to see that the future citation of *Junior Books* could serve any useful purpose. In *D & F Estates Ltd v Church Commissioners* [1988] 2 All E.R. 992 the House of Lords applied the dissenting dicta of Lord Brandon, not the decision of the majority. They held that, in the absence of a contractual relationship between the parties, the cost of repairing a defect in a chattel or structure which was discovered before the defect had caused personal injury or physical damage was not recoverable in negligence. The lessees of a block of flats could not recover from the builders the cost of work necessary to remedy negligent plastering work. This was pure economic loss. It would probably have been different if the negligently applied plaster had fallen off and injured a plaintiff's person or property.

The Law Commission (Law Com. No.242, para.2.14) write of *Junior Books*, "The owners' claim can again [like *White v Jones*] be viewed as being one by a third party beneficiary of a contract (here between the sub-contractor and the head contractor) to enforce the benefit which was contracted for." But in para.7.17 (iii) the Commission states ". . . we do not think that in normal circumstances an owner would be able to sue a sub-contractor for breach of the latter's contract with the head-contractor. This is because, even if the sub-contractor has promised to confer a benefit on the expressly designated owner, the parties have deliberately set up a chain of sub-contracts which are well understood in the construction industry as ensuring that a party's remedies lie against the other contracting party only . . . on a proper construction of the contract—construed in the light of the surrounding circumstances (that is, the existence of the connected head-contract and the background practice and understanding of the construction industry)—the contracting parties (for example the head-contractor and the sub-contractor) did not intend the third party to have the right of enforceability. For similar reasons we consider that [s.1(1)(b) of the Act] would not normally give a purchaser of goods from a retailer a right to sue the manufacturer (rather than the retailer) for breach of contract as regards the quality of the goods."

2. PRIVITY AND DEFENCES

13–003   The cases examined so far concern the question whether C can sue on, or because of, a contract made by A and B. The following cases are concerned with the question whether C can rely on the contract made by A and B when he is sued. They happen to be mainly concerned with contracts for the carriage of goods, particularly carriage by sea. They involve a bill of lading which, according to Lord Blackburn on Sale, 275—

"is a writing signed on behalf of the owner of the ship in which goods are embarked, acknowledging the receipt of the goods, and undertaking to deliver them at the end of the voyage, subject to such conditions as may be mentioned in the bill of lading."

There is some debate as to whether the bill contains the contract of carriage or is merely evidence of its terms (see Debattista, 'The Bill of Lading as the Contract of Carriage' (1982) 45 MLR 652) but that is not material for present purposes. The reader will find that the shipper (the person who sends the goods) and the consignee (the person to whom they are sent) tend to be treated as if they were one and the same, vis-à-vis the carrier. This is because the delivery of the bill of lading transferred not only the ownership in the goods but also the contractual relationship with the carrier from shipper to consignee. The Bills of Lading Act 1855 s.1, which was in force at the time the cases were decided, provided:

"Every consignee of goods named in a bill of lading, and every endorsee of a bill of lading, to whom the property in the goods therein mentioned shall pass upon or by reason of such consignment or endorsement, shall have transferred to and vested in him all rights of suit, and be subject to the same liabilities in respect of such goods as if the contract contained in the bill of lading had been made with himself."

The 1855 Act has been replaced by the Carriage of Goods by Sea Act 1992 which provides by s.2(1) that the lawful holder of a bill of lading, or the consignee under a waybill or a ship's delivery order—

"shall (by virtue of becoming the holder of the bill or, as the case may be, the person to whom delivery is to be made) have transferred to and vested in him all rights of suit under the contract of carriage as if he had been a party to that contract."

It is no longer necessary for the third party to have acquired the property in the goods. It is sufficient that he is lawfully in possession of the bill of lading.

It will be noted that the Contracts (Rights of Third Parties) Act 1999 confers no rights on a third party to these contracts, except that a third party may rely on s.1 to avail himself of an exclusion or limitation of liability clause in such a contract: s.6(5), (6) and (7).

It should also be noted that a feature of the cases in this group is that they involve the law of bailment as well as that of contract. A bailment arises when the owner of goods (the bailor) gives possession of the goods to another (the bailee) for some specified purpose, while retaining ownership for himself. A delivers goods to B to be carried to a named place, or to be stored in a warehouse, or to be repaired, or to be cleaned. There will, of course, usually be a contract between A and B as well as a bailment. It is when B makes a sub-bailment to C, and C damages or loses the goods, that a problem arises. Unless B was acting as A's agent in making a contract with C, there is no privity of contract between A and C. C may however owe a duty of care to A under the law of the tort of negligence. The question arises whether C can rely on the terms on which B accepted the goods from A to exclude or limit his liability. In the leading case of *Scruttons* which follows, the majority considered only the law of contract. Only Lord Denning, in his dissenting speech, invoked the law of bailment which led him to differ from the majority. But in *The Pioneer Container*, below, the Privy Council (four Law Lords and Sir Thomas Eichelbaum) applied Lord Denning's opinion, expressed obiter in *Morris v Martin*, below. The importance of his Lordship's full and brilliant analysis in *Scruttons* is therefore enhanced.

The law of bailment is, of course, irrelevant where the question is one of liability for injury to the person.

SCRUTTONS LTD v MIDLAND SILICONES LTD

House of Lords [1962] A.C. 446; [1962] 2 W.L.R. 186; 106 S.J. 34; [1962] 1 All E.R. 1

13-004   A drum of chemicals was shipped to the plaintiffs (the consignees) on a ship owned by United States Lines Inc (the carrier) under a bill of lading which incorporated the United States Carriage of Goods by Sea Act 1936, and limited the liability of the carrier for damage to $500. The defendants, a stevedoring company, were engaged by the carrier to discharge their vessels in London and to act as agents in the delivery of goods to consignees, by a contract which limited the liability of the stevedores to $500. They negligently dropped the drum, causing damage to the value of £593. The plaintiffs sued the defendants in tort, claiming £593. Diplock J held ([1959] 2 Q.B. 171) that the plaintiffs could recover that sum, rejecting the defendants' arguments that they were protected by the bill of lading. He held that the bill of lading did not purport to govern the relations between the consignees and the stevedores; that it was impossible to say that the stevedores were undisclosed principals of the carrier; that the *Elder, Dempster* case[1] was not an authority for the doctrine of "vicarious immunity from liability for torts" laid down by Scrutton L.J. in *Mersey Shipping & Transport Co Ltd v Rea Ltd* ((1925) 21 Lloyd's Rep. at 378); that if, as in the Elder, Dempster case A invites B to do something to A's goods which B is under no antecedent contractual duty to do, it may be reasonable to imply an agreement between A and B as to the terms on which that thing shall be done; but, as the plaintiffs in the present case never invited the defendants to do anything, no contract between them could be implied; that Denning LJ's observations in the *Snipes Hall* case ([1949] 2 K.B. 500; [1949] 2 All E.R. 179), in *White v John Warwick & Co Ltd* ([1953] 1 W.L.R. 1285; [1953] 2 All E.R. 1021) and *Adler v Dickson* ([1955] 1 Q.B. 158; [1954] 3 All E.R. 397) were obiter and seemed in direct conflict with *Dunlop v Selfridge* (above, para.12–004) and *Cosgrove v Horsfall* (below, para.13–017) which were binding on him; and that the defendants could not limit their liability to the plaintiffs in tort by relying on a contract between the plaintiffs and a third party to which they were not parties and for which they gave no consideration to the plaintiffs. The Court of Appeal (Hodson, Pearce and Upjohn LJJ) affirmed the decision. The defendants now appealed to the House of Lords.

Viscount Simonds made a speech dismissing the appeal.

LORD REID

Although I may regret it, I find it impossible to deny the existence of the general rule that a stranger to a contract cannot in a question with either of the contracting parties take advantage of provisions of the contract, even where it is clear from the contract that some provision in it was intended to benefit him. That rule appears to have been crystallised a century ago in *Tweddle v Atkinson* [above, para.12–004] and finally established in this House in *Dunlop Pneumatic Tyre Co Ltd v Selfridge & Co Ltd* [above]. There are, it is true, certain well-established exceptions to that rule—though I am not sure that they are really exceptions and do not arise from other principles. But none of these in any way touches the present case.

The actual words used by Lord Haldane in the *Dunlop* case were made the basis of an argument that,

---

[1]   [1924] A.C. 522. The plaintiffs sued the charterers and owners of the ship, Grelwen, for damage caused by bad stowage to oil shipped by the plaintiffs on the Grelwen. The bills of lading issued by the charterers provided that 'the shipowners' should not be liable for any damage caused by bad stowage. It was not disputed that the term 'shipowners' included the charterers but it was argued that the clause could not protect the owners from liability for the negligence of their servants since "they neither knew nor cared anything about the bills of lading." Allowing an appeal from the Court of Appeal where Scrutton LJ dissented, the House of Lords held that the owners were protected. The precise juristic basis for this rule remains obscure; but it will be noted that the situation in which it operates is a highly specialised one: the master of the ship who takes possession of the goods shipped is the servant of the shipowners, who thus acquire possession directly from the shipper. While the shipowners are exempt, it does not by any means necessarily follow that the master or any member of the crew would be exempt if he were sued personally for his negligence: Cf. Jenkins LJ at [1955] 1 Q.B. 194.

although a stranger to a contract may not be able to sue for any benefit under it, he can rely on the contract as a defence if one of the parties to it sues him in breach of his contractual obligation—that he can use the contract as a shield though not as a sword. I can find no justification for that. If the other contracting party can prevent the breach of contract well and good, but if he cannot I do not see how the stranger can. As was said in *Tweddle v Atkinson*, the stranger cannot "take advantage" from the contract.

It may be that in a roundabout way the stranger could be protected. If A, wishing to protect X, gives to X an enforceable indemnity, and contracts with B that B will not sue X, informing B of the indemnity, and then B does sue X in breach of his contract with A, it may be that A can recover from B as damages the sum which he has to pay X under the indemnity, X having had to pay it to B. But there is nothing remotely resembling that in the present case.

The appellants in this case seek to get round this rule in three different ways. In the first place, they say that the decision in *Elder, Dempster & Co Ltd v Paterson, Zochonis & Co Ltd* ([1924] A.C. 522) establishes an exception to the rule sufficiently wide to cover the present case. I shall later return to consider this case. Secondly, they say that through the agency of the carrier they were brought into contractual relation with the shipper and that they can now found on that against the consignees, the respondents. And thirdly, they say that there should be inferred from the facts an implied contract, independent of the bill of lading, between them and the respondents. It was not argued that they had not committed a tort in damaging the respondents' goods.

I can see a possibility of success of the agency argument if (first) the bill of lading makes it clear that the stevedore is intended to be protected by the provisions in it which limit liability, (secondly) the bill of lading makes it clear that the carrier, in addition to contracting for these provisions on his own behalf, is also contracting as agent for the stevedore that these provisions should apply to the stevedore, (thirdly) the carrier has authority from the stevedore to do that, or perhaps later ratification by the stevedore would suffice, and (fourthly) that any difficulties about consideration moving from the stevedore were overcome. And then to affect the consignee it would be necessary to show that the provisions of the Bills of Lading Act 1855, apply.

But again there is nothing of that kind in the present case. I agree with your Lordships that "carrier" in the bill of lading does not include stevedore, and if that is so I can find nothing in the bill of lading which states or even implies that the parties to it intended the limitation of liability to extend to stevedores. Even if it could be said that reasonable men in the shoes of these parties would have agreed that the stevedores should have this benefit, that would not be enough to make this an implied term of the contract. And even if one could spell out of the bill of lading an intention to benefit the stevedore, there is certainly nothing to indicate that the carrier was contracting as agent for the stevedore in addition to contracting on his own behalf. So it appears to me that the agency argument must fail.

And the implied contract argument seems to me to be equally unsound. From the stevedores' angle, they are employed by the carrier to deal with the goods in the ship. They can assume that the carrier is acting properly in employing them, and they need not know whom the goods belong to. There was in their contract with the carrier a provision that they should be protected, but that could not by itself bind the consignee. They might assume that the carrier would obtain protection for them against the consignee and feel aggrieved when they found that the carrier did not or could not do that. But a provision in the contract between them and the carrier is irrelevant in a question between them and the consignee. Then from the consignees' angle they would know that stevedores would be employed to handle their goods, but if they read the bill of lading they would find nothing to show that the shippers had agreed to limit the liability of the stevedores. There is nothing to show that they ever thought about this or that if they had they would have agreed or ought as reasonable men to have agreed to this benefit to the stevedores. I can find no basis in this for implying a contract between them and the stevedores. It cannot be said that such a contract was in any way necessary for business efficiency.

So this case depends on the proper interpretations of the *Elder, Dempster* case. What was there decided is clear enough. The ship was under time charter, the bill of lading made by the shippers and the charterers provided for exemption from liability in the event which happened and this exemption was held to enure to the benefit of the shipowners who were not parties to the bill of lading but whose servant the master caused damage to the shippers' goods by his negligence. The decision is binding on us but I agree that the decision by itself will not avail the present appellants because the facts of this case are very different from those in the *Elder, Dempster* case. For the appellants to succeed it would be necessary to find from the speeches in this House a ratio decidendi which would cover this case and then to follow that ratio decidendi . . .

It can hardly be denied that the ratio decidendi of the *Elder, Dempster* decision is very obscure. A number of eminent judges have tried to discover it, hardly any two have reached the same result, and none of the explanations hitherto given seems to me very convincing. If I had to try, the result might depend on whether or not I was striving to obtain a narrow ratio. So I turned to the decision itself. Two quite separate points were involved in the case. The first was whether the damage to the cargo was caused by bad stowage or by the ship being unseaworthy. This was very fully considered and the decision was bad stowage. On the conditions in the bill of lading this clearly freed the charterer of liability. The other question was whether those conditions were also available as a defence to the shipowner. From the report of the case it would seem that this was not very fully argued, and none of the three noble Lords who spoke devoted more than a page of print to it. They cannot have thought that any important question of law or any novel principle was involved. Lord Finlay said that a decision against the shipowner would be absurd and the other noble Lords probably thought the same. They must all have thought that they were merely applying an established principle to the facts of the particular case.

But when I look for such a principle I cannot find it, and the extensive and able arguments of counsel in this case have failed to discover it . . .

(Having discussed the case and the dissenting judgment of Scrutton L.J. in the Court of Appeal [1923] 1 K.B. 420, his Lordship proceeded): I must treat the decision as an anomalous and unexplained exception to the general principle that a stranger cannot rely for his protection on provisions in a contract to which he is not a party. The decision of this House is authoritative in cases of which the circumstances are not reasonably distinguishable from those which gave rise to the decision. The circumstances in the present case are clearly distinguishable in several respects. Therefore I must decide this case on the established principles of the law of England apart from that decision and on that basis I have no doubt that this appeal must be dismissed.
Lord Keith of Avonholme made a speech dismissing the appeal.

LORD DENNING

[Having referred to the statement of Scrutton LJ in *Mersey Shipping and Transport Co, Ltd v Rea, Ltd* (1925) 21 Lloyd's Rep. at p.378 that "where there is a contract which contains an exemption clause, the servants or agents who act under that contract have the benefit of the exemption clause," his Lordship proceeded:] My Lords, it is said that, in stating this proposition, for once Homer nodded and that this great master of our commercial law—and the members of this House too—overlooked the "fundamental principle" that no one who is not a party to a contract can sue or be sued upon it or take advantage of the stipulations or conditions that it contains. I protest they did nothing of the kind. You cannot understand the *Elder, Dempster* case without some knowledge of the previous law and I would draw the attention of your Lordships to it.

First of all let me remind your Lordships that this "fundamental principle" was a discovery of the nineteenth century. Lord Mansfield and Buller J. knew nothing of it. But in the nineteenth century it was carried to the most extravagant lengths. It was held that, where a duty to use reasonable care arose out of a contract, no one could sue or be sued for a breach of that contract except a party to it, see *Winterbottom v Wright* ((1842) 10 M. & W. 109), *Alton v Midland Ry.* ((1865) 19 C.B.(n.s.) 213). In the nineteenth century if a goods owner had sought to sue stevedores for negligence, as he has in this case, he would have failed utterly. The reason being that the duty of the stevedores to use reasonable care arose out of their contract with the carrier; and no one could sue them for a breach of that duty except the other party to the contract, namely, the carrier. If the goods were damaged, the only remedy of the owner of the goods was against the carrier with whom he contracted, and not against the stevedores with whom he had no contract. If proof were needed that the doctrine was carried so far, it is provided by the many cases in the middle of the nineteenth century where the owner of goods sent them by railway for "through transit" to a destination on another line. The first carrier carried them safely over his line but they were damaged by the negligence of the second carrier. It was repeatedly held that the goods owner had no remedy against the second carrier: for the simple reason that he had no contract with him. The owner's only remedy was against the first carrier with whom he contracted, see *Scothorn v South Staffordshire Ry.* ((1853) 8 Exch. 341): and not against the second carrier with whom he had no contract, see *Mytton v Midland Ry.* ((1859) 4 H. & N. 615), *Coxon v Great Western Ry.* ((1860) 5 H. & N. 274). If the first carrier was exempted from liability by the conditions of the contract, the goods owner had no remedy at all: none against the first carrier because he was protected by the conditions: and none against the second carrier because he was "not liable at all." It was so held by this House in *Bristol and Exeter Ry. v Collins* ((1859) 7 H.L.Cas. 194). See especially what Lord Chelmsford said with the entire agreement of Lord Brougham and what Lord Cranworth said.

What an irony is here! This "fundamental principle" which was invoked 100 years ago for the purpose of holding that the agents of the carrier were "not liable at all" is now invoked for the purpose of holding that they are inescapably liable, without the benefit of any of the conditions of carriage. How has this come about?

The reason is because in the nineteenth century negligence was not an independent tort. If you wished to sue a man for negligence, you had to show some special circumstances which put him under a duty of care towards you. You might do it by reason of a contract, by a bailment, by his inviting you on to his premises on business, by his leaving about a thing which was dangerous in itself, and in other ways. But apart from some such special circumstances, there was no general duty to use care . . . Suppose in those days that you tried to show that the defendant was under a duty of care, then if you could only show it by reason of contract, your remedy lay only in contract and not in tort. But if you could show it, not only by reason of contract, but also for some other reason, as for instance by reason of his inviting you to his premises, you could sue either in contract or in tort. It was by a development of this principle that, in the "through transit" cases, the courts eventually found a way of making the second carrier liable. It was held that if, on through transit, the second carrier accepted a person as a passenger, the second carrier was under a duty, irrespective of contract, to carry him with reasonable care . . . Likewise, if a second carrier accepted goods for carriage, so that they were lawfully on his premises, he was under a duty to the owner to use reasonable care, although there was no contract between them . . . But when the courts found this way of making the second carrier liable, they did not thereby open a way by which the injured person could escape the conditions of carriage. If he had agreed that the carriage was to be "at owner's risk" for the whole journey, he was held to his agreement, even when he sued the second carrier in tort . . . the only acceptable explanation of the "through transit" cases, to my mind, is that the second carrier falls within Scrutton L.J.'s proposition, being an "agent," that is, a sub-contractor employed to carry out the contract to the first carrier, and so entitled to the benefit of the conditions.

This brings me to the *Elder, Dempster* case itself . . . It is said that the decision is anomalous and contrary to principle, but that is only because you are looking at it through the spectacles of 1961 and not those of 1924. Since the decision of *Donoghue v Stevenson* ([1932] A.C. 562) in 1932 we have had negligence established as an independent tort in itself. Small wonder, then, that nowadays it is said that the tortfeasor cannot rely for his protection on provisions in a contract to which he was not a party. But the very point in the *Elder, Dempster* case was that the negligence there was not an independent tort in itself. It was negligence in the very course of performing the contract—done, it is true, by the sub-contractor and not by the principal—but if you permit the owner of the goods to sue the sub-contractor in tort for what is in truth a breach of the contract of carriage, then at least you should give him the protection of the contract. Were it otherwise there would be an easy way round the conditions of the contract of carriage. That is how the judges in the *Elder, Dempster* case looked at it and I am not prepared to say they were wrong. I am sure that the profession looked at it, too, at that time in the same way. If the draftsmen of the Hague Rules had thought in those days that the goods owner could get round the exceptions by suing the stevedores or the master in tort, they would surely have inserted provisions in those Rules to protect them. They did not do so because they did not envisage their being made liable at all.

But if you look at the *Elder, Dempster* case with the spectacles of 1961, then there is a way in which it can be supported. It is this: Even though negligence is an independent tort, nevertheless it is an accepted principle of the law of tort that no man can complain of an injury if he has voluntarily consented to take the risk of it on himself. This consent need not be embodied in a contract. Nor does it need consideration to support it. Suffice it that he consented to take the risk of injury on himself. So in the case of through transit, when the shipper of goods consigns them "at owner's risk" for the whole journey, his consent to take the risk avails the second carrier as well as the first, even though there is no contract between the goods owner and the second carrier. Likewise in the *Elder, Dempster* case the shipper, by exempting the charterers from bad stowage, may be taken to have consented to exempt the shipowners also. But I am afraid that this reasoning would not avail the stevedores in the present case: for the simple reason that the bill of lading is not expressed so as to protect the stevedores but only the "carrier." The shipper has therefore not consented to take on himself the risk of the negligence of the stevedores and is not to be defeated on that ground. But if the bill of lading were expressed in terms by which the owner of the goods consented to take on himself the risk of loss in excess of $500, whether due to the negligence of the carrier or the stevedores, I know of no good reason why his consent, if freely given, should not be binding on him . . .

I suppose, however, that I must be wrong about all this: because your Lordships, I believe, take a different view. But it means that I must go on to consider the second question, namely, whether the stevedores can avail themselves of the protection clause in their own "stevedoring contract." Here your Lordships are untrammelled by authority. The cases in the High Court of Australia and in the United States Supreme Court do not touch the point. The stevedores in those two cases, for aught that appears, had agreed to do their work on a "bald" stevedoring contract "with unrestricted liability": where as here they stipulated that they should "have such protection as is afforded by the terms, conditions and exceptions of the bill of lading."

It is said here again that the owners of the goods cannot be affected by the "stevedoring contract" to which they were not parties: but it seems to me that we are now in a different branch of the law. When considering the contract between the carrier and the stevedores, it is important to remember that the carrier of goods, like a hirer, is a bailee: and the law of bailment is governed by somewhat different principles from those of contract or of tort: for "bailment," as Sir Percy Winfield said, "is more fittingly regarded as a distinct branch of the Law of Property, under the title Possession than as appropriate to either the law of contract or the law of tort," see *The Province of the Law of Tort*, p. 100. One special feature of the law of bailment is that the bailee can make a contract in regard to the goods which will bind the owner, although the owner is no party to the contract and cannot sue or be sued upon it . . .

Applying this principle, the question is: Did the owners of the goods impliedly authorise the carrier to employ the stevedores on the terms that their liability should be limited to $500? I think they did. Put in simple language, the shipper said to the carrier: "Please carry these goods to London and deliver them to the consignee. You may take it that they are not worth more than $500 so your liability is limited to $500. If they were worth more, we would declare it to you." The carrier carries them to London and says to the stevedores: "Please deliver these goods to the consignee. They have not been declared as being in excess of $500, so you need not insure them for more. You are to have the same protection as I have, namely, your liability is limited to $500." It is quite plain that the consignee cannot sue the carrier for more than $500, and the carrier cannot sue the stevedores for more than $500. But can the consignee turn round and say to the stevedores: "Although the goods were not declared as being worth more than $500, yet they were worth in fact $1,500 and I can make you liable for it"? I do not think our law permits him to do this. The carrier simply passed on the self-same limitation as he himself had, and this must have been within his implied authority. It seems to me that when the owner of goods allows the person in possession of them to make a contract in regard to them, then he cannot go back on the terms of the contract, if they are such as he expressly or impliedly authorised, that is to say, consented to be made, even though he was no party to the contract and could not sue or be sued upon it. It is just the same as if he stood by and watched it being made. And his successor in title is in no better position.

I would allow the appeal.

Lord Morris made a speech dismissing the appeal.

Questions

13–005

1. If the clause in the bill of lading did not protect the stevedores because it was not expressed to protect them, but only the carrier, then seemingly it would not satisfy the provisions of s.1(1) of the 1999 Act. How should the carrier amend the clause in the bill of lading if he wished the protection to apply to any stevedore whom he might employ?

2. If Lord Denning is right about the effect of the 'stevedoring contract', the stevedore is protected against the action by the consignee, without resort to the 1999 Act. If Lord Denning is wrong about that, could the stevedoring contract protect the stevedore against the consignee under the 1999 Act? Does the Act enable the contracting parties to impose any burden or disadvantage on a third party?

NEW ZEALAND SHIPPING COMPANY LTD v A M SATTERTHWAITE & CO LTD: THE EURYMEDON

Privy Council [1975] A.C. 154; [1974] 2 W.L.R. 865; [1974] 1 All E.R. 1015

13–006   The question was whether the stevedore could obtain the benefit of a provision discharging the carrier from all liability unless action was brought within one year after delivery of the goods. The bill of lading between the consignors and the carrier contained the following provision: "It is hereby expressly agreed that no servant or agent of the Carrier (including every independent contractor from time to time employed by the Carrier) shall in any circumstances whatsoever be under any liability whatsoever to the Shipper, Consignee or Owner . . . and . . . every exemption, limitation, condition and liberty herein contained . . . shall also be available and shall extend to protect every such servant or agent of the Carrier . . . and for the purpose of all the foregoing provisions of this clause the Carrier is or shall be deemed to be acting as agent or trustee on behalf of and for the benefit of all persons who are or might be his agents from time to time (including independent contractors as aforesaid) . . ."

Reversing the New Zealand Court of Appeal and restoring the judgment of Beattie J., the Privy Council (Viscount Dilhorne and Lord Simon of Glaisdale dissenting) held that it could. Lord Wilberforce, delivering the majority opinion, said that the question was whether the contract satisfied the four propositions which Lord Reid declared to be necessary to argue that the carriers acted as agents for the stevedore [above, para.13–004].

LORD WILBERFORCE

It was on this point that the Court of Appeal differed from Beattie J., holding that it had not been shown that any consideration for the shippers' promise as to exemption moved from the promisee, that is, the stevedore.

If the choice, and the antithesis, is between a gratuitous promise and a promise for consideration, as it must be, in the absence of a tertium quid, there can be little doubt which, in commercial reality, this is. The whole contract is of a commercial character, involving service on one side, rates of payment on the other, and qualifying stipulations as to both. The relations of all parties to each other are commercial relations entered into for business reasons of ultimate profit. To describe one set of promises, in this context, as gratuitous, or nudum pactum, seems paradoxical and is prima facie implausible. It is only the precise analysis of this complex of relations into the classical offer and acceptance, with identifiable consideration, that seems to present difficulty, but this same difficulty exists in many situations of daily life, for example, sales at auction; supermarket purchases; boarding an omnibus; purchasing a train ticket; tenders for the supply of goods; offers of reward; acceptance by post; warranties of authority by agents; manufacturers' guarantees; gratuitous bailments; bankers' commercial credits. These are all examples which show that English law, having committed itself to a rather technical and schematic doctrine of contract, in application takes a practical approach, often at the cost of forcing the facts to fit uneasily into the marked slots of offer, acceptance and consideration.

In their Lordships' opinion the present contract presents much less difficulty than many of those above referred to. It is one of carriage from Liverpool to Wellington. The carrier assumes an obligation to transport the goods and to discharge at the port of arrival. The goods are to be carried and discharged, so the transaction is inherently contractual. It is contemplated that a part of this contract, viz., discharge, may be performed by independent contractors—viz., the stevedore. By clause 1 of the bill of lading the shipper agrees to exempt from liability the carrier, his servants and independent contractors in respect of the performance of this contract of carriage. Thus, if the carriage, including the discharge, is wholly carried out by the carrier, he is exempt. If part is carried out by him, and part by his servants, he and they are exempt. If part is carried out by him and part by an independent contractor, he and the independent contractor are exempt. The exemption is designed to cover the whole carriage from loading to discharge, by whomsoever it is performed: the performance attracts the exemption or immunity in favour of whoever the performer turns out to be. There is possible more than one way of analysing this business transaction into the necessary components; that which their Lordships would accept is to say that the bill of lading brought into existence a bargain initially unilateral but capable of becoming mutual, between the shippers and the stevedore, made through the carrier as agent. This became a full contract when the stevedore performed services by discharging the goods. The performance of these services for the benefit of the shipper was the consideration for the agreement by the shipper that the stevedore should have the benefit of the exemptions and limitations contained in the bill of lading. The conception of a "unilateral" contract of this kind was recognised in *Great Northern Railway Co v Witham* [above, Ch.2] and is well established. This way of regarding the matter is very close to, if not identical to, that accepted by Beattie J. in the Supreme Court; he analysed the transaction as one of an offer open to acceptance by action such as was found in *Carlill v Carbolic Smoke Ball Co* [above, Ch.2]. But whether one describes the shipper's promise to exempt as an offer to be accepted by performance or as a promise in exchange for an act seems in the present context to be a matter of semantics. The words of Bowen L.J. in *Carlill v Carbolic Smoke Ball Co*, ". . . why should not an offer be made to all the world which is to ripen into a contract with anybody who comes forward and performs the condition?" seem to bridge both conceptions: he certainly seems to draw no distinction between an offer which matures into a contract when accepted and a promise which matures into a contract after performance, and, though in some special contexts (such as in connection with the right to withdraw) some further refinement may be needed, either analysis may be equally valid. On the main point in the appeal, their Lordships are in substantial agreement with Beattie J.

The following other points require mention:

1. In their Lordships' opinion, consideration may quite well be provided by the stevedore, as suggested, even though (or if) it was already under an obligation to discharge to the carrier. (There is no direct evidence of the existence or nature of this obligation, but their Lordships are prepared to assume it.) An agreement to do an act which the promisor is under an existing obligation to a third party to do, may quite well amount to valid consideration and does so in the present case: the promisee obtains the benefit of a direct obligation which he can enforce. This proposition is illustrated and supported by *Scotson v Pegg* [above, Ch.10] which their Lordships consider to be good law.

2. The consignee is entitled to the benefit of, and is bound by, the stipulations in the bill of lading by his acceptance of it and request for delivery of the goods thereunder. This is shown by *Brandt v Liverpool, Brazil and River Plate Steam Navigation Co Ltd* ([1924] 1 K.B. 575 CA) and a line of earlier cases. The Bills of Lading Act, 1855, s.1 (in New Zealand the Mercantile Law Act, 1908, s.13) gives a partial statutory recognition to this rule, but, where the statute does not apply, as it may well not do in this case, the previously established law remains effective.

3. The stevedore submitted, in the alternative, an argument that, quite apart from contract, exemptions from, or limitation of, liability in tort may be conferred by mere consent on the part of the party who may be injured. As their Lordships consider that the stevedore ought to succeed in contract, they prefer to express no opinion on this argument: to evaluate it requires elaborate discussion.

4. A clause very similar to the present was given effect by a United States District Court in *Carle and Montanari Inc v American Export Isbrandtsen Lines Inc* ([1968] 1 Lloyd's Rep. 260). The carrier in that case contracted, in an exemption clause, as agent for, inter alias, all stevedores and other independent contractors and although it is no doubt true that the law in the United States is more liberal than ours as regards third party contracts, their Lordships see no reason why the law of the Commonwealth should be more restrictive and technical as regards agency contracts. Commercial consideration should have the same force on both sides of the Pacific.

In the opinion of their Lordships, to give the stevedore the benefit of the exemptions and limitations contained in the bill of lading is to give effect to the clear intentions of a commercial document and can be given within existing principles. They see no reason to strain the law or the facts in order to defeat these intentions. It should not be overlooked that the effect of denying validity to the clause would be to encourage actions against servants, agents and independent contractors in order to get round exemptions (which are almost invariable and often compulsory) accepted by shippers against carriers, the existence, and presumed efficacy, of which is reflected in the rates of freight. They see no attraction in this consequence.

VISCOUNT DILHORNE (dissenting)

The clause does not in my opinion either expressly or impliedly contain an offer by the shippers to the carriers to enter into an agreement whereby if the appellants performed services in relation to the goods the shippers would give them the benefit of every exemption from, and limitation of, liability contained in the bill of lading. I see no difficulty in expressing such an offer in clear and unequivocal language, and if the clause contained such an offer, I would have been in favour of allowing the appeal.

What the clause records is not an offer but an agreement, and one agreement only, made between the shippers and the carriers acting in a dual capacity, on their own behalf and on behalf of all persons who were or might be their servants or employed by them as independent contractors, and an agreement to which all such persons are or are to be deemed to be parties.

I agree with Turner P. in thinking that the terms of clause 1 cannot be read as constituting such an offer. If the terms of the expressed agreement fail to constitute a legally binding contract between the shippers and the appellants, to read them as merely constituting an offer by the shippers capable of acceptance by conduct by the appellants is to rewrite the clause.

LORD SIMON OF GLAISDALE (dissenting)

The difference between the two ways of putting the case can be illustrated by two simple types of unilateral contract. In the first, A says to B, "If you will dig over my kitchen garden next Tuesday I will give you £2." B replies, "Agreed! If I dig over your kitchen garden next Tuesday I will get £2 from you." Though there has been what the stevedore's second proposition calls "a bargain," neither party is contractually bound at this stage, and A can, at any reasonable period before the time for performance, communicate the withdrawal of his offer without incurring liability. But, if the offer is not so withdrawn, and if B on Tuesday does dig over A's kitchen garden (the mode of performance being clearly indicated), the contract is complete and A is bound to pay B £2. The acceptance is verbal, and performance furnishes the consideration moving from B. In the second type, A may say to B, "If you dig over my kitchen garden next Tuesday, I will pay you £2." B does not verbally communicate his acceptance of the offer, A having impliedly waived such requirement. But if A does not communicate any withdrawal of his offer, and if B on Tuesday does dig over A's kitchen garden, the offer is accepted by the stipulated mode of performance, which also provides the consideration: A is bound to pay B £2. This latter type of unilateral contract—the *Carlill* type contract—is that propounded in the stevedore's third proposition; the former type of unilateral contract in the stevedore's second proposition. As counsel for the stevedore rightly submitted, they are mutually exclusive. Nevertheless, both require an offer, and one stipulating a mode of performance. Here, for the reasons given in the Court of Appeal and heretofore, there was no offer, and no sufficient stipulation of a mode of performance which would constitute acceptance. Counsel for the stevedore relied for his second proposition on *Great Northern Railway Co v Witham* [above, Ch.2] a well-known case the soundness of which has never been doubted. But it is far removed from the instant.

Questions

1. In *Port Jackson Stevedoring Pty Ltd v Salmond & Spraggon Pty (Australia) Ltd* [1980] 1 W.L.R.   **13–007**
138; [1980] 3 All E.R. 257, PC the Board said, obiter, that *Satterthwaite* was not only a decision in principle that the so-called Himalaya clause is capable of conferring on a third person falling within the description, "servant or agent of the Carrier (including every independent contractor from time to time employed by the Carrier)", defences and immunities conferred by the bill of lading, but also that stevedores employed by the carrier may and normally will come within that protection. Thus, it involved no new principle. Its importance, quoting an Australian court, lay in "the manner in which on the bare facts of the case their Lordships were able to discern a contract between the shipper and the stevedore." Nevertheless, did their Lordships discern a contract which was not really there?

2. Is there any real difference between Lord Simon's examples of two types of unilateral contract? He says of the first example, "The acceptance is verbal" and that "neither party is contractually bound at this stage." But, if acceptance is the act of concluding a contract, this is not an "acceptance" in the sense in which that term is used in the law relating to the formation of contracts. Is not B's reply, "Agreed . . ." merely a declaration that he intends to accept the offer, which has no effect in law? Is it not just as if someone declared an intention to search for a lost dog and claim the reward? In neither case is A under any obligation until B has dug the garden.

3. If the decision is right, the stevedore does not need to rely on the 1999 Act, could he do so if he wished? See s.6(1) of the Act.

THE MAHKUTAI

Privy Council [1996] A.C. 650; [1996] 3 W.L.R. 1; [1996] 3 All E.R. 502

Shipowners [C] chartered their vessel to time charterers [B] who sub-chartered it to shippers [A] for the   **13–008**
carriage of a cargo from Jakarta to China. The bill of lading issued by the time charterers [B] included a "Himalaya clause" stating that the "subcontractors" were to have the benefit of "all exceptions, limitations, provisions, conditions and liberties herein benefiting the carrier as if such provisions were expressly made for their benefit." An "exclusive jurisdiction clause" stated that all disputes were to be settled under Indonesian law. A dispute having arisen, the cargo owners arrested the ship in Hong

Kong. The shipowners, who were not parties to the bill of lading, claiming to be "sub-contractors," applied for a stay, relying on the exclusive jurisdiction clause.

The Privy Council explained that the basis of *The Eurymedon* and *The New York Star* was a bilateral agreement between the stevedores and the shippers, entered into through the agency of the shipowners, which, though initially unsupported by consideration, became enforceable when consideration was supplied by the stevedores' performance of their duties. Assuming but not deciding that the shipowners [C] were "subcontractors," that, nevertheless, they could not take advantage of the exclusive jurisdiction clause in the bill of lading which was a contract between A and B. The exclusive jurisdiction clause was different from clauses in the bill which were purely for the protection of the carrier involving mutual rights and obligations.

LORD GOFF

[Having examined the swing of "The pendulum of judicial opinion" from the *Elder Dempster* case through *Midland Silicones* to *The Eurymedon* and *The New York Star*, and noted the criticisms which have been made of the two latter cases:] Nevertheless, there can be no doubt of the commercial need of some such principle as this, and not only in cases concerned with stevedores; and the bold step taken by the Privy Council in *The Eurymedon*, and later developed in *The New York Star*, has been widely welcomed. But it is legitimate to wonder whether that development is yet complete. Here their Lordships have in mind not only Lord Wilberforce's discouragement of fine distinctions, but also the fact that the law is now approaching the position where, provided that the bill of lading contract, clearly provides that (for example) independent contractors such as stevedores are to have the benefit of exceptions and limitations contained in that contract, they will be able to enjoy the protection of those terms as against the cargo owners. This is because (1) the problem of consideration in these cases is regarded as having been solved on the basis that a bilateral agreement between the stevedores and the cargo owners, entered into through the agency of the shipowners, may, though itself unsupported by consideration, be rendered enforceable by consideration subsequently furnished by the stevedores in the form of performance of their duties as stevedores for the shipowners; (2) the problem of authority from the stevedores to the shipowners to contract on their behalf can, in the majority of cases, be solved by recourse to the principle of ratification; and (3) consignees of the cargo may be held to be bound on the principle in *Brandt & Co v Liverpool Brazil and River Plate Steam Navigation Co Ltd* [1924] 1 K.B. 575, All E.R. 656. Though these solutions are now perceived to be generally effective for their purpose, their technical nature is all too apparent; and the time may well come when, in an appropriate case, it will fall to be considered whether the courts should take what may legitimately be perceived to be the final, and perhaps inevitable, step in this development and recognise in these cases a fully-fledged exception to the doctrine of privity of contract, thus escaping from all the technicalities with which courts are now faced in English law. It is not far from their Lordships' minds that, if the English courts were minded to take that step, they would be following in the footsteps of the Supreme Court of Canada (see *London Drugs Ltd v Kuehne & Nagel International Ltd* (1992) 97 D.L.R. (4th) 261) and, in a different context, the High Court of Australia (see *Trident General Insurance Co Ltd v McNiece Bros Pty. Ltd* (1988) 165 C.L.R. 107). Their Lordships have given consideration to the question whether they should face up to this question in the present appeal. However, they have come to the conclusion that it would not be appropriate for them to do so, first because they have not heard argument specifically directed towards this fundamental question, and second because, as will become clear in due course, they are satisfied that the appeal must in any event be dismissed.

It should be noted that, in the Law Commission's opinion, *The Mahkutai* would be decided in the same way under the 1999 Act (Law Com. No 242, para.2.35). The exclusive jurisdiction clause is not "an exclusion or limitation of liability" provision within the meaning of s.6(5).)

Question

13–009   1. A bilateral contract, by definition, is one which involves mutual rights and obligations. If a bilateral contract was an acceptable basis for the imposition of liability on C in *The Eurymedon*, why was it not so in *The Mahkutai*? Is it because the particular term (the exclusive jurisdiction clause) in *The Mahkutai* was one which could be invoked by either party whereas the exclusion clause was for the benefit of one party only?

MORRIS v CW MARTIN & SONS LTD

Court of Appeal [1966] 1 Q.B. 716; [1965] 3 W.L.R. 276; [1965] 2 All E.R. 725

13–010

The plaintiff sent a mink stole to Beder, a furrier, to be cleaned. With the plaintiff's consent Beder sent the fur to the defendants, well-known and reputable cleaners. Beder made the contract with the defendants as principal and not as agent for the plaintiff. It contained exempting clauses. The defendants' servant, whose duty it was to clean the fur, stole it from their premises. It was never recovered. The plaintiff failed in the county court on the ground that the servant's act was not done in the course of his employment. The Court of Appeal held, following *Lloyd v Grace, Smith & Co* [1912] A.C. 716 and overruling *Cheshire v Bailey* [1905] 1 K.B. 237, that the servant's act was done in the course of his employment. Lord Denning MR, having so held, went on:

LORD DENNING MR

Now comes the question: Can the defendants rely, as against the plaintiff, on the exempting conditions although there was no contract directly between them and her? There is much to be said on each side. On the one hand, it is hard on the plaintiff if her just claim is defeated by exempting conditions of which she knew nothing and to which she was not a party. On the other hand, it is hard on the defendants if they are held liable to a greater responsibility than they agreed to undertake. As long ago as 1601 Lord Coke advised a bailee to stipulate specially that he would not be responsible for theft, see *Southcote's Case* (1601) 4 Co Rep. 83b, a case of theft by a servant. It would be strange if his stipulation was of no avail to him. The answer to the problem lies, I think, in this: the owner is bound by the conditions if he has expressly or impliedly consented to the bailee making a sub-bailment containing those conditions, but not otherwise. Suppose the owner of a car lets it out on hire, and the hirer sends it for repair, and the repairer holds it for a lien. The owner is bound by the lien because he impliedly consented to the repairs being done, since they were reasonably incidental to use of the car: see *Tappenden v Argus* [1964] 2 Q.B. 185. So also if the owner of a ship accepts goods for carriage on a bill of lading containing exempting conditions (that is, a "bailment upon terms") the owner of the goods (although not a party to the contract) is bound by those conditions if he impliedly consented to them as being in "the known and contemplated form": see the words of Lord Sumner in *Elder, Dempster & Co v Paterson, Zochonis & Co Ltd* [1924] A.C. 522 which were regarded by Dixon C. J. and Fullagar J. as stating the ratio decidendi: see *Wilson v Darling Island Stevedoring & Lighterage Co Ltd* (1956) 95 C.L.R. 43; [1956] 1 Lloyds' Rep. 346 with whose judgment Viscount Simonds entirely agreed in *Scruttons Ltd v Midland Silicones Ltd* [1962] A.C. 446, 472, and also the cases to which I referred in that case [1962] A.C. 446, 489, 491.

In this case the plaintiff agreed that Beder should send the fur to the defendants, and by so doing I think she impliedly consented to his making a contract for cleaning on the terms usually current in the trade. But when I come to study the conditions I do not think they are sufficient to protect the cleaners. We also construe such conditions strictly. Clause 9 applies only to "goods belonging to customers," that is, goods belonging to Beder, and not to goods belonging to his customers such as the plaintiff. The conditions themselves draw a distinction between "customer" and "his own customer": see clause 16. Clause 14 only applied to "the loss of or damage to the goods during processing." The loss here was not during processing. It was before or after processing.

Diplock and Salmon L.JJ. agreed that the exemption clauses were inapplicable to the facts of the present case and reserved the question whether they would have protected the defendants had they been applicable; but Salmon L.J. said that he was "strongly attracted" by the view of the Master of the Rolls.

Appeal Allowed.

13–011   Would the 1999 Act have helped the defendants? Could the contract between Beder and the defendants impose any burden on the plaintiff?

13–012   In *Harris Ltd v Continental Express Ltd and Another* [1961] 1 Lloyds' Rep. 251 (Paull J) the plaintiffs entered into a contract with forwarding agents, X, for the dispatch of the plaintiffs' goods by X's postal service. X had a contract with the second defendants, Y, under which Y lent vans to X for use in X's business and supplied drivers. It was provided that Y should not be responsible for goods carried and that X should indemnify them in all claims relating thereto. The plaintiffs' goods were collected in a van bearing X's name and coloured in the manner of X's own vans, but in fact owned by Y and driven by Y's servant. Owing to the negligence of Y's servant, the goods were stolen.

The plaintiffs' action against X failed because of a clause in the contract between the plaintiffs and X providing that X should not be liable in any circumstances whatsoever for any theft of the goods. The plaintiffs' action in negligence against Y succeeded. The contract between X and Y could not in any way affect the plaintiffs. But, in third-party proceedings brought by Y against X, Y was entitled to an indemnity from X under the terms of the contract between them. Thus X had to pay in the end.

It will be noted that the plaintiffs thought that they were dealing with X throughout. If this had been the case, of course they would have failed. It was purely fortuitous, so far as they were concerned, that X had employed a sub-contractor; and thus purely fortuitous that they were able to recover damages which, in the end, were paid by X. But why should not the *Elder Dempster* case (above) have applied? See also *Johnson Matthey & Co Ltd v Constantine Terminals Ltd* [1976] 2 Lloyd's Rep. 215 and Beatson, 1977 Can. Bar Rev. 746.

THE PIONEER CONTAINER KH ENTERPRISE v PIONEER CONTAINER

Privy Council [1994] 2 All E. R. 250

13–013   The plaintiffs (A) contracted with carriers (B) for the carriage of B's goods from Taiwan to Hong Kong by bills of lading which provided that B was entitled to sub-contract "on any terms" the whole or any part of the carriage. B sub-contracted the carriage to the defendants (C) on bills of lading which provided that the contract was governed by Chinese law and any dispute was to be determined in Taiwan ("the exclusive jurisdiction clause"). The ship sank and the question was whether A could sue C in Hong Kong. It was accepted that there was no contract between A and C. The Hong Kong Court of Appeal held that A was bound by the exclusive jurisdiction clause. The Privy Council, applying the principle stated by Lord Denning in *Morris v Martin*, dismissed A's appeal. C became a bailee of the goods for reward and both A and B had concurrently the rights of a bailor against C. The obligation owed by C to A (as well as to B) was that of a bailee for reward, (A bailee for reward owes a higher obligation than a gratuitous bailee) although the reward was payable not by A but by B. It would be inconsistent to impose on the bailee two different standards of care in respect of the goods entrusted to him.

LORD GOFF

In *Morris v C W Martin & Son*, [1966] 1 Q.B. 716 at 729 Lord Denning M.R. expressed his opinion on this point in clear terms, though on the facts of the case his opinion was obiter. He said:

"The answer to the problem lies, I think, in this: the owner is bound by the conditions if he has expressly or impliedly consented to the bailee making a sub-bailment containing those conditions, but not otherwise."

. . . In order to decide whether . . . to accept the principle so stated by Lord Denning M.R., it is necessary to consider the relevance of the concept of "consent" in this context. It must be assumed that, on the facts of the case, no direct contractual relationship has been created between the owner and the sub-bailee, the only contract created by the sub bailment being that between the bailee and the sub-bailee. Even so, if the effect of the sub-bailment is that the sub-bailee voluntarily receives into his custody the goods of the owner and so assumes towards the owner the responsibility of a bailee, then to the extent that the terms of the sub-bailment are consented to by the owner, it can properly be said that the owner has authorised the bailee so to regulate the duties of the sub-bailee in respect of the goods entrusted to him, not only towards the bailee but also towards the owner. . . .

Such a conclusion, finding its origin in the law of bailment rather than the law of contract, does not depend for its efficacy either on the doctrine of privity of contract or on the doctrine of consideration. That this may be so appears from the decision of the House of Lords in *Elder Dempster & Co Ltd v Paterson Zochonis & Co Ltd* [above, para.13–004, fn]. In that case, shippers of cargo on a chartered ship brought an action against the shipowners for damage caused to the cargo by bad stowage, for which the shipowners were responsible. It is crucial to observe that the cargo was shipped under charterers' bills of lading, so that the contract of carriage contained in or evidenced by the bills of lading was between the shippers and the charterers. The shipowners nevertheless sought to rely, as against the shippers, upon an exception in the bill of lading which protected the charterers from liability for damage due to bad stowage. It was held that the shipowners were entitled to do so, the preferred reason upon which the House so held . . . being found in the speech of Lord Sumner where he said ([1924] AC 522 at 564 . . .):

". . . in the circumstances of this case the obligations to be inferred from the reception of the cargo for carriage to the United Kingdom amount to a bailment upon terms, which include the exceptions and limitations of liability stipulated in the known and contemplated form of bill of lading."

Of course, there was in that case a bailment by the shippers direct to the shipowners, so that it was not necessary to have recourse to the concept of sub-bailment. Even so, notwithstanding the absence of any contract between the shippers and the shipowners, the shipowners' obligations as bailees were effectively subject to the terms upon which the shipowners implicitly received the goods into their possession. Their Lordships do not imagine that a different conclusion would have been reached in the *Elder Dempster* case if the shippers had delivered the goods, not directly to the ship, but into the possession of agents of the charterers who had, in their turn, loaded the goods on board; because in such circumstances, by parity of reasoning, the shippers may be held to have impliedly consented that the sub-bailment to the shipowners should be on terms which included the exemption from liability for bad stowage.

. . . once it is recognised that the sub-bailee, by voluntarily taking the owner's goods into his custody, ipso facto becomes the bailee of those goods vis-à-vis the owner, it must follow that the owner's rights against the sub-bailee will only be subject to terms of the sub-bailment if he has consented to them, i.e. if he has authorised the bailee to entrust the goods to the sub-bailee on those terms. Such consent may, as Lord Denning M.R. pointed out, be express or implied; and in this context the sub-bailee may also be able to invoke, where appropriate, the principle of ostensible authority . . .

Their Lordships wish to add that this conclusion . . . produces a result which in their opinion is both principled and just. They incline to the opinion that a sub-bailee can only be said for these purposes to have voluntarily taken into his possession the goods of another if he has sufficient notice that a person other than the bailee is interested in the goods so that it can properly be said that (in addition to his duties to the bailee) he has, by taking the goods into his custody, assumed towards that other person the responsibility for the goods which is characteristic of a bailee. This they believe to be the underlying principle. Moreover, their Lordships do not consider this principle to impose obligations on the sub-bailee which are onerous or unfair, once it is recognised that he can invoke against the owner terms of the sub-bailment which the owner has actually (expressly or impliedly) or even ostensibly authorised. In the last resort the sub bailee may, if necessary and appropriate, be able to invoke against the bailee the principle of warranty of authority.

13–014

1. Does the failure of the majority in *Scruttons Ltd* to consider the law of bailment mean that that case was decided per incuriam?

2. Has the *Elder Dempster* case, written off by Lord Reid as "an anomalous and unexplained exception", now been rehabilitated as an authority on general principle?

NORWICH CITY COUNCIL v HARVEY AND OTHERS

Court of Appeal [1989] 1 W.L.R. 828; [1989] 1 All E.R. 1180

13–015   The plaintiffs employed contractors to extend a swimming pool. The contract provided (clause 20) that the risk of loss or damage by fire should be on the employer who was required to maintain adequate insurance. The contractor sub-contracted roofing work to the second defendant. The invitation to the sub-contractor to tender identified the main contract and expressly stated that clause 20 would apply. It stated: ". . . acceptance of this order binds the Sub-contractors . . . to the same terms and conditions as those of the Main contract."

The sub-contractor's employee, the first defendant, while using a blow torch set fire to the building. It was not disputed that, if the sub-contractors owed any duty to take care to avoid damage by fire to plaintiffs' property, they were in breach. Garland J held that there was no privity of contract between the plaintiffs and the sub-contractors and that the main contractor was not acting as agent or trustee for the sub-contractors; but that the duty of care which the defendants would otherwise have owed had been so qualified by the terms of the contracts that it would not be just and reasonable to hold that the defendants owed any duty to the plaintiffs to avoid damage by fire. The plaintiffs appealed.

MAY LJ

I trust I do no injustice to the plaintiffs' argument in this appeal if I put it shortly in this way. There is no dispute between the employer and the main contractor that the former accepted the risk of fire damage: see *James Archdale & Co Ltd v Comservices Ltd* [1954] 1 All E.R. 210, [1954] 1 W.L.R. 459 and *Scottish Special Housing Association v Wimpey Construction UK Ltd* [1986] 2 All E.R. 957, [1986] 1 W.L.R. 995. However clause 20[C] does not give rise to any obligation on the employer to indemnify the sub-contractor. That clause is primarily concerned to see that the works were completed. It was intended to operate only for the mutual benefit of the employer and the main contractor. If the judge and the sub-contractors are right, the latter obtain protection which the rules of privity do not provide. Undoubtedly the sub-contractors owed duties of care in respect of damage by fire to other persons and in respect of other property (for instance the lawful visitor, employees of the employer or other buildings outside the site); in those circumstances it is impracticable juridically to draw a sensible line between the plaintiffs on the one hand and others on the other to whom a duty of care was owed. The employer had no effective control over the terms on which the relevant sub-contract was let and no direct contractual control over either the sub-contractors or any employee of theirs.

In addition, the plaintiffs pointed to the position of the first defendant, the sub-contractors' employee. Ex hypothesi he was careless and, even if his employers are held to have owed no duty to the building employers, on what grounds can it be said that the employee himself owed no such duty? In my opinion, however, this particular point does not take the matter very much further. If in principle the sub-contractors owed no specific duty to the building owners in respect of damage by fire, then neither in my opinion can any of their employees have done so.

In reply the defendants contend that the judge was right to hold that in all the circumstances there was no duty of care on the sub-contractors in this case. Alternatively they submit that the employers' insurers have no right of subrogation to entitle them to maintain this litigation against the sub-contractors . . .

[His Lordship discussed the cases on duty of care in the law of tort.]

In the instant case it is clear that as between the employer and the main contractor the former accepted the risk of damage by fire to its premises arising out of and in the course of the building works. Further, although there was no privity between the employer and the sub-contractor, it is equally clear from the documents passing between the main contractors and the sub-contractors to which I have already referred that the sub-contractors contracted on a like basis. In *Scottish Special Housing Association v Wimpey Construction UK Ltd* [1986] 2 All E.R. 957, [1986] 1 W.L.R. 995 the House of Lords had to consider whether, as between the employer and main contractors under a contract in precisely the same terms as those of the instant case, it was in truth intended that the employer should bear the whole risk of damage by fire, even fire caused by the contractor's negligence. The position of sub-contractors was not strictly in issue in the *Scottish Housing* case, which I cannot think the House did not appreciate, but having considered the terms of clauses 18, 19 and 20[C] of the same standard form as was used in the instant case Lord Keith, in a speech with which the remainder of their Lordships agreed, said ([1986] 2 All E.R. 957 at 959, [1986] 1 W.L.R. 995 at 999): "I have found it impossible to resist the conclusion that it is intended that the employer shall bear the whole risk of damage by fire, including fire caused by the negligence of the contractor or that of sub-contractors."

As Lord Keith went on to point out, a similar conclusion was arrived at by the Court of Appeal in England in *James Archdale & Co Ltd v Comservices Ltd* [1954] 1 All E.R. 210, [1954] 1 W.L.R. 459 on the construction of similarly but not identically worded corresponding clauses in a predecessor of the standard form used in the Scottish Housing and instant cases. Again the issue only arose in the earlier case as between employer and main contractor, but approaching the question on the basis of what is just and reasonable I do not think that the mere fact that there is no strict privity between the employer and the sub-contractor should prevent the latter from relying on the clear basis on which all the parties contracted in relation to damage to the employer's building caused by fire, even when due to the negligence of the contractors or sub-contractors.

Appeal Dismissed.

Questions

1. Were the sub-contractors insured against the loss? If not, may they not reasonably have omitted to insure in reliance on clause 20? Should that be relevant? Would it have assisted the defence of the first defendant, their employee?   **13–016**

2. Assuming that the plaintiffs fulfilled their obligation to insure, the action was brought for the benefit, not of the Norwich City Council, but for that of the insurers. If the action had succeeded, future sub-contractors in the same situation would have been well advised to insure against the same risk. Is that a result which the law should strive to avoid?

3. Can the decision be reconciled with *Scruttons Ltd v Midland Silicones*, which was cited in argument but not mentioned by the court? Is it easier for the court to hold that a duty of care in tort is negatived than to hold that a limitation clause is effective?

4. What do you think of the proposition that the sub-contractors had no duty to take care not to burn down the building? Suppose that the plaintiffs had discovered that the sub-contractors were following a dangerous practice. Would they have had no remedy?

Points for reflection

In *Cosgrove v Horsfall* (1945) 62 T.L.R. 140 CA, a bus driver was held liable to a passenger travelling on a free pass containing a term that neither the company nor its servants would be liable to him for injury, however caused; the driver "was not a party to and has no right by virtue of the licence or contract." In *Adler v Dickson* [1955] 1 Q.B. 158 CA, the captain and boatswain of a P. & O. steamship, Himalaya, were held liable for their negligence in causing injury to a passenger, notwithstanding a   **13–017** clause in the ticket that the company should not be liable for any injury. Denning LJ agreed in the result but, differing from his brethren, thought that the servants would have had a good defence if the clause had, in express terms, purported to cover them. (Such a clause is now commonly known as a 'Himalaya clause'.) This view is inconsistent with the speeches of the majority in *Scruttons Ltd v Midland Silicones Ltd* but in that case, too, it will be noted, the clause did not in express terms purport to cover the stevedores. (Cf. Furmston, 'Return to *Dunlop v Selfridge*?' (1960) 23 M.L.R. 373). And see *NZ Shipping Co v Satterthwaite* (above) and *Port Jackson v Salmond & Spraggon* (above).

In *Adler v Dickson* both Denning and Morris LJJ said that an injured party could be deprived of his rights at common law only by a contract. This is a difficult proposition to sustain (and Lord Denning seems to have had second thoughts in *Scruttons Ltd v Midland Silicones Ltd* above). Consider *Wilkie v LPTB* [1947] 1 All E.R. 258. In *Ashdown v Samuel Williams & Sons Ltd* [1957] 1 Q.B. 409 CA, it was held that an occupier had excluded his liability for the negligence of his servants towards a licensee by giving proper notice to her of the terms on which she might cross his land. The rules about notice laid down in *Parker v South Eastern Ry.* (above, Ch.7) were held to be equally applicable to the case of a non-contractual licence. No question was raised in that case as to the possible liability of the occupier's servants for their negligence; and *Cosgrove v Horsfall* clearly suggests that they would not be protected. See also *White v Blackmore* [1972] 2 Q.B. 651; [1972] 3 W.L.R. 296 CA.

----

3. ENFORCEMENT OF THE CONTRACT BY A CONTRACTOR FOR THE BENEFIT OF A NON-CONTRACTOR

13–018   In the situations represented by Cases 1 and 2 (above, Ch.12), there remains the possibility that B may be able to sue A for the benefit of C. If the contract is a specifically enforceable one, B may be able to obtain a decree that A carry out the contract for the benefit of C. If the contract is not specifically enforceable, B will be able to recover damages from A if A fails, in breach of contract, to confer the promised benefit on C. For example, in *Dunlop v Selfridge* (above), Selfridge's refusal to pay £5 to Dunlop was clearly a breach of contract with Dew for which Dew could have recovered damages. The difficulty is that B (in that case, Dew) will usually have suffered no damage and so, prima facie, will be entitled only to nominal damages. (See, however Lord Pearce in *Beswick v Beswick*, below. Where B has contracted as trustee for C the contractual right against A belongs in law to B but in equity to C and B can then recover the substantial damages which belong in equity to C and C himself may sue).

BESWICK v BESWICK

House of Lords [1968] A.C. 58; [1967] 2 All E.R. 1197; [1967] 3 W.L.R. 932

13–019   Peter Beswick was assisted in his business of coal merchant by his nephew, the defendant. In March 1962, when Peter was over seventy and in ill-health, he entered into an agreement with the defendant under which he assigned the business to the defendant in consideration of the defendant employing him as consultant for the remainder of his life at £6 10s. 0d a week and paying an annuity of £5 a week to his widow after his death, to be charged on the business. Peter died in November 1963. The defendant paid the widow the first £5 but thereafter refused to pay any more. The widow sued as administratrix of her husband's estate and in her personal capacity for arrears of the annuity, for a declaration and for specific performance of the agreement. Burgess VC in the Chancery Court of the County Palatine of Lancaster dismissed the action: [1965] 3 All E.R. 858. The plaintiff appealed. The Court of Appeal (Denning MR, Danckwerts and Salmon LJJ) allowed the appeal, declaring that the agreement to pay the annuity should be specifically enforced. The defendant appealed to the House of Lords. It was not argued in the House that the widow was entitled to enforce her claim at common law in her own name.

LORD REID

[Having stated the facts and the arguments of the appellant:] the respondent's first answer is that the common law has been radically altered by section 56(1) of the Law of Property Act 1925, and that that section entitles her to sue in her personal capacity and recover the benefit provided for her in the agreement although she was not a party to it.

[Having considered the background to s.56, particularly s.5 of the Real Property Act 1845 which it replaced, his Lordship proceeded:]

"A person may take an immediate or other interest in land or other property, or the benefit of any condition, right of entry, covenant or agreement over or respecting land or other property, although he may not be named as a party to the conveyance or other instrument. . . ."

If the matter stopped there it would not be difficult to hold that section 56 does not substantially extend or alter the provisions of section 5 of the Act of 1845. But more difficulty is introduced by the definition section of the Act of 1925 (section 205) which provides:

"(1) In this Act unless the context otherwise requires, the following expressions have the meanings hereby assigned to them respectively, that is to say: . . . "Property includes any thing in action, and any interest in real or personal property."

[His Lordship discussed earlier authorities on s.56.]

I can now return to consider the meaning and scope of section 56. It refers to any "agreement over or respecting land or other property." If "land or other property" means the same thing as "tenements or hereditaments" in the Act of 1845 then this section simply continues the law as it was before the Act of 1925 was passed, for I do not think that the other differences in phraseology can be regarded as making any substantial change. So any obscurities in section 56 are obscurities which originated in 1845 . . .

Perhaps more important is the fact that the section does not say that a person may take the benefit of an agreement although he was not a party to it: it says that he may do so although he was not named as a party in the instrument which embodied the agreement . . . if the definition [of "property" in s.205(1), above] is applied the result is to make section 56 go far beyond the pre-existing law. Holding that the section has such an effect would involve holding that the invariable practice of Parliament has been departed from per incuriam, so that something has got into this consolidation Act which neither the draftsman nor parliament can have intended to be there. I am reinforced in this view by two facts. The language of section 56 is not at all what one would have expected if the intention had been to bring in all that the application of the definition would bring in and, secondly, section 56 is one of twenty-five sections which appear in the Act under the cross-heading "Conveyances and other Instruments." The other twenty-four sections come appropriately under that heading and so does section 56 if it has a limited meaning: but, if its scope is extended by the definition of property, it would be quite inappropriately placed in this part of the Act. For these reasons I am of opinion that section 56 has no application to the present case.

The respondent's second argument is that she is entitled in her capacity of administratrix of her deceased husband's estate to enforce the provision of the agreement for the benefit of herself in her personal capacity, and that a proper way of enforcing that provision is to order specific performance. That would produce a just result, and, unless there is some technical objection, I am of opinion that specific performance ought to be ordered . . . This appeal should be dismissed.

Lords Hodson and Guest delivered speeches holding that section 56 excludes the definition of "property" in section 205(1) and is confined to real property; but that the respondent was entitled to a decree of specific performance.

LORD PEARCE

My Lords, if the annuity had been payable to a third party in the lifetime of Beswick senior and there had been default, he could have sued in respect of the breach. His administratrix is now entitled to stand in his shoes and to sue in respect of the breach which has occurred since his death. It is argued that the estate can recover only nominal damages and that no other remedy is open, either to the estate or to the personal plaintiff. Such a result would be wholly repugnant to justice and common sense. And if the argument were right it would show a very serious defect in the law.

In the first place, I do not accept the view that damages must be nominal. Lush L.J. in *Lloyd's v Harper* [below] said:

"Then the next question which, no doubt, is a very important and substantial one, is, that Lloyd's, having sustained no damage themselves, could not recover for the losses sustained by third parties by reason of the default of Robert Henry Harper as an underwriter. That, to my mind, is a startling and alarming doctrine, and a novelty, because I consider it to be an established rule of law that where a contract is made with A for the benefit of B, A can sue on the contract for the benefit of B, and recover all that B could have recovered if the contract had been made with B himself."

(See also *Drimmie v Davies* [1899] 1 I.R. 176.) I agree with the comment of Windeyer J. in the case of *Coulls v Bagot's Executor and Trustee Co, Ltd* (1967) 40 A.L.J.R. 471, 486, in the High Court of Australia that the words of Lush L.J. cannot be accepted without qualification and regardless of context and also with his statement:

"I can see no reason why in such cases the damages which A would suffer upon B's breach of his contract to pay C $500 would be merely nominal: I think that in accordance with the ordinary rules for the assessment of damages for breach of contract they could be substantial. They would not necessarily be $500; they could I think be less or more."

In the present case I think that the damages, if assessed, must be substantial. It is not necessary, however, to consider the amount of damages more closely since this is a case in which, as the Court of Appeal rightly decided, the more appropriate remedy is that of specific performance.

The administratrix is entitled, if she so prefers, to enforce the agreement rather than accept its repudiation, and specific performance is more convenient than an action for arrears of payment followed by separate actions as each sum falls due. Moreover, damages for breach would be a less appropriate remedy since the parties to the agreement were intending an annuity for a widow; and a lump sum of damages does not accord with this. And if (contrary to my view) the argument that a derisory sum of damages is all that can be obtained be right, the remedy of damages in this case is manifestly useless.

The present case presents all the features which led the equity courts to apply their remedy of specific performance. The contract was for the sale of a business. The defendant could on his part clearly have obtained specific performance of it if Beswick senior or his administratrix had defaulted. Mutuality is a ground in favour of specific performance.

Moreover, the defendant on his side has received the whole benefit of the contract and it is a matter of conscience for the court to see that he now performs his part of it. Kay J. said in *Hart v Hart* (1881) 18 Ch.D. 670 at p. 685:

". . . when an agreement for valuable consideration . . . has been partially performed, the court ought to do its utmost to carry out that agreement by a decree for specific performance."

What, then, is the obstacle to granting specific performance? It is argued that since the widow personally had no rights which she personally could enforce the court will not make an order which will have the effect of enforcing those rights. I can find no principle to this effect. The condition as to payment of an annuity to the widow personally was valid. The estate (though not the widow personally) can enforce it. Why should the estate be barred from exercising its full contractual rights merely because in doing so it secures justice for the widow who, by a mechanical defect of our law, is unable to assert her own rights? Such a principle would be repugnant to justice and fulfil no other object than that of aiding the wrongdoer. I can find no ground on which such a principle should exist.

[Having discussed previous authorities, his Lordship continued:]

Recently in *Coulls v Bagot's Executor and Trustee Co, Ltd* the learned Chief Justice of Australia, Sir Garfield Barwick, in commenting on the report of the Court of Appeal's decision in the present case, said:

"I would myself, with great respect, agree with the conclusion that where A promises B for a consideration supplied by B to pay C that B may obtain specific performance of A's promise, at least where the nature of the consideration given would have allowed the debtor to have obtained specific performance. I can see no reason whatever why A in those circumstances should not be bound to perform his promise. That C provided no part of the consideration seems to me irrelevant."

It is argued that the court should be deterred from making the order because there will be technical difficulties in enforcing it. In my opinion, the court should not lightly be deterred by such a consideration from making an order which justice requires. But I do not find this difficulty.

R.S.C., Ord. 45, r. 9(1), provides under the heading "Execution by or against a person not being a party":

"Any person not being a party to a cause or matter, who obtains any order or in whose favour any order is made, shall be entitled to enforce obedience to the order by the same process as if he were a party."

This would appear by its wide terms to enable the widow for whose benefit the annuity is ordered to enforce its payment by the appointment of a receiver, by writ of fi. fa., or even by judgment summons. I see no reason to limit the apparent meaning of the words of the rule, which would appear to achieve a sensible purpose.

In my opinion, the plaintiff as administratrix is entitled to a decree of specific performance. [His Lordship went on to hold that s.56 had no relevance to the case. He was inclined to the view of the section expressed by Lord Upjohn.]

Lord Upjohn [having held that the plaintiff was entitled to a decree of specific performance and having considered the history behind s.56:] Bearing in mind the wide import of the word "property" apart from any definition, I find it difficult in the context to limit that word to an interest in real property. Without expressing any concluded view, I think it may be that the true answer is that Parliament (as sometimes happens in consolidation statutes) inadvertently did alter the law in section 56 by abrogating the old common law rule in respect of contracts affecting personal property as well as real property. But it cannot have done more. Parliament per incuriam it may be, went back to the position under the Act of 1845 but I am convinced that it never intended to alter the fundamental rule laid down in *Tweddle v Atkinson* [above, Ch.12].

The real difficulty is as to the true scope and ambit of the section. My present views, though obiter and tentative, are these. Section 56, like its predecessors, was only intended to sweep away the old common law rule that in an indenture inter partes the covenantee must be named as a party to the indenture to take the benefit of an immediate grant or the benefit of a covenant; it intended no more. So that for the section to have any application it must be to relieve from the consequences of the common law, and in my opinion three conditions must be satisfied. If all of them are not satisfied then the section has no application and the parties are left to their remedies at common law.

First let me assume for a moment that the agreement in this case is an indenture inter partes under seal—does section 56 help B? Plainly not. C did not purport to covenant with or make any grant to B; he only covenanted with A. Had C purported to covenant with B to pay the annuity to B though B was not a party, then any difficulty B might have had in suing might be saved by section 56.

The narrow view which I take of section 56 is, I think, supported by the observations of Simonds J. (as he then was) in *White v Bijou Mansions* [1937] Ch. 610 when he said:

"Just as under section 5 of the Act of 1845 only that person could call it in aid who, although not a party, was a grantee or covenantee, so under section 56 of this Act only that person can call it in aid, who, although not named as a party to the conveyance or other instrument, is yet a person to whom that conveyance or other instrument purports to grant some thing or with which some agreement or covenant is purported to be made."

See to the same effect Wynn-Parry J. in *Re Miller's Agreement* [1947] Ch. 615. That was another example of the familiar case where, upon the dissolution of a partnership, the continuing partners covenanted with the retiring partner to pay as from his death annuities to his three daughters. the learned judge said:

"In my view the plaintiffs [the daughters] are not persons to whom the deed purports to grant something, or with whom some agreement or covenant is purported to be made. . . ."

So B does not satisfy this condition.

The second condition is that the reference to the "conveyance or other instrument" in the section is, in my opinion, limited to documents under seal. This does no violence to the definitions of "conveyance" or "instrument" in section 205 of the Law of Property Act.

The third condition is that, in my opinion, the section refers only to documents strictly inter partes (*Cooker v Child* (1673) 2 Lev. 74).

The agreement satisfies none of these conditions.

Section 56 does not help the appellant, but, for reasons given earlier, I would dismiss this appeal.

Appeal Dismissed.

Questions

13-020

1. Lord Pearce, above, seems to have been alone in thinking that substantial damages might have been recoverable. In a simple contract by A with B to pay C £500, how would the damages be estimated? On the basis of B's loss of gratification at the benefit to C? How could that be evaluated? Or on the basis of the consideration supplied to A by B and now 'wasted'? Cf. the cases on damages for wasted expenditure, below Ch.19.

2. If the deceased had appointed an executor who had declined to sue the nephew, would the widow have had any remedy?

3. Suppose the hypothetical executor had agreed to release the nephew from his obligation to pay the annuity, in consideration of the payment of £100, which he had then applied for the benefit of those entitled (not the widow) under the supposed will. Would the widow have had any redress? Cf. *Re Schebsman* [1944] Ch. 83.

4. Would s.56, in the opinion of any of the judges, have enabled the plaintiff in *Tweddle v Atkinson* (above) to succeed?

5. Might the widow now have been able to rely on the 1999 Act?

6. C grants a lease to B who grants an underlease to A. A covenants with B (a) to keep the premises in repair and to permit C and B to enter the premises and to view the state of repair; (b) to remedy any defects within 3 months of being given notice or to reimburse B or C for doing so. In *Amsprop Trading Ltd v Harris Distribution Ltd* [1997] 2 All E.R. 990 the question was whether C could enforce the covenant to repair directly against A. C relied on s.56 of the Law of Property Act 1925. Neuberger J, considering *Beswick v Beswick*, held that s.56 allowed a person who was not named as a party to a covenant to sue, only if the covenant purported to be made with him. It was not enough to show that the covenant was made for his benefit. Would C have a better chance of success under the 1999 Act?

JACKSON V HORIZON HOLIDAYS LTD

Court of Appeal [1975] 1 W.L.R. 1468; [1975] 3 All E.R. 92

13-021 The plaintiff entered into a contract for a holiday for himself, his wife and two children, in Ceylon. The price including air fares was £1,200. The holiday provided failed to comply with the description given by the defendants in important respects. The judge, following *Jarvis v Swan's Tours Ltd* below para.19–022, awarded £1,100 damages. He said that he could only consider the distress to the plaintiff, not that to the wife and children. The defendants appealed against the amount of the damages.

LORD DENNING MR

[Dealing with a submission that the plaintiff was entitled to damages for his wife and children:]

We have had an interesting discussion as to the legal position when one person makes a contract for the benefit of a party. In this case it was a husband making a contract for the benefit of himself, his wife and children. Other cases readily come to mind. A host makes a contract with a restaurant for a dinner for himself and his friends. The vicar makes a contract for a coach trip for the choir. In all these cases there is only one person who makes the contract. It is the husband, the host, or the vicar, as the case may be. Sometimes he pays the whole price himself. Occasionally he may get a contribution from the others. But in any case it is he who makes the contract. It would be a fiction to say that the contract was made by all the family, or all the guests, or all the choir, and that he was only an agent for them. Take this very case. It would be absurd to say that the twins of three years old were parties to the contract or that the father was making the contract on their behalf as if they were principals. It would equally be a mistake to say that in any of these instances there was a trust. The transaction bears no resemblance to a trust. There was no trust fund and no trust property. No, the real truth is that in each instance, the father, the host or the vicar, was making a contract himself for the benefit of the whole party. In short, a contract by one for the benefit of third persons.

What is the position when such a contract is broken? At present the law says that the only one who can sue is the one who made the contract. None of the rest of the party can sue, even though the contract was made for their benefit. But when that one does sue, what damages can he recover? Is he limited to his own loss? Or can he recover for the others? Suppose the holiday firm puts the family into a hotel which is only half built and the visitors have to sleep on the floor? Or suppose the restaurant is fully booked and the guests have to go away, hungry and angry, having spent so much on fares to get there? Or suppose the coach leaves the choir stranded half-way and they have to hire cars to get home? None of them individually can sue. Only the father, the host or the vicar can sue. He can, of course, recover his own damages. But can he not recover for the others? I think he can. The case comes within the principle stated by Lush L.J. in *Lloyd's v Harper* ". . . I consider it to be an established rule of law that where a contract is made with A. for the benefit of B., A. can sue on the contract for the benefit of B. and recover all that B. could have recovered if the contract had been made with B. himself." It has been suggested that Lush L.J. was thinking of a contract in which A. was trustee for B. But I do not think so. He was a common lawyer speaking of the common law. His words were quoted with considerable approval by Lord Pearce in *Beswick v Beswick*. I have myself often quoted them. I think they should be accepted as correct, at any rate so long as the law forbids the third persons themselves to sue for damages. It is the only way in which a just result can be achieved. Take the instance I have put. The guests ought to recover from the restaurant their wasted fares. The choir ought to recover the cost of hiring the taxis home. There is no one to recover for them except the one who made the contract for their benefit. He should be able to recover the expense to which they have been put, and pay it over to them. Once recovered, it will be money had and received to their use. (They might even, if desired, be joined as plaintiffs.) If he can recover for the expense, he should also be able to recover for the discomfort, vexation and upset which the whole party have suffered by reason of the breach of contract, recompensing them accordingly out of what he recovers.

Applying the principles to this case, I think that the figure of £1,100 was about right. It would, I think, have been excessive if it had been awarded only for the damage suffered by Mr Jackson himself. But when extended to his wife and children I do not think it is excessive . . .

I would therefore dismiss this appeal.

ORR LJ

I agree.

James L.J. delivered judgment dismissing the appeal.

Appeal Dismissed.

Question

George, the secretary of the University Law Society arranged the Society's annual dinner at the Majestic Hotel. All the diners suffered food poisoning but there was no negligence on the part of the Hotel. All the members of the Society paid for their meals but their guests, Box and Cox LJJ, did not. What damages can be recovered and by whom?   **13–022**

Points for reflection

In *Woodar Investment Development Ltd v Wimpey Construction UK Ltd* [1980] 1 W.L.R. 277; 1 All E.R. 571; Lord Wilberforce 'explained' *Jackson* as follows: **13–023**

"The majority of the Court of Appeal followed, in the case of Goff L.J. with expressed reluctance, its previous decision in *Jackson v Horizon Holidays Ltd*. I am not prepared to dissent from the actual decision in that case. It may be supported either as a broad decision on the measure of damages [per James LJ] or possibly as an example of a type of contract—examples of which are persons contracting for family holidays, ordering meals in restaurants for a party, hiring a taxi for a group— calling for special treatment. As I suggested in *New Zealand Shipping Co Ltd v A.M. Satterthwaite & Co, Ltd*, there are many situations of daily life which do not fit neatly into conceptual analysis, but which require some flexibility in the law of contract. *Jackson's* case may well be one.

I cannot however agree with the basis on which Lord Denning M.R. put his decision in that case. The extract on which he relied from the judgment of Lush L.J. in *Lloyd's v Harper* (1880) 16 Ch.D. 290, 321 was part of a passage in which the Lord Justice was stating as an 'established rule of law' that an agent (sc. an insurance broker) may sue on a contract made by him on behalf of the principal (sc. the assured) if the contract gives him such a right, and is no authority for the proposition required in Jackson's case, still less for the proposition required here, that, if Woodar made a contract for a sum of money to be paid to Transworld, Woodar can, without showing that it has itself suffered loss or that Woodar was agent or trustee for Transworld, sue for damages for non-payment of that sum. That would certainly not be an established rule of law, nor was it quoted as such authority by Lord Pearce in *Beswick v Beswick*."

Lord Russell of Killowen, while dissenting from the decision, said:

"I do not criticise the outcome of Jackson's case: the plaintiff had bought and paid for a high class family holiday, he did not get it, and therefore was entitled to substantial damages for the failure to supply him with one. It is to be observed that the order of the Court of Appeal as drawn up did not suggest that any part of the damages awarded to him were 'for the use and benefit of' any member of his family. It was a special case quite different from the instant case on the Transworld point.

I would not, my Lords, wish to leave the Jackson case without adverting with respectful disapproval to the reliance there placed by Lord Denning M.R.—not for the first time—on an extract taken from the judgment of Lush L.J. in *Lloyd's v Harper*. That case was plainly a case in which a trustee or agent was enforcing the rights of a beneficiary or principal, there being therefore a fiduciary relationship.

[His Lordship cited Lord Denning's discussion of *Lloyd's v Harper*.]

I have already indicated that in all the other judgments the matter proceeded upon a fiduciary relationship between A and B: and Lush L.J. in the same passage makes it plain that he does also; for he says: 'It is true that the person [B] who employed him [the broker A] has a right, if he pleases, to take action himself and sue upon the contract made by the broker for him, for he [B] is a principal party to the contract.'

To ignore that passage is to divorce the passage quoted by Lord Denning from the fiduciary context in which it was uttered, the context of principal and agent, a field with which it may be assumed Lush L.J. was familiar. I venture to suggest that the brief quotation should not be used again as support for a proposition which Lush L.J. cannot have intended to advance."

For other aspects of *Woodar* see below, Ch.18. See also Rose, 1977, Can. Bar. Rev. 333.

DARLINGTON BOROUGH COUNCIL v WILTSHIER NORTHERN LTD AND ANOTHER

Court of Appeal [1995] 1 W.L.R. 68; [1995] 3 All E. R. 895

W entered into contracts with MG, a finance company, to build, and built, a recreational centre for the Council on the Council's land. The Council resorted to this method of financing the project to avoid government restrictions on borrowing. In accordance with an agreement with the Council, MG assigned to the Council all rights and causes of action against W arising out of the contracts with MG. The Council claimed that the building work was defective. As assignee of MG's rights, they would be able to recover only such damages as MG might have recovered. On a preliminary issue as to the Council's right of action, Judge Newcy QC held that MG, having no proprietary right in the Centre and not being liable for the cost of repairs, could have recovered only nominal damages. The Council appealed.

13–024

> Dillon L.J. said that he would allow the appeal by the direct application of the rule in *Dunlop v Lambert* (1839) 6 Cl. & F. 600 HL (discussed by Steyn L.J., below) as applied in a building contract context in Lord Browne-Wilkinson's speech in *Linden Gardens Trust Ltd v Lenesta Sludge Disposals Ltd* [1994] A.C. 85 at 114–115; and added that if, before any assignment, MG had sued in its own name it would have recovered damages as constructive trustee for the Council, by analogy to *Lloyds v Harper*.

STEYN LJ

[Having discussed the need for reform of the law (now effected by the 1999 Act) and the issues in the present case, his Lordship continued] That brings me to the speech of Lord Browne-Wilkinson in the *Linden Gardens* case [1994] A.C. 85. In his speech Lord Browne-Wilkinson rested his decision on the exception to the rule that a plaintiff can only recover damages for his own loss which was enunciated in *The Albazero* [1977] A.C. 774 in the context of carriage of goods by sea, bills of lading and bailment. The relevant passage from Lord Diplock's speech in *The Albazero* reads, at p. 847:

> "The only way in which I find it possible to rationalise the rule in *Dunlop v Lambert* so that it may fit into the pattern of the English law is to treat it as an application of the principle, accepted also in relation to policies of insurance upon goods, that in a commercial contract concerning goods where it is in the contemplation of the parties that the proprietary interests in the goods may be transferred from one owner to another after the contract has been entered into and before the breach which causes loss or damage to the goods, an original party to the contract, if such be the intention of them both, is to be treated in law as having entered into the contract for the benefit of all persons who have or may acquire an interest in the goods before they are lost or damaged, and is entitled to recover by way of damages for breach of contract the actual loss sustained by those for whose benefit the contract is entered into."

Clearly, this passage did not exactly fit the material facts in the *Linden Gardens* case. But Lord Browne-Wilkinson extracted the rationale of the decision and by analogy applied it to the purely contractual situation in *Linden Gardens*. He particularly justified this extension of the exception in *The Albazero* by invoking Lord Diplock's words in *The Albazero*:

> "there may still be occasional cases in which the rule would provide a remedy where no other would be available to a person sustaining loss which under a rational legal system ought to be compensated by the person who has caused it."

Lord Browne-Wilkinson's conclusion was supported by all members of the House of Lords, although, it is right to say, Lord Griffiths wished to go further. Relying on the exception recognised in the *Linden Gardens* case, as well as on the need to avoid a demonstrable unfairness which no rational legal system should tolerate, I would rule that the present case is within the rationale of Lord Browne-Wilkinson's speech. I do not say that the relevant passages in his speech precisely fit the material facts of the present case. But it involves only a very conservative and limited extension to apply it by analogy to the present case. For these reasons I would hold that the present case is covered by an exception to the general rule that a plaintiff can only recover damages for his own loss.

Waite L.J. agreed with Dillon and Steyn L.JJ. that the appeal be allowed by the direct application of the rule in *Dunlop v Lambert* and also on the constructive trust ground mentioned by Dillon L.J.

Appeal Allowed.

Point for reflection

13-025   In one of the most complex cases of recent years, *Alfred McAlpine Construction Ltd v Panatown Ltd* [2001] A.C. 518, an important limit to the *Linden Gardens* exception was established. In *Panatown*, the question was the standard one: namely, whether, where A (McAlpine), who has contracted with B (Panatown), is in breach of contract, B may recover damages for the losses suffered by C (a third-party, having no contract with A, but on whose land the contracted building work has been carried out). However, the twist in this case was that A had entered into a duty of care deed with C, the effect of which was to give C an independent and direct line of recourse against A. In these circumstances, the majority of the House of Lords held that there was no reason to resort to the *Linden Gardens* exception; accordingly, B had no right to recover from A anything more than its own financial losses.

----

4. PRIVITY OF CONTRACT AND THE TRUST CONCEPT

13-026   If it can be shown that, in a contract made by A and B whereby A undertakes to do something for C, B was acting as trustee for C (that is, holding his contractual rights in trust for C) then C can directly enforce A's obligation in equity. Originating in the Old Court of Chancery (Cf. *Tomlinson v Gill* (1756) Amb. 330 and *Gregory and Parker v Williams* (1817) 3 Mer. 582), the principle was accepted after the Judicature Act 1873, in *Lloyd's v Harper* (above). In this case, Lloyd's and a creditor of an insolvent underwriter were allowed to sue on a guarantee which had been given to Lloyd's by a person then deceased, in respect of the liabilities which might be incurred by the underwriter. Whether or not Lush LJ in that case was a "common lawyer speaking of the common law" (as Lord Denning says (supra)), it is clear that Fry J at first instance and James and Cotton LJJ in the Court of Appeal proceeded on the basis that there was a trust. The possibility of implying a trust in a contract made by A for the benefit of C was confirmed by the acceptance of the concept by the House of Lords in *Les Affréteurs Réunis Société Anonyme v Leopold Walford (London) Ltd*, below, though there are abundant instances of the use of the concept before that decision. In *Walford's* case, indeed, it was held by the House of Lords that C could sue in his own name without joining the other contracting party. While it is a convenient way of in fact allowing a third party to secure an enforceable benefit under a contract, the use of the concept depends upon the readiness of the court to construe a trust in such cases. Hence there has been a number of seemingly inconsistent decisions (see, for example, *Re Flavell* (1883) 25 Ch.D.89 and *Re Englebach's Estate* [1924] 2 Ch. 348) showing the doctrine of the implied trust to be one of uncertain application—on this, see Corbin, 'Contracts for the Benefit of Third Persons' 46 LQR 12 and Williams, 'Contracts for Third Parties' 7 MLR 123.

Historically, the turning point in the use of the trust concept was *Vandepitte v Preferred Accident Insurance Corporation of New York* [1933] A.C. 70, a decision of the Judicial Committee of the Privy Council. In that case, V had incurred injuries in a motor accident and recovered judgment against B, a minor who had been driving her father's vehicle with his permission. B's father had insured his car with the respondent company which undertook to indemnify him and those driving his car with his permission. A British Columbia statute provided that where someone recovered judgment for injury or damage against an insured person and the judgment was unsatisfied, the judgment creditor could proceed against the insurers for the amount of the judgment. V's judgment against B remaining unsatisfied, V brought the present action against the respondents, arguing that B was insured by them, either as a party directly to the insurance contract which had been effected by her father or as cestui que trust of the promise of indemnity made by the respondents in the contract with B's father. The Judicial Committee of the Privy Council rejected both contentions.

B could be a direct party to the insurance contract only if she had had animus contrahendi but she had had no part in the contract which had been concluded entirely by her father and the respondents; on the second contention in the words of Lord Wright, "the intention to constitute a trust must be affirmatively proved; the intention cannot necessarily be inferred from the mere general words of the policy . . ."

There followed a long period in which the trust concept was scarcely mentioned in the context of third party beneficiaries of a contract. Thus, Lord Greene M.R. in *Re Schebsman* [1944] Ch. 83—the first case fairly to raise the issue after *Vandepitte*—said, "it is not legitimate to import into the contract the idea of a trust when the parties have given no indication that such was their intention. To interpret this contract as creating a trust would, in my judgment, be to disregard the dividing line between the case of a trust and the simple case of a contract made between two persons for the benefit of a third." Subsequent cases have shown a similar disregard for the trust concept: for example, *Green v Russell* [1959] 2 Q.B. 229, where an employer, B, insured the life of his employee, C, with A who agreed to pay the insurance money to C's representatives; the Court of Appeal held that neither C nor his representatives had any right in law or equity to recover the insurance money. The concept does not even appear in *Beswick v Beswick* in the House of Lords (above). Not the least reason why the trust concept has found relatively little favour is the irrevocability of a trust. If the court finds that a trust in favour of C has been created by a contract between A and B, it is in effect saying that A and B have put it out of their power to alter or modify their own positions in the future.

Nevertheless, the trust concept cannot be regarded as defunct (see the opinions of Dillon and Waite LJJ in the *Darlington* case, above). But the Law Commission thought it most unlikely that the case will herald a swing back to the old approach to trusts of a promise: Law Com. No.242, para.2.9. In *A. Tomlinson (Hauliers) Ltd v Hepburn* [1966] A.C. 451, the plaintiffs entered into a contract with Imperial Tobacco subsidiary, Players, whereby they agreed to carry goods and to insure them comprehensively while in transit. The plaintiffs insured the goods with the defendant. Two lorry loads of cigarettes were stolen without any fault on the part of the plaintiffs. The plaintiffs claimed the full value of the goods lost. The defendant contended that the policy covered only the liability which the plaintiffs might incur to Players; and they incurred none.

The Court of Appeal [1966] 1 Q.B. 21, affirming Roskill J, decided for the plaintiffs. They held that, where B and C each has an insurable interest in goods and B effects a policy covering the totality of the insurable interest, intending to insure C's as well as his own interest, B may sue on the policy as trustee for C. Distinguishing *Green v Russell* (above), Pearson LJ said (at 51): "The distinguishing feature of the present case . . . is that where two persons, bailor and bailee, having [sic] concurrent interests in the same goods, so that it would be reasonable and natural and economical for one of them to insure for the benefit of both. In the sphere of insurance on goods, it would be unrealistic and productive of injustice to require from the party taking out the insurance an express declaration or conscious assumption of trusteeship. The existence of the intention is sufficient."

Affirming the decision, the House of Lords ([1966] A.C. 451) regarded the case as one depending on a special rule governing the insurance of goods by a bailee for the benefit of a bailor rather than as an application of the trust concept. Lord Reid said (at 470–471): "No doubt the principle preventing just quaesitum tertio has been firmly established for at least half a century. But it does not appear to me to be a primeval or necessary principle of the law of England. We must uphold it until it is altered.

But I do not think that we are bound to be astute to extend it on a logical basis so as to cut down an exception, if it be an exceptions . . .". Lord Pearce drew attention to the special position of the bailee of goods who has a right to sue for conversion and said (at 480): "It would seem irrational, therefore, if he could not also insure for their full value." However the dictum of Pearson LJ be regarded in the future, the circumstances of 'insurance of goods' cases are manifestly distinguishable from the *Vandepitte, Re Schebsman, Beswick* situations.

But while rejecting the possible enforcement of the contract by the intended third party beneficiary himself these later cases have established that the performance of the agreement by the contracting party for the benefit of the third party—although it would have been unenforceable by that party—is in itself a valid performance of the contract with the other contracting party. This has had peripheral consequences illustrated by *Re Schebsman* (infra) and *Re Miller's Agreement* [1947] Ch. 615. In that case, a deed of dissolution of partnership between A, B, and C, on the retiral of A, provided that A transferred his share of the goodwill to B and C in consideration of a lump sum and an annuity for life and a covenant that B and C would pay certain annuities to A's daughters. B and C entered into a covenant to pay annuities as from A's death. On A's death, B, and C did pay the annuities to A's daughters. The question was whether the daughters were liable to pay estate and succession duty in respect of the annuities. Wynn-Parry J, holding that the covenants, being res inter alios acta, gave the daughters no interest in property that would be protected in a court of law or equity, held that the payments to them by B and C were gratuitous and so attracted neither duty.

5. The Imposition of Burdens on Third Parties

13-027   It would be surprising if a contract between A and B could impose burdens or obligations on C and the general principle is that it cannot do so (but cf. *Morris v Martin*, above) The only established exceptions to this rule are part of the law of property rather than that of contract. Covenants in a lease are binding not only on the original parties but also on their successors in title: Landlord and Tenant (Covenants) Act 1995. In addition, covenants restricting the use of land are binding in equity not only on the original covenantor but also on subsequent purchasers of the land with notice of the covenant, provided that the covenantee has retained other land for the benefit of which the covenant was taken. This is the doctrine of *Tulk v Moxhay* (1848) 2 Ph. 74. In *Taddy v Sterious* [1904] 1 Ch. 354 Swinfen Eady J declined to extend a similar principle to goods. The plaintiffs, manufacturers of tobacco, attached a notice to each packet stating that it was sold on the express condition that retailers would not sell it below stipulated prices, adding that:

"acceptance of the goods will be deemed a contract between the purchaser and Taddy & Co that he will observe these stipulations. In the case of a purchase by a retail dealer through a wholesale dealer, the latter shall be deemed to be the agent of Taddy & Co."

The defendants who had purchased through a wholesaler with notice of the conditions were held not bound by them.

Suppose that a publisher of paperback books inserts the following notice in the front of the book:

"This book is sold subject to the condition that it shall not, by way of trade or otherwise, be lent, re-sold, hired out, or otherwise circulated without the publisher's prior consent in any form of binding or cover other than that in which it is published and without a similar condition including this condition being imposed on the subsequent purchaser."

Would this notice be binding on C who purchases the book from a retailer and wishes to re-bind it and use it in a private lending library. In *De Mattos v Gibson* (1858) 4 De G. & J. 276 at 282 the following broad principle of 'reason and justice' was enunciated:

"Reason and justice seem to prescribe that, at least as a general rule, where a man, by gift or purchase, acquires property from another, with knowledge of a previous contract, lawfully and for valuable consideration made by him with a third person, to use and employ the property for a particular purpose in a specified manner, the acquirer shall not, to the material damage of the third person, in opposition to the contract and inconsistently with it, use and employ the property in a manner not allowable to the giver or seller. This rule, applicable alike in general as I conceive to moveable and immoveable property, and recognised and adopted, as I apprehend, by the English law, may, like other general rules, be liable to exceptions arising from special circumstances; but I see at present no room for any exception in the instance before us."

The validity of this principle is, to say the least, controversial. It has received its fullest judicial consideration in the following judgment of Browne-Wilkinson J. (The case subsequently went to the Court of Appeal and the House of Lords [1981] 2 W.L.R. 893; [1981] 2 All E.R. 449, which decided the case on other grounds, not affecting this aspect of Browne-Wilkinson J's opinion. The facts of the case are omitted.)

SWISS BANK CORPORATION v LLOYDS BANK LTD

Chancery Division [1979] 3 W.L.R. 201; [1979] 2 All E.R. 853

BROWNE-WILKINSON J

How then do the authorities stand? In *De Mattos v Gibson* itself the plaintiff had chartered a ship from its owner Curry. Curry had subsequently charged the ship to Gibson, who had actual notice of the charterparty. Curry got into financial difficulties and was unable to continue the voyage. Gibson was proposing to sell the ship of which he had taken possession. In the action the plaintiff claimed an injunction against Gibson restraining him from interfering with the charterparty. The plaintiff applied for an interim injunction, which was granted on appeal. The grounds for the decision of Knight Bruce L.J. were those set out in the passage [quoted, above]. The decision of Turner L.J. was founded entirely on balance of convenience, but one of the three questions he said would have to be decided at the trial was whether the plaintiff, even if not entitled to specific performance of the charterparty, was entitled to an injunction to restrain a breach of the charterparty. In due course the action came on for trial before Page Wood V.-C. (from whose decision there was an appeal to the Lord Chancellor). Lord Chelmsford L.C. held that no injunction should be granted against Gibson. He referred expressly to the three questions posed by Turner L.J., and after holding that the charterparty could not be specifically performed, said that Gibson having taken with full knowledge of the charter could be restrained from doing any act which would have the immediate effect of preventing its performance. But Lord Chelmsford L.C. went on to show that on the facts there was no real possibility of Curry performing the charterparty whatever Gibson did, and therefore there was no question of any act by Gibson constituting an interference by Gibson with the plaintiff's contractual rights. In my judgment that case is an authority binding on me that a person taking a charge on property which he knows to be subject to a contractual obligation can be restrained from exercising his rights under the charge in such a way as to interfere with the performance of that contractual obligation. In my judgment the *De Mattos v Gibson* principle is merely the equitable counterpart of the tort. But two points have to be emphasised about the decision in *De Mattos v Gibson*: first, the ship was acquired with actual knowledge of the plaintiff's contractual rights; secondly, that no such injunction will be granted against the third party if it is clear that the original contracting party cannot in any event perform his contract. It is this second point which in my judgment accounts for the fact that the *De Mattos v Gibson* principle is not applicable to restrictive covenants: the original contracting party (even if traceable) could not carry out his contract relating to the land, or the chattel once he had parted with it.

13-028

In *Lord Strathcona Steamship Co Ltd v Dominion Coal Co* [1926] A.C. 108 the facts were that a ship which was the subject-matter of a charterparty to Dominion was sold to Strathcona expressly subject to the rights of Dominion under the charterparty. The Privy Council held that an injunction could be granted restraining Strathcona from interfering with Dominion's rights under the charterparty. It will be noted that the *Strathcona* case is of the type I considered under category (b) above, that is, Strathcona bought expressly subject to Dominion's rights. And certainly one ground of decision is that, in the circumstances, Strathcona was a constructive trustee. It is not clear to me whether this was the only ground of decision since the passages in the judgment dealing with *De Mattos v Gibson* (which was held to be good law) certainly seem to proceed on the basis of knowing interference with another's contract. The Privy Council accepted that, in order to get an injunction, the plaintiff had to have a continuing interest in the property but undoubtedly held that a bare contractual right, as opposed to a property interest, was a sufficient interest for this purpose.

There are parts of the judgment in the *Strathcona* case which I find difficult to follow but in my judgment it certainly decides (i) that *De Mattos v Gibson* is good law and (ii) that an injunction can be granted to restrain a subsequent purchaser of a chattel from using it so as to cause a breach of a contract of which he has express notice.

In *Port Line Ltd v Ben Line Steamers Ltd* [1958] 2 Q.B. 146, 168 Diplock J. stated that he thought the *Strathcona* case was wrongly decided and refused to follow it. In that case Port had chartered a vessel from Silver. Silver then sold to Ben but subject to an immediate recharter by Ben to Silver. Under the charterparty between Port and Silver the requisitioning of the vessel did not determine the charter; under the charterparty between Ben and Silver it did. The vessel was requisitioned and Port was claiming from Ben compensation received by Ben for the requisition. It is important to notice that Port could only succeed if it showed either that it had a positive right to possession of the vessel or that Ben was accountable for the compensation as constructive trustee. Diplock J. was not concerned with the question whether Port was entitled to a negative injunction to restrain the tort.

It is not necessary for me to express any view as to whether the *Strathcona* case was rightly decided so far as it was a decision based on constructive trusteeship, which was all that Diplock J. was concerned with: the *Strathcona* case itself decided that there was no right to specific performance of the charterparty. However, although I of course differ from Diplock J. with diffidence, in my judgment the *Strathcona* case was rightly decided on the basis that Dominion was entitled to an injunction against Strathcona to prevent Strathcona from interfering with the contract between Dominion and the original charterer. Diplock J. explained *De Mattos v Gibson* on that ground and gave as an alternative ground for his decision that actual, as opposed to constructive, notice was necessary in such a case. To that extent his decision supports my own view.

In my judgment there is in any event a decision of the Court of Appeal which is binding on me, namely *Manchester Ship Canal Co v Manchester Racecourse Co* [1901] 2 Ch. 37. In that case the racecourse company had granted the canal company a right of first refusal over certain land. The racecourse company, without giving proper effect to such a right of first refusal, had entered into a contract to sell the land to a third party, Trafford. The Court of Appeal held (whether rightly or wrongly does not for this purpose matter) that the right of first refusal did not create any property interest in the land, but even so granted an injunction against Trafford restraining them from completing their contract to purchase. The Court of Appeal founded its decision expressly on the basis that Trafford, having full knowledge, was proposing to do something which would cause a breach of the contract between the canal company and the racecourse company, that is, to commit the tort. In my judgment this is a decision of the Court of Appeal that the court will restrain a person from enforcing his contractual rights so as to cause a breach of another contract of which he had full knowledge when he entered into his own contract. As such, it covers the present case. But it is to be noted that Trafford in that case had actual knowledge, as opposed to constructive notice, of the contract between the canal company and the racecourse company.

In *Binions v Evans* [1972] Ch. 359, 371 Megaw L.J. indicated that he thought the case could properly have been decided on the basis that an injunction to restrain the tort should be granted. This again supports the existence of the jurisdiction.

What then are the authorities which suggest that the *De Mattos v Gibson* principle is not good law? In my judgment apart from the *Port Line* case they are all cases falling within category (a) above; that is to say not cases in which the plaintiff sought an injunction to restrain the defendant from committing the tort but cases where the plaintiff was seeking to make the defendant positively perform a contract to which he was not a party. In particular, it is in my judgment, clear that the remarks of Scrutton J. (as he then was) in *London County Council v Allen* [1914] 3 K.B. 642 and Scrutton L.J. in *Barker v Stickney* [1919] 1 K.B. 121 are to be read in their context as cases where the plaintiff was seeking to enforce performance of the contract against the defendant who was not a party to the contract. So far as I can see, in neither of those cases was there any consideration of the rights of the plaintiff to a negative injunction restraining the defendant from causing someone else to breach the contract with the plaintiff.

Therefore, in my judgment the authorities establish the following propositions. (i) The principle stated by Knight Bruce L.J. in *De Mattos v Gibson* is good law and represents the counterpart in equity of the tort of knowing interference with contractual rights. (ii) A person proposing to deal with property in such a way as to cause a breach of a contract affecting that property will be restrained by injunction from so doing if when he acquired that property he had actual knowledge of that contract. (iii) A plaintiff is entitled to such an injunction even if he has no proprietary interest in the property: his right to have his contract performed is a sufficient interest. (iv) There is no case in which such an injunction has been granted against a defendant who acquired the property with only constructive, as opposed to actual, notice of the contract. In my judgment constructive notice is not sufficient, since actual knowledge of the contract is a requisite element in the tort.

----

6. Exceptions to the Doctrine of Privity

Some of the cases which are often treated as exceptions to the doctrine of privity are not really excep-   **13–029**
tions. *The Eurymedon* and *The New York Star* (above) do not create exceptions because the courts found, however deviously and improbably, that there was a separate contract between the shipper or consignee and the stevedore. Nor do the cases on collateral contracts such as *Shanklin v Detel Products* (below, Ch.15). In all these cases, C is found to be a contracting party, not the beneficiary of a contract between A and B. Whether the trust cases, above, and the doctrine of the undisclosed principal in the law of agency should be regarded as 'exceptions' is a matter of taste. Genuine exceptions to the rule so far encountered are:

1. The Contracts (Rights of Third Parties) Act 1999.

2. The *Elder Dempster* case, above.

3. The principle that a contract by the bailee in relation to the bailed goods may be binding on the bailor: *The Pioneer Container*, above.

4. The principle that a bailor can sue on a contract of insurance of the bailed goods made by the bailee for the benefit of the bailor: above.

   In addition, the following exceptions or quasi-exceptions should be noted.

5. The principle that, where A and B, when making a contract concerning B's goods or land, contemplate that B's proprietary interest may be transferred to another, (C), before the breach causes loss or damage, B may recover the loss sustained by C: *Dunlop v Lambert* as applied in the *Linden Gardens* and *Darlington* cases, above.

6. Assignment of contractual obligations. Both at law under the Law of Property Act 1925 s.136, and in equity it is possible for B to assign to C certain rights arising under a contract between A and B which C may then enforce against A.

7. Certain covenants in land law. Covenants in a lease of land granted by A to B bind successors in title of either party: Landlord and Tenant (Covenants) Act 1995. And see *Tulk v Moxhay*, above.

8. Statutory exceptions. In some cases Parliament has intervened to overcome what were seen to be injustices and inconveniences arising from the privity rule. The following are examples.

Married Women's Property Act 1882 s.11

13–030   A policy of assurance effected by any man on his own life and expressed to be for the benefit of his wife, or of his children, or of his wife and children, or any of them, or by any woman on her own life, and expressed to be for the benefit of her husband, or of her children, or of her husband and children, or any of them, shall create a trust in favour of the objects therein named, and the moneys payable under any such policy shall not, so long as any object of the trust remains unperformed, form part of the estate of the insured, or be subject to his or her debts

Marine Insurance Act 1906 s.14(2)

13–031   A mortgagee, consignee, or other person having an interest in the subject-matter insured may insure on behalf and for the benefit of other persons interested as well as for his own benefit

Law of Property Act 1925

13–032   **47**(1)—Where after the date of any contract for sale or exchange of property, money becomes payable under any policy of insurance maintained by the vendor in respect of any damage to or destruction of property included in the contract, the money shall, on completion of the contract, be held or receivable by the vendor on behalf of the purchaser and paid by the vendor to the purchaser on completion of the sale or exchange, or as soon thereafter as the same shall be received by the vendor.

56(1)—A person may take an immediate or other interest in land or other property, or the benefit of any condition, right of entry, covenant or agreement over or respecting land or other property, although he may not be named as a party to the conveyance or other instrument.

Public Passenger Vehicles Act 1981 s.29

13–033   A contract for the conveyance of a passenger in a public service vehicle shall, so far as it purports to negative or to restrict the liability of a person in respect of a claim which may be made against him in respect of the death of, or bodily injury to, the passenger while being in, entering or alighting from the vehicle, or purports to impose any conditions with respect to the enforcement of any such liability, be void.

It should be noted that this section, like its predecessor, under the Road Traffic Acts of 1930 and 1960, applies only to an exclusion clause in a contract, and so was held to have no application to a clause in a mere licence: *Wilkie v LPTB* [1946] 1 All E.R. 650, KBD. Whether a 'Free Pass' constitutes a contract or a licence might be a difficult question: *Gore v Van Der Lann* [1967] 2 Q.B. 31 CA.

Because the Unfair Contract Terms Act 1977 s.2 invalidates any contract term or notice excluding or restricting liability for death or personal injury resulting from negligence, this distinction should no longer present a problem. The provision is invalid, whether in a contract or a licence. A contract or notice purporting to exclude liability for negligent damage to property would be valid, if reasonable: Unfair Contract Terms Act 1971 s.2(2). It might then be relied on, under the 1999 Act by a third party for whose benefit it was made, e.g. the (allegedly) negligent bus conductor employed by Liverpool Corporation in *Gore v Van Der Lann* [1967] 2 Q.B. 31.

Road Traffic Act 1988 s.148(7)

13–034   Notwithstanding anything in any enactment, a person issuing a policy of insurance under section 145 of this Act shall be liable to indemnify the persons or classes of persons specified in the policy in respect of any liability which the policy purports to cover in the case of those persons or classes of persons.

Defective Premises Act 1972

13–035   See below, Ch.16.

Points for reflection

An agreement of June 17, 1946, between the Minister of Transport and the Motor Insurers' Bureau   **13–036**
contained the following provision:

"If judgment in respect of any liability which is required to be covered by a policy of insurance or a security (hereinafter called 'a contract of insurance') under Part II of the Road Traffic Act 1930, is obtained against any person or persons in any court in Great Britain, whether or not such person or persons be in fact covered by a contract of insurance or if judgment in respect of any liability which is not so required to be covered by reason only of the provisions of subsection (4) of section 35 of the said Act is in fact covered by a contract of insurance and any such judgment is not satisfied in full within seven days from the date upon which the person or persons in whose favour the judgment was given became or would apart from the provisions of the Courts (Emergency Powers) Act 1939, or similar legislation have become entitled to enforce it, then M.I.B. will, subject to the provisions of clauses 5 and 6 of these presents, pay or satisfy or cause to be paid or satisfied to or to the satisfaction of the person or persons in whose favour the judgment was given any sum payable or remaining payable thereunder in respect of the aforesaid liability including taxed costs (or such proportion thereof as is attributable to the aforesaid liability) whatever may be the cause of the failure of the judgment debtor to satisfy the judgment."

In *Hardy v Motor Insurers' Bureau* [1964] 2 Q.B. 745 at 757, Lord Denning MR said of the above agreement:

"This was, on the face of it, a contract between two parties for the benefit of a third person. No point is taken by the Motor Insurers' Bureau that it is not enforceable by the third person. I trust no such point will ever be taken."

See now Motor Insurers' Bureau (Compensation of Victims of Untraced Drivers) 1972 and Motor Insurers' Bureau (Compensation of Victims of Uninsured Drivers) 1988 (HMSO).

----

7. NETWORK CONTRACTS

Before we leave the doctrine of privity of contract, some attention should be paid to the idea of   **13–037**
"network contracts" or "contracts with network effects". Initially, the idea was that, where contractors A, B, C, and D and so on, were linked together in some common business enterprise or project—for example, in a franchise or a construction project—then, in such a network, the usual restrictions on third-party claims and defences should be relaxed. This might mean, for example, that franchisee B could enforce the contract between franchisor A and fellow franchisee C and D; or that sub-contractor C could rely on defences in the head contract between A and B. Although some of the restrictions imposed by the principle of privity of contract have now been relaxed in English law (both by legislation and in the case-law), it is clear that "network contracts" have some attraction over and above their easing of third-party problems. Quite apart from bringing the law more closely into alignment with networking forms of economic organisation and business practice, the idea would allow for the heightening of cooperative contractual obligations and it should facilitate

a more appropriate framing of questions concerning the fairness of exclusion and limitation clauses in connected contracts.[2]

That said, it is arguable that the need for recognising 'network contracts' or 'contracts with network effects' has been overtaken—at any rate, in commercial contracting—by the contextual approach to the interpretation of business contracts (Chapter 17) and by the new contextualism more generally.

We can get the flavour of networks by looking at the contractual arrangements that support the modern use of credit cards; and then we can consider whether a contextual approach makes it unnecessary to adopt the idea of networks explicitly.

A. Credit card networks and OFT v Lloyds TSB

13–038   Modern credit card arrangements involve a cluster of connected contracts—contracts between card-holders and card-issuers, together with the various contracts that connect card issuers to retailers with whom card-holders contract. Such clusters of connected contracts look like possible candidates for "network effects". Indeed, long before the idea of network contracts had crystallised, section 75(1) of the Consumer Credit Act 1974 introduced special measures that were designed to give consumers greater confidence in using their credit cards. Stated simply, in relation to a broad range of consumer transactions, the legislation enabled card-holders to pass over to their card-issuers the problems that they might have with defaulting retailers—in effect, the card-issuer was put in the shoes of the card-holder to take up any contractual claim against the retailer which, in turn, impacted on the contractual terms and conditions connecting card-issuers to retailers. However, as the use of credit cards expanded, and as their use spread overseas and into online marketplaces, questions were raised about the scope of the protection introduced in 1974. In *OFT v Lloyds TSB* [2007] UKHL 48, the question was whether section 75(1) continues to apply where a UK consumer, using a credit card issued by a UK card-issuer, deals with a foreign supplier. Even though it was argued that a protective scheme with application to foreign suppliers would expose UK card-issuers to some 29 million suppliers worldwide, and even though the credit infrastructure no longer maps neatly on to the tripartite debtor-creditor-supplier template of the 1970s, the House of Lords ruled that section 75(1) so applies.

Using the language of networks, Lord Mance (at para.23) describes the changing, and strongly connected, nature of the credit card infrastructure in the following way:

"Large-scale consolidation has led to card issuers becoming members of one of the two main international credit card networks, VISA and MasterCard. Under the rules of these networks, certain card issuers are authorised to act as 'merchant acquirers' . . . They contract with suppliers . . . to process all such supply transactions made with cards of the relevant network . . . Suppliers do not become members of the network, but contract with merchant acquirers to honour the cards of the network . . . Where the merchant acquirer is itself the issuer of the card used in a particular transaction, the transaction is tripartite . . . But in the more common (and in the case of a foreign

---

[2]   See, e.g., Fabrizio Cafaggi, 'Contractual Networks and the Small Business Act: Towards European Principles?' (2008) 4 *European Review of Contract Law* 493; Fabrizio Cafaggi (ed), *Contractual Networks, Inter-Firm Cooperation and Economic Growth* (Cheltenham: Edward Elgar, 2011); Marc Amstutz and Gunther Teubner (eds), *Networks: Legal Issues of Multilateral Cooperation* (Oxford: Hart, 2009); Gunther Teubner, '"And if I by Beelzebub Cast Out Devils. . .": An Essay on the Diabolics of Network Failure' (2009) 10 *German Law Journal* 395; and Gunther Teubner, *Networks as Connected Contracts* (Oxford: Hart, 2011) (translated by Michelle Everson, and with an exceptionally helpful introduction by Hugh Collins).

transaction inevitable) case of use of a card issued by a card issuer other than the merchant acquirer who acquired the particular supplier, the network operates as a clearing system, through which the merchant acquirer is reimbursed by the card issuer . . ."

Although 1970s-style three-party networks have been overtaken by four-party networks, a network remains a network; and the House did not view these changes as affecting the legislative intention that consumers should be given the protection envisaged by s.75(1).

We should not overstate the significance of the court talking the talk of networks. Credit card arrangements are networked; such is the economic reality; but it does not follow that there is a special doctrinal coding for networks. In the *OFT v Lloyds TSB* case, the fact that networks are involved is not seen as legally significant; it is simply a matter of whether the legislative purposes encompass credit card-supported transactions with foreign suppliers. To put the legal significance of networks to the test, we would need to see how the House would have dealt with a credit card dispute in the absence of any special legislative measures.

We can derive some assistance from Clayton Gillette's examination of the US case-law where card-holders' information is compromised by criminals who have hacked into the systems of merchants who have (in breach of contract) retained the relevant details.[3] In the US jurisprudence, where third-parties within the network try to enforce the merchants' contractual obligations, their prospects depend typically upon the willingness of the courts to stretch a traditional third-party beneficiary rule. Although courts exhibit varying degrees of (un)willingness to stretch this rule, they fully understand that it is not practicable to join every card-holder contractually to every merchant so that the merchants' obligations can be enforced directly; and it is clear that the value of the network is enhanced where merchants adhere to their obligations. Gillette concludes:

" [T]hose charged with interpretation of contracts should take the presence and purpose of the network into account in determining the reach of explicit obligations and should vindicate the intent of all participants by imposing cooperative obligations under the same circumstances in which parties would have required them if explicit contract had been available."[4]

The question is: how is this best to be done? The third-party beneficiary rule does have some flexibility but a culture of cautious use can hinder its application. "Networks" might be the answer; but, in the UK, the obvious thought is that contextualism holds the key to the progressive development of the commercial law.

B. Is contextualism the answer?

On the face of it, a contextual approach should quickly direct the courts to a networked setting in which a particular transaction is located; and, from this, it should be possible to articulate the expectations of contractors that, in that networked setting, are reasonable. Arguably for some time, this is what the courts have actually been doing (albeit without saying as much) in some of the leading commercial cases. For instance, is this not precisely the way in which we should now understand Lord Wilberforce's remarks in cases such as *The Eurymedon* (above) and the *New York Star* [1980] 3 All E.R. 257?

13–039

---

[3]   Clayton Gillette, 'Contractual Networks, Contract Design, and Contract Interpretation: The Case of Credit Cards' in Grundmann, Cafaggi, and Vettori (eds), *The Organizational Contract: From Exchange to Long-Term Network Cooperation in European Contract Law* (Ashgate, 2013) p.77.

[4]   above, at p.95.

Nevertheless, from the fact that contextualism might invite a court to take into account a background of connected contracts, it does not follow that this invitation will be accepted or, even if it is accepted, that the background will be translated as having network effects. Consider, for example, the Court of Appeal's decision in *Tekdata Interconnections Ltd v Amphenol Ltd* [2009] EWCA Civ 1209 (below). *Tekdata* is not a case involving third-party issues; rather it is a "battle of the forms" case (see Ch.3) in a context of connected supply contracts. In *Tekdata*, T sent a purchase order to A stating that the purchase was to be on T's terms and conditions. In response to this purchase order from T, A sent an acknowledgment stating that A's terms and conditions applied. Whose terms prevailed? The trial judge accepted Tekdata's argument that, in the context of long-term trade between itself and Amphenol, it was understood that T's terms applied. By contrast, the Court of Appeal held that, because Amphenol had had the 'last shot' at introducing its terms, it was A's terms that applied. However, on a more fine-grained analysis, we might detect a difference between the approaches of Longmore LJ and Dyson LJ. Whereas the latter seems to be reluctant to embrace contextualism (see below, especially paras 25-27), the former seems to be more willing to view the dispute in its context (see below, para.16) but he does not find in the setting compelling evidence of an implicit understanding that Tekdata's terms should apply.

TEKDATA INTERCONNECTIONS LTD v AMPHENOL LTD

[2009] EWCA Civ 1209

LORD JUSTICE LONGMORE

Introduction

13-040
1. This appeal raises the question whether in what is sometimes called "the battle of forms", there can be circumstances in which a traditional offer and acceptance analysis can be displaced by reference to the conduct of the parties over a long-term relationship. An offer to buy containing the purchaser's terms which is followed by an acknowledgement of purchase containing the seller's terms which is followed by delivery will (other things being equal) result in a contract on the seller's terms. If, however, it is clear that the neither party ever intended the seller's terms to apply and always intended the purchaser's terms to apply, it is conceptually possible to arrive at the conclusion that the purchaser's terms are to apply. It will be a rare case where that happens. Do the facts of this appeal amount to that rare case?

The Facts
2. The parties to this dispute are part of a chain of suppliers to Rolls Royce as ultimate purchasers. Rolls Royce need engine control systems for installation in their aero engines. They bought such systems from a company called Goodrich who themselves bought cable assembly items such as cable harnesses for internal wiring from Tekdata Interconnections Ltd ("Tekdata") in Stoke-on-Trent. In order to manufacture these harnesses Tekdata acquired connectors from Amphenol Ltd ("Amphenol") who originally manufactured them at premises in Nottinghamshire but later, in about August 2005, moved to Whitstable in Kent. They in turn acquired material, such as electronic filters, for the connectors from a firm known as Oxley in Ulverston in Cumbria. The dispute has arisen between Tekdata and Amphenol (to whom I shall as relevant refer as "Buyers" and "Sellers"). Tekdata claim that certain connectors were delivered late and were not fit for the purpose or of merchantable quality. They say that the contract of purchase was on the terms of their purchase orders (or, more accurately, revisions to purchase orders already placed); Amphenol defend by saying that the contracts were on the terms of their (Amphenol's) acknowledgement of the purchase orders and that those terms exclude or limit their liability for any breaches of contract. It fell to HHJ Simon Brown QC sitting in the Birmingham Mercantile Court to decide, on a preliminary issue, whose terms (if either) applied.
3. Tekdata and Amphenol have been doing business for many years; for most (if not all of that time) the supply of connectors had been controlled by Goodrich who required Tekdata to purchase the connectors from Amphenol to a specification required by Goodrich and at a price determined by Goodrich. Goodrich had a long term supply contract with Tekdata although that contract had formally expired by August 2005 when problems started to arise. It emerged in the course of disclosure in the proceedings that Amphenol also had a

long term contract with Goodrich pursuant to which they agreed to supply connectors to Tekdata for the price determined by Goodrich but Tekdata were unaware of that contract until it was disclosed in the proceedings.

4. The contractual obligations in relation to any particular equipment bought from Amphenol began with a Purchase Order generated by Tekdata. That stated that the purchase was to be on Tekdata's own terms and conditions. It contained a delivery date which was 26 weeks from the date of the order since Tekdata themselves had 28 weeks from the date of Goodrich's order to supply the harnesses to Goodrich.

5. According to Tekdata's financial manager Mr Downing, whose evidence the judge in general accepted, Tekdata then expected the purchase order to be automatically actioned and assumed that the items covered by the purchase order would be delivered by the relevant dates.

6. Mr Downing thus thought that a contract came into existence as soon as Amphenol received the purchase order and that such contract was on the terms of that purchase order. That could not, however, be the legal position unless there was some prior overarching contract whereby Amphenol were obliged to supply connectors as and when Tekdata (or perhaps Goodrich) chose to order them and there was no evidence of such a contract, despite the considerable evidence that the parties had enjoyed a business relationship that went back for over 20 years.

7. The judge found that Amphenol acknowledged the purchase orders by sending an acknowledgment to Tekdata. In law it could only be at that date at earliest that a contract for the purchase and sale of the specified connectors came into existence. The acknowledgment, however, stated that Amphenol's terms and conditions were to apply and the traditional view would be that, if no further documentation passed between the parties and if Tekdata took delivery of the connectors, the contract would be on the terms of Amphenol's acknowledgement. The judge, however, held that it was never intended that Amphenol's terms should apply because the parties had always intended that Tekdata's terms were to apply. He seems to have concluded, although he did not expressly say so, that the clause (at the bottom right hand corner of the acknowledgement) about the application of Amphenol's terms was to be ignored and that the contract came into existence when the acknowledgment was returned to Tekdata.

8. There were 13 grounds of appeal but, in the course of oral argument they boiled down to the following two questions.

9. Was it open to Judge to accept Tekdata's arguments?

When I gave permission to appeal, I was troubled by this question because there was no sign in the pleadings that Tekdata wished to rely not on the traditional offer and acceptance analysis but rather on the conduct of the parties not only over their long-term relationship over 20 years but also after the conclusion of the relevant contracts. But I am now satisfied that Tekdata's skeleton argument made it sufficiently clear that (right or wrong) Tekdata wished to rely on the parties' overall relationship and that they would say that it was always their intention that Tekdata's terms were to apply. Any objection to this approach could and should have been taken at the time but was not and the Judge was therefore right to have proceeded to determine the second question.

10. Was it right to analyse the overall relationship and come to the conclusion which the Judge did?

Mr Tomson for Amphenol said the Judge was not so entitled and the traditional offer and acceptance analysis should be applied. The Judge relied on *Butler Machine Tool Company v Excell-O Corporation* [1979] 1WLR 401 in which Thesiger J had not applied that traditional analysis and said that the seller's quotation terms should prevail over the terms incorporated by the buyer's order because the seller's terms expressly said that they should prevail over any other terms. Lord Denning MR said (404 F-G):

> "I have much sympathy with the judge's approach to this case. In many of these cases our traditional analysis of offer, counter-offer, rejection, acceptance and so forth is out of date. This was observed by Lord Wilberforce in *New Zealand Shipping Co. Ltd. V A. M. Satterthwaite & Co Ltd* [1975] AC 154, 167. The better way is to look at all the documents passing between the parties— and glean from them, or from the conduct of the parties, whether they have reached agreement on all material points—even though there may be differences between the forms and conditions printed on the back of them."

Applying that guidance he concluded that the contract was made when the seller returned a slip attached to the buyer's purchase order accepting the order on the buyer's terms. Mr Tomson pointed out that:

(1) in the end the traditional offer of acceptance analysis was applied even by Lord Denning.
(2) the other members of the court applied the traditional analysis, Lawton LJ saying expressly (405G) that the battle of forms had to be conducted in accordance with set rules;
(3) *Butler*'s case was, therefore, no precedent for abandoning the traditional analysis.

11. I agree with Mr Tomson's submissions on the aspect of the case, while accepting that, as Lord Denning said, there will be cases when one must glean from documents passing between the parties and from their conduct whether agreement has been reached. The way in which I would put it is to say that the traditional offer and acceptance analysis must be adopted unless the documents passing between the parties and their conduct show that their common intention was that some other terms were intended to prevail.

12. I have already indicated that a traditional analysis would conclude that the terms on Amphenol's acknowledgment would be the terms, on which the parties contracted.

13. In this case the Judge gave weight to the following countervailing factors

i)   The fact that the connectors were items of considerable sophistication which were to be fitted into engine control systems destined for use in Rolls-Royce aero engines. Any departure from agreed times of delivery or, even more importantly, the quality of degree of materials and workmanship as specified in the purchase order could have catastrophic consequences not only for Rolls-Royce business arrangements, but also for the general travelling public. (Para 23 of the Judgment);

ii) The connected fact that there had, a short time before the purchase orders were concluded, been in existence contractual commitments by Amphenol to the party beyond Tekdata in the chain of purchases (Goodrich in their previous incarnation of TRW Limited). They were the instigators not only of the specification for the connectors but also of the requirement that Tekdata had to obtain the connectors from Amphenol. The contractual commitment assumed by Amphenol to TRW/Goodrich was contained in what was called a Long Term Purchase Agreement dated 8th August 2001 which had expired on 30 June 2004, two months before the first relevant revisions to the relevant purchase orders had been made. That agreement committed Amphenol to make their supplies on terms which largely corresponded to those of Tekdata even if they were not identical. (paras 24-27 of Judgment);

iii) The fact that at no time before Amphenol served their Defence did they mention their own terms. (paras 36-48 of the judgment).

14. The Judge appears to have relied on all these matters in coming to the conclusion that the parties must have intended Tekdata's conditions to apply rather than Amphenol's conditions as set out in the last document passing between the parties before the individual contracts were made. The crucial paragraphs are para 31 and part of para 53 as follows:-

"31. I am satisfied that there was never any suggestion put forward to either of [the parties] that the terms and conditions of Amphenol were extant between the parties. Indeed, it would defy common sense in this particular commercial arrangement for the Amphenol terms and conditions to be part of any of these supplies. It would not be acceptable with everybody depending upon each other for time not to be of the essence, you can deliver the goods more or less when you like, or when it was imposed upon you by your own supplier, and also it would defy common sense for there to be no requirements for conformity to certain standards. Indeed, in one of the documents there is quite clearly identified that the Defendants signed up to and signed off something as conforming with one of the appropriate standards.
53. . . .. . .and it was well known between the parties, and certainly well known to those in the Defendant's office, Mrs Hagan and Mr Dolton, that those particular [Tekdata] conditions would be applied. Any attempt to say otherwise, in my judgment is wrong. I do not accept their evidence on that."

15. This reasoning is, in my judgment, not satisfactory. In the first place the use of the word "would" no less than 4 times shows that the Judge is concentrating more on what he thinks ought to have happened between the parties rather than (as he ought to have done) on what did happen. It is only by ascertaining what did happen between the parties, that it is possible to ascertain their objective intention. Secondly, the purported finding of fact that it was well known to Mrs Hagan and Mr Dolton that Tekdata's conditions would be applied is unexplained and has no basis in the evidence. It was never put to either witness that they knew Tekdata's conditions would be applied whatever that may mean. They did not give evidence that they "knew" otherwise so there was no such evidence to reject. The most that their evidence amounted to (in fact Mrs Hagan only, since Mr Dolton did not give any relevant evidence on this topic) was that she considered Amphenol's conditions applied and told her manager that that was her view. The Judge was perfectly entitled to reject her evidence as to that but it does not remotely follow that she "well knew" Tekdata's conditions "would be applied".

16. The fact that the judge's reasoning is open to criticism, does not, of course, mean that his ultimate conclusion is wrong and the question remains whether the factors on which he relied were individually or cumulatively able to displace the traditional offer and acceptance analysis. I certainly agree with the Judge that

the context of the parties' relationship was very important but, having given the matter the best consideration I can, I do not consider that the factors on which he relied justified his conclusion.

17. The fact that delivery times and quality control are essential and, indeed, fundamental to the good relationship of the parties is no doubt true but it must be true in many commercial relationships. This is a matter that can not be more than a background factor. It is much strengthened by the fact that Amphenol had a long term purchase agreement with Goodrich who were in a position to require Tekdata to obtain the connectors from Amphenol and even to name the price at which they were to be supplied. But Goodrich did not purport to require Tekdata to contract with Amphenol on any particular terms. What gives one pause is that Amphenol did in fact contract with Goodrich on terms that were similar to the terms on the reverse of Tekdata's purchase order forms. But they were not identical and Tekdata never (as far as the evidence went) knew that Amphenol had had a long term purchase agreement with Goodrich let alone what the terms of that agreement were. (The document only became known to Tekdata after Amphenol had disclosed it in the course of these proceedings.) The fact that there is no precise matching between the terms of the long term purchase agreement and Tekdata's own terms is shown by the detailed provision for liquidated damages in the event of delay in the Goodrich/Amphenol agreement which have no counterpart in Tekdata's own terms. It thus appears that the parties had an opportunity to agree a single set of terms, if they wanted to, but that was something which they conspicuously did not do; this detracts from the importance that it might otherwise have been appropriate to accord to the long term purchase agreement.

18. The Judge was also influenced by the fact that Amphenol were prepared to and did sign a certificate of conformance in respect to the connectors as Tekdata's conditions required them to do. Why should they do this unless they agreed that the contract was to be on Tekdata's terms? Again this has some force but not conclusive force since parties to contracts often do things in the course of a performance which is working well, which they might not strictly be obliged to do.

19. Much the greater part of the judgment is taken up by setting out the terms of the correspondence which took place after dispute had arisen and by pointing out that Amphenol made no reference to their terms and conditions, but only relied on them once the defence was served. It seems that this may have had the greatest impact for the judge. It is, of course, possible to rely on post –contract correspondence when one has to determine what the terms of a contract are (rather than what those terms mean) see *Great Northern Railways v Avon Insurance* [2001] 2 Lloyd's Rep 649 at paragraph 29. But again, one has to be careful about reading too much into such correspondence. At the stage of trying to sort a dispute out, it may well be counter-productive to refer to one's terms and conditions. Reasonable business men do not necessarily start resolving their problems by making legal assertions and counter assertions. That is left for the lawyers later. The terms of the post-dispute correspondence do not, to my mind, carry the matter very far.

20. In paras 2-110 and 111 of *Chitty on Contracts* (30th ed) Professor Sir Guenther Treitel points out that the traditional offer and acceptance analysis is not always without its difficulties. Having referred to three specific cases of (1) multilateral contracts, (2) references to third parties and (3) sale of land, he cites the words of Lord Denning MR in Butler and his similar words in the earlier case of *Gibson v Manchester City Council* [1978] 1 WLR 520, 523. He then says of these comments:

"But such an outright rejection of the traditional analysis is open to the objection that it provides too little guidance for the courts (or their parties or their legal advisers) in determining whether an agreement has been reached"

and I might add 'on what terms'. The fact that *Gibson* was reversed by the House of Lords [1979] 1 WLR 294 adds considerable force to this comment of that very distinguished author.

21. So, although I am not saying that the context of a long term relationship and the conduct of the parties can never be so strong as to displace the result which a traditional offer and acceptance analysis would dictate, I do not consider the circumstances are sufficiently strong to do so in this present case. Indeed I think it will always be difficult to displace the traditional analysis, in a battle of forms case, unless it can be said there was a clear course of dealing between the parties. That was never proved. For my part, I would allow this appeal and order that it is the terms and conditions of the Appellants that apply to the contracts contained in or evidenced by the purchase orders referred to in the Particulars of Claim.

LORD JUSTICE DYSON

22. I agree with the judgment of Longmore LJ.

23. The so-called "last shot" doctrine has been explained in *Chitty on Contracts* (30th edition) at para 2-037 as meaning that where conflicting communications are exchanged, each is a counter-offer, so that if a contract

results at all (eg from an acceptance by conduct) it must be on the terms of the final document in the series leading to the conclusion of the contract. This doctrine has been criticised in *Anson's Law of Contract* (28th edition) at p 39 as depending on chance and being potentially arbitrary as well as on the ground that, unless and until the counter-offer is accepted, there is no contract even though both buyer and seller may firmly believe that a contract has been made.

24. The paradigm battle of the forms occurs where A offers to buy goods from B on its (A's) conditions and B accepts the offer but only on its own conditions. As is pointed out in *Cheshire, Fifoot & Furmston's Law of Contract* (15th ed.) at p 210, it may be possible to analyse the legal situation that results as being that there is (i) a contract on A's conditions; (ii) a contract on B's conditions; (iii) a contract on the terms that would be implied by law, but incorporating neither A's nor B's conditions; (iv) a contract incorporating some blend of both parties' conditions; or (v) no contract at all.

25. In my judgment, it is not possible to lay down a general rule that will apply in all cases where there is a battle of the forms. It always depends on an assessment of what the parties must objectively be taken to have intended. But where the facts are no more complicated than that A makes an offer on its conditions and B accepts that offer on its conditions and, without more, performance follows, it seems to me that the correct analysis is what Longmore LJ has described as the "traditional offer and acceptance analysis", ie that there is a contract on B's conditions. I accept that this analysis is not without its difficulties in circumstances of the kind to which Professor Treitel refers in the passage quoted at [20] above. But in the next sentence of that passage, Professor Treitel adds: "For this reason the cases described above are best regarded as exceptions to a general requirement of offer and acceptance". I also accept the force of the criticisms made in *Anson*. But the rules which govern the formation of contracts have been long established and they are grounded in the concepts of offer and acceptance. So long as that continues to be the case, it seems to me that the general rule should be that the traditional offer and acceptance analysis is to be applied in battle of the forms cases. That has the great merit of providing a degree of certainty which is both desirable and necessary in order to promote effective commercial relationships.

26. In the present case, it was not contended on behalf of Amphenol that there was no contract between it and Tekdata. The issue was whose conditions were incorporated into the contract. On behalf of Tekdata, it is submitted that the acknowledgement of order by which Tekdata's offer was accepted "subject to the terms and conditions as printed overleaf" was in law an unqualified acceptance of Tekdata's offer (including its conditions). It is said that the words "subject to the terms and conditions as printed overleaf" were not intended to have, and did not in fact have, any contractual effect and were to be ignored.

27. In my judgment, such a conclusion could only be reached if Tekdata could show that the parties had expressly agreed that these words were to be ignored or if such an agreement was necessarily to be inferred from the circumstances of the case. I acknowledge that this is a high hurdle for Tekdata to surmount, but anything less would lead to an uncertainty which is inimical to commercial relationships.

28. Mr Chapple does not say that there was any express agreement that the words on the face of Amphenol's acknowledgement of order were to be ignored and the judge made no finding to that effect. Nor did the judge ask himself whether there were facts which gave rise to the necessary inference that this is what the parties must have agreed. He held the parties must have intended that Tekdata's conditions should apply for a number of reasons all of which were founded in what he described as "reasonable commonsense" (para 19). At para 31, he said that it "would defy common sense in this particular commercial arrangement for the Amphenol terms and conditions to be party (sic) of any of these supplies". At para 56, he said that he justified his conclusion by reference to the context, the conduct of the parties in how they operated the contract "and one has to say that with the experience of a Mercantile Judge looking at how commercial parties in the aviation industry would behave and were behaving at this particular time."

29. I agree with the reasons given by Longmore LJ at [17] to [19] above that none of the factors relied on by the judge for concluding that Tekdata's conditions were incorporated justified his conclusion. Whether considered individually or in combination, they did not give rise to the necessary inference that the parties must have intended the words on the face of Amphenol's acknowledgement of order to have no effect and to contract on Tekdata's conditions.

30. In particular, the judge placed far too much reliance on the correspondence that was written after the dispute had arisen. I agree with Longmore LJ that post-contractual behaviour may be admissible to prove the terms of a contract. An obvious example is where there is an issue as to whether a term was orally agreed and in post-contractual correspondence the party who denies the existence of the term admits that it was agreed. But in a battle of the forms case where it is not suggested that there was any oral agreement as to which conditions should apply, I find it difficult to see how subsequent cor-

respondence can shed light on the question of whose conditions were intended to apply, particularly, as Longmore LJ says, if the correspondence is written at the stage of trying to resolve a dispute. The question of whose conditions were intended to apply must be determined objectively on the basis of the proper interpretation of the documents which comprise the contract viewed objectively in their context. The focus must always be on what the parties must be taken, objectively, to have intended at the time when the contract was made.

31. I would add that I do not consider that the judge's reasoning gained any weight from his rather magisterial remark at para 56 based on his experience as a Mercantile Judge.

32. For these reasons as well as those given by Longmore LJ, I would allow this appeal.

LORD JUSTICE PILL

33. I agree that the appeal should be allowed.

34. I agree with Dyson LJ, at paragraph 30, that the focus must always be on what the parties must be taken, objectively, to have intended at the time when the contract was made.

35. The surrounding circumstances may throw light on their intentions. The judge was entitled to look for indications that Amphenol never intended, in their business dealings with Tekdata, that the terms and conditions printed on the reverse of their acknowledgement of orders should apply. If that was their state of mind, it could readily be inferred that they intended Tekdata's terms and conditions to apply and that, viewed objectively, was what the parties intended.

36. While not formulating it in quite that way, that appears to have been, at least in part, the approach of the judge. At paragraph 35 he posed these questions:

"Did the Defendants actually believe that by their conduct their own terms and conditions were appropriate, were extant in this case? Did they in fact rely upon them? This is a question where we can look at the conduct of the parties in some detail"

37. In answering those questions in Tekdata's favour, the judge attached considerable weight to the conduct of Amphenol after the dispute arose and in particular their failure, in correspondence, to place reliance on their terms and conditions. I agree with the analysis of that correspondence by Longmore LJ, at paragraph 19. Amphenol's letters demonstrate serious attempts to deal in a practical way with problems which had arisen with a customer of long standing. A conclusion that Amphenol had never intended their terms and conditions to apply cannot fairly be inferred from the terms of their letters.

38. To justify his conclusion, the judge also made findings of fact at paragraph 53:

"And it was well known between the parties, and certainly well known to those in the [appellant's] office, Mrs Hagan and Mr Dolton, that those particular conditions [Tekdata's] would be applied. Any attempt to say otherwise, in my judgment, is wrong."

These findings of fact were not justified for the reasons given by Longmore LJ at paragraph 15. There was no basis for them.

39. Thus while I would accept that in a "battle of forms" there could be a case in which a court would be entitled to conclude that one of the parties had not intended that printed terms and conditions attached to its acknowledgement would apply, the evidence did not justify such a finding against Amphenol in this case. Overall, I agree with Longmore LJ's and Dyson LJ's conclusions that, on the evidence in this case, there was, for the reasons they give, no basis for a finding in Tekdata's favour.

In *Contract Law and Contract Practice* (2013), Catherine Mitchell suggests that an opportunity to recognise networks (via context) was missed in *Tekdata*. For, although the dispute involved a set of connected supply chain contracts, the Court of Appeal "interpreted the network as a series of transactions taking place on express terms that could be analysed separately and in isolation" (at 58). According to Mitchell, by taking this approach, the court made a "stark error", namely imposing "the discrete contract model on the network and regard[ing] an isolated instance of transacting as the prime focus for the legal analysis, ignoring the other aspects of the relationship and its 20-year history and the expectations amongst participants to which this would give rise" (at 59). If we accept this critique of *Tekdata*, contextualism might be the answer not only to network issues but also to the long-standing question about the battle of the forms.

Further reading

John N. Adams and Roger Brownsword, 'Privity and the Concept of a Network Contract' (1990) 10 *Legal Studies* 12

Roger Brownsword, *Contract Law: Themes for the Twenty-First Century* (Oxford: Oxford University Press, 2006) Ch.9 (for the interface between contract and tort law)

Roger Brownsword, 'Contracts in a Networked World' in Larry di Matteo et al (eds) *Commercial Contract Law: Transatlantic Perspectives* (Cambridge: Cambridge University Press, 2012) p.116

B.S. Markesinis, 'An Expanding Tort Law—the Price of a Rigid Contract Law' (1987) 103 LQR 354

Simon Whittaker, 'Privity of Contract and the Law of Tort: the French Experience' (1995) 15 OJLS 327

PART III

OBLIGATIONS ARISING FROM THE CONTRACT AND ITS FORMATION

14

MISREPRESENTATION

LEARNING OBJECTIVES

By the end of this chapter, you should:

- **understand the requirements for a representation (or, exceptionally, silence) to be actionable as a misrepresentation;**
- **understand the nature and limits of "rescission" as the traditional remedy that is available to a misrepresentee;**
- **understand how the Misrepresentation Act 1967 strengthened the position of a misrepresentee;**
- **appreciate the importance of s.2(1) of the Act in opening the way to a claim in damages that does not depend on proof of fraud and you should have considered whether it is overprotective of the misrepresentee;**
- **be familiar with the post-Act jurisprudence and the tricky questions of interpretation and application that have arisen in the case-law.**

INTRODUCTION

It is common for one party to make statements during the course of negotiations for a contract with the object and perhaps the effect of inducing the other party to enter into a contract. Such statements might be characterised as (i) mere sales talk (that is, as statements that are not intended to have any kind of legal effect and that no reasonable person would assume are to be taken seriously), (ii) mere opinion (also, as such, of no legal effect), (iii) statements of fact (which if false might be actionable as misrepresentations), (iv) promises which might form the basis of a collateral contract (see Ch.15), or (v) promises that have been incorporated as terms of the principal contract so that, if such promises are unfulfilled, an action for breach of contract will lie (the circumstances in which such statements become part of a contract are considered in detail in Ch.15).

14–001

In this chapter, we are concerned with statements that are held not to form part of a contract. For example, where a contract of sale has been reduced to writing, assurances which were given by the seller as to his land or his goods, as the case may be, will probably be held not to form part of the contract if they are not referred to in the document. The parol evidence rule, though subject to many exceptions, will generally apply to exclude evidence which would add to, vary or contradict the written document. However, a statement which induces a contract without forming part of it is not necessarily devoid of legal effect. Crucially, a statement of fact that is false will be actionable as a misrepresentation where the misrepresentor intends it to be acted on and where it is reasonably relied on by the misrepresentee.

In all cases of misrepresentation, the misrepresentee has the paper possibility of avoiding the contract by invoking the somewhat fragile equitable remedy of rescission (coupled with an indemnity, the nature of which is considered below in section 6 of the chapter). However, until the reconfiguration of the modern law in the 1960s, claims for damages were available only in the tort of deceit. To succeed in deceit, the misrepresentee had to show that the misrepresentation was made fraudulently (that is, the maker knew it was false or was reckless whether it was true or false: *Derry v Peek* (1889) 14 App.Cas. 337 at 374, per Lord Herschell)—and proving fraud was an uphill struggle. If the misrepresentation was made non-fraudulently (that is, the maker believed it to be true, whether reasonably or not) damages were not available; and, it was to compensate for this restriction that the collateral contract was utilised (see *Esso v Mardon*, below, Ch.15).

The legal position was transformed after, first, the decision of the House of Lords in *Hedley Byrne v Heller & Partners* (below, section 3) and, then, the enactment of the Misrepresentation Act, 1967 (below, section 7). In *Hedley Byrne*, it was established that, in certain circumstances, damages might be recovered at common law for financial losses occasioned by acting on negligent advice (so-called liability for negligent mis-statement). More importantly, at any rate for present purposes, s.2(1) of the Misrepresentation Act provided that a misrepresentee has a right to recover damages unless the misrepresentor can show that the representation was made with a belief in its truth and with reasonable grounds for such a belief. In practice, nowadays, this means that the obvious recourse for a misrepresentee is to claim damages under the Act and put the burden of disproving negligence on to the misrepresentor. If the misrepresentor succeeds in showing an honest and reasonable belief in the truth of the statement, the misrepresentee's only remedy continues to be that of rescission.

Given that the modern law is so configured, the principal questions are: (i) whether the statement at issue is a misrepresentation; and (ii) if so, whether (a) rescission and/or (b) damages (for fraud or under the Act) are available to the misrepresentee.

The law in this chapter is presented in seven sections. In the first section, the ingredients of an actionable misrepresentation—a false statement of fact that is intended to be acted upon and that is relied on by the representee—are considered. In the second section, the general principle that mere silence is not actionable is reviewed. Section three highlights the decision of the House of Lords in *Hedley Byrne v Heller & Partners*, in which the scope of liability for negligence was extended to include cases where A makes a careless statement to B who then reasonably foreseeably relies on the statement and suffers financial loss. Although *Hedley Byrne* is a landmark in the modern development of the law of negligence, it intersects with liability for misrepresentations in contract law and it was a significant part of the context in which the Misrepresentation Act 1967 took effect. Before the 1967 Act opened up the availability of damages for a non-fraudulent misrepresentation, the standard remedy was rescission. In section four, the focus is on the bars to this remedy; in section five, it is on the way in which the innocent party should signal that the remedy is being exercised; and, in section six, it is on the remedy of 'indemnity' which might be available alongside rescission. Finally, in section seven, we get to the Misrepresentation Act 1967 and the unfolding of the modern law in which the assessment and recovery of damages for misrepresentation, together with attempts to exclude such claims, move to the centre of the stage.

1. The Elements of a Misrepresentation

REDGRAVE v HURD

Court of Appeal (1881) 20 Ch.D. 1; 51 L.J.Ch. 113; 45 L.T. 485; 30 W.R. 251

14-002   The plaintiff, a solicitor, inserted in the Law Times an advertisement offering to "take as partner an efficient lawyer and advocate, about forty, who would not object to purchase advertiser's suburban residence . . ." The defendant replied to the advertisement, and had two interviews with the plaintiff, at which, as Fry J found, the plaintiff had represented that his business was bringing in either about £300 a year, or from £300 to £400 a year. At a third interview the plaintiff produced summaries of business done in 1877, 1878 and 1879. These summaries showed gross receipts not quite amounting to £200 a year. The defendant asked how the difference was made up and the plaintiff produced a quantity of letters and papers which, he stated, related to other business which he had done. The defendant did not examine the books and papers thus produced, but only looked cursorily at them, and ultimately agreed to purchase the house and take a share in the business for £1,600. Fry J came to the conclusion that the letters and papers, if examined, would have shown business of only £5 or £6 a year.

The defendant signed a written agreement to purchase the house for £1,600 and paid £100 deposit. Finding, as he alleged, that the practice was utterly worthless, he refused to complete, and the plaintiff brought an action for specific performance. The defendant alleged that he was induced to enter into the contract by misrepresentations, and counterclaimed for rescission of the contract.

Fry J gave judgment for the plaintiff, holding that the defendant must be taken not to have relied on the oral representations as to the value of the business: "If he had intended to rely upon that parol representation . . . having the materials before him, he would have made some inquiry into it": and that he "must be taken to have accepted the statements which were in those papers." The defendant appealed.

JESSEL MR

As regards the rescission of a contract, there was no doubt a difference between the rules of courts of equity and the rules of courts of common law—a difference which, of course, has now disappeared by the operation of the Judicature Act, which makes the rules of equity prevail. According to the decisions of courts of equity it was not necessary, in order to set aside a contract obtained by material false representation, to prove that the party who obtained it knew at the time when the representation was made that it was false. It was put in two ways, either of which was sufficient. One way of putting the case was, "A man is not to be allowed to get a benefit from a statement which he now admits to be false. He is not to be allowed to say, for the purpose of civil jurisdiction, that when he made it he did not know it to be false; he ought to have found that out before he made it." The other way of putting it was this: "Even assuming that moral fraud must be shown in order to set aside a contract, you have it where a man, having obtained a beneficial contract by a statement which he now knows to be false, insists upon keeping that contract. To do so is a moral delinquency: no man ought to seek to take advantage of his own false statements." The rule in equity was settled, and it does not matter on which of the two grounds it was rested. As regards the rule of common law there is no doubt it was not quite so wide. There were, indeed, cases in which, even at common law, a contract could be rescinded for misrepresentation, although it could not be shown that the person making it knew the representation to be false. They are variously stated, but I think, according to the later decisions, the statement must have been made recklessly and without care whether it was true or false, and not with the belief that it was true. But, as I have said, the doctrine in equity was settled beyond controversy, and it is enough to refer to the judgment of Lord Cairns in the *Reese River Silver Mining Co v Smith*, L.R. 4 HL 64, in which he lays it down in the way which I have stated.

There is another proposition of law of very great importance which I think it is necessary for me to state, because, with great deference to the very learned judge from whom this appeal comes, I think it is not quite accurately stated in his judgment. If a man is induced to enter into a contract by a false representation it is not a sufficient answer to him to say, "If you had used due diligence you would have found out that the statement was untrue. You had the means afforded to you of discovering its falsity, and did not choose to avail yourself of them." I take it to be a settled doctrine of equity, not only as regards specific performance but also as regards rescission, that this is not an answer unless there is such delay as constitutes a defence under the Statute of Limitations. That, of course, is quite a different thing. Under the statute delay deprives a man of his right to rescind on the ground of fraud, and the only question to be considered is from what time the delay is to be reckoned. It had been decided, and the rule was adopted by the statute, that the delay counts from the time when by due diligence the fraud might have been discovered. Nothing can be plainer, I take it, on the authorities in equity than that the effect of false representation is not got rid of on the ground that the person to whom it was made has been guilty of negligence. One of the most familiar instances in modern times is where men issue a prospectus in which they make false statements of the contracts made before the formation of a company, and then say that the contracts themselves may be inspected at the offices of the solicitors. It has always been held that those who accepted those false statements as true were not deprived of their remedy merely because they neglected to go and look at the contracts. Another instance with which we are familiar is where a vendor makes a false statement as to the contents of a lease, as, for instance, that it contains no covenant preventing the carrying on of the trade which the purchaser is known by the vendor to be desirous of carrying on upon the property. Although the lease itself might be produced at the sale, or might have been open to the inspection of the purchaser long previously to the sale, it has been repeatedly held that the vendor cannot be allowed to say, "You were not entitled to give credit to my statement." It is not sufficient, therefore, to say that the purchaser had the opportunity of investigating the real state of the case, but did not avail himself of that opportunity. It has been apparently supposed by the learned judge in the court below that the case of *Attwood v Small*, 6 Cl. & F. 232, conflicts with that proposition. He says this: "He inquired into it to a certain extent, and if he did that carelessly and inefficiently it is his own fault. As in *Attwood v Small*, those directors and agents of the company who made ineffectual inquiry into the business which was to be sold to the company were nevertheless held by their investigation to have bound the company, so here, I think, the defendant who made a cursory investigation into the position of things on February 17 must be taken to have accepted the statements which were in those papers." I think that those remarks are inaccurate in law, and are not borne out by the case to which the learned judge referred.

[His Lordship then considered the speeches in *Attwood v Small*.]

. . . the two grounds taken by Lord Brougham are that there was no misrepresentation, and that the purchaser did not rely on the representations. He agreed in one with Lord Cottenham and in the other with Lord Devon. The three grounds taken by the three noble Lords, one of which grounds was taken by one only of the Lords, and each of the others by two, were that there was no fraud—that there was actual knowledge of the facts before the contract, and that no reliance was placed upon the representation. In no way, as it appears to me, does the decision, or any of the grounds of decisions, in *Attwood v Small*, support the proposition that it is a good defence to an action for rescission of a contract on the ground of fraud that the man who comes to set aside the contract inquired to a certain extent, but did it carelessly and inefficiently, and would, if he had used reasonable diligence, have discovered the fraud . . .

. . . the learned judge came to the conclusion either that the defendant did not rely on the statement, or that if he did rely upon it he had shown such negligence as to deprive him of his title to relief from this court. As I have already said, the latter proposition is in my opinion not founded in law, and the former part is not founded in fact; I think also it is not founded in law, for when a person makes a material representation to another to induce him to enter into a contract, and the other enters into the contract, it is not sufficient to say that the party to whom the representation is made does not prove that he entered into the contract relying upon the representation. If it is a material representation calculated to induce him to enter into the contract, it is an inference of law that he was induced by the representation to enter into it, and in order to take away his title to be relieved from the contract on the ground that the representation was untrue, it must be shown either that he had knowledge of the facts contrary to the representation, or that he stated in terms, or showed clearly by his conduct, that he did not rely on the representation. If you tell a man, "You may enter into partnership with me, my business is bringing in between £300 and £400 a year," the man who makes that representation must know that it is a material inducement to the other to enter into the partnership, and you cannot investigate as to whether it was more or less probable that the inducement would operate on the mind of the party to whom the representation was made. Where you have neither evidence that he knew facts to show that the statement was untrue, or that he said or did anything to show that he did not actually rely upon the statement, the inference remains that he did so rely, and the statement being a material statement, its being untrue is a sufficient ground for rescinding the contract.

Baggallay and Lush LJJ delivered concurring judgments.

Appeal Allowed.

Points for reflection

14–003

1. The presumption that a party, A, relied on a representation made by the other party, B, if a reasonable person would naturally have done so, was applied in *County NatWest Bank Ltd v Barton*, *The Times*, July 29, 1999. If it appeared that A had already made up his mind on the issue before the misrepresentation was made, B was not liable unless A continued in his decision in reliance on the misrepresentation.

2. The principle in *Redgrave v Hurd* was considered in *Peekay Intermark Ltd v Australia and New Zealand Banking Group Ltd* [2006] EWCA Civ 386. The court confirmed that it is no bar to a claim that the misrepresentee could have found out the true state of affairs. However, the controversial case is that in which the misrepresentee not only could have found out, but (on any reasonable view) should have done so. The question, then, is whether it is fair to hold a misrepresentor (particularly an honest and careful misrepresentor) liable in such circumstances.

BISSET v WILKINSON

Privy Council [1927] A.C. 177; 96 L.J.P.C. 12; 136 L.T. 97; 42 T.L.R. 727

The respondent purchased from the appellant two blocks of land in New Zealand for the purpose   14–004
of sheep-farming. During the negotiations the appellant told the respondent that, if the place was worked properly, it would carry two thousand sheep. The respondent, it was admitted, bought the place believing that it would carry two thousand sheep. As both parties were aware, the appellant had not and, so far as appeared, no other person had at any time carried on sheep-farming on the land. In an action for rescission for misrepresentation, Sim J said:

"In ordinary circumstances, any statement made by an owner who has been occupying his own farm as to its carrying capacity would be regarded as a statement of fact. . . . This, however, is not such a case. . . . In these circumstances . . . the defendants were not justified in regarding anything said by the plaintiff as to the carrying capacity as being anything more than an expression of his opinion on the subject."

Their Lordships concurred in this view of the matter, and therefore held that the purchaser had no right to rescind the contract,

". . . since an erroneous opinion stated by the party affirming the contract, though it may have been relied upon and have induced the contract on the part of the party who seeks rescission, gives no title to relief unless fraud is established . . . If a reasonable man with the vendor's knowledge could not have come to the conclusion he stated, the description of that conclusion as an opinion would not necessarily protect him against rescission for misrepresentation, but what was actually the capacity in competent hands of the land the purchasers purchased had never been, and never was practically ascertained."

ECONOMIDES v COMMERCIAL UNION

Court of Appeal [1997] 3 W.L.R. 1066; [1997] 3 All E.R. 636

14–005   In 1991 E's parents moved into E's flat bringing their valuables with them. When E renewed his household insurance in January 1991 he stated that, "to the best of my knowledge and belief," the value of the contents, including his parents' valuables (which his father told him were worth about £4,000) was £16,000; and that the valuables were worth not more than one-third of the total sum. E's father seriously underestimated the worth of the parents' valuables. In October 1991 the flat was burgled. It emerged that the true value of the contents was £40,000 and the property stolen was worth £31,000. The insurers repudiated liability, alleging misrepresentation and non-disclosure. E's claim was dismissed and he appealed.

SIMON BROWN LJ

. . . Ms Kinsler [for the respondent] submits that Bowen L.J.'s dictum in *Smith v Land and House Property Corp* (1884) 28 Ch.D. 7 at 15[1]—that "if the facts are not equally known to both sides, then a statement of opinion by the one who knows the facts best involves very often a statement of a material fact, for he impliedly states that he knows facts which justify his opinion"—can be seen to apply equally in an insurance context as in the general law (see in particular the *Highlands* case [1987] 1 Lloyd's Rep. 515). I understand her to submit, indeed, that it applies with particular force in an insurance context given that contracts of insurance are based on the utmost good faith and that the insured will always know far more about the facts than the insurer. Given that inevitable inequality of knowledge, she argues, the respondent here was entitled to assume that the appellant had reasonable grounds to support his valuation of the contents and that he was not merely relying, however honestly, on father's say-so.

Mr Bartlett [for the appellant] submits that the approach adopted by the judge below and urged afresh by Ms Kinsler on appeal is fundamentally flawed. His starting point is s. 20 of the Marine Insurance Act 1906—one of a group of sections which it is now established apply equally to non-marine as to marine insurance (see *PCW Syndicates v PCW Reinsurers* [1996] 1 WLR 1136). The relevant subsections of s. 20 are:

"(3)   A representation may be either a representation as to a matter of fact, or as to a matter of expectation or belief.
(4)   A representation as to a matter of fact is true, if it be substantially correct, that is to say, if the difference between what is represented and what is actually correct would not be considered material by a prudent insurer.
(5)   A representation as to a matter of expectation or belief is true if it be made in good faith . . ."

Mr Bartlett relies in particular on sub-s. 1(5), notwithstanding what Steyn J. said about it in the passage cited above from the *Highlands* case.[2] He accepts, as inevitably he must, that the appellant had to have some basis for his statement of belief in this valuation; he could not simply make a blind guess: one cannot believe to be true that which one has not the least idea about. But, he submits, and this is the heart of the argument, the basis of belief does not have to be an objectively reasonable one. What the appellant's father told him here was a sufficient basis for his representation: he was under a duty of honesty, not a duty of care.

In my judgment, these submissions are well-founded. This case seems to me very different from those relied on by the respondent.

The representation in *Smith v Land and House Property Corp* (1884) 28 Ch.D. 7 at 15, as Bowen L.J. expressly stated—

---

[1]   The plaintiffs put up for sale a hotel stating that it was let to "Mr Frederick Fleck (a most desirable tenant)". The defendants agreed to buy the hotel. Fleck went bankrupt and the defendants refused to complete. The Court of Appeal held that they could rescind for misrepresentation, rejecting the plaintiffs' argument that they had merely expressed an opinion. They knew he only paid rent under pressure and that rent was overdue.

[2]   Steyn J said that an express representation of belief implied a representation that there were reasonable grounds for that belief, notwithstanding s.20(5) of the Marine Insurance Act.

"amounts at least to an assertion that nothing has occurred in the relations between the landlords and the tenant which can be considered to make the tenant an unsatisfactory one. That is an assertion of a specific fact."

In the event, it was held to be an untrue assertion of fact.

Similarly, the representation of opinion in the *Credit Lyonnnais* case [1996] 1 Lloyd's Rep. 200 can be seen on analysis to have been not merely without foundation but actually contrary to the representor's experience. As stated in *Chitty on Contracts* para. 6–004 (one of the paragraphs relied on by Longmore J.):

". . . in certain circumstances a statement of opinion or of intention may be regarded as a statement of fact, and therefore as a ground for avoiding a contract if the statement is false. Thus, if it can be proved that the person who expressed the opinion did not hold it, or could not, as a reasonable man having his knowledge of the facts, honestly have held it, the statement may be regarded as a statement of fact."

Brown v Raphael [1958] Ch. 636 seems to me to fall into a different category. The representation there, purporting as it did to come from the vendor's solicitors, would inevitably carry with it the implication that there were reasonable grounds to support the belief, not least given that the true situation could readily have been discovered. The case is in no way inconsistent with the appellant's submissions here. After all, Bowen L.J.'s dictum in *Smith v Land and House Property Corp* (1884) 28 Ch.D. 7 at 15 is only that "a statement of opinion by one who knows the facts best involves very often a statement of a material fact, for he impliedly states that he knows facts which justify his opinion" (my emphasis); he did not say that that is invariably so. And of course, *Brown v Raphael* was not an insurance case so that s. 20(5) of the 1906 Act was not in play.

Ionides' case—decided before Smith's case but which, Ms Kinsler submits, assumes the principle therein stated to be correct—is, I think, to be explained rather on the basis that the representor there was held not entitled to rely on a belief which ignored the letter of advice in his possession. The passage relied on is, in any event, obiter.

What then of the *Highlands'* case, the case at the very forefront of Ms Kinsler's submissions? This passage too is, of course, obiter, Steyn J. having already decided that the words amounted to a representation of fact. More to the point, however, is it correct? Can one in an insurance context, consistently with s. 20(5) of the 1906 Act, find in a representation of belief an implied representation that there are reasonable grounds for that belief? In my judgment, not.

I accept, of course, that, as in *Smith's* case, what may at first blush appear to be a representation merely of expectation or belief can on analysis be seen in certain cases to be an assertion of a specific fact. In that event, the case is governed by sub-ss. (3) and (4) rather than sub-s. (5) of s. 20. And I accept too, as already indicated, that there must be some basis for a representation of belief before it can be said to be made in good faith. But if what Steyn J. was saying—which is not altogether easy to discern—was that all who propose insurance must have reasonable grounds for their (ex hypothesi honest) representations of belief, as was found to be required of the particular vendor in *Brown v Raphael*, I would respectfully disagree. In my judgment, the requirement is rather, as s. 20(5) states, solely one of honesty.

There are practical and policy considerations too. What, would amount to reasonable grounds for belief in this sort of situation? What must a householder seeking contents insurance do? Must he obtain professional valuations of all his goods and chattels? The judge below held:

". . . it would have been necessary for him to make substantially more inquiries than he did make before he could be said to have reasonable grounds for his belief. It is not necessary to specify what those inquiries might have involved."

The problem with not specifying them, however, is that householders are left entirely uncertain of the obligations put on them and at risk of having insurers seek to avoid liability under the policies. There would be endless scope for dispute. In my judgment, if insurers wish to place on their assured an obligation to carry out specific inquiries or otherwise take steps to provide objective justification for their valuations, they must spell out these requirements in the proposal form.

I would hold, therefore, that the sole obligation on the appellant when he represented to the respondent on renewal that he believed the full contents value to be £16,000 was that of honesty. That obligation the judge apparently found him to have satisfied. Certainly, given that the appellant was at the time aged 21, given that the figure for the increase in cover was put forward by his father, and given that father was a retired senior police officer, inevitably better able than the appellant himself to put a valuation on the additional contents, there would seem to me every reason to accept the appellant's honesty.

In these circumstances it is unnecessary to consider whether, as Mr Bartlett submits in the alternative, the appellant had in fact reasonable grounds for his belief, reasonable that is from an objective standpoint. Suffice it to say that I found little merit in Ms Kinsler's argument that the appellant should at the very least have insisted on examining all the additional valuables for himself and have formed his own view on their worth. That seems to me wholly unrealistic.

Peter Gibson L.J. agreed and Sir Iain Glidewell concurred in the result.

Appeal Allowed.

Questions

14-006
1. A statement that the value of the contents was £16,000 would have been false. But was the statement, "to the best of my knowledge and belief, the value was £16,000" true or false? Does it matter how unreasonable the belief is?

2. Is there a material difference between findings (i) X did not hold the opinion he stated and (ii) X could not, as a reasonable man, *having his knowledge of the facts*, honestly have held it? Is there any difference if we omit the italicised words from (ii)? See citation from *Chitty on Contracts*, above. Suppose X, being a stupid or naive man, did hold that belief. Is he dishonest, as the court in *Economides* requires? Is his statement, "To the best of my knowledge and belief", then true or false?

3. Must we take it that the vendors in *Smith v Land and House Property Corp*, above, were lying?

4. Consider *The Mihalis Angelos*, below Ch.20 where Lord Denning MR said: "The owners were quite wrong in saying that [*The Mihalis Angelos*] was 'expected ready to load on 1st July' at Haiphong. They had no reasonable grounds for any such expectation." The owners were guilty, not merely of a misrepresentation, but also of a breach of condition. The owners may in fact have had such an unreasonable expectation. Is that case distinguishable from *Economides*? Does the commercial setting justify a distinction? See also *Esso Petroleum v Mardon*, below, Ch.15.

SPICE GIRLS v APRILIA WORLD SERVICE BV

[2002] EWCA Civ 15 CA

THE VICE-CHANCELLOR

This is the judgment of the court.

Introduction

14-007
1. On 24th February 1998 the Spice Girls, a well-known group of girl singers then consisting of five members, embarked on a tour of Europe. The claimant ("SGL"), a company owned by them and through which their services were exploited, had instructed agents ("KLP") to obtain sponsors for the tour. The agents made contact with Aprilia Spa ("Aprilia"), a company incorporated in Italy and a manufacturer of motorcycles. On 4th March 1998 heads of agreement were reached between SGL and Aprilia for the latter to sponsor the Spice Girls tour of Europe, due to end on 29th May 1998, and, on a more limited basis, the tour of the United States then planned for the period from 15th June to 31st August 1998. The sponsorship was announced on 8th March 1998.

2. The terms of the heads of agreement were substantially performed by all parties until given contractual effect by an agreement in writing dated 6th May 1998 ("the Agreement") made between SGL and Aprilia World

Service BV ("AWS"), a member of the Aprilia Group incorporated in the Netherlands. In the period between the conclusion of the heads of agreement and the execution of the Agreement two significant events occurred. The first is a fax sent on 30th March 1998 by KLP to Aprilia in which confirmation was given of the commitment of the Spice Girls to their involvement with Aprilia. The second is the filming in London on 4th May 1998 of a TV commercial ("the commercial shoot") in which all five Spice Girls participated which was designed to implant in the minds of the public an association between the products of Aprilia, primarily air-cooled motor scooters, and the Spice Girls.

3. The Agreement signed on 6th May 1998 described the Spice Girls as "currently consisting" of the five named members. It provided for AWS to pay £400,000 by three instalments, two of which had already been paid, and £112,500 as a non-returnable advance against royalties payable in respect of motor scooters manufactured and sold by the Aprilia Group bearing the name Sonic Spice. On 31st May 1998 it was announced that Ms Geri Halliwell, professionally known as Ginger Spice, had left the Spice Girls on 27th May 1998.

4. In a letter dated 8th June 1998 AWS informed SGL that it did not consider the departure of Ms Halliwell to constitute a breach of contract. Nevertheless AWS refused to pay either the third instalment or the advance against royalties. These proceedings were commenced by SGL on 22nd October 1998. SGL claimed payment of £212,500 being the balance of the third instalment and the non-returnable advance together with VAT and interest. The original defence and counterclaim of AWS relied on an express or implied representation and/or implied term or collateral warranty that SGL was unaware of any matter which might give AWS reason to believe that the Spice Girls might cease to consist of all five members during the minimum term of the Agreement. It was contended that SGL was aware of such matter and that AWS would give particulars thereof after discovery in the action.

5. In October 1999 Ms Geri Halliwell published her autobiography entitled "If Only". She disclosed that on both 3rd and 9th March 1998 she had informed the other four members of the Spice Girls that she intended to leave the Spice Girls at the end of the US tour in September 1998. She also revealed that at a meeting at Wembley Arena on 25th April 1998 she informed both the other members of the Spice Girls and their solicitor/manager of her intention.

6. In the light of these revelations AWS amended its defence and counterclaim so as to extend and particularise its contention that the Agreement had been induced by misrepresentation. AWS relied on the fax dated 30th March 1998, the description of the group in the Agreement as "currently consisting" of the five members, the participation of all the Spice Girls in the commercial shoot and the revelations in Ms Halliwell's autobiography with regard to the communication of her intentions to the other members of the group on 3rd and 9th March and 25th April 1998.

9. The action was tried by Arden J. from 7th to 14th February 2000. She gave judgment on 24th February 2000. She concluded that any claim for breach of contract was precluded by the letter from AWS of 8th June 1998. There is no appeal in respect of that conclusion. The judge also decided that SGL was liable to AWS under s.2(1) Misrepresentation Act 1967 in respect only of misrepresentations by conduct arising from the participation of all five Spice Girls in the commercial shoot on 4th May 1998 and their approval of promotional material depicting the five Spice Girls intended for use in connection with Aprilia's scooters at any time during the period of the Agreement. She rejected all the other misrepresentations on which AWS relied. Both SGL and AWS contend that those decisions are wrong. . . .

10. Accordingly the issues for our determination are:

(1) whether SGL is liable to AWS under s.2(1) Misrepresentation Act 1967 either on the narrow basis accepted by the judge but challenged by SGL or the wider basis for which AWS contends . . .

The Representation

51. At the outset it is necessary to reiterate certain well-established principles. First, though the representation must be one of fact representations as to the future or of opinion frequently contain implied representations with regard to the present or to the knowledge of the representor. Spencer Bower, Turner and Handley on Actionable Misrepresentation 4th Ed. paras 26 to 28. Second, a representation once made is likely to have continuing effect. So if made for the purpose of an intended transaction it will continue until the transaction is completed or abandoned or the representation ceases to be operative on the mind of the representee. *With v O'Flanagan* [1936] 1 Ch. 575, 585. Spencer Bower, Turner and Handley 4th Ed. paras 61 and 62. Third, if at a time when it is continuing the representor discovers that the representation was false when made or has become false since he should correct it. The principle is most clearly expounded in the judgment of Romer L.J. in *With v O'Flanagan* [1936] 1 Ch. 575, 586 where he said

"If A with a view to inducing B to enter into a contract makes a representation as to a material fact, then if at a later date and before the contract is actually entered into, owing to a change of circumstances, the representation then made would to the knowledge of A be untrue and B subsequently enters into the contract in ignorance of that change of circumstances and relying upon that representation, A cannot hold B to the bargain. There is ample authority for that statement and, indeed, I doubt myself whether any authority is necessary, it being, it seems to me, so obviously consistent with the plainest principles of equity."

An alternative formulation, with which Römer L.J. agreed, appears in the judgment of Lord Wright M.R. at page 583. After citing with approval the judgment of Turner L.J. in *Traill v Baring* 4 De G.J.& S 318, 329 he said that "the position is based on a duty to communicate the change of circumstances". Fourth, the meaning and effect of a statement or of conduct must be ascertained in the light of the circumstances pertaining at the time. Those circumstances will include the course of the negotiations and any earlier representations.

52. The representation for which AWS has contended ever since it amended its defence and counterclaim in December 1999 is that

"SGL did not know and had no reasonable grounds to believe at or before the time of entry into the agreement that any of the Spice Girls had an existing declared intention to leave the group during the minimum term of the Agreement", i.e. before March 1999.

This was accepted by the judge (J1 para 112) but only in respect of the commercial shoot on 4th May 1998 and "other promotional material depicting the five Spice Girls which was intended to be used at any time during the period of the agreement".

53. In our view the judge took too limited a view of the effect of the course of the negotiations as a whole and the specific documents and conduct relied on. We have already described the course of negotiations in some detail. Accordingly at this stage it is sufficient to highlight the most salient facts and events.

54. First, shortly after the conclusion of the heads of agreement on 4th March 1998 SGL supplied the logos, images and designs depicting each of the Spice Girls which were to be used by Aprilia in the promotion of the scooters. It must have been quite obvious from all such material and the judge's finding quoted in paragraph 19 above that the same five girls were required for all of them. AWS was entitled to use them throughout the period of 12 months for which the heads of agreement and, subsequently, paragraphs 10.8–10.10 and 13 of the Agreement provided. As we understand it such material was consistently used thereafter so as to generate a connection in the public eye between the Spice Girls and the scooters. In our view the representation contended for is necessarily implicit in that conduct from early March 1998 onwards. In, seemingly, connecting such material only to the commercial shoot on 4th May 1998, in our view, the judge seriously understated its significance.

55. Second, the events of 9th March 1998 were such as to bring to the attention of four of the other five directors of SGL the fact that Ms Halliwell had declared her intention to leave in September 1998. It follows that the representation implicit in the approval and use of the promotional material was false when made, or to the extent it was made before 9th March, became false on 9th March 1998. The fact that the other Spice Girls mistakenly as it turned out did not take Ms Halliwell seriously is immaterial.

56. Third, the subsequent events merely served to affirm, not correct, the initial representation and its falsity. Thus, the photocalls in Madrid, Munich and Paris held on or between 16th and 26th March may have been unsatisfactory to Ms Fuzzi but they took place and their effect was no different to the other promotional material. There were five Spice Girls each with her "distinct and individual image, style and personality".

57. Fourth, the fax of 30th March 1998 was sent by Mr Pettett in the light of the information given to him by Ms Halliwell and the tour manager at Arnhem on 27th March 1998. For the reasons we have already explained (paragraph 27 above) we do not agree with the judge's narrow construction of that document. In our view it was an express assurance that each Spice Girl was fully committed to all the matters contained in the heads of agreement and in the draft agreement then circulating for the full term of 12 months. There is implicit in such assurance the representation for which AWS contends. That representation was false when made because of the declaration of intention made by Ms Halliwell on 9th March 1998 and never qualified or withdrawn. The fact that Mr Pettett did not consider that he was making such a representation is irrelevant. *Greenwood v Leather Shod Wheel Co* [1900] 1 Ch 421, 434. Knowledge of the fax is to be attributed to SGL because KLP was its agent. *Krakowski v Eurolink Properties Ltd* [1995] 183 CLR 563, 582–4.

58. Fifth, the events of the meeting held at Wembley on 25th April 1998 demonstrated quite conclusively the falsity of all the representations previously made. Whichever formulation of the principle enunciated in *With v O'Flanagan* is adopted and whatever view is taken of the declaration made by Ms Halliwell on 9th March

1998 it is quite clear that SGL could no longer deal with AWS on the previous basis without disclosing Ms Halliwell's expressed intention. Certainly this was the view of Mr Morrison. [Day 2 page 45 lines 12–19]

59. Sixth, it is clear that far from correcting the previous misrepresentations SGL continued and affirmed them. There was the draft agreement originally issued on 24th March and reissued on 30th April. No doubt the phrase "currently comprising" points primarily to the present (whether at the time of the draft or as of the imminent time when the Agreement was executed) and in that limited sense was true. But to our minds, in the context of the surrounding circumstances, it was concerned with an agreement which would continue into the future, in much the same sense as the conduct of SGL in approving the promotional material or of the Spice Girls in participating in the commercial shoot, in each case, for future use. In these two latter senses there was implicit in the representation derived from the conduct of SGL in circulating the draft agreement with the phrase "currently comprising" the representation for which AWS contends. It follows that, in that context, to say that the Spice Girls currently comprised the five named individuals without going on to say that one of them was going to leave within the period of the Agreement was false when made. What was omitted rendered that which was actually stated false or misleading in the context in which it was made: see Chitty on Contracts, 1999 28th Ed, vol 1, para 6–016.

60. Seventh, as the judge held, participation in the commercial shoot necessarily carried the same implication and was likewise false. It did nothing to correct the previous misrepresentations, indeed it gave them additional force.

61. SGL contended that the conduct relied on by Arden J. could not give rise to the misrepresentation she found. Counsel pointed out that both the approval of the promotional material and participation in the commercial shoot on 4th May were required by the terms of the Agreement. Reliance was placed on the fact that Ms Halliwell did not appreciate that the deal with AWS could not be terminated before March 1999. It was also suggested that the description of the group as "currently comprising" showed that there was no representation as to their future composition.

62. We do not accept those submissions. The fact that the Spice Girls were doing what the, as yet unsigned, Agreement required appears to us to support, not negate, a conclusion that the representations alleged are to be implied. The knowledge of Ms Halliwell as to the terms of the prospective Agreement is irrelevant because whether any and if so what representation is to be implied is to be determined objectively in the light of what was said and done. For the reasons we have already given we consider that the description "currently comprising" supports the conclusions at which we have arrived.

63. Whilst it is necessary to give each episode separate consideration it is also necessary to have regard to their cumulative effect. This is not a case of an isolated representation made at an early stage of ongoing negotiations. It is the case of a series of continuing representations made throughout two months' negotiations leading to the Agreement. Later representations gave added force to the earlier ones; earlier representations gave focus to the later ones. It is in this context, not the much more limited one the judge adopted, that the submissions for SGL as to inducement and reliance must be considered.

Inducement and Reliance

64. S.2(1) Misrepresentation Act 1967 provides that

". . . if the person making the misrepresentation would be liable to damages in respect thereof had the misrepresentation been made fraudulently, that person shall be so liable notwithstanding that the misrepresentation was not made fraudulently.."

It is not disputed that the statute requires the representation to have induced the representee to enter into the contract. In addition SGL submits that the statutory analogy with damages in fraud introduces the additional requirement that the representation as understood was intended by the representor to induce the contract.

65. Arden J. relied on *Smith v Chadwick* (1884) 9 AC 187, 196 for the proposition that inducement and reliance may be inferred from the purpose of the representor, the nature of the statement and the fact that the contract was entered into. She referred to the evidence of both Ms Fuzzi and Sr Brovazzo to the effect that AWS would not have entered into the Agreement if they had known that Ms Halliwell had declared an existing intention to leave in September 1998. She pointed out that unless AWS did enter into the Agreement it could not obtain the benefit of the promotional material or the commercial shoot. We have quoted her conclusion in paragraph 43 above.

66. These conclusions were challenged by SGL on the grounds that it had not been established that AWS understood the representations in the sense contended for by AWS (*E.A. Grimstead & Son Ltd v McGarrigan* Court of Appeal 27th October 1999 unreported), or that SGL intended to induce AWS to sign the Agreement in

reliance on representations so understood (*Nautamix BV v Jenkins of Retford* [1975] FSR 385 a case in fraud). SGL submits that there was no evidence that AWS relied on the representations in that sense; in particular AWS relied on the commercial success of the Spice Girls to keep them together. SGL contends that there was no evidence from any individual in AWS to the effect that AWS would have withdrawn from the negotiations had the representation not been made. It is suggested that AWS was committed too far to justify any implication of withdrawal.

67. We do not accept these submissions. The representation bears the meaning in which it would be reasonably understood by the representee, that is to say, the natural and ordinary meaning which would be conveyed to a normal person. *Akerhielm v De Mare* [1959] AC 789. In the circumstances no one at AWS gave any consideration at the time to what representations were to be implied into the statements and conduct of the Spice Girls. But this is not a case in which the representations were ambiguous, so that the problem exemplified in *E.A. Grimstead & Son Ltd v McGarrigan* does not arise. There is no reason to think that AWS did not understand the representations in the sense alleged. The judge so inferred with regard to approval of promotional material and participation in the commercial shoot. We would do likewise in relation to the other representations to which we have referred.

68. It is not disputed that the various misrepresentations to which we have referred were made intentionally in the sense that the express statements and conduct in which they were implicit, if not express, were not accidental. In addition they were made in the context of a commercial relationship arising from heads of agreement already concluded which both parties hoped would reach fruition in a concluded and fully performed agreement. The various representations we have found to have been made were all such as to induce a normal person to act as AWS did. In those circumstances any requisite intention on the part of the representor will be presumed. *Smith v Chadwick* (ibid) p.190. In particular we cannot accept that SGL did not intend AWS to do exactly as it did, namely sign the Agreement, when it, SGL, failed to disclose to AWS immediately after the meeting on 25th April 1998 that Ms Halliwell definitely intended to leave in September 1998. Accordingly, in our view the conditions to which Oliver J. referred in *Nautamix BV v Jenkins of Retford* were satisfied, whatever may be the relevance of the intention of the representor in a case outside fraud but within S2(1).

69. It remains to consider whether the misrepresentations we have found to have been made did induce AWS to sign the Agreement. SGL contends that no witness for AWS was called to give evidence to that effect. It is true that both Ms Fuzzi and Sr Brovazzo indicated that AWS would not have entered into the Agreement if they had known that Ms Halliwell would leave in September 1998 but that, counsel contended, is not the same as testifying that AWS entered into the contract in reliance on the representation. Moreover, SGL contended, the evidence of Ms Fuzzi appeared to be that AWS was so far committed to the sponsorship deal by 4th May 1998 that it would not have withdrawn even if it had known of Ms Halliwell's intentions.

70. It is sufficient that the misrepresentation is a material inducement, it does not have to be the only one. In *Smith v Chadwick* (ibid.) page 196 Lord Blackburn said:

"I do not think it is necessary, in order to prove [damage], that the plaintiff should always be called as a witness to swear that he acted upon the inducement. At the time when Pasley v Freeman was decided, and for many years afterwards he could not be so called. I think that if it is proved that the defendants with a view to induce the plaintiff to enter into a contract made a statement to the plaintiff of such a nature as would be likely to induce a person to enter into a contract, it is a fair inference of fact that he was induced to do so by the statement."

Lord Blackburn went on to point out that the inference was one of fact not law and that if no evidence is given as to reliance in fact that was ground for not drawing the inference.

71. Arden J. did draw the inference that if the representations contained in the fax of 30th March 1998 had not been made Aprilia would have pulled out at that stage. We have already quoted her finding to that effect in paragraph 24 above. As we have pointed out that finding is significant because it recognises the importance of the views of Ms Fuzzi to any decision AWS was likely to make. It is true that over the next five weeks AWS paid £300,000 towards the fee due to SGL and took further steps to put the Spice Sonic scooter into production. Even so the judge concluded that the representation arising from participation in the commercial shoot on 4th May 1998 was a material inducement to AWS to sign the Agreement two days later.

72. In our view the judge was entitled to conclude that the representations, express or implied, in both the fax of 30th March 1998, which continued, and participation in the commercial shoot on 4th May 1998 were material inducements to AWS to enter into the Agreement on 6th May 1998. Signature to the Agreement on 6th May 1998 bound AWS to pay to SGL £100,000 as the third instalment of the fee and £112,500 as the non-returnable advance against royalties on the Spice Sonic scooters. It is inconceivable, and Ms Fuzzi did

not say, that AWS would have entered into those commitments had it been told of Ms Halliwell's declared intention to leave in September 1998. It might have entered into some other agreement with a view to cutting its losses but that was not alleged by SGL and is inconsistent with the evidence of Ms Fuzzi [Day 2 pages 30 and 31].

73. For all these reasons, while we consider that the judge took too narrow a view as to what representations were made and when, we do not accept the submissions for SGL that s.2(1) Misrepresentation Act 1967 is inapplicable. Subject to proof of damage, we conclude that SGL is liable to AWS under that provision. The conclusion of Arden J. that AWS sustained consequential damage of £39,669, being the cost of the scooters and moto bikes supplied pursuant to the Agreement, may depend on our conclusion on the issue whether in assessing the damages to which AWS is entitled credit should be given for any benefit derived therefrom and if so how much. To that issue we now turn.

---

2. SILENCE AND MISREPRESENTATION

14–008

In *Banque Financiere v Westgate Insurance Co* [1989] 2 All E.R. 952 at 1010, (affirmed on other grounds by the House of Lords, [1990] 2 All E.R. 947) Slade LJ, quoting from Blackburn J in *Smith v Hughes* (above, Ch.5) and citing Lord Atkin's example in *Bell v Lever Bros* (below, Ch.23) of the horse, the picture, the lease and the garage, said:

"The general principle that there is no obligation to speak within the context of negotiations for an ordinary commercial contract (though qualified by the well-known special principles relating to contracts uberrimae fidei, fraud, undue influence, fiduciary duty etc.) is one of the foundations of our law of contract, and must have been the basis of many decisions over the years. There are countless cases in which one party to a contract has in the course of negotiations failed to disclose a fact known to him which the other party would have regarded as highly material, if it had been revealed. However, ordinarily in the absence of misrepresentation, our law leaves that other party entirely without remedy."

That said, the law does not leave insurance companies without a remedy where the insured has failed to make a full disclosure. Both the general rule (that non-disclosure is not actionable as a misrepresentation) and the exception (that insurers can avoid policies where the insured, even quite innocently, has failed to make full disclosure) invite the criticism that this is not in line with the principles of fair dealing.

WALES v WADHAM

Family Division [1977] 1 W.L.R. 199; [1977] 2 All E.R. 125

14–009

On February 15, 1973, Wales and his wife (now Mrs Wadham) reached a compromise agreement whereby he would pay her £13,000 out of his half-share of the proceeds of the sale of their matrimonial home if she would not make any further claim for maintenance. (Cf. Matrimonial Causes Act 1973, above, Ch.10). The agreement was embodied in a consent order made on July 6 on the grant to the wife of a decree nisi. Wales sought rescission of the agreement on the ground, inter alia, that he would not have entered into the agreement on February 15 had he known that his wife then intended to remarry. The agreement was intended to commute his liability for periodical payments, a liability which, in the event, he would never have had. She had stated on several occasions in 1971 that she would never remarry. She did not reveal her intention to marry Mr Wadham because she did not wish him to be involved in the divorce proceedings.

TUDOR EVANS J

It is submitted that even if the wife's statement that she would never remarry was honestly held, she was under a duty to tell the husband of her changed circumstances, but that she failed to do so. Counsel has referred me to *With v O'Flanagan* [1936] Ch. 575 in the Court of Appeal. In that case, during the course of negotiations for the sale of a medical practice, the vendor made representations to the purchaser, about the existing nature of the practice which, by the time when the contract was signed, were untrue. The value of the practice had declined in the meantime because of the vendor's inability to attend to it through illness. Lord Wright M.R. quoted, with approval, observations of Fry J. in *Davies v London and Provincial Marine Insurance Co* (1878) 8 Ch.D. 469, 475 where he said:

> "So again, if a statement has been made which is true at the time, but which during the course of negotiations becomes untrue, then the person who knows that it has become untrue is under an obligation to disclose to the other the change of circumstances."

The representations in both of these cases related to existing fact and not to a statement of intention in relation to future conduct. A statement of intention is not a representation of existing fact, unless the person making it does not honestly hold the intention he is expressing, in which case there is a misrepresentation of fact in relation to the state of that person's mind. That does not arise on the facts as I have found them. On the facts of this case, the wife made an honest statement of her intention which was not a representation of fact, and I can find no basis for holding that she was under a duty in the law of contract to tell the husband of her change of mind. Counsel for the wife submits that, apart from any other consideration, the wife's objection to remarriage after divorce and her specific statements to the husband that she would not remarry, do not have the quality of representations in the sense that at her age she could not seriously be taken as representing that she would never change her mind. I accept that submission. It seems to me that when after a marriage which had lasted for some 26 years the wife told the husband she would never marry again she was not representing to the husband that, she then being barely 50, she would never change her mind. The wife's objections to remarriage on religious grounds could not, in themselves, amount to a representation. They were simply general opinions expressed during the existence of the marriage, and not in any way made in contemplation by either party of a contract. With respect to the specific statements, as I have said, I am satisfied that the wife made them in an attempt to save her marriage and I am satisfied she was not representing that she would never change her mind.

I must now consider the submission of the husband that the contract in this case was one requiring uberrima fides. Such contracts are an exception to the common law rule that a party may remain silent about material facts when negotiating a contract, and that such silence does not amount to a misrepresentation. I have been referred to *Bell v Lever Bros Ltd* [1932] A.C. 161, 232, where Lord Thankerton said:

> "The most familiar of these exceptions is found in the case of policies of insurance, as to which Blackburn J. says, in Fletcher v Krell (1873) 42 L.J.Q.B. 55, 'mercantile custom has established the rule with regard to concealment of material facts in policies of assurance, but in other cases there must be an allegation of moral guilt or fraud.' Other exceptions are found in case of trustee and cestui que trust and of a company issuing a prospectus and an applicant for shares, but the number of exceptions is limited, and no authority has been cited which extends the exceptions to cover a case such as the present."

Further examples are contracts of partnership and suretyship but there is no case in which the principle has been extended to contracts between a husband and wife, although counsel for the husband has referred to a number of authorities in the 19th century concerned with deeds of separation, in which he submits the duty to disclose has been recognised. I shall refer to these cases at a later stage. The first submission is that the contract in the present case is similar to a contract of insurance. It is pointed out that contracts of insurance are speculative in nature in the sense that an insurer can only compute his risk on the basis of what he is told by the proposed assured. I have been referred to an early case, *Carter v Boehm* (1766) 3 Burr. 1905 at 1909, where Lord Mansfield C. J. said:

> "Insurance is a contract upon speculation. The special facts, upon which the contingent chance is to be computed, lie most commonly in the knowledge of the insured only: the under-writer trusts to his representation, and proceeds upon confidence that he does not keep back any circumstance in his knowledge, to mislead the under-writer into a belief that the circumstance does not exist . . ."

It is said that the husband in the present case was computing or compromising in a single sum a future and uncertain liability to maintain the wife and that the likelihood of the wife's remarriage was a material fact in the computation which should have been disclosed. I cannot accept that there is any analogy between a contract of insurance and the contract in the present case. In contracts of insurance, the material facts on which the insurer decides whether to assume the risk and, if so, on what terms, lie exclusively within the knowledge of the insured. Contracts requiring uberrima fides are based on the fact that, from the very necessity of the case, only one party possesses knowledge of all the material facts. In the case of life assurance, for example, only the proposed assured can know the state of his health, past or present. The contract in the present case was one in which material facts on both sides were withheld. Neither side made full disclosure. The husband admitted in cross-examination that he did not disclose his income. Nor was anything said about Mrs Turner's financial position.[3] The wife stated in evidence that although she knew the sources of the husband's capital assets, that is his interest in Dean Cottage and his share capital, she had no real idea of his income although she pressed him for details . . . On the wife's side, she did not disclose that between the end of October 1972, when the husband made the offer, and February 1973, when counsel agreed the terms in settlement of all the wife's claims for ancillary relief for maintenance, that she had an arrangement to marry Mr Wadham. No questions were asked of the wife's financial position nor whether she intended to marry at any time in the future. It seems to me that the negotiations and the agreement reached was a compromise without full disclosure on either side. I can find no similarity at all to a contract of insurance.

Judgment for the Wife.

Question

Is it true to say that a statement of intention is not a representation of existing fact where the person making it honestly holds the intention expressed? It is not a misrepresentation because it is true; but that does not prevent it being a representation of fact. Is *With v O'Flanagan* properly distinguishable?

14–010

LAMBERT v CO-OPERATIVE INSURANCE SOCIETY LTD

Court of Appeal [1975] 2 Lloyd's Rep. 485

In April 1963 Mrs Lambert signed a proposal form for an insurance policy to cover her own and her husband's jewellery. Her answers to questions on the form were filled in by an agent of the insurance company. No questions were asked about previous convictions and Mrs Lambert gave no information about them. She knew that her husband had been convicted some years earlier of stealing cigarettes and fined £25. The company issued a policy providing that it should be void if there was an omission to state any fact material to the risk. The policy was renewed from year to year, the last application to renew being made in March 1972. In December 1971 the husband had been convicted of conspiracy to steal and theft and sentenced to 15 months imprisonment. Mrs Lambert knew of the conviction but did not disclose it and the policy was renewed. On April 30, 1972, seven items of the insured jewellery, valued at £311, were lost or stolen. Mrs Lambert's claim was repudiated on the grounds (i) that she had failed to disclose her husband's first conviction; (ii) that she had failed to disclose his second conviction. Judge Ranking dismissed the wife's claim on the ground that the 1971 conviction was a material fact and that a prudent insurer, knowing of it, would not have continued the risk.

The plaintiff appealed.

14–011

---

[3]   The husband left the wife to live with Mrs Turner.

MACKENNA J

Everyone agrees that the assured is under a duty of disclosure and that the duty is the same when he is applying for a renewal as it is when he is applying for the original policy. The extent of that duty is the matter in controversy. There are, at least in theory, four possible rules or tests which I shall state. (1) The duty is to disclose such facts only as the particular assured believes to be material. (2) It is to disclose such facts as a reasonable man would believe to be material. (3) It is to disclose such facts as the particular insurer would regard as material. (4) It is to disclose such facts as a reasonable or prudent insurer might have treated as material.

Section 18 of the Marine Insurance Act, 1906, chooses the fourth. Sub-section (1) of that section provides that:

"The assured must disclose to the insurer, before the contract is concluded, every material circumstance which is known to the assured, and the assured is deemed to know every circumstance which, in the ordinary course of business, ought to be known by him. If the assured fails to make such disclosure, the insurer may avoid the contract."

Sub-section (2) is in these words:

"Every circumstance is material which would influence the judgment of a prudent insurer in fixing the premium, or determining whether he will take the risk."

There is no obvious reason why there should be a rule in marine insurance different from the rules in other forms of insurance and, in my opinion, there is no difference. [His Lordship examined various authorities, concluding with the Report of the Law Reform Committee (Cmnd. 62 of 1957)].

After stating their decision to exclude marine insurance from the scope of their inquiries, because of the lack of interest by the general public in the subject, the committee went on to state their view about non-disclosure. I quote from paragraph 4 of the report.

The effect of non-disclosure may be considered first, since it is a consequence of the general law relating to insurance contracts and does not involve any express term or condition. We take it to be well settled law (a) that the duty of disclosure of material facts—or the rule of uberrima fides as it is often called—applies to all classes of insurance, and (b) that the question in every case is whether the fact not disclosed was material to the risk, and not whether the insured, whether reasonably or otherwise, believed or understood it to be so.

Further, we see no reason to doubt that the definition of "material," adopted by the Privy Council in *Mutual Life Insurance Co of New York v Ontario Metal Products Co Ltd* for the purposes of life assurance—namely that the fact, if disclosed, might have led a reasonable insurer to decline the risk or to stipulate for a higher premium—would be applied in all classes of insurance. This definition is substantially the same as that laid down in the Marine Insurance Act, 1906, and has been adopted by an English Court as a definition of materiality for the purpose of subsections (3) and (5) of section 10 of the Road Traffic Act 1934.

That last reference is of course to the *Zurich General Accident and Liability Insurance Co v Morrison*. The report continues:

"The practical effect of the law on this point is that insurers are entitled to repudiate liability wherever they can show that a fact within the knowledge of the insured was not disclosed which, according to current insurance practice, would have affected their judgment of the risk. Whether the insuring public at large is aware of this it is difficult to say; but it seems to us to follow from the accepted definition of materiality that a fact may be material to insurers, in the light of the great volume of experience of claims available to them, which would not necessarily appear to a proposer for insurance, however honest and careful, to be one which he ought to disclose. [—They went on to recommend a change in the law. I will quote the first of three recommendations in paragraph 14 of the report:—] (1) That for the purpose of any contract of insurance no fact should be deemed material unless it would have been considered material by a reasonable insured."

We are, in effect, invited to say that the committee misunderstood the matter and that what they proposed as a change in the law is the existing rule. I am not prepared to accept this invitation. Recognising that there are expressions in some of the cases which favour the appellant's argument, I think the committee got it right and that their statement of the existing law was correct . . . I cannot say that the Judge's view was wrong. I am content to act upon his finding of fact which is, I think, sufficiently supported by evidence, and to take the law as stated by the Law Reform Committee.

I would only add to this long judgment the expression of my personal regret that the Committee's recommendation has not been implemented. The present case shows the unsatisfactory state of the law. Mrs Lambert is unlikely to have thought that it was necessary to disclose the distressing fact of her husband's recent conviction when she was renewing the policy on her little store of jewellery. She is not an under-writer and has presumably no experience in these matters. The defendant company would act decently if, having established the point of principle, they were to pay her. It might be thought a heartless thing if they did not, but that is their business, not mine. I would dismiss the appeal.

Lawton and Cairns L.JJ. delivered judgments dismissing the appeal.

It should be noted that, in *Economides*, above, Simon Brown LJ said that the test for non-disclosure was the same as for misrepresentation, i.e. a test of honesty. Discussing s.18(1) of the Marine Insurance Act 1906, above, he said: "It is clearly established that an assured such as this appellant, effecting insurance cover as a private individual and not 'in the ordinary course of business', must disclose only material facts known to him; he is not to have ascribed to him any form of deemed or constructive knowledge."

A. The Duty to Disclose: Mutuality; and Remedies

The duty of disclosure of facts which are material to the risk in insurance contracts is mutual, that is,   **14–012**
it is imposed on the insurer as well as the insured. In *Banque Financière v Westgate Insurance* [1990] 2 All E.R. 947 at 960 HL, Lord Jauncey said that the duty is limited to facts which are material to the risk insured, that is, facts which would influence a prudent insurer in deciding whether to accept the risk and, if so, on what terms, and a prudent insured in entering into the contract on the terms proposed by the insurer; but that there is no duty to disclose supervening facts which come to the knowledge of either party after the conclusion of the contract. There have been no reported cases involving the failure of an insurer to disclose material facts to an insured. The example given by Lord Mansfield in *Carter v Boehm* (1766) 3 Burr. 1905 at 1909, is of an insurer who insured a ship knowing that she had already arrived. Another example would be the insurance against fire of a house which the insurer knew had been demolished.

In *Banque Financière*, Steyn J had held that an action for damages lies for breach of the obligation of utmost good faith in an insurance contract—a proposition for which there was no previous author-ity—but the Court of Appeal decided that no such action lies. There was some suggestion in earlier cases that the duty of disclosure rests upon an implied promise in the contract that full disclosure had been made. If that were so, the non-disclosure would be a breach of contract as soon as the contract came into existence and an action for damages would lie. But the court (at 993–996) held that the duty is imposed by law and arises entirely outside the contract. (A holding followed in *Bank of Novia Scotia v Hellenic Mutual* [1989] 3 All E.R. 628 at 659 CA) Nor was there any authority to the effect that non-disclosure constitutes a tort and the court was not prepared to create a new one. The court assumed (at 1001), without deciding, that any conduct which is capable of giving rise to an estoppel by conduct is capable of giving rise to a claim for misrepresentation; but mere silence, even where there is a duty to speak does not constitute a misrepresentation, (at 1003). For the purposes of the 1967 Act (below) a misrepresentation must be 'made.' This is not apt to include a failure to make a statement which ought to have been made, (see 1004).

B. Materiality and Inducement

A circumstance is material if a prudent insurer would consider it in deciding whether to accept the risk   **14–013**
and, if so, on what terms, even though, after that consideration, the circumstance would not affect

his decision on either of these matters: The House of Lords so held in *Pan Atlantic Insurance Co Ltd v Pine Top Insurance Co Ltd* [1994] 3 All E.R. 581 HL (Lords Templeman and Lloyd dissenting), rejecting the "decisive influence test"; but they went on to hold unanimously, applying the "actual inducement test", that an insurer can avoid a policy for a misrepresentation or non-disclosure only if (a) it was material and (b) it induced the making of the policy on the relevant terms. So the duty of the insured to disclose extends to facts which the prudent insurer would take into account even though they would, in the end, have no influence on his decision. But a failure to disclose such a fact would have no effect unless the particular insurer, being of more than ordinary prudence, would either have refused to take the risk or charged a higher premium if he had known of the fact. So the assured must disclose facts which a prudent insurer might think material; but his failure to do so will have no effect unless the particular insurers would have so considered it.

Law Commission Working Paper No. 73: Insurance Law—Non-disclosure and breach of warranty

[After referring to judicial criticism of the law in *Lambert v Co-op. Ins.*, the Law Commission go on[4]:]

38. It has been pointed out that many laymen are not aware that a duty of disclosure exists and that it may be very difficult if not impossible for those who are aware of the duty to know what information would be regarded as material by a prudent insurer. One writer has observed that the duty imposes an especially heavy burden on insureds who hold a policy which is renewable year by year as they are most unlikely to realise that the duty arises on each successive renewal. Another has raised the problem of the extent of the duty to an insured when he applies over the telephone for the issue of a cover-note by an insurer.

39. The general rule of the present law whereby an insured is not relieved of his duty of disclosure even where the insurer has asked questions of him in a proposal form, has been criticised on the ground that the insured may well have been led to suppose that no further information was required to be disclosed by him.

40. In endeavouring to ascertain the materiality of particular facts, the courts will hear the expert evidence of other insurers; such evidence will be produced by the insurer who will select its expert witnesses. Some judicial doubt has been cast on the cogency of such evidence. For instance, it has been thought odd that an insurer who would not himself have regarded a non-disclosed fact as material should be able to call evidence that a prudent insurer would have done so.

41. Criticism has also been directed to judicial decisions as to the materiality of particular types of fact. It will suffice to mention two such decisions. One is *Regina Fur v Bossom* [1957] 2 Lloyd's Rep. 466 in which an insurer was held entitled to repudiate on the grounds of the insured's failure to disclose a conviction that had taken place 23 years earlier. Another is *Locker & Woolf Ltd v Western Australian Insurance Co* [1936] 1 K.B. 408 in which the non-disclosed fact held to be material was a previous rejection with regard to an entirely different type of insurance from that which was being applied for.

42. We are impressed by these criticisms and have reached the conclusion that the law as to non-disclosure should be reformed.

See the Law Commission's Report, Law Com. No.104, (Cmnd. 8064). This report has never been implemented. Consumer contracts, however, are now subject to the Unfair Terms in Consumer Contract Regulations below, Ch.22.

3. Damages for Innocent Misrepresentation at Common Law

HEDLEY BYRNE & CO v HELLER & PARTNERS

House of Lords [1964] A.C. 465; [1963] 3 W.L.R. 101; [1963] 2 All E.R. 575; [1963] 1 Lloyd's Rep. 485

14-014   Hedley Byrne were a firm of advertising agents who had placed advertising orders for £8,000–£9,000 on behalf of a client, Easipower Ltd. They wanted to know whether Easipower Ltd was creditworthy,

---

4   Footnotes are omitted.

and asked their bank, the National Provincial, to find out. The National Provincial got in touch with Heller & Partners, Easipower's bankers. Heller told the National Provincial, "in confidence and without responsibility on our part," that Easipower were good for £100,000 per annum on advertising contracts. Hedley Byrne relied on this statement in placing further orders on behalf of Easipower Ltd and, as a result, lost more than £17,000 when Easipower went into liquidation. They sought to recover this loss as damages. McNair J held that Heller were negligent but that they owed no duty of care to Hedley Byrne. The Court of Appeal affirmed that there was no duty of care and did not find it necessary to decide whether Heller was negligent. Hedley Byrne appealed.

Lords Reid, Morris, Hodson and Devlin made speeches dismissing the appeal.

LORD PEARCE

My Lords, Viscount Haldane L.C. in *Nocton v Lord Ashburton* [1914] A.C. 932 at 948 said:

> "Although liability for negligence in word has in material respects been developed in our law differently from liability for negligence in act, it is none the less true that a man may come under a special duty to exercise care in giving information or advice. I should accordingly be sorry to be thought to lend countenance to the idea that recent decisions have been intended to stereotype the cases in which people can be held to have assumed such a special duty. Whether such a duty has been assumed must depend on the relationship of the parties, and it is at least certain that there are a good many cases in which that relationship may be properly treated as giving rise to a special duty of care in statement."

The law of negligence has been deliberately limited in its range by the courts' insistence that there can be no actionable negligence in vacuo without the existence of some duty to the plaintiff. For it would be impracticable to grant relief to everybody who suffers damage through the carelessness of another.

The reason for some divergence between the law of negligence in word and that of negligence in act is clear. Negligence in word creates problems different from those of negligence in act. Words are more volatile than deeds. They travel fast and far afield. They are used without being expended and take effect in combination with innumerable facts and other words. Yet they are dangerous and can cause vast financial damage . . .

Denning L.J. in his dissenting judgment in *Candler v Crane, Christmas & Co* [1951] 2 K.B. at 179 . . . reached the conclusion that in respect of reports and work that resulted in such reports there was a duty of care laid on

> "those persons such as accountants, surveyors, valuers and analysts, whose profession and occupation it is to examine books, accounts, and other things and to make reports on which other people—other than their clients—rely in the ordinary course of business."

The duty is in his opinion owed (apart from contractual duty to their employer)

> "to any third person to whom they themselves show the accounts, or to whom they know their employer is going to show the accounts so as to induce him to invest money or take some other action on them."

He excludes strangers of whom they have heard nothing and to whom their employer without their knowledge may choose to hand their accounts, and continues:

> "The test of proximity in these cases is: did the accountants know that the accounts were required for submission to the plaintiff and use by him?"

. . . I agree with those words. In my opinion they are consonant with earlier cases and with the observations of Lord Haldane.

It is argued that so to hold would create confusion in many aspects of the law and infringe the established rule that innocent misrepresentation gives no right to damages. I cannot accept that argument. The true rule is that innocent misrepresentation per se gives no right to damages. If the misrepresentation was intended by the parties to form a warranty between two contracting parties, it gives on that ground a right to damages (*Heilbut, Symons & Co v Buckleton*). If an innocent misrepresentation is made between parties in a fiduciary relationship it may, on that ground, give a right to claim damages for negligence. There is also in my opinion a duty of care created by special relationships which, though not fiduciary, give rise to an assumption that care as well as honesty is demanded.

Was there such a special relationship in the present case as to impose on the respondents a duty of care to the appellants as the undisclosed principals for whom National Provincial Bank Ltd was making the inquiry? The answer to that question depends on the circumstances of the transaction. If, for instance, they disclosed a casual social approach to the inquiry no such special relationship or duty of care would be assumed (see *Fish v Kelly* (1864) 17 C.B. (n.s.) 194). To import such a duty the representation must normally, I think, concern a business or professional transaction whose nature makes clear the gravity of the inquiry and the importance and influence attached to the answer. It is conceded that Salmon J rightly found a duty of care in *Woods v Martins Bank Ltd* [1959] 1 Q.B. 55, but the facts in that case were wholly different from those in the present case. A most important circumstance is the form of the inquiry and of the answer. Both were here plainly stated to be without liability. Counsel for the appellants argues that those words are not sufficiently precise to exclude liability for negligence. Nothing, however, except negligence could, in the facts of this case, create a liability (apart from fraud, to which they cannot have been intended to refer and against which the words would be no protection since they would be part of the fraud). I do not, therefore, accept that, even if the parties were already in contractual or other special relationship, the words would give no immunity to a negligent answer. But in any event they clearly prevent a special relationship from arising. They are part of the material from which one deduces whether a duty of care and a liability for negligence was assumed. If both parties say expressly (in a case where neither is deliberately taking advantage of the other) that there shall be no liability, I do not find it possible to say that a liability was assumed . . .

I would, therefore, dismiss the appeal.

Appeal Dismissed.

----

4. LOSING THE RIGHT TO RESCIND

LEAF v INTERNATIONAL GALLERIES

Court of Appeal [1950] 2 K.B. 86; 66 T.L.R. (Pt. 1) 1031; [1950] 1 All E.R. 693

14-015 In March 1944 the plaintiff purchased from the defendants a picture called "Salisbury Cathedral" for £85. At the time of purchase the defendants represented that the picture was painted by John Constable, but when, five years later, the plaintiff tried to sell it, he was informed that it was not by Constable. Thereupon he returned it to the defendants and asked them to refund the £85. The plaintiff brought an action for rescission. The county court judge found that the defendants had made an innocent misrepresentation and that the picture had not been painted by Constable. He gave judgment for the defendant, holding, on the authority of *Angel v Jay*, below, that the equitable remedy of rescission was not available in the case of an executed contract.

DENNING LJ

The question is whether the plaintiff is entitled to rescind the contract on the ground that the picture in question was not painted by Constable. I emphasise that it is a claim to rescind only: there is no claim in this action for damages for breach of condition or breach of warranty. The claim is simply one for rescission. At a very late stage before the county court judge counsel did ask for leave to amend by claiming damages for breach of warranty, but it was not allowed. No claim for damages is before us at all. The only question is whether the plaintiff is entitled to rescind.

The way in which the case is put by Mr Weitzman, on behalf of the plaintiff, is this: he says that this was an innocent misrepresentation and that in equity he is, or should be, entitled to claim rescission even of an executed contract of sale on that account. He points out that the judge has found that it is quite possible to restore the parties to their original position. It can be done by simply handing back the picture to the defendants.

In my opinion, this case is to be decided according to the well-known principles applicable to the sale of goods. This was a contract for the sale of goods. There was a mistake about the quality of the subject-matter, because both parties believed the picture to be a Constable; and that mistake was in one sense essential or fundamental. But such a mistake does not avoid the contract: there was no mistake at all about the subject-matter of the sale. It was a specific picture, "Salisbury Cathedral." The parties were agreed in the same terms on the same subject-matter, and that is sufficient to make a contract: see *Solle v Butcher* [below, Ch.23].

There was a term in the contract as to the quality of the subject-matter: namely, as to the person by whom the picture was painted–that it was by Constable. That term of the contract was, according to our terminology, either a condition or a warranty. If it was a condition, the buyer could reject the picture for breach of the condition at any time before he accepted it, or is deemed to have accepted it; whereas, if it was only a warranty, he could not reject it at all but was confined to a claim for damages.

I think it right to assume in the buyer's favour that this term was a condition, and that if he had come in proper time he could have rejected the picture; but the right to reject for breach of condition has always been limited by the rule that, once the buyer has accepted, or is deemed to have accepted, the goods in performance of the contract, then he cannot thereafter reject, but is relegated to his claim for damages: see section 11(1)(c) of the Sale of Goods Act 1893 [See now s.11(4) of the 1979 Act below, para.16–014], and *Wallis, Son & Wells v Pratt & Haynes* [1910] 2 K.B. 1003; [1911] A.C. 394 [below, Ch.20].

The circumstances in which a buyer is deemed to have accepted goods in performance of the contract are set out in section 35 of the Act, which says that the buyer is deemed to have accepted the goods, amongst other things, "when, after the lapse of a reasonable time, he retains the goods without intimating to the seller that he has rejected them." In this case the buyer took the picture into his house and, apparently, hung it there, and five years passed before he intimated any rejection at all. That, I need hardly say, is much more than a reasonable time. It is far too late for him at the end of five years to reject this picture for breach of any condition. His remedy after that length of time is for damages only, a claim which he has not brought before the court.

Is it to be said that the buyer is in any better position by relying on the representation, not as a condition, but as an innocent misrepresentation? . . .

Although rescission may in some cases be a proper remedy, it is to be remembered that an innocent misrepresentation is much less potent than a breach of condition; and a claim to rescission for innocent misrepresentation must at any rate be barred when a right to reject for breach of condition is barred. A condition is a term of the contract of a most material character, and if a claim to reject on that account is barred, it seems to me a fortiori that a claim to rescission on the ground of innocent misrepresentation is also barred.

So, assuming that a contract for the sale of goods may be rescinded in a proper case for innocent misrepresentation, the claim is barred in this case for the self-same reason as a right to reject is barred. The buyer has accepted the picture. He had ample opportunity for examination in the first few days after he had bought it. Then was the time to see if the condition or representation was fulfilled. Yet he has kept it all this time. Five years have elapsed without any notice of rejection. In my judgment he cannot now claim to rescind. His only claim, if any, as the county court judge said, was one for damages, which he has not made in this action. In my judgment, therefore, the appeal should be dismissed.

Jenkins L.J. and Evershed M.R. delivered concurring judgments.

PEYMAN v LANJANI

Court of Appeal [1985] Ch. 457; [1985] 2 W.L.R. 154; [1984] 3 All E.R. 703

The plaintiff entered into an agreement to purchase from the defendant the lease of a restaurant for £55,000 to be paid by the plaintiff selling his house to the defendant for £32,000, the balance to be paid in cash. The defendant had obtained the landlord's consent to the assignment to him of the lease by fraud ("the first impersonation"). On February 9, when the plaintiff was reluctant to proceed with the transaction, he learned of the impersonation. The solicitor who was acting for both parties urged him to proceed. A month later the plaintiff consulted new solicitors who advised him that the defendant's title was defective because of the fraud and that he had a right to rescind; and the plaintiff gave notice to the defendant of his intention to do so. The judge held that the plaintiff had affirmed the contract because on February 22, after he knew of the impersonation, he had proceeded with the contract, taken possession of the restaurant and paid £10,000 to the defendant.

The plaintiff appealed. The Court of Appeal held that the plaintiff was not deprived of his right to rescind because, knowing of the facts which give rise to the right to rescind, he proceeded with the contract, unless he also knew that he had the right to rescind. The plaintiff (an Iranian who spoke no

14–016

English) did not know he had such a right. As he did not know he had such a right, he could not be said to have elected to affirm the contract by his actions.

SLADE LJ

Where the other stated conditions for the operation of the common law doctrine of "election" are present, a person may be held to his election even though the other party has not in any way acted to his detriment in reliance on the relevant communication; the mere facts of the unequivocal act or statement, coupled with the communication thereof to the other party, suffice to bring the doctrine into play. For this reason, if no other, as appears from the judgments of Stephenson and May L.JJ. a clear distinction has to be drawn between election on the one hand and estoppel or waiver by conduct on the other hand.

The relevant argument in the present case has primarily been directed to election. Before us it has been common ground that the injured party to a contract who has a right of rescission cannot be said to have elected to affirm it at a time before he became aware of the facts which give rise to this right. However, as Stephenson L.J. has demonstrated, statements of the highest authority seem at first sight to give conflicting answers to the question whether knowledge of the existence of the legal right to rescind is also a condition precedent to an effective election.

Lord Blackburn in *Kendall v Hamilton* (1879) 4 App.Cas. 504 at 542, said: ". . . there cannot be election until there is knowledge of the right to elect." For the reasons given by Stephenson and May L.JJ., I am of the opinion that this statement, which was cited by Lord Porter in *Young v Bristol Aeroplane Co Ltd* [1946] A.C. 163 at 186 as being the foundation of the principle of election, still correctly represents the law. With Stephenson and May L.JJ., I do not think that a person (such as Mr Peyman in the present case) can be held to have made the irrevocable choice between rescission and affirmation which election involves unless he had knowledge of his legal right to choose and actually chose with that knowledge.

I would like to make a few observations as to the practical consequences of this court's decision on this point, as I see them. If A wishes to allege that B, having had a right of rescission, has elected to affirm a contract, he should in his pleadings, so it seems to me, expressly allege B's knowledge of the relevant right to rescind, since such knowledge will be an essential fact on which he relies. The court may, and no doubt often will, be asked to order A to give further and better particulars of the allegation (see RSC Ord. 18, r. 12(4)). In many cases the best particulars that A will be able to give will be to invite the court to infer knowledge from all the circumstances. However strong that prima facie inference may be, it will still be open to the court at the trial, after hearing evidence as to B's true state of mind, to hold on the balance of probabilities that he did not in fact have the requisite knowledge. In the latter event A's plea that B has elected will fail. Yet it should not be thought that injustice to A will necessarily follow. For, if A has acted to his detriment in reliance of [sic] an apparent election by B, he will in most cases be able to plead and rely on an estoppel by conduct, in the alternative. If, on the other hand, A has not acted to his detriment in reliance on any such apparent election, justice would not seem to preclude B from sheltering behind his ignorance of his legal rights. These brief observations may perhaps serve to highlight the distinction between election and estoppel.

Since Mr Peyman had no knowledge of his legal right to rescind the restaurant agreement, until he consulted new solicitors, his conduct in entering into possession of the restaurant and paying £10,000 to Mr Lanjani, for this reason if no other, cannot in my opinion have amounted to an election to affirm the contract; the only remaining question can be whether Mr Peyman by that conduct has estopped himself from relying on his right to rescind.

However, even if I am wrong in thinking that knowledge of the relevant legal right is a precondition to an effective election, the result on the facts of the present case is, in my opinion, still the same for these reasons. Whatever knowledge may be requisite, the passages which I have cited above . . . in my opinion make it quite clear that a person who has the right to rescind a contract cannot be treated as having elected to affirm it unless and until he has done an unequivocal act, or made an unequivocal statement, which demonstrates to the other party to the contract that he still intends to proceed with it, notwithstanding the relevant breach. An unequivocal act or unequivocal statement on the part of Mr Peyman is no less necessary if Mr Lanjani is to rely on an estoppel by conduct.

The judge considered that the arrangements by which Mr Peyman took possession of the restaurant and paid Mr Lanjani £10,000 of the purchase price did amount to "an unequivocal affirmation of the contract." He thought that Mr Lanjani acted on this affirmation by giving up possession of the restaurant and going away to Iran. Mr Peyman, he considered, by these arrangements, "accepted the title through his solicitor . . . and that as between him and Mr Lanjani is that."

This conduct of Mr Peyman on February 22, 1979 undeniably indicated that, at least for the time being, he intended to proceed with the restaurant agreement. In my opinion, however, this does not by itself suffice to indicate any relevant final choice on his part. The question is whether his conduct on February 22, 1979 would have led Mr Lanjani and his legal advisers reasonably to infer he did not intend to object to the particular defect in title which had arisen through the first impersonation.

For my part, I do not think that Mr Lanjani or his legal advisers could reasonable have drawn any such inference . . .

Point for reflection

Compare the principles stated by Lord Denning in *Leaf v International Galleries*, above, governing rescission of a contract for the sale of goods, and see Lord Goff in *The Kanchenjunga* [1990] 1 Lloyd's Rep. 391 at 398:   **14–017**

"Generally . . . it is a prerequisite of election that the party making the election must be aware of the facts which have given rise to the existence of his new right. This may not always be so. For example, in the law of sale of goods, where goods have been tendered to the buyer which are not in conformity with the contract, he may, if he has had a reasonable opportunity to examine them, be deemed in certain circumstances to have accepted them, thereby electing not to exercise his right to reject them, even though he has not actually examined the goods and discovered the defect (see sections 34 and 35 of the Sale of Goods Act 1979). This may flow from the fact that he has waived his right to examine them—yet another example of waiver. I add in parenthesis that, for present purposes, it is not necessary for me to consider certain cases in which it has been held that, as a prerequisite of election, the party must be aware not only of the facts giving rise to his rights but also of the rights themselves, because it is not in dispute here that the owners were aware both of the relevant facts and of their relevant rights."

----

5. How to Rescind

TSB BANK v CAMFIELD

Court of Appeal [1995] 1 W.L.R. 430; [1995] 1 All E.R. 951

ROCH LJ

The right to set aside or rescind the transaction is that of the representee, not that of the court. The court's   **14–018**
role in a disputed case will be to decide whether the representee has lawfully rescinded the transaction or is entitled to rescind it. Normally, if the representee is entitled to rescind the legal charge, that will have been effected by the representee's pleading that the transaction has been or should be set aside; that is to say, the transaction would have been set aside before the matter reaches the court. The court is not being asked to grant equitable relief; nor is it, in my view, granting equitable relief to which terms may be attached.

If this analysis (which, as I understand it, is the analysis adopted by Ferris J. in *Allied Irish Bank v Byrne* (February 1, 1994, unreported)) is correct, then the provisions of the Misrepresentation Act 1967 become, in my view, of the utmost significance. Section 1 of that Act is in terms consistent with the right to rescind for misrepresentation being that of the person to whom the misrepresentation has been made. Section 2(2) gives the court power, where such a person has rescinded or is entitled to rescind a contract, to declare the contract subsisting and to award damages in lieu of rescission in certain circumstances. That implies that but for that subsection the court does not have the power to declare the contract to be subsisting when, as in this case, the representee has exercised her right to set aside the transaction.

Question

It is often stated that equitable remedies are discretionary. Is this true of rescission for misrepresentation? (Compare the doctrine of rescission for mistake to be found in *Solle v Butcher*, below, Ch.23.   **14–019**

Note, however that rescission for misrepresentation or undue influence is subject to the restitution by the rescinding party of benefits which he has received from the other (restitutio in integrum), below. See also *Dunbar Bank Plc v Nadeem* [1998] 3 All E.R. 876, below, Ch.26).

CAR AND UNIVERSAL FINANCE CO LTD V CALDWELL

[1965] 1 Q.B. 525; [1964] 2 W.L.R. 600; [1964] 1 All E.R. 290

14–020   The defendant sold his car on January 12, 1960, to Norris who took it away leaving a deposit of £10 and a cheque for £965. The cheque was dishonoured when the defendant presented it the next day. He immediately informed the police and the Automobile Association of the fraudulent transaction. Subsequently Norris sold the car to X who sold it to Y who sold it to Z who sold it to the plaintiffs. In interpleader proceedings one of the issues to be tried was whether the defendant's conduct and representations on or about January 13 amounted to a rescission of the contract of sale. Lord Denning MR held that, where a seller of goods had a right to avoid a contract for fraud, he sufficiently exercised his election if, on discovering the fraud, he immediately took all possible steps to regain the goods, even though he could not find the purchaser or communicate with him; and that the contract of sale was therefore rescinded on January 13. The plaintiffs appealed.

Sellers LJ delivered judgment dismissing the appeal.

UPJOHN LJ

Where one party to a contract has an option unilaterally to rescind or disaffirm it by reason of the fraud or misrepresentation of the other party, he must elect to do so within a reasonable time, and cannot do so after he has done anything to affirm the contract with knowledge of the facts giving rise to the option to rescind. In principle and on authority, however, he must, in my judgment, in the ordinary course communicate his intention to rescind to the other party. This must be so because the other party is entitled to treat the contractual nexus as continuing until he is made aware of the intention of the other to exercise his option to rescind. So the intention must be communicated and an uncommunicated intention, for example, by speaking to a third party or making a private note, will be ineffective. The textbooks to which we were referred are unanimous on the subject. "If a party elects to rescind he must within a reasonable time manifest that election by communicating to the other party his intention to rescind the transaction and claim no interest under it. The communication need not be formal provided it is a distinct and positive repudiation of the transaction": *Kerr on Fraud and Mistake* (7th ed., 1952), p. 530. See also *Benjamin on Sale* (8th ed., 1950), p. 441; *Pollock on Contracts* (13th ed., 1950), p. 467.

Mr Caplan, for the plaintiffs, of course also relies strongly on the well-known words of Lord Blackburn in *Scarf v Jardine*, 7 App.Cas. 345, 349, 360, to the effect that in general an election must be communicated to the other side, though that was not a case of contract. Further, with all respect to the judgment of Lord Denning M.R., Lord Hatherley's observations in *Reese River Silver Mining Co v Smith* (1869) L.R. 4 HL 64, 74, in my view support the same conclusion.

Such in my view must be the general principle. Does it admit of any exception? Mr Caplan concedes that there is one: Where the subject-matter of the contract is a transfer of property, then the party entitled to do so may disaffirm the contract by retaking possession of the property. Mr Caplan, however, submits this is really a method of communication, though for my part I do not see how that can be true of every case that can be suggested. Is there any other exception? Mr Caplan submits not and that, apart from recaption, there should be a universal rule of law that communication is essential to break the nexus. On the facts of this case it is clear that Norris intended quite deliberately to disappear and render it impossible for the defendant to communicate with him or to recover the car. While I appreciate Mr Caplan's argument that this point can only arise in cases between the vendor and a third party, I agree with Sellers L.J. that this problem must be solved by consideration of the rights between the two contracting parties. Admittedly one of two innocent parties must suffer for the fraud of a third, but that cannot be helped and does not assist to solve the problem. One thing is quite clear—that neither Lord Blackburn nor Lord Hatherley in the cases above mentioned nor the textbook writers had in mind circumstances remotely resembling these. It is indeed strange that there is no authority in point.

If one party, by absconding, deliberately puts it out of the power of the other to communicate his intention to rescind which he knows the other will almost certainly want to do, I do not think he can any longer insist on his right to be made aware of the election to determine the contract. In these circumstances communication is a useless formality. I think that the law must allow the innocent party to exercise his right of rescission otherwise than by communication or repossession. To hold otherwise would be to allow a fraudulent contracting party by his very fraud to prevent the innocent party from exercising his undoubted right. I would hold that in circumstances such as these the innocent party may evince his intention to disaffirm the contract by overt means falling short of communication or repossession.

We heard much interesting argument on the position where one party makes an innocent misrepresentation which entitles the other to elect to rescind and then innocently so acts that the other cannot find him to communicate his election to him. I say nothing about that case and would leave it to be decided if and when it arises. I am solely concerned with the fraudulent rogue who deliberately makes it impossible for the other to communicate with him or to retake the property.

Mr Caplan further argued that even if, in the circumstances of the case, communication to Norris was not necessary, yet what the plaintiff did on January 13, when the cheque was dishonoured, did not amount to an unequivocal election to disaffirm; and it was further said that he could have done more to contact Norris. On the facts of this case I do not see what the plaintiff could reasonably have done, nor how he could have made his position plainer.

Davies L.J. delivered judgment dismissing the appeal.

Appeal Dismissed.

Points for reflection

1. The Law Reform Committee (Twelfth Report (Transfer of Title to Chattels), Cmnd. 2958, para.16) **14–021** thought that the decision in the above case:

> "goes far to destroy the value of section 23 of the Sale of Goods Act, 1893 [see 1979 Act], which provides that where the seller of goods has a voidable title which has not been avoided at the time of sale, the buyer acquires a good title to the goods provided he buys them in good faith and without notice of the seller's defect of title. We think that unless and until notice of the rescission of the contract is communicated to the other contracting party an innocent purchaser from the latter should be able to acquire a good title. No doubt this will mean that the innocent purchaser will do so in the great majority of cases since it will usually be impracticable for the original owner of the goods to communicate with the rogue who has deprived him of them."

Why should the innocent purchaser's rights depend on whether or not notice has been given to his seller since, by definition, the innocent purchaser knows nothing of it?

2. The party who seeks rescission must be in a position to restore whatever benefits he has received under the contract. If he is not, he can no longer rescind. "If you are fraudulently induced to buy a cake you may return it and get back the price; but you cannot both eat your cake and return your cake," per Crompton J in the course of the argument in the next case.

CLARKE v DICKSON

Queen's Bench (1858) 120 E.R. 463; El.Bl. & El. 148

14-022   In 1853 the plaintiff was induced to take shares in a company by the misrepresentation of the defendants. In 1857 the company was in bad circumstances and was, with the plaintiff's assent, registered as a company with limited liability. It was afterwards wound up and, during the winding up, the plaintiff discovered the falsity of the representations for the first time. He brought an action to recover the money which he had paid for the shares. The Court of Queen's Bench held that the action failed.

CROMPTON J

> When once it is settled that a contract induced by fraud is not void, but voidable at the option of the party defrauded, it seems to me to follow that, when that party exercises his option to rescind the contract, he must be in a state to rescind; that is, he must be in such a situation as to be able to put the parties into their original state before the contract. Now here I will assume, what is not clear to me, that the plaintiff bought his shares from the defendants and not from the company, and that he might at one time have had a right to restore the shares to the defendants if he could, and demand the price from them. But then what did he buy? Shares in a partnership with others. He cannot return those; he has become bound to those others. Still stronger, he has changed their nature: what he now has and offers to restore are shares in a quasi corporation now in process of being wound up. That is quite enough to decide this case. The plaintiff must rescind in toto or not at all; he cannot both keep the shares and recover the whole price. That is founded on the plainest principles of justice. If he cannot return the article he must keep it, and sue for his real damage in an action on the deceit. Take the case I put in the argument, of a butcher buying live cattle, killing them, and even selling the meat to his customers. If the rule of law were as the plaintiff contends, that butcher, might, upon discovering a fraud on the part of the grazier who sold him the cattle, rescind the contract and get back the whole price: but how could that be consistent with justice? The true doctrine is, that a party can never repudiate a contract after, by his own act, it has become out of his power to restore the parties to their original condition.

Point for reflection

14-023   In *O'Sullivan v Management Agency* [1985] 3 All E.R. 351, 365, Dunn LJ, after a detailed examination of the case law, concluded that the case-law shows that the principle of restitutio in integrum is not applied with its full rigour in equity in relation to transactions entered into by persons in breach of a fiduciary relationship, and that such transactions may be set aside even though it is impossible to place the parties precisely in the position in which they were before. However, this is subject to the proviso that the court can achieve practical justice between the parties by obliging the wrongdoer to give up his profits and advantages, while at the same time compensating him for any work that he has actually performed pursuant to the transaction. *Erlanger v New Sombrero Phosphate Co* (1878) 3 App. Cas. 1218 is a striking example of the application of this principle.

----

6. THE RIGHT TO INDEMNITY

14-024   For an innocent but 'negligent' misrepresentation the injured party may now recover damages as well as rescind the contract: see the Misrepresentation Act 1967, below. In the rare case where a contract is rescinded for an innocent non-negligent misrepresentation, the injured party may not recover damages (unless the misrepresentation has become a term of the contract), but he has a right to indemnity.

NEWBIGGING v ADAM

Court of Appeal (1886) 34 Ch.D. 582; 56 L.J.Ch. 275; 55 L.T. 794; 35 W.R. 597; 3 T.L.R. 259

The plaintiff was induced by the defendants by innocent misrepresentations to enter into a contract of partnership. The plaintiff bound himself to bring in £10,000 to the capital of the firm. Of this, he brought in £9,700 and also paid, in discharge of the liabilities of the partnership, £324. The business proved unsuccessful. In an action for the dissolution of the partnership Bacon VC ordered the defendants to repay the sums brought into the partnership by the plaintiff, and to indemnify him against all liabilities to which he had become or might become liable on account of the partnership. The defendants appealed and argued that this order amounted to giving the plaintiff damages for innocent misrepresentation.

14–025

BOWEN LJ

If we turn to the question of misrepresentation, damages cannot be obtained at law for misrepresentation which is not fraudulent, and you cannot, as it seems to me, give in equity any indemnity which corresponds with damages. If the mass of authority there is upon the subject were gone though I think it would be found that there is not so much difference as is generally supposed between the view taken at common law and the view taken in equity as to misrepresentation. At common law it has always been considered that misrepresentations which strike at the root of the contract are sufficient to avoid the contract on the ground explained in *Kennedy v Panama, New Zealand, and Australian Royal Mail Company*, L.R. 2 Q.B. 580; but when you come to consider what is the exact relief to which a person is entitled in a case of misrepresentation it seems to me to be this, and nothing more, that he is entitled to have the contract rescinded, and is entitled accordingly to all the incidents and consequences of such rescission. It is said that the injured party is entitled to be replaced in status quo. It seems to me that when you are dealing with innocent misrepresentation you must understand that proposition that he is to be replaced in status quo with this limitation—that he is not to be replaced in exactly the same position in all respects, otherwise he would be entitled to recover damages, but is to be replaced in his position so far as regards the rights and obligations which have been created by the contract into which he has been induced to enter. That seems to me to be the true doctrine . . .

[His Lordship then considered the case of *Redgrave v Hurd* (above) and continued:] . . . the Master of the Rolls . . . treats the relief as being the giving back by the party who made the misrepresentation of the advantages he obtained by the contract. Now those advantages may be of two kinds. He may get an advantage in the shape of an actual benefit, as when he receives money; he may also get an advantage if the party with whom he contracts assumes some burthen in consideration of the contract. In such a case it seems to me that complete rescission would not be effected unless the misrepresenting party not only hands back the benefits which he has himself received—but also reassumes the burthen which under the contract the injured person has taken upon himself. Speaking only for myself I should not like to lay down the proposition that a person is to be restored to the position which he held before the misrepresentation was made, nor that the person injured must be indemnified against loss which arises out of the contract, unless you place upon the words "out of the contract" the limited and special meaning which I have endeavoured to shadow forth. Loss arising out of the contract is a term which would be too wide. It would embrace damages at common law, because damages at common law are only given upon the supposition that they are damages which would naturally and reasonably follow from the injury done. I think *Redgrave v Hurd* shows that it would be too wide, because in that case the court excluded from the relief which was given the damages which had been sustained by the plaintiff in removing his business, and other similar items. There ought, as it appears to me, to be a giving back and a taking back on both sides, including the giving back and taking back of the obligations which the contract has created, as well as the giving back and the taking back of the advantages. There is nothing in the case of *Rawlins v Wickham*, 3 De G. & J. 304, which carries the doctrine beyond that. In that case, one of three partners having retired, the remaining partners introduced the plaintiff into the firm, and he, under his contract with them, took upon himself to share with them the liabilities which otherwise they would have borne in their entirety. That was a burthen which he took under the contract and in virtue of the contract. It seems to me, therefore, that upon this principle indemnity was rightly decreed as regards the liabilities of the new firm. I have not found any case which carries the doctrine further, and it is not necessary to carry it further in order to support the order now appealed from. A part of the contract between the plaintiff and Adam & Co was that the plaintiff should become and continue for five years partner in a new firm and bring in £10,000. By this very contract he was to pledge his credit with his partners in the new firm for the business transactions of the new firm. It was a burthen or liability imposed on him by the very contract. It seems to me that the £9,000 odd, and, indeed, all the moneys brought in by him or expended by him for the new firm up to the £10,000 were part of the actual moneys which he undertook by the true contract with Adam & Co to pay. Of course he ought to be indemnified as regards that. I think, also, applying the same doctrine, he ought to be indemnified against all the liabilities of the firm, because they were liabilities which under the contract he was bound to take upon himself.

Cotton and Fry L.JJ. delivered concurring judgments.

Appeal Dismissed.

On appeal, the House of Lords varied the decision of the Vice Chancellor, there having been financial adjustments between the parties: 13 App.Cas. 308.

WHITTINGTON v SEALE-HAYNE

Chancery Division (1900) 82 L.T. 49; 16 T.L.R. 181

14–026   The plaintiffs, breeders of prize poultry, were induced to take a lease of the defendant's premises by the defendant's oral innocent representation that the premises were in a thoroughly sanitary condition. Under the lease the plaintiff covenanted to execute all such works as might be required by any local or public authority. Owing to the insanitary condition of the premises the water supply was poisoned, the plaintiff's manager and his family became very ill, and the poultry either died or became valueless for breeding purposes. The plaintiffs sought indemnity against the following losses: value of stock lost, £750; loss of profit on sales, £100; loss of breeding season, £500; removal of storage and rent, £75; services on behalf of the manager, £100.

Farwell J rescinded the lease, and, following the judgment of Bowen LJ in *Newbigging v Adam*, held that the plaintiff could recover the rents, rates, and repairs under the covenants in the lease but nothing more.

----

7. MISREPRESENTATION ACT 1967

14–027   As we highlighted in the introductory remarks to this chapter, the Misrepresentation Act 1967, extends the availability of damages for misrepresentation. To this extent, it is one of the cornerstones of the modern law. But, this was not the full extent of the reforms that the Act introduced. Indeed, the Act made important changes in the law relating to misrepresentation in three areas: (a) rescission of contracts; (b) damages; and (c) the effect of exception clauses.

A. Rescission

14–028   As will be apparent from the preceding cases, an innocent misrepresentation has long been a ground for rescission of a contract provided that two conditions were satisfied:

(a) It was a misrepresentation of fact and not of law or opinion. Failure to fulfil a promise or a statement of intention was not a misrepresentation, but a misstatement of present intention was.

(b) It misled the representee and he contracted relying on its truth. He could not rescind if he never knew of it, or knew it to be untrue, or did not believe it, or if he was entirely uninfluenced by it.

The Act extends the right to rescind in two respects:

i. Where a Misrepresentation is Incorporated as a Term

The law before the Act was clear enough where a misrepresentation made in the course of negotia- **14–029**
tions was not subsequently incorporated into the contract. It might happen, however that it was so
incorporated. Suppose that Seller tells Buyer, "the horse is sound", and thereby induces him to contract. The horse is not sound. All the conditions are fulfilled to entitle Buyer to rescind. But suppose
that they then enter into a written contract which states as one of its terms, "Seller warrants the horse
to be sound." This term, according to the traditional theory (which is now known to be inadequate
(see below, Ch.20.) but which will suffice for present purposes) is to be classified as either a condition or a warranty. The distinction is that if the term is a condition, breach of it entitles the injured
party to terminate the contract; if the term is a warranty, breach of it does not. If the term were held
to have the status of a condition, there was no problem—the buyer could return the horse if it was
unsound. If, however, the term were held to have the status merely of a warranty, there was an apparent conflict, the misrepresentation rules stating that Buyer could return the horse, the rules relating
to terms saying that he could not. Such authority as there was (and there was not much) suggested
that the rules relating to terms prevailed; with the anomalous result that Buyer might be worse off
if the misrepresentation was incorporated into the contract than if it were left outside as a "mere
representation."

　This absurdity, if it ever was the law, is repealed by s.1(a). If a misrepresentation during negotiations
would otherwise give rise to a right to rescind, it does not fail to do so because the misrepresentation
has become incorporated as a term of the contract. In that case, if the term is a warranty, the contract
may not be terminated for breach but it may be rescinded for misrepresentation.

ii. Where the Contract has been Performed

Section 1(b) is also concerned with preserving to the representee a right of rescission which would, **14–030**
before the Act, have been lost. Once again there was no conclusive authority for saying what the law
was, but there was at least respectable authority for the proposition that when a contract was performed (or 'executed') any right of rescission for innocent misrepresentation, which had existed up to
that moment, ceased to exist. In Angel v Jay [1911] 1 K.B. 666 a lessor innocently misrepresented during
negotiations for a lease that the drains were in good order. The lease for a term of three years was
executed and the tenant occupied the premises. He then discovered the falsity of the representation
and sought to rescind the lease. It was held by a divisional court that he could not do so; the right to
rescind the contract for the lease terminated on the execution of the lease. Earlier, the same doctrine
had been held applicable to a contract for the sale of shares in a company, so that a right to rescind
the contract for innocent misrepresentation was lost when the shares were transferred. Under the
Misrepresentation Act, in neither of these cases would the right to rescind be lost merely on the ground
that the contract had been performed. But it should be noted that failure to rescind within a reasonable
time after discovering the truth would be held to be evidence of an affirmation of the contract.

　Section 1(b) is more far-reaching than the clause proposed by the Law Reform Committee. They
recommended that contracts for the sale of land should be excepted from this provision—that is, they
thought that such contracts should not be capable of rescission after execution. Their view was:

> ". . . in the case of sales of land finality should be the predominant consideration. The vendor
> will often have spent the proceeds of sale on the purchase of another house and so be unable

to repay them. The purchase of a house is commonly linked with the raising of a mortgage and perhaps a sequence of other transactions. Rescission of one sale may thus start a chain reaction. The purchaser who buys a house in reliance on the vendor's representations and without an adequate survey, like one who buys without fully investigating the title, must know that he is taking a risk."

In spite of this, and against the advice of all of the professional bodies consulted, the government decided against excluding contracts for the sale of land. The difficulties feared do not seem in fact to have arisen. It must be remembered that the court will order rescission only where the parties can be restored to substantially the position they were in before the contract. If the vendor has spent the proceeds on another house and is unable to repay them, it seems most improbable that rescission will be ordered. The purchaser certainly does not wish to give up the house without getting his money back; and to require the vendor to re-sell his new house in order to pay back the price of his old one would probably be thought too harsh. The case for refusing rescission in these circumstances is greatly strengthened by the new discretionary power given by the Act to award damages in lieu of rescission for innocent misrepresentation. Where the vendor has agreed to buy another house "subject to contract" the rescission of his contract to sell may certainly set up a chain reaction—but this frequently happens anyway, since the vendor may withdraw at will from the arrangement. If the vendor has entered into a binding contract to purchase another property, he of course remains bound, whether his contract to sell be rescinded or not.

The other objection to the extension of the new section to land was that contracts for the sale of land are contracts in which the principle of caveat emptor ought to apply in its full rigour, since the prudent buyer has the title investigated by his solicitor and the property inspected by his surveyor. But the solicitor and the surveyor may in fact be misled by the vendor or his agents, just as the purchaser himself may be; and it has never been regarded as an answer to a claim for rescission that the party who has been misled could have found out the truth if only he had been more diligent.

B. Damages

14–031   Damages have always been recoverable at common law for a fraudulent misrepresentation through the action of deceit—an action in tort. If a vendor represents that the drains of a house are in good order, when either he knows that they are not in good order, or he is aware that he does not know whether they are in good order or not, he commits a fraudulent misrepresentation. If, however, he genuinely believes that the drains are in good order, whether his belief is based on reasonable grounds or not, his misrepresentation is categorised as innocent. Until 1964 it was thought that no damages could be recovered at common law for a non-fraudulent misrepresentation—the only possible remedy was rescission of the contract. The decision of the House of Lords in *Hedley Byrne & Co v Heller & Partners* [1964] A.C. 465 (above) established that, in some circumstances, damages might be recoverable if it were proved that the innocent misrepresentation was made negligently; but the extent of this rule remains very uncertain.

The Misrepresentation Act now provides that damages may be recovered for innocent misrepresentation in two situations:

(a) Under s.2(1) where the representor is unable to prove that he had reasonable grounds to believe that the misrepresentation was true—that is, he is unable to disprove negligence: though he can prove that he honestly believed the drains to be in good order, he cannot prove that he had reasonable grounds for that belief.

(b) Under s.2(2) where the representee has rescinded or is asking for rescission; and the court holds that he is entitled to rescission but that it would be more equitable to award damages. Here damages may be awarded even though the representor's belief was honest and based on reasonable grounds. The point is that the more drastic remedy of rescission is being refused in the representor's own interest.

i. Damages for Misrepresentation not Reasonably Believed to be True

An action for damages for innocent misrepresentation will lie under s.2(1) where the following four conditions are satisfied: **14–032**

1. The action is brought by a party to a contract against a party to that contract.

2. A misrepresentation was made by the defendant to the plaintiff before the contract was entered into and the defendant cannot prove that he had reasonable grounds to believe and did believe that it was true. (The misrepresentation may have been made by an agent; but the agent is not personally liable under the subsection, according to Mustill J in *The Skopas* [1983] 2 All E.R. 1).

3. As a result, the plaintiff suffered loss.

4. The defendant would have been liable in damages had the misrepresentation been made fraudulently.

This last seems a strange and circuitous way of making innocent misrepresentations actionable. Suppose that the defendant has said that the drains are in good order, honestly believing this to be true. The Act now requires us to ask, what would have been the position had he made this statement not believing it to be true? This sends us to the law of the tort of deceit which is thus incorporated by reference into the Act.

  This fiction, if applied literally, could lead to some very curious results. Suppose Vendor says in all good faith: "In my opinion, the drains are in good order." They are not. Since this is a mere expression of opinion it is not such a misrepresentation as would have given rise to a right to rescind or to liability in any shape or form before the Act. If, however, we are now required to pretend that Vendor was fraudulent, he will be liable in damages; if, knowing the drains are in bad condition, he says, "In my opinion, the drains are in good order," he is lying and, if the Purchaser buys the property relying on such a fraudulent statement of opinion, Vendor is liable in deceit. If this be correct, the perfectly innocent Vendor, who has cautiously made it clear that he is doing no more than expressing an opinion, might find himself liable to pay damages.

  The only way to avoid this result is to give a narrow meaning to 'misrepresentation.' That is, to construe it as meaning such misrepresentations as would formerly have given rise to a right to rescind—and thus to exclude misrepresentations of law or opinion. This would seem to be the preferable course.

  Section 2(1) appears to create a new statutory tort, with the consequence that the tort and not the contract rules concerning damages apply. In two cases Lord Denning MR expressed the opinion that the contractual measure of damages applies but the Court of Appeal has now decided that the tort rules apply: *Chesnau v Interhome Ltd* (1983) 134 N.L.J. 341; *Royscot Trust Ltd v Maidenhead Honda Centre* [1991] 3 All E.R. 294. In the latter case the court had to decide the further point, whether the tortious measure is that of fraudulent misrepresentation (deceit) or that of negligent (*Hedley Byrne*, above) misrepresentation. A number of contrary academic opinions notwithstanding, the court held that the "plain words of the section require the court to apply the rules of fraudulent misrepresentation."

In *Smith New Court Securities Ltd v Scrimgeour Vickers Ltd* [1996] 4 All E.R. 769, 793 HL, Lord Steyn referred to *Royscot* and said: "The question is whether the rather loose wording of the statute compels the court to treat a person who was morally innocent as if he was guilty of fraud when it comes to the measure of damages. There has been trenchant criticism of the *Royscot* case (see Richard Hooley 'Damages and the Misrepresentation Act 1967' (1991) 107 L.Q.R. 547–551). Since this point does not directly arise in the present case, I express no concluded view of the correctness of the *Royscot* case."

Whereas in contract the object of the damage is usually to put the plaintiff in the position he would have been in had the contract been performed, in tort it is to put him in the position he would have been in had the tort not been committed. In *Royscot* the court applied *Doyle v Olby Ltd* [1969] 2 Q.B. 158 CA, where Lord Denning said:

"In contract, the damages are limited to what may reasonably be supposed to have been in the contemplation of the parties. In fraud, they are not so limited. The defendant is bound to make reparation for all the actual damage directly flowing from the fraudulent inducement. The person who has been defrauded is entitled to say: 'I would not have entered into this bargain at all but for your representation. Owing to your fraud, I have not only lost all the money I paid you, but, what is more, I have been put to a large amount of extra expense as well and suffered this or that extra damages.' All such damages can be recovered: and it does not lie in the mouth of the fraudulent person to say that they could not reasonably have been foreseen."

This is all very well where the defendant has really been guilty of fraud; but is it fair where, as under s.2(1), the fraud is entirely fictional? Assuming that *Hedley Byrne* damages are less severe, is it defensible that a tortfeasor who is proved to have been negligent should be better off than one who is deemed a tortfeasor because he cannot satisfy the court that he had reasonable grounds to believe that his representation was true?

In *Yam Seng Pte Limited v International Trade Corporation Limited* [2013] EWHC 111 (QB) (above, Ch.2), the principal question was whether Yam Seng were justified in terminating for alleged breach by ITC. However, in addition to claiming that ITC were in breach, Yam Seng argued that, in the pre-contractual dealings, ITC misrepresented the situation by stating that they had "recently signed" a licence agreement to manufacture and sell Manchester United fragrances when, in fact, the licence agreement was yet to be signed. Leggatt J held that, subject to one caveat, this met the criteria for a claim under s.2(1) (including that ITC did not believe, and had no reasonable ground to believe, that the representation was true). The caveat, however, was whether the misrepresentation caused any loss to Yam Seng. For ITC, it was argued that, in the absence of the misrepresentation, Yam Seng would have delayed entering into the contract with ITC (waiting for confirmation that the licence agreement had actually been signed) but would then have entered into the contract and suffered much the same loss that they actually did suffer. In other words, ITC argued that a comparison should be made between two narratives: between the facts as they actually were (including ITC's misrepresentation) and the facts as they would have been if the misrepresentation had not been made (this latter being the counterfactual narrative). Having reviewed a confusing series of cases, Leggatt J held that it was open to ITC to argue that such a comparison should be made but that the burden was on them to show that, in the counterfactual narrative, Yam Seng's loss would have been no different.

YAM SENG PTE LIMITED V INTERNATIONAL TRADE CORPORATION LIMITED

[2013] EWHC 111 (QB)

LEGGATT J

208. The argument made by Mr Eaton Turner on behalf of ITC was that the misrepresentations made in this case did not cause loss because Yam Seng would still have lost money if it had not entered into the Agreement. The only effect of the misrepresentations, Mr Eaton Turner submitted, was to accelerate the making of the contract. If Mr Presswell had waited before approaching Mr Tuli until he had signed a licence agreement with Manchester United Merchandising Limited, the likelihood is that a distribution agreement would still have been concluded with Yam Seng in similar terms to the agreement actually made; the only difference would have been that the contract period would have commenced a few months later. In that event, Mr Eaton Turner submitted, there is no reason to think that the sales and profits would have been materially different from the results actually achieved. Thus, the likelihood is that Yam Seng would still have suffered a loss similar to that which it in fact suffered.

14–033

Relevance of Alternative Transactions

209. This argument raises a question of principle: in assessing damages for fraudulent misrepresentation or under section 2(1), is it relevant to consider what, if any, other transaction the claimant would have entered into if the misrepresentation had not been made? One approach would be to say that it is not. It might be said that where the claimant has been induced to enter into a contract by misrepresentation the object of an award of damages is simply to restore the claimant to the position before the contract was made: there is no warrant for going further and examining what the claimant would or would not have done if it had not made the contract and then bringing into account in assessing damages the financial consequences of such hypothetical alternative transactions. This approach finds support in a dictum of Hobhouse LJ in *Downs v Chappell* [1997] 1 WLR 426 at 441:

> "In general, it is irrelevant to inquire what the representee would have done if some different representation had been made to him or what other transactions he might have entered into if he had not entered into the transaction in question. Such matters are irrelevant speculations."

210. This statement was cited and applied by May J in *Slough Estates plc v Welwyn Hatfield District Council* [1996] 2 PLR 50. In that case the plaintiffs were induced by fraudulent misrepresentations to invest in a property development. During the period of the investment property values fell. The plaintiffs recovered damages calculated as the difference between all their costs incurred in relation to the development and all their receipts plus the value of the property at the time of assessment. Applying the dictum of Hobhouse LJ in *Downs v Chappell* quoted above, May J considered that it was irrelevant to inquire whether if they had not entered into the transaction the plaintiffs would have invested in another development and incurred a loss as a result of the fall in property values. Commenting on the defendant's objection that the damages awarded amounted to a windfall, he said (at 124):

> "If, as I conceive, the policy of the law is to transfer the whole foreseeable risk of a transaction induced by fraud to the fraudulent defendant, and if, as I conceive, the court does not speculate what, if any, different transaction the plaintiff might have done if the fraudulent representation had not been made, damages on this basis are not to be regarded as a windfall, but the proper application of the policy of the law."

211. Another case where the court refused to speculate about what the claimant would have done if the representation had not been made is *Naughton v O'Callaghan* [1990] 3 All ER 191. In that case the plaintiffs were induced to buy a thoroughbred yearling colt by a misrepresentation as to the colt's pedigree. As part of their damages the plaintiffs claimed costs incurred in training and keeping the colt before the misrepresentation was discovered. The defendant argued that the expenditure would have been incurred anyway as the plaintiffs would, if they had not bought this particular yearling, have bought another one at the same sale. The plaintiffs accepted this but said that had they bought a different horse it might have paid for its keep and reaped for them rich rewards. Waller J said:

> "I have concluded that the plaintiffs are entitled to ask the court to look simply at the contract they made in reliance on the representation which induced them to enter into that bargain. They are entitled to say

that there must be no speculation one way or the other about what would have happened if they had not purchased this horse and if no misrepresentation had been made to them."

212. Nevertheless, there is a line of cases in which courts have inquired and taken account in assessing damages of what other transaction the claimant would have entered into if no misrepresentation had been made.

213. In *East v Maurer* [1991] 1 WLR 461 the plaintiffs bought a hairdressing salon from the defendant in reliance on a fraudulent misrepresentation that the defendant did not intend to carry on operating another salon which he also owned in the same area. The business lost money as customers deserted it for the defendant's other salon. The Court of Appeal held that the plaintiffs were entitled to recover as damages not only the trading losses they sustained in running the salon and the capital loss suffered on its eventual resale, but also the profits which they could reasonably have expected to make if they had instead bought another similar hairdressing business in a different part of the town.

214. In *Clef Acquitaine SARL v Laporte Materials (Barrow) Ltd* [2001] QB 488, the Court of Appeal went a step further. In that case the plaintiffs entered into two distributorship agreements with the defendant which were in fact profitable. However, the judge found that, but for the defendant's deceit during the negotiations, the agreements would have contained more favourable terms as to price and the profits made by the plaintiffs would consequently have been greater. The Court of Appeal held that the plaintiffs were entitled to recover as damages the additional profits which they would have made in those circumstances.

215. In *4 Eng Ltd v Harper* [2009] Ch 91 damages were awarded on a loss of a chance basis for the lost opportunity of entering into another, more profitable transaction. The claimant was induced by fraudulent misrepresentations to buy a company from the defendant which turned out to be worthless. David Richards J found that there was another company which the claimant would have sought to buy if it had not bought the company in question and that there was a good chance, which he assessed at 80 per cent, that the owners of that company would have been agreed to sell it to the claimant. On this basis he awarded as damages 80% of the income and capital gain which the claimant would have received from such an investment, assessed at the date of trial.

216. In all these cases the hypothetical alternative transaction which the claimant would otherwise have entered into was one which would have been profitable. Should account also be taken of a transaction which would probably have resulted in a loss? Chitty on Contracts (31st Edn) at para 6-064 suggests not, citing an observation of Lord Steyn in *Smith New Court* at 283 that:

". . . it is not necessary for the judge to embark on a hypothetical reconstruction of what the parties would have agreed had the deceit not occurred."

Similarly, *Clerk & Lindsell on Torts* (20th Edn) at para 18-45 states that:

"where a defendant deceives the claimant into entering a business transaction, the claimant is entitled to recover the loss he suffers as a result, without reference to the fact that he might otherwise have invested his money in some other unprofitable way and lost it anyway."

The editors add in a footnote, however, that such an attitude is difficult to defend and that:

"if the claimant can increase his recovery by showing he would have invested his money profitably, by parity of reasoning the defendant ought to be able to reduce his exposure by showing that, but for his deceit, the claimant would have lost it in any case."

217. In my view such an attitude would be not merely difficult but impossible to defend. In circumstances where it is established that the claimant can recover a profit that would have been obtained from entering into some other transaction, it must in principle be equally relevant to take account of any loss. Nor in my view does the case law justify any different conclusion. In particular:

(1)   The dictum of Hobhouse LJ in *Downs v Chappell* quoted above begins with the words "in general". It cannot therefore have been intended to state a rule of law—all the more so since it immediately follows a reference to *East v Maurer* where the plaintiffs were awarded profits which they would have been made if they had entered into a different transaction.

(2)   The observation of Lord Steyn in *Smith New Court* quoted in Chitty is taken out of context. The hypothetical reconstruction which Lord Steyn was disapproving was a reconstruction of the kind suggested separately by Hobhouse LJ in *Downs v Chappell* of what the claimant would have done if the representation had been true; Lord Steyn's observation should not be interpreted as a statement

that it is never relevant to consider what alternative transaction would have been entered into if the representation had not been made—not least since Lord Steyn (at 282) specifically approved *East v Maurer* as showing that "an award based on the hypothetical profitable business in which the plaintiff would have engaged but for deceit is permissible: it is classic consequential loss."

(3)   The statements of Hobhouse LJ in *Downs v Chappell* and of Lord Steyn in *Smith New Court* were both considered by the Court of Appeal in *Clef Aquitaine* and explained by Simon Brown LJ in the way I have indicated above.

(4)   There is no difference in principle between an alternative transaction which would have been more profitable and one which would have been less profitable than the actual transaction such that it can be relevant to take account of the former but not the latter.

(5)   The evidential burden will be on the defendant, however, to show that if the misrepresentation had not been made the claimant would have incurred a loss. In seeking to discharge this burden, the defendant (unlike the claimant) does not have the benefit of the principle that if the financial outcome of the alternative transaction is uncertain the court will make reasonable assumptions in its favour (for example by allowing damages to be calculated on a loss of a chance basis) to assist in the proof of loss.

(6)   Unless the defendant can demonstrate with a reasonable degree of certainty, therefore, both the fact that the claimant would probably have suffered a loss from entering into an alternative transaction and the amount of that loss, the damages will not be reduced on that account. In this respect there is a disparity, but a principled one, between hypothetical transactions which would have made the claimant worse off and those which would have made the claimant better off.

(7)   *Slough Estates* and *Naughton v O'Callaghan* are both consistent with this analysis. In those cases there was evidence which justified a very general inference that the claimant would quite likely have suffered some loss if it had not entered into the contract in question (by investing in another property development or buying another horse). But there was no way of estimating with any certainty or precision what loss, if any, the claimant would have incurred from any such transaction. As it was the defendant rather than the claimant who wished to rely on such a loss, that difficulty was insuperable and meant that there was no quantifiable loss which could be taken into account.

Conclusions on Right to Damages for Misrepresentation

218. I therefore consider that in this case it would in principle be open to ITC to show that, if the misrepresentations regarding ITC's legal right to manufacture and sell the Manchester United products had not been made and the Agreement had not been concluded, Yam Seng would nevertheless have entered into a similar contract at a later date and lost money. However, in order to reduce the damages recoverable by Yam Seng on this basis, it would be necessary for ITC to quantify a sum of money which the court can conclude with reasonable confidence that Yam Seng would have lost. That is not an exercise which ITC has attempted to undertake, nor which I would be able to undertake.

219. I think it likely that, if the misrepresentations had not been made, a distribution agreement would have been concluded between ITC and Yam Seng a few months later than the Agreement was in fact concluded, after ITC had acquired the relevant licences. In that event, however, there would not have been the same delay after the contract was made in producing the deodorant and 50ml EDT. Nor would Yam Seng have been encouraged to market the full range of products including the toiletries for as long as it did, if at all, in the expectation that they would be produced. Nor can it be assumed that the contract would have been terminated prematurely because of breaches of contract by ITC as the Agreement was. It is safe to assume that in those circumstances the expenditure incurred and sales made by Yam Seng would have been different from the actual figures. What exactly the differences would have been, however, and what would have been the net financial outcome of such a hypothetical contract is not a matter about which I can properly speculate.

220. I conclude that Yam Seng is entitled to recover as damages for misrepresentation its net loss incurred as a result of entering into the Agreement without any reduction on account of the possibility that, if no misrepresentation had been made, Yam Seng might still have entered into a similar agreement at a later date and lost money anyway.

----

ii. Damages in Lieu of Rescission

14–034   Damages under s.2(1) may, presumably, be recovered where the contract is rescinded as well as where it is not—as is the case with fraudulent misrepresentation. Damages under s.2(2) may be recovered 'in lieu' of rescission (i.e., where the court refuses rescission or (a new concept) reconstitutes a rescinded contract). Does this imply that, where rescission is barred, the jurisdiction to award damages in lieu is also barred? In *Government of Zanzibar v British Aerospace (Lancaster House) Ltd* [2000] 1 W.L.R. 2333—a case in which the misrepresentee's right of rescission was barred—Judge Raymond Jack QC took the view that the language of s.2(2) clearly indicated that the jurisdiction to award damages in lieu of rescission presupposed that rescission is available. In taking this view, Judge Jack declined to follow the view taken by Jacob J. in *Thomas Witter Ltd v TBP Industries Ltd* [1996] 2 All E.R. 573 (to the effect that the jurisdiction does not depend upon an extant right of rescission). Unless the intention underlying s.2(2) was to give the victim of a non-negligent innocent misrepresentation an enhanced remedy (over and above rescission), Judge Jack's view seems the more persuasive.

In *William Sindall Plc v Cambridgeshire County Council* [1994] 3 All E.R. 932 WS in 1988 bought land for development from CCC for over £5 million. In 1990 WS discovered that a sewer was buried under the land which, unless it could be re-routed, would prevent the proposed development. They purported to rescind the contract for misrepresentation and mistake. (As to mistake, see below, Ch.23). The judge held that WS were entitled to rescind for innocent misrepresentation, and, declining to exercise his discretion under s.2(2) to award damages in lieu of rescission, ordered CCC to repay the full purchase price with interest. In 1990 the property was worth less than half the price paid. The cost of diverting the sewer was £18,000. The Court of Appeal held that there had been no misrepresentation but considered, obiter, how the discretion under s.2(2) should have been applied if there had been.

Hoffmann LJ said that there were three particular matters to which the court must have regard:

(i)   The importance of the representation in relation to the subject-matter of the contract. In this case, a defect which would cost £18,000 to rectify was of relatively minor importance in the context of a £5 million sale.

(ii) The loss which would be caused by the misrepresentation if the contract were upheld. Section 2(2) gave power to award damages which would not previously have been recoverable. Whereas s.2(1) was concerned with damage flowing from having entered into the contract, s.2(2) was concerned with the damage caused by the property being not what it was represented to be; and should never exceed the sum which would have been awarded if the representation had been a warranty.

(iii) The loss which would be caused to CCC by rescission. They would have to return about £8 million (purchase price plus interest) in exchange for land worth less than £2 million.

Accordingly, he would have exercised his discretion to award damages in lieu of rescission.

C. Avoidance of Provisions Excluding Liability for Misrepresentation

14–035   The effect of s.3 is that a term purporting to exclude liability for misrepresentation is ineffective, unless the party relying on it satisfies the court that it was a fair and reasonable term to be included, in the following actions:

(a) Under s.2(1) for an innocent negligent misrepresentation.

(b) Under s.2(2) for an innocent misrepresentation whether negligent or not.

If the misrepresentation is a fraudulent one, liability may not be avoided. A clause purporting to exclude liability for fraudulent misrepresentation is probably void at common law and s.3 is unlikely to be construed as giving the court a discretion to uphold such a clause.

Whether s.3 is applicable at all to an action for breach of contract, as distinct from an action for fraudulent, negligent or innocent misrepresentation, is a more difficult question. Suppose that a misrepresentation is later incorporated into a contract in which there is a clause excluding liability for both misrepresentation and breach of contract. If the plaintiff claims damages under s.2(1) or rescission for misrepresentation, then, clearly, the clause may be struck down under s.3. But what if he claims damages for breach of contract or to avoid for breach of condition? One view is that the defendant still cannot rely on the exclusion clause. "The point is that the section does not invalidate a provision only to the extent that it excludes or restricts a liability or remedy arising from a misrepresentation; it invalidates the whole provision, though subject to the discretion of the court" (Atiyah and Treitel, 30 M.L.R. at p.383.)

If there are two exclusion clauses, one excluding liability for misrepresentation and the other excluding liability for breach of contract, it is clear that these will be separate 'provisions' and that s.3 applies only to the first and not to the second. Against the view stated above, it might be argued that it would be absurd that it should make any difference whether substantially the same provisions are put into one clause of a contract rather than into two: and that a single clause which purports to exclude liability (a) for misrepresentation and (b) for breach of contract really constitutes two 'provisions', the former being valid and the second invalid. (Cf. the cases on severance of void provisions, below, Ch.27).

If this view be correct, s.3 does not limit the right of a party to a contract to exclude liability for contractual promises as to matters of fact, whether or not they amounted to misrepresentation before the conclusion of the contract. Whether this view is correct or not, s.3 does not limit a party's right to exclude liability for contractual promises as to future conduct. In a great many contracts, this will not matter, because the purported exclusion of contractual liability will be subject to the same 'fair and reasonable' test of the Unfair Contract Terms Act 1977, below, Ch.22). But, whereas s.3 applies to all contracts, the 1977 Act does not. Where the contract is one of those excluded by the 1977 Act, the scope of s.3 is material. The Law Reform Committee proposed that provisions excluding liability for negligent misrepresentations should be entirely void. It was apparently thought that such a rule might work hardly against a party relying on an exclusion clause in a big commercial contract negotiated at arm's length (foreign buyers were referred to in Parliament); and the draft clause was amended in the interests of the party seeking to exclude liability. He may be able to do so, notwithstanding his negligence, to the extent that the court thinks it fair and reasonable.

For criminal sanctions for false statements, see Theft Act 1968 ss.15 and 16, Theft Act 1978 ss.1 and 2, and Trade Descriptions Act 1968, generally.

HOWARD MARINE & DREDGING CO LTD v A OGDEN & SONS (EXCAVATIONS) LTD

Court of Appeal [1978] Q.B. 574; [1978] 2 W.L.R. 515; [1978] 2 All E.R. 1134; [1978] 1 Lloyd's Rep. 334

The defendants wished to hire two sea-going barges to carry earth and dump it at sea. On April 10, 1974, the plaintiffs quoted a price for the hire of two barges in a letter which stated that the cubic capacity of each was 850 cubic metres but made no mention of weight. At a meeting on July 11 the

14–036

plaintiffs' representative, O'Loughlin, was asked about the carrying capacity in tonnes and replied that it was about 1,600 tonnes. The answer was given honestly but was wrong. It was based on O'Loughlin's recollection of the deadweight figure given in Lloyd's Register of 1,800 tonnes. This was wrong, the true figure being 1,195 tonnes. The correct figure was given in shipping documents which O'Loughlin had seen but forgotten. The defendants hired the barges but the work was held up because of their limited carrying capacity. They refused to pay the hire. The plaintiffs withdrew the barges and sued for the outstanding payments. The defendants counterclaimed damages, inter alia, for misrepresentation under the Misrepresentation Act 1967 s.2(1).

LORD DENNING MR (Dissenting)

Held (1) that there was no collateral warranty; (2) that there was nothing to give rise to a duty of care so as to make the plaintiffs liable for negligence at common law; and, having cited s.2(1) of the Misrepresentation Act 1967, he examined the judge's finding that O'Loughlin was not negligent.

It seems to me that, when one examines the details, the judge's view was entirely justified. He found that Mr O'Loughlin's state of mind was this. Mr O'Loughlin had examined Lloyd's register and had seen there that the deadweight capacity of each barge was 1,800 tonnes. That figure stuck in his mind. The judge found that "the 1,600 tonnes was arrived at by knocking off what he considered a reasonable margin for fuel, and so on, from the 1,800 tonnes summer deadweight figure in Lloyd's Register, which was in the back of his mind." The judge said that Mr O'Loughlin had seen at some time the German shipping documents and had seen the deadweight figure of 1,055.135 tonnes, but it did not register. All that was in his mind was the 1,800 tonnes in Lloyd's Register which was regarded in shipping circles as the bible. That afforded reasonable ground for him to believe that the barges could each carry 1,600 tonnes payload; and that is what Mr O'Loughlin believed.

So on this point, too, I do not think we should fault the judge. It is not right to pick his judgment to pieces, by subjecting it (or the shorthand note) to literal analysis. Viewing it fairly, the judge (who had section 2(1) in front of him) must have been of opinion that the burden of proof was discharged.

The Exception Clause

If I be wrong so far, however, there remains the exception clause in the charterparty. It was, as I have said, included throughout all the negotiations; and no objection was ever taken to it. The important words are:

"... Charterers acceptance of handing over the vessel shall be conclusive that [she is] ... in all respects fit for the intended and contemplated use by the Charterers and in every other way satisfactory to them."

In the old days we used to construe such an exception clause strictly against the party relying on it; but there is no need, and I suggest no warrant, any longer for construing it so strictly. The reason is that now by section 3 of the Misrepresentation Act 1967 the provision is of no effect except to the extent that the court may allow reliance on it as being fair and reasonable in the circumstances of the case. Under this section the question is not whether the provision itself is reasonable, but only whether "reliance on it [is] fair and reasonable in the circumstances of the case."[5]

If the clause itself is reasonable, that goes a long way towards showing that reliance on it is fair and reasonable. It seems to me that the clause was itself fair and reasonable. The parties here were commercial concerns and were of equal bargaining power. The clause was not foisted by one on the other in a standard printed form. It was contained in all the drafts which passed between them, and it was no doubt given close consideration by both sides, like all the other clauses, some of which were amended and others not. It was a clause common in charterparties of this kind; and is familiar in other commercial contracts, such as construction and engineering contracts ... It is specially applicable in cases where the contractor has the opportunity of checking the position for himself. It tells him that he should do so; and that he should not rely on any information given beforehand, for it may be inaccurate. Thus it provides a valuable safeguard against the consequences of innocent misrepresentation.

Even if the clause were somewhat too wide (I do not think it is), nevertheless this is, I think, a case where it would be fair and reasonable to allow reliance on it. Here is a clause by which Ogdens accepted that the barges were "in all respects fit for the intended and contemplated use by the charterers." Ogdens had had full inspec-

---

5   Note that, under the amended s.3, the test is the requirement of reasonableness in s.11(1) of the Unfair Contract Terms Act—whether the term was a fair and reasonable one to be included.

tion and examination of the barges. They had had an "on-hire condition" survey by their surveyors. Any expert could have given them a reliable estimate as to the dead-weight capacity. Yet they seek to say that the barges were not fit for the use for which they intended them, in that they were of too low carrying capacity. And in support of their case they have no written representation to go on. They only have two telephone conversations and one interview, as to which there is an acute conflict of evidence. It is just such conflicts which commercial men seek to avoid by such a clause as this. I would do nothing to impair its efficacy. I would allow Howards to rely on it . . .

BRIDGE LJ

[having held that there was no evidence of a collateral warranty, cited s.2(1) of the Misrepresentation Act 1967 and continued:] The first question then is whether Howards would be liable in damages in respect of Mr O'Loughlin's misrepresentation if it had been made fraudulently, that is to say, if he had known that it was untrue. An affirmative answer to that question is inescapable. The judge found in terms that what Mr O'Loughlin said about capacity of the barges was said with the object of getting the hire contract for Howards, in other words with the intention that it should be acted on. This was clearly right. Equally clearly the misrepresentation was in fact acted on by Ogdens. It follows, therefore, on the plain language of the 1967 Act that, although there was no allegation of fraud, Howards must be liable unless they proved that Mr O'Loughlin had reasonable ground to believe what he said about the barges' capacity.

It is unfortunate that the learned judge never directed his mind to the question whether Mr O'Loughlin had any reasonable ground for his belief. The question he asked himself, in considering liability under the 1967 Act, was whether the innocent misrepresentation was negligent. He concluded that if Mr O'Loughlin had given the inaccurate information in the course of the April telephone conversations he would have been negligent to do so but that in the circumstances obtaining at the Otley interview in July there was no negligence. I take it that he meant by this that on the earlier occasions the circumstances were such that he would have been under a duty to check the accuracy of his information, but on the later occasions he was exempt from such duty. I appreciate the basis of this distinction, but it seems to me, with respect, quite irrelevant to any question of liability under the 1967 Act. If the representee proves a misrepresentation which, if fraudulent, would have sounded in damages, the onus passes immediately to the representor to prove that he had reasonable ground to believe the facts represented. In other words the liability of the representor does not depend on his being under a duty of care the extent of which may vary according to the circumstances in which the representation is made. In the course of negotiations leading to a contract the 1967 Act imposes an absolute obligation not to state facts which the representor cannot prove he had reasonable ground to believe . . .

I am fully alive to the dangers of trial by transcript and it is to be assumed that Mr O'Loughlin was perfectly honest throughout. But the question remains whether his evidence, however benevolently viewed, is sufficient to show that he had an objectively reasonable ground to disregard the figure in the ship's documents and to prefer the Lloyd's Register figure. I think it is not. The fact that he was more interested in cubic capacity could not justify reliance on one figure of deadweight capacity in preference to another. The fact that the deadweight figure in the ship's documents was a freshwater figure was of no significance since, as he knew, the difference between freshwater and sea water deadweight capacity was minimal. Accordingly I conclude that Howards failed to prove that Mr O'Loughlin had reasonable ground to believe the truth of his misrepresentation to Mr Redpath.

Having reached a conclusion favourable to Ogdens on the issue of liability under the Misrepresentation Act 1967, I do not find it necessary to express a concluded view on the issue of negligence at common law. As at present advised I doubt if the circumstances surrounding the misrepresentation at the Otley interview were such as to impose on Howards a common law duty of care for the accuracy of the statement. If there was such a duty, I doubt if the evidence established a breach of it.

There remains the question whether Howards can escape from their liability under the 1967 Act in reliance on clause I of the charterparty, which provides: . . .

[see above].

A clause of this kind is to be narrowly construed. It can only be relied on as conclusive evidence of the charterers' satisfaction in relation to such attributes of the vessel as would be apparent on an ordinary examination of the vessel. I do not think deadweight capacity is such an attribute. It can only be ascertained by an elaborate calculation or by an inspection of the ship's documents. But even if, contrary to this view, the clause can be read as apt to exclude liability for the earlier misrepresentation, Howards still have to surmount the restrictions imposed by section 3 of the 1967 Act, which provides: . . .

[His Lordship quoted the section.]

What the learned judge said in this matter was: "If the wording of the clause is apt to exempt from responsibility for negligent misrepresentation as to carrying capacity, I hold that such exemption is not fair and reasonable . . ." The judge having asked himself the right question and answered it as he did in the exercise of the discretion vested in him by the 1967 Act, I can see no ground on which we could say that he was wrong.

I would accordingly allow the appeal to the extent of holding that Ogdens have established liability against Howards under section 2(1) of the 1967 Act for any damages they have suffered as a result of Mr O'Loughlin's misrepresentation at the Otley interview in the terms as found by the learned judge.

SHAW LJ

[Having held that there was no evidence of a warranty, but (differing from the other members of the court and Bristow J) that Ogden had a cause of action in negligence at common law continued:]

There remains the issue raised by the claim under section 2(1) of the Misrepresentation Act 1967. I do not regard the telephone conversation of April and the interview of July 11, 1974 as being so casual as to give rise to no legal consequences. Certainly I find myself unable to dismiss what was said at the interview in July as inconsequential. I share the opinion expressed in this regard in the judgment of Bridge L.J. which is based on the finding of the learned judge. I entirely agree, furthermore, with Bridge L.J.'s analysis of the evidence, together with the learned judge's findings in this regard, and I agree also with the views expressed by Bridge L.J. as to the operation and effect of the relevant provisions of the 1967 Act. I cannot do better than respectfully to adopt his reasoning without seeking to repeat it and I agree with his conclusions.

On this ground as well as in relation to the claim based on negligence at common law I would allow the appeal.

Appeal Allowed.

In *Howard Marine*, the clause in question did not go as far as saying that the hirers had not placed any reliance on the owners' representations. However, what would be the legal position if a clause were drafted in a way that either denied that the owners had made any actionable representations (e.g., "It is expressly agreed that the written Agreement supersedes any previous discussions, correspondence, or representations between the parties") or declared that the hirers had not relied on any representations made by the owners? How easy would it be to persuade a court that such an express agreement or declaration precludes (i.e., 'estops') a party from alleging the facts on which to base an action for misrepresentation? Would a court seriously entertain that such a provision could stick when, as the parties know full well, the actuality is that there have been material representations, inducement, and reliance? Can a contract so rewrite history? Moreover, how readily would a court accept that a provision of this kind falls outwith the scope of section 3 of the Act because, quite simply, it does not purport to exclude or restrict liability for a misrepresentation?

Broadly speaking, the modern case-law—at any rate, from *Peekay Intermark v Australia and New Zealand Banking Group* [2006] EWCA Civ 386 onwards—suggests that the courts are perfectly comfortable with provisions of this kind where they are found in transactions between competent commercial contractors; but if they are used to defeat the reasonable expectations of a consumer contractor, that is probably another matter. As Christopher Clarke J neatly expresses it in *Raiffeisen Zentralbank Osterriech AG v The Royal Bank of Scotland* (below), the law needs to "accommodate the car dealer as well as the bond dealer" (para.305).

The background to the *Raiffeisen Zentralbank Osterriech* case was that RBS, having lent a large sum of money to Enron, then syndicated the loan to other banks. RZB was one of these other banks, its loan amounting to £10 million. Following the collapse of Enron, RZB claimed that it had been induced to enter into the loan agreement by misrepresentations made by RBS. In response, RBS relied on a number of provisions ('the relevant provisions') which it argued established that no representations had been made or that RZB were estopped from contending that such representations were made.

RAIFFEISEN ZENTRALBANK OSTERREICH AG v THE ROYAL BANK OF SCOTLAND

[2010] EWHC 1392 (Comm)

CHRISTOPHER CLARKE J

230. Parties to a contract may agree that a particular state of affairs is to be the basis upon which they are contracting, regardless of whether or not that state of affairs is true. A line of authority establishes that such an agreement may give rise to a contractual estoppel, precluding the assertion of facts inconsistent with those that have been agreed to form the basis of the contract. If that is done the question arises as to whether or not the agreement constitutes an attempted exclusion of liability for misrepresentation to which section 3 of the Misrepresentation Act 1967 applies.

14–037

231. The chain of authority is now extended; but in several of the cases not all the relevant earlier authority appears to have been cited, with the result that the status of some of the authorities is less clear than it might be.

232. In *Colchester Borough Council v Smith* [1991] Ch 448 the Council claimed possession of land in respect of which T asserted a title by adverse possession. By clause 4 of an agreement in 1983 T had agreed that he had had no title to any part of the land except for the tenancy under the agreement. Ferris J held that T was estopped by contract and by convention from asserting to the contrary and from relying on the provisions of the Limitation Act 1939 as a defence. In so doing he referred to a passage in the 3rd edition of *Spencer Bower and Turner, Estoppel by Representation*, para 158 in which the author had said that:

> "A convention of the parties, which binds them to adhere to an assumed state of facts, may amount to an express contract, in which case each party contracts with the other to be estopped. Burroughs Adding Machine Ltd v Aspinall (1925) 41 TLR 276 C.A. is an example . . .. It is not proposed to discuss estoppel by contract in this chapter, which is concerned with a type of estoppel by convention in which estoppel arises not as a matter of contract, but from a convention of the parties having less than contractual force. But it has been of interest to notice, by way of introduction to the subject , that there may be an estoppel whereby parties are precluded, as a matter of contract, and not of a mere recital, from setting up a version of the facts different from that which they have agreed to assume."

Ferris J accepted the submission that clause 4 was an example of a *"perhaps rare"* type of the estoppel described in *Spencer Bower* as arising from contract. His decision was affirmed by the Court of Appeal: [1992] Ch 421.

233. In *William Sindall Plc v Cambridgeshire County Council* [1994] 1 WLR 1016 property was sold under a contract which incorporated the National Conditions of Sale (20th ed) including condition 14 and special condition 17:

> "14. Without prejudice to the duty of the vendor to disclose all latent easements and latent liabilities known to the vendor to affect the property , the property is sold subject to any rights of way and water, rights of common and other rights, easements, quasi-easements, liabilities and pubic rights affecting the same.
>
> 17. The purchaser shall be deemed to purchase with full notice of and subject to: . . .. (e) all easements, quasi-easements rights and privileges (whether of a public or private nature) now affecting the property but without any obligation on the part of the vendor to define the same."

Hoffmann LJ, with whom the other members of the Court of Appeal agreed, held that the judge had been wrong to treat those conditions as exclusion clauses which had to satisfy the test of reasonableness in accordance with section 3, saying:

> "In my judgment they are nothing of the kind. Section 3 deals with provisions which exclude or restrict a party's liability for 'any misrepresentation made by him before the contract was made'. The clauses in question do not exclude a liability for misrepresentation but go to the question of whether there was a misrepresentation in the first place. They qualify the obligations to convey as beneficial owner and give vacant possession and therefore qualify any representation which could be implied from having undertaken those obligations."

234. A contractual estoppel is not the same as an estoppel by representation, sometimes known as an eviden-tial estoppel, the nature of which is well established. A number of authorities have considered the extent to which such an estoppel may effectively prevent a liability from arising.

235. In *Lowe v Lombank* [1960] 1 WLR 196, a 65 year old widow bought a Standard motor car on hire purchase for less than £ 300. The salesman described it as "perfect" or "near perfect". In fact it was unroad-worthy and dangerous. Clause 9 (ii) of the HP agreement, which she did not read and he did not explain, provided that the hirer acknowledged and agreed that he had examined the goods prior to the signing of the agreement; that they were of merchantable quality and that he had not *"made known to the owners expressly or by implication the particular purpose for which the goods are required and that the goods are reasonably fit for the purpose for which they are in fact required"*. She also signed a delivery receipt which contained a statement that she acknowledged that she had read the whole agreement and that she had examined the goods and that they were in good order and condition.

236. Diplock J, giving the judgment of the Court of Appeal said:

> "[Clause 9 (ii)] is expressed to be an acknowledgement, that is to say a representation by the plaintiff that she had not made known by implication that the car was required for a particular purpose, and also as an agreement that she had not made that purpose known to the defendants. Insofar as [clause 9 (ii)] was a representation it could operate only as an estoppel preventing the plaintiff from asserting the contrary, but Mr Roche expressly disclaims reliance upon it as an estoppel, no doubt for the very good reason that there was no evidence (and it is difficult to see how there could have been truthful evidence) that the defendants believed in the truth of the representation. To call it an agreement as well as an acknowledgment by the plaintiff cannot convert a statement as to past facts, known by both parties to be untrue, into a contractual obligation, which is essentially a promise by the promisor to the promisee that acts will be done in the future or that facts exist at the time of the promise or will exist in the future. To say that the hirer "agreed" that he has not done something in the past means no more than that the hirer, at the request of the owner, repre-sents that he has not done that thing in the past. If intended by the hirer to be acted upon by the person to whom the representation is made, believed to be true by such person and acted upon by such person to his detriment, it can give rise to an estoppel; it cannot give rise to any positive contractual obligation. Although contained in the same document as the contract, it is not a contractual promise.
>
> There lies the fallacy in Mr Roche's contention. Whether or not the plaintiff made known to the defend-ants by implication the particular purpose for which she required the car is a pure question of fact as to the state of knowledge of the defendants to be inferred in the light of all the circumstances, including the terms of the contract itself. On this issue the rule of construction relied on by Mr Roche that you cannot imply in a contract a promise, which is inconsistent with an express provision, is irrelevant for the inference to be drawn from the terms of the contract that the defendants knew the particular purpose for which the plaintiff required the car is not an implied promise, nor is the representation in clause 9 (ii) of the contract an express promise."

237. The Court held that the acknowledgement in the delivery receipt did not work as an estoppel since it failed all three of the tests namely that the statement relied on must be:

(a)   clear and unambiguous;
(b)   intended by the hirer to be acted upon by the defendants or that she had so conducted herself that a reasonable man in the position of the defendants would take the representation to be true and believe that it was meant that they should act upon it; and
(c)   that the defendants in fact believed it to be true and were induced by such belief to act upon it.

238. In *Peekay Intermark v Australia and New Zealand Banking Group* [2006] EWCA Civ 386; [2006] 2 Lloyd's Rep 511 the customer asserted that, contrary to express representations in the written contract, it had not understood the investment it was acquiring because it had been described incorrectly to him by the defendant in a conversa-tion before he contracted to purchase the investment. The agent of the customer had confirmed by his signature that he had read and understood a Risk Disclosure Statement which read:

> "You should also ensure that you fully understand the nature of the transaction and contractual relationship into which you are entering"

and

> "The issuer assumes that the customer is aware of the risks and practices described herein, and that prior to each transaction the customer has determined that such transaction is suitable for him."

239. The Court of Appeal held that, where parties to a contract have agreed that a certain state of affairs will form the basis of their transactions, they are estopped by their contract from asserting that the true facts were different. At paras 56 and 57 Moore-Bick LJ, with whom Chadwick and Collins LJJ agreed, said this:

> "56 There is no reason in principle why parties to a contract should not agree that a certain state of affairs should form the basis for the transaction, whether it be the case or not. For example, it may be desirable to settle a disagreement as to an existing state of affairs in order to establish a clear basis for the contract itself and its subsequent performance. Where parties express an agreement of that kind in a contractual document neither can subsequently deny the existence of the facts and matters upon which they have agreed, at least so far as concerns those aspects of their relationship to which the agreement was directed. The contract itself gives rise to an estoppel: see *Colchester Borough Council v Smith* [1991] Ch 448, affirmed on appeal [1992] Ch 421.
>
> 57 It is common to include in certain kinds of contracts an express acknowledgment by each of the parties that they have not been induced to enter the contract by any representations other than those contained in the contract itself. The effectiveness of a clause of that kind may be challenged on the grounds that the contract as a whole, including the clause in question, can be avoided if in fact one or other party was induced to enter into it by misrepresentation. However, I can see no reason in principle why it should not be possible for parties to an agreement to give up any right to assert that they were induced to enter into it by misrepresentation, provided that they make their intention clear, or why a clause of that kind, if properly drafted, should not give rise to a contractual estoppel of the kind recognised in *Colchester Borough Council v Smith* . . . However, that particular question does not arise in this case. A clause of that kind may (depending on its terms) also be capable of giving rise to an estoppel by representation if the necessary elements can be established: see *EA Grimstead & Son Ltd v McGarrigan* (CA) [1999] EWCA Civ 3029.

240. Chadwick LJ observed (para 70):

> "The Risk Disclosure Statement was a contractual document . . . ANZ accepted the investment instruction in that letter on the basis of the investor's confirmation that it had read and understood the terms of the statement. That confirmation, as it seems to me, operated as a contractual estoppel to prevent Peekay from asserting in litigation that it had not, in fact read and understood the Risk Disclosure Statement. And if it had read and understood the Risk Disclosure statement, it must be taken to have accepted that ANZ would assume that it fully understood the nature of the transaction into which it was entering, was aware of the risks, and had determined that the transaction was suitable for its purposes. Given that, Peekay could not be heard to say that Mr Pawani had assumed that the FTCs which he had signed on its behalf did not need to be read and understood."

241. The decision that there could be a contractual estoppel was not obiter. One of the bases of the dismissal of the claim was that, in the light of what he had agreed, the claimant could not assert that he had not satisfied himself that the transaction was suitable for him or that he had assumed that he did not need to read or understand the final terms and conditions. These were or included matters of past fact.

242. *Lowe v Lombank* was not cited nor referred to in the judgments. Moore-Bick, LJ referred to *Grimstead v McGarrigan* (which proceeded on *Lowe v Lombank* lines) and Chadwick LJ gave the leading judgment in *Grimstead* and *Watford Electronics Ltd v Sanderson CFL Ltd* [2001] EWCA Civ 317. The Court must necessarily have had the *Lowe v Lombank* type of estoppel in mind; but it is less clear to what extent it had in mind what Diplock J had said about the effect of agreements as to what had happened in the past. Section 3 of the Misrepresentation Act was not in issue.

243. In *Springwell* [*JP Morgan Chase Bank (formerly Chase Manhattan Bank) v Springwell Navigation Corpn* [2008] EWHC 1186 (Comm)] Gloster J applied the principle of contractual estoppel from *Peekay* in a context similar to the present. Springwell had claimed that, notwithstanding certain contractual representations and acknowledgments of fact in the Relevant Provisions in that case (such as that Springwell was a sophisticated investor, that the transaction had been conducted on an execution only basis, that Springwell had not received any advice from Chase in relation to the relevant transactions and had not relied on any advice from Chase) Chase was in fact advising it on a regular basis and had even referred to itself as Springwell's adviser in certain internal documents.

244. Gloster J held that Springwell could not set these facts up against the agreed facts which had formed the terms of its contract with Chase. It could not challenge the contractually agreed position that it was a sophisticated investor, that it was making its own analysis of the investments, and that it was not relying on the bank to advise it or on any representation made by the bank. Gloster J held that the basis of a contractual estoppel is a

contractual representation, warranty or agreement forming the agreed and binding basis on which the parties will conduct their dealings (para 567). She accepted Chase's submissions that contractual estoppel is a separate species of estoppel from estoppel by representation, that it does not require detrimental reliance and that it can arise from an agreement or representation about past facts (para 556).

245. She noted that the reasoning of all three judges in Peekay was "firmly rooted in, and consistent with, the importance of freedom of contract and contractual certainty" and held that the principle extends to cover "any other form of contractual statement, for instance as to sophistication or non-reliance on advice generally" (para 559) and said:

> "In conclusion on this topic, I see nothing inappropriate or commercially offensive about Chase being permitted to rely on the statements contained in the Relevant Provisions, even if it could be said that in some respects they did not accurately reflect every aspect of the dealing relationship. All of the relevant terms of the contractual documentation fall squarely within the Peekay analysis, as contractual representations (and in some cases, warranties) or "agreements" as to the basis upon which the business was to be conducted. Thus, for example, where the contract provided that, by placing an order, Springwell represented . . . that it was a sophisticated investor and that it had independently and without reliance on Chase made a decision to acquire the instrument, that was not a mere statement of historical fact, but a contractual representation forming the agreed and binding basis upon which the parties would transact every future purchase. The same analysis applies in respect of every clause in every document to which Springwell takes this objection. The fact that some statements are expressed in the language of representation or acknowledgement cannot, in my view, make any difference to the analysis that the statements give rise to a contractual estoppel."

246. Gloster J's approach was applied by Aikens J, as he then was, in *Trident Turboprop (Dublin) Ltd v First Flight Couriers Ltd* [2008] EWHC 1686 (Comm); [2009] 1 All ER (Comm) 16, at para 36, affirmed [2009] EWCA Civ 290. In that case the parties to a lease agreement of commercial aircraft had included a clause whereby the defendant:

> "agree[d] and acknowledge[d] that save as expressly stated in this Agreement and the other Transaction Documents to which [the claimant] is a party [the claimant] has not and shall not be deemed to have made any warranties or representations, express or implied, about the aircraft."

247. Aikens J held that parties who agree such a clause are agreeing that no representations were made by the claimant or if any representations were made, then it was "deemed" that they were not. He referred to *Colchester BC v Smith* and *Peekay* and the commercial convenience for parties to a contract to agree that a certain state of affairs (e.g. that no pre-contractual representations were made) is the case, so as to provide a clear basis for the contract itself. In *Trident*, as he held, the parties had agreed to base their contractual relations on the footing that there had been no representations *"even if it was not in fact the case that there had been no representations"* (para 36). Subject to the potential application of section 3 of the Misrepresentation Act, Trident could rely on the clause to defeat the misrepresentation.

248. In *Titan Steel Wheels Limited v Royal Bank of Scotland Plc* [2010] EWHC 211 (Comm) there were allegations of mis-selling of forward currency contracts. The relevant contractual provisions were again similar to those in issue in the present case (see paras 30-32 of the judgment). On a preliminary issue Steel J applied the *Peekay* analysis and found that no duty of care arose:

> ". . . I conclude that the terms outlined, taken as a whole, are only consistent with the conclusion that Titan and the Bank were agreeing to conduct their dealings on the basis that the Bank was not acting as an advisor nor undertaking any duty of care regardless of what recommendations, suggestions or advice were tendered . . ." (para 85)

249. Referring to *Peekay*, *Springwell* and *Trident*, Steel J concluded *"I detect no basis upon which a different analysis would be justified in the present case"* (para 89). He noted that it was no answer to say that the bank was not protected if it did in fact give advice (para 91) because the terms in question went much further than to relieve the Bank from any obligation to give advice: they provided that any statements were not to be treated as advice nor could they be relied on by the claimant and the parties had agreed that if the Bank did give advice it was not to be treated as accepting any responsibility. He adopted Gloster J's exhaustive analysis in *Springwell* (para 97).

Discussion

250. The authorities to which I have referred, other than *Lowe v Lombank*, show that parties can agree that their dealings shall be conducted on a particular basis of fact (including as to what has or has not occurred)

even if the true facts are different and that, if they do, a contractual estoppel will arise. It is not easy to reconcile that position with the apparently absolute statement in *Lowe v Lombank* that a statement as to past facts known to be untrue cannot be converted into a contractual obligation and is not a contractual promise. If *Lowe v Lombank* means that an agreement that something has not happened is incapable of being a contractual obligation or promise, and is no more than a representation, which is ineffective unless the three *Lowe v Lombank* conditions have been fulfilled, then it cannot found a contractual estoppel.

251. The distinction between past and present facts is not without difficulty. If a party agrees that he is entering into a contract in reliance on three identified representations which are the only representations that have been made to him, his agreement may be said to relate partly to the present (his reliance at the moment of contract) and partly to the past (what he has been told). It would be somewhat curious if such an agreement operated as a contractual estoppel only in respect of the claimant's agreement as to what he relied on at the moment of contracting but not in respect of his agreement as to the limits of what he had been told.

252. Gloster J observed that in *Lowe v Lombank* all that the Court of Appeal had to decide was that the false statement in the agreement as to non-notification of purpose fell foul of section 8 (3) of the HP A 1938 and suggested that in reality Diplock, J was regarding the so-called agreement as no more than a sham provision as was "*shortly*" to be recognised by the Court of Appeal including himself, now Diplock LJ, in *Snook v London and West Riding Investment Ltd* [1967] 2 QB 786. The Court of Appeal in *Lowe v Lombank* did not, however, decide the case on the basis of section 8 (3), nor did it decide that the agreement was a sham. It is by no means clear that it was. The finance company had every intention that the contract should take effect in accordance with its terms.

253. Nevertheless I do not regard myself as bound by *Lowe v Lombank* to conclude that an agreement that no representations have been made or relied on (or as to any other past fact) can never amount to a contractual estoppel. There is no intrinsic reason why that should be so. There is good reason for allowing businessmen to agree with each other the basis of fact (including past fact) upon which they are to do business. In *Lowe* itself Counsel had "*expressly disclaim[ed] reliance upon [the clause] as an estoppel*". The argument which Diplock J addressed was that Mrs Lowe could not be regarded as having made known to the finance company that she wanted the car in order to use it safely on the road because it was impossible to imply into a contract a term inconsistent with an express term, so that the implication, otherwise apparent from the terms of the contract, that the car was wanted for use on the road, did not arise.

254. But, as the Court held:

"Whether or not the plaintiff made known to the defendants by implication the particular purpose for which she required the car is a pure question of fact as to the state of knowledge of the defendants to be inferred in the light of all the circumstances, including the terms of the contract itself. On this issue, the rule of construction relied on by Mr. Roche that you cannot imply in a contract a promise, which is inconsistent with an express promise, is irrelevant, for the inference to be drawn from the terms of the contract that the defendants knew the particular purpose for which the plaintiff required the car is not an implied promise, nor is the representation in clause 9 (ii) of the contract an express promise."

255. In circumstances where no reliance had been placed on estoppel in argument I decline to take the last phrase of that citation as a decision that a contractual estoppel (which may not be the same as a contractual promise or obligation) in relation to past facts can never arise. If, contrary to my view, *Lowe v Lombank* so holds, then I regard the decision as (a) wrong and (b) reached per incuriam in the light of *Colchester Borough Council*, itself affirmed on appeal, and following *Burroughs Adding Machine Ltd v Aspinall*, a decision of the Court of Appeal which accepted the effectiveness of a provision whereby statements of account given to a salesman were deemed to be accepted as correct and were to be binding on him in the absence of objection within 30 days of receipt. The statements given omitted certain sales to banks which the salesmen contended were commissionable. I believe that I should follow the later decision of the Court of Appeal in *Peekay*, which has itself been followed in several subsequent first instance decisions— *Bottin International Investments Ltd v Vonson* [2006] EWHC 3112; *Donegal International v Republic of Zambia* [2007] EWHC 197; [2007] 1 Lloyd's Rep 397; *Springwell; Trident; Titan Steel Wheels; Food Co UK LLP v Henry Boot Developments Ltd* [2010] EWHC 358.

256. In any event, whilst some of the Relevant Provisions relate to the past, the Confidentiality Agreement itself relates to the future by providing that the Arranger will be making no representations, so that the question of the effect of an agreement as to past facts does not arise.

[Christopher Clarke J then dealt with some questions arising on the construction of the relevant provisions]

The Misrepresentation Act 1967

271. Section 3 of the Misrepresentation Act 1967, as amended, provides as follows:

"Avoidance of provision excluding liability for misrepresentation.

If a contract contains a term which would exclude or restrict —
(a)   any liability to which a party to a contract may be subject by reason of any misrepresentation made by him before the contract was made; or
(b)   any remedy available to another party to the contract by reason of such a misrepresentation,

that term shall be of no effect except in so far as it satisfies the requirement of reasonableness as stated in section 11 (1) of the Unfair Contract Terms Act 1977; and it is for those claiming that the term satisfies that requirement to show that it does."

272. The relevant questions are, therefore, (a) whether the Relevant Provisions exclude or restrict any liability to which RBS is subject by reason of any misrepresentation made by it or any remedy available to RZB by reason of such misrepresentation; and (b) if and to the extent that they do, whether or not RBS has established that they satisfy the requirement of reasonableness.

273. Section 3 does not affect the logically prior question as to whether, having regard to the terms of the Confidentiality Agreement and the IM, a banker in RZB's position would have understood RBS to be making representations in the IM, and what representations, if any, were impliedly made.

The authorities on section 3

274. In *Cremdean Properties Ltd v Nash* [1977] 241 EG 837 certain tender documents were alleged to contain representations in reliance on which the plaintiffs had submitted an offer as required by the tender. The first defendant relied upon a notice on the final page of the special conditions of sale which provided that the particulars given were believed to be correct but their accuracy was not guaranteed and any error should not annul the sale or be a grounds for compensation and that:

"(b) any intending purchaser must satisfy himself by inspection or otherwise as to the correctness of each of the statements contained in those particulars."

275. Fox J, as he then was, held that if there was a misrepresentation, a provision which sought to exclude or restrict liabilities or remedies arising from that misrepresentation was within the mischief of the section 3 and it did not make any difference what the form of that provision was. If there was a representation and the defendant had to rely on the notice to relieve him from the consequences of that misrepresentation, section 3 would prohibit that reliance. He also decided that, upon the assumption that there had been misrepresentations as alleged, the notice was no answer to the first defendant's liability, although he accepted, as a purely factual matter, that the notice might be material in determining whether there was a misrepresentation and whether the plaintiff had relied on it. He rejected an argument that paragraph (b) meant that the first defendant could be under no liability because the plaintiffs were by the notice put on inquiry and told to check the facts for themselves.

276. In the Court of Appeal [1977] 2 EGLR 80, 244 EG 547 Bridge LJ held that paragraph (b) did not amount even to a purported annulment of the existence of any representation embodied in the earlier parts of the document. Having done so he said that he would:

". . . go further and say that if the ingenuity of the draftsman could devise language which would have that effect, I am extremely doubtful whether the court would allow it to operate so as to defeat section 3. Supposing the vendor included a clause which the purchaser was required, and did, agree to in some terms as "notwithstanding any statement of fact included in these particulars the vendor shall be conclusively determined to have made no representation within the meaning of the Misrepresentation Act 1967", I should have thought that that was only a form of words the intended and actual effect of which was to exclude or restrict liability, and I should not have thought that the courts would have been ready to allow such ingenuity in the form of language to defeat the plain purpose at which section 3 is aimed."

277. Scarman LJ agreed:

". . . in particular with the observations that my Lord made about the submissions put to the court by Mr Maurice . . . Nevertheless, the case for the appellant does have an audacity and a simple logic which I confess I find attractive. It runs thus: a statement is not a representation unless it is also a statement that what is stated is true. If in context a statement contains no assertion express or implied that its content is accurate there is no representation. Ergo, there can be no misrepresentation; ergo, the Misrepresentation

Act 1967 cannot apply to it. Humpty Dumpty would have fallen for this argument. If we were to fall for it, the Misrepresentation Act would be dashed to pieces, which not all the King's lawyers could put together again."

and held that the notice, fairly construed was:

"a warning to the would-be purchaser to check the facts; that is to say, not to rely on [the representation]. It is because the statement contains the representation that the warning is given. Since the statement was false, there was a false representation; the Act therefore applies."

278. In *Thomas Witter v T.B.P Industries Ltd* [1992] 2 All ER 573 Jacob J had to construe a clause by which a party acknowledged that he had not been induced to enter the agreement by any representation except those contained or referred to in a schedule. He held that the representation relied on was within the schedule and that, even if the clause had exclusionary effect, it was neither fair nor reasonable. He appears to have taken it for granted that such a clause came within section 3.

279. In *E A Grimstead & Son Ltd v McGarrigan* [1999] EWCA Civ 3029 Chadwick LJ held that an acknowledgment of non-reliance was capable of operating as an evidential estoppel, subject to the *Lowe v Lombank* constraints. He held that, in the absence of evidence from Mr McGarrigan that he entered into the agreement on the basis that the purchaser from him was not relying on whatever representations he had made, he could not rely on the estoppel.

280. Chadwick LJ assumed, without deciding, that such a clause fell within section 3 and said:

"There are, as it seems to me, at least two good reasons why the courts should give effect to an acknowledgment of non-reliance in a commercial contract between experienced parties of equal bargaining power—a fortiori, where those parties have the benefit of professional advice. First, it is reasonable to assume that the parties desire commercial certainty. They want to order their affairs on the basis that the bargain between them can be found within the document which they have signed. They want to avoid the uncertainty of litigation based on allegations as to the content of oral discussions at pre-contractual meetings. Second, it is reasonable to assume that the price to be paid reflects the commercial risk which each party—or, more usually, the purchaser—is willing to accept. The risk is determined, in part at least, by the warranties which the vendor is prepared to give. The tighter the warranties, the less the risk and (in principle, at least) the greater the price the vendor will require and which the purchaser will be prepared to pay. It is legitimate, and commercially desirable that both parties should be able to measure the risk, and agree the price, on the basis of the warranties which have been given and accepted."

281. In *Government of Zanzibar v British Aerospace (Lancaster House) Ltd* [2000] 1 WLR 2333 a clause in a contract for the sale of a jet aircraft provided as follows (the letters being those inserted by the judge for ease of exposition):

"[A] The parties have negotiated this contract on the basis that the terms and conditions set out herein represent the entire agreement between them relating in any way whatsoever to the aircraft and the initial and continuing spares which for the subject matter of this contract and [B] accordingly they agree that all liabilities for and remedies in respect of any representations made are excluded save in so far as provided in this contract. [C] The parties further agree that neither party has placed any reliance whatsoever on any representations agreements statements or understandings whether oral or in writing made prior to the date of this contract other than those expressly incorporated or recited in this contract"

282. Judge Raymond Jack QC, as he then was, held that Part C of the clause came within section 3, whether looked at as a warranty or an estoppel. He held Part C was:

"a term [of the contract] which would exclude or restrict—(a) any liability to which a party to [the] contract may be subject by reason of any misrepresentation made by him before the contract was made"

"A term which negates a reliance which in fact existed is a term which excludes a liability which the represent or would otherwise be subject to by reason of the misrepresentation. If that were wrong, it would mean that section 3 could always be defeated by including an appropriate non-reliance clause in the contract, however unreasonable that might be."

283. In *Watford Electronics* a contract for the supply of certain equipment contained the following term:

"14 Entire Agreement
The parties agree that these terms and conditions (together with any other terms and conditions expressly incorporated in the Contract) represent the entire agreement between the parties relating to the sale and

purchase of the Equipment and that no statement or representations made by either party have been relied upon by the other in agreeing to enter into the Contract".

284. The issue before the Court of Appeal was whether two other provisions, one excluding liability for consequential losses and the other limiting liability to the price, were unreasonable. For that purpose it was necessary to decide what types of claim the two provisions related to. The judge had held that they covered both contractual and misrepresentation claims. Clause 14 of the contract was relevant to the issue because it bore on the question whether the provisions were limited (as the Court decided that they were) to contractual claims. Chadwick LJ held that the second half of the clause could operate as an evidential estoppel, subject to proof of the three requirements in *Lowe v Lombank;* and that it was not "*in substance an exclusion clause to which section 3 of the Misrepresentation Act is applicable*", as the judge had wrongly held.

285. Chadwick LJ went on to say:

". . . there is no reason why the parties should have intended, by the words which they have used in the first sentence of the limit of liability clause to exclude liability for negligent pre-contract misrepresentation. Liability in damages under the Misrepresentation Act 1967 can arise only where the party who has suffered the damage has relied upon the representation. Where both parties to the contact have acknowledged in the document itself that they have not relied upon any pre-contract representation, it would be bizarre (unless compelled to do so by the words which they have used) to attribute to them an intention to exclude a liability which they must have thought could never arise."

286. I cannot perceive any relevant distinction between clause 14 in *Watford Electronics* and clause [C] in *Government of Zanzibar*. It seems to me that, if there had in fact been reliance on the representations pleaded in *Watford Electronics*, the effect of clause 14 would have been to exclude liability as it did in *Government of Zanzibar*. If, therefore, the clause had been relied upon as a contractual, as opposed to an evidential estoppel, it would have fallen within section 3.

287. There is an important distinction between a provision which makes clear that no (or only a qualified) representation is being made and one which purports to exclude a representation that has been made. Toulson J, as he then was, considered this distinction in *IFE v Goldman Sachs*.

288. In that case Goldman Sachs had sent a Syndicate Information Memorandum ("SIM") to the claimant and others inviting them to participate in the syndication of a mezzanine facility. The SIM stated that the information in it had been derived from many sources and was not to form the basis of any contract; that Goldman Sachs had not independently verified the information and gave no representation, warranty or undertaking, express or implied and did not accept responsibility for its accuracy; and that the information was not to be assumed to have been updated and did not constitute a representation by any person that the information would be updated. The SIM gave a rosy view of the company in question.

289. The claimant contended that these statements were properly to be characterised as attempts to exclude liability for misrepresentation to which section 3 of the Misrepresentation Act 1967 applied. It also sought to invoke section 2 of the Unfair Contract Terms Act 1977 ("UCTA").

290. Toulson J observed that the question was whether the challenged clauses were properly to be understood, not as excluding a liability for misrepresentation, but rather as going to the question whether the alleged representation was made at all. If the latter, neither the Misrepresentation Act 1967, section 3, nor UCTA section 2, had any relevance to them: *William Sindall plc v Cambridgeshire County Council* [1994] 1 WLR 1016 at 1034 per Hoffmann LJ.

291. He rejected the claimant's challenge to the clauses holding that the question was one of substance and not form (para 68) so that a party cannot by a carefully chosen form of wording circumvent the statutory controls on exclusion of liability for a representation which on a proper analysis has been made.

292. He gave the example of the seller of a car who says to a buyer "*I have serviced the car since it was new, it has had only one owner and the clock reading is accurate*". Such statements would be representations and would remain so even if the seller had added the words "*but those statements are not statements on which you can rely*".

293. By contrast, if the seller of the car said "*The clock reading is 20,000 miles, but I have no knowledge whether the reading is true or false*" the position would be different because the qualifying words could not fairly be regarded as an attempt to exclude liability for a false representation arising from the first half of the sentence.

294. On the facts of that case he held that (paras 70-71):

"The statements in the SIM . . . went to the scope of the representations being made and cannot properly be characterised for the purposes of either Act as attempts to exclude liability for misrepresentation . . . The relevant paragraphs of the SIM are not in my view to be characterised in substance as a notice excluding or restricting a liability for negligence, but more fundamentally as going to the issue whether there was a relationship between the parties (amounting to or equivalent to that of professional adviser and advisee). . ."

295. On appeal the Court of Appeal took exactly the same approach in characterising the clauses as determining the basis of the parties' relationship: [2007] EWCA Civ 811 at para 28 (per Waller LJ).

296. In *Springwell*, which involved clauses similar to those in the present case, Gloster J found that (with the exception of a small number of genuine exclusion clauses, which were immaterial) most of the relevant provisions did not engage the Misrepresentation Act or UCTA. She found (paras 669-671) that the effect of the particular clauses was to preclude any representation, whether of fact or opinion, being made at all because Springwell and JP Morgan Chase had contracted on the express basis that Springwell was taking its own decision to enter into the transactions, independently and without reliance on the bank, and because the latter was not assuming any responsibility for statements of fact or opinion that were made.

297. Having pointed out the distinction between clauses which exclude liability and clauses which define the terms upon which the parties are conducting their business, in other words clauses which prevent an obligation from arising in the first place, she referred to *Tudor Grange Holdings v Citibank*, in which Sir Nicholas Browne-Wilkinson, V-C, stated that:

"The Act of 1977 [UCTA] is normally regarded as being aimed at exemption clauses in the strict sense, that is to say, clauses in a contract which aim to cut down prospective liability arising in the course of the performance of the contract in which the exemption clause is contained."

298. She accepted that:

"terms which simply define the basis upon which services will be rendered and confirm the basis upon which parties are transacting business are not subject to section 2 of UCTA. Otherwise, every contract which contains contractual terms defining the extent of each party's obligations would have to satisfy the requirement of reasonableness."

299. She went on to hold that the contractual documents showed that the bank was only prepared to allow Springwell's representative access to the bank's representative on the basis that, in accordance with the contractual documentation, Springwell was contractually precluded from bringing a claim in misrepresentation and that the bank was not assuming any responsibility for any statements that were made (para 675). The effect of this, in Gloster J's view was that (para 675):

"Having contracted to trade with Chase on those terms, it is not, in my judgment, now open to Springwell to seek to elevate those trading discussions into pre-contractual representations or statements in relation to which it is contended that Chase assumed a duty of care."

300. In *Peart Stevenson Associates Ltd v Brian Holland* [2008] EWHC 1868 HHJ Richard Seymour QC discerned a difference in approach between *Cremdean* and *Watford Electronics*, the former holding that a form of words which however expressed had the effect of preventing a party to the contract from pursuing a claim for damages of misrepresentation came within section 3, and the latter providing that section 3 would not be applicable if a *Lowe v Lombank* estoppel operated. But he did not consider it necessary to decide between the two because on either basis the claim, which involved fraudulent misrepresentations, failed.

301. In *Trident* Aikens J had to consider whether section 3 applied. In the first part of the relevant clause—clause 19.1—FFCL had agreed and acknowledged that, save as expressly stated in the lease agreement, Trident should not have any liability in relation to the description, satisfactory quality, fitness for any use or purpose, condition or design of the Aircraft. The second part of the clause provided that:

"The Lessee [i.e. FFCL] also agrees and acknowledges that save as expressly stated in this Agreement and the other Transaction Documents to which the Lessor is a party, the Lessor has not and shall not be deemed to have made any warranties or representations, express or implied, about the aircraft, including but not limited to matters referred to above."

Clause 19.2 provided:

"The Lessee [FFCL] gives up any rights against the Lessor [Trident] regarding any warranty or representation, except in respect of any warranty or representation expressly made in this Agreement or the other Transaction Documents to which the Lessor is a party. The Lessee cannot make any claim against the Lessor at any time after Delivery relating to the condition of the Aircraft."

302. He acknowledged the force of the logic in Chadwick LJ's statements in *Watford Electronics* but held:

"However, the effect of a clause must always depend on its exact wording. In this case the first half of cl 19.1 undoubtedly contemplates that FFCL might assert that Trident was liable in relation to the description, merchantability, satisfactory quality or fitness for any use or purpose of the aircraft. Clause 19.2 expressly contemplates that FFCL, as lessee, would but for the clause, have rights in respect of representations. Therefore, I have concluded that both cl 19.1 and 19.2 do fall within the scope of s 3 of the 1967 Act because they both purport to exclude or restrict liability for misrepresentation."

303. He then went on to find that because the relevant contracts were "*international supply contracts*" for the purpose of section 26 of the 1967 Act, they were outside its ambit.

Discussion

304. As Aikens J said, the effect of any clause must depend on its wording, which usually takes one or other of the following forms:

(a)   X agrees with Y that Y is not giving, or has not given, or is deemed not to have given, any representations of any kind (or is only giving certain specified representations); or that he does not intend anything he has said to be relied on;

(b)   X agrees with Y that he is not entering into the contract as a result of any representations by Y; or that he has not relied and does not rely upon any representations and/or that he has exercised an independent judgment and/or has sought independent advice;

(c)   X agrees with Y that Y is not acting as an adviser or assuming any responsibility.

In the drafting the word "*representations*" is often followed by one or more of "*warranties, assurances, statements, undertakings etc*". In some cases X may acknowledge rather than agree.

305. Although contractual estoppel clauses are increasingly common, particularly in the case of complex financial instruments or investments, their use is not restricted to that field. They may also be used in everyday contracts made with consumers or between businesses great and small. Any interpretation of section 3 must accommodate the car dealer as well as the bond dealer.

306. Suppose, to take a version of Toulson J's example, a car is sold. The dealer says "*I have serviced the car since it was new, it has had only one owner and the clock reading is accurate*". He is not fraudulent but mistaken, carelessly confusing one car for another, in relation to which the statement is true. Relying on his statement the buyer purchases the car. Without it he would not have done so. The car has had several owners, no known service history, and the clock reading is substantially inaccurate. The contract of sale provides (in one of many paragraphs on the back of the form which the buyer does not read and to which his attention is not directed) that the buyer is entering into the contract on the basis that no representations have been made to, or relied on by, the purchaser.

307. In that example there has been a clear statement of fact, on a matter said to be within the representor's personal knowledge, which was in fact intended to induce the contract, upon which the purchaser in fact relied, which is false. If section 3 has no application in respect of a contractual estoppel there is no further control mechanism on its operation, which does not require detrimental reliance. The seller (and any other similar seller) may, subject to any applicable consumer protection laws, make non-fraudulent misrepresentations of that type with impunity.

308. In such a situation section 3 is, as it seems to me, applicable because, on those facts, there has been what the person to whom the statement was made would reasonably understand to be a representation, which was intended to be and was in fact relied on. The clause seeks to avoid liability for what, absent the clause, would be a clear liability in misrepresentation. The situation might be different in the unlikely scenario that before he contracts the buyer sees the clause and, eyes wide open, agrees that he is not relying on what he may have been told.

309. Such a conclusion is consistent with that reached in *Cremdean* by Fox J (if there is a misrepresentation, any clause, whatever its form, which excludes liability is within the mischief of section 3) and, tentatively, by the Court of Appeal (a purported annulment of the existence of any representation cannot by artful draftsmanship operate to exclude the operation of the Act).

310. As has already been said, the essential question is whether the clause in question goes to whether the alleged representation was made (or, I would add, was intended to be understood and acted on as a representation), or whether it excludes or restricts liability in respect of representations made, intended to be acted on and in fact acted on; and that question is one of substance not form.

311. Everything must depend on the facts. In some cases the effect of the clause will be to show that what might otherwise have been a representation of fact to be relied on is no more than a statement of belief, or of opinion, or a statement of what the maker has been told, or a statement of a very limited character ("the clock says 20,000 but I do not know whether that is true"). Thus in *IFE Fund* Goldman Sachs supplied information from others in an information memorandum. The representations alleged were said to be implicit in what was said in that memorandum. Goldman Sachs' non acceptance of responsibility was apt to make it plain that it was not itself making any representations about the accuracy of the information.

312. Similarly the clause in question may show that no representation is in fact being made, or rebut any suggestion of an implicit statement of fact contained within an express statement, particularly one of opinion (where the existence of an implied statement of fact and the nature of that statement is debatable: see *BG Plc v Nelson Groups Services (Maintenance) Ltd* [2002] EWCA Civ 547). Thus in *William Sindall* the argument that a vendor who sold as "*beneficial owner*" implicitly represented that he had a good right to convey free from encumbrances failed because the court held that the provision that the purchaser should be deemed to purchase with full notice of and subject to all easements qualified the obligation to convey as beneficial owner and any representation which could be *implied* from that expression.

Basis clauses

313. In *Springwell* Gloster J took the view that terms which simply defined the basis upon which the parties were transacting business did not fall within section 2 of UCTA; otherwise, as she said, all contractual terms that did so would have to satisfy the test of reasonableness. It is obviously advantageous that commercial parties of equal bargaining power should be able to agree what responsibility they are taking (or not taking) towards each other without having to satisfy some reasonableness test. At the same time there is a danger that the "*ingenuity of the draftsman*" will insert into a myriad of contracts a clause to the effect that the basis upon which the parties are contracting is that no representations have been made, are intended to be relied on or have been relied on, as a means of evading liability which is intended to be impregnable.

314. In this respect the key question, as it seems to me, is whether the clause attempts to rewrite history or parts company with reality. If sophisticated commercial parties agree, in terms of which they are both aware, to regulate their future relationship by prescribing the basis on which they will be dealing with each other and what representations they are or are not making, a suitably drafted clause may properly be regarded as establishing that no representations (or none other than honest belief) are being made or are intended to be relied on. Such parties are capable of distinguishing between statements which are to be treated as representations on which the recipient is entitled to rely, and statements which do not have that character, and should be allowed to agree among themselves into which category any given statement may fall.

315. Per contra, to tell the man in the street that the car you are selling him is perfect and then agree that the basis of your contract is that no representations have been made or relied on, may be nothing more than an attempt retrospectively to alter the character and effect of what has gone before, and in substance an attempt to exclude or restrict liability.

[Christopher Clarke J went on to hold that the relevant provisions did not purport to exclude liability so as to fall within section 3; and, even if they did fall within section 3, they satisfied the reasonableness test].

322. The undesirability of refusing to give effect to the Relevant Provisions seems to me particularly applicable here. Both parties are large commercial concerns. The transaction into which RZB entered was an arm's length transaction entered into after mature deliberation. RZB was and is a very large Austrian bank; an experienced participant in the syndicated lending market (in which Mr Stuart-Prince had worked extensively) with experience in structured finance transactions. It had previously participated in syndicated loan facilities for Enron. The Relevant Provisions were in no way unusual. On the contrary, they were in a form habitually used in the market. The IM and the Confidentiality Agreement were presented, and in the case of the latter signed and agreed, at the outset.

323. The Relevant Provisions are a means of allocating risk and of avoiding disputes as to, inter alia, the debatable ambit of implied representations. That risk may involve the lender not being informed of something of which it (but not the Arranger) thinks it ought to have been told. RBS was entitled to expect that the provisions would take effect in accordance with their terms. The likelihood is that, if RZB wanted to participate in the Facility it would have to sign up to the Relevant Provisions. But it was in no sense obliged to engage in this particular form of structured finance, or to enter into the Syndication Agreement, or to deal with Enron or RBS.

It was legitimate for RBS to agree terms which sought (unsuccessfully as it happened) to avoid the prospect of a detailed review, years after the transaction, of the history of its negotiation.

Finally, it should be noted that provisions of this kind would not avail a *fraudulent* party (see, para.325).

Further reading

P.S. Atiyah and G.H. Treitel, 'Misrepresentation Act 1967' (1967) 30 MLR 369
Michael Bridge, 'Innocent Misrepresentation in Contract' (2004) 57 *Current Legal Problems* 277

15

REPRESENTATIONS, TERMS AND COLLATERAL CONTRACTS

LEARNING OBJECTIVES

By the end of this chapter, you should:

- **understand the criteria that determine whether a promise made during the negotiation of a contract is incorporated as a term of the contract;**
- **understand why it matters whether a promise is characterised as a "mere representation" or as a term of the contract;**
- **understand the idea of a 'collateral contract' and appreciate its significance as a device (prior to the Misrepresentation Act 1967) to make available damages for a non-fraudulent misrepresentation.**

INTRODUCTION

In the introductory remarks to the previous chapter, we noted that statements made during the course of negotiations for a contract might or might not have legal effect and might or might not form part of a contract. In this chapter, we are concerned with two legal issues that relate to these remarks: first, whether a promise has been incorporated as a term of the principal contract (so that, if that promise is not fulfilled, an action for breach of contract will lie); and, secondly, whether a promise, although not incorporated as a term of the principal contract, is nevertheless the basis for a so-called "collateral contract" (for breach of which a claim for damages will lie).

    There are three sections in this chapter. In the first, there is a short overview of the general landscape of representations and terms; in the second, the cases deal with the question of whether a representation made during the lead-up to a contract is or is not a part of that contract; and, in the third, the case-law on collateral contracts is set out.

15-001

1. REPRESENTATIONS AND TERMS: A SHORT OVERVIEW

Many of the cases in this chapter are concerned with the question whether a particular statement or "representation" is, or is not, part of the contract. If it is not part of the contract, it is commonly described as a "mere representation". In spite of the remedies for negligent misrepresentation that are provided by the Misrepresentation Act, it will frequently be important to determine whether a statement has, or has not, become part of the contract. For example, the defendant may be able to prove that he believed on reasonable grounds that his misrepresentation was true, in which case he will not be liable for damages under the Act. His honest and reasonable belief will

15-002

not, however, afford him a defence if he is held to have given a contractual undertaking as to its truth.

The problem of determining the extent of the contractual obligation is not at an end when we have classified all the statements that have been made as either mere representations or contractual terms. A contract may be held to include terms which have never been put into words, whether written or oral; these are "implied terms" and they are just as much a part of the contractual obligation as the express terms. The circumstances in which the courts will imply terms are considered in detail in Ch.16 below.

Even when both the express and implied terms have been ascertained, the interpreter's task is not necessarily at an end, for terms differ in their nature. Traditionally, they were divided into two categories: conditions and warranties. Conditions are the essential promises in a contract, while warranties are of a subsidiary nature. Breach of either kind of term entitles the injured party to sue for damages. The importance of the distinction is that, in the case of a breach of condition, the injured party has the additional remedy of terminating the contract, if he so wishes. If the claimant is suing for damages it will not be necessary for the court to determine whether the term alleged to be broken is a condition or a warranty; the damages will be the same in either case. The two words are commonly loosely used by the courts, especially in the older cases: and the fact that either word is used must not be taken to mean that the court has evaluated the terms as an essential or subsidiary one unless the question of its value was actually in issue. The value of the term will be in issue in two main types of case: (i) where the claimant seeks to terminate the contract for breach, there having been no actionable misrepresentation, and (ii) where there is a clause in the contract excluding liability for warranties but not conditions.

Following the decision of the Court of Appeal in *Hong Kong Fir Shipping Co Ltd v Kawasaki Kisen Kaisha Ltd* (below, Ch.20), it is commonly thought that we must allow for a third category of terms a breach of which may or may not entitle the injured party to rescind, depending on the nature of the breach and its effect: these are so-called "innominate" or "intermediate" terms. Another view is that there are only two categories: conditions, any breach of which justifies termination of the contract; and warranties, breach of which justifies termination only if the effect of the breach is to deprive the other party of the consideration for which he bargained. See Ormrod LJ in the *Hansa Nord* [1976] Q.B. 44 and Lord Devlin, 'The Treatment of Breach of Contract' [1966] CLJ 192 at 202. The "Guide", below, adopts the former view.

The law concerning misrepresentation and terms of the contract may have been improved by the Misrepresentation Act, but it has certainly become more complicated. The following "Guide" may assist the reader in considering the subsequent cases. It should be noted that the terms "rescind" and "avoid" are often used in books, cases and statutes to mean either (i) to nullify the contract ab initio or (ii) to nullify the contract from the moment of "rescission" or "avoidance"; but in this "Guide", 'rescind' means to nullify the contract ab initio and 'terminate' means to bring the contract to an end from the moment of the act of termination—usually on notice by P (the representee) to D (the representor).

Guide

i. Where the Misrepresentation Leads to the Conclusion of a Contract

15-003   (1) Where the misrepresentation is a term of the contract. The term may be:

      (a) a condition. If so, P may recover *damages*, and *terminate* the contract for breach.

      (b) a warranty. If so, P may recover *damages* but he may not *terminate* the contract for breach.

    (c) an innominate term. If so, P may recover *damages* and, if the breach and its consequences are sufficiently grave, *terminate* the contract for breach.

P may alternatively *rescind* the contract for misrepresentation, even though the misrepresentation has become a term of the contract and the contract has been performed: Misrepresentation Act, 1967 s.1; *and* recover *damages* under s.2 of that Act as in (2) below.

(2) Where the misrepresentation is not a term of the contract:

P may recover damages under s.2(1) of the Misrepresentation Act, 1967 and rescind the contract, unless D can prove that he had reasonable grounds to believe and did believe the facts represented to be true. If D can so prove, P's only remedy is rescission in equity and an indemnity (but damages might be awarded in lieu of rescission, if it were equitable to do so, under s.2(2) of the Misrepresentation Act 1967).

ii. Where the Misrepresentation does not Lead to the Conclusion of a Contract

P may recover damages: **15-004**

    (a) for deceit, if he can prove that the misrepresentation was made fraudulently: *Derry v Peek* (1889) 14 App.Cas. 337; or

    (b) under *Hedley Byrne & Co v Heller and Partners* [1964] A.C. 465, if he can prove that D had assumed, and was in breach of, a duty to exercise care in making the representation.

(There is no practical advantage to P in pursuing these common law remedies where the misrepresentation leads to a contract since, by doing so, he (P) would incur the onus of proof which lies on D where action is brought under s.2(1) of the Misrepresentation Act; but a plaintiff may sue in deceit instead of under the Act if he wishes: *Archer v Brown* [1984] 2 All E.R. 267 (Peter Pain J)).

2. MERE REPRESENTATION OR CONTRACTUAL TERM?

The problem to be considered in this section is the extent of the *contractual* obligation. Assuming   **15-005** that a contract has been concluded, there may still be a problem of ascertaining what promises have been made by each party and which of these promises have effect as part of the finalised contract.

If the contract is an oral one, this may involve an examination of a long history of negotiations. For instance, the offer and acceptance in a contract for the sale of a car may consist simply of the buyer saying, "I offer you £5,000 for the car"; and the seller saying "I accept". It is unlikely, however, that this is the whole contract between the parties. During previous negotiations the buyer may have received assurances that the car is a 2010 model, that the seller has owned it since it was new, that it has a reconditioned engine, that it has done a certain mileage, and so on. Such assurances will, as the seller knows, have contributed to the buyer's decision to make his offer and been present to his mind when he did so. If they are false, they amount to misrepresentations with the consequences which we have considered in the previous chapter; but it may very well be that they amount to contractual undertakings by the seller. When the contract has been reduced to writing, the parol evidence rule applies to exclude evidence which would add to, vary or contradict the terms of the document. Generally, therefore, we will be confined to interpreting the document. But this rule is subject to important exceptions and cases will be considered in which, by one means or another, the court succeeds certainly in adding to, and perhaps varying or even contradicting, the document, by reference to the negotiations which precede it.

Where the courts have to classify a statement as a mere (or mis) representation or as a contractual term, they need to set the statement in question in its particular context, asking "Who said what to whom, and in what setting?" For example, was the statement made by one expert (or professional) to another, by an expert to a non-expert, or by a non-expert to an expert? Concomitantly, they need to consider whether it was reasonable for one party to rely on the statement—possibly, for example, the courts might judge that it is more reasonable for a non-expert to rely on a statement made by an expert than the other way round. The first group of cases (*Oscar Chess*, *Harlingdon*, and *Dick Bentley*) illustrate how the courts view these potential indicators of what is to be treated as a mere representation and what as a contractual term.

OSCAR CHESS LTD v WILLIAMS

15-006

Court of Appeal [1957] 1 W.L.R. 370; 101 S.J. 186; [1957] 1 All E.R. 325

In March 1954 the defendant's mother acquired a second-hand Morris car on the footing that it was a 1948 model. The registration book showed that it was first registered on April 13, 1948, with five changes of ownership between 1948 and 1954. In May 1955 the defendant acquired a new car on hire-purchase terms through the plaintiffs who took the Morris in part exchange. The defendant described the car as a 1948 Morris and produced the registration book. The plaintiffs' salesman, who was familiar with the car, having often had lifts in it, checked the current price for a 1948 Morris in Glass's Guide which was £290 and made the defendant an allowance for that sum against the price of the new car.

Eight months later the plaintiffs discovered that the car was not made in 1948 but in 1939, the appearance of the model not having changed in the meantime. If they had known that it was a 1939 model they would have allowed only £175. They brought an action to recover £115 as damages for breach of an express term that the car was a 1948 model. The county court judge found that it was a condition of the contract that the car was a 1948 model. The defendant appealed.

DENNING LJ

[Stated the facts set out above, and said that in describing the car as a 1948 Morris the defendant was perfectly innocent; he honestly believed it was a 1948 model; and so no doubt did the previous sellers. Someone in 1948 must have fraudulently altered the log-book, but he could not now be traced. His Lordship continued:] I entirely agree with the judge that both parties assumed that the Morris was a 1948 model and that this assumption was fundamental to the contract. But this does not prove that the representation was a term of the contract. The assumption was based by both of them on the date given in the registration book as the date of first registration. They both believed it was a 1948 model whereas it was only a 1939 one. They were both mistaken and their mistake was of fundamental importance.

The effect of such a mistake is this: It does not make the contract a nullity from the beginning, but it does in some circumstances enable the contract to be set aside in equity. If the buyer had come promptly, he might have succeeded in getting the whole transaction set aside in equity on the ground of this mistake[1]: see *Solle v Butcher* [below, Ch.23]; but he did not do so and it is too late for him to do it: see *Leaf v International Galleries* [above, Ch.14]. His only remedy is in damages, and to recover these he must prove a warranty.

In saying that he must prove a warranty, I use the word "warranty" in its ordinary English meaning to denote a binding promise. Everyone knows what a man means when he says "I guarantee it" or "I warrant it" or "I give you my word on it." He means that he binds himself to it. That is the meaning it has borne in English law for 300 years from the leading case of *Chandelor v Lopus* (1603) Cro.Jac. 4 onwards. During the last fifty years, however, some lawyers have come to use the word "warranty" in another sense. They use it to denote a

---

subsidiary term in a contract as distinct from a vital term which they call a "condition." In so doing they depart from the ordinary meaning, not only of the word "warranty" but also of the word "condition." There is no harm in their doing this, so long as they confine this technical use to its proper sphere, namely, to distinguish between a vital term, the breach of which gives the right to treat the contract as at an end, and a subsidiary term which does not. But the trouble comes when one person uses the word "warranty" in its ordinary meaning and another uses it in its technical meaning. When Holt C. J., in *Crosse v Gardner* (1689) Carth. 90 (as glossed by Buller J. in *Pasley v Freeman* (1789) 3 Term Rep. 51, 57) and *Medina v Stoughton* (1700) 1 Salk. 210, made his famous ruling that an affirmation at the time of a sale is a warranty, provided it appears on evidence to be so intended, he used the word "warranty" in its ordinary English meaning of a binding promise: and when Lord Haldane L.C. and Lord Moulton in 1913 in *Heilbut, Symons & Co v Buckleton* [below], adopted his ruling, they used it likewise in its ordinary meaning. These different uses of the word seem to have been the source of confusion in the present case. The judge did not ask himself, "Was the representation (that it was a 1948 Morris) intended to be a warranty?" He asked himself, "Was it fundamental to the contract?" He answered it by saying that it was fundamental; and therefore it was a condition and not a warranty. By concentrating on whether it was fundamental, he seems to me to have missed the crucial point in the case which is whether it was a term of the contract at all. The crucial question is: was it a binding promise or only an innocent misrepresentation? The technical distinction between a "condition" and a "warranty" is quite immaterial in this case, because it is far too late for the buyer to reject the car. He can at best only claim damages. The material distinction here is between a statement which is a term of the contract and a statement which is only an innocent misrepresentation. This distinction is best expressed by the ruling of Lord Holt: Was it intended as a warranty or not? using the word warranty there in its ordinary English meaning: because it gives the exact shade of meaning that is required. It is something to which a man must be taken to bind himself.

In applying Lord Holt's test, however, some misunderstanding has arisen by the use of the word "intended." It is sometimes supposed that the tribunal must look into the minds of the parties to see what they themselves intended. That is a mistake. Lord Moulton made it quite clear that "The intention of the parties can only be deduced from the totality of the evidence." The question whether a warranty was intended depends on the conduct of the parties, on their words and behaviour, rather than on their thoughts. If an intelligent bystander would reasonably infer that a warranty was intended, that will suffice. And this, when the facts are not in dispute, is a question of law. That is shown by *Heilbut, Symons & Co v Buckleton* [below] itself, where the House of Lords upset the finding by a jury of a warranty.

It is instructive to take some recent instances to show how the courts have approached this question. When the seller states a fact which is or should be within his own knowledge and of which the buyer is ignorant, intending that the buyer should act on it, and he does so, it is easy to infer a warranty: see *Couchman v Hill* [below], where the farmer stated that the heifer was unserved, and *Harling v Eddy* [below], where he stated that there was nothing wrong with her. So also if he makes a promise about something which is or should be within his own control: see *Birch v Paramount Estates Ltd* (unreported), decided on October 2, 1956, in this court, where the seller stated that the house would be as good as the show house. But if the seller, when he states a fact, makes it clear that he has no knowledge of his own but has got his information elsewhere and is merely passing it on, it is not so easy to imply a warranty. Such a case was *Routledge v McKay* [1954] 1 W.L.R. 615, 636, where the seller "stated that it was a 1942 model and pointed to the corroboration found in the book," and it was held that there was no warranty.

Turning now to the present case, much depends on the precise words that were used. If the seller says "I believe it is a 1948 Morris. Here is the registration book to prove it," there is clearly no warranty. It is a statement of belief, not a contractual promise. But if the seller says "I guarantee that it is a 1948 Morris. This is borne out by the registration book, but you need not rely solely on that. I give you my own guarantee that it is," there is clearly a warranty. The seller is making himself contractually responsible, even though the registration book is wrong.

In this case much reliance was placed by the judge on the fact that the buyer looked up Glass's Guide and paid £290 on the footing that it was a 1948 model: but that fact seems to me to be neutral. Both sides believed the car to have been made in 1948 and in that belief the buyer paid £290. That belief can be just as firmly based on the buyer's own inspection of the log-book as on a contractual warranty by the seller.

Once that fact is put on one side I ask myself: What is the proper inference from the known facts? It must have been obvious to both that the seller had himself no personal knowledge of the year when the car was made. He only became owner after a great number of changes. He must have been relying on the registration book. It is unlikely that such a person would warrant the year of manufacture. The most he would do would be to state his belief, and then produce the registration book in verification of it. In these circumstances the intelligent bystander would, I suggest, say that the seller did not intend to bind himself so as to warrant that it was a 1948 model. If the seller was asked to pledge himself to it, he would at once have said "I cannot do that. I have only the log-book to go by, the same as you."

The judge seems to have thought that there was a difference between written contracts and oral contracts. He thought that the reason why the buyer failed in *Heilbut, Symons & Co v Buckleton* and *Routledge v McKay* was because the sales were afterwards recorded in writing, and the written contracts contained no reference to the representation. I agree that that was an important factor in those cases. If an oral representation is afterwards recorded in writing, it is good evidence that it was intended as a warranty. If it is not put into writing, it is evidence against a warranty being intended. But it is by no means decisive. There have been many cases where the courts have found an oral warranty collateral to a written contract such as *Birch v Paramount Estates*. But when the purchase is not recorded in writing at all it must not be supposed that every representation made in the course of the dealing is to be treated as a warranty. The question then is still: Was it intended as a warranty? In the leading case of *Chandelor v Lopus* in 1603 a man by word of mouth sold a precious stone for £100 affirming it to be a bezar stone whereas it was not. The declaration averred that the seller affirmed it to be a bezar stone, but did not aver that he warranted it to be so. The declaration was held to be ill because "the bare affirmation that it was a bezar stone, without warranting it to be so, is no cause of action." That has been the law from that day to this and it was emphatically reaffirmed by the House of Lords in *Heilbut, Symons & Co v Buckleton*.

One final word: It seems to me clear that the motor-dealers who bought the car relied on the year stated in the log-book. If they had wished to make sure of it, they could have checked it then and there, by taking the engine number and chassis number and writing to the makers. They did not do so at the time, but only eight months later. They are experts, and, not having made that check at the time, I do not think they should now be allowed to recover against the innocent seller who produced to them all the evidence he had, namely, the registration book. I agree that it is hard on the dealers to have paid more than the car is worth: but it would be equally hard on the seller to make him pay the difference. He would never have bought the Hillman at all unless he had got the allowance of £290 for the Morris. The best course in all these cases would be to "shunt" the difference down the train of innocent sellers until one reaches the rogue who perpetrated the fraud: but he can rarely be traced, or if he can, he rarely has the money to pay the damages. So one is left to decide between a number of innocent people who is to bear the loss. That can only be done by applying the law about representations and warranties as we know it: and that is what I have tried to do. If the rogue can be traced, he can be sued by whomsoever has suffered the loss: but if he cannot be traced, the loss must lie where it falls. It should not be inflicted on innocent sellers, who sold the car many months perhaps many years before and have forgotten all about it and have conducted their affairs on the basis that the transaction was concluded. Such a seller would not be able to recollect after all this length of time the exact words he used, such as whether he said "I believe it is a 1948 model," or "I warrant it is a 1948 model." The right course is to let the buyer set aside the transaction if he finds out the mistake quickly and comes promptly before other interests have irretrievably intervened; otherwise the loss must lie where it falls: and that is, I think, the course prescribed by law. I would allow this appeal accordingly.

Hodson L.J. delivered a concurring judgment.

Morris L.J. dissented, holding that the defendant's statement amounted to a condition in the contract. He said: The statement related to a vitally important matter: it described the subject-matter of the contract then being made and the statement directed the parties to, and was the basis of, their agreement as to the price to be paid or credited to the defendant. In the language of Scott L.J. [in *Couchman v Hill*, below] it seems to me that the statement made by the defendant was "an item in the description" of what was being sold and that it constituted a substantial ingredient in the identity of the thing sold.

Question

15-007   Might the result in the above case have been different if the seller had been the car dealer and the buyer the layman? Consider what effect, if any, the Misrepresentation Act or the Unfair Contract Terms Act might have on this case.

HARLINGDON & LEINSTER ENTERPRISES LTD v CHRISTOPHER HULL FINE ART LTD

Court of Appeal [1990] 3 W.L.R. 13; [1990] 1 All E.R. 737

In 1984 Hull, the owner of the defendant company, was asked to dispose of two oil paintings which were described in an auction catalogue of 1980 as the work of Gabriele Münter (1877–1962), an artist of the German expressionist school. Hull, who specialised in British contemporary artists had no training, experience or knowledge which would enable him to identify a painting as the work of Münter. He took the paintings to Christies who expressed interest. Earlier he had been told that the plaintiff company had a good reputation as dealers in German art and in fact they had a special interest in buying and selling German expressionist paintings. Hull telephoned the plaintiffs that he had two paintings by Münter to sell. They expressed interest and sent their Mr Runkel to view them. Hull told Runkel he did not know much about the paintings, he had never heard of Münter and thought little of the paintings. He made it absolutely plain that he was not an expert in them and "to a certain extent" made it clear that he was relying on Runkel. Runkel saw a copy of the 1980 catalogue and asked no questions about the provenance of the paintings. There was some bargaining as to price but Runkel agreed to the asking price of £6,000 for one of the paintings, provided he could find a customer. When he did so, Hull made out an invoice:

15-008

"GABRIELE MU¨NTER (1877–1962)
Dorfstrasse in Oberbayern December 3rd, 1984
oil on board
£6,000"

In February 1985 the customer discovered that the painting was not by Münter but was a forgery. The plaintiffs took it back and refunded the price. The defendants refused to take it back. The plaintiffs sued, alleging a breach of a contract; (i) for the sale of goods by description (Sale of Goods Act s.13(1), below, Ch.16); (ii) that the painting was of merchantable quality (s.14(2)); (iii) that the painting would be reasonably fit for a particular purpose (s.14(3)); and (iv) a misrepresentation under the Misrepresentation Act 1967. The judge held in favour of the defendants on all four points. Only the first and second were pursued in the Court of Appeal. The concept of "merchantable quality" in the Sale of Goods Act has now been replaced by that of "satisfactory quality" and judgments on that issue are therefore omitted.

NOURSE LJ

[Having cited certain authorities:]
It is suggested that the significance which some of these authorities attribute to the buyer's reliance on the description is misconceived. I think that that criticism is theoretically correct. In theory it is no doubt possible for a description of goods which is not relied on by the buyer to become an essential term of a contract for their sale. But in practice it is very difficult, and perhaps impossible, to think of facts where that would be so. The description must have a sufficient influence in the sale to become an essential term of the contract and the correlative of influence is reliance. Indeed, reliance by the buyer is the natural index of a sale by description. It is true that the question must, as always, be judged objectively and it may be said that previous judicial references have been to subjective or actual reliance. But each of those decisions, including that of Judge Oddie in the present case, can be justified on an objective basis. For all practical purposes, I would say that there cannot be a contract for the sale of goods by description where it is not within the reasonable contemplation of the parties that the buyer is relying on the description. For those purposes, I think that the law is correctly summarised in these words of Benjamin, p. 641, which should be understood to lay down an objective test:

"Specific goods may be sold as such . . . where, though the goods are described, the description is not relied upon, as where the buyer buys the goods such as they are."

In giving his decision on this question Judge Oddie said:

"There can clearly be a sale by description where the buyer has inspected the goods if the description relates to something not apparent on inspection. Every item in a description which constitutes a substantial ingredient in the identity of the thing sold is a condition."

Later, having said that he had not been referred to any similar case where a sale in reliance on a statement that a painting was by a particular artist had been held to be a sale by description, the judge continued:

"In my judgment such a statement could amount to a description and a sale in reliance on it to a sale by description within the meaning of the 1979 Act. However, on the facts of this case I am satisfied that the description by Mr Hull before the agreement was not relied on by Mr Runkel in making his offer to purchase which was accepted by Mr Hull. I conclude that he bought the painting as it was. In these circumstances there was not in my judgment a sale by description."

I agree. On a view of their words and deeds as a whole the parties could not reasonably have contemplated that the defendants were relying on the plaintiff's statement that the painting was by Gabriele Münter. On the facts which he found the judge could not, by a correct application of the law, have come to any other decision.

STUART-SMITH LJ (DISSENTING)

In my judgment the matter can be tested in this way. If following the telephone conversation Mr Runkel had arrived at the defendants' gallery, seen the painting, bargained about the price and agreed to buy it, it seems to me beyond argument that it would have been a sale by description. And indeed counsel for the defendants was at one time disposed to concede as much. Had the invoice been a contractual document, as it frequently is, again it seems to me clear that the sale would have been a sale by description. In fact the invoice was written out subsequently to the oral contract; but the judge held, rightly as it seems to me, that it gave effect to what had been agreed. It was cogent evidence of the oral contract.

How does it come about that what would otherwise be a sale by description in some way ceased to be one? It can only be as a result of the conversation between Mr Hull and Mr Runkel before the bargain was actually struck. If Mr Hull had told Mr Runkel that he did not know one way or the other whether the painting was by Münter in spite of the fact that he had so described it or that he could only say that the painting was attributed to Münter, and that Mr Runkel must make up his mind for himself on this point, I can well see that the effect of what had previously been said about the identity of the painter might have been cancelled or withdrawn and was no longer effective at the time of the contract. But Mr Hull did not say that, as the judge found. And I cannot see that this is the effect of what was said. Merely to say that he knew nothing of the painter and did not like her paintings does not in any way to my mind necessarily mean that he was cancelling or withdrawing what he had previously said, based as it was on the auction catalogue. Nor does the fact that it was recognised that the plaintiffs were more expert in German expressionist art than Mr Hull advance the matter. It would, in my judgment, be a serious defect in the law if the effect of a condition implied by statute could be excluded by the vendor's saying that he was not an expert in what was being sold or that the purchaser was more expert than the vendor. That is not the law; it has long been held that conditions implied by statute can only be excluded by clear words. There is nothing of that kind in this case.

SLADE L.J.

While some judicial dicta seem to support the view that there can be no sale by description unless there is actual reliance on the description by the purchaser, I am not sure that this is strictly correct in principle. If a party to a contract wishes to claim relief in respect of a misrepresentation as to a matter which did not constitute a term of the contract, his claim will fail unless he is able to show that he relied on this representation in entering into the contract; in general, however, if a party wishes to claim relief in respect of a breach of a term of the contract (whether it be a condition or warranty) he need prove no actual reliance.

Nevertheless, where a question arises whether a sale of goods was one by description, the presence or absence of reliance on the description may be very relevant in so far as it throws light on the intentions of the parties at the time of the contract. If there was no such reliance by the purchaser, this may be powerful evidence that the parties did not contemplate that the authenticity of the description should constitute a term of the contract, in other words, that they contemplated that the purchaser would be buying the goods as they were. If, on the other hand, there was such reliance (as in *Varley v Whipp* [1900] 1 Q.B. 513, where the purchaser had never seen the goods) this may be equally powerful evidence that it was contemplated by both parties that the correctness of the description would be a term of the contract (so as to bring it within section 13(1)).

So far as it concerns section 13(1), the issue for the court in the present case was and is, in my judgment, this: on an objective assessment of what the parties said and did at and before the meeting at Motcomb Street, and of all the circumstances of the case, is it right to impute to them the common intention that the authenticity of the attribution to Gabriele Münter should be a term of the contract of sale? The proper inferences to be drawn from the evidence and the findings of primary fact by the judge are matters on which different minds can take different views, as the cogent judgments of Nourse and Stuart-Smith L.JJ. have shown. However, I for my part feel no doubt that the answer to the crucial issue is, No . . .

I do not say that in the present case section 13 has been excluded by any contract term: my analysis of the position is that the contract was not one for the sale of goods by description. Nevertheless, in my judgment, the provisions of the 1977 Act support the view that the very fact that two parties to the negotiations for the sale of a specific chattel are dealers in that class of chattel is a relevant factor in considering whether or not an attribution of origin made by one dealer to the other during the course of negotiation should be treated as rendering the transaction a "sale by description."

The form of the invoice subsequently made out in favour of the plaintiffs does not, in my judgment, assist the plaintiffs' case. By that time the contract had already been concluded. While the reference to Gabriele Münter in the invoice is quite consistent with the parties having made the origin of the picture a term of the contract, it can equally well be read as merely a convenient mode of reference to a particular picture which both parties knew to have been attributed to Gabriele Münter (and indeed both still thought to be her work).

Appeal Dismissed.

Questions

1. *Oscar Chess v Williams* (above) is not mentioned in the report. Was it not a powerful authority in favour of the seller?   **15-009**

2. Would it have been different if the buyer had been not an art dealer but, say, a stockbroker, buying a picture for his house? (In a consumer sale liability for breach of the undertaking as to description implied by s.13 cannot be excluded: Unfair Contract Terms Act 1977 s.6(2); but this only applies where the contract is "a contract for the sale of goods by description.")

3. The judges suggest that a description may be an essential term though it is not in fact relied on; but can it be a term if the seller makes it clear that his description is not to be relied on? (On the relation between description and reliance, see the discussion of this case by M. G. Bridge, *The Sale of Goods* (Oxford University Press, 1997) pp.288–289).

4. Might it have been argued that, in the absence of any undertaking that the picture was by Münter, the contract was void for failure of a common assumption which was the foundation of the contract (below, Ch.23), that is, that the picture was by Münter? Or that, if not void, it was voidable for common mistake as to an essential quality (*Solle v Butcher*, below, Ch.23)? The fact that the buyer was not relying on the seller would be irrelevant. (The judge found that Hull and Runkel both believed the painting was by Münter and, if either had not believed that, the deal would not have been made.)

DICK BENTLEY PRODUCTIONS LTD AND ANOTHER v HAROLD SMITH (MOTORS) LTD

Court of Appeal [1965] 1 W.L.R. 623; [1965] 2 All E.R. 65

Bentley asked Smith, a car dealer, to find him a "well-vetted" Bentley car. Smith found a car which he told Bentley had done only 20,000 miles since it had been fitted with a replacement engine and gear   **15-010** box. This statement was untrue and, on the car proving unsatisfactory, Bentley sued and recovered damages for breach of warranty. Smith appealed.

LORD DENNING MR

I endeavoured to explain in *Oscar Chess Ltd v Williams* [above] that the question whether a warranty was intended depends on the conduct of the parties, on their words and behaviour, rather than on their thoughts. If an intelligent bystander would reasonably infer that a warranty was intended, that will suffice. What conduct, then? What words and behaviour, lead to the inference of a warranty?

Looking at the cases once more, as we have done so often, it seems to me that if a representation is made in the course of dealings for a contract for the very purpose of inducing the other party to act on it, and it actually induces him to act on it by entering into the contract, that is prima facie ground for inferring that the representation was intended as a warranty. It is not necessary to speak of it as being collateral. Suffice it that the representation was intended to be acted on and was in fact acted on. But the maker of the representation can rebut this inference if he can show that it really was an innocent misrepresentation, in that he was in fact innocent of fault in making it, and that it would not be reasonable in the circumstances for him to be bound by it. [His Lordship referred to the *Oscar Chess* case and continued:] . . . in the present case it is very different. The inference is not rebutted. Here we have a dealer, Mr Smith, who was in a position to know, or at least to find out, the history of the car. He could get it by writing to the makers. He did not do so. Indeed it was done later. When the history of this car was examined, his statement turned out to be quite wrong. He ought to have known better. There was no reasonable foundation for it. . . .

DANCKWERTS LJ

I agree with the judgment of Lord Denning M. R.

SALMON LJ

I agree. I have no doubt at all that the learned county court judge reached a correct conclusion when he decided that Mr Smith gave a warranty to the second plaintiff, Mr Bentley, and that that warranty was broken. Was what Mr Smith said intended and understood as a legally binding promise? If so, it was a warranty and as such may be part of the contract of sale or collateral to it. In effect, Mr Smith said: "If you will enter into a contract to buy this motor car from me for £1,850, I undertake that you will be getting a motor car which has done no more than twenty thousand miles since it was fitted with a new engine and a new gear box." I have no doubt at all that what was said by Mr Smith was so understood and was intended to be so understood by Mr Bentley . . .

Appeal Dismissed.

Question

15-011   When a seller warrants the quality of his goods, is it relevant, in an action on the warranty, whether he had reasonable grounds to believe his statement to be true or whether he was "completely innocent of any fault"? Suppose Smith had taken reasonable steps to find out the history of the car and been misinformed. Would the statement to Bentley have been any less a warranty? M. G. Bridge, *The Sale of Goods*, p.375, writes: "Negligence of the maker of a statement and reasonable reliance by the other party have become the motive forces in the inference of warranty, though a breach of warranty may occur where all due care has been taken." Has the seller's negligence any proper part to play in determining whether he has made a promise? Cf. *Harlingdon v Leinster*, above. Cf. the case where the buyer is suing on s.2(1) of the Misrepresentation Act 1967. Are the *Oscar Chess* and *Dick Bentley* cases properly distinguishable? Cf. *Beale v Taylor* [1967] 1 W.L.R. 1193 and note by K.L. Koh [1968] CLJ 11.

Further guidance as to the circumstances in which a pre-contractual statement is to be treated as a mere representation and when is it to be treated as a term may be derived from a series of cases concerning the sale of animals. In *Schawel v Reade* [1913] 2 Ir. Rep. 81 HL, the owner of a horse said to a potential buyer who was examining it, "You need not look for anything. The horse is perfectly sound. If there was anything the matter with the horse I would tell you." The buyer thereupon terminated the examination and three weeks later bought the horse. It was unfit for stud purposes. The jury answered in the affirmative the judge's question: "Did the defendant at the time of the sale represent to the plaintiff in order that the plaintiff might purchase the horse, that the horse was fit for stud purposes and did the plaintiff act upon that representation in the purchase of the horse?" The House of Lords held that the jury's answer amounted to a finding of a warranty. Lords MacNaghten and Atkinson said that the question contained all the ingredients of a warranty. Lord Moulton said that the essence of a warranty is that it is made plain by the words and actions that it is intended that the responsibility for soundness shall rest upon the vendor; and the vendor, at the conversation three weeks before the sale, could not have indicated more clearly that he intended to take upon himself the responsibility of the fitness of the horse.

In an earlier case, *Hopkins v Tanqueray* (1854) 15 C.B. 130 an almost identical conversation took place the day before the sale by auction at Tattersalls of a horse, California. The seller was emphatic: "I assure you he is perfectly sound in every respect"; and the buyer responded, "If you say so, I am perfectly satisfied." He bought the horse at the auction. It was unsound. The Court of Common Pleas found that there was no evidence to support the jury's finding that there was a warranty embodied in the contract of sale. The explanation seems to be that both parties knew at the time of the conversation that the sale was to be by auction at Tattersalls, that the well-known course of business there is that sales are without a warranty and that the parties could not have intended a warranty since they could not have supposed that the buyer would be in a better position than other bidders at the sale. The court expressed doubts about the legality of a private warranty at a public auction without a warranty; but the decision is that no warranty was intended.

In *Couchman v Hill* [1947] K.B. 554 the plaintiff purchased a heifer at an auction. The heifer was described in the catalogue as "unserved" but the catalogue and the exhibited conditions of sale made it clear that the accuracy of any description was not guaranteed and the lots were to be sold with all errors of description. The plaintiff required an unserved heifer for service by his own bull. Before the sale when the heifers were in the ring he asked both the defendant, the owner, and the auctioneer if they could confirm that the heifer was unserved. They both answered, "Yes." After the plaintiff had bought the heifer it was found to be in calf and died from carrying a calf at too young an age. The Court of Appeal ruled that the answers of the defendant and auctioneer amounted to an offer of a warranty overriding the conditions of sale, that the offer was accepted by the plaintiff's bid and that the misdescription amounted to a breach of condition, which the plaintiff was entitled to treat as a breach of warranty and recover damages. *Hopkins v Tanqueray* was not cited and an editorial note in the Law Reports questioned whether a private bargain for a warranty could be upheld when it is publicly announced that the sale is without warranty.

Question

In the modern law, the context in which any statement is made together with the expectations that would be reasonably entertained are the key considerations. Viewing the above cases from a modern perspective, are the decisions any easier to explain? If not, does this suggest that the cases are simply inconsistent or that there are limits to the explanatory power of the modern approach?

15-012

HARLING v EDDY

Court of Appeal [1951] 2 K.B. 739; [1951] 2 T.L.R. 245; 95 S.J. 501; [1951] 2 All E.R. 212

15-013   The defendant put up a heifer for sale at Ashford Cattle Market on June 30, 1950. Condition 12 of the printed conditions of sale provided: "No animal . . . is sold with a 'warranty' unless specially mentioned at the time of offering, and no warranty so given shall have any legal force or effect unless the terms thereof appear on the purchaser's account." When the heifer appeared in the auction ring no one made a bid, owing to her unpromising appearance. Thereupon the defendant said that there was nothing wrong with the heifer, that he would absolutely guarantee her in every respect, and that he would be willing to take her back if she turned out not to be what he stated she was. Bidding then began and the heifer was knocked down to the plaintiff. Within three months the heifer had died from advanced tuberculosis.

EVERSHED MR

[After stating the facts:] The real question is whether the statement which the defendant made at the sale immediately before the bidding entitles the plaintiff now to say that the animal was not, as the defendant stated her to be, sound in every respect, and that he now takes advantage of the offer which the defendant made and claims from the defendant the price paid for the animal, or equivalent damages. The real difficulty arises from the circumstance that condition 12, prima facie, seems intended to render nugatory any mere warranty given at the sale. The first answer, in my judgment, to the defence based on condition 12 is that, in the circumstances, this statement by the defendant was a condition.

It has been said many times, and particularly in *Wallis, Son & Wells v Pratt & Haynes* [below, Ch.20], that whether any statement is to be regarded as a condition or a warranty must depend upon the intention to be inferred from the particular statement. A statement that an animal is sound in every respect would, prima facie, be but a warranty; but in this case the judge quite clearly found as a fact that the defendant went further: he promised that he would take the animal back if she were no good . . .

The defendant's statement having, therefore, included words to the effect, "If there is anything wrong I will take it back," it seems to me quite plain that the words which he used could not have been intended merely as a warranty; for a warranty would give no right of rejection to the purchaser. The final words involve necessarily a right in the purchaser to reject, that is, to return the animal; and they convert the statement, to my mind, from a warranty into a condition.

If, then, it is a condition, what would be the right of the plaintiff? Mr Laskey has argued forcibly that the plaintiff must at least exercise his right of rejection in due time. He plainly purported to do so on September 21, when he called upon the defendant to take the animal back. In my judgment, in the circumstances of the case, the period between July 1 and the middle of September would not be unreasonable; but, however that may be, it is plain also from *Wallis, Son & Wells v Pratt & Haynes* that a person entitled to the benefit of a condition, as was the plaintiff here, can turn the condition, in effect, into a warranty by claiming damages as for breach of warranty instead of his exercising his right or rejection. By the time this claim had been formulated, the animal was dead, and the plaintiff could, in truth, not do otherwise than he has done here—namely, to claim damages; and in my judgment he was entitled to treat the condition to that extent as though it were a warranty.

If that is right, the question still remains whether condition 12 of the conditions apply. In my opinion, the answer is No. Condition 12 is limited in its terms to a statement which is a mere warranty and is not a condition, and the second part of it, ". . . and no warranty so given shall have any legal force or effect . . ." can only refer to the warranty previously mentioned, namely, a statement which is a warranty and no more. In other words, condition 12 cannot be relied on by the defendant to defeat the right of the plaintiff to sue for damages for the breach of the condition.

[His Lordship then considered *Couchman v Hill*]

The terms of the printed conditions in this case differ from the terms of the printed conditions in *Couchman v Hill* [above], and the language used by the two defendants differs also. Bearing the facts in mind, and in particular the initial silence which greeted the entry of this animal into the ring, and the fact that bidding only began when the defendant's statement had been made, the question may properly be formulated thus: did the defendant imply by this statement that the animal should be sold on the faith of what he stated, to the exclusion of the printed condition 12, or of any other condition which might be found in the auction particulars which would of itself appear to exclude any oral statement? Mr Laskey argued that neither party may have had in mind, when this particular incident occurred, what were the exact terms of the conditions of sale. I should, however, suppose that, both being experienced in the buying and selling of cattle, they would be aware, according to common practice, that there would be stultifying conditions of some kind in the auction particulars.

If that were the question to be posed, in my judgment it should be answered affirmatively on the facts as found by the judge. I therefore, for my part, would hold that, even if the language used here were a warranty only and not a condition, the plaintiff nevertheless would be entitled to succeed.

[His Lordship then discussed a question of pleading which arose at the trial, and continued:] Before leaving *Couchman v Hill* I would like to say one further word about it. To the report in the All England Law Reports there is an editorial note referring to a case of 100 years ago, *Hopkins v Tanqueray* [above], relating to the sale of a horse at Tattersalls. In that case the seller and the buyer happened to have met not at the sale, but the day before it, and the conversation which is related in this note formed no part of the transaction which occurred at the sale itself. At this meeting between the seller and the buyer a statement was made about the soundness of the horse, and later the auction took place. The question in that case was whether what had passed in that previous conversation could affect a stultifying condition in the auction particulars. But the court in *Hopkins v Tanqueray* found that what was said—the promise made by the seller in his private conversation—formed no part of the contract: the contract was formed as a result of the sale at the auction and comprehended the conditions set out in the auction particulars. It is plain, therefore, that that case is wholly distinguishable from *Couchman v Hill*, and equally from this case. I say that because the note to which I have alluded suggests that, had *Hopkins v Tanqueray* been referred to at the time of the hearing in this court of *Couchman v Hill*, the later decision might have been different. I do not think so. Having considered this editorial note, it seems to me that the earlier case was entirely distinguishable from *Couchman v Hill*, and to my mind there is no reason for suggesting that *Couchman v Hill* was otherwise than rightly decided on the issues raised before the court. It binds this court in any case; but I desire to express my entire concurrence with that decision, without, however, committing myself either way on the question whether a private bargain for a warranty, as distinguished from a public bargain, as the bargain was in this case, is assailable on the ground of illegality.

DENNING LJ (Concurring)

The decision of this court in *Couchman v Hill* is to the same effect. *Hopkins v Tanqueray* is distinguishable because there was no warranty. I have before me Scott L.J.'s copy of the All England Law Reports containing the report of *Couchman v Hill*, and I can see that he has noted in his own handwriting: "*Hopkins v Tanqueray*, a case of a conversation a day before the sale is distinguishable. My attention was drawn to it by the editor of the Law Reports, February 22, 1947."

Roxburgh J. concurred.

Questions

1. Does this case settle the question whether a private bargain for a warranty is enforceable when it has been publicly announced that the sale is to be without warranty? How could Evershed MR express his "entire concurrence" with *Couchman v Hill* without committing himself on the question? What should be the answer to the question?

   15-014

2. A racehorse, Scattercash, is to be sold by auction without a warranty. Al alone has received a private assurance as to Scattercash's fitness from the owner. When the bidding reaches £10,000, all the bidders except Al and Ben fall out. Al would fall out too, if he had not received the warranty. He continues to bid up to £14,000. Ben bids £14,500 and the horse is knocked down to him. He then learns the truth. Is the contract binding?

3. Is *Hopkins v Tanqueray* distinguishable because the conversation took place the day before the sale? Cf. *Schawel v Reade*, above, and note that the jury found that the representation made

three weeks earlier was made "at the time of the sale." Does it matter when the words were uttered if the buyer was reasonably relying on them at the time of the sale?

4. Consider the effect of the Misrepresentation Act 1967 and the Unfair Contract Terms Act 1977 ss.6 and 12(2).

----

3. COLLATERAL CONTRACTS

15-015 The idea of a so-called 'collateral contract' is that of a contract that is ancillary to a main contract; so there are two contracts, the main contract and a collateral contract. Typically, some key statements made in the negotiation of the main contract become terms of the collateral contract and are, thus, actionable as warranties (breach of which sounds in damages). Clearly, there is some considerable artificiality in this reconstruction of the negotiations—not least by treating the act of entering into the main contract as the consideration that supports the warranty given under the collateral contract. Why, we might wonder, should the law engage in such conceptual gymnastics? Quite simply, the collateral contract is a device that is designed to enable a meritorious claimant, who would otherwise be denied a remedy in damages, to recover financial compensation (see Lord Denning MR's remarks in *Esso v Mardon*, below).

HEILBUT, SYMONS & CO v BUCKLETON

House of Lords [1913] A.C. 30; 82 L.J.K.B. 245; 107 L.T. 769

VISCOUNT HALDANE LC

15-016 My Lords, the appellants, who were rubber merchants in London in the spring of 1910 underwrote a large number of shares in a company called the Filisola Rubber and Produce Estates Ltd, a company which was promoted and registered by other persons about that time. They instructed a Mr Johnston, who was the manager of their Liverpool business, to obtain applications for shares in Liverpool. Johnston, who had seen a draft prospectus in London but had at the time no copy of the prospectus, mentioned the company to several people in Liverpool, including a Mr Wright, who sometimes acted as broker for the respondent. On April 14 the respondent telephoned to Johnston from Wright's office. As to what passed there is no dispute. The respondent said: "I understand you are bringing out a rubber company." The reply was: "we are." The respondent then asked whether Johnston had any prospectuses, and his reply was in the negative. The respondent then asked "if it was all right," and Johnston replied: "We are bringing it out," to which the respondent rejoined: "That is good enough for me." He went on to ask how many shares he could have, and to say that he would take almost any number. He explained in his evidence in chief that his reason for being willing to do this was that the position the appellants occupied in the rubber trade was of such high standing that "any company they should see fit to bring out was a sufficient warranty" to him "that it was all right in every respect." Afterwards, as the result of the conversation, a large number of shares were allotted to the respondent. [The contract was embodied on two letters dated April 15, the day after the conversation].

About this time the rubber boom of 1910 was at its height and the shares of the Filisola Company were, and for a short time remained, at a premium. Later on it was discovered that there was a large deficiency in the rubber trees which were said in the prospectus to exist on the Filisola Estate, and the shares fell in value. The respondent brought an action against the appellants for fraudulent misrepresentation, and alternatively for damages for breach of warranty that the company was a rubber company whose main object was to produce rubber.

The action was tried at Liverpool Assizes before Lush J. and a special jury. The jury found that there was no fraudulent representation by the appellants or Johnston, but they found that the company could not be properly described as a rubber company, and that the appellants or Johnston, or both, had warranted that the company was a rubber company . . .

It is contrary to the general policy of the law of England to presume the making of such a collateral contract in the absence of language expressing or implying it, and I think the learned judge who tried the case ought to have informed the jury that on the issue of warranty there was no case to go to it, and that on this issue he and the Court of Appeal ought to have given judgment for the appellants. The strongest presentation of the case for the respondents seems to me that of Farwell L.J. to the effect that there was a contract that the shares should be shares in a rubber company, and that the jury has found that the company was not a rubber company. But even on the basis of this finding I do not think that the account given by the learned Lord Justice of the transaction properly describes it. The respondent did not ask the technical question whether the company of which he had heard vaguely was correctly described as a rubber company. That he was not thinking of this point seems to me clear from the fact that when he received the letters informing him that he was to have shares in the Filisola Rubber and Produce Estates (a description which was in accordance with that in the prospectus) he made no further inquiry. What he from the first wanted to know was whether Johnston thought the company was "all right," a question to which Johnston simply replied that the appellants were bringing it out, an answer which, to my mind, simply conveyed that a firm of their standing would not be bringing it out if they did not believe it to be all right. From the evidence of the respondents, which immediately follows in the passage I have quoted, it seems to me plain that this was accepted by the respondent as the answer he wanted . . .

Neither the respondent nor Johnston appears to have had any question in his mind other than whether some company dealing with rubber, as to the identity of which there was no question raised, was being brought out by the appellants. For the respondent says that the position of the appellants in the rubber trade was such that "any company that they should see fit to bring out was a sufficient warranty" to him "that it was all right in every respect." His interest was in the shares for which he was minded to apply, and all he was really asking for was the assurance I have mentioned. Had Johnston thought that he was being asked to do anything else than answer the question whether the appellants were bringing out the company, he might well have refused to pledge himself, and I do not believe that either he or the respondent, regard being had to the character of the conversation, was thinking of any other question. But if not, there was in point of law no evidence to go to the jury on the issue as to warranty, and this issue ought not to have been submitted to it. In reality the only contract entered into seems to have been the contract reduced into writing by the two letters of April 15 for procuring an allotment of shares in what was described as the Filisola "Rubber and Produce Estates" Company. . . .

LORD MOULTON

[Having stated the facts, went on:]
It is evident, both on principle and on authority, that there may be a contract the consideration for which is the making of some other contract. "If you will make such and such a contract I will give you one hundred pounds," is in every sense of the word a complete legal contract. It is collateral to the main contract, but each has an independent existence, and they do not differ in respect of their possessing to the full the character and status of a contract. But such collateral contracts must from their very nature be rare. The effect of a collateral contract such as that which I have instanced would be to increase the consideration of the main contract by £100, and the more natural and usual way of carrying this out would be by so modifying the main contract and not by executing a concurrent and collateral contract. Such collateral contracts, the sole effect of which is to vary or add to the terms of the principal contract, are therefore viewed with suspicion by the law. They must be proved strictly. Not only the terms of such contracts but the existence of an animus contrahendi on the part of all the parties to them must be clearly shown. Any laxity on these points would enable parties to escape from the full performance of the obligations of contracts unquestionably entered into by them and more especially would have the effect of lessening the authority of written contracts by making it possible to vary them by suggesting the existence of verbal collateral agreements relating to the same subject-matter. There is in the present case an entire absence of any evidence to support the existence of such a collateral contract . . .

In the history of English law we find many attempts to make persons responsible in damages by reason of innocent misrepresentations, and at times it has seemed as though the attempts would succeed . . .

On the common law side of the court the attempts to make a person liable for an innocent misrepresentation have usually taken the form of attempts to extend the doctrine of warranty beyond its limits and to find that a warranty existed in cases where there was nothing more than an innocent misrepresentation. The present case is, in my opinion, an instance of this. But in respect of the question of the existence of a warranty the courts have had the advantage of an admirable enunciation of the true principle of law which was made in very early days by Holt C. J. with respect to the contract of sale. He says: "An affirmation at the time of the sale is a warranty, provided it appears on evidence to be so intended." So far as decisions are concerned, this has, on the whole, been consistently followed in the courts of common law. But from time to time there have been dicta inconsistent with it which have, unfortunately, found their way into textbooks and have given rise to confusion and uncertainty in this branch of the law. For example, one often sees quoted the dictum of Bayley J. in *Cave v Coleman*, 3 Man. & Ry. 2, where, in respect of a representation made verbally during the sale of a horse, he says that, "being made in the course of dealing, and before the bargain was complete, it amounted to a warranty"—a proposition that is far too sweeping and cannot be supported. A still more serious deviation from the correct principle is to be found in a passage in the judgment of the Court of Appeal in *De Lassalle v Guildford* [1901] 2 K.B. 215, 221, which was cited to us in the argument in the present case. In discussing the question whether a representation amounts to a warranty or not the judgment says: "In determining whether it was so intended, a decisive test is whether the vendor assumes to assert a fact of which the buyer is ignorant, or merely states an opinion or judgment upon a matter of which the vendor has no special knowledge, and on which the buyer may be expected also to have an opinion and to exercise his judgment."

With all deference to the authority of the court that decided that case, the proposition which it thus formulates cannot be supported. It is clear that the court did not intend to depart from the law laid down by Holt C. J. and cited above, for in the same judgment that dictum is referred to and accepted as a correct statement of the law. It is, therefore, evident that the use of the phrase, "decisive test," cannot be defended. Otherwise it would be the duty of a judge to direct a jury that if a vendor states a fact of which the buyer is ignorant, they must, as a matter of law, find the existence of a warranty, whether or not the totality of the evidence shows that the parties intended the affirmation to form part of the contract; and this would be inconsistent with the law as laid down by Holt C. J. It may well be that the features thus referred to in the judgment of the Court of Appeal in that case may be criteria of value in guiding a jury in coming to a decision whether or not a warranty was intended; but they cannot be said to furnish decisive tests, because it cannot be said as a matter of law that the presence or absence of those features is conclusive of the intention of the parties. The intention of the parties can only be deduced from the totality of the evidence, and no secondary principles of such a kind can be universally true.

Order of the Court of Appeal Reversed and Judgment Entered for the Appellants.

Questions

15-017
1. What did the respondent want to know when he telephoned? On what matter or matters was he seeking assurance? Did he make it clear to Johnston that it was of importance to him to know whether it was a 'rubber' company?

2. Was Johnston negligent in describing the company as a 'rubber company' (assuming this was a misdescription)? Would negligence in such circumstances afford a remedy today? Cf. *Hedley Byrne & Co v Heller & Partners* [1964] A.C. 465 and the Misrepresentation Act.

A warranty is often described as a "collateral" term of a contract. By this is meant that it relates to the subject-matter of another promise made by the warrantor and exists, side by side with that promise, in a single contract. In the Sale of Goods Act 1979 (s.61(1)):

"'Warranty' . . . means an agreement with reference to goods which are the subject of a contract of sale, but collateral to the main purpose of such contract, the breach of which gives rise to a claim for damages, but not to a right to reject the goods and treat the contract as repudiated."

Suppose that A promises to sell a horse to B and warrants that it is sound. The warranty is subordinate to A's promise to sell the horse in the sense that it is only made because of that promise. In normal circumstances it would be pointless for A to give B a warranty of the soundness of A's horse unless A also transferred the property in the horse (or hired it, etc.) to B (cf., however, *Shanklin Pier Ltd v Detel Products Ltd*, below). Though "collateral", a warranty is generally part of a single contract containing the main promise. Suppose that Buckleton had obtained from Johnston a firm assurance that the company was a rubber company in the technical sense and that, subsequently, an oral contract had been concluded for the sale of the shares. It would surely not have been unreasonable to say that it was a term in that contract that the shares were shares in a rubber company. In fact, the contract was concluded in writing and the judges were no doubt inhibited by the parol evidence rule from holding that the representation amounted to a warranty in that written contract (though see Ch.16 on Implied Terms, below). Buckleton's counsel therefore argued that the warranty was contained in a separate contract; that is, "If you will buy shares in the company, I will promise you that it is a rubber company." Buckleton's entering into the main contract for the purchase of the shares would then have been the consideration for the promise. Had this contention been made out, a quite distinct and separate contract would have come into existence at the same moment as the main contract.

Such a contract, existing side by side with the main contract, is described as "a collateral contract."[2] It is clearly quite a different concept from an ordinary warranty which is not a separate contract. The epithet "collateral" is applied to both concepts and it is not always clear to which the courts are referring. The collateral contract is an extremely useful device, particularly in that the parol evidence rule is no bar to its use.

Collateral contracts of this kind were well known before *Heilbut v Buckleton*. In *Morgan v Griffith* (1871) L.R. 6 Ex. 70 and *Erskine v Adeane* (1873) L.R. 8 Ch.App. 756 lessors were held liable to their tenants for failing to keep down the game on the demised land although they had refused to allow any promise that they would do so to be inserted in the leases, when it was proved that the tenant in each case declined to sign the lease until he had such an undertaking and signed on the faith of it. In *De Lassalle v Guildford* a tenant had declined to hand over his counterpart of a lease until he had the landlord's oral assurance that the drains were in good order and was held entitled to damages for breach of that undertaking. The decision appears to be sound in spite of Lord Moulton's observations on the dicta of A. L. Smith MR. For another type of collateral contract, see *Warlow v Harrison*, above, Ch.2 and cf. *Howard Marine v Ogden*, above, Ch.14.

Heilbut v Buckleton (and especially Lord Moulton's judgment) is almost always cited when the question of warranty or no warranty is in issue. Yet in spite of Lord Moulton's suspicion of collateral contracts, the courts have made liberal use of them over the years. It has been held that there may even be a contract collateral to a contract for the sale of land required by s.2 of the Law of Property (Miscellaneous Provisions) Act 1989, above, Ch.4, to be in writing and to incorporate all the terms expressly agreed in one document: *Record v Bell* [1991] 4 All E.R. 471 Ch D. See also *Webster v Higgin* [1948] 2 All E.R. 127, *Couchman v Hill* (above), *Harling v Eddy* (above), *City and Westminster Properties Ltd v Mudd* (below), *Esso v Mardon* (below), *Bowerman v ABTA*, above, Ch.3, and *Strongman Ltd v Sincock* (below, Ch.27). Cf. *Evans v Merzario* [1976] 1 W.L.R. 1078.

CITY AND WESTMINSTER PROPERTIES (1934) LTD v MUDD

[1959] Ch. 129; [1958] 3 W.L.R. 312; 102 S.J. 582; [1958] 2 All E.R. 733

In 1941 the defendant became the tenant of a lock-up shop for three years. He was allowed by the landlords (the plaintiffs) to sleep in the shop. In 1944 the plaintiffs granted the defendant a second lease for three years, in which the defendant covenanted not to use the premises except as a shop

15-018

---

[2] This proposition should be considered in the light of *Bell v Lever Bros* (below, Ch.23) and *Smith v Hughes* (above, Ch.5).

for his business as an antique dealer. He continued to sleep there and fitted up the basement as a residence. The plaintiffs knew that he slept there but not that the premises were his residence. In 1947 a draft of a new lease was prepared which contained covenants by the lessee not to use the premises as a place for lodging, dwelling or sleeping. The defendant objected to this clause and his solicitors deleted it from the draft but the plaintiffs insisted on retaining it, fearing that to permit the defendant to reside on the premises might bring them within the Rent Restriction Acts. The defendant told the plaintiffs' agent that he would not sign a lease with a clause about not sleeping there. The agent then told the defendant orally that, if he would sign the lease, the plaintiffs would not object to his sleeping there. In consequence the defendant was willing to complete and the lease and counterpart were exchanged. The words about lodging dwelling or sleeping were omitted—according to the plaintiffs' solicitor, through inadvertence in his office. The covenant to use the premises for trade purposes only, however, remained.

In 1956 the defendant applied for a new lease for 21 years. The plaintiffs noticed that he was living there and brought an action for forfeiture of the lease, alleging a breach of the covenant not to use the premises except for trade purposes.

Harman J. held that he was not entitled to use the negotiations and the drafts as an aid to construction (the defendant having relied on the omission of the words "lodging, dwelling or sleeping" as evidence that he was to be allowed to sleep there. Nor was the defendant entitled to rectification for there was no common intention that a clause permitting him to reside should be inserted in the lease. Nor did the fact that the plaintiffs knew that the defendant was sleeping there amount to a release of the covenant or a new letting. The learned judge continued:

HARMAN J

There remains the so-called question of estoppel. This, in my judgment, is a misnomer and the present case does not raise the controversial issue of the *Central London Property Trust v High Trees, Ltd* decision [above, para.11–002]. This is not a case of a representation made after contractual relations existed between the parties to the effect that one party to the contract would not rely on his rights. If the defendant's evidence is to be accepted, as I hold it is, it is a case of a promise made to him before the execution of a lease that if he would execute it in the form put before him, the landlord would not seek to enforce against him personally the covenant about using the property as a shop only. The defendant says that it was in reliance on this promise that he executed the lease and entered on the onerous obligations contained in it. He says, moreover, that but for the promise made he would not have executed the lease, but would have moved to other premises available to him at the time. If these be the facts, there was a clear contract acted upon by the defendant to his detriment and from which the Plaintiffs cannot be allowed to resile. The case is truly analogous to *Re William Porter & Co Ltd* [1937] 2 All E.R. 361 . . .

The plea that this was a mere licence retractable at the plaintiff's will does not bear examination. The promise was that as long as the defendant personally was tenant, so long would the landlords forbear to exercise the rights which they would have if he signed the lease. He did sign the lease on this promise and is therefore entitled to rely on it so long as he is personally in occupation of the shop.

Judgment for the Defendant.

Questions

1. Would the application of the *High Trees* doctrine have protected the defendant as effectively as the collateral contract?

2. In *Henderson v Arthur* [1907] 1 K.B. 10, an action on a covenant in a lease for payment of the rent quarterly in advance, the lessee's defence was that, antecedently to the execution of the lease, the lessor had agreed to take a bill payable at three months for each quarter's rent in advance as it became due. The Court of Appeal, reversing Lord Alverstone CJ, held that the evidence of

the agreement was inadmissible. Collins M. R. said: ". . . to admit evidence of such an agreement as being so available would be to violate one of the first principles of the law of evidence; because, in my opinion, it would be to substitute the terms of an antecedent parol agreement for the terms of a subsequent formal contract under seal dealing with the same subject-matter. I do not see how, in this case, the covenant in the lease and the antecedent parol agreement can co-exist and the subsequent deed has the effect of wiping out any previous agreement dealing with the same subject-matter . . . it is not a merely collateral agreement, but provides in another and contradictory manner for doing what was subsequently provided for by the lease."

3. Is *Mudd's* case reconcilable with *Henderson v Arthur*? Is there a difference between an antecedent agreement (which is wiped out) and a coincident agreement (which is not)?

4. In *W v Essex County Council and Another* [1998] 3 All E.R. 111 CA, the plaintiffs agreed in writing with the council to foster G, a 15-year old boy. The terms of the agreement were fixed by statute. Because they were concerned for their own young children the plaintiffs had made it clear to the council, before signing the agreement, that they were not willing to accept an adolescent who was known or suspected to be a sexual abuser. They were assured that no such adolescent would be placed with them. Three years earlier G had been cautioned for an indecent assault on his sister. He abused the plaintiffs' children. They sued in negligence and for breach of an express or implied term of the fostering agreement. The claim in contract was dismissed: "A contract is essentially an agreement that is freely negotiated. If there is a statutory obligation to enter into a form of agreement the terms of which are laid down, at any rate in their most important respects, there is no contract" (per Stuart-Smith LJ). If the plaintiffs were saying (as appears to be the case) "We will sign this agreement only if you assure us . . ." why was there not a contract collateral to the statutory agreement? The terms of the adoption agreement were prescribed, but the plaintiffs were not obliged to enter into the agreement at all. Was it material that the statutory agreement was not a contract? Was not signing that agreement at the council's request consideration for the council's assurance? The collateral contract cases do not appear to have been cited. Should they have been? (An appeal to the House of Lords was allowed on grounds not affecting the point discussed above: [2000] 2 All E.R. 237).

SHANKLIN PIER LTD v DETEL PRODUCTS LTD

King's Bench Division [1951] 2 K.B. 854; 95 S.J. 563; [1951] 2 All E.R. 471, [1951] 2 Lloyd's Rep. 187

The plaintiffs, the owners of a pier, entered into a contract with contractors to have the pier repainted with two coats of bituminous paint. The plaintiffs had the right, under this contract, to vary the specification. A director of the defendant company went to Shanklin with the object of securing for his company the contract for supplying the paint. He assured the plaintiffs' representatives that a certain paint manufactured by the defendants and known as DMU would have a life of at least seven to ten years. On the faith of this representation the plaintiffs amended their specification by the substitution of DMU. That paint was bought by the contractors from the defendants and applied to the pier but it proved to be unsatisfactory and lasted only about three months. The plaintiffs, by their statement of claim, alleged that, in consideration of the plaintiffs' specifying that the contractors should use for repainting the pier two coats of a paint known as DMU, the defendants warranted that the paint would be suitable for repainting the pier and would have a life of from seven to ten years.

15-020

MCNAIR J

This case raises an interesting and comparatively novel question whether or not an enforceable warranty can arise as between parties other than parties to the main contract for the sale of the article in respect of which the warranty is alleged to have been given . . . [His Lordship then stated the facts, and reviewed the evidence about the negotiations which led to the contract for DMU paint.]

In the result, I am satisfied that, if a direct contract of purchase and sale of the DMU had then been made between the plaintiffs and the defendants, the correct conclusion on the facts would have been that the defendants gave to the plaintiffs the warranties substantially in the form alleged in the statement of claim. In reaching this conclusion, I adopt the principles stated by Holt C. J. in *Crosse v Gardner* (1689) Comb. 142, and *Medina v Stoughton* (1700) 1 Salk. 210, that an affirmation at the time of sale is a warranty, provided it appear on evidence to have been so intended.

Counsel for the defendants submitted that in law a warranty could give rise to no enforceable cause of action except between the same parties as the parties to the main contract in relation to which the warranty was given. In principle, this submission seems to me to be unsound. If, as is elementary, the consideration for the warranty in the usual case is the entering into of the main contract in relation to which the warranty is given, I see no reason why there may not be an enforceable warranty between A and B supported by the consideration that B should cause C to enter into a contract with A or that B should do some other act for the benefit of A.

Judgment for the Plaintiffs.

Point for reflection

15-021   The principle of the *Shanklin Pier* case was applied to the common transaction in which a dealer induced his customer to take goods by representations about the goods whereupon the customer entered into a contract of credit sale or hire-purchase, not with the dealer, but with a finance company to which the dealer sold the goods. In *Andrews v Hopkinson* [1957] 1 Q.B. 289, the dealer said, "It's a good little bus. I would stake my life on it. You will have no trouble with it." The plaintiff entered into a written contract with a finance company to take the car on hire-purchase. The car was unroadworthy. McNair J held that there was a warranty by the dealer, enforceable by the customer. The consideration given by the customer was the entry into the hire-purchase agreement. Notice that the warranty was probably enforceable only against the dealer and not against the finance company. Consider the effect upon such transactions of s.14(3) of the Sale of Goods Act 1979.

WELLS (MERSTHAM) LTD v BUCKLAND SAND AND SILICA LTD

Queen's Bench Division [1964] 2 W.L.R. 453; [1964] 1 All E.R. 41; 108 S.J. 177

15-022   The plaintiffs were chrysanthemum growers and the defendants, sand merchants. The plaintiffs' manager visited the defendants and was assured by their manager that deliveries of sand could be relied on as conforming to an analysis which showed that the sand had a low iron oxide content. Subsequently the plaintiffs placed an order for the defendants' sand with a third party (in order to save transport costs) who bought the sand from the defendants and resold it to the plaintiffs. The third party did not tell the defendants that the sand was for the plaintiffs and the defendants did not know that it was for horticultural purposes. The sand did not correspond with the analysis, having a high iron oxide content which caused damage agreed at £2,500 to the plaintiffs. Having held that a warranty was intended that the sand conformed to the analysis, Edmund Davies J went on:

EDMUND DAVIES J

Then does it make any difference that, the warranty having been given to the plaintiffs, all the purchases other than the first were made by the plaintiffs from a third party? If that question demands in law an affirmative answer, the result would not be justice, for, as I have said, it was purely fortuitous that all the loads were not sold by the defendants direct to the plaintiffs. But in my judgment such an affirmative answer is not required, as several reported decisions indicate. Thus, in *Brown v Sheen and Richmond Car Sales Ltd* [1950] 1 All E.R. 1102, *Shanklin Pier Ltd v Detel Products Ltd* [above] and *Andrews v Hopkinson* [1957] 1 Q.B. 289, all tried at first instance, and *Yeoman Credit Ltd v Odgers* [1962] 1 W.L.R. 215, the warranty given by the defendant was held enforceable notwithstanding that the main contract was subsequently entered into between the plaintiff and a third party. As McNair J. said in the second case, "If, as is elementary, the consideration for the warranty in the usual case is the entering into of the main contract in relation to which the warranty is given, I see no reason why there may not be an enforceable warranty between A and B supported by the consideration that B should cause C to enter into a contract with A or that B should do some other act for the benefit of A." And if Clark gave the warranty I have found he did, it would be absurd in the circumstances of the case to regard that warranty as being impliedly restricted to orders placed directly by the plaintiffs with the defendants.

As between A (a potential seller of goods) and B (a potential buyer), two ingredients, and two only, are in my judgment required in order to bring about a collateral contract containing a warranty: (1) a promise or assertion by A as to the nature, quality or quantity of the goods which B may reasonably regard as being made animo contrahendi, and (2) acquisition by B of the goods in reliance on that promise or assertion. As K. W. Wedderburn expresses it in "Collateral Contracts" in *Cambridge Law Journal*, 1959, at p. 79: ". . . the consideration given for the promise is no more than the act of entering into the main contract. Going ahead with that bargain is a sufficient price for the promise, without which it would not have gone ahead at all." And a warranty may be enforceable notwithstanding that no specific main contract is discussed at the time it is given, though obviously an animus contrahendi (and, therefore, a warranty) would be unlikely to be inferred unless the circumstances show that it was within the present contemplation of the parties that a contract based upon the promise would shortly be entered into. Furthermore, the operation of the warranty must have a limitation in point of time which is reasonable in all the circumstances. But none of these considerations gives rise to difficulty in the present case.

Judgment for the Plaintiffs for £2,500.

Questions

1. What consideration did the plaintiffs supply to the defendants? When did the warranty become binding?

2. Suppose the third party had held a stock of the defendants' sand and had supplied the plaintiffs from that: would there still have been a warranty?

3. Suppose the plaintiffs had already held stocks of the defendants' sand and had sent their manager to find out if it was suitable for growing chrysanthemums: could the plaintiffs have recovered damages? (Cf. *Hedley Byrne & Co v Heller & Partners* [1964] A.C. 465, above, Ch.14.)

4. Is the case the same as those cited by Edmund Davies J? In each of those cases a transaction with a third party was clearly contemplated by the party giving the warranty. Should this make a difference?

5. Henry advertises on television that his sand (which can be obtained from any gardening shop) is ideal for growing chrysanthemums. In reliance on the advertisement, several hundred people buy Henry's sand. Because of its high iron oxide content, their chrysanthemums die. Advise Henry. Cf. *Bowerman v ABTA*, above, Ch.3.

15-023

ESSO PETROLEUM CO LTD v MARDON

Court of Appeal [1976] 2 W.L.R. 583; [1976] 2 All E.R. 5

15-024   Esso's experienced representative told Mardon that Esso estimated that the throughput of petrol on a certain site would reach 200,000 gallons in the third year of operation and so persuaded Mardon to enter into a tenancy agreement in April 1963 for three years. Mardon did all that could be expected of him as tenant but the site was not good enough to achieve a throughput of more than 60,000–70,000 gallons. In July 1964 Mardon gave notice to quit but Esso granted him a new tenancy at a reduced rent. Mardon continued to lose money and by August 1966 was unable to pay for petrol supplied. Esso claimed possession of the site and money due. Mardon claimed damages in respect of the representation alleging that it amounted (i) to a warranty; (ii) to a negligent misrepresentation. Lawson J rejected the claim for breach of warranty but held Esso liable in negligence. The Court of Appeal affirmed the finding of negligence under the principle of *Hedley Byrne v Heller* [1964] A.C. 465: above, Ch.14. (The Misrepresentation Act 1967 was inapplicable because the misrepresentation was made before the Act came into force). On the issue of warranty:

LORD DENNING MR

   Ever since *Heilbut Symons & Co v Buckleton* [above] we have had to contend with the law as laid down by the House of Lords that an innocent misrepresentation gives no right to damages. In order to escape from that rule, the pleader used to allege—I often did it myself—that the misrepresentation was fraudulent, or alternatively a collateral warranty. At the trial we nearly always succeeded on collateral warranty. We had to reckon, of course, with the dictum of Lord Moulton that "such collateral contracts must from their very nature be rare." But more often than not the court elevated the innocent misrepresentation into a collateral warranty; and thereby did justice—in advance of the Misrepresentation Act, 1967. I remember scores of cases of that kind, especially on the sale of a business. A representation as to the profits that had been made in the past was invariably held to be a warranty. Besides that experience, there have been many cases since I have sat in this court where we have readily held a representation—which induces a person to enter into a contract—to be a warranty sounding in damages. I summarised them in *Dick Bentley Products Ltd v Harold Smith (Motors) Ltd* [1965] 2 All E.R. 65 at 67; [1965] 1 W.L.R. 623 at 627 [above] . . . .
   Counsel for Esso retaliated, however, by citing *Bisset v Wilkinson* [above, Ch.14] where the Privy Council said that a statement by a New Zealand farmer that an area of land "would carry 2,000 sheep" was only an expression of opinion. He submitted that the forecast here of 200,000 gallons was an expression of opinion and not a statement of fact; and that it could not be interpreted as a warranty or promise.
   Now, I would quite agree with counsel for Esso that it was not a warranty—in this sense—that it did not guarantee that the throughput would be 200,000 gallons. But, nevertheless, it was a forecast made by a party, Esso, who had special knowledge and skill. It was the yardstick (the "e a c") by which they measured the worth of a filling station. They knew the facts. They knew the traffic in the town. They knew the throughput of comparable stations. They had much experience and expertise at their disposal. They were in a much better position than Mr Mardon to make a forecast. It seems to me that if such a person makes a forecast—intending that the other should act on it and he does act on it—it can well be interpreted as a warranty that the forecast is sound and reliable in this sense that they made it with reasonable care and skill. It is just as if Esso said to Mr Mardon: "Our forecast of throughput is 200,000 gallons. You can rely on it as being a sound forecast of what the service station should do. The rent is calculated on that footing." If the forecast turned out to be an unsound forecast, such as no person of skill or experience should have made, there is a breach of warranty. Just as there is a breach of warranty when a forecast is made "expected to load" by a certain date if the maker has no reasonable grounds for it: see *Samuel Sanday v Keighley Maxted & Co* ((1922) 27 Com.Cas. 296); or bunkers "expected 600/700 tons": see *The Pantanassa* ([1958] 2 Lloyd's Rep. 449 at 455–457) by Diplock J. It is very different from the New Zealand case where the land had never been used as a sheep farm and both parties were equally able to form an opinion as to its carrying capacity.
   In the present case it seems to me that there was a warranty that the forecast was sound, that is that Esso had made it with reasonable care and skill. That warranty was broken. Most negligently Esso made a "fatal

error" in the forecast they stated to Mr Mardon, and on which he took the tenancy. For this they are liable in damages.

Ormrod and Shaw L.JJ. delivered judgments allowing the appeal.

Appeal Allowed.

Further reading

K.W. Wedderburn, 'Collateral Contracts' [1959] CLJ 58

16

IMPLIED TERMS

LEARNING OBJECTIVES

By the end of this chapter, you should:

- **be familiar with the leading cases on the implication of terms;**
- **understand that there is a difference between implying a term in a particular contract (terms implied in fact) and implying a term as standard in a certain class of contracts (whether because of statutory provision or common law decisions);**
- **understand that, while the modern law is pulled towards meeting reasonable expectations, there has been resistance to the idea that judges should be able to imply terms simply because they think it is reasonable to do so;**
- **appreciate the significance of the decision in *Attorney General of Belize v Belize Telecom Ltd* in (a) extending the scope of contextualist thinking (b) elaborating the idea of reasonable expectations in relation to the implication of terms (in fact) (c) rendering more coherent the various tests for the implication of terms and (d) opening the way for the implication of a higher level of cooperative obligation than admitted by the traditional tests (especially the test of "necessary implication").**

INTRODUCTION

In one of the key cases of the modern era, *Suisse Atlantique Societe d'Armement SA v NV Rotterdamsche Kolen Centrale* (below, Ch.21), the claimants, the Swiss owners of the motor vessel, *General Guisen*, argued that they had not received the performance that they reasonably expected from the defendant charterers, a Dutch company. It was the owners' contention that the charterers had deliberately taken their time with loading and discharging the vessel because it made economic sense for them to pay demurrage at the agreed rate rather than pay the freight rates set by the contract. This, the owners contended, amounted to a breach of an implied term of cooperation. Quite how much co-operation a commercial contractor might reasonably expect where its economic interests are in conflict with the economic interests of a co-contractor is moot. At all events, the owners' argument received no judicial support. Quite simply, it was ruled, the only performance that the owners could reasonably expect was the performance that they had contracted for. There was no express term in the charter setting a minimum or other number of voyages; and, even allowing for some flexibility in commercial dealings, the proposed term could not be accepted so long as a test of 'business efficacy' sets the standard for the implication of terms.

The *Suisse Atlantique* case, soon to be overtaken by legislative control over unfair contract terms (see Ch.22), represents something of a last stand in support of the classical values of freedom of contract and sanctity of contract (see Roger Brownsword, 'Suisse Atlantique', in Charles Mitchell and

Paul Mitchell (eds), *Landmark Cases in the Law of Contract* (Oxford: Hart, 2008), p.299). At the root of these values is the idea that contractors deal with one another in an entirely self-interested way. Hence, where one contractor argues that a particular term should be implied—and where the basis of the implication is not that this is a statutory requirement, or in line with settled custom and practice, or something of that kind—the classical view is that the implication can only be made where neither party, taking a self-interested view, would object; or, to put this another way, a term will be implied only where both parties, acting in an entirely self-interested fashion, would readily accept the implication as 'necessary' (or, as essential for business efficacy, as essential for the contract to work).

Although the classical law has had to yield much ground to modern notions of fair and reasonable dealing, there is still resistance to the kind of argument for cooperation, by implication, that was made in *Suisse Atlantique*. In one case after another, and especially in *Liverpool City Council v Irwin* (below), the courts have emphasised (albeit using a range of expressions) that terms are to be implied in fact only where the parties (assuming a self-interested approach to the deal) would have readily signed up to them when the contract was made. However, as more recent cases such as *Scally* (below) and *Equitable Life v Hyman* (below) indicate, the modern courts are prepared to imply terms that clearly reflect the parties' reasonable expectations. Once these expectations are anchored to the context of the parties' dealings and the norms of the sector in which they trade, the door is open to a quite different approach to the implication of terms. This door was emphatically opened by the Privy Council in the *Belize* case (below).

The cases in this chapter are divided in two sections: in the first section, the cases by and large reflect the traditional approach to implied terms, setting a high threshold before accepting that a term is to be implied; by contrast, in the second section, the approach evinced by the cases is distinctly modern.

1. The Traditional Approach

Glanville Williams, Language and the Law, 61 L.Q.R., 401

16-002   The courts will generally enforce consequences logically implied in the language of contracts, wills, statutes, and other legal documents and transactions. The point now to be noticed is that the legal doctrine of implied terms goes much farther than this. Judges are accustomed to read into documents and transactions many terms that are not logically implied in them. As an academic matter non-logical implication may be classified into three kinds: (i) of terms that the parties (the plural shall throughout include the singular) probably had in mind but did not trouble to express; (ii) of terms that the parties, whether or not they actually had them in mind, would probably have expressed if the question had been brought to their attention; and (iii) of terms that the parties, whether or not they had them in mind or would have expressed them if they had foreseen the difficulty, are implied by the court because of the court's view of fairness or policy or in consequence of rules of law. Of these three kinds of non-logical implication (i) is an effort to arrive at actual intention; (ii) is an effort to arrive at hypothetical or conditional intention—the intention that the parties would have had if they had foreseen the difficulty; (iii) is not concerned with the intention of the parties except to the extent that the term implied by the court may be excluded by an expression of positive intention to the contrary . . . .

The view may perhaps be held that this particular process is not very happily called "implication". It is not so much the interpretation of a pre-existing and expressed intent as legislation amending or supplementing the expressed intent. Terms so read into the contract might better be called "constructive" than "implied". However, this is simply a question of nomenclature; and in any case no fixed nomenclature can be maintained in practice, because terms of classes (i), (ii) and (iii) merge into each other. There is no legal difference between the three classes, and the only practical difference is that the courts are more ready to imply terms of class (i) than of classes (ii) and (iii). Terms of classes (ii) and (iii) are mainly of specified types and are comparatively rarely added to, though it is always open to the court to add to them . . .

It is a matter of taste whether implied terms of classes (ii) and (iii) be styled implied terms or rules of law. They are in fact merely rules of law that apply in the absence of an expression of contrary intent: whether we choose to call them implied terms or not is simply a matter of terminology. Our terminology as we now have it is not consistent, for there are some rules of law that are indistinguishable from implied terms in their practical effect, yet which are never called implied terms. Such, for instance, are the rules of interpretation. So, also we do not say that the rule that a contract is voidable for innocent misrepresentation is an implied term, although it can be derogated from by agreement; yet some judges and writers have been known to declare that the law of frustration, the duty to disclose in contracts uberrimae fidei, and even part of the law of mistake in contract, rest upon implied terms or conditions. With all respect to those who hold a contrary opinion, it is submitted that the question is purely terminological and has (or should have) no practical importance.

HUTTON v WARREN

Exchequer of Pleas (1836) 1 M. & W. 466; 2 Gale 71; 1 Tyr. & G. 646; 5 L.J.Ex. 234; 150 E.R. 517

The defendant was the landlord, and the plaintiff the tenant of a certain farm. At Michaelmas 1833 **16–003** the defendant gave the plaintiff notice to quit at the Lady Day following. In October 1833 the defendant insisted that the plaintiff was bound to continue to cultivate the farm in due course of husbandry according to the custom of the country, and gave him formal notice to that effect. The plaintiff quitted in accordance with the notice and now alleged that he was entitled to a fair allowance for seeds and labour on the arable land. It was proved that by the custom of the country a tenant was bound to farm according to a certain course of husbandry for the whole of his tenancy, and, on quitting, was entitled to a fair allowance for seeds and labour on the arable land. The judgment of the court was delivered by Parke B:

PARKE B

We are of opinion that this custom was, by implication, imported into the lease. It has long been settled, that, in commercial transactions, extrinsic evidence of custom and usage is admissible to annex incidents to written contracts, in matters with respect to which they are silent. The same rule has also been applied to contracts in other transactions of life, in which known usages have been established and prevailed; and this has been done upon the principle of presumption that, in such transactions, the parties did not mean to express in writing the whole of the contract by which they intended to be bound, but a contract with reference to those known usages. Whether such a relaxation of the strictness of the common law was wisely applied, where formal instruments have been entered into, and particularly leases under seal, may well be doubted; but the contrary has been established by such authority, and the relations between landlord and tenant have been so long regulated upon the supposition that all customary obligations, not altered by the contract, are to remain in force, that it is too late to pursue a contrary course; and it would be productive of much inconvenience if this practice were now to be disturbed.

The common law, indeed, does so little to prescribe the relative duties of landlord and tenant, since it leaves the latter at liberty to pursue any course of management he pleases, provided he is not guilty of waste, that it is by no means surprising that the courts should have been favourably inclined to the introduction of those regulations in the mode of cultivation which custom and usage have established in each district to be the most beneficial to all parties . . .

[Parke B referred to a number of cases including *Senior v Armitage*, reported in Holt's Nisi Prius Cases 197, where the question was whether a tenant was entitled to compensation for seeds and labour. He continued:] Mr Holt appears to have stated the case too strongly when he said that the court held the custom to be operative, "unless the agreement in express terms excluded it"; and probably he has not been quite accurate in attributing a similar opinion to the Lord Chief Baron Thompson, who presided on the second trial. It would appear that the court held that the custom operated, unless it could be collected from the instrument, either expressly or impliedly, that the parties did not mean to be governed by it.

On the second trial, the Lord Chief Baron Thompson held that the custom prevailed, although the written instrument contained an express stipulation that all the manure made on the farm should be left at the end of the tenancy, without any compensation being paid. Such a stipulation certainly does not exclude by implication the tenant's right to receive a compensation for seed and labour . . .

The question then is, whether, from the terms of the lease now under consideration it can be collected that the parties intended to exclude the customary obligations to make allowances for seed and labour.

The only clause relating to the management of the farm (except the covenant to repair) is one which stipulated that the plaintiff shall spend and consume on the farm three-fourths of the hay and straw arising not only from the farm itself, but from the demised tithes of the whole parish, and spread the manure, leaving such as should not be spread at the end of the term for the use of the landlord, on paying a reasonable price for the same. This provision introduces and has a principal reference to a subject to which the custom of the country does not apply at all, namely, the tithes, and imposes a new obligation on the tenant dehors that custom, and then qualifies that obligation by an engagement on the landlord's part to give a remuneration, by re-purchasing a part of the produce in a particular event. It is by no means to be inferred from this provision that this is the only compensation which the tenant is to receive on quitting. If, indeed, there had been a covenant by the tenant to plough and sow a certain portion of the demised land in the last year, being such as the custom of the country required, he being paid on quitting for the ploughing, or to plough, sow, and manure, he being paid for the manuring, the principle of expressum facit cessare tacitum, which governed the decision in *Webb v Plummer* (1819) 2 B. & Ald. 746, would have applied; but that is not the case here. The custom of the country as to the obligation of the tenant to plough and sow, and the corresponding obligation of the landlord to pay for such ploughing and sowing in the last year of the term, is in no way varied. The only alteration made in the custom is, that the tenant is obliged to spend more than the produce of the farm on the premises being paid for it in the same way as he would have been for that which the custom required him to spend.

Point for reflection

16–004 By way of comparison, in *Les Affréteurs Réunis Société Annonyme v Leopold Walford (London) Ltd* [1919] A.C. 801; 121 L.T. 393 HL, above, Ch.13, Bailhache J held that there was a custom in the shipping trade that a chartering broker's commission was payable only in respect of hire duly earned under the charterparty. He therefore rejected W's claim for commission as broker in effecting a charter of SS. Flore since the ship was requisitioned by the French Government and never entered upon service under the charterparty. The charterparty, however, provided that the commission should be payable "on signing this charter (ship lost or not lost)"; and the Court of Appeal and the House of Lords held that the custom could have no application since it was inconsistent with the express terms of the charterparty.

THE MOORCOCK

Court of Appeal (1889) 14 P.D. 64; 58 L.J.P. 73; 60 L.T. 654; 37 W.R. 439

16–005 The appellants were wharfingers possessed of a wharf abutting on, and a jetty extending into, the River Thames. The respondent was the owner of the steamship Moorcock.

In November 1887 it was agreed between the appellants and the respondent that the vessel should be discharged and loaded at the wharf, and for that purpose should be moored alongside the jetty where she would take the ground at low water.

No charge was made in respect of the vessel being moored alongside, or lying at, the jetty but the shipowner paid for the use of the cranes in discharging the cargo, and rates were payable to the appellants on all goods landed, shipped, or stored.

Whilst the Moorcock was lying moored at the extremity of the jetty discharging her cargo, the tide ebbed and, when she ceased to be waterborne, she sustained damage, owing to the centre of the vessel settling on a ridge of hard ground beneath the mud.

Butt J came to the conclusion that there was no warranty by the wharfingers that the place was safe for the vessel to lie in, and that the evidence negatived any express representation by them that the place was suitable for the vessel, but the learned judge held that as the use of the wharfingers' premises by the owner of the Moorcock required that the vessel should take the ground when moored alongside the jetty, there was an implied representation by the wharfingers that they had taken reasonable care to ascertain that the bottom of the river at the jetty was in such a condition as not to endanger the vessel.

The defendants appealed.

BOWEN LJ

The question which arises here is whether when a contract is made to let the use of this jetty to a ship which can only use it, as is known by both parties, by taking the ground, there is any implied warranty on the part of the owners of the jetty, and if so, what is the extent of the warranty. Now, an implied warranty, or, as it is called, a covenant in law, as distinguished from an express contract or express warranty, really is in all cases founded on the presumed intention of the parties, and upon reason. The implication which the law draws from what must obviously have been the intention of the parties, the law draws with the object of giving efficacy to the transaction and preventing such a failure of consideration as cannot have been within the contemplation of either side; and I believe if one were to take all the cases, and they are many, of implied warranties or covenants in law, it will be found that in all of them the law is raising an implication from the presumed intention of the parties with the object of giving to the transaction such efficacy as both parties must have intended that at all events it should have. In business transactions such as this, what the law desires to effect by the implication is to give such business efficacy to the transaction as must have been intended at all events by both parties who are business men; not to impose on one side all the perils of the transaction, or to emancipate one side from all the chances of failure, but to make each party promise in law as much, at all events, as it must have been in the contemplation of both parties that he should be responsible for in respect of those perils or chances.

Now what did each party in a case like this know? For if we are examining into their presumed intention we must examine into their minds as to what the transaction was. Both parties knew that this jetty was let out for hire, and knew that it could only be used under the contract by the ship taking the ground. They must have known that it was by grounding that she used the jetty; in fact, except so far as the transport to the jetty of the cargo in the ship was concerned, they must have known, both of them, that unless the ground was safe the ship would be simply buying an opportunity of danger, and that all consideration would fail unless some care had been taken to see that the ground was safe. In fact the business of the jetty could not be carried on except upon such a basis. The parties also knew that with regard to the safety of the ground outside the jetty the shipowner could know nothing at all, and the jetty owner might with reasonable care know everything. The owners of the jetty, or their servants, were there at high and low tide, and with little trouble they could satisfy themselves, in case of doubt, as to whether the berth was reasonably safe. The ship's owner, on the other hand, had not the means of verifying the state of the jetty, because the berth itself opposite the jetty might be occupied by another ship at any moment.

Now the question is how much of the peril of the safety of this berth is it necessary to assume that the shipowner and the jetty owner intended respectively to bear—in order that such a minimum of efficacy should be secured for the transaction, as both parties must have intended it to bear? Assume that the berth outside had been absolutely under the control of the owners of the jetty, that they could have repaired it and made it fit for the purpose of the unloading and the loading. If this had been the case, then the case of *The Mersey Docks Trustees v Gibbs*, L.R. 1 HL 93, shows that those who owned the jetty, who took money for the use of the jetty, and who had under their control the locus in quo, would have been bound to take all reasonable care to prevent danger to those who were using the jetty—either to make the berth outside good, or else not to invite ships to go there—either to make the berth safe, or to advise persons not to go there. But there is a distinction in the present instance. The berth outside the jetty was not under the actual control of the jetty owners. It is in the bed of the river, and it may be said that those who owned the jetty had no duty cast upon them by statute or common law to repair the bed of the river, and that they had no power to interfere with the bed of the river, unless under the licence of the Conservators. Now it does make a difference, it seems to me, where the entire control of the locus in quo—be it canal, or be it dock, or be it river berth—is not under the control of the persons who are taking toll for accommodation which involves its user, and, to a certain extent, the view must be modified of the necessary implication which the law would make about the duties of the parties receiving the remuneration. This must be done exactly for the reason laid down by Lord Holt in his judgment in *Coggs v Bernard*, Ld.Raym. 909, 918, where he says: "it would be unreasonable to charge persons with a trust further than the nature of the thing puts it in their power to perform." Applying that modification, which is one of reason, to this case, it may well be said that the law will not imply that the persons who have not the control of the place have taken reasonable care to make it good, but it does not follow that they are relieved from all responsibility. They are on the spot. They must know that the jetty cannot be used unless reasonable care is taken, if not to make it safe, at all events to see whether it is safe. No one can tell whether reasonable safety has been secured except themselves, and I think if they let out their jetty for use they at all events imply that they have taken reasonable care to see whether the berth, which is the essential part of the use of the jetty, is safe, and if it is not safe, and if they have not taken such reasonable care, it is their duty to warn persons with whom they have dealings that they have not done so. This is a business transaction as to which at any moment the parties may make any bargain they please, and either side may by the contract throw upon the other the burden of the unseen and existing danger. The question is what inference is to be drawn where the parties are dealing with each other on the assumption that the negotiations are to have some fruit, and where they say nothing about the burden of this kind of unseen peril, leaving the law to raise such inferences as are reasonable from the very nature of the transaction. So far as I am concerned I do not wish it to be understood that I at all consider this is a case of any duty on the part of the owners of the jetty to see to the access to the jetty being kept clear. The difference between access to the jetty and the actual use of the jetty seems to me, as Mr Finlay says it is, only a question of degree, but when you are dealing with implications which the law directs, you cannot afford to neglect questions of degree, and it is just that difference of degree which brings one case on the line and prevents the other from approaching it. I confess that on the broad view of the case I think that business could not be carried on unless there was an implication to the extent I have laid down, at all events in the case where a jetty like the present is so to be used, and, although the case is a novel one, and the cases which have been cited do not assist us, I feel no difficulty in drawing the inference that this case comes within the line.

Lord Esher M.R. and Fry L.J. delivered judgment to the same effect.

Question

16–006   Bowen LJ speaks in this case of an implied warranty. Might he have held the term to be a condition if that had been necessary to the decision? Did the wharfingers impliedly promise (a) that the berth was safe; (b) that they had taken reasonable steps to make it safe; (c) that they had taken reasonable steps to find out whether it was safe? Does the court imply only the minimum term necessary to give the contract business efficacy? Was that particular term necessary? Cf. *Re Charge Card Services Ltd*, above, Ch.2.

REIGATE v UNION MANUFACTURING CO

Court of Appeal [1918] 1 K.B. 592, 605, 87 L.J.K.B. 724; 118 L.T. 479

16–007   In this case, the Court of Appeal held that where, in consideration of the plaintiff investing £1,000 in the capital of the defendant company, the company had appointed him their sole agent for the sale of certain goods for seven years, no term could be implied that the company could terminate the agency at any time by ceasing to carry on business. According to Scrutton LJ (at 605): "If this matter had been mooted at the time when the contract had been negotiated, I expect that the parties would at once have disagreed as to what the position was. Unless we are satisfied that it is an implication which must necessarily have been in the minds of both parties, we cannot imply a term which they have not expressed, especially when I see that they have thought sufficiently about the matter to express two conditions on which the agreement is to be determined, first the obvious one on the death of the agent; and secondly, by six months' notice after the expiration of seven years."

SCRUTTON LJ

The first thing is to see what the parties have expressed in the contract; and then an implied term is not to be added because the court thinks it would have been reasonable to have inserted it in the contract. A term can only be implied if it is necessary in the business sense to give efficacy to the contract; that is, if it is such a term that it can confidently be said that if at the time the contract was being negotiated someone had said to the parties, "What will happen in such a case?" they would both have replied: "Of course, so and so will happen; we did not trouble to say that; it is too clear." Unless the court comes to some such conclusion as that, it ought not to imply a term which the parties themselves have not expressed.

SHIRLAW v SOUTHERN FOUNDRIES LTD

Court of Appeal [1939] 2 K.B. 206, 227; 108 L.J.K.B. 747; 160 L.T. 353; 55 T.L.R. 611; 83 S.J. 357; [1939] 2 All E.R. 113

MACKINNON LJ

I recognise that the right or duty of a court to find the existence of an implied term or implied terms in a written contract is a matter to be exercised with care; and a court is too often invited to do so upon vague and uncertain grounds. Too often also such an invitation is backed by the citation of a sentence or two from the judgment of Bowen L.J. in *The Moorcock* [above]. They are sentences from an extempore judgment as sound and sensible as all the utterances of that great judge; but I fancy that he would have been rather surprised if he could have foreseen that these general remarks of his would come to be a favourite citation of a supposed principle of law, and I even think that he might sympathise with the occasional impatience of his successors when *The Moorcock* is so often flushed for them in that guise.

16–008

For my part, I think that there is a test that may be at least as useful as such generalities. If I may quote from an essay which I wrote some years ago, I then said: "Prima facie that which in any contract is left to be implied and need not be expressed is something so obvious that it goes without saying; so that, if, while the parties were making their bargain, an officious bystander were to suggest some express provision for it in their agreement, they would testily suppress him with a common 'Oh, of course!'"

At least it is true, I think, that, if a term were never implied by a judge unless it could pass that test, he could not be held to be wrong.

Applying the above test, MacKinnon LJ held that there were implied terms in a company's contract, appointing the plaintiff, a director, to be its managing director for 10 years, (i) that the company would not remove him during that time from his directorship, since such removal would automatically terminate his appointment as managing director; and (ii) that the company would not alter its articles of association so as to create a right in itself or another to remove him. Goddard LJ agreed, but Greene MR dissented on the first point. The House of Lords ([1940] A.C. 701) dismissed an appeal by a majority of three to two; but none of their Lordships held that term (ii) (above) should be implied; and, of the majority, Lord Wright stated that the removal of the plaintiff from his directorship was a breach of an express, not an implied term. Cf. *General Publicity Services Ltd v Best's Brewery Ltd* [1951] 2 T.L.R. 875 CA; [1951] W.N. 507.

For interesting applications of MacKinnon LJ's test, see *Forbes v Kemsley Newspapers, Ltd* [1951] 2 T.L.R. 656 and *Spring v National Amalgamated Stevedores and Dockers Society* [1956] 1 W.L.R. 585 at 598–599. See also *Trollope & Colls Ltd v NW Hospital Board* [1973] 2 All E.R. 260.

LIVERPOOL CITY COUNCIL v IRWIN AND ANOTHER

House of Lords [1977] A.C. 239; [1976] 2 W.L.R. 562; [1976] 2 All E.R. 39

The plaintiff owned a tower block containing about 70 flats. Access was by a common staircase and two lifts. Tenants were provided with an internal chute for the discharge of rubbish. In July 1966 the defendants became tenants of a flat. The tenancy agreement imposed obligations on the tenant but said nothing of the obligations of the landlord. The conditions of the block deteriorated seriously, partly because of the activities of vandals and lack of cooperation by the tenants. The defendants and other tenants refused to pay rent by way of protest at the conditions. The plaintiff sought an order for

16–009

possession and the defendants counterclaimed alleging, inter alia, a breach of an implied covenant for quiet enjoyment. The judge granted the order for possession but awarded the defendants £10 damages on their counterclaim. The plaintiff appealed. The Court of Appeal allowed the appeal. Roskill and Ormrod LJJ held that no covenant could be implied, since it was not necessary to do so. Lord Denning MR held that the court could imply a term if it was reasonable to do so; that a term should be implied that the council would take reasonable care to keep the lifts and staircase reasonably fit for use; but that there was no evidence that they had not done so. The defendants' appeal to the House of Lords was dismissed.

LORD WILBERFORCE

I consider first the appellants' claim insofar as it is based on contract. The first step must be to ascertain what the contract is. This may look elementary, even naive, but it seems to me to be the essential step and to involve, from the start, an approach different, if simpler, from that taken by the members of the Court of Appeal. We look first at documentary material. As is common with council lettings there is no formal demise or lease or tenancy agreement. There is a document headed "Liverpool Corporation, Liverpool City Housing Department" and described as "Conditions of Tenancy". This contains a list of obligations on the tenant—he shall do this, he shall not do that, or he shall not do that without the corporation's consent. This is an amalgam of obligations added to from time to time, no doubt, to meet complaints, emerging situations, or problems as they appear to the council's officers. In particular there have been added special provisions relating to multi-storey flats which are supposed to make the conditions suitable to such dwellings. We may note under "Further special notes" some obligations not to obstruct staircases and passages, and not to permit children under 10 to operate any lifts. I mention these as a recognition of the existence and relevance of these facilities. At the end there is a form for signature by the tenant stating that he accepts the tenacy. On the landlords' side there is nothing, no signature, no demise, no covenant; the contract takes effect as soon as the tenants sign the form and are let into possession.

We have then a contract which is partly, but not wholly, stated in writing. In order to complete it, in particular to give it a bilateral character, it is necessary to take account of the actions of the parties and the circumstances. As actions of the parties, we must note the granting of possession by the corporation and reservation by it of the "common parts"—stairs, lifts, chutes, etc. As circumstances we must include the nature of the premises, viz. a maisonette for family use on the ninth floor of a high block, one which is occupied by a large number of other tenants, all using the common parts and dependent on them, none of them having any expressed obligation to maintain on repair them.

To say that the construction of a complete contract out of these elements involves a process of "implication" may be correct: it would be so if implication means the supplying of what is not expressed. But there are varieties of implications which the courts think fit to make and they do not necessarily involve the same process. Where there is, on the face of it, a complete, bilateral contract, the courts are sometimes willing to add terms to it, as implied terms; this is very common in mercantile contracts where there is an established usage; in that case the courts are spelling out what both parties know and would, if asked, unhesitatingly agree to be part of the bargain. In other cases, where there is an apparently complete bargain, the courts are willing to add a term on the ground that without it the contract will not work—this is the case, if not of *The Moorcock* [above] itself on its facts, at least of the doctrine of *The Moorcock* as usually applied. This is, as was pointed out by the majority in the Court of Appeal, a strict test—though the degree of strictness seems to vary with the current legal trend, and I think that they were right not to accept it as applicable here. There is a third variety of implication, that which I think Lord Denning M.R. favours, or at least did favour in this case, and that is the implication of reasonable terms. But though I agree with many of his instances, which in fact fall under one or other of the preceding heads, I cannot go so far as to endorse his principle; indeed, it seems to me, with respect, to extend a long, and undesirable, way beyond sound authority.

The present case, in my opinion, represents a fourth category or, I would rather say, a fourth shade on a continuous spectrum. The court here is simply concerned to establish what the contract is, the parties not having themselves fully stated the terms. In this sense the court is searching for what must be implied.

What then should this contract be held to be? There must first be implied a letting, that is, a grant of the right of exclusive possession to the tenants. With this there must, I would suppose, be implied a covenant for quiet enjoyment, as a necessary incident of the letting. The difficulty begins when we consider the common parts. We start with the fact that the demise is useless unless access is obtained by the staircase; we can add that, having regard to the height of the block, and the family nature of the dwellings, the demise would be useless without a lift service; we can continue that there being rubbish chutes built in to the structures and no other means of disposing of light rubbish there must be a right to use the chutes. The question to be answered—and it is the only question in this case—is what is to be the legal relationship between landlord and tenant as regards these matters.

There can be no doubt that there must be implied (i) an easement for the tenants and their licensees to use the stairs, (ii) a right in the nature of an easement to use the lifts and (iii) an easement to use the rubbish chutes.

But are these easements to be accompanied by any obligation on the landlord, and what obligation? There seem to be two alternatives. The first, for which the corporation contends, is for an easement coupled with no legal obligation, except such as may arise under the Occupiers' Liability Act, 1957, as regards the safety of those using the facilities, and possibly such other liability as might exist under the ordinary law of tort. The alterative is for easements coupled with some obligation on the part of the landlords as regards the maintenance of the subject of them, so that they are available for use.

My Lords, in order to be able to choose between these, it is necessary to define what test is to be applied, and I do not find this difficult. In my opinion such obligation should be read into the contract as the nature of the contract itself implicitly requires, no more, no less; a test in other words of necessity. The relationship accepted by the corporation is that of landlord and tenant; the tenant accepts obligations accordingly, in relation, inter alia, to the stairs, the lifts and the chutes. All these are not just facilities, or conveniences provided at discretion; they are essentials of the tenancy without which life in the dwellings, as a tenant, is not possible. To leave the landlord free of contractual obligation as regards these matters, and subject only to administrative or political pressure, is, in my opinion, totally inconsistent with the nature of this relationship. The subject-matter of the lease (high-rise blocks) and the relationship created by the tenancy demands, of its nature, some contractual obligation on the landlord.

I do not think that this approach involves any innovation as regards the law of contract. The necessity to have regard to the inherent nature of a contract and of the relationship thereby established was stated in this House in *Lister v Romford Ice & Cold Storage Co Ltd* ([1957] A.C. 555). That was a case between master and servant and of a search for an "implied term." Viscount Simonds made a clear distinction between a search for an implied term such as might be necessary to give "business efficacy" to the particular contract and a search, based on wider considerations, for such a term as the nature of the contract might call for, or as a legal incident of this kind of contract. If the search were for the former, he said ([1957] A.C. at 576): "I should lose myself in the attempt to formulate it with the necessary precision." We see an echo of this in the present case, when the majority in the Court of Appeal, considering a "business efficacy term," that is, a "*Moorcock*" ((1889) 14 P.D. 64) term, found themselves faced with five alternative terms and therefore rejected all of them. But that is not, in my opinion, the end, or indeed the object, of the search.

We have some guidance in authority for the kind of term which this typical relationship (of landlord and tenant in multi-occupational dwellings) requires in *Miller v Hancock*. There Bowen L.J. said ([1893] 2 Q.B. 177 at 180, 181):

"The tenants could only use their flats by using the staircase. The defendant, therefore, when he let the flats, impliedly granted to the tenants an easement over the staircase, which he retained in his own occupation, for the purpose of the enjoyment of the flats so let. Under those circumstances, what is the law as to the repairs of the staircase? It was contended by the defendant's counsel that, according to the common law, the person in enjoyment of an easement is bound to do the necessary repairs himself. That may be true with regard to easements in general, but it is subject to the qualification that the grantor of the easement may undertake to do the repairs either in express terms or by necessary implication. This is not the mere case of a grant of an easement without special circumstances. It appears to me obvious, when one considers what a flat of this kind is, and the only way in which it can be enjoyed, that the parties to the demise of it must have intended by necessary implication, as a basis without which the whole transaction would be futile, that the landlord should maintain the staircase, which is essential to the enjoyment of the premises demised, and should keep it reasonably safe for the use of the tenants, and also of those persons who would necessarily go up and down the stairs in the ordinary course of business with the tenants; because, of course, a landlord must know when he lets a flat that tradesmen and other persons having business with the tenant must have access to it. It seems to me that it would render the whole transaction inefficacious and absurd if an implied undertaking were not assumed on the part of the landlord to maintain the staircase so far as might be necessary for the reasonable enjoyment of the demised premises."

Certainly that case, as a decision concerning a claim by a visitor, has been overruled (*Fairman v Perpetual Investment Building Society* ([1923] A.C. 74)). But I cite the passage for its common sense as between landlord and tenant, and you cannot overrule common sense . . .

I accept, of course, the argument that a mere grant of an easement does not carry with it any obligation on the part of the servient owner to maintain the subject-matter. The dominant owner must spend the necessary money, for example, in repairing a drive leading to his house. And the same principle may apply when a landlord lets an upper floor with access by a staircase; responsibility for maintenance may well rest on the tenant. But there is a difference between that case and the case where there is an essential means of access, retained in the landlord's occupation, to units in a building of multi-occupation; for unless the obligation to maintain is, in a defined manner, placed on the tenants, individually or collectively, the nature of the contract, and the circumstances, require that it be placed on the landlord.

It remains to define the standard. My Lords, if, as I think, the test of the existence of the term is necessity the standard must surely not exceed what is necessary having regard to the circumstances. To imply an absolute obligation to repair would go beyond what is a necessary legal incident and would indeed be unreasonable. An obligation to take reasonable care to keep in reasonable repair and usability is what fits the requirements of the case. Such a definition involves—and I think rightly—recognition that the tenants themselves have their responsibilities. What it is reasonable to expect of a landlord has a clear relation to what a reasonable set of tenants should do for themselves . . .

I would hold therefore that the corporation's obligation is as I have described. And in agreement, I believe, with your Lordships, I would hold that it has not been shown in this case that there was any breach of that obligation. On the main point therefore I would hold that the appeal fails.

My Lords, it will be seen that I have reached exactly the same conclusion as that of Lord Denning M.R., with most of whose thinking I respectfully agree. I must only differ from the passage in which, more adventurously, he suggested that the courts had power to introduce into contracts any terms they thought reasonable or to anticipate legislative recommendations of the Law Commission. A just result can be reached, if I am right, by a less dangerous route.

LORD SALMON

[Having cited the passage of the judgment of Bowen LJ in *Miller v Hancock* quoted by Lord Wilberforce, continued:] Could it in reality have been contemplated by the corporation or its tenants that the corporation undertook no responsibility to take, at any rate, reasonable care to keep the lifts in order and the staircases lit? No doubt the tenants also owed a duty to use the lifts and staircases reasonably; indeed, so much was clearly implied in the printed terms of the tenancy. Can a pregnant woman accompanied by a young child be expected to walk up 15, or for that matter nine, storeys in the pitch dark to reach her home? Unless the law, in circumstances such as these, imposes an obligation on the corporation at least to use reasonable care to keep the lifts working properly and the staircase lit, the whole transaction becomes inefficacious, futile and absurd. I cannot go so far as Lord Denning M.R. and hold that the courts have any power to imply a term into a contract merely because it seems reasonable to do so. Indeed, I think that such a proposition is contrary to all authority. To say, as Lord Reid ([1969] 1 A.C. 454 at 465) said in *Young and Marten, Ltd v McManus Childs, Ltd* that "no warranty ought to be implied in a contract unless it is in all the circumstances reasonable" is, in my view, quite different from saying that any warranty or term which is, in all the circumstances, reasonable ought to be implied in a contract. I am confident that Lord Reid meant no more than that unless a warranty or term is in all the circumstances reasonable there can be no question of implying it into a contract, but before it is implied much else besides is necessary, for example, that without it the contract would be inefficacious, futile and absurd . . .

I find it difficult to think of any term which it could be more necessary to imply than one without which the whole transaction would become futile, inefficacious and absurd as it would do if in a 15-storey block of flats or maisonettes, such as the present, the landlords were under no legal duty to take reasonable care to keep the lifts in working order and the staircases lit.

It may be that further codification of the law of landlord and tenant is desirable. The recommendations of the Law Commission referred to in the Court of Appeal may be translated into Acts sooner or later—perhaps much later. I respectfully agree with Lord Denning M.R. that, in the meantime, the law should not be condemned to sterility and that the judges should take care not to abdicate their traditional role of developing the law to meet even the advent of tower blocks . . . Since, however, only an absolute obligation was pleaded against the corporation to which it had a complete answer, I do not think it would be right for the reasons I have already given to find against it on the ground that it failed to take reasonable care. I would accordingly dismiss the appeal insofar as it relates to the lifts and staircase.

Questions

1. Why was the *Moorcock* doctrine considered inapplicable?

2. If the contract without the implied term would have been "futile, inefficacious and absurd", how could it be that the Liverpool Council (as a reasonable council) would not have agreed to it if it had been proposed by the officious bystander? Is it to be assumed that they intended a futile, inefficacious and absurd contract?

3. Did not Bowen LJ in the passage from *Miller v Hancock* (approved by a majority of the House) apply the "business efficacy" principle?

4. If the test was necessity, but not necessity to give business efficacy, for what purpose was the term required to be "necessary"?

5. Why should the House be persuaded of the necessity for a general rule implying a term into a class of contracts when it was not persuaded of the necessity for implying the term into that particular contract? What are the "wider considerations" applicable in stating a general rule? Did the House lay down a rule which they thought reasonable rather than necessary?

6. Does not the *Moorcock* itself establish a rule for a class of contracts—wharfingers' contracts?

7. In *Scally v Southern Health and Social Services Board* (below), the House of Lords held that the defendant employers had an implied contractual obligation to take reasonable steps to bring to the attention of their employees the existence of an opportunity to enhance their pension entitlements? Lord Bridge presents such an implication as being both reasonable and "necessary". How convincing is this? How is *Scally* to be reconciled with *Liverpool City Council v Irwin*?

SCALLY v SOUTHERN HEALTH AND SOCIAL SERVICES BOARD

House of Lords [1992] 1 A.C. 294

LORD BRIDGE

Will the law then imply a term in the contract of employment imposing such an obligation on the employer? The implication cannot, of course, be justified as necessary to give business efficacy to the contract of employment as a whole. I think there is force in the submission that, since the employee's entitlement to enhance his pension rights by the purchase of added years is of no effect unless he is aware of it and since he cannot be expected to become aware of it unless it is drawn to his attention, it is necessary to imply an obligation on the employer to bring it to his attention to render efficacious the very benefit which the contractual right to purchase added years was intended to confer. But this might be stretching the doctrine of implication for the sake of business efficacy beyond its proper reach. A clear distinction is drawn in the speeches of Viscount Simonds in *Lister v Romford Ice and Cold Storage Co Ltd* . . . and Lord Wilberforce in *Liverpool City Council v Irwin* [above] between the search for an implied term necessary to give business efficacy to a particular contract and the search, based on wider considerations, for a term which the law will imply as a necessary incident of a definable category of contractual relationship. If any implication is appropriate here, it is, I think, of this latter type. . . . [The category of contractual relationship needs to be defined with sufficient precision]. I would define it as the relationship of employer and employee where the following circumstances obtain: (1) the terms of the contract of employment have not been negotiated with the individual employee but result from negotiation with a representative body or are otherwise incorporated by reference; (2) a particular tem of the contract makes available to the employee a valuable right contingent upon action being taken by him to avail himself of its benefit; (3) the employer cannot, in all the circumstances, reasonably be expected to be aware of the term unless it

16–010

16–011

is drawn to his attention. I fully appreciate that the criterion to justify an implication of this kind is necessity, not reasonableness. But I take the view that it is not merely reasonable, but necessary, in the circumstances postulated, to imply an obligation on the employer to take reasonable steps to bring the term of the contract in question to the employee's attention, so that he may be in a position to enjoy its benefit.

Question

16-012   How close is Lord Bridge coming to saying that a term will be implied to protect the reasonable expectations of the employees? Does *Scally* invite a re-assessment of the principle that terms will only be implied where it is necessary to do so? Compare *Paragon Finance Plc v Nash* [2001] EWCA Civ 1466 and *Crossley v Faithful & Gould Holdings Ltd* [2004] EWCA Civ 293.

In *Liverpool City Council v Irwin* [1977] A.C. at 254 Lord Cross said:

"When it implies a term in a contract the court is sometimes laying down a general rule that in all contracts of a certain type—sale of goods, master and servant, landlord and tenant, and so on— some provision is to be implied unless the parties have expressly excluded it."

This passage has been quoted in more recent cases to show that only express exclusion will keep the term out: *The Maira* [1989] 1 All E.R. 213 at 219 CA; *Elawadi v Bank of Credit and Commerce SA* [1989] 1 All E.R. 242 at 251, Hutchison J. Cf. the discussion by Parke B. of *Senior v Armitage* in *Hutton v Warren*, above. Did Lord Cross, like Mr Holt, put the case too strongly by allowing only for express exclusion? What if the clear implication of the contract is that the alleged term is not to apply?

MALIK v BANK OF CREDIT AND COMMERCE INTERNATIONAL SA (IN LIQUIDATION)

House of Lords [1998] A.C. 20; [1997] 3 W.L.R. 95; [1997] 3 All E.R. 1.

LORD NICHOLLS

16-013   [With whose speech Lord Goff and Lord Mackay agreed:]

My Lords, this is another case arising from the disastrous collapse of Bank of Credit and Commerce International SA (BCCI) in the summer of 1991. Thousands of people around the world suffered loss. Depositors lost their money, employees lost their jobs. Two employees who lost their jobs were Mr Raihan Nasir Mahmud and Mr Qaiser Mansoor Malik. They were employed by BCCI in London. They claim they lost more than their jobs. They claim that their association with BCCI placed them at a serious disadvantage in finding new jobs. So in March 1992 they sought to prove for damages in the winding up of BCCI. The liquidators rejected this "stigma" head of loss in their proofs. Liability for notice money and statutory redundancy pay was not in dispute.

Mr Mahmud had worked for the bank for 16 years. At the time of his dismissal he was manager of the bank's Brompton Road branch. Mr Malik was employed by the bank for 12 years. His last post was as the head of deposit accounts and customer services at BCCI's Leadenhall branch. On 3 October 1991 they were both dismissed by the provisional liquidators, on the ground of redundancy . . .

Before this House, as in the courts below, the issue is being decided on the basis of an agreed set of facts . . . [The agreed facts were as follows:]

(a) the applicants were employees of BCCI [the bank]; (b) BCCI operated in a corrupt and/or dishonest manner; (c) the applicants were innocent of any involvement in BCCI's corruption and/or dishonesty; (d) following the collapse of BCCI, its corruption and/or dishonesty has become widely known; (e) in consequence, the applicants are now at a handicap on the labour market because they are stigmatized by reason of their previous employment by BCCI; (f) the applicants have suffered a loss in consequence of (e) above.]

In the Court of Appeal and in your Lordships' House the parties were agreed that the contracts of employment of these two former employees each contained an implied term to the effect that the bank would not, without reasonable and proper cause, conduct itself in a manner likely to destroy or seriously damage the relationship of confidence and trust between employer and employee. Argument proceeded on this footing, and ranged round the type of conduct and other circumstances which could or could not constitute a breach of this implied term. The submissions embraced questions such as the following: whether the trust-destroying conduct must be directed at the employee, either individually or as part of a group; whether an employee must know of the employer's trust-destroying conduct while still employed; and whether the employee's trust must actually be undermined. Furthermore, and at the heart of this case, the submissions raised an important question on the damages recoverable for breach of the implied term, with particular reference to the decisions in *Addis v Gramophone Co Ltd* [1909] A.C. 488 [below, para.19–018], and *Withers v General Theatre Corp Ltd* [1933] 2 K.B. 536.

A Dishonest and Corrupt Business

These questions are best approached by focusing first on the particular conduct of which complaint is made. The bank operated its business dishonestly and corruptly. On the assumed facts, this was not a case where one or two individuals, however senior, were behaving dishonestly. Matters had gone beyond this. They had reached the point where the bank itself could properly be identified with the dishonesty. This was a dishonest business, a corrupt business. It is against this background that the position of an innocent employee has to be considered. In my view, when an innocent employee of the bank learned the true nature of the bank's business, from whatever source, he was entitled to say: "I wish to have nothing more to do with this organisation. I am not prepared to help this business, by working for it. I am leaving at once." This is my intuitive response to the case of all innocent employees of the business, from the most senior to the most junior, from the most long serving to the most recently joined. No one could be expected to have to continue to work with and for such a company against his wish.

This intuitive response is no more than a reflection of what goes without saying in any ordinary contract of employment. namely, that in agreeing to work for an employer the employee, whatever his status, cannot be taken to have agreed to work in furtherance of a dishonest business. This is as much true of a doorkeeper or cleaner as a senior executive or branch manager.

An Implied Obligation

Two points can be noted here. First, as a matter of legal analysis, the innocent employee's entitlement to leave at once must derive from the bank being in breach of a term of the contract of employment which the employee is entitled to treat as a repudiation by the bank of its contractual obligations. That is the source of his right to step away from the contract forthwith.

In other words, and this is the necessary corollary of the employee's right to leave at once, the bank was under an implied obligation to its employees not to conduct a dishonest or corrupt business. This implied obligation is no more than one particular aspect of the portmanteau, general obligation not to engage in conduct likely to undermine the trust and confidence required if the employment relationship is to continue in the manner the employment contract implicitly envisages.

Second, I do not accept the liquidators' submission that the conduct of which complaint is made must be targeted in some way at the employee or a group of employees. No doubt that will often be the position, perhaps usually so. But there is no reason in principle why this must always be so. The trust and confidence required in the employment relationship can be undermined by an employer, or indeed an employee, in many different ways. I can see no justification for the law giving the employee a remedy if the unjustified trust-destroying conduct occurs in some ways but refusing a remedy if it occurs in others. The conduct must, of course, impinge on the relationship in the sense that, looked at objectively, it is likely to destroy or seriously damage the degree of trust and confidence the employee is reasonably entitled to have in his employer. That requires one to look at all the circumstances.

Breach

The objective standard just mentioned provides the answer to the liquidators' submission that unless the employee's confidence is actually undermined there is no breach. A breach occurs when the proscribed conduct takes place: here, operating a dishonest and corrupt business. Proof of a subjective loss of confidence in the employer is not an essential element of the breach, although the time when the employee learns of the misconduct and his response to it may affect his remedy.

Remedies

(1) Acceptance of Breach as Repudiation

The next step is to consider the consequences which flow from the bank being in breach of its obligation to its innocent employees by operating a corrupt banking business. The first remedy of an employee has already been noted. The employee may treat the bank's conduct as a repudiatory breach, entitling him to leave. He is not compelled to leave. He may choose to stay. The extent to which staying would be more than an election to remain, and would be a waiver of the breach for all purposes, depends on the circumstances.

I need say no more about waiver in the present case. The assumed facts do not state whether the appellants first learned of the corrupt nature of BCCI after their dismissal on 3 October 1991, or whether they acquired this knowledge earlier, in the interval of three months between the appointment of the provisional liquidators on 5 July 1991 and 3 October 1991. If anything should turn on this, the matter can be investigated further in due course.

In the nature of things, the remedy of treating the conduct as a repudiatory breach, entitling the employee to leave, can only avail an employee who learns of the facts while still employed. If he does not discover the facts while his employment is still continuing, perforce this remedy is not open to him. But this does not mean he has no remedy. In the ordinary course breach of a contractual term entitles the innocent party to damages.

(2) Damages

Can an employee recover damages for breach of the trust and confidence term when he first learns of the breach after he has left the employment? The answer to this question is inextricably bound up with the further question of what damages are recoverable for a breach of this term. In turn, the answer to this further question is inextricably linked with one aspect of the decision in *Addis v Gramophone Co Ltd*.

At first sight it seems almost a contradiction in terms that an employee can suffer recoverable loss if he first learns of the trust-destroying conduct after the employment contract has already ended for other reasons. But of the many forms which trust-destroying conduct may take, some may have continuing adverse financial effects on an employee even after his employment has ceased. In such a case the fact that the employee only learned of the employer's conduct after the employment had ended ought not, in principle, to be a bar to recovery. If it were otherwise, an employer who conceals a breach would be better placed than an employer who does not.

Premature Termination Losses

This proposition calls for elaboration. The starting point is to note that the purpose of the trust and confidence implied term is to facilitate the proper functioning of the contract. If the employer commits a breach of the term, and in consequence the contract comes to an end prematurely, the employee loses the benefits he should have received had the contract run its course until it expired or was duly terminated. In addition to financial benefits such as salary and commission and pension rights, the losses caused by the premature termination of the contract (the premature termination losses) may include other promised benefits, for instance, a course of training, or publicity for an actor or pop star. Prima facie, and subject always to established principles of mitigation and so forth, the dismissed employee can recover damages to compensate him for these promised benefits lost to him in consequence of the premature termination of the contract.

It follows that premature termination losses cannot he attributable to a breach of the trust and confidence term if the contract is terminated for other reasons, for instance, for redundancy or if the employee leaves of his own volition. Since the trust destroying conduct did not bring about the premature termination of the contract, ex hypothesi the employee did not sustain any loss of pay and so forth by reason of the breach of the trust and confidence term. That is the position in the present case.

Lord Steyn made a concurring speech with which Lords Goff, Mackay and Mustill agreed.

[The Court of Appeal had dismissed Malik's appeal on the ground that damages were not recoverable in contract for damage to or loss of an existing reputation, except in certain limited situations which did not apply here. The House unanimously allowed the appeal. This aspect of the case is considered in *Johnson v Unisys Ltd* below, Ch.19].

SALE OF GOODS ACT 1979

(As Amended by the Sale and Supply of Goods Act 1994)

Conditions and Warranties

Stipulations about time

10.—(1) Unless a different intention appears from the terms of the contract, stipulations as to time of payment are not of the essence of a contract of sale.   **16–014**

(2) Whether any other stipulation as to time is or is not of the essence of the contract depends on the terms of the contract.

(3) In a contract of sale "month" prima facie means calendar month.

Part II

When condition to be treated as warranty

11.—(1) This section does not apply to Scotland.

(2) Where a contract of sale is subject to a condition to be fulfilled by the seller, the buyer may waive the condition, or may elect to treat the breach of the condition as a breach of warranty and not as a ground for treating the contract as repudiated.

(3) Whether a stipulation in a contract of sale is a condition, the breach of which may give rise to a right to treat the contract as repudiated, or a warranty, the breach of which may give rise to a claim for damages but not to a right to reject the goods and treat the contract as repudiated, depends in each case on the construction of the contract; and a stipulation may be a condition, though called a warranty in the contract.

(4) Where a contract of sale is not severable and the buyer has accepted the goods or part of them, the breach of a condition to be fulfilled by the seller can only be treated as a breach of warranty, and not as a ground for rejecting the goods and treating the contract as repudiated, unless there is an express or implied term of the contract to that effect.

[(5) Repealed]

(6) Nothing in this section affects a condition or warranty whose fulfilment is excused by law by reason of impossibility or otherwise.

(7) Paragraph 2 of Schedule 1 below applies in relation to a contract made before April 22, 1967 or (in the application of this Act to Northern Ireland) July 28, 1967.

Implied terms about title, etc.

12.—(1) In a contract of sale, other than one to which subsection (3) below applies, there is an implied term on the part of the seller that in the case of a sale he has a right to sell the goods, and in the case of an agreement to sell he will have such a right at the time when the property is to pass.

(2) In a contract of sale, other than one to which subsection (3) below applies, there is also an implied term that—

(a) the goods are free, and will remain free until the time when the property is to pass, from any charge or encumbrance not disclosed or known to the buyer before the contract is made, and

(b) the buyer will enjoy quiet possession of the goods except so far as it may be disturbed by the owner or other person entitled to the benefit of any charge or encumbrance so disclosed or known.

(3) This subsection applies to a contract of sale in the case of which there appears from the contract or is to be inferred from its circumstances an intention that the seller should transfer only such title as he or a third person may have.

(4) In a contract to which subsection (3) above applies there is an implied term that all charges or encumbrances known to the seller and not known to the buyer have been disclosed to the buyer before the contract is made.

(5) In a contract to which subsection (3) above applies there is also an implied term that none of the following will disturb the buyer's quiet possession of the goods, namely—

(a) the seller;

(b) in a case where the parties to the contract intend that the seller should transfer only such title as a third person may have, that person;

(c) anyone claiming through or under the seller or that third person otherwise than under a charge or encumbrance disclosed or known to the buyer before the contract is made.

(5A) As regards England and Wales and Northern Ireland, the term implied by subsection (1) above is a condition and the terms implied by subsections (2), (4) and (5) above are warranties.

(6) Paragraph 3 of Schedule 1 below applies in relation to a contract made before May 18, 1973.

Sale by description

13.—(1) Where there is a contract for the sale of goods by description, there is an implied term that the goods will correspond with the description.

(1A) As regards England and Wales and Northern Ireland, the term implied by subsection (1) above is a condition.

(2) If the sale is by sample as well as by description it is not sufficient that the bulk of the goods corresponds with the sample if the goods do not also correspond with the description.

(3) A sale of goods is not prevented from being a sale by description by reason only that, being exposed for sale or hire, they are selected by the buyer.

(4) Paragraph 4 of Schedule 1 below applies in relation to a contract made before May 18, 1973.

Implied terms about quality or fitness

14.—(1) Except as provided by this section and section 15 below and subject to any other enactment, there is no implied term about the quality or fitness for any particular purpose of goods supplied under a contract of sale.

(2) Where the seller sells goods in the course of a business, there is an implied term that the goods supplied under the contract are of satisfactory quality.

(2A) For the purposes of this Act, goods are of satisfactory quality if they meet the standard that a reasonable person would regard as satisfactory, taking account of any description of the goods, the price (if relevant) and all the other relevant circumstances.

(2B) For the purposes of this Act, the quality of goods includes their state and condition and the following (among others) are in appropriate cases aspects of the quality of goods—

(a) fitness for all the purposes for which goods of the kind in question are commonly supplied,

(b) appearance and finish,

(c) freedom from minor defects,

(d) safety, and

(e) durability.

(2C) The term implied by subsection (2) above does not extend to any matter making the quality of goods unsatisfactory—

(a) which is specifically drawn to the buyer's attention before the contract is made,

(b) where the buyer examines the goods before the contract is made, which that examination ought to reveal, or

(c) in the case of a contract for sale by sample, which would have been apparent on a reasonable examination of the sample.

(3) Where the seller sells goods in the course of a business and the buyer, expressly or by implication, makes known—

    (a) to the seller, or

    (b) where the purchase price or part of it is payable by instalments and the goods were previously sold by a credit-broker to the seller, to that credit-broker,

any particular purpose for which the goods are being bought, there is an implied term that the goods supplied under the contract are reasonably fit for that purpose, whether or not that is a purpose for which such goods are commonly supplied, except where the circumstances show that the buyer does not rely, or that it is unreasonable for him to rely, on the skill or judgment of the seller or credit-broker.

(4) An implied term about quality or fitness for a particular purpose may be annexed to a contract of sale by usage.

(5) The preceding provisions of this section apply to a sale by a person who in the course of a business is acting as agent for another as they apply to a sale by a principal in the course of a business, except where that other is not selling in the course of a business and either the buyer knows that fact or reasonable steps are taken to bring it to the notice of the buyer before the contract is made.

(6) As regards England and Wales and Northern Ireland, the terms implied by subsections (2) and (3) above are conditions.

(7) Paragraph 5 of Schedule 1 below applies in relation to a contract made on or after May 18, 1973 and before the appointed day, and paragraph 6 in relation to one made before May 18, 1973.

(8) In subsection (7) above and paragraph 5 of Schedule 1 below references to the appointed day are to the day appointed for the purposes of those provisions by an order of the Secretary of State made by statutory instrument. . . .

Modification of remedies for breach of condition in non-consumer Cases.

15A.—(1) Where in the case of a contract of sale—

    (a) the buyer would, apart from this subsection, have the right to reject goods by reason of a breach on the part of the seller of a term implied by section 13, 14 or 15 above, but

    (b) the breach is so slight that it would be unreasonable for him to reject them,

then, if the buyer does not deal as consumer, the breach is not to be treated as a breach of condition but may be treated as a breach of warranty.

(2) This section applies unless a contrary intention appears in, or is to be implied from, the contract.

(3) It is for the seller to show that a breach fell within subsection (1)(b) above.

(4) This section does not apply to Scotland.

55.—(1) Where a right, duty or liability would arise under a contract of sale of goods by implication of law, it may (subject to the Unfair Contract Terms Act 1977) be negatived or varied by express agreement, or by the course of dealing between the parties, or by such usage as binds both parties to the contract.

(2) An express term does not negative a term implied by this Act unless inconsistent with it.

(3) Paragraph 11 of Schedule 1 below applies in relation to a contract made on or after May 18, 1973 and before February 1, 1978, and paragraph 12 in relation to one made before May 18, 1973.

Two points should be noted. First, provisions corresponding to ss.12, 13, 14, 15 (Sale by sample) and 55 of the Sale of Goods Act are to be found, for hire-purchase contracts, in the Supply of Goods (Implied Terms) Act 1973 ss.8–12; for other contracts for the transfer of property in goods (such as contracts for work and materials or barter), in the Supply of Goods and Services Act 1982 ss.2–5 and 16; and, for contracts for the hire of goods, in ss.7–10 and 16 of the same Act. Similar provisions for goods exchanged for trading stamps are in the Trading Stamps Act 1964, as amended by the Supply of Goods (Implied Terms) Act 1973. Secondly, following several reviews of the clarity, simplicity, and adequacy of the remedies available to consumers for breach of the statutory implied terms in contracts for the sale of goods (including, Law Commission, *Consumer Remedies for Faulty Goods* [LCCP No 1880 (2008)]), a consolidated regime of rights and remedies is laid out in the Consumer Rights Act 2015. In addition to laying out the standard rights that consumers have in contracts for goods and for services (for example, the well-known right that goods should be of satisfactory quality and that they should be reasonably fit for the purpose; and the right that services should be supplied with reasonable care and skill), the Act makes provision for the rights that consumers have under digital content contracts (concerning, for example, quality, fitness and content matching description). The remedial regime in the Act involves a complex mix of short-term and longer-term rights of rejection, rights to repair or replacement, and a right to a reduction of the price. No doubt, it is too soon to know whether the Act will achieve its objectives but it seems unlikely that the "average consumer", defined by the Act as one who is "reasonably well-informed, observant and circumspect", will be much the wiser.

Points for reflection

16–015   What is the legal position with regard to the implication of terms in the sale or lease of land and houses? At common law, there is no implied term in a contract for the sale or lease of land that the land is fit for any particular purpose: for example, for building upon or for cultivation. Where there is a contract for the sale (or letting) of a piece of land with a house on it there is no implied term that the house is fit for human habitation.

Subject to some statutory exceptions, the maxim caveat emptor is applied rigorously and it is for the buyer or his surveyor to inspect the house and make up his own mind as to its fitness. In the case of a lease of furnished premises, however, there is an implied condition that the premises are fit for human habitation at the beginning of the tenancy; so if the house is infested with bugs (*Smith v Marrable* (1843) 11 M. & W. 5) or if the drainage is out of order (*Wilson v Finch-Hatton* (1877) 2 Ex.D. 336) or if it was recently occupied by a person suffering from pulmonary tuberculosis (*Collins v Hopkins* [1923] 2 K.B. 617), the tenant may rescind the contract. But there is no implied undertaking that the premises will continue fit during the term; so that where a person living in the same house as the demised premises caught scarlet fever after the commencement of the term, this did not constitute a breach of contract by the landlord (*Sarson v Roberts* [1895] 2 Q.B. 395). The reason for the distinction between furnished and unfurnished premises is obscure. Even where, as in *Wilson v Finch-Hatton*, the defect is only in the building and not in the furniture, the tenant's right depends on the fact that the building was furnished.

Where the defect in unfurnished premises is one easily discoverable on inspection it is, perhaps, reasonable that there should be no warranty; but where it is not discoverable the reasonableness of the rule is more doubtful. Professor Glanville Williams suggests (5 M.L.R. 194, 199) that the law ought to be that the condition as to reasonable fitness is implied in leases of both furnished and unfurnished premises, "unless in either case the lessor has reason to believe that the lessee is taking it with his eyes open." At present, there is no implied contractual duty; but, if the vendor is the builder, he may be liable in tort to the purchaser or a visitor to the premises who is injured as a result of negligent construction.

Where the contract is to sell, not a completed house, but a piece of land on which the seller agrees to erect a house, or complete a partially built house, then a term is implied at common law that the house, when completed, will be reasonably fit for human habitation: *Miller v Cannon Hill Estates Ltd*

[1931] 2 K.B. 113; *Jennings v Taverner* [1955] 1 W.L.R. 932. See also the Defective Premises Act 1972, infra.

DEFECTIVE PREMISES ACT 1972

Duty to build dwellings properly

1.—(1) A person taking on work for or in connection with the provision of a dwelling (whether the dwelling is provided by the erection or by the conversion or enlargement of a building) owes a duty— **16–016**

    (a) if the dwelling is provided to the order of any person, to that person; and

    (b) without prejudice to paragraph (a) above, to every person who acquires an interest (whether legal or equitable) in the dwelling;

to see that the work which he takes on is done in a workman-like or, as the case may be, professional manner, with proper materials and so that as regards that work the dwelling will be fit for habitation when completed.

(2) A person who takes on any such work for another on terms that he is to do it in accordance with instructions given by or on behalf of that other shall, to the extent to which he does it properly in accordance with those instructions, be treated for the purposes of this section as discharging the duty imposed on him by subsection (1) above except where he owes a duty to that other to warn him of any defects in the instructions and fails to discharge that duty.

(3) A person shall not be treated for the purposes of subsection (2) above as having given instructions for the doing of work merely because he has agreed to the work being done in a specified manner, with specified materials or to a specified design. . . .

6.—(3) Any term of an agreement which purports to exclude or restrict, or has the effect of excluding or restricting, the operation of any of the provisions of this Act, or any liability arising by virtue of any such provision, shall be void.

LYNCH v THORNE

Court of Appeal [1956] 1 W.L.R. 303; 100 S.J. 225; [1956] 1 All E.R. 744

The plaintiff agreed to purchase from the defendant, a builder, a plot of land with a partially erected **16–017** house on it. The defendant agreed to complete the house in accordance with the plan and specification produced by the defendant and attached to the agreement. The specification provided that the walls were to be nine-inch brick walls. The house was built precisely in accordance with specification, with sound material and good workmanship, but turned out to be unfit for human habitation because rain penetrated the walls. Of three architects who gave evidence one would have expected a nine-inch wall to allow driving rain to penetrate and the other two were not at all surprised that it did. The defendant appealed from the judgment of a county court judge, awarding damages for breach of an implied warranty that the house when completed would be reasonably fit for human habitation.

EVERSHED MR

Where there is a written contract expressly setting forth the bargain between the parties it is, as a general rule, also well established that you only imply terms under the necessity of some compulsion. It was thus that Lord Russel of Killowen expressed himself in *Luxor (Eastbourne) Ltd v Cooper* [above, Ch.3], and similarly Scrutton L.J. in the case to which Mr Garland referred us of *Reigate v Union Manufacturing Co (Ramsbottom) Ltd* [above]. I am, however, prepared to assume for the purposes of this judgment that, whether or not it can be said that any necessity so compels in the case where a vendor contracts to sell the land and also to complete the building, in such a case prima facie there is an implied covenant on the vendor builder's part that he will complete the house so as to make it habitable. Still, such a term prima facie to be implied must, according to well-established principle, always yield to the express letter of the bargain . . .

Here there was an express contract as to the way in which the house was to be completed. The express provisions were exactly complied with, and any variation from them which would have rendered this wall water proof would (as Parker L.J. observed during the course of the argument) have been a deviation from the express language of the contract.

Mr Garland has sought to avoid that result in one of two ways. He has said, first, as I have followed him: even though there is here an express contract precisely prescribing the way in which this work is to be done, still there is an overriding promise or warranty that the edifice, when built in strict accordance with those terms, will be a habitable house. That seems to me to involve an extension of the principle of implied terms for which I can find no authority, and which indeed seems to me to be in direct conflict with the authorities to which I have already referred. Then, secondly, he says—and Mr Garland uses this rather to emphasise and support the main contention already stated: after all, the plaintiff, the unfortunate Mr Lynch, no expert himself in the mysteries of architecture and house building, relied, and the judge found that he relied, upon the skill and judgment of the defendant, the builder. I am unable to derive from that fact the conclusion which commended itself to the judge. Of course, if a skilled person promises to do a job, that is, to produce a particular thing, whether a house or a motor-car or a piece of machinery, and he makes no provision as a matter of bargain as to the precise structure or articles he will create, then it may well be that the buyer of the structure or article relies upon the judgment and skill of the other party to produce that which he says he will produce. But that, after all, is only another way of formulating the existence in such circumstances of an implied warranty. On the other hand, if two parties elect to make a bargain which specifies in precise detail what one of them will do, then, in the absence of some other express provision, it would appear to me to follow that the bargain is that which they have made; and so long as the party doing the work does that which he has contracted to do, that is the extent of his obligation. For the plaintiff obviously one cannot help feeling a great deal of sympathy; but a grown adult man is presumably capable of taking competent skilled advice if he wants to; and if he elects not to do so but to make a bargain in precise terms with someone else, then, though no doubt he does rely upon the skill of the other party in a sense, he only does so in the sense that he assumes that the other party, as was the fact in this case, will do the job he has promised to do competently and, at best, that he believes that the house he is going to build will be a habitable house. But that is far short of importing into the transaction any such overriding condition or warranty as that for which Mr Garland has contended. It would appear almost to involve the result that because the plaintiff elected not to take advice himself, therefore there was some duty of care thrust upon the defendant which should more properly have been borne by somebody engaged by the plaintiff. These considerations seem to me to find no place in the authorities, as I have understood them, and since, as I think, there was here what Romer L.J. has called an express contract as to the way in which the house was to be completed, I can find no room for an implied warranty, the only effect of the operation of which would, so far as I can see, be to create an inconsistency with the express language of the bargain made.

Birkett and Parker L.JJ. delivered concurring judgments.

Appeal Allowed.

Questions

16–018   1. In *Harbutt's Plasticine v Wayne Tank* (below, Ch.19) the defendants supplied machinery using 'Durapipe' in accordance with the specification in the contract. Durapipe was unsuitable for the purpose and the court said that stainless steel pipes should have been specified. It would have been a breach of the express contract to supply stainless steel pipes (per Widgery LJ [1970] 1 Q.B. at 471, and see Cross LJ at p.474). The court held that the defendants were liable for the faulty specification, thus holding that the defendants promised both (i) to do the work according to a particular specification, and (ii) (impliedly) that the work so done would be reasonably fit for the purpose for which it was done. It was impossible to fulfil both promises; work done in accordance with the specification was inevitably unfit for the purpose. Did not the court in *Harbutt* do what it held to be impossible in *Lynch v Thorne*? In *Basildon DC v JE Lesser Ltd* [1985]

1 All E.R. 20 at 27, Judge John Newey distinguished *Lynch v Thorne* "in which the court concentrated its attention on the agreed defective plan and did not consider whether if the builder was its author he was in breach of an implied term either on account of its faults or in failing to warn against the use of it." See also, *Cullinane v British Rema* [1954] Q.B. 292 and *Baldry v Marshall* [1925] 1 K.B. 90 CA.

2. In the latter case the plaintiff asked the defendants, specialists in the sale of Bugatti cars, about the Bugatti eight-cylinder, saying that he wanted a car suitable for touring purposes. The defendants said the Bugatti would be suitable. The plaintiff entered into a contract to buy a Bugatti "fully equipped and finished to standard specification as per the car inspected." A car similar to that inspected and apparently complying with specification was delivered, but it was not suitable for touring purposes. The plaintiff succeeded in an action for breach of s.14(1) of the Sale of Goods Act 1893 (s.14(3) of the 1979 Act, above). Is this case reconcilable with the reasoning in *Lynch v Thorne*?

3. How is the position in *Lynch v Thorne* affected by the Defective Premises Act 1972, above?

WETTERN ELECTRIC LTD v WELSH DEVELOPMENT AGENCY

Queen's Bench Division [1983] Q.B. 796; [1983] 2 W.L.R. 897; [1983] 2 All E.R. 629

The defendants gave the plaintiffs a licence to occupy a factory unit for 12 months. Serious structural defects made the premises unsafe and the plaintiffs had to leave. They claimed damages for loss of production, etc., relying on an implied term that the premises would be reasonably suitable for their purposes.

16–019

JUDGE NEWEY QC

My view is that it is possible for terms as to fitness for purpose to be implied in licences, but that, except perhaps in relation to safety, there are none which the courts imply prima facie in the way that such terms are implied in sale of goods, hire and the like. If any term as to suitability was to be implied in the contractual licence in this case it must, I think, be on the application of the test propounded in *The Moorcock*, as clarified by *Reigate v Union Manufacturing Co (Ramsbotton) Ltd* and by *Liverpool City Council v Irwin*, [above] or because it is necessary to complete an incomplete contract as in *Irwin*, or both . . .

Asking, as *The Moorcock* test requires, whether it was necessary in order to give efficacy to the licence agreement that the defendant should have warranted as set out in (a) of the issue that unit 7 was of sound construction or reasonably fit for the purposes required by the plaintiffs, namely the manufacture of plastics and composite materials, I think that the answer must be Yes. The sole purpose of the licence was to enable the plaintiffs to have accommodation in which to carry on and expand their business while their existing factory was being enlarged. If anyone had said to the plaintiff and the defendants' directors and executives at the time when the licence was being granted, "Will the premises be sound and suitable for the plaintiffs' purposes?" they would assuredly have replied, "Of course; there would be no point in the licence if that were not so." The term was required to make the contract workable.

The defendants' letter of June 21, 1979 which the plaintiffs were required to approve was not unlike the conditions of tenancy which the tenants in *Liverpool City Council v Irwin* were required to sign. In each case the terms provided were one-sided. If I had not thought that a warranty of soundness and suitability for the plaintiffs' purposes was to be implied on the application of *The Moorcock* test, I would have thought that an identical term would have had to be implied in order to complete the contract as the parties must clearly have intended.

16-020   1. Why should a term be implied in a licence when it would not be implied in a lease? Is it not odd that "a mere licensee" should be better off than a lessee?

2. What is the difference between implying a term (i) to give business efficacy to the contract and (ii) 'to complete the contract'? Are not both operations "to complete the contract"?

WILLIAM CORY & SON LTD v LONDON CORPORATION

Court of Appeal [1951] 2 K.B. 476; [1951] 2 T.L.R. 174; 115 J.P. 371; 95 S.J. 465; [1951] 2 All E.R. 85;
[1951] 1 Lloyd's Rep. 475

16-021   London Corporation, acting as sanitary authority under the Public Health (London) Act 1936, made a contract in 1936 with the claimants, barge and lighter owners, for the removal of refuse from the city to Essex. In April 1948 the corporation, acting as port public health authority, sealed by-laws to come into effect on November 1, 1950, which made regulations as to coamings and coverings far more onerous than those contained in the contract of 1936. The claimants alleged that the sealing of this by-law amounted to a repudiation of the contract by anticipatory breach (on which, see Ch.18) and they claimed rescission. The corporation did not dispute that the passing of the by-law made the contract commercially impossible of performance as from November 1, 1950, and the contract was frustrated as from that date. The Court of Appeal, affirming Goddard LCJ, held that there had been no repudiation of the contract by anticipatory breach.

LORD ASQUITH

The claimants argue that it is an implied term of every, or almost every, contract between A and B (and certainly of this contract) that A shall not prevent or disable B from performing the contract and vice versa, and that this was just what the corporation did by the act in question. In general, no doubt, it is true that a term is necessarily implied in any contract whose other terms do not repel the implication, that neither party shall prevent the other from performing it, and that a party so preventing the other is guilty of a breach.

But an act cannot be a breach of a term of the contract—express or implied—(let alone a repudiation) unless the term in question is valid. There can be no breach, if the term in question is illegal, contrary to public policy, or (in the case of a corporation) ultra vires the contracting party, or for some other reason waste paper, because in such a case there is no binding obligation, and only a binding obligation can be violated . . .

If the suggested term were express, it would have to take some such form as this: "True we are charged by Parliament with the duty of making such by-laws with reference to refuse as may be called for from time to time by considerations of public health. But even if these considerations call, and call peremptorily, for a provision not less stringent than that made by the 1948 by-laws, even if a second plague of London is likely to occur, unless such provision is made, we undertake in such an event to neglect or violate our statutory duty so far as the requirement of such a by-law may exceed the requirements imposed by clause 1 of our contract with the claimants." Such a contractual provision would seem to be plainly invalid.

16-022   With regard to performance rendered impossible by a party's own act, consider *Thompson v Asda-MFI Group Plc* [1988] 2 All E.R. 722. There, the plaintiff, as an employee of Wades Ltd, a wholly owned subsidiary of Asda, was eligible to acquire, and did acquire for £1, share options under a scheme established for the benefit of the employees of Asda and its subsidiaries. The rules of the scheme provided that the option should lapse if the holder should cease to hold the office or employment by virtue of which he was eligible to participate in the scheme. In January 1985 Asda sold Wades and informed the plaintiff that, in accordance with the rules of the scheme, his options had lapsed. The plaintiff sued for damages for wrongful repudiation of the share option agreement, relying on the principle that a party to a contract cannot take advantage of his own acts to avoid his obligations, or to defeat the rights of the other party, under the contract. Scott J, having extensively reviewed the authorities held that the action failed:

> ". . . the law is now, in my judgment, as stated by Lord Diplock in *Cheall v Association of Professional Executive Clerical and Computer Staff* [1983] 2 A.C. 180 at 189. In order to attract the principle that a party is not entitled to rely on his own acts as fulfilling a condition subsequent and bringing a contract to an end, the act must be a breach of duty and (per Lord Diplock)—
>
>> '. . . the duty must be one that is owed to the other party under that contract; breach of a duty whether contractual or non-contractual owed to a stranger to the contract does not suffice.'
>
> . . . In this area of the law of contract English law proceeds, in my view, by means of implied terms. If a term can be implied that a party will not do an act that, if done, would prevent the fulfilment of a condition precedent, then the doing of that act will be a breach of contract; if a term can be implied that a party will not do an act that, if done, would cause a condition subsequent to be fulfilled, then the doing of that act will be a breach of contract. But if a suitable term cannot be implied into the contract then in my judgment, the contract will take effect according to its tenor. The condition precedent will fail and the condition subsequent will be fulfilled.
>
> In the present case, Asda was entitled to sell its shareholding in Wades. The sale did not represent any breach of duty owed to the plaintiff. Nor, for that matter, was the sale wrongful in any other sense. A term to the effect that Asda would not sell its Wades shares cannot be implied into the rules. So the rules take effect as they stand . . ."

In the light of this, would it be reasonable to hold that a term was necessarily implied in the share option contract that Asda would not sell Wades because that sale would defeat the option agreement? Cf. *General Publicity Services Ltd v Best's Brewery Ltd* [1951] 2 T.L.R. 875.

If the principle is (as commonly stated) that a person cannot take advantage of his own wrong (as distinct from "his own act") was there any "wrong" by Asda? Cf. *Micklefield v SAC Technology Ltd* [1991] 1 All E.R. 275 Ch.D., where an employee was wrongfully dismissed shortly before becoming entitled to exercise a share option but the principle was nevertheless held to be excluded by the terms of the scheme.

In *Alghussein Establishment v Eton College* [1991] 1 All E.R. 267 the House of Lords found it unnecessary to decide whether there is "an absolute rule of law and morality which prevents a party taking advantage of his own wrong whatever the terms of the contract"; and Lord Jauncey said that for his part he had no doubt that the weight of authority favoured the view that the principle is a rule of construction rather than a rule of law. An agreement with a developer ('the Tenant') provided (cl.4, proviso) that "if for any reason due to the wilful default of the Tenant the development shall remain uncompleted on the 29th day of September 1983 the lease shall forthwith be granted . . .". The Tenant claimed that, if they were in "wilful default", the landlord was bound to grant them a lease. The court suspected that the word "not" had been missed out of the relevant clause but there was no claim for rectification and the word could not be inserted. Reading the contract as a whole and applying the rule of construction, the House held that the Tenant was not entitled to invoke the proviso to cl.4.

Cases of this kind should be compared with those where a contract has become impossible of performance by reason of a frustrating event which is alleged to have been self-induced (see Ch.24).

Why should the nature of the fault differ according to whether the "condition subsequent" is express (as in *Thompson v Asda*) or implied (as in frustration)?

----

2. IMPLIED TERMS: REASONABLE EXPECTATIONS AND CONTEXTUALISM

EQUITABLE LIFE ASSURANCE SOCIETY v HYMAN

House of Lords [2002] 1 AC 408

LORD STEYN

My Lords,

16–023   The need to plan for retirement is for many a high priority. One of the most attractive methods of personal saving in the United Kingdom has been life assurance policies with profits. The tax advantages associated with them have encouraged their use as a method of saving for retirement by the self-employed and those in non-pensionable employment. Provided that policyholders take their retirement benefits in the form of a taxable annuity, they are entitled to tax relief on premiums. It is, however, a fact of life that the level of such retirement benefits is dependent on variable investment returns and annuity rates. This was the contextual scene against which the Society, and other life offices, sold policies containing guaranteed minimum annuity rates. On the face of it this may have seemed to investors an attractive way of reducing uncertainties in retirement.

Against this background a dispute arose out of the decisions of the directors of the Society of calculating final bonuses so as to allocate to a with-profits policyholder, whose policy contains provision for guaranteed annuity rates ("GARs"), a different final bonus at the maturity of the policy, depending on whether the policyholder ("the GAR policyholder") elects:

(a)   to take the annuity to which the guaranteed annuity rates apply under the policy; or

(b)   to take an alternative benefit, whether an annuity with the society, calculated at current rates, or an annuity with some other pension provider, likewise calculated at current rates called "taking benefits in fund form."

The purpose and effect of this practice is to equalise, so far as possible, the total value irrespective of the election the policyholder makes. The ground upon which the society seeks to justify this differential policy is article 65 of the articles of association of the Society which provides that the directors "shall apportion the amount of [the] declared surplus by way of bonus among the holders of participating policies on such principles, and by such methods, as they may from time to time determine." By mid-December 1998 a number of GAR policyholders had complained to the Personal Investment Authority Ombudsman. At the request of the Society he relinquished jurisdiction of the complaints to the High Court. By an originating summons dated 15 January 1999 the Society sought declarations affirming the validity of the decisions of the directors to apply differential bonuses to GAR policyholders for the stated purpose. On 5–7 July 1999 the action came on for trial before Sir Richard Scott V.-C. On 9 September he gave judgment granting declarations affirming the validity of the decisions of the directors. Mr. Hyman, a representative policyholder, appealed to the Court of Appeal. On 21 January 2000 the Court of Appeal allowed the appeal by a 2:1 majority: *Equitable Life Assurance Society v Hyman* [2000] 2 W.L.R. 798.

The final resolution of the dispute will affect many policyholders. As at the beginning of 1999 there were about 90,000 policyholders holding with-profits policies of the Society that contained guaranteed annuity rates. Some 27,000 GAR policies had matured since October 1993. By contrast, there were about 290,000 non-GAR policyholders. Some 20,000 of these policies had matured since October 1993. These figures demonstrate the direct importance of the case. It may, however, be that the question before the House is also of wide commercial importance . . .

It is common ground that a fall in current annuity rates led to the decision of the directors which is under challenge. Before October 1993 the Society's current annuity rates were always above the guaranteed annuity rates. The operation of the GAR provisions produced retirement benefits of a lower value than those which could be obtained by the with-profits policyholders electing to take their benefits in fund form and using those benefits to purchase an annuity at current rates (either from the Society or from another life office). The policyholders therefore elected to take the latter option. In October 1993, as a result of falling interest rates, the GARs began for the first time to exceed the Society's current annuity rates. This position continued until May 1994 when current rates again exceeded GARs. In May 1995 GARs once again began to exceed current rates. Thereafter, GARs continued to exceed current rates by an increasing amount. By September 1998 GARs were approximately 25% higher than current annuity rates. It is an agreed prediction that if and insofar as interest rates remain low, conditions in which GARs are liable to exceed current rates are likely to persist. The fall in market annuity rates to a level below those guaranteed has made the guarantees expensive to honour. The directors' response to the fall in current annuity rates below GARs was to allot different levels of final bonus to policyholders with GARs depending upon whether or not they wished to elect to take benefits in fund form or the contractual annuity calculated by reference to the GARs in their policies. The reasoning behind this decision was apparently that the differential policy achieves fairness between GAR and non-GAR policyholders by equalising the financial result of different forms of policy. This course of action was first adopted in an amending directors' bonus resolution made on 22 December 1993.

The originating summons

Against the background sketched in outline, the Society issued the originating summons already mentioned
. . .

The approach to be adopted

My Lords, much of the argument focused on the minutiae of the policy. The detailed provisions are, as I have pointed out, set out in the judgment of Lord Woolf. It is important, however, as Lord Woolf observed to keep firmly in mind what the real issue is, namely whether the Society is entitled to declare a differential final bonus because the current annuity rates have fallen below the GAR: at p. 807H. Insofar as it is necessary to rule on the effect of the terms of the policy *taken by itself*, I would uphold the submissions of counsel for Mr. Hyman. He put the matter as follows. The terms of the policy require the guaranteed rates in Table B of the policy to be used to calculate the contractual annuity. The effect of the Society's current practice is that they are not. The rates in Table B are conveniently referred to as the "guaranteed" rates. They are the rates which must be used in computing the annuity. The alternative of taking an annuity at the Society's current market rate arises only if the contractual annuity is renounced. What the Society currently does is to start from a capital fund attributable to the policyholder and to calculate an annuity from that capital fund *at current annuity rates*. It then grants that annuity to a policyholder who wishes to take his annuity at the higher contractual rate. This means that the contractual annuity rate is not being used as an element in the calculation of the contractual annuity. The only annuity rate which determines the annuity is the current rate. The only function of the contractual annuity rate is to calculate what the final bonus would have to be in order to justify the payment of no more than an annuity at the current rate. Unless the policyholder has elected to take a current rate annuity this is inconsistent with the rights of the GAR policyholder. While I accept this description of the position under the policy, it does not conclude the matter in favour of GAR policyholders. After all, participating policyholders become members of the Society. Their policies must be read subject to the powers and decisions of the directors in respect of the declaration and payment of final bonuses. If properly construed the powers of the directors under article 65 are wide enough to override the terms of the guaranteed annuity rates, the GAR policyholders can have no valid complaint. On the other hand, if article 65 expressly or impliedly contains a prohibition on directors exercising their discretion to override or undermine guaranteed annuity rates, the Society's practice is invalid. Beyond that there can be no liability on the Society. It follows that there are not two separate principal issues but only one. In the circumstances of the present case one never reaches the question whether the power was exercised for an improper or collateral purpose: see *Howard Smith Ltd v Ampol Petroleum Ltd* [1974] A.C. 821. Everything hinges on the meaning of article 65.

The meaning of article 65

It is necessary to distinguish between the processes of interpretation and implication. The purpose of interpretation is to assign to the language of the text the most appropriate meaning which the words can legitimately bear. The language of article 65(1) contains no relevant express restriction on the powers of the directors. It is impossible to assign to the language of article 65(1) by construction a restriction precluding the directors from overriding GARs. To this extent I would uphold the submissions made on behalf of the Society. The critical question is whether a relevant restriction may be implied into article 65(1). It is certainly not a case in which a term can be implied by law in the sense of incidents impliedly annexed to particular forms of contracts. Such standardised implied terms operate as general default rules: see *Scally v Southern Health and Social*

Services Board [1992] 1 A.C. 294. If a term is to be implied, it could only be a term implied from the language of article 65 read in its particular commercial setting. Such implied terms operate as ad hoc gap fillers. In *Luxor (Eastbourne) Ltd v Cooper* [1941] A.C. 108, 137 Lord Wright explained this distinction as follows:

> "The expression 'implied term' is used in different senses. Sometimes it denotes some term which does not depend on the actual intention of the parties but on a rule of law, such as the terms, warranties or conditions which, if not expressly excluded, the law imports, as for instance under the Sale of Goods Act and the Marine Insurance Act. . . . But a case like the present is different because what it is sought to imply is based on an intention imputed to the parties from their actual circumstances."

It is only an individualised term of the second kind which can arguably arise in the present case. Such a term may be imputed to parties: it is not critically dependent on proof of an actual intention of the parties. The process "is one of construction of the agreement as a whole in its commercial setting": *Banque Bruxelles Lambert S.A. v Eagle Star Insurance Co Ltd* [1997] A.C. 191, 212E, *per* Lord Hoffmann. This principle is sparingly and cautiously used and may never be employed to imply a term in conflict with the express terms of the text. The legal test for the implication of such a term is a standard of strict necessity. This is how I must approach the question whether a term is to be implied into article 65(1) which precludes the directors from adopting a principle which has the effect of overriding or undermining the GARs.

The enquiry is entirely constructional in nature: proceeding from the express terms of article 65, viewed against its objective setting, the question is whether the implication is strictly necessary. My Lords, as counsel for the GAR policyholders observed, final bonuses are not bounty. They are a significant part of the consideration for the premiums paid. And the directors' discretions as to the amount and distribution of bonuses are conferred for the benefit of policyholders. In this context the self-evident commercial object of the inclusion of guaranteed rates in the policy is to protect the policyholder against a fall in market annuity rates by ensuring that if the fall occurs he will be better off than he would have been with market rates. The choice is given to the GAR policyholder and not to the Society. It cannot be seriously doubted that the provision for guaranteed annuity rates was a good selling point in the marketing by the Society of the GAR policies. It is also obvious that it would have been a significant attraction for purchasers of GAR policies. The Society points out that no special charge was made for the inclusion in the policy of GAR provisions. So be it. This factor does not alter the reasonable expectations of the parties. The supposition of the parties must be presumed to have been that the directors would not exercise their discretion in conflict with contractual rights. These are the circumstances in which the directors of the Society resolved upon a differential policy which was designed to deprive the relevant guarantees of any substantial value. In my judgment an implication precluding the use of the directors' discretion in this way is strictly necessary. The implication is essential to give effect to the reasonable expectations of the parties. The stringent test applicable to the implication of terms is satisfied.

In substantial agreement with Lord Woolf M.R. I would hold that the directors were not entitled to adopt a principle of making the final bonuses of GAR policyholders dependent on how they exercised their rights under the policy. In adopting the principle of a differential policy in respect of GAR policyholders the directors acted in breach of article 65(1).

The "ring fencing" Issue

There remains the suggestion by Waller L.J. that the Society could lawfully have declared a differential bonus which varied not according to the form in which the benefits were taken, but according to whether the policy did or did not include GARs. It is agreed that the House should deal with this issue. If the suggestion of Waller L.J. is sound in law, the directors could in that way erode the substantial value of the guarantees by different means. If my conclusion on the principal arguments is right, it must follow that this suggested route is not open to the Society. After all, the object would still be to eliminate as far as possible any benefit attributable to the inclusion of a GAR in the policy. In my view such a device is precluded by the very term which I have held to be implied in article 65. I would hold that the suggested course is not open to the Society.

Disposal of the appeal

I would dismiss the appeal of the Society. Given the terms of this judgment I do not consider that any declaratory relief need be granted by the House.

In a potentially landmark decision in *Attorney General of Belize v Belize Telecom Ltd* (below), the Privy Council (led by Lord Hoffmann) applied new contextualist thinking to transform the basis for the implication of terms. The question in *Belize* was whether two 'special C' directors of Belize

Telecom, appointed by (and subject to removal by) a party with a particular qualifying holding of C shares in the company, retained their position as members of the board of directors when the appointing party no longer had the qualifying share holding. Article 112 of the company's articles of association expressly provided for vacation of a director in the event of bankruptcy, lunacy, and so on; but it made no provision for the circumstances that actually arose. The question was whether a term providing for the vacation of the directorship in these circumstances (i.e. where the appointment was tied to a particular specified shareholding that no longer existed) should be implied. The Supreme Court of Belize held that such a term should be implied; but the Court of Appeal of Belize, applying a test of necessity, ruled that there was no ground for such an implication. Taking a radically different approach, the Privy Council held (at para.21) that "in every case in which it is said that some provision ought to be implied in an instrument, the question for the court is whether such a provision would spell out in express words what the instrument, read against the relevant background, would reasonably be understood to mean." In other words, the contextualist approach to the interpretation of terms that started with the *Investors Compensation* case in 1998 (see Ch.17) now also controlled the implication of terms. Applying this approach, the Privy Council found that, in the particular context, the term argued for should be implied—the tenure of the special C directors made sense only so long as the underlying pattern of shareholding met the qualifying criteria.

ATTORNEY GENERAL OF BELIZE & OTHERS v BELIZE TELECOM LTD & ANOR (BELIZE)

[2009] UKPC 10

LORD HOFFMANN

16. Before discussing in greater detail the reasoning of the Court of Appeal, the Board will make some general observations about the process of implication. The court has no power to improve upon the instrument which it is called upon to construe, whether it be a contract, a statute or articles of association. It cannot introduce terms to make it fairer or more reasonable. It is concerned only to discover what the instrument means. However, that meaning is not necessarily or always what the authors or parties to the document would have intended. It is the meaning which the instrument would convey to a reasonable person having all the background knowledge which would reasonably be available to the audience to whom the instrument is addressed: see *Investors Compensation Scheme Ltd v West Bromwich Building Society* [1998] 1 WLR 896, 912-913. It is this objective meaning which is conventionally called the intention of the parties, or the intention of Parliament, or the intention of whatever person or body was or is deemed to have been the author of the instrument.

17. The question of implication arises when the instrument does not expressly provide for what is to happen when some event occurs. The most usual inference in such a case is that nothing is to happen. If the parties had intended something to happen, the instrument would have said so. Otherwise, the express provisions of the instrument are to continue to operate undisturbed. If the event has caused loss to one or other of the parties, the loss lies where it falls.

18. In some cases, however, the reasonable addressee would understand the instrument to mean something else. He would consider that the only meaning consistent with the other provisions of the instrument, read against the relevant background, is that something is to happen. The event in question is to affect the rights of the parties. The instrument may not have expressly said so, but this is what it must mean. In such a case, it is said that the court implies a term as to what will happen if the event in question occurs. But the implication of the term is not an addition to the instrument. It only spells out what the instrument means.

19. The proposition that the implication of a term is an exercise in the construction of the instrument as a whole is not only a matter of logic (since a court has no power to alter what the instrument means) but also well supported by authority. In *Trollope & Colls Ltd v North West Metropolitan Regional Hospital Board* [1973] 1 WLR 601, 609 Lord Pearson, with whom Lord Guest and Lord Diplock agreed, said:

16-024

"[T]he court does not make a contract for the parties. The court will not even improve the contract which the parties have made for themselves, however desirable the improvement might be. The court's function is to interpret and apply the contract which the parties have made for themselves. If the express terms are perfectly clear and free from ambiguity, there is no choice to be made between different possible meanings: the clear terms must be applied even if the court thinks some other terms would have been more suitable. An unexpressed term can be implied if and only if the court finds that the parties must have intended that term to form part of their contract: it is not enough for the court to find that such a term would have been adopted by the parties as reasonable men if it had been suggested to them: it must have been a term that went without saying, a term necessary to give business efficacy to the contract, a term which, though tacit, formed part of the contract which the parties made for themselves."

20. More recently, in *Equitable Life Assurance Society v Hyman* [2002] 1 AC 408, 459, Lord Steyn said:

"If a term is to be implied, it could only be a term implied from the language of [the instrument] read in its commercial setting."

21. It follows that in every case in which it is said that some provision ought to be implied in an instrument, the question for the court is whether such a provision would spell out in express words what the instrument, read against the relevant background, would reasonably be understood to mean. It will be noticed from Lord Pearson's speech that this question can be reformulated in various ways which a court may find helpful in providing an answer—the implied term must "go without saying", it must be "necessary to give business efficacy to the contract" and so on—but these are not in the Board's opinion to be treated as different or additional tests. There is only one question: is that what the instrument, read as a whole against the relevant background, would reasonably be understood to mean?

22. There are dangers in treating these alternative formulations of the question as if they had a life of their own. Take, for example, the question of whether the implied term is "necessary to give business efficacy" to the contract. That formulation serves to underline two important points. The first, conveyed by the use of the word "business", is that in considering what the instrument would have meant to a reasonable person who had knowledge of the relevant background, one assumes the notional reader will take into account the practical consequences of deciding that it means one thing or the other. In the case of an instrument such as a commercial contract, he will consider whether a different construction would frustrate the apparent business purpose of the parties. That was the basis upon which Equitable *Life Assurance Society v Hyman* [2002] 1 AC 408 was decided. The second, conveyed by the use of the word "necessary", is that it is not enough for a court to consider that the implied term expresses what it would have been reasonable for the parties to agree to. It must be satisfied that it is what the contract actually means.

23. The danger lies, however, in detaching the phrase "necessary to give business efficacy" from the basic process of construction of the instrument. It is frequently the case that a contract may work perfectly well in the sense that both parties can perform their express obligations, but the consequences would contradict what a reasonable person would understand the contract to mean. Lord Steyn made this point in the *Equitable Life* case (at p. 459) when he said that in that case an implication was necessary "to give effect to the reasonable expectations of the parties."

24. The same point had been made many years earlier by Bowen LJ in his well known formulation in *The Moorcock* (1889) 14 PD 64, 68:

"In business transactions such as this, what the law desires to effect by the implication is to give such business efficacy to the transaction as must have been intended at all events by both parties who are business men"

25. Likewise, the requirement that the implied term must "go without saying" is no more than another way of saying that, although the instrument does not expressly say so, that is what a reasonable person would understand it to mean. Any attempt to make more of this requirement runs the risk of diverting attention from the objectivity which informs the whole process of construction into speculation about what the actual parties to the contract or authors (or supposed authors) of the instrument would have thought about the proposed implication. The imaginary conversation with an officious bystander in *Shirlaw v Southern Foundries (1926) Ltd* [1939] 2 KB 206, 227 is celebrated throughout the common law world. Like the phrase "necessary to give business efficacy", it vividly emphasises the need for the court to be satisfied that the proposed implication spells out what the contact would reasonably be understood to mean. But it carries the danger of barren argument over how the actual parties would have reacted to the proposed amendment. That, in the Board's opinion, is

irrelevant. Likewise, it is not necessary that the need for the implied term should be obvious in the sense of being immediately apparent, even upon a superficial consideration of the terms of the contract and the relevant background. The need for an implied term not infrequently arises when the draftsman of a complicated instrument has omitted to make express provision for some event because he has not fully thought through the contingencies which might arise, even though it is obvious after a careful consideration of the express terms and the background that only one answer would be consistent with the rest of the instrument. In such circumstances, the fact that the actual parties might have said to the officious bystander "Could you please explain that again?" does not matter.

26. In *BP Refinery (Westernport) Pty Ltd v Shire of Hastings* (1977) 180 CLR 266, 282-283 Lord Simon of Glaisdale, giving the advice of the majority of the Board, said that it was "not . . . necessary to review exhaustively the authorities on the implication of a term in a contract" but that the following conditions ("which may overlap") must be satisfied:

> "(1) it must be reasonable and equitable; (2) it must be necessary to give business efficacy to the contract, so that no term will be implied if the contract is effective without it; (3) it must be so obvious that 'it goes without saying' (4) it must be capable of clear expression; (5) it must not contradict any express term of the contract"

27. The Board considers that this list is best regarded, not as series of independent tests which must each be surmounted, but rather as a collection of different ways in which judges have tried to express the central idea that the proposed implied term must spell out what the contract actually means, or in which they have explained why they did not think that it did so. The Board has already discussed the significance of "necessary to give business efficacy" and "goes without saying". As for the other formulations, the fact that the proposed implied term would be inequitable or unreasonable, or contradict what the parties have expressly said, or is incapable of clear expression, are all good reasons for saying that a reasonable man would not have understood that to be what the instrument meant.

In paras 21-27 of his speech, Lord Hoffmann repeatedly reduces the many common formulations for the implication of terms to a single test: namely, whether the instrument, read as a whole against the relevant background, would reasonably be understood to have the meaning that the proposed implied terms would give it. This raises the question of whether the classical standard of necessity is still applicable. In the post-*Belize* case-law—for example, in *Mediterranean Salvage and Towage Limited v Seamar Trading and Commerce Inc (The Reborn)* [2009] EWCA Civ 531, *Eastleigh Borough Council v Town Quay Developments Ltd* [2009] EWCA Civ 1391, *Groveholt Ltd v Hughes* [2010] EWCA Civ 538, and to a limited extent in *Consolidated Finance Limited v McCluskey* [2012] EWCA Civ 1325— the courts seemed uncertain how to answer this question. However, a strong signal was given by Arden LJ in *Stena Line v Merchant Navy Ratings Pension Fund Trustees Limited* [2011] EWCA Civ 543, at para.36 (which she repeated in the *Consolidated Finance* case), when she underlined the importance of Lord Hoffmann's speech in improving the coherence of the law:

> "In *Belize*, the Privy Council analysed the case law on the implication of terms and decided that the implication of terms is, in essence, an exercise in interpretation. This development promotes the internal coherence of the law by emphasising the role played by the principles of interpretation not only in the context of the interpretation of documents *simpliciter* but also in the field of the implication of terms. Those principles are the unifying factor. The internal coherence of the law is important because it enables the courts to identify the aims and values that underpin the law and to pursue those values and aims so as to achieve consistency in the structure of the law."

If this is indeed the modern path of the law, then necessity is no longer the standard and, arguably, this is an important step forward.

Question

How should the court proceed when the context gives no clear indication in reflection to the point at issue (compare *Dear v Jackson* [2013] EWCA Civ 89)?

Further reading

Hugh Collins, 'Implied Duty to Give Information During Performance of Contracts' (1992) 55 MLR 556
Richard Hooley, 'Implied Terms after *Belize Telecom*' (2014) 73 CLJ 315

17

INTERPRETATION OF TERMS

LEARNING OBJECTIVES

By the end of this chapter, you should:

- understand that, in the modern law, commercial contracts are to be interpreted "contextually" rather than "literally";
- be familiar with the leading cases on contextual interpretation;
- understand that the interpretation of contracts is where the modern ideas of "contextualism", the protection of "reasonable expectations" and decision-making in line with "commercial realities" and "commercial sense" are most strongly rooted;
- have a view on whether contextualism takes the law in the right direction or whether, as its critics assert, it jeopardises traditional values (especially the value of certainty and calculability).

INTRODUCTION

Given that a high percentage of contractual disputes turn on the interpretation of terms, we might expect there to be a considerable jurisprudence of interpretation of contracts (rather in the way that there is a considerable jurisprudence of statutory interpretation). However, until quite recently, the jurisprudence, such as it was, treated a literal approach as governing: judges simply read contractual terms in a plain, straightforward and natural way—or, at any rate, this was the practice unless terms were interpreted *contra proferentem* as a means of correcting for an imbalance in bargaining power, or to limit a deviation from a reasonably expected performance, or to regulate exception or indemnity clauses, or something of that kind (e.g., see *HIH Casualty and General Insurance Ltd v Chase Manhattan Bank* [2003] UKHL 6, and Ch.21 below).[1]

17–001

In recent years, however, this traditional approach has been swept away by a series of House of Lords' rulings, amply confirmed by the Supreme Court in *Rainy Sky S.A. v Kookmin Bank* [2011] UKSC 50 (below). At the root of this major doctrinal development is the House's decision in *Investors Compensation Scheme Ltd v West Bromwich Building Society* [1998] 1 All E.R. 98, where Lord Hoffmann declared that, in relation to commercial contracts, "contextual" interpretation should be preferred to an abstracted "literalism". Text, so to speak, has been replaced by context (or by text in context); and, as Professor McLauchlan has put it, contextualism "is rapidly becoming the bible for the courts in contract interpretation disputes" (2000) 19 N.Z.U.L.R. 147.

---

[1] Of course, where the provisions of a contract are ambiguous or vague, literalism needs some supplementation, typically by resorting to the "reasonableness" of a particular interpretation. See, e.g., *Gillespie Bros v Roy Bowles Transport Ltd* [1973] Q.B. 400, at 421 (Buckley LJ).

Whereas literalism treats the words of a contractual agreement as having an abstracted life, or meaning, of their own (any context to be supplied being minimal), the fundamental feature of contextualism is that it seeks out the meaning that fits best with the context. In *Mannai Investments Co Ltd v Eagle Star Life Assurance Co Ltd* [1997] 3 All E.R. 352, where Lord Hoffmann prefigured the key aspects of his approach in *Investors*, he sketched his understanding of the relevance of context as follows:

> "The meaning of words, as they would appear in a dictionary, and the effect of their syntactical arrangement, as it would appear in a grammar, is part of the material which we use to understand a speaker's utterance. But it is only a part; another part is our knowledge of the background against which the utterance was made. It is that background which enables us, not only to choose the intended meaning when a word has more than one dictionary meaning but also . . . to understand a speaker's meaning, often without ambiguity, when he has used the wrong words." (at 376)

Context, thus, plays an important corrective part in the process of interpretation. Hence, in *Mannai* itself, where a tenant purported to give notice to determine leases on January 12, 1995, when (to comply strictly with the terms of the leases) the tenant should have specified January 13, 1995, it mattered little why this mistake had been made. The critical point, as the majority ruled in *Mannai*, was that the landlord, receiving the notice, would have realised, *in this particular context*, that the tenant was intending to give notice in accordance with the terms of the lease and that a slip had been made in specifying January 12 rather than January 13.

Similarly, in *Total Gas Marketing Ltd v Arco British Ltd* [1998] 2 Lloyd's Rep. 209, at 221, Lord Steyn (who, along with Lord Hoffmann has been the principal author of the new contextualism) summarised the key idea in the following way: "[questions of interpretation] must be considered in the light of the contractual language, the contractual scheme, the commercial context and the reasonable expectations of the parties."

The case-law and discussion in this chapter is in three sections. In the first section, the focus is on the *Investors Compensation* case itself, the root authority on new contextualist interpretation. The case-law following *Investors Compensation*, leading to the recent Supreme Court decision in *Rainy Sky v Kookmin Bank*, is set out in the second section. In the final section, some stock-taking is undertaken.

1. THE *INVESTORS COMPENSATION* CASE

17–002   The background to the litigation in *Investors Compensation* was quite complex but, stated shortly, the setting was as follows. In the late 1980s, financial advisers in conjunction with a number of building societies marketed so-called "home income plans". Typically, these plans were sold to elderly homeowners who hoped to realise income by mortgaging their homes. Unfortunately, these income plans proved to be disastrous investments as a result of which those who invested in such plans had claims (in negligence and for breach of statutory duty under the Financial Services Act 1986) against their financial advisers as well as possible claims against the building societies and solicitors who had dealt with the mortgages. Where investors had unsatisfied claims against financial advisers belonging to the Financial Intermediaries, Managers and Brokers Regulatory Association (FIMBRA), they could seek compensation under a scheme set up by the FSA 1986. This scheme was administered by a management company, the Investors Compensation Scheme Ltd (the ICS).

The litigation in *Investors* itself focused on the position of a number of investors who, having come to grief after receiving advice about home income plans from a firm called Fisher Prew-Smith, had claimed compensation under the statutory compensation scheme (which generally covered between half and three-quarters of their losses). Under the terms of the compensation scheme, the ICS treated the investors' claims as having been assigned to the company and it commenced action against the relevant building society, the West Bromwich Building Society. However, the investors, too, proceeded against the building society. Faced with competing claims for damages, by the ICS and by the investors, the building society raised the question of whether (and, if so, to what extent) the investors' claims had been assigned to the ICS. In contrast with the legalistic terminology of the standard form claims agreement made between the investors and the ICS, an accompanying explanatory note tried to put matters more straightforwardly. This note, having dealt with the assignment of claims against Fisher Prew-Smith, then (in para.4) said that it was to be agreed that "ICS should be able to use any rights which you now have against anyone else in relation to the claim." This seemingly general assignment of third party claims was mirrored in the claims agreement under which the investors agreed to "assign absolutely to ICS each and every Third Party Claim and the benefit thereof . . ." Section 3(b) of the same claims agreement, however, provided for an exception to the assignment of third party claims. According to s.3(b), the investors did not assign:

> "Any claim (whether sounding in rescission for undue influence or otherwise) that you [ie the investor] have or may have against the West Bromwich Building Society in which you claim an abatement of sums which you would otherwise have to repay to that Society in respect of sums borrowed by you from that Society in connection with the transaction and dealings giving rise to the claim (including interest on any such sums)."

Once s.3(b) was brought into the equation, the question was whether the investors had reserved "any claim" against the building society in which they sought a reduction of the amounts due under the mortgage loans (as the investors submitted), or a narrower range of claims sounding in rescission (as the ICS contended).

At first instance, Evans-Lombe J preferred the interpretation argued for by the ICS. In effect, on this view, a contextually corrected reading of s.3(b) would provide for the narrow reservation of "Any claim sounding in rescission (whether for undue influence or otherwise)". And, the majority of the House, led by Lord Hoffmann, shared this view. However, the Court of Appeal and Lord Lloyd (dissenting in the House of Lords) preferred the investors' reading of s.3(b), holding that the broader reading was both more natural and more plausible.

INVESTORS COMPENSATION SCHEME v WEST BROMWICH BUILDING SOCIETY

[1998] 1 W.L.R. 896; [1998] 1 All E.R. 98 HL

LORD HOFFMANN

My Lords, I start with the construction of Section 3(*b*). Evans-Lombe J. followed his own decision in the earlier **17-003** *Cheltenham and Gloucester* case and I shall first summarise his reasoning and then that of Leggatt L.J. in the Court of Appeal. Evans-Lombe J. focused on the words "any claim (whether sounding in rescission for undue influence or otherwise) that you have . . . against the . . . Society in which you claim an abatement of sums which you would otherwise have to repay to that Society . . ." According to ordinary rules of syntax, "any claim" is the antecedent of "that you have" and the words "or otherwise" in the adjectival parenthesis mean that it does not limit the breadth of "any claim." It follows that claims of any description are reserved as long as they amount to claims for an "abatement" of what is owing to the Society. There are various ways in which the amount owing might be abated but one would be on account of a set-off against the Society's liability for damages. Thus the syntax of the words following "any claim" points to a wide meaning of "abatement" which includes the effect of cross-claims.

Evans-Lombe J. then turned to the background against which the language in the Claim Form had been used. Two features seemed to him odd. First, the building society and the solicitors were the only solvent parties against which the investors were likely to have any claim. As between the building society and the solicitors, the former would certainly be the prime target. It had profited from the Home Income Plans by lending money at enhanced rates of interest on safe security (maximum of 50 per cent. of value) at a time when lenders were falling over themselves to lend as much money as possible. One might expect that I.C.S., having paid compensation to the investor, would take over his claim against the building society. If not, the investor might well be over-compensated. Other provisions of the form, like clause 7, seemed to assume that I.C.S. would do the suing and account to the investor for the net recovery in excess of the compensation paid. But there was no provision for the investor having to pay anything back to I.C.S. This pointed to I.C.S. being entitled to any recoverable damages.

Secondly, the parenthesis seemed very strange against the background of the law. If it was exhaustive, why was "sounding in rescission for undue influence" singled out? What about rescission on other grounds, or claims for breach of statutory or common law duty? It was rather like providing in a lease of a flat that the tenant should not keep "any pets (whether neutered Persian cats or otherwise)." Something seemed to have gone wrong.

Considerations of this kind led the judge to conclude in the *Cheltenham and Gloucester* case that the wider construction of "any claim" and "abatement" led to a "ridiculous commercial result which the parties to the Claim Forms were quite unlikely to have intended" and that it was clear that "the drafting of the second paragraph of Section 3(*b*) was mistaken." He therefore concluded that the meaning intended by the parties was that the investor should retain any claim for an abatement of his debt which arose out of a claim for rescission, whether for undue influence or otherwise. This could be fitted easily into the scheme of the law because the old equitable remedy of rescission included, as part of the restitutio in integrum, an accounting for benefits and indemnity against liabilities which could result in an abatement of the mortgage debt. Such a remedy was quite separate from a common law action for misrepresentation or breach of statutory duty. But the learned judge seems to have had some misgivings about his interpretation: he said that was doing violence to the natural meaning of the words and altering the drafting of the paragraph in a way "more appropriate to rectification than the process of construction." In the present case, however, the judge adhered to his construction and gave some additional reasons.

In the Court of Appeal, Leggatt L.J. said, on the authority of *Alice Through the Looking Glass*, that the judge's interpretation was "not an available meaning of the words." "Any claim (whether sounding in rescission for undue influence or otherwise)" could not mean "Any claim sounding in rescission (whether for undue influence or otherwise)" and that was that. He was unimpressed by the alleged commercial nonsense of the alternative construction.

My Lords, I will say at once that I prefer the approach of the learned judge. But I think I should preface my explanation of my reasons with some general remarks about the principles by which contractual documents are nowadays construed. I do not think that the fundamental change which has overtaken this branch of the law, particularly as a result of the speeches of Lord Wilberforce in *Prenn v Simmonds* [1971] 1 W.L.R. 1381, 1384–1386 and *Reardon Smith Line Ltd v Yngvar Hansen-Tangen* [1976] 1 W.L.R. 989, is always sufficiently appreciated. The result has been, subject to one important exception, to assimilate the way in which such documents are interpreted by judges to the common sense principles by which any serious utterance would be interpreted in ordinary life. Almost all the old intellectual baggage of "legal" interpretation has been discarded. The principles may be summarised as follows:

(1) Interpretation is the ascertainment of the meaning which the document would convey to a reasonable person having all the background knowledge which would reasonably have been available to the parties in the situation in which they were at the time of the contract.

(2) The background was famously referred to by Lord Wilberforce as the "matrix of fact," but this phrase is, if anything, an understated description of what the background may include. Subject to the requirement that it should have been reasonably available to the parties and to the exception to be mentioned next, it includes absolutely anything which would have affected the way in which the language of the document would have been understood by a reasonable man.

(3) The law excludes from the admissible background the previous negotiations of the parties and their declarations of subjective intent. They are admissible only in an action for rectification. The law makes this distinction for reasons of practical policy and, in this respect only, legal interpretation differs from the way we would interpret utterances in ordinary life. The boundaries of this exception are in some respects unclear. But this is not the occasion on which to explore them.

(4) The meaning which a document (or any other utterance) would convey to a reasonable man is not the

same thing as the meaning of its words. The meaning of words is a matter of dictionaries and grammars; the meaning of the document is what the parties using those words against the relevant background would reasonably have been understood to mean. The background may not merely enable the reasonable man to choose between the possible meanings of words which are ambiguous but even (as occasionally happens in ordinary life) to conclude that the parties must, for whatever reason, have used the wrong words or syntax. (see *Mannai Investments Co Ltd v Eagle Star Life Assurance Co Ltd* [1997] 2 W.L.R. 945

(5) The "rule" that words should be given their "natural and ordinary meaning" reflects the common sense proposition that we do not easily accept that people have made linguistic mistakes, particularly in formal documents. On the other hand, if one would nevertheless conclude from the background that something must have gone wrong with the language, the law does not require judges to attribute to the parties an intention which they plainly could not have had. Lord Diplock made this point more vigorously when he said in *The Antaios Compania Neviera S.A. v Salen Rederierna A.B.* 19851 A.C. 191, 201:

"... if detailed semantic and syntactical analysis of words in a commercial contract is going to lead to a conclusion that flouts business commonsense, it must be made to yield to business commonsense."

If one applies these principles, it seems to me that the judge must be right and, as we are dealing with one badly drafted clause which is happily no longer in use, there is little advantage in my repeating his reasons at greater length. The only remark of his which I would respectfully question is when he said that he was "doing violence" to the natural meaning of the words. This is an over-energetic way to describe the process of interpretation. Many people, including politicians, celebrities and Mrs. Malaprop, mangle meanings and syntax but nevertheless communicate tolerably clearly what they are using the words to mean. If anyone is doing violence to natural meanings, it is they rather than their listeners ...

Finally, on this part of the case, I must make some comments upon the judgment of the Court of Appeal. Leggatt L.J. said that his construction was "the natural and ordinary meaning of the words used." I do not think that the concept of natural and ordinary meaning is very helpful when, on any view, the words have not been used in a natural and ordinary way. In a case like this, the court is inevitably engaged in chosing between competing unnatural meanings. Secondly, Leggatt L.J. said that the judge's construction was not an "available meaning" of the words. If this means that judges cannot, short of rectification, decide that the parties must have made mistakes of meaning or syntax, I respectfully think he was wrong. The proposition is not, I would suggest, borne out by his citation from *Alice Through the Looking Glass*. Alice and Humpty Dumpty were agreed that the word "glory" did not mean "a nice knock-down argument." Anyone with a dictionary could see that. Humpty Dumpty's point was that "a nice knock-down argument" was what *he* meant by using the word "glory." He very fairly acknowledged that Alice, as a reasonable young woman, could not have realised this until he told her, but once he had told her, or if, without being expressly told, she could have inferred it from the background, she would have had no difficulty in understanding what he meant ...

My Lords, I think that if the rights of the investor are properly analysed, it will become clear that clause 6 of Section 4 of the Claim Form is a complete and effectual assignment of the whole of the investor's claim to compensation and damages to I.C.S. Section 3(*b*) may well have been unnecessary, but this conclusion seems to me preferable to attributing to the parties an intention, as, in their different ways, the judge and the Court of Appeal have done, to do six impossible things before breakfast and then regretfully saying that they could not be done. I would therefore allow the appeal ...

LORD LLOYD

The question of construction

A useful starting point for ascertaining the meaning of section 3(*b*) of the Claim Form is to put oneself in the position of the ordinary investor to whom the Claim Form is addressed. This was the approach adopted by the House in *Porter v National Union of Journalists* [1980] I.R.L.R. 404. The question in that case concerned the proper construction of the rules of the N.U.J. Lord Diplock said, at p. 407:

"I turn to the interpretation of the relevant rules, bearing in mind that their purpose is to inform the members of the N.U.J. of what rights they acquire and obligations they assume vis-à-vis the union and their fellow members, by becoming and remaining members of it. The readership to which the rules are addressed consists of ordinary working journalists, not judges or lawyers versed in the semantic technicalities of statutory draftsmanship."

The purpose of the Claim Form was to inform the investor in relatively non-technical language what his rights and liabilities were to be on receipt of compensation under the scheme. No doubt the investor would start by reading the Explanatory Note, as he is invited to do before signing section 4. He would notice that the first three paragraphs of the explanatory note are all dealing with his right to claim against the defaulting firm, Fisher Prew-Smith. This would not surprise him. For it was the firm of Fisher Prew-Smith which led him into his disastrous investment. He would well understand that I.C.S. might wish to recover some or all of its outlay from that firm: see paragraph 2 of the explanatory note. He might then turn to section 4 itself. He would at once notice that the heading of section 4 refers specifically to "*Rights against Participant Firm*". Next he would find that the first five paragraphs of section 4 are all dealing with the claim against Fisher Prew-Smith. He would infer that the claim against Fisher Prew-Smith was of primary importance to I.C.S.; otherwise it would hardly have been given such prominence.

Next he would read paragraph 4 of the Explanatory Note. He would note that he was to give up his rights against "anyone else" in relation to the claim (i.e. the claim against Fisher Prew-Smith). The examples given are any rights he might have against a director of Fisher Prew-Smith "or any persons also responsible" for causing his loss. He might or might not at that stage envisage a claim against W.B.B.S.; probably not. Certainly the reference to "other persons" in the context of the directors of Fisher Prew-Smith does not serve to highlight a possible claim against W.B.B.S. If he were in doubt, he would turn to paragraph 6 of section 4, note the definition of Third Party Claim in paragraph 12, and so come to section 3(*b*).

On a quick reading of section 3(*b*) our hypothetical reasonable investor would notice that it excludes from the definition of Third Party Claim any claim which he might have against W.B.B.S. for an "abatement" of sums due under his mortgage. The benefit of any such claim was to enure to him absolutely. In other words it was *not* to pass to I.C.S. under any circumstances. He would probably not pause over the words in brackets, recognising that words in brackets do not ordinarily govern the meaning of the rest of the sentence, especially if the parenthesis starts with the word "whether" and ends with the words "or otherwise." He might well, in passing, understand the words in brackets as being the equivalent of "whether or not sounding in rescission for undue influence." He would then come to "abatement." This would strike him as an unusual word in the context. So he would turn to his lawyer (who is assumed to be at his elbow) and ask him whether abatement has some special meaning in law. His lawyer would reply that abatement has a technical meaning in the law of nuisance, and in connection with contracts for the sale of goods and the provision of services. But otherwise it simply means reduction. It has no technical meaning in relation to rescission. Counsel were unable to point to a single case in which the word had been used in that connection. So the investor would understand that if he still owed money on his mortgage, as would almost always be the case, he would retain the right to sue W.B.B.S. in order to reduce his outstanding debt. Again, this would not surprise him. For in most cases he would not have recovered full compensation from I.C.S., and in some cases nothing like full compensation. Certainly he would wish to have all defences available should W.B.B.S. start proceedings against him for recovery of the loan.

So the position would be that he, the investor, would retain his right to sue W.B.B.S. for a reduction of the mortgage debt, but I.C.S. would obtain the right to sue Fisher Prew-Smith and "Third Parties" other than W.B.B.S., on the understanding that I.C.S. would re-assign those rights on request, should they not be needed: see paragraph 5 of the Explanatory Note. This would strike the investor as fair and reasonable. At this stage our hypothetical investor would feel that he understood his rights and obligations well enough and would sign section 4.

Is there, then, any reason why the courts should not give section 3(*b*), and the Claim Form as a whole, the same meaning as the investor? (I shall refer to this as "the plain meaning.") The objections fall into two groups. The first group of objections relate to the language of section 3(*b*); the second group of objections relate to the legal and commercial consequences of adopting the plain meaning. I suspect that none of these objections would occur to anyone other than a lawyer.

The meaning of the language

The objection to the plain meaning is the inclusion of the words "for undue influence" after "rescission"; for any lawyer would know that there are other grounds on which the investor might claim rescission, for example, on the ground of misrepresentation. Why, therefore, should the draftsman have specifically included one of the grounds on which the investor might claim rescission, but not others?

We do not know the answer to this question. It may be that if one had access to the preliminary drafts of the Claim Form, or to the mind of the draftsman himself, the answer would emerge clearly enough. It may be that a claim for rescission on the ground of undue influence was, for some reason, uppermost in the draftsman's mind; so he put the words in. But we cannot go into the draftsman's mind. We having nothing to go on but the words he has used. The inclusion of undue influence is odd, but not so odd as to obscure the meaning. "Or oth-erwise" must relate back to "whether sounding in rescission." Any other construction would leave "whether" hanging in the air. So "or otherwise" covers claims in contract and tort. It is not limited to other grounds for claiming rescission. The drafting is slovenly. But I do not have any great difficulty with the meaning.

It is said that the plain meaning would make the words in brackets otiose. So indeed it would. But words in brackets are often otiose, especially brackets in the format "(whether . . . or otherwise)." They show that the general words which precede the parenthesis are not limited to any particular kind of claim, but cover all claims so long as they are claims for reduction of sums due.

What are the alternatives? Mr. Vos submits that section 3(b) means "any claims sounding in rescission (whether for undue influence or otherwise) in which you claim an abatement . . ." I agree with Evans-Lombe J. that such a construction does violence to the language. I know of no principle of construction (whether by reference to what Lord Wilberforce said in *Prenn v Simmons* [1971] 1 W.L.R. 1381, 1384–1386 or otherwise) which would enable the court to take words from within the brackets, where they are clearly intended to underline the width of "any claim," and place them outside the brackets where they have the exact opposite effect. As Leggatt L.J. said in the Court of Appeal, such a construction is simply not an available meaning of the words used; and it is, after all, from the words used that one must ascertain what the parties meant. Purposive interpretation of a contract is a useful tool where the purpose can be identified with reasonable certainty. But creative interpretation is another thing altogether. The one must not be allowed to shade into the other.

So with great respect to those taking a different view, I do not regard the present case as raising any question of ambiguity, or of choosing between two possible interpretations. The construction advocated by the inves-tors, though it gives rise to the oddity which I have mentioned, is a permissible construction of the words used. The I.C.S.'s construction is not.

Nor does the I.C.S. construction avoid one of the main objections which is raised against the investors' construction. If "whether sounding in rescission for undue influence or otherwise" is otiose on the investors' construction, so also is "whether for undue influence or otherwise" on the I.C.S.'s construction. Indeed the objection is all the greater, since a claim for rescission would necessarily result in an abatement, if by abate-ment is meant the financial adjustment which takes place in any event on rescission of a contract, and which would in this case be limited (if Mr. Vos's argument is correct) to repayment of W.B.B.S.'s charges and an adjustment in the rate of interest on the loan. On that view, clause 3(b) would be an elaborate way of saying very little indeed.

The legal and commercial consequences

If Evans-Lombe J. is right that the investors' construction is the more natural meaning of section 3(b) and if, a fortiori, the Court of Appeal is right that the I.C.S.'s construction is not even a possible meaning of the language used, then it would take a very strong case indeed before I would reject the former meaning in favour of the latter. As Lord Mustill said in *Charter Reinsurance Co Ltd v Fagan* [1996] 2 W.L.R. 726, 758–759:

> "If . . . the words 'actually paid' can only as a matter of language and context mean what the syndicates maintain, I would hesitate long before giving them any other meaning, just because the result would be extraordinary."

What then are the consequences of the investors' construction which are said to be so extraordinary, or so "very unreasonable" (the expression used by Lord Reid in *Wickman Machine Tool Sales Ltd v L. Schuler A.G.* [1974] A.C. 235, 251), and which Evans-Lombe J. described as producing a ridiculous result? I start with the commercial consequences. It is said that I.C.S. would have wanted to take over the investors' claim against W.B.B.S., as well as their claim against Fisher Prew-Smith, since W.B.B.S. would be worth suing, whereas Fisher Prew-Smith, being insolvent, would not. Secondly it is said that the investors would have little incen-tive to sue W.B.B.S., once they had received compensation from I.C.S. A third objection was that the investors would not be entitled to claim on their own behalf, once they had accepted compensation. This third objection is now accepted as being wrong in law, and is no longer relied on.

By way of answer to the second objection, Mr. Strauss pointed out that since, in the generality of cases, investors had received only between half and three-quarters of their losses by way of compensation, they would have every incentive to look elsewhere for a remedy. Over 500 investors have in fact done so, by bringing claims against Cheltenham and Gloucester, W.B.B.S. and other building societies. So it does not look as if the investors have been shy or backward in pursuing their rights.

As to the first objection, the structure and language of the Claim Form, and the express provisions of section 54(2)(e) of the Act, do not suggest that claims against participant firms were expected to be valueless. (It is common ground that "person" in section 54(2)(e) means, and means only, the participant firm.) It is true that Fisher Prew-Smith are in liquidation. But other participant firms are not. Moreover the building societies are not the only third parties likely to be worth suing. It must not be forgotten that I.C.S. has brought proceedings against 197 firms of solvent solicitors. In any event it is not for the court to speculate on what the parties would have wanted. I accept, of course, as Mr. Vos observed, that I.C.S. is not a charity. But it is far from being an ordinary commercial organisation. Its raison d'etre is the compensation of investors.

Even so, if I.C.S. had undertaken to compensate the investors in full then one might perhaps have expected I.C.S. to insist on a transfer of all third party rights. But that is not what has happened. It is common ground that investors have retained rights of some kind against W.B.B.S. That being so it would seem to me as likely as not, commercially, that the agreement would provide for the investors to retain the whole of their rights against W.B.B.S., including the right to claim damages in reduction of their loans. Such a consequence cannot be regarded as "ridiculous" or "extraordinary" or "very unreasonable."

Various other so-called anomalies are mentioned in Mr. Vos's written submissions by way of reply. For example, a conscientious investor who had used his compensation to pay off his mortgage would lose his rights against W.B.B.S., since there would then be no sum to be abated, whereas a less conscientious investor who had spent his compensation on a holiday would retain his rights in full. I agree with Mr. Vos that there are theoretical anomalies on the investors' construction, though how likely they would be to arise in practice is another question. Where I disagree with him is in his evaluation of these anomalies. In my judgment they fall far short of the sort of absurdity which would justify the rejection of what I have called the plain meaning of section 3(b). They do not prompt the comment "whatever else the parties may have had in mind, they cannot have meant *that*."

As for the legal consequences, the difficulties are all on the other side. Both Evans-Lombe J. and the Court of Appeal were of the view that the splitting of mutually inconsistent remedies in respect of a single cause of action against W.B.B.S. meant that the purported assignment was void for uncertainty, as well as being contrary to public policy. My noble and learned friend, Lord Hoffmann has found a way round that difficulty. But the difficulty does not arise at all on the investors' construction. If the whole of the investors' rights against W.B.B.S. are retained, the question of splitting remedies, and "dividing the indivisible" simply does not arise.

For the above reasons I would hold that on the true construction of the Claim Form the investors' claims against W.B.B.S. have been retained by the investors, and have not been assigned to I.C.S. It follows that the question whether if there had been an assignment, it would have been valid or invalid does not call for an answer. In the result, therefore, I would uphold the reasoning of the Court of Appeal and dismiss the main appeal.

----

2. After Investors Compensation

17-004   The disagreements, in both *Mannai Investment* and *Investors Compensation*, hint at the difficulties that courts might have in applying a contextual approach to particular sets of facts. Particular contexts might speak too little or too much to the interpretive point at issue. We see precisely this problem in *Bank of Credit and Commerce International SA v Ali* (below).

In *BCCI v Ali*, the background was that, following reorganisation by the bank, a number of employees (including one Mr Naeem) were made redundant. Mr Naeem's basic redundancy package purported to settle in full all known claims arising from the termination of his employment. However, the bank offered Mr Naeem the option of receiving a further payment, equivalent to one month's salary of £2,772, if he would sign a general release (on ACAS form COT 3). Having talked this through with an officer from ACAS, Mr Naeem duly signed in July 1990. About one year later, application was made to wind up the bank and it became clear that the business had been carried on in a dishonest and corrupt manner. In the wake of the collapse of the bank, one of the questions to arise was whether the bank's ex-employees might be entitled to so-called stigma damages; but it was not until 1998 that the House of Lords ruled that such claims were sustainable in principle (see *Mahmud v Bank of Credit and Commerce International SA* [1998] A.C. 20). In turn, this gave rise to the question whether, if Mr Naeem were now to seek stigma damages, his claim would be barred by the general release that he had signed eight years earlier and at a time when a claim for stigma damages was not, as such, known to English law.

Two principal questions arose for decision: (1) whether, contextually interpreted, the terms of the general release covered a claim (such as that for stigma damages) that was unknown to the law at the time of the agreement; and (2) whether, if the general release applied to stigma damages, it would be unfair or unconscionable for the bank to rely on it. On the first question, their Lordships were divided, holding 4 to 1 (with Lord Hoffmann dissenting) that the release properly interpreted did not bar such an unknown claim. On the second question, which was still a live issue for Lord Hoffmann, his Lordship held that there was no reason why the bank should not rely on the release for which they had bargained. In the extracts which follow (from Lord Nicholls' majority speech and from Lord Hoffmann's dissenting speech), it is largely the first issue that is discussed.

BANK OF CREDIT AND COMMERCE INTERNATIONAL SA (IN COMPULSORY LIQUIDATION) v MUNAWAR ALI, SULTANA RUNI KHAN AND OTHERS

House of Lords [2001] UKHL 8

LORD NICHOLLS OF BIRKENHEAD

22. This appeal raises a question of interpretation of a general release. By a general release I mean an agreement containing widely drawn general words releasing all claims one party may have against the other. The release given by Mr Naeem was of this character. Mr Naeem accepted a payment from BCCI "in full and final settlement of all or any claims . . . of whatsoever nature that exist or may exist".

23. The circumstances in which this general release was given are typical. General releases are often entered into when parties are settling a dispute which has arisen between them, or when a relationship between them, such as employment or partnership, has come to an end. They want to wipe the slate clean. Likewise, the problem which has arisen in this case is typical. The problem concerns a claim which subsequently came to light but whose existence was not known or suspected by either party at the time the release was given. The emergence of this unsuspected claim gives rise to a question which has confronted the courts on many occasions. The question is whether the context in which the general release was given is apt to cut down the apparently all-embracing scope of the words of the release.

24. In times past the common law courts and the Court of Chancery differed in their approach to this question. In particular, the Court of Chancery was readier to admit extrinsic evidence as an aid to interpretation than were the common law courts. Sir Frederick Pollock summarised the matter thus in the first edition of his work *Principles of Contract* (1876), p 414:

"We have seen that courts of law as well as courts of equity have assumed a power to put a restricted construction on general words when it appears on the face of the instrument that it cannot have been the real intention of the parties that they should be taken in their apparent general sense. But courts of equity will do the like if the same conviction can be arrived at by evidence external to the instrument. . . . This jurisdiction is exercised chiefly in dealing with releases."

25. This difference in approach is now a matter of historic interest and no more. It is part of the history of the law of interpretation, described vividly in *Wigmore on Evidence* (1981), vol 9, paragraph 2461, as "the history of progress from a stiff and superstitious formalism to a flexible rationalism". Today there is no question of a document having a legal interpretation as distinct from an equitable interpretation.

26. Further, there is no room today for the application of any special "rules" of interpretation in the case of general releases. There is no room for any special rules because there is now no occasion for them. A general release is a term in a contract. The meaning to be given to the words used in a contract is the meaning which ought reasonably to be ascribed to those words having due regard to the purpose of the contract and the circumstances in which the contract was made. This general principle is as much applicable to a general release as to any other contractual term. Why ever should it not be?

17–005

27. That said, the typical problem, as I have described it, which arises regarding general releases poses a particular difficulty of its own. Courts are accustomed to deciding how an agreement should be interpreted and applied when unforeseen circumstances arise, for which the agreement has made no provision. That is not the problem which typically arises regarding a general release. The wording of a general release and the context in which it was given commonly make plain that the parties intended that the release should not be confined to known claims. On the contrary, part of the object was that the release should extend to any claims which might later come to light. The parties wanted to achieve finality. When, therefore, a claim whose existence was not appreciated does come to light, on the face of the general words of the release and consistently with the purpose for which the release was given the release is applicable. The mere fact that the parties were unaware of the particular claim is not a reason for excluding it from the scope of the release. The risk that further claims might later emerge was a risk the person giving the release took upon himself. It was against this very risk that the release was intended to protect the person in whose favour the release was made. For instance, a mutual general release on a settlement of final partnership accounts might well preclude an erstwhile partner from bringing a claim if it subsequently came to light that inadvertently his share of profits had been understated in the agreed accounts.

28. This approach, however, should not be pressed too far. It does not mean that once the possibility of further claims has been foreseen, a newly emergent claim will always be regarded as caught by a general release, whatever the circumstances in which it arises and whatever its subject matter may be. However widely drawn the language, the circumstances in which the release was given may suggest, and frequently they do suggest, that the parties intended or, more precisely, the parties are reasonably to be taken to have intended, that the release should apply only to claims, known or unknown, relating to a particular subject matter. The court has to consider, therefore, what was the type of claims at which the release was directed. For instance, depending on the circumstances, a mutual general release on a settlement of final partnership accounts might properly be interpreted as confined to claims arising in connection with the partnership business. It could not reasonably be taken to preclude a claim if it later came to light that encroaching tree roots from one partner's property had undermined the foundations of his neighbouring partner's house. Echoing judicial language used in the past, that would be regarded as outside the "contemplation" of the parties at the time the release was entered into, not because it was an unknown claim, but because it related to a subject matter which was not "under consideration".

29. This approach, which is an orthodox application of the ordinary principles of interpretation, is now well established. Over the years different judges have used different language when referring to what is now commonly described as the context, or the matrix of facts, in which a contract was made. But, although expressed in different words, the constant theme is that the scope of general words of a release depends upon the context furnished by the surrounding circumstances in which the release was given. The generality of the wording has no greater reach than this context indicates.

30. The cases are legion. A few well known examples will suffice. As long ago as 1750 Lord Hardwicke L.C. said that it was common in equity to restrain a general release to "what was under consideration at the time of giving it": see *Cole v Gibson*, 1 VesSen 503, 507. A century later, in 1839, Lord Langdale M.R. said that the _general words of a release are to be restrained by "the contract and the intention of the parties, that contract and intention appearing by the deed itself or from any other proper evidence that may be adduced upon the occasion": see *Lindo v Lindo*, 1 Beav 496, 506. In 1870 Lord Westbury said that the "general words in a release are limited always to that thing or those things which were specially in the contemplation of the parties at the time when the release was given": see *Directors of the London and South Western Railway Co v Blackmore*, LR 4 HL 610, 623. In 1926 Bankes L.J. emphasised the "necessity of ascertaining what the parties were contracting about before the court can determine the true meaning" of a release: see *Richmond v Savill* [1926] 2 KB 530, 540. In 1954 Dixon C. J., Fullagar, Kitto and Taylor J. J., in a joint judgment in the High Court of Australia, said that the general words of a release are confined to "the true purpose of the transaction ascertained from the scope of the instrument and the external circumstances": see *Grant v John Grant & Sons Pty Ltd*, 91 CLR 112, 130.

31. This judgment in the High Court of Australia in *Grant's* case contained also the observation that the surrounding circumstances to be taken into account include the state of knowledge of the respective parties concerning the existence, character and extent of the liability in question and "the actual intention of the releasor" For many years the accepted wisdom has been that evidence of the actual intention of the parties is not admissible on the interpretation of a written agreement, although such evidence is admissible for other purposes, for example, on a claim for rectification. In *Investors Compensation Scheme Ltd v West Bromwich Building Society* [1998] 1 WLR 896, 913, my noble and learned friend Lord Hoffmann pointed out that the exclusion from evidence of the previous negotiations of the parties and their declarations of subjective intent is for reasons of

practical policy. He added that the boundaries of this exception are in some respects unclear. Whether these reasons of practical policy still hold good today in all circumstances has become increasingly the subject of debate in recent years. The debate is still continuing: see the recent observations of Thomas J. in the Court of Appeal of New Zealand in paragraphs 59 to 95 of his judgment in *Yoshimoto v Canterbury Golf International Ltd* (27 November 2000). This is not the moment to pursue this topic, important though it is, because the point does not arise on this appeal. I desire, however, to keep the point open for careful consideration on a future occasion.

Sharp practice
32. Thus far I have been considering the case where both parties were unaware of a claim which subsequently came to light. Materially different is the case where the party to whom the release was given knew that the other party had or might have a claim and knew also that the other party was ignorant of this. In some circumstances seeking and taking a general release in such a case, without disclosing the existence of the claim or possible claim, could be unacceptable sharp practice. When this is so, the law would be defective if it did not provide a remedy.

33. That is not the present case. Although BCCI through its officers may be fixed with knowledge of the corrupt activities taking place within the bank, officers of BCCI and, through them, BCCI itself were not aware that these activities might give bank employees a claim for damages for breach of their contracts of employment. In *Mahmud v Bank of Credit and Commerce International SA* [1998] AC 20 the House developed or, put more bluntly, changed the law. The House decided that, as a matter of law, corrupt and dishonest activities by an employer are capable of giving rise to a claim in damages. But that decision was in June 1997, seven years after Mr Naeem had signed his release form. In these circumstances there can be no question of BCCI having indulged in anything approaching sharp practice in this case. This being so, I prefer to leave discussion of the route by which the law provides a remedy where there has been sharp practice to a case where that issue arises for decision. That there is a remedy in such cases I do not for one moment doubt.

The present case
34. I turn to the interpretation of the release signed by Mr Naeem. Clearly, BCCI and Mr Naeem are to be regarded as having intended not to confine the release signed by Mr Naeem to known claims. Specific payments were made in settlement in full of all known claims. Mr Naeem's redundancy package comprised four weeks' pay, an ex gratia payment equal to two weeks' pay, three weeks' pay in lieu of notice, and statutory redundancy pay. These items totalled £7,138. An additional amount, equal to a further one month's pay, £2,772, was paid in exchange for his signing the general release (ACAS form COT 3). Plainly, the general release was intended to "mop up" any other claims which Mr Naeem might have. BCCI was making a specific additional payment in order to be rid of the possibility of having to face any further claims from Mr Naeem. Unfair dismissal is the most obvious example. The release specifically mentioned any application Mr Naeem could make to the industrial tribunal. But the release is not confined to a claim for unfair dismissal. It would include also matters such as a claim for wrongful dismissal.

35. Equally clearly the release is confined to claims arising out of the employment relationship. The release cannot reasonably be regarded as embracing any claim the employee might have as a depositor or borrower. I am inclined to think that the release is to be construed even more narrowly as restricted to claims arising out of the *ending* of the employment relationship. What if it later came to light that due to a clerical error Mr Naeem had been significantly underpaid while employed? It would be surprising if Mr Naeem could not pursue such a claim. Whether this is so or not, I consider these parties are to be taken to have contracted on the basis of the law as it then stood. To my mind there is something inherently unattractive in treating these parties as having intended to include within the release a claim which, *as a matter of law*, did not then exist and whose existence could not then have been foreseen. This employee signed an informal release when he lost his job, in return for an additional month's pay. The ambit of the release should be kept within reasonable bounds. Mr Naeem cannot reasonably be regarded as having taken upon himself the risk of a subsequent retrospective change in the law. A claim arising out of such a change cannot be regarded as having been within the contemplation of the parties. I too would dismiss this appeal.

LORD HOFFMANN

36. . . . There are two issues in this case. First, does the respondent's claim fall within the description of claims which he agreed to release? If it does, then the second point is whether in the circumstances BCCI is entitled to rely upon the agreement.

37. . . . [the] first issue raises an ordinary question of construction. What would a reasonable person have understood the parties to mean by using the language of the document against all the background which would reasonably have been available to them at time? . . .

38. The language of the document is very wide. The impression it conveys is that the draftsman meant business. He has gone to some trouble to avoid leaving anything out. He uses traditional style: pairs of words like "full and final settlement", "all or any claims", "that exist or may exist" and phrases like "whether under statute, common law or in equity" and "of whatsoever nature". Admittedly, he could have gone further. *Tudor Grange Holdings Ltd v Citibank NA* [1992] Ch 53, 57 contains an even more elaborate release and I have seen American documents in which the release covers an entire page. But most people in this country would regard this as overkill. The modern English tradition, while still erring on the side of caution, is to avoid the grosser excesses of verbiage and trust to the judges to use common sense to get the message. I think that this tendency should be encouraged. So I think that anyone who was simply reading the document without preconceptions would accept that the draftsman was not leaving deliberate gaps. It does not however follow that the language was to be read completely literally. There may be limitations in scope to be inferred from the background, limitations from context which the draftsman may have thought too obvious to mention. But that is a different matter from saying that he did not use enough words.

39. The background is however very important. I should in passing say that when, in *Investors Compensation Scheme Ltd v West Bromwich Building Society* [1998] 1 WLR 896, 913, I said that the admissible background included "absolutely anything which would have affected the way in which the language of the document would have been understood by a reasonable man", I did not think it necessary to emphasise that I meant anything which a reasonable man would have regarded as *relevant*. I was merely saying that there is no conceptual limit to what can be regarded as background. It is not, for example, confined to the factual background but can include the state of the law (as in cases in which one takes into account that the parties are unlikely to have intended to agree to something unlawful or legally ineffective) or proved common assumptions which were in fact quite mistaken. But the primary source for understanding what the parties meant is their language interpreted in accordance with conventional usage: "we do not easily accept that people have made linguistic mistakes, particularly in formal documents". I was certainly not encouraging a trawl through "background" which could not have made a reasonable person think that the parties must have departed from conventional usage.

40. What is the relevant background in this case? To start with, there are three matters to which I attach considerable importance. First, there was no dispute between the parties. No doubt Mr Naeem and his union were opposed to the whole idea of making him redundant. But, given that he was being made redundant, there was no dispute about the legal consequences. Mr Naeem had a claim to salary in lieu of notice and redundancy pay which BCCI did not contest. Secondly, there was no element of compromise. All his claims known to the parties were paid in full; in fact, more than in full because there was an ex gratia increase over the statutory redundancy pay. Thirdly, the release was not simply in consideration of a settlement or compromise. It was not, as often happens, a mere ancillary tidying up. BCCI paid a separate consideration of some £2,700 specifically for the release.

41. The absence of a dispute is important because most of the authorities on the construction of releases concern documents which were intended to settle disputes. In such a case, the scope of the dispute provides a limiting background context to the document. It is easy to infer that although the parties used very wide language—"all claims" and so forth—they meant all claims arising out of the matters in dispute. It would go without saying that they were not intending to include claims of an altogether different character. A good example is the decision of the House of Lords in *Directory of the London and South Western Railway Co v Blackmore*, LR 4 HL 610. In 1861 the railway company used its statutory powers to buy some of Mr Blackmore's land for railway purposes. In 1864 they had a dispute over their boundary. This was settled by an agreement that he should build a wall to be maintained at their joint expense. The agreement included a release of claims in general terms. In 1866 the railway company decided that it did not need the land it had taken and proposed to sell it as surplus land. Mr Blackmore claimed that, as the person from whom it had been taken, he had a statutory right of pre-emption under the Land Clauses Consolidation Act 1845. The railway company argued (rather faintly, it would seem, by their second counsel) that it fell within the description of claims which he surrendered when settling the boundary dispute. Lord Hatherley L.C., who gave the leading judgment, did not even bother to address this point. Lord Westbury picked it up. He said, at p 623:

"The general words in a release are limited always to that thing or those things which were specially in the contemplation of the parties at the time when the release was given."

42. This is rather a sweeping statement. It is almost always dangerous to say "always". But, in cases of a release given in connection with the settlement of a dispute, it is a fair generalisation.

43. There may also be cases in which there is no dispute but the parties enter into a compromise of undisputed claims. This happens when an insolvent debtor enters into a composition with his creditors. In such a case, an ancillary release is also likely to be construed as releasing any further claim on the debts which are being compromised but not as extending to claims which did not fall within the terms of the composition. The best example is *Lyall v Edwards*, 6 H & N 337. Edwards and Matthie were East India and colonial brokers who suspended payment and entered into a compromise with their creditors, including the plaintiffs. The creditors agreed by a deed of composition that the assets of the partnership should be realised, a dividend paid to creditors and the defendants then given a release in general terms. After executing the deed, the plaintiffs found that they had a claim for the conversion of 22 chests of indigo of which they had not known and for which they had not claimed in the composition. The Court of Exchequer held that a replication in these terms was a good answer to the plea of release. Martin B. said, at p 347:

"The replication is founded on the equitable doctrine that if a release is given for a particular purpose, and it is understood by the parties that its operation is to be limited to that purpose, but it turns out that the terms of the release are more extensive than was intended, a court of equity will interfere and confine it to that which was in the contemplation of the parties at the time it was executed."

44. I shall have to come back later to the question of why Martin B. calls this an "equitable doctrine" rather than an illustration of the general proposition that language always takes meaning from context. It requires a certain amount of historical explanation. But nowadays, if the context satisfies the court that a release was "understood by the parties . . . to be limited" in some way, then that, as an ordinary matter of construction, is what the document means. The decision in *Lyall v Edwards* makes perfectly good sense as an example of contextual construction.

45. In the present case, however, there is no context of a particular dispute being settled or particular claims being compromised. So the generalisations in *Directors of the London and South Western Railway Co v Blackmore*, (1870) LR 4 HL 610 and *Lyall v Edwards*, 6 H & N 337 are of little assistance. We are dealing with similar forms of words, but in a radically different situation. Nevertheless, although there was no dispute or compromise, that does not mean that there was no context whatever. The parties were making an agreement for the termination of Mr Naeem's employment. One would therefore expect that when the release referred to all his claims, it meant claims arising out of the employment relationship. He agreed that he would not make any claims in his capacity as a former employee. I doubt, however, whether a reasonable person would have understood the parties to be dealing with claims he might coincidentally have in some other capacity—for example, as a depositor with the bank.

46. It may also be that a reasonable person would regard the release as applicable only to *financial* claims and not, for example, to claims for personal injury. This is a rather more difficult question, on which there is something to be said on both sides, and I shall return to it later. But what seems to me quite impossible is to exclude financial claims arising out of the employment relationship on the grounds that they were unknown, or not within the specific contemplation of the parties. Not only is there no context of compromise or dispute which suggests this, but there is an extremely strong indication which points the other way.

47. The counter-indication, as it seems to me, is the fact that after payment of the known claims in full, BCCI paid £2,772.50 specifically for the release in the COT-3 form. This may be taken as representative of the sums paid to the 900 employees who were made redundant. So BCCI paid some £2.5m for the releases. The reasonable man is bound to ask himself: what was it paying for? If it was intended that the release should be confined to claims within the contemplation of the parties, it was getting no consideration whatever. Why did it bother to insist on the forms being signed? In my view, one of the first principles of construction is to try to give some business sense to the agreement. To exclude unknown claims makes the release nonsensical. Nor do I think it is realistic to attribute to the parties an intention to make fine distinctions between different kinds of unknown claims; for example, between those which were conceivable but not conceived of and those which (perhaps because of what was then thought to be the law) were not even conceivable. To regard such claims as nevertheless included in the class of those released does not seem to me extravagant. On the contrary, the more improbable the claim, the more likely it is that the reasonable employee would be willing to part with it for ready money. And the construction gives effect to the object of BCCI, which must have been to draw a final line under the employment relationship.

48. For these reasons, I think that Miss Booth, who appeared for Mr Naeem before Lightman J. [1999] ICR

1068, was realistic and right to concede that as a matter of construction her client's claim fell within the terms of the release. Lightman J. proceeded on this assumption . . .

63. Before leaving the question of construction, I must deal with some subsidiary arguments which Mr Allen made. The first was what I might call the all-or-nothing argument. If I have understood it correctly, it went as follows. BCCI's construction depends upon a literal reading of the release clause. It involves reading any claim to mean absolutely any claim whatever. But BCCI concedes that context would almost certainly limit the clause to claims arising out of the employment relationship. In so doing, they have sold the pass and allowed Mr Naeem to put forward a different principle of limitation for which the context provides no support—indeed, which the separate consideration for the release actually contradicts—namely that it does not apply to claims which were unknown to the parties, or at any rate those which were entirely unknown or unimaginable. A similar argument is advanced on the basis of the concession that it was arguable that the release did not apply to personal injury claims. I find it difficult to deal with this argument because it seems to me so entirely irrational.

64. The following conversation may be imagined. A motorist is stopped by a park warden driving down a road which is signposted "No cars allowed". He says "But I am driving a green car". The warden points out that it is nevertheless a car. The motorist says "But the words cannot be read literally. Do you suggest that they forbid children's toy cars?" The warden concedes that the context suggests a prohibition for the protection of pedestrians frequenting the park and that it does not apply to toy cars. "And what about police cars going to an emergency? Surely there is an implied exception for emergency vehicles?" "Yes, perhaps there is". "Well then" says the motorist "if it cannot be read literally, why should it apply to green cars?"

65. The fact is that BCCI is not contending for a literal meaning. It is contending for a contextual meaning, but submitting that while the context excludes claims outside the employee relationship, it includes unknown claims. As for personal injuries, I agree with Mr Jeans who appeared for BCCI that this is a debatable area. Mr Allen, who has considerable experience of the use of the COT-3 form, told us that in industries in which long-term industrial injury claims are common, it is customary to have a specific clause excluding personal injury claims from the release. This would suggest that the parties otherwise expect that they would or might be caught by the general words. I am not sure that Mr Naeem would have been entitled to bring a claim after leaving his employment on the ground that he was suffering from repetitive strain injury caused by his use of the BCCI computer. BCCI might be entitled to say that it paid the extra money in return for not having to hear from Mr Naeem in his capacity as employee again. If, however, a court decided that it did not come within the class of claims released, it would not be on the ground that it had not been known at the time to the parties. On the contrary, one would be much more likely to conclude that the parties intended to exclude such a claim from the release if it was known to the parties. If both parties knew that Mr Naeem had a personal injury claim which was potentially worth, say, £30,000, the court would be reluctant to interpret the agreement as amounting to its release in consideration of less than £3,000. But the principle of exclusion would have to be that personal injury claims, as such, were outside the scope of the agreement. It would not support the exclusion of claims for some entirely different reason.

66. Another suggestion was that the clause should not be construe to release claims arising out of a wrongful act of BCCI. This was put forward by analogy with the construction of exemption clauses, on which there is authority for saying that they should prima facie not be read to exempt a contracting party from liability for negligence. I have already referred to the change which has taken place in the court's approach to exemption clauses. But in any case, there seems to me no real analogy. The reason for the traditional hostility of the courts to exemption clauses was that they often amounted to taking with one hand what had been given with the other. A contracting party undertook various obligations and then provided that he was not to be liable if he failed to perform them. But the release in this case is quite different. BCCI is paying a sum of money specifically to buy its release from any possible future claim by the employee. If there was such a claim, it was almost bound to be founded upon some wrongful act of BCCI—a breach of contract or statutory obligation, or else a tort. It is hard to imagine what other kind of claim there could be. So the release involved the employee taking a sum of money in return for giving up the speculative possibility that he might have such a claim. This has nothing in common with an exemption clause.

67. Finally it was submitted that although, for the reasons I have advanced, the release applied to unknown claims, it should not be read as applying to claims of which the employer actually knew, and in particular claims which he knew were unknown to the employee. There are two forms in which this argument can be put. One, as I have already said, was that adopted by Sir Richard Scott V.-C. [2000] ICR 1410. It involved relying as background upon the actual fact that BCCI knew of its own misconduct and knew that it was unknown to the employee. But these facts, whatever argument they may support to preclude BCCI from relying on the

agreement, cannot affect its construction. They are not admissible background. An alternative is to put the proposition in general terms: no release of unknown claims should be construed to extend to claims which were known to the party obtaining the benefit of the release but not to the other party. My difficulty with this proposition is, that it involves another artificial rule of construction. In view of the principles upon which the beneficiary of a release can be precluded from relying upon it because he has been guilty of sharp practice, to which I shall in a moment refer, I think that it is unnecessary to create such a rule of construction. There is again an analogy with exemption clauses and the 1977 Act.

68. My Lords, I turn now to the question of whether BCCI is entitled to rely upon the terms of the release . . .

73. It follows that in my opinion the stigma claim falls within the description of claims which Mr Naeem agreed to release and there is no reason why BCCI should not rely upon the release. My Lords, I do not think that there is any injustice in this result. Of course I sympathise with Mr Naeem, who, after a long and unblemished career in banking in Pakistan and then, from 1974, in this country, found himself made redundant at the difficult age of 49. But this is regrettably a very common occurrence. The claim that his subsequent difficulties in finding another job are attributable to his having worked for BCCI is however extremely speculative. In *Mahmud's* case, at p 53 Lord Steyn drew attention to the formidable practical obstacles to such a claim presented by the limiting principles of causation, remoteness and mitigation. So it has turned out. In 1999 Lightman J. tried five representative cases out of the 369 which had been commenced by former BCCI employees. None of them succeeded in proving that his unemployment was attributable to stigma. Four of the cases tried by Lightman J. appear to have concerned employees who were dismissed by the liquidators when the bank collapsed in 1991. By contrast, Mr Naeem and the others made redundant in 1990 face the additional hurdle of having to explain why their unemployment is attributable to stigma when they were unable to find jobs for a year before any stigma attached to them. The present position is that this vastly expensive litigation, which has been twice to the House of Lords and given rise to two lengthy trials before Lightman J., has produced benefits for no one except the lawyers involved and has been at the expense, not of the fraudulent villains but of the public and the unfortunate creditors of BCCI.

74. Mr Naeem says that despite all his difficulties, he should be entitled to have his day in court. He should not be struck out merely because he accepted £2,772 for a general release in 1990. In *Mahmud's* case Lord Nicholls of Birkenhead said, at pp 41–42, that he was:

> "conscious that the outcome of the present appeals may be seen by some as opening the door to speculative claims, to the detriment of admitted creditors. Claims of handicap in the labour market, and the other ingredients of the cause of action now under consideration, may give rise to lengthy and costly investigations and, ultimately, litigation. If the claims eventually fail, liquidators may well be unable to recover their costs from the former employees . . . I am aware of the dangers here, but it could not be right to allow 'floodgates' arguments of this nature to stand in the way of claims which, as a matter of ordinary legal principle, are well founded."

75. In general, I would respectfully agree. Justice is a matter of individual right which cannot be subjected to an ordinary utilitarian calculation. But there are limits. There are some people who assume that life itself is literally priceless; that no expense for the purpose of saving a life can possibly be too much. But the fact is that resources even for these purposes are not unlimited. Choices have to be made: see the judgment of Sir Thomas Bingham M.R. in *R v Cambridge Health Authority, Ex parte B* [1995] 1 WLR 898. Similarly there comes a point at which the object of achieving perfect justice for everyone has to be tempered by some consideration of the resources required to investigate every possible claim. In the present case, this point does not arise. The House has decided that the stigma claims should go forward and so they must. But I see no reason in justice to add to the expense by giving the language of the release a strained construction which will require BCCI to answer claims from which it paid to be free.

76. I would allow the appeal and restore the judgment of Lightman J.

By contrast, in the more recent case of *Rainy Sky S.A. v Kookmin Bank* (below), the divisions in judicial opinion did not originate in different readings of the commercial context so much as in rival approaches to interpretation (textual in the Court of Appeal as against contextual in the Supreme Court). The dispute in the case centred on the construction of a shipbuilder's refund guarantees (advance payment bonds) that were given pursuant to six shipbuilding contracts. When, in 2008 and early 2009, the shipbuilders experienced financial difficulties, the buyers sought a refund of the instalments paid, claiming that this was covered by the guarantees. The shipbuilders as well as the guarantor bank refused to make the refund; and, by the time that the dispute had reached the appeal courts, the question was whether the guarantees, as drafted, applied in these circumstances. Simon J held that the guarantees applied but his decision was reversed by the majority of the Court of Appeal (with Sir Simon Tuckey dissenting). On final appeal, the Supreme Court, applying a contextual approach, held unanimously that, the drafting of the guarantees notwithstanding, the buyers' reasonable expectation was that the guarantees would apply. No other construction was consistent with the commercial purpose of the guarantees.

RAINY SKY S.A. v KOOKMIN BANK

[2011] UKSC 50

LORD CLARKE

The Bonds

17–006   7. I begin with the Bonds because it was common ground that all depends upon the true construction of the Bonds and that the terms and meaning of the Contracts are only relevant to the extent that they inform the true construction of the Bonds. The paragraphs in the letter comprising the Bonds were not numbered but both the Judge and the Court of Appeal referred to them by number for convenience of reference and I will do the same. As so numbered the relevant parts of each Bond were these:

"[1] We refer to the . . . Contract entered into between . . . the Builder and yourselves for the construction and delivery of . . . the 'Vessel' to be delivered before [31 July 2009]. Other terms and expressions used in this Bond shall have the same meaning as in the Contract, a copy of which has been provided to us.

[2] Pursuant to the terms of the Contract, you are entitled, upon your rejection of the Vessel in accordance with the terms of the Contract, your termination, cancellation or rescission of the Contract or upon a Total Loss of the Vessel, to repayment of the pre-delivery instalments of the Contract Price paid by you prior to such termination or a Total Loss of the Vessel (as the case may be) and the value of the Buyer's Supplies delivered to the Shipyard (if any) together with interest thereon at the rate of . . . (7%) per annum (or . . . (10%) per annum in the case of a Total Loss of the Vessel) from the respective dates of payment by you of such instalments to the date of remittance by telegraphic transfer of such refund.

[3] In consideration of your agreement to make the pre-delivery instalments under the Contract and for other good and valuable consideration (the receipt and adequacy of which is hereby acknowledged), we hereby, as primary obligor, irrevocably and unconditionally undertake to pay to you, your successors and assigns, on your first written demand, all such sums due to you under the Contract (or such sums which would have been due to you but for any irregularity, illegality, invalidity or unenforceability in whole or in part of the Contract) PROVIDED THAT the total amount recoverable by you under this Bond shall not exceed US $[26,640,000] . . . plus interest thereon at the rate of . . . (7%) per annum (or . . . (10%) per annum in the case of a Total Loss of the Vessel) from the respective dates of payment by you of such instalments to the date of remittance by telegraphic transfer of such refund.

[4] Payment by us under this Bond shall be made without any deduction or withholding, and promptly on receipt by us of a written demand (substantially in the form attached) signed by two of your directors stating that the Builder has failed to fulfil the terms and conditions of the Contract and as a result of such failure, the amount claimed is due to you and specifying in what respects the Builder has so failed and the amount claimed. Such claim and statement shall be accepted by us as evidence for the purposes of this Bond alone that this amount claimed is due to you under this Bond.

[5] Our liability under this Bond shall not be affected by . . . (v) any insolvency, re-organisation or dissolution of the Builder, or (vi) any other matter or thing which may operate to discharge or reduce our liability hereunder.. . ."

8. The Bonds further provided that they were assignable, that they were governed by English law and that all disputes arising out of them were to be determined by the Commercial Court.

9. The resolution of the issue between the parties depends upon the true construction of paragraph [3]. The Bank promised to pay on demand "all such sums due to you under the Contract". The question is what was meant by "such sums". Only two possibilities were suggested. The Buyers said (and the Judge and

Sir Simon Tuckey held) that the expression "such sums" referred back to the "pre-delivery instalments" in the first line. They said that the purpose of the Bond was to guarantee the refund of pre-delivery instalments and that the promise was therefore to refund pre-delivery instalments. By contrast the Bank said (and Thorpe and Patten LJJ held) that the expression "such sums" was a reference back to the sums referred to in paragraph [2], namely the repayment of the pre-delivery instalments paid prior to a termination of the Contract or a Total Loss of the vessel and the value of the Buyer's Supplies in the case of a Total Loss. On the Buyers' analysis the Bond guaranteed pre-delivery instalments which were repayable under Article XII.3 in the case of any insolvency event, whereas on the Bank's analysis it did not. . . .

The correct approach to construction

14. For the most part, the correct approach to construction of the Bonds, as in the case of any contract, was not in dispute. The principles have been discussed in many cases, notably of course, as Lord Neuberger MR said in *Pink Floyd Music Ltd v EMI Records Ltd* [2010] EWCA Civ 1429; [2011] 1 WLR 770 at para 17, by Lord Hoffmann in *Mannai Investment Co Ltd v Eagle Star Life Assurance Co Ltd* [1997] AC 749, passim, in *Investors Compensation Scheme Ltd v West Bromwich Building Society* [1998] 1 WLR 896, 912F-913G and in *Chartbrook Ltd v Persimmon Homes Ltd* [2009] 1 AC 1101, paras 21-26. I agree with Lord Neuberger (also at para 17) that those cases show that the ultimate aim of interpreting a provision in a contract, especially a commercial contract, is to determine what the parties meant by the language used, which involves ascertaining what a reasonable person would have understood the parties to have meant. As Lord Hoffmann made clear in the first of the principles he summarised in the *Investors Compensation Scheme* case at page 912H, the relevant reasonable person is one who has all the background knowledge which would reasonably have been available to the parties in the situation in which they were at the time of the contract.

15. The issue between the parties in this appeal is the role to be played by considerations of business common sense in determining what the parties meant. Sir Simon Tuckey said at para 19 of his judgment that there was no dispute about the principles of construction and the Bank so submitted in its skeleton argument. However, I do not think that is quite correct.

16. At para 18 Sir Simon identified the question of construction substantially as set out in para 9 above and said at para 19:

"There is no dispute about the principles of construction to be applied in order to answer this question. The court must first look at the words which the parties have used in the bond itself. The shipbuilding contract is of course the context and cause for the bond but is nevertheless a separate contract between different parties. If the language of the bond leads clearly to a conclusion that one or other of the constructions contended for is the correct one, the Court must give effect to it, however surprising or unreasonable the result might be. But if there are two possible constructions, the Court is entitled to reject the one which is unreasonable and, in a commercial context, the one which flouts business common sense. This follows from the House of Lords decisions in *Wickman Machine Tools Sales Limited v Schuler AG* [1974] AC 235, where at 251 Lord Reid said:

'The fact that a particular construction leads to a very unreasonable result must be a relevant consideration. The more unreasonable the result, the more unlikely it is that the parties can have intended it, and if they do intend it the more necessary it is that they shall make that intention abundantly clear.'

and *The Antaios* [1984] AC 191, where at 201 Lord Diplock said:

'If detailed and syntactical analysis of words in a commercial contract is going to lead to a conclusion that flouts business common sense it must yield to business common sense.'"

17. As I read his judgment, Patten LJ did not put the question in quite the same way. This can be seen from paras 35 to 44 of his judgment. At para 35 he referred to Sir Simon Tuckey's approach at para 19 (as quoted above). He also referred to para 18(iii) of the Judge's judgment, where the Judge described the Bank's construction of the Bond as having the surprising and uncommercial result of the guarantee not being available to meet the Builder's repayment obligations in the event of insolvency. Patten LJ noted that the Judge appeared to have taken that into account as a factor in favour of the Buyers' construction of paragraph [3] of the Bonds. Patten LJ added that the Judge's approach was the same as that of Sir Simon Tuckey.

18. Patten LJ then referred to the cases mentioned above and expressed his conclusion in principle thus at para 42:

"In this case (as in most others) the Court is not privy to the negotiations between the parties or to the commercial and other pressures which may have dictated the balance of interests which the contract strikes. Unless the most natural meaning of the words produces a result which is so extreme as to suggest that it was unintended, the Court has no alternative but to give effect it its terms. To do otherwise would be to risk imposing obligations on one or other party which they were never willing to assume and in circumstances which amount to no more than guesswork on the part of the Court."

19. Finally, at paras 43 and 44, Patten LJ quoted from the speeches of Lord Wilberforce in *Prenn v Simmonds* [1971] 1 WLR 1381, 1384-5 and of Lord Hoffmann in *Chartbrook* at para 20, where they discussed the reason for the rule excluding evidence of pre-contractual negotiations. In particular they stressed the irrelevance of the parties' subjective intentions and noted that the mere fact that a term in the contract appears to be particularly unfavourable to one party or the other is irrelevant. As Lord Hoffmann put it, the term may have been agreed in exchange for some concession made elsewhere in the transaction or it may simply have been a bad bargain.

20. I entirely accept those caveats. However, it seems to me to be clear that the principle stated by Patten LJ in para 42 is different from that stated by the Judge in his para 18(iii) and by Sir Simon Tuckey in para 19. It is not in my judgment necessary to conclude that, unless the most natural meaning of the words produces a result so extreme as to suggest that it was unintended, the court must give effect to that meaning.

21. The language used by the parties will often have more than one potential meaning. I would accept the submission made on behalf of the appellants that the exercise of construction is essentially one unitary exercise in which the court must consider the language used and ascertain what a reasonable person, that is a person who has all the background knowledge which would reasonably have been available to the parties in the situation in which they were at the time of the contract, would have understood the parties to have meant. In doing so, the court must have regard to all the relevant surrounding circumstances. If there are two possible constructions, the court is entitled to prefer the construction which is consistent with business common sense and to reject the other.

22. This conclusion appears to me to be supported by Lord Reid's approach in *Wickman* quoted by Sir Simon Tuckey and set out above. I am of course aware that, in considering statements of general principle in a particular case, the court must have regard to the fact that the precise formulation of the proposition may be affected by the facts of the case. Nevertheless, there is a consistent body of opinion, largely collated by the Buyers in an appendix to their case, which supports the approach of the Judge and Sir Simon Tuckey.

23. Where the parties have used unambiguous language, the court must apply it. This can be seen from the decision of the Court of Appeal in *Co-operative Wholesale Society Ltd v. National Westminster Bank plc* [1995] 1 EGLR 97. The court was considering the true construction of rent review clauses in a number of different cases. The underlying result which the landlords sought in each case was the same. The court regarded it as a most improbable commercial result. Where the result, though improbable, flowed from the unambiguous language of the clause, the landlords succeeded, whereas where it did not, they failed. The court held that ordinary principles of construction applied to rent review clauses and applied the principles in *The Antaios (Antaios Compania Naviera SA v Salen Rederierna AB)* [1985] AC 191. After quoting the passage from the speech of Lord Diplock cited above, Hoffmann LJ said, at p 98:

"This robust declaration does not, however, mean that one can rewrite the language which the parties have used in order to make the contract conform to business common sense. But language is a very flexible instrument and, if it is capable of more than one construction, one chooses that which seems most likely to give effect to the commercial purpose of the agreement."

24. The court also comprised Leggatt and Simon Brown LJJ. Simon Brown LJ at p 101 said that, having regard to the improbable result for which the landlords contended, only the most unambiguous of such clauses could properly be found to bear the landlords construction and that in the case of only one of the leases did the clause "unambiguously . . . achieve the improbable result for which the landlords contend". The case is of interest because Simon Brown LJ considered that, of the other three cases, one unambiguously failed to achieve the result sought by the landlords, whereas, of the other two, he said this at p 102:

"For my part, I would accept that the more obvious reading of both favours the landlord's construction. I am persuaded, however, that they are capable of being, and therefore, for the reasons already given, should be, construed differently."

That case is therefore an example of the adoption and application of the principle endorsed by the Judge and by Sir Simon Tuckey. See also *International Fina Services AG v Katrina Shipping Ltd, The Fina Samco* [1995] 2

Lloyd's Rep. 344, where Neill LJ said at page 350 it was necessary when construing a commercial document to strive to attribute to it a meaning which accords with business common sense.

25. In 1997, writing extra-judicially ("Contract Law: Fulfilling the reasonable expectations of honest men") in 113 LQR 433, 441 Lord Steyn expressed the principle thus:

"Often there is no obvious or ordinary meaning of the language under consideration. There are competing interpretations to be considered. In choosing between alternatives a court should primarily be guided by the contextual scene in which the stipulation in question appears. And speaking generally commercially minded judges would regard the commercial purpose of the contract as more important than niceties of language. And, in the event of doubt, the working assumption will be that a fair construction best matches the reasonable expectations of the parties."

I agree. He said much the same judicially in *Society of Lloyd's v Robinson* [1999] 1 All ER (Comm) 545, 551:

"Loyalty to the text of a commercial contract, instrument, or document read in its contextual setting is the paramount principle of interpretation. But in the process of interpreting the meaning of the language of a commercial document the court ought generally to favour a commercially sensible construction. The reason for this approach is that a commercial construction is likely to give effect to the intention of the parties. Words ought therefore to be interpreted in the way in which a reasonable commercial person would construe them. And the reasonable commercial person can safely be assumed to be unimpressed with technical interpretations and undue emphasis on niceties of language"

26. Similar assistance is at hand nearer at home. In *Gan Insurance Co Ltd v Tai Ping Insurance Co Ltd* [2001] CLC 1103, 1118-1119; [2011] EWCA Civ 1047; [2001] 2 All ER (Comm) 299, Mance LJ said:

"13. Construction, as Sir Thomas Bingham MR said in *Arbuthnott v Fagan* [1995] CLC 1396 at p 1400 is thus 'a composite exercise, neither uncompromisingly literal nor unswervingly purposive'. To para (5), one may add as a coda words of Lord Bridge in *Mitsui Construction Co Ltd v A-G of Hong Kong* (1986) 33 BLR 14, cited in my judgment in *Sinochem International Oil (London) Ltd v Mobil Sales and Supply Corp* [2000] CLC 878 at p 885. Speaking of a poorly drafted and ambiguous contract, Lord Bridge said that poor drafting itself provides:

'no reason to depart from the fundamental rule of construction of contractual documents that the intention of the parties must be ascertained from the language that they have used interpreted in the light of the relevant factual situation in which the contract was made. But the poorer the quality of the drafting, the less willing the court should be to be driven by semantic niceties to attribute to the parties an improbable and unbusinesslike intention, if the language used, whatever it may lack in precision, is reasonably capable of an interpretation which attributes to the parties an intention to make provision for contingencies inherent in the work contracted for on a sensible and businesslike basis.'

. . .

16 . . . in my judgment the subclause has no very natural meaning and is, at the least, open to two possible meanings or interpretations—one the judge's, the other that it addresses two separate subject-matters. In these circumstances, it is especially important to undertake the exercise on which the judge declined to embark, that is to consider the implications of each interpretation. In my opinion, a court when construing any document should always have an eye to the consequences of a particular construction, even if they often only serve as a check on an obvious meaning or a restraint upon adoption of a conceivable but unbusiness-like meaning. In intermediate situations, as Professor Guest wisely observes in *Chitty on Contracts* (28th edn) vol 1, para. 12-049, a 'balance has to be struck' through the exercise of sound judicial discretion."

27. More generally, in *Homburg Houtimport BV v Agrosin Private Ltd: The Starsin* [2004] 1 AC 715, para 10 Lord Bingham referred to

"the rule to which Lord Halsbury LC alluded in *Glynn v Margetson & Co* [1893] AC 351, 359, 'that a business sense will be given to business documents. The business sense is that which businessmen, in the course of their ordinary dealings, would give the document.'"

28. Three other cases merit brief reference. The same approach was adopted by Arden LJ in *In the Matter of Golden Key Ltd (In Receivership)* [2009] EWCA Civ 636, paras 29 and 42 and by this Court in *In Re Sigma Finance Corporation (in administrative receivership)* [2009] UKSC 2; [2010] 1 All ER 571, where Lord Mance said at para 12 that the resolution of an issue of interpretation in a case like the present was an iterative process, involving

checking each of the rival meanings against other provisions of the document and investigating its commercial consequences.

29. Finally, it is worth setting out two extracts from the judgment of Longmore LJ in *Barclays Bank plc v HHY Luxembourg SARL* [2010] EWCA Civ 1248; [2011] 1 BCLC 336, paras 25 and 26:

> "25. The matter does not of course rest there because when alternative constructions are available one has to consider which is the more commercially sensible. On this aspect of the matter Mr Zacaroli has all the cards. . . .
>
> 26. The judge said that it did not flout common sense to say that the clause provided for a very limited level of release, but that, with respect, is not quite the way to look at the matter. If a clause is capable of two meanings, as on any view this clause is, it is quite possible that neither meaning will flout common sense. In such circumstances, it is much more appropriate to adopt the more, rather than the less, commercial construction."

30. In my opinion Longmore LJ has there neatly summarised the correct approach to the problem. That approach is now supported by a significant body of authority. As stated in a little more detail in para 21 above, it is in essence that, where a term of a contract is open to more than one interpretation, it is generally appropriate to adopt the interpretation which is most consistent with business common sense. For these reasons I prefer the approach of the Judge and Sir Simon Tuckey to that of Patten LJ, which is to my mind significantly different on this point.

Application to the facts

31. As indicated above, two possible interpretations of paragraph [3] of the Bonds were advanced. It was conceded on behalf of the Bank in the Court of Appeal that both constructions were arguable. I did not understand Mr Guy Philipps QC to resile from that position on behalf of the Bank in this Court. In any event, in my judgment there are indeed two possible interpretations.

32. The strength of the Bank's interpretation is that it is not easy to see the point of paragraph [2] of the Bonds if the Buyers' interpretation of paragraph [3] is correct. On the other hand, the Buyers' interpretation is straightforward. It is that, reduced to its essentials, the Bank's promise in paragraph [3] was that "in consideration of your [i.e. the Buyers'] agreement to make the pre-delivery instalments . . . we hereby, as primary obligor, promise to pay to you, your successors and assigns, on your first written demand, all such sums due to you under the Contract . . .". In the absence of paragraph [2] there could be no doubt that the reference to 'such sums' was a reference to the 'pre-delivery instalments' at the beginning of paragraph [3]. That makes perfect sense because one would naturally expect the parties to agree (and the Buyers' financiers to insist) that, in the event, for example, of the insolvency of the Builders, the Buyers should have security for the repayment of the pre-delivery instalments which they had paid.

33. The question is whether the presence of paragraph [2] leads to a different conclusion. It was submitted with force by Mr Philipps on behalf of the Bank that it did. He correctly submitted that paragraph [3] must be construed in its context and that part of the context was paragraph [2], which was of course the immediately preceding paragraph. He submitted that the only purpose there can have been for including paragraph [2] in the Bonds was to identify the scope of paragraph [3]. He further submitted that no other sensible explanation for the inclusion of paragraph [2] had been advanced on behalf of the Buyers.

34. I accept the submission that no very good reason was advanced on behalf of the Buyers for the inclusion of paragraph [2] in the Bonds. The best they could do was to say that it was a preamble to the operative provision in paragraph [3], that it simply set out some of the Buyers' rights under the Contracts and that it was not intended to identify the scope of the Bank's liability under the Bonds. Patten LJ accepted at para 50 that the Buyers' construction was arguable but said that, in his view, it was not the meaning that the document would convey to a reasonable person reading it with knowledge of the terms of the Contracts. This must I think mean that he took the view that, although it was arguable that it had that effect, it did not in fact do so. Otherwise the Buyers' construction could not in any relevant sense have been said to be arguable and Patten LJ would surely not have described it as such. Patten LJ made this clear in para 51 (quoted below), where he described the alternative constructions as not being in any way evenly balanced. The position is thus that, although he regarded both constructions as arguable in the sense that the Bonds might convey either construction to a reasonable person reading the Bonds with knowledge of the terms of the Contracts, in his view the Bank's construction was plainly to be preferred. If Patten LJ went further later in para 51, where he said that the fact that cover for the insolvency of the Builder was desirable did not justify a departure from what would otherwise be "the natural and obvious construction

of the bond", I respectfully disagree because I do not regard the Bank's construction as being the natural and ordinary meaning of the Bonds. . . .

40. In all these circumstances, because of the difficulties in construing para [2] as setting out the sums due under the Bond, if I were focusing only on the language of the clause, I would be inclined to prefer the Buyers' construction to that of the Bank. I note in passing in this regard that the construction advanced by the Bank was something of an afterthought. However, I recognize that, on the Buyers' construction, it is not easy to see why paragraph [2] was included in the Bond at all, and that the Bank's construction is arguable. This case is therefore a good example of the kind of case referred to in the authorities to which I have referred. Since the language of paragraph [3] is capable of two meanings it is appropriate for the court to have regard to considerations of commercial common sense in resolving the question what a reasonable person would have understood the parties to have meant.

41. As noted at para 17 above, at his para 18(iii) the Judge described the Bank's construction of the Bonds as having what he called the surprising and uncommercial result that the Buyers would not be able to call on the Bonds on the happening of the event, namely insolvency of the Builder, which would be most likely to require the first class security. I agree with Sir Simon Tuckey that an appellate court is entitled to take account of the fact that an experienced judge of the Commercial Court reached that conclusion. In any event, Sir Simon Tuckey expressed essentially the same view in strong terms at para 30:

"On the Bank's construction the Bonds covered each of the situations in which the Buyers were entitled to a return or refund of the advance payments which they had made under the contracts apart from the insolvency of the Builder. No credible commercial reason has been advanced as to why the parties (or the Buyers' financiers) should have agreed to this. On the contrary, it makes no commercial sense. As the judge said, insolvency of the Builder was the situation for which the security of an advance payment bond was most likely to be needed. The importance attached in these contracts to the obligation to refund in the event of insolvency can be seen from the fact that they required the refund to be made immediately. It defies commercial common sense to think that this, among all other such obligations, was the only one which the parties intended should not be secured. Had the parties intended this surprising result I would have expected the contracts and the bonds to have spelt this out clearly but they do not do so."

I agree.

42. Patten LJ's view to the contrary is summarised at para 51:

"For the reasons which I have given, I do not regard the alternative constructions of paragraph (3) advanced on this appeal as being in any way evenly balanced. I also agree with Mr Philipps that it is impermissible to speculate on the reasons for omitting repayments in the event of insolvency from the bond. Although the judge is right to say that cover for such event was, objectively speaking, desirable, that is not sufficient in itself to justify a departure from what would otherwise be the natural and obvious construction of the bond. There may be any number of reasons why the Builder was unable or unwilling to provide bank cover in the event of its insolvency and why the Buyer was prepared to take the risk. This is not a case in which the construction contended for would produce an absurd or irrational result in the sense described in the cases I have referred to and merely to say that no credible commercial reason has been advanced for the limited scope of the bond does, in my view, put us in real danger of substituting our own judgment of the commerciality of the transaction for that of those who were actually party to it."

43. As Hoffmann LJ put it, after quoting from Lord Diplock's speech in *The Antaios* [1985] AC 191, if the language is capable of more than one construction, it is not necessary to conclude that a particular construction would produce an absurd or irrational result before having regard to the commercial purpose of the agreement. See, for example, per Hoffmann LJ quoted at para 23 above, where he said:

"But language is a very flexible instrument and, if it is capable of more than one construction, one chooses that which seems most likely to give effect to the commercial purpose of the agreement."

See also the quotation from Longmore LJ at para 29 above, where he said that, if a clause is capable of two meanings, it is quite possible that neither meaning will flout common sense, but that, in such a case, it is much more appropriate to adopt the more, rather than the less, commercial construction.

44. In para 51 Patten LJ appears to have accepted that no credible commercial reasons were advanced for the limited scope of the Bonds being advanced by the Bank. Mr Philipps submitted that it was not necessary for the Bank to address the question but I have no doubt that if he or the Bank had been able to think of a credible

reason for excluding repayments in the event of the Builder's insolvency, such a reason would have been at the forefront of the Bank's case.

45. In these circumstances I would, if necessary, go so far as to say that the omission of the obligation to make such re-payments from the Bonds would flout common sense but it is not necessary to go so far. I agree with the Judge and Sir Simon Tuckey that, of the two arguable constructions of paragraph [3] of the Bonds, the Buyers' construction is to be preferred because it is consistent with the commercial purpose of the Bonds in a way in which the Bank's construction is not.

46. I note that Thorpe LJ was initially inclined to agree with the conclusions of the Judge but, in the event, agreed with Patten LJ without giving any independent reasons of his own.

Conclusion

47. For these reasons I would allow the appeal and restore the order of the Judge.

----

3. TAKING STOCK

17–007   Following *Investors Compensation*, we can no longer complain about a lack of jurisprudence in the matter of contractual interpretation. Some of this jurisprudence relates to 'big picture' questions concerning the function and purpose of the modern law of contract; some of it relates to matters of doctrinal detail. At all levels, though, this is a chapter of the law that is now under intense scrutiny. If we were to take stock, our key points would be the following:

(1) Contextual interpretation starts as a relatively modest corrective to literalism (the underlying principle being that it defeats reasonable expectations if one contractor, who has perfectly well understood the other's intended meaning is permitted to rely on the uncorrected and unintended literal meaning of the term). This extends into the more general proposition that, where reference to the context indicates that something has gone wrong in the drafting, then it defeats reasonable expectations if the literal meaning of the contract is applied. And, as *Rainy Sky* highlights, this extends into the even more general proposition that, in all cases, interpretation of a commercial contract has to be through a contextual lens—or, as John Wightman has neatly put it, the interpretation of contracts is "inherently contextual" (see 'Contract in a Pre-Realist World: Professor Macaulay, Lord Hoffmann and the Rise of Context in the English Law of Contract' in Jean Braucher, John Kidwell, and William C. Whitford (eds), *Revisiting the Contracts Scholarship of Stewart Macaulay* (Oxford: Hart, 2013) 377, 384). The significance of such a broad contextual approach for the range of readings that are 'available' or 'possible' is sharply drawn out by Lord Neuberger in *Pink Floyd Music Ltd v EMI Records Ltd* [2010] EWCA Civ 1429, at para.18, when he says:

"[W]hile one may proceed on the prima facie assumption that the words at issue mean what they naturally say, they cannot be interpreted in a vacuum. The words must be interpreted by reference to what a reasonable person (who is informed with business common sense, the knowledge of the parties, including of course of the other provisions of the contract, and the experience and expertise enjoyed by the parties, at the time of the contract) would have understood by the provision. So construed, the words of a provision may have a meaning which is not that which they may appear to have if read out of context, or the meaning which they may appear to have had at first sight. Indeed, it is clear that there will be circumstances where the words in question are attributed a meaning which they simply cannot have as a matter of ordinary linguistic analysis, because the notional reasonable person would be satisfied that something had gone wrong in the drafting."

Hence, if we adopt full-blooded contextualism, the range of "possible" interpretations will be given by the context, not by playing around with the language. To be sure, in particular cases, contextualists can end up relying on the language of the contract—just as literalists can feed contextual considerations into their judgments of reasonableness where the text is unclear—but, for contextualists, text-in-context is where the process of interpretation starts.

(2) If the obvious attraction of contextualism is that it improves the chances of aligning, so to speak, the "paper deal" with what the contractors actually understand the "real deal" to be, then a less obvious attraction is that the flexibility given by contextualism spares courts the need to press other doctrines into service in order to relieve against an unacceptable literal reading of a contract. For example, in *Lloyds TSB Foundation for Scotland v Lloyds Banking Group Plc (Scotland)* [2013] UKSC 3, the question was "how a covenant should be construed and understood as applying in a novel legal and accounting context, which was not foreseen or foreseeable—or was, according to uncontradicted expert evidence, 'unthinkable'—when the covenant was entered into" (para.1). Dating back to a deed in 1986 (which was subsequently varied), the covenant required that, for each relevant accounting period, Lloyds Banking Group should pay to the Foundation either "(a) an amount equal to one-third of 0.1946 per cent of the Pre-Tax Profits (after deducting Pre-Tax Losses)" or "(b) the sum of £38,920" whichever were the greater. Over the years, the rules of accounting practice changed so that when, in 2008, Lloyds rescued HBOS (paying half its book value), the anticipated but as yet unrealised net gain was shown as a profit (amounting to £1 billion). The Foundation, taking a literal or "mechanical" view of the covenant, argued that, for the purposes of calculating the payment due under the covenant, the "profit" on the HBOS acquisition should be treated as part of the "pre-tax profits". However, applying a contextual approach, the Supreme Court took a different view. According to Lord Mance (at para.22):

> "Here, the landscape, matrix and aim of the 1997 Deed as well as its predecessors could not be clearer. They were, when made, and could only have been, concerned with and aimed at realised profits or losses before the taxation which would fall on group companies . . . In the light of the legal position of the 1980s and 1990s . . . the change [in the accounting rules] was wholly outside the parties' original contemplation, and something which they would not have accepted, had they foreseen it."

Accordingly, set in context, the only reasonable reading of the covenant was that it related to realised profits (on which, unlike unrealised profits, dividends could be paid).

(3) Set against the attractions of contextualism, the obvious problem is that, while some contexts will be transparent and the expectations of the parties will be clear, others will be more opaque and contested. Accordingly, one of the principal challenges for contextualism and its supporters is to find an acceptable strategy for dealing with cases where the particular context fails to offer unequivocal standards of reasonableness to inform the reasonable person's understanding of the contractual documents. In such cases, we might find the judges appealing to what would be ridiculous, unrealistic, nonsensical, and inherently unattractive (in other words, to standards that determine what is reasonable or unreasonable *in any context*) in order to induce a particular resolution of the question. However, as critics of contextualism rightly caution, there is a danger that contextualism becomes another name for construing the contract until one arrives at the result one wants.

(4) Regardless of whether contextualism does better than literalism in serving the purposes of contract law (whatever they might be), the doctrinal details of contextualism continue to be addressed. In particular, there is a standing question about the boundaries of the "context" that limits the operation of contextual interpretation. Writing extra-judicially, Lord Nicholls suggested that the rule which precludes reliance on pre-contractual dealings in order to shed light on the intended meaning of a contract is no longer sustainable (see, 'My Kingdom for a Horse: The Meaning of Words' (2005) 121 LQR 577); and in *Proforce Recruit Ltd v The Rugby Group Ltd* [2006] EWCA Civ 69, Mummery LJ (at paras 34–36) endorsed this view. However, in *Chartbrook Limited v Persimmon Homes Limited* [2009] UKHL 38, the House of Lords apparently drew a line under this debate by maintaining this particular restriction (see above Ch.5). Another nice point arose, more recently, in *Cherry Tree Investments Ltd v Landmain Ltd* [2012] EWCA Civ 736, where the Court of Appeal was called on to decide how far the "context" can extend where the dispute is located within the setting of a public register (on which third parties might reasonably be expected to rely). The facts were that Landmain had charged a property in London to Dancastle in return for a loan of £635,000. Alongside the charge the parties had entered into a "facility agreement" which provided that Dancastle's power of sale arose on execution of the charge and was exercisable at any time after such execution. While the charge was registered against the property at the Land Registry, the facility agreement was not. Pursuant to the power of sale, Dancastle sold the property to Cherry Tree. However, Landmain argued that, by reference to the charge as registered, this was a potentially wrongful sale and that it should remain as the registered proprietor. Taking a different view from the trial judge, the majority of the Court of Appeal (Lewison and Longmore LJJ) held that the facility agreement could *not* be treated as part of the context. Granted, this agreement was very much part of the background as between Landmain and Dancastle; but it was not disclosed on the face of the register—a register on which third parties might entirely reasonably rely. Dissenting, Arden LJ argued that the key limiting principle was that the rights of third parties should not be prejudicially affected (and she held that, on the facts, there was no such prejudice). See, further, Matthew Barber and Rod Thomas, 'Contractual Interpretation, Registered Documents and Third Party Effects' (2014) 77 MLR 597.

(5) In other common law jurisdictions, contextualism has received mixed reviews. For example, in Australia—in *Pacific Carriers Limited v BNP Paribas* (2004) 218 C.L.R. 451 and *Toll (FGCR) Pty Ltd v Alphapharm Pty Ltd* (2004) 219 C.L.R. 165—the High Court seems to have aligned itself with the spirit of Lord Hoffmann's approach (see The Honourable J. J. Spigelman AC (Chief Justice of New South Wales), 'From Text to Context: Contemporary Contractual Interpretation' *http://www.lawlink.nsw.gov.au* [accessed November 19, 2008]); but, in the US law reviews, there is an extensive debate about whether New York's literalism is superior to California's contextualism.[2] In England, contextualism is the new orthodoxy but, elsewhere, the jury is out.

(6) Finally, and perhaps most importantly, in English law, contextualism is not confined to matters of contractual interpretation. As we have seen already (in Ch.16), after the *Belize Telecom* case, contextualism also governs the implication of terms. Moreover, following *Transfield Shipping Inc*

---

[2]   See. e.g., Alan Schwartz and Robert E. Scott, 'Contract Interpretation Redux' (2010) 119 YLJ 926 (for a minimal evidentiary base; formalism); and Shawn J. Bayern, 'Rational Ignorance, Rational Closed-Mindedness, and Modern Economic Formalism in Contract Law' (2009) 97 *California Law Review* 943 (for a maximal evidentiary base; contextualism).

v Mercator Shipping Inc [2008] UKHL 48 (below, Ch.19), it seems not only that many of the rules of the general law of contract are simply defaults but that they can be displaced by the implicit contextual expectations of the parties. In *Transfield Shipping*, where the context was one of late redelivery of a chartered vessel and where the question of law concerned the application of the remoteness rules, Lord Hoffmann said (at para.9):

"The case therefore raises a fundamental point of principle in the law of contractual damages: is the rule that a party may recover losses which were foreseeable ('not unlikely') an external rule of law, imposed upon the parties to every contract in default of express provision to the contrary, or is it a prima facie assumption about what the parties may be taken to have intended, no doubt applicable in the great majority of cases but capable of rebuttal in cases in which the context, surrounding circumstances or general understanding in the relevant market shows that a party would not reasonably have been regarded as assuming responsibility for such losses?"

Drawing a parallel with the contextual approach to the interpretation of contracts, Lord Hoffmann preferred the latter view. And, applying such a view, Lord Hoffmann found that, relative to background market expectations in the shipping sector, "it is clear that [the parties] would have considered losses arising from the loss of the following fixture a type or kind of loss for which the charterer was not assuming responsibility" (para.23). In other words, the usual (default) rule for the recovery of consequential losses was displaced not by the parties' express contrary intention (which would be nothing new) but by the implicit contextual expectations of contractors in the shipping market. The general significance of this particular extension of contextualism can hardly be over-stated.

Further reading

Roger Brownsword 'After *Investors*: Interpretation, Expectation and the Implicit Dimension of the "New Contextualism"' in David Campbell, Hugh Collins, and John Wightman (eds) *The Implicit Dimension of Contract* (Oxford: Hart Publishing, 2003), p.103

Lord Grabiner QC, 'The Iterative Process of Contractual Interpretation' (2012) 128 LQR 41

Stewart Macaulay, 'The Real and the Paper Deal: Empirical Pictures of Relationships, Complexity and the Urge for Transparent Simple Rules' (2003) 66 MLR 44

Catherine Mitchell, *Contract Law and Contract Practice* (Oxford: Hart Publishing, 2013)

Jonathan Morgan, *Contract Law Minimalism* (Cambridge: Cambridge University Press, 2013) (for a sustained critique of contextualism)

Alan Schwartz and Robert E. Scott, 'Contract Interpretation Redux' (2010) 119 YLJ 926

Robert E. Scott, 'The Promise and the Peril of Relational Contract Theory' in Jean Braucher, John Kidwell, and William C. Whitford (eds), *Revisiting the Contracts Scholarship of Stewart Macaulay* (Oxford: Hart, 2013) p.105

PART IV

REMEDIES

18

PERFORMANCE AND RESCISSION

LEARNING OBJECTIVES

By the end of this chapter, you should:

- understand that, in the event of a repudiatory breach, the law generally permits the innocent party to elect between "accepting the breach as repudiatory" or "affirming the contract";
- be familiar with the case-law from *White and Carter* onwards, setting the conditions on affirming the contract;
- have a view about whether (and in which circumstances) an innocent party should be permitted to elect to affirm and to provide an unwanted performance;
- understand the limited circumstances in which a court will make an order for specific performance of a contract;
- appreciate that, before issuing an injunction to prevent a breach, a court will take care that this does not amount to a disguised order for (unacceptable) specific performance.

INTRODUCTION

A contractor who claims a court-based remedy will usually argue that the defendant has failed to perform the contract, that the defendant *actually is* in breach; and, in English law, where the claimant's case is made out, the standard remedial response will be an award of damages (see Ch.19). However, what is the legal position if the defendant is not yet in breach of contract but the claimant has reason to believe (on the basis of indications given by the defendant) that, when the time for performance comes, the defendant will not perform? What is the legal position, in other words, where the claimant pleads an anticipatory breach of contract? What, too, is the legal position if the claimant, not wanting damages (or the payment of the agreed price), asks the court to order specific performance of the contract or to issue an injunction to restrain a breach? In what circumstances will a court make orders of this kind? These are the questions that are the focus of this chapter.

The cases are divided into four sections. In the first section, there is a general introduction to the law on anticipatory breach, including the important idea that the innocent party has the right to elect whether to keep the contract alive or to treat it as at an end (the so-called "elective" theory). The case-law in the second section starts with the decision of the House of Lords in *White & Carter (Councils) Ltd v McGregor* [1962] A.C. 413 (below). There, the majority of the House held that the innocent party is entitled to elect to treat the contract as alive even though this means that an unwanted performance is rendered—or, at any rate, the innocent party is so entitled provided that there is a legitimate reason for continuing with the contract. Predictably, what counts as such a reason has troubled later courts. In the third section, the question is whether the elective theory applies in the context of employment contracts, a question recently addressed by the Supreme Court in *Société Générale v Geys* [2012] UKSC 63 (below). Finally, in section four, it is the law on the remedies of specific performance and injunction that is reviewed.

1. ANTICIPATORY BREACH

FROST v KNIGHT

Exchequer Chamber (1872) L.R. 7 Exch. 111; 41 L.J. Ex. 78; 26 L.T. 77; 20 W.R. 471

18–002   The defendant promised to marry the plaintiff on the death of the defendant's father. During his father's lifetime the defendant announced his intention of not fulfilling his promise and broke off the engagement. The plaintiff, without waiting for the father's death, sued for breach of contract.[1] The Court of Exchequer, Martin B dissenting, made absolute a rule to arrest a judgment in favour of the plaintiff. The case was brought on error before the Court of Exchequer Chamber.

COCKBURN CJ

. . . The law with reference to a contract to be performed at a future time, where the party bound to performance announces prior to the time his intention not to perform it, as established by the cases of *Hochster v De la Tour*, 2 E. & B. 678,[2] and *The Danube and Black Sea Co v Xenos* on the one hand, and *Avery v Bowden*, 5 E. & B. 714,[3] *Reid v Hoskins*, 6 E. & B. 953, and *Barwick v Buba*, 2 C.B. (n.s.) 563, on the other, may be thus stated. The promisee, if he pleases, may treat the notice of intention as inoperative, and await the time when the contract is to be executed, and then hold the other party responsible for all the consequences of non-performance: but in that case he keeps the contract alive for the benefit of the other party as well as his own; he remains subject to all his own obligations and liabilities under it, and enables the other party not only to complete the contract, if so advised, notwithstanding his previous repudiation of it, but also to take advantage of any supervening circumstances which would justify him in declining to complete it.

On the other hand, the promisee may, if he thinks proper, treat the repudiation of the other party as a wrongful putting an end to the contract, and may at once bring his action as on a breach of it; and in such action he will be entitled to such damages as would have arisen from the non-performance of the contract at the appointed time, subject, however, to abatement in respect of any circumstances which may have afforded him the means of mitigating his loss.

Considering this to be now settled law, notwithstanding anything that may have been held or said in the cases of *Philpotts v Evans*, 5 M. & W. 475, and *Ripley v McClure*, 4 Ex. at p. 359, we should have had no difficulty in applying the principle of the decision in *Hochster v De la Tour* to the present case, were it not for the difference which undoubtedly exists between that case and the present, viz., that, whereas there the performance of

---

[1]   The action for breach of promise of marriage was abolished by the Law Reform (Miscellaneous Provisions) Act 1970 s.1(1); but the principles enunciated in this case are of general application in the law of contract.

[2]   In *Hochster v de la Tour* the defendant, on April 12, 1852, agreed to engage the plaintiff as a courier, on June 1, 1852, to travel on the Continent of Europe. On May 11, 1852, the defendant wrote to the plaintiff that he had changed his mind, and did not require the plaintiff's services. The plaintiff commenced an action on May 22. The defendant's counsel objected that there could be no breach of contract before June 1. Lord Campbell CJ said that ". . . where there is a contract to do an act on a future day, there is a relation constituted between the parties in the meantime by the contract, and that they impliedly promise that in the meantime neither will do anything to the prejudice of the other inconsistent with that relation . . . from the day of the hiring till the day when the employment was to begin, they were engaged to each other; and it seems to be a breach of an implied contract if either of them renounces the engagement . . .".

[3]   In *Avery v Bowden* the defendant chartered the plaintiff's ship, Lebanon and agreed to load her with a cargo at Odessa within 45 days. The ship proceeded to Odessa and remained there a great part of the 45 days. The defendant told the captain of the ship that he had no cargo for him, and repeatedly advised him to go away. The captain remained at the port in the hope that the defendant would fulfil his contract. Before the 45 days had elapsed, the Crimean War broke out, rendering the performance of the contract thereafter illegal. The plaintiff's action failed. It would have been otherwise if, assuming the defendant's action amounted to a repudiation (which the court doubted), the plaintiff had sailed away before the declaration of war.

the contract was to take place at a fixed time, here no time is fixed, but the performance is made to depend on a contingency, namely, the death of the defendant's father during the lifetime of the contracting parties. It is true that in every case of a personal obligation to be fulfilled at a future time, there is involved the possible contingency of the death of the party binding himself, before the time of performance arrives; but here we have a further contingency depending on the life of a third person, during which neither party can claim performance of the promise. This being so, we thought it right to take time to consider whether an action would lie before the death of the defendant's father had placed the plaintiff in a position to claim the fulfilment of the defendant's promise.

After full consideration we are of opinion that, notwithstanding the distinguishing circumstances to which I have referred, this case falls within the principle of *Hochster v De la Tour*, and that, consequently, the present action is well brought.

The considerations on which the decision in *Hochster v De la Tour* is founded are that the announcement of the contracting party of his intention not to fulfil the contract amounts to a breach, and that it is for the common benefit of both parties that the contract shall be taken to be broken as to all its incidents, including non-performance at the appointed time; as by an action being brought at once, and the damages consequent on non-performance being assessed at the earliest moment, many of the injurious effects of such non-performance may possibly be averted or mitigated.

It is true, as is pointed out by the Lord Chief Baron, in his judgment in this case, that there can be no actual breach of a contract by reason of non-performance so long as the time for performance has not yet arrived. But, on the other hand, there is—and the decision in *Hochster v De la Tour* proceeds on that assumption—a breach of the contract when the promisor repudiates it and declares he will no longer be bound by it. The promisee has an inchoate right to the performance of the bargain, which becomes complete when the time for performance has arrived. In the meantime he has a right to have the contract kept open as a subsisting and effective contract. Its unimpaired and unimpeached efficacy may be essential to his interests. His rights acquired under it may be dealt with by him in various ways for his benefit and advantage. Of all such advantage the repudiation of the contract by the other party, and the announcement that it never will be fulfilled, must of course deprive him. It is therefore quite right to hold that such an announcement amounts to a violation of the contract in omnibus, and that upon it the promisee, if so minded, may at once treat it as a breach of the entire contract, and bring his action accordingly.

The contract having been thus broken by the promisor, and treated as broken by the promisee, performance at the appointed time becomes excluded, and the breach by reason of the future non-performance becomes virtually involved in the action as one of the consequences of the repudiation of the contract; and the eventual non-performance may therefore, by anticipation, be treated as a cause of action, and damages be assessed and recovered in respect of it, though the time for performance may yet be remote.

It is obvious that such a course must lead to the convenience of both parties; and though we should be unwilling to found our opinion on grounds of convenience alone, yet the latter tend strongly to support the view that such an action ought to be admitted and upheld. By acting on such a notice of the intention of the promisor, and taking timely measures, the promisee may in many cases avert, or at all events materially lessen, the injurious effects which would otherwise flow from the non-fulfilment of the contract; and in assessing the damages for breach of performance, a jury will of course take into account whatever the plaintiff has done, or has had the means of doing, and as a prudent man, ought in reason to have done, whereby his loss has been, or would have been, diminished.

It appears to us that the foregoing considerations apply to the case of a contract the performance of which is made to depend on a contingency, as much as to one in which the performance is to take place at a future time; and we are, therefore, of opinion that the principle of the decision of *Hochster v De la Tour* is equally applicable to such a case as the present . . .

Keating and Lush J. J. concurred in the judgment of the Chief Justice, and Byles J. delivered a judgment to the same effect.

Judgment Reversed.

A. 'Accepting' an Anticipatory Breach

18–003   The breach occurs when the contract is repudiated.[4] But an anticipatory breach differs from other breaches of contract in that the injured party, A, must "accept" it before he can sue for damages. If A elects to keep the contract alive, the repudiating party, B, may yet perform, in which case A will suffer no loss. Because the word 'accept' has been traditionally used, it has sometimes been assumed that something like offer and acceptance in the formation of contract is required. In *Denmark Productions Ltd v Boscobel Productions Ltd* [1968] 3 All E.R. 513 at 527 Winn LJ said:

> "It seems to me that the process of ending or indeed of varying a contract by repudiation is the converse of that of making the same contract; each process operates by offer and acceptance or their equivalents; each is essentially bilateral. Where A and B are parties to an executory contract, if A intimates by word or conduct that he no longer intends, or is unable, to perform it, or to perform it in a particular manner, he is, in effect, making an offer to B to treat the contract as resolved or varied so far as it relates to the future."

Insofar as this relates to repudiation as distinct from variation, this seems an inappropriate analogy. Suppose that in *Hochster v De la Tour* (above) the plaintiff (P), on receiving the defendant (D)'s letter of May 11, had immediately offered his services to X and, without a word to D, gone off to South America. D, meanwhile, having changed his mind, on May 30, delivers to P's address items to be taken to Europe. P has accepted the fact that the contract is at an end but done nothing to accept any "offer" by D. Is it really to be said that P is now liable to D for damages for breach of contract? P is surely entitled to take D at his word. As Lord Campbell CJ said at p.690, "It seems strange that the defendant, after renouncing the contract, and absolutely declaring that he will never act under it, should be permitted to object that faith is given to his assertion and that an opportunity is not left to him of changing his mind."

Or suppose that in, *Frost v Knight*, D, having contracted to marry P on the death of D's father, writes to P during father's lifetime, "I wouldn't marry you if you were the last woman on earth," whereupon P promptly marries another. Not unnaturally, she does not reply to D. Next day, father dies and D calls upon P to marry him. Could D really have succeeded (before 1970) in an action for breach of promise? Surely, "acceptance" here simply means acceptance of the fact that the contract is at an end.

There is however an ambiguity in the word "repudiation". A fundamental breach of contract is sometimes described as a repudiatory breach. The party, A, who has committed such a breach, far from declaring the contract to be at an end, may be very anxious that it should continue. Then, B, if he wishes to terminate the contract must notify A to that effect See *Car and Universal Finance Co Ltd v Caldwell*, above, Ch.14.

Vitol SA v Norelf Ltd [1995] 3 All E.R. 971 raises the question of whether an innocent party can accept a repudiation of the contract merely by failing to perform his own obligations under it. The case concerned a contract for the sale by N to V of a cargo to be loaded on the Santa Clara. V, believing that loading was unlikely to be completed until well outside the contractual period sent N a telex stating "In view of the breach of this condition we must reject the cargo and repudiate the contract." V was apparently in error in supposing that there had been a breach of condition by N because it was not disputed that this telex was an anticipatory breach of contract by V. On March 11 N informed V that

---

[4]   J. C. Smith, 'Anticipatory Breach of Contract', in *Contemporary Issues in Commercial Law (Essays in Honour of Professor A. G. Guest* (ed. E. Z. Lomnicka and C. J. G. Morse) (London: Sweet & Maxwell, 1997), p.175 (Hereafter 'Smith, Anticipatory Breach').

loading had been completed; and on March 15 N resold the cargo. There was no further communication between them until N claimed damages of US $1 million, the difference between the contract price and resale price. The arbitrator took the view that, until V's breach was accepted by N, it was of no effect but that N's failure to take any further steps to perform the contract, as by tendering a bill of lading, a failure which was apparent to V, constituted a sufficient communication of acceptance. On appeal to the Queen's Bench Division, Phillips J held that all he had to decide was whether mere failure to perform contractual obligations can ever constitute acceptance of an anticipatory breach by the other party. He held that it could, and dismissed V's appeal. The Court of Appeal disagreed. A failure to perform contractual obligations was not sufficiently clear and unequivocal to amount to acceptance of a repudiation because it was equally consistent with misunderstanding, indecision or inadvertence by the innocent party. Because of their limited jurisdiction on appeal from an arbitrator, the question whether the resale was an acceptance of the breach was not considered by the courts. In principle, however, it seems that the resale of the cargo must have put an end to the contract, no less than the supposed marriage in the above example based on *Frost v Knight*.

B. The Nature and Extent of the Threatened Breach

The threatened breach may be of (i) the whole contract, or (ii) a condition, or (iii) an innominate term, or (iv) a warranty. Clearly threat (i) entitles the other party to terminate the contract. It might be expected that threat (ii) would have the same effect, whatever the extent of the threatened breach, since any actual breach justifies termination. Where, however, there is an express term for terminating the contract on the occurrence of a particular breach it appears that only the actual breach, not the threat of it, justifies termination: *The Afovos* [1983] 1 All E.R. 449 HL Lord Diplock, with whom the whole House agreed, said that the doctrine of anticipatory breach applies only to a fundamental breach, meaning, apparently, a breach which would deprive the other party of substantially the whole benefit of the contract—which is not true of every breach of condition. In the case of (iii) the answer presumably depends on the extent of the threatened breach: see *Federal Commerce, etc v Molena Apha Inc* [1979] A.C. 757 where the majority of their Lordships held that the relevant clause was an innominate term and proceeded to consider whether the threatened breach of it was so fundamental as to amount to a repudiation of the contract. Cf. *Torvald Klaveness v Arni*, below. As for case (iv), given that the actual breach of a mere warranty (by definition) does not justify termination, the threatened breach can hardly do so.

18–004

Points for reflection

1. *Specific Performance*. A party who declines to accept an anticipatory breach as putting an end to the contract can bring no action for damages until the time for performance arrives and the other party fails to perform. But, if the contract is one capable of specific performance, an action for that remedy will lie at once: *Hasham v Zenab* [1960] A.C. 316, PC. By a written contract, the defendant agreed to sell the plaintiff a plot of land in Nairobi. A few minutes after signing the contract, the defendant repudiated it by tearing it up. The last day for completion was August 19 and the plaintiff instituted proceedings on July 2. It was held that the institution of the proceedings was not premature. There was a fallacy in equating a right to sue for specific performance with a cause of action at law. The purchaser had an equitable interest in the land which would have enabled him to get an injunction to prevent the vendor disposing of it. All he needed to show were circumstances justifying the intervention of a court of equity.

18–005

2. *"Anticipatory breach" is a present breach.* In *The Mihalis Angelos* (below, Ch.20) the Court of Appeal considered what would be the position if they were wrong in holding that C had properly terminated the contract on July 17. In that event, C, by declaring on July 17 that he would not provide a cargo when the ship arrived, was guilty of an anticipatory breach of contract. But since the ship could not possibly have been ready to load by July 20 he could and would have rightly cancelled the charterparty on that day. Mocatta J at first instance had nevertheless held that S was entitled to ±4,000 damages for the anticipatory breach. His view was that "the assumed and, in law, inevitable failure to perform is one at the date in the future when performance would have been required had there been no anticipatory breach"; and that damages had to be assessed in relation to that assumed future breach. This was wrong.

Lord Denning said:

> "The words 'anticipatory breach' are misleading. The cause of action is not the future breach. It is the renunciation itself . . . the damages must be assessed by compensating the injured party for the loss he has suffered by the renunciation. One must take into account all contingencies which might have reduced or extinguished that loss . . . if the defendant has, under the contract, an option which would reduce or extinguish the loss, it will be assumed that he would exercise it . . . In short, the plaintiff must be compensated for such loss as he would have suffered if there had been no renunciation . . . Seeing that the charterers would, beyond doubt, have cancelled, I am clearly of opinion that the shipowners suffered no loss and would be entitled at most to nominal damages."

Question

18–006   It is clear that the term of the contract which is broken by anticipatory breach is a condition, for the breach entitles the injured party to terminate (not "rescind") the contract as well as to sue for damages. What is the promise which is broken in these cases? Cf. Montrose in (1937) 15 Can.Bar Rev. 309, 315: "The time for performance does not affect the inception of the promise: an obligation comes into existence as soon as the contract is concluded. This is shown in English law by the action for an anticipatory breach of contract." What is this obligation?

WOODAR INVESTMENT DEVELOPMENT LTD v WIMPEY CONSTRUCTION UK LTD

House of Lords [1980] 1 W.L.R. 277; [1980] 1 All E.R. 571

18–007   Woodar contracted to sell to Wimpey 14 acres of land for development. It was provided by cl.E(a)(iii) that Wimpey should be entitled to rescind the contract if prior to completion a statutory authority "shall have commenced" compulsorily to acquire the property. As both parties knew, the Minister had commenced compulsory purchase proceedings for 2.3 acres of the property before the time of the contract. Land prices fell dramatically. Wimpey purported to rescind, relying on cl.E(a)(iii), Woodar claimed a declaration that Wimpey were not entitled to rescind and Wimpey counterclaimed for a declaration that they had validly rescinded the contract. Woodar then brought a second action claiming that the notice of rescission and the counterclaim amounted to a repudiation which they accepted and claimed damages. The two actions were consolidated. The trial judge held that Wimpey were not entitled to rescind: cl.E(a)(iii) applied only to compulsory purchase proceedings commenced after the date of the contract. This finding was not challenged in the higher courts. The judge awarded

£462,000 damages. The Court of Appeal affirmed his decision but reduced the damages to £272,943. Wimpey appealed.

LORD WILBERFORCE

My Lords . . . in considering whether there has been a repudiation by one party, it is necessary to look at his conduct as a whole. Does this indicate an intention to abandon and to refuse performance of the contract? In the present case, without taking Wimpey's conduct generally into account, Woodar's contention, that Wimpey had repudiated, would be a difficult one. So far from repudiating the contract, Wimpey were relying on it and invoking one of its provisions, to which both parties had given their consent. And unless the invocation of that provision were totally abusive, or lacking in good faith, (neither of which is contended for), the fact that it has proved to be wrong in law cannot turn it into a repudiation. At the lowest, the notice of rescission was a neutral document consistent either with an intention to preserve, or with an intention to abandon, the contract, and I will deal with it on this basis, more favourable to Woodar. In order to decide which is correct Wimpey's conduct has to be examined.

One point can, in my opinion, be disposed of at once. Woodar, in March 1974, started proceedings against Wimpey: this is one of the actions consolidated in the litigation before us. They claimed a declaration that Wimpey's notice of rescission was not valid, and Wimpey, by their defence asserted the contrary and they counterclaimed for a declaration to that effect. Woodar now contend that if the original notice did not amount to a repudiation, the defence and counterclaim did. I regard this contention as hopeless. Wimpey's pleading carried the matter no further: it simply rested the matter on the contract. It showed no intention to abandon the contract whatever the result of the action might be. If the action were to succeed (that is if Wimpey lost) there was no indication that Wimpey would not abide by the result and implement the contract.

The facts indicative of Wimpey's intention must now be summarised. It is clear in the first place that, subjectively, Wimpey in 1974 wanted to get out of the contract. Land prices had fallen, and they thought that if the contract was dissolved, they could probably acquire it at a much lower price. But subjective intention is not decisive: it supplied the motive for serving the notice of rescission; there remains the question whether, objectively regarded, their conduct showed an intention to abandon the contract.

In early 1974 there was a possibility that some planning permission might be granted. If it were, and unless Wimpey could take valid objection to it, completion would (under the conditions) have to follow in two months. Therefore, if a notice of rescission were to be given, it had to be served without delay, that is before the planning permission arrived. In this situation, Wimpey's advisers arranged a meeting with a Mr Cornwell, who was acting for Woodar, or as an intermediary with power to commit Woodar, to discuss the matter. This took place on March 7, 1974 and is recorded as a disclosed aide memoire dated the next day. This document was prepared by Wimpey, and we have not had the benefit of Mr Cornwell's evidence on it: he died before the trial. But the rest of the correspondence is fully in line with it and I see no reason to doubt its general accuracy. After recording each side's statement of position, the document contained, inter alia, these passages: "He [Mr Cornwell] stated that if we attempted to rescind the contract, then he would take us to court and let the judge decide whether the contract could be rescinded on the point we were making." This "point" was undoubtedly that relating to the compulsory purchase of the 2.5 (sic) acres. The aide memoire continues:

> "I told him that our Legal Department would be serving the Notice to Rescind the Contract within a short while—this would ensure that the company was fully protected and was prudent. He assured me that he would accept it on that basis and not regard it as a hostile act."

The notice was then served on March 20, 1974. On March 22, Woodar's solicitors wrote that they did not accept its validity. On May 30, 1974 Mr Cornwell wrote a long letter to Sir Godfrey Mitchell, president of Wimpey. I refer to one passage:

> ". . . within a few days of the original meeting, a notice of rescission was served upon the vendor company by your organisation that the contract was to be rescinded. Simultaneously with that notice of rescission, proceedings were instituted and there the matter remains so far as the legal situation is concerned and both parties, from the legal point of view, must now await the decision of the court as to the validity of the claim made by Messrs. George Wimpey & Co Limited that they are entitled to rescind this contract upon the grounds which they have so stated."

On June 4, 1974 Mr Cornwell wrote again: "All I need say now is that we will retire to our battle stations and it goes without saying I am sure that you will abide by the result as I will."

568   Performance and Rescission

My Lords, I cannot find anything which carries the matter one inch beyond, on Wimpey's part an expressed reliance on the contract (in condition E(a)(iii)), on Woodar's side an intention to take the issue of the validity of the notice (nothing else) to the courts, and an assumption, not disputed by Wimpey, that both sides would abide by the decision of the court. This is quite insufficient to support the case for repudiation . . .

My Lords, in my opinion, it follows, as a clear conclusion of fact, that Wimpey manifested no intention to abandon, or to refuse future performance of, or to repudiate the contract. And the issue being one of fact, citation of other decided cases on other facts is hardly necessary. I shall simply state that the proposition that a party who takes action relying simply on the terms of the contract and not manifesting by his conduct an ulterior intention to abandon it is not to be treated as repudiating it, is supported by *James Shaffer Ltd v Findlay Durham & Brodie* [1953] 1 W.L.R. 106 and *Sweet & Maxwell Ltd v Universal News Services Ltd* [1964] 2 Q.B. 699.

In contrast to these is the case in this House of *Federal Commerce and Navigation Co Ltd v Molena Alpha Inc* [1979] A.C. 757 at 780 which fell on the other side of the line. Of that I said:

"The two cases relied on by the owners (*James Shaffer Ltd v Findlay Durham & Brodie* and *Sweet & Maxwell Ltd v Universal News Services Ltd*) . . . would only be relevant here if the owners' action had been confined to asserting their own view, possibly erroneous, as to the effect of the contract. They went, in fact, far beyond this when they threatened a breach of contract with serious consequences."

Spettabile Consorzio Veneziano di Armamento e Navigazione v Northumberland Shipbuilding Co Ltd (1919) 121 L.T. 628, though in some factual respects distinguishable from the present, is nevertheless, in my opinion, clear support for Wimpey.

In my opinion, therefore, Wimpey are entitled to succeed on the repudiation issue, and I would only add that it would be a regrettable development of the law of contract to hold that a party who bona fide relies on an express stipulation in a contract in order to rescind or terminate a contract should, by that fact alone, be treated as having repudiated his contractual obligations if he turns out to be mistaken as to his rights. Repudiation is a drastic conclusion which should only be held to arise in clear cases of a refusal, in a matter going to the root of the contract, to perform contractual obligations. To uphold Woodar's contentions in this case would represent an undesirable extension of the doctrine.

LORD SALMON (DISSENTING)

I do not understand how Wimpey's honest belief in a bad point of law can in any way avail them. In *Federal Commerce Navigation Co Ltd v Molena Alpha Inc* [1978] Q.B. 927, 979 Lord Denning M.R. said:

"I have yet to learn that a party who breaks a contract can excuse himself by saying that he did it on the advice of his lawyers; or that he was under an honest misapprehension. Nor can he excuse himself on those grounds from the consequences of a repudiation."

I gratefully adopt that passage which seems to me to be particularly apt in the present case. It certainly was never questioned in your Lordships' House when the appeal from the decision of the Court of Appeal in the *Federal Commerce* case was dismissed . . .

[His Lordship quoted from other cases.]

I do not recall that any of these definitions of a repudiation of a contract have ever, until now, been questioned. The fact that a party to a contract mistakenly believes that he has the right to refuse to perform it cannot avail him. Nor is there any authority for the proposition that if a party to a contract totally refuses to perform it, this refusal is any the less a repudiation of the contract because he honestly but mistakenly believes that he is entitled by a condition of the contract to refuse to perform it.

It would indeed be unfortunate if the law were otherwise. A mistake in the construction of a contractual condition, even such a glaringly obvious mistake as the present, can apparently easily be made especially perhaps when the market price has fallen far below the contract price. It is acknowledged in this case that the mistake was an honest one. If, however, a case arose in which a mistake of this kind was alleged to be an honest mistake, but not acknowledged to be so, it would be extremely difficult, if not impossible to prove the contrary . . .

Lord Russell made a dissenting speech

Lord Keith and Scarman made speeches allowing the appeal.

Appeal Allowed.

Questions

1. Would the answer have been different if it had been proved that Wimpey knew very well that, in   **18-008**
the circumstances, cl.E(a)(iii) did not entitle them to rescind? Should it make any difference? The
loss suffered by Woodar would be the same.

2. Wimpey purported to rely on an express provision in the contract. Would it have been different if
they had purported to determine the contract in the mistaken belief that Woodar had committed a breach of condition or fundamental breach?

3. Does the decision depend on the fact that it concerned a conveyancing transaction? See J.
W. Carter [1980] C.L.J. 256: ". . . in a commercial charterparty or sale of goods . . . there will usually
be no room for nice considerations as to whether or not a promisor has acted in good faith."

4. "In this case, Woodar did mitigate and resold the land in 1975 for £330,000. However, it must
follow from the House of Lords decision that this resale was wrongful. If Wimpey's notice of
rescission was not repudiatory, the contract was still alive and Woodar committed an anticipatory breach by selling the land" (see A. Nicol and R. Rawlings (1980) 43 MLR 696 at 698).
Suppose that the price of land had then shot up. Could Wimpey have recovered damages from
Woodar?

----

2. White & Carter and a "Legitimate Interest" in Performing

WHITE & CARTER (COUNCILS) LTD v McGREGOR

House of Lords (Scotland) [1962] A.C. 413; [1962] 2 W.L.R. 17; [1961] 3 All E.R. 1178; 1962 S.C.(HL) 1

The facts appear sufficiently in the speech of Lord Reid.

LORD REID

My Lords, the pursuers supply to local authorities litter bins which are placed in the streets. They are allowed   **18-009**
to attach to these receptacles plates carrying advertisements, and they make their profit from payments made
to them by the advertisers. The defender carried on a garage in Clydebank and in 1954 he made an agreement
with the pursuers under which they displayed advertisements of his business on a number of these bins. In June
1957 his sales manager made a further contract with the pursuers for the display of these advertisements for a
further period of three years. The sales manager had been given no specific authority to make this contract and
when the defender heard of it later on the same day he at once wrote to the pursuers to cancel the contract.
The pursuers refused to accept this cancellation. They prepared the necessary plates for attachment to the
bins and exhibited them on the bins from November 2, 1957, onwards.

The defender refused to pay any sums due under the contract and the pursuers raised the present action in
the Sheriff Court craving payment of £196 4s., the full sum due under the contract for the period of three years.
After sundry procedure the Sheriff-Substitute on March 15, 1960, dismissed the action. He held that the sales
manager's action in renewing the contract was within his apparent or ostensible authority and that is not now
disputed. The ground on which he dismissed the action was that in the circumstances an action for implement
of the contract was inappropriate. He relied on the decision in *Langford & Co, Ltd v Dutch*, (1952), S.C. 15, and
cannot be criticised for having done so.

The pursuers appealed to the Court of Session and on November 2, 1960, the Second Division refused the
appeal. The present appeal is taken against their interlocutor of that date. That interlocutor sets out detailed

findings of fact and, as this case began in the Sheriff Court, we cannot look beyond those findings. The pursuers must show that on those findings they are entitled to the remedy which they seek.

The case for the defender (now the respondent) is that, as he repudiated the contract before anything had been done under it, the appellants were not entitled to go on and carry out the contract and sue for the contract price: he maintains that in the circumstances the appellants' only remedy was damages, and that, as they do not sue for damages, this action was rightly dismissed.

The contract was for the display of advertisements for a period of 156 weeks from the date when the display began. This date was not specified but admittedly the display began on November 2, 1957, which seems to have been the date when the former contract came to an end. The payment stipulated was 2s. per week per plate together with 5s. per annum per plate, both payable annually in advance, the first payment being due seven days after the first display. The reason why the appellants sued for the whole sum due for the three years is to be found in clause 8 of the conditions: "In the event of an instalment or part thereof being due for payment, and remaining unpaid for a period of four weeks or in the event of the advertiser being in any way in breach of this contract then the whole amount due for the 156 weeks or such part of the said 156 weeks as the advertiser shall not yet have paid shall immediately become due and payable."

A question was debated whether this clause provides a penalty or liquidated damages, but on the view which I take of the case it need not be pursued. The clause merely provides for acceleration of payment of the stipulated price if the advertiser fails to pay an instalment timeously. As the respondent maintained that he was not bound by the contract he did not pay the first instalment within the time allowed. Accordingly, if the appellants were entitled to carry out their part of the contract notwithstanding the respondent's repudiation, it was hardly disputed that this clause entitled them to sue immediately for the whole price and not merely the first instalment.

The general rule cannot be in doubt. It was settled in Scotland at least as early as 1848 and it has been authoritatively stated time and again in both Scotland and England. If one party to a contract repudiates it in the sense of making it clear to the other party that he refuses or will refuse to carry out his part of the contract, the other party, the innocent party, has an option. He may accept that repudiation and sue for damages for breach of contract, whether or not the time for performance has come; or he may if he chooses disregard or refuse to accept it and then the contract remains in full effect . . .

I need not refer to the numerous authorities. They are not disputed by the respondent but he points out that in all of them the party who refused to accept the repudiation had no active duties under the contract. The innocent party's option is generally said to be to wait until the date of performance and then to claim damages estimated as at that date. There is no case in which it is said that he may, in face of the repudiation, go on and incur useless expense in performing the contract and then claim the contract price. The option, it is argued, is merely as to the date as at which damages are to be assessed.

Developing this argument, the respondent points out that in most cases the innocent party cannot complete the contract himself without the other party doing, allowing or accepting something, and that it is purely fortuitous that the appellants can do so in this case. In most cases by refusing co-operation the party in breach can compel the innocent party to restrict his claim to damages. Then it was said that, even where the innocent party can complete the contract without such co-operation, it is against the public interest that he should be allowed to do so. An example was developed in argument. A company might engage an expert to go abroad and prepare an elaborate report and then repudiate the contract before anything was done. To allow such an expert then to waste thousands of pounds in preparing the report cannot be right if a much smaller sum of damages would give him full compensation for his loss. It would merely enable the expert to extort a settlement giving him far more than reasonable compensation.

[His Lordship then considered *Langford & Co, Ltd v Dutch*, (1952), S.C. 15, and continued:] *Langford & Co, Ltd v Dutch* is indistinguishable from the present case. Quite properly the Second Division followed it in this case as a binding authority and did not develop Lord Cooper's reasoning: they were not asked to send this case to a larger court. We must now decide whether that case was rightly decided. In my judgment it was not. It could only be supported on one or other of two grounds. It might be said that, because in most cases the circumstances are such that an innocent party is unable to complete the contract and earn the contract price without the assent or co-operation of the other party, therefore in cases where he can do so he should not be allowed to do so. I can see no justification for that.

The other ground would be that there is some general equitable principle or element of public policy which requires this limitation of the contractual rights of the innocent party. It may well be that, if it can be shown that a person has no legitimate interest, financial or otherwise, in performing the contract rather than claiming damages, he ought not to be allowed to saddle the other party with an additional burden with no benefit to himself. If a party has no interest to enforce a stipulation, he cannot in general enforce it: so it might be said that, if a party has no interest to insist on a particular remedy, he ought not to be allowed to insist on it. And, just as a party is not allowed to enforce a penalty, so he ought not to be allowed to penalise the other party by taking one course when another is equally advantageous to him. If I may revert to the example which I gave of a company engaging an expert to prepare an elaborate report and then repudiating before anything was done, it might be that the company could show that the expert had no substantial or legitimate interest in carrying out the work rather than accepting damages: I would think that the de minimis principle would apply in determining whether his interest was substantial, and that he might have a legitimate interest other than an immediate financial interest. But if the expert had no such interest then that might be regarded as a proper case for the exercise of the general equitable jurisdiction of the court. But that is not this case. Here the respondent did not set out to prove that the appellants had no legitimate interest in completing the contract and claiming the contract price rather than claiming damages; there is nothing in the findings of fact to support such a case, and it seems improbable that any such case could have been proved. It is, in my judgment, impossible to say that the appellants should be deprived of their right to claim the contract price merely because the benefit to them, as against claiming damages and reletting their advertising space, might be small in comparison with the loss to the respondent: that is the most that could be said in favour of the respondent. Parliament has on many occasions relieved parties from certain kinds of improvident or oppressive contracts, but the common law can only do that in very limited circumstances. Accordingly, I am unable to avoid the conclusion that this appeal must be allowed and the case remitted so that decree can be pronounced as craved in the initial writ.

Lord Morton of Henryton made a dissenting speech.

LORD KEITH OF AVONHOLM

. . . Much argument and citation of authority was advanced on the topic of anticipatory repudiation. That, in my view, was largely beside the point. There is no doubt that there was here an anticipatory repudiation, for the contract was repudiated by the defender the very day it was made and some months before it could come into operation. But the pursuers did not choose to act on that repudiation and sue the defender for what has sometimes been called an anticipatory breach. The real question at issue is what were the rights of parties when the contract fell to be put into operation, the defender having maintained his repudiation throughout . . .

Repudiation of a contract is nothing but a breach of contract. Except where it is accepted as an anticipatory breach and as a ground for a claim of damages, a repudiation can never be said to be accepted by the other party except in the sense that he acquiesces in it and does not propose to take any action. Otherwise he founds on it as a cause of action.

The late Professor Gloag in his work on *Contract* (2nd ed.), p. 592, considering the rights arising on breach of contract, said: "The primary rights of the creditor in a contractual obligation may be said to be to secure performance by invoking the assistance of the court to compel it, or, where that remedy is inappropriate, to obtain compensation damages." . . . in the case of a repudiation of a contract when performance is tendered, or due to be given by the other party, the repudiation cannot be said to be writ in water. It gives rise immediately to a cause of action. This does not involve acceptance of the repudiation. There has been a breach of contract which the complaining party denies the other had any right to commit. I know of no authority for saying that the offended party can go quietly on as if the contract still continued to be fully operative between both parties. He is put to his remedy at the date of the breach. It has been said that when an anticipatory repudiation is not treated as a cause of action the contract remains alive. It does until the contract would become operative, when the repudiation, if still maintained, then becomes a cause of action and all pleas and defences then existing are available to the respective parties.

The party complaining of the breach also has a duty to minimise the damage he has suffered, which is a further reason for saying that after the date of breach he cannot continue to carry on his part of an executory contract. A breach of a contract of employment will serve to illustrate the nature of this duty. A person is engaged to serve for a certain period, say three months, to commence at a future date. When that date arrives the prospective employer wrongfully refuses to honour the engagement. The servant is not entitled to see out the three months and then sue the recalcitrant employer for three months' wages. He must take steps by seeking other employment to minimise his loss. It is true, of course, that a servant cannot invoke a contract to force himself on an unwilling master, any more than a master can enforce the service of an unwilling servant. But if the appellants' contention is sound, it is difficult to see why, by parity of reasoning, it should not apply to a person who keeps himself free to perform the duties of his contract of service during the whole period of the contract and is prevented from doing so by the refusal of the other contracting party. Yet in *Hochster v De la Tour*, from which the whole law about anticipatory repudiation stems, Lord Campbell plainly indicated that if the courier in that case, instead of accepting as he did the repudiation of his engagement as a cause of action, before it was due to commence, had waited till the lapse of the three months of the engagement he could not have sued as for a debt. The jury, he said, would be entitled to look at all that might "increase or mitigate the loss of the plaintiff down to the day of trial." There is no difference in this matter between the law of England and the law of Scotland (*Ross v M'Farlane* (1894) 21 R. 396) . . .

I find the argument advanced for the appellants a somewhat startling one. If it is right it would seem that a man who has contracted to go to Hong Kong at his own expense and make a report, in return for remuneration of £10,000, and who, before the date fixed for the start of the journey and perhaps before he has incurred any expense, is informed by the other contracting party that he has cancelled or repudiates the contract, is entitled to set off for Hong Kong and produce his report in order to claim in debt the stipulated sum. Such a result is not, in my opinion, in accordance with principle or authority, and cuts across the rule that where one party is in breach of contract the other must take steps to minimise the loss sustained by the breach. (Cf. below.)

It may also be put in another way, that the pursuers are precluded from carrying on with their performance by the notice from the defender, albeit in breach of contract, that he does not intend to pay them if they do. Lord President Dunedin said very much this in *Johannesburg Municipal Council v D. Stewart & Co* (1909) Ltd, (1909), S.C. 860, 877, in the following passage: "When two parties are bound together under contract, of course each must perform to the other his mutual stipulations. If one of the parties is in breach of a stipulation of the contract, what is the position of the other? . . . If the stipulation which is broken goes to the root and essence of the contract, the other party is entitled to say—now you have so broken the contract that I am entitled to say that it is at an end through your fault, I shall not perform any more of my stipulations, because you have precluded me, and I shall claim damages."

There remains for consideration the alternative case made for the appellants upon condition 8 of the contract. Their claim is, that in respect of the defender's repudiation and breach of contract he is liable in damages, and that under the clause the damages are fixed at three years' rent which, they say, is liquidated damages, and not a penalty. But the clause, in my opinion, is only intended to take effect after the contract comes in operation. This is clear in the first event mentioned in the clause, because there can be no failure of payment until the advertising plates have been displayed in terms of the agreement. This could not happen on the hypothesis, which must be accepted on this part of the case, that the pursuers were not entitled to go on with the contract. The clause is, in my opinion, just a debt clause ancillary to the conditions for the payment of rent and providing for instant payment of the whole rent in the event of failure in punctual payment of the instalments. No very convincing suggestions were given as to what was meant to be covered by the second event. But, in my opinion, this also must refer to some breaches in the course of performance of the contract, which will again involve instant payment of the full rent. I fail to see how the clause can be at one and the same time a contractual clause sounding in payment of debt and a damages clause for repudiation of the contract. The clause accordingly has, in my opinion, no operation here, and I find it unnecessary to consider whether, if it had, it is a clause for liquidated damages, or for a penalty.

I would dismiss the appeal.

Lord Hodson, with whom Lord Tucker concurred, made a speech allowing the appeal.

Appeal Allowed.

Questions

18–010

1. Would it have made any difference if the contract had been that the defenders should supply the pursuers with details of the advertisements and the defenders had repudiated and declined to do so? See *Finelli et al v Dee et al.* (1968) 67 D.L.R. (2d) 393.

2. Would it have made any difference if cl.8 had been omitted from the contract?

Problems

1. A delivers his car to B's garage and B accepts A's instructions to install a new engine. Before B has started the work, A countermands his instructions. B refuses to return the car and installs the new engine. Advise A.

    18-011

2. A contracts with B that he will deliver his car to B's garage on June 1 and pay £100 for the installation of new engine. A refuses to deliver the car. Advise B.

HOUNSLOW LONDON BOROUGH COUNCIL v TWICKENHAM GARDEN DEVELOPMENTS LTD

Chancery Division [1971] Ch. 233; [1970] 3 W.L.R. 538; [1970] 3 All E.R. 326; 69 L.G.R. 109

The defendant contractor was employed by the borough to do building work on the borough's land. The contract provided that if the contractor failed to proceed diligently with the work, the architect might give him notice specifying the default and, if the default continued for 14 days, the borough might by notice determine the contract. The contractor was given possession of the site in 1966 and in January 1970 the borough gave notice under the above procedure to determine the contract. The contractor refused to accept the repudiation of the contract and continued with the work. The borough issued a writ claiming damages for trespass and an injunction, and, by notice of motion, sought an order restraining the contractor until judgment in the action from entering, remaining or otherwise trespassing on the site.

18-012

Megarry J held that the licence given to the contractor to carry out works on the site was created by the contract and was in terms irrevocable, unless the notices were valid, and equity would not assist the borough to revoke the licence in breach of contract. The borough was not entitled to an injunction unless there was a high degree of assurance that the validity of the notices would be established at the trial; and the judge felt no such assurance.

MEGARRY J

The contractor relied, inter alia, on *White and Carter (Councils) Ltd v McGregor*. Megarry J. referred to the "Hong Kong" example and continued: The examples discussed in argument before me applied the doctrine to cases concerning land. A contract to erect buildings on land is let; a few days later the landowner unexpectedly learns that he can obtain a far more advantageous planning permission for developing the land, and he thereupon repudiates the contract; but the contractor insists on performing it, even though the landowner must then either abandon the more valuable development and accept the far less profitable buildings or else pull those buildings down when they have been completed and then carry out the more fruitful scheme. Another landowner lets a contract to erect an extravagant building which his wealth can afford; before much work has been done his fortune collapses, and he can pay for the building only by using all that is left to him; yet the contractor insists on performing the contract. A third landowner contracts with an artist to paint extensive frescoes in a new building over a period of two years; the landowner then receives a handsome offer for the unadorned building, provided vacant possession is delivered forthwith; yet the artist insists on painting on for the rest of the two years.

Examples such as these suggest that there may well be limits to the doctrine. Lord Morton and Lord Keith both stressed the duty to mitigate damages: and he who is bound to mitigate can hardly be entitled to insist on aggravating. However, theirs were dissenting speeches which rejected the doctrine in toto. Accordingly I must turn to the speech of Lord Reid. Although it was his voice, with the voices of Lord Tucker and Lord Hodson, that carried the day, two important limitations appear in Lord Reid's speech. First, he pointed out that the peculiarity of the case was that the agents could perform the contract without any co-operation by the proprietor.

He said at [1962] A.C. 413, 429: "Of course, if it had been necessary for the defender to do or accept anything before the contract could be completed by the pursuers, the pursuers could not and the court would not have compelled the defender to act, the contract would not have been completed and the pursuers' only remedy would have been damages."

This, I think, was in effect an acceptance of the argument to which Lord Reid had referred on p. 428: "the respondent points out that in most cases the innocent party cannot complete the contract himself without the other party doing, allowing or accepting something, and that it is purely fortuitous that the appellants can do so in this case. In most cases by refusing co-operation the party in breach can compel the innocent party to restrict his claim to damages."

The other limitation, cautiously expressed, at p. 431, was that "it may well be" that if a person has no legitimate financial or other interest in performing the contract rather than claiming damages, "he ought not to be allowed to saddle the other party with an additional burden with no benefit to himself": and this principle might apply to the example of the expert report. However, no such absence of a legitimate interest in the agents had been established, and so the possible principle did not apply.

It seems to me that the decision is one which I should be slow to apply to any category of case not fairly within the contemplation of their Lordships. The case before me is patently one in which the contractor cannot perform the contract without any co-operation by the borough. The whole machinery of the contract is geared to acts by the architect and quantity surveyor, and it is a contract that is to be performed on the borough's land. True, the contractor already has de facto possession or control of the land, there is no question of the borough being required to do the act of admitting the contractor into possession, and so in that respect the contractor can perform the contract without any "co-operation" by the borough. But I do not think that the point can be brushed aside so simply. Quite apart from questions of active co-operation, cases where one party is lawfully in possession of property of the other seem to me to raise issues not before the House of Lords in *White and Carter (Councils), Ltd v McGregor* (above). Suppose that A, who owns a large and valuable painting, contracts with B, a picture restorer, to restore it over a period of three months. Before the work is begun, A receives a handsome offer from C to purchase the picture, subject to immediate delivery of the picture in its unrestored state, C having grave suspicions of B's competence. If the work of restoration is to be done in A's house, he can effectually exclude B by refusing to admit him to the house: without A's "co-operation" to this extent B cannot perform his contract. But what if the picture stands in A's locked barn, the key of which he has lent to B so that he may come and go freely, or if the picture has been removed to B's premises? In these cases can B insist on performing his contract, even though this makes it impossible for A to accept C's offer? In the case of the barn, A's co-operation may perhaps be said to be requisite to the extent of not barring B's path to the barn or putting another lock on the door: but if the picture is on B's premises, no active co-operation by A is needed. Nevertheless, the picture is A's property, and I find it difficult to believe that Lord Reid intended to restrict the concept of "co-operation" to active co-operation. In *White and Carter (Councils), Ltd v McGregor* no co-operation by the proprietor, either active or passive, was required: the contract could be performed by the agents wholly without reference to the proprietor or his property. The case was far removed from that of a property owner being forced to stand impotently aside while a perhaps ill-advised contract is executed on property of his which he has delivered into the possession of the other party, and is powerless to retrieve.

Accordingly, I do not think that *White and Carter (Councils) Ltd v McGregor* has any application to the case before me. I say this, first, because a considerable degree of active co-operation under the contract by the borough is requisite, and second, because the work is being done to property of the borough. I doubt very much whether the White case can have been intended to apply where the contract is to be performed by doing acts to property owned by the party seeking to determine it. I should add that it seems to me that the ratio of the White case involves acceptance of Lord Reid's limitations, even though Lord Tucker and Lord Hodson said nothing of them: for without Lord Reid there was no majority for the decision of the House. Under the doctrine of precedent, I do not think that it can be said that a majority of a bare majority is itself the majority.

ATTICA SEA CARRIERS CORPORATION v FERROSTAAL POSEIDON BULK REEDEREI GMBH THE PUERTO BUITRAGO

Court of Appeal [1976] 1 Lloyd's L.Rep. 250

18–013   The charterers chartered the Puerto Buitrago from the shipowners for a period of 17 months. Clause 15, "Conditions on Redelivery," provided that the charterer should return the vessel in the same good order and condition as on delivery, ordinary wear and tear excepted, and should do all necessary repairs. The vessel developed engine trouble and was eventually towed to Kiel. Repairs were estimated to cost $2 million and the value of the vessel when repaired would be $1 million. Charterers admitted liability for $400,000 of repairs and redelivered vessel unrepaired. The shipowners refused to accept redelivery contending that the charterers were bound to repair the vessel and to pay the charter hire until it was repaired. They relied on *White & Carter v McGregor*.

LORD DENNING MR

[Referred to that case and continued:] The decision has been criticised in a leading textbook (Cheshire & Fifoot (8th edn), pp.600 and 601). It is said to give a "grotesque" result. Even though it was a Scots case, it would appear that the House of Lords, as at present constituted, would expect us to follow it in any case that is precisely on all fours with it. But I would not follow it otherwise. It has no application whatever in a case where the plaintiff ought, in all reason, to accept the repudiation and sue for damages—provided that damages would provide an adequate remedy for any loss suffered by him. The reason is because, by suing for the money, the plaintiff is seeking to enforce specific performance of the contract—and he should not be allowed to do so when damages would be an adequate remedy. Take a servant, who has a contract for six months certain, but is dismissed after one month. He cannot sue for his wages for each of the six months by alleging that he was ready and willing to serve. His only remedy is damages. Take a finance company which lets a machine or motor-car on hire purchase, but the hirer refuses to accept it. The finance company cannot sue each month for the instalments. Its only remedy is in damages: see *National Cash Register Co v Stanley*, [1921] 3 K.B. 292; *Karsales (Harrow) v Wallis*, [1956] 1 W.L.R. 936 (2nd point). So here, when the charterers tendered redelivery at the end of the period of the charter—in breach of the contract to repair—the shipowners ought in all reason to have accepted it. They cannot sue for specific performance—either of the promise to pay the charter hire, or of the promise to do the repairs—because damages are an adequate remedy for the breach. What is the alternative which the shipowners present to the charterers? Either the charterers must pay the charter hire for years to come, whilst the vessel lies idle and useless for want of repair. Or the charterers must do repairs which would cost twice as much as the ship would be worth when repaired—after which the shipowners might sell it as scrap, making the repairs a useless waste of money. In short, on either alternative, the shipowners seek to compel specific performance of one or other of the provisions of the charter—with most unjust and unreasonable consequences—when damages would be an adequate remedy. I do not think the law allows them to do this. I think they should accept redelivery and sue for damages. The charterers are, we are told, good for the money. That should suffice.

Orr and Browne L.JJ. agreed.

CLEA SHIPPING CORP v BULK OIL INTERNATIONAL LTD THE ALASKAN TRADER

Queen's Bench Division (Commercial Court) [1984] 1 All E.R. 129

By a charter dated October 19, 1979 the owners chartered the Alaskan Trader to charterers for a period **18–014** of approximately 24 months. After nearly a year the ship suffered an engine breakdown whereupon the charterers said they had no further use for it. The owners repaired it and on April 7, 1981 informed the charterers that the ship was again at their disposal. The charterers considered the charter-party to have ended and declined to give the master any instructions; but the owners maintained the ship at anchor with a full crew ready to sail until the time charter expired in December 1981. The question was whether the charterers could recover the hire paid for the period April to December 1981. An arbitrator held that the owners had no legitimate interest in pursuing a claim for hire rather than damages.

LLOYD J

[Having examined the authorities:] In addition to arguing that what Lord Reid had said about legitimate interest was only a quotation from counsel, and in any event obiter, arguments with which I have already dealt, counsel for the owners submitted that Lord Reid was, quite simply, wrong. It seems to me that it would be difficult for me to take that view in the light of what was said by all three members of the Court of Appeal in *The Puerto Buitrago* [above]. Whether one takes Lord Reid's language, which was adopted by Orr and Browne L.JJ.

in *The Puerto Buitrago*, or Lord Denning M.R.'s language in that case ("in all reason"), or Kerr J.'s language in *The Odenfeld* [1978] 2 Lloyd's Rep. 357 ("wholly unreasonable . . . quite unrealistic, unreasonable and untenable"), there comes a point at which the court will cease, on general equitable principles, to allow the innocent party to enforce his contract according to its strict legal terms. How one defines that point is obviously a matter of some difficulty, for it involves drawing a line between conduct which is merely unreasonable (see per Lord Reid in *White & Carter v McGregor* criticising the Lord President in *Langford & Co Ltd v Dutch*) and conduct which is wholly unreasonable (see per Kerr J. in The Odenfeld at 374). But however difficult it may be to define the point, that there is such a point seems to me to have been accepted both by the Court of Appeal in *The Puerto Buitrago* and by Kerr J. in *The Odenfeld*.

I turn last to the alternative ground on which the arbitrator based his decision, that this was a contract which called for co-operation between the parties, and therefore fell within Lord Reid's first limitation. Counsel for the charterers argued that a time charter is a contract for services, to be performed by the owners through the master and crew, and through the use of their vessel. As a contract for services, it is, as Lord Diplock pointed out in *The Scaptrade* [1983] 2 All E.R. 763 at 766, [1983] 3 W.L.R. 203 at 207—

"the very prototype of a contract of which before the fusion of law and equity a court would never grant specific performance . . ."

As in any other contract for services the owners earn their remuneration by performing the services required. If they are wrongfully prevented from performing any services, then, as in any other contract for services, the only remedy lies in damages. The fact that the owners' remuneration in this case, called hire, is payable in advance makes no difference. Counsel for the owners, on the other hand, argued that the owners earned their hire simply by holding the vessel and the services of their master and crew at the charterers' disposal. He concedes that in the case of master and servant, where the master has wrongfully dismissed the servant, the servant cannot earn remuneration by holding himself at the disposal of his master. He is confined to his remedy in damages. But counsel for the owners submits that a time charter is different. In view of my decision on the legitimate interest point, it is unnecessary for me to decide between these rival arguments, or to explore the nature of a time charter contract any further. All I will say is that, at first blush, there seemed much to be said for the argument of counsel for the charterers. I say no more, because in *The Odenfeld* Kerr J. found a similar argument unimpressive.

For the reasons I have given I would dismiss the owners' appeal and uphold the award.

Appeal Dismissed.

REICHMAN v BEVERIDGE

Court of Appeal [2006] EWCA Civ 1659

18–015   In January 2000, the two defendants (Beveridge and Gauntlett), then in partnership as practising solicitors, entered into a 5-year lease of office premises with the claimant landlords. The defendants ceased to practise in February 2003. Having no further use for the office premises, they did not pay the rent that was due in March 2003, nor thereafter. In January 2004, the landlords sued for the rent that was due. The essence of the defendants' response was that the principles of contract law now apply to leases in such a way that a landlord is required to take reasonable steps to reduce its loss and, in particular, that it is not open to a landlord simply to proceed as though the lease is subsisting and sue for the rent. At a preliminary hearing of the question of "whether it is necessary as a matter of law for a landlord to mitigate his loss when seeking to recover arrears of rent", District Judge Kubiak held that the landlord is under no such duty; and, on appeal, her ruling was confirmed by His Honour Judge Reid QC. The defendants appealed to the Court of Appeal.

Lloyd LJ reviewed the case-law after *White and Carter*, namely: *The Puerto Buitrago* (above); *Gator Shipping Corporation v Trans-Asiatic Oil Ltd, The Odenfeld* [1978] 2 Lloyd's Reports 357 where, at 374, Kerr J emphasised that "any fetter on the innocent party's right of election whether or not to accept a repudiation will only be applied in extreme cases, viz., where damages would be an adequate remedy and where an election to keep the contract alive would be wholly unreasonable"; *The Alaskan*

Trader (above); and *Ocean Marine Navigation Ltd v Koch Carbon Inc, The Dynamic* [2003] EWHC 1936 (Comm), where Simon J followed the orthodox view that any fetter applies only in extreme cases. Summarising the law, Lloyd LJ continued:

> "17. There is, therefore, a very limited category of cases in which, although the innocent party to a contract has not accepted a repudiation by the other party, and although the innocent party is able to continue to perform all his obligations under the contract despite the absence of co-operation from the other party, nevertheless the court will not allow the innocent party to enforce his full contractual right to maintain the contract in force and sue for the contract price. The characteristics of such cases are that an election to keep the contract alive would be wholly unreasonable and that damages would be an adequate remedy, or that the landlord would have no legitimate interest in making such an election. Mr Gauntlett seeks to establish that a case where the tenant has not only failed to pay rent and all other sums due under the lease, but has also abandoned the demised premises is, or may be, within this category of cases."

Having reviewed the question of whether English law fully protects the landlord's expectation interest (in the way that it would if the landlord were a straightforward contractor), Lloyd LJ continued:

LLOYD LJ

28. If it is still the law of England that damages for the loss of future rent cannot be recovered after the landlord has taken back possession of the premises following a tenant's default, as seems to me to be the case, then damages cannot be an adequate remedy for the landlord in the circumstances suggested by Mr Gauntlett, and one of the conditions for the intervention of equity so as to fetter the landlord's ability to hold the tenant to the lease is not satisfied. Even if it is not clear that this is the position under English law, the uncertainty of the position at law would be relevant to the reasonableness or otherwise of the landlord's conduct. The landlord could not be criticised for wishing to avoid embarking on litigation which might have to go to the House of Lords before the point was settled . . .

30. The important point is whether it could be said that a landlord was acting wholly unreasonably in failing to take steps to find an alternative tenant to whom to let in place of the defaulting tenant, rather than leaving the lease in place and suing for the rent as it falls due. That is to be considered against the background of the rights and obligations under the lease. If the lease remains in force, the landlord is entitled to the rent and other sums falling due. Of course, if the tenant is in default there may be a question whether the landlord will in fact recover the sums due in full, but if so the same would be true of any claim for damages to which he may be entitled if the lease is brought to an end. No doubt if the rental market has improved the landlord will forfeit and re-let at a profit, so the question is only likely to arise if the landlord would not be able to re-let easily or only at a lower rent. In that case, as already discussed, the landlord cannot under English law expect to be able to sue the tenant for damages in respect of the difference between the lower rent under a new letting and the rent to which he would have been entitled under the original lease. His right to the original rent comes to an end as soon as he takes possession in a way which is inconsistent with the continuance of the original tenancy. Leaving aside the *Walls v Atcheson* approach, the landlord had, in the present case, no relevant right to go into the premises under the lease (or not until only 6 months of the term remained, in July 2004). There may be some scope for saying that steps preparatory to re-letting can be taken without amounting to a re-entry such as to forfeit the lease, as in *Oastler v Henderson* (1877) 2 QBD 575, for example, but the landlord would be entitled to take a cautious line on that, knowing that the tenant would wish to argue that the lease had been determined sooner rather than later . . .

Conclusion

39. Mr Gauntlett urged on us a modern approach to the relationship between landlord and tenant, focussing on principles of contract law, and a policy approach which would not leave premises empty, after the tenants had abandoned them and while the landlord waited for the end of the lease, so as to avoid the waste of useful space and to ensure that property is put to beneficial use. As to the latter factor, if there is enough demand for the space, the market rent may exceed that payable under the lease in which case the landlord will no doubt

terminate the lease and re-let at a profit. Equally, the tenant can attempt to find an assignee or sub-tenant to use the premises; it is not only the landlord who can take steps to fill the space.

40. Leaving aside policy issues of that kind, it seems to me that Mr Gauntlett's submissions fail to take account of the present state of English law as to the consequences of the premature termination of a tenancy, or of the very limited scope for the intervention of equity as explained in *White and Carter* and subsequent cases. Having regard to the way in which that has been explored and explained in the cases, in particular *The Odenfeld* (see paragraph [16 ii)] above), it seems to me impossible to say that a tenant could successfully invoke equity in that way. First, it seems to me very far from clear, to say the least, that the landlords were acting unreasonably in not taking their own steps to find a new tenant, rather than leaving it to the tenants to propose one, or in rejecting a proposal made by the tenants. Given the extremely limited nature of the test ("wholly unreasonable"), it would have to be a most extraordinary case for a tenant to be able to show that the land-lord's conduct could properly be characterised in this way. Secondly, if it be the case that in 2003 the market rent was lower than that reserved by the lea se, damages would not be an adequate remedy for the landlords if they terminated the lease by way of forfeiture and then re-let at a lower rent, because under English law as it stands they could not recover damages to compensate for the loss of rent. If, on the other hand the market rent was the same or higher, it should have been possible for the tenants to take their own steps to find an assignee. If they had found an assignee (or subtenant) whom the landlords had refused to accept on reasonable terms, that may have been a different matter; they would have had a statutory remedy under the Landlord and Tenant Act 1985, and there would have been a number of different steps open to them. In the present case, so far as we know, the tenants did not seek to establish that the landlords' refusal to agree to an assignment to a possible new tenant was in breach of the statutory obligation.

41. It is also to be noted that it is for the party in breach to establish that the innocent party's conduct is wholly unreasonable and that damages would be an adequate remedy. Mr Gauntlett's position seems to be that any landlord, knowing that the tenants have abandoned the premises, ought to take steps to re-let, and therefore to terminate the tenancy, and look to the tenant for damages to cover any resulting loss. It does not seem to me that this could be right. It cannot follow from what Lord Reid said in *White and Carter*. It is clear from that and the later cases that it would be extremely rare for this principle to apply, whereas Mr Gauntlett seeks to apply it to what must be a very common set of circumstances.

42. With the benefit of the industry and learning of Miss Tipples, the argument in this court has been much fuller than it was before District Judge Kubiak or His Honour Judge Reid Q.C. With that benefit, I have come to the same conclusion as each of them did, namely that, on the present state of English law, the contention which Mr Gauntlett wishes to advance by way of defence on quantum is not open to him. I do not decide whether or not repudiation plays any, and if so what, part in the English law of landlord and tenant. That is not directly in issue before us, and it would be wrong to decide it unnecessarily. There is, however, no case in English law that shows that a landlord can recover damages from a former tenant in respect of loss of future rent after termination, and there is at least one case which decides that he cannot. In those circumstances, either damages are not an adequate remedy for the landlord, or at least the landlord would be acting reason-ably in taking the view that he should not terminate the lease because he may well not be able to recover such damages. In principle, moreover, if the landlord chooses to regard it as up to the tenant to propose an assignee, sub-tenant or, if he wishes, a substitute tenant under a new tenancy, rather than take the initiative himself, that is not unreasonable, still less wholly unreasonable.

43. For those reasons, what Lord Reid said in *White and Carter*, as developed in the later cases cited above, does not apply to the position in which the present parties found themselves after the Defendants had aban-doned the premises. I would therefore dismiss this appeal.

Point for reflection

18–016   In *E-nik Limited v Department for Communities and Local Government* [2012] EWHC 3027 (Comm) the Department contracted with the claimant supplier for the provision of IT consultancy services. Under clause 2.1 of the contract, the Department undertook "to purchase [a] minimum of 500 days of Consultancy from the Supplier per year based on project requirement, additional days will be required once the purchased days have been exhausted." Applying *Rainy Sky v Kookmin Bank*, (above Ch.17), Burton J held that clause 2.1 would make no commercial sense if it meant, as the Department argued, that if their project requirements did not require at least 500 days of consultancy services, then there was no obligation to purchase a minimum of 500 days' services from the claimant. Rather, the Department was committed to purchasing at least 500 days' services from the claimant each year; and, even if no services were actually required, the claimant was justified in billing the Department accordingly. On the evidence, it was clear that the claimant was ready and willing to supply services and that, applying *White and Carter (Council) Ltd v McGregor*, he was entitled to act in this way.

----

3. CONTRACTS OF EMPLOYMENT AND THE "ELECTIVE" THEORY

In *Société Générale v Geys* [2012] UKSC 63, one of the questions was whether, where one of the parties to an employment contract commits a repudiatory breach of contract, the contract comes to an end *automatically* or does so only if the innocent party elects to accept the repudiation as putting an end to the contract. In other words, in contracts of employment, does the usual "elective" rule apply or is there a special exception that means that, irrespective of the innocent party's wishes, the contract is at an end? The extensive and inconsistent case-law on this question lent support to both views.

18–017

In support of the automatic termination view, for example, one might point to *Vine v National Dock Labour Board* [1956] 1 Q.B. 658 at 674, where Jenkins LJ said, obiter, "In the ordinary case of master and servant . . . the repudiation or the wrongful dismissal puts an end to the contract, and a claim for damages arises. It is necessarily a claim for damages and nothing more. The nature of the bargain is such that it can be nothing more." In the House of Lords Viscount Kilmuir agreed, saying, ". . . if the master wrongfully dismisses the servant, either summarily or by giving insufficient notice, the employment is effectively terminated, albeit in breach of contract." In *Sanders v Ernest A. Neale Ltd* [1974] 3 All E.R. 327 Sir John Donaldson P said that "the repudiation of a contract of employment is an exception to the general rule. It terminates the contract without the necessity for acceptance by the injured party." The basis for the alleged exception appears to lie in the fact that the contract for personal services cannot be specifically enforced.

Against this view, however, in *Decro-Wall International SA v Practitioners in Marketing Ltd* [1971] 2 All E.R. 216 Salmon and Sachs LJJ expressed their doubts about the automatic termination theory (though Salmon LJ had appeared to accept that the contract was terminated by breach in *Denmark Productions Ltd v Boscobel Productions Ltd* [1969] 1 Q.B. 699). In *Thomas Marshall (Exports) Ltd v Guinle* [1978] 3 All E.R. 193 Megarry VC held that a contract of service was not terminated when repudiated by the employee and granted an injunction restraining the employee from soliciting orders from the employer's customers and from disclosing his trade secrets. The Vice Chancellor thought it impossible to reconcile the opinions in the preceding paragraph with the cases deciding that an employee who had repudiated his contract could be restrained by injunction from acting in breach of it: *Lumley v Wagner* (1852) 1 De G.M. & G. 604, *Warner Bros Pictures Inc v Nelson* [1937] 1 K.B. 209. The "automatic determination" cases had not dealt with the question whether, by repudiation, the servant could release himself not only from any further obligations to serve but also from other restrictions, imposed by the contract or implied by law only while the contract exists.

Most significantly, perhaps, in *Gunton v London Borough of Richmond* [1980] 3 All E.R. 577 the Court of Appeal held that the wrongful dismissal of an employee did not put an end to the contract of service. The ordinary principles of contract apply. The fact that a contract of personal service cannot be specifically enforced makes no difference for there are innumerable contracts to which specific performance is inapplicable (cf. *Frost v Knight*, above): ". . . the servant cannot sue in debt under the contract for remuneration in respect of any period after the wrongful dismissal, because the right to receive remuneration and the obligation to render services are mutually inter-dependent"—per Buckley LJ. [But do not both the right and the obligation continue, if the servant can elect to keep the contract alive?] ". . . the servant must come under an immediate obligation to mitigate his damages and so must almost invariably be bound to seek other employment . . ."—per Buckley LJ. [But is not seeking other employment accepting the repudiation and, if he is obliged to seek other employment, is he not thereby obliged to accept the repudiation?] Brightman LJ, agreeing that the servant could not sue for wages, said that the status or relationship of master and servant was determined, but not the contract.

Shaw LJ, dissenting on this point, said that the practical basis for according an election to the injured party has no reality in relation to a contract of service where there is a total repudiation which is at once destructive of the contractual relationship. To preserve the bare contractual relationship is an empty formality. It might be different where the repudiation is "oblique", for example where the employer seeks to change the nature of the work required to be done.

Faced with these conflicting views, in *Geys*, the majority of the Supreme Court (Lord Sumption dissenting) preferred to treat the usual elective rule as applicable to contracts of employment. On the facts of *Geys*, where a bank's initial dismissal of an employee was a repudiatory breach, and where the employee (despite having been taken at once to clear his desk and escorted from the building) could be treated as not having accepted the repudiation, this made a difference of several million euros to the "compensation payment" made. The majority's thinking is captured by Lord Hope at para.15: "The automatic theory can operate to the disadvantage of the injured party in a way that enables the wrongdoer to benefit from his own wrong. The law should seek to avoid such an obvious injustice. Where there is a real choice as to the direction of travel, the common law should favour the direction that is least likely to to do harm to the injured party."

While it is arguable that the majority's support for the elective theory in *Geys* is in line with *White and Carter (Council) Ltd v McGregor*, the principle does not give the innocent party an unfettered right to treat the contract as subsisting. On the facts of *Geys*, there was no way that the employee could carry out his work without the employing bank's cooperation—and, quite clearly, the bank was not cooperating; and what, we might wonder, was the employee's "legitimate interest" in treating the contract as subsisting (other than the several million euros at stake)? Lord Sumption (dissenting) opens his speech in a way that clearly indicates his view of where the merits and good sense lie:

LORD SUMPTION

108. Mr Geys is a lucky man. He had a responsible and highly paid job with an entitlement to participate in a profit-sharing bonus scheme dependent on the performance of his division, in addition to discretionary bonuses. The other side of the coin was that he had no contractual job security. Under his contract of employment, his employers, Société Générale ("SG"), were entitled to dismiss him at any time without cause either upon three months' notice or "with immediate effect by making a payment to you in lieu of notice." This is what happened to Mr Geys. He was called to a meeting on 29 November 2007 and given a letter informing him that SG had decided to terminate his employment with immediate effect and that the "appropriate termination documentation" would follow. In accordance with the time-honoured ritual, he was then taken to clear his desk and escorted from the building by security staff. There could not have been the slightest doubt that his employment relationship with SG was at an end. He cannot have supposed that he had been dismissed for cause, for no cause was stated. The only reasonable inference was that SG was purporting to dismiss him summarily without cause, as they were entitled in principle to do.

109. Fortunately for Mr Geys, SG did not understand their own contract. It is common ground that if they had handed him a cheque for his payment in lieu of notice at the meeting on 29 November, his dismissal would have taken effect according to his contract at once. Because the right to terminate with immediate effect is exercisable "by making a payment in lieu of notice", it is common ground that the purported dismissal with immediate effect on 29 November was a repudiatory breach of contract by SG. They were not entitled to dismiss him with

immediate effect from 29 November, but only with effect from the payment in lieu. It was, however, a repudiation of the most technical kind. There was no doubt about SG's right to dismiss him with immediate effect if they set about it in the right way. For this reason, as I understand the majority to accept, SG's mistake in itself caused him no loss. It made a practical difference of only three weeks and a legal difference of just over five. It made a practical difference of three weeks because the payment in lieu was in fact received on 18 December by Mr Geys' bank on his behalf. If knowledge of the payment by Mr Geys himself was required (which I doubt), he had it by his own admission when he consulted his account on-line some time in late December. As he accepted in cross-examination, he saw the payment from SG and realised that "it had to be—thought would probably be, yes, compensation pay of—in lieu. That is the best guess one could have." In the circumstances, it could not have been anything else. SG's mistake made a legal difference of just over five weeks because the majority of this Court is of the opinion that the payment, although received by Mr Geys' bank on his behalf on 18 December, was by a term to be implied into the contract ineffective to bring it to an end until 6 January, when SG unequivocally told him what he had already appreciated in late December, namely that the payment was in lieu of notice.

110. The result is that although the employment relationship was dead for all practical purposes from 29 November, and Mr Geys contributed nothing to SG's fortunes after that date, he is in a position to argue that technically the contract limped on as a formal "shell" or "husk" (to use the terms deployed in argument) into January 2008. The financial consequences of this, if it is right, are considerable. The effect of paragraph 5.15(b)(iii) and (iv) of the contract is that if Mr Geys' "employment terminates" after 31 December 2007, he is entitled to a "Compensation Payment" assessed by reference to the aggregate of his bonus awards for the calendar years 2006 and 2007, whereas if it terminates on or before that date, it will be assessed by reference to his awards in 2005 and 2006, which were substantially lower. The figures are disputed, but the result is likely to be that SG's breach, although it has caused Mr Geys no substantial loss, will have brought him a windfall amounting to several million euros. Rarely can form have triumphed so completely over substance.

Point for reflection

In *Hare v Murphy Bros Ltd* [1973] I.C.R. 331, NIRC the plaintiff, a foreman employed by the defendants, **18–018** was sentenced in June 1971 to 12 months' imprisonment for unlawful wounding. On his release in February 1972 the defendants told him that there was no job for him. He claimed compensation for unfair dismissal. It was held that the sentence of imprisonment was "a breach by him of his contract of so serious a nature, bearing in mind the length of time during which he would be away from work and importance of his position as foreman, that it went to the root and constituted a repudiation of his contract of employment." The contract had come to an end as a result of the repudiation and the consequent sentence of imprisonment, so there could be no unfair dismissal in February 1972.

However, in *F C Shepherd & Co Ltd v Jerrom* [1986] 3 All E.R. 589, the Court of Appeal held that Hare's case was not a binding authority on this point. The contract of an apprentice who had been sentenced to borstal training had come to an end, not because the apprentice had repudiated it, but because it had been frustrated by the sentence of the court. It was not open to the apprentice, who alleged that he had been unfairly dismissed, to claim that this was a self-induced frustration and so not effective to terminate the contract (see above) because he could not be allowed to take advantage of his own wrong.

----

4. Specific Performance and Injunction

Examples of cases concerning the principles according to which specific performance is granted or **18–019** refused are *Gibson v Manchester City Council* (above, Ch.2), *Tamplin v James* (above, Ch.5), *Denny v Hancock* (above, Ch.5), *Beswick v Beswick* (above, Ch.13), and *Redgrave v Hurd* (above, Ch.14). The leading modern case is *Co-operative Insurance Society Ltd v Argyll Stores (Holdings) Ltd* (below).

Where a court will decline to order specific performance (for example, in relation to a contract of employment or a contract for services), care will be taken to ensure that an injunction does not become a disguised or indirect order for specific performance. In principle, there is a clear distinction between ordering that services be rendered in accordance with the contract and ordering that acts that are inconsistent with the terms of the contract not be taken (see, e.g., *Lumley v Wagner* (1852) 1 De G.M. & G. 604, and *Warner Bros Pictures Inc v Nelson* [1937] 1 K.B. 209). However, where the practical effect of a restraining order is to compel performance of the contract, this might be seen as militating against the grant of an injunction (see, e.g., *Warren v Mendy* [1989] 1 W.L.R. 853; but, compare, *LauritzenCool AB v Lady Navigation Inc* [2005] EWCA Civ 579).

CO-OPERATIVE INSURANCE SOCIETY LTD v ARGYLL STORES (HOLDINGS) LTD

House of Lords [1998] A.C. 1, [1997] 2 W.L.R. 898, [1997] 3 All E.R. 297

18–020 The defendants were tenants for 35 years from August 1979 of a property comprising 30 per cent of the total letting area of the Hillsborough Shopping Centre, Sheffield. It was the anchor unit in the centre and played a key role. The lease required the defendants to keep the demised premises open for retail trade during the usual hours of business. The current rent was £140,000 a year. After the property had made a loss of £70,000 in its last trading year the defendants decided in May 1995 to sell it (together with 26 other supermarkets), well knowing of the "keep open" covenant. The plaintiff landlord wrote asking the defendant to keep open for trading until an assignee could be found. The defendants did not respond and, on May 19, 1995, stripped out the shop. It would cost £1 million to reinstate. Judge Maddocks QC gave summary judgment for damages to be assessed but refused an order for specific performance. The plaintiff appealed.

The Court of Appeal (Leggatt and Roch LJJ, Millett LJ dissenting) allowed an appeal and ordered specific performance of the covenant during the remainder of the term, i.e. until August 3, 2014. On appeal to the House of Lords, Lords Browne-Wilkinson, Slynn, Hope and Clyde said that they agreed with the speech of Lord Hoffmann.

LORD HOFFMANN

[Having considered (1) The issue, (2) The facts and (3) The trial, continued:]

(4) The settled practice

There is no dispute about the existence of the settled practice to which the judge referred. It is sufficient for this purpose to refer to *Braddon Towers Ltd v International Stores Ltd* (1979) [1987] 1 E.G.L.R. 209 at 213, where Slade J. said:

"Whether or not this may be properly described as a rule of law, I do not doubt that for many years practitioners have advised their clients that it is the settled and invariable practice of this court never to grant mandatory injunctions requiring persons to carry on business."

But the practice has never, so far as I know, been examined by this House and it is open to CIS to say that it rests upon inadequate grounds or that it has been too inflexibly applied. Specific performance is traditionally regarded in English law as an exceptional remedy, as opposed to the common law damages to which a successful plaintiff is entitled as of right. There may have been some element of later rationalisation of an untidier history, but by the nineteenth century it was orthodox doctrine that the power to decree specific performance was part of the discretionary jurisdiction of the Court of Chancery to do justice in cases in which the remedies available at common law were inadequate. This is the basis of the general principle that specific performance will not be ordered when damages are an adequate remedy. By contrast, in countries with legal systems based on civil law, such as France, Germany and Scotland, the plaintiff is prima facie entitled to specific performance. The cases in which he is confined to a claim for damages are regarded as the exceptions. In practice, however, there is less difference between common law and civilian systems than these general statements might lead one to suppose. The principles on which English judges exercise the discretion to grant specific performance are reasonably well settled and depend on a number of considerations, mostly of a practical nature, which are of very general application. I have made no investigation of civilian systems, but a priori I would expect that judges take much the same matters into account in deciding whether specific performance would be inappropriate in a particular case.

The practice of not ordering a defendant to carry on a business is not entirely dependent upon damages being an adequate remedy. In *Dowty Boulton Paul Ltd v Wolverhampton Corp.* [1971] 1 W.L.R. 204 at 211, 212 Pennycuick V.-C. refused to order the corporation to maintain an airfield as a going concern because:

"It is very well established that the court will not order specific performance of an obligation to carry on a business . . . It is unnecessary in the circumstances to discuss whether damages would be an adequate remedy to the company."

Thus the reasons which underlie the established practice may justify a refusal of specific performance even when damages are not an adequate remedy.

The most frequent reason given in the cases for declining to order someone to carry on a business is that it would require constant supervision by the court. In *J. C. Williamson Ltd v Lukey* (1931) 45 C.L.R. 282 at 297–298 Dixon J. said flatly: "Specific performance is inapplicable when the continued supervision of the Court is necessary in order to ensure the fulfilment of the contract."

There has, I think, been some misunderstanding about what is meant by continued superintendence. It may at first sight suggest that the judge (or some other officer of the court) would literally have to supervise the execution of the order. In *C. H. Giles & Co Ltd v Morris* [1972] 1 W.L.R. 307 at 318 Megarry J. said that "difficulties of constant superintendence" were a "narrow consideration" because—

"there is normally no question of the court having to send its officers to supervise the performance of the order . . . Performance . . . is normally secured by the realisation of the person enjoined that he is liable to be punished for contempt if evidence of his disobedience to the order is put before the court . . ."

This is, of course, true but does not really meet the point. The judges who have said that the need for constant supervision was an objection to such orders were no doubt well aware that supervision would in practice take the form of rulings by the court, on applications made by the parties, as to whether there had been a breach of the order. It is the possibility of the court having to give an indefinite series of such rulings in order to ensure the execution of the order which has been regarded as undesirable.

Why should this be so? A principal reason is that, as Megarry J. pointed out in the passage to which I have referred, the only means available to the court to enforce its order is the quasi-criminal procedure of punishment for contempt. This is a powerful weapon; so powerful, in fact, as often to be unsuitable as an instrument for adjudicating upon the disputes which may arise over whether a business is being run in accordance with the terms of the court's order. The heavy-handed nature of the enforcement mechanism is a consideration which may go to the exercise of the court's discretion in other cases as well, but its use to compel the running of a business is perhaps the paradigm case of its disadvantages and it is in this context that I shall discuss them.

The prospect of committal or even a fine, with the damage to commercial reputation which will be caused by a finding of contempt of court, is likely to have at least two undesirable consequences. First, the defendant, who ex hypothesi did not think that it was in his economic interest to run the business at all, now has to make decisions under a sword of Damocles which may descend if the way the business is run does not conform to the terms of the order. This is, as one might say, no way to run a business. In this case, the Court of Appeal ([1996] Ch. 286) made light of the point because it assumed that, once the defendant had been ordered to run the business, self-interest and compliance with the order would thereafter go hand in hand. But, as I shall explain, this is not necessarily true.

Secondly, the seriousness of a finding of contempt for the defendant means that any application to enforce the order is likely to be a heavy and expensive piece of litigation. The possibility of repeated applications over a period of time means that, in comparison with a once and for all inquiry as to damages, the enforcement of the remedy is likely to be expensive in terms of cost to the parties and the resources of the judicial system.

This is a convenient point at which to distinguish between orders which require a defendant to carry on an activity, such as running a business over a more or less extended period of time, and orders which require him to achieve a result. The possibility of repeated applications for rulings on compliance with the order which arises in the former case does not exist to anything like the same extent in the latter. Even if the achievement of the result is a complicated matter which will take some time, the court, if called upon to rule, only has to examine the finished work and say whether it complies with the order . . .

This distinction between orders to carry on activities and to achieve results explains why the courts have in appropriate circumstances ordered specific performance of building contracts and repairing covenants (see *Wolverhampton Corp v Emmons* [1901] 1 K.B. 515 (building contract) and *Jeune v Queens Cross Properties Ltd* [1974] Ch. 97 (repairing covenant)). It by no means follows, however, that even obligations to achieve a result will always be enforced by specific performance. There may be other objections, to some of which I now turn.

One such objection, which applies to orders to achieve a result and a fortiori to orders to carry on an activity, is imprecision in the terms of the order. If the terms of the court's order, reflecting the terms of the obligation, cannot be precisely drawn, the possibility of wasteful litigation over compliance is increased. So is the oppression caused by the defendant having to do things under threat of proceedings for contempt. The less precise the order, the fewer the signposts to the forensic minefield which he has to traverse. The fact that the terms of a contractual obligation are sufficiently definite to escape being void for uncertainty, or to found a claim for damages, or to permit compliance to be made a condition of relief against forfeiture, does not necessarily mean that they will be sufficiently precise to be capable of being specifically performed. So in *Wolverhampton Corp v Emmons* [1901] 1 K.B. 515 at 525 Romer L.J. said that the first condition for specific enforcement of a building contract was—

> "that the particulars of the work are so far definitely ascertained that the Court can sufficiently see what is the exact nature of the work of which it is asked to order the performance."

Similarly in *Morris v Redland Bricks Ltd* [1970] A.C. 652 at 666 Lord Upjohn stated the following general principle for the grant of mandatory injunctions to carry out building works:

> ". . . the court must be careful to see that the defendant knows exactly in fact what he has to do and this means not as a matter of law but as a matter of fact, so that in carrying out an order he can give his contractors the proper instructions."

Precision is of course a question of degree and the courts have shown themselves willing to cope with a certain degree of imprecision in cases of orders requiring the achievement of a result in which the plaintiffs' merits appeared strong; like all the reasons which I have been discussing, it is, taken alone, merely a discretionary matter to be taken into account (see Spry Equitable Remedies (4th edn, 1990) p. 112). It is, however, a very important one . . .

There is a further objection to an order requiring the defendant to carry on a business, which was emphasised by Millett L.J. in the Court of Appeal (see [1996] 3 All E.R. 934 at 948–950, [1996] Ch. 286 at 303–305). This is that it may cause injustice by allowing the plaintiff to enrich himself at the defendant's expense. The loss which the defendant may suffer through having to comply with the order (for example, by running a business at a loss for an indefinite period) may be far greater than the plaintiff would suffer from the contract being broken. As Professor R. J. Sharpe explains in "Specific Remedies for Contract Breach" (ed. Reiter and Swan Studies in Contract Law (1980)) p. 129:

> "In such circumstances, a specific decree in favour of the plaintiff will put him in a bargaining position vis-á-vis the defendant whereby the measure of what he will receive will be the value to the defendant of being released from performance. If the plaintiff bargains effectively, the amount he will set will exceed the value to him of performance and will approach the cost to the defendant to complete."

This was the reason given by Lord Westbury L.C. in *Isenberg v East India House Estate Co Ltd* (1863) 3 De G.J. & S. 263 at 273, 46 E.R. 637 at 641 for refusing a mandatory injunction to compel the defendant to pull down part of a new building which interfered with the plaintiff's light and exercising instead the Court of Chancery's recently acquired jurisdiction under the Chancery Amendment Act 1858 (Lord Cairns's Act) to order payment of damages:

> "I hold it . . . to be the duty of the Court in such a case as the present not, by granting a mandatory injunction, to deliver over the Defendants to the Plaintiff bound hand and foot, in order to be made subject to any extortionate demand that he may by possibility make, but to substitute for such mandatory injunction an inquiry before itself, in order to ascertain the measure of damage that has been actually sustained."

The cumulative effect of these various reasons, none of which would necessarily be sufficient on its own, seems to me to show that the settled practice is based on sound sense. Of course the grant or refusal of specific performance remains a matter for the judge's discretion. There are no binding rules, but this does not mean that there cannot be settled principles, founded on practical considerations of the kind which I have discussed, which do not have to be re-examined in every case, but which the courts will apply in all but exceptional circumstances. As Slade J. said in the passage which I have quoted from *Braddon Towers Ltd v International*

Stores Ltd (1979) [1987] 1 E.G.L.R. 209 at 213, lawyers have no doubt for many years advised their clients on this basis. In the present case, Leggatt L.J. remarked that there was no evidence that such advice had been given (see [1996] Ch. 286 at 294). In my view, if the law or practice on a point is settled, it should be assumed that persons entering into legal transactions will have been advised accordingly. I am sure that Leggatt L.J. would not wish to encourage litigants to adduce evidence of the particular advice which they received. Indeed, I doubt whether such evidence would be admissible.

Appeal Allowed.

Questions

1. Professor Gareth Jones writes: "It is difficult to envisage how Co-operative could ever prove what loss it suffered from Argyll's breach of covenant. Here then is a situation where the injured party is not indifferent whether he is awarded damages or granted specific performance. On the other hand, there is much force in Lord Hoffmann's argument that the difficulties of supervision would be considerable, spawning further litigation and the sanction of contempt a draconian one. Furthermore there are the economic arguments already rehearsed. ['If the consequence (of the decision of the Court of Appeal) is to compel a considerable number of "big" businesses to run the stores for a significant period of time at a loss, the result will be an inefficient allocation of economic resources', Jones and Goodhart, *Specific Performance* (2nd edn 1996), p.54.] Co-operative Insurance is a difficult case which I am told, would be decided very differently in France and Germany. But, on balance, the conclusion of the House of Lords is more to be welcomed than deplored" [1997] 56 C.L.J. 488, 490–491. Do you agree?   **18-021**

2. *The Principles of European Contract Law, 1998 art.9: 102: Non-monetary Obligations* provides as follows:

    "(1) The aggrieved party is entitled to specific performance of an obligation other than one to pay money, including the remedying of a defective performance.

    (2) Specific performance cannot, however, be obtained where:

        (a) performance would be unlawful or impossible; or
        (b) performance would cause the obligor unreasonable effort or expense; or
        (c) the performance consists in the provision of services or work of a personal character or depends upon a personal relationship; or
        (d) the aggrieved party may reasonably obtain performance from another source.

    (3) The aggrieved party will lose the right to specific performance if it fails to seek it within a reasonable time after it has or ought to have become aware of the non-performance."

    Does this suggest that the result in *Co-operative* would be different under European law? Would performance have caused Argyll unreasonable effort or expense?

Further reading

J.C. Smith, 'Anticipatory Breach of Contract' in E. Lomnicka and CJG Morse (eds), *Contemporary Issues in Commercial Law: Essays in Honour of A.G. Guest* (London: Sweet & Maxwell, 1994) p.175

19

DAMAGES

LEARNING OBJECTIVES

By the end of this chapter, you should:

- understand that the standard remedy for breach of contract is an award of damages and that the usual measure is the so-called "expectation" measure (the object of which is to put the innocent party in the same position as if the contract had been performed);
- be familiar with the case-law in which the courts have grappled with the interpretation and application of the apparently simple idea of putting the innocent party "in the same position as if the contract had been performed";
- have critically reflected on how the court should choose between a "cost of cure" and a "diminution in value" award;
- have a view on how the court should respond to cases where there is a calculating breach which causes no financial loss to the innocent party;
- should be familiar with the case-law on "reliance"-based recovery (particularly in order to recover wasted expenditure);
- be able to place the modern development of awards of damages for disappointment (starting with *Jarvis v Swan's Tours*) in the context of the protection of consumer contractors;
- understand the requirement placed upon the innocent party to take reasonable steps to mitigate the loss;
- be familiar with the leading cases on remoteness of damage and understand that this part of the law places limits on the innocent party's right to recover compensation for consequential and indirect losses;
- appreciate the potential significance of the *Transfield Shipping* case in reshaping the modern commercial law of contract;
- understand the distinction between penalties and liquidated damages clauses.

INTRODUCTION

The standard remedy sought by a claimant alleging a breach of contract is *damages* to compensate for the loss occasioned by the breach. Damages are designed to offer the victim financial *compensation* related to the loss (not, as some lay people might imagine, a figure plucked out of the air or simply nominated by the claimant). The usual starting point is that damages should be measured by reference to the claimant's so-called "expectation loss". This basic rule as to the measure of damages is generally expressed in the following way: namely, that the object of an award of damages for breach of contract is to put the innocent party in the same position as if the contract had been performed (see *Robinson v Harman* (1848) 1 Exch 850).

19–001

Typically, the expectation measure is more generous than the so-called "reliance" measure (which is designed to restore the claimant to the position that obtained before the contract was made); but, where the breach occasions no tangible loss, the expectation measure can be less generous than a restitutionary measure (which is designed to reverse an unjust enrichment).

Although the expectation measure is a relatively generous award, the law trims the recovery of damages in two principal ways. First, according to the principle of mitigation of damage, victims of a breach of contract are required to respond to the breach in a responsible way, taking reasonable steps to minimise their losses post-breach, and not unreasonably aggravating their losses. Secondly, there is the principle of remoteness of damage, this being a principle that places quite tight limits on recovery for consequential losses that are indirect, or unanticipated, or unlikely, or beyond the defendant's reasonable contemplation, or some such boundary-marker.

The cases in this chapter are divided into six sections. In the first section, the cases relate to the interpretation and application of the expectation measure; in the second, the cases probe the adequacy of the expectation measure—for example, in circumstances where the award of such damages in no way deters an egregious breach by the defendant, or where the claimant suffers disappointment but no tangible financial loss; in the third, the focus is on questions of (claimant) contribution and causation (another damage-limiting doctrine); in the fourth, the focus is on the principle of mitigation; in the fifth, the cases deal with remoteness; and, in the sixth section, the focus is on the distinction between penalty clauses (which are not enforceable, being treated as contrary to public policy) and liquidated damages clauses (which are enforceable).

1. THE EXPECTATION MEASURE

19–002   It has been said on more than one occasion that, while it is very easy to state the basic compensatory principle of seeking to award damages that will put the innocent party in the same position as if the contract had been performed, it is a deceptively difficult principle to apply. What precisely is "the same position" and what would have been the position had the contract been performed?

In what follows, two such difficulties are highlighted. First, in *Golden Strait Corporation v Nippon Yusen Kubishka Kaisha: The Golden Victory* [2007] UKHL 12, the question was whether expectation damages are to be calculated in the light of (i) what is known at the date of breach (including what might be speculated to have happened if there had been no breach) or (ii) what is known by the court when (at a later time) it makes its assessment of damages. In some cases, the subsequent knowledge will favour the claimant; but, in *The Golden Victory*, the subsequent knowledge favoured the contract breakers (so that, if the later time applied, the claimants' damages would be reduced). In a split 3/2 decision, the House of Lords preferred the later time as being more faithful to the principle that the claimant should be compensated for their actual loss. As Lord Scott put it (at para.38): "The arguments of the Owners [claimants] offend the compensatory principle. They are seeking compensation exceeding the value of the contractual benefits of which they were deprived." So, the rule seems to be that the claimant is entitled to be placed in the same situation, with respect to damages, as if the contract had been performed, taking into account everything that is actually known about what would have happened had the contract continued to run. Secondly, in *Ruxley Electronics & Construction Ltd v Forsyth* [1996] A.C. 344, the House faced the question of whether expectation damages are to be assessed on the basis of the cost of cure or the diminution in value. In many instances, it will make no practical difference whether the former or the latter is applied. However, where the cost of cure exceeds the reduction in market value, there might be an argument that the higher level of expenditure is wasteful and unreasonable. In *Ruxley*, the majority of the Court of Appeal held that the cost of cure award was appropriate no matter that some might judge it disproportionate in the circumstances. However, the House of Lords, restoring the trial judge's award, rejected cost of cure as unreasonable and awarded a sum that reflected reduction in value coupled with loss of amenity.

A. Calculation at the Date of Breach or in the Light of Post-Breach Information?

GOLDEN STRAIT CORPORATION v NIPPON YUSEN KUBISHKA KAISHA

House of Lords [2007] UKHL 12

LORD BINGHAM OF CORNHILL

My Lords,

19–003

1. The issue in this appeal concerns the assessment of damages for loss of charter hire recoverable by a shipowner where a charterer repudiates a time charter of a vessel during its currency and he accepts that repudiation, there being an available market in which the shipowner can, at or shortly after the date of acceptance of repudiation, charter out the vessel for the balance of the charter term. The dispute between the parties turns on the date at which the quantification of damages is to be made. The shipowners contend that the quantification should be made when, the repudiation having been made and accepted, they charter out (or may reasonably be expected to charter out) the vessel. Events occurring later, not affecting the value of the contractual right which the owner has lost at that time, are irrelevant. The charterers contend that the quantification should be made as of the date on which the damages actually fall to be assessed, taking account of any event which has by then occurred which affects the value of what the owners lost as a result of his repudiation. The maritime arbitrator who was the original decision-maker in this case (Mr Robert Gaisford) would have preferred to accept the owners' contention, but felt constrained by first instance authority to accept the charterers'. His decision was upheld by Langley J. in the Commercial Court ([2005] EWHC 161 (Comm), [2005] 1 All ER (Comm) 467) and by Auld and Tuckey L.JJ. and Lord Mance in the Court of Appeal ([2005] EWCA Civ 1190, [2006] 1 WLR 533). A majority of my noble and learned friends also agree with that decision. I have the misfortune to differ. I give my reasons for doing so, unauthoritative though they must be, since in my respectful opinion the existing decision undermines the quality of certainty which is a traditional strength and major selling point of English commercial law, and involves an unfortunate departure from principle.

The facts

2. By a time charterparty on an amended Shelltime 4 form dated 10 July 1998 Golden Strait Corporation, a Liberian company, as owners chartered their tanker *Golden Victory* to Nippon Yusen Kubishika Kaisha of Tokyo as charterers for a period of 7 years with one month more or less in charterers' option. The charterparty provided for payment of a minimum guaranteed base charter hire rate per day, increasing over the 7 years of the charter, but subject to a specified reduction if market rates should fall to a certain level. The owners were also to receive a share of operating profits earned by the charterers during the term of the charter above the base charter rate. The charterparty provided (in clause 33) that both owners and charterers should have the right to cancel the charter if war or hostilities were to break out between any two or more of a number of countries including the United States, the United Kingdom and Iraq. The charter was subject to English law and jurisdiction and there was an arbitration clause.

3. On 14 December 2001 the charterers repudiated the charter by redelivering the vessel to the owners. The owners accepted the repudiation three days later, on 17 December, when the charter had nearly four years to run. The owners claimed damages. The charterers did not accept the claim. The matter was referred to arbitration and the arbitrator was asked to decide whether (and if so when) the charterers had repudiated the charter, whether (and if so when) the owners had accepted the repudiation, and what was the earliest date on which the vessel could be redelivered under the charter. By an Interim Declaratory Award dated 16 September 2002 the arbitrator resolved the first two issues in the owners' favour, as summarised above. He found 6 December 2005 to be the earliest date for contractual redelivery of the vessel. This date was significant as the terminal date of the owners' claim for damages.

4. The charterers sought unsuccessfully to challenge this Award on appeal, and negotiations then followed for redelivery of the vessel to the charterers on the same terms (so far as material) as before, with settlement of damages for the period between the accepted repudiation and the redelivery. The charterers made an offer to that effect on 7 February 2003. At that stage the owners, according to evidence recited by the arbitrator in

the Reasons for his Second Declaratory Arbitration Award (para 8), had received legal advice that if they pro-ceeded to arbitration of their damages claim the arbitrator would ignore a later event of war and the charterers' option to cancel and would award the owners damages for the entire four year period between 17 December 2001 and 6 December 2005. The owners' consultant considered that an event 15 months after the repudiation was irrelevant and that (para 10) "it would be sheer stupidity and not mitigation for us to enter into a charter well below the current market with a clause which entitled the charterer to cancel if there was a war, which seemed to be about to happen". The owners rejected the charterers' offer.

5. The matter then returned to the arbitrator, who was asked to decide three further questions. The first was whether the owners had failed to mitigate their loss by not accepting the charterers' offer of 7 February 2003 to take the vessel back on charter on the same terms as before. In his Second Declaratory Arbitration Award dated 27 October 2004 he held that they had not. There is no appeal against this ruling. The second issue was that which gives rise to this appeal. It was whether the events (described as the outbreak of the Second Gulf War) in March 2003 placed a temporal limit on the damages recoverable by the owners for the charterers' repudiation of the charterparty such that no damages were recoverable for the period from 21 March 2003 onwards. This issue the arbitrator reluctantly decided in the charterers' favour. The owners say that he was wrong to do so. The third issue was not explored in the reference and is irrelevant for present purposes.

6. In his reasons for deciding the first of these issues as he did, the arbitrator correctly summarised the law on mitigation of damage where there is an available market, as it was agreed, and the arbitrator found, was the case here.

7. In his reasons for deciding the second issue as he did, the arbitrator concluded that the Second Gulf War, which effectively began on 20 March 2003, fell within clause 33, as it plainly did. He then considered the likeli-hood of the Second Gulf War occurring when judged from mid-December 2001 by a reasonably well-informed person. This was an issue on which both sides called expert evidence. He judged (para 59) that at 17 December 2001 such a person would have considered war or large-scale hostilities between the United States or the United Kingdom and Iraq to be not inevitable or even probable but merely a possibility. But by the date of the Award, the war had occurred and the judge accepted the charterers' evidence that if the charterparty had still been in force on 20 March 2003 they would have exercised their right to cancel under clause 33. He had to decide whether that conclusion put a limit on the period of the owners' recoverable loss or whether, as he put it, "the question is what was the value of the contract that the Owners lost on the date it was lost". He observed (para 55) that

"if the Second Gulf War was no more than a possibility on 17 December 2001, it cannot be doubted that what the Owners lost at that date was a charterparty with slightly less than four years to run. For example, had the Charterers not repudiated the Charterparty but the Owners had sold the vessel with her charter on that day, the value they would have received would surely have been calculated on that basis."

He favoured the owners' position (para 56)

"since it seems to me to be the more orthodox approach and supported by cogent reasons for maintaining it. In essence, it does not seem to me that it can be right that the value of that which the Owners have lost (and which is calculable on the date of breach in the then prevailing circumstances) should thereafter vary according to when a determination is made in proceedings to enforce their rights and in perhaps quite dif-ferent circumstances."

But (para 56) he felt constrained to follow Timothy Walker J.'s decision in BS & N Ltd (BVI) v Micado Shipping Ltd (Malta) ("The Seaflower") [2000] 2 Lloyd's Rep 37 which he found to be in point and indistinguishable.

Principle

8. The repudiation of a contract by one party ("the repudiator"), if accepted by the other ("the injured party"), brings the contract to an end and releases both parties from their primary obligations under the contract. The injured party is thereupon entitled to recover damages against the repudiator to compensate him for such financial loss as the repudiator's breach has caused him to suffer. This is elementary law.

9. The damages recoverable by the injured party are such sum as will put him in the same financial position as if the contract had been performed. This is the compensatory principle which has long been recognised as the governing principle in contract. Counsel for the charterers cited certain classical authorities to make good this proposition, but it has been enunciated and applied times without number and is not in doubt. It does not, however, resolve the question whether the injured party's loss is to be assessed as of the date when he

suffers the loss, or shortly thereafter, in the light of what is then known, or at a later date when the assessment happens to be made, in the light of such later events as may then be known.

10. An injured party such as the owners may not, generally speaking, recover damages against a repudiator such as the charterers for loss which he could reasonably have avoided by taking reasonable commercial steps to mitigate his loss. Thus where, as here, there is an available market for the chartering of vessels, the injured party's loss will be calculated on the assumption that he has, on or within a reasonable time of accepting the repudiation, taken reasonable commercial steps to obtain alternative employment for the vessel for the best consideration reasonably obtainable. This is the ordinary rule whether in fact the injured party acts in that way or, for whatever reason, does not. The actual facts are ordinarily irrelevant. The rationale of the rule is one of simple commercial fairness. The injured party owes no duty to the repudiator, but fairness requires that he should not ordinarily be permitted to rely on his own unreasonable and uncommercial conduct to increase the loss falling on the repudiator. I take this summary to reflect the ruling of Robert Goff J. in *Koch Marine Inc v D'Amica Società di Navigazione ARL (The "Elena D'Amico")* [1980] 1 Lloyd's Rep 75. That case concerned the measure of damages recoverable by a charterer for breach of a time charter during its currency by an owner. While taking care to avoid laying down an inflexible or invariable rule, the judge held (p 89, col 2) that if, at the date of breach, there is an available market, the normal measure of damages will be the difference between the contract rate and the market rate for chartering in a substitute ship for the balance of the charter period. An analogy was drawn with section 51(3) of the Sale of Goods Act 1893. Neither party challenged this decision, which has always been regarded as authoritative. It does however assume that the injured party knows, or can ascertain, what the balance of the charter period is.

11. It is a general, but not an invariable, rule of English law that damages for breach of contract are assessed as at the date of breach. Authority for this familiar proposition may be found in *Jamal v Moolla Dawood Sons & Co* [1916] AC 175, 179; *Miliangos v George Frank (Textiles) Ltd* [1976] AC 443, 468; *Johnson v Agnew* [1980] AC 367, 400–401; *Dodd Properties (Kent) Ltd v Canterbury City Council* [1980] 1 WLR 433, 450–451, 454–455, 457; *County Personnel (Employment Agency) Ltd v Alan R Pulver & Co* [1987] 1 WLR 916, 925–926; *Chitty on Contracts*, 29th ed (2004), vol 1, para 26–057; Professor S. M. Waddams, "The Date for the Assessment of Damages", (1981) 97 LQR 445, 446. The Sale of Goods Acts of 1893 and 1979 both give effect to this prima facie rule in section 51(3) of the respective Acts in the case of refusal or neglect by a seller to deliver goods to a buyer where there is an available market.

The argument

12. While not, I think, challenging the general correctness of the principles last stated, the charterers dispute their applicability to the present case. Their first ground for doing so is in reliance on what, from the name of the case in which this principle has been most clearly articulated, has sometimes been called "the *Bwllfa* principle". It is that where the court making an assessment of damages has knowledge of what actually happened it need not speculate about what might have happened but should base itself on the known facts. In non-judicial discourse the point has been made that you need not gaze into the crystal ball when you can read the book. I have, for my part, no doubt that this is in many contexts a sound approach in law as in life, and it is true that the principle has been judicially invoked in a number of cases. But these cases bear little, if any, resemblance to the present. In *Bwllfa and Merthyr Dare Steam Collieries (1891) Limited v Pontypridd Waterworks Company* [1903] AC 426 a coalowner claimed statutory compensation against a water undertaking which had, pursuant to statutory authority, prevented him mining his coal over a period during which the price of coal had risen. The question was whether the coal should be valued as at the beginning of the period or at its value during the currency of the period. The coalowner was entitled to "full compensation" and the House upheld the latter measure. In doing so, it was at pains to distinguish the case from one of sale or property transfer: see Lord Halsbury L.C., pp 428–429; Lord Macnaghten, p 431; Lord Robertson, p 432. *In re Bradberry* [1943] Ch 35, where the principle was invoked, concerned the valuation of an annuity in the course of administering an estate. The claim in *Carslogie Steamship Co Ltd v Royal Norwegian Government* [1952] AC 292 was a claim by shipowners for loss of time during repairs of damage caused by a collision. After the collision the ship had suffered heavy weather damage, which required the ship to be detained for repair of that damage. It was common ground that the ship would have been detained for the same period if the collision had never occurred (p 313). In *In Re Thoars Deceased* ([2002] EWHC 2416(Ch), unreported, 15 November 2002) the principle was invoked in the course of deciding whether a policy of life insurance had been transferred at an undervalue within the meaning of section 339 of the Insolvency Act 1986. The principle was again invoked in *McKinnon v F Survey Ltd* ([2003] EWHC 475 (Ch), unreported, 14 January 2003), a claim against negligent surveyors in which the court was asked to assume, for purposes of a preliminary issue, that the property had not been the

subject of movement at the date of valuation and had not been subject to movement since, but that it would not have been possible to establish these facts until after the purchase of the property. In *Aitchison v Gordon Durham & Company Limited* (unreported, 30 June 1995) the Court of Appeal applied the principle where a joint venture agreement to develop land had been broken and the court took account of what actually happened to decide what the claimant's profit would have been. I do not think it necessary to discuss these cases, since it is clear that in some contexts the court may properly take account of later events. None of these cases involved repudiation of a commercial contract where there was an available market.

13. The charterers further submit that even if, as a general rule, damages for breach of contract (or tort, often treated as falling within the same rule) are assessed as at the date of the breach or the tort, the court has shown itself willing to depart from this rule where it judges it necessary or just to do so in order to give effect to the compensatory principle. I accept that this is so. But it is necessary to consider the cases in which the court departs from the general rule. Some are personal injury claims, of which *Curwen v James* [1963] 1 WLR 748 and *Murphy v Stone-Wallwork (Charlton) Ltd* [1969] 1 WLR 1023 may serve as examples. *Dudarec v Andrews* [2006] EWCA Civ 256, [2006] 1 WLR 3002 was in form a negligence claim against solicitors, but damages were sought for the loss of a chance of success in a personal injuries action struck out for want of prosecution seven years earlier, and the issue was similar to that in a personal injuries action. It is unnecessary to consider the extent to which, in the light of *Baker v Willoughby* [1970] AC 467 and *Jobling v Associated Dairies Ltd* [1982] AC 794, the breach date principle applies to the assessment of personal injury damages in tort. The court has also departed from the general rule in cases where, on particular facts, it was held to be reasonable for the injured party to defer taking steps to mitigate his loss and so reasonable to defer the assessment of damage. *Radford v De Froberville* [1977] 1 WLR 1262 and *Dodd Properties (Kent) Ltd v Canterbury City Council* [1980] 1 WLR 433 are examples. In both cases the general rule was acknowledged and reasons given for departing from it. *County Personnel (Employment Agency) Ltd v Alan Pulver & Co* [1987] 1 WLR 916 was a claim against solicitors whose negligent advice had saddled the plaintiffs with a ruinous underlease, from which the plaintiffs had had to buy themselves out. The ordinary diminution in value measure of damage was held to be wholly inapt on the particular facts. Again, reasons were given for departing from the normal rule. In *Miliangos v George Frank (Textiles) Ltd* [1976] AC 443 the effect of inflation led the House to sanction a departure from the rule that losses sustained in a foreign currency must be converted into sterling at the date of breach. The plaintiff in *Re-Source America International Ltd v Platt Site Services Ltd* [2005] EWCA Civ 97, [2005] 2 Lloyd's Rep 50 was bailee of spools used to carry optic fibre cables which it was to refurbish. The spools were destroyed by fire. It was held to be entitled to recover the cost of replacing the spools, subject to a deduction based on the saved cost of refurbishment. The Court of Appeal took account of what happened after the fire. It was expressly found (para 5) that there was no available market in used spools, so the plaintiff could not have mitigated its loss by replacing them. *Sally Wertheim v Chicoutimi Pulp Company* [1911] AC 301, cited by the charterers, was not a case of non-delivery or refusal to deliver, but of delayed delivery. The goods, although delivered late, were received and there was no accepted repudiation. The case would not have fallen under section 51(3) of the 1893 Act. The buyer made a claim for damages, based on the difference between the market price at the place of delivery when the goods should have been delivered and the market price there when the goods were in fact delivered. It was apparent on the figures that this claim, if successful, would have yielded the plaintiff a much larger profit than if the contract had not been broken, and he was compensated for his actual loss. None of these cases, as is evident, involves the accepted repudiation of a commercial contract such as a charterparty. It is necessary to consider some cases more similar to the present case to which the House was referred.

14. Considerable attention has been paid to the decision of the Court of Appeal (Lord Denning M.R., Edmund Davies and Megaw L.JJ.) in *Maredelanto Compania Naviera SA v Bergbau-Handel GmbH ("The Mihalis Angelos")* [1971] 1 QB 164. The case concerned a voyage charterparty by which the ship was fixed to sail to Haiphong and there load a cargo for delivery in Europe. In the charterparty dated 25 May 1965 the owners stated that the ship was "expected ready to load under this charter about July 1, 1965". The charterparty also provided, in the first sentence of the cancelling clause, "Should the vessel not be ready to load (whether in berth or not) on or before July 20, 1965, charterers have the option of cancelling this contract, such option to be declared, if demanded, at least 48 hours before vessel's expected arrival at port of loading". On 17 July 1965 the ship was at Hong Kong still discharging cargo from her previous voyage. It was physically impossible for her to finish discharging and reach Haiphong by 20 July. The charterers gave notice cancelling the charter. The owners treated this as a repudiation and claimed damages, which were the subject of arbitration and of an appeal to Mocatta J. On further appeal, there were three issues. The first was whether the "expected readiness" clause was a condition of which the owners were in breach, entitling the charterers to terminate the charter

contract. All three members of the court decided this issue in favour of the charterers and against the owners. The second issue was whether (if the answer to the first issue was wrong) the charterers had repudiated the contract by cancelling on 17 July, three days before the specified 20 July deadline. Lord Denning held that they had not, but Edmund Davies and Megaw L.JJ. held that they had. The third issue was as to the damage suffered by the owners, on the assumption that the charterers' premature cancellation had been a repudiation. Lord Denning, in agreement with the arbitrators, who were themselves agreed, held that they had suffered no damage (p 197):

> "Seeing that the charterers would, beyond doubt, have cancelled, I am clearly of opinion that the shipowners suffered no loss: and would be entitled at most to nominal damages."

Edmund Davies L.J. agreed (p 202):

> "One must look at the contract as a whole, and if it is clear that the innocent party has lost nothing, he should recover no more than nominal damages for the loss of his right to have the whole contract completed."

Megaw L.J. (at pp 209–210) stated:

> "In my view, where there is an anticipatory breach of contract, the breach is the repudiation once it has been accepted, and the other party is entitled to recover by way of damages the true value of the contractual rights which he has thereby lost; subject to his duty to mitigate. If the contractual rights which he has lost were capable by the terms of the contract of being rendered either less valuable or valueless in certain events, and if it can be shown that those events were, at the date of acceptance of the repudiation, predestined to happen, then in my view the damages which he can recover are not more than the true value, if any, of the rights which he has lost, having regard to those predestined events."

It is evident that all members of the court were viewing the case as from the date of acceptance of the repudiation (although only Megaw L.J. said so in terms). They were not taking account of later events. They were recognising, as was obvious on the facts as found, that the value of the contractual right which the owners had lost, as of the date of acceptance of the repudiation, was nil because the charter was bound to be lawfully cancelled three days later.

15. If, as I think, the Court of Appeal's decision on the third issue in the *Mihalis Angelos* was entirely orthodox, so was the decision of Mustill J. in *Woodstock Shipping Co v Kyma Compania Naviera SA ("The Wave")* [1981] 1 Lloyd's Rep 521. This concerned a time charter for 24 months, 3 months more or less at charterers' option. The owners repudiated the charter and the charterers accepted their repudiation on 2 August 1979. In assessing the charterers' loss, and allowing for their ability to obtain a substitute fixture in the available market shortly after the date of the accepted repudiation, in accordance with the ruling in the *Elena D'Amico*, above, the judge compared the charterparty rate with the market rate in the early days of September 1979, declining to speculate whether market rates in September 1981 would induce the charterers to exercise their three month option one way or the other.

16. *SIB International SRL v Metallgesellschaft Corporation ("The Noel Bay")* [1989] 1 Lloyd's Rep 361 concerned a voyage charterparty. The charterers repudiated the charterparty and the owners accepted the repudiation on 3 June 1987. On appeal to the Court of Appeal, Staughton L.J. accepted (p 364, col 2) the submission of counsel that the value of the contract which the owners lost "must be assessed as at June 3, the date when repudiation was accepted". He went on to quote, with approval, the passage from the judgment of Megaw L.J. in the *Mihalis Angelos* which I have set out in para 14 above.

17. *Kaines (UK) Ltd v Osterreichische Warrenhandelsgesellschaft Austrowaren Gesellschaft m.b.H.* [1993] 2 Lloyd's Rep 1 concerned not a charterparty but a contract for the sale and purchase of crude oil. The sellers repudiated and at 17.28 hours on 18 June 1987 the buyers accepted the repudiation. Steyn J. held that the buyers should have replaced the oil in the market by, at latest, 19 June, and their damages were assessed accordingly. It was an anticipatory repudiation. Both the judge and the Court of Appeal in dismissing the appeal cited with approval (pp 7, 10) a passage in Treitel, *The Law of Contract*, 7th ed (1987), p 742:

> "Under this [mitigation] rule, the injured party may, and if there is a market generally will, be required to make a substitute contract; and his damages will be assessed by reference to the time when the contract should have been made. This will usually be the time of acceptance of the breach (or such reasonable time thereafter as may be allowed under the rules stated above) . . ."

The Court of Appeal observed (p 11) that the judge's finding on the date when the buyers should have bought in a substitute cargo "fixes the level of the plaintiffs' damages on the facts of this case irrespective of what the plaintiffs did or failed to do at the time" and (p 13) "crystallises the position so far as the basis of a capital award of damages is concerned".

18. The buyers in *North Sea Energy Holdings NV v Petroleum Authority of Thailand* [1999] 1 Lloyd's Rep 483 repudiated an oil purchase agreement and the sellers accepted their repudiation. The sellers could not, however, show that they would have been able to obtain the oil to sell, and the Court of Appeal accordingly held that they were not entitled to substantial damages. In reaching this conclusion the court cited and applied part of Megaw L.J.'s statement in the *Mihalis Angelos* which I have quoted in para 14 above.

19. *BS & N Ltd (BVI) v Micado Shipping Ltd (Malta) ("The Seaflower")* [2000] 2 Lloyd's Rep 37 concerned a time charterparty dated 20 October 1997 for a period of 11 months, maximum 12 months at charterers' option. The charterparty referred to various major oil company approvals including that of Mobil all on the point of expiring and provided that if during the charter term the owners lost one of these approvals they should reinstate the same within 30 days failing which the charterers would be at liberty to cancel the charterparty. It also contained a guarantee by the owners to obtain an approval from Exxon within 60 days of the charter date. The vessel was duly delivered but the owners had not obtained an Exxon approval from Exxon and did not do so within 60 days from the charter date. On 30 December 1997 the charterers fixed the vessel to load a cargo of Exxon products. On the same date the charterers asked the owners if they had obtained the Exxon approval and gave notice requiring the owners to obtain it by 5 January 1998. The owners replied that the vessel would be ready for Exxon inspection by late January or early February. The charterers responded by terminating the charter and redelivering the vessel. At an initial hearing Aikens J. held that the 60-day guarantee was an innominate term, not a condition. Thus the charterers were not entitled to terminate, and had repudiated the charterparty, which the owners had accepted. In proceedings initiated by the charterers, the owners counterclaimed for damages for wrongful termination of the charter, quantified as the difference between the daily hire rates in the charter and the alternative employment found for the vessel for the rest of the charter period. The charterers met this claim by contending that the owners would have lost their Mobil approval on 27 January 1998 and would not have been able to regain it within 30 days, namely 26 February: therefore the charterers would be contractually entitled to cancel, and the owners' damages should end then. Timothy Walker J. discerned a difference between the three judgments in the *Mihalis Angelos*, discounting Megaw L.J.'s formulation as that of a minority, but found on the facts, as established at 30 December 1997, that the owners would have lost the Mobil approval on 27 January 1998. This conclusion he found to be supported by evidence of what actually happened after 30 December. He concluded that it was inevitable that the charter would have come to an end on 26 February, and limited the owners' damages accordingly. This was, as I read the judgment, a conclusion he regarded as inevitable on 30 December. It does not appear that there was argument about the permissibility of relying on evidence of what happened later, and the judge cannot have supposed that he was deciding any issue of principle. The result of this case was perhaps less obvious than that on the third issue in the *Mihalis Angelos*, but it was a judgment, on different facts, to very much the same effect. It was quite unlike the present case, because early termination was very clearly predictable on the date when the repudiation was accepted, and the judge only relied on evidence of later events to fortify his conclusion on that point. I do not think he would have reached a different conclusion had he not received that evidence.

20. *Dampskibsselskabet "Norden" A/S v Andre & Cie SA* [2003] EWHC 84 (Comm), [2003] 1 Lloyd's Rep 287 is a recent example of the application of the general rule. A forward freight swap agreement was treated as terminated because of the defendants' breach of solvency guarantees. It was common ground by the end of the trial that the injured party's loss was to be measured by the difference between the contract rate and the market rate after the date of termination. Toulson J. recorded this agreement, observing (p 292, col 2) that "The availability of a substitute market enables a market valuation to be made of what the innocent party has lost, and a line thereby to be drawn under the transaction". This is what the general rule is intended to achieve.

21. In support of their argument that damages should be assessed as of the date of actual assessment, the charterers contend that their claim attributable to loss of profit share would in any event have to be deferred. Neither the arbitrator nor the judge mentioned this point, from which it seems safe to infer that the point was not at that stage relied on. But Lord Mance, giving the leading judgment in the Court of Appeal, did refer to it (para 25), and counsel for the owners accepted in argument that the assessment of the profit share loss would have had to be deferred. I am far from convinced that counsel was right to accept this. It would of course be very difficult to calculate loss of profit prospectively over a four year period, but an injured party can recover damages for the loss of a chance of obtaining a benefit (see Treitel, 11th ed, (2003), pp 955–957) and the

difficulty of accurate calculation is not a bar to recovery. Even if counsel is right on this point and I am wrong, this would not in my view be sufficient to displace the general rule in this context.

Conclusion

22. The thrust of the charterers' argument was that the owners would be unfairly over-compensated if they were to recover as damages sums which, with the benefit of hindsight, it is now known that they would not have received had there been no accepted repudiation by the charterers. There are, in my opinion, several answers to this. The first is that contracts are made to be performed, not broken. It may prove disadvantageous to break a contract instead of performing it. The second is that if, on their repudiation being accepted, the charterers had promptly honoured their secondary obligation to pay damages, the transaction would have been settled well before the Second Gulf War became a reality. The third is that the owners were, as the arbitrator held (see para 7 above), entitled to be compensated for the value of what they had lost on the date it was lost, and it could not be doubted that what the owners lost at that date was a charterparty with slightly less than four years to run. This was a clear and, in my opinion, crucial finding, but it was not mentioned in either of the judgments below, nor is it mentioned by any of my noble and learned friends in the majority. On the arbitrator's finding, it was marketable on that basis. I can readily accept that the value of a contract in the market may be reduced if terminable on an event which the market judges to be likely but not certain, but that was not what the arbitrator found to be the fact in this case. There is, with respect to those who think otherwise, nothing artificial in this approach. If a party is compensated for the value of what he has lost at the time when he loses it, and its value is at that time for any reason depressed, he is fairly compensated. That does not cease to be so because adventitious later events reveal that the market at that time was depressed by the apprehension of risks that did not eventuate. A party is not, after all, obliged to accept a repudiation: he can, if he chooses, keep the contract alive, for better or worse. By describing the prospect of war in December 2001 as "merely a possibility", the expression twice used by the arbitrator in paragraph 59 of his reasons, the arbitrator can only have meant that it was seen as an outside chance, not affecting the marketable value of the charter at that time.

23. There is, however, a further answer which I, in common with the arbitrator, consider to be of great importance. He acknowledged the force of arguments advanced by the owners based on certainty ("generally important in commercial affairs"), finality ("the alternative being a running assessment of the state of play so far as the likelihood of some interruption to the contract is concerned"), settlement ("otherwise the position will remain fluid"), consistency ("the idea that a party's accrued rights can be changed by subsequent events is objectionable in principle") and coherence ("the date of repudiation is the date on which rights and damages are assessed"). The judge was not greatly impressed by the charterers' argument along these lines, observing (paras 13, 35) that although certainty is a real and beneficial target, it is not easily achieved, and the charterparty contained within it the commercial uncertainty of the war clause. Lord Mance similarly said (para 24):

> "Certainty, finality and ease of settlement are all of course important general considerations. But the element of uncertainty, resulting from the war clause, meant that the owners were never entitled to absolute confidence that the charter would run for its full seven-year period. They never had an asset which they could bank or sell on that basis. There is no reason why the transmutation of their claims to performance of the charter into claims for damages for non-performance of the charter should improve their position in this respect."

I cannot, with respect, accept this reasoning. The importance of certainty and predictability in commercial transactions has been a constant theme of English commercial law at any rate since the judgment of Lord Mansfield C. J. in *Vallejo v Wheeler* (1774) 1 Cowp 143, 153), and has been strongly asserted in recent years in cases such as *Scandinavian Trading Tanker Co AB v Flota Petrolera Ecuatoriana ("The Scaptrade")* [1983] QB 529, 540–541, [1983] 2 AC 694, 703–704; *Homburg Houtimport BV v Agrosin Private Ltd* [2003] UKHL 12, [2004] 1 AC 715, 738; *Jindal Iron and Steel Co Ltd v Islamic Solidarity Shipping Co Jordan Inc ("The Jordan II")* [2004] UKHL 49, [2005] 1 WLR 1363, 1370. Professor Sir Guenter Treitel Q.C. read the Court of Appeal's judgment as appearing to impair this quality of certainty ("Assessment of Damages for Wrongful Repudiation", (2007) 123 LQR 9–18) and I respectfully share his concern.

24. On my reading of *The Seaflower* (see para 19 above), I do not think the arbitrator was bound by that decision to reach the conclusion he did. If he was, I respectfully think the judge was wrong to analyse the *Mihalis Angelos* as he did in that case. But on the facts Timothy Walker J. was entitled to value the owners' charter in that case at two months' purchase as of the repudiation acceptance date. In the present case, by contrast,

the arbitrator found four years' purchase (less a few days) as the true market value of the charterparty on the repudiation acceptance date.

25. For these reasons and those given by my noble and learned friend Lord Walker of Gestingthorpe, with which I wholly agree, I would, for my part, have allowed the owners' appeal.

LORD SCOTT OF FOSCOTE

[Having summarised the facts, Lord Scott continued:]

28. Two important matters that have, or may have, a bearing on the answer to the question are now common ground. First, it is common ground that, if the charterparty had still been on foot when, in March 2003, hostilities between the USA and the UK on one side and Iraq on the other side began, the Charterers would have exercised their clause 33 right to terminate the charterparty. Second, it is common ground that as at 17 December 2001 the chance that any hostilities triggering the clause 33 right of termination would break out was no more than a possibility and certainly not a probability.

29. My Lords, the answer to the question at issue must depend on principles of the law of contract. It is true that the context in this case is a charterparty, a commercial contract. But the contractual principles of the common law relating to the assessment of damages are no different for charterparties, or for commercial contracts in general, than for contracts which do not bear that description. The fundamental principle governing the quantum of damages for breach of contract is long established and not in dispute. The damages should compensate the victim of the breach for the loss of his contractual bargain. The principle was succinctly stated by Parke B. in *Robinson v Harman* 1 Ex 850 at 855 and remains as valid now as it was then.

"The rule of the common law is, that where a party sustains a loss by reason of a breach of contract, he is, so far as money can do it, to be placed in the same situation, with respect to damages, as if the contract had been performed."

If the contract is a contract for performance over a period, whether for the performance of personal services, or for supply of goods, or, as here, a time charter, the assessment of damages for breach must proceed on the same principle, namely, the victim of the breach should be placed, so far as damages can do it, in the position he would have been in had the contract been performed.

30. If a contract for performance over a period has come to an end by reason of a repudiatory breach but might, if it had remained on foot, have terminated early on the occurrence of a particular event, the chance of that event happening must, it is agreed, be taken into account in an assessment of the damages payable for the breach. And if it is certain that the event will happen, the damages must be assessed on that footing. In *The Mihalis Angelos* [1971] 1 QB 164, Megaw L.J. referred to events "predestined to happen". He said, at p.210, that:

". . . if it can be shown that those events were, at the date of acceptance of the repudiation, predestined to happen, then . . . the damages which [the claimant] can recover are not more than the true value, if any, of the rights which he has lost, having regard to those predestined events."

Another way of putting the point being made by Megaw L.J. is that the claimant is entitled to the benefit, expressed in money, of the contractual rights he has lost, but not to the benefit of more valuable contractual rights than those he has lost. In *Wertheim v Chicoutimi Pulp Co* [1911] AC 301, Lord Atkinson referred, at 307, to:

". . . the general intention of the law that, in giving damages for breach of contract, the party complaining should, so far as it can be done by money, be placed in the same position as he would have been in if the contract had been performed"

and, in relation to a claim by a purchaser for damages for late delivery of goods where the purchaser had, after the late delivery, sold the goods for a higher price than that prevailing in the market on the date of delivery, observed, at 308, that:

". . . the loss he sustains must be measured by that price, unless he is, against all justice, to be permitted to make a profit by the breach of contract, be compensated for a loss he never suffered, and be put, as far as money can do it, not in the same position in which he would have been if the contract had been performed, but in a much better position."

31. The result contended for by the appellant in the present case is, to my mind, similar to that contemplated by Lord Atkinson in the passage last cited. If the charterparty had not been repudiated and had remained on foot, it would have been terminated by the Charterers in or shortly after March 2003 when the Second Gulf War

triggered the clause 33 termination option. But the Owners are claiming damages up to 6 December 2005 on the footing, now known to be false, that the charterparty would have continued until then. It is contended that because the Charterers' repudiation and its acceptance by the Owners preceded the March 2003 event, the rule requiring damages for breach of contract to be assessed at the date of breach requires that event to be ignored.

32. That contention, in my opinion, attributes to the assessment of damages at the date of breach rule an inflexibility which is inconsistent both with principle and with the authorities. The underlying principle is that the victim of a breach of contract is entitled to damages representing the value of the contractual benefit to which he was entitled but of which he has been deprived. He is entitled to be put in the same position, so far as money can do it, as if the contract had been performed. The assessment at the date of breach rule can usually achieve that result. But not always. In *Miliangos v Frank (Textiles) Ltd* [1976] AC 443 Lord Wilberforce at 468 referred to "the general rule" that damages for breach of contract are assessed as at the date of breach but went on to observe that:

"... It is for the courts, or for arbitrators, to work out a solution in each case best adapted to giving the injured plaintiff that amount in damages which will most fairly compensate him for the wrong which he has suffered ..."

and, when considering the date at which a foreign money obligation should be converted into sterling, chose the date that "gets nearest to securing to the creditor exactly what he bargained for". If a money award of damages for breach of contract provides to the creditor a lesser or a greater benefit than the creditor bargained for, the award fails, in either case, to provide a just result.

33. In *Dodd Properties v Canterbury City Council* [1980] 1 WLR 433, Megaw L.J., commenting on the "general rule" to which Lord Wilberforce had referred in the *Miliangos* case, said, at 451, that it was "clear" that the general rule was "subject to many exceptions and qualifications". In *County Personnel Ltd v Alan R Pulver & Co* [1987] 1 WLR 916, Bingham L.J., as my noble and learned friend then was, said at 926 that the general rule that damages were assessed at the date of the breach "should not be mechanistically applied in circumstances where assessment at another date may more accurately reflect the overriding compensatory rule." In *Lavarack v Woods of Colchester Ltd* [1967] 1 QB 278, the Court of Appeal held that damages for wrongful dismissal could not confer on an employee extra benefits that the contract did not oblige the employer to confer and Diplock L.J. (as he then was) said at 294, that:

"... the first task of the assessor of damages is to estimate as best he can what the plaintiff would have gained in money or money's worth if the defendant had fulfilled his legal obligations and had done no more. Where there is an anticipatory breach by wrongful repudiation, this can at best be an estimate, whatever the date of the hearing. It involves assuming that what has not occurred and never will occur has occurred or will occur, i.e. that the defendant has since the breach performed his legal obligations under the contract and, if the estimate is made before the contract would otherwise have come to an end, that he will continue to perform his legal obligations thereunder until the due date of its termination. But the assumption to be made is that the defendant has performed or will perform his legal obligations under his contract with the plaintiff and nothing more."

This passage was cited and applied by Waller L.J. in giving his judgment, concurred in by Roch and Ward L.JJ., in *North Sea Energy Holdings NV v Petroleum Authority of Thailand* [1999] 1 Lloyd's Rep 483 at 494/5.

34. The assessment at the date of breach rule is particularly apt to cater for cases where a contract for the sale of goods in respect of which there is a market has been repudiated. The loss caused by the breach to the seller or the buyer, as the case may be, can be measured by the difference between the contract price and the market price at the time of the breach. The seller can re-sell his goods in the market. The buyer can buy substitute goods in the market. Thereby the loss caused by the breach can be fixed. But even here some period must usually be allowed to enable the necessary arrangements for the substitute sale or purchase to be made (see e.g. *Kaines v Österreichische* [1993] 2 Lloyd's Rep 1). The relevant market price for the purpose of assessing the quantum of the recoverable loss will be the market price at the expiration of that period.

35. In cases, however, where the contract for sale of goods is not simply a contract for a one-off sale, but is a contract for the supply of goods over some specified period, the application of the general rule may not be in the least apt. Take the case of a three year contract for the supply of goods and a repudiatory breach of the contract at the end of the first year. The breach is accepted and damages are claimed but before the assessment of the damages an event occurs that, if it had occurred while the contract was still on foot, would have been a frustrating event terminating the contract, e.g. legislation prohibiting any sale of the goods. The contractual

benefit of which the victim of the breach of contract had been deprived by the breach would not have extended beyond the date of the frustrating event. So on what principled basis could the victim claim compensation attributable to a loss of contractual benefit after that date? Any rule that required damages attributable to that period to be paid would be inconsistent with the overriding compensatory principle on which awards of contractual damages ought to be based.

36. The same would, in my opinion, be true of any anticipatory breach the acceptance of which had terminated an executory contract. The contractual benefit for the loss of which the victim of the breach can seek compensation cannot escape the uncertainties of the future. If, at the time the assessment of damages takes place, there were nothing to suggest that the expected benefit of the executory contract would not, if the contract had remained on foot, have duly accrued, then the quantum of damages would be unaffected by uncertainties that would be no more than conceptual. If there were a real possibility that an event would happen terminating the contract, or in some way reducing the contractual benefit to which the damages claimant would, if the contract had remained on foot, have become entitled, then the quantum of damages might need, in order to reflect the extent of the chance that that possibility might materialize, to be reduced proportionately. The lodestar is that the damages should represent the value of the contractual benefits of which the claimant had been deprived by the breach of contract, no less but also no more. But if a terminating event had happened, speculation would not be needed, an estimate of the extent of the chance of such a happening would no longer be necessary and, in relation to the period during which the contract would have remained executory had it not been for the terminating event, it would be apparent that the earlier anticipatory breach of contract had deprived the victim of the breach of nothing. In the *Bwllfa* case [1903] AC 426, Lord Halsbury at 429 rejected the proposition that "because you could not arrive at the true sum when the notice was given, you should shut your eyes to the true sum now you do know it, because you could not have guessed it then" and Lord Robertson said at 432, that "estimate and conjecture are superseded by facts as the proper media concludendi" and, at 433, that "as in this instance facts are available, they are not to be shut out". Their Lordships were not dealing with a contractual, or tortious, damages issue but with the quantum of compensation to be paid under the Waterworks Clauses Act 1847. Their approach, however, is to my mind as apt for our purposes on this appeal as to theirs on that appeal.

37. My noble and learned friend Lord Bingham, in what has been rightly described as a strong dissent, has referred (in para 9) to the overriding compensatory principle that the injured party is entitled to such damages as will put him in the same financial position as if the contract had been performed. On the facts of the present case, however, the contract contained clause 33 and would not have required any performance by the Charterers after March 2003. It should follow that, in principle, the owners, the injured party, are not entitled to any damages in respect of the period thereafter. As at the date of the Owners' acceptance of the Charterers' repudiation of the charterparty, the proposition that what at that date the Owners had lost was a charterparty with slightly less than four years to run requires qualification. The charterparty contained clause 33. The Owners had lost a charterparty which contained a provision that would enable the Charterers to terminate the charterparty if a certain event happened. The event did happen. It happened before the damages had been assessed. It was accepted in argument before your Lordships that the Owners' charterparty rights would not, in practice, have been marketable for a capital sum. The contractual benefit of the charterparty to the Owners, the benefit of which they were deprived by the repudiatory breach, was the right to receive the hire rate during the currency of the charterparty. The termination of the charterparty under clause 33 would necessarily have brought to an end that right.

38. The arguments of the Owners offend the compensatory principle. They are seeking compensation exceeding the value of the contractual benefits of which they were deprived. Their case requires the assessor to speculate about what might happen over the period 17 December 2001 to 6 December 2005 regarding the occurrence of a clause 33 event and to shut his eyes to the actual happening of a clause 33 event in March 2003. The argued justification for thus offending the compensatory principle is that priority should be given to the so-called principle of certainty. My Lords there is, in my opinion, no such principle. Certainty is a desideratum and a very important one, particularly in commercial contracts. But it is not a principle and must give way to principle. Otherwise incoherence of principle is the likely result. The achievement of certainty in relation to commercial contracts depends, I would suggest, on firm and settled principles of the law of contract rather than on the tailoring of principle in order to frustrate tactics of delay to which many litigants in many areas of litigation are wont to resort. Be that as it may, the compensatory principle that must underlie awards of contractual damages is, in my opinion, clear and requires the appeal in the case to be dismissed. I wish also to express my agreement with the reasons given by my noble and learned friends Lord Carswell and Lord Brown of Eaton-under-Heywood for coming to the same conclusion.

Points for reflection

In *Novasen S.A. v Alimenta S.A.* [2013] EWHC 345 (Comm), there were questions concerning the applicability of *The Golden Victory* to sale of goods contracts as well as whether a particular form of contract issued by the Federation of Oils, Seeds and Fats Association (FOSFA) had excluded *The Golden Victory*. Briefly, the dispute arose when the sellers under a FOSFA contract failed, because of an export prohibition in Senegal, to ship the goods on time. The trade tribunal held that the buyers were entitled to recover damages measured by the difference between the contract price and the market price at the date of breach. However, relying on *The Golden Victory*, the argument for the sellers was that, in the light of subsequent events, they would have been released from their obligations anyway. On the question of whether *The Golden Victory* applied to sale of goods contracts, Popplewell J said:

19–004

12. The [contract in *The Golden Victory*] was not one of sale of goods. It concerned the period element of the assessment of damages applicable to a long term time charter, in respect of which the rate of hire to be applied over the relevant period was accepted to be the market/contract differential at or close to the date of breach, irrespective of future market fluctuation. Although the statements of principle by the majority were expressed in wide terms, it might be open to question whether the same principles are applicable to a one off contract for the sale of commodities where there is an available market. In his recent decision in *Bunge SA v Nidera SA*, [2013] EWHC 84 (Comm), Mr Justice Hamblen, who had been counsel for the unsuccessful owners in *The Golden Victory*, expressed the view that this remained an open question. In that case he held that the GAFTA Default Clause (which is in materially different terms to the FOSFA Default Clause) had the result of crystallising the assessment of damages at the date of breach in the way in which the minority in *The Golden Victory* would have held the common law to apply. Whether the same result would have been reached in the absence of the clause was therefore a question which did not need to be decided. Hamblen J said:

> '54. . . . I would not accept that it is settled law that *The Golden Victory* approach applies to a one off sale of goods contract such as this. The majority in *The Golden Victory* recognised that they were departing from the general rule that damages in respect of a marketable commodity fall to be assessed by reference to the available market price at the date of breach, but considered that the compensatory principle justified them so doing in the circumstances. However, *The Golden Victory* concerned a period contract and the departure from the general rule was only adopted in relation to the period element of the damages claimed, not the applicable hire rate. Further, as the Board observed, Lord Scott at paragraph 34 recognised that the assessment at the date of breach rule "is particularly apt" in sale of goods cases, as is reflected in the Sale of Goods Act. At paragraph 35 he drew a distinction between a one-off sale and "a contract for the supply of goods over some specified period". It is also to be noted that Benjamin treats *The Golden Victory* as being relevant to sale of goods cases because it's "reasoning could apply to long term contracts for the sale of goods"— para.19–170.
> 55. Although there are passages in the majority judgments in *The Golden Victory* which are put in very general terms, I would for my part regard it as very much an open question whether The Golden Victory approach would apply in a one-off sale of goods contract where there is an available market and damages fall to be assessed in accordance with the Sale of Goods Act. There is in such a case no difficulty about valuing what has been lost. The innocent party has been compensated for what he has lost at the time he loses it. Having had a mitigation opportunity which can be valued without difficulty by reference to the market there is no need or warrant to consider subsequent events. Fixing the damages by reference to market value promotes certainty and predictability and helps inform the innocent party's decision whether or not to terminate. However, the matter was not fully argued and since it is not necessary to decide it on this appeal I do not propose to do so.'"

As for the question of whether the FOSFA default provisions had excluded or fine-tuned the principles of *The Golden Victory*, Popplewell J said:

"17   . . . . The majority of the House of Lords in *The Golden Victory* decided that this compensatory principle should take precedence over considerations of certainty and finality in that case. If, as is not contested, those principles would apply equally to the contract and breach in this case, so that considerations of certainty and finality would not be sufficient to confer on the Buyers an entitlement at law to recover where with hindsight it can be seen that no loss has occurred, it would require, in my judgment, clear words if the parties wished to achieve the opposite result. Considerations of certainty and finality are undoubtedly matters which might lead parties to wish to do so. But the starting point, in commercial dealings as in the law, is that a party claiming damages for breach of contract should be entitled to recover no more than the loss occasioned by the breach. . . .

23.   In this way the clause [in question] seems to me to strike a balance between the common law position and commercial considerations of certainty and finality. It achieves a greater measure of certainty than the common law affords, by providing that if the buyer chooses to go into the market to buy against the defaulting seller, he will be able to recover the price differential between contract and repurchase price, or between contract and market price if the latter is lower. To that extent it meets what I have ventured to suggest may be one of the most important of the considerations of certainty and finality which concern purchasers (or sellers in the converse situation). But if the buyer chooses not to buy against the default, and so not to put himself in a position of having an equivalent bargain to that which he has lost, his damages are those provided by law and in particular may be nominal if subsequent events demonstrate that the value of his lost rights was nil because the seller could have terminated the contract without liability. That might not be considered a surprising consequence of the commercial decision not to replace the lost bargain. In those circumstances the buyer is inevitably at the whim of future events to determine whether his financial position turns out more or less favourably than if he had replaced the lost bargain. The effect of subsequent events on his lost bargain might sensibly be seen as an acceptable uncertainty inherent in his decision not to replace the lost bargain, or at least one which from the seller's point of view should not override the compensatory principle."

B. Cost of Cure or Diminution in Value?

RUXLEY ELECTRONICS AND CONSTRUCTION LTD v FORSYTH

House of Lords [1996] A.C. 344; [1995] 3 W.L.R 118; [1995] 3 All E.R. 268

19–005   F contracted with R to build a swimming pool, with a maximum depth of 7ft 6in in F's garden. After the pool was complete, F discovered that the maximum depth was only 6ft 9in F refused to pay the outstanding balance of the contract price. R sued for it and F counterclaimed for breach of contract. The judge found that the pool as constructed was perfectly safe for diving and that the shortfall in depth had not decreased its value; the only practicable way to achieve a pool of the specified depth would be to demolish the existing pool and build a new one at a cost of £21,560; he was not satisfied that F intended to build a pool at that cost; to do so would be wholly disproportionate to the disadvantage of having the shallower pool; and he awarded damages for loss of amenity of £2,500. The Court of Appeal, (Staughton and Mann LJJ, Dillon LJ dissenting), allowed F's appeal: the only way F could achieve his contractual object was to rebuild the pool which was accordingly a reasonable venture. R appealed to the House of Lords.

F's counsel, Jacob, QC, argued that the award to his client of £2,500 was contrary to principle and unsupported by authority; that the judge had only two alternatives: to award the cost of rebuilding or the loss of value—i.e. nothing; and since F had undoubtedly suffered a loss the judge was bound to award the cost of rebuilding.

Lord Keith, Lord Bridge and Lord Jauncey delivered opinions allowing the appeal.

LORD MUSTILL

There are not two alternative measures of damage, at opposite poles, but only one: namely the loss truly suffered by the promisee. In some cases the loss cannot be fairly measured except by reference to the full cost of repairing the deficiency in performance. In others, and in particular those where the contract is designed to fulfil a purely commercial purpose, the loss will very often consist only of the monetary detriment brought about by the breach of contract. But these remedies are not exhaustive, for the law must cater for those occasions where the value of the promise to the promisee exceeds the financial enhancement of his position which full performance will secure. This excess, often referred to in the literature as the "consumer surplus" (see e.g. the valuable discussion by Harris, Ogus and Phillips, "Contract Remedies and the Consumer Surplus" (1979) 95 LQR 581) is usually incapable of precise valuation in terms of money, exactly because it represents a personal, subjective and non-monetary gain. Nevertheless, where it exists the law should recognise it and compensate the promisee if the misperformance takes it away. The lurid bathroom tiles, or the grotesque folly instanced in argument by my noble and learned friend Lord Keith of Kinkel, may be so discordant with general taste that in purely economic terms the builder may be said to do the employer a favour by failing to instal[l] them. But this is too narrow and materialistic a view of the transaction. Neither the contractor nor the court has the right to substitute for the employer's individual expectation of performance a criterion derived from what ordinary people would regard as sensible. As my Lords have shown, the test of reasonableness plays a central part in determining the basis of recovery, and will indeed be decisive in a case such as the present when the cost of reinstatement would be wholly disproportionate to the non-monetary loss suffered by the employer. But it would be equally unreasonable to deny all recovery for such a loss. The amount may be small, and since it cannot be quantified directly there may be room for difference of opinion about what it should be. But in several fields the judges are well accustomed to putting figures to intangibles, and I see no reason why the imprecision of the exercise should be a barrier, if that is what fairness demands.

. . . The judgment of the trial judge acknowledges that the employer has suffered a true loss and expresses it in terms of money. Since there is no longer any issue about the amount of the award, as distinct from principle, I would simply restore his judgment by allowing the appeal.

Lord Lloyd, having cited the judgment of Cardozo J. in *Jacob & Youngs Inc v Kent* (1921) 230 N.Y. 239: Cardozo J.'s judgment is important because it establishes two principles which I believe to be correct and which are directly relevant to the present case: first, the cost of reinstatement is not the appropriate measure of damages if the expenditure would be out of all proportion to the good to be obtained, and secondly, the appropriate measure of damages in such a case is the difference in value, even though it would result in a nominal award.

The first of these principles is contrary to Staughton L.J.'s view that the plaintiff is entitled to reinstatement, however expensive, if there is no cheaper way of providing what the contract requires. The second principle is contrary to the whole thrust of Mr Jacob's argument that the judge had no alternative but to award the cost of reinstatement, once it became apparent that the difference in value produced a nil result . . .

[Having cited various authorities, Lord Lloyd continued]. It seems to me that in the light of these authorities . . . Mr McGuire Q.C. [counsel for R] was right when he submitted, and Dillon L.J. was right when he held, that mitigation is not the only area in which the concept of reasonableness has an impact on the law of damages.

If the court takes the view that it would be unreasonable for the plaintiff to insist on reinstatement, as where, for example, the expense of the work involved would be out of all proportion to the benefit to be obtained, then the plaintiff will be confined to the difference in value. If the judge had assessed the difference in value in the present case at, say, £5,000, I have little doubt that the Court of Appeal would have taken that figure rather than £21,560. The difficulty arises because the judge has, in the light of the expert evidence, assessed the difference in value as nil. But that cannot make reasonable what he has found to be unreasonable . . .

How then does Mr Jacob seek to support the majority judgment? It can only be, I think, by attacking the judge's finding of fact that the cost of rebuilding the pool would have been out of all proportion to the benefit to be obtained. Mr Jacob argues that this was not an ordinary commercial contract but a contract for a personal preference. This was the line taken by Mann L.J. in the Court of Appeal . . .

I am far from saying that personal preferences are irrelevant when choosing the appropriate measure of damages ("predilections" was the word used by Ackner L.J. in *GW Atkins Ltd v Scott* (1980) 7 Const LJ 215 at 221, adopting the language of Oliver J. in *Radford v De Froberville* [1977] 1 WLR 1262). But such cases should not be elevated into a separate category with special rules. If, to take an example mentioned in the course of argument, a landowner wishes to build a folly in his grounds, it is no answer to a claim for defective workmanship that many people might regard the presence of a well-built folly as reducing the value of the estate. The eccentric landowner is entitled to his whim, provided the cost of reinstatement is not unreasonable. But the difficulty of that line of argument in the present case is that the judge, as is clear from his judgment, took Mr Forsyth's personal preferences and predilections into account. Nevertheless, he found as a fact that the cost of reinstatement was unreasonable in the circumstances. The Court of Appeal ought not to have disturbed that finding . . .

In the present case the judge found as a fact that Mr Forsyth's stated intention of rebuilding the pool would not persist for long after the litigation had been concluded. In these circumstances it would be "mere pretence" to say that the cost of rebuilding the pool is the loss which he has in fact suffered. This is the critical distinction between the present case and the example given by Staughton L.J. of a man who has had his watch stolen. In the latter case, the plaintiff is entitled to recover the value of the watch because that is the true measure of his loss. He can do what he wants with the damages. But if, as the judge found, Mr Forsyth had no intention of rebuilding the pool, he has lost nothing except the difference in value, if any.

Addis v Gramophone Co Ltd [below] established the general rule that in claims for breach of contract, the plaintiff cannot recover damages for his injured feelings. But the rule, like most rules, is subject to exceptions. One of the well-established exceptions is when the object of the contract is to afford pleasure, as, for example, where the plaintiff has booked a holiday with a tour operator. If the tour operator is in breach of contract by failing to provide what the contract called for, the plaintiff may recover damages for his disappointment (see *Jarvis v Swans Tours Ltd* (below) and *Jackson v Horizon Holidays Ltd* [above, Ch.13].

This was, as I understand it, the principle which Judge Diamond applied in the present case. He took the view that the contract was one "for the provision of a pleasurable amenity". In the event, Mr Forsyth's pleasure was not so great as it would have been if the swimming pool had been 7ft 6in deep. This was a view which the judge was entitled to take. If it involves a further inroad on the rule in *Addis v. Gramophone Co Ltd* then so be it. But I prefer to regard it as a logical application or adaptation of the existing exception to a new situation. I should, however, add this note of warning. Mr Forsyth was, I think, lucky to have obtained so large an award for his disappointed expectations. But as there was no criticism from any quarter as to the quantum of the award as distinct from the underlying principle, it would not be right for your Lordships to interfere with the judge's figure.

Appeal Allowed.

Questions

19–006

1. Might the result have been different if the judges had not been sceptical about F's professed intention to rebuild the pool? If the Court of Appeal's decision had stood, and F had decided not to rebuild, he would have had a pool, as valuable and as good for all practical purposes, as the pool contracted for, and a windfall of £21,560. Would that have been a just result?

2. What if, on discovering the shortfall, F had immediately contracted with another builder to rebuild the pool with a depth of 7ft 6in?

3. F argued at the trial that this was an "entire contract". The judge held that it was not because the price was payable by a deposit and thereafter by instalments. The point was not argued on appeal. Suppose the price had been payable in a lump sum on completion. Could F have refused to pay anything? If he had paid before discovering the shortfall, could he have recovered his money? Cf. the *Liddesdale* case, Ch.20, below. If it would have been different, should the fact that the price is payable in a lump sum be so significant?

4. The contract as originally entered into was for a pool 6ft 6in deep. Subsequently at F's request R agreed to make it 7ft 6in without extra charge. The point was apparently never taken; but could

R have contended that the original contract stood, there being no consideration for the promise to provide the extra depth?

5. In *White Arrow Express Ltd v Lamey's Distribution Ltd* [1995] N.L.J. 1504 CA, Bingham MR, having stated that, unless a plaintiff could show that his financial position had been injured, he could recover only nominal damages, gave the following examples.

> "If A hired and paid in advance for a four-door saloon at £200 a day and received delivery of a two-door saloon available for £100 a day, he suffered loss.
>
> If B ordered and paid in advance for a five-course meal costing £50 and was served with a three-course meal costing £30, he suffered loss.
>
> If C agreed and paid in advance to be taught the violin by a world famous celebrity at £500 an hour and was in the event taught by a musical nonentity whose charging rate was £25 an hour, he suffered loss."

Bingham MR said that it would defy common sense to suggest that A, B and C had suffered no loss and were not financially disadvantaged by the breach. They would be entitled to damages amounting to the difference between the price paid, or, if it was lower, the market value of what was contracted for, and the market value of what was obtained. What is the difference between these cases and *Ruxley*?

6. In *Abrahams v Reiach (Herbert) Limited* [1922] 1 K.B. 477, a firm of publishers, in breach of contract, failed to publish a book. The contract did not specify the number of copies to be printed. The publishers, relying on the principle that damages should be assessed on the basis of what would have been a minimally compliant contractual performance, argued that 1,500 copies should be treated as the relevant figure. At the agreed royalty rate, this converted into damages of £25. The trial judge awarded the plaintiff authors £500 (representing 30,000 copies). The Court of Appeal reduced the award to £100. Which sum best reflected the authors' expectation loss? See, for discussion, *Durham Tees Valley Airport Limited v Bmibaby Limited* [2010] EWCA Civ 485.

----

2. Expectation, Reliance, Restitution

A. The Objects of an Award of Damages

SURREY COUNTY COUNCIL AND ANOTHER v BREDERO HOMES LTD

Court of Appeal [1993] 3 All E.R. 705

In 1980 two councils sold freehold land to the defendant (B) for £1.25 million, subject to B's obtaining planning permission to develop the land in accordance with the councils' scheme. B obtained planning permission and the land was transferred, B covenanting with the councils to develop the land in accordance with that permission. B, in breach of the covenant, subsequently obtained planning permission to build, and did build, a larger number of houses on the site, thus making a greater profit. The councils, though aware of the breach, did not seek an injunction or specific performance of the covenants. After B had sold all the houses, the councils sued for damages equal to the amount that they might have extracted from B in return for agreeing to the more profitable development. Ferris J held that they were entitled only to nominal damages. The councils appealed.

19–007

DILLON LJ

Delivered judgment dismissing the appeal.

STEYN LJ

An award of compensation for breach of contract serves to protect three separate interests. The starting principle is that the aggrieved party ought to be compensated for loss of his positive or expectation interests. In other words, the object is to put the aggrieved party in the same financial position as if the contract had been fully performed. But the law also protects the negative interest of the aggrieved party. If the aggrieved party is unable to establish the value of a loss of bargain he may seek compensation in respect of his reliance losses. The object of such an award is to compensate the aggrieved party for expenses incurred and losses suffered in reliance of the contract. These two complementary principles share one feature. Both are pure compensatory principles. If the aggrieved party has suffered no loss he is not entitled to be compensated by invoking these principles. The application of these principles to the present case would result in an award of nominal damages only.

There is, however, a third principle which protects the aggrieved party's restitutionary interest. The object of such an award is not to compensate the plaintiff for a loss, but to deprive the defendant of the benefit he gained by the breach of contract. The classic illustration is a claim for the return of goods sold and delivered where the buyer has repudiated his obligation to pay the price. It is not traditional to describe a claim for restitution following a breach of contract as damages. What matters is that a coherent law of obligations must inevitably extend its protection to cover certain restitutionary interests. How far that protection should extend is the essence of the problem before us . . .

The introduction of restitutionary remedies to deprive cynical contract breakers of the fruits of their breaches of contract will lead to greater uncertainty in the assessment of damages in commercial and consumer disputes. It is of paramount importance that the way in which disputes are likely to be resolved by the courts must be readily predictable. Given the premise that the aggrieved party has suffered no loss, is such a dramatic extension of restitutionary remedies justified in order to confer a windfall in each case on the aggrieved party? I think not. In any event such a widespread availability of restitutionary remedies will have a tendency to discourage economic activity in relevant situations. In a range of cases such liability would fall on underwriters who have insured relevant liability risks. Inevitably underwriters would have to be compensated for the new species of potential claims. Insurance premiums would have to go up. That, too, is a consequence which militates against the proposed extension. The recognition of the proposed extension will in my view not serve the public interest. It is sound policy to guard against extending the protection of the law of obligations too widely. For these substantive and policy reasons I regard it as undesirable that the range of restitutionary remedies should be extended in the way in which we have been invited to do so . . .

I would dismiss the appeal.

Rose L.J. delivered judgment dismissing the appeal

Appeal Dismissed.

ATTORNEY GENERAL v BLAKE

House of Lords [2001] A.C. 268

LORD NICHOLLS OF BIRKENHEAD

19-008   My Lords,

George Blake is a notorious, self-confessed traitor. He was employed as a member of the security and intelligence services for 17 years, from 1944 to 1961. In 1951 he became an agent for the Soviet Union. From then until 1960 he disclosed valuable secret information and documents gained through his employment. On 3 May 1961 he pleaded guilty to five charges of unlawfully communicating information contrary to section 1(1)(c) of the Official Secrets Act 1911. He was sentenced to 42 years' imprisonment. This sentence reflected the extreme gravity of the harm brought about by his betrayal of secret information.

In 1966 Blake escaped from Wormwood Scrubs prison and fled to Berlin and then to Moscow. He is still there, a fugitive from justice. In 1989 he wrote his autobiography. Certain parts of the book related to his activities as a secret intelligence officer. By 1989 the information in the book was no longer confidential, nor was its disclosure damaging to the public interest. On 4 May 1989 Blake entered into a publishing contract with Jonathan Cape Ltd He granted Jonathan Cape an exclusive right to publish the book in this country in return for royalties. Jonathan Cape agreed to pay him advances against royalties: £50,000 on signing the contract, a further £50,000 on delivery of the manuscript, and another £50,000 on publication. Plainly, had Blake not been an infamous spy who had also dramatically escaped from prison, his autobiography would not have commanded payments of this order.

The book, entitled *No Other Choice*, was published on 17 September 1990. Neither the security and intelligence services nor any other branch of the Government were aware of the book until its publication was announced. Blake had not sought any prior authorisation from the Crown to disclose any of the information in the book relating to the Secret Intelligence Service. Jonathan Cape has, apparently, already paid Blake about £60,000 under the publishing agreement. In practice that money is irrecoverable. A further substantial amount, in the region of £90,000, remains payable. These proceedings concern this unpaid money.

The proceedings

On 24 May 1991 the Attorney General commenced an action against Blake, with a view to ensuring he should not enjoy any further financial fruits from his treachery. The writ and statement of claim sought relief on a variety of grounds. The trial took place before Sir Richard Scott V.-C. Blake was not represented at the trial. He had sought unsuccessfully to have access to the further money due and owing to him by the publisher for the purpose of funding his defence. He was refused legal aid. But the court had the assistance of leading and junior counsel as amici curiae. At the trial the Crown rested its claim exclusively on one cause of action: that in writing the book and authorising its publication Blake was in breach of fiduciary duties he owed the Crown. The Vice-Chancellor rejected this claim and dismissed the action: see [1997] Ch. 84. The Vice-Chancellor accepted that former members of the intelligence and security services owed a lifelong duty of non-disclosure in respect of secret and confidential information. But the law did not impose a duty which went beyond this.

The Crown appealed. Blake was not represented on the hearing of the appeal but, once again, the court had the assistance of leading and junior counsel as amici curiae. The Court of Appeal, comprising Lord Woolf M.R., Millett and Mummery L.JJ., allowed the appeal: see [1998] Ch. 439. The court upheld Sir Richard Scott V.-C.'s ruling on the breach of fiduciary claim. On this appeal to your Lordships' House the Attorney General has not sought to challenge that decision. However, the Court of Appeal permitted the Attorney General to amend his statement of claim and advance a public law claim. In making this claim the Attorney General asserted, not a private law right on behalf of the Crown, but a claim for relief in his capacity as guardian of the public interest. In this latter capacity the Attorney General may, exceptionally, invoke the assistance of the civil law in aid of the criminal law. Typically this occurs where an offence is frequently repeated in disregard of an inadequate penalty: see *Gouriet v. Union of Post Office Workers* [1978] A.C. 435. In the present case Blake's disclosure of the information in his autobiography to his publishers was a breach of section 1(1) of the Official Secrets Act 1989:

> "A person who is or has been . . . a member of the security and intelligence services . . . is guilty of an offence if without lawful authority he discloses any information . . . relating to security or intelligence which is or has been in his possession by virtue of his position as a member of any of those services . . ."

If Blake's disclosure occurred before this Act came into force on 1 March 1990, the disclosure was an offence under comparable provisions in section 2(1) of the Official Secrets Act 1911. The Court of Appeal held that the jurisdiction of the civil courts, on an application of the Attorney General, was not limited to granting an injunction restraining the commission or repeated commission of an offence. Lord Woolf said, at p. 462:

> "If, as here, a criminal offence has already been committed, the jurisdiction extends to enforcing public policy with respect to the consequences of the commission of that crime, e.g. restraining receipt by the criminal of a further benefit as a result of or in connection with that crime. . . .
>
> This is an exceptional case in which the Attorney General is entitled to intervene by instituting civil proceedings, in aid of the criminal law, to uphold the public policy of ensuring that a criminal does not retain profit directly derived from the commission of his crime."

The court made an order in the following terms:

"That the defendant George Blake be restrained until further order from receiving or from authorising any person to receive on his behalf any payment or other benefit resulting from or in connection with the exploitation of *No Other Choice* in any form or any information therein relating to security and intelligence which is or has been in his possession by virtue of his position as a member of the Secret Intelligence Service."

Blake appealed against this decision of the Court of Appeal. On the hearing of this appeal by your Lordships he was represented by counsel and solicitors acting pro bono. I wish to pay tribute to the thoroughness with which counsel and solicitors prepared the appeal and the expertise with which Mr. Clayton presented it to your Lordships.

The private law claim

In the course of his judgment Lord Woolf made some interesting observations, at [1998] Ch. 439, 455G to 459D, on a matter which had not been the subject of argument either in the Court of Appeal or before the Vice-Chancellor. The point arose out of the amendments made to the statement of claim in the course of the proceedings in the Court of Appeal. On 16 August 1944 Blake signed an Official Secrets Act declaration. This declaration included an undertaking:

". . . I undertake not to divulge any official information gained by me as a result of my employment, either in the press or in book form. I also understand that these provisions apply not only during the period of service but also after employment has ceased."

This undertaking was contractually binding. Had Blake not signed it he would not have been employed. By submitting his manuscript for publication without first obtaining clearance Blake committed a breach of this undertaking. The Court of Appeal suggested that the Crown might have a private law claim to "restitutionary damages for breach of contract", and invited submissions on this issue. The Attorney General decided that the Crown did not wish to advance argument on this point in the Court of Appeal. The Attorney General, however, wished to keep the point open for a higher court. The Court of Appeal expressed the view, necessarily tentative in the circumstances, that the law of contract would be seriously defective if the court were unable to award restitutionary damages for breach of contract. The law is now sufficiently mature to recognise a restitutionary claim for profits made from a breach of contract in appropriate situations. These include cases of "skimped" performance, and cases where the defendant obtained his profit by doing "the very thing" he contracted not to do. The present case fell into the latter category: Blake earned his profit by doing the very thing he had promised not to do.

This matter was pursued in your Lordships' House. Prompted by an invitation from your Lordships, the Attorney General advanced an argument that restitutionary principles ought to operate to enable the Crown to recover from Blake his profits arising from his breach of contract. It will be convenient to consider this private law claim first.

This is a subject on which there is a surprising dearth of judicial decision. By way of contrast, over the last 20 years there has been no lack of academic writing. This includes valuable comment on the Court of Appeal dicta in the present case: by Janet O'Sullivan, "Reflections on the Role of Restitutionary Damages to protect contractual expectations" (to be published), and Catherine Mitchell, "Remedial Inadequacy in Contract and the Role of Restitutionary Damages" (1999) 15 J.C.L. 133. Most writers have favoured the view that in some circumstances the innocent party to a breach of contract should be able to compel the defendant to disgorge the profits he obtained from his breach of contract. However, there is a noticeable absence of any consensus on what are the circumstances in which this remedy should be available. Professor Burrows has described this as a devilishly difficult topic: see "No Restitutionary Damages for Breach of Contract" [1993] L.M.C.L.Q.R. 453. The broad proposition that a wrongdoer should not be allowed to profit from his wrong has an obvious attraction. The corollary is that the person wronged may recover the amount of this profit when he has suffered no financially measurable loss. As Glidewell L.J. observed in *Halifax Building Society v Thomas* [1996] Ch. 217, 229, the corollary is not so obviously persuasive. In these choppy waters the common law and equity steered different courses. The effects of this are still being felt.

Interference with rights of property

So I turn to established, basic principles. I shall first set the scene by noting how the court approaches the question of financial recompense for interference with rights of property. [Having discussed the property cases, as well as cases involving breach of trust and breach of fiduciary duty, and awards of damages under Lord Cairns' Act, his Lordship continued:]

Breach of contract

Against this background I turn to consider the remedies available for breaches of contract. The basic remedy is an award of damages. In the much quoted words of Baron Parke, the rule of the common law is that where a party sustains a loss by reason of a breach of contract, he is, so far as money can do it, to be placed in the same position as if the contract had been performed: *Robinson v Harman* (1848) 1 Ex. 850, 855. Leaving aside the anomalous exception of punitive damages, damages are compensatory. That is axiomatic. It is equally well established that an award of damages, assessed by reference to financial loss, is not always "adequate" as a remedy for a breach of contract. The law recognises that a party to a contract may have an interest in performance which is not readily measurable in terms of money. On breach the innocent party suffers a loss. He fails to obtain the benefit promised by the other party to the contract. To him the loss may be as important as financially measurable loss, or more so. An award of damages, assessed by reference to financial loss, will not recompense him properly. For him a financially assessed measure of damages is inadequate.

The classic example of this type of case, as every law student knows, is a contract for the sale of land. The buyer of a house may be attracted by features which have little or no impact on the value of the house. An award of damages, based on strictly financial criteria, would fail to recompense a disappointed buyer for this head of loss. The primary response of the law to this type of case is to ensure, if possible, that the contract is performed in accordance with its terms. The court may make orders compelling the party who has committed a breach of contract, or is threatening to do so, to carry out his contractual obligations. To this end the court has wide powers to grant injunctive relief. The court will, for instance, readily make orders for the specific perfor-mance of contracts for the sale of land, and sometimes it will do so in respect of contracts for the sale of goods. In *Beswick v Beswick* [1968] A.C. 58 the court made an order for the specific performance of a contract to make payments of money to a third party. The law recognised that the innocent party to the breach of contract had a legitimate interest in having the contract performed even though he himself would suffer no financial loss from its breach. Likewise, the court will compel the observance of negative obligations by granting injunctions. This may include a mandatory order to undo an existing breach, as where the court orders the defendant to pull down building works carried out in breach of covenant.

All this is trite law. In practice, these specific remedies go a long way towards providing suitable protection for innocent parties who will suffer loss from breaches of contract which are not adequately remediable by an award of damages. But these remedies are not always available. For instance, confidential information may be published in breach of a non-disclosure agreement before the innocent party has time to apply to the court for urgent relief. Then the breach is irreversible. Further, these specific remedies are discretionary. Contractual obligations vary infinitely. So do the circumstances in which breaches occur, and the circumstances in which remedies are sought. The court may, for instance, decline to grant specific relief on the ground that this would be oppressive.

An instance of this nature occurred in *Wrotham Park Estate Co Ltd v Parkside Homes Ltd* [1974] 1 W.L.R. 798. For social and economic reasons the court refused to make a mandatory order for the demolition of houses built on land burdened with a restrictive covenant. Instead, Brightman J. made an award of damages under the jurisdiction which originated with Lord Cairns' Act. The existence of the new houses did not diminish the value of the benefited land by one farthing. The judge considered that if the plaintiffs were given a nominal sum, or no sum, justice would manifestly not have been done. He assessed the damages at five per cent of the developer's anticipated profit, this being the amount of money which could reasonably have been demanded for a relaxation of the covenant.

In reaching his conclusion the judge applied by analogy the cases mentioned above concerning the assess-ment of damages when a defendant has invaded another's property rights but without diminishing the value of the property. I consider he was right to do so. Property rights are superior to contractual rights in that, unlike contractual rights, property rights may survive against an indefinite class of persons. However, it is not easy to see why, as between the parties to a contract, a violation of a party's contractual rights should attract a lesser degree of remedy than a violation of his property rights. As Lionel Smith has pointed out in his article *Disgorgement of the Profits of Contract: Property, Contract and "Efficient Breach"* 24 Can. B.L.J. 121, it is not clear why it should be any more permissible to expropriate personal rights than it is permissible to expropriate property rights.

I turn to the decision of the Court of Appeal in *Surrey County Council v Bredero Homes Ltd* [1993] 1 W.L.R. 1361. A local authority had sold surplus land to a developer and obtained a covenant that the developer would develop the land in accordance with an existing planning permission. The sole purpose of the local authority in imposing the covenant was to enable it to share in the planning gain if, as happened, planning permission was subsequently granted for the erection of a larger number of houses. The purpose was that the developer would have to apply and pay for a relaxation of the covenant if it wanted to build more houses. In breach of covenant the developer completed the development in accordance with the later planning permission, and the local authority brought a claim for damages. The erection of the larger number of houses had not caused any financial loss to the local authority. The judge awarded nominal damages of £2, and the Court of Appeal dismissed the local authority's appeal.

This is a difficult decision. It has attracted criticism from academic commentators and also in judgments of Sir Thomas Bingham M.R. and Millett L.J. in *Jaggard v Sawyer* [1995] 1 W.L.R. 269. I need not pursue the detailed criticisms. In the *Bredero* case Dillon L.J. himself noted, at p. 1364, that had the covenant been worded differently, there could have been provision for payment of an increased price if a further planning permission were forthcoming. That would have been enforceable. But, according to the *Bredero* decision, a covenant not to erect any further houses without permission, intended to achieve the same result, may be breached with impunity. That would be a sorry reflection on the law. Suffice to say, in so far as the *Bredero* decision is inconsistent with the approach adopted in the *Wrotham Park* case, the latter approach is to be preferred.

The *Wrotham Park* case, therefore, still shines, rather as a solitary beacon, showing that in contract as well as tort damages are not always narrowly confined to recoupment of financial loss. In a suitable case damages for breach of contract may be measured by the benefit gained by the wrongdoer from the breach. The defendant must make a reasonable payment in respect of the benefit he has gained. In the present case the Crown seeks to go further. The claim is for all the profits of Blake's book which the publisher has not yet paid him. This raises the question whether an account of profits can ever be given as a remedy for breach of contract. The researches of counsel have been unable to discover any case where the court has made such an order on a claim for breach of contract. In *Tito v Waddell (No. 2)* [1977] Ch. 106, 332, a decision which has proved controversial, Sir Robert Megarry V.-C. said that, as a matter of fundamental principle, the question of damages was "not one of making the defendant disgorge" his gains, in that case what he had saved by committing the wrong, but "one of compensating the plaintiff." In *Occidental Worldwide Investment Corp. v Skibs A/S Avanti* [1976] 1 Lloyd's Rep. 293, 337, Kerr J. summarily rejected a claim for an account of profits when ship owners withdrew ships on a rising market.

There is a light sprinkling of cases where courts have made orders having the same effect as an order for an account of profits, but the courts seem always to have attached a different label. A person who, in breach of contract, sells land twice over must surrender his profits on the second sale to the original buyer. Since courts regularly make orders for the specific performance of contracts for the sale of land, a seller of land is, to an extent, regarded as holding the land on trust for the buyer: *Lake v. Bayliss* [1974] 1 W.L.R. 1073. In *Reid-Newfoundland Co v Anglo-American Telegraph Co, Ltd* [1912] A.C. 555 a railway company agreed not to transmit any commercial messages over a particular telegraph wire except for the benefit and account of the telegraph company. The Privy Council held that the railway company was liable to account as a trustee for the profits it wrongfully made from its use of the wire for commercial purposes. In *British Motor Trade Association v Gilbert* [1951] 2 All E.R. 641 the plaintiff suffered no financial loss but the award of damages for breach of contract effectively stripped the wrongdoer of the profit he had made from his wrongful venture into the black market for new cars.

These cases illustrate that circumstances do arise when the just response to a breach of contract is that the wrongdoer should not be permitted to retain any profit from the breach. In these cases the courts have reached the desired result by straining existing concepts. Professor Peter Birks has deplored the "failure of jurisprudence when the law is forced into this kind of abusive instrumentalism": see (1993) 109 L.Q.R. 518, 520. Some years ago Professor Dawson suggested there is no inherent reason why the technique of equity courts in land contracts should not be more widely employed, not by granting remedies as the by-product of a phantom "trust" created by the contract, but as an alternative form of money judgment remedy. That well known ailment of lawyers, a hardening of the categories, ought not to be an obstacle: see "Restitution or Damages" (1959) 20 Ohio L.J. 175.

My conclusion is that there seems to be no reason, in principle, why the court must in all circumstances rule out an account of profits as a remedy for breach of contract. I prefer to avoid the unhappy expression "restitutionary damages". Remedies are the law's response to a wrong (or, more precisely, to a cause of action). When, exceptionally, a just response to a breach of contract so requires, the court should be able to grant the discretionary remedy of requiring a defendant to account to the plaintiff for the benefits he has received from his breach of contract. In the same way as a plaintiff's interest in performance of a contract may render it just and equitable for the court to make an order for specific performance or grant an injunction, so the plaintiff's interest in performance may make it just and equitable that the defendant should retain no benefit from his breach of contract.

The state of the authorities encourages me to reach this conclusion, rather than the reverse. The law recognises that damages are not always a sufficient remedy for breach of contract. This is the foundation of the court's jurisdiction to grant the remedies of specific performance and injunction. Even when awarding damages, the law does not adhere slavishly to the concept of compensation for financially measurable loss. When the circumstances require, damages are measured by reference to the benefit obtained by the wrongdoer. This applies to interference with property rights. Recently, the like approach has been adopted to breach of contract. Further, in certain circumstances an account of profits is ordered in preference to an award of damages. Sometimes the injured party is given the choice: either compensatory damages or an account of the wrongdoer's profits. Breach of confidence is an instance of this. If confidential information is wrongfully divulged in breach of a non-disclosure agreement, it would be nothing short of sophistry to say that an account of profits may be ordered in respect of the equitable wrong but not in respect of the breach of contract which governs the relationship between the parties. With the established authorities going thus far, I consider it would be only a modest step for the law to recognise openly that, exceptionally, an account of profits may be the most appropriate remedy for breach of contract. It is not as though this step would contradict some recognised principle applied consistently throughout the law to the grant or withholding of the remedy of an account of profits. No such principle is discernible.

The main argument against the availability of an account of profits as a remedy for breach of contract is that the circumstances where this remedy may be granted will be uncertain. This will have an unsettling effect on commercial contracts where certainty is important. I do not think these fears are well founded. I see no reason why, in practice, the availability of the remedy of an account of profits need disturb settled expectations in the commercial or consumer world. An account of profits will be appropriate only in exceptional circumstances. Normally the remedies of damages, specific performance and injunction, coupled with the characterisation of some contractual obligations as fiduciary, will provide an adequate response to a breach of contract. It will be only in exceptional cases, where those remedies are inadequate, that any question of accounting for profits will arise. No fixed rules can be prescribed. The court will have regard to all the circumstances, including the subject matter of the contract, the purpose of the contractual provision which has been breached, the circumstances in which the breach occurred, the consequences of the breach and the circumstances in which relief is being sought. A useful general guide, although not exhaustive, is whether the plaintiff had a legitimate interest in preventing the defendant's profit-making activity and, hence, in depriving him of his profit.

It would be difficult, and unwise, to attempt to be more specific. In the Court of Appeal Lord Woolf, M.R. suggested there are at least two situations in which justice requires the award of restitutionary damages where compensatory damages would be inadequate: see [1998] Ch. 439, 458. Lord Woolf was not there addressing the question of when an account of profits, in the conventional sense, should be available. But I should add that, so far as an account of profits is concerned, the suggested categorisation would not assist. The first suggested category was the case of "skimped" performance, where the defendant fails to provide the full extent of services he has contracted to provide. He should be liable to pay back the amount of expenditure he saved by the breach. This is a much discussed problem. But a part refund of the price agreed for services would not fall within the scope of an account of profits as ordinarily understood. Nor does an account of profits seem to be needed in this context. The resolution of the problem of cases of skimped performance, where the plaintiff does not get what was agreed, may best be found elsewhere. If a shopkeeper supplies inferior and cheaper goods than those ordered and paid for, he has to refund the difference in price. That would be the outcome of a claim for damages for breach of contract. That would be so, irrespective of whether the goods in fact served the intended purpose. There must be scope for a similar approach, without any straining of principle, in cases where the defendant provided inferior and cheaper services than those contracted for.

The second suggested category was where the defendant has obtained his profit by doing the very thing he contracted not to do. This category is defined too widely to assist. The category is apt to embrace all express negative obligations. But something more is required than mere breach of such an obligation before an account of profits will be the appropriate remedy.

Lord Woolf, at [1998] Ch. 439, 457, 458, also suggested three facts which should not be a sufficient ground for departing from the normal basis on which damages are awarded: the fact that the breach was cynical and deliberate; the fact that the breach enabled the defendant to enter into a more profitable contract elsewhere; and the fact that by entering into a new and more profitable contract the defendant put it out of his power to perform his contract with the plaintiff. I agree that none of these facts would be, by itself, a good reason for ordering an account of profits.

The present case

The present case is exceptional. The context is employment as a member of the security and intelligence services. Secret information is the lifeblood of these services. In the 1950s Blake deliberately committed repeated breaches of his undertaking not to divulge official information gained as a result of his employment. He caused untold and immeasurable damage to the public interest he had committed himself to serve. In 1990 he published his autobiography, a further breach of his express undertaking. By this time the information disclosed was no longer confidential. In the ordinary course of commercial dealings the disclosure of non-confidential information might be regarded as venial. In the present case disclosure was also a criminal offence under the Official Secrets Acts, even though the information was no longer confidential. Section 1 of the Official Secrets Act 1989 draws a distinction in this regard between members of the security and intelligence services and other Crown servants. Under section 1(3) a person who is or has been a Crown servant is guilty of an offence if without lawful authority he makes "a damaging disclosure" of information relating to security or intelligence. The offence is drawn more widely in the case of a present or past member of the security and intelligence services. Such a person is guilty of an offence if without lawful authority he discloses "any information" relating to security or intelligence which is or has been in his possession by virtue of his position as a member of those services. This distinction was approved in Parliament after debate when the legislation was being enacted.

Mr. Clayton submitted that section 1(1) is drawn too widely and infringes article 10 of the European Convention of Human Rights. Section 1(1) criminalises disclosure of information when no damage results. It focuses on the status of the individual who makes the disclosure, rather than on the nature of the information itself. A non-damaging disclosure by a member of the security and intelligence services is criminal, but the identical non-damaging disclosure by a Crown servant is not.

This argument was raised for the first time in this House. Your Lordships are not equipped with the material necessary to decide the point. In the event this does not matter, because there is in the present case another consideration which is sufficient for the purposes of the Attorney General. When he joined the Secret Intelligence Service Blake expressly agreed in writing that he would not disclose official information, during or after his service, in book form or otherwise. He was employed on that basis. That was the basis on which he acquired official information. The Crown had and has a legitimate interest in preventing Blake profiting from the disclosure of official information, whether classified or not, while a member of the service and thereafter. Neither he, nor any other member of the service, should have a financial incentive to break his undertaking. It is of paramount importance that members of the service should have complete confidence in all their dealings with each other, and that those recruited as informers should have the like confidence. Undermining the willingness of prospective informers to co-operate with the services, or undermining the morale and trust between members of the services when engaged on secret and dangerous operations, would jeopardise the effectiveness of the service. An absolute rule against disclosure, visible to all, makes good sense.

In considering what would be a just response to a breach of Blake's undertaking the court has to take these considerations into account. The undertaking, if not a fiduciary obligation, was closely akin to a fiduciary obligation, where an account of profits is a standard remedy in the event of breach. Had the information which Blake has now disclosed still been confidential, an account of profits would have been ordered, almost as a matter of course. In the special circumstances of the intelligence services, the same conclusion should follow even though the information is no longer confidential. That would be a just response to the breach. I am reinforced in this view by noting that most of the profits from the book derive indirectly from the extremely serious and damaging breaches of the same undertaking committed by Blake in the 1950s. As already mentioned, but for his notoriety as an infamous spy his autobiography would not have commanded royalties of the magnitude Jonathan Cape agreed to pay.

As a footnote I observe that a similar conclusion, requiring the contract-breaker to disgorge his profits, was reached in the majority decision of the United States Supreme Court in *Snepp v United States* (1980) 444 U.S. 507. The facts were strikingly similar. A former employee of the Central Intelligence Agency, whose conditions of employment included a promise not to divulge any information relating to the agency without pre-publication clearance, published a book about the agency's activities in Vietnam. None of the information was classified, but an agent's violation of his non-disclosure obligation impaired the agency's ability to function properly. The court considered and rejected various forms of relief. The actual damage was not quantifiable, nominal damages were a hollow alternative, and punitive damages after a jury trial would be speculative and unusual. Even if recovered they would bear no relation to either the government's irreparable loss or Snepp's unjust gain. The court considered that a remedy which required Snepp "to disgorge the benefits of his faithlessness", was swift and sure, tailored to deter those who would place sensitive information at risk and, since the remedy reached only funds attributable to the breach, it could not saddle the former agent with exemplary damages out of all proportion to his gain. In order to achieve this result the court "imposed" a constructive trust on Snepp's profits. In this country, affording the plaintiff the remedy of an account of profits is a different means to the same end.

The form of the order
The Attorney General's entitlement to an account of Blake's profits does not, in this case, confer on the Crown any proprietary interest in the debt due to Blake from Jonathan Cape. The Crown is entitled, on the taking of the account, to a money judgment which can then be enforced by attachment of the debt in the usual way. These formal steps may be capable of being short-circuited. Despite the niceties and formalities once associated with taking an account, the amount payable under an account of profits need not be any more elaborately or precisely calculated than damages. But in this case there is a complication. Blake has brought third party proceedings against Jonathan Cape, seeking payment of £90,000 (less tax). In the third party proceedings Jonathan Cape has sought to deduct legal expenses incurred in resisting a defamation claim and in resisting the Crown's claim. Accordingly, the appropriate form of order on this appeal is a declaration that the Attorney General is entitled to be paid a sum equal to whatever amount is due and owing to Blake from Jonathan Cape under the publishing agreement of 4 May 1989. The injunction granted by the Court of Appeal will remain in force until Jonathan Cape duly makes payment to the Attorney General. I would dismiss this appeal.

The public law claim
The public law claim, advanced by the Attorney General as guardian of the public interest, arises only if the Crown as Blake's former employer has no private law claim in respect of the royalties. Accordingly, having regard to the conclusion already reached on the private law claim, the public law claim does not call for decision. . . .

LORD HOBHOUSE OF WOODBOROUGH

My Lords,

When he opened this appeal, Mr Clayton, to whose *pro bono* services on behalf of the appellant George Blake I too would wish to pay tribute, warned your Lordships against being drawn into making bad law in order to enable an intuitively just decision to be given against a traitor. It is therefore particularly important to be clear what are the facts which have given rise to the Attorney-General's claim in the present case. They are not materially in dispute.

Between 1944 and 1961, Blake was employed by the Crown as a member of the Secret Intelligence Service. As such he was subject to the provisions of the Official Secrets Act 1911. In August 1944 he signed the requisite declaration under the Act. The declaration which he signed included the added sentence:

> "I understand that the above clauses [2 and 3] of the Official Secrets Act 1911 and 1920 cover also articles published in the press and in book form and I undertake not to divulge any official information gained by me as a result of my employment either in the press or in book form."

It is common ground in the present case that these words amounted to a contractual undertaking by Blake in favour of the Crown and that the Crown had a legitimate interest in asking for this undertaking in aid of the criminal provisions quoted earlier in the document. It was not a commercial document and its purpose was not to protect any commercial interest of the Crown or any right of the Crown commercially to exploit such information. Its purpose and justification was to support and reinforce the provisions of the criminal law to which Blake became subject by reason of his entering the employment of the Crown and signing the statutory declaration. It is that justification which prevented the undertaking from amounting to an unlawful restraint of trade and would now have to be relied upon to justify the infringement of his freedom to impart information . . .

The Private Law Claim: Restitutionary Damages
It is with some hesitation that I enter upon this field at all in view of your Lordships' so far unanimous opinion save so as to record my dissent. The subject is a profound one which has attracted much attention among the academic writers for some time. Neither the subject nor the opinions of my noble and learned friends

Lord Nicholls and Lord Steyn could be done justice in many fewer pages than their opinions will occupy. However I do not believe that it is helpful (or courteous to Mr Clayton) that I should add nothing at all. Exceptional though this case is, courts hereafter will have to consider its relevance to the decisions of other cases which will surely come before them. I will however confine myself to what I regard as the minimum of explanatory comment (with the inevitable consequence of some simplification).

The concepts of restitution and compensation are not the same though they will on occasions fulfil the same need. Restitution is analogous to property; it concerns wealth or advantage which ought to be returned or transferred by the defendant to the plaintiff. It is a form of specific implement. Its clearest form is an order for the return or transfer of property which belongs in law or in equity to the plaintiff. Property includes an interest in property. Then there are rights recognised in equity such as those which arise from a fiduciary relationship. These rights give rise to restitutionary remedies including the remedy of account which, depending on the circumstances, could also derive from a common law relationship such as agency. Then, again, there are the rights now grouped under the heading of the law of restitution or unjust enrichment. These are still truly restitutionary concepts leading to restitutionary remedies. Typically they require the payment of money by the person unjustly enriched to the person at whose expense that enrichment has taken place. In so far as the appropriate remedy is the payment of money or the delivery up of a chattel or goods is concerned the common law could provide it; insofar as it required some other remedy or the recognition of an equitable right, the chancery jurisdiction had to be invoked.

The essential of such rights and their enforcement was the procuring by the courts of the *performance* by the defendant of his obligations. The plaintiff recovers what he is actually entitled to not some monetary substitute for it. If what the plaintiff is entitled to is wealth expressed in monetary terms, the order will be for the payment of money but this does not alter the character of the remedy or of the right being recognised. He gets the money because it was his property or he was in some other way entitled to it. It is still the enforced performance of an obligation. The same is the case where an injunction is granted or a decree of specific performance or the ordering of an account.

It is this class of rights which the Crown is unable to invoke as a result of the judgment of the Vice-Chancellor upheld by the Court of Appeal. There is no obligation of Blake left to perform or which now can be enforced. That time passed with the failure to apply for an injunction in 1989 or 1990. The Crown has no right to an injunction to stop the payment of the royalty to Blake and procure its payment to the Crown instead. The Crown has no right to the royalty and does not now assert one.

The law, including equity, provides extensive and effective remedies for protecting and enforcing property rights. It is no criticism of the law that they are not available now to the Crown. The Crown does not have the substantive rights to support such remedies.

Two further points need to be briefly mentioned. There are cases which are treated as so closely analogous to proprietary rights that they are covered by remedies which are appropriate to such rights. The contractual right in *Reid-Newfoundland Co v Anglo-American Telegraph Co Ltd* [1912] AC 555 was held to have created a trust. In *Reading v Att-Gen* [1951] AC 507, restitutionary remedies were awarded against an army sergeant who used his army uniform and army vehicle to enable him to assist smugglers. The money he was paid by the smugglers was held to be money for which he must account to his employer in the same way as if he had received a bribe: see per Asquith L.J. in the Court of Appeal. These cases would have assisted the Crown had they succeeded on the facts before Scott V.-C. The other point is that where a court declines to grant an injunction it may award damages in lieu. This does not alter the principles which are applicable nor does it provide the Crown with a remedy in the present case; but it is relevant to the understanding of the authorities.

The Crown has to allege a breach of contract. This is not a claim to the performance of any obligation save in the sense used by Lord Diplock that contractual obligations are correctly understood as being the obligation to perform or pay damages for failing to do so—the primary and secondary obligation: *Photo Production Ltd v Securicor Transport Ltd* [1980] AC 827. The claim is for damages in order to put the plaintiff in the same position as if the contract had been performed. It is a *substitute* for performance. That is why it is necessarily compensatory. The error is to describe compensation as relating to a loss as if there has to be some identified physical or monetary loss to the plaintiff. In the vast majority of cases this error does not matter because the plaintiff's claim can be so described without distortion. But in a minority of cases the error does matter and cases of the breach of negative promises typically illustrate this category.

But, before coming to them, I would like to refer to *Ruxley Electronics and Construction Ltd v Forsyth* [1996] AC 344. This was the case of the swimming pool. The defendant had contracted to build for the plaintiff a swimming pool of a specified depth. The pool was not of that depth. The defendant had broken his contract. The plaintiff was entitled to damages. The value of his property was affected either not at all or only marginally.

The swimming pool was serviceable. But the plaintiff was entitled to a deeper pool. The *prima facie* measure of damages would have been the cost of increasing the depth of the pool to the stipulated depth—a considerable sum. But this sum was so disproportionate that the courts refused to award it. It would be unreasonable for the plaintiff to incur that expense. His damages must be assessed at a lower figure. The speech of Lord Mustill (pp. 359–61) is illuminating. The loss is a reasonable valuation of what the plaintiff ought to have had but did not get. It is not just the amount (if any) by which his property has a lower market value than that it would have had if the contract had been performed. In the present case, by 1989, Blake's undertaking had no remaining value to the Crown.

The question of negative covenants typically arise in relation to land and covenants not to build. A complication is that they usually involve a proprietary right of the plaintiff which he is *prima facie* entitled to enforce as such. Where the plaintiff has failed to obtain or failed to apply for an injunction, he has to be content with a remedy in damages. What has happened in such cases is that there has either actually or in effect been a compulsory purchase of the plaintiff's right of refusal. (The award of damages in tort for the conversion or detinue of goods is also an example of compulsory purchase as is demonstrated by the common law rule that the payment of the damages vests the title in the goods in the defendant.) What the plaintiff has lost is the sum which he could have exacted from the defendant as the price of his consent to the development. This is an example of compensatory damages. They are damages for breach. They do not involve any concept of restitution and so to describe them is an error. The error comes about because of the assumption that the only loss which the plaintiff can have suffered is a reduction in the value of the dominant tenement. It is for this reason that I agree with my noble and learned friend Lord Nicholls that the decision in *Wrotham Park Estate Co Ltd v Parkside Homes Ltd* [1974] 1 WLR 798 is to be preferred to that in *Surrey C.C. v Bredero Homes Ltd* [1993] 1 WLR 1361: see also *Jaggard v Sawyer* [1995] 1 WLR 269. I would however add that the order proposed by your Lordships does not reflect this principle; it goes further. It does not award to the Crown damages for breach of contract assessed by reference to what would be the reasonable price to pay for permission to publish. It awards the Crown damages which equal the whole amount owed by Jonathan Cape to Blake. That is a remedy based on proprietary principles when the necessary proprietary rights are absent.

The principle of compensation is both intellectually sound as the remedy for breach and provides the just answer. The examples discussed in my noble and learned friend's speech do not on the correct analysis disclose the supposed need to extend the boundaries of remedies for breach of contract. The reason why the Crown should not recover damages in the present case derives from the exceptional public law nature of the undertaking which Blake gave. If the relationship had been a commercial one it is probable that by 1989 the undertaking would be regarded as spent or no longer enforcible, but if still enforcible the breach of it would have supported compensatory damages on the "compulsory purchase" basis.

The examples given by my noble and learned friend are examples of compensatory damages. Lord Halsbury's dining-room chair is no different unless the error which I have identified is made. He would have lost the use of the chair and it, like other such amenity-value assets, can be assessed by reference to the sum which has been expended on its acquisition and/or maintenance or interest upon its capital value during the period of deprivation. The supposed problem arises from asking the wrong question not from receiving the wrong answer.

I must also sound a further note of warning that if some more extensive principle of awarding non-compensatory damages for breach of contract is to be introduced into our commercial law the consequences will be very far reaching and disruptive. I do not believe that such is the intention of your Lordships but if others are tempted to try to extend the decision of the present exceptional case to commercial situations so as to introduce restitutionary rights beyond those presently recognised by the law of restitution, such a step will require very careful consideration before it is acceded to.

My Lords, Mr Clayton was right to say that the exceptional facts of this case have been critical to its decision. The policy which is being enforced is that which requires Blake to be punished by depriving him of any benefit from anything connected with his past deplorable criminal conduct. Your Lordships consider that this policy can be given effect to without a departure from principle. I must venture to disagree. I would allow the appeal and dismiss the cross-appeal.

B . Taking Stock

19–009   Since the decision in *Blake*, courts and commentators have struggled both to stabilise and to ration-
alise the legal position. Distinctions between "compensatory" and "gains-based" remedies have been
made and then criticised (see, e.g., *WWF-World Wide Fund for Nature v World Wrestling Federation
Entertainment Inc* [2007] EWCA Civ 286); further distinctions have been suggested between damages
that, in their nature, involve restitution, disgorgement, and penalty; and the occasions for the exceptional relief in *Blake* have been considered. Stated shortly, the current position seems to be as follows.

First, there is support for the view that, in cases such as *Wrotham Park*, *Bredero* and *Blake*, where
the defendant profits from a breach of contract but without causing the innocent party to suffer a
straightforward financial loss, the demands of justice might require some (special) corrective adjustment of the parties' post-breach position. However, the not uncommon case of a commercial contractor breaking a contract in order to take advantage of a better offer that is now available in the market
(the case of an efficient breach), is not one that requires special treatment, see *AB Corporation v CD
Company (The "Sine Nomine")* [2002] 1 Lloyd's Rep 805).

Secondly, in some of these special cases, a more imaginative application of the expectation principle (protecting the innocent party's interest in performance) might suffice to achieve the required
degree of correction. In effect, the innocent party is compensated for the loss of opportunity to bargain
for a release from the strict terms of the contract (see, e.g., *Experience Hendrix LLC v PPX Enterprises
Inc* [2003] EWCA Civ 323, and *Lane v O'Brien Homes* [2004] EWHC 303, QB). Where such an approach
can be applied then, as Lord Hobhouse points out in *Blake*, contract law can keep faith with its defining
and distinctive compensatory principles.

Thirdly, there might be cases where, exceptionally, justice requires a more dramatic corrective
adjustment—for example, in a case such as *Blake* itself where the Crown would never have bargained
for release from the terms of the contract. In such cases, where the terms of the contract are categorically non-negotiable, an order for an account of profits might be appropriate.

C. Recovery of Wasted Expenditure

McRAE v THE COMMONWEALTH DISPOSALS COMMISSION

High Court of Australia 84 C.L.R. 377; [1951] Argus L.R. 771

19–010   The facts are given below, in para.23–010. The plaintiffs recovered the expenditure which they had
incurred in sending a salvage expedition to look for the tanker.

DIXON AND FULLAGAR JJ

Mr Tait (for the Commission) contended that . . . it could not be held that the alleged damage flowed from
the alleged breach. Let it be supposed, he said in effect, that the plaintiffs acted reasonably in what they
did, and let it be supposed that the Commission ought reasonably to have contemplated that they would
so act. Still, he said, the plaintiffs are faced with precisely the same difficulty with which they are faced if
the case is regarded as a simple and normal case of breach by non-delivery. Suppose there had been a
tanker at the place indicated. Non constat that the expenditure incurred by the plaintiffs would not have
been equally wasted. If the promise that there was a tanker in situ had been performed, she might still have
been found worthless or not susceptible of profitable salvage operations or of any salvage operations at all.
How, then, he asked, can the plaintiffs say that their expenditure was wasted because there was no tanker
in existence?

The argument is far from being negligible. But it is really, we think, fallacious. If we regard the case as a
simple and normal case of breach by non-delivery, the plaintiffs have no starting-point. The burden of proof

is on them, and they cannot establish that they have suffered any damage unless they can show that a tanker delivered in performance of the contract would have had some value, and this they cannot show. But when the contract alleged is a contract that there was a tanker in a particular place, and the breach assigned is that there was no tanker there, and the damages claimed are measured by expenditure incurred on the faith of the promise that there was a tanker in that place, the plaintiffs are in a very different position. They have now a starting-point. They can say: (1) this expense was incurred; (2) it was incurred because you promised us that there was a tanker; (3) the fact that there was no tanker made it certain that this expense would be wasted. The plaintiffs have in this way a starting-point. They make a prima facie case. The fact that the expense was wasted flowed prima facie from the fact that there was no tanker; and the first fact is damage, and the second fact is breach of contract. The burden is now thrown on the Commission of establishing that, if there had been a tanker, the expense incurred would equally have been wasted. This, of course, the Commission cannot establish. The fact is that the impossibility of assessing damages on the basis of a comparison between what was promised and what was delivered arises not because what was promised was valueless but because it is impossible to value a non-existent thing. It is the breach of contract itself which makes it impossible even to undertake an assessment on that basis. It is not impossible, however, to undertake an assessment on another basis, and, in so far as the Commission's breach of contract itself reduces the possibility of an accurate assessment, it is not for the Commission to complain.

HAYES AND ANOTHER v JAMES & CHARLES DODD (A FIRM)

Court of Appeal [1990] 2 All E.R. 815

In 1982 the plaintiffs were considering the purchase of new and larger premises for their motor business. Access for vehicles at the rear of the property which they had in view was critical to the success of the business. The owners of the land over which the access ran asserted that there was no right of way. The defendants who were the plaintiffs' solicitors informed them that the right of way was secure and in reliance on that assurance the plaintiffs purchased the property. There was no right of way and within days of completion the access was blocked with disastrous consequences to the plaintiffs' business. After 12 months they closed it down and attempted unsuccessfully to sell the property as a single unit. Eventually they sold a maisonette on the property in 1986 and the workshop a year later. The defendants appealed on the quantum of damages.

19–011

STAUGHTON LJ

The first question in this appeal relates to the basis on which damages should be assessed. Like Hirst J. I start with the principle stated by Lord Blackburn in *Livingstone v Rawyards Coal Co* (1880) 5 App.Cas. 25 at 39:

". . . you should as nearly as possible get at that sum of money which will put the party who has been injured, or who has suffered, in the same position as he would have been in if he had not sustained the wrong for which he is now getting his compensation or reparation."

One must therefore ascertain the actual situation of the plaintiffs and compare it with their situation if the breach of contract had not occurred.

What then was the breach of contract? It was not the breach of any warranty that there was a right of way: the defendant solicitors gave no such warranty. This is an important point: see *Perry v Sidney Phillips & Son (a firm)* [1982] 3 All E.R. 705. The breach was of the solicitors' promise to use reasonable skill and care in advising their clients. If they had done that, they would have told the plaintiffs that there was no right of way; and it is clear that, on the receipt of such advice, the plaintiffs would have decided not to enter into the transaction at all. They would have bought no property, spent no money and borrowed none from the bank.

That at first sight is the situation which one should compare with the actual financial state of the plaintiffs. I will call this the "no-transaction method." There are, however, authorities which show that instead one takes for the first element in the comparison the situation which the plaintiff would have been in if the transaction had gone through in accordance with his legitimate expectations. This I call the "successful-transaction method." Thus, in *Perry's* case, the plaintiff recovered from negligent surveyors the difference between the value of the house at the date when he bought it if it had not been defective and its actual value at that date.

However, it appears to have been found, or assumed, in that case that the plaintiff would still have bought the house if he had been given correct advice as to its condition, albeit at a lower price. It was not a case where he would never have entered into the transaction at all . . .

The difference between the two methods is unlikely to be of importance in a case which concerns some commodity that is readily saleable, such as peas or beans, and if there is no difficulty or delay in ascertaining that a breach has occurred. A plaintiff who has agreed to buy beans at the current market price and has received a quantity which is defective can sell them forthwith and realise their actual value. If he intended to perform a profitable sub-contract, he can buy other beans in the market for that purpose. In such a case it makes no difference whether damages are assessed on the no-transaction method, so that he recovers the price paid less the sum realised on disposition of the defective beans, or on the successful-transaction method, which gives him the difference between the value of sound beans and the value of defective beans.

However, this case is not concerned with a readily saleable commodity: it took the plaintiffs nearly five years from the date of their purchase to dispose of the maisonette, and another year expired before they were free from the obligations imposed by the lease of the workshop and yard. During all that period they were incurring expenses, such as rent and other items, together with interest on the money which they had borrowed from the bank. Furthermore, they did not receive, until the first year had almost expired, any acknowledgment by the defendants that there was in fact no right of way; that only happened on July 6, 1983, whereas they had completed their purchase on July 28, 1982, and the right of way had first been challenged two days later.

I am quite satisfied that Hirst J. was entitled to award damages in this case on the no-transaction basis, and that he was right to do so. Indeed it may well be that the plaintiffs were, as he held, entitled to elect between that method and the successful-transaction method; but I need not express any concluded view on that. So they should recover all the money which they spent, less anything which they subsequently recovered, provided always that they acted reasonably in mitigating their loss. But they were quite properly denied any sum for the profit which they would have made if they had operated their business successfully.

[Staughton L.J. considered the damages under various heads and came to "G. Mental distress."]

Hirst J. awarded £1,500 to each of the plaintiffs under this head. There can be no doubt, and it was accepted in this court, that each of them suffered vexation and anguish over the years to a serious extent, for which the sum awarded was but modest compensation. There is, however, an important question of principle involved.

For my part I would have wished for a rather more elaborate argument than we received on this point, before deciding it, since the law seems to be in some doubt. But I would be most reluctant to impose on the plaintiffs, on top of their other misfortunes, two or three days of scholarly argument whether and in what circumstances damages can be awarded for mental distress consequent on breach of contract in a business transaction, possibly at their expense, when the sum involved is only £3,000 or roughly 3 per cent of their total claim. The difficulty is that almost any other case where a plaintiff claims to have suffered mental distress would present a similar problem, that the individual plaintiff ought not to be expected to bear the burden and perhaps also the cost of an elaborate argument. If, as I think, the law needs clarification, it is to be hoped that a case can be found where that will be provided by the House of Lords. Or it may be that the Law Commission can supply it.

Like the judge, I consider that the English courts should be wary of adopting what he called "the United States practice of huge awards." Damages awarded for negligence or want of skill, whether against professional men or anyone else, must provide fair compensation, but no more than that. And I would not view with enthusiasm the prospect that every shipowner in the Commercial Court, having successfully claimed for unpaid freight or demurrage, would be able to add a claim for mental distress suffered while he was waiting for his money.

In a sense, the wrong done to the plaintiffs in this action, for which they seek compensation under this head, lay in the defendants' failure to admit liability at an early stage. On July 6, 1983 the defendants acknowledged that there was no right of way, but denied negligence. Had they on that very day admitted liability and tendered a sum on account of damages, or offered interim reparation in some other form, the anxiety of the plaintiffs, and their financial problems, could have been very largely relieved. But liability was not admitted until January 1987. I believe that in one or more American states damages are awarded for wrongfully defending an action. But there is no such remedy in this country so far as I am aware . . .

I am not convinced that it is enough to ask whether mental distress was reasonably foreseeable as a consequence, or even whether it should reasonably have been contemplated as not unlikely to result from a breach of contract. It seems to me that damages for mental distress in contract are, as a matter of policy, limited to certain classes of case. I would broadly follow the classification provided by Dillon L.J. in *Bliss v South East Thames Regional Health Authority* [1987] I.C.R. 700 at 718:

"... where the contract which has been broken was itself a contract to provide peace of mind or freedom from distress ..."

It may be that the class is somewhat wider than that. But it should not, in my judgment, include any case where the object of the contract was not comfort or pleasure, or the relief of discomfort, but simply carrying on a commercial activity with a view to profit. So I would disallow the item of damages for anguish and vexation.

Sir George Waller and Purchas L.J. delivered judgments to similar effect.

C & P HAULAGE (A FIRM) v MIDDLETON

Court of Appeal [1983] 1 W.L.R. 1461; [1983] 3 All E.R. 94

The appellant was granted by the respondents a contractual licence to occupy premises for the purposes of his business on a renewable six-monthly basis. It was expressly provided that any fixtures he put in were not to be removed at the end of the licence. Ten weeks before the end of a six-month period, he was unlawfully ejected by the respondents. He was given temporary permission by the local authority to use his own home for the work which he continued to do until well after the six-month term would have expired. He claimed the cost of the improvements he had made to the premises. The judge awarded only nominal damages. He appealed.

19–012

ACKNER LJ

The case which I have found of assistance—and I am grateful to counsel for their research—is a case in the *British Columbia Supreme Court: Bowlay Logging Ltd v Domtar Ltd* [1978] 4 W.W.R. 105. Berger J, in a very careful and detailed judgment, goes through various English and American authorities and refers to the leading textbook writers, and I will only quote a small part of his judgment. At the bottom of p. 115 he refers to the work of Professor L. L. Fuller and William R. Perdue, Jr., in "The Reliance Interest in Contract Damages: 1" (1936), 46 *Yale Law Jour*. 52 and their statement, at p. 79: "We will not in a suit for reimbursement for losses incurred in reliance on a contract knowingly put the plaintiff in a better position than he would have occupied had the contract been fully performed." Berger J., at p. 116, then refers to *L. Albert & Son v Armstrong Rubber Co* (1949) 178 F.2d 182 in which Learned Hand C. J., speaking for the Circuit Court of Appeals, Second Circuit: "held that on a claim for compensation for expenses in part performance the defendant was entitled to deduct whatever he could prove the plaintiff would have lost if the contract had been fully performed." What Berger J. had to consider was this, p. 105: "The parties entered into a contract whereby the plaintiff would cut timber under the defendant's timber sale, and the defendant would be responsible for hauling the timber away from the site of the timber sale. The plaintiff claimed the defendant was in breach of the contract as the defendant had not supplied sufficient trucks to make the plaintiff's operation, which was losing money, viable, and claimed not for loss of profits but for compensation for expenditures. The defendant argued that the plaintiff's operation lost money not because of a lack of trucks but because of the plaintiff's inefficiency, and, further, that even if the defendant had breached the contract the plaintiff should not be awarded damages because its operation would have lost money in any case."

This submission was clearly accepted because the plaintiff was awarded only nominal damages, and Berger J. said, at p. 117: "The law of contract compensates a plaintiff for damages resulting from the defendant's breach; it does not compensate a plaintiff for damages resulting from his making a bad bargain. Where it can be seen that the plaintiff would have incurred a loss on the contract as a whole, the expenses he has incurred are losses flowing from entering into the contract, not losses flowing from the defendant's breach. In these circumstances, the true consequence of the defendant's breach is that the plaintiff is released from his obligation to complete the contract—or in other words, he is saved from incurring further losses. If the law of contract were to move from compensating for the consequences of breach to compensating for the consequences of entering into contracts, the law would run contrary to the normal expectations of the world of commerce. The burden or risk would be shifted from the plaintiff to the defendant. The defendant would become the insurer of the plaintiff's enterprise. Moreover, the amount of the damages would increase not in relation to the gravity or consequences of the breach but in relation to the inefficiency with which the plaintiff carried out the contract. The greater his expenses owing to inefficiency, the greater the damages. The fundamental principle upon which damages are measured under the law of contract is restitutio in integrium. The principle contended for here by the plaintiff would entail the award of damages not to compensate the plaintiff but to punish the defendant."

It is urged here that the garage itself was merely an element in the defendant's business; it was not a profit-making entity on its own. Nevertheless, if as a result of being kept out of these premises the defendant had found no other premises to go to for a period of time, his claim would clearly have been a claim for such loss of profit as he could establish his business suffered.

In my judgment, the approach of Berger J. is the correct one. It is not the function of the courts where there is a breach of contract knowingly, as this would be the case, to put a plaintiff in a better financial position than if the contract had been properly performed. In this case the defendant who is the plaintiff in the counterclaim, if he was right in his claim, would indeed be in a better position because, as I have already indicated, had the contract been lawfully determined as it could have been in the middle of December, there would have been no question of his recovering these expenses.

Fox L.J. agreed, pointing out that the case was different from *Anglia Television v Reed* and *Lloyd v Stanbury*, infra, in that, in the present case, it was equally likely that the expenditure would be wasted if there had been no breach. The reality was that the appellant had made a very unsatisfactory and dangerous bargain.

Appeal Dismissed—Judgment for the Appellant for Nominal Damages of £10.

Points for reflection

19–013

1. In *CCC Films Ltd v Impact Quadrant Films Ltd* [1984] 3 All E.R. 298 the plaintiffs paid the defendants $12,000 for a licence to exploit, distribute and exhibit three films. In breach of contract, the defendants failed to deliver the films. The plaintiffs were unable to produce any evidence of loss of profits and instead claimed to recover the $12,000 as wasted expenditure. Hutchinson J held that the onus lay on the defendants to prove that, if they had not broken their contract, the plaintiffs would not have succeeded in recouping their expenditure. He followed Berger J in the *Bowlay Logging* case, above, and *Albert v Armstrong Rubber*, above, quoting from the judgment of Learned Hand CJ:

    "In cases where the venture would have proved profitable to the promisee there is no reason why he should not recover his expenses. On the other hand, on those occasions in which the performance would not have covered the promisee's outlay, such a result imposes the risk of the promisee's contract upon the promisor. We cannot agree that the promisor's default in performance should under this guise make him an insurer of the promisee's venture; yet it does not follow that the breach should not throw upon him the duty of showing that the value of the performance would in fact have been less than the promisee's outlay. It is often very hard to learn what the value of the performance would have been; and it is a common expedient, and a just one, in such situations to put the peril of the answer upon that party who by his wrong has made the issue relevant to the rights of the other. On principle therefore the proper solution would seem to be that the promisee may recover his outlay in preparation for the performance, subject to the privilege of the promisor to reduce it by as much as he can show that the promisee would have lost, if the contract had been performed."

    Compare the position where the question is whether the promisee acted reasonably to mitigate the damage.

2. Damages may be recovered for costs incurred before the contract was entered into if they are—

    (i)   legal costs of approving and executing the contract; or

    (ii) costs of performing an act required to be done by the contract, notwithstanding that the act is performed in anticipation of the contract: *Lloyd v Stanbury* [1971] 1 W.L.R. 535; [1971] 2 All E.R. 267 (Brightman J); or

(iii) "such as would reasonably be in the contemplation of the parties as likely to be wasted if the contract was broken": *Anglia Television v Reed* [1972] 1 Q.B. 60; [1971] 3 All E.R. 690 C.A.

In *Lloyd v Stanbury* [1971] W.L.R. 535 the defendant agreed to sell part of his land including a farmhouse to the plaintiff. The defendant intended to build a bungalow on the remaining land and the contract provided that the plaintiff should provide a caravan for use of the defendant until the bungalow was built. While the contract was in draft, the plaintiff moved a caravan to the land. Contracts were exchanged and the plaintiff went into occupation, but the defendant wrongly refused to complete. Held, that the plaintiff was entitled to damages under head (i), above, and under head (ii) for costs of removing the caravan.

The plaintiff did not recover damages for cost of installation of a power circuit and erection of a television aerial at the farmhouse while he was in occupation because it will not usually be regarded as being in the contemplation of the parties that a buyer will spend money on improving the property before it has been conveyed to him. (Contrast *Mason v Burningham* [1949] 2 K.B. 545 CA, where the buyer of a second-hand typewriter, who had to return it to the true owner because the seller had no title to it, was held entitled to recover not only the price of the typewriter but also the cost of having it overhauled. Having the typewriter overhauled was the "ordinary and natural thing" to do in the circumstances.)

In *Anglia Television v Reed* [1972] 1 Q.B. 60 the plaintiffs incurred expense in preparation for filming a television play. Subsequently they entered into a contract with the defendant to play the leading role. The defendant repudiated the contract. The plaintiffs tried hard to find a substitute but failed. They abandoned the play. Held: they were entitled to recover the whole of the wasted expenditure—"[R] must have known perfectly well that much expenditure had already been incurred on director's fees and the like. He must have contemplated—or, at any rate, it is reasonably to be imputed to him—that if he broke his contract, all that expenditure would be wasted, whether or not it was incurred before or after the contract"—per Lord Denning.

3. In *Omak Maritime Limited v Mamola Challenger Shipping Company* [2010] EWHC 2026, the question was whether the additional profit made by the claimant shipowners in responding to the defendant charterers' repudiatory breach should be brought into account where the owners sought recovery of their wasted expenses, namely various expenses (including the installation of a crane) incurred in preparing the vessel for the charterers' needs. Resisting the owners' claim, the charterers argued that, because the owners were able to re-let the vessel at a much higher rate than the contract rate, they were actually in a better position than if the contract had been performed and this, it was submitted, should preclude recovery of damages for the wasted expenses. Against this, the owners argued that 'reliance' claims for wasted expenses were to be distinguished from "expectation" claims for loss of profit; and that the principle of not putting the innocent party overall in a better position than if the contract had been performed did not apply to wasted expenditure claims. Teare J sketched the rival arguments as follows:

> "9. Mr. Young [for the charterers] submitted that the tribunal's decision [in favour of the owners] was wrong in law. His argument was simple. The Owners had in fact suffered no loss by reason of the Charterers' breach because the market rate of hire was higher than the charter rate of hire and therefore the Owners 'more than recuperated the losses they claim in this arbitration'. In those circumstances the

decision to award any damages to the Owners (other than nominal damages) breached the principle that awards of damages for breach of contract are compensatory (see *The Golden Strait Corpn. v NYKK ('The Golden Victory')* [2007] 2 AC 353) and are designed to put the innocent party in the position he would have been in had the contract been performed (see *Robinson v Harman* (1848) 1 Exch.850) rather than the position he would have been in had no contract been made (see *C&P Haulage v Middleton* [1983] 1 WLR 1461). Where the innocent party receives a benefit which flows directly from the breach that benefit must be taken into account in assessing damages for that breach (see *British Westinghouse v Underground Electric Railways* [1912] AC 673.)

10. Mr. Brenton [for the owners] submitted that the tribunal's decision was right in law. His argument was, perhaps, not as simple but was nevertheless principled. Where the law protects a party's 'negative' or 'reliance' interest, as where wasted expenditure is claimed, the benefit flowing from the substitute employment cannot be taken into account to reduce or extinguish a claim for wasted expenditure. *Robinson v Harman* does not require that benefit to be taken into account since it is concerned with the protection of a party's 'positive' or 'expectation' interest. It is only when the law is protecting that interest that it is appropriate to compare a party's actual position with the position had the contract been performed. *Robinson v Harman* does not provide a rational and sensible explanation for the award of damages in a wasted expenditure case. Mr. Brenton accepted that the principle in *British Westinghouse* applied to claims for injury to a claimant's negative interest but submitted that, properly applied, it did not prevent the claimant from recovering expenditure wasted as a result of the breach of contract. By entering into the charterparty the Owners not only committed themselves to expenditure which was wasted by the Charterers' breach but also gave up the opportunity to charter the vessel at the market rate. That sacrifice was also wasted by the breach. By chartering the vessel out at the market rate after the charterparty had been terminated the Owners ensured that their sacrifice had in fact caused them no loss from the date on which the vessel was employed at the market rate. But such earnings did not compensate them for their expenditure which had been incurred before that date and which therefore remained 'wasted'."

Discussing the rival views, Teare J said:

"13. The principle enunciated by Baron Parke in *Robinson v Harman* was restated in *Wertheim v Chicoutimi Pulp* [1911] AC 301 at pp.307-308 and in *British Westinghouse v Undergrounds Railways* [1912] AC 673. It has recently been said to be the "fundamental principle governing the quantum of damages for breach of contract"; see *The Golden Strait Corpn. v NYKK ('The Golden Victory')* [2007] 2 AC 353 at para.29 per Lord Scott.

14. A corollary of that principle is that an award of damages for breach of contract should not put the claimant in a better position than he would have been in had the contract been performed; see *Wertheim v Chicoutimi Pulp* [1911] AC 301 at p.308.

15. In a typical claim for damages for breach of contract on the expectancy basis both expected profits and necessary expenses will be taken into account. The claimant will claim a sum equal to the benefit he expected to earn from performance of the contract less the costs he would have had to have incurred in order to earn that benefit, which costs would include not only any sum he would have had to pay to the party in breach but also any expenses he would have had to incur in preparation for performance of the contract. Damages calculated in that way would put the clamant in the position he would have been in had the contract been performed. The measure of loss thus compensates for the loss of bargain and in doing so takes account of the expenses the claimant would have incurred in reliance on the contract being performed. To ignore those expenses when assessing damages would put the claimant in a better position than he would have been in had the contract been performed. Equally, if those expenses had already been incurred at the date on which the contract was repudiated, to award those expenses in addition to damages for loss of bargain would put the claimant in a better position than he would have been in had the contract been performed.

16. The principle is closely related to the well recognised principles of mitigation. If, as illustrated by *Wertheim v Chicoutimi Pulp,* the effects of mitigation are ignored, the claimant will end up in a better position than he would have been in had the contract been performed . . .

19. The law of damages permits a claimant to seek damages on the reliance basis rather than upon the expectancy basis. He may 'elect' to claim damages by reference to the expenses incurred by him in reliance on the contract being performed; see *Cullinane v British Rema* [1954] 1 QB 292 and *Anglia Television v Reed* [1972] 1 QB 60.

20. In the present case the claimant, having abandoned his claim to damages on the expectancy basis, claimed damages in the sum of the expenses incurred by him in reliance on the contract being performed. There

is no dispute that damages may be claimed on that basis but the question raised by Mr. Brenton's submission is whether and if so how the principle in *Robinson v Harman* applies so as ensure that the claimant is not put in a better position than he would have been in had the contract been performed.

21. There is considerable authority, both in other common law jurisdictions and in this jurisdiction, for the proposition that the recovery of damages on a reliance basis is governed by Baron Parke's principle in *Robinson v Harman*. Given the fundamental nature of that principle that is not surprising . . .

26. In *Anglia Television v Reed* [1972] 1 QB 60 an actor had agreed to play the leading role in a television play to be produced by the plaintiffs. He repudiated the contract and the production was abandoned. The plaintiffs claimed their wasted expenditure. The issue before the Court of Appeal was whether such damages extended to expenditure incurred before, as well as after, the contract was made. It was held that they did so long as it was reasonably within the contemplation of the parties that they were likely to be wasted if the contract were broken. Lord Denning said that the plaintiffs had to elect between claiming loss of profits or expenses thrown away.

27. Neither *Cullinane v British Rema* nor *Anglia Television v Reed* expressly dealt with the question whether wasted expenditure could be recovered in circumstances where an award of damages on that basis might put the claimant in a better position than he would have been in had the contract been performed . . .

30. In *C&P Haulage v Middleton* [1983] 1 WLR 1461 the English Court of Appeal followed the approach of Chief Judge Learned Hand in *L. Albert & Son v Armstrong Rubber Co.* and of Berger J in *Bowlay Logging Limited v Domtar Limited* and refused to award damages by reference to wasted expenses where the expenses would have been wasted in any event by reason of the terms of the contract. Ackner LJ, having also referred to *Cullinane v British Rema* and *Anglia Television v Reed*, said at p.1467:

> 'It is not the function of the courts where there is a breach of contract knowingly, as this would be the case, to put a plaintiff in a better financial position than if the contract had been properly performed.'

31. Fox LJ agreed and noted at p.1468:

> ' . . . while it is true that the expenditure could in a sense be said to be wasted in consequence of the breach of contract, it was equally likely to be wasted if there had been no breach, because the plaintiffs . . . could terminate the license at quite short notice. A high risk of waste was from the very first inherent in the nature of the contract itself, breach or no breach. The reality of the matter is that the waste resulted from what was, on the defendant's side, a very unsatisfactory and dangerous bargain.'

32. That reasoning mirrored the reasoning of Berger J in *Bowlay Logging Limited v Domtar Limited*.

33. No question of the burden of proof arose in *C&P Haulage v Middleton* because reliance was placed on a term of the license to show that the contract was a bad bargain. In *CCC Films (London) Ltd v Impact Quadrant Films Ltd* [1985] 1 QB 16 Hutchinson J had to consider the burden of proof and in particular whether it was right to modify the general rule as to the onus of proof in the manner suggested by Chief Judge Learned Hand in *L. Albert & Son v Armstrong Rubber Co.* He concluded at p.39-40 that it was:

> 'Even without the assistance of such authorities, I should have held on principle that the onus was on the defendant. It seems to me that at least in these cases where the plaintiff's decision to base his claim on abortive expenditure was dictated by the practical impossibility of proving loss of profit rather then by unfettered choice, any other rule would largely, if not entirely, defeat the object of allowing this alternative method of formulating a claim. This is because, notwithstanding the distinction to which I have drawn attention between proving a loss of net profit and proving in general terms the probability of sufficient returns to cover expenditure, in the majority of contested cases impossibility of proof of the first would probably involve like impossibility in the case of the second. It appears to me to be eminently fair that in such cases where the plaintiff has by the defendant's breach been prevented from exploiting the chattel or the right contracted for and, therefore, putting to the test the question of whether he would have recouped his expenditure, the general rule as to the onus of proof of damage should be modified in this manner.'

> . . .

35. Mr. Brenton accepts, as he must in the light of the above authorities, that there are authorities which seek to explain reliance loss as a species of expectation loss but he submits that there are others which treat such loss as "an independent form of loss". He further submits that the expectation loss principle cannot provide a rational and sensible explanation for the award of damages in wasted expenditure cases.

36. The first authority relied upon by Mr. Brenton is *Cullinane v British Rema* and in particular the passage in the judgment of Lord Evershed MR at p.303:

'As a matter of principle also it seems to me that a person who has obtained a machine . . . which was unable to perform a particular function which it was warranted to perform, may adopt one of two courses. He may . . . claim to recover the capital loss he has incurred . . . A claim of that kind puts the plaintiff in the same position as though he had never made the contract at all . . . But, alternatively . . . he may, in my judgment, make his claim on the basis of the profit which he has lost because the machine as delivered fell short in its performance of that which it was warranted to do . . .'

37. It is arguable that this passage suggests that the basis of a claim for wasted expenditure is to put the claimant in the same position in which he would have been in had the contract not been made. This is a different basis from that stated by Baron Parke in *Robinson v Harman*. However, Lord Evershed MR did not address the question whether damages in the amount of wasted expenditure could be awarded where to do so would put the claimant in a better position than he would have been in had the contract been performed. That question was addressed by the Court of Appeal in *C&P Haulage v Middleton* in which case Ackner LJ expressly held that the court could not put a plaintiff in a better financial position than he would have been in had the contract been performed. I am not therefore persuaded that the dicta of Lord Evershed MR relied upon by Mr. Brenton should be regarded as authority for the proposition that the jurisprudential basis for awarding damages for wasted expenditure is different from Baron Parke's principle in *Robinson v Harman* . . .

42. I consider that the weight of authority strongly suggests that reliance losses are a species of expectation losses and that they are neither, to use Mr. Brenton's phrase, 'fundamentally different' nor awarded on a different 'juridical basis of claim'. That they are a species of expectation losses is supported by the decision of the Court of Appeal in *C&P Haulage v Middleton* and by very persuasive authorities in the United States, Canada and Australia.

43. Mr. Brenton nevertheless invites me to prefer his submission because the expectation loss analysis does not provide a rational and sensible explanation for the award of damages in wasted expenditure cases.

44. It seems to me that the expectation loss analysis does provide a rational and sensible explanation for the award of damages in wasted expenditure cases. The expenditure which is sought to be recovered is incurred in expectation that that the contract will be performed. It therefore appears to me to be rational to have regard to the position that the claimant would have been in had the contract been performed.

45. If there were an independent principle pursuant to which expenditure incurred in expectation of the performance of a contract was recoverable without regard to what the position would have been had the contract been performed the defendant would in effect underwrite the claimant's decision to enter the contract. If the contract was unwise from his point of view, because his expenses were likely to exceed any gross profit, it is difficult to understand why the defendant should pay damages in an amount equal to that expenditure. His breach has not caused that loss. The claimant's expenditure should only be recoverable where the likely gross profit would at least cover that expenditure.

46. This was the approach of Chief Judge Learned Hand in *L. Albert & Son v Armstrong Rubber* and of Berger J in *Bowlay Logging v Domtar*. That approach was followed and approved in *C & P Haulage v Middleton*.

47. The authorities therefore state a rational and sensible explanation for the view that the expectation loss principle underpins the award of damages in wasted expenditure cases. In some cases a contract can be shown to be a bad bargain. In other cases it may not be possible to show one way or the other whether the likely gross profits would at least equal the expenditure. In that latter type of case the question arises as to which party should bear the evidential burden of proof. Should the burden be on the claimant to show that the likely profits would at least equal his expenditure or on the defendant to show that the likely profits would not at least equal the claimant's expenditure ? The authorities to which I have referred, in particular *L. Albert & Son v Armstrong Rubber* and *CCC Films (London) Ltd. v Impact Quadrant Films Ltd.* provide a rational and sensible explanation for the view that that burden should be on the defendant . . .

Conclusion

64. I am therefore unpersuaded by Mr. Brenton's submission that the tribunal's decision was correct in law, notwithstanding the obvious care and skill with which his submission was presented. I am persuaded that the tribunal's decision was wrong in law. The tribunal said that:

'to take the Charterers' position and look at the net overall position is to mix this basis of claim with a claim based on the difference between contract and market rates inasmuch as the latter contains within it the concept of what the vessel should have earned overall from substitute employment as compared with what would have been earned under the Charterparty'.

65. The tribunal's error was to regard a claim for wasted expenses and a claim for loss of profits as two separate and independent claims which could not be 'mixed'. But the weight of authority clearly shows that both claims are illustrations of, and governed by, the fundamental principle stated by Baron Parke in *Robinson v Harman*. That principle requires the court to make a comparison between the claimant's position and what it would have been had the contract been performed. Where steps have been taken to mitigate the loss which would otherwise have been caused by a breach of contract that principle requires the benefits obtained by mitigation to be set against the loss which would otherwise have been sustained. To fail to do so would put the claimant in a better position than he would have been in had the contract been performed.

66. It follows that the appeal must be allowed and the award set aside.

Question

Is the loss of pre-contract expenditure caused by the breach of contract? Does not a party who incurs expenditure before a contract has been concluded do so at his own risk? See A. I. Ogus (1972) 35 M.L.R. 423.

19–014

JOHNSON AND ANOTHER v AGNEW

House of Lords [1980] A.C. 367; [1979] 2 W.L.R. 487; [1979] 1 All E.R. 883; (1979) 38 P. & C.R. 424

The vendors agreed to sell a house and land which were subject to separate mortgages. The purchaser failed to complete on January 21, 1974, which had been fixed as the final date by a notice making time of the essence. The vendor obtained an order for specific performance on June 27 but it was not drawn up and entered until November 26. By then the mortgagees of the house had obtained an order for possession. On March 7, 1975 the mortgagees of the land also obtained an order for possession and they contracted to sell the land on April 3. The vendors who had taken no action to enforce the order for specific performance were not in a position to convey the land after April 3. The vendors sought a declaration that they entitled to treat the contract as repudiated, and damages.

19–015

The House of Lords held that, where it becomes impossible to enforce an order for specific performance, the plaintiff has a right to ask the court to discharge the order and terminate the contract. The contract is then not rescinded ab initio but remains in existence until terminated: *Heyman v Darwins Ltd* [1942] A.C. 356, 359, below, Ch.21. The court will grant such an order only when it is just to do so, as it was in the present case where the non-completion and ultimate impossibility of completion was the fault of the purchaser.

LORD WILBERFORCE

It is now necessary to deal with questions relating to the measure of damages. The Court of Appeal, while denying the vendors' right to damages at common law, granted damages under Lord Cairns's Act. Since on the view which I take, damages can be recovered at common law, two relevant questions now arise: (1) whether Lord Cairns's Act provides a different measure of damages from the common law? If so, the respondents would be in a position to claim the more favourable basis to them; and (2) if the measure of damages is the same, on what basis they should be calculated?

Since the decision of this House, by a majority, in *Leeds Industrial Co-operative Society Ltd v Slack* [1924] A.C. 851, it is clear that the jurisdiction to award damages in accordance with section 2 of Lord Cairns's Act (accepted by the House as surviving the repeal of the Act) may arise in some cases in which damages could not be recovered at common law; examples of this would be damages in lieu of a quia timet injunction and damages for breach of a restrictive covenant to which the defendant was not a party. To this extent the Act created a power to award damages which did not exist before at common law. But apart from these, and similar cases where damages could not be claimed at all at common law, there is sound authority for the proposition that the Act does not provide for the assessment of damages on any new basis. The wording of section 2 that damages "may be assessed in such manner as the court shall direct" does not so suggest, but clearly refers only to procedure.

In *Ferguson v Wilson* (1866) L.R. 2 Ch.App. 77, 88 Turner L.J., sitting in a court which included Cairns L.J. himself, expressed the clear opinion that the purpose of the Act was to enable a court of equity to grant those damages which another court might give; a similar opinion was strongly expressed by Kay J. in *Rock Portland Cement Co v Wilson* (1882) 48 L.T. 386, and *Fry on Specific Performance* (6th ed.) 602 is of the same opinion. In *Wroth v Tyler* [1974] Ch. 36 however, Megarry J., relying on the words "in lieu of specific performance," reached the view that damages under the Act should be assessed as on the date when specific performance could have been ordered, in that case as at the date of the judgment of the court. This case was followed in *Grant v Dawkins* [1973] 1 W.L.R. 1406. If this establishes a different basis from that applicable at common law, I could not agree with it, but in *Horsler v Zorro* [1975] Ch. 302, 316, Megarry J. went so far as to indicate his view that there is no inflexible rule that common law damages must be assessed as at the date of the breach. Furthermore, in *Malhotra v Choudhury* [1978] 3 W.L.R. 825 the Court of Appeal expressly decided that, in a case where damages are given in substitution for an order for specific performance, both equity and the common law would award damages on the same basis, in that case as on the date of judgment. On the balance of these authorities and also on principle, I find in the Act no warrant for the court awarding damages differently from common law damages, but the question is left open on what date such damages, however awarded, ought to be assessed.

The general principle for the assessment of damages is compensatory, that is that the innocent party is to be placed, so far as money can do so, in the same position as if the contract had been performed. Where the contract is one of sale, this principle normally leads to assessment of damages as at the date of the breach, a principle recognised and embodied section 51 of the Sale of Goods Act 1893. But this is not an absolute rule; if to follow it would give rise to injustice, the court has power to fix such other date as may be appropriate in the circumstances.

In cases where a breach of a contract for sale has occurred, and the innocent party reasonably continues to try to have the contract completed, it would to me appear more logical and just rather than tie him to the date of the original breach, to assess damages as at the date when (otherwise than by his default) the contract is lost. Support for this approach is to be found in the cases. In *Ogle v Earl Vane* (1867) L.R. 2 Q.B. 275 the date was fixed by reference to the time when the innocent party, acting reasonably, went into the market; in *Hickman v Haynes* (1875) L.R. 10 C.P. 598 at a reasonable time after the last request of the defendants (the buyers) to withhold delivery. In *Radford v de Froberville* [1977] 1 W.L.R. 1262, where the defendant had covenanted to build a wall, damages were held measurable as at the date of the hearing rather than at the date of the defendant's breach, unless the plaintiff ought reasonably to have mitigated the breach at an earlier date.

In the present case if it is accepted, as I would accept, that the vendors acted reasonably in pursuing the remedy of specific performance, the date on which that remedy became aborted (not by the vendors' fault) should logically be fixed as the date on which damages should be assessed. Choice of this date would be in accordance both with common law principle, as indicated in the authorities I have mentioned, and with the wording of the Act "in substitution for . . . specific performance." The date which emerges from this is April 3, 1975, the first date on which mortgagees contracted to sell a portion of the property. I would vary the order of the Court of Appeal by substituting this date for that fixed by them, viz. November 26, 1974. The same date (April 3, 1975) should be used for the purpose of limiting the respondents' right to interest on damages. Subject to these modifications I would dismiss the appeal.

Points for reflection

19-016   In *Wroth v Tyler* the defendant contracted to sell a bungalow for £6,050. He failed to complete on the date fixed. The value of the house on that day was £7,500. Megarry J refused the plaintiff an order for specific performance on the ground that the defendant could give vacant possession only if he took legal proceedings against his wife which would not necessarily succeed. The plaintiff was however entitled to damages "in substition for such . . . specific performance" under the Chancery Amendment Act 1858 (Lord Cairns' Act). The value of the house at the date of judgment was £11,500. Megarry J held that damages assessed at the date of breach in accordance with the "normal rule" would be £1,500 which would not be a true substitute for a decree to convey land which, at the time of decree, was worth £5,500 more than the contract price. Whatever the position at common law, the appropriate damages under Lord Cairns' Act were £5,500. But see *Johnson v Agnew*, above.

It was sufficient to satisfy the rules in *Hadley v Baxendale* that a rise in the price of houses was in the contemplation of the parties when the contract was made. It was immaterial that they may not have contemplated a rise which nearly doubled the price. The "second rule" in *Hadley v Baxendale* required contemplation of a head or type of damage, not its quantum. Cf. *Parsons v Uttley Ingham*, above.

Question

In *Howard-Jones v Tate* [2011] EWCA Civ 1330, Tate failed in breach of contract to provide "a new directly metered single phase electricity supply" and "a separately metered water supply" to the property that Howard-Jones had bought from Tate. The Recorder found that these breaches went to the root of the contract, rendering the property unsuitable for Howard-Jones who intended to use the property to carry on his business as a motor trader. He held, however, that Mr Howard-Jones was not entitled to rescind the contract ab initio but, rather, was entitled to recover damages. Was the Recorder right to deny the remedy of rescission?

19–017

D. Damages for Distress and Disappointment

ADDIS v GRAMOPHONE COMPANY LTD

House of Lords [1909] A.C. 488; 78 L.J.K.B. 1122; 101 L.T. 466

The plaintiff was employed by the defendants at a salary of £15 per week and commission on the trade done. He could be dismissed by six months' notice. The defendants gave him six months' notice but, at the same time, appointed a successor and prevented the plaintiff from acting as manager. The jury awarded £340 in respect of lost commission and £600 in respect of wrongful dismissal. The House of Lords (Lord Loreburn LC and Lords James, Atkinson, Gorrell and Shaw) held that he was entitled only to the commission and salary which he had lost.

19–018

LORD ATKINSON

. . . The damages plaintiff sustained by this illegal dismissal were (1) the wages for the period of six months during which his formal notice would have been current; (2) the profits or commission which would, in all reasonable probability, have been earned by him during the six months had he continued in the employment; and possibly (3) damages in respect of the time which might reasonably elapse before he could obtain other employment. He has been awarded a sum possibly of some hundreds of pounds, not in respect of any of these heads of damage, but in respect of the harsh and humiliating way in which he was dismissed, including, presumably, the pain he experienced by reason, it is alleged, of the imputation upon him conveyed by the manner of his dismissal. This is the only circumstance which makes the case of general importance, and this is the only point I think it necessary to deal with . . .

I have always understood that damages for breach of contract were in the nature of compensation, not punishment, and that the general rule of law applicable to such cases was that in effect stated by Cockburn C. J. in *Engel v Fitch* (1868) L.R. 3 Q.B. 314, 330, in these words: "By the law of England as a general rule a vendor who from whatever cause fails to perform his contract is bound, as was said by Lord Wensleydale in the case referred to, to place the purchaser, so far as money will do it, in the position he would have been in if the contract had been performed. If a man sells a cargo of goods not yet come to hand, but which he believes to have been consigned to him from abroad, and the goods fail to arrive, it will be no answer to the intended purchaser to say that a third party who had engaged to consign the goods to the seller has deceived or disappointed him. The purchaser will be entitled to the difference between the contract price and the market price."

In *Sikes v Wild* (1861) 1 B. & S. 587, at p. 594, Lord Blackburn says: "I do not see how the existence of misconduct can alter the rule of law by which damages for breach of contract are to be assessed. It may render the contract voidable on the ground of fraud or give a cause of action for deceit, but surely it cannot alter the effect of the contract itself."

. . . in actions of tort motive, if it may be taken into account to aggregate [sic] damages, as it undoubtedly may be, it may also be taken into account to mitigate them, as may also the conduct of the plaintiff himself who seeks redress. Is this rule to be applied to actions of breach of contract? There are few breaches of contract more common than those which arise where men omit or refuse to repay what they have borrowed, or to pay for what they have bought. Is the creditor or vendor who sues for one of such breaches to have the sum he recovers lessened if he should be shown to be harsh, grasping, or pitiless, or even insulting, in enforcing his demand, or lessened because the debtor has struggled to pay, has failed because of misfortune, and has been suave, gracious, and apologetic in his refusal? On the other hand, is that sum to be increased if it should be shown that the debtor could have paid readily without any embarrassment, but refused with expression of contempt and contumely, from a malicious desire to injure his creditor?

Few parties to contracts have more often to complain of ingratitude and baseness than sureties. Are they, because of this, to be entitled to recover from the principal, often a trusted friend, who has deceived and betrayed them, more than they paid on that principal's behalf? If circumstances of aggravation are rightly to be taken into account in actions of contract at all, why should they not be taken into account in the case of the surety, and the rules and principles applicable to cases of tort applied to the full extent?

In many other cases of breach of contract there may be circumstances of malice, fraud, defamation, or violence, which would sustain an action of tort as an alternative remedy to an action for breach of contract. If one should select the former mode of redress, he may, no doubt, recover exemplary damages, or what is sometimes styled vindictive damages; but if he should choose to seek redress in the form of an action for breach of contract, he lets in all the consequences of that form of action: *Thorpe v Thorpe* (1832) 3 B. & Ad. 580. One of these consequences is, I think, this: that he is to be paid adequate compensation in money for the loss of that which he would have received had his contract been kept, and no more.

I can conceive nothing more objectionable and embarrassing in litigation than trying in effect an action of libel or slander as a matter of aggravation in an action for illegal dismissal, the defendant being permitted, as he must in justice be permitted, to traverse the defamatory sense, rely on privilege, or raise every point which he could raise in an independent action brought for the alleged libel or slander itself.

Questions

19–019   1. Does the case decide that only damages for pecuniary loss are recoverable in contract? Could the plaintiff in *Hobbs v L & SW Ry* (1875) L.R. 10 Q.B. 111 recover damages for inconvenience today?

2. Does the case decide that damages for loss of reputation can never be recovered in contract?

JOHNSON v UNISYS LTD

House of Lords [2001] UKHL 13

19–020   The plaintiff was unfairly dismissed because the required disciplinary procedures were not adhered to and was awarded compensation for unfair dismissal by an industrial tribunal. He brought an action for wrongful dismissal in the county court claiming that, because of the manner in which he had been dismissed, he had suffered a mental breakdown and been unable to work, suffering a loss of earnings of more that £400,000. The judge struck out the claim holding that an unfair dismissal could not amount to a breach of the implied duty of trust and confidence or any other implied duties of an employer. The Court of Appeal unanimously dismissed the appeal as did the House of Lords.

LORD STEYN

My Lords,

I. Addis's case

3. The head note of the decision of the House of Lords in *Addis v Gramophone Co Ltd* [1909] AC 488 purports to state the ratio decidendi of that case as follows: where a servant is wrongfully dismissed from his employment the damages for the dismissal cannot include compensation for the manner of his dismissal, for his injured feelings, or for the loss he may sustain from the fact that the dismissal of itself makes it more difficult for him to obtain fresh employment. This statement of the law was based on an observation in the speech of Lord Loreburn L.C. A majority of the Law Lords expressed agreement with this speech. On the other hand, only Lord Loreburn specifically referred to the unavailability of special damages for loss of employment prospects. The other Law Lords concentrated on the non-pecuniary aspects of the case. The headnote is arguably wrong insofar as it states that the House decided that a wrongfully dismissed employee can never sue for special damages for loss of employment prospects arising from the harsh and humiliating manner of the dismissal: see *MacGregor on Damages*, 16th ed, (1997), para 1242. Nevertheless, the statement of the law encapsulated in the controversial headnote has exercised an influence over this corner of the law for more than 90 years. It has had a restrictive impact on the damages which an employee may recover for financial loss actually suffered as a result of the manner of wrongful dismissal.

4. It is instructive to consider how this decision was viewed in 1909. Sir Frederic Pollock, the editor of the Law Quarterly Review, was not impressed. In a case note he contrasted "an artificial rule or mere authority" to "the rationale of the matter": (1910) 26 LQR, 1–2. Citing cases contrary to what was perceived to be the *Addis* rule, and "said to be exceptions," he plainly thought that as a matter of legal principle the decision was questionable. He said:

> "In the case of wrongful dismissal, a harsh and humiliating way of doing it, by the imputation which such a dismissal conveys, may make it very difficult for the servant to obtain a new situation. That was how the court looked at it in *Maw v Jones* [25 QBD 107]; not as a mere personal slight or affront. So in *Addis v Gramophone Co* The plaintiff was dismissed summarily from an important post in India, and the whole management taken out of his hands in a way which could not but import obloquy among the commercial community of India, and as a result permanent loss. It was no mere rudeness or want of consideration. But the majority of the House of Lords thought the damages in question were really for defamation, and could be recovered only in a separate action."

The supposed rule in *Addis* has been controversial for a long time. When the first edition of Treitel's classic book on contract was published some 40 years ago the author described the exclusion of any claim by an employee for financial loss to reputation as hard to justify: *The Law of Contract*, (1962), pp 606–607. In the 10th edition of the same work Sir Guenter Treitel Q.C., remained of the same view and was able to cite further decisions in which damages were awarded for financial loss of employment prospects or for injury to reputation resulting from a breach of contract: see pp 921–924.

5. During the course of the last century a fundamental alteration in the relationship between employer and employee has come about. And in the economic sphere that relationship has also drastically altered. This is the context in which the question of public importance now before the House is whether *Addis's* case precludes the recovery by an employee of special damages for financial loss in respect of damage to his employment prospects resulting from the manner of a wrongful dismissal. It was on this basis that the Appeal Committee granted leave to appeal rather than the particular features of the claim under consideration.

II. The background to the dispute

6. In outline the facts are as follows. The employee is now 52 years of age. With a gap of 3 years he was employed by the employers in the software computer industry from 1971 to 1994. In 1992 he became a director of the company. Over the years he suffered from work-related stress and the employers were aware of his particular psychological vulnerability. In January 1994 the employers made allegations against him regarding his conduct. On 17 January 1994 he was asked to attend a meeting. No specific allegations were put to him. Later that day he was summarily dismissed. He lodged an internal appeal. On 3 March 1994 his dismissal was confirmed. Shortly thereafter he made a complaint of unfair dismissal to

an industrial tribunal (now called an employment tribunal). By decisions made on 20 February 1995 and 26 July 1995 the tribunal upheld his complaint and awarded him compensation, subject to a finding that he had contributed by 25% to his dismissal. Applying the statutory maximum the employee was awarded £11,691.88.

7. It is agreed that as "a result of the circumstances and the fact of his dismissal the [employee] suffered a major psychiatric illness, involving, inter alia, in-patient treatment from March to August 1994". In addition the employee had to undergo hypnotherapy every three weeks until January 1996; he was re-admitted twice in 1996 to hospital, thereafter he had to undergo intensive psychotherapy and visit a psychiatric nurse; and he had to take anti depressant drugs for depression, mood swings and alcohol dependency. His health has remained severely affected. Despite repeated applications for jobs he remains unemployed. The main obstacles facing him in seeking employment is the time he spent in hospital following his dismissal and the substantial period he has now been out of work in a rapidly developing industry.

III. The proceedings

8. In August 1997 the employee instituted proceedings in the County Court for breach of contract and negligence on the ground of the manner of his dismissal. He alleged that his employers never informed him of the complaints against him. He relied on an implied term of his contract that his employers would not without reasonable and proper cause conduct themselves in such a way so as to damage the relationship of trust and confidence between the parties. The employee further alleged that the manner of his dismissal and the circumstances leading up to it had caused his mental breakdown and inability to find work, with the result that he would suffer a loss of earnings in excess of £400,000.

IV. The decisions

9. The case came before a judge on an application to strike out the action. The judge viewed the case as in substance one seeking damages for unfair dismissal. He considered that the employee was seeking to circumvent the unfair dismissal legislation. He relied on the law as stated in the headnote in Addis's case. He held that an unfair dismissal could not by itself ground any action to recover financial loss caused by the manner of the employee's dismissal. He struck out the action.

10. The employee appealed. The Court of Appeal gave him an opportunity to amend his particulars of claim. Re-amended particulars of claim were produced. The Court of Appeal indicated that, if the appeal was successful, leave to amend would be given. But Lord Woolf M.R., with whom Hutchison and Tuckey L.JJ. agreed, dismissed the appeal in a closely reasoned reserved judgment: [1999] 1 All E R 854. Lord Woolf expressed agreement with the views of the judge. Lord Woolf held that, despite the form of the re-cast pleading, the substance of the employee's complaint was as to the manner in which he had been dismissed. He proceeded on the basis that the headnote in Addis's case correctly stated the effect of that decision. That is not surprising for the contrary was not argued in the Court of Appeal. He examined in detail the impact of the speeches in Mahmud v Bank of Credit and Commerce International SA [1980] AC 20 on the decision of the House in Addis's case and concluded that the House had merely distinguished Addis's case and had not departed from it. He observed, at p 861J, that Addis's case precluded the recovery of damages for the manner of dismissal of an employee while Mahmud's case was concerned with the recovery of damages for an anterior breach. He drew a distinction, at p 859D, between express and constructive dismissal. Applying the rule in Addis's case, Lord Woolf held that the employee had no sustainable claim. Lord Woolf further held that, having regard to the circumstances, the prospects of the plaintiff overcoming the issue of remoteness were unreal: p 862A–B.

V. The issues

11. It is necessary to explain the shape of the case. First, it must be assumed that as a result of the circumstances and fact of his dismissal the plaintiff suffered a major psychiatric illness, involving, inter alia, in patient treatment in a mental hospital from March to August 1994; that subsequently he was hospitalised and treated as I have set out; and that in consequence he has been unable to find a job. Secondly, the claim is brought in contract and, alternatively, in tort. Thirdly, the claim in contract is based on a term implied in contracts of employment, namely that an employer shall not, without reasonable and proper cause, conduct himself in a manner calculated and likely to destroy or seriously damage the relationship of trust and confidence between employer and employee: see Mahmud's case at p 45F–G. Fourthly, in the alternative, the re-amended particulars of claim put forward additional negative and positive implied terms. At the hearing of the appeal counsel for the employee explained that these implied terms were based on dicta in decided cases but he was content

to regard these as instances of the application of the general obligation of mutual trust and confidence. The contractual claim is therefore squarely based on a breach of the implied obligation of mutual trust and confidence between employer and employee. The re-amended particulars of claim allege a breach of the implied obligation in that the employers failed:

"(i) to put allegations to the plaintiff;
(ii) to accord the plaintiff an opportunity to defend himself;
(iii) to provide a full explanation of allegations against the plaintiff
(iv) to comply with the defendant's disciplinary procedures and the rules of natural justice . . ."

The consequences of the breach allegedly involved the employee's mental breakdown and consequent total inability to find employment. Having regard to his previous earnings he claims a sum of the order of £400,000. Fifthly, it is important to note that the claim is solely for the recovery of special damages for financial loss. The separate question whether an employee may recover compensation for anxiety and mental stress arising from the manner of his dismissal was not raised before the judge or before the Court of Appeal. It is not an issue before the House and it would be wrong to express any view on it.

12. It will also be necessary to consider the issue of remoteness, namely whether the employee has any realistic prospect of establishing that his loss is not too remote.

13. As I have explained the claim is framed in contract and tort. Having regard to the particular circumstances of this case, if the claim in contract is held to be unsustainable the fate of the claim in tort must inevitably be the same. I propose therefore to concentrate on the potential sustainability of the claim in contract.

14. It is convenient to start by examining the following issues:

(1) What is the effect of the decision in *Addis's* case?
(2) Even if it is not part of the ratio decidendi of *Addis's* case does the observation of Lord Loreburn L.C. (and the headnote) correctly state the law?
(3) What was the impact of *Mahmud's* case on *Addis's* case?

Depending on the answer to these questions it will then be necessary to examine the further arguments in detail and to consider the impact of the conclusions on the disposal of the case.

VI. *The effect of Addis's case*

15. It is necessary to examine what was decided in *Addis's* case. The speeches in *Addis's* case are not easy to understand. Two of their Lordships spoke in terms of exemplary damages: see Lord James of Hereford, at p 492; and Lord Collins, diss, at p 497 and pp 500–501. That could not have been an issue. In English law such damages have never and cannot be awarded for breach of any contract. That part of the discussion in the speeches in *Addis's* case can safely be put to one side. The context of the dispute has often been described. For my part it is sufficient to adopt the description of the case by Sir Frederic Pollock that the plaintiff "was dismissed summarily from an important post in India, and the whole management taken out of his hands in a way which could not but import obloquy among the commercial community of India, and as a result permanent loss". The critical observation on the law of Lord Loreburn L.C., at p 491, was undeniably to the effect stated in the headnote. On the other hand, *MacGregor on Damages* 16th ed, para 1242 has argued that the other Law Lords in the majority confined themselves to the non-pecuniary aspects of the case. Accordingly, it is said, the headnote may not reflect the ratio decidendi of the case. Lord James of Hereford in his substantive reasons discussed the availability of general damages for injury to feelings. But he did say, at p 492, that he agreed with "the entirety of the judgment delivered by my noble and learned friend on the Woolsack". In my view he endorsed the relevant part of the speech of Lord Loreburn L.C. On the other hand, Lord Atkinson (at p 493), Lord Gorrell (at p 502) and Lord Shaw of Dunfermline (at p 505) at most expressed general concurrence. In *Broome v Cassel & Co Ltd* [1972] AC 1027, 1087B Lord Reid observed:

"Concurrence with the speech of a colleague does not mean acceptance of every word which he has said. If it did there would be far fewer concurrences than there are."

When one turns to the substantive reasons given by Lord Atkinson, Lord Gorrell and Lord Shaw of Dunfermline, one finds that they dealt exclusively with the non-pecuniary aspects of the case. Only one of the Law Lords who sat in the case can realistically be regarded as having evinced a clear endorsement of Lord Loreburn's observation so far as it ruled out special damages for loss of employment prospects flowing from the manner of a wrongful dismissal.

16. Given the apparently harsh and humiliating manner of the dismissal, it is surprising that the other Law Lords did not consider this aspect. Indeed Lord Atkinson expressly said it was not "necessary" to deal with it. The explanation may be the view taken of the pleadings: see Lord Atkinson's complaint, at p 493, about the "unscientific form" of the pleadings and "the loose manner in which the proceeding's at trial were conducted". Despite assumptions to the contrary (including in particular my assumption in *Mahmud's* case at pp 50D–51D) it is nevertheless tolerably clear that the ratio decidendi of *Addis's* case does not preclude the recovery of special damages flowing from the manner of a wrongful dismissal.

VII. The correctness of the observation of Lord Loreburn L.C.

17. It is still necessary to consider whether the observation of Lord Loreburn L.C., although not reflecting the ratio decidendi of *Addis's* case, was nevertheless correct. This is so for two reasons. First my interpretation of *Addis's* case may not be correct. Secondly, the proposition of Lord Loreburn L.C. may be correct in all its constituent parts. As Sir Frederick Pollock explained in his case note in the Law Quarterly Review Lord Loreburn enunciated a special and restrictive rule precluding the recovery of special damages in respect of financial loss flowing from the manner of wrongful dismissal. It was viewed as contrary to legal principle in 1909. In modern times it has been widely criticised as being in conflict with general principles of contract law. In *Mahmud's* case Lord Nicholls of Birkenhead and I dealt with this point and it is unnecessary to cover the same ground again. But perhaps I may add that I am not aware of any modern academic writer, addressing the subject, who has tried to defend the relevant restrictive rule of Lord Loreburn L.C. One is entitled to pose the question: Why was the contract of employment singled out for a special rule to the disadvantage of employees?

18. *Addis's* case was decided in the heyday of a judicial philosophy of market individualism in respect of what was then called the law of master and servant. The idea that in the eyes of the law the position of a servant was a subordinate one seemed natural and inevitable. And in *Addis's* case it may have been the background to the adoption of a special restrictive rule denying in all cases to employees the right to recover financial loss which naturally flowed from the manner of their wrongful dismissal. Since 1909 there has been a fundamental change in legal culture. A good illustration is the decision of the House in *Scally v Southern Health and Social Services Board* [1992] 1 AC 294. In *Scally's* case a contract negotiated by trade unions conferred on an employee a valuable right contingent on him taking up the right in a prescribed manner. He was unaware of the right. The House of Lords held that there was an obligation implied by law as an incident of a contract of employment, as opposed to implied in fact, to bring the term to the notice of the employee. Such a decision would have been unthinkable at the time of *Addis's* case. In *Spring v Guardian Assurance Plc* [1995] 2 AC 296, 335B, Lord Slynn of Hadley noted "the changes which have taken place in the employer—employee relationship, with far greater duties imposed on the employer than in the past, whether by statute or by judicial decision, to care for the physical, financial and even psychological welfare of the employee". One of the most important of those developments is the evolution since the mid seventies of the obligation of trust and confidence in contracts of employment and its unanimous and unequivocal endorsement in *Mahmud's* case. The orthodox view is that this implied obligation may be displaced or qualified but only by express agreement or necessary implication: compare, however, a different view in *Brodie, "Beyond Exchange: The New Contract of Employment"*, (1998) 27 ICJ 79, 82–83.

19. Since 1909 our knowledge of the incidence of stress related psychiatric and psychological problems of employees, albeit still imperfect, has greatly increased. What could in the early part of the last century dismissively be treated as mere "injured feelings" is now sometimes accepted as a recognisable psychiatric illness. The outlines of the gradual development of the law in this area are well known: see, for example, *McLoughlin v O'Brian* [1983] 1 AC 410; *Frost v Chief Constable of South Yorkshire Police* [1999] 2 AC 455. Nowadays courts generally accept that they must act on the best medical insight of the day. Specifically, this realism has taken root in the field of employment law: *Walker v Northumberland County Council* [1995] ICR 702 HC; *Gogay v Hertfordshire County Council* [2000] IRLR 703. These considerations are testimony to the need for implied terms in contracts of employment protecting employees from harsh and unacceptable employment practices. This is particularly important in the light of the greater pressures on employees due to the progressive deregulation of the labour market, the privatisation of public services, and the globalisation of product and financial markets: see Brendan J. Burchell and others, "Job Insecurity and Work Intensification", (1999), a report published for the Joseph Rowntree Foundation, at pp 60–61. This report documents a phenomenon during the last two decades "of an extraordinary intensification of work pressures". The report states as a major cause the fact that the "quantity of work required of individuals has increased because of under-staffing so that hours of work have lengthened and, more importantly, the pace of work has intensified". Inevitably, the incidence of psychiatric injury due to excessive stress has increased. The need for protec-

tion of employees through their contractual rights, express and implied by law, is markedly greater than in the past.

20. It is no longer right to equate a contract of employment with commercial contracts. One possible way of describing a contract of employment in modern terms is as a relational contract. If (contrary to my view) the headnote of *Addis's* case correctly states the ratio decidendi of *Addis's* case I would now be willing to depart from it. That is not a particularly bold step. Indeed, in *Mahmud's* case the House took that step.

VIII. The impact of Mahmud's case on Addis's case

21. It is necessary to return to the analysis by Lord Woolf of the difference between *Addis's* case and *Mahmud's* case. Lord Woolf held that the relevant part of the rule in *Addis's* case deals with the consequences of wrongful dismissal whereas *Mahmud's* case concerned a breach of the obligation of mutual trust and confidence during the subsistence of a contract. It is, noteworthy that the implied obligation of mutual trust and confidence was developed in a series of constructive dismissal cases: see *Hepple & O'Higgins, Employment Law*, 4th ed (1981) pp 134–135, paras 291–292. It cannot therefore be confined to breaches during the subsistence of the contract. The development of the implied obligation of mutual trust and confidence as it has evolved was unanimously endorsed by the House as "workable" and "sound" in *Mahmud's* case: see Lord Nicholls, at p 35A, and in my speech at p 46. It was held in *Mahmud's* case that the employees in that case would have been entitled to accept a breach of such an obligation as repudiatory and to claim damages: Lord Nicholls, at p 38B–D and my speech at p 48. If the employees had discovered the corrupt conduct of employers during the subsistence of the contract, they would on the law as stated in *Mahmud's* case have been entitled to terminate the contract and sue for damages. Not only is this an inevitable result of the logic of the decision in *Mahmud's* case but it had the express unanimous endorsement of the House. "Pecuniary loss brought about by a loss of reputation caused by a breach of contract [does not] preclude the plaintiffs from recovering in respect of that pecuniary loss" (*Foaminol Laboratories Ltd v British Artid Plastics Ltd* [1941] 2 All ER 393, 400): Lord Nicholls, at p 40F–G; my speech at p 52C–H. Damages for wrongful dismissal are governed not by a special rule applicable to employment contracts but by ordinary principles of contract law: see *Mahmud's* case, at p 39D; and also informative comment in two major new publications, namely *English Private Law*, ed Professor Birks (2000), vol 2, para 1860–1861, per Professor Burrows; *Butterworths Common Law Series, The Law of Contract*, ed Professor Furmston (1999), para 8.59. The consequence is that "[c]ases previously regarded as exceptional can now be seen as examples of the general rule": *Anson's Law of Contract*, 27th ed (1998) ed J. Beatson, pp 562–563. In *Mahmud's* case the House embarked on a process of synthesis. To this extent therefore the observation of Lord Loreburn L.C., which rules out in all cases a claim for financial loss resulting from the manner of a wrongful dismissal, is qualified by the unanimous decision of the House in *Mahmud's* case. In my respectful view the reasoning of the Court of Appeal is not correct.

IX. The contrary arguments of the employers

22. *The statutory dimension*. Counsel for the employers argued that *Addis's* case has been a cornerstone of the law of employment for nearly a century. He submitted that the law as stated in *Addis's* case was the background against which Parliament introduced the unfair dismissal legislation in its original form by the Industrial Relations Act 1971: see the Employment Protection Act 1975 and the Employment Rights Act 1996 for subsequent reforms of the system. In support of this submission he pointed to paragraph 522 of the Report of the Royal Commission on Trade Unions and Employers Associations (1965–1968), Cmnd 3623, June 1968, commonly described as the Donovan Report. It reads as follows:

"An employee has protection at common law against 'wrongful' dismissal, but this protection is strictly limited; it means that if an employee is dismissed without due notice he can claim the payment of wages he would have earned for the period of notice. From this payment will be deducted any amount which he earned (or through his fault failed to earn) during the period of notice. Beyond this, the employee has no legal claim at common law, whatever hardship he suffers as a result of his dismissal. Even if the way in which he is dismissed constitutes an imputation on his honesty and his ability to get another job is correspondingly reduced he cannot—except through an action for defamation—obtain any redress (see the decision of the House of Lords in *Addis v Gramophone Co* [1909] AC 486)."

He argued further that, even if it would otherwise be right to depart from *Addis's* case in the respect under consideration, it would be wrong to do so in the face of the elaborate statutory scheme governing unfair dismissal created by Parliament. In my opinion this argument ought not to prevail. In *West Midland Baptist (Trust)*

Association (Inc) v Birmingham Corporation [1970] AC 874, Lord Reid put such arguments in context. He said, at p 898F:

> "But the mere fact that an enactment shows that Parliament must have thought that the law was one thing does not preclude the courts from deciding that the law was in fact something different. This has been stated in a number of cases including *Inland Revenue Commissioners v Dowdall, O'Mahoney & Co Ltd* [1952] AC 401. No doubt the position would be different if the provisions of the enactment were such that they would only be workable if the law was as Parliament supposed it to be."

It cannot be said that the unfair dismissal legislation would be unworkable if the House departs from *Addis's* case.

23. The unfair dismissal legislation must be put in context. At the time of the Donovan Report collective bargaining was seen as the main form of protection of individuals. It apparently covered about 83% of the workforce in 1980. It has, however, been contracting steadily. It fell to 35% in 1998. In the result individual legal rights have now become the main source of protection of employees: see Brown, Deakin, Nash and Oxenbridge, "The Employment Contract: From Collective Procedures to Individual Rights" (2000) 38, British Journal of Industrial Relations, 611, 613–616. At the time of the Donovan Report reinstatement was envisaged as a major remedy: paras 551–552. In practice, however, only about 3% of applicants are reinstated: see *Davies and Friedland, Labour Legislation and Public Policy*, (1993), p 210, citing statistics dating from 1987/8. My understanding is that about 3% still represents the reinstatement figure. Not surprisingly, the award of compensation by a tribunal has to be the primary remedy. The 1971 Act in section 116 adopted the formula, which appears with minor changes in the current law, that the compensation should be "such amount as the . . . tribunal considers just and equitable in all the circumstances, having regard to the loss sustained by the aggrieved party in consequence of the matters to which the complaint relates, in so far as the loss was attributable to action taken by or on behalf of the party in default". *Hugh Collins, Justice in Dismissal*, (1992), pp 218–223 has shown how the award of compensation, by reason of artificial limits, has markedly failed to meet the aim of corrective justice in accordance with the employee's contractual rights. One of those limits was the requirement of the unfair dismissal system that such cases had to be resolved in accordance with a very expeditious timetable. Initially, the claim had generally to be lodged within four weeks, that being a period within which the seriousness of damage to employment prospects would often not have become clear: see sections 22, 106(4) and (5) read with schedule 6, para 5 of the Industrial Relations Act 1971. Even now section 111(2) of the Employment Rights Act 1996 provides that such claims must generally be lodged within 3 months, that still being a period within which the seriousness of damage to employment prospects may not have become clear. More importantly, the low statutory limit on the award of compensation made the attainment of corrective justice impossible. At the inception of the statutory regime section 118(1) of the Industrial Relations Act 1971 placed a limit on the maximum amount of compensation of two years pay or £4,160 (whichever was the lesser). In 1975 the alternative way of expressing the limit was abolished. The monetary limit was from time to time increased. In April 1998 it reached £12,000. In October 1999 the maximum was increased to £50,000. It is now index-linked. It has been pointed out that allowing for inflation, £4,160 in 1971 is now worth about £50,000: HC Research Paper 98/99. The statutory system was therefore always only capable of meeting the requirements of cases at the lower end of seriousness. Manifestly, it was always incapable, for example, of affording any significant financial compensation to employees with substantial salaries and pension entitlements in cases where they suffered a serious loss of employment prospects due to the manner of their dismissal. In such cases, inter alia, the artificial statutory limits from the inception inhibited significant compensation. If Parliament is deemed to have been aware of the *Addis* decision, one must also deem Parliament to have been aware that the system it was creating was only capable of dealing effectively and justly with less serious cases where the threshold of a breach of contract was not necessarily established. Moreover, the changing nature of the relationship between employer and employee, and numerous judicial inroads in case law on *Addis's* case were already well documented before 1971. The third edition of *Treitel, The Law of Contract*, was published in 1970. *Treitel* observed, at p 813, that "the rule may be that *general* damages cannot be recovered for injury to reputation by a non-trader, but that *special* damages can be recovered for actual loss resulting from such injury" (author's emphasis). In my view the headnote in *Addis's* case (and its recitation in the Donovan Report) in respect of special damages is based on a misconception. But at the very least the relevant part of the rule in *Addis's* case was controversial. In all these circumstances it is unrealistic to say that Parliament would have assumed the common law as reflected in the headnote in *Addis's* case to be set in stone and incapable of principled development. I would therefore reject this argument.

24. *Conflict with express terms.* Counsel for the employers was asked to place the employment contract of the employee before the House. It was done. It revealed that either party was able to terminate the contract by giving four weeks' notice. This proved to be a platform for an argument for striking out the claim which was not considered by the judge or by the Court of Appeal. It was also not raised in the agreed statement of facts and issues or in the written cases. Nevertheless, relying on the notice provision, counsel for the employers submitted that to apply the implied obligation of mutual trust and confidence in relation to a dismissal is to bring it into conflict with the express terms of the contract. He said orthodox contract law does not permit such a result. His argument approached the matter as if one was dealing with the question whether a term can be implied *in fact* in the light of the express terms of the contract. This submission loses sight of the particular nature of the implied obligation of mutual trust and confidence. It is not a term implied in fact. It is an overarching obligation implied by law as an incident of the contract of employment. It can also be described as a legal duty imposed by law: *Treitel, The Law of Contract,* 10th ed, p 190. It requires at least express words or a necessary implication to displace it or to cut down its scope. Prima facie it must be read consistently with the express terms of the contract. This emerges from the seminal judgment of Sir Nicolas Browne-Wilkinson V.-C., in *Imperial Group Pension Trust Ltd v Imperial Tobacco Ltd* [1991] ICR 524. It related to an employer's express contractual right to refuse amendments under a pension scheme. The Vice Chancellor held that the employer's express rights were subject to the implied obligation that they should not be exercised so as to destroy or seriously damage the relationship of trust and confidence between the company and its employees and former employees. The employer's blanket refusal was unlawful. The decision did not involve trust law and the employer was not treated as a fiduciary. It was decided on principles of contract law. The Vice Chancellor described the implied obligation of trust and confidence as "the implied obligation of good faith". It could also be described as an employer's obligation of fair dealing. In the same way an employer's express right to transfer an employee may be qualified by the obligation of mutual trust and confidence: see *United Bank v Akhtar* [1989] IRLR 507, *Sweet & Maxwell's Encyclopaedia of Employment Law,* vol 1 paras 1.5101 and 1.5107. The interaction of the implied obligation of trust and confidence and express terms of the contract can be compared with the relationship between duties of good faith or fair dealing with the express terms of notice in a contract. They can live together. In any event, the argument of counsel for the employers misses the real point. The notice provision in the contract is valid and effective. Nobody suggests the contrary. On the other hand, the employer may become liable in damages if he acts in breach of the independent implied obligation by dismissing the employee in a harsh and humiliating manner. There is no conflict between the express and implied terms. I would therefore dismiss this argument.

25. *Unfair dismissal.* Counsel for the employers further argued that in substance the claim, based on a failure to follow disciplinary procedures, is one for unfair dismissal. This is a misdescription of the claim. It is not a claim for unfair dismissal but one based on allegations of breach of the obligation of mutual trust and confidence. Counsel also said that a tribunal's award may include compensation for a breach in respect of the manner of a wrongful dismissal. That is so. But it is equally obvious that as at 1971, and afterwards, such amount would have been fairly nominal. Of course, an employee must not be allowed to recover the same damages twice. But such adjustments in common law damages can be and are often made.

26. *Inapplicability to termination.* Counsel for the employers also argued that the implied obligation of trust and confidence is restricted to unacceptable conduct by the employer during the relationship. It is a legalistic point. It ignores the purpose of the obligation. The implied obligation aims to ensure fair dealing between employer and employee, and that is as important in respect of disciplinary proceedings, suspension of an employee and dismissal as at any other stage of the employment relationship. In my view this argument ought not to be accepted.

27. *Floodgates.* Counsel for the employers further submitted that in virtually every case there could be a claim based on the manner of dismissal. He said there would be an enormous proliferation of claims in the County Court. These predictions are too alarmist. In *Mahmud's* case it was held, at p 39H, that the mere fact of dismissal could not of itself handicap an employee in the labour market. On the other hand, if the employer acts in a harsh and oppressive manner that inflicts unnecessary and substantial financial damage on the employee there is no principled reason why an employee should not put forward a claim for such loss. I would therefore reject the floodgates argument.

X. *The cause of action*
28. In my view the employee has a reasonable cause of action based on a breach of the implied obligation of trust and confidence.

XI. Remoteness

29. Leaving aside legal objections, there are formidable evidential difficulties in the way of the employee. It was suggested at the hearing that the claim would at trial inevitably fail on causation. The difficulty is real: How would the employee prove that his psychiatric condition was caused by the manner of his dismissal rather than the fact of his dismissal? On the facts, which must be assumed to be correct, I am however inclined to think that it would not be right to strike out the claim on this ground. But remoteness presents an even more formidable difficulty for the employee even at this stage. This issue must be judged at the date of the re-employment of the employee in 1990. The allegations of the knowledge of the employers before that date are set out in the pleadings as follows:

> "during the plaintiff's posting to Paris and his work on a conference in Barcelona in 1985, the defendant's servant or agent, Keith Binks, was made aware that the plaintiff was under extreme stress and was at risk of suffering psychological injury.
>
> At the end of 1985 the plaintiff saw his GP who prescribed anti-depressants and wrote to the defendant requesting that the plaintiff be given time off work as a result of work-related stress. The defendant allowed the plaintiff some time off work as a result. The defendant's doctor was aware of the plaintiff's psychological condition as a result of a meeting with the plaintiff prior to his return to work in 1986. Further, in 1987 the defendant was aware of the plaintiff's special psychological needs, as was evidenced by its offering him one-to-one counselling because of his medical condition and impending redundancy."

Taking into account what the employer is alleged to have known, as well as the lapse of time, I would not dissent from the view of Lord Woolf M.R. that there is no realistic prospect that the employee will be able to overcome this obstacle.

XII. Disposal

30. For the reasons I have given I would dismiss the appeal.

LORD HOFFMANN

[Having summarised the background to the case, Lord Hoffmann continued:]

35. My Lords, the first question is whether the implied term of trust and confidence upon which Mr Johnson relies, and about which in a general way there is no real dispute, or any of the other implied terms, applies to a dismissal. At common law the contract of employment was regarded by the courts as a contract like any other. The parties were free to negotiate whatever terms they liked and no terms would be implied unless they satisfied the strict test of necessity applied to a commercial contract. Freedom of contract meant that the stronger party, usually the employer, was free to impose his terms upon the weaker. But over the last 30 years or so, the nature of the contract of employment has been transformed. It has been recognised that a person's employment is usually one of the most important things in his or her life. It gives not only a livelihood but an occupation, an identity and a sense of self-esteem. The law has changed to recognise this social reality. Most of the changes have been made by Parliament. The Employment Rights Act 1996 consolidates numerous statutes which have conferred rights upon employees. European law has made a substantial contribution. And the common law has adapted itself to the new attitudes, proceeding sometimes by analogy with statutory rights.

36. The contribution of the common law to the employment revolution has been by the evolution of implied terms in the contract of employment. The most far reaching is the implied term of trust and confidence. But there have been others. For example, in *W A Goold (Pearmak) Ltd v McConnell* [1995] IRLR 516, Morison J. (sitting in the Employment Appeal Tribunal) said that it was an implied term of the contract of employment that an employer would reasonably and promptly afford employees an opportunity to obtain redress of grievances. He inferred such a term from what is now section 3 of the Employment Rights Act 1996, which requires that an employee be provided with a written statement of the particulars of his employment, including a note of how he may apply if he has any grievances. So statute and common law have proceeded hand in hand.

37. The problem lies in extending or adapting any of these implied terms to dismissal. There are two reasons why dismissal presents special problems. The first is that any terms which the courts imply into a contract must be consistent with the express terms. Implied terms may supplement the express terms of the contract but cannot contradict them. Only Parliament may actually override what the parties have agreed. The second reason is that judges, in developing the law, must have regard to the policies expressed by Parliament in legislation. Employment law requires a balancing of the interests of employers and employees, with proper regard not only to the individual dignity and worth of the employees but also to the general economic interest. Subject

to observance of fundamental human rights, the point at which this balance should be struck is a matter for democratic decision. The development of the common law by the judges plays a subsidiary role. Their traditional function is to adapt and modernise the common law. But such developments must be consistent with legislative policy as expressed in statutes. The courts may proceed in harmony with Parliament but there should be no discord.

38. My Lords, I shall consider first the problem posed by the express terms of the contract. In developing the implied term of trust and confidence and other similar terms applicable to the continuing employment relationship, the courts were advancing across open country. No express provision that BCCI would be entitled to conduct a fraudulent business, or that the employer in *W A Goold (Pearmak) Ltd v McConnell* would have no grievance procedure, stood in their way. But the employer's right to dismiss the employee is strongly defended by the terms of the contract. In the present case, Mr Johnson's contract provided:

> "If you decide to leave UNISYS you are required to give the company four weeks notice, equally, the company may terminate your employment on four weeks notice . . . In the event of gross misconduct, the company may terminate your employment without notice."

39. The effect of such a provision at common law was stated with great clarity by McLachlin J. of the Supreme Court of Canada in *Wallace v United Grain Growers Ltd* (1997) 152 DLR (4th) 1, 39:

> "The action for wrongful dismissal is based on an implied obligation in the employment contract to give reasonable notice of an intention to terminate the relationship (or pay in lieu thereof) in the absence of just cause for dismissal. . . A 'wrongful dismissal' action is not concerned with the wrongness or rightness of the dismissal itself. Far from making dismissal a wrong, the law entitles both employer and employee to terminate the employment relationship without cause. A wrong arises only if the employer breaches the contract by failing to give the dismissed employee reasonable notice of termination. The remedy for this breach of contract is an award of damages based on the period of notice which should have been given."

40. Likewise in *Malloch v Aberdeen Corporation* [1971] 1 WLR 1578, 1581 Lord Reid said:

> "At common law a master is not bound to hear his servant before he dismisses him. He can act unreasonably or capriciously if he so chooses but the dismissal is valid. The servant has no remedy unless the dismissal is in breach of contract and then the servant's only remedy is damages for breach of contract."

41. The action for wrongful dismissal could therefore yield no more than the salary which should have been paid during the contractual period of notice. In the present case Mr Johnson's letter of engagement referred to Terms and Conditions of Employment contained in the company's Employee Handbook, which stipulated expressly that "The company reserves the right to make payment in lieu of notice". Unisys exercised that right.

42. My Lords, in the face of this express provision that Unisys was entitled to terminate Mr Johnson's employment on four weeks notice without any reason, I think it is very difficult to imply a term that the company should not do so except for some good cause and after giving him a reasonable opportunity to demonstrate that no such cause existed.

43. On the other hand, I do not say that there is nothing which, consistently with such an express term, judicial creativity could do to provide a remedy in a case like this. In *Wallace v United Grain Growers Ltd* (1997) 152 DLR (4th) 1, 44–48, McLachlin J. (in a minority judgment) said that the courts could imply an obligation to exercise the power of dismissal in good faith. That did not mean that the employer could not dismiss without cause. The contract entitled him to do so. But in so doing, he should be honest with the employee and refrain from untruthful, unfair or insensitive conduct. He should recognise that an employee losing his or her job was exceptionally vulnerable and behave accordingly. For breach of this implied obligation, McLachlin J. would have awarded the employee, who had been dismissed in brutal circumstances, damages for mental distress and loss of reputation and prestige.

44. My Lords, such an approach would in this country have to circumvent or overcome the obstacle of *Addis v Gramophone Co Ltd* [1909] AC 488, in which it was decided that an employee cannot recover damages for injured feelings, mental distress or damage to his reputation, arising out of the manner of his dismissal. Speaking for myself, I think that, if this task was one which I felt called upon to perform, I would be able to do so. In *Mahmud v Bank of Credit and Commerce International SA* [1998] AC 20, 51 Lord Steyn said that the true ratio of *Addis's* case was the damages were recoverable only for loss caused by a breach of contract, not for loss caused by the manner of its breach. As McLachlin J. said in the passage I have quoted, the only loss caused by a wrongful dismissal flows from a failure to give proper notice or make payment in lieu. Therefore, if wrongful dismissal is the only cause of action, nothing can be recovered for mental distress or damage to

reputation. On the other hand, if such damage is loss flowing from a breach of another implied term of the contract, *Addis's* case does not stand in the way. That is why in *Mahmud's* case itself, damages were recoverable for financial loss flowing from damage to reputation caused by a breach of the implied term of trust and confidence.

45. In this case, Mr Johnson says likewise that his psychiatric injury is a consequence of a breach of the implied term of trust and confidence, which required Unisys to treat him fairly in the procedures for dismissal. He says that implied term now fills the gap which Lord Shaw of Dunfermline perceived and regretted in *Addis's* case (at pp 504–505) by creating a breach of contract additional to the dismissal itself.

46. It may be a matter of words, but I rather doubt whether the term of trust and confidence should be pressed so far. In the way it has always been formulated, it is concerned with preserving the continuing relationship which should subsist between employer and employee. So it does not seem altogether appropriate for use in connection with the way that relationship is terminated. If one is looking for an implied term, I think a more elegant solution is McLachlin J's implication of a separate term that the power of dismissal will be exercised fairly and in good faith. But the result would be the same as that for which Mr Johnson contends by invoking the implied term of trust and confidence. As I have said, I think it would be possible to reach such a conclusion without contradicting the express term that the employer is entitled to dismiss without cause.

47. I must however make it clear that, although in my opinion it would be jurisprudentially possible to imply a term which gave a remedy in this case, I do not think that even if the courts were free of legislative constraint (a point to which I shall return in a moment) it would necessarily be wise to do so. It is not simply an incremental step from the duty of trust and confidence implied in *Mahmud v Bank of Credit and Commerce International SA* [1998] AC 20. The close association between the acts alleged to be in breach of the implied term and the irremovable and lawful fact of dismissal give rise to special problems. So, in *Wallace v United Grain Growers Ltd* (1997) 152 DLR (4th) 1, the majority rejected an implied duty to exercise the power of dismissal in good faith. Iacobucci J. said, at p 28, that such a step was better left to the legislature. It would be "overly intrusive and inconsistent with established principles of employment law".

48. Some of the potential problems can be illustrated by the facts of this case, in which Mr Johnson claims some £400,000 damages for the financial consequences of psychiatric damage. This form of damage notoriously gives rise at the best of times to extremely difficult questions of causation. But the difficulties are made greater when the expert witnesses are required to perform the task of distinguishing between the psychiatric consequences of the fact of dismissal (for which no damages are recoverable) and the unfair circumstances in which the dismissal took place, which constituted a breach of the implied term. The agreed statement of facts records that for the purposes of this appeal against a strike-out it is accepted that Mr Johnson's psychiatric illness was caused by "the circumstances and the fact" of his dismissal. At a trial, however, it would be necessary to decide what was caused by what.

49. Another difficulty is the open-ended nature of liability. Mr Johnson's case is that Unisys had knowledge of his psychological fragility by reason of facts lodged in the corporate memory in 1985–87 and therefore should have foreseen when he was engaged that a failure to comply with proper disciplinary procedures on dismissal might result in injury which deprived him of the ability ever to work again. On general common law principles it seems to me that if the necessary term is implied and these facts are made out, the claim should succeed. It may be that such liability would be grossly disproportionate to the employer's degree of fault. It may be likely to inhibit the future engagement of psychologically fragile personnel. But the common law decides cases according to principle and cannot impose arbitrary limitations on liability because of the circumstances of the particular case. Only statute can lay down limiting rules based upon policy rather than principle. In this connection it is interesting to notice that although the majority in *Wallace v United Grain Growers Ltd* were unwilling to accept an implied term as to the manner of dismissal, they treated it as relevant to the period of notice which should reasonably have been given. McLachlin J. said that this was illogical and so perhaps it is. But one can understand a desire to place some limit upon the employer's potential liability under this head.

50. It follows, my Lords, that if there was no relevant legislation in this area, I would regard the question of whether judges should develop the law by implying a suitable term into the contract of employment as finely balanced. But now I must consider the statutory background against which your Lordships are invited to create such a cause of action.

[Having considered the statutory background, Lord Hoffmann concluded:]

66. My Lords, given this background to the disciplinary procedures, I find it impossible to believe that Parliament, when it provided in section 3(1) of the 1996 Act that the statement of particulars of employment

was to contain a note of any applicable disciplinary rules, or the parties themselves, intended that the inclusion of those rules should give rise to a common law action in damages which would create the means of circumventing the restrictions and limits which Parliament had imposed on compensation for unfair dismissal. The whole of the reasoning which led me to the conclusion that the courts should not imply a term which has this result also in my opinion supports the view that the disciplinary procedures do not do so either. It is I suppose possible that they may have contractual effect in determining whether the employer can dismiss summarily in the sense of not having to give four weeks' notice or payment in lieu. But I do not think that they can have been intended to qualify the employer's common law power to dismiss without cause on giving such notice, or to create contractual duties which are independently actionable.

67. I would dismiss the appeal.

Question

Why should damages not be recoverable for wrongful dismissal in a manner which injures the employee's reputation and makes it difficult or impossible for him to get a job, when damages are recoverable for a breach causing similar results which occurs during the course of the employment? If A, a senior officer of the X Co is wrongly dismissed at a time when the company is rocked by fraud, so that the public believe A must be involved in it, should he be any less entitled to damages for his resulting inability to get another job than Mr Malik of BCCI?

19-021

JARVIS v SWAN'S TOURS

Court of Appeal [1973] 1 Q.B. 233; [1972] 3 W.L.R. 954; [1973] 1 All E.R. 71

Defendants, travel agents, advertised in glowing terms a houseparty in Switzerland, promising "a great time." The plaintiff booked the holiday with the defendants and paid £63.45. He went during his annual fortnight's holiday. There were only 13 guests there during the first week and none during the second. The hotel proprietor could not speak English. The holiday failed to comply with the description in the brochure in numerous respects. The county court judge awarded £31.72 damages. The plaintiff appealed.

19-022

LORD DENNING MR

What is the legal position? I think that the statements in the brochure were representations or warranties. The breaches of them give Mr Jarvis a right to damages. It is not necessary to decide whether they were representations or warranties; because, since the Misrepresentation Act, 1967, there is a remedy in damages for misrepresentation as well as for breach of warranty.

The one question in the case is: what is the amount of damages? The judge seems to have taken the difference in value between what he paid for and what he got. He said that he intended to give "the difference between the two values and no other damages" under any other head. He thought that Mr Jarvis had got half of what he paid for. So the judge gave him half the amount which he had paid, namely, £31.72. Mr Jarvis appeals to this court. He says that the damages ought to have been much more. . .

What is the right way of assessing damages? It has often been said that on a breach of contract damages cannot be given for mental distress. Thus in *Hamlin v Great Northern Railway Co* ((1856) 1 H. & N. 408 at 411) Pollock C.B. said that damages cannot be given "for the disappointment of mind occasioned by the breach of contract." And in *Hobbs v London & South Western Railway Co.* ((1875) L.R. 10 Q.B. 111 at 122) Mellor J. said that— ". . . for the mere inconvenience, such as annoyance and loss of temper, or vexation, or for being disappointed in a particular thing which you have set your mind upon, without real physical inconvenience resulting, you cannot recover damages." The courts in those days only allowed the plaintiff to recover damages if he suffered physical inconvenience, such as, having to walk five miles home, as in *Hobbs'* case; or to live in an overcrowded house: see *Bailey v Bullock* ([1950] 2 All E.R. 1167).

I think that those limitations are out of date. In a proper case damages for mental distress can be recovered in contract, just as damages for shock can be recovered in tort. One such case is a contract for a holiday, or any other contract to provide entertainment and enjoyment. If the contracting party breaks his contract, damages can be given for the disappointment, the distress, the upset and frustration caused by the breach. I know that it is difficult to assess in terms of money, but it is no more difficult than the assessment which the courts have to make every day in personal injury cases for loss of amenities. Take the present case. Mr Jarvis has only a fortnight's holiday in the year. He books it far ahead, and looks forward to it all that time. He ought to be compensated for the loss of it.

A good illustration was given by Edmund Davies L.J. in the course of the argument. He put the case of a man who has taken a ticket for Glyndbourne. It is the only night on which he can get there. He hires a car to take him. The car does not turn up. His damages are not limited to the mere cost of the ticket. He is entitled to general damages for the disappointment he has suffered and the loss of the entertainment which he should have had. Here, Mr Jarvis's fortnight's winter holiday has been a grave disappointment. It is true that he was conveyed to Switzerland and back and had meals and bed in the hotel. But that is not what he went for. He went to enjoy himself with all the facilities which the defendants said he would have. He is entitled to damages for the lack of those facilities, and for his loss of enjoyment . . . I think the damages in this case should be the sum of £125.

Edmund-Davies L.J., having stated that he did not accept the observations of Mellor J. in Hobbs' case: Be that as it may, Mellor J. was dealing with a contract of carriage and the undertaking of the railway company was entirely different from that of the defendants in the present case. These travel agents made clear by their lavishly illustrated brochure with its ecstatic text that what they were contracting to provide was not merely air travel, hotel accommodation and meals of a certain standard. To quote the assurance which they gave regarding the Morlialp House Party Centre, "No doubt you will be in for a great time, when you book this houseparty holiday." The result was that they did not limit themselves to the obligation to ensure that an air passage was booked, that hotel accommodation was reserved, that food was provided and that these items would measure up the standards they themselves set up. They went further than that. They assured and undertook to provide a holiday of a certain quality, with "Gemutlichkeit" (that is to say, geniality, comfort and cosiness) as its overall characteristics, and "a great time," the enjoyable outcome which would surely result to all but the most determined misanthrope. . . .

Stephenson L.J. delivered judgment allowing the appeal.

Appeal Allowed; Damages of £125 Awarded.

Questions

19–023   1. Was Lord Denning right in saying that the damages would be the same under s.2(1) of the Misrepresentation Act? See above, para.14–031.

2. Should damages for vexation and disappointment be recoverable for breach of contract generally? Or is a contract to provide pleasure different. cf. *Addis v Gramophone Co Ltd* (above); *Jackson v Horizon Holidays* (above, Ch.13) and *Hayes v Dodd* (above).

FARLEY v SKINNER

House of Lords [2001] UKHL 49

LORD STEYN

19–024   My Lords,

1. The central question is whether a buyer, who employed a surveyor to investigate whether a property in the countryside was seriously affected by aircraft noise, may in principle recover non-pecuniary damages against

the surveyor for the latter's negligent failure to discover that the property was so affected. The trial judge answered this question in the affirmative. A two-member Court of Appeal disagreed on it. The point was then re-argued before a three-member Court of Appeal. By a majority the Court of Appeal reversed the decision of the trial judge and ruled that there was no right to recover non-pecuniary damages in such cases. The second Court of Appeal was deluged with authorities. So was the House on the present appeal. The hearings of what was a comparatively simple case took up an exorbitant amount of time. This circumstance underlines the importance, in the quest for coherent and just solutions in such cases, of simple and practical rules.

I. Riverside House, aircraft noise and the surveyor

2. In 1990 the plaintiff, a successful businessman, contemplated retirement. He owned a flat in London, a house in Brighton and a property overseas. He wanted to buy a gracious country residence. He became interested in a beautiful property known as Riverside House in the village of Blackboys in Sussex which was situated some 15 miles from Gatwick International Airport. The property is in the heart of the countryside. There is a stream running through the middle of it. The property has a croquet lawn, tennis court, orchard, paddock and swimming pool. Although the attractive house required modernisation and refurbishment, it appeared to be ideal for the plaintiff. There was, however, one question mark over the transaction. For the plaintiff a property offering peace and tranquillity was the raison d'être of the proposed purchase. He wanted to be reasonably sure that the property was not seriously affected by aircraft noise.

3. The plaintiff engaged as his surveyor the defendant, who had been in practice as a sole practitioner for some years. The surveyor had to investigate the usual matters expected of a surveyor who inspects a property. In addition the plaintiff also specifically asked the surveyor to investigate, amongst other things, whether the property would be affected by aircraft noise. The plaintiff told the surveyor that he did not want a property on a flight path. The surveyor accepted these instructions.

4. On 17 December 1990 the surveyor sent his report to the plaintiff. From the plaintiff's point of view it was a satisfactory report. About aircraft noise the surveyor reported:

"You have also asked whether we felt the property might be affected by aircraft noise, but we were not conscious of this during the time of our inspection, and think it unlikely that the property will suffer greatly from such noise, although some planes will inevitably cross the area, depending on the direction of the wind and the positioning of the flight paths."

Comforted by this reassuring report the plaintiff decided to buy the property. The purchase price was £420,000 (which included £45,000 for chattels). The purchase was completed on 28 February 1991.

5. In the next few months the plaintiff caused the house to be modernised and refurbished at a total cost of about £125,000. During this period he was unaware that there was a significant problem associated with aircraft noise. On 13 June 1991 the plaintiff and his partner (who had a 32.74% beneficial interest) moved in. Since 1991 they had lived there three to four days a week for seven to nine months of the year.

6. After he moved in the plaintiff quickly discovered that the property was indeed affected by aircraft noise. In fact, the property was not far away from a navigation beacon (the Mayfield Stack) and at certain busy times, especially in the morning, the early evening, and at weekends, aircraft waiting to land at Gatwick would be stacked up maintaining a spiral course around the beacon until there was a landing slot at the airport. Aircraft frequently passed directly over, or nearly over, the position of the house. The impact of aircraft noise on the tranquillity of the property was marked. The property was undoubtedly affected by aircraft noise.

7. It is common ground that the plaintiff's enjoyment of the property was diminished by aircraft noise at those times when he was enjoying the amenities of the property outdoors and aircraft were stacked up, maintaining their spiral course around the beacon, waiting for a landing slot at the airport. Nevertheless, after initial vacillation, the plaintiff decided not to sell the property and he does not presently intend to do so.

[Having summarised the proceedings in the High Court and before the Court of Appeal, Lord Steyn continued:]

IV. The law

14. The judgments in the Court of Appeal and the arguments before the House took as their starting point the propositions enunciated by Bingham L.J. in *Watts v Morrow* [1991] 1 WLR 1421. In that case the Court of Appeal had to consider a claim for damages for distress and inconvenience by a buyer of a house against his surveyor who had negligently failed to report defects in the house. Bingham L.J. observed, at p 1445:

"(1) A contract-breaker is not in general liable for any distress, frustration, anxiety, displeasure, vexation, tension or aggravation which his breach of contract may cause to the innocent party. This rule is not, I think, founded on the assumption that such reactions are not foreseeable, which they surely are or may be, but on considerations of policy.

(2) But the rule is not absolute. Where the very object of a contract is to provide pleasure, relaxation, peace of mind or freedom from molestation, damages will be awarded if the fruit of the contract is not provided or if the contrary result is procured instead. If the law did not cater for this exceptional category of case it would be defective. A contract to survey the condition of a house for a prospective purchaser does not, however, fall within this exceptional category.

(3) In cases not falling within this exceptional category, damages are in my view recoverable for physical inconvenience and discomfort caused by the breach and mental suffering directly related to that inconvenience and discomfort. If those effects are foreseeably suffered during a period when defects are repaired I am prepared to accept that they sound in damages even though the cost of the repairs is not recoverable as such. But I also agree that awards should be restrained, and that the awards in this case far exceeded a reasonable award for the injury shown to have been suffered." (Numbering introduced).

As Stuart-Smith L.J. pointed out in the present case [2000] Lloyd's Rep PN 516, 519–522, the propositions of Bingham L.J. have often been cited and applied.

15. But useful as the observations of Bingham L.J. undoubtedly are, they were never intended to state more than broad principles. In *Broome v Cassell & Co Ltd* [1972] AC 1027 Lord Reid commented, at p 1085:

"experience has shown that those who have to apply the decision [*Rookes v Barnard* [1964] AC 1129] to other cases and still more those who wish to criticise it seem to find it difficult to avoid treating sentences and phrases in a single speech as if they were provisions in an Act of Parliament. They do not seem to realise that it is not the function of . . . judges to frame definitions or to lay down hard and fast rules. It is their function to enunciate principles and much that they say is intended to be illustrative or explanatory and not to be definitive."

Bingham L.J. would have had this truth about judicial decision making well in mind. So interpreted the passage cited is a helpful point of departure for the examination of the issues in this case. Specifically, it is important to bear in mind that *Watts v Morrow* [1991] 1 WLR 1421 was a case where a surveyor negligently failed to discover defects in a property. The claim was not for breach of a specific undertaking to investigate a matter important for the buyer's peace of mind. It was a claim for damages for inconvenience and discomfort resulting from breach. In *Watts v Morrow* [1991] 1 WLR 1421 therefore there was no reason to consider the case where a surveyor is in breach of a distinct and important contractual obligation which was intended to afford the buyer information confirming the presence or absence of an intrusive element before he committed himself to the purchase.

V. Recovery of non-pecuniary damages

16. The examination of the issues can now proceed from a secure foothold. In the law of obligations the rules governing the recovery of compensation necessarily distinguish between different kinds of harm. In tort the requirement of reasonable foreseeability is a sufficient touchstone of liability for causing death or physical injury: it is an inadequate tool for the disposal of claims in respect of psychiatric injury. Tort law approaches compensation for physical damage and pure economic loss differently. In contract law distinctions are made about the kind of harm which resulted from the breach of contract. The general principle is that compensation is only awarded for financial loss resulting from the breach of contract: *Livingstone v Rawyards Coal Co* (1880) 5 AppCas 25, 39, per Lord Blackburn. In the words of Bingham L.J. in *Watts* as a matter of legal policy "a contract breaker is not *in general* liable for any distress, frustration, anxiety, displeasure, vexation, tension or aggravation which his breach of contract may cause to the innocent party" (my emphasis). There are, however, limited exceptions to this rule. One such exception is damages for pain, suffering and loss of amenities caused to an individual by a breach of contract: see *McGregor on Damages*, 16th ed, para 96, pp 56–57. It is not material in the present case. But the two exceptions mentioned by Bingham L.J., namely where the very object of the contract is to provide pleasure (proposition (2)) and recovery for physical inconvenience caused by the breach (proposition (3)), are pertinent. The scope of these exceptions is in issue in the present case. It is, however, correct, as counsel for the surveyor submitted, that the entitlement to damages for mental distress caused by a breach of contract is not established by mere foreseeability: the right to recovery is dependent on the case falling fairly within the principles governing the special exceptions. So far there is no real disagreement between the parties.

VI. The very object of the contract: The framework

17. I reverse the order in which the Court of Appeal considered the two issues. I do so because the issue whether the present case falls within the exceptional category governing cases where the very object of the contact is to give pleasure, and so forth, focuses directly on the terms actually agreed between the parties. It is concerned with the reasonable expectations of the parties under the specific terms of the contract. Logically, it must be considered first.

18. It is necessary to examine the case on a correct characterisation of the plaintiff's claim. Stuart-Smith L.J. [2000] Lloyd's Rep PN 516, 521 thought that the obligation undertaken by the surveyor was "one relatively minor aspect of the overall instructions." What Stuart-Smith and Mummery LJ.J. would have decided if they had approached it on the basis that the obligation was a major or important part of the contract between the plaintiff and the surveyor is not clear. But the Court of Appeal's characterisation of the case was not correct. The plaintiff made it crystal clear to the surveyor that the impact of aircraft noise was a matter of importance to him. Unless he obtained reassuring information from the surveyor he would not have bought the property. That is the tenor of the evidence. It is also what the judge found. The case must be approached on the basis that the surveyor's obligation to investigate aircraft noise was a major or important part of the contract between him and the plaintiff. It is also important to note that, unlike in *Addis v Gramophone Co Ltd* [1909] AC 488, the plaintiff's claim is not for injured feelings caused by the breach of contract. Rather it is a claim for damages flowing from the surveyor's failure to investigate and report, thereby depriving the buyer of the chance of making an informed choice whether or not to buy resulting in mental distress and disappointment.

19. The broader legal context of *Watts v Morrow* [1991] 1 WLR 1421 must be borne in mind. The exceptional category of cases where the very object of a contract is to provide pleasure, relaxation, peace of mind or freedom from molestation is not the product of Victorian contract theory but the result of evolutionary developments in case law from the 1970s. Several decided cases informed the description given by Bingham L.J. of this category. The first was the decision of the sheriff court in *Diesen v Samson* 1971 SLT (Sh Ct) 49. A photographer failed to turn up at a wedding, thereby leaving the couple without a photographic record of an important and happy day. The bride was awarded damages for her distress and disappointment. In the celebrated case of *Jarvis v Swans Tours Ltd* [1973] QB 233, the plaintiff recovered damages for mental distress flowing from a disastrous holiday resulting from a travel agent's negligent representations: compare also *Jackson v Horizon Holidays Ltd* [1975] 1 WLR 1468. In *Heywood v Wellers* [1976] QB 446, the plaintiff instructed solicitors to bring proceedings to restrain a man from molesting her. The solicitors negligently failed to take appropriate action with the result that the molestation continued. The Court of Appeal allowed the plaintiff damages for mental distress and upset. While apparently not cited in *Watts v Morrow* [1991] 1 WLR 1421, *Jackson v Chrysler Acceptances Ltd* [1978] RTR 474 was decided before *Watts v Morrow*. In *Jackson's* case the claim was for damages in respect of a motor car which did not meet the implied condition of merchantability in section 14 of the Sale of Goods Act 1893. The buyer communicated to the seller that one of his reasons for buying the car was a forthcoming touring holiday in France. Problems with the car spoilt the holiday. The disappointment of a spoilt holiday was a substantial element in the award sanctioned by the Court of Appeal.

20. At their Lordships' request counsel for the plaintiff produced a memorandum based on various publications which showed the impact of the developments already described on litigation in the county courts. Taking into account the submissions of counsel for the surveyor and making due allowance for a tendency of the court sometimes not to distinguish between the cases presently under consideration and cases of physical inconvenience and discomfort, I am satisfied that in the real life of our lower courts non-pecuniary damages are regularly awarded on the basis that the defendant's breach of contract deprived the plaintiff of the very object of the contract, viz pleasure, relaxation, and peace of mind. The cases arise in diverse contractual contexts, eg the supply of a wedding dress or double glazing, hire purchase transactions, landlord and tenant, building contracts, and engagements of estate agents and solicitors. The awards in such cases seem modest. For my part what happens on the ground casts no doubt on the utility of the developments since the 1970s in regard to the award of non-pecuniary damages in the exceptional categories. But the problem persists of the precise scope of the exceptional category of case involving awards of non-pecuniary damages for breach of contract where the very object of the contract was to ensure a party's pleasure, relaxation or peace of mind.

21. An important development for this branch of the law was *Ruxley Electronics and Construction Ltd v Forsyth* [1996] AC 344. The plaintiff had specified that a swimming pool should at the deep end have a depth of 7 feet 6 inches. The contractor failed to comply with his contractual obligation: the actual depth at the deep end was the standard 6 feet. The House found the usual "cost of cure" measure of damages to be wholly disproportionate to the loss suffered and economically wasteful. On the other hand, the House awarded the

moderate sum of £2,500 for the plaintiff's disappointment in not receiving the swimming pool he desired. It is true that for strategic reasons neither side contended for such an award. The House was, however, not inhibited by the stance of the parties. Lord Mustill and Lord Lloyd of Berwick justified the award in carefully reasoned judgments which carried the approval of four of the Law Lords. It is sufficient for present purposes to mention that for Lord Mustill, at p 360, the principle of pacta sunt servanda would be eroded if the law did not take account of the fact that the consumer often demands specifications which, although not of economic value, have value to him. This is sometimes called the "consumer surplus": see Harris, Ogus and Philips, "Contract Remedies and the Consumer Surplus" (1979) 95 LQR 581. Lord Mustill rejected the idea that "the promisor can please himself whether or not to comply with the wishes of the promisee which, as embodied in the contract, formed part of the consideration for the price". Lords Keith of Kinkel and Bridge of Harwich agreed with Lord Mustill's judgment and with Lord Lloyd of Berwick's similar reasoning. Labels sometimes obscure rather than illuminate. I do not therefore set much store by the description "consumer surplus". But the controlling principles stated by Lord Mustill and Lord Lloyd are important. It is difficult to reconcile this decision of the House with the decision of the Court of Appeal [2000] Lloyd's Rep PN 516 in the present case. I will in due course return to the way in which the majority attempted to distinguish *Ruxley Electronics and Construction Ltd v Forsyth* [1996] AC 344. At this stage, however, I draw attention to the fact that the majority in the Court of Appeal, at p 521, regarded the relevant observations of Lord Mustill and Lord Lloyd as obiter dicta. I am satisfied that the principles enunciated in *Ruxley's* case in support of the award of £2,500 for a breach of respect of the provision of a pleasurable amenity have been authoritatively established.

VII. The very object of the contract: The arguments against the plaintiff's claim
22. Counsel for the surveyor advanced three separate arguments each of which he said was sufficient to defeat the plaintiff's claim. First, he submitted that even if a major or important part of the contract was to give pleasure, relaxation and peace of mind, that was not enough. It is an indispensable requirement that the object of the entire contract must be of this type. Secondly, he submitted that the exceptional category does not extend to a breach of a contractual duty of care, even if imposed to secure pleasure, relaxation and peace of mind. It only covers cases where the promiser guarantees achievement of such an object. Thirdly, he submitted that by not moving out of Riverside House the plaintiff forfeited any right to recover non-pecuniary damages.

23. The first argument fastened onto a narrow reading of the words "the very object of [the] contract" as employed by Bingham L.J. in *Watts v Morrow* [1991] 1WLR 1421, 1445. Cases where a major or important part of the contract was to secure pleasure, relaxation and peace of mind were not under consideration in *Watts v Morrow*. It is difficult to see what the principled justification for such a limitation might be. After all, in 1978 the Court of Appeal allowed such a claim in *Jackson v Chrysler Acceptances Ltd* [1978] RTR 474 in circumstances where a spoiled holiday was only one object of the contract. Counsel was, however, assisted by the decision of the Court of Appeal in *Knott v Bolton* (1995) 11 Const LJ 375 which in the present case the Court of Appeal treated as binding on it. In *Knott v Bolton* an architect was asked to design a wide staircase for a gallery and impressive entrance hall. He failed to do so. The plaintiff spent money in improving the staircase to some extent and he recovered the cost of the changes. The plaintiff also claimed damages for disappointment and distress in the lack of an impressive staircase. In agreement with the trial judge the Court of Appeal disallowed this part of his claim. Reliance was placed on the dicta of Bingham L.J. in *Watts v Morrow* [1991] 1 WLR 1421, 1445.

24. Interpreting the dicta of Bingham L.J. in *Watts v Morrow* narrowly the Court of Appeal in *Knott v Bolton* ruled that the central object of the contract was to design a house, not to provide pleasure to the occupiers of the house. It is important, however, to note that *Knott v Bolton* was decided a few months before the decision of the House in *Ruxley Electronics and Construction Ltd v Forsyth* [1996] AC 344. In any event, the technicality of the reasoning in *Knott v Bolton*, and therefore in the Court of Appeal judgments in the present case, is apparent. It is obvious, and conceded, that if an architect is employed only to design a staircase, or a surveyor is employed only to investigate aircraft noise, the breach of such a distinct obligation may result in an award of non-pecuniary damages. Logically the same must be the case if the architect or surveyor, apart from entering into a general retainer, concludes a separate contract, separately remunerated, in respect of the design of a staircase or the investigation of aircraft noise. If this is so the distinction drawn in *Knott v Bolton* and in the present case is a matter of form and not substance. David Capper, "Damages for Distress and Disappointment—The Limits of *Watts v Morrow*" (2000) 116 LQR 553, 556) has persuasively argued:

"A ruling that intangible interests only qualify for legal protection where they are the "very object of the contract" is tantamount to a ruling that contracts where these interests are merely important, but not the central object of the contract, are in part unenforceable. It is very difficult to see what policy objection there can be to parties to a contract agreeing that these interests are to be protected via contracts where the central object is something else. If the defendant is unwilling to accept this responsibility he or she can say so and either no contract will be made or one will be made but including a disclaimer."

There is no reason in principle or policy why the scope of recovery in the exceptional category should depend on the object of the contract as ascertained from all its constituent parts. It is sufficient if a major or important object of the contract is to give pleasure, relaxation or peace of mind. In my view *Knott v Bolton* 11 Const L.J. 375 was wrongly decided and should be overruled. To the extent that the majority in the Court of Appeal relied on *Knott v Bolton* their decision was wrong.

25. That brings me to the second issue, namely whether the plaintiff's claim is barred by reason of the fact that the surveyor undertook an obligation to exercise reasonable care and did not guarantee the achievement of a result. This was the basis upon which Hale L.J. after the first hearing in the Court of Appeal thought that the claim should be disallowed. This reasoning was adopted by the second Court of Appeal and formed an essential part of the reasoning of the majority. This was the basis on which they distinguished *Ruxley Electronics and Construction Ltd v Forsyth* [1996] AC 344. Against the broad sweep of differently framed contractual undertakings, and the central purpose of contract law in promoting the observance of contractual promises, I am satisfied that this distinction ought not to prevail. It is certainly not rooted in precedent. I would not accept the suggestion that it has the pedigree of an observation of Ralph Gibson L.J. in *Watts v Morrow* [1991] 1 WLR 1421, 1442B–D: his emphasis appears to have been on the fact that the contract did not serve to provide peace of mind, and so forth. As far as I am aware the distinction was first articulated in the present case. In any event, I would reject it. I fully accept, of course, that contractual guarantees of performance and promises to exercise reasonable care are fundamentally different. The former may sometimes give greater protection than the latter. Proving breach of an obligation of reasonable care may be more difficult than proving breach of a guarantee. On the other hand, a party may in practice be willing to settle for the relative reassurance offered by the obligation of reasonable care undertaken by a professional man. But why should this difference between an absolute and relative contractual promise require a distinction in respect of the recovery of non-pecuniary damages? Take the example of a travel agent who is consulted by a couple who are looking for a golfing holiday in France. Why should it make a difference in respect of the recoverability of non-pecuniary damages for a spoiled holiday whether the travel agent gives a guarantee that there is a golf course very near the hotel, represents that to be the case, or negligently advises that all hotels of the particular chain of hotels are situated next to golf courses? If the nearest golf course is in fact 50 miles away a breach may be established. It may spoil the holiday of the couple. It is difficult to see why in principle only those plaintiffs who negotiate guarantees may recover non-pecuniary damages for a breach of contract. It is a sing[u]larly unattractive result that a professional man, who undertakes a specific obligation to exercise reasonable care to investigate a matter judged and communicated to be important by his customer can in Lord Mustill's words in *Ruxley Electronics and Construction Ltd v Forsyth* [1996] AC 344, 360 "please himself whether or not to comply with the wishes of the promisee which, as embodied in the contract, formed part of the consideration for the price". If that were the law it would be seriously deficient. I am satisfied that it is not the law. In my view the distinction drawn by Hale L.J. and by the majority in the Court of Appeal between contractual guarantees and obligations of reasonable care is unsound.

26. The final argument was that by failing to move out the plaintiff forfeited a right to claim non-pecuniary damages. This argument was not advanced in the Court of Appeal. It will be recalled that the judge found as a fact that the plaintiff had acted reasonably in making "the best of a bad job". The plaintiff's decision also avoided a larger claim against the surveyor. It was never explained on what legal principle the plaintiff's decision not to move out divested him of a claim for non-pecuniary damages. Reference was made to a passage in the judgment of Bingham L.J. in *Watts v Morrow* [1991] 1 WLR 1421, 1445C. Examination showed, however, that the observation, speculative as it was, did not relate to the claim for non-pecuniary damages: see the criticism of Professor M. P. Furmston, "Damages—Diminution in Value or Cost of Repair?—Damages for Distress" (1993) 6 JCL 64, 65. The third argument must also be rejected.

27. While the dicta of Bingham L.J. are of continuing usefulness as a starting point, it will be necessary to read them subject to the three points on which I have rejected the submissions made on behalf of the surveyor.

VIII. Quantum

28. In the surveyor's written case it was submitted that the award of £10,000 was excessive. It was certainly high. Given that the plaintiff is stuck indefinitely with a position which he sought to avoid by the terms of his contract with the surveyor I am not prepared to interfere with the judge's evaluation on the special facts of the case. On the other hand, I have to say that the size of the award appears to be at the very top end of what could possibly be regarded as appropriate damages. Like Bingham L.J. in *Watts v Morrow* [1991] 1 WLR 1421, 1445H I consider that awards in this area should be restrained and modest. It is important that logical and beneficial developments in this corner of the law should not contribute to the creation of a society bent on litigation.

IX. Conclusion

29. In agreement with the reasoning of Clarke L.J. I would therefore hold that the decision of the majority in the Court of Appeal was wrong. I would also reject the subsidiary written argument of counsel for the surveyor that the plaintiff was not entitled to his costs at trial.

X. Inconvenience and discomfort

30. It is strictly unnecessary to discuss the question whether the judge's decision can be justified on the ground that the breach of contract resulted in inconvenience and discomfort. It is, however, appropriate that I indicate my view. The judge had a great deal of evidence on aircraft noise at Riverside House. It is conceded that noise can produce a physical reaction and can, depending on its intensity and the circumstances, constitute a nuisance. Noise from aircraft is exempted from the statutory nuisance system and in general no action lies in common law nuisance by reason only of the flight of aircraft over a property: see section 6(1) of the Civil Aviation Act 1982 and *McCracken, Jones, Pereira and Payne, Statutory Nuisance*, 2001, 10.33. The existence of the legislation shows that aircraft noise could arguably constitute a nuisance. In any event, aircraft noise is capable of causing inconvenience and discomfort within the meaning of Bingham L.J.'s relevant proposition. It is a matter of degree whether the case passes the threshold. It is sufficient to say that I have not been persuaded that the judge's decision on this point was not open to him on the evidence which he accepted. For this further reason, in general agreement with Clarke L.J., I would rule that the decision of the Court of Appeal was wrong.

XI. Disposal

31. I would allow the appeal and restore the judge's decision.

LORD SCOTT OF FOSCOTE

My Lords,

62. This is a case with simple facts, a short question and, in my respectful opinion, a simple answer. [Having summarised the facts, Lord Scott continued] . . .

73. . . . The issue on appeal was whether, in law, Mr Farley was entitled to contractual damages for impairment of his enjoyment of Riverside House. My noble and learned friend, Lord Steyn, has described the course of proceedings in the Court of Appeal and it suffices for me to say that two Lords Justices held that he was, three held that he was not, and it is now for your Lordships to resolve the issue.

74. The reason why such an apparently straightforward issue has caused such division of opinion is because it has been represented as raising the question whether and when contractual damages for mental distress are available. It is highly desirable that your Lordships should resolve the present angst on this subject and avoid the need in the future for relatively simple claims, such as Mr Farley's, to have to travel to the appellate courts for a ruling.

75. In my opinion, the issue can and should be resolved by applying the well known principles laid down in *Hadley v Baxendale* (1854) 9 Exch 341 (as restated in *Victoria Laundry Ltd v Newman Industries Ltd* [1949] 2 KB 528) in the light of the recent guidance provided by Bingham L.J. in *Watts v Morrow* [1991] 1 WLR 1421 and by this House in *Ruxley Electronics and Construction Ltd v Forsyth* [1996] AC 344.

76. The basic principle of damages for breach of contract is that the injured party is entitled, so far as money can do it, to be put in the position he would have been in if the contractual obligation had been properly performed. He is entitled, that is to say, to the benefit of his bargain: see *Robinson v Harman* (1848) 1 Exch 850, 855.

77. In *Ruxley Electronics and Construction Ltd v Forsyth* [1996] AC 344 builders had agreed to construct a swimming pool with a diving area 7 feet 6 inches deep. The pool when constructed had a depth of only

6 feet. The cost of rebuilding the pool to the contractual depth would have been £21,560. But the trial judge, having heard the evidence, concluded that the pool owner did not have the intention of using the damages to reconstruct the pool. He found also that the residential property of which the pool formed part had suffered no diminution in value by reason of the lack of one foot of depth in the pool's diving area. Nonetheless the pool owner claimed the £21,500 as damages. The builders, on the other hand, contended that, on the facts as found, the pool owner had suffered no loss and the damages should be nil. The trial judge accepted neither contention but instead awarded the £2,500 expressed as compensation for "a loss of amenity brought about by the shortfall in depth" (see at p 363). The Court of Appeal [1994] 1 WLR 650 set aside the £2,500 award and substituted an award of the cost of rebuilding, ie the £21,560. This House restored the trial judge's order.

78. Lord Mustill [1996] AC 344, 360 referred to situations where, in the carrying out of building works on residential property, there had been minor deviations from the contractual specifications but where the deviations had not reduced the value of the property below the value it would have had if the work had been properly carried out. He went on:

"Yet the householder must surely be entitled to say that he chose to obtain from the builder a promise to produce a particular result because he wanted to make his house more comfortable, more convenient and more conformable to his own particular tastes; not because he had in mind that the work might increase the amount which he would receive if, contrary to expectation, he thought it expedient in the future to exchange his home for cash. To say that in order to escape unscathed the builder has only to show that to the mind of the average onlooker, or the average potential buyer, the results which he has produced seem just as good as those which he had promised would make a part of the promise illusory, and unbalance the bargain. In the valuable analysis contained in *Radford v De Froberville* [1977] 1 WLR 1262, Oliver J. emphasised, at p 1270, that it was for the plaintiff to judge what performance he required in exchange for the price. The court should honour that choice. Pacta sunt servanda. If the plaintiff's argument leads to the conclusion that in all cases like the present the employer is entitled to no more than nominal damages, the average householder would say that there must be something wrong with the law."

Lord Lloyd of Berwick, to the same effect, said, at p 374:

"What is then to be the position where, in the case of a new house, the building does not conform in some minor respect to the contract, as, for example, where there is a difference in level between two rooms, necessitating a step. Suppose there is no measurable difference in value of the complete house, and the cost of reinstatement would be prohibitive. Is there any reason why the court should not award by way of damages for breach of contract some modest sum, not based on difference in value, but solely to compensate the buyer for his disappointed expectations? Is the law of damages so inflexible . . . that it cannot find some middle ground in such a case? I do not give a final answer to that question in the present case. But it may be it would have afforded an alternative ground for justifying the judge's award of damages."

79. *Ruxley's* case establishes, in my opinion, that if a party's contractual performance has failed to provide to the other contracting party something to which that other was, under the contract, entitled, and which, if provided, would have been of value to that party, then, if there is no other way of compensating the injured party, the injured party should be compensated in damages to the extent of that value. Quantification of that value will, in many cases be difficult and may often seem arbitrary. In *Ruxley's* case the value placed on the amenity value of which the pool owner had been deprived was £2,500. By that award, the pool owner was placed, so far as money could do it, in the position he would have been in if the diving area of the pool had been constructed to the specified depth.

80. In *Ruxley's* case the breach of contract by the builders had not caused any consequential loss to the pool owner. He had simply been deprived of the benefit of a pool built to the depth specified in the contract. It was not a case where the recovery of damages for consequential loss consisting of vexation, anxiety or other species of mental distress had to be considered.

81. In *Watts v Morrow* [1991] 1 WLR 1921, however, that matter did have to be considered. As in the present case, the litigation in *Watts v Morrow* resulted from a surveyor's report. The report had negligently failed to disclose a number of defects in the property. The clients, who had purchased the property in reliance on the report, remedied the defects and sued for damages. The judge awarded them the costs of the repairs and also general damages of £4,000 each for "distress and inconvenience" (p 1424). As to the cost of repairs, the Court of Appeal substituted an award of damages based on the difference between the value of the property as the surveyor's report had represented it to be and the value as it actually was. Nothing, for present purposes, turns on that. As to the damages for "distress and inconvenience" the Court of Appeal

upheld the award in principle but held that the damages should be limited to a modest sum for the physical discomfort endured and reduced the award to £750 for each plaintiff. Bingham L.J., at p 1445, in an important passage, set out the principles to be applied where contractual damages for distress and inconvenience are claimed:

"A contract-breaker is not in general liable for any distress, frustration, anxiety, displeasure, vexation, tension or aggravation which his breach of contract may cause to the innocent party. This rule is not, I think, founded on the assumption that such reactions are not foreseeable, which they surely are or may be, but on considerations of policy.

But the rule is not absolute. Where the very object of a contract is to provide pleasure, relaxation, peace of mind or freedom from molestation, damages will be awarded if the fruit of the contract is not provided or if the contrary result is procured instead. If the law did not cater for this exceptional category of case it would be defective. A contract to survey the condition of a house for a prospective purchaser does not, however, fall within this exceptional category.

In cases not falling within this exceptional category, damages are in my view recoverable for physical inconvenience and discomfort caused by the breach and mental suffering directly related to that inconvenience and discomfort."

82. In the passage I have cited, Bingham L.J. was dealing with claims for consequential damage consisting of the intangible mental states and sensory experiences to which he refers. Save for the matters referred in the first paragraph, all of which reflect or are brought about by the injured party's disappointment at the contract breaker's failure to carry out his contractual obligations, and recovery for which, if there is nothing more, is ruled out on policy grounds, Bingham L.J.'s approach is, in my view, wholly consistent with established principles for the recovery of contractual damages.

83. There are, however, two qualifications that I would respectfully make to the proposition in the final paragraph of the cited passage that damages "for physical inconvenience and discomfort caused by the breach" are recoverable.

84. First, there will, in many cases, be an additional remoteness hurdle for the injured party to clear. Consequential damage, including damage consisting of inconvenience or discomfort, must, in order to be recoverable, be such as, at the time of the contract, was reasonably foreseeable as liable to result from the breach: see *McGregor on Damages*, 16th ed (1997), para 250, pp 159–160.

85. Second, the adjective "physical", in the phrase "physical inconvenience and discomfort", requires, I think, some explanation or definition. The distinction between the "physical" and the "non-physical" is not always clear and may depend on the context. Is being awoken at night by aircraft noise "physical"? If it is, is being unable to sleep because of worry and anxiety "physical"? What about a reduction in light caused by the erection of a building under a planning permission that an errant surveyor ought to have warned his purchaser-client about but failed to do so? In my opinion, the critical distinction to be drawn is not a distinction between the different types of inconvenience or discomfort of which complaint may be made but a distinction based on the cause of the inconvenience or discomfort. If the cause is no more than disappointment that the contractual obligation has been broken, damages are not recoverable even if the disappointment has led to a complete mental breakdown. But, if the cause of the inconvenience or discomfort is a sensory (sight, touch, hearing, smell etc) experience, damages can, subject to the remoteness rules, be recovered.

86. In summary, the principle expressed in *Ruxley Electronics and Construction Ltd v Forsyth* [1996] AC 344 should be used to provide damages for deprivation of a contractual benefit where it is apparent that the injured party has been deprived of something of value but the ordinary means of measuring the recoverable damages are inapplicable. The principle expressed in *Watts v Morrow* [1991] 1 WLR 1421 should be used to determine whether and when contractual damages for inconvenience or discomfort can be recovered.

87. These principles, in my opinion, provide the answer, not only to the issue raised in the present case, but also to the issues raised in the authorities which were cited to your Lordships.

88. In *Hobbs v London and South Western Railway Co* (1875) LR 10 QB 111 the claim was for consequential damage caused by the railway company's breach of contract. Instead of taking the plaintiff, his wife and two children to Hampton Court, their train dumped them at Esher and they had to walk five miles or so home in the rain. The plaintiff's wife caught a cold as a result of the experience. The plaintiff was awarded damages for the inconvenience and discomfort of his and his family's walk home but his wife's cold was held to be too remote a consequence. The plaintiff's recovery of damages attributable, in part, to the discomfort suffered

by his wife and children was in accordance with principle. The contractual benefit to which he was entitled was the carriage of himself and his family to Hampton Court. It was reasonable in my opinion, to value that benefit, of which he had been deprived by the breach of contract, by reference to the discomfort to the family of the walk home. This was, in my view, a *Ruxley Electronics and Construction Ltd v Forsyth* [1996] AC 344 case.

89. *Jarvis v Swans Tours Ltd* [1973] QB 233 was a case in which the plaintiff had contracted for a holiday with certain enjoyable qualities. He had been given a holiday which lacked those qualities. His holiday had caused him discomfort and distress. The trial judge awarded him £31.72, one half of the price of the holiday. This must, I think have been the value attributed by the judge to the contractual benefit of which the plaintiff had been deprived. But on the plaintiff's appeal against so low an award, the Court of Appeal allowed him £125.

90. Somewhat different reasons were given by the three members of the court. Lord Denning M.R. said, at pp 237–238:

"In a proper case damages for mental distress can be recovered in contract . . . One such case is a contract for a holiday, or any other contract to provide entertainment and enjoyment. If the contracting party breaks his contract, damages can be given for the disappointment, the distress, the upset and frustration caused by the breach."

The reference in this passage to the "contract for a holiday, or any other contract to provide entertainment and enjoyment" is consistent with an intention to compensate the plaintiff for the contractual benefit of which he had been deprived. The reference, however, to "the disappointment, the distress . . ." etc reads like a reference to consequential damage.

91. Edmund Davies L.J. based his decision on the defendant's failure to provide a holiday of the contractual quality". He held that the amount of damages was not limited by the price for the holiday. He said, at p 239:

"The court is entitled, and indeed bound, to contrast the overall quality of the holiday so enticingly promised with that which the defendants in fact provided."

He regarded the plaintiff's vexation and disappointment as relevant matters to take into account in "determining what would be proper compensation for the defendants' marked failure to fulfil their undertaking". This was a *Ruxley Electronics and Construction Ltd v Forsyth* [1996] AC 344 approach. Stephenson L.J., at p 240, based his decision on the "reasonable contemplation of the parties . . . as a likely result of [the holiday contract] being so broken". He said, at pp 240–241, that where there are contracts "in which the parties contemplate inconvenience on breach which may be described as mental: frustration, annoyance, disappointment . . ." damages for breach should take that inconvenience into account. This was a *Watts v Morrow* [1991] 1 WLR 1421 approach.

92. *Jackson v Horizon Holidays Ltd* [1975] 1 WLR 1468 was a case brought by another disappointed holiday-maker. He had booked a holiday for himself, his wife and children. Its quality turned out to be substantially below contractually justified expectations. The plaintiff recovered £1,100 damages as compensation not only for his own discomfort but also for the discomfort experienced by his wife and children. In my opinion, the justification for such an award is that the plaintiff was entitled to be compensated for the value of the contracted benefit of which he had been deprived. This case, like *Jarvis v Swans Tours Ltd,* [1973] QB 233, 239 per Edmund Davies L.J., and like *Hobbs v London and South Western Railway Co* LR 10 QB 111 is a *Ruxley Electronics and Construction Ltd v Forsyth* [1996] AC 344 type of case.

93. *Knott v Bolton* 11 Const LJ 375 is, in my opinion, inconsistent with *Ruxley's* case and should now be regarded as having been wrongly decided. The plaintiffs had been deprived of the wide staircase and gallery and baronial entrance hall to which they were contractually entitled and had to put up with lesser facilities. A value should, in my opinion, have been placed on the benefit of which they had been deprived.

94. In *Heywood v Wellers* [1976] QB 446 a firm of solicitors was sued for failure to provide adequate legal services to the plaintiff in connection with proceedings to protect her from molestation by an ex boyfriend. The failure had the result that the plaintiff continued to suffer molestation. She was awarded damages as compensation for the vexation, anxiety and distress that the continuing molestation had caused her. This, in my opinion, is a clear example of compensation for consequential loss within the reasonable contemplation of the parties at the time of the contract as liable to be caused by the solicitors' failure to deal properly with the anti-molestation proceedings.

95. Contrast *Cook v S* [1967] 1 All ER 299 and *Hayes v James & Charles Dodd* [1990] 2 All ER 815, both

solicitors' negligence cases where it was claimed that the solicitors' failure to provide the services to which the plaintiffs had been contractually entitled had caused the plaintiffs anguish, distress and vexation.

96. In *Cook v S* Lord Denning M.R. said, at p 302:

"if anything goes [wrong] with the litigation owing to the solicitor's negligence . . . [it] can be foreseen that there will be injured feelings; mental distress; anger and annoyance. But for none of these can damages be recovered."

As Bingham L.J. pointed out in *Watts v Morrow* [1991] 1 WLR 1421, 1445, these damages are ruled out on public policy grounds.

97. In *Hayes v James & Charles Dodd* Staughton L.J. said, at p 824, that contractual damages for mental distress were, as a matter of policy limited to certain classes of case and that the classes—

"should not . . . include any case where the object of the contract was not comfort or pleasure, or the relief [from] discomfort, but simply carrying on a commercial activity with a view to profit."

So he disallowed the claim for damages for anguish and vexation.

98. In my opinion, the distinction between commercial contracts and other contracts is too imprecise to be satisfactory. I think the decision of Staughton L.J. was plainly correct for the reason that the commercial character of the contract required a negative answer to the question whether the anguish and vexation caused by the breach and for which recovery was sought was within the reasonable contemplation of the parties at the time of the contract (see also Lord Reid's point in *C Czarnikow Ltd v Koufos* [1969] 1 AC 350, 383 that the loss in question should, to be recoverable, be "not very unusual and easily foreseeable").

99. In *Perry v Sydney Phillips & Son* [1982] 1 WLR 1297, contractual damages for distress and discomfort caused to the plaintiff by having to live for a while in a house with a leaking roof and defective drains were awarded as compensation for a surveyor's negligent failure to draw attention to these defects in his report. The Court of Appeal adopted a foreseeability approach.

100. In *R v Investors Compensation Scheme Ex parte Bowden* [1994] 1 WLR 17, 28 decided after *Watts v Morrow* [1991] 1 WLR 1421 had been reported, Mann L.J. said this:

"Unless the very object of the contract is as stated by Bingham L.J. [at p 1445], then a contract breaker is not liable to compensate for mental and physical distress consequent upon his breach of contract."

101. This statement is not, in my opinion, accurate. It concentrates only on the first part and ignores the second part of Bingham L.J.'s proposition. I agree with Mann L.J. that a contract relating to the investment of money is not such a contract as Bingham L.J. had in mind as a contract "the very object" of which is to provide pleasure etc. But if a breach of any contract has caused physical inconvenience or discomfort that is within the recognised rules of remoteness and mental distress is a part of that inconvenience or discomfort, it would, in my opinion, in principle be recoverable.

102. Mr Simpson referred to *Johnson v Gore Wood & Co* [2001] 2 WLR 72, which he said was indistinguishable from the present case. The case raised a number of difficult issues which have nothing whatever to do with the present case but the case did involve also a claim for damages for mental distress caused by solicitors' negligence. The alleged negligence was the solicitors' failure to advise Mr Johnson, the client, about various financial matters. Mr Johnson claimed, among other heads of damage, damages "for the mental distress and anxiety which he has suffered" as a result of the alleged negligence. Lord Bingham of Cornhill cited, at p 96, the first two paragraphs of the passage from his own judgment in *Watts v Morrow* [1991] 1 WLR 1421, 1445 that I have cited at paragraph 20 above. He referred to *Ruxley Electronics and Construction Ltd v Forsyth* [1996] AC 344 and said, at p 97:

"It is undoubtedly true that many breaches of contract cause intense frustration and anxiety to the innocent party."

103. He did not, however, think that Mr Johnson's claim for damages for mental distress and anxiety came within the established principles for the recovery of such damages.

104. The decision in *Johnson v Gore Wood & Co* [2001] 2 WLR 72 is, in my view, plainly distinguishable from the present. It was not, in my view, remotely arguable that Mr Johnson's alleged mental distress was a consequence that, at the time he retained the solicitors, was reasonably in the contemplation of the parties as liable to result from a breach.

105. It is time for me to turn to the present case and apply the principles expressed in *Ruxley Electronics and*

Construction Ltd v Forsyth [1996] AC 344 and *Watts v Morrow* [1991] 1 WLR 1421. In my judgment, Mr Farley is entitled to be compensated for the "real discomfort" that the judge found he suffered. He is so entitled on either of two alternative bases.

106. First, he was deprived of the contractual benefit to which he was entitled. He was entitled to information about the aircraft noise from Gatwick bound aircraft that Mr Skinner, through negligence, had failed to supply him with. If Mr Farley had, in the event, decided not to purchase Riverside House, the value to him of the contractual benefit of which he had been deprived would have been nil. But he did buy the property. And he took his decision to do so without the advantage of being able to take into account the information to which he was contractually entitled. If he had had that information he would not have bought. So the information clearly would have had a value to him. Prima facie, in my opinion, he is entitled to be compensated accordingly.

107. In these circumstances, it seems to me, it is open to the court to adopt a *Ruxley Electronics and Construction Ltd v Forsyth* [1996] AC 344 approach and place a value on the contractual benefit of which Mr Farley has been deprived. In deciding on the amount, the discomfort experienced by Mr Farley can, in my view, properly be taken into account. If he had had the aircraft noise information he would not have bought Riverside House and would not have had that discomfort.

108. Alternatively, Mr Farley can, in my opinion, claim compensation for the discomfort as consequential loss. Had it not been for the breach of contract, he would not have suffered the discomfort. It was caused by the breach of contract in a causa sine qua non sense. Was the discomfort a consequence that should reasonably have been contemplated by the parties at the time of contract as liable to result from the breach? In my opinion, it was. It was obviously within the reasonable contemplation of the parties that, deprived of the information about aircraft noise that he ought to have had, Mr Farley would make a decision to purchase that he would not otherwise have made. Having purchased, he would, having become aware of the noise, either sell—in which case at least the expenses of the re-sale would have been recoverable as damages—or he would keep the property and put up with the noise. In the latter event, it was within the reasonable contemplation of the parties that he would experience discomfort from the noise of the aircraft. And the discomfort was "physical" in the sense that Bingham L.J. in *Watts v Morrow* [1991] 1 WLR 1421, 1445 had in mind. In my opinion, the application of *Watts v Morrow* principles entitles Mr Farley to damages for discomfort caused by the aircraft noise.

109. I would add that if there had been an appreciable reduction in the market value of the property caused by the aircraft noise, Mr Farley could not have recovered both that difference in value and damages for discomfort. To allow both would allow double recovery for the same item.

110. Whether the approach to damages is on *Ruxley Electronics and Construction Ltd v Forsyth* [1996] AC 344 lines, for deprivation of a contractual benefit, or on *Watts v Morrow* [1991] 1 WLR 1421 lines, for consequential damage within the applicable remoteness rules, the appropriate amount should, in my opinion, be modest. The degree of discomfort experienced by Mr Farley, although "real", was not very great. I think £10,000 may have been on the high side. But in principle, in my opinion, the judge was right to award damages and I am not, in the circumstances, disposed to disagree with his figure.

111. For the reasons I have given and for the reasons contained in the opinion of my noble and learned friend, Lord Steyn, I would allow the appeal and restore the judge's order.

Question

Consider the facts of *Hamilton Jones v David & Snape (A Firm)* [2003] EWHC 3147, Ch. There, the contract was between the claimant, who feared that her husband might try to remove their children from the jurisdiction, and the defendant solicitors. The claimant's worst fears were realised when, as a result of the solicitors' negligence, the husband was able to take the children to Tunisia where he was awarded custody. Was this contract sufficiently for the claimant's peace of mind to qualify as one falling under the *Farley* principles?

19-025

----

3. Causation and Contribution

A. The Negligent Valuation Cases

19-026   In a clutch of cases involving the negligent valuation of property that stands as security for a loan, the courts have grappled with some complex issues concerning the extent of the valuers' liability. For example, in the Bank Bruxelles litigation, reported as *South Australia Asset Management Corporation v York Montague Ltd* [1997] A.C. 191, a loan of £11m was advanced on a property that was valued at £15m. However, the valuation was negligently carried out, the property having an actual value of only £5m. Provided that the borrower repaid the loan, the negligent overvaluation would cause no loss to the lenders; but, if the borrower defaulted and if the security needed to be realised, the lenders would suffer a loss. Where the lenders suffer such a loss, the so-called basic loss of the lender needs to be assessed. Essentially, this involves a calculation that compares (a) what the lender's position would have been if the valuers had fulfilled their duty of care with (b) what the lender's position actually is (see Lord Nicholls in *Nykredit Mortgage Bank Plc v Edward Erdman (No.2)* [1997] 1 W.L.R. 1627 at 1631). In the negligent valuation jurisprudence, however, two complications tend to arise. First, the effect of the overvaluation is exacerbated by a fall in property values—for example, in *South Australia Asset Management Corporation*, the property was sold for just under half its actual value at the time of the loan. Secondly, the lender might have contributed to the loss by failing to exercise due care in checking the loan application or due caution in its general lending policy.

With regard to the first of these complications, it was decided in *South Australia Asset Management Corporation* that the scope of the valuers' liability should be limited to the extent of the negligent overvaluation. This means that where the lender's basic loss is less than the amount of the negligent overvaluation, the lender will recover its loss in full. However, where the lender's basic loss exceeds the amount of the negligent overvaluation, the lender will recover its losses only up to the level indicated by the amount of the negligent overvaluation. Some refer to this as the SAAMCO cap.

Turning to the second complication, where the lender has been careless, there is a nice question as to whether any reduction for contributory negligence should be made against the lender's basic loss or the lender's loss as limited by the SAAMCO cap. Where the lender's basic loss falls within the amount of the negligent overvaluation, so that the SAAMCO cap is not going to come into play, it seems obvious that the reduction should be applied to the lender's basic loss. However, where the lender's basic loss exceeds the amount of the negligent overvaluation, so that the SAAMCO cap is in play, it is not clear whether the reduction should be applied to the amount of the lender's basic loss or to the amount of recoverable loss set by the SAAMCO cap. In *Platform Home Loans Ltd v Oyston Shipways Ltd* [2000] 2 A.C. 190, below, the majority of the House of Lords held that the reduction for the lender's contributory negligence should be set against the basic loss.

PLATFORM HOME LOANS LTD v OYSTON SHIPWAYS LTD

House of Lords [2000] 2 A.C. 190

LORD MILLETT

19-027   My Lords,
In 1990 the appellant advanced £1,050,000 on the security of land valued by the respondents at £1,500,000. The advance represented 70 per cent. of valuation. The judge found that the land had been negligently overvalued, and that the true value of the land at the date of the advance was only £1,000,000. In 1994, following a catastrophic collapse of the property market, the appellant realised its security for £435,000, thereby

incurring a loss of £615,000. After taking into account interest paid by the appellant and payments received from the borrower together with a sum of £40,000 which the appellant conceded was deductible because of a failure on its part to mitigate its loss, the overall loss on the transaction amounted to £611,748. The amount of the overvaluation (£500,000) was less than this, and accordingly this latter sum would have represented the amount of damages recoverable by the appellant in the absence of contributory negligence on its part: see *South Australia Asset Management Corporation v York Montague Ltd* [1997] A.C. 191 and *Nykredit Mortgage Bank Plc v Edward Erdman Group Ltd (No. 2)* [1997] 1 W.L.R. 1627 ("Nykredit").

The judge made two findings of contributory negligence. He found that the appellant was negligent in making the loan without having obtained from the borrower information required by its own form. The judge also found that the appellant was imprudent in advancing as much as 70 per cent. of valuation. He did not make any finding on the amount which a prudent mortgage lender would have advanced, whether 65 per cent. or 60 per cent. of valuation, but he expressed himself in terms which showed that, of the two items of contributory negligence, he considered the overlending to be much the more potent cause of loss.

Having found that the appellant had itself contributed to the loss, the judge applied a broad brush to the assessment of damages. Taking both findings of contributory negligence together, he assessed their combined contribution to the loss at 20 per cent. There is no appeal from this assessment, though it is to be observed that, in respect of the second and more serious finding of contributory negligence, there was no need to apply a broad brush; the consequences of advancing too high a proportion of valuation can be precisely calculated. 5 per cent. of £1.500,000 is £75,000; for every 5 per cent. of valuation which the appellant advanced in excess of what was prudent it increased its loss by that amount.

Having thus found that 20 per cent. of the loss or damage (£611,748) which the appellant had suffered as a result of the transaction was the result of its own fault, the judge awarded damages of £489,398. This figure represented 80 per cent. of £611,748 and, being less than the amount of the overvaluation, represented a loss which was entirely within the scope of the respondents' duty of care.

The Court of Appeal rejected the appellant's argument that no imprudence in their lending policy could constitute contributory negligence, and held that the judge was entitled to find that the appellant was partly responsible for the overall loss of £611,748 which it had incurred on the transaction. It accepted the judge's assessment of the contribution which the appellant's own negligence made to the loss at 20 per cent. and held that he was entitled to apportion the damages accordingly. But it varied the order made by the judge. Instead of awarding the appellant damages of £489,398, representing the 80 per cent. of the overall loss of £611,748 which was not attributable to its own fault, as the judge had done, it reduced the award to £400,000, being 80 per cent. of the respondents' overvaluation of £500,000. The remarkable consequence is that, if the award stands, the appellant will bear more than one third of a loss for which it was only 20 per cent. to blame.

It is necessary to recapitulate what this House has laid down in relation to the assessment of damages in cases of the present kind. Two calculations are required. The first is a calculation of the loss incurred by the lender as a result of having entered into the transaction. This is an exercise in causation. The main component in the calculation is the difference between the amount of the loan and the amount realised by enforcing the security.

The second calculation has nothing to do with questions of causation: see *Nykredit* at p. 1638 *per* Lord Hoffmann. It is designed to ascertain the maximum amount of loss capable of falling within the valuer's duty of care. The resulting figure is the difference between the negligent valuation and the true value of the property at the date of valuation. The recoverable damages are limited to the lesser of the amounts produced by the two calculations.

It is to be observed that neither amount is an element or component of the other. Either may be the greater, for they are the results of completely different calculations. In mathematical terms, they bear the same relationship to each other as $a-b$ does to $c-d$. The figure produced by the second calculation is simply the amount of the overvaluation. It is not the loss or any part of it, and cannot be equated with the amount of the loss sustained by the lender in consequence of the overvaluation. The two are the same only in a case where the lender has advanced 100 per cent. of valuation.

Section 1(1) of the Law Reform (Contributory Negligence) Act 1945 applies "where any person suffers damage as the result partly of his own fault and partly of the fault of another". The appellant submits that, as a result of the respondents' negligent overvaluation, it suffered damage of £500,000, and that it is inappropriate to reduce the damages in order to reflect fault on its part which played no part in their breach of duty.

Now if the premise were correct, viz. that the £500,000 represented all or any part of the damage suffered by the appellant, then the conclusion would follow. But, as I have already pointed out, it is not correct. The £500,000 is merely the amount of the overvaluation. The damage which the appellant suffered as a result of the transaction which they entered into in consequence of the overvaluation is not £500,000 but £611,748. This is the damage referred to in section 1(1). This damage was due to the insufficiency of the security. The sufficiency of any security, however, depends on a combination of two factors: the value of the security and the amount of the advance. If the respondents had given a lower valuation, or if the appellant had lent a lower proportion of valuation, then in either case the appellant's loss would have been less. Accordingly, the loss of £611,748 which the appellant suffered was partly as a result of its own fault and partly of the fault of the respondents within the meaning of section 1(1) of the Act.

Where the subsection applies, "the damages recoverable in respect" of that damage are to be reduced "to such extent as the court thinks just and equitable having regard to the claimant's share in the responsibility for the damage." In the present case, the damage in question was £611,748, the appellant's share in the responsibility for that damage was 20 per cent., and the damages which would have been recoverable if there had been no contributory negligence would have been £500,000. The Court of Appeal seem to have assumed that, if the appellant was 20 per cent. responsible for the damage of £611,748, it must be just and equitable to reduce the amount of the damages that would otherwise be recoverable to the same extent. Normally, no doubt, that is so; but then normally the amount of the damages which would otherwise be recoverable and the amount of the damage are the same. But in the present case this ignores the fact that the result of the appellant's own imprudence has been to cause it to suffer a measure of irrecoverable loss. This ought to be reflected in the apportionment of the overall loss. Deeper analysis shows that it may be appropriate to do this by first reducing the amount of the irrecoverable damages until they are exhausted, and only then reducing the amount of the recoverable damages.

As I have already pointed out, 5 per cent. of £1,500,000 is £75,000. It follows that if a prudent lender would have advanced only 65 per cent. of valuation instead of 70 per cent., it would have suffered a loss of (£611,748–75,000) = £536,748, and would have recovered damages of £500,000. It cannot be right to award damages of £500,000 to a lender who prudently lends 65 per cent. of valuation and yet reduce the damages to £425,000 to a lender because he has imprudently lent more than 65 per cent. of valuation. It is sufficient that he should bear the whole of the additional loss of £75,000 himself. Likewise, it cannot be right to award damages of (£611,748–150,000) = £461,748 to a lender who has prudently lent only 60 per cent. of valuation and yet reduce the damages to £350,000 to a lender because he has imprudently lent more than 60 per cent. of valuation. In each case the lender has lent too much and he must bear the whole of the resulting additional loss himself. This may result in his suffering a reduction in the amount of the damages which can be recovered from the valuer, but it need not do so.

Where the lender's negligence has caused or contributed directly to the overvaluation, then it may be appropriate to apply the reduction to the amount of the overvaluation as well to the overall loss. Where, however, the lender's imprudence was partly responsible for the overall loss but did not cause or contribute to the overvaluation, it is the overall loss alone which should be reduced, possibly but not necessarily leading to a consequential reduction in the damages. When the consequences of the lender's imprudence cannot be calculated, the judge will have to do the best he can to assess the parties' respective contributions. But the court should not speculate when it can calculate.

In the present case the appellant was found to be at fault in two respects. Neither of them caused or contributed to the overvaluation. The judge assessed the appellant's share in the responsibility for the overall damage at 20 per cent. and reduced the damages to £489,398 accordingly. In my opinion this was the right approach. The amount of damages which the judge awarded properly reflected the 80 per cent. of the overall loss for which the respondents have been found to be responsible and which, being less than the amount of the overvaluation, fell wholly within the scope of their duty of care.

I would allow the appeal and restore the award of damages made by the judge.

B. Supervening Events

BEOCO LTD v ALFA LAVAL CO LTD AND ANOTHER

Court of Appeal [1994] 4 All E.R. 464

19–028   Alfa (A) installed a heat exchanger in Beoco (B)'s factory. Twenty months later on August 24, 1988 the exchanger was found to be cracked. B employed the second defendant (X) to repair the defect. The repair was only partially successful and the exchanger failed a pressure test. B nevertheless put it back into use without an inspection, which would have revealed that it was defective. Two months later it exploded causing damage to B's plant and loss of production.

Chadwick J held that (i) A was liable for breach of warranty because the exchanger had defects which were latent until the cracks appeared; (ii) X was liable for breach of contract in failing to repair it properly; but (iii) the cause of the explosion was B's recklessness in failing to carry out the proper tests to ascertain that the repair had been successful. He gave judgment against A for damages, to be assessed, for the loss which B would have incurred in replacing or repairing the exchanger if the explosion had not occurred. The first ground of appeal concerned the pleadings in the case.

STUART-SMITH LJ

The second ground of appeal raises an interesting point of law upon which there does not appear to be any authority directly in point. Can the plaintiff recover damages which he would have incurred by way of loss of profit on lost production during the period necessary to repair the defect in goods or materials supplied by the defendant and caused by his breach of contract, where because of some supervening event those repairs are not carried out or are subsumed in other more extensive repairs?

The supervening event in this case was the negligence of the plaintiff's engineers, who when they discovered the hitherto latent defect in the heat exchanger, put it back into service without making proper tests to see that the repair had been correctly carried out, in circumstances where they knew of the risk of explosion if it was not. But the supervening event might equally have been caused by the breach of contract or negligence of the second defendant, if it had been responsible for making all proper tests before the heat exchanger was put back into service; or it may have been some extraneous event, like a fire in the factory for which no one could be held to blame.

It is common ground in this case that the first defendant is liable for the cost of making good the defective casing of the heat exchanger. This is because what was damaged in the explosion was not a sound heat exchanger with 18 years' life in it, but a defective one with much less. The plaintiff's loss caused by the explosion was therefore much less than it would otherwise have been. And it could have recovered from its insurers, or the second defendant as the case may be, only the value of the defective heat exchanger.

Mr Knight submits that the same principle should apply to the loss of profit which could have resulted during the time taken to make good the defect. The cause of action for damages for breach of contract arises at the time of the breach, even though this may not be quantifiable until later. On 24 August 1988, therefore, the plaintiff had a claim against the defendant for breach of contract, the measure of which was the cost of repair and the as yet unquantified claim for lost profit. It is immaterial, he submits, that that loss was never in fact incurred or quantified because of the explosion.

Although there do not appear to be any cases in contract, there are a number of authorities in tort which bear upon the point.

[Having examined the authorities in the law of tort, Stuart-Smith L.J. held that the same principles applied in contract and that the question he posed in the first paragraph, above, should be answered in the negative.]

Peter Gibson and Balcombe L.JJ. agreed.

Appeal Allowed.

C. Contributory Negligence

BARCLAYS BANK Plc v FAIRCLOUGH BUILDING LTD

Court of Appeal [1995] Q.B. 214; [1995] 1 All E.R. 289

The defendant (F) contracted with the plaintiff (B) to carry out work on B's premises, including the cleaning of roofs. In breach of an express term that F would execute the work in an expeditious, efficient and workmanlike manner, F's sub-contractor caused the premises to become contaminated with asbestos, requiring remedial work costing £4 million. B owed a duty to its employees to prevent

19–029

the premises becoming contaminated. B's safety officer and architect failed to take steps to prevent the contamination. F relied on the Contributory Negligence Act 1945. The judge found that F was the party primarily at fault; the fault of B was a failure to prevent F from committing that fault; and he reduced B's damages by 40 per cent. B appealed.

BELDAM LJ

Section 4 of the 1945 Act defines "fault" as follows:

> "'fault' means negligence, breach of statutory duty or other act or omission which gives rise to a liability in tort or would, apart from this Act, give rise to the defence of contributory negligence."

It is generally agreed that the first part of the definition relates to the defendant's fault and the second part to the plaintiff's but debate has focused on the words "or other act or omission which gives rise to a liability in tort" in the first part and "other act or omission which . . . would, apart from this Act, give rise to the defence of contributory negligence" in the second part. It has been argued that, merely because the plaintiff frames his cause of action as a breach of contract, if the acts or omissions on which he relies could equally well give rise to a liability in tort, the defendant is entitled to rely on the defence of contributory negligence. Examples frequently cited are claims for damages against an employer or by a passenger against a railway or bus company where the plaintiff may frame his action either in tort or in contract and the duty relied on in either case is a duty to take reasonable care for the plaintiff's safety.

Contributory negligence has been a defence in such actions for many years. So it is argued that in all cases in which the contractual duty broken by a defendant is the same as and is co-extensive with a similar duty in tort, the defendant may now rely upon the defence. An opposing view based upon the second part of the definition is that if the plaintiff framed his action for breach of contract, contributory negligence at common law was never regarded as a defence to his claim and so cannot be relied on under the 1945 Act.

Under the first part of the definition, if the plaintiff claims damages for breach of a contractual term which does not correspond with a duty in tort to take reasonable care, the defendant's acts or omissions would not give rise to a liability in tort and accordingly no question of contributory negligence could arise.

These arguments have led courts to classify contractual duties under three headings.

(1) Where a party's liability arises from breach of a contractual provision which does not depend on a failure to take reasonable care.
(2) Where the liability arises from an express contractual obligation to take care which does not correspond to any duty which would exist independently of the contract.
(3) Where the liability for breach of contract is the same as, and co-extensive with, a liability in tort independently of the existence of a contract.

This analysis was adopted by Hobhouse J. in *Forsikringsaktieselskapet Vesta v Butcher* [1986] 2 All E.R. 488 at 508 and by the Court of Appeal ([1988] 2 All E.R. 43, [1989] A.C. 852). The judgments in the Court of Appeal in that case assert that in category (3) cases the Court of Appeal is bound by the decision in *Sayers v Harlow UDC* [1958] 2 All E.R. 342, [1958] 1 W.L.R. 623 to admit the availability of the defence.

Since I do not regard the case before the court as being in that category, I am content to accept that decision . . .

In my judgment therefore in the present state of the law contributory negligence is not a defence to a claim for damages founded on breach of a strict contractual obligation. I do not believe the wording of the 1945 Act can reasonably sustain an argument to the contrary. Even if it did, in the present case the nature of the contract and the obligation undertaken by the skilled contractor did not impose on the bank any duty in its own interest to prevent the contractor from committing the breaches of contract. To hold otherwise would, I consider, be equivalent to implying into the contract an obligation on the part of the bank inconsistent with the express terms agreed by the parties. The contract clearly laid down the extent of the obligations of the bank as architect and of the contractor. It was the contractor who was to provide appropriate supervision on site, not the architect.

SIMON BROWN LJ

The very imposition of a strict liability upon the defendant is to my mind inconsistent with an apportionment of the loss. And not least because of the absurdities that the contrary approach carries in its wake. Assume a defendant, clearly liable under a strict contractual duty. Is his position to be improved by demonstrating that besides breaching that duty he was in addition negligent? Take this very case. Is this contract really to be construed so that the respondents are advantaged by an assertion of their own liability in nuisance or trespass as well as in contract? Are we to have trials at which the defendant calls an expert to implicate him in tortious liability, whilst the plaintiffs' expert seeks paradoxically to exonerate him? The answer to all these questions is surely No. Whatever arguments exist for apportionment in other categories of case—and these are persuasively deployed in the 1993 Law Commission Report, Contributory Negligence as a Defence in Contract (Law Com. No. 219)—to my mind there are none in the present type of case and I for my part would construe the contract accordingly.

Nourse L. S. agreed with Beldam L.J.

Appeal Allowed.

4. MITIGATION OF DAMAGE

PAYZU LTD v SAUNDERS

King's Bench Division: Court of Appeal [1919] 2 K.B. 581; 89 L.J.K.B. 17; 121 L.T. 563; 35 T.L.R. 657

A contract for the sale of goods by the defendant to the plaintiffs provided that delivery should be as required over a period of nine months and that payment be made within one month of delivery. The plaintiffs failed to make prompt payment for the first instalment. The defendant, in breach of contract (cf. s.10 of the Sale of Goods Act 1979, above, para.16–014), refused to deliver any more instalments under the contract, but offered to deliver the goods at the contract price if the plaintiffs would agree to pay cash with each other. The plaintiffs refused to do so and brought an action for breach of contract. They claimed the difference between the contract price and the market price which had risen.

19–030

MCCARDIE J

. . . Now a serious question of law arises on the question of damages. I find as a fact that the defendant was ready and willing to supply the goods to the plaintiffs at the times and prices specified in the contract, provided the plaintiffs paid cash on delivery. Mr Matthews argued with characteristic vigour and ability that the plaintiffs were entitled to ignore that offer on the ground that a person who has repudiated a contract cannot place the other party to the contract under an obligation to diminish his loss by accepting a new offer made by the party in default.

The question is one of juristic importance. What is the rule of law as to the duty to mitigate damages? I will first refer to the judgment of Cockburn C. J. in *Frost v Knight* [above, Ch.18], where he said: "In assessing the damages for breach of performance, a jury will of course take into account whatever the plaintiff has done, or has had the means of doing, and, as a prudent man, ought in reason to have done, whereby his loss has been, or would have been, diminished." This rule is strikingly exemplified in *Brace v Calder* [1895] 2 Q.B. 253. There the plaintiff claimed damages for wrongful dismissal. He had been employed as manager of a business carried on by four persons in partnership. In the course of his employment two of the partners retired, and the business continued to be carried on by the two remaining partners. The plaintiff resented his technical dismissal which resulted from the dissolution of the partnership, and declined to serve the two remaining partners; and he brought an action against the original firm claiming damages for wrongful dismissal. There was a difference of opinion in the Court of Appeal as to whether the plaintiff had been wrongly dismissed, but the members of the court were unanimously of opinion that the plaintiff as a prudent, reasonable man should have accepted the offer of the two remaining partners to retain him in their service, and that he was therefore entitled to nominal damages only. I think that the substance of the rule which I have indicated was also laid down by the House of Lords in *British Westinghouse Electric and Manufacturing Co v Underground Electric Railways Co of London* [1912] A.C. 673, 689, when Lord Haldane said: "The fundamental basis is thus compensation for pecuniary loss naturally flowing from the breach; but this first principle is qualified by a second, which imposes on a plaintiff the duty of taking all reasonable steps to mitigate the loss consequent on the breach, and debars him from claiming any part of the damage which is due to his neglect to take such steps."

The question, therefore, is what a prudent person ought reasonably to do in order to mitigate his loss arising from a breach of contract. I feel no inclination to allow in a mercantile dispute an unhappy indulgence in far-fetched resentment or an undue sensitiveness to slights or unfortunately worded letters. Business often gives rise to certain asperities. But I agree that the plaintiffs in deciding whether to accept the defendant's offer were fully entitled to consider the terms in which the offer was made, its bona fides or otherwise, its relation to their own business methods and financial position, and all the circumstances of the case; and it must be remembered that an acceptance of the offer would not preclude an action for damages for the actual loss sustained. Many illustrations might be given of the extraordinary results which would follow if the plaintiffs were entitled to reject the defendant's offer and incur a substantial measure of loss which would have been avoided by their acceptance of the offer. The plaintiffs were in fact in a position to pay cash for the goods, but instead of accepting the defendant's offer, which was made perfectly bona fide, the plaintiffs permitted themselves to sustain a large measure of loss which as prudent and reasonable people they ought to have avoided . . .

Judgment for Plaintiffs.

The plaintiffs appealed on the question of damages.

Banks LJ delivered judgment dismissing the appeal.

BANKS LJ

Scrutton L.J. I am of the same opinion. Whether it be more correct to say that a plaintiff must minimise his damages, or to say that he can recover no more than he would have suffered if he had acted reasonably, because any further damages do not reasonably follow from the defendant's breach, the result is the same . . . Mr Matthews has contended that in considering what steps should be taken to mitigate the damage all contractual relations with the party in default must be excluded. That is contrary to my experience. In certain cases of personal service it may be unreasonable to expect a plaintiff to consider an offer from the other party who has grossly injured him; but in commercial contracts it is generally reasonable to accept an offer from the party in default. However, it is always a question of fact. About the law there is no difficulty.

Eve J. delivered judgment dismissing the appeal.

Appeal Dismissed.

It should be noted that, where the question is whether the claimant acted reasonably to mitigate the damage, it appears that the onus of proof is on the defendant to satisfy the court that he did not do so, notwithstanding a ruling to the contrary in *Selvanayagam v University of West Indies* [1983] 1 W.L.R. 585, PC. See Kemp (1983) 99 L.Q.R. 497. Cf. *CCC Films Ltd v Impact Quadrant Films Ltd*, above.

THE SOLHOLT

Court of Appeal [1983] Lloyds' Rep. 605; [1983] Com. L.R. 114

19–031   The respondents agreed to sell the Solholt to appellants for $5 million, delivery not later than August 31, 1979, failing which buyers were to have right of cancellation. Sellers were unable to deliver until after August 31 and buyers exercised right of cancellation on September 3, 1979 although market value of vessel was now $5.5 million. Buyers then offered to buy for $4.75 million but the offer was not accepted and buyers claimed damages. Staughton J held that the prima facie measure of damages was the difference between the market value and the contract price, that is, $.5 million, but dismissed buyers' claim on the ground that they had failed to mitigate their loss by negotiating a further contract for purchase at the original contract price. The buyers appealed.

SIR JOHN DONALDSON MR

A plaintiff is under no duty to mitigate his loss, despite the habitual use by the lawyers of the phrase "duty to mitigate." He is completely free to act as he judges to be in his best interests. On the other hand, a defendant is not liable for all loss suffered by the plaintiff in consequence of his so acting. A defendant is only liable for such part of the plaintiff's loss as is properly to be regarded as caused by the defendants' breach of duty. As Viscount Haldane, L.C., put it in *British Westinghouse Electric and Manufacturing Co Ltd v Underground Electric Railways Co of London Ltd*, [1912] A.C. 673 at p. 689:

> "The fundamental basis is thus compensation for pecuniary loss naturally flowing from the breach; but this first principle is qualified by a second, which imposes on a plaintiff the duty of taking all reasonable steps to mitigate the loss consequent on the breach, and debars him from claiming any part of the damage which is due to his neglect to take such steps."

As we have already accepted as being trite law, the buyers had an unfettered right in the circumstances of this case to affirm the original contract of sale or to cancel it. No question of mitigation arose at that stage. They decided to cancel and in consequence they suffered a loss of U.S. $500,000. As a matter of causation, this loss, unless avoidable by some reasonable further action, was directly attributable to the sellers' breach of contract. The learned Judge held that it was in fact avoidable by further action and that such action would have been reasonable. It is nothing to the point that this further action might, in effect, have reversed the cancellation of the old contract. We say might because the new contract which the learned Judge held that the buyers could and should have made might not have been on the same terms as to price although, on the evidence, he held that it would have been.

Whether a loss is avoidable by reasonable action on the part of the plaintiff is a question of fact not law. This was decided in *Payzu Ltd v Saunders* [above].

[His Lordship discussed *Payzu v Saunders* and *Strutt v Whitnell* [1975] 2 All E.R. 510 and continued:] We therefore turn to the evidence. The buyers are in the business of shipowning and there is no suggestion that there was any material change in their circumstances or intentions between the time when they agreed to buy the vessel and the time when they cancelled. They wanted a vessel then, and there is no suggestion that they did not want one at the beginning of September, 1979. If they could have found a different but identical ship, clearly it would have been reasonable that they should have bought it and the price of that purchase would have established the measure of their loss. However there is no suggestion that any such vessel was available. This left them with the alternative of buying Solholt. The buyers might have been able to allege and prove that she had some fatal defect which made her unsuitable for their purposes, but no such suggestion was made. On the contrary, the buyers recognised that she remained suitable for their purposes and offered to buy her for U.S. $4.75 million. Had that offer been accepted, their loss of U.S. $500,000 would have been extinguished and they would have made an incidental profit of U.S. $250,000. But it was rejected and they did nothing further . . . Dicta in the judgments in [*Strutt v Whitnell*] are undoubtedly helpful to the buyers. If the House of Lords ever had to consider the decision, it might well hold that the judgments totally confuse the proposition that in deciding whether to rescind or affirm a contract the innocent party need have no regard to considerations of mitigation of loss with the proposition that, having made such an election, he will be able to recover such loss as was unavoidable following that election and that in some, perhaps exceptional, circumstances it may be reasonable at a stage after the decision to rescind or affirm the contract to adopt a course of action which will nullify the effect of that decision. However, no such comment is open to us in this Court. In this Court all that can be said is that the decision has to be reconciled with that in *Payzu Ltd v Saunders* and that this can only be done by treating it as a decision turning on reasonableness and its own special facts. We so regard it. [His Lordship found nothing in the evidence to contradict Staughton J.'s conclusion that the buyers had failed to take reasonable steps to mitigate their loss by offering $5 million dollars, an offer which would have been accepted.]

Appeal Dismissed.

Question

What would have been the position in *The Solholt* if the buyers, at the time of the breach, had decided they no longer wanted a ship?   **19–032**

PILKINGTON v WOOD

[1953] Ch. 770; [1953] 2 All E.R. 810; 97 S.J. 572

19–033 The plaintiff, because of the negligence of the defendant, his solicitor, bought a house with a defective title. Harman J held that the plaintiff was entitled to recover the difference between the market value of the property at the time of breach with a good title and its value at that time with a defective title. He rejected the defendant's contention that the plaintiff should have mitigated his damage by suing the vendor on the covenant for title implied under s.76 of and Sch.2 to the Law of Property Act 1925, provided that (1) an adequate indemnity against costs were offered; (2) the vendor appeared to be solvent; and (3) there was a good prima facie right of action. Harman J said it might be conceded that the indemnity would be adequate and that the vendor was a man of substance, but it was clear that he would resist the claim. He went on:

HARMAN J

> I do not propose to attempt to decide whether an action against Colonel Wilks [the vendor] would lie or be fruitful. I can see it would be one attended with no little difficulty. I am of opinion that the so-called duty to mitigate does not go so far as to oblige the injured party, even under an indemnity, to embark on a complicated and difficult piece of litigation against a third party. The damage to the plaintiff was done once and for all directly the voidable conveyance to him was executed. This was the direct result of the negligent advice tendered by his solicitor, the defendant, that a good title had been shown; and, in my judgment, it is no part of the plaintiff's duty to embark on the proposed litigation in order to protect his solicitor from the consequences of his own carelessness.

Question

19–034 In *Southcott Estates Inc v Toronto Catholic District School Board* [2012] 2 S.C.R. 675, the Canadian Supreme Court was called on to decide whether the appellant single-purpose company, incorporated specifically for the purpose of purchasing a particular parcel of land within the TCDSB's property, with no assets other than money advanced to it by its parent company for the deposit relating to the purchase, was excused from mitigating its loss (by seeking to find alternative land) when the respondent vendors breached the contract. The court having refused to order specific performance, the appellants argued that they were not required to mitigate because the parcel of school land for which they had contracted was the only land that they sought to purchase; accordingly, they had never intended to try to mitigate their loss and, indeed, they had taken no steps to try to do so. How would you expect the Supreme Court to decide this point of law?

Points for reflection

19–035 1. It will be recalled that where there has been an anticipatory breach of contract, the injured party has an option either to accept the breach as putting an end to the contract and to sue at once for damages or to treat the breach as entirely inoperative and to await the time for performance (Ch.18). If the injured party adopts the former course, then he is under "a duty" (so-called—see *The Solholt*, above) to mitigate the damage. So where a person who has agreed to buy goods at a future date declares that he will not accept them when that date arrives, the seller who accepts the breach may be under "a duty" to sell the goods at the first opportunity, if that is the course which a reasonable business man who desired to mitigate the loss would take: *Roth & Co v Tayson, Townsend & Co* (1895) 1 Com.Cas. 240. The loss must not be increased by any act which the plaintiff ought not to have done or by the omission to do any act which the plaintiff ought to have done. The standard required of the injured party is not a strict one; his duty is only not to act unreasonably: the wrongdoer has no right to expect from the man whom he has wronged the utmost amount of diligence, the utmost amount of skill and the most accurate conclusion in a matter of judgment: *Dunkirk Colliery Co v Lever* (1880) 41 L.T. 633, per James LJ.

The position may be different, however, where the injured party declines to accept the breach as putting an end to the contract. Here there may be no need to mitigate: *White & Carter (Councils) Ltd v McGregor* (above, Ch.18). In *Tredegar Iron and Coal Co Ltd v Hawthorn Bros & Co* (1902) 18 T.L.R. 716 the defendants had contracted to buy coal at 16s. a ton from the plaintiffs, to be delivered in February. On February 16, the defendants repudiated the contract; but they procured and communicated to the plaintiffs an offer from a third party to buy the coal at 16s. 3d. a ton. The plaintiffs refused this offer and insisted on the performance of the contract. The defendants having failed to take delivery, the plaintiffs ultimately sold the coal for only 15s. a ton. The Court of Appeal, reversing Phillimore J, held that the plaintiffs were entitled to damages amounting to 1s. a ton. The repudiation, not having been accepted as such, was a nullity and there was no breach of contract until the expiration of the time for the delivery of the goods.

2. Where property is damaged by breach of contract, is the plaintiff entitled to (i) the cost of reinstating the property, or (ii) the difference in value of the property before and after breach?

The answer seems to depend on whether, in all the circumstances, the reasonable course for the plaintiff is to reinstate the property or to buy new property. In *Harbutt's* case (above, Ch.16) the plaintiff recovered the cost of reinstatement—£30,000 more than the difference in value of the old mill before and after the fire. "[The plaintiffs] had no choice. They were bound to replace it as soon as they could, not only to keep their business going, but also to mitigate the loss of profit (for which they would be able to charge the defendants)"—per Lord Denning. "It was reasonable for the plaintiffs to rebuild their factory, because there was no other way in which they could carry on their business and retain their labour force"—Widgery LJ. The plaintiffs did not have to give credit under the heading of "betterment" because the new factory was modern in design and materials. "To do so would be the equivalent of forcing the plaintiffs to invest their money in the modernising of their plant which might be highly inconvenient for them"—per Widgery LJ. (If they had added extra accommodation, it would have been different.)

On the other hand, "If the article damaged is a motor-car of popular make the plaintiff cannot charge the defendant with the cost of repair when it is cheaper to buy a similar car on the market"—per Widgery LJ. See the discussion in Street, *Principles of the Law of Damages*, pp.210–212, and of this aspect of *Harbutt* in (1970) 86 L.Q.R. 524. *Harbutt* was followed in *Dominion Mosaics Co Ltd v Trafalgar Trucking Co Ltd* [1990] 2 All E.R. 246 CA.

Problem

Needle, a tailor, enters into a contract with Nash to make him a suit for £200. Before Needle has started to make the suit, Nash informs him that he no longer wants it and will not take delivery of it. Needle nevertheless makes the suit which, since Nash is of an unusual build, cannot be disposed of elsewhere. The cost to Needle of the labour and materials for making the suit was £100. Advise him.

19–036

5. REMOTENESS OF DAMAGE

19–037   The starting point for any discussion of the limits on recovery that are set by the doctrine of remoteness is Baron Alderson's guidance in *Hadley v Baxendale* (1854) 9 Ex. 341 (Ex Ct). There, at 354, the range of recoverable loss was expressed in the following terms:

> "Where two parties have made a contract which one of them has broken, the damages which the other party ought to receive in respect of such breach of contract should be such as may fairly and reasonably be considered either arising naturally, i.e. according to the usual course of things, from such breach of contract itself, or such as may reasonably be supposed to have been in the contemplation of both parties, at the time they made the contract, as the probable result of the breach of it."

Accordingly, a defendant seeking to limit its liability for losses caused by the breach might argue that some of the losses were not of the kind that would be the ordinary and obvious consequence of the breach, and nor was the defendant privy to information that would alert it to the risk of such losses. In the *Victoria Laundry* case (below), the Court of Appeal sought to restate this principle in terms of what was reasonably foreseeable given the state of the defendant's knowledge (that is, the knowledge that the defendant would normally be taken to have together with any additional special knowledge of the claimant's circumstances). However, in *The Heron II* (below), this restatement, implying that the range of recovery for breach of contract was co-extensive with losses that were reasonably foreseeable, was corrected. There, the House of Lords insisted that the range of recovery in contract claims is more restricted. Defendants are not liable for losses that are merely reasonably foreseeable; rather the loss must be of a kind that the parties would contemplate as a fairly likely result of the breach. Despite the high-level judicial attention given to the precise formulation of the remoteness test, its application still presents difficulties (see, e.g., *Parsons v Uttley Ingham*, below, *Jackson v RBS*, below, and the *Transfield Shipping* case, below).

VICTORIA LAUNDRY (WINDSOR) LTD v NEWMAN INDUSTRIES LTD

Court of Appeal [1949] 2 K.B. 528; 65 T.L.R. 274; 93 S.J. 371; [1949] 1 All E.R. 997

19–038   The plaintiffs, launderers and dyers, wanted a boiler of much greater capacity than the one they possessed in order to expand their business. The defendants, engineers, agreed to sell to the plaintiffs for £2,150 a large boiler then installed on the defendants' premises. Delivery was arranged for June 5, 1946. The boiler was damaged while being dismantled by third parties employed by the defendants and delivery was delayed until November 8, 1946. The plaintiffs claimed as damages for loss of profit due to the defendants' breach of contract:

1. £16 a week for the very large number of new customers whom they could and would have taken on—the demand for laundry services at that time being insatiable.

2. £262 a week which they could and would have earned under dyeing contracts with the Ministry of Supply.

Streatfeild J awarded £110 under certain minor heads, but held that, under the second rule in *Hadley v Baxendale* (1854) 9 Ex. 341, the defendants were not liable for loss of profits because the special object for which the plaintiffs were acquiring the boiler had not been drawn to the defendants' attention.

The plaintiffs appealed.

The judgment of the court (Tucker, Asquith and Singleton LJJ) was delivered by Asquith LJ. After stating the facts and emphasising that the defendants knew that the plaintiffs were launderers and dyers and that they required the boiler for immediate use in their business, the learned judge continued:

ASQUITH LJ

The authorities on recovery of loss of profits as a head of damage are not easy to reconcile. At one end of the scale stand cases where there has been non-delivery or delayed delivery of what is on the face of it obviously a profit-earning chattel; for instance, a merchant or passenger ship: see *Fletcher v Tayleur* (1855) 17 C.B. 21; *Re Trent and Humber Company, ex p. Cambrian Steam Packet Company* (1868) L.R. 6 Eq. 396; or some essential part of such a ship; for instance, a propeller, in *Wilson v General Ironscrew Company* (1878) 47 L.J.Q.B. 23, or engines, *Saint Line v Richardson* [1940] 2 K.B. 99. In such cases loss of profit has rarely been refused. A second and intermediate class of case in which loss of profit has often been awarded is where ordinary mercantile goods have been sold to a merchant with knowledge by the vendor that the purchaser wanted them for resale; at all events, where there was no market in which the purchaser could buy similar goods against the contract on the seller's default, see, for instance, *Borries v Hutchinson* (1865) 18 C.B.(n.s.) 445. At the other end of the scale are cases where the defendant is not a vendor of the goods, but a carrier, see, for instance, *Hadley v Baxendale* and *Gee v Lancashire and Yorkshire Ry.*, 6 H. & N. 211. In such cases the courts have been slow to allow loss of profit as an item of damage. This was not, it would seem, because a different principle applies in such cases, but because the application of the same principle leads to different results. A carrier commonly knows less than a seller about the purposes for which the buyer or consignee needs the goods, or about other "special circumstances" which may cause exceptional loss if due delivery is withheld.

Three of the authorities call for more detailed examination. First comes *Hadley v Baxendale* itself. Familiar though it is, we should first recall the memorable sentence in which the main principles laid down in this case are enshrined: "Where two parties have made a contract which one of them has broken, the damages which the other party ought to receive in respect of such breach of contract should be such as may fairly and reasonably be considered as either arising naturally, that is according to the usual course of things, from such breach of contract itself, or such as may reasonably be supposed to have been in the contemplation of both parties, at the time they made the contract, as the probable result of the breach of it." The limb of this sentence prefaced by "either" embodies the so-called "first" rule; that prefaced by "or" the "second." In considering the meaning and application of these rules, it is essential to bear clearly in mind the facts on which *Hadley v Baxendale* proceeded. The head note is definitely misleading in so far as it says that the defendant's clerk, who attended at the office, was told that the mill was stopped and that the shaft must be delivered immediately. The same allegation figures in the statement of facts which are said on p. 344 to have "appeared" at the trial before Crompton J. If the Court of Exchequer had accepted these facts as established, the court must, one would suppose, have decided the case the other way round; must, that is, have held the damage claimed was recoverable under the second rule. But it is reasonably plain from Alderson B.'s judgment that the court rejected this evidence, for on p. 355 he says: "We find that the only circumstances here communicated by the plaintiffs to the defendants at the time when the contract was made were that the article to be carried was the broken shaft of a mill and that the plaintiffs were the millers of that mill," and it is on this basis of fact that he proceeds to ask, "How do these circumstances show reasonably that the profits of the mill must be stopped by an unreasonable delay in the delivery of the broken shaft by the carrier to the third person?" *British Columbia Sawmills v Nettleship* (1868) L.R. 3 C.P. 499 annexes to the principle laid down in *Hadley v Baxendale* a rider to the effect that where knowledge of special circumstances is relied on as enhancing the damage recoverable, that knowledge must have been brought home to the defendant at the time of the contract and in such circumstances that the defendant impliedly undertook to bear any special loss referable to a breach in those special circumstances. The knowledge which was lacking in that case on the part of the defendant was knowledge that the particular box of machinery negligently lost by the defendants was one without which the rest of the machinery could not be put together and would therefore be useless.

Cory v Thames Ironworks Company, L.R. 3 Q.B. 181, 187—a case strongly relied on by the plaintiffs—presented the peculiarity that the parties contemplated respectively different profit-making uses of the chattel sold by the defendant to the plaintiff. It was the hull of a boom derrick, and was delivered late. The plaintiffs were coal merchants, and the obvious use, and that to which the defendants believed it was to be put, was that of a coal store. The plaintiffs, on the other hand, the buyers, in fact intended to use it for transhipping coals from colliers to barges, a quite unprecedented use for a chattel of this kind, one quite unsuspected by the sellers and one calculated to yield much higher profits. The case accordingly decides, inter alia, what is the measure of damage recoverable when the parties are not ad idem in their contemplation of the use for which the article is needed. It was decided that in such a case no loss was recoverable beyond what would have resulted if the intended use had been that reasonably within the contemplation of the defendants, which in that case was the "obvious" use. This special complicating factor, the divergence between the knowledge and contemplation of the parties respectively, has somewhat obscured the general importance of the decision, which is in effect that the facts of the case brought it within the first rule of *Hadley v Baxendale* and enabled the plaintiff to recover loss of such profits as would have arisen from the normal and obvious use of the article. The "natural consequence," said Blackburn J., of not delivering the derrick was that £420 representing those normal profits was lost. Cockburn C. J., interposing during the argument, made the significant observation: "No doubt in order to recover damage arising from a special purpose the buyer must have communicated the special purpose to the seller; but there is one thing which must always be in the knowledge of both parties, which is that the thing is bought for the purpose of being in some way or other profitably applied." This observation is apposite to the present case. These three cases have on many occasions been approved by the House of Lords without any material qualification.

What propositions applicable to the present case emerge from the authorities as a whole, including those analysed above? We think they include the following:

(1) It is well settled that the governing purpose of damages is to put the party whose rights have been violated in the same position, so far as money can do so, as if his rights had been observed: *Sally Wertheim v Chicoutimi Pulp Company* [1911] A.C. 301. This purpose, if relentlessly pursued, would provide him with a complete indemnity for all loss de facto resulting from a particular breach, however improbable, however unpredictable. This, in contract at least, is recognised as too harsh a rule. Hence.

(2) In cases of breach of contract the aggrieved party is only entitled to recover such part of the loss actually resulting as was at the time of the contract reasonably foreseeable as liable to result from the breach.

(3) What was at the time reasonably so foreseeable depends on the knowledge then possessed by the parties or, at all events, by the party who later commits the breach.

(4) For this purpose, knowledge "possessed" is of two kinds; one imputed, the other actual. Everyone, as a reasonable person, is taken to know the "ordinary course of things" and consequently what loss is liable to result from a breach of contract in that ordinary course. This is the subject-matter of the "first rule" in *Hadley v Baxendale*. But to this knowledge, which a contract-breaker is assumed to possess whether he actually possesses it or not, there may have to be added in a particular case knowledge which he actually possesses, of special circumstances outside the "ordinary course of things," of such a kind that a breach in those special circumstances would be liable to cause more loss. Such a case attracts the operation of the "second rule" so as to make additional loss also recoverable.

(5) In order to make the contract-breaker liable under either rule it is not necessary that he should actually have asked himself what loss is liable to result from a breach. As has often been pointed out, parties at the time of contracting contemplate not the breach of the contract, but its performance. It suffices that, if he had considered the question, he would as a reasonable man have concluded that the loss in question was liable to result (see certain observations of Lord du Parcq in the recent case of *Monarch Steamship Co Ltd v A/B Karlshamns Oljefabriker* [1949] A.C. 196).

(6) Nor, finally, to make a particular loss recoverable, need it be proved that upon a given state of knowledge the defendant could, as a reasonable man, foresee that a breach must necessarily result in that loss. It is enough if he could foresee it was likely so to result. It is indeed enough, to borrow from the language of Lord du Parcq in the same case, at p. 158, if the loss (or some factor without which it would not have occurred) is a "serious possibility" or a "real danger." For short, we have used the word "liable" to result. Possibly the colloquialism "on the cards" indicates the shade of meaning with some approach to accuracy.

If these, indeed, are the principles applicable, what is the effect of their application to the facts of this case? We have, at the beginning of this judgment, summarised the main relevant facts. The defendants were an engineering company supplying a boiler to a laundry. We reject the submission for the defendants that an engineering company knows no more than the plain man about boilers or the purposes to which they are commonly put by different classes of purchasers, including laundries. The defendant company were not, it is true, manufacturers of this boiler or dealers in boilers, but they gave a highly technical and comprehensive description of this boiler to the plaintiffs by letter of January 19, 1946, and offered both to dismantle the boiler at Harpenden and re-erect it on the plaintiffs' premises. Of the uses or purposes to which boilers are put, they would clearly know more than the uninstructed layman. Again, they knew they were supplying the boiler to a company carrying on the business of laundrymen and dyers, for use in that business. The obvious use of a boiler, in such a business, is surely to boil water for the purpose of washing or dyeing. A laundry might conceivably buy a boiler for some other purpose; for instance, to work radiators or warm bath water for the comfort of its employees or directors, or to use for research, or to exhibit in a museum. All these purposes are possible, but the first is the obvious purpose which, in the case of a laundry, leaps to the average eye. If the purpose then be to wash or dye, why does the company want to wash or dye, unless for purposes of business advantage, in which term we, for the purposes of the rest of this judgment, include maintenance or increase of profit, or reduction of loss? (We shall speak henceforward not of loss of profit, but of "loss of business.") No commercial concern commonly purchases for the purposes of its business a very large and expensive structure like this—a boiler 19 feet high and costing over £2,000—with any other motive, and no supplier, let alone an engineering company, which has promised delivery of such an article by a particular date, with knowledge that it was to be put into use immediately on delivery, can reasonably contend that it could not foresee that loss of business (in the sense indicated above) would be liable to result to the purchaser from a long delay in the delivery thereof. The suggestion that, for all the supplier knew, the boiler might have been needed simply as a "standby", to be used in a possibly distant future, is gratuitous . . .

[His Lordship then quoted from the judgment of Streatfeild J and continued:] The answer to this reasoning has largely been anticipated in what has been said above, but we would wish to add: First, that the learned judge appears to infer that because certain "special circumstances" were, in his view, not "drawn to the notice of" the defendants and therefore, in his view, the operation of the "second rule" was excluded, ergo nothing in respect of loss of business can be recovered under the "first rule." This inference is, in our view, no more justified in the present case than it was in the case of *Cory v Thames Ironworks Company*. Secondly, that while it is not wholly clear what were the "special circumstances" on the non-communication of which the learned judge relied, it would seem that they were, or included, the following: (a) the "circumstance" that delay in delivering the boiler was going to lead "necessarily" to loss of profits. But the true criterion is surely not what was bound "necessarily" to result, but what was likely or liable to do so, and we think that it was amply conveyed to the defendants by what was communicated to them (plus what was patent without express communication) that delay in delivery was likely to lead to "loss of business"; (b) the "circumstance" that the plaintiffs needed the boiler "to extend their business." It was surely not necessary for the defendants to be specifically informed of this, as a precondition of being liable for loss of business. Reasonable persons in the shoes of the defendants must be taken to foresee without any express intimation that a laundry which, at a time when there was a famine of laundry facilities, was paying £2,000 odd for plant and intended at such a time to put such plant "into use" immediately, would be likely to suffer in pocket from five months' delay in delivery of the plant in question, whether they intended by means of it to extend their business, or merely to maintain it, or to reduce a loss; (c) the "circumstance" that the plaintiffs had the assured expectation of special contracts, which they could only fulfil by securing punctual delivery of the boiler. Here, no doubt, the learned judge had in mind the particularly lucrative dyeing contracts to which the plaintiffs looked forward and which they mention in para. 10 of the statement of claim. We agree that in order that the plaintiffs should recover specifically and as such the profits expected on these contracts, the defendants would have had to know, at the time of their agreement with the plaintiffs, of the prospect and terms of such contracts. We also agree, that they did not in fact know these things. It does not, however, follow that the plaintiffs are precluded from recovering some general (and perhaps conjectural) sum for loss of business in respect of dyeing contracts to be reasonably expected, any more than in respect of laundering contracts to be reasonably expected.

Thirdly, the other point on which Streatfeild J. largely based his judgment was that there is a critical difference between the measure of damages applicable when the defendant defaults in supplying a self-contained profit-earning whole and when he defaults in supplying a part of that whole. In our view, there is no intrinsic magic, in this connection, in the whole as against a part. The fact that a part only is involved is only significant in so far as it bears on the capacity of the supplier to foresee the consequences of non-delivery . . .

Appeal Allowed.

Question

19–039   In *Parsons v Uttley Ingham* and *Wroth v Tyler*, (above) it was held that what must be contemplated is damage of a particular type, not its degree or quantum. Was the damage caused by loss of the particularly lucrative dyeing contracts different in "type" from that caused by the loss of other, less lucrative, dyeing contracts?

THE HERON II

House of Lords [1969] 1 A.C. 350; [1967] 3 W.L.R. 1491; [1967] 3 All E.R. 686; [1967] 2 Lloyd's Rep. 259

LORD REID

19–040   My Lords, by charterparty of October 15, 1960, the respondents chartered the appellant's vessel, Heron II, to proceed to Constanza, there to load a cargo of 3,000 tons of sugar; and to carry it to Basrah, or, in the charterers' option, to Jeddah. The vessel left Constanza on November 1. The option was not exercised and the vessel arrived at Basrah on December 2. The umpire has found that "a reasonably accurate prediction of the length of the voyage was 20 days." But the vessel had in breach of contract made deviations which caused a delay of nine days.

It was the intention of the respondent charterers to sell the sugar "promptly after the arrival at Basrah and after the inspection by merchants." The appellant shipowner did not know this, but he was aware of the fact that there was a market for sugar at Basrah. The sugar was in fact sold at Basrah in lots between December 12 and 22 but shortly before that time the market price had fallen partly by reason of the arrival of another cargo of sugar. It was found by the umpire that if there had not been this delay of nine days the sugar would have fetched £32 10s. per ton. The actual price realised was only £31 2s. 9d. per ton. The charterers claim that they are entitled to recover the difference as damage for breach of contract. This shipowner admits that he is liable to pay interest for nine days on the value of the sugar and certain minor expenses but denies that fall in market value can be taken into account in assessing damages in this case.

McNair J., following the decision in *The Parana*[1] (1877) 2 P.D. 118, decided this question in favour of the appellant. He said:

"In those circumstances it seems to me almost impossible to say that the shipowner must have known that the delay in prosecuting the voyage would probably result, or be likely to result, in this kind of loss."

The Court of Appeal by a majority (Diplock and Salmon L.JJ., Sellers L.J. dissenting) reversed the decision of the trial judge. The majority held that *The Parana* laid down no general rule, and, applying the rule (or rules) in *Hadley v Baxendale* as explained in *Victoria Laundry (Windsor) Ltd v Newman Industries Ltd* [above], they held that the loss due to fall in market price was not too remote to be recoverable as damages.

It may be well first to set out the knowledge and intention of the parties at the time of making the contract so far as relevant or argued to be relevant. The charterers intended to sell the sugar in the market at Basrah on arrival of the vessel. They could have changed their mind and exercised their option to have the sugar delivered at Jeddah, but they did not do so. There is no finding that they had in mind any particular date as the likely date of arrival at Basrah or that they had any knowledge or expectation that in late November or December there would be a rising or a falling market. The shipowner was given no information about these matters by the charterers. He did not know what the charterers intended to do with the sugar. But he knew there was a market in sugar at Basrah, and it appears to me that, if he had thought about the matter, he must have realised that at least it was not unlikely that the sugar would be sold in the market at market price on arrival. He must also be held to have known that in any ordinary market prices are apt to fluctuate from day to day: but he had

---

[1]   The facts of *The Parana* appear below.

no reason to suppose it more probable that during the relevant period such fluctuation would be downwards rather than upwards—it was an even chance that the fluctuation would be downwards.

So the question for decision is whether a plaintiff can recover as damages for breach of contract a loss of a kind which the defendant, when he made the contract, ought to have realised was not unlikely to result from a breach of contract causing delay in delivery. I use the words "not unlikely" as denoting a degree of probability considerably less than an even chance but nevertheless not very unusual and easily foreseeable.

For over a century everyone has agreed that remoteness of damage in contract must be determined by applying the rule (or rules) laid down by a court including Parke, Martin and Alderson B. B. in *Hadley v Baxendale*; but many different interpretations of that rule have been adopted by judges at different times. So I think that one ought first to see just what was decided in that case, because it would seem wrong to attribute to that rule a meaning which, if it had been adopted in that case, would have resulted in a contrary decision of that case.

In *Hadley v Baxendale* the owners of a flour mill at Gloucester, which was driven by a steam engine, delivered to common carriers, Pickford & Co, a broken crank shaft to be sent to engineers in Greenwich. A delay of five days in delivery there was held to be in breach of contract, and the question at issue was the proper measure of damages. In fact the shaft was sent as a pattern for a new shaft and until it arrived the mill could not operate. So the owners claimed £300 as loss of profit for the five days by which resumption of work was delayed by this breach of contract; but the carriers did not know that delay would cause loss of this kind. Alderson B. delivering the judgment of the court said:

"... we find that the only circumstances here communicated by the plaintiffs to the defendants at the time the contract was made were that the article to be carried was the broken shaft of a mill and that the plaintiffs were the millers of that mill. But how do these circumstances show reasonably that the profits of the mill must be stopped by an unreasonable delay in the delivery of the broken shaft by the carrier to the third person? Suppose the plaintiffs had another shaft in their possession put up or putting up at the time, and that they only wished to send back the broken shaft to the engineer who made it; it is clear that this would be quite consistent with the above circumstances, and yet the unreasonable delay in the delivery would have no effect upon the intermediate profits of the mill. Or, again, suppose that at the time of the delivery to the carrier the machinery of the mill had been in other respects defective, then, also the same result would follow."

Then, having said that in fact the loss of profit was caused by the delay, he continued:

"But it is obvious that, in the great multitude of cases of millers sending off broken shafts to third persons by a carrier under ordinary circumstances, such consequences would not, in all probability, have occurred ..."

Alderson B. clearly did not and could not mean that it was not reasonably foreseeable that delay might stop the resumption of work in the mill. He merely said that in the great multitude—which I take to mean the great majority—of cases this would not happen. He was not distinguishing between results which were foreseeable and unforeseeable, but between results which were likely because they would happen in the great majority of cases, and results which were unlikely because they would only happen in a small minority of cases. He continued:

"It follows, therefore, that the loss of profits here cannot reasonably be considered such a consequence of the breach of contract as could have been fairly and reasonably contemplated by both the parties when they made this contract."

He clearly meant that a result which will happen in the great majority of cases should fairly and reasonably be regarded as having been in the contemplation of the parties, but that a result which, though foreseeable as a substantial possibility, would happen only in a small minority of cases should not be regarded as having been in their contemplation. He was referring to such a result when he continued:

"For such loss would neither have flowed naturally from the breach of this contract in the great multitude of such cases occurring under ordinary circumstances, nor were the special circumstances, which, perhaps, would have made it a reasonable and natural consequence of such breach of contract, communicated to or known by the defendants."

I have dealt with the latter part of the judgment before coming to the well-known rule, because the court were there applying the rule and the language which was used in the latter part appears to me to throw considerable light on the meaning which they must have attached to the rather vague expressions used in the rule itself. The rule is that the damages:

"... should be such as may fairly and reasonably be considered either arising naturally, that is, according to the usual course of things, from such breach of contract itself, or such as may reasonably be supposed to have been in the contemplation of both parties at the time they made the contract as the probable result of the breach of it."

I do not think that it was intended that there were to be two rules or that two different standards or tests were to be applied. The last two passages which I quoted from the end of the judgment applied to the facts before the court, which did not include any special circumstances communicated to the defendants; and the line of reasoning there is that, because in the great majority of cases loss of profit would not in all probability have occurred, it followed that this could not reasonably be considered as having been fairly and reasonably contemplated by both the parties, for it would not have flowed naturally from the breach in the great majority of cases.

I am satisfied that the court did not intend that every type of damage which was reasonably foreseeable by the parties when the contract was made should either be considered as arising naturally, that is, in the usual course of things, or be supposed to have been in the contemplation of the parties. Indeed the decision makes it clear that a type of damage which was plainly foreseeable as a real possibility but which would only occur in a small minority of cases cannot be regarded as arising in the usual course of things or be supposed to have been in the contemplation of the parties: the parties are not supposed to contemplate as grounds for the recovery of damage any type of loss or damage which, on the knowledge available to the defendant, would appear to him as only likely to occur in a small minority of cases.

In cases like *Hadley v Baxendale* or the present case it is not enough that in fact the plaintiff's loss was directly caused by the defendant's breach of contract. It clearly was so caused in both. The crucial question is whether, on the information available to the defendant when the contract was made, he should, or the reasonable man in his position would, have realised that such loss was sufficiently likely to result from the breach of contract to make it proper to hold that the loss flowed naturally from the breach or that loss of that kind should have been within his contemplation.

The modern rule in tort is quite different and it imposes a much wider liability. The defendant will be liable for any type of damage which is reasonably foreseeable as liable to happen even in the most unusual case, unless the risk is so small that a reasonable man would in the whole circumstances feel justified in neglecting it; and there is good reason for the difference. In contract, if one party wishes to protect himself against a risk which to the other party would appear unusual, he can direct the other party's attention to it before the contract is made, and I need not stop to consider in what circumstances the other party will then be held to have accepted responsibility in that event. In tort, however there is no opportunity for the injured party to protect himself in that way, and the tortfeasor cannot reasonably complain if he has to pay for some very unusual but nevertheless foreseeable damage which results from his wrongdoing. I have no doubt that today a tortfeasor would be held liable for a type of damage as unlikely as was the stoppage of Hadley's Mill for lack of a crank shaft: to any one with the knowledge the carrier had that may have seemed unlikely, but the chance of it happening would have been seen to be far from negligible. But it does not at all follow that *Hadley v Baxendale* would today be differently decided.

[His Lordship then considered some of the authorities, in particular *Re R & H Hall Ltd and W H Pim (Jnr.) and Co's Arbitration* (1928) 139 L.T. 50, and continued:]

It may be that there was nothing very new in this, but I think that *Hall's* case must be taken to have established that damages are not to be regarded as too remote merely because, on the knowledge available to the defendant when the contract was made, the chance of the occurrence of the event which caused the damage would have appeared to him to be rather less than an even chance. I would agree with Lord Shaw that it is generally sufficient that that event would have appeared to the defendant as not unlikely to occur. It is hardly ever possible in this matter to assess probabilities with any degree of mathematical accuracy. But I do not find in that case, or in cases which preceded it, any warrant for regarding as within the contemplation of the parties any event which would not have appeared to the defendant, had he thought about it, to have a very substantial degree of probability.

Then it has been said that the liability of defendants has been further extended by *Victoria Laundry (Windsor) Ltd v Newman Industries Ltd*. I do not think so . . . A large part of the profits claimed would have resulted from some specially lucrative contracts which the plaintiffs could have completed if they had had the boiler: that was rightly disallowed because the defendants had no knowledge of these contracts. Asquith L.J. said:

> "It does not, however, follow that the plaintiffs are precluded from recovering some general (and perhaps conjectural) sum for loss of business in respect of dyeing contracts to be reasonably expected, any more than in respect of laundering contracts to be reasonably expected."

It appears to me that this was well justified on the earlier authorities. It was certainly not unlikely on the information which the defendants had when making the contract that delay in delivering the boiler would result in loss of business: indeed it would seem that that was more than an even chance. And there was nothing new in holding that damages should be estimated on a conjectural basis. This House had approved of that as early as 1813 in *Hall v Ross* (1813) 1 Dow. 201.

What is said to create a "landmark," however, is the statement of principles by Asquith L.J. This does to some extent go beyond the older authorities and in so far as it does so, I do not agree with it. In para. (2) it is said that the plaintiff is entitled to recover "such part of the loss actually resulting as was at the time of the contract reasonably foreseeable as liable to result from the breach." To bring in reasonable forseeability appears to me to be confusing measure of damages in contract with measure of damages in tort. A great many extremely unlikely results are reasonably foreseeable: it is true that Asquith L.J. may have meant foreseeable as a likely result, and if that is all he meant I would not object farther than to say that I think that the phrase is liable to be misunderstood. For the same reason I would take exception to the phrase "liable to result" in para.(5). Liable is a very vague word, but I think that one would usually say that when a person foresees a very improbable result he foresees that it is liable to happen.

I agree with the first half of para.(6). For the best part of a century it has not been required that the defendant could have foreseen that a breach of contract must necessarily result in the loss which has occurred; but I cannot agree with the second half of para.(6). It has never been held to be sufficient in contract that the loss was foreseeable as "a serious possibility" or "a real danger" or as being "on the cards." It is on the cards that one can win £100,000 or more for a stake of a few pence—several people have done that; and anyone who backs a hundred to one chance regards a win as a serious possibility—many people have won on such a chance. Moreover, The *Wagon Mound (No. 2); Overseas Tankship (U.K.) Ltd v Miller Steamship Co Pty. Ltd* [1967] 1 A.C. 617 could not have been decided as it was unless the extremely unlikely fire should have been foreseen by the ship's officer as a real danger. It appears to me that in the ordinary use of language there is a wide gulf between saying that some event is not unlikely or quite likely to happen and saying merely that it is a serious possibility, a real danger, or on the cards. Suppose one takes a well-shuffled pack of cards, it is quite likely or not unlikely that the top card will prove to be a diamond: the odds are only three to one against; but most people would not say that it is quite likely to be the nine of diamonds for the odds are then fifty-one to one against. On the other hand I think that most people would say that there is a serious possibility or a real danger of its being turned up first and, of course, it is on the cards. If the tests of "real danger" or "serious possibility" are in future to be authoritative, then the *Victoria Laundry* case would indeed be a landmark because it would mean that *Hadley v Baxendale* would be differently decided today. I certainly could not understand any court deciding that, on the information available to the carrier in that case, the stoppage of the mill was neither a serious possibility nor a real danger. If those tests are to prevail in future, then let us cease to pay lip service to the rule in *Hadley v Baxendale*. But in my judgment to adopt these tests would extend liability for breach of contract beyond what is reasonable or desirable. From the limited knowledge which I have of commercial affairs I would not expect such an extension to be welcomed by the business community, and from the legal point of view I can find little or nothing to recommend it.

[His Lordship then examined the case of *Monarch Steamship Co, Ltd v A/B Karlshamns Oliefabriker* [1949] A.C. 196.]

It appears to me that, without relying in any way on the *Victoria Laundry* case, and taking the principle that had already been established, the loss of profit claimed in this case was not too remote to be recoverable as damages. So it remains to consider whether the decision in *The Parana* established a rule which, though now anomalous, should nevertheless still be followed. In that case owing to the defective state of the ship's engines a voyage which ought to have taken sixty-five to seventy days took 127 days, and as a result a cargo of hemp fetched a much smaller price than it would have done if there had been no breach of contract. The Court of Appeal held, however, that the plaintiffs could not recover this loss as damages. The vital part of their judgment was as follows:

"In order that damages may be recovered, we must come to two conclusions—first that it was reasonably certain that the goods would not be sold until they did arrive; and secondly, that it was reasonably certain that they would be sold immediately after they arrived, and that that was known to the carrier at the time when the bills of lading were signed."

If that was the right test then the decision was right, and I think that that test was in line with a number of cases decided before or about that time (1877); but, as I have already said, so strict a test has long been obsolete; and, if one substitutes for "reasonably certain" the words "not unlikely" or some similar words denoting a much smaller degree of probability, then the whole argument in the judgment collapses.

For the reasons which I have given I would dismiss this appeal.

Lords Morris, Hodson, Pearce and Upjohn also made speeches dismissing the appeal.

Lord Morris thought the "illuminating judgment" of the Court of Appeal in the *Victoria Laundry* case a most valuable analysis of the rule in *Hadley v Baxendale* which it neither added to nor modified. Lord Hodson thought the phrase, "liable to result", used by the Court of Appeal in *Victoria Laundry*, perhaps a colourless expression but one on which he could not improve. Lord Pearce thought there was nothing startling or novel about the *Victoria Laundry* case; ". . . it represented (in felicitous language) the approximate view of *Hadley v Baxendale* taken by many judges in trying ordinary cases of breach of contract." Lord Upjohn thought that the *Victoria Laundry* case did not alter the law.

All of their Lordships, however, deprecated the use of the phrase, "on the cards", as not having a sufficiently clear meaning (Lord Morris) and as capable of denoting a most improbable and unlikely event (Lord Upjohn).

Problems and questions

19–041

1. Baxendale negligently drops Hadley's mill shaft while performing a contract to carry it to Greenwich. In consequence, the operation of Hadley's mill has to be suspended for a month. Baxendale was unaware that Hadley did not have a spare shaft. Advise Hadley whether he should sue in contract or in tort.

2. If the defendants in the *Victoria Laundry* case were guilty of a tort (for example the ownership in the boiler had passed to the plaintiffs before it was negligently dropped) might the plaintiffs have recovered the loss on the "particularly lucrative dyeing contracts"?

3. Should *Hadley v Baxendale* be decided the same way today in the light of the interpretation now put upon that case?

SALE OF GOODS ACT 1979

Damages for non-acceptance: section 50

19–042

(2) The measure of damages is the estimated loss directly and naturally resulting, in the ordinary course of events, from the buyer's breach of contract.

(3) Where there is an available market for the goods in question the measure of damages is prima facie to be ascertained by the difference between the contract price and the market or current price at the time or times when the goods ought to have been accepted or (if no time was fixed for acceptance) at the time of the refusal to accept.

Damages for non-delivery: section 51

(2) The measure of damages is the estimated loss directly and naturally resulting, in the ordinary course of events, from the seller's breach of contract.

(3) Where there is an available market for the goods in question the measure of damages is prima facie to be ascertained by the difference between the contract price and the market or current price of the goods at the time or times when they ought to have been delivered or (if no time was fixed) then at the time of the refusal to deliver.

Points for reflection

In *WL Thompson v Robinson (Gunmakers) Ltd* [1955] Ch.177 the defendants refused to accept delivery of a "Vanguard" car which they had contracted to buy from the plaintiffs. The plaintiffs returned the car to the suppliers who took it back free from any claim for damages. The plaintiffs claimed as damages their loss of profit. The defendants said that the plaintiffs had suffered no loss of profit and that the damages should be nominal. It was admitted that there was no shortage of Vanguard cars to meet all immediate demands in the locality. It was held by Upjohn J that the plaintiffs' loss was the loss of their bargain and they were entitled to recover the loss of profit. Section 50(3) did not apply because there was no available market.

19–043

In *Charter v Sullivan* [1957] 2 Q.B. 117 the facts were similar except that the car was a Hillman and the plaintiff could sell all the Hillman cars that he could get. The Court of Appeal held that the plaintiff was entitled only to nominal damages, for he had shown no "loss directly and naturally resulting from the defendant's breach of contract." Cf. *Re Vic Mill* [1913] 1 Ch.465; *Interoffice Telephones Ltd v Robert Freeman Co Ltd* [1958] 1 Q.B. 190.

In *Lazenby Garages Ltd v Wright* [1976] 1 W.L.R. 459 the defendant repudiated a contract to buy a secondhand BMW car for £1,670. The sellers who had paid £1,325 for the car claimed £345 as lossof profit. They resold it for £1,770. The trial judge held that there was a 50:50 chance that the sellers would have sold another car and awarded £172.50. The Court of Appeal held that *Thompson v Robinson* was inapplicable to the sale of a secondhand car. There was no "available market" for secondhand cars. Each car is unique. It was not proved that the buyer must have contemplated that the seller would sell one car fewer. The sellers had suffered no loss.

Would it have been different if the second buyer had been about to buy another car from the sellers when the BMW became available because of the defendant's breach of contract?

M. G. Bridge, *The Sale of Goods*, 590, writes "In cases like *Lazenby Garages Ltd*, the practical answer is that the seller ought to demand a deposit and forfeit it if the buyer defaults."

Problem

Alfred, a painter of portraits, takes a month to paint a portrait and charges 1,000 guineas. He is fully booked up for the next two years. Bertrand, who has contracted to sit for his portrait in two months' time, repudiates the contract. Advise Alfred.

19–044

H PARSONS (LIVESTOCK) LTD v UTTLEY INGHAM & CO LTD

Court of Appeal [1978] Q.B. 791; [1977] 3 W.L.R. 990; [1978] 1 All E.R. 525; [1977] 2 Lloyd's Rep. 522

19-045 The plaintiffs, pig farmers, bought from the defendants, manufacturers of bulk food storage hoppers, a hopper which the defendants agreed to erect at the plaintiffs' farm. The hopper was described as "fitted with ventilated top." The defendants sealed the ventilator for the purpose of carriage and, after erecting it, forgot to unseal it. As the ventilator was 28 feet above ground, the plaintiffs could not detect that it was closed. Because of the lack of ventilation the pignuts stored in the hopper became mouldy. As a result of eating mouldy nuts many of the plaintiffs' pigs suffered a rare type of intestinal infection, E coli, of which 254 of them died. The plaintiffs brought an action for breach of contract of the sale of the hopper, claiming the value of the pigs, £10,000, and lost sales and turnover amounting to a further £10,000–£20,000. The defendants argued that the plaintiffs were entitled only to the extra cost of bagged food (used while the mouldy nuts were taken away for examination), £18.02. Swanwick J found that the parties could not reasonably be supposed to have contemplated that there was a serious possibility that the illness which in fact occurred would result from the breach of contract but he held that the death and sickness of the pigs were the direct result of a breach of s.14(1) of the Sale of Goods Act 1893 (see now s.14(3) of the Sale of Goods Act 1979, above, Ch.16) and that the damages claimed were recoverable under s.53(2) of that Act.

LORD DENNING MR

[Having discussed *The Heron II* and observed that in the law of tort there was emerging a distinction between economic loss and physical damage:]

It seems to me that in the law of contract, too, a similar distinction is emerging. It is between loss of profit consequent on a breach of contract and physical damage consequent on it.

Loss of profit cases

I would suggest as a solution that in the former class of case, loss of profit cases, the defaulting party is only liable for the consequences if they are such as, at the time of the contract, he ought reasonably to have contemplated as a serious possibility or real danger. You must assume that, at the time of the contract, he had the very kind of breach in mind, such a breach as afterwards happened, as for instance, delay in transit, and then you must ask: ought he reasonably to have contemplated that there was a serious possibility that such a breach would involve the plaintiff in loss of profit? If Yes, the contractor is liable for the loss unless he has taken care to exempt himself from it by a condition in the contract as, of course, he is able to do if it was the sort of thing which he could reasonably contemplate. The law on this class of case is now covered by the three leading cases of *Hadley v Baxendale* (above), *Victoria Laundry (Windsor) Ltd v Newman Industries Ltd* (above) and *The Heron II*, (above). These were all "loss of profit" cases, and the test of "reasonable contemplation" and "serious possibility" should, I suggest, be kept to that type of loss or, at any rate, to economic loss.

Physical damage cases

In the second class of case, the physical injury or expense case, the defaulting party is liable for any loss or expense which he ought reasonably to have foreseen at the time of the breach as a possible consequence, even if it was only a slight possibility. You must assume that he was aware of his breach, and then you must ask: ought he reasonably to have foreseen, at the time of the breach, that something of this kind might happen in consequence of it? This is the test which has been applied in cases of tort, ever since *The Wagon Mound* cases [1961] A.C. 388 and [1967] 1 A.C. 617. But there is a long line of cases which support a like test in cases of contract. One class of case which is particularly apposite here concerns latent defects in goods. In modern words: "product liability." In many of these cases the manufacturer is liable in contract to the immediate party for a breach of his duty to use reasonable care, and is liable in tort to the ultimate consumer for the same want of reasonable care. The ultimate consumer can either sue the retailer in contract and pass the liability up the chain to the manufacturer, or he can sue the manufacturer in tort and thus by-pass the chain. The liability of the manufacturer ought to be the same in either case. In nearly all these cases the defects were outside the range of anything that was in fact contemplated, or could reasonably have been contemplated by the manufacturer or by anyone down the chain to the retailers. Yet the manufacturer and others in the chain have been held liable for the damage done to the ultimate user, as for instance the death of the young pheasants in *Henry Kendall & Sons (a firm) v William Lillico & Sons Ltd* [1969] 2 A.C. 31 and of the mink in *Ashington Piggeries Ltd v Christopher Hill Ltd* [1972] A.C. 441. Likewise the manufacturers and retailers were held liable for the dermatitis caused to the wearer in the woollen underwear case of *Grant v Australian Knitting Mills Ltd* [1936] A.C. 85, even though they had not the faintest suspicion of any trouble. So were the manufacturers down the chain to the subcontractors for the disintegrating roofing-tiles in *Young and Marten Ltd v McManus Childs Ltd* [1969] 1 A.C. 454.

Another familiar class of case is where the occupier of premises is under the common duty of care, both in pursuance of a contract with a visitor or under the Occupiers Liability Act 1957. If he fails in that duty and a visitor is injured, the test of remoteness must be the same no matter whether the injured person enters by virtue of a contract or as a visitor by permission without a contract. No matter whether in contract or tort, the damages must be the same. Likewise when a contractor is doing work on premises for a tenant, and either the tenant or a visitor is injured, the test of remoteness is the same no matter whether the person injured is a tenant under the contract or a visitor without a contract; see *A.C. Billings & Sons Ltd v Riden* [1958] A.C. 620.

Yet another class of case is where a hospital authority renders medical services in contract to a paying patient and gratuitously to another patient without any contract. The paying patient can sue in contract for negligence. The poor patient can sue in tort; see *Cassidy v Ministry of Health* [1951] 3 K.B. at 359, 360. The test of remoteness should be the same whether the hospital authorities are sued in contract or in tort; see *Esso Petroleum Co Ltd v Mardon* [above, para.15–024].

Instances could be multiplied of injuries to persons or damage to property where the defendant is liable for his negligence to one man in contract and to another in tort. Each suffers like damage. The test of remoteness is, and should be, the same in both.

Coming to the present case, we were told that in some cases the makers of these hoppers supply them direct to the pig farmer under contract with him, but in other cases they supply them through an intermediate dealer who buys from the manufacturer and resells to the pig farmer on the self-same terms, in which the manufacturer delivers, direct to the pig farmer. In the one case the pig farmer can sue the manufacturer in contract. In the other in tort. The test of remoteness should be the same. It should be the test in tort.

Conclusion

The present case falls within the class of case where the breach of contract causes physical damage. The test of remoteness in such cases is similar to that in tort. The contractor is liable for all such loss or expense as could reasonably have been foreseen, at the time of the breach, as a possible consequence of it. Applied to this case, it means that the makers of the hopper are liable for the death of the pigs. They ought reasonably to have foreseen that, if the mouldy pig nuts were fed to the pigs, there was a possibility that they might become ill. Not a serious possibility. Nor a real danger. But still a slight possibility. On that basis the makers were liable for the illness suffered by the pigs. They suffered from diarrhoea at the beginning. This "triggered off" the deadly E coli. That was a far worse illness than could then be foreseen. But that does not lessen this liability. The type or kind of damage was foreseeable even though the extent of it was not; see *Hughes v Lord Advocate* [1963] A.C. 837. The makers are liable for the loss of the pigs that died and of the expenses of the vet, and such like. But not for the loss of profits on future sales or future opportunities of gain; see *Simon v Pawson & Leafs Ltd* (1932) 38 Com.Cas. 151.

So I reach the same result as Swanwick J., but by a different route. I would dismiss the appeal.

Orr L.J. said that he would dismiss the appeal for the reasons to be given by Scarman L.J.

SCARMAN LJ

My conclusion in the present case is the same as that of Lord Denning M.R. but I reach it by a different route. I would dismiss the appeal. I agree with him in thinking it absurd that the test for remoteness of damage should, in principle, differ according to the legal classification of the cause of action, though one must recognise that parties to a contract have the right to agree on a measure of damages which may be greater or less than the law would offer in the absence of agreement. I also agree with him in thinking that, notwithstanding the interpretation put on some dicta in The Heron II, the law is not so absurd as to differentiate between contract and tort save in situations where the agreement, or the factual relationship, of the parties with each other requires it in the interests of justice. I differ from him only to this extent: the cases do not, in my judgment, support a distinction in law between loss of profit and physical damage. Neither do I think it necessary to develop the law judicially by drawing such a distinction. Of course (and this is a reason for refusing to draw the distinction in law) the type of consequence, loss of profit or market or physical injury, will always be an important matter of fact in determining whether in all the circumstances the loss or injury was of a type which the parties could reasonably be supposed to have in contemplation. [His Lordship quoted Swanwick J.'s conclusion:]

"On this interpretation the inevitable conclusion from the findings I have already made would be that this hopper was not reasonably fit for that purpose and that this caused the nuts to become toxic and that the illness of the pigs was a direct and natural consequence of such breach and toxicity, and that the plaintiffs do not have to prove that the toxicity or its results were foreseeable to either party. To put it another way, once the question of foreseeability of the breach is eliminated, as it is by the absolute warranty, the consequences of the breach flow naturally from it."

Counsel for the defendant criticises strongly this part of the judgment. He says it is based on a misunderstanding of *Hadley v Baxendale*; and he referred us to the well-known passage in Lord Reid's speech in *The Heron II*, where he said that it is not enough that in fact the plaintiff's loss was directly caused by the defendant's breach of contract. Lord Reid said:

"The crucial question is whether, on the information available to the defendant when the contract was made, he should, or the reasonable man in his position would, have realised that such loss was sufficiently likely to result from the breach of contract to make it proper to hold that the loss flowed naturally from the breach or that loss of that kind should have been within his contemplation."

Notwithstanding his choice of language, I think the judge was making the approach which, according to Lord Reid, is the correct one. He was saying, in effect, that the parties to this contract must have appreciated that, if, as happened in the event, the hopper, unventilated, proved not to be suitable for the storage of pig nuts to be fed to the plaintiffs' pigs, it was not unlikely, there was a serious possibility, that the pigs would become ill. The judge put it in this way:

"The natural result of feeding toxic food to animals is damage to their health and maybe death, which is what occurred, albeit from a hitherto unknown disease and to particularly susceptible animals. There was therefore no need to invoke the question of reasonable contemplation in order to make the defendants liable."

The judge in this critical passage of his judgment is contrasting a natural result, that is one which people placed as these parties were would consider as a serious possibility, with a special, specific result, that is E coli disease, which, as he later found, the parties could not at the time of contract reasonably have contemplated as a consequence. He distinguishes between "presumed contemplation" based on a special knowledge from ordinary understanding based on general knowledge and concludes that the case falls within the latter category. He does so because he has held that the assumption, or hypothesis, to be made is that the parties had in mind at the time of contract not a breach of warranty limited to the delivery of mouldy nuts but a warranty as to the fitness of the hopper for its purpose. The assumption is of the parties asking themselves not what is likely to happen if the nuts are mouldy but what is likely to happen to the pigs if the hopper is unfit for storing nuts suitable to be fed to them. While, on his finding, nobody at the time of contract could have expected E coli to ensue from eating mouldy nuts, he is clearly, and, as a matter of common sense, rightly, saying that people would contemplate, on the second assumption, the serious possibility of injury and even death among the pigs.

And so the question becomes; was he right to make the assumption he did? In my judgment, he was (see *Grant v Australian Knitting Mills Ltd* [1936] A.C. 85, esp. at 98, 99, and particularly the well-known passage in the speech of Lord Wright).

I would agree with Mr McGregor in his work on *Damages* that—

"in contract as in tort, it should suffice that, if physical injury or damage is within the contemplation of the parties, recovery is not to be limited because the degree of physical injury or damage could not have been anticipated."

This is so, in my judgment, not because there is, or ought to be, a specific rule of law governing cases of physical injury but because it would be absurd to regulate damages in such cases on the necessity of supposing the parties had a prophetic foresight as to the exact nature of the injury that does in fact arise. It is enough if on the hypothesis predicated physical injury must have been a serious possibility. Though in loss of market or loss of profit cases the factual analysis will be very different from cases of physical injury, the same principles, in my judgment, apply. Given the situation of the parties at the time of contract, was the loss of profit, or market, a serious possibility, something that would have been in their minds had they contemplated breach?

It does not matter, in my judgment, if they thought that the chance of physical injury, loss of profit, loss of market, or other loss as the case may be, was slight or that the odds were against it provided they contemplated as a serious possibility the type of consequence, not necessarily the specific consequence, that ensued on breach. Making the assumption as to breach that the judge did, no more than common sense was needed for them to appreciate that food affected by bad storage conditions might well cause illness in the pigs fed on it.

Appeal Dismissed. Leave to Appeal to the House of Lords Granted.

Questions

1. If there had been only a slight possibility of injury to the pigs, would the plaintiff have succeeded?   **19-046**

2. Did Scarman LJ correctly interpret the findings of Swanwick J? See 94 L.Q.R. 171.

3. Was the illness which occurred of the same type as an illness which might have been contemplated? See Hadjihambis, 41 M.L.R. 483.

4. Why does it help the plaintiffs to consider the consequences of the hopper being unfit instead of the consequences of the nuts being mouldy? The first consequence of the hopper being unfit was that the nuts were mouldy; so is there any difference? Or are we supposed to consider some other type of unfitness which the parties would have known was likely to cause serious injury— but was not present?

5. Should the rules relating to damages be the same in contract and tort? The same negligent act is commonly both a breach of contract and a tort. See *Midland Bank Trust Co Ltd v Hett, Stubbs and Kemp* [1978] 3 W.L.R. 167.

Points for reflection

In *Wroth v Tyler*, above, Megarry J applied a principle similar to that stated by *McGregor on Damages*   **19-047** to a case of economic loss. In *Brown v KMR Services Ltd* [1994] 4 All E.R. 385 at 399, where a Lloyd's "name" sued his agent for breach of contract in negligently placing him with a high-risk syndicate, Gatehouse J, following *Parsons v Uttley Ingham*, said: "It is most unlikely that any professional member of Lloyd's foresaw the magnitude of the financial disasters that struck in the middle-to-late 1980's . . . But losses of the type that occurred were undoubtedly foreseeable and in fact foreseen even though their scale was not. That is enough for the plaintiff . . . The plaintiff's losses were the natural and obvious result of his being a member of the "disaster" syndicates."

CHAPLIN v HICKS

Court of Appeal [1911] 2 K.B. 786; 80 L.J.K.B. 1292; 105 L.T. 285; 27 T.L.R. 458

The defendant by an advertisement in the Daily Express newspaper offered theatrical engage-   **19-048** ments for three years to twelve ladies, four at £5, four at £4 and four at £3 per week. Applicants were to submit photographs and a fee of one shilling. The readers of the newspaper in each of ten districts were to select the five whom they considered the most beautiful. The defendant would then select from the fifty chosen by the districts the twelve to fill the places offered. Six thousand photographs were submitted. The plaintiff topped the pole in her district but was not given a reasonable opportunity of presenting herself for final selection. At the trial before Pickford J the jury awarded £100 damages. On appeal it was argued that the damages were too remote and unassessable.

FLETCHER MOULTON LJ

[Having held that the damages were not too remote:] Then the learned counsel takes up a more hopeful position. He says that the damages are difficult to assess, because it is impossible to say that the plaintiff would have obtained any prize. This is the only point of importance left for our consideration. Is expulsion from a limited class of competitors an injury? To my mind there can be only one answer to that question; it is an injury and may be a very substantial one. Therefore the plaintiff starts with an unchallengeable case of injury, and the damages given in respect of it should be equivalent to the loss. But it is said that the damages cannot be arrived at because it is impossible to estimate the quantum of the reasonable probability of the plaintiff's being a prize-winner. I think that, where it is clear that there has been actual loss resulting from the breach of contract, which it is difficult to estimate in money, it is for the jury to do their best to estimate; it is not necessary that there should be an absolute measure of damages in each case. There are no doubt well-settled rules as to the measure of damages in certain cases, but such accepted rules are only applicable where the breach is one that frequently occurs. In such cases the Court weighs the pros and cons and gives advice, and I may almost say directions, to the jury as regards the measure of damages. This is especially the case in actions relating to the sale of goods of a class for which there is an active and ready market. But in most cases it may be said that there is no recognized measure of damages, and that the jury must give what they think to be an adequate solatium under all the circumstances of the case. Is there any such rule as that, where the result of a contract depends on the volition of an independent party, the law shuts its eyes to the wrong and says that there are no damages? Such a rule, if it existed, would work great wrong. Let us take the case of a man under a contract of service to serve as a second-class clerk for five years at a salary of £200 a year, which expressly provides that, at the end of that period, out of every five second-class clerks two first-class clerks will be chosen at a salary of £500 a year. If such a clause is embodied in the contract, it is clear that a person thinking of applying for the position would reckon that he would have the advantage of being one of five persons from whom the two first-class clerks must be chosen, and that that might be a very substantial portion of the consideration for his appointment. If, after he has taken the post and worked under the contract of service, the employers repudiate the obligation, is he to have no remedy? He has sustained a very real loss, and there can be no possible reason why the law should not leave it to the jury to estimate the value of that of which he has been deprived. Where by contract a man has a right to belong to a limited class of competitors, he is possessed of something of value, and it is the duty of the jury to estimate the pecuniary value of that advantage if it is taken from him. The present case is a typical one. From a body of six thousand, who sent in their photographs, a smaller body of fifty was formed, of which the plaintiff was one, and among that smaller body twelve prizes were allotted for distribution; by reason of the defendant's breach of contract she has lost all the advantage of being in the limited competition, and she is entitled to have her loss estimated. I cannot lay down any rule as to the measure of damages in such a case; this must be left to the good sense of the jury. They must of course give effect to the consideration that the plaintiff's chance is only one out of four and that they cannot tell whether she would have ultimately proved to be the winner. But having considered all this they may well think that it is of considerable pecuniary value to have got into so small a class, and they must assess the damages accordingly.

This consideration decides the case, but I wish to refer to the decision of Jelf J. in *Sapwell v Bass* [1910] 2 K.B. 486. That decision was, in my opinion, right on the facts of the particular case. The plaintiff had acquired by contract a right to send a mare during the following year to a renowned stallion belonging to the defendant, and the defendant broke his contract. The right to send the mare was coupled with the payment of a fee of 300 guineas. Jelf J. held that for the breach of contract the plaintiff was only entitled to nominal damages. The ground of the decision was that there was no evidence to shew that the right was worth more to the plaintiff than the 300 guineas which he would have had to pay for the services of the stallion, and that there was therefore no evidence that the damages were more than nominal. If, however, the learned judge meant to hold that there were no damages for breach of an undertaking to serve the mare, there is, in my opinion, no justification for such a view. The contract gave the plaintiff a right of considerable value, one for which many people would give money; therefore to hold that the plaintiff was entitled to no damages for being deprived of such a right because the final result depended on a contingency or chance would have been a misdirection. This appeal must be dismissed.

Vaughan Williams and Farwell L.JJ. delivered judgment dismissing the appeal.

JACKSON v ROYAL BANK OF SCOTLAND

House of Lords [2005] UKHL 3

LORD HOPE OF CRAIGHEAD

My Lords,

3. This is an appeal about the damages to be awarded to the former partners of a business partnership for a breach of contract as a result of which the relationship of that business with its principal customer was terminated. The claim is for the loss of the opportunity to earn further profits from that relationship. It raises issues about the proper approach to remoteness where damages are claimed for breach of contract and about the quantum of the damages.

4. The claimants are James Jackson and the late Barrie Stewart Davies, who carried on business in partnership. They traded under the name of Samson Lancastrian ("Samson"). Samson imported goods from the Far East, including Thailand, and sold them to customers in the United Kingdom. Its principal customer in this country was another business partnership which traded under the name Economy Bag. The partners in this business were Mr Taylor and Mr Holt. The products which Economy Bag sold to its wholesale and retail customers included dog chews. By coincidence the bankers to both Samson and Economy Bag were the Royal Bank of Scotland Plc ("the Bank"). The Bank is the respondent in this appeal . . .

9. The relationship [between Samson and Economy Bag] came to an end unexpectedly as a result of a breakdown in [the] arrangements for which the Bank were responsible. In January 1993 Economy Bag asked the Bank to open a transferable letter of credit in favour of Samson in the sum of US$50,976 for a consignment of dog chews that it had ordered on 7 January 1993. The Bank complied with this request. They issued the letter of credit to Samson on 22 January 1993. On 1 February 1993 Samson instructed the Bank to transfer the credit to Pet Products [the Thai supplier] in the sum of US$43,932.50 and to debit its account with the Bank with the transfer charges. The transaction proceeded normally until 15 March 1993, when the Bank in error sent a completion statement and other documents including Pet Products' invoice to Economy Bag instead of to Samson. The effect of the Bank's error was to reveal to Economy Bag the substantial profit that Samson was making on these transactions. On this occasion it amounted to a mark-up of 19% on the amount payable to Pet Products by Samson, excluding the 5% handling charge. This was as much, if not more than, the amount of the profit that Economy Bag was making on its transactions with its own distributors.

10. Mr Taylor was angry when he discovered the size of the mark-up. He decided to cut Samson out of Economy Bag's system for importing the dog chews from Thailand. He terminated their relationship. Four contracts that were already on foot were performed. But thereafter Economy Bag bought its dog chews from Pet Products direct. In the year ending March 1994 it purchased 15 shipments from Pet Products worth US$257,944. Between March 1994 and March 1995 it purchased 28 shipments worth US$468,296. Between March 1995 and March 1996 it purchased 23 shipments worth US$462,467. Between March 1996 and March 1997 it purchased 25 shipments worth US$645,429. Mr Taylor's evidence at the trial in 1998 was that its business was still continuing on that scale, and that it also did business with other suppliers in the Far East which would have been done through Samson if their relationship had continued.

11. As for Samson, the loss of its business with Economy Bag had disastrous consequences. It deprived it of its principal source of income. It had to cease trading. The partnership was dissolved.

The issues

12. The judge, H.H. Judge Kershaw Q.C., held that the Bank was in breach of an obligation of confidence under its contract with Samson not to disclose to Economy Bag any of the documents relating to its purchase of goods from Pet Products. These documents included the invoice by Pet Products to Samson. It was the disclosure of this document to Economy Bag that revealed the amount of the profit that Samson was making on the transaction. There was no appeal against that part of his judgment. It was common ground in the Court of Appeal that the Bank was in breach of its contract with Samson when it disclosed the invoice to Economy Bag.

13. The judge then found that Samson was entitled to damages for loss of the opportunity to earn profits from its trading relationship. He held that there was a significant chance that Samson's trading relationship with Economy Bag would have continued for a further four years. But in view of the uncertainties he reduced the profit which had been projected by Samson for each of these years for the purposes of his award, and he increased the amount of the reduction year by year. The implication of his judgment was that after the end of the fourth year Samson's chance of obtaining repeat business was so speculative as not to sound in damages.

14. Three points were in issue in the Court of Appeal. The first was whether the relationship between Samson and Economy Bag was that of buyer and seller, as Samson contended and the judge found, or was that of agent and principal. Mr Taylor's evidence was that he regarded Samson, not Pet Products, as Economy Bag's supplier. The expert witnesses were agreed that, while transferable letters of credit may be used where the relationship between the applicant and the first beneficiary is that of agent and principal, they are also in practice used for the benefit of middle-men. The Court of Appeal held that there was no justifiable basis for interfering with the findings of the trial judge on this point, and it is no longer in issue. The third point related to the rate of interest ordered by the judge on his award of damages. The rate of interest which he awarded was found to be excessive, and it was reduced by the Court of Appeal. There is no challenge to its decision on this point.

15. The second point however remains in issue. It is whether the judge was correct in his findings on causation, remoteness and quantum. The Court of Appeal rejected the Bank's submissions that the claim for the loss of repeat business was too remote and that in any event the relationship between Samson and Economy Bag was so unstable that, if any award were to be made, it should be simply one of general damages. But it held that the judge was in error in his approach to quantum.

16. Potter L.J., with whom Nourse L.J. and Ferris J. agreed, said in para 33 of his judgment that there was no sufficient basis on which the judges could have awarded damages for a period anything like as long as four years. He said that the judge should have focused on the Bank's limited knowledge of the facts at the date of the breach. Had he done so he would have concluded that the Bank could reasonably foresee a substantial loss of business in relation to orders likely to be placed by Economy Bag in the near future but with a cut-off point far shorter than the four year period. In para 34 he said that the award of damages should be limited to a period of one year from the date of the breach, all other loss being regarded as too remote.

17. For the appellants Miss Andrews Q.C. submitted that the decision of the Court of Appeal to limit the award to a period of one year was based on an error of principle and that it should be set aside. But she said that the judge too was in error, as there was no real justification for his finding that Samson's trading relationship with Economy Bag would have lasted for only four years. The Bank's liability, she said, was open-ended. It ought not to have been subjected to an arbitrary cut-off point. Figures had been submitted which would have justified an award extending over a period of six years, and the judge ought to have made an award for loss of repeat orders over that entire period. Mr Hapgood Q.C., presenting the Bank's cross-appeal, said that the proper conclusion from the facts was that there was no foreseeable loss at all. In any event any attempt to assess Samson's actual loss was so speculative that any award should be confined to one of general damages . . .

The issues relating to damages

25. The way in which the Court of Appeal dealt with the case suggests it misunderstood the effect of the rules that were identified in *Hadley v Baxendale* (1854) 9 Exch 341, 354. They are very familiar to every student of contract law. Most would claim to be able to recite them by heart. But it may be helpful, as background to the discussion that follows, if I were to set out the rules again here:

> "Where two parties have made a contract which one of them has broken, the damages which the other party ought to receive in respect of such breach of contract should be such as may fairly and reasonably be considered either arising naturally, ie according to the usual course of things, from such breach of contract itself, or such as may reasonably be supposed to have been in the contemplation of both parties, at the time they made the contract, as the probable result of the breach of it."

The first rule, prefaced by the word "either", is the rule that applies in this case. It is the ordinary rule. Everyone is taken to know the usual course of things and consequently to know what loss is liable to result from a breach of the contract if things take their usual course. But the way the second rule is expressed, prefaced by the word "or", shows the principle that underlies both limbs. It refers to what was in the contemplation of the parties at the time they made their contract.

26. As Asquith L.J. said in *Victoria Laundry (Windsor) Ltd v Newman Industries Ltd* [1949] 2 KB 528, 539 in cases of breach of contract the aggrieved party is only entitled to recover such part of the loss actually resulting as was at the time of the contract reasonably foreseeable as likely to result from the breach. In tort, the question whether loss was reasonably foreseeable is addressed to the time when the tort was committed. In contract, the question is addressed to the time when the parties made their contract. Where knowledge of special circumstances is relied on, the assumption is that the defendant undertook to bear any special loss

which was referable to those special circumstances. It is assumed too that he had the opportunity to seek to limit his liability under the contract for ordinary losses in the event that he was in breach of it.

27. The Bank's primary argument on damages was that the loss of the repeat business on which Samson based its claim was too remote. This was because it was not in the Bank's reasonable contemplation that the disclosure of the profit that Samson was making would lead to the termination by Economy Bag of its trading relationship with Samson. Their relationship, it was said, was based on mutual trust and confidence. There was no reason for the Bank to think that breach of its duty of confidence to Samson would result in any loss at all. The real reason for the loss of repeat business was Mr Taylor's anger when he detected the amount of the mark-up. This was something that could not have been predicted.

28. The trial judge rejected that argument, and the Court of Appeal did so too for the reasons explained by Potter L.J. in paras 25 and 26 of his judgment. The judge proceeded to examine the figures for the profit which Samson projected on the basis of the figures relating to Economy Bag's trade in dog chews for the four years from March 1993 to March 1997 which I have set out in para 10 above. Holding that there was a significant chance that Samson's business relationship with Economy Bag would have continued for some time, but that the likelihood of its coming to an end would have increased as time passed, he attributed what he said was an appropriate sum by way of each year in which the claimants had shown that damages should be awarded as follows: 1993–1994 $27,000; 1994–1995 $42,000; 1995–1996 $29,000; 1996–1997 $26,500. His total award, prior to the addition of interest, was $124,500.

29. The Court of Appeal applied the first rule in *Hadley v Baxendale* 9 Exch 341 as explained by Asquith L.J. in *Victoria Laundry* [1949] 2 KB 528. Potter L.J. said that loss of the chance or opportunity of repeat business should in principle be available, and that the issue in this case was for how long it was or should have been in the reasonable contemplation of the parties that the trading relationship would continue. In para 29 he referred to the statement by Evans L.J. in *Kpohraror v Woolwich Building Society* [1996] 4 All ER 119, 127J–128A that the starting point for any application of *Hadley v Baxendale* is the extent of the shared knowledge of both parties when the contract was made. In para 31 he observed that the claim, as presented at the trial, was one for loss of business profits made up of specific transactions none of which had yet been concluded at the time of the Bank's breach. It depended on the chance or contingency that Economy Bag would act so as to enable Samson to make that profit as explained in *Allied Maples Group Ltd v Simmons & Simmons* [1995] 1 WLR 1602 where, at p 1614C, Stuart-Smith L.J. said that the plaintiff must prove as a matter of causation that he had a real substantial chance as opposed to a speculative one. Thus far the judgment proceeded on orthodox lines, and there are no grounds for criticism.

30. But at the end of para 31 and the beginning of para 32, in a passage where he identified the approach that he then took to this issue, Potter L.J. said:

"31 . . . That principle however, properly regarded is a principle or method of *quantification*, and not a rule as to *remoteness*, of damage. It is thus subject to, and may be constrained by, the rules as to remoteness laid down in *Hadley v Baxendale*, so that, whatever the judge's view of the percentage chance that, but for the Bank's breach, Samson would *in fact* have been Economy Bag's supplier in the respect of the transactions in the following years, the cut-off point for the Bank's liability was the end of such period as was within the reasonable contemplation of the Bank at the time of breach. [emphasis in the original]

32. As to that, the Bank's knowledge of the background and details of Samson's trading relationship was limited to the period of time and the individual transactions conducted *prior to breach*." [emphasis added]

31. In para 33 Potter L.J. said that it seemed to him that there was no sufficient basis on which the judge could or should have predicated his award covering a period anything like as long as four years. In para 34 he said that the judge could and should have approached the case on the broad basis that, while it could reasonably be contemplated that the established relationship of Samson and Economy Bag would have continued for a time, and thus that some award of damages for future business fell to be made, that time should in all the circumstances be limited to a period of one year from the date of the breach, all loss thereafter being regarded as too remote. In para 35 he said:

"On the assumption that the evidence (as I read it) showed that, but for the Bank's error, Samson was virtually certain to have retained Economy Bag's business in dog chews for the year 1993/94, the loss of profit on the figures adopted by the judge would have been $38,831, to which should be added 5% commission, less overheads, giving a total of $47,278.15. I would round down that figure to $45,000 to reflect the small degree of uncertainty inherent in even the closest of trading relationships and would award that sum together with interest by way of general damages for loss of profit."

32. Miss Andrews submitted that the Court of Appeal fell into error at this point. All that the claimant had to show was that at the time of the contract the contract-breaker should have contemplated that damage of the kind suffered would have occurred as a result of his breach. Once it had decided, correctly, that it was a natural and probable consequence of the Bank's breach that Samson would suffer a loss of repeat business, there was no cut-off point. The Bank's liability was open-ended, as it had not limited its liability by the contract to any particular period. The restriction which the Court of Appeal had imposed ex post facto on the Bank's liability cut across the rules in *Hadley v Baxendale* 9 Exch 341, which allocated risk between the parties at the time of the contract when they were still in a position to make provision for it in their bargain if they wished to do so.

Was the loss of repeat business too remote?

33. Mr Hapgood accepted that the proper time to which to look on the question of remoteness was the time when the parties entered into the contract. But he said that it would have been quite impossible at that stage to say what it would have taken to get Economy Bag to take action to dispose of the mark-up which was being charged by Samson. The parties' reasonable contemplation would have been that, as Economy Bag knew the identity of the supplier and where it could be contacted, no loss would flow from the disclosure to it of the amount of Samson's mark-up. The courts below, when dealing with the issue of remoteness, had fallen into the error of treating use of transferable letters of credit as a means of concealing the supplier's identity. That was not so in this case, as the seller's identity was known all along. He conceded that there had been a breach of contract. But he said that the information which was released when they provided Economy Bag with Pet Products prices could not reasonably be regarded as confidential, and that on the facts of this case there was no loss that was foreseeable.

34. I am unable to accept this argument. It is closely linked to the issue about the Bank's breach of contract which I dealt with earlier. There was no evidence that the parties contemplated at the time of the contract that knowledge of the supplier's identity and its contact details would lead inevitably to knowledge of the prices which were being charged by it. The fact that Economy Bag had the means of obtaining the information if it chose to do is beside the point. The effect of the contract that the Bank entered into was that it was obliged not to pass this information on, and Samson had an obvious and legitimate commercial interest in maintaining its confidentiality. There is no reason at all to suppose that, if it had been asked at the time of the contract, Samson would have agreed to the release of this information by the Bank to Economy Bag. I would hold in agreement both with the trial judge and the Court of Appeal, whose concurrent findings on the relevant facts I would regard as conclusive on this issue, that the loss of repeat orders from Economy Bag was not too remote. As soon as the confidential information was released there was no repeat business. The claimants are entitled to an award of damages to put them in the same position as they would have been if there had been no breach of contract. The question that remains is one of assessment. I would reject Mr Hapgood's contention that the matter is so speculative that the award should confined to one of general damages.

How is that loss to be quantified?

35. The first question is whether the Court of Appeal was wrong to limit the period for which damages were recoverable by reference to what was within the reasonable contemplation of the Bank at the time of the breach. Potter L.J. said in para 31 that, whatever the judge's view was of the percentage chance that Samson would in fact in the following years have been Economy Bag's supplier of dog chews, the Bank's reasonable contemplation at the date of the breach introduced a cut-off point beyond which the Bank was not liable. He said that this was the effect of the rule as to remoteness in *Hadley v Baxendale* 9 Exch 341.

36. In my opinion there are two errors in this approach to the assessment of damages. This first may appear to be the somewhat technical point, that it is the date of the making of the contract, not the date of the breach, that was identified as the relevant date in *Hadley v Baxendale*. I say that it may appear to be somewhat technical because in this case the date of the making of the contract and the date of the breach were only about two months apart. There is no evidence that the facts that were relevant to what the Bank had in reasonable contemplation changed to any significant extent between 22 January 1993 when the letter of credit was issued and 15 March 1993 when the Bank sent Pet Products' invoice to Economy Bag. But the error was an error of principle. The choice of dates is more important than the differences, if any, in those facts. The parties have the opportunity to limit their liability in damages when they are making their contract. They have the opportunity at that stage to draw attention to any special circumstances outside the ordinary course of things which they ought to have in contemplation when entering into the contract. If no cut-off point is provided by the contract, there is no arbitrary limit that can be set to the amount of the damages once the test of remoteness according to one or other of the rules in *Hadley v Baxendale* has been satisfied.

37. The second error flows from the first. The Bank did not include any provision in the letter of credit limiting its liability for the loss of repeat business to any particular period. So the only limit on the period of its liability is that which the trial judge identified. This is when, on the facts, the question whether any loss has been sustained has become too speculative to permit the making of any award. He held that as time passed it was increasing likely that Economy Bag would have acquired the motive and the means to squeeze Samson's profit margins and would ultimately have ended their business relationship. Miss Andrews did not challenge this approach, although she contended that the judge should have extended his award over a longer period. It seems to me that it is amply supported by the facts of the case. Samson were in a precarious position. Mr Taylor knew who the suppliers were and he had met Mr Veerachai. He knew where he could be contacted. It was only a matter of time before the harsh reality of doing business persuaded him that he should take a closer interest in what his arrangements with Samson were costing him and ask himself whether those costs could be cut down and perhaps eliminated.

38. These errors lie at the heart of the Court of Appeal's decision to limit the Bank's liability to a period of one year. For this reason I would hold that its decision cannot stand. I would allow the appeal and set aside its assessment of the amount to be awarded to the appellants as damages. . .

43. . . . I would hold that the award which the judge made, on a reducing basis extending over a four year period, is as good an estimate as can now be made of the effect on Samson's profits of the Bank's breach of contract.

TRANSFIELD SHIPPING INC v MERCATOR SHIPPING INC

House of Lords [2008] UKHL 48

The background to this case was that the charterers of a single-deck bulk carrier were in breach of **19–050** contract by being some nine days late in redelivering the vessel to the owners. As a result of this late redelivery, the owners were put in a difficult position in relation to a new fixture of the vessel that had been agreed with another charterer. In order to retain this fixture, the owners agreed to reduce the daily rate by $8,000. The question was whether the owners were entitled to recover the loss of $8,000 per day for the duration of the new charter (a sum of $1,364,584.37) or merely the difference between the market rate and the charter rate for the nine days late redelivery (a sum of $158,301.17). The majority of the arbitrators and the lower appeal courts held that the owners were entitled to the higher amount: their reasoning was that the charterers must have known that the owners were likely to arrange a new onward charter, that market rates fluctuate, and that late delivery might reduce the profitability of the onward charter (i.e., the forward fixture). However, the House of Lords held unanimously (albeit with some hesitation) that the owners were restricted to the lesser sum.

BARONESS HALE OF RICHMOND

My Lords,

88. Ship-owners let out their ship for a period of five to seven months, to end no later than midnight on 2 May 2004. The charterers notified the ship-owners that the ship would be back no later than then. The ship-owners therefore contracted to let the ship to new charterers for a period of about four to six months, promising that they could have the ship no later than 8 May 2004. The agreed price of hire was $39,500 a day. The ship was delayed on its last voyage and the owners did not get their ship back until 11 May 2004. The new charterers agreed to take the ship, but by then the market had fallen and they would only take it at a reduced price of $31,500 a day. Are the first charterers liable to pay only for the use of the ship for the number of days that they were late at the market rate then prevailing? Or are they liable to pay the difference between what the owners would have got from the new charter had the ship been returned in time and what the owners in fact got?

89. My Lords, this could be an examination question. Although the context is a specialised one, the answer has mainly to be found in the general principles to be derived from the well-known authorities to which your Lordships have all referred, principally *Hadley v Baxendale* (1854) 9 Exch 341, *Victoria Laundry (Windsor) Ltd v Newman Industries Ltd* [1949] 2 KB 528 and, above all, *C Czarnikow Ltd v Koufos (The Heron II)* [1969] 1 AC 350. There is no obviously right answer: two very experienced commercial judges have reached one answer, your Lordships have reached another. There is no obviously just answer: the charterer's default undoubtedly caused

the owner's loss, but a loss for which no-one has ever had to pay before. The examiners would surely have given first class marks to all the judges who have answered the question so far.

90. In common with my noble and learned friend, Lord Hope of Craighead, I was at first inclined to agree with the very full and thoughtful judgments in the courts below which arrived at the second answer. Their careful reviews of the shipping cases show that, although the normal measure of damages is undoubtedly the first, there is no case in which a claim to the second has been rejected. The fact that no-one has thought to make such a claim before now does not mean that it is unfounded. The question was unlikely to arise if the last voyage on which the charterer wished to send the ship was illegitimate, because the owner could then refuse to undertake it and the first charter would come to a premature end (or he might undertake it without prejudice as happened in *The Gregos* [1995] 1 Lloyd's Rep 1). And until the decision in *The Peonia* [1991] 1 Lloyd's Rep 100 it would not arise if the last voyage was legitimate, because the charterer was not liable at all for delay which was not his fault. So the novelty of the claim is no answer. It is not novel in principle. The object of damages for breach of contract is to put the claimants in the position in which they would have been had the contract been properly performed. Had this contract not been broken in the way that it was, the claimants would have had the benefit of the next fixture at the original rate. Putting them in the position in which they would have been had the contract been performed in accordance with its terms entails paying them the difference. No-one has suggested that it was at all unusual or unlikely for the owners to commit their ship to a new fixture to begin as soon as possible after the ship was free from the first. It was conceded before the arbitrators that missing dates for a subsequent fixture was a "not unlikely" result of late redelivery. Both parties would have been well aware of that at the time when the contract was made. They would also have been well aware that a new charter was likely to commit that particular ship rather than to allow the ship-owner to go into the market and find a substitute to fulfil his next commitment if his ship was late back. Charterparties allowing the owner to substitute a different vessel are unusual. Above all, if the parties wish to exclude liability for consequential loss of this kind then it will be very simple to insert such a clause into future charterparties. It would take a much more complicated piece of drafting, following some complicated negotiations, to impose liability for this sort of loss. To rule out a whole class of loss, simply because the parties had not previously thought about it, risks as much uncertainty and injustice as letting it in.

91. That argument cuts both ways. We are looking here at the general principles which limit a contract breaker's liability when the contract itself does not do so. The contract breaker is not inevitably liable for all the loss which his breach has caused. Loss of the type in question has to be "within the contemplation" of the parties at the time when the contract was made. It is not enough that it should be foreseeable if it is highly unlikely to happen. It would not then arise "in the usual course of things": see *The Heron II* [1969] 1 AC 350, 385, per Lord Reid. So one answer to our question, given as I understand it by my noble and learned friend, Lord Rodger of Earlsferry, is that these parties would not have had this particular type of loss within their contemplation. They would expect that the owner would be able to find a use for his ship even if it was returned late. It was only because of the unusual volatility of the market at that particular time that this particular loss was suffered. It is one thing to say, as did the majority arbitrators, that missing dates for a subsequent fixture was within the parties' contemplation as "not unlikely". It is another thing to say that the "extremely volatile" conditions which brought about this particular loss were "not unlikely".

92. Another answer to the question, given as I understand it by my noble and learned friends, Lord Hoffmann and Lord Hope, is that one must ask, not only whether the parties must be taken to have had this *type of loss* within their contemplation when the contract was made, but also whether they must be taken to have had *liability for this type of loss* within their contemplation then. In other words, is the charterer to be taken to have undertaken legal responsibility for this type of loss? What should the unspoken terms of their contract be taken to be? If that is the question, then it becomes relevant to ask what has been the normal expectation of parties to such contracts in this particular market. If charterers would not normally expect to pay more than the market rate for the days they were late, and ship-owners would not normally expect to get more than that, then one would expect something extra before liability for an unusual loss such as this would arise. That is essentially the reasoning adopted by the minority arbitrator.

93. My Lords, I hope that I have understood this correctly, for it seems to me that it adds an interesting but novel dimension to the way in which the question of remoteness of damage in contract is to be answered, a dimension which does not clearly emerge from the classic authorities. There is scarcely a hint of it in *The Heron II*, apart perhaps from Lord Reid's reference, at p 385, to the loss being "sufficiently likely to result from the breach of contract *to make it proper* to hold that the loss flowed naturally from the breach or that loss of that kind should have been within his contemplation" (emphasis supplied). In general, *The Heron II* points the other way, as it emphasises that there are no special rules applying to charterparties and that the law of

remoteness in contract is not the same as the law of remoteness in tort. There is more than a hint of it in the judgment of Waller L.J. in *Mulvenna v Royal Bank of Scotland Plc* [2003] EWCA Civ 1112, but in the context of the "second limb" of *Hadley v Baxendale* where knowledge of an unusual risk is posited. To incorporate it generally would be to introduce into ordinary contractual liability the principle adopted in the context of liability for professional negligence in *South Australia Asset Management Corp v York Montague Ltd* [1997] AC 191, 211. In an examination, this might well make the difference between a congratulatory and an ordinary first class answer to the question. But despite the excellence of counsels' arguments it was not explored before us, although it is explored in academic textbooks and other writings, including those cited by Lord Hoffmann in paragraph 11 of his opinion. I note, however, that the most recent of these, Professor Robertson's article on "The basis of the remoteness rule in contract" (2008) 28 Legal Studies 172 argues strongly to the contrary. I am not immediately attracted to the idea of introducing into the law of contract the concept the scope of duty which has perforce had to be developed in the law of negligence. The rule in *Hadley v Baxendale* asks what the parties must be taken to have had in their contemplation, rather than what they actually had in their contemplation, but the criterion by which this is judged is a factual one. Questions of assumption of risk depend upon a wider range of factors and value judgments. This type of reasoning is, as Lord Steyn put it in *Aneco Reinsurance Underwriting Ltd v Johnson & Higgins Ltd* [2002] 1 Lloyd's Rep 157, para 186, a "deus ex machina". Although its result in this case may be to bring about certainty and clarity in this particular market, such an imposed limit on liability could easily be at the expense of justice in some future case. It could also introduce much room for argument in other contractual contexts. Therefore, if this appeal is to be allowed, as to which I continue to have doubts, I would prefer it to be allowed on the narrower ground identified by Lord Rodger, leaving the wider ground to be fully explored in another case and another context.

Points for reflection

1. In *Supershield Limited v Siemens Building Technologies FE Limited* [2010] EWCA Civ 7, the Court of Appeal accepted that the logic of Lord Hoffmann's contextual approach in *Transfield Shipping* is that the usual rule in *Hadley v Baxendale* may be displaced by an implicit background expectation that points to a less extensive ("exclusionary") or, equally, a more extensive ("inclusionary") recovery for consequential losses. According to Toulson LJ, *Transfield Shipping* (and, similarly, the earlier decision of the House of Lords in *South Australia Asset Management Corp v York Montague Ltd* [1997] A.C. 191) had modified the standard rule in the following way (see para.43):

   19-051

   Hadley v Baxendale remains a standard rule but it has been rationalised on the basis that it reflects the expectation to be imputed to the parties in the ordinary case, i.e. that a contract breaker should ordinarily be liable to the other party for damage resulting from his breach if, but only if, at the time of making the contract a reasonable person in his shoes would have had damage of that kind in mind as not unlikely to result from a breach. However, *South Australia* and *Transfield Shipping* are authority that there may be cases where the court, on examining the contract and the commercial background, decides that the standard approach would not reflect the expectation or intention reasonably to be imputed to the parties.

   While, in both *South Australia* and *Transfield Shipping*, the effect of bringing in the commercial background was "exclusionary", in *Supershield*, the question was whether the new approach may also operate with "inclusionary" effect, so as to increase the contract-breaker's liability beyond the standard level. To this, Toulson LJ confirmed (at para.43) that "the same principle may have an inclusionary effect. If, on the proper analysis of the contract against its commercial background, the loss was within the scope of the duty, it cannot be regarded as too remote, even if it would not have occurred in ordinary circumstances."

2. Where (as in *Supershield*) the commercial background speaks clearly to the parties' expectations with regard to their liability for consequential loss, the application of contextualism is relatively straightforward. However, what if the background is less clear? In *John Grimes Partnership Ltd*

v Gubbins [2013] EWCA 37, the question was whether a firm of consultant engineers whose breach of contract led to a delay of some 15 months in relation to a proposed housing development, was liable to compensate the client for the reduced value of the development (the price of houses having fallen by some 14% during the intervening period). The client, relying on the standard rules, argued that this loss was within the reasonable contemplation of the engineers and, thus, was not too remote; the engineers, relying on *Transfield Shipping* (and cases such as *South Australia*) argued that they had not assumed responsibility for losses arising from fluctuations in the housing market. However, the weakness in the engineers' argument was that, on the facts, "there was no evidence . . . to show that there was some general understanding or expectation in the property world that a party in this engineer's position would not be taken to have assumed responsibility for losses arising from movement in the property market where there had been delay in breach of contract" (para.26). How should a court proceed where there is no clear evidence of a settled understanding in a particular market about the limits of consequential loss liability? One option is to treat the standard rules on remoteness as defaults which have not been disapplied; and another is to assess, under conditions of uncertainty, the more likely reading of the parties' understanding of their risks and liabilities. The Court of Appeal in *Gubbins* ruled against the engineers, apparently treating the standard rules as applicable by dint of presumed intention and implication.

----

6. Penalties and Liquidated Damages

19–052   The parties to a contract may anticipate the possibility of a breach and include a term in their agreement that a certain sum shall be paid to the injured party by the party in default in the event of a specified breach or breaches. If the sum fixed is a genuine estimate of the actual damage likely to be suffered by the injured party in the event of the specified breach, then it is recoverable and is known as "liquidated damages". If it is not a genuine estimate of the amount of damage likely to be caused but is much less, it may still be liquidated damages, for a party may properly limit his liability: *Cellulose Acetate Silk Co v Widnes Foundry* (1925) Ltd [1933] A.C. 20. But if the sum fixed is greater than any loss which the injured party could suffer as a result of the breach and, therefore, is intended to operate as a threat to keep a potential defaulter to his bargain, it is described as a "penalty". Courts of Equity gave relief against penalties and allowed the injured party to recover no more than his actual loss. Where, for example, a hire-purchase agreement provided that if, as the result of a breach by the hirer, the latter terminated the agreement, the hirer should pay, as compensation for depreciation, 75 per cent of the total sum due under the agreement, the Court of Appeal held that this was a penalty and irrecoverable. If the hirer had failed to pay the first instalment, the latter, according to the agreement, would have recovered a car that had hardly depreciated at all and 75 per cent of its value; and, on the actual facts of the case, he would have been £136 better of as a result of the breach than if the agreement had been carried out: *Lamdon Trust Co v Hurrel* [1955] 1 W.L.R. 391.

If a claimant sues for a penalty he can recover no more than the sum stipulated, even though he has suffered damage in excess of that sum. But it is open to him to ignore the penalty clause and sue for damages in which case he can recover the whole of his loss: *Wall v Rederiaktiebolaget Luggude* [1915] 3 K.B. 66 and *Jobson v Johnson*, below.

DUNLOP PNEUMATIC TYRE CO LTD v NEW GARAGE AND MOTOR CO LTD

House of Lords [1915] A.C. 79; 83 L.J.K.B. 1574; 111 L.T. 862; 30 T.L.R. 625

The appellants, manufacturers, supplied their goods to the respondents (dealers) under an agreement whereby the respondents, in consideration of a trade discount, undertook not to tamper with marks on the goods, not to sell below list prices, not to supply certain persons named by the appellants, not to exhibit or export any of the goods, and to pay £5 "by way of liquidated damages and not as a penalty" for every item of the goods sold or offered in breach of the agreement.

19–053

The respondents sold a tyre manufactured by the appellants below list price. There was evidence that the whole of the appellants' business was carried on through the trade, that all their customers were required to sign agreements of this nature, and that the probable effect of underselling by any one customer was to compel other customers to deal elsewhere. The Court of Appeal (Vaughan Williams and Swinfen Eady LJJ, Kennedy LJ dissenting), reversing the finding of a master, held that the £5 was a penalty and that the plaintiffs were entitled to nominal damages only. The House of Lords (Lords Dunedin, Atkinson, Parker and Parmoor) held, assuming without deciding that the sum of £5 applied to all the undertakings in the agreement, that it was liquidated damages.

LORD DUNEDIN

. . . I shall content myself with stating succinctly the various propositions which I think are deducible from the decisions which rank as authoritative:

1. Though the parties to a contract who use the words "penalty" or "liquidated damages" may prima facie be supposed to mean what they say, yet the expression used is not conclusive. The court must find out whether the payment stipulated is in truth a penalty or liquidated damages. This doctrine may be said to be found passim in nearly every case.

2. The essence of a penalty is a payment of money stipulated as in terrorem of the offending part; the essence of liquidated damages is a genuine covenanted pre-estimate of damage (*Clydebank Engineering and Shipbuilding Co v Don Jose Ramos Yzquierdo y Castaneda* [1905] A.C. 6).

3. The question whether a sum stipulated is penalty or liquidated damages is a question of construction to be decided upon the terms and inherent circumstances of each particular contract, judged of as at the time of the making of the contract, not as at the time of the breach (*Public Works Commissioner v Hills* [1906] A.C. 368 and *Webster v Bosanquet* [1912] A.C. 394).

4. To assist this task of construction various tests have been suggested, which if applicable to the case under consideration may prove helpful, or even conclusive. Such are:

(a) It will be held to be a penalty if the sum stipulated for is extravagant and unconscionable in amount in comparison with the greater loss that could conceivably be proved to have followed from the breach. (Illustration given by Lord Halsbury in *Clydebank* case.)

(b) It will be held to be a penalty if the breach consists only in not paying a sum of money, and the sum stipulated is a sum greater than the sum which ought to have been paid (*Kemble v Farren* 6 Bing. 141). This, though one of the most ancient instances, is truly a corollary to the last test. Whether it had its historical origin in the doctrine of the common law that when A promised to pay B a sum of money on a certain day and did not do so, B could only recover the sum with, in certain cases, interest, but could never recover further damages for non-timeous payment, or whether it was a survival of the time when equity reformed unconscionable bargains merely because they were unconscionable—a subject which much exercised Jessel M.R. in *Wallis v Smith*, 21 Ch.D. 243—is probably more interesting than material.

(c) There is a presumption (but no more) that it is penalty when "a single lump sum is made payable by way of compensation, on the occurrence of one or more or all of several events, some of which may occasion serious and others but trifling damage" (Lord Watson in *Lord Elphinstone v Monkland Iron and Coal Co*, 11 App.Cas. 332).

On the other hand:

(d) It is no obstacle to the sum stipulated being a genuine pre-estimate of damage, that the consequences of the breach are such as to make precise pre-estimation almost an impossibility. On the contrary, that is just the situation when it is probable that pre-estimated damage was the true bargain between the parties (*Clydebank* case, Lord Halsbury; Webster v Bosanquet, Lord Mersey).

Turning now to the facts of the case, it is evident that the damage apprehended by the appellants owing to the breaking of the agreement was an indirect and not a direct damage. So long as they got their price from the respondents for each article sold, it could not matter to them directly what the respondents did with it. Indirectly it did. Accordingly, the agreement is headed "Price Maintenance Agreement," and the way in which the appellants would be damaged if prices were cut is clearly explained in evidence by Mr Baisley, and no successful attempt is made to controvert that evidence. But though damage as a whole from such a practice would be certain, yet damage from any one sale would be impossible to forecast. It is just, therefore, one of those cases where it seems quite reasonable for parties to contract that they should estimate that damage at a certain figure, and provided that figure is not extravagant there would seem no reason to suspect that it is not truly a bargain to assess damages, but rather a penalty to be held in terrorem.

Points for reflection

19–054   Penalties and liquidated damages have one thing in common: they are both sums of money which, by the terms of the contract, are payable on the occurrence of a breach of contract. If a contract provides that a sum of money shall become payable on the occurrence of some event other than a breach of contract, then this sum cannot be either a penalty or liquidated damages as these concepts have been traditionally understood and, prima facie, the sum will be recoverable in full whether it bears any relation to any loss which may have been suffered by the party suing or not. For example, if A promises B that, if B, having used one of A's carbolic smoke balls three times daily for two weeks, catches influenza, he (A) will pay £100—or £10,000—B can, on the happening of the event, recover the specified sum even though it vastly exceeds the injury which B has suffered through catching influenza. The position might well be different if A had promised B that, if B used the smoke ball as specified, he would not catch influenza and that if B did, A would pay him a certain sum. The money would then be payable on a breach of contract and the question would arise whether it was a penalty or liquidated damages.

In *Alder v Moore* [1961] 2 Q.B. 57 CA, the defendant, a professional footballer, was insured by his Union against permanent total disablement from playing professional football. He suffered an injury which the underwriters were satisfied amounted to permanent total disablement. As required by the policy, he signed a declaration that he would take no part, as a playing member, in any form of professional football and that "in the event of infringement of this condition, he will be subject to a penalty of the amount paid him in settlement of his claim."

Four months later the defendant started playing professional football again and the underwriters sued to recover £500. The defence was that the clause was a penalty and that the underwriters had suffered no damage through his playing football again. The Court of Appeal, allowing an appeal from Paull J, held that, notwithstanding the use of the term "penalty", this was a contract for the payment of a certain sum in a certain event which was not a breach of contract (there was no "contractual ban upon the defendant from playing professional football again"—per Slade J) and, that event having happened, the sum was payable. Devlin LJ dissenting, took the view that the underwriters had called the clause "a penalty" so there was an onus on them to satisfy the court that they did not mean what they said; that the underwriters had in fact exacted a promise from the defendant that he would not play football again and he was not prepared to rewrite this as a contingent promise to pay in the event of his playing football again.

The problem has arisen in an acute form in hire-purchase agreements which commonly provide that, if the hirer determines the agreement, he will bring his payments up to a specified sum as compensation for depreciation of the goods. If the hirer exercises his option to return the goods this is not a breach of contract—it is the exercise of a contractual right—and no question of penalty or liquidated damages prima facie arises. If, however, the hirer repudiates the contract, and the owner resumes possession, there is clearly a breach of contract and the sum specified is recoverable only if it amounts to liquidated damages and not a penalty.

BRIDGE v CAMPBELL DISCOUNT CO LTD

House of Lords [1962] A.C. 600; [1962] 2 W.L.R. 439; [1962] 1 All E.R. 385

The hirer of a car under a hire-purchase agreement paid an initial sum of £105 and one monthly instalment. He then informed the finance company that he could not keep up the payments and returned the car to them. By cl.6 the hirer had a right to terminate the hiring at any time and return the car but, if he did so, by cl.9, he was required to pay, "by way of agreed compensation for depreciation" such sum as would make his total payments up to two-thirds of the purchase price. Under this clause, the company claimed £206 3s. 4d.

19–055

The Court of Appeal, allowing an appeal from the county court judge, held that the amount claimed was not a penalty but was the sum payable as compensation to the company for the hirer's exercise of his right under cl.6. The House of Lords interpreted the hirer's conduct as a repudiation of the contract and not the exercise of his right under cl.6 and, accordingly, held that this was a claim for a penalty.

VISCOUNT SIMONDS

[Having stated that he dissented from the interpretation put upon the hirer's conduct by their Lordships and preferred the view of the Court of Appeal, went on:] Clause 6 is not a penal clause. It confers on the hirer a right for which he agrees to pay a price. He need not exercise it if he does not want to . . . I must dissent, as Harman L.J. did, from the suggestion that there is a general principle of equity which justifies the court in relieving a party to any bargain if in the event it operates hardly against him. In particular cases, for example, of expectant heirs or of fiduciary relationship, a court of equity (and now any court) will if the circumstances justify it grant relief. So also if there Is duress or fraud "which unravels all." In the present case there is nothing which would justify the court in granting relief to a hirer who exercised his rights under clause 6. [His Lordship went on to say that if, as the majority held, the hirer had committed a breach of contract, he agreed that the claim was for a penalty.]

Lord Morton said that if the appellant had exercised his option under clause 6, he would have agreed with the Court of Appeal; but that he thought the appellant had broken his contract and that clause 9 was a penal provision.

LORD RADCLIFFE

. . . Having regard to the view that your Lordships have taken as to the true facts of the case, our decision does not, I take it, conclude the question of an owner's rights under such agreements, when the hiring is determined under a hirer's option or by an event specified in the contract but not involving a breach. Such questions are closely related to what we have to consider here, but it does not follow that the legal arguments that sustain the hirer, when he is sued on breach, would be capable of sustaining him in these other situations. Indeed, although I wish to decide nothing, I appreciate that the doctrine of penalties can only be applied to those situations by the construction of almost a new set of arguments that would not arise naturally out of the arguments and considerations that have prevailed with courts, either of equity or of common law, when relieving against penalties in the past. "Unconscionable" must not be taken to be a panacea for adjusting any contract between competent persons when it shows a rough edge of one side or the other, and equity lawyers are, I notice, sometimes both surprised and discomfited by the plenitude of jurisdiction, and the imprecision of rules that are attributed to "equity" by their more enthusiastic colleagues . . .

LORD DENNING

[Having pointed out that, according to the view of the Court of Appeal, if Bridge, finding himself unable to keep up the payments and being a conscientious man, gave notice of termination and returned the car, he was liable to pay the "penal sum of £206 3s. 4d. without relief of any kind," went on:] Let no one mistake the injustice of this. It means that equity commits itself to this absurd paradox: it will grant relief to a man who breaks his contract but will penalise the man who keeps it. If this be the state of equity today, then it is in sore need of an overhaul, so as to restore its first principles. But I am quite satisfied that such is not the state of equity today. This can be brought within long-established principles without recourse to any new equity. From the very earliest times equity has relieved not only against penalties for breach of contract, but also against penalties for non-performance of a condition . . .

If I am wrong about all this, however, and there is no jurisdiction to grant the relief unless the hirer is in breach, then I would be prepared to hold in this case Bridge was in breach . . .

LORD DEVLIN

[Having held that the case was one of breach of contract and that the sum claimed was penal, went on:] When your Lordships have determined that clause 9(b), when it comes into operation as the result of a breach, is a penalty clause, your Lordships must also have determined that the clause contained no genuine estimate of the loss caused to the owner by depreciation and no genuine agreement that a sum should be paid in respect of it. There is no half-way house between a penalty and liquidated damages. However large the sum stipulated may be, if it is a genuine, covenanted pre-estimate of damage it is not stipulated as in terrorem and so cannot be a penalty. If, therefore, your Lordships had taken clause 9(b) at its face value and had supposed that, as it states, there was really an agreement about the sum to be paid as compensation for depreciation (I do not mean necessarily a separate collateral agreement; an estimate in which the defendant acquiesced would serve the purpose) the plaintiffs would inevitably have succeeded in their claim . . .

My Lords, I do not see how an agreement can be genuine for one purpose and a sham for another. If it is a sham, it means that it was never made and does not exist; if it does not exist, it must be ignored altogether . . .

On this comparatively narrow ground I should (if I had construed the letter of September 3 as the exercise of an option) have held that the defendant was nevertheless entitled to succeed . . .

Appeal Allowed.

Question

19–056   Z, a footballer, being apparently disabled, received £500 from an insurance company. Having started to play football again, he is sued for the return of the money. Advise him, assuming that, when he received the £500, he signed a form which stated: "I undertake that I will not in the future play football and, should I do so, will repay the insurance moneys." Would it be different if the form read: "I undertake that, if I should play football in the future, I will refund the insurance moneys"?

The Law Commission Working Paper No.61: Penalty Clauses and Forfeiture of Monies Paid

19–057   The Law Commission having referred to the paradox stated by Lord Denning in *Bridge v Campbell Discount* (above), continue:

22. Our provisional view is that the court should have the power to deal with such clauses in the same way whether or not they come into operation by breach. There is however a problem of some difficulty, and that centres on the statutory description of contractual provisions to which this power will apply, since we do not envisage the power being confined to minimum payment clauses in hire-purchase agreements. It would not, we think, be possible to confer such a power in relation to all contractual provisions calling for payment of a sum of money for it is not our intention that every price payable under a contract should be subject to judicial control . . .

25. The South African Conventional Penalties Act 1962 equates stipulations which provide that a party is to remain liable for the performance of some obligation upon withdrawal from an agreement with stipula-

tions for penalties or liquidated damages.[2] A provision on these lines might deal with clauses which come into operation on a voluntary termination of an agreement, but we think that the phrase "upon withdrawal from an agreement" is too narrow to cover all the circumstances in which penalty clauses might come into operation.

Proposal for reform

26. A more acceptable approach would, we think, be this. There are in essence two separate matters which are being considered. There is first the contractual obligation which is being challenged as penal—typically (though not necessarily) an obligation to pay money in specified circumstances. Such an obligation might arise, for example, on the non-performance of some other act, or on the termination of an agreement voluntarily or on death or bankruptcy. The second matter is the act or result which is the true purpose of the contract, although its non-performance or non-fulfilment may not constitute a breach of the contract. Our proposal is that the rules as to penalties should be applied wherever the object of the disputed contractual obligation is to secure the act or result which is the true purpose of the contract. If, for example, a building contract were to provide for completion of the building by a certain date unless delayed by bad weather there would be no breach of contract if completion were delayed by bad weather. If the contract were also to provide that the builder should pay £50 for every day's delay caused by bad weather, the recoverability of the specified sum would depend on its being a genuine pre-estimate of the loss caused by delay. We should welcome views on this provisional proposal.

JOBSON v JOHNSON

Court of Appeal [1989] 1 W.L.R. 1026; [1989] 1 All E.R. 621

The defendant agreed to buy shares in Southend United Football Club for £351,688 by an initial payment of £40,000 and six half-yearly instalments of £51,948. Clause 6(b) of the agreement provided that if the defendant defaulted on the second or any subsequent instalment, he must return the shares to the seller for £40,000. The defendant paid £140,000 and the shares were transferred to him. He then defaulted and the plaintiff, the assignee of the seller, obtained an order for specific performance of the agreement to re-transfer the shares. The defendant appealed arguing that cl.6(b) was a penalty clause and unenforceable.

19-058

Dillon LJ delivered judgment allowing the appeal to the extent indicated below.

NICHOLLS LJ

Equitable relief

In considering this appeal it is right to have in mind that the legal principles applicable today regarding penalty clauses in contracts and those applicable regarding relief from forfeiture stem from a common origin. A penalty clause in a contract, as that expression is normally used today, is a provision which, on breach of the contract, requires the party in default to make a payment to the innocent party of a sum of money which, however it may be labelled, is not a genuine pre-estimate of the damage likely to be sustained by the innocent party, but is a payment stipulated in terrorem of the party in default. For centuries equity has given relief against such provisions by not permitting the innocent party to recover under the penal provision more than his actual loss. In *Wyllie v Wilkes* (1780) 2 Doug K.B. 519 at 522–523, Lord Mansfield observed that in the reign of Henry VIII Sir Thomas More had attempted unsuccessfully to persuade the judges to give relief in respect of money bonds:

---

[2]   Act No.15 of 1962, as amended by Act No.102 of 1967. On the Act, see P. M. A. Hunt in [1962] Annual Survey of South African Law, p.94 and C. I. Belcher (1964) 81 S.A.L.J. 80. See also B. A. Hepple (1961) 78 S.A.L.J. 445 on the Bill which led to the Act.

"For he summoned them to a conference concerning the granting relief at law, after the forfeiture of bonds, upon payment of principal, interest, and costs; and when they said they could not relieve against the penalty, he swore by the body of God, he would grant an injunction."

Likewise with forfeiture. Take the simple case of a provision for forfeiture of a lease on non-payment of rent. That provision was regarded by equity as a security for the rent. So that, where conscience so required, equity relieved against the forfeiture on payment of the rent with interest. Again with mortgages: . . .

Penalty clauses

The particular procedure by which the Court of Chancery prevented a party seeking payment under a penalty clause in a contract, including a bond, from recovering more than his actual loss seems to have differed a little according to whether the penalty was intended to secure only a payment of money on a specified date or was intended to secure the performance of an obligation other than a payment of money. The details are not material for the purpose of this appeal . . .

Thus today, when law and equity are administered concurrently in the same courts, and the rules of equity prevail whenever there is any conflict or variance between the rules of equity and the rules of the common law with reference to the same matter (section 49 of the Supreme Court Act 1981), a penalty clause in a contract is, in practice, a dead letter. An obligation to make a money payment stipulated in terrorem will not be enforced beyond the sum which represents the actual loss of the party seeking payment, namely, principal, interest and, if appropriate, costs, in those cases where (to use modern terminology) the primary obligation is to pay money, or where the primary obligation is to perform some other obligation, beyond the sum recoverable as damages for breach of that obligation. (For convenience I shall hereafter refer to that sum as "the actual loss of the innocent party.") Hence normally there is no advantage in suing on the penalty clause. In *Wall v Rederiaktiebolaget Luggude* [1915] 3 K.B. 66 at 73 Bailhache J. concluded his examination of the history of this matter in the context of a penalty clause in a charterparty with these words:

"This being the state of the law as I understand it, one easily sees why in charterparty cases no one sues on the penalty clause now. You cannot under it recover more than the proved damages, and if the proved damages exceed the penal sum you are restricted to the lower amount. As the penalty clause may be disregarded it always is disregarded and has become a dead letter, or from another point of view a 'brutum fulmen' . . ."

Although in practice a penalty clause in a contract as described above is effectively a dead letter, it is important in the present case to note that, contrary to the submissions of counsel for the defendant, the strict legal position is not that such a clause is simply struck out of the contract, as though with a blue pencil, so that the contract takes effect as if it had never been included therein. Strictly, the legal position is that the clause remains in the contract and can be sued on, but it will not be enforced by the court beyond the sum which represents, in the events which have happened, the actual loss of the party seeking payment. There are many cases which make this clear . . .

Accordingly, once a court becomes aware that the amount claimed by the plaintiff is a penalty arising on default of payment of a specific sum of money the legal consequence which follows, as day follows night, is that the amount claimed will be scaled down by the court to a sum equal to the unpaid principal, with interest and costs. That consequence, albeit having its historical origin in equity, is not dependent on the court exercising a discretion to grant or withhold relief having regard to all the circumstances. It is a consequence which for many years has followed automatically, regardless of the circumstances of the default.

In this respect, as the law has developed, a distinction has arisen between the enforcement of penalty clauses in contracts and the enforcement of forfeiture clauses. A penalty clause will not be enforced beyond the sum which equals the actual loss of the innocent party. A forfeiture clause, of which a right of re-entry under a lease on non-payment of rent is the classic example, may also be penal in its effect. Such a clause frequently subjects the defaulting party, in the event of non-payment of rent or breach of some other obligation, to a sanction which damnifies the defaulting party, and benefits the other party, to an extent far greater than the actual loss of the innocent party. For instance, the lease may be exceedingly valuable and the amount of unpaid rent may be small. But in such a case the court will lend its aid in the enforcement of the forfeiture, by making an order for possession, subject to any relief which in its discretion the court may grant to the party in default. Normally the granting of such relief is made conditional on the payment of the rent with interest and costs. If that condition is not complied with, and subject to any further application by the tenant or other person in default for yet more time, the forfeiture provision will be enforced. Thus the innocent party is in a better position when seeking to enforce a forfeiture clause than when seeking to enforce a penalty clause in a contract . . .

Property and not money

I return to penalty clauses. The scaling-down exercise which is carried out automatically by equity is straightforward when the penalty clause provides for payment of a sum of money. More difficult, and more unusual, is the case where the penal obligation triggered by the breach is an obligation to transfer property to the party not in default, as under clause 6(b). Even in such a case there is no difficulty where the value of the property at the time when the court is making its order does not exceed the actual loss of the innocent party. In that event there can be no more objection to the court specifically enforcing the obligation to transfer the property than there would be to the court making an order for the payment of a sum of money stipulated in a (pecuniary) penalty clause where, in the event, that sum does not exceed the actual loss of the innocent party. The difficulty arises where the value of the property agreed to be transferred exceeds the actual loss of the innocent party. A precisely comparable scaling-down exercise would not provide an acceptable solution, at any rate where the property consists of a single piece of land, or a block of shares in a company such as Southend United Football Club Ltd, whose shares are not traded in one of the securities markets. It could not be right to order specific performance of clause 6(b) in part only, namely in respect of the reduced number of shares whose value does not exceed the actual loss of the plaintiff. That, indeed, would be to make a new bargain for the parties.

In the present case we do not know what is the current value of the shares comprised in clause 6(b), even in approximate terms. I shall return later to the question of what, in that circumstance, can and should be done. For the moment it is sufficient to note that, apart from the difference between shares and money, clause 6(b) possesses all the essential characteristics of a penalty clause. In principle, and subject to the complication arising from the difficulty of "scaling-down" an obligation to transfer shares, there can be no difference between an obligation to pay a stipulated sum of money arising on a default and an obligation to transfer specified property arising on a default. The essential vice is the same in each case. In principle, so far as this can be achieved, the parties' respective positions should be no better, or worse, than they would be if clause 6(b) had stipulated for payment of money rather than a transfer of shares.

[The court offered the plaintiff two alternative forms of relief: (a) an order for the sale of the shares by the court and payment of the unpaid instalments and interest to the plaintiff out of the proceeds or (b) an inquiry as to the value of the shares and, if it did not exceed the amount of the unpaid instalments and interest by £40,000, an order for specific performance of the agreement. Kerr L.J., thinking neither alternative offered sufficient justice to the plaintiff, would have offered a third alternative.]

Appeal Allowed to the Extent Indicated in the Judgments of Dillon and Nicholls L.JJ.

It should be noted that the more recent jurisprudence on penalty clauses suggests that, in the context of commercial contracts where the parties enjoy equal bargaining power, the courts will be slow to declare that an agreed damages clause (e.g., for late delivery or late payment) is to be treated as penal. However, it cannot be taken for granted that the courts will not intervene. For example, in *Jeancharm Ltd t/a Beaver International v Barnet Football Club Ltd* [2003] EWCA Civ 58, the Court of Appeal held unanimously that a late payment "penalty" of 5 per cent per week (amounting to an annual rate of some 260 per cent) was penal. Although this provision was matched by a clause setting a daily deduction of 20p per garment for late delivery, the court rejected the argument that the latter clause could be used to justify the former. As Peter Gibson LJ put it:

"[T]he authorities show that one concentrates on the relevant clause said to be a penalty, and, on the application of the test so clearly laid down in *Dunlop*, in my judgment it is plain that in this case the interest clause far exceeds anything that could be said to be a genuine pre-estimate of actual loss and amounts to a penalty."

Two penal wrongs, then, do not make a right.

Further reading

Brian Coote, 'Contract Damages, Ruxley and the Performance Interest' [1997] 56 CLJ 537

Richard Danzig, '*Hadley v Baxendale*: A Study in the Industrialization of the Law' (1975) 4 *Journal of Legal Studies* 249

M. P. Furmston, 'Damages—Diminution in Value or Cost of Repair? Damages for Distress' (1993) 6 JCL 64

Lon L. Fuller and William Perdue, 'The Reliance Interest in Contract Damages' (1936) 46 *Yale Law Journal* 52 and 373

D. Harris, A. Ogus and J. Philips, 'Contract Remedies and the Consumer Surplus' (1979) 95 LQR 581

Charles Mitchell, '*Johnson v Agnew* (1979)' in Charles Mitchell and Paul Mitchell (eds) *Landmark Cases in the Law of Contract* (Oxford: Hart, 2008) p.351

Andrew Robertson, 'The Basis of the Remoteness Rule in Contract' (2008) 28 Legal Studies 172

Charlie Webb, 'Performance and Compensation: An Analysis of Contract Damages and Contractual Obligation' (2006) 26 OJLS 41

20

WITHDRAWAL

LEARNING OBJECTIVES

By the end of this chapter, you should:

- understand that, in the event of certain kinds of breach, the innocent party may have the option of withdrawing from the contract;
- be familiar with the traditional case-law that identifies the relevant trigger for the option of withdrawal as a breach of "condition" (as opposed to a breach of a mere "warranty");
- be familiar with the modern case-law (from the *Hong Kong Fir Shipping* case onwards) in which the courts have identified the trigger for the option of withdrawal, not as the breach of a particular class of term, but by reference to the seriousness of the consequences of the breach;
- have critically reflected on the threshold set by the modern law for the innocent party to have the option of withdrawal;
- have formed a view about whether the right to withdraw may be abused by an innocent party and, if so, how this is best addressed;
- be familiar with the case-law on "entire" contracts and the doctrine of substantial performance.

INTRODUCTION

In any relationship, termination (or withdrawal) is a last resort; and so it is, too, in contractual relation-ships. As we have seen (in Chs 18 and 19), the standard remedy for breach of contract is the payment of damages. The right to withdraw for breach (the right to discontinue performance, to end the relation-ship) is available only in rather limited cases. Broadly speaking, this right arises where: **20–001**

- it is expressly reserved by legislation (as in legislation regulating sale of goods);

- it is conferred by express contractual provision;

- it is recognised by virtue of settled commercial expectation;

- it arises by implication given the seriousness of the breach (striking at the root of the contract);

- it is appropriate in the light of the grave consequences of the breach that has taken place.

In all these cases, it is arguable that the governing principle is that the right to withdraw becomes available only when damages would no longer be an adequate remedy.

One might wonder why the innocent party might wish to opt for withdrawal. Some possible answers include:

- Because non-performance leaves the contractor with no alternative other than to seek a substitute supplier.

- Because the performance is so defective that it cannot possibly be accepted and must be rejected.

- Because all confidence in the contract-breaker (or in the product) has been lost. Compare *J & H Ritchie Ltd v Lloyd Ltd* [2007] UKHL 9.

- Because, all things considered, it is best to give up on the deal.

- Because a better deal is available outside the contract; or because, following withdrawal, a better deal can be negotiated with the original contractor.

In general, these reasons fit with the governing principle that the option to withdraw should only become available when damages are no longer an adequate remedy. However, the final reason reveals an opportunistic line of thinking that is quite different; and one of the major fault lines in English law turns on whether the courts (or legislators) are prepared to regulate and restrict such opportunism.

The benchmark for the classical approach to such opportunism is *Arcos Ltd v EA Ronaasen and Son* [1933] A.C. 470. There, the House of Lords held that the buyers were entitled to reject a consignment of timber on the ground that it failed to correspond to the contractual specification. On one view, this was perfectly straightforward because s.13 of the then applicable Sale of Goods Act 1893 gave the buyers the option of rejection where goods fail to correspond with the contract description. However, the timber that was delivered was actually perfectly adequate for the buyers' purposes and the real reason for the buyers' action was that, the market price for timber having fallen, they could now buy timber at a lower price on the open market. In other words, the buyers were looking for an excuse to get out of the contract. So far as the House of Lords was concerned, on a falling market, it was simply business as usual for a buyer to take advantage of the opportunity presented by a seller's breach. In general, this view should be contrasted with the approach taken in the *Hong Kong Fir Shipping* case (below) and by the House in *Schuler v Wickman* (below); and, in particular, it needs to be read alongside the change effected by s.15A Sale and Supply of Goods Act 1994 (below).

The chapter is divided into three sections. In the first section, there is a commentary together with some case-law on the nature of a "condition" and of "conditional contracts". The second section sets out the leading cases on the characterisation of particular terms of a contract as "warranties" or "conditions", whether determined by a traditional approach or by the consequential test that was introduced by the *Hong Kong Fir Shipping* case. In the third section, we consider some cases that assess the legal consequences of a failure by A to satisfy completely a condition that sets the threshold for B's obligation to pay for A's services (as in so-called "entire" contracts).

1. THE NATURE OF A CONDITION

20-002   The word "condition" is used in many senses. Stoljar ((1953) 69 LQR 485) discerns no fewer than 12 senses of the term. So far, the word has been used in this book mainly as meaning a promise in a contract of so important a nature that a breach of it entitles the other party to terminate the contract as well as to sue for damages. In this sense, the word is contrasted with "warranty" which, it will be recalled, also means a promise, but one of a subsidiary nature, the breach of which entitles the injured party to damages only and not to terminate the contract.[1] It is time now to consider some of the further uses of the term "condition".

A . Conditions Precedent, Conditions Subsequent, and Concurrent Conditions

The word "condition" may be used in the law of contract to describe some fact or event on the existence or occurrence of which some or all of the rights and duties under the contract are made to depend. It is not necessary that anyone should promise that that fact or event exists or will occur, but, if it does not exist or occur, the rights and duties dependent on it will be inoperative. When Mrs Carlill had used the smoke ball for two weeks (above, Ch.2) she had a contract with the Carbolic Smoke Ball Company. But the company was under no duty to do anything until a certain event occurred—that is, Carlill caught influenza. Catching influenza was, then, a condition of the company's obligation to pay £100. Notice that it was not held that the company promised that she would not catch influenza.[2] Notice also that Carlill did not promise that she would, or would not do so. This was not an "act" by her, but simply the happening of an event. As this was a unilateral contract, only one party undertook any obligation. In a bilateral contract the obligations of either or both parties may be made subject to a condition. It has been seen (above, Ch.4) that the Sale of Goods Act 1979 s.9, provides that where the parties to a contract for the sale of goods agree that the price is to be fixed by a third party and the third party cannot or does not fix the price, the agreement is thereby avoided. Here the fixing of the price is a condition of the obligations of both parties. Again, there is no promise by either buyer or seller that the third party will fix the price. The proper interpretation of this situation would seem to be that there is a contract as soon as the parties have completed their agreement but no duties to perform arise unless and until the specified event, in this case the fixing of the price, occurs. The specified event may be an act by one of the parties: see *Trans Trust SPRL v Danubian Trading Co Ltd* (below); and see *Bentworth Finance Ltd v Lubert and Another* [1968] 1 Q.B. 680. That party is not necessarily obliged to do the act; but, if he does not, the contract will never become operative.

These are examples of conditions precedent, because the condition must be fulfilled before the obligation exists or becomes operative. By contrast, so-called conditions subsequent are said to occur where the happening of the event operates to destroy an existing obligation. True examples of such conditions are hard to find. The example usually given is *Head v Tattersall* (1871) L.R. 7 Ex. 7, where A sold a horse to B and warranted that it had been hunted with the Bicester hounds. There was an express condition that if the horse did not answer the description it could be returned before five o'clock on the following Wednesday. It was held that B, on finding that the horse did not answer the description, could return it within the time limited, although in the meantime it had suffered an injury (in no way B's fault) which reduced its value. It is difficult to see, however, that this condition was subsequent to anything. At the time of the making of the contract, the condition either was or was not fulfilled. The true interpretation of the contract would seem to be that not having been hunted with the Bicester hounds was a condition precedent to B's right to reject the horse. In fact, he had such a right from the moment the contract was made though he did not know it until he discovered

20–003

---

[1]   Notice that "terminate" does not mean "rescind". Recission avoids the contract ab initio, termination avoids it only for the future: rights and obligations already incurred are unaffected. "The failure to distinguish between discharge by breach and rescission ab initio has led many courts astray and continues to do so" (*Hurst v Bryk* [2000] 2 All E.R. 193 at 199–200 HL, per Lord Millett).

[2]   It was argued, [1892] 2 Q.B. 484 at 486, before Hawkins J, that the defendants warranted that the plaintiff would not catch influenza, with liquidated damages in the event of breach; but that was not the decision. (cf. *Lambert v Lewis* [1980] 1 All E.R. 978 at 1002.)

the horse's lack of connection with the Bicester hounds (compare Stoljar ((1953) 69 LQR 485, 510). Perhaps a better example is the "promissory warranty" in a contract of marine insurance because the effect of a breach of that warranty by the insured is that, while the contract may survive, the insurer is automatically discharged from liability as from the date of the breach (see *The Good Luck* [1991] 3 All E.R. 1 HL, applying the Marine Insurance Act 1906, s.33(3)). In *The Good Luck*, when the ship, in breach of such a warranty, entered a prohibited zone in the Persian Gulf, the insurer's obligations automatically ceased. Unlike the ordinary case of breach of condition, the termination of the obligations is not dependent on any decision by the insurer. But even in this case, the House used the language of condition precedent, citing Lord Blackburn in *Thomson v Weems* (1884) 9 App.Cas. 671 at 684: "compliance with that warranty is a condition precedent to the attaching of the risk."

Conditions subsequent are sometimes confused with limitations—that is, clauses defining the extent of the promise. In the *High Trees* case (above, Ch.11) the plaintiff's promise not to demand the full rent was held to be subject to an implied limitation in that it was only to be operative while the war-time conditions prevailed. In *Wyatt v Kreglinger* (above, Ch.10) the entry of the plaintiff into the wool trade was a limitation on the defendants' promise (void, as it turned out, for another reason) to pay the pension. The distinction is that a condition subsequent avoids the liability ab initio, so that the promise is treated as never having been made (Montrose, 15 Can.Bar Rev. 319). But in *High Trees* it was certainly not intended that the plaintiffs should be able to demand arrears of rent on the cessation of war-time conditions (notice that whether that intention should be effective is a different question and one to which Denning J devoted most of his judgment). Nor, in *Wyatt v Kreglinger*, was it the intention that the plaintiff's right to the pension he had already received should be avoided on his subsequent entry into the wool trade. Both these clauses, then, were limitations and not conditions subsequent. When this distinction is borne in mind conditions subsequent become even harder to find and Stoljar's conclusion that "the famous condition subsequent is nothing but a ghost" is hard to resist ((1953) 69 LQR 485, 508).

Conditions are sometimes also described as "concurrent". For example, s.28 of the Sale of Goods Act provides that "Payment and delivery are concurrent conditions". This would appear to mean that the seller's obligation to deliver is conditional on the price having been paid and that the buyer's obligation to pay the price is conditional on the goods having been delivered. If this were the case, clearly the statute would have created a legal stalemate in which neither party is bound to act. In fact, however, the Act goes on to explain what it means: ". . . that is to say, the seller must be ready and willing to give possession of the goods to the buyer in exchange for the price, and the buyer must be ready and willing to pay the price in exchange for possession of the goods." This makes it clear that the seller's readiness and willingness to give possession is a condition precedent to the buyer's duty to pay the price and vice versa. The truth is that the so-called "concurrent condition" is "an elliptical expression for a condition precedent where performances are due at the same time." (Restatement of Contracts, p.363.)

It is clear that in describing as "conditions" both (a) the essential as opposed to the subsidiary promises in a contract and (b) those facts or events on the occurrence of which the duty to perform contractual promises depends, we are using the same word to describe two very different things. The distinction between a condition, strictly so-called, and a promise is clearly explained by Professor Montrose (see 'Conditions, Warranties and Other Contractual Terms' 15 Can.Bar Rev. 308, 323):

"I promise you £5 if you go to Rome: you promise to go to Rome. There are two terms of the contract, the subject-matter of which is going to Rome: there is a condition annexed by my promise and there is your promise. Each has a distinct function and so your going to Rome has a dual operation. It is a fulfilment of the condition annexed to my promise and also the performance of your promise. I must pay you the £5 not because you have performed your promise as such, but because such performance operates as a fulfilment of the condition annexed to my promise. Likewise, of course, your not going to Rome has a dual operation. There is a failure of the condition annexed to my promise and you have committed a breach of your promise. Because of the failure of the condition I do not have to pay you £5: because of the non-performance of your promise you are liable to me in damages. The event which brings about the failure of the condition operates also as a breach of your promise. Failure of the condition is followed by your liability to pay damages but is not the cause of it. The breach of your promise is followed by release from my promise but is not the cause of it."

The English usage which describes an essential promise in a contract as a condition is misleading, not because there is not a condition in the contract, but because the term is applied to the wrong thing. A offers B an old picture, of unknown authorship, for £1000. After examining it and forming the opinion that it is a Constable, B says: "I will give you £1000 for it provided it is a genuine Constable." A accepts. Clearly B's promise is subject to a condition and equally clearly A gives no undertaking as to the authorship of the picture. There is a condition, but no promise. Now if the facts were that A had given an assurance that the picture was by Constable, without which he knew B would not have contracted, the same condition would have been present, for B clearly did not intend to pay unless the painting was a Constable; but, in addition, there is now a promise by A for which he could be held liable in damages.

Professor Williston (Selections from Williston, *Contracts*, subs.665) described the use of the word "condition" to mean a certain kind of promise as "astonishing", expressing the opinion that "the difference between conditions and promises is so radical in its consequences that there is no excuse for a nomenclature which fails to recognise the distinction." The usage is nevertheless well established and was defended by Stephenson LJ in *Wickman Sales v Schuler* [1972] 1 W.L.R. 840 at 859–861 and the student of English law must be on his guard to ascertain in which sense the term is being used in any case.

PYM v CAMPBELL

Queen's Bench (1856) 6 El. & Bl. 379; 119 E.R. 903

The plaintiff alleged that the defendants agreed in writing to purchase a share in an invention of the plaintiff's. The defendants gave evidence that they had agreed on the price at which the invention should be purchased, if bought at all, and had arranged for a meeting at which the plaintiff was to explain his invention to two engineers appointed by the defendants. If they approved, the machine should be bought. At the appointed time the defendants and the two engineers, Fergusson and Abernethie, attended, but the plaintiff did not come and the engineers went away. Shortly after they were gone the plaintiff arrived. Fergusson was found, and expressed a favourable opinion; but Abernethie could not then be found. It was then proposed that, as the parties were all present, and might find it troublesome to meet again, an agreement should be then drawn up and signed which, if Abernethie approved of the invention, should be the agreement, but, if Abernethie did not approve, should not be one. Abernethie did not approve of the invention when he saw it; and the defendants contended that there was no bargain.

The Lord Chief Justice told the jury that, if they were satisfied that, before the paper was signed, it was agreed amongst them all that it should not operate as an agreement until Abernethie approved of the invention, they should find for the defendants. Verdict for the defendants. The plaintiff obtained a rule nisi for a new trial on the ground of misdirection.

20–004

ERLE J

I think that this rule ought to be discharged. The point made is that this is a written agreement, absolute on the face of it, and that evidence was admitted to show it was conditional: and if that had been so it would have been wrong. But I am of opinion that the evidence showed that in fact there was never any agreement at all. The production of a paper purporting to be an agreement by a party, with his signature attached, affords a strong presumption that it is his written agreement; and, if in fact he did sign the paper animo contrahendi, the terms contained in it are conclusive, and cannot be varied by parol evidence: but in the present case the defence begins one step earlier: the parties met and expressly stated to each other that, though for convenience they would then sign the memorandum of the terms, yet they were not to sign it as an agreement until Abernethie was consulted. I grant the risk that such a defence may be set up without ground; and I agree that a jury should therefore always look on such a defence with suspicion: but, if it be proved that in fact the paper was signed with the express intention that it should not be an agreement, the other party cannot fix it as an agreement upon those so signing. The distinction in point of law is that evidence to vary the terms of an agreement in writing is not admissible, but evidence to show that there is not an agreement at all is admissible.

Crompton J. and Lord Campbell C. J. delivered concurring judgments.

Rule Discharged.

Questions

20–005

1. Was it accurate to say that there was never any agreement at all? Was there (a) any disagreement? (b) any outstanding matter on which agreement was required? Cf. Corbin, *Contracts*, Vol.I, 66. For the parol evidence rule, see above Ch.14.

2. Suppose that the defendant had announced that he would not buy the invention, whatever the result of Abernethie's inspection and before he had had a reasonable opportunity to carry it out. Would the plaintiff have had any remedy? Compare the case where the parties to a sale of goods agree that the price is to be fixed by a third party. The Sale of Goods Act 1979 s.9(2), provides that if either the seller or the buyer prevents the fixing of the price, the party not in fault may maintain an action for damages against the party in fault. What is the cause of action in such a case?

3. Suppose that the defendant had said that, notwithstanding Abernethie's disapproval, he wanted the invention. Would the plaintiff have been bound to sell it? Cf. *Aquis Estates Ltd v Minton* [1975] 3 All E.R. 1043 CA; *Heron Ltd v Moss* [1974] 1 All E.R. 421 (Brightman J).

4. In *Wood Preservation Ltd v Prior* [1969] 1 W.L.R. 1077; [1969] 1 All E.R. 364 CA B agreed to buy from S, Ltd the whole of the shares in the WP Co Ltd subject to the production within one month of a letter from a German Co, giving an assurance that it would continue certain rights in favour of WP Ltd. The question (for tax purposes) was: Did the beneficial ownership in the shares pass before the condition was satisfied or (as in fact happened) was waived? S, Ltd said it did not pass because there was no binding contract until the condition was waived. Held: there was a binding contract; S, Ltd could have been restrained by injunction from selling the shares to anyone else; it could not declare any bonus or dividend; and it would have been bound to transfer the shares if B had waived the condition. S, Ltd was no longer "beneficial owner"; its ownership was a mere legal shell.

Cf. *Pym v Campbell*: could not the seller in that case have been similarly restrained from selling to another, pending Abernethie's inspection? And could not the buyer have waived the condition of Abernethie's approval, since it was exclusively for the buyer's benefit?

MARTEN v WHALE

Court of Appeal [1917] 2 K.B. 480; 86 L.J.K.B. 1305; 117 L.T. 137; 33 T.L.R. 330

20–006

The plaintiff and one Thacker entered into an agreement by which Thacker agreed to sell and the plaintiff to buy a plot of land for the sum of £385, "subject to purchaser's solicitors' approval of title and restrictions." In consideration of that transaction the plaintiff agreed to sell and Thacker to buy a motor-car for £300, "completion of such sale and purchase to be carried out simultaneously with above transaction." The plaintiff let Thacker have the car "on loan," and Thacker sold it to the defendant who bought in good faith and without notice of the plaintiff's rights. Subsequently, the plaintiff's solicitors refused to approve the restrictions in connection with the land. If Thacker was a person who had "agreed to buy" the car then he had given a good title under s.25(2) of the Sale of Goods Act 1893 [s.25(1) of the 1979 Act]. In an action to recover the car and damages for its detention Rowlatt J gave judgment for the defendant. The plaintiff appealed.

SCRUTTON LJ

The plaintiff contends that Thacker only agreed to buy the car if the plaintiff carried through the transaction for the purchase of the land from Thacker, which transaction the plaintiff might at his option repudiate, and that, as the carrying through of the transaction as to the land was at the plaintiff's option, it cannot be said that the plaintiff had entered into a binding agreement to sell, and that Thacker had "agreed to buy," the car. On the other hand, the defendant says that the sale of the car was to be carried out whether or not the sale of the land went through. If that is so, it is clear that Thacker had agreed to buy. The defendant further says that, if the two parts of the agreement are interdependent, the matter did not rest only on the plaintiff's option; that the plaintiff had to appoint a solicitor, and the solicitor had to give an honest opinion as to approving of the restrictions, and that therefore there was an agreement to buy the car. I am inclined to think that the two parts of the document are dependent on each other, and I will deal with the case upon this assumption. What is the nature of the transaction? I cannot read the first part of the document as giving the plaintiff a mere option. There is an implied provision that the plaintiff shall appoint a solicitor and shall consult him in good faith, and that the solicitor shall give his honest opinion. That is not an option; it is a conditional contract, and I agree with Swinfen Eady L.J. that a conditional agreement to buy is an agreement to buy within the Act.
    Swinfen Eady L. J and Bray J. delivered judgment to the same effect.

Appeal Dismissed.

Questions

1. If the plaintiff had refused to appoint a solicitor would Thacker have had any remedy? If the solicitor, appointed in good faith, had given his honest opinion disapproving of title and restrictions would Thacker have had any remedy? (Assume that Thacker had not behaved dishonestly.) Cf. *Ee v Kakar*, above, Ch.4.

20–007

2. If there was a conditional contract in this case, was there not one also in *Pym v Campbell*?

3. Was it a contract for sale of goods or an exchange of land for a car and £85?

B . Conditional Contracts

20-008 The agreements in *Pym v Campbell* and *Marten v Whale* may properly be described as "conditional contracts" because both parties were bound, subject to a condition, the approval of Abernethie in the one case and the solicitor in the other. It will be noted that Scrutton LJ distinguished a conditional contract from an option. The grantor of an option for consideration or under seal has undertaken an obligation but the grantee, of course, has not. The essence of the option is that the grantee has a choice whether to become bound or not. But in *Spiro v Glencrown Properties* (above, Ch.4) Hoffmann J held that the grant of an option to purchase land was "a contract for the sale of an interest in land"— "An option to buy land can properly be described as a contract for the sale of that land conditional upon the exercise of the option." The grantor may fairly be said to have made a conditional contract to sell—his obligation to sell is dependent on an event outside his control and it may be thought immaterial that the event is the act, not of a third party as in *Marten v Whale*, but of the other party to the proposed contract. But can the grantee be said to have made any sort of contract to buy? Like any offeree, he is entirely free to accept or not as he thinks fit.

TRANS TRUST SPRL v DANUBIAN TRADING CO LTD

[1952] 2 Q.B. 297; [1952] 1 T.L.R. 1066; 96 S.J. 312; [1952] 1 All E.R. 970; [1952] 1 Lloyd's Rep. 348

20-009 The defendants contracted to buy a quantity of steel from the plaintiffs. It was provided that payment by the defendants should be by cash against shipping documents from a confirmed credit to be opened at a named bank. The defendants never opened the credit and eventually repudiated the contract. McNair J awarded the plaintiffs their loss of profit on the transaction as damages for breach of contract. The defendants' appeal against the award of damages was dismissed.

DENNING LJ

[Referring to the provision for the opening of the confirmed credit, said:] What is the legal position of such a stipulation? Sometimes it is a condition precedent to the formation of a contract, that is, it is a condition which must be fulfilled before any contract is concluded at all. In those cases the stipulation "subject to the opening of a credit" is rather like a stipulation "subject to contract." [See above, Ch.4.] If no credit is provided, there is no contract between the parties. In other cases a contract is concluded and the stipulation for a credit is a condition which is an essential term of the contract. In those cases the provision of the credit is a condition precedent, not to the formation of a contract, but to the obligation of the seller to deliver the goods. If the buyer fails to provide the credit, the seller can treat himself as discharged from any further performance of the contract and can sue the buyer for damages for not providing the credit.

The first question is: what was the nature of the stipulation in this case? When the buyers sent their order, they stated in writing on September 25, 1950, that a "credit will be opened forthwith." . . . The statement was a firm promise by the buyers by which they gave their personal assurance that a credit would be opened forthwith . . . the stipulation for a credit was not a condition precedent to the formation of any contract at all. It was a condition which was an essential term of a contract actually made. [The judgments in this case were concerned mainly with the measure of damages recoverable.]

Questions

20-010 There seem to be three possible situations:

(a) the buyer undertakes that a credit will be opened;

(b) the buyer undertakes that he will use reasonable diligence to procure the opening of a credit: Cf. *Re Anglo-Russian Merchant Traders Ltd* [1917] 2 K.B. 679;

(c) the buyer says that he will open a credit if he thinks fit.

Is any of these cases the same in legal effect as a stipulation "subject to contract"? In the third case is there any contract at all (i) before the buyer opens a credit? (ii) after he does so?

Problem

A agrees to sell goods to B, "subject to the opening of a credit by B." Before B has had a reasonable opportunity to open the credit, A repudiates the contract. B has to buy the goods at a higher price elsewhere. Has he any remedy?   20-011

----

2. CONDITIONS, WARRANTIES AND INNOMINATE TERMS

It is commonly said that, for the purposes of determining the remedies available for a breach, the   20-012
terms of a contract may be classified into two principal categories, namely conditions and warranties. Where the term that is broken is classified as a condition, the innocent party has the option of withdrawing from the contract as well as making a claim for damages; but, if the term in question is a warranty, the option of withdrawal is no longer available, the innocent party being restricted to a remedy in damages.

In principle, contractors who wish to withdraw (for example, purchasers who wish to reject goods) should know where they stand by reference to this distinction and its application to their transaction. However, consider the facts of *J & H Ritchie Ltd v Lloyd Ltd* [2007] UKHL 9, where Ritchie purchased a quite complex piece of farming equipment (a seed drill and power harrow) from Lloyd. When he first used the equipment, Ritchie noticed that the harrow's drive chain was causing some vibration. Fearing that there might be a serious problem with the harrow, Ritchie took the matter up with Lloyd's. At this stage, without knowing the nature and extent of the problem, it would have been difficult to advise Ritchie with confidence that he had the right to reject the harrow (in fact, the harrow did have a serious defect and Ritchie would have been perfectly entitled to withdraw). Sensibly, Ritchie agreed that the harrow should be taken back by Lloyd's so that their fitter could inspect the machine. When Lloyd's stripped down the equipment, they identified the problem (some missing bearings) and put it right. The equipment was now absolutely fine and they informed Ritchie that the harrow was repaired "to factory gate specification" and ready for collection. However, for some reason, Lloyd's refused to tell Ritchie what the problem had been. Moreover, when Ritchie found out informally what the problem had been, Lloyd's refused to provide an engineer's report to certify that the harrow was undamaged as a result of having been used without the bearings. In the light of all this, Ritchie decided to reject the equipment. Did he have the right to withdraw? In the lower courts, the case went first one way and then the other; but the House of Lords decided unanimously that Ritchie was entitled to withdraw—not from the initial sales agreement as such but from the subsequent agreement for inspection and repair. According to the Law Lords, it was implicit in this inspection and repair agreement that Lloyd's would tell Ritchie what they had found to be wrong with the machine and what they had done to repair it. So, on the facts, Lloyd's were in breach of the inspection and repair agreement. Precisely why this justified Ritchie in rejecting the machine is not made clear. Given that the machine was, in fact, fully repaired, Lloyd's breach did not obviously deprive Ritchie of the benefit of the secondary bargain and nor did it go to the root of what was a repairing contract. On the other hand, the Law Lords underline the significance of Ritchie being able to make an "informed choice" about whether to accept the machine and Lloyd's breach certainly deprived Ritchie of this opportunity. Taking this latter line, it was of the essence (i.e., it was a condition) of the inspection and repair agreement that Lloyd's should keep Ritchie informed.

While *Ritchie v Lloyd* might be viewed as an isolated instance of a difficulty in applying the distinction between a condition and a warranty, the law in relation to some everyday questions about the details of a buyer's remedies is far from clear. In particular, if the basic rule is that a buyer may return faulty goods and have the price refunded provided that this is done within a reasonable time, it is important that there is a clear understanding of what constitutes such a time (see Law Commission, *Consumer Remedies for Faulty Goods* (LCCP No.188) (2008)). If one of the principal intended functions of contract law is to give buyers, whether businesses or consumers, confidence (by assuring them that, where they have a problem with a supplier or with the goods supplied, they have a simple legal remedy), then the present state of the law gives rise to considerable cause for concern. So far as consumer buyers are concerned, the recent Consumer Rights Act seeks to respond to this problem. The Act does nothing (and does not attempt to do anything) to assist business buyers such as Ritchie; but the more urgent question is whether it will succeed in assisting consumers—in particular, the question is whether anyone other than specialist consumer lawyers will understand the Act's remedial regime which features short-term and final rights to reject, as well as rights to repair or replacement, and sometimes to a reduction in the price.

As if this were not bad enough, the decision of the Court of Appeal in the *Hong Kong Fir Shipping* case (below) introduced a more general complexity. There, the court remarked that, at the point of contractual formation, some terms cannot be classified as conditions or warranties; rather, it is only when the term is broken that one can make the classificatory judgment—that judgment being guided by the seriousness of the consequences of the breach. On this view, while a term might appropriately be classified on some occasions as a warranty (because the consequences of the breach are not so serious), on others precisely the same term might be classified as a condition (because the consequences of the breach are serious). How far the *Hong Kong Fir Shipping* approach impinges on straightforward classification remains a difficult matter for the courts (see *Bunge v Tradax*, below).

WALLIS, SON & WELLS v PRATT AND HAYNES

Court of Appeal [1910] 2 K.B. 1003; House of Lords [1911] A.C. 394; 80 L.J.K.B. 1058; 105 L.T. 146; 27 T.L.R. 431; 55 S.J. 496

20–013   The defendants sold to the plaintiffs by sample a quantity of seed described as "common English sainfoin." Seed equal to sample was delivered, and a portion of it was resold by the plaintiffs as common English sainfoin. When it came up, it was found to be, not common English, but giant sainfoin, a seed which is indistinguishable but of inferior quality. The plaintiffs reasonably and properly settled a claim brought against them by the sub-purchaser and sued to recover the amount so paid. The defendants relied on a term in the written contract: "Sellers give no warranty, express or implied, as to growth, description, or any other matters . . .". Bray J gave judgment for the plaintiffs, but was reversed by the Court of Appeal. Vaughan Williams and Farwell LJJ held that the plaintiffs, having accepted and resold the seed, had put it out of their power to treat the description of the article sold as common English sainfoin as a condition, and could treat it only as a warranty, but that the condition relied on by the defendants excluded all liability for breach of warranty. The decision of the Court of Appeal was reversed by the House of Lords, on the grounds given by Fletcher Moulton LJ, dissenting in the Court of Appeal.

FLETCHER MOULTON LJ

> . . . A party to a contract who has performed, or is ready and willing to perform, his obligations under that contract is entitled to the performance by the other contracting party of all the obligations which rest upon him. But from a very early period of our law it has been recognised that such obligations are not all of equal

importance. There are some which go so directly to the substance of the contract or, in other words, are so essential to its very nature that their non-performance may fairly be considered by the other party as a substantial failure to perform the contract at all. On the other hand, there are other obligations which, though they must be performed, are not so vital that a failure to perform them goes to the substance of the contract. Both classes are equally obligations under the contract, and the breach of any one of them entitles the other party to damages. But in the case of the former class he has the alternative of treating the contract as being completely broken by the non-performance and (if he takes the proper steps) he can refuse to perform any of the obligations resting upon himself and sue the other party for a total failure to perform the contract. Although the decisions are fairly consistent in recognising the distinction between the two classes of obligations under a contract there has not been a similar consistency in the nomenclature applied to them. I do not, however, propose to discuss this matter, because later usage has consecrated the term "condition" to describe an obligation of the former class and "warranty" to describe an obligation of the latter class. I do not think that the choice of terms is happy, especially so far as regards the word "condition," for it is a word which is used in many other connections and has considerable variety of meaning. But its use with regard to the obligations under a contract is well known and recognised, and no confusion need arise if proper regard be had to the context.

This usage has been followed in the codification of the law of the contract of sale in the Sale of Goods Act. The word "condition" is used in the text of the Act, though no formal definition is given to it. But in the interpretation clause "warranty" is expressly defined in the followed terms: " 'Warranty' as regards England and Ireland means an agreement with reference to goods which are the subject of a contract of sale, but collateral to the main purposes of such contract, the breach of which gives rise to a claim for damages, but not to a right to reject the goods and treat the contract as repudiated." It is clear from this definition that a breach of warranty entitles the other contracting party to damages only. In contrast to this the additional right in the case of a breach of a condition is fully recognised in section 11. In all this the Act adopts the well-settled law that existed at the date when it was passed . . .

Now it is admitted that the vendors committed a breach of this contract in that they delivered seed of giant sainfoin, which is a different article of inferior value. Inasmuch as by the law the obligation to deliver the kind of goods stipulated for in a contract of sale is an obligation which has the status of a condition, this breach gave to the purchasers the choice of the two remedies, either of rejecting the goods and treating the contract as repudiated or suing for damages for delivery of the inferior article. But the purchasers resold the goods in ignorance of the breach (the two kinds of seed bearing a close resemblance to one another in appearance), and by the fact that they have resold the goods they have prevented themselves from exercising the higher right. They must, therefore, content themselves with suing for damages for breach on the vendors' part of the obligation which lay upon them under the contract. This they are doing, and we are asked to say whether their claim is a good one.

I confess that for my own part I can see no possible answer to it . . .

Point for reflection

Fletcher Moulton LJ went on to reject the argument that, as the vendors could not now reject the goods, the condition had become a warranty and was caught by the exclusion clause. He pointed out that s.11(1) of the Sale of Goods Act 1893 (s.11(4) of the 1979 Act, above, Ch.16) does not say that a condition becomes a warranty but only that the "higher remedy" is no longer available. Once a condition, always a condition, apparently.

20–014

L SCHULER AG v WICKMAN MACHINE TOOL SALES LTD

House of Lords [1974] A.C. 235; [1973] 2 W.L.R. 683; [1973] 2 All E.R. 39; [1973] 2 Lloyd's Rep. 53

Schuler agreed to give the claimants Wickman sole selling rights of presses manufactured by Schuler for four and a half years. Clause 7(b) of the agreement provided that "It shall be a condition of this agreement that (i) [Wickman] shall send its representative to visit" the six largest UK motor

20–015

manufacturers "at least once in every week" to solicit orders. No other term in the 20 clauses was described as a condition. Clause 11 provided that either party might determine the agreement if the other committed a "material breach" of its obligations and failed to remedy it within 60 days of being required to do so in writing. Wickman committed material breaches of cl.7(b) in the first eight months but these were waived by the respondents. In the next six months they committed some immaterial breaches but Schuler terminated the contract, relying on cl.11. Wickman claimed damages. Schuler's amended defence relied on Wickman's breach of the "express condition" in cl.7(b). The arbitrator construed "condition" in cl.7(b) as referable to cl.11 and awarded in favour of Wickman. Mocatta J held the word, "condition," gave Schuler the right to repudiate the agreement if Wickman committed a single breach of the visiting obligation. Wickman's appeal to the Court of Appeal was allowed, Stephenson LJ dissenting. Schuler appealed to the House of Lords.

LORD REID

In the ordinary use of the English language "condition" has many meanings, some of which have nothing to do with agreements. In connection with an agreement it may mean a pre-condition: something which must happen or be done before the agreement can take effect. Or it may mean some state of affairs which must continue to exist if the agreement is to remain in force. The legal meaning on which Schuler rely is, I think, one which would not occur to a layman; a condition in that sense is not something which has an automatic effect. It is a term the breach of which by one party gives to the other an option either to terminate the contract or to let the contract proceed and, if he so desires, sue for damages for the breach.

Sometimes a breach of a term gives that option to the aggrieved party because it is of a fundamental character going to the root of the contract, sometimes it gives that option because the parties have chosen to stipulate that it shall have that effect. Blackburn J. said in *Bettini v Gye* [below]: "Parties may think some matter, apparently of very little importance, essential; and if they sufficiently express an intention to make the literal fulfilment of such a thing a condition precedent, it will be one."

In the present case it is not contended that Wickman's failures to make visits amounted in themselves to fundamental breaches. What is contended is that the terms of clause 7 "sufficiently express an intention" to make any breach, however small, of the obligation to make visits a condition so that any such breach shall entitle Schuler to rescind the whole contract if they so desire.

Schuler maintains that the use of the word "condition" is in itself enough to establish this intention. No doubt some words used by lawyers do have a rigid inflexible meaning. But we must remember that we are seeking to discover intention as disclosed by the contract as a whole. Use of the word "condition" is an indication—even a strong indication—of such an intention but it is by no means conclusive. The fact that a particular construction leads to a very unreasonable result must be a relevant consideration. The more unreasonable the result the more unlikely it is that the parties can have intended it, and if they do intend it the more necessary it is that they shall make that intention abundantly clear.

Clause 7(b) requires that over a long period each of the six firms shall be visited every week by one or other of two named representatives. It makes no provision for Wickman being entitled to substitute others even on the death or retirement of one of the named representatives. Even if one could imply some right to do this, it makes no provision for both representatives being ill during a particular week. And it makes no provision for the possibility that one or other of the firms may tell Wickman that they cannot receive Wickman's representative during a particular week. So if the parties gave any thought to the matter at all they must have realised the probability that in a few cases out of the 1,400 required visits a visit as stipulated would be impossible. But if Schuler's contention is right failure to make even one visit entitles them to terminate the contract however blameless Wickman might be. This is so unreasonable that it must make me search for some other possible meaning of the contract. If none can be found then Wickman must suffer the consequences. But only if that is the only possible interpretation.

If I have to construe clause 7 standing by itself then I do find difficulty in reaching any other interpretation. But if clause 7 must be read with clause 11 the difficulty disappears. The word "condition" would make any breach of clause 7(b), however excusable, a material breach. That would then entitle Schuler to give notice under clause 11(a)(i) requiring the breach to be remedied. There would be no point in giving such a notice if Wickman were clearly not in fault but if it were given Wickman would have no difficulty in showing that the breach had been remedied. If Wickman were at fault then on receiving such a notice they would have to amend their system so that they could show that the breach had been remedied. If they did not do that within the period of the notice then Schuler would be entitled to rescind.

In my view, that is a possible and reasonable construction of the contract and I would therefore adopt it. The contract is so obscure that I can have no confidence that this is its true meaning but for the reasons which I have given I think that it is the preferable construction. It follows that Schuler were not entitled to rescind the contract as they purported to do. So I would dismiss this appeal.

I must add some observations about a matter which was fully argued before your Lordships. The majority of the Court of Appeal ([1972] 1 W.L.R. 840) were influenced by a consideration of actings subsequent to the making of the contract. In my view, this was inconsistent with the decision of this House in *James Miller and Partners Ltd v Whitworth Street Estates* (Manchester) Ltd [above, Ch.6]. . . . We were asked by Wickman to reconsider that decision on this point and I have done so. As a result I see no reason to change the view which I expressed in that case.

Lords Morris, Simon and Kilbrandon made speeches dismissing the appeal.

LORD WILBERFORCE

Does clause 7(b) amount to a "condition" or a "term?" (to call it an important or material term adds, with all respect, nothing but some intellectual assuagement). My Lords, I am clear in my own mind that it is a condition, but your Lordships take the contrary view. On a matter of construction of a particular document, to develop the reasons for a minority opinion serves no purpose. I am all the more happy to refrain from so doing because the judgments of Mocatta J., Stephenson L.J. and indeed of Edmund Davies L.J. on construction, give me complete satisfaction and I could in any case add little of value to their reasons. I would only add that, for my part, to call the clause arbitrary, capricious or fantastic, or to introduce as a test of its validity the ubiquitous reasonable man (I do not know whether he is English or German) is to assume, contrary to the evidence, that both parties to this contract adopted a standard of easy-going tolerance rather than one of aggressive, insistent punctuality and efficiency. This is not an assumption I am prepared to make, nor do I think myself entitled to impose the former standard on the parties if their words indicate, as they plainly do, the latter. I note finally, that the result of treating the clause, so careful and specific in its requirements, as a term is, in effect, to deprive the appellants of any remedy in respect of admitted and by no means minimal breaches. The arbitrator's finding that these breaches were not "material" was not, in my opinion, justified in law in the face of the parties' own characterisation of them in their document: indeed the fact that he was able to do so, and so leave the appellants without remedy, argues strongly that the legal basis of his finding—that clause 7(b) was merely a term—is unsound.

I would allow this appeal.

Appeal Dismissed.

Points for reflection

By way of comparison, consider *The Chikuma* [1981] 1 All E.R. 652. There, a time charter provided, ". . . failing the punctual and regular payment of the hire . . . the Owners shall be at liberty to withdraw the vessel. . .". An Instalment of hire fell due on January 22, 1976. On that day the charterers caused the owners' bank to be credited with the amount of the hire but on terms that interest would not begin to run until January 26. If the owners had withdrawn the money, as they could have done, on January 22, they would probably have had to pay interest on it to their bank until January 26. The House of Lords, restoring a judgment of Robert Goff J and allowing an appeal from the Court of Appeal, held that there was no payment in cash, as the contract required, on January 22 and the owners had acted within their rights in withdrawing the ship on January 24. Lord Bridge, with whom all their Lordships agreed, said:

> "It has often been pointed out that shipowners and charterers bargain at arm's length. Neither class has such a preponderance of bargaining power as to be in a position to oppress the other.

20–016

They should be in a position to look after themselves by contracting only on terms which are acceptable to them. Where, as here, they embody in their contracts common form clauses, it is, to my mind, of overriding importance that their meaning and legal effect should be certain and well understood. The ideal at which the courts should aim, in construing such clauses, is to produce a result such that in any given situation both parties seeking legal advice as to their rights and obligations can expect the same clear and confident answer from their advisers and neither will be tempted to embark on long and expensive litigation in the belief that victory depends on winning the sympathy of the court. This ideal may never be fully attainable, but we shall certainly never even approximate to it unless we strive to follow clear and consistent principles and steadfastly refuse to be blown off course by the supposed merits of individual cases."

20–017   For many years writers on the law of contract assumed that there were only two classes of contractual term and that every term was either a condition or a warranty. The Sale of Goods Act 1893 seems to have been drafted on this assumption. The Sale and Supply of Goods Act 1994 replaced the words "condition" and "warranty" by "term"; but then made clear that, for English, but not Scots, law, every implied term was either a condition or a warranty. Whether an injured party had a right to determine the contract depended, according to this theory, on the nature of the term which had been broken. If it was a condition he could do so. If it was a warranty, he could not. The nature of the term was settled when the contract was made. The nature and consequences of the breach were immaterial. That principle is qualified by the 1994 Act s.15A, in non-consumer cases: in such cases, a breach of a condition by the seller which is so slight that it would be unreasonable to reject the goods is to be "treated as a breach of warranty".

This was the theory at common law; but, in practice, the courts seem often to have had regard to the effect of the breach in deciding whether the injured party could treat the contract as at an end. Standard examples of a warranty and a condition, used in the pre-1962 editions of Anson and Cheshire and Fifoot, were the cases of *Bettini v Gye* (1876) 1 QBD 183 and *Poussard v Spiers* (1876) 1 QBD 351. In each case, the plaintiff singers failed to make themselves available on the day on which their presence was first required. The defendant in each case terminated the contract and the plaintiff sued for damages. Bettini was required by his contract to be present six days before the first performance for rehearsals and arrived three days late. His engagement was to sing in theatres, halls and drawing-rooms from March 30 to July 13, 1875. His failure to arrive on time clearly did not prevent the contract from being substantially carried out. If the engagement had been a very short one it might have been different. The Queen's Bench Division thought the failure did not go to the root of the matter. The defendant was not entitled to dismiss the plaintiff. Madame Poussard was taken ill five days before the first performance. Her illness appeared to be a serious one of uncertain duration and it was held that the defendant was justified in terminating her contract and engaging another artiste.

Bettini was considered by the writers to have committed a breach of warranty and Poussard a breach of condition. Yet, it seems implausible that Poussard, who had fallen ill, was in any kind of *breach*; she surely would not have been liable in damages if the defendant had counter-claimed. At all events, in neither case did the court scrutinise the contract at the time it was made and identify a term as a condition or warranty. It looked at the effect of the failure to perform in the circumstances existing at the time of the failure. Thus, if a temporary substitute for Poussard, capable of performing the part adequately, could have been obtained on reasonable terms, the defendant would not have been justified in dismissing her. The plaintiff's failure went to the root of the matter because no such substitute was available. The term broken seems to have been the same in both cases—the promise to be available on a certain day. The difference was in the nature and effect of the non-performance of the term.

Another example is *Aerial Advertising Co v Batchelor's Peas Ltd* [1938] 2 All E.R. 788. The plaintiffs contracted to advertise the defendants' product by flying an aircraft trailing a banner reading "Eat Batchelor's Peas." The pilot flew over Salford main square on Armistice Day during the two minute silence, causing outrage. The defendants terminated the contract. Atkinson J held that they were entitled to do so. Further flights might have re-kindled public anger so it was unreasonable to expect them to continue. The term of the contract that was broken seems to have been that which required the pilot to consult the defendants as to where he was going each day. Clearly, on any other day, a breach of the same term would have been relatively innocuous. It was not the nature of the term that was important so much as the nature of the breach and its effect.

The "innominate term", a term which is neither a condition nor a warranty, is thus not a recent invention. The courts utilised the concept for many years before they or the writers identified it as such. The *Hong Kong Fir* case seems to have been the first in which it was expressly recognised.

HONG KONG FIR SHIPPING CO LTD v KAWASAKI KISEN KAISHA LTD

Court of Appeal [1962] 2 Q.B. 26; [1962] 2 W.L.R. 474; [1962] 1 All E.R. 474; [1961] 2 Lloyd's Rep. 478

20–018

By a time charter the plaintiffs agreed to let and the defendants to hire the vessel Hong Kong Fir for 24 months from the date of delivery "she being fitted in every way for ordinary cargo service." The vessel was delivered and sailed from Liverpool to Newport News, USA, and loaded a cargo for Osaka. The engine room staff were inefficient and the engines were very old with the result that she was held up for repairs for five weeks on her way to Osaka where it was found that further repairs, requiring 15 weeks to complete, were necessary to make her seaworthy. The charterparty still had 20 months to run. The charterers repudiated the contract and the owners sued for wrongful repudiation.

Salmon J found that the vessel was unseaworthy, having regard to her engine room staff, but that the owners' breach of contract did not entitle the charterers to rescind the contract and that the contract was not frustrated. The charterers appealed to the Court of Appeal.

Sellers and Upjohn LJJ delivered judgment dismissing the appeal.

DIPLOCK LJ

Every synallagmatic[3] contract contains in it the seeds of the problem: in what event will a party be relieved of his undertaking to do that which he has agreed to do but has not yet done? The contract may itself expressly define some of these events, as in the cancellation clause in a charterparty; but, human prescience being limited, it seldom does so exhaustively and often fails to do so at all. In some classes of contracts such as sale of goods, marine insurance, contracts of affreightment evidenced by bills of lading and those between parties to bills of exchange, Parliament has defined by statute some of the events not provided for expressly in individual contracts of that class; but where an event occurs the occurrence of which neither the parties nor Parliament have expressly stated will discharge one of the parties from further performance of his undertakings, it is for the court to determine whether the event has this effect or not.

The test whether an event has this effect or not has been stated in a number of metaphors all of which I think amount to the same thing: does the occurrence of the event deprive the party who has further undertakings still to perform of substantially the whole benefit which it was the intention of the parties as expressed in the contract that he should obtain as the consideration for performing those undertakings?

---

3   "Synallagmatic" means "bilateral".

This test is applicable whether or not the event occurs as a result of the default of one of the parties to the contract, but the consequences of the event are different in the two cases. Where the event occurs as a result of the default of one party, the party in default cannot rely upon it as relieving himself of the performance of any further undertakings on his part, and the innocent party, although entitled to, need not treat the event as relieving him of the further performance of his own undertakings. This is only a specific application of the fundamental legal and moral rule that a man should not be allowed to take advantage of his own wrong. Where the event occurs as a result of the default of neither party, each is relieved of the further performance of his own undertakings, and their rights in respect of undertakings previously performed are now regulated by the Law Reform (Frustrated Contracts) Act, 1943 [below, Ch.24].

This branch of the common law has reached its present stage by the normal process of historical growth, and the fallacy in Mr Ashton Roskill's contention that a different test is applicable when the event occurs as a result of the default of one party from that applicable in cases of frustration where the event occurs as a result of the default of neither party lies, in my view, from a failure to view the cases in their historical context. The problem: in what event will a party to a contract be relieved of his undertaking to do that which he has agreed to do but has not yet done? has exercised the English courts for centuries, probably ever since assumpsit emerged as a form of action distinct from covenant and debt and long before even the earliest cases which we have been invited to examine; but until the rigour of the rule in *Paradine v Jane* [below, Ch.24] was mitigated in the middle of the last century by the classic judgments of Blackburn J. in *Taylor v Caldwell* [below, Ch.24] and Bramwell B. in *Jackson v Union Marine Insurance Co Ltd* [below, Ch.24], it was in general only events resulting from one party's failure to perform his contractual obligations which were regarded as capable of relieving the other party from continuing to perform that which he had undertaken to do . . .

Once it is appreciated that it is the event and not the fact that the event is a result of a breach of contract which relieves the party not in default of further performance of his obligations, two consequences follow. (1) The test whether the event relied upon has this consequence is the same whether the event is the result of the other party's breach of contract or not, as Devlin J. pointed out in *Universal Cargo Carriers Corporation v Citati* [1957] 2 Q.B. 401, 434.[4] (2) The question whether an event which is the result of the other party's breach of contract has this consequence cannot be answered by treating all contractual undertakings as falling into one of two separate categories: "conditions" the breach of which gives rise to an event which relieves the party not in default of further performance of his obligations, and "warranties" the breach of which does not give rise to such an event.

Lawyers tend to speak of this classification as if it were comprehensive, partly for the historical reasons which I have already mentioned and partly because Parliament itself adopted it in the Sale of Goods Act 1893, as respects a number of implied terms in contracts for the sale of goods and has in that act used the expressions "condition" and "warranty" in that meaning. But it is by no means true of contractual undertakings in general at common law.

No doubt there are many simple contractual undertakings, sometimes express but more often because of their very simplicity ("It goes without saying") to be implied, of which it can be predicated that every breach of such an undertaking must give rise to an event which will deprive the party not in default of substantially the whole benefit which it was intended that he should obtain from the contract. And such a stipulation, unless the parties have agreed that breach of it shall not entitle the non-defaulting party to treat the contract as repudiated, is a "condition."[5] So too there may be other simple contractual undertakings of which it can be predicated that no breach can give rise to an event which will deprive the party not in default of substantially the whole benefit which it was intended that he should obtain from the contract; and such a stipulation, unless the parties have agreed that breach of it shall entitle the non-defaulting party to treat the contract as repudiated, is a "warranty."

There are, however, many contractual undertakings of a more complex character which cannot be categorised as being "conditions" or "warranties," if the late nineteenth-century meaning adopted in the Sale of Goods Act, 1893, and used by Bowen L.J. in *Bentsen v Taylor, Sons & Co* [1893] 2 Q.B. 274, 280, be given to those terms. Of such undertakings all that can be predicated is that some breaches will and others will not give rise to an event which will deprive the party not in default of substantially the whole benefit which it was intended that he should obtain from the contract; and the legal consequences of a breach of such an undertaking,

---

[4]   But see *Bunge v Tradax*, below.

[5]   The passage from the beginning of this paragraph is criticised in *Bunge v Tradax*, below. It is not true that every breach of condition deprives the injured party of substantially the whole benefit of the contract.

unless provided for expressly in the contract, depend upon the nature of the event to which the breach gives rise and do not follow automatically from a prior classification of the undertaking as a "condition" or a "warranty." For instance, to take Bramwell B.'s example in *Jackson v Union Marine Insurance Co Ltd* itself, breach of an undertaking by a shipowner to sail with all possible dispatch to a named port does not necessarily relieve the charterer of further performance of his obligation under the charterparty, but if the breach is so prolonged that the contemplated voyage is frustrated it does have this effect . . .

As my brethren have already pointed out, the shipowner's undertaking to tender a seaworthy ship has, as a result of numerous decisions as to what can amount to "unseaworthiness," become one of the most complex of contractual undertakings. It embraces obligations with respect to every part of the hull and machinery, stores and equipment and the crew itself. It can be broken by the presence of trivial defects easily and rapidly remediable as well as by defects which must inevitably result in a total loss of the vessel.

Consequently the problem in this case is, in my view, neither solved nor soluble by debating whether the shipowner's express or implied undertaking to tender a seaworthy ship is a "condition" or a "warranty." It is like so many other contractual terms an undertaking one breach of which may give rise to an event which relieves the charterer of further performance of his undertakings if he so elects and another breach of which may not give rise to such an event but entitle him only to monetary compensation in the form of damages. It is, with all deference to Mr Ashton Roskill's skilful argument, by no means surprising that among the many hundreds of previous cases about the shipowner's undertaking to deliver a seaworthy ship there is none where it was found profitable to discuss in the judgments the question whether that undertaking is a "condition" or a "warranty"; for the true answer, as I have already indicated, is that it is neither, but one of that large class of contractual undertakings one breach of which may have the same effect as that ascribed to a breach of "condition" under the Sale of Goods Act, 1893, and a different breach of which may have only the same effect as that ascribed to a breach of "warranty" under that act . . .

What the judge had to do in the present case, as in any other case where one party to a contract relies upon a breach by the other party as giving him a right to elect to rescind the contract, and the contract itself makes no express provision as to this, was to look at the events which had occurred as a result of the breach at the time at which the charterers purported to rescind the charterparty and to decide whether the occurrence of those events deprived the charterers of substantially the whole benefit which it was the intention of the parties as expressed in the charterparty that the charterers should obtain from the further performance of their own contractual undertakings.

One turns therefore to the contract, the Baltime 1939 charter, of which Sellers L.J. has already cited the relevant terms. Clause 13, the "due diligence" clause, which exempts the shipowners from responsibility for delay or loss or damage to goods on board due to unseaworthiness, unless such delay or loss or damage has been caused by want of due diligence of the owners in making the vessel seaworthy and fitted for the voyage, is in itself sufficient to show that the mere occurrence of the events that the vessel was in some respect unseaworthy when tendered or that such unseaworthiness had caused some delay in performance of the charterparty would not deprive the charterer of the whole benefit which it was the intention of the parties he should obtain from the performance of his obligations under the contract—for he undertakes to continue to perform his obligations notwithstanding the occurrence of such events if they fall short of frustration of the contract and even deprives himself of any remedy in damages unless such events are the consequence of want of due diligence on the part on the shipowner.

The question which the judge had to ask himself was, as he rightly decided, whether or not at the date when the charterers purported to rescind the contract, namely, June 6, 1957, or when the shipowners purported to accept such rescission, namely, August 8, 1957, the delay which had already occurred as a result of the incompetence of the engine-room staff, and the delay which was likely to occur in repairing the engines of the vessel and the conduct of the shipowners by that date in taking steps to remedy these two matters, were, when taken together, such as to deprive the charterers of substantially the whole benefit which it was the intention of the parties they should obtain from further use of the vessel under the charterparty.

In my view, in his judgment—on which I would not seek to improve—the judge took into account and gave due weight to all the relevant considerations and arrived at the right answer for the right reasons.

Appeal Dismissed.

Question

20–019   Is the shipowner's obligation to tender a seaworthy ship a single obligation or a "bundle of obligations of varying importance"? If the latter, is it necessary to modify the traditional categorisation of all terms as either conditions or warranties?

BUNGE CORPORATION, NEW YORK V TRADAX EXPORT SA, PANAMA

Court of Appeal [1980] 1 Lloyd's Rep. 294; [1981] 2 All E.R. 513

20–020   A contract for the sale of 5,000 long tons, 5 per cent more or less, of soya bean flour, required the buyers to give at least 15 consecutive days' notice of probable readiness of vessel(s) and of approximate quantity to be loaded. A Gulf port of loading was then to be nominated by the seller. The buyer gave notice on June 17, 1975, less than 15 days before the end of the shipment period, June 30. On June 20 the seller repudiated the contract. The market price having fallen by $60 per metric ton, the seller claimed and was awarded damages of $317,500 by the umpire whose decision was upheld by the Trade Association appeal board but reversed by Parker J. Parker J held that the term requiring 15 days' notice was an innominate term and that the breach did not go to the root of the contract. The Court of Appeal (Megaw, Browne and Brightman LJJ) allowed the seller's appeal, holding that the term was a condition.

MEGAW LJ

I come back to the purpose of the notice of probable readiness term in the present contract. The commercial reasons why advance notice is required are, I think obvious. The sellers have to nominate the loading port. Is loading going to be possible, and if possible convenient, at Port A, or Port B, or Port C? Until the probable date of readiness is known, it may be impossible to answer those questions. Until they are answered, the sellers cannot perform their contractual duty of nominating the port. When the port is decided, arrangements have to be made to have the contract quantity (to be defined by the buyers by reference to "5 per cent. more or less") of the contract goods available when the vessel is ready. What is involved in making such arrangements? It may involve, or include, buying goods, arranging for them to be moved by road, rail or water from wherever they may be; for warehousing them or moving them from one warehouse to another. Of course, in any given case, some or all of these tasks may be simply achieved, or their achievement may be possible in less than 15 days, in order to have the goods ready for loading where and when the vessel is ready for loading. It obviously cannot be predicated that 14 days' notice, instead of 15 days, would necessarily and in all circumstances cause sellers serious difficulties in respect of a contract containing these terms. What can and should be accepted is that the parties have agreed that, for the purposes of this contract, the reasonable time required to enable the sellers to perform their contractual obligations as to delivery of the goods is 15 days' notice of the probable readiness of the vessel to load . . .

[Having quoted Diplock LJ in *Hong Kong Fir*, above "No doubt there are many simple contractual undertakings, sometimes express but more often because of their very simplicity ('It goes without saying') to be implied, of which it can be predicated that every breach of such an undertaking must give rise to an event which will deprive the party not in default of substantially the whole benefit which it was intended that he should obtain from the contract. And such a stipulation, unless the parties have agreed that breach of it shall not entitle the non-defaulting party to treat the contract as repudiated, is a 'condition.'"]

If that statement is intended to be a definition of the requirements which must always be satisfied, in all types of contract and all types of clauses, in order that a term may qualify as a condition, I would very respectfully express the view that it is not a correct statement of the law . . .

[Having quoted from *United Scientific v Burnley Council* [1978] A.C. 904:]

In the light of what was said by their Lordships in that case, I think it can fairly be said that in mercantile contracts stipulations as to time not only may be, but usually are, to be treated as being "of the essence of the contract," even though this is not expressly stated in the words of the contract. It would follow that in a mercantile contract it cannot be predicated that, for time to be of the essence, any and every breach of the term as to time must necessarily cause the innocent party to be deprived of substantially the whole of the benefit which it was intended that he should have . . .

[Having referred again to Diplock LJ in *Hong Kong Fir*:]

In its literal sense, the words there used would mean that the test whether a term is a condition is whether every breach of such an undertaking must give rise to an event which will deprive the party not in default of substantially the whole benefit which it was intended that he should obtain from the contract (I underline various words to which I have given emphasis in reading it.) If this is a definition of the requirements which, in English law, must always be fulfilled before any contractual term (in the absence, of course, of express words) can achieve the legal status of a condition, then the term with which we are here concerned would not pass the test. The view which I have expressed that it is a condition would necessarily be wrong.

There are various reasons why I do not think that this was intended to be a literal, definitive and comprehensive statement of the requirements of a condition; and also, if it were, why, with great respect, I do not think that it represents the law as it stands today.

First, if it were intended to cover terms as to time in mercantile contracts, how could the requirements be said to be met in respect of stipulations in contracts of types in which, as Lord Diplock has recently said, time may be of the essence: for example, in respect of a stipulated time for delivery? It could never be said, as I see it, in any real sense, that any breach of such a stipulation must necessarily cause the innocent party to be deprived of substantially all the benefit.

Secondly, and following on what I have just said, I do not see how any contractual term, whether as to time or otherwise, could ever pass the test. Conditions would no longer exist in the English law of contract. For it is always possible to suggest hypothetically some minor breach or breaches of any contractual term which might, without undue use of the imagination, be wholly insufficient to produce serious effects for the innocent party, let alone the loss of su[b]stantially all the benefit.

Thirdly, English law does recognise as conditions contractual terms which do not pass that test. For example, *Bowes v Shand* (1877) 2 App.Cas. 455 and, I think, a substantial number of other cases which are binding, at least, on this Court.

Fourthly, it is clear law, reaffirmed by the House of Lords since Hong Kong Fir was decided, that where there has been a breach of a condition the innocent party is entitled to elect whether or not to treat the contract as repudiated. . . . How could this right of election be anything other than a legal fiction, a chimera, if the election can arise only in circumstances in which, as a result of the breach, an event has happened which will deprive the innocent party of substantially the whole benefit which it was intended that he should receive? This test, it is to be observed, is regarded (*Hong Kong Fir*, above) as applying also where the term is an intermediate term, except that you then look to what has actually happened in order to see if the innocent party has lost substantially all the benefit. So, again, if the test be right, the former principle of English law that the innocent party has the right to elect is no longer anything but an empty shadow, for a right to elect to continue a contract, with the result that the innocent party will be bound to continue to perform his own contractual obligations, when he will, by definition, have lost substantially all his benefit under the contract, does not appear to me to make sense.

Fifthly, the same considerations as I have set out in the previous paragraph apply if the test be that a breach of contract gives a right to the innocent party to treat it as a repudiation only if the events which in fact have flowed from the breach would, if they had come about otherwise than by a breach of contract, amount to frustration of the contract. Lord Radcliffe's classical definition of frustration in *Davis Contractors Ltd v Fareham Urban District Council* [below, Ch.24], is:

". . . without default of either party a contractual obligation has become incapable of being performed because the circumstances in which performance is called for would render it a thing radically different from that which was undertaken by the contract. Non haec in foedera veni.[6] It was not this that I promised to do

---

6   Sir John Megaw in a letter to *The Times*, December 20, 1980, refers to this quotation and asks "Have those eminent jurists, beginning with Lord Cairns in 1876, who have used that quotation to throw light on the circumstances in which a contract is frustrated, considered the context? Do the words not come, only slightly distorted, from the Aeneid, Book 4,

. . . There must be . . . such a change in the significance of the obligation that the thing undertaken would, if performed, be a different thing from that contracted for."

If that, with the substitution of "default" for "no default" as being the cause of "the different thing," were the universal test which must be applied before there can be a condition or a breach of condition, then there can never be an election by the innocent party to proceed with the contract, despite the other party's default. For, as appears dramatically in the Virgilian quotation, it would not be the same contract. Yet the law has never ceased to recognise that there may be a right of election, when the innocent party is faced with a repudiatory breach, to keep the contract alive: the same contract, not a different one, as it would, necessarily and invariably, be on the frustration test.

Counsel for the sellers submitted that the test of a condition suggested in the paragraph which I have quoted, at least if it fell to be treated in its literal sense and as a comprehensive definition of the requirements of a condition, in all types of contracts and all types of contractual stipulations, is not a part of the ratio decidendi of the *Hong Kong Fir* case. I would, with very great respect, feel obliged to agree. Lord Justice Upjohn, in the opening words of his judgment, said that he—

". . . [entirely agreed] with the judgment which has just been delivered."

That judgment was the judgment of Lord Justice Sellers. As I understand it, the ratio of the judgment of Lord Justice Sellers, as to the test of a condition, is to be found in the paragraph in which he said:

"The formula for deciding whether a stipulation is a condition or a warranty is well recognised; the difficulty is in its application. It is put in a practical way by Lord Justice Bowen in *Bentsen v Taylor Sons & Co* [1893] 2 Q.B. 274, at p. 281: 'There is no way of deciding that question except by looking at the contract in the light of the surrounding circumstances, and then making up one's mind whether the intention of the parties, as gathered from the instrument itself, will best be carried out by treating the promise as a warranty sounding only in damages, or as a condition precedent by the failure to perform which the other party is relieved of his liability.'"

Applying that test for the reasons which I have sought to give I would hold that the term here in question is a condition.

The decision of the Court of Appeal was affirmed by the House of Lords, [1981] 1 W.L.R. 711; [1981] 2 All E.R. 513; [1981] 2 Ll.R. 1.

LORD WILBERFORCE

[Having referred to the "inescapable conclusion" of the Court of Appeal in *Hong Kong Fir* that the obligation of seaworthiness was not a condition:] Diplock L.J. then generalised this particular consequence into the analysis which has since become classical. The fundamental fallacy of the appellants' argument lies in attempting to apply this analysis to a time clause such as the present in a mercantile contract, which is totally different in character. As to such a clause there is only one kind of breach possible, namely to be late, and the questions which have to be asked are: first, what importance have the parties expressly ascribed to this consequence? and, second, in the absence of expressed agreement, what consequence ought to be attached to it having regard to the contract as a whole?

The test suggested by the appellants was a different one. One must consider, they said, the breach actually committed and then decide whether that default would deprive the party not in default of substantially the whole benefit of the contract. They even invoked certain passages in the judgment of Diplock L.J. in *Hong Kong Fir* to support it. One may observe in the first place that the introduction of a test of this kind would be commercially most undesirable. It would expose the parties, after a breach of one, two, three, seven and other numbers of days, to an argument whether this delay would have left time for the seller to provide the goods. It would make it, at the time, at least difficult, and sometimes impossible, for the supplier to know whether he could do so. It would fatally remove from a vital provision in the contract that certainty which is the most indispensable quality of mercantile contracts, and lead to a large increase in arbitrations. It would confine the seller, perhaps after arbitration and reference through the courts, to a remedy in damages which might be extremely difficult

---

lines 338 and 339: 'nec . . . haec in foedera veni?' If so, they are a part of Aeneas's shabby excuses for his planned desertion of Queen Dido. Hardly, perhaps, the most attractive basis for a doctrine which involves releasing people from their contracts!"

to quantify. These are all serious objections in practice. But I am clear that the submission is unacceptable in law. The judgment of Diplock L.J. does not give any support and ought not to give any encouragement to any such proposition; for beyond doubt it recognises that it is open to the parties to agree that, as regards a particular obligation, any breach shall entitle the party not in default to treat the contract as repudiated. Indeed, if he were not doing so he would, in a passage which does not profess to be more than clarificatory, be discrediting a long and uniform series of cases, at least from *Bowes v Shand* (1877) 2 App.Cas. 455 onwards, which have been referred to by my noble and learned friend Lord Roskill. It remains true, as Roskill L.J. has pointed out in *Cehave NV v Bremer Handelsgesellschaft mbH* [1976] Q.B. 44 at 70–71, that the courts should not be too ready to interpret contractual clauses as conditions. And I have myself commended, and continue to commend, the greater flexibility in the law of contracts to which *Hong Kong Fir* points the way (see *Reardon Smith Line Ltd v Hansen-Tangen* [1976] 3 All E.R. 570 at 576, [1976] 1 W.L.R. 989 at 998). But I do not doubt that, in suitable cases, the courts should not be reluctant, if the intentions of the parties as shown by the contract so indicate, to hold that an obligation has the force of a condition, and that indeed they should usually do so in the case of time clauses in mercantile contracts. To such cases the "gravity of the breach" approach of *Hong Kong Fir* would be unsuitable. I need only add on this point that the word "expressly" used by Diplock L.J. in *Hong Kong Fir* [1962] 1 All E.R. 474 at 487, [1962] 2 Q.B. 26 at 70 should not be read as requiring the actual use of the word "condition"; any term or terms of the contract, which, fairly read, have the effect indicated, are sufficient. Lord Diplock himself has given recognition to this in this House (see *Photo Production Ltd v Securicor Transport Ltd* [1980] A.C. 827 at 849). I therefore reject that part of the appellants' argument which was based on it, and I must disagree with the judgment of the trial judge in so far as he accepted it. I respectfully indorse, on the other hand, the full and learned treatment of this issue in the judgment of Megaw L.J. in the Court of Appeal.

LORD SCARMAN

I read the *Hong Kong Fir* case as being concerned as much with the construction of the contract as with the consequences and effect of breach. The first question is always, therefore, whether, on the true construction of a stipulation and the contract of which it is part, it is a condition, an innominate term, or only a warranty. If the stipulation is one which on the true construction of the contract the parties have not made a condition, and breach of which may be attended by trivial, minor or very grave consequences, it is innominate, and the court (or an arbitrator) will, in the event of dispute, have the task of deciding whether the breach that has arisen is such as the parties would have said, had they been asked at the time they made their contract, "It goes without saying that, if that happens, the contract is at an end."

Where, therefore, as commonly happens, the parties do not identify a stipulation as a condition, innominate term or warranty, the court will approach the problem of construction in the way outlined by Upjohn L.J. [1962] 2 Q.B. 26 at 63–64:

"Where, however, on the true construction of the contract, the parties have not made a particular stipulation a condition, it would be unsound and misleading to conclude that, being a warranty, damages is a sufficient remedy."

Unless the contract makes it clear, either by express provision or by necessary implication arising from its nature, purpose and circumstances ("the factual matrix" as spelt out for example, by Lord Wilberforce in his speech in *Reardon Smith Line Ltd v Hansen-Tangen* [1976] 1 W.L.R. 989 at 995–997), that a particular stipulation is a condition or only a warranty, it is an innominate term the remedy for a breach of which depends on the nature, consequences and effect of the breach.

[After some hesitation, Lord Scarman concluded that the term in the present case was not an innominate term but a condition.]

Question

Diplock LJ says that a breach gives rise to a right to terminate a contract only if the event caused by the breach is so fundamental that, if it had happened without breach, it would have frustrated the contract. (For frustration, see Ch.24, below.) *Bunge* makes it clear that this is not so regarding breach of a condition. Is it true for breach of an innominate term? Was the event in the *Aerial Advertising* case, above, such that, if it had occurred without breach (that is, if the pilot had flown over Salford with the approval of Batchelors and produced the same wrath on the part of the populace), the contract would

20–021

have been frustrated? Would a party having the right to terminate for breach of an innominate term ever exercise his option to affirm if, ex hypothesi, the contract were frustrated?

THE MIHALIS ANGELOS

Court of Appeal [1971] 1 Q.B. 164; [1970] 3 W.L.R. 601; [1970] 3 All E.R. 125; [1970] 2 Lloyd's Rep. 43

20-022   In a charterparty a shipowner (S) undertook that the ship, "expected ready to load . . . about July 1, 1965," would proceed to Haiphong and there load a cargo, the charterer (C) to have the option of cancelling the charter if the ship was not ready to load by July 20.

On July 17, C, being unable to get a cargo, cancelled the charter, alleging that it was frustrated. It was accepted at the trial that the charter was not frustrated merely by C's inability to procure a cargo, but it was argued that C was entitled to avoid the contract on July 17 by reason of a breach of contract by S—that is, that he had impliedly promised that he had reasonable grounds for his expectation that the ship would be ready to load on July 1, and that there were no such grounds. Mocatta J held that there was a breach of this term, but the term was not a condition and the breach was not so fundamental as to afford a right to terminate the contract.

The Court of Appeal held that the term was a condition and that C had properly avoided the contract even though he had done so on the ground that the contract was frustrated when this was not the case. "The fact that a contracting party gives a bad reason for determining it does not prevent him from afterwards relying on a good reason when he discovers it"—per Lord Denning, following *British & Beningtons Ltd v Cachar Tea Co Ltd* [1923] A.C. 48.

MEGAW LJ

[Discussing the term "expected ready to load . . .":] In my judgment, such a term in a charterparty ought to be regarded as being a condition of the contract, in the old sense of the word "condition"; that is that when it has been broken, the other party can, if he wishes, by intimation to the party in breach, elect to be released from performance of his further obligations under the contract; and he can validly do so without having to establish that, on the facts of the particular case, the breach has produced serious consequences which can be treated as "going to the root of the contract" or as being "fundamental," or whatever other metaphor may be thought appropriate for a frustration case.

I reach that conclusion for four interrelated reasons. First, it tends towards certainty in the law. One of the essential elements of law is some measure of uniformity. One of the important elements of the law is predictability. At any rate in commercial law, there are obvious and substantial advantages in having, where possible, a firm and definite rule for a particular class of legal relationship; for example as here, the legal categorisation of a particular, definable type of contractual clause in common use. It is surely much better, both for shipowners and charterers (and, incidentally, for their advisers), when a contractual obligation of this nature is under consideration, and still more when they are faced with the necessity for an urgent decision as to the effects of a suspected breach of it, to be able to say categorically: "If a breach is proved, then the charterer can put an end to the contract," rather than that they should be left to ponder whether or not the courts would be likely, in the particular case, when the evidence had been heard, to decide that in the particular circumstances the breach was or was not such as "to go to the root of the contract." Where justice does not require greater flexibility, there is everything to be said for, and nothing against, a degree of rigidity in legal principle.

Second, it would, in my opinion, only be in the rarest case, if ever, that a ship-owner could legitimately feel that he had suffered an injustice by reason of the law having given to a charterer the right to put an end to the contract because of the breach by the ship-owner of a clause such as this. If a ship-owner has chosen to assert contractually, but dishonestly or without reasonable grounds, that he expects his vessel to be ready to load on such and such a date, wherein does the grievance lie? Third, it is, as Mocatta J. held, clearly established by authority binding on this court that where a clause "expected ready to load" is included in a contract for the sale of goods to be carried by sea, that clause is a condition, in the sense that any breach of it enables the buyer to reject the goods without having to show that the dishonest or unreasonable expectation of the seller has in fact been prejudicial to the buyer . . .

It would, in my judgment, produce an undesirable anomaly in our commercial law if such a clause—"expected ready to load"—were to be held to have a materially different legal effect where it is contained in a charterparty from that which it has when it is contained in a sale of goods contract . . .

The fourth reason why I think that the clause should be regarded as being a condition when it is found in a charterparty is that that view was the view of Scrutton L.J. so expressed in his capacity as the author of Scrutton on Charterparties.

Points for reflection

1. In *The Naxos* [1990] 3 All E.R. 641, the principle that a stipulation as to time in a mercantile contract will usually be interpreted as a condition, was applied by the House of Lords to a clause requiring the seller of sugar to have it available at the port of loading immediately on the arrival of the ship. Lord Brandon, dissenting, pointed out that two other stipulations as to time, breach of which would result in delay in loading the ship (the buyer's obligation to present the ship, and the seller's obligation to complete loading, within a specified time), were clearly intended to be only warranties. He continued:

   20–023

   "In each case what matters to the party to whom the obligation is owed is the result of the breach, namely delay in the loading of the ship, and not the form or nature of the obligation itself. It seems to me that the logical way to interpret the contract . . . is to classify all the obligations of either party, the breach of which would cause delay in the loading of the ship, in the same way, that is to say as warranties and not as conditions."

2. In *Torvald Klaveness A/S v Arni Maritime Corp* [1994] 4 All E.R. 998 HL the term in question was that specifying the date for the redelivery of a ship under a time charter. In the Court of Appeal, Simon Brown LJ said that this was clearly established not to be a condition properly so called. In the House of Lords, Lord Mustill, with whom the majority agreed, said ". . . although it is well established that certain obligations under charterparties do have the character of conditions I would not for my part wish to enlarge the category unduly, given the opportunity which this provides for a party to rely on an innocuous breach as a means of escaping from an unwelcome bargain." He inclined to the view that this particular obligation is "innominate" and that a short delay in redelivery would not justify the termination of the contract. (The vessel was in fact redelivered eight days late).

   The charterer had given an order for a voyage which, in the circumstances then existing, could have been performed within the charter period. After circumstances had so changed that this was impossible, they persisted in it. Lord Mustill said that "the charterer's persistence in [the original order] after it had become invalid showed that they did not intend to perform their obligations under the charter. That is to say, they 'evinced an intention no longer to be bound' by the charter. This was an anticipatory breach entitling the owners to treat the contract as ended." What if the anticipated breach had been a delay of only one day?

3. In *Rice (t/a Garden Guardian) v Great Yarmouth Borough Council, The Times*, July 26, 2000, the contract provided in cl.23.2.1:

   "If the Contractor commits a breach of any of its obligations under the Contract . . . the Council may . . . terminate the Contractor's employment under the Contract by notice in writing having immediate effect."

Faced with an argument for termination based on this clause, Hale LJ said:

> "The problem with the council's argument in this case is that clause 23.2.1 does not characterise any particular term as a condition or indicate which terms are to be considered so important that any breach will justify termination. It appears to visit the same draconian consequences upon any breach, however small, of any obligation, however small . . . [T]he notion that [cl.23.2.1] would entitle the council to terminate a contract such as this at any time for any breach of any term flies in the face of commercial common sense."

Compare, too, *South Oxfordshire DC v Sita UK Ltd* [2006] EWHC 2459, where the scale and extent of the performance required under the District Council's waste management contract militated against a finding of repudiatory breach by the contractor.

Question

20–024   Smith agrees to sell a house to Jones for a purchase price of £500,000. A deposit of £50,000 is to be paid at the time that the formal contracts are signed and exchanged; and the balance of £450,000 is to be paid on completion (this being no later than 28 days after the contracts are exchanged). Before Smith completes the sale to Jones, Brown offers Smith £600,000 for the house. Advise Smith whether he may withdraw from the sale to Jones where:

(i)   Jones fails to pay the deposit on time (see *Samarenko v Dawn Hill House Limited* [2011] EWCA Civ 1445);

(ii)   Jones pays the deposit on time but pays the balance of £450,000 one hour after the deadline for payment has passed (see *Union Eagle Limited v Golden Achievement Limited* [1997] AC 514).

In (i) would it make any difference if the contract provided that the deposit should be paid once Jones had obtained a satisfactory planning permission and Jones then failed to pay the deposit on time?

In (ii), if Smith is legally entitled to withdraw and does withdraw from the sale, is Smith entitled to keep the deposit that Jones has paid?

----

3. Partial or Substituted Performance of Conditions

20–025   The problems considered in this section may be summarised as follows. Where A and B have contracted that the performance of a defined act by A shall be a condition of the liability of B, and A either partly performs that act but fails to complete it or completely performs a similar but not identical act, what are the rights of the parties? Can B repudiate his own obligations under the contract and yet retain any benefit which A's performance may have conferred on him without payment? Does it make any difference that the part of the act which A failed to do was large or very small, or that the act completely performed differed widely or only slightly from the defined act?

CUTTER v POWELL

King's Bench (1795) 6 T.R. 320; 2 Sm.L.C., 13th edn, 1; 3 R.R. 185; 101 E.R. 573

20–026   To assumpsit for work and labour done by the intestate, the defendant pleaded the general issue. And at the trial at Lancaster the jury found a verdict for the plaintiff for £31 10s. subject to the opinion of this court on the following case.

The defendant being at Jamaica subscribed and delivered to T. Cutter, the intestate, a note, whereof the following is a copy:

> "Ten days after the ship Governor Parry, myself master, arrives at Liverpool, I promise to pay to Mr T. Cutter the sum of thirty guineas, provided he proceeds, continues and does his duty as second mate in the said ship from hence to the port of Liverpool. Kingston, July 31, 1793."

The ship Governor Parry sailed from Kingston on August 2, 1793, and arrived in the port of Liverpool on October 9 following. T. Cutter went on board the ship on July 31, 1793, and sailed in her on August 2, and proceeded, continued and did his duty as second mate in her from Kingston until his death, which happened on September 20 following, and before the ship's arrival in the port of Liverpool. The usual wages of a second mate of a ship on such a voyage, when shipped by the month out and home is four pounds per month: but when seamen are shipped by the run from Jamaica to England, a gross sum is usually given. The usual length of a voyage from Jamaica to Liverpool is about eight weeks.

It was argued for the plaintiff, the intestate's widow, that she was entitled to recover a proportionable part of the wages on a quantum meruit for work and labour done during that part of the voyage that he lived and served the defendant. The defendant replied that where there is an express contract between the parties they cannot resort to an implied one; that this was an entire and indivisible contract, and the intestate's continuing to perform his duty during the whole voyage was a condition precedent to his recovering anything.

LORD KENYON CJ

> I should be extremely sorry that in the decision of this case we should determine against what had been the received opinion in the mercantile world on contracts of this kind, because it is of great importance that the laws by which the contracts of so numerous and so useful a body of men as the sailors are supposed to be guided should not be overturned. Whether these kind of notes are much in use among the seamen, we are not sufficiently informed; and the instances now stated to us from Liverpool are too recent to form anything like usage. But it seems to me at present that the decision of this case may proceed on the particular words of this contract and the precise facts here stated, without touching marine contracts in general. That where the parties have come to an express contract none can be implied has prevailed so long as to be reduced to an axiom in the law. Here the defendant expressly promised to pay the intestate 30 guineas, provided he proceeded, continued and did his duty as second mate in the ship from Jamaica to Liverpool; and the accompanying circumstances disclosed in the case are that the common rate of wages is four pounds per month, when the party is paid in proportion to the time he serves: and that this voyage is generally performed in two months. Therefore if there had been no contract between these parties, all that the intestate could have recovered on a quantum meruit for the voyage would have been eight pounds; whereas here the defendant contracted to pay 30 guineas provided the mate continued to do his duty as mate during the whole voyage, in which case the latter would have received nearly four times as much as if he were paid for the number of months he served. He stipulated to receive the larger sum if the whole duty were performed, and nothing unless the whole of that duty were performed: it was a kind of insurance. On this particular contract my opinion is formed at present; at the same time I must say that if we were assured that these notes are in universal use, and that the commercial world have received and acted upon them in a different sense, I should give up my own opinion.

> [The concurring judgments of Ashurst, Grose and Lawrence JJ are omitted.]

It should be noted that the rights of seamen in respect of wages are now regulated by legislation.

Points for reflection

20-027
1. A quantum meruit action may be contractual or quasi-contractual. It is contractual where there is a real contract, but no price has been fixed for the plaintiff's services or other consideration supplied by him. It is quasi-contractual where the plaintiff, not relying on a contract, claims the value of a benefit conferred by him on a defendant who had an option to accept or reject it (see *Sumpter v Hedges*, below) and accepted it. So where the plaintiff rendered services in pursuance of a supposed contract which turned out to be void he could recover the value of his services in quantum meruit: *Craven-Ellis v Canons Ltd* [1936] 2 K.B. 403. Since, however, the action is based on an implied promise, it cannot lie where there is in existence an inconsistent express contract: *Britain v Rossiter* (1879) 11 QBD 123.

2. Is it arguable that the defendant's note to Cutter was merely an offer of a unilateral contract which Cutter never succeeded in accepting? This would be analogous to the case of the offeree who, through no fault of his own, fails to complete the walk to York. Or do the words, "duty as second mate", and the circumstances imply that Cutter undertook obligations such that this was a bilateral contract?

3. In connection with *Cutter v Powell*, see also the Frustrated Contracts Act ss.1(3), 2(3), (below Ch.24).

VIGERS v COOK

Court of Appeal [1919] 2 K.B. 475; 88 L.J.K.B. 1132; 121 L.T. 357; 35 T.L.R. 605

20-028 The plaintiff, a funeral undertaker, contracted with the defendant for the conduct of the funeral of the defendant's son. By the terms of the contract the coffin was to be taken into a certain church where a part of the funeral service was to be read over the body. The body was in an advanced state of decomposition. The plaintiff supplied a lead coffin, in which he left a vent for the escape of gas resulting from decomposition, and the coffin with the body in it was taken to a mortuary. Owing to a complaint by the mortuary authorities of an offensive smell from the coffin, the plaintiff had the vent closed, in consequence of which by the time the funeral had reached the church the coffin had burst and was leaking, and the smell was so offensive that it was impossible to take the coffin into the church, and the service had to be read without it. In consequence the defendant refused to pay the plaintiff's bill. The county court judge found that the plaintiff had broken his contract and disallowed the cost of the lead coffin and the plaintiff's profits, and gave judgment for the plaintiff for the reduced sum of £42 as upon a quantum meruit. The defendant appealed to a divisional court (A. T. Lawrence and Lush JJ) which held that this was one entire contract, to conduct the service in a proper manner, and as this had not been done, the plaintiff could recover nothing. The plaintiff appealed to the Court of Appeal.

BANKES LJ

In my opinion the contract which was made between the parties included, as I have said, as an essential term the conveying of the body into the church for a part of the service, subject to this condition, that the body was in such a state as to permit of that being done. The body in this coffin was not in that state, but the onus was on the plaintiff to establish that it was not in that state owing to no default on his part. In my opinion he did not discharge that onus. In considering whether he discharged the onus it is necessary to see what it was prima facie possible for him to have done. When on August 3 the body left the mortuary for Richmond the plaintiff knew that there was within the coffin a very considerable accumulation of gas, such an accumulation as raised a question of doubt whether it could safely be removed on that journey. He considered it, and came to the conclusion that the risk could be safely taken. Assuming he had come to the conclusion that the risk could not safely be taken, as it turned out it could not, what was it possible to have done? It was possible to reopen the aperture and allow the gas to escape. Whether it was practicable was a different question, and the onus rested upon the plaintiff to prove that, though possible, it was not practicable. No evidence was given on that point. Another question arose which it was necessary to consider. Assuming it to be both possible and practicable to reopen the aperture, would the condition of things with the aperture reopened have been equally offensive as it was with the coffin burst, or at any rate so offensive that the body could not have been carried into the church? There again the onus rested upon the plaintiff. It may well be that the condition of things was such that, even if the hole had been reopened, it would not have been possible, reverently and decently, to take the body into the church. At present that is left unsettled. In these two matters I think that, although the plaintiff down to the time of the closing of the aperture did nothing other than what a competent and careful undertaker would do, in the difficult circumstances which arose when he felt it necessary to close the aperture, he has not shown that it was owing to no fault on his part that one essential term of his contract was not fulfilled; and it being one entire contract, in my opinion he fails in proving that he is entitled to any portion of the one entire price which was payable for the entire contract.

Scrutton and Atkin L.JJ. agreed.

Questions

Why did the court consider that this case turned on whether the plaintiff was negligent or not, when nothing was said about negligence in *Cutter v Powell*?   **20–029**

It is possible for a contract to allow alternative modes of performance, depending upon some condition: for example, "The concert will be held on the lawn if it is fine; but in the hall if it is wet." Might it not be that it was implicit in the contract in *Vigers v Cook* that if, after all proper steps had been taken, the condition of the body made it impossible to take the coffin into church, then the coffin should be left outside? If so, would not Vigers, then, have fully performed his contract if he had been able to show that he was not negligent? (On the question of burden of proof on the negligence issue, compare the *Constantine Steamship* case, below, Ch.24).

SUMPTER v HEDGES

Court of Appeal [1898] 1 Q.B. 673; 67 L.J.Q.B. 545; 78 L.T. 378; 46 W.R. 454

The plaintiff, a builder, contracted with the defendant to erect certain buildings upon the defendant's   **20–030** land for £565. The plaintiff did part of the work to the value of about £333 and received payment of part of the price. He then informed the defendant that he had no money and could not go on with the work. The defendant finished the buildings on his own account, using for that purpose certain materials which the plaintiff had left on the site. In an action for work done and materials provided Bruce J found that the plaintiff had abandoned the contract and gave judgment for him for the value of the materials used by the defendant, but allowed him nothing for the work done. The plaintiff appealed.

A. L. Smith and Chitty LJJ gave judgment dismissing the appeal

COLLINS LJ

I agree. I think the case is really concluded by the finding of the learned judge to the effect that the plaintiff had abandoned the contract. If the plaintiff had merely broken his contract in some way so as not to give the defendant the right to treat him as having abandoned the contract, and the defendant had then proceeded to finish the work himself, the plaintiff might perhaps have been entitled to sue on a quantum meruit on the ground that the defendant had taken the benefit of the work done. But that is not the present case. There are cases in which, though the plaintiff has abandoned the performance of a contract, it is possible for him to raise the inference of a new contract to pay for the work done on a quantum meruit from the defendant's having taken the benefit of that work, but, in order that that may be done, the circumstances must be such as to give an option to the defendant to take or not to take the benefit of the work done. It is only where the circumstances are such as to give that option that there is any evidence on which to ground the inference of a new contract. Where, as in the case of work done on land, the circumstances are such as to give the defendant no option whether he will take the benefit of the work or not, then one must look to other facts than the mere taking the benefit of the work in order to ground the inference of a new contract. In this case I see no other facts on which such an inference can be founded. The mere fact that a defendant is in possession of what he cannot help keeping, or even has done work upon it, affords no ground for such an inference. He is not bound to keep unfinished a building which in an incomplete state would be a nuisance on his land. I am therefore of opinion that the plaintiff was not entitled to recover for the work which he had done.

Appeal Dismissed.

SALE OF GOODS ACT 1979

Delivery of wrong quantity.

20–031   **30.**—(1) Where the seller delivers to the buyer a quantity of goods less than he contracted to sell, the buyer may reject them, but if the buyer accepts the goods so delivered he must pay for them at the contract rate.

(2)   Where the seller delivers to the buyer a quantity of goods larger than he contracted to sell, the buyer may accept the goods included in the contract and reject the rest, or he may reject the whole.

(2A)   A buyer who does not deal as consumer may not—

(a)   where the seller delivers a quantity of goods less than he contracted to sell, reject the goods under subsection (1) above, or
(b)   where the seller delivers a quantity of goods larger than he contracted to sell, reject the whole under subsection (2) above,

if the shortfall or, as the case may be, excess is so slight that it would be unreasonable for him to do so.

(2B)   It is for the seller to show that a shortfall or excess fell within subsection (2A) above.

Section 30(1) and (2) enacted the rule of the common law, requiring strict performance as a condition. Delivery of 143 bottles, instead of the gross contracted for, entitled the buyer to reject. In a consumer contract, it still does (and see now s.25 of the Consumer Rights Act 2015). The consumer may reject, however unreasonable it is for him to do so. But, for other contracts, s.30(2)A, inserted by the Sale and Supply of Goods Act 1994, reduces the term regarding quantity, in effect to an innominate term.

APPLEBY v MYERS

Exchequer Chamber (1867) L.R. 2 C.P. 651; 36 L.J.C.P. 331; 16 L.T. 669

20–032   The plaintiffs contracted with the defendant to erect a steam engine and machinery on premises in the possession of the defendant. The specification divided the work into 10 different parts and stated the price to be charged for each part. The contract concluded with these words: "We offer to make and erect the whole of the machinery . . . and to put it to work, for the sums above named respectively, and to keep the whole in order, under fair wear and tear, for two years from the date of completion. . . ." The total cost of the works to be done amounted to £459. When all parts of the work were far advanced towards completion, though none of them had been absolutely completed, an accidental fire entirely destroyed the premises and the works which had been erected thereon. The plaintiff sued to recover £419 for work done and materials provided. The judgment of the Court of

Common Pleas in favour of the plaintiff was reversed by the Court of Exchequer Chamber. Blackburn J, delivering the judgment of the court (Martin B, Blackburn J, Bramwell B, Shee and Lush JJ), held, differing from the court below, that there was no absolute promise or warranty by the defendant that the premises should continue in a fit state to enable the plaintiffs to perform the work upon them. The destruction of the premises excused both parties, but gave a cause of action to neither. He went on:

BLACKBURN J

> Then it was argued before us, that, inasmuch as this was a contract of that nature which would in pleading be described as a contract for work, labour, and materials, and not as one of bargain and sale, the labour and materials necessarily became the property of the defendant as soon as they were worked into his premises and became part of them, and therefore were at his risk. We think that, as to a great part at least of the work done in this case, the materials had not become the property of the defendant; for, we think that the plaintiffs, who were to complete the whole for a fixed sum, and keep it in repair for two years, would have had a perfect right, if they thought that a portion of the engine which they had put up was too slight, to change it and substitute another in their opinion better calculated to keep in good repair during the two years, and that without consulting or asking the leave of the defendant. But, even on the supposition that the materials had become unalterably fixed to the defendant's premises, we do not think that, under such a contract as this, the plaintiffs could recover anything unless the whole work was completed. It is quite true that materials worked by one into the property of another become part of that property. This is equally true, whether it be fixed or movable property. Bricks built into a wall become part of the house; thread stitched into a coat which is under repair, or planks and nails and pitch worked into a ship under repair, become part of the coat or the ship; and therefore, generally, and in the absence of something to show a contrary intention, the bricklayer, or tailor, or shipwright, is to be paid for the work and materials he has done and provided, although the whole work is not complete. It is not material whether in such a case the non-completion is because the shipwright did not choose to go on with the work, as was the case in *Roberts v Havelock*, 3 B. & Ad. 404, or because in consequence of a fire he could not go on with it, as in *Menetone v Athawes*, 3 Burr. 1592. But, though this is the prima facie contract between those who enter into contracts for doing work and supplying materials, there is nothing to render it either illegal or absurd in the workman to agree to complete the whole, and be paid when the whole is complete, and not till then: and we think that the plaintiffs in the present case had entered into such a contract. Had the accidental fire left the defendant's premises untouched, and only injured a part of the work which the plaintiffs had already done, we apprehend that it is clear the plaintiffs under such a contract as the present must have done that part over again, in order to fulfil their contract to complete the whole and "put it to work for the sums above named respectively." As it is, they are, according to the principle laid down in *Taylor v Caldwell* [below, Ch.24], excused from completing the work; but they are not therefore entitled to any compensation for what they have done, but which has, without any fault of the defendant, perished. The case is in principle like that of a shipowner who has been excused from the performance of his contract to carry goods to their destination, because his ship has been disabled by one of the excepted perils, but who is not therefore entitled to any payment on account of the part-performance of the voyage, unless there is something to justify the conclusion that there has been a fresh contract to pay freight pro rata.

It is important to note that this case must now be considered in the light of the Frustrated Contracts Act 1943. See especially ss.1(3) and 2(3), below, Ch.24.

FORMAN & CO PROPRIETARY LTD v THE SHIP "LIDDESDALE"

Privy Council [1900] A.C. 190; 69 L.J.P.C. 44; 82 L.T. 33]; 9 Asp.M.C. 45

The Liddesdale ran aground and sustained damage off the coast of Western Australia. The p laintiffs contracted with the shipowner to effect certain specified repairs for a fixed sum. The plaintiffs did do repairs which were good work, and which added value to the ship; but the work was not—and the plaintiffs did not assert that it was—the stipulated work. The plaintiffs did allege that it was equivalent to the stipulated work, or something better. For example, the plaintiffs had used iron girders where their contract required steel. The iron girders were more expensive and, the plaintiffs alleged, to the advantage of the ship—though the defendants denied this. The Privy Council held that the plaintiffs

20–033

could recover nothing; they could not recover under the express contract, because they had not done what they had undertaken to do; nor under an implied contract for the work actually done, because there had been no acquiescence in, or ratification of that work by the defendants. "The mere fact that the defendant took the ship which was his own property and made the best he could of it cannot give the plaintiffs any additional right. It is not like the case of an acceptance of goods which were not previously the property of the acceptor . . ."

HOENIG v ISAACS

Court of Appeal [1952] 1 T.L.R. 1360; [1952] 2 All E.R. 176

20–034   The plaintiff was an interior decorator and furniture designer. The defendant, the owner of a one-room flat, employed the plaintiff to decorate it and provide it with furniture, including bedstead and wardrobe and bookcase fitments, for a sum of £750, the terms of payment being "net cash, as the work proceeds; and balance on completion." On April 12, 1950, the defendant paid £150, and on April 19 he paid a further £150. On August 28, the plaintiff said that he had carried out the work in compliance with the contract and requested payment of the balance of £450. The defendant replied complaining of faulty design and bad workmanship, but he sent the plaintiff a further £100, entered into occupation of the flat, and used the furniture. On a claim by the plaintiff for the balance of £350, the defendant alleged that the plaintiff had failed to perform his contract, and, alternatively, that the work was done negligently, unskilfully, and in an unworkmanlike manner. The official referee held that the door of a wardrobe required replacing, and that a bookshelf, which was too short, would have to be remade, which would require alterations being made to a bookcase. The defendant contended that this was an entire contract which had not been performed, and, therefore, the plaintiff could not recover. The official referee held that there had been a substantial compliance with the contract and that the defendant was liable for £350 less the cost of remedying the defects which he assessed at £55 18s. 2d., and he gave judgment for £294 1s. 10d.

SOMERVELL LJ

[Having stated the facts, continued:] Counsel for the defendant submits that the decision of the official referee is wrong in law. He submits that this is an entire contract which, on the findings of fact, has not been performed. On the well-known principle applied to the facts of that case in *Cutter v Powell* [above] he submitted that the plaintiff cannot, therefore, recover on his contract. He was not concerned to dispute that on this basis the plaintiff might on the facts of this case be entitled to recover on a quantum meruit. Such a claim has never been put forward. If it were, he submits that the amount recoverable would be the fair value of what was done and delivered. The learned official referee found that there had been a substantial compliance with the contract. Counsel submits that, if his first point is right, this does not enable the pla[i]ntiff to succeed. If necessary, he submits that on his findings of fact the learned official referee was wrong as a matter of law in holding that there had been substantial compliance. [His Lordship referred to the official referee's findings as to the wardrobe door, the bookshelf, and the bookcase, and continued:] If any issue arises whether the breaches were substantial, I think it must be based on the items to which I have referred, bearing in mind, of course, that there were some additional minor defects.

The official referee regarded the principle laid down in *H. Dakin & Co Ltd v Lee* [1916] 1 K.B. 566 as applicable. The contract in that case was for repairs to a house. The official referee before whom the case came in the first instance found that the work as completed did not accord with the contract in certain respects. He proceeded to hold that the plaintiff could not recover any part of the contract price or any sum in respect of the contract work. This decision was reversed in the Divisional Court and their decision was affirmed by this court. In support of the official referee's decision it was argued that the plaintiff could not recover either on the contract or on a quantum meruit. No new contract on the latter basis could be implied from the fact that the defendant by continuing to live in her house had enjoyed the benefit of what had been done.

In *Eshelby v Federated European Bank Ltd* [1932] 1 K.B. 423, Greer L.J. ([1932] 1 K.B. 431) clearly felt some difficulty about *H. Dakin & Co Ltd v Lee* as possibly inconsistent with *Cutter v Powell*, and the cases following that decision and deciding that where work is to be done for a sum named neither that sum nor any part of it can be recovered while the work remains undone. We were referred to a number of these cases and I have considered those authorities and others. Each case turns on the construction of the contract. In *Cutter v Powell* the condition for the promissory note sued on was that the sailor should proceed to continue and do his duty as second mate in the ship from Jamaica to the port of Liverpool. The sailor died before the ship reached Liverpool and it was held his estate could not recover either on the contract or on a quantum meruit. It clearly decided that his continuing as mate during the whole voyage was a condition precedent to payment. It did not decide that if he had completed the main purpose of the contract, namely, serving as mate for the whole voyage, the defendant could have repudiated his liability by establishing that in the course of the voyage the sailor had, possibly through inadvertence, failed on some occasion in his duty as mate whereby some damage had been caused. In these circumstances, the court might have applied the principle applied to ordinary contracts for freight. The shipowner can normally recover nothing unless the goods are carried to their agreed destination. On the other hand, if this is done, his claim is not defeated by the fact that some damage has been done to the goods in transit which has resulted from a breach of the contract. The owner of the goods has his remedy by cross-action: *Dakin v Oxley* (1864) 15 C.B.(n.s.) 646; 143 E.R. 938. The damage might, of course, be so great as to raise the question whether what was agreed to be carried had substantially arrived. *Sinclair v Bowles* (1829) 9 B. and Co 92; 109 E.R. 35, is often cited as an illustration of the *Cutter v Powell* principle. The plaintiff had undertaken to repair chandeliers and make them "complete" or "perfect." This he, quite plainly on the evidence and findings of the jury, failed to do. It may, perhaps, be regarded as a case where, on the construction of the contract, having regard to the subject-matter, there was no scope for terms collateral to the main purpose.

The principle that fulfilment of every term is not necessarily a condition precedent in a contract for a lump sum is usually traced back to a short judgment of Lord Mansfield C. J. in *Boone v Eyre* (1779) 1 Hy. Bl. 273n. the sale of the plantation with its slaves. Lord Mansfield said: ". . . where mutual covenants go to the whole of the consideration on both sides, they are mutual conditions, the one precedent to the other. But where they go only to a part, where a breach may be paid for in damages, there the defendant has a remedy on his covenant, and shall not plead it as a condition precedent." One is very familiar with the application of this principle in the law relating to the sale of goods. Quoad stipulations which are conditions, the *Cutter v Powell* principle is applicable. If they are not all performed the other party can repudiate, but there will not have been, as there was in *Cutter v Powell*, a partial performance. But there may be other terms, collateral to the main purpose, the breach of which in English law gives rise to a claim for damages, but not to a right to reject the goods and treat the contract as repudiated: see definition of warranty, Sale of Goods Act, 1893, s.62(1).

In a contract to erect buildings on the defendant's land for a lump sum, the builder can recover nothing on the contract if he stops before the work is completed in the ordinary sense—in other words, abandons the contract. He is also usually in a difficulty in recovering on a quantum meruit because no new contract can be inferred from the mere fact that the defendant remains in possession of his land: *Sumpter v Hedges*. In *Appleby v Myers* while the work was in progress the premises and the work so far done on them were destroyed by fire and the court held both parties excused. At the end of his judgment Blackburn J., after referring to *Cutter v Powell*, *Sinclair v Bowles*, and that line of cases, said: ". . . the plaintiffs, having contracted to do an entire work for a specific sum, can recover nothing unless the work be done . . ." In *H. Dakin & Co Ltd v Lee* Lord Cozens-Hardy M.R., I think, had this principle in mind when he said: "The work was finished—and when I say this I do not wish to prejudice matters, but I cannot think of a better word to use at the moment."

The question here is whether in a contract for work and labour for a lump sum payable on completion the defendant can repudiate liability under the contract on the ground that the work though "finished" or "done" is in some respects not in accordance with the contract. *H. Dakin & Co Ltd v Lee* is, of course, binding on us, but counsel for the defendant submitted that it was an exception to a general rule applying to contracts such as that in issue here and should be confined within as narrow limits as possible. I agree with the learned editor of the notes to *Cutter v Powell* in *Smith's Leading Cases*, (13th ed.), Vol. 2, p. 21, that *H. Dakin & Co Ltd v Lee*, so far from being an exception, reaffirmed the true position on the construction of this class of contract on which doubts had been thrown by taking certain observations out of their context. . . .

The learned official referee regarded *H. Dakin & Co Ltd v Lee* as laying down that the price must be paid subject to set-off or counterclaim if there was a substantial compliance with the contract. I think on the facts of this case where the work was finished in the ordinary sense, though in part defective, this is right. It expresses in a convenient epithet what is put from another angle in the Sale of Goods Act, 1893. The buyer cannot reject if he proves only the breach of a term collateral to the main purpose. I have, therefore, come to the conclusion that the first point of counsel for the defendant fails.

The learned official referee found that there was substantial compliance. Bearing in mind that there is no appeal on fact, was there evidence on which he could so find? The learned official referee having, as I hold, properly directed himself, this becomes, I think, a question of fact. The case on this point was, I think, near the border line, and if the finding had been the other way I do not think we could have interfered. Even if I had felt we could interfere, the defendant would be in a further difficulty. The contract included a number of chattels. If the defendant wished to repudiate his liability under the contract he should not, I think, have used those articles, which he could have avoided using. On this view, though it is not necessary to decide it, I think he put himself in the same position as a buyer of goods who by accepting them elects to treat a breach of condition as a breach of warranty.

I now come to the final question, the measure of damages. It seems from the argument that the defendant regards the price of £750 as excessive irrespective of any relief by way of reduction of price or on his counter-claim. He was anxious to put the plaintiff in the position of having to sue on a quantum meruit for the value of the work done and he was anxious to tender evidence designed, no doubt, to show that the work done was worth much less than £750. The learned official referee excluded this evidence. The measure he applied was the cost of putting the work in accordance with the contract and on this basis such evidence was rightly excluded. The defendant is bound, he held, to pay for the furniture supplied less the cost of putting right the defects. This I think is, as the learned official referee thought, in accordance with *H. Dakin & Co Ltd v Lee*. Lord Cozens-Hardy M.R. there said: ". . . the builders are entiled to recover the contract price, less so much as it is found ought to be allowed in respect of the items which the official referee has found to be defective." This seems to follow what was said by Parke B. in *Mondel v Steel*. In dealing with the procedural point he said that the defendant need not bring a cross-action but can diminish the price ". . . by showing how much less the subject-matter of the contract was worth, by reason of the breach of contract."

Denning and Romer L.JJ. delivered concurring judgments.

Appeal Dismissed.

Points for reflection

20–035

1. In *Bolton v Mahadeva* [1972] 1 W.L.R. 1009 the Court of Appeal applied the rule to defeat an action by a contractor for the agreed price of £560 for the installation of a combined heating and domestic hot water system. The county court judge, though he assessed the deficiencies at £174, held that there had been substantial performance. Cairns LJ said: "If a central heating system when installed is such that it does not heat the house adequately and is such, further, that fumes are given out, so as to make living rooms uncomfortable, and if the putting right of these defects is not something which can be done by some slight amendment of the system, then I think that the contract is not substantially performed." Sachs LJ said: "This rule does not work hardly upon a contractor if only he is prepared to remedy the defects before seeking to resort to litigation to recover the lump sum. It is entirely the fault of the contractor in this instant case that he has placed himself in a difficulty by his refusal, on December 4, 1969, to remedy the defects of which complaint was being made."

2. Of the various plaintiffs, Cutter, Vigers, Sumpter, Appleby, and Forman & Co, who were in breach of contract? Who were excused because the contract became impossible of performance without fault? Where the contract has become impossible of performance without the plaintiff's fault he may now have a remedy under s.1(3) and 2(3) of the Frustrated Contracts Act 1943, below, Ch.24. Where the plaintiff was in breach of contract, however, the Act does not help him. The plight of the party in breach of contract is one of the matters considered by the Law Commission in Working Paper No.65 (1975) and in its Report, *Pecuniary Restitution on Breach of Contract* Law Com. No.121, (1983). It is recommended that the party who has failed to complete and who would have no right to recover under the present law should be entitled to recover

from the other party to the contract a sum representing the value of what he has done under the contract to that person who has had the benefit of it, whether he is a party to the contract or not. The court would have no discretion to reduce or disallow the claim, because of the conduct of the party in breach but the sum awarded would not exceed the proportion of the sum payable on completion as is equal to the proportion of the work done to that promised. The party not in breach would be able to counterclaim for damages and the normal rules relating to remoteness and mitigation would apply.

Further reading

Anthony Beck, 'The Doctrine of Substantial Performance: Conditions and Conditions Precedent' (1975) 38 MLR 413

Roger Brownsword, 'Retrieving Reasons, Retrieving Rationality? A New Look at the Right to Withdraw for Breach of Contract' (1992) 5 *Journal of Contract Law* 83

Michael Bridge, '*Reardon Smith Lines Ltd v Yngvar Hansen-Tangen, The Diana Prosperity* (1976)' in Charles Mitchell and Paul Mitchell (eds), *Landmark Cases in the Law of Contract* (Oxford: Hart, 2008) p.321

Donal Nolan, '*Hongkong Fir Shipping Co v Kawasaki Kisen Kaisha Ltd, The Hongkong Fir* (1961)' in Charles Mitchell and Paul Mitchell (eds), *Landmark Cases in the Law of Contract* (Oxford: Hart, 2008) p.269

John Randall, 'Express Termination Clauses in Contracts' (2014) 73 CLJ 113

Samuel J. Stoljar, 'The Great Case of *Cutter v Powell*' (1956) 34 Can. Bar Rev. 288

Glanville Williams, 'Partial Performance of Entire Contracts' (1941) 57 L.Q.R. 373

PART V

EXCLUSION OF LIABILITY AND UNFAIR TERMS

21

EXCLUSION CLAUSES

LEARNING OBJECTIVES

By the end of this chapter, you should:

- **understand the concept of an exclusion or exemption clause;**
- **be familiar with the common law strategies for controlling exclusion clauses that are judged to be unfair or unreasonable (particularly by stringent application of the rules for the incorporation of terms and by restrictive interpretation);**
- **appreciate the limitations of these strategies and the difficulty of adjusting for context (particularly to take account of whether the exclusion clause is in a commercial contract or in a consumer contract, in a standard form contract or not, and so on);**
- **have a view about the need for bespoke statutory control over unfair terms.**

INTRODUCTION

"Exclusion" or "exemption" or "exceptions" or "limitations" clauses are terms which exclude or   21–001
limit, or purport to exclude or limit, a liability which would otherwise arise at common law, or by statute, or under the terms of a contract. Such a clause may exclude or limit a liability which would otherwise arise under the express or implied terms of a contract, but the effect of these clauses is not confined to contractual liability. Duties imposed by the common law or by statute may sometimes be excluded by the terms of a contract or, indeed, by a notice not having contractual effect. The common law of bailment imposes duties on the bailee to take proper care of the goods but this duty might be restricted or excluded by a contract or notice accompanying the bailment; and, in some circumstances, a statutory duty or obligation may be restricted, modified or excluded by agreement or otherwise. An exclusion clause in a contract or, indeed, in a notice not forming part of a contract, may thus amount to a defence to an action for a breach of a common law or statutory duty.

Suppliers of goods and services have often sought to exclude or limit their possible legal liability by the inclusion of far-reaching exclusion clauses in their standard forms of contract. The courts have long been hostile to such clauses. They are not freely negotiated but are in effect imposed by the one party on the other. The supplier declares that he will contract on his standard terms and no other and his customer frequently has to accept those terms or go without the service he wants. There is no "equality of bargaining power"; the deal is non-negotiable, being offered on a "take it or leave it" basis. Because of their sympathy with the weaker party, the courts have sometimes applied the rules concerning the formation and interpretation of contracts strictly in his favour, resolving any doubts against the stronger party. Thus, techniques for controlling the unacceptable application of exclusion clauses have included—

(1) holding the clause not to be part of the contract because notice of it was insufficient or too late. The relevant cases are to be found above, Ch.7;

(2) construing the clause strictly against the person relying on it (contra proferentem) and holding it inapplicable to the events which have occurred; and

(3) creating a doctrine of "fundamental breach"—to the effect that a person who has committed a breach of a fundamental term or a fundamental breach of an innominate term is precluded from relying on any exemption clause, at least if the contract has been terminated as a result of the breach. The House of Lords has now twice stated that there is no rule of law to this effect—it is only an aspect of the rule of strict construction. The first case, *Suisse Atlantique*, below, was restrictively interpreted or ignored altogether by lower courts; but, the second, *Photo Production v Securicor*, below, has been more effective.

Injustice arising from the use of exclusion clauses has attracted the attention of Parliament from time to time and the reader has encountered examples of statutes which invalidate such clauses in particular circumstances. Attention is drawn to the following:

(1) Road transport: Public Passenger Vehicles Act 1981 s.29.

(2) Liability for misrepresentation: Misrepresentation Act 1967 s.3.

(3) Defective Premises Act 1972 s.6.

However, the use of exclusion clauses in both consumer and commercial contracts was systematically addressed in the Unfair Contract Terms Act 1977; and the Unfair Terms in Consumer Contracts Regulations 1999 deal more broadly with the control of unfair terms but only in consumer contracts. The Act came into force on February 1, 1978, and applies to contracts made on or after (but not before) that date and to liability for loss or damage suffered on or after (but not before) that date. Its title is misleading in two respects. First, it is not concerned with all contract terms which might be thought "unfair" but with only exclusion (and limitation) clauses and indemnity clauses. Secondly, it is not confined to contractual terms. It applies, also, to cases where there is no contractual relationship between the parties and an attempt is made to exclude tortious or other liability by means of a notice or other disclaimer. (Cf. *Ashdown v Samuel Williams*, above, Ch.13).

The Regulations apply only to terms in consumer contracts which have not been individually negotiated and, for these purposes, only natural persons, not limited companies or other corporations, are consumers. However, the overlapping protection given to consumer contractors by, first the Act and then the Regulations invites some confusion; and, in an attempt to clean up and clarify the law relating to the control of unfair terms in consumer contracts, the Consumer Rights Act 2015 now restates these controls (see Ch.22).

Far-reaching though these enactments are, the common law continues to be of importance because (i) some very important classes of contracts are outside the scope of the legislation; and (ii) where an enactment provides that an exclusion clause is valid if it is fair and reasonable the claimant may argue (a) that it is not part of the contract at all or (b) that, on its true construction, it does not apply to the situation which has arisen—in which case it is ineffective even if it is a reasonable clause. That said, with the legislative controls in place, the common law principles are not applied with the same degree of strictness as before. On this, consider the observations of Lord Wilberforce in the *Securicor* case, below, and of Lord Denning in *Mitchell v Finney Lock Seeds*, below.

The case-law in this chapter is divided into two sections. First, in a short section, a simple illustration is given of the ad hoc way in which, before unfair terms were subjected to broad legislative controls, judges could protect consumers against unfair practices; and, secondly, in the main body of the chapter, the case-law on the interpretation of exclusion clauses is set out.

1. THE EFFECT OF MISREPRESENTATION

CURTIS v CHEMICAL CLEANING AND DYEING CO

Court of Appeal [1951] 1 K.B. 805; [1951] 1 T.L.R. 452; 95 S.J. 253; [1951] 1 All E.R. 631

The plaintiff took a white satin wedding dress to the shop of the defendants for cleaning. On being requested by a shop assistant to sign a paper headed "Receipt," the plaintiff asked why her signature was required and was told that it was because the defendants would not accept liability for certain specified risks, including the risk of damage by or to the beads and sequins with which the dress was trimmed. The plaintiff then signed the "Receipt" which, in fact, contained the following condition: "This article is accepted on condition that the company is not liable for any damage howsoever arising." When the dress was returned there was a stain on it which could not be explained.   **21–002**

The county court judge found for the plaintiff. The defendants appealed.

DENNING LJ

[Having referred to *L'Estrange v Graucob*, (above) and asked, "what is a sufficient misrepresentation?" went on:] In my opinion any behaviour, by words or conduct, is sufficient to be a misrepresentation if it is such as to mislead the other party about the existence or extent of the exemption. If it conveys a false impression, that is enough. If the false impression is created knowingly, it is a fraudulent misrepresentation; if it is created unwittingly, it is an innocent misrepresentation; but either is sufficient to disentitle the creator of it to the benefit of the exemption. In *R. v Kylsant (Lord)* [1932] 1 K.B. 442 it was held that a representation might be literally true but practically false, not because of what it said, but because of what it left unsaid; in short, because of what it implied. This is as true of an innocent misrepresentation as it is of a fraudulent misrepresentation. When one party puts forward a printed form for signature, failure by him to draw attention to the existence or extent of the exemption clause may in some circumstances convey the impression that there is no exemption at all, or at any rate not so wide an exemption as that which is in fact contained in the document. The present case is a good illustration. The customer said in evidence: "When I was asked to sign the document I asked why? The assistant said I was to accept any responsibility for damage to beads and sequins. I did not read it all before I signed it." In those circumstances, by failing to draw attention to the width of the exemption clause, the assistant created the false impression that the exemption only related to the beads and sequins, and that it did not extend to the material of which the dress was made. It was done perfectly innocently, but nevertheless a false impression was created. It was probably not sufficiently precise and unambiguous to create an estoppel: *Low v Bouverie* [1891] 3 Ch. 82, but nevertheless it was a sufficient misrepresentation to disentitle the cleaners from relying on the exemption, except in regard to beads and sequins . . .

In my opinion when the signature to a condition, purporting to exempt a person from his common law abilities, is obtained by an innocent misrepresentation, the party who has made that misrepresentation is disentitled to rely on the exemption . . . I therefore agree that the appeal should be dismissed.

[The judgment of Somervell L.J. is omitted. Singleton L.J. agreed.]

Appeal Dismissed.

Questions

1. What would have been the position if only the beads and sequins had been damaged?   **21–003**

2. What would have been the position if the plaintiff had signed the document without asking for an explanation of it?

3. The Conditions of Acceptance approved by the National Federation of Dyers and Cleaners included the following term: "None of our agents or employees has any authority to alter, vary or qualify in any way these terms and conditions." Would this term have protected the defendants in the *Curtis* case? Consider *Overcombe Estates v Glencombe Properties Ltd* [1974] 2 All E.R. 511 and UTCC Regs 5(1) and Sch.3, sub-para.1(n).

----

2. The Interpretation of the Clause

21–004   Regulation 7 of the Unfair Terms in Consumer Contracts Regulations 1999 provides:

"Written contracts.

(1) A seller or supplier shall ensure that any written term of a contract is expressed in plain, intelligible language.

(2) If there is any doubt about the meaning of a written term, the interpretation most favourable to the consumer shall prevail but this rule shall not apply in proceedings brought under regulation 12. [Injunctions to prevent continued use of unfair terms]."

The first half of this provision seems little more than a pious exhortation to sellers and suppliers; but the second half is, in substance, the contra proferentem rule of construction which, in English law, applies not only to sale and supply contracts with consumers but to contracts generally. See particularly the examples discussed below.

"ISTROS" (OWNERS) v F W DAHLSTROEM & CO

King's Bench Division [1931] 1 K.B. 247; 18 Asp.M.L.C. 177

21–005   A charterparty provided by cl.8: "Captain to prosecute all voyages with utmost dispatch . . ."; and by cl.12: "Owners only to be responsible . . . for delay . . . if . . . caused by want of due diligence on the part of owners or their manager in making steamer seaworthy and fitted for the voyage, or any other personal act or omission, or default of owners or their manager." The captain failed to prosecute the voyage with the utmost dispatch and the charterer withheld part of the hire in respect of the delay. An umpire ordered that the sum withheld should be paid; and the question for the court was whether this award was right in law.

WRIGHT J

> In my opinion the award is right in law and I, therefore, order that it shall stand. Clause 12 appears to me, so far as the facts of this particular case are concerned, to be quite clear. There has been no want of due diligence on the part of the owner or his manager in making the ship seaworthy and fitted for the voyage, and there has been no other personal act, or omission, or default on the part of either of them. Any neglect or default that there has been, has been that of the owner's servants. The umpire has found that there was neglect or default by the master and that that caused the delay. That seems to me to come within the precise words of clause 12.
>
> It is not necessary here to consider whether every possible case that may arise under clause 8 of a failure on the part of the captain to prosecute all voyages with utmost dispatch is covered by clause 12. I have not in my mind at this moment any specific type of a breach of clause 8 by act of the captain for which, notwithstanding clause 12, the owner would be responsible. There may be such cases, but it seems to me that clause 12 must receive effect where the case comes within its clear terms.

If the effect is to render th e owner free from any liability for loss or delay where there is a failure on the part of the captain to prosecute the voyage with the utmost dispatch, then I think that the owner is entitled to the full benefit of that clause. Clause 8, it may be said, has then no practical effect. It has a practical effect to the extent that it contains clear recognition of the duty of the captain so to act, and the effect of clause 12 is not to modify or qualify the existence of that duty, although it may operate if an action is brought against the owner for damages as a defence. In one sense, every exception clause is pro tanto inconsistent with the primary or express obligation which at law or by contract rest upon an owner or a master in respect of the goods entrusted to his charge and the duties arising under a charterpar[t]y, but, notwithstanding those obligations, exception clauses must receive in due course, if their language and the circumstances require it, their appropriate effect as a shield to a claim for damages.

I see nothing in the circumstances of this case to prevent the owner from relying here on the protection afforded to him by clause 12 of the charterparty.

Award Upheld.

Questions

1. In what sense was the captain under a duty to prosecute the voyage with the utmost dispatch?   **21–006**

2. Was the failure of the captain a breach of contract by the owners?

Points for reflection

For a criticism of the approach to exception clauses adopted by Wright J in the above case, see Brian   **21–007** Coote, *Exception Clauses*, especially Chs 1 and 8. Professor Coote's view is that "Instead of being mere shields to claims based on breach of accrued rights, exception clauses substantively delimit the rights themselves" (p.17); that is, that in the above case, it ought to have been held that there was no right to performance with the utmost dispatch—and, therefore, of course, no duty so to perform. Coote divides exception clauses into two classes: "Type A: exception clauses whose effect, if any, is upon the accrual of particular primary rights. . . . Type B: exception clauses which qualify primary or secondary rights without preventing the accrual of any particular primary right" (p.9). Examples of Type A are that in the above case and those in *Harling v Eddy* (above, Ch.15), *Wallis v Pratt* (above, Ch.20), *Andrews v Singer* (below) and *Thompson v LMS* (above, Ch.7). It will be found that in each of these cases the object of the clause was to exclude entirely an obligation which would otherwise arise. Type B clauses, however, merely limit the time within which a claim might be brought, as in *Smeaton Hanscomb v Setty* [1953] 1 W.L.R. 1468 or limit the amount which might be recovered on a claim, as in *Parker v SE Ry* (above, Ch.7), *Scruttons v Midland Silicones* (above, Ch.13) and *Alderslade v Hendon Laundry* (below).

Coote concedes, however, that the current approach of the courts even to clauses of Type A is to regard them as no more than shields to breaches of accrued rights and duties.

See now, Photo *Production v Securicor*, below.

ANDREWS BROS LTD v SINGER & CO LTD

Court of Appeal [1934] 1 K.B. 17; 103 L.J.K.B. 90; 150 L.T. 172; 39 Com.Cas. 96; 50 T.L.R. 33

The plaintiffs entered into a contract to buy "new Singer cars" from the defendants. Clause 5 of the   **21–008** contract provided: "All cars sold by the company are subject to the terms of the warranty set out in Schedule 3 of this agreement and all conditions, warranties and liabilities implied by common law, statute or otherwise are excluded." (Cf. *L'Estrange v Graucob*, above, para.6–002) The plaintiffs succeeded in an action for damages before Goddard J on the ground that one of the cars delivered, having run a considerable mileage, was not a new car. The defendants appealed.

SCRUTTON LJ

... The judge has found, and his view is not now contested, that the car tendered in this case was not a new Singer car. Does then clause 5 prevent the vendors being liable in damages for having tendered and supplied a car which is not within the express terms of the contract? Clause 5 says this: "All conditions, warranties and liabilities implied by statute, common law or otherwise are excluded." There are well-known obligations in various classes of contracts which are not expressly mentioned but are implied. During the argument Greer L.J. mentioned an apt illustration, namely, where an agent contracts on behalf of A he warrants that he has authority to make the contract on behalf of A although no such warranty is expressed in the contract. Mr Pritt relied on section 13 of the Sale of Goods Act, 1893, which provides that "where there is a contract for the sale of goods by description, there is an implied condition that the goods shall correspond with the description ..." and from that he says it follows that this particular condition comes within the words employed by the section. That, I think, is putting a very strained meaning on the word "implied" in the section. Where goods are expressly described in the contract and do not comply with that description, it is quite inaccurate to say there is an implied term; the term is expressed in the contract. Suppose the contract is for the supply of a car of 1932 manufacture, and a car is supplied which is of 1930 manufacture, there has not been a breach of an implied term; there has been a breach of an express term of the contract. It leads to a very startling result if it can be said that clause 5 allows a vendor to supply to a purchaser an article which does not comply with the express description of the article in the contract, and then, though the purchaser did not know of the matter which prevented the article supplied from complying with the express terms of the contract, to say, "We are under no liability to you because this is a condition implied by statute and we have excluded such liability."

In my view there has been in this case a breach of an express term of the contract. If a vendor desires to protect himself from liability in such a case he must do so by much clearer language than this, which, in my opinion, does not exempt the defendants from liability where they have failed to comply with the express term of the contract. For these reasons I think Goddard J. came to a correct conclusion, and this appeal therefore fails.

Greer L.J. delivered a concurring judgment and Eve J. agreed.

Question

21–009   In *L'Estrange v Graucob* the clause provided: "This agreement contains all the terms and conditions under which I agree to purchase the machine specified above and any express or implied condition, statement, or warranty, statutory or otherwise not stated herein is hereby excluded." Scrutton LJ referred to *Wallis v Pratt* (above, Ch.20) and *Andrews v Singer* and said: "The clause here in question would seem to have been intended to go further than any of the previous clauses, and in order to avoid the result of these decisions, to include all terms denoting collateral stipulations." The document stated that the contract was for "One Six Column Junior Ilam Automatic Machine." The machine supplied did not work satisfactorily but it does not appear that it did not comply with the description. Would the clause have protected the seller if it had not so complied—if, for example, a Five Column Junior Ilam Automatic Machine had been supplied?

Benjamin on Sale (8th edn, by Finnemore and James, 1950), p.622

21–010   [Referring to *Andrews v Singer* the editors wrote:] It is a little curious that the judgment in this case give a hint that the defendants might have protected themselves by a more carefully chosen wording. It is submitted that by no words can a seller avoid the strict legal consequences of a sale by description. He cannot do it by excluding all implied conditions; and it is difficult to see how he can exclude an express condition. A man cannot in one and the same contract expressly include a term (whether condition or warranty) and also exclude it; there would be no contract at all. Of course he may say that he gives no guarantee, whether condition or warranty, but that would not touch the description. Once it is established that a certain phrase is a description, and the contract is a sale by description, that is the contract, and the sale is of described goods and of nothing else. The defendant in the present case might have said: "We will appoint you agent to sell new Singer cars, but we do not bind ourselves that the cars will always be new; they may occasionally be as good as new," but then it follows that "new" would have been no part of the description. Once the court has decided that the sale was a sale by description of "new Singer cars" then nothing else could satisfy the contract and by no artifice could the seller avoid the obligation to provide new Singer cars. Startling results would follow otherwise, for, if the seller can ignore one of the three descriptive words, he can ignore the others; the article need not be a Singer car, or even a car. The seller might supply a second-hand pedal bicycle or a child's perambulator! In a sale by description one is selling a described thing or things and that is fundamental and one need not really consider conditions or warranties express or implied as ordinarily understood. A contract for the sale of one thing can never be performed by the supply of another. The questions in cases of this kind will be: (1) Was this a sale by description? (2) What was the description? The answer to the second question gives the subject-matter of the contract. Scrutton L.J. said, "In my opinion this was a contract for the sale of a new Singer car" and, it is submitted, that concluded the matter.

Point for reflection

In *White v John Warwick & Co Ltd* [1953] 1 W.L.R. 1285 the plaintiff hired a tradesman's cycle from the defendants under a written agreement which provided that "nothing in this agreement shall render the owners liable for any personal injuries." While the plaintiff was riding the cycle the saddle tilted forward and he was injured. The Court of Appeal held that the defendants were liable in negligence. In the absence of the exemption clause, the defendants might have been liable in contract for supplying a defective machine even if they were not negligent. The operation of the clause had to be confined to that stricter liability. (For a valuable note on this case, see L. C. B. Gower, 17 MLR 155.)   **21-011**

HOLLIER v RAMBLER MOTORS (AMC), LTD

Court of Appeal [1972] 2 W.L.R. 401; [1972] 1 All E.R. 399; [1972] R.T.R. 190

For the facts and the judgment on the first point in the case, see above, Ch.7.

SALMON LJ

The principles are stated by Scrutton L.J. with his usual clarity in *Rutter v Palmer* [1922] 2 K.B. 87, 92[1]: "For the present purposes a rougher test will serve. In construing an exemption clause certain general rules may be applied: First the defendant is not exempted from liability for the negligence of his servants unless adequate words are used; secondly, the liability of the defendant apart from the exempting words must be ascertained; then the particular clause in question must be considered; and if the only liability of the party pleading the exemption is a liability for negligence, the clause will more readily operate to exempt him."   **21-012**

Scrutton L.J. was far too great a lawyer, and had far too much robust common sense, if I may be permitted to say so, to put it higher than that "if the only liability of the party pleading the exemption is a liability for negligence, the clause will more readily operate to exempt him." He does not say that "if the only liability of the party pleading the exemption is a liability for negligence, the clause will necessarily exempt him." After all, there are many cases in the books dealing with exemption clauses, and in every case it comes down to a question of construing the alleged exemption clause which is then before the court. It seems to me that in *Rutter v Palmer*, although the word "negligence" was never used in the exemption clause, the exemption clause would have conveyed to any ordinary, literate and sensible person that the garage in that case was inserting a clause in the contract which excluded their liability for the negligence of their drivers. The clause

---

[1]   The plaintiff left his car with the defendant, a dealer, for sale on commission. The defendant's driver, when showing the car to a prospective purchaser, negligently collided with a lamp-post.

being considered in that case—and it was without any doubt incorporated in the contract—was: "Customers' cars are driven by your staff at customers' sole risk." Any ordinary man knows that when a car is damaged it is not infrequently damaged because the driver had driven it negligently. He also knows, I suppose, that if he sends it to a garage and a driver in the employ of the garage takes the car on the road for some purpose in connection with the work which the customer has entrusted the garage to do, the garage could not conceivably be liable for the car being damaged in an accident unless the driver was at fault. It follows that no sensible man could have thought that the words in that case had any meaning except that the garage would not be liable for the negligence of their own drivers. That is a typical case where, on the construction of the clause in question, the meaning for which the defendant was there contending was the obvious meaning of the clause.

The next case to which I wish to refer is the well-known case of *Alderslade v Hendon Laundry, Ltd* [1945] 1 K.B. 189. In that case articles were sent by the plaintiff to the defendants' laundry to be washed, and they were lost. In an action by the plaintiff against the defendants for damages, the defendants relied on the following condition to limit their liability: "The maximum amount allowed for lost or damaged articles is 20 times the charge made for laundering." Again, this was a case where negligence was not expressly excluded. The question was: what do the words mean? I have no doubt that they would mean to the ordinary housewife who was sending her washing to the laundry that, if the goods were lost or damaged in the course of being washed through the negligence of the laundry, the laundry would not be liable for more than 20 times the charge made for the laundering. I say that for this reason. It is, I think, obvious that when a laundry loses or damages goods it is almost invariably because there has been some neglect or default on the part of the laundry. It is said that thieves break in and steal, and the goods (in that case handkerchiefs) might have been stolen by thieves. That of course is possible, but I should hardly think that a laundry would be a great allurement to burglars. It is a little far-fetched to think of burglars breaking into a laundry to steal the washing when there are banks, jewellers, post offices, factories, offices and homes likely to contain money and articles far more attractive to burglars. I think that the ordinary sensible housewife, or indeed anyone else who sends washing to the laundry, who saw that clause must have appreciated that almost always goods are lost or damaged because of the laundry's negligence, and, therefore, this clause could apply only to limit the liability of the laundry, when they were in fault or negligent.

Mr Tuckey has drawn our attention to the way in which the matter was put by Lord Greene M.R. in delivering the leading judgment in this court, and he contends that Lord Greene M.R. was in fact making a considerable extension to the law as laid down by Scrutton L.J. in the case to which I have referred. For this proposition he relies on the following passage in Lord Greene M.R.'s judgment at p. 192: "The effect of those authorities can I think be stated as follows: where the head of damage in respect of which limitation of liability is sought to be imposed by such a clause is one which rests on negligence and nothing else, the clause must be construed as extending to that head of damage, because it would otherwise lack subject-matter."

If one takes that word "must" au pied de la lettre that passage does support Mr Tuckey's contention. However, we are not here construing a statute, but a passage in an unreserved judgment of Lord Greene M.R., who was clearly intending no more than to restate the effect of the authorities as they then stood. It is to be observed that MacKinnon L.J., who gave the other judgment in this court, set out the rule or principle which he said was very admirably stated by Scrutton L.J. in *Rutter v Palmer* [1922] 2 K.B. 87. He said at p. 195: "Applying that principle to the facts of the case, I think that the clause in question does avail to protect the proprietors of the laundry in respect of liability for negligence, which must be assumed to be the cause of these handkerchiefs having disappeared."

And clearly it did, for the reasons I have already given. I do not think that Lord Greene M.R. was intending to extend the law in the sense for which Mr Tuckey contends. If it were so extended, it would make the law entirely artificial by ignoring that rules of construction are merely our guides and not our masters; in the end you are driven back to construing the clause in question to see what it means. Applying the principles laid down by Scrutton L.J., they lead to the result at which the court arrived in *Alderslade v Hendon Laundry Ltd* [1945] 1 K.B. 189. In my judgment these principles lead to a very different result in the present case. The words are: "The company is not responsible for damage caused by fire to customer's cars on the premises." What would that mean to any ordinarily literate and sensible car owner? I do not suppose that any such, unless he is a trained lawyer, has an intimate or, indeed, any knowledge of the liability of bailees in law. If you asked the ordinary man or woman: "Supposing you send your car to the garage to be repaired, and there is a fire, would you suppose that the garage would be liable?" I should be surprised if many of them did not answer, quite wrongly; "Of course they are liable if there is a fire." Others might be more cautious and say; "Well, I had better ask my solicitor," or, "I do not know. I suppose they may well be liable." That is the crucial difference, to my mind, between the present case and *Alderslade v Hendon Laundry, Ltd* and *Rutter v Palmer*. In those two cases, any ordinary man or woman reading the conditions would have known that all that was being excluded was the negligence of the laundry, in the one case, and the garage, in the other. But here I think the ordinary man or woman would be equally surprised and horrified to learn that if the garage was so negligent that a fire was caused which damaged their car, they would be without remedy because of the words in the condition. I can quite understand that the ordinary man or woman would consider that, because of these words, the mere fact that there was a fire would not make the garage liable. Fire can occur from a large variety of causes, only one of which is negligence on the part of the occupier of the premises, and that is by no means the most frequent cause. The ordinary man would I think say to himself: "Well, what they are telling me is that if there is a fire due to any cause other than their own negligence they are not responsible for it." To my mind, if the defendants were seeking to exclude their responsibility for a fire caused by their own negligence, they ought to have done so in far plainer language than the language here used.

[Salmon L.J. then discussed *Olley v Marlborough Court, Ltd* (above, Ch.7) which the court had also considered on the basis that the notice did become part of the contract and that the defendants were not common inn-keepers (who, in the absence of agreement to the contrary, are subject to strict liability in respect of the goods of guests).]

Denning L.J. said at p. 550: "Ample content can be given to the notice by construing it as a warning that the hotel company is not liable, in the absence of negligence. As such it serves a useful purpose. It is a warning to the guest that he must do his part to take care of his things himself, and, if need be, insure them. It is unnecessary to go further and to construe the notice as a contractual exemption of the hotel company from their common law liability for negligence."

Similarly, I think, in this case the words at the bottom of this form can be given ample content by construing them as a warning in the sense that I have already indicated. It seems plain that if the notice in the bedroom of the hotel had read as follows: "Proprietors will not hold themselves responsible for articles lost or stolen, nor for the damage or destruction of articles caused by fire," and then there had been a full stop, and the notice went on to say that to avoid articles being lost or stolen they should be handed to the manageress for safe custody, by a parity of reasoning the court must have come to the conclusion that the notice would not have excluded the hotel proprietors from liability for the loss of articles by a fire caused by their own negligence.

Stamp L.J. and Latey J. delivered judgment allowing the appeal.

Appeal Allowed.

Questions

1. Would the clause in *Hollier* have protected the defendant if the plaintiff's car had been damaged **21–013** by negligent driving? Cf. the discussion of *Rutter v Palmer*. Could the clause be so construed that one half of it excluded liability for negligence while the other did not?

2. Lord Greene's statement in *Alderslade* (above) related to limitation of liability. Was it not correct for limitation, as distinct from exclusion of liability? A limitation clause cannot have the declaratory function attributed by the court to an exclusion clause. There could be no point in limiting a liability which could never arise. If the only liability which could arise would be in negligence, does it not follow that the clause, if it has any meaning at all, must, as Lord Greene said, apply to liability in negligence?

Points for reflection

21-014   The courts distinguish between cases where, in the absence of any exclusion clause, (i) the defendant may be held liable only if he is negligent (N) and (ii) the defendant may be held liable if he is negligent or even if he is not (strict liability (SL)). This may be illustrated diagramatically:

(i)   (ii)

| N | | N | SL |

If the clause is held to be not merely declaratory of the position at common law but to be intended to affect the relationship between the parties and is not expressed to cover negligence then it will be construed to limit or exclude the liability for negligence in (i) because there is nothing else for it to apply to; but to exclude only the strict liability in (ii); thus;

(i)   (ii)

There is the possibility, however, that the defendant may have been guilty of something worse than negligence; for example, being the bailee of a fur coat for cleaning, he has given it away to his girl-friend. No reasonable man would suppose that even the most far-reaching clause in a dry-cleaning contract entitled the cleaner to do that. Imagine reaction to a suggestion by the officious bystander that this was what they were agreeing to. There is thus the possibility of a third type of liability which, for want of a better term, may be called fundamental breach (FB). A complete diagram of potential liability is then as follows:

(i)   (ii)

| FB | N | | FB | N | SL |

If we apply the exclusion clause envisaged above to this situation we reach the following result:

(i)   (ii)

| FB | N | | FB | N | SL |

Where goods have been lost, there may be no direct evidence of either negligence or of fundamental breach and the question of onus of proof is then of crucial importance.

In *Woolmer v Delmer Price* [1955] 1 Q.B. 291 the plaintiff left a mink coat with the defendants for storage or resale. The defendants failed to comply with a demand for the return of the coat and were unable to adduce satisfactory evidence as to what had happened to it. In an action in detinue the defendants relied on a clause in their receipt, "All goods left at customer's risk." McNair J said that it must be assumed that there was negligence on the part of the launderer in the *Alderslade* case (above) whereas in the present case it was not proved whether the loss did or did not occur through negligence. The coat might have been sold in mistake and its sale mistakenly recorded as that of another coat (but this surely would amount to negligence) or it may have been put into store at a place not permitted by the contract which would have been a fundamental breach. The implication is that if the defendants had been able to prove that they lost the coat through negligence, they would have been protected by the clause.

In *Hunt & Winterbotham v BRS (Parcels) Ltd* [1962] 1 Q.B. 617, which concerned a contract of carriage, the Court of Appeal agreed that the onus was on the carrier to show that the loss of the goods was not due to his negligence but said that was a very different thing from saying that he must also prove the absence of any fundamental breach. There was, however, no allegation of fundamental breach in that case.

LEVISON AND ANOTHER v PATENT STEAM CARPET CLEANING CO LTD

Court of Appeal [1978] Q.B. 69; [1977] 3 W.L.R. 90; [1977] 3 All E.R. 498

The plaintiffs telephoned the defendants and asked them to collect a carpet for cleaning. It was a Chinese carpet worth £900. At the defendant's van driver's request, Mr L signed the defendant's order form. He did not read it. By cl.2(a), the maximum value of the carpet, based on its area, was deemed to be £40. Clause 5 provided "All merchandise is expressly accepted at the owner's risk" and recommended owners to insure their goods. The carpet was lost. The plaintiffs recovered £900 damages. The defendants appealed, contending that they were exempt from liability for negligence by virtue of cl.5, that on a balance of probabilities the loss was due to their negligence, not a fundamental breach, and the burden of proving that the loss was due to fundamental breach lay on the plaintiffs.

21–015

Lord Denning MR said that, on the construction of the contract, the liability of the defendants was limited to £40; but that, notwithstanding *Suisse Atlantique*, the doctrine of fundamental breach still applied to standard form contracts where there was inequality of bargaining power. [But see *Photo Productions v Securicor,* below.] His Lordship continued:

LORD DENNING MR

This brings me to the crux of the case: on whom is the burden of proof? Take the present case. Assuming that clause 2(a) or clause 5, or either of them, limits or exempts the cleaners from liability for negligence, but not for a fundamental breach. On whom is the burden to prove that there was fundamental breach?

On principle, I should have thought that the burden was on the cleaners to prove that they were not guilty of a fundamental breach. After all, Mr Levison does not know what happened to it. The cleaners are the ones who know, or should know, what happened to the carpet, and the burden should be on them to say what it was. It was so held by McNair J. in *Woolmer v Delmer Price Ltd* [above]; and by me in *J. Spurling Ltd v Bradshaw* [1956] 1 W.L.R. at 466, and by the East African Court of Appeal in *United Manufacturers Ltd v WAF Co Ltd*. A contrary view was expressed by this court in *Hunt & Winterbotham (West of England) Ltd v B.R.S. (Parcels) Ltd* [above]; and there is a long line of shipping cases in which it has been held that, if a shipowner makes a prima facie case that the cause of the loss was one of the excepted perils, the burden is on the shipper to prove that it was not covered by the exception: see the cases from *The Glendarroch* [1894] p. 266, and *Munro, Brice & Co v War Risks Association Ltd* [1918] 2 K.B. 78, to which there may be added *Joseph Constantine Steamship Line Ltd v Imperial Smelting Corp Ltd, The Kingswood* [below, Ch.24].

It is, therefore, a moot point for decision. On it I am clearly of opinion that, in a contract of bailment, when a bailee seeks to escape liability on the ground that he was not negligent or that he was excused by an exception or limitation clause, then he must know what happened to the goods. He must prove all the circumstances known to him in which the loss or damage occurred. If it appears that the goods were lost or damaged without any negligence on his part, then, of course, he is not liable. If it appears that they were lost or damaged by a slight breach, not going to the root of the contract, he may be protected by the exemption or limitation clause. But, if he leaves the cause of loss or damage undiscovered and unexplained, then I think he is liable: because it is then quite likely that the goods were stolen by one of his servants; or delivered by a servant to the wrong address; or damaged by reckless or wilful misconduct; all of which the offending servant will conceal and not make known to his employer. Such conduct would be a fundamental breach against which the exemption or limitation clause will not protect him.

The cleaning company in this case did not show what had happened to the carpet. They did not prove how it was lost. They gave all sorts of excuses for non-delivery and eventually said it had been stolen. Then I would ask: by whom it was stolen? Was it by one of their servants? or with his connivance? Alternatively, was it delivered by one of their servants to the wrong address? In the absence of any explanation, I would infer that it was one of these causes. In none of them would the cleaning company be protected by the exemption or limitation clause.

Orr L.J. and Sir David Cairns held that the words of clause 5 exempted the defendants from liability for negligence but were not sufficiently clear or strong to exempt them from liability for so fundamental or radical a breach as, say, misdelivery of the carpet; and they agreed with Lord Denning that the onus of proving that the loss was not due to fundamental breach was on the defendants and that they had not discharged it.

Appeal Dismissed.

Questions

21–016
1. Suppose that the carpet had been misdelivered because of a mistake by the van driver, Why would not that be negligence and so covered by cl.5?

2. Suppose that the carpet was stolen by one of the defendants' employees. The defendants may have been negligent in employing him, or they may not. Should the company be held to have committed "a fundamental breach" when the company—the directors and managerial staff— were not even negligent?

3. Consider the effect of the Unfair Contract Terms Act s.2(2) and s.3 and of reg.6 of the Regulations. Is it unreasonable or unfair for a cleaning company to say that they will accept a carpet only if the owner agrees to take the risk, against which they advise him to insure? Cf. S. M. Males [1978] CLJ 24, 26: ". . . even if the defendants had pointed out the exemption clause, why should Mr Levison have worried? He was insured. Indeed, knowing himself to be insured, he had no need even to bother to read the form." Does the decision benefit anyone but the insurance company?

SZE HAI TONG BANK LTD v RAMBLER CYCLE CO LTD

Privy Council [1959] A.C. 576; [1959] 3 W.L.R. 214; 103 S.J. 567; [1959] 3 All E.R. 182; [1959] 2 Lloyd's Rep. 114

21–017   The respondent shipped goods under a bill of lading which required delivery "unto order or his or their assigns" and provided that the responsibility of the carrier should cease absolutely after the goods had been discharged from the ship. After the goods had been discharged into a warehouse in Singapore the carrier-agents released them to the consignee without requiring production of the bill of lading. The consignee never paid for the goods. The carrier was held liable for breach of contract and conversion of the goods.

LORD DENNING

. . . it is contended that [the exemption clause] is wide enough to absolve the shipping company from responsibility for the act of which the Rambler Cycle Co complains, that is to say, the delivery of the goods to a person who, to their knowledge, was not entitled to receive them. If the exemption clause upon its true construction absolved the shipping company from an act such as that, it seems that by parity of reasoning they would have been absolved if they had given the goods away to some passer-by or had burnt them or had thrown them into the sea. If it had been suggested to the parties that the condition exempted the shipping company in such a case, they would both have said: "Of course not." There is, therefore, an implied limitation on the clause, which cuts down the extreme width of it: and, as matter of construction, their Lordships decline to attribute to it the unreasonable effect contended for.

But their Lordships go further. If such an extreme width were given to the exemption clause, it would run counter to the main object and intent of the contract. For the contract, as it seems to their Lordships, has, as one of its main objects, the proper delivery of the goods by the shipping company "unto order or his or their assigns," against production of the bill of lading. It would defeat this object entirely if the shipping company were at liberty, at its own will and pleasure, to deliver the goods to somebody else, not entitled at all, without being liable for the consequences. The clause must therefore be modified to the extent necessary to enable effect to be given to the main object and intent of the contract: see *Glynn v Margetson & Co* [1893] A.C. 351, 357; *G. H. Renton & Co Ltd v Palmyra Trading Corp of Panama* [1956] 1 Q.B. 462, 501.

To what extent is it necessary to limit or modify the clause? It must at least be modified so as not to permit the shipping company deliberately to disregard its obligations as to delivery. For that is what has happened here. The shipping company's agents in Singapore acknowledged: "We are doing something we know we should not do." Yet they did it. And they did it as agents in such circumstances that their acts were the acts of the shipping company itself. And they deliberately disregarded one of the prime obligations of the contract. No court can allow so fundamental a breach to pass unnoticed under the cloak of a general exemption clause: see *The Cap Palos* [1909] A.C. 369.

The self-same distinction runs through all the cases where a fundamental breach has disentitled a party from relying on an exemption clause. In each of them there will be found a breach which evinces a deliberate disregard of his bounden obligations. Thus, in *Bontex Knitting Works Ltd v St. John's Garage* (1943) 60 T.L.R. 44, the lorry driver left the lorry unattended for an hour, in breach of an express agreement for immediate delivery. In *Alexander v Railway Executive* [1951] 2 K.B. 882 the cloak-room official allowed an unauthorised person to have access to the goods, in breach of the regulations in that behalf. In *Karsales (Harrow) Ltd v Wallis* [1956] 1 W.L.R. 936 the agent of the finance company delivered a car which would not go in breach of its obligation to deliver one that would go . . . It might have been different if the servant had merely been negligent or inadvertent.

Points for reflection

Exclusion or limitation? In the introductory remarks to this chapter, "exclusions" and "limitations"   **21–018** were treated as belonging to the same species of contract clause. And, indeed, from the viewpoint of the claimant, it may matter little whether the defendant is seeking to exclude liability or limit it to a nominal amount. Nevertheless, there are three important distinctions between a clause which purports to exclude liability altogether and one which purports to limit liability.

1. An exclusion clause may be inconsistent with an express term (and therefore have to give way to it) whereas a limitation clause may be quite compatible with the same express term. Thus—

    (i) "We undertake to exercise due care . . ." and
    (ii) "We are not to be liable for our negligence . . ."

    are inconsistent in that (ii), if valid, destroys (i) as a contractual undertaking. But

    (i) "We undertake to exercise due care . . ." and
    (ii) "If we fail to exercise due care our liability shall be limited to £1,000"

    are perfectly compatible (although the distinction is eroded in practice as the limit on liability is reduced, e.g. to a mere £1).

2. An exclusion clause may have the merely declaratory function attributed by the court to the clause in *Hollier v Rambler Motors* above, so that the clause has no effect on the rights and duties of the parties; but a limitation clause cannot be declaratory and therefore must limit at least some kind of liability which might arise.

3. A limitation clause is not to be construed as rigidly and strictly as an exclusion clause.

AILSA CRAIG FISHING CO LTD v MALVERN FISHING CO LTD AND ANOTHER

House of Lords [1983] 1 W.L.R. 964; [1983] 1 All E.R. 101

21-019   Securicor agreed to provide a security service to Ailsa Craig Ltd's fishing boats in Aberdeen harbour. Because of negligence consisting in a total or partial failure to provide the service contracted for, a fishing boat belonging to Ailsa Craig sank and took with it another boat belonging to Malvern. The contract contained both an exclusion and a limitation clause. The Court of Session held that liability had been limited but not excluded. Ailsa Craig appealed against that decision insofar as it held that liability had been limited. The House of Lords unanimously dismissed the appeal.

LORD FRASER

[Having referred to the strict principles to be applied when construing exclusion clauses went on:]
   In my opinion these principles are not applicable in their full rigour when considering the effect of clauses merely limiting liability. Such clauses will of course be read contra proferentem and must be clearly expressed, but there is no reason why they should be judged by the specially exacting standards which are applied to exclusion and indemnity clauses. The reason for imposing such standards on these clauses is the inherent improbability that the other party to a contract including such a clause intended to release the proferens from a liability that would otherwise fall upon him. But there is no such high degree of improbability that he would agree to a limitation of the liability of the proferens, especially when, as explained in condition (4) (i) of the present contract, the potential losses that might be caused by the negligence of the proferens or its servants are so great in proportion to the sums that can reasonably be charged for the services contracted for. It is enough in the present case that the clause must be clear and unambiguous.

SUISSE ATLANTIQUE SOCIÉTÉ D'ARMEMENT MARITIME SA v NV ROTTERDAMSCHE KOLEN CENTRALE

House of Lords [1967] 1 A.C. 361; [1966] 2 W.L.R. 944; [1966] 2 All E.R. 61

21-020   By a charterparty dated December, 1956, the respondents agreed to charter a vessel from the appellants for the carriage of coal from the United States to Europe. The charter was to remain in force for a total of two years' consecutive voyages. The vessel had with all possible dispatch to sail and proceed to a port in the United States and, having loaded a cargo of coal, proceed with all possible dispatch to a port in Europe. She had to be loaded at a specified rate per running day and, if she was detained beyond the loading time, the respondents were to pay $1,000 a day demurrage. Similarly, if she were detained longer than was required to unload her at the stipulated rate per day and that was not due to strikes, etc., or other causes beyond the control of the respondents, the respondents, who were to discharge the cargo, were to pay demurrage at the rate of $1,000 a day. In September, 1957, the appellants regarded themselves as entitled to treat the charterparty as repudiated by reason of the respondents' delays in loading and discharging the vessel. That was not accepted by the respondents, and, in October, 1957, the appellants and respondents agreed, without prejudice to their dispute, that from thenceforward the charterparty would be carried out. Between then and the end of the charter the vessel made eight round voyages. The appellants alleged that, due to delays in loading and unloading for which the respondents were responsible, the vessel did not make as many voyages as she should have done, with the result that they were deprived of the freights they would have earned on the additional voyages and, after giving credit for the demurrage payments received by them, claimed damages from the respondents in respect of voyages which, they said, ought to have been completed between October 19, 1957, and the end of the charterparty. The appellants contended that, if the delays for which the respondents were responsible were such as to entitle the appellants to treat the charterparty as repudiated, the demurrage provisions did not apply and they were entitled to recover the full loss that they had suffered.

Mocatta J gave judgment in favour of the respondents and the appellants' appeal to the Court of Appeal was dismissed. The appellants appealed to the House of Lords.

Viscount Dilhorne and Lords Reid, Hodson and Upjohn delivered opinions in favour of the respondents.

LORD WILBERFORCE

. . . The appellants' main argument in law is formulated as follows: First, they say that a breach of contract which goes to the root of the contract or which conflicts with its main purpose is a deviation from or a repudiation or fundamental breach of such contract. Secondly, they contend that exceptions clauses do not apply to breaches which are deviations from or repudiations or fundamental breaches of the contract. These propositions contain in themselves implicitly or explicitly several distinct lines of argument. It is necessary to separate the strands before attempting to examine them. It is convenient first to segregate the reference to what is sometimes (and conveniently) described as the main purpose rule. This is a rule of construction, a classic statement of which is found in Lord Halsbury's speech in *Glynn v Margetson* [1893] A.C. 351 at p. 357: it can be summed up in his words:

> "Looking at the whole of the instrument, and seeing what one must regard, as its main purpose, one must reject words, indeed whole provisions, if they are inconsistent with what one assumes to be the main purpose of the contract."

The decision in that case was that printed words in a document intended to be used in a variety of contracts of affreightment between a variety of ports ought to be restricted so as to be consistent with the purpose of the particular charterparty which was for a voyage from Malaga to Liverpool. There is no difficulty as to this, and I shall consider in due course whether it has any application to the relevant clause (that is, the demurrage clause) in the contract.

Next for consideration is the argument based on "fundamental breach" or, which is presumably the same thing, a breach going "to the root of the contract.". . .

The conception . . . of "fundamental breach" as one which, through ascertainment of the parties' contractual intention, falls outside an exceptions clause is well recognised and comprehensible. Is there any need, or authority, in relation to exceptions clauses, for extension of it beyond this? In my opinion there is not. The principle that the contractual intention is to be ascertained—not just grammatically from words used, but by consideration of those words in relation to commercial purpose (or other purpose according to the type of contract)—is surely flexible enough, and though it may be the case that adhesion contracts give rise to particular difficulties in ascertaining or attributing a contractual intent, which may require a special solution, those difficulties need not be imported into the general law of contract nor be permitted to deform it.

The only new category of "fundamental breach" which in this context I understand to have been suggested is one of "deliberate" breaches. This most clearly appears in the Privy Council case of *Sze I Iai Tong Bank Ltd v Rambler Cycle Co Ltd* [above]. The decision itself presents no difficulty and seems to have been based on construction: it was that an exceptions clause referring to "discharge" of the goods did not apply to a discharge wholly outside the contract, a case I would have thought well within the principle of the "deviation" cases. But the appellants rely on one passage in the judgment of the Board which seems to suggest that "deliberate" breaches may, of themselves, form a separate category, citing three previous English decisions. Two of them *Alexander v Railway Executive* [1951] 2 K.B. 882 and *Karsales (Harrow) Ltd v Wallis* [1956] 1 W.L.R. 936 (on which I have already commented) are straightforward cases of "total departure" from what is contractually contemplated and present no difficulty. The third *Bontex Knitting Works Ltd v St. John's Garage* (1943) 60 T.L.R. 44, does not appear to be based on the deliberate character of the breach. The decision may be justified on the basis that there was a breach of contract equivalent to a deviation, but if it goes beyond this I would regard it as of doubtful validity. The "deliberate" character of a breach cannot, in my opinion, of itself give to a breach of contract a "fundamental" character, in either sense of that word. Some deliberate breaches there may be of a minor character which can appropriately be sanctioned by damages: some may be, on construction, within an exceptions clause (for example, a deliberate delay for one day in loading). This is not to say that "deliberateness" may not be a relevant factor: depending on what the party in breach "deliberately" intended to do, it may be possible to say that the parties never contemplated that such a breach would be excused or limited; and a deliberate breach may give rise to a right for the innocent party to refuse further performance because it indicates the other party's attitude towards future performance. All these arguments fit without difficulty into the general principle: to create a special rule for deliberate acts is unnecessary and may lead astray.

I now come to the facts of the present case. First, it is necessary to decide what is the legal nature of the demurrage clause: is it a clause by which damages for breach of the contract are agreed in advance, a liquidated damages clause as such provisions are commonly called, or is it, as the appellants submit, a clause limiting damages? If it is the latter, the appellants are evidently a step nearer the point when they can invoke cases in which clauses of exception, or exemption, do not apply to particular breaches of contract. The appellants' strongest argument here rests on the discrepancy which they assert to exist between the demurrage rate of $1,000 per diem and the freight rate for which the charterparty provides. The extent of the discrepancy is said to be shown by the difference between the appellants' claim for lost freight (which is of the order of $900,000 on one calculation and $600,000 on another) and the amount which they would receive under the demurrage provision, which is approximately $150,000. So, the argument runs, the $1,000 per diem cannot be a pre-estimate of damage: it must be a limit in the charterer's favour.

I am unable to accept this. Leaving aside that the figures quoted for lost freight represent merely the owners' claim, it must be borne in mind that the $1,000-a-day figure has to cover a number of possible events. There might have been delay for one day or a few days beyond the laytime, in which case the owners might, and probably would, lose nothing in the way of freight and only suffer through increased overheads in port. Even if a case were to arise where freight was lost, over a period of two years circumstances might well change which would affect adversely the owners' anticipated rate of profit. So I am far from satisfied that any such discrepancy has been shown between the agreed figure and reality as requires the conclusion that the clause is not what on its face it purports to be—particularly when one bears in mind that each side derives an advantage from having the figure fixed and so being assured of payment without the expense and difficulty of proof.

The form of clause is, of course, not decisive, nor is there any rule of law which requires that demurrage clauses should be construed as clauses of liquidated damages; but it is the fact that the clause is expressed as one agreeing a figure and not as imposing a limit: and as a matter of commercial opinion and practice demurrage clauses are normally regarded as liquidated damage clauses. (This has the authority of *Scrutton on Charter-parties* (10th and following editions), and see *Chandris v Isbrandtsen Moller Co Inc* [1951] 1 K.B. 240 at p. 249, per Devlin J.)

The clause being, then, one which fixes, by mutual agreement, the amount of damages to be paid to the owners of the vessel if "longer detained" than is permitted by the contract, is there any reason why it should not apply in the present case in either of the assumed alternatives, that is, either that the aggregated delays add up to "frustrating" breach of contract, or that the delays were "deliberate" in the special sense? In answering these questions it is necessary to have in mind what happened. It appears that there was an initial dispute between the owners and the charterers in which the owners claimed that they were entitled to treat the charterers as having repudiated the charterparty. This dispute was resolved by an agreement on October 8, 1957, under which the charterers agreed to pay an agreed sum as demurrage, leaving it to arbitration to decide whether the owners' claim was correct and, if so, what damages they should recover. It was further agreed that the charterparty should be performed for the remainder of the agreed two-year period. The manner in which it was performed is set out in a schedule to the consultative case. There were eight voyages in all, the last terminating on March 7, 1959, three days before the termination date. It is as regards these eight voyages that it is claimed that the delays in question occurred. During the whole of the period, although the periods spent in port on either side of the Atlantic (in fact at Rotterdam and, in every case but the first, Newport News) must have been known to the owners, who must also have been in a position to ascertain the availability of cargo and of loading and discharging facilities, the owners took no steps which would indicate that they regarded the charterparty as repudiated: they did not sail their vessel away but allowed it to continue with further voyages and took demurrage at the agreed rate for the delays. So there is no question here of any termination of the contract having taken place. Is there, then, any basis upon which the owners can escape from their bargain as regards detention of the vessel? In my opinion there is not. The arbitrators can (on the assumptions required) only find that the breach of contract falls within one, or other, or both of the two stated categories, namely, that they "frustrate the commercial purpose of the charterparty," or that the delays were "deliberate" (in the special sense). In either case, why should not the agreed clause operate? Or what reason is there for limiting its application to such delays as fall short of such as "frustrate the commercial purpose" or such as are not "deliberate"? I can see no such reason for limiting a plain contractual provision, nor is there here any such conflict between the demurrage clause and the main purpose of the contract as to bring into play the doctrine of *Glynn v Margetson & Co.* On a consideration of the nature of this clause, together with the events which took place, and in particular the fact that the owners did not during its currency put an end to the contract, I reach the conclusion that the owners are clearly bound by it and can recover no more than the appropriate amount of demurrage.

Points for reflection

If the first dispute had not been resolved by the agreement of October 8, 1957, and the owners had sailed their ship away, it is plain that the clause in the charterparty would have had no further application; the charterers would not have been able to detain the ship when loading or unloading. The owners (assuming that they were justified in repudiating) would presumably have recovered as damages the difference between the profit they would have made under the charterparty and that which they made by employing the ship on other work. The application of the particular clause depended on the fact that the contract was affirmed. In *Harbutt's Plasticine Ltd v Wayne Tank and Pump Co Ltd* [1970] 1 Q.B. 447 the Court of Appeal wrongly deduced from this, and from certain dicta in the case, that the doctrine of fundamental breach was excluded only where the contract continued in existence after the breach. If the contract came to an end as a result of the breach, the effect was to avoid the exclusion clause ab initio, though it was (and is) well established that both frustration and avoidance for breach are not retrospective but terminate the contract only from the occurrence of the frustrating event or the act of avoidance. The contract "remains alive for the awarding of damages either for previous breaches, or for the breach which constitutes the repudiation": *Heyman v Darwins* [1942] A.C. 356 at 379, per Lord Wright. In that case the House held that an arbitration clause in a contract applied when one party had repudiated the contract and the other had accepted the breach. *Harbutt's* case (on this point) was overruled by the next case.

21–021

PHOTO PRODUCTION LTD v SECURICOR TRANSPORT LTD

House of Lords [1980] A.C. 827; [1980] 2 W.L.R. 283; [1980] 1 All E.R. 556

In 1968, for a fee of £8 15s. 0d. a week the defendants agreed to provide security services, including night patrols, at the plaintiff's factory. The defendants' employee, Musgrove, while carrying out a night patrol, deliberately started a small fire which got out of control and destroyed the factory and stock, together valued at £615,000. There was no evidence that the defendants were negligent in employing Musgrove. In an action for damages, the defendants relied on the following clause in the contract.

21–022

> "Under no circumstances shall the company [Securicor] be responsible for any injurious act or default by any employee of the company unless such act or default could have been foreseen and avoided by the exercise of due diligence on the part of the company as his employer; nor, in any event, shall the company be held responsible for (a) any loss suffered by the customer through burglary, theft, fire or any other cause, except in so far as such loss is solely attributable to the negligence of the company's employees acting within the course of their employment. . . ."

MacKenna J dismissed the action. The Court of Appeal allowed an appeal, following the *Harbutt's Plasticine* case and holding that a fundamental breach of the contract had brought it to an end and that it followed that the exemption clause could no longer be relied on. Alternatively, the clause was to be construed so as not to apply to the event which had occurred. The defendants appealed.

Lord Wilberforce said that the ratio decidendi of the *Suisse Atlantique* case was correctly summarised in the headnote: "That the question whether an exceptions clause was applicable where there was a fundamental breach of contract was one of the true construction of the contract."

LORD WILBERFORCE

[Having discussed the speeches in *Suisse Atlantique*, continued:]

1. The doctrine of "fundamental breach" in spite of its imperfections and doubtful parentage has served a useful purpose. There was a large number of problems, productive of injustice, in which it was worse than unsatisfactory to leave exception clauses to operate. Lord Reid referred to these in the *Suisse Atlantique* case, pointing out at the same time that the doctrine of fundamental breach was a dubious specific. But since then Parliament has taken a hand. it has passed the Unfair Contract Terms Act 1977. This Act applies to consumer contracts and those based on standard terms and enables exception clauses to be applied with regard to what is just and reasonable. It is significant that Parliament refrained from legislating over the whole field of contract. After this Act, in commercial matters generally, when the parties are not of unequal bargaining power, and when risks are normally borne by insurance, not only is the case for judicial intervention undemonstrated, but there is everything to be said, and this seems to have been Parliament's intention, for leaving the parties free to apportion the risks as they think fit and for respecting their decisions.

At the stage of negotiation as to the consequences of a breach, there is everything to be said for allowing the parties to estimate their respective claims according to the contractual provisions they have themselves made, rather than for facing them with a legal complex so uncertain as the doctrine of fundamental breach must be. What, for example, would have been the position of the respondents' factory if instead of being destroyed it had been damaged, slightly or moderately or severely? At what point does the doctrine (with what logical justification I have not understood) decide, ex post facto, that the breach was (factually) fundamental before going on to ask whether legally it is to be regarded as fundamental? How is the date of "termination" to be fixed? Is it the date of the incident causing the damage, or the date of the innocentparty's election, or some other date? All these difficulties arise from the doctrine and are left unsolved by it.

At the judicial stage there is still more to be said for leaving cases to be decided straightforwardly on what the parties have bargained for rather than upon analysis, which becomes progressively more refined, of decisions in other cases leading to inevitable appeals. The learned judge was able to decide this case on normal principles of contractual law with minimal citation of authority. I am sure that most commercial judges have wished to be able to do the same: see *Trade and Transport Inc v Iino Kaiun Kaisha Ltd* [1973] 1 W.L.R. 210, 232, per Kerr J. In my opinion they can and should.

2. The case of *Harbutt* must clearly be overruled. It would be enough to put that upon its radical inconsistency with the *Suisse Atlantique* case [above]. But even if the matter were res integra I would find the decision to be based upon unsatisfactory reasoning as to the "termination" of the contract and the effect of "termination" on the plaintiff's claim for damage. I have, indeed, been unable to understand how the doctrine can be reconciled with the well accepted principle of law, stated by the highest modern authority, that when in the context of a breach of contract one speaks of "termination," what is meant is no more than that the innocent party or, in some cases, both parties, are excused from further performance. Damages, in such cases, are then claimed under the contract, so what reason in principle can there be for disregarding what the contract itself says about damages—whether it "liquidates" them, or limits them, or excludes them? These difficulties arise in part from uncertain or inconsistent terminology. A vast number of expressions are used to describe situations where a breach has been committed by one party of such a character as to entitle the other party to refuse further performance: discharge, rescission, termination, the contract is at an end, or dead, or displaced; clauses cannot survive, or simply go. I have come to think that some of these difficulties can be avoided; in particular the use of "rescission," even if distinguished from rescission ab initio, as an equivalent for discharge, though justifiable in some contexts (see *Johnson v Agnew* [1980] A.C. 367) may lead to confusion in others. To plead for complete uniformity may be to cry for the moon. But what can and ought to be avoided is to make use of these confusions in order to produce a concealed and unreasoned legal innovation: to pass, for example, from saying that a party, victim of a breach of contract, is entitled to refuse further performance, to saying that he may treat the contract as at an end, or as rescinded, and to draw from this the proposition, which is not analytical but one of policy, that all or (arbitrarily) some of the clauses of the contract lose, automatically, their force, regardless of intention.

If this process is discontinued the way is free to use such words as "discharge" or "termination" consistently with principles as stated by modern authority which *Harbutt's* case disregards. I venture with apology to relate the classic passages. In *Heyman v Darwins Ltd* [1942] A.C. 356, 399 Lord Porter said:

"To say that the contract is rescinded or has come to an end or has ceased to exist may in individual cases convey the truth with sufficient accuracy, but the fuller expression that the injured party is thereby absolved from future performance of his obligations under the contract is a more exact description of the position. Strictly speaking, to say that on acceptance of the renunciation of a contract the contract is rescinded is incorrect. In such a case the injured party may accept the renunciation as a breach going to the root of the whole of the consideration. By that acceptance he is discharged from further performance and may bring an action for damages, but the contract itself is not rescinded."

And similarly Lord Macmillan at p. 373: see also Boston Deep Sea Fishing and Ice Co v Ansell (1888) 39 Ch.D. 339, 361, per Bowen L.J. In *Lep Air Services Ltd v Rolloswin Investments Ltd* [1973] A.C. 331, 350, my noble and learned friend, Lord Diplock, drew a distinction (relevant for that case) between primary obligations under a contract, which on "rescission" generally come to an end, and secondary obligations which may then arise. Among the latter he includes an obligation to pay compensation, that is, damages. And he states in terms that this latter obligation "is just as much an obligation arising from the contract as are the primary obligations that it replaces." My noble and learned friend has developed this line of thought in an enlightening manner in his opinion which I have now had the benefit of reading.

These passages I believe to state correctly the modern law of contract in the relevant respects: they demonstrate that the whole foundation of *Harbutt's* case is unsound . . .

3. I must add to this, by way of exception to the decision not to "gloss" the *Suisse Atlantique* [1967] 1 A.C. 361 a brief observation on the deviation cases, since some reliance has been placed upon them, particularly upon the decision of this House in *Hain Steamship Co Ltd v Tate and Lyle Ltd* (1936) 155 L.T. 177 (so earlier than the *Suisse Atlantique*) in the support of the *Harbutt* doctrine. I suggested in the *Suisse Atlantique* that these cases can be regarded as proceeding upon normal principles applicable to the law of contract generally viz., that it is a matter of the parties' intentions whether and to what extent clauses in shipping contracts can be applied after a deviation, that is, a departure from the contractually agreed voyage or adventure. It may be preferable that they should be considered as a body of authority sui generis with special rules derived from historical and commercial reasons. What on either view they cannot do is to lay down different rules as to contracts generally from those later stated by this House in *Heyman v Darwins Ltd* [1942] A.C. 356 . . .

4. It is not necessary to review fully the numerous cases in which the doctrine of fundamental breach has been applied or discussed. Many of these have now been superseded by the Unfair Contract Terms Act 1977. Others, as decisions, may be justified as depending upon the construction of the contract (see *Levison v Patent Steam Carpet Cleaning Co Ltd* [above]), in the light of well known principles such as that stated in *Alderslade v Hendon Laundry Ltd* [above].

In this situation the present case has to be decided. As a preliminary, the nature of the contract has to be understood. Securicor undertook to provide a service of periodical visits for a very modest charge which works out at 26p. per visit. It did not agree to provide equipment. It would have no knowledge of the value of the plaintiffs' factory: that, and the efficacy of their fire precautions, would be known to the respondents. In these circumstances nobody could consider it unreasonable, that as between these two equal parties the risk assumed by Securicor should be a modest one, and that the respondents should carry the substantial risk of damage or destruction.

The duty of Securicor was, as stated, to provide a service. There must be implied an obligation to use due care in selecting their patrol-men, to take care of the keys and, I would think, to operate the service with due and proper regard to the safety and security of the premises. The breach of duty committed by Securicor lay in a failure to discharge this latter obligation. Alternatively it could be put upon a vicarious responsibility for the wrongful act of Musgrove—viz., starting a fire on the premises: Securicor would be responsible for this upon the principle stated in *Morris v C. W. Martin & Sons Ltd* [above, Ch.13]. This being the breach, does condition 1 apply? It is drafted in strong terms, "Under no circumstances" . . . "any injurious act or default by any employee." These words have to be approached with the aid of the cardinal rules of construction that they must be read contra proferentem and that in order to escape from the consequences of one's own wrongdoing, or that of one's servant, clear words are necessary. I think that these words are clear. The respondents in fact relied upon them for an argument that since they exempted from negligence they must be taken as not exempting from the consequence of deliberate acts. But this is a perversion of the rule that if a clause can cover something other than negligence, it will not be applied to negligence. Whether, in addition to negligence, it covers other, for example, deliberate, acts, remains a matter of construction requiring, of course, clear words. I am of opinion that it does, and being free to construe and apply the clause, I must hold that liability is excluded. On this part of the case I agree with the judge and adopt his reasons for judgment. I would allow the appeal.

Lord Diplock made a speech allowing the appeal.

Lord Salmon made a speech allowing the appeal. He agreed with Lord Wilberforce's analysis of Suisse Atlantique.

Lords Keith of Kinkel and Scarman agreed with Lord Wilberforce.

Appeal Allowed.

Questions

21–023

1. Does the decision support Professor Coote's theory of the construction of exemption clauses? Did the judges decide that the clause excluded liability for a breach that had been committed or that it excluded a duty and so prevented a breach being committed? See Palmer and Yates [1981] C.L.J. 108.

2. Was the House right to assume that there was equality of bargaining power? Should the result have been different if the plaintiffs had been a new, struggling, small business? See A. Nicol and R. Rawlings (1980) 43 M.L.R. 567.

3. The first half of the exemption clause (above) clearly exempted the defendants from either a duty or a liability for breach of a duty; but what about the second half? Did it not implicitly restrict the first half? Or does it apply to foreseeable acts or defaults?

Further reading

John N. Adams and Roger Brownsword, 'The Unfair Contract Terms Act: A Decade of Discretion' (1988) 104 LQR 94
Brian Coote, *Exception Clauses* (Cambridge: Cambridge University Press, 1964)
N Palmer and D Yates, 'The Future of the Unfair Contract Terms Act 1977' [1981] CLJ 108
David Yates, *Exclusion Clauses in Contracts* (London: Sweet and Maxwell, 1978)

22

UNFAIR TERMS

LEARNING OBJECTIVES

By the end of this chapter, you should:

- be familiar with the principal legislative provisions that are designed to control unfair or unreasonable contract terms (including the Consumer Rights Act 2015);
- be familiar with the leading cases on the interpretation of the legislative controls;
- appreciate that it is in these various controls that we find the sharpest distinction between the regulation of consumer contracts and the more limited control over commercial contracts;
- reflect on whether this raft of legislative interventions has succeeded in bringing contract law more into alignment with the reasonable expectations of consumer and business contractors.

INTRODUCTION

One of the key developments in the modern law of contract was the control that the courts began to exert (in the middle years of the last century) over terms that were perceived to be unfair or unreasonable, especially so in non-negotiated standard form consumer contracts. This control was exercised in various ad hoc ways—for example, by making it difficult for terms to be incorporated by notice, by strict interpretation of terms and by developing a (now discredited) doctrine of fundamental breach (see Ch.21). These legal responses were purely instrumental and, in a legal regime that was committed to a robustly individualistic understanding of the principles of freedom and sanctity of contract, there was an obvious tension. Legislative intervention eased these difficulties. Accordingly, nowadays, it is the unfair contract terms legislation that provides the principal point of reference in an unfair terms case; and, indeed, in relation to unfair terms in *consumer* contracts, it now largely falls to the Office of Fair Trading rather than to the courts to take the lead in ensuring fair dealing.

22-001

The principal legislative enactments are the Unfair Contract Terms Act 1977 and the Unfair Terms in Consumer Contracts Regulations 1999. At the time of the enactment of the Regulations, there was a view that the law would be clearer and more accessible if the Act and the Regulations were properly integrated. It took some years for that view to be accepted. However, early in 2014, the Government introduced the Consumer Rights Bill, which is designed precisely to consolidate, clarify, and simplify the rights and remedies of consumer contractors. In effect, those parts of the Unfair Contract Terms Act that apply to consumer contracts have been put together with the Regulations and re-expressed in what is now the Consumer Rights Act 2015. This means that the Unfair Contract Terms Act continues to control exclusion, limitation, and indemnity clauses in commercial contracts; and that unfair terms in consumer contracts will be regulated by the new Consumer Rights Act.

In order to review this body of legislation and its associated jurisprudence, this chapter is divided into the following three main sections: first, the salient features of the legislative scheme (that is, the Unfair Contract Terms Act 1977 and the Unfair Terms in Consumer Contracts Regulations 1999) are set out; secondly, the judicial interpretation and application of the cornerstone legislative tests of fairness are considered; and thirdly the main provisions of the Consumer Rights Act 2015 are given.

1. THE SALIENT FEATURES OF THE LEGISLATIVE SCHEME

22–002   As we explained in Ch.21, the Unfair Contract Terms Act 1977 was primarily a response to exclusion clauses, particularly where they appear in standard form contracts. In some cases, these clauses gave rise to such a degree of concern that the Act declares that, even if they appear in the contract, they simply cannot be relied on (they are, so to speak, "black-listed"). In most cases, however, the question is whether the clause in question is judged to be one that was fair and reasonable to be included in the contract; if it is so judged, then it may be relied on. Given that the Act applies to both commercial and consumer contractors, and given the particular concern about the vulnerability of the latter, it is probably correct to assume that the Act has been used more aggressively in the protection of consumers than as a ground for interfering with the allocation of risk in commercial contracts. We can also detect in the Act the unmistakable signs of the general law of contract bifurcating so that separate regulatory regimes are developed for, respectively, commercial and consumer contracts.

In the European Community, while there was a deep respect for the background market principle of freedom of contract, there was little hesitation in regulating the consumer marketplace. At minimum, so the Commission thought, consumers should have basic rights applicable throughout the European market—and, predictably, this included the right to be protected against unfair terms that were imposed by suppliers into the consumer markets. This line of thinking led to the adoption of Council Directive 93/13/EEC on unfair contract terms. The original version of the Regulations which implement this Directive came into force on July 1, 1995. Those Regulations were revoked and re-enacted with modifications and additions by the 1999 Regulations which came into force on October 1, 1999. Unlike the Unfair Contract Terms Act, the Regulations do not "black-list" any terms. Rather, the central control is the test set out in Regulation 5(1) which treats a term as unfair if "contrary to the requirement of good faith, it causes a significant imbalance in the parties' rights and obligations arising under the contract, to the detriment of the consumer" (see below)—a test re-enacted by s.62(4) of the Consumer Rights Act. Under the 1995 Regulations the Director General of Fair Trading had an obligation to consider any complaint about the fairness of a contract term drawn up for general use and a power to apply for an injunction to prevent the continued use of such a term. That continues, but the 1999 Regulations provide for the first time that a qualifying body named in Sch.1 (statutory regulators, trading standards departments and the Consumers' Association) shall have a similar power, provided they give the Director the required notice of their intention. The Regulations also create a new power for the Director and the qualifying bodies to require traders to produce copies of their standard contracts and give information about their use.

The Regulations, as we have remarked, were enacted without any revision of, and on top of the statutory protection against unfair terms already existing in English law, such as the Misrepresentation Act 1967 s.3 and the 1977 Act. The result is that the 1977 Act and the Regulations overlap in a rather disorderly way. Some types of contract are covered by both enactments, some only by one and some only by the other. Section 26 and Sch.1 to the Act specify types of contract to which the Act does not apply. The Regulations apply only to contracts between a seller or supplier and a consumer. (For a summary of the principal differences between these overlapping regimes, together with a proposed unification of the regimes, see The Law Commission and the Scottish Law Commission's joint report on *Unfair Terms in Contracts* (Law Com. No.292, Scot Law Com. No.199) (Cm 6464, February 2005) below).

A. *Terms Affected by the Act and Terms Affected by the Regulations*

i. The Act

Part I of the Act applies to terms which exclude or restrict liability and s.13(1) states "to the extent that [Pt I] prevents the exclusion or restriction of liability it also prevents—   **22-003**

(a) making the liability or its enforcement subject to restrictive or onerous conditions;

(b) excluding or restricting any right or remedy in respect of the liability, or subjecting any person to any prejudice in consequence of his pursuing any such right or remedy;

(c) excluding or restricting rules of evidence or procedure; and (to that extent) sections 2 and 5 to 7 also prevent excluding or restricting liability by reference to terms and notices which exclude or restrict the relevant obligation or duty."

Clauses requiring claims or complaints to be made within a specified time or in a specified form would be covered by para.(a). Paragraph (b) would apply to clauses excluding the right to rescind or avoid a contract or to withhold part of the price because of defects in the goods or services supplied. A clause stating that a customer's signature should be conclusive proof that goods comply with a contract or have a particular value would fall foul of para.(c).

Agreements to submit differences to arbitration, on the other hand, are not to be treated as excluding or restricting liability (s.13(2)) and so are unaffected by the Act. While a clause which limits the amount of damages payable on a breach of contract is covered, a clause which fixes the amount is probably not, and is valid if it is a liquidated damages clause but void if it is a penalty clause.

An agreement to settle an action for damages is an agreement to exclude or restrict liability but it relates to an existing liability, whereas the Act is concerned with prospective liability—liability which the parties contemplate might arise under a contract which they are about to enter into. Though s.15 provides that the Act does not affect the validity of such a settlement in Scotland and there is no corresponding provision for England, it has been held that the Act is not intended to, and does not, apply to such a settlement: *Tudor Grange Holdings Ltd v Citibank NA* [1991] 4 All E.R. 1, Ch D, Browne-Wilkinson VC.

ii. The Regulations

The Regulations, on the other hand, apply to all terms in consumer contracts except—   **22-004**

"(i) terms which have been individually negotiated (reg.5(1));

(ii) terms defining the main subject-matter of the contract (reg.6(2)(a)); and

(iii) terms fixing the price or remuneration where its adequacy is in issue (reg.6(2)(b))."

Following the decision of the House of Lords in *Director General of Fair Trading v First National Bank* (below), it seemed that the courts would apply reg.6(2)(a) very restrictively; in other words, they would not allow the category of "core" terms, defining the main subject matter of the contract, to spread in a way that would frustrate the spirit and intent of the Regulations. See, further, *Bairstow Eves London Central Ltd v Smith* [2004] EWHC 263, and Elizabeth Macdonald, 'Bank Charges and the Core Exemption: *Office of Fair Trading v Abbey National Plc*' (2008) 71 MLR 987. However, the Supreme Court's decision in *Office of Fair Trading v Abbey National Plc and Others* [2009] UKSC 6 (below), which focuses on reg.6(2)(b), indicates that the interpretation of the regulation is tricky and that some caution is in order.

It appears that the Regulations may apply to an arbitration clause or a liquidated damages clause; but not to a contract for the settlement of a dispute because that could hardly be called a consumer contract.

A long "indicative and non-exhaustive list of terms which may be regarded as unfair" is provided in Sch.2; and a similar strategy is adopted in the Consumer Rights Act 2015.

iii. Consumer Contracts

22-005   Though the terminology differs, the definition of a consumer contract seems to be substantially the same for the purposes of the Act and the Regulations. Section 12(1) of the Act provides that—

"a party to a contract 'deals as consumer' in relation to another party if—

(a) he neither makes the contract in the course of a business nor holds himself out as doing so; and
(b) The other party does make the contract in the course of a business . . ."

Under reg.3 a "consumer" is "a natural person who . . . is acting for purposes which are outside his trade, business or profession"; and a "seller or supplier" is any legal or natural person "who . . . is acting for purposes relating to his trade, business or profession, whether publicly or privately owned." (As defined by s.2(3) of the Consumer Rights Act 2015, a consumer "means an individual acting for purposes that are wholly or mainly outside that individual's trade, business, craft or profession.")

So a corporation, not being a "natural person", cannot benefit from the consumer provisions of the Regulations but it may be protected by the Act. It takes a stretch of the imagination to treat a limited company as making a contract otherwise than in the course of its business; but precisely this stretch was made in both *R & B Customs Brokers Co v United Dominions Trust Ltd* [1988] 1 W.L.R. 321 and *Feldaroll Foundry Plc v Hermes Leasing (London) Ltd* [2004] EWCA Civ 747. More plausibly, perhaps, a corporation which is a charity could be a "consumer" for the purposes of the Act but not the Regulations.

iv. Avoidance of Liability for Negligence

22-006   Both enactments apply to an attempt to avoid liability to a consumer for negligence but the Act also protects persons who are not consumers. Where death or personal injury is caused by negligence, the Act rules out absolutely any exclusion or restriction of liability whereas, under the Regulations, it is only a term "which may be regarded as unfair": Sch.2 para.1(a). So the injured consumer, or his personal representatives if he is dead, will be protected by the Act and there is no room for the application of the Regulations. Where the term purports to exclude or limit liability for damage to property caused by negligence, it will be invalid under the Act unless it is shown to satisfy the "requirement of reasonableness" and, under the Regulations, unless it is shown not to be an "unfair term" within the meaning of reg.5. It is not clear that there is any material difference between the two tests. Compare Sch.2 of the Act ("Guidelines" for the Application of Reasonableness Test) with Sch.2 of the Regulations. As the Act is the more generally applicable enactment, we will concentrate particularly on it.

v. The Effect of the Act on Liability for Negligence

Negligence is defined by s.1(1) to include the breach of any duty to take reasonable care or exercise reasonable skill arising out of a contract or imposed by the common law or the Occupier's Liability Act 1957. The common law duty will include duties imposed by the tort of negligence and the law of bailment (see Palmer, 128 N.L.J. 887). In order to satisfy the requirement of reasonableness, a contract term must be a fair and reasonable one to be included having regard to the circumstances which were, or ought reasonably to have been, known to or in the contemplation of the parties when the contract was made: s.11(1). In the case of a notice not having contractual effect the requirement is that it should be fair and reasonable to allow reliance on it, having regard to all the circumstances obtaining when the liability arose or (but for the notice) would have arisen: s.11(3). Where the term or notice purports to restrict liability to a specified sum of money, the court must have regard to the resources which the defendant could expect to have to meet the liability and how far it was open to him to cover himself by insurance: s.11(4). The onus is on the party relying on the term to establish that it satisfies the requirement of reasonableness: s.11(5). Where a term, considered as a whole, is unreasonable, a party cannot rely on a part of the term which, considered in isolation, might be reasonable: *Stewart Gill Ltd v Horatio Myer & Co Ltd* [1992] 2 All E.R. 257.

    A notice may be relevant evidence that the defendant has satisfied a duty of care by giving warning of a danger; but a term or notice may not negative a duty which would otherwise arise: s.13(1), which provides that ss.2 and 5 to 7 prevent the exclusion or restriction of an obligation or duty to the same extent as they prevent the exclusion or restriction of liability for breach of the duty or obligation: *Smith v Eric S Bush*, below. So the words, "without responsibility on our part," which saved the defendants in *Hedley Byrne v Heller* from liability would not be effective unless the defendants persuaded the court (as they well might and as an estate agent succeeded in doing in *McCullagh v Lane Fox and Partners Ltd*, *The Times*, December 22, 1995) that the disclaimer satisfied the requirement of reasonableness. (For discussion of s.13(1), see Palmer and Yates, [1981] CLJ 108, 126–134.)

    Section 2(3) of the Act imposes some restriction on the defence to an action in negligence that the plaintiff had voluntarily assumed the risk—volenti non fit injuria. At one time it was held that a warning on the dashboard in front of the passenger seat of a private car that the passenger travelled at his own risk was effective: *Buckpitt v Oates* [1968] 1 All E.R. 1145; *Bennett v Tugwell* [1971] 2 All E.R. 248. These decisions were reversed by s.148(3) of the Road Traffic Act 1972 which invalidated agreements between drivers and passengers that negatived or restricted liability for personal injury or death caused while driving on a road. That section, now replaced by s.149 of the Road Traffic Act 1988, provides a more effective protection to the passenger than the Unfair Contract Terms Act because it is not confined to business liability—it would apply to the commercial traveller picking up a hitchhiker whether he was on his way to secure an order or to the races. If a similar notice were displayed otherwise than in a motor vehicle while driving on a road, reliance on those decisions by a "business" defendant would now be subject to the provision in s.2(3) that a person's agreement to or awareness of such a notice is not of itself to be taken as indicating his voluntary assumption of any risk. It is difficult to see what would be enough, if this is not.

22–007

B. Avoidance of Liability in Contract (Other than Breaches Consisting in Negligence)

i. Consumer Contracts

22–008   Here both the Act (s.3) and the Regulations operate in favour of a consumer. A term which has been individually negotiated with a consumer is, however, liable to be held invalid only under the Act, not (see reg.5) under the Regulations. On the other hand, there are two limitations in the Act which are not in the Regulations:

(i)   Where the contract is one of sale or hire-purchase, or one under which the title to goods passes, it is a consumer transaction for the purposes of the Act only if the goods are of a type ordinarily supplied for private use or consumption. A natural person who bought a steam-roller for his private collection would probably not be able to rely on the Act, but could rely on the Regulations.

(ii)   Sales by auction or competitive tender are not, in any circumstances, to be regarded as consumer transactions for the purposes of the Act, but they may be under the Regulations. A buyer of a car at an auction sale might now successfully argue that a term relating to the condition of the car was unfair.

ii. Non-Consumer Contracts on Written Standard Terms

22–009   The Act, but not the Regulations, operates in favour of one who is not a consumer but who is dealing on the other party's written standard terms of business. So a limited company or a businessman may invoke the protection of the Act where he has accepted the other party's written standard terms. The party proffering the standard terms is, ex hypothesi, making the contract in the course of a business but the other party may or may not be. Clearly, terms will not fail to qualify as 'standard' because particular matters are negotiated—price, time of performance, etc. If the whole of the written terms have been specially drafted for the particular contract, clearly they are not 'standard'. Standard terms may be prepared by a trade or professional organisation, for example, the RIBA, or by the individual contractor. Standard terms are not necessarily signed. Parties may agree to contract on the terms stated in a catalogue, price list, sold note, ticket, etc.

The effect of s.3. The effect of s.3 is that the business party in a consumer contract or the party proffering the standard terms cannot—

(a)   when in breach of contract, exclude or restrict liability, except insofar as the contract term satisfies the requirement or reasonableness; or

(b)   claim to be entitled to render a contractual performance substantially different from that which was reasonably expected of him, or to tender no performance at all except insofar as the contract term authorising him to do so satisfies the requirement of reasonableness.

Paragraph (a) is applicable only when the defendant is in breach. If the term in question excludes the alleged promise there is no breach. See *Photo Production v Securicor*, above Ch.21 (s.13, which prevents the exclusion or restriction of obligations does not apply to s.3). If, on the other hand, the term purports to exclude liability for breach of the promise, it is caught by the paragraph and is ineffective unless it satisfies the requirement of reasonableness.

However, the importance of the freedom of the defendant to exclude a promise under (a) is much diminished, if not entirely eliminated by para.(b). The different performance or non-performance contemplated by (b) is not a breach of contract—if it were it would be covered by (a). Paragraph (b) assumes that there are two ways of performing the contract. Each is a "contractual performance" but only one is "reasonably expected". Performing the contract in the other way will be a statutory breach of contract unless the term authorising it satisfies the requirement of reasonableness.

Suppose that standard terms provide—

"(i) Accommodation will be provided in the Majestic Hotel . . .

(xi) If accommodation in the Majestic Hotel is not available it will be provided in another hotel of comparable quality."

If clause (xi) is held to be an attempt to exclude liability for breach of a promise to provide accommodation in the Majestic, it is caught by para.(a) and is inoperative unless it satisfies the requirement of reasonableness; but if it is held to provide for an alternative mode of performance of the contract and the plaintiff reasonably expected to be accommodated in the Majestic, it is caught by para.(b) and is a statutory breach of contract unless the defendant shows that the term satisfies the requirement of reasonableness. Potentially, s.3(2)(b) offers an important peg on which to hang an argument for review of what are plainly expressed terms of a contract (on the ground that the terms unfairly or unreasonably authorise a performance that is out of line with the recipient's reasonable expectations)—for an exploration of this potential, see Roger Brownsword and John MacGowan 'Credit Card Fraud' (1997) 147 N.L.J. 1806–1808 (with response by Susan Ward at (1998) 148 N.L.J. 7–8; and reply to Susan Ward at (1998) 148 N.L.J. 133). There is some support for developing this potential in *Timeload Ltd v British Telecommunications Plc* [1995] EMLR 459; but for a much more conservative approach, see *Peninsula Business Services Ltd v Sweeney* [2004] I.R.L.R. 49.

The provision in s.9(1), that an exclusion clause which is required to be reasonable survives the termination of the contract either by breach or the exercise of a right to avoid it, was designed to overrule one aspect of *Harbutt's Plasticine v Wayne Tank* (above, Ch.21). Since that case was overruled in *Photo Production Ltd v Securicor* the subsection may, with one possible qualification, be regarded as a declaration of the common law. The qualification is that the subsection appears to acknowledge that a contract may be terminated by breach, a proposition not previously recognised; though it may be noted that in *Photo Production* Lord Wilberforce said, ". . . when in the context of a breach of contract one speaks of 'termination' what is meant is no more than that the innocent party or, in some cases, both parties, are excused from further performance."

Section 9(2) makes it clear that a party who, after breach, affirms the contract, may recover damages despite an exclusion clause which does not satisfy the requirement of reasonableness.

iii. Contracts under which Possession or Ownership of Goods Passes

Section 6 relates to terms implied under the Sale of Goods Act 1979 and the Supply of Goods (Implied Terms) Act 1973, which governs contracts of hire-purchase; and s.7 relates to other contracts under which ownership or possession of goods passes—for example, barter, hiring or contracts for work and materials. Section 6 provides that liability for breach of the terms of s.12 of the Sale of Goods Act can never be excluded or restricted; and that liability for breach of the terms of ss.13, 14 and 15 can never be excluded or restricted against a consumer and, as against others, only insofar as the clause satisfies the test of reasonableness. The same rules apply to the corresponding provisions of the Supply of Goods Act. Where these provisions apply, there is no room for the application of the Regulations.

Section 7 makes the same provision for the other contracts, with one exception. The supplier may

22-010

exclude liability for failure to give a good title if the term satisfies the requirement of reasonableness. But the new s.3(A) introduced by the Supply of Goods and Services Act 1982 substantially removes this exception because it prohibits the exclusion of liability for failure to give a good title under contracts within that Act, which include most of the contracts to which s.7 applies.

"Guidelines" for the application by the court of the reasonableness test under ss.6 and 7 are set out in Sch.2.

iv. Secondary Contracts

22–011 It appears that s.10, precluding "Evasion by means of secondary contract", does not apply to secondary contracts between the same contracting parties. So an agreement to compromise a contractual dispute falling within ss.2 or 3 of the Act cannot be struck down on the ground that it is unreasonable: *Tudor Grange Holdings Ltd v Citibank NA* [1991] 4 All E.R. 1, 13, Ch D, Browne-Wilkinson VC. The section applies where a contract between A and B contains no exemption clause but a second contract between A and C contains terms precluding A from exercising rights against B under the first contract. A is not bound by those terms.

If, in the example of the Majestic Hotel, above, the parties enter into a second contract providing that the accommodation will be provided in the Imperial, it seems that that will be binding, though accommodation in the Imperial would not have satisfied the first contract.

v. Guarantees of Consumer Goods

22–012 Section 5 is concerned with the relationship between a manufacturer or distributor of goods and the consumer. It does not apply as between the parties to a contract under or in pursuance of which ownership or possession of goods passes. So, if goods are manufactured by A, distributed by B, and retailed by C to the consumer, D, the section may apply as between A and D or between B and D but not as between C and D. D will have ample remedies against C under the Sale of Goods Act. The section is concerned with saving D's rights in tort against A and B, or under any collateral contract with A or B.

A or B may offer D a guarantee of the goods in consideration of D's surrendering his potential rights of action under *Donoghue v Stevenson* [1932] A.C. 562 or under any collateral contract there may be. Any such purported surrender of rights is invalidated by the section. If death or personal injury is caused, the term or notice is invalid under s.2 of the Act. Reliance need be placed on s.5 only in respect of damage to property or such other economic loss as may be recoverable at common law.

The section does not create any new liability. If goods merely prove useless in consumer use, s.5 does not give any remedy to the consumer against the manufacturer or distributor with whom he has no contract. Indeed, it has been suggested (see Rogers and Clark, *Current Law Statutes*) that such rights as the consumer may formerly have acquired under the guarantee have been lost since the consideration for the guarantee (the surrender of the consumer's common law rights) may have been removed because that surrender is now void.

(Consider the definition of "consumer use". Is a car supplied to an employee in 'consumer use' if he is allowed to use it for private as well as business purposes?)

vi. Indemnity Clauses

22–013 Section 4 applies only in favour of consumers (see s.12). A consumer may not be required by contract to indemnify any other person against a liability incurred by that other for negligence or breach of contract—unless it is shown that the requirement of reasonableness is satisfied. Suppose that D, the owner of a car ferry, obtains from P, the owner of a car, a promise to indemnify D, or D's servants, against claims arising from the negligent manoeuvring of the car. If injury is caused to a third party (whether to person or property) P can be required to indemnify D only if D shows the clause to be reasonable. If personal injury or death is caused to P himself, the clause appears to be void since s.2(1) prevents exclusion of liability and s.13(1)(b) prevents "subjecting a person to any prejudice in consequence of his pursuing any such right or remedy." A person is clearly subjected to prejudice in pursuing a remedy if he is required immediately to repay what is recovered by exercising the remedy. If the clause is void by s.2 it can hardly be saved by s.4, even if reasonable. (See John N. Adams and Roger Brownsword (1982) JBL 200 and (1988) JBL 146.)

The Law Commission and the Scottish Law Commission's joint report on *Unfair Terms In Contracts* (Law Com. No.292, Scot Law Com. No.199) (Cm. 6464, February 2005) summarises the principal differences between UCTA and the UTCCR as follows:

"2.6 UCTA:

(1)   applies only to exclusion and limitation of liability clauses and indemnity clauses;

(2)   makes certain exclusions or restrictions of no effect at all;

(3)   subjects others to a reasonableness test;

(4)   contains guidelines for the application of the reasonableness test;

(5)   puts the burden of proving that a term within its scope is reasonable on the party seeking to rely on the clause;

(6)   often applies whether the terms were negotiated or were in a "standard form";

(7)   does not apply to certain types of contract even when they are consumer contracts;

(8)   has effect only between the immediate parties;

(9)   has separate provisions for Scotland; and

(10)   applies to terms and notices excluding certain liabilities in tort [delict].

UCTA also applies to contracts between businesses and certain "private" contracts for the sale of goods where neither of the two parties is a business.

2.7   In contrast, the UTCCR:

(1)   apply to any kind of term other than the definition of the main subject matter of the contract and the adequacy of the price;

(2)   do not make any particular type of term of no effect at all;

(3)   subject the terms to a fairness test;

(4)   do not contain detailed guidelines as to how that test should be applied, but contain a so-called "grey" list of terms which "may be regarded" as unfair;

(5)   leave the burden of establishing that the clause is unfair on the consumer;

(6)   apply only to "non-negotiated" terms;

(7)   apply to consumer contracts of all kinds;

(8) are not only effective between the parties but empower various bodies to take action to prevent the use of unfair terms; and

(9) apply to the UK as a whole.

They do not apply to business or private contracts."

The Law Commissions recommend, inter alia, that:

(a) there should be a single (unified) piece of unfair contract terms legislation covering the whole of the United Kingdom;

(b) there should be no significant reduction in *consumer* protection; terms which are automatically of no effect under UCTA should continue to be of no effect under the new unified legislation; any term in a consumer contract, with the exception of a "core" term, should be open to challenge irrespective of whether the term was individually negotiated; the applicable test would be a "fair and reasonable" test (with no express reference to "good faith"); the test would consider the transparency of the term, its substance and effect, and the circumstances in existence at the time that the contract was made; the burden of proving that a term is fair and reasonable would rest on the business contractor;

(c) there should be a special regime for small business contractors (businesses with nine or fewer employees) who are parties to contracts with a value of no more than £500,000; such small business contractors would have the right to challenge a "non-core" standard term of a contract provided that the term had not been modified in favour of the small business as a result of negotiation; the applicable test would be the "fair and reasonable" test; the small business would bear the burden of showing unfairness; and

(d) broadly speaking, the current regime would apply to business contracts with the new "fair and reasonable" test being applicable.

2. JUDICIAL INTERPRETATION AND APPLICATION OF THE LEGISLATION

A. The Regulations: Good Faith and Significant Imbalance

DIRECTOR GENERAL OF FAIR TRADING v FIRST NATIONAL BANK PLC

House of Lords [2001] UKHL 52

LORD BINGHAM

22–014   My Lords,

1. First National Bank Plc ("the bank") is licensed to carry on consumer credit business. It is a major lender in the market and has lent large sums to borrowers under credit agreements regulated under the Consumer Credit Act 1974. Such agreements are made on its printed form which contains a number of standard terms. The Director General of Fair Trading ("the Director"), in exercising powers conferred on him by regulation 8 of the Unfair Terms in Consumer Contracts Regulations 1994 (SI 1994/3159) ("the regulations"), sought an injunction to restrain use of or reliance on one such standard term on the ground that it was unfair. The bank resisted the Director's application on two grounds. The first, rejected by Evans-Lombe J. at first instance ([2000] 1 WLR 98) and the Court of Appeal (Peter Gibson, Waller and Buxton L.JJ.) ([2000] QB 672), was that the fairness provisions of the regulations did not apply to the term in question. The second, accepted by the judge but partially

rejected by the Court of Appeal, was that the term in question was not unfair. In this appeal to the House the bank again relies on both these arguments. The Director seeks to uphold the decision of the Court of Appeal but contends that the term was more fundamentally unfair than the Court of Appeal held it to be. Thus there are two broad questions before the House:

(1) Do the fairness provisions of the regulations apply to the term in question?
(2) If so, is the term unfair and, if it is, on what ground?

2. By its standard form of regulated credit agreement the bank agrees to make a sum of money available to the borrower for a specified period in consideration of the borrower's agreement to repay that sum by specified instalments on specified dates with interest at a specified rate. Condition 4 of the bank's standard form provided that:

"The rate of interest will be charged on a day to day basis on the outstanding balance and will be debited to the Customer's account monthly in arrears . . ."

and provided that the rate of interest might be varied. Condition 8 of the agreement was in these terms:

"Time is of the essence for making all repayments to FNB as they fall due. If any repayment instalment is unpaid for more than 7 days after it became due, FNB may serve a notice on the Customer requiring payment before a specified date not less than 7 days later. If the repayment instalment is not paid in full by that date, FNB will be entitled to demand payment of the balance on the Customer's account and interest then outstanding together with all reasonable legal and other costs charges and expenses claimed or incurred by FNB in trying to obtain the repayment of the unpaid instalment of such balance and interest. *Interest on the amount which becomes payable shall be charged in accordance with Condition 4, at the rate stated in paragraph D overleaf (subject to variation) until payment after as well as before any judgement (such obligation to be independent of and not to merge with the judgement).*"

Emphasis has been added to the last sentence of this condition, since it is to that sentence alone that the Director's objection relates. I shall refer to this sentence as "the term".

3. The bank's stipulation that interest shall be charged until payment after as well as before any judgment, such obligation to be independent of and not to merge with the judgment, is readily explicable. At any rate since *In re Sneyd; Ex p Fewings* (1883) 25 Ch D 338, not challenged but accepted without demur by the House of Lords in *Economic Life Assurance Society v Usborne* [1902] AC 147, the understanding of lawyers in England has been as accurately summarised by the Court of Appeal at p 682 of the judgment under appeal:

"It is trite law in England that once a judgment is obtained under a loan agreement for a principal sum and judgment is entered, the contract merges in the judgment and the principal becomes owed under the judgment and not under the contract. If under the contract interest on any principal sum is due, absent special provisions the contract is considered ancillary to the covenant to pay the principal, with the result that if judgment is obtained for the principal, the covenant to pay interest merges in the judgment. Parties to a contract may agree that a covenant to pay interest will not merge in any judgment for the principal sum due, and in that event interest may be charged under the contract on the principal sum due even after judgment for that sum."

4. To ensure that they were able to recover not only the full sum of principal outstanding but also any interest accruing on that sum after judgment as well as before, it became the practice for lenders to include in their credit agreements a term to the effect of the term here in issue. If such a provision had not been included, a lender seeking to enforce a loan agreement against a borrower in the High Court would suffer prejudice only to the extent that the statutory rate of interest on judgment debts at the material time is lower than the contractual interest rate, because the High Court has, since 1838, had power to award statutory interest on a judgment debt until payment.

5. But a lender seeking to enforce a regulated credit agreement is in a different position. He is obliged by section 141 of the 1974 Act to sue in the county court. Until the Lord Chancellor, exercising his power under section 74 of the County Courts Act 1984, made the County Courts (Interest on Judgment Debts) Order 1991 (SI 1991/1184), the county court lacked power to award statutory interest on any judgment debt and, when such a general power was conferred by the order, judgments given in proceedings to recover money due under agreements regulated by the 1974 Act were expressly excluded from its scope. It was further provided in the order:

"3   Where under the terms of the relevant judgment payment of a judgment debt—

  (a) is not required to be made until a specified date, or
  (b) is to be made by instalments,

interest shall not accrue under this Order—

  (i)   until that date, or
  (ii) on the amount of any instalment, until it falls due,

as the case may be."

6. Thus a lender under a regulated credit agreement who obtains judgment against a defaulting borrower in the county court will be entitled to recover the principal outstanding at the date of judgment and interest accrued up to that date but will not be entitled to an order for statutory interest after that date, and even if the court had power to award statutory post-judgment interest it could not do so, in any case where an instalment order had been made, unless there had been a default in the due payment of any instalment. The lender may recover post-judgment interest only if he has the benefit of an independent covenant by the borrower entitling him to recover such interest. There is nothing to preclude inclusion of such a covenant in a regulated credit agreement, unless it falls foul of the fairness requirement in the regulations.

7. Section 71 of the County Courts Act 1984 conferred a general power on the county court, where any judgment was given or order made for payment of a money sum, to order that the money might be paid "by such instalments payable at such times as the court may fix". The 1974 Act also conferred on the county court three powers relevant for present purposes. First, the court was empowered to make a time order. Sections 129 and 130 of the Act, so far as relevant, provided:

"129.   (1) If it appears to the court just to do so—
  . . .

  (c) in an action brought by a creditor or owner to enforce a regulated agreement or any security, or recover possession of any goods or land to which a regulated agreement relates,

the court may make an order under this section (a "time order").
  (2) A time order shall provide for one or both of the following, as the court considers just—

  (a) the payment by the debtor or hirer or any surety of any sum owed under a regulated agreement or a security by such instalments, payable at such times, as the court, having regard to the means of the debtor or hirer and any surety, considers reasonable;
  . . .
130.   (1) Where in accordance with rules of court an offer to pay any sum by instalments is made by the debtor or hirer and accepted by the creditor or owner, the court may in accordance with rules of court make a time order under section 129(2) (a) giving effect to the offer without hearing evidence of means. . .

Secondly, section 136 provided:

"136. The court may in an order made by it under this Act include such provision as it considers just for amending any agreement or security in consequence of a term of the order."

Thirdly, by sections 137, 138 and 139 of the Act the county court was given power to reopen credit agreements "so as to do justice between the parties" if it found a credit bargain to be "extortionate". A credit bargain was defined as extortionate if it

"(a) requires the debtor or a relative of his to make payments (whether unconditionally, or on certain contingencies) which are grossly exorbitant, or
  (b) otherwise grossly contravenes ordinary principles of fair dealing."

In determining whether a credit bargain was extortionate regard was to be had to such evidence as might be adduced concerning interest rates prevailing at the time the bargain was made, a number of factors relating to the debtor and the circumstances of the transaction and "any other relevant considerations".

8. The provisions of the regulations directly at issue in these proceedings must be considered in more detail below. It should however be noted that the regulations were made to give effect in the United Kingdom to Council Directive 93/13/EEC (OJ 1993, L95, p 29) on unfair terms in consumer contracts ("the directive"). (They were superseded by further regulations in 1999, but these are to very much the same effect, do not govern this

case and need not be further considered). It is common ground that the regulations should be construed so as to give effect to the directive, to which resort may properly be made for purposes of construction. Regulation 5, giving effect to article 6 of the directive, provides:

"(1) An unfair term in a contract concluded with a consumer by a seller or supplier shall not be binding on the consumer.
(2) The contract shall continue to bind the parties if it is capable of continuing in existence without the unfair term."

Thus the Director's challenge, although addressed only to the bank's use of and reliance on the term, if upheld, may well invalidate any similar term in any other regulated agreement made by any other lender with any borrower. The questions at issue are accordingly of general public importance.

(1) The applicability of the regulations

9. Regulation 3(2) of the regulations provides:

"In so far as it is in plain, intelligible language, no assessment shall be made of the fairness of any term which—

(a) defines the main subject matter of the contract, or
(b) concerns the adequacy of the price or remuneration, as against the goods or services sold or supplied."

This gives effect, almost word for word, to article 4(2) of the directive, although some light may be shed on its meaning by the 19th recital to the directive:

"Whereas, for the purposes of this Directive, assessment of unfair character shall not be made of terms which describe the main subject matter of the contract nor the quality/price ratio of the goods or services supplied; whereas the main subject matter of the contract and the price/quality ratio may nevertheless be taken into account in assessing the fairness of other terms; whereas it follows, *inter alia*, that in insurance contracts, the terms which clearly define or circumscribe the insured risk and the insurer's liability shall not be subject to such assessment since these restrictions are taken into account in calculating the premium paid by the consumer".

10. In reliance on regulation 3(2)(b) Lord Goodhart Q.C., on behalf of the bank, submitted that no assessment might be made of the fairness of the term because it concerns the adequacy of the bank's remuneration as against the services supplied, namely the loan of money. A bank's remuneration under a credit agreement is the receipt of interest. The term, by entitling the bank to post-judgment interest, concerns the quantum and thus the adequacy of that remuneration. This was the more obviously true if, as Lord Goodhart submitted, the merger rule as commonly understood is unsound. Where judgment is given for outstanding principal payable under a loan agreement and interest accrued up to the date of judgment, those claims (he accepted) are merged in the judgment. That is a conventional application of the principle of res judicata. But no claim for future interest has been the subject of adjudication by the court and such a claim cannot be barred as res judicata. The borrower's covenant to pay interest on any part of the principal loan outstanding thus survives such a judgment, and *In re Sneyd*, above, was wrong to lay down any contrary principle. Lord Goodhart adopted the observation of Templeman L.J. in *Ealing London Borough Council v El Isaac* [1980] 1 WLR 932 at 937:

"I do not for myself understand how a debt payable with interest until actual repayment can be merged in a judgment without interest or with a different rate of interest payable thereafter."

11. To this submission Mr Crowe, representing the Director, gave two short answers. First, condition 8, of which the term forms part, is a default provision. Its purpose, and its only purpose, is to prescribe the consequences of a default by the borrower. It does not lay down the rate of interest which the bank is entitled to receive and the borrower bound to pay. It is an ancillary term, well outside the bounds of regulation 3(2)(b). Secondly, there is no merger "rule" but only a rule of construction. It is a question of construction of any given agreement whether the borrower's covenant to pay interest is or is not to be understood as intended to continue after judgment. But whatever the correct approach to merger, it is an irrelevance. Even if a bank's borrower's covenant to pay interest is ordinarily to be taken, as in Scotland (see *Bank of Scotland v Davis* 1982 SLT 20), to continue until the full sum of principal is repaid, after as before judgment, the term remains part of a default provision and not one falling within the provisions of regulation 3(2)(b).

12. In agreement with the judge and the Court of Appeal, I do not accept the bank's submission on this issue. The regulations, as Professor Sir Guenter Treitel Q.C. has aptly observed (*The Law of Contract*, 10th ed, 1999, p 248) "are not intended to operate as a mechanism of quality or price control" and regulation 3(2) is of "crucial importance in recognising the parties' freedom of contract with respect to the essential features of their bargain" (*ibid*, at p 249). But there is an important "distinction between the term or terms which express the substance of the bargain and 'incidental' (if important) terms which surround them" (*Chitty on Contracts*, 28th ed, 1999, "Unfair Terms in Consumer Contracts", p 747, para 15–025). The object of the regulations and the directive is to protect consumers against the inclusion of unfair and prejudicial terms in standard-form contracts into which they enter, and that object would plainly be frustrated if regulation 3(2)(b) were so broadly interpreted as to cover any terms other than those falling squarely within it. In my opinion the term, as part of a provision prescribing the consequences of default, plainly does not fall within it. It does not concern the adequacy of the interest earned by the bank as its remuneration but is designed to ensure that the bank's entitlement to interest does not come to an end on the entry of judgment. I do not think the bank's argument on merger advances its case. It appears that some judges in the past have been readier than I would be to infer that a borrower's covenant to pay interest was not intended to extend beyond the entry of judgment. But even if a borrower's obligation were ordinarily understood to extend beyond judgment even in the absence of an independent covenant, it would not alter my view of the term as an ancillary provision and not one concerned with the adequacy of the bank's remuneration as against the services supplied. It is therefore necessary to address the second question.

(2) Unfairness

13. Regulation 4 of the regulations is entitled "Unfair terms" and provides:

"(1) In these Regulations, subject to paragraphs (2) and (3) below, 'unfair term' means any term which contrary to the requirement of good faith causes a significant imbalance in the parties' rights and obligations under the contract to the detriment of the consumer.

(2) An assessment of the unfair nature of a term shall be made taking into account the nature of the goods or services for which the contract was concluded and referring, as at the time of the conclusion of the contract, to all circumstances attending the conclusion of the contract and to all the other terms of the contract or of another contract on which it is dependent.

(3) In determining whether a term satisfies the requirement of good faith, regard shall be had in particular to the matters specified in Schedule 2 to these Regulations.

(4) Schedule 3 to these Regulations contains an indicative and non-exhaustive list of the terms which may be regarded as unfair."

Schedule 2 to the regulations provides:

"In making an assessment of good faith, regard shall be had in particular to:

(a) the strength of the bargaining positions of the parties;
(b) whether the consumer had an inducement to agree to the term;
(c) whether the goods or services were sold or supplied to the special order of the consumer, and
(d) the extent to which the seller or supplier has dealt fairly and equitably with the consumer."

Each of (a), (b) and (c) also appear in Schedule 2 to the Unfair Contract Terms Act 1977 among the guidelines for application of the reasonableness test laid down by that statute, suggesting that some similarity of approach in applying the two tests may be appropriate. In a case such as the present, where the fairness of a term is challenged in the absence of any individual consumer, little attention need be paid to (b) and (c). It may however be assumed that any borrower is in a much weaker bargaining position than a large bank contracting on its own standard form. (d) applies a general test of fair and equitable dealing between supplier and consumer. Schedule 3 contains a list of indicative and illustrative terms which may because of their object or effect be regarded as unfair. Examples are terms which have the object or effect of "(e) requiring any consumer who fails to fulfil his obligation to pay a disproportionately high sum in compensation", "(i) irrevocably binding the consumer to terms with which he had no real opportunity of becoming acquainted before the conclusion of the contract", or "(k) enabling the seller or supplier to alter unilaterally without a valid reason any characteristics of the product or service to be provided". It is not suggested that the term falls within any specific entry in the list. It is common ground that fairness must be judged as at the date the contract is made, although account may properly be taken of the likely effect of any term which is then agreed and said to be unfair.

14. The 15th and 16th recitals to the directive are relevant. They provide:

"Whereas it is necessary to fix in a general way the criteria for assessing the unfair character of contract terms;

Whereas the assessment, according to the general criteria chosen, of the unfair character of terms, in particular in sale or supply activities of a public nature providing collective services which take account of solidarity among users, must be supplemented by a means of making an overall evaluation of the different interests involved; whereas this constitutes the requirement of good faith; whereas, in making an assessment of good faith, particular regard shall be had to the strength of the bargaining positions of the parties, whether the consumer had an inducement to agree to the term and whether the goods or services were sold or supplied to the special order of the consumer; whereas the requirement of good faith may be satisfied by the seller or supplier where he deals fairly and equitably with the other party whose legitimate interests he has to take into account".

Article 3(1) of the directive is the counterpart of regulation 4(1), and is in terms which are for present purposes indistinguishable. The directive has no annex to the effect of Schedule 2 to the regulations, but has an annex in terms identical to those of Schedule 3.

15. The trial judge first asked himself whether the term was inherently unfair and concluded that it was not because a borrower, to whom the effect of the term had been fully explained, would not have regarded it as unfair that he would be obliged, in the event of his default, to pay interest on the full sum owed to the lender until complete repayment, even if the court permitted him to pay by instalments extending over a substantial period ([2000] 1 WLR 98 at 108C–H). The judge then considered whether the term was unfair because a defaulting borrower would not expect to bear an interest charge over and above any instalments ordered by the court, and whether the term deprived the consumer of a benefit or advantage which he might reasonably expect to receive. The judge resolved these issues in favour of the bank (pp 108–111), observing (at p 111H) that

"if the provisions of sections 129 and 136 of the Act of 1974 are correctly used by the courts the inclusion of the provisions of clause 8 need not operate to impose on a borrower post judgment interest where it would not be appropriate and just to do so."

16. The Court of Appeal differed from the judge on the question of unfairness. In the judgment of the court it was said ([2000] QB 672 at 688):

"In our judgment the relevant term is unfair within the meaning of the Regulations of 1994 to the extent that it enables the bank to obtain judgment against a debtor under a regulated agreement and an instalment order under section 71 of the Act of 1984 without the court considering whether to make a time order, or, if it does and makes a time order, whether also to make an order under section 136 to reduce the contractual interest rate. The bank, with its strong bargaining position as against the relatively weak position of the consumer, has not adequately considered the consumer's interests in this respect. In our view the relevant term in that respect does create unfair surprise and so does not satisfy the test of good faith; it does cause a significant imbalance in the rights and obligations of the parties by allowing the bank to obtain interest after judgment in circumstances when it would not obtain interest under the Act of 1984 and the Order of 1991, and no specific benefit to compensate the borrower is provided; and it operates to the detriment of that consumer who has to pay the interest.".

The Court of Appeal did not grant an injunction but instead accepted undertakings offered by the bank (subject to appeal) which would bring to the borrower's attention the powers of the court under sections 129 and 136 of the 1974 Act and ensure that a claim to post judgment contractual interest would not be enforced by the bank after the court had made an instalment order unless the court's attention had previously been drawn to its powers under sections 129 and 136 and it had considered whether to exercise those powers.

17. The test laid down by regulation 4(1), deriving as it does from article 3(1) of the directive, has understandably attracted much discussion in academic and professional circles and helpful submissions were made to the House on it. It is plain from the recitals to the directive that one of its objectives was partially to harmonise the law in this important field among all member states of the European Union. The member states have no common concept of fairness or good faith, and the directive does not purport to state the law of any single member state. It lays down a test to be applied, whatever their pre-existing law, by all member states. If the meaning of the test were doubtful, or vulnerable to the possibility of differing interpretations in differing member states, it might be desirable or necessary to seek a ruling from the European Court of Justice on its interpretation. But the language used in expressing the test, so far as applicable in this case, is in my opinion clear and not reasonably capable of differing interpretations. A term falling within the scope of the regulations

is unfair if it causes a significant imbalance in the parties' rights and obligations under the contract to the detriment of the consumer in a manner or to an extent which is contrary to the requirement of good faith. The requirement of significant imbalance is met if a term is so weighted in favour of the supplier as to tilt the parties' rights and obligations under the contract significantly in his favour. This may be by the granting to the supplier of a beneficial option or discretion or power, or by the imposing on the consumer of a disadvantageous burden or risk or duty. The illustrative terms set out in Schedule 3 to the regulations provide very good examples of terms which may be regarded as unfair; whether a given term is or is not to be so regarded depends on whether it causes a significant imbalance in the parties' rights and obligations under the contract. This involves looking at the contract as a whole. But the imbalance must be to the detriment of the consumer; a significant imbalance to the detriment of the supplier, assumed to be the stronger party, is not a mischief which the regulations seek to address. The requirement of good faith in this context is one of fair and open dealing. Openness requires that the terms should be expressed fully, clearly and legibly, containing no concealed pitfalls or traps. Appropriate prominence should be given to terms which might operate disadvantageously to the customer. Fair dealing requires that a supplier should not, whether deliberately or unconsciously, take advantage of the consumer's necessity, indigence, lack of experience, unfamiliarity with the subject matter of the contract, weak bargaining position or any other factor listed in or analogous to those listed in Schedule 2 of the regulations. Good faith in this context is not an artificial or technical concept; nor, since Lord Mansfield was its champion, is it a concept wholly unfamiliar to British lawyers. It looks to good standards of commercial morality and practice. Regulation 4(1) lays down a composite test, covering both the making and the substance of the contract, and must be applied bearing clearly in mind the objective which the regulations are designed to promote.

18. In support of his contention that the term is unfair the Director adduced evidence of complaints made to him by a number of borrowers. Some of these disclose a very highly unsatisfactory state of affairs. In one case a husband and wife borrowed £3,000 plus £443.70 for insurance to finance improvements to their home. The principal was repayable over a five-year term by instalments of £84.89 plus £8.98 insurance. The borrowers fell into arrear and judgment was given for £3,953.11. The court ordered this sum to be paid by monthly instalments of £4.18, at which rate (it was calculated) the judgment debt would take 78 years to clear. Meanwhile, under the contract, interest would continue to accrue even if the instalments were fully and punctually paid. The bank's deponent described these borrowers as "a good example of customers who demonstrated an ability easily to pay the instalments for home improvements when the credit was granted but thereafter appeared to have undertaken many other financial commitments which seriously prejudiced their ability to pay" the bank. A financial statement prepared on these borrowers some months before the county court judgment is consistent with that assertion.

19. For the Director, reliance was placed on the provisions in the 1991 order which denied the court power to order payment of statutory interest on money judgments given under regulated agreements and precluded entitlement to interest in any case where payment by instalments had been ordered and the instalments had been fully and punctually paid. It was argued that the term was unfair because it denied the borrower the protection which those provisions afforded. It was argued, in the alternative, that the term was unfair for the more limited reason upheld by the Court of Appeal.

20. In judging the fairness of the term it is necessary to consider the position of typical parties when the contract is made. The borrower wants to borrow a sum of money, often quite a modest sum, often for purposes of improving his home. He discloses an income sufficient to finance repayment by instalments over the contract term. If he cannot do that, the bank will be unwilling to lend. The essential bargain is that the bank will make funds available to the borrower which the borrower will repay, over a period, with interest. Neither party could suppose that the bank would willingly forgo any part of its principal or interest. If the bank thought that outcome at all likely, it would not lend. If there were any room for doubt about the borrower's obligation to repay the principal in full with interest, that obligation is very clearly and unambiguously expressed in the conditions of contract. There is nothing unbalanced or detrimental to the consumer in that obligation; the absence of such a term would unbalance the contract to the detriment of the lender.

21. It seems clear, as the judge pointed out ([2000] 1 WLR 98 at 111) that a secured lender who does not obtain a money judgment but instead proceeds for possession and sale under the mortgage may obtain interest at the contract rate provided for in the mortgage down to the date when he is actually repaid, and in my opinion there is nothing unbalanced or detrimental to the consumer in that result either.

22. Should it then be said that the provisions of the 1991 order render the term unfair, providing as it does for a continuing obligation to pay interest after judgment notwithstanding the payment of instalments by the borrower in accordance with a court order? It is, I think, pertinent that the 1974 Act, which laid down a number of stipulations with which regulated agreements must comply, did not prohibit terms providing for post-

judgment interest even though it required claims to enforce regulated agreements to be brought in the county court which could not at the time award statutory interest in any circumstances. The 1974 Act was passed to protect consumers and such a prohibition would no doubt have been enacted had it been recognised as a necessary or desirable form of protection. The Crowther Committee, on whose report (Cmnd. 4596, March 1971) the Act was based, did not recommend such a prohibition; indeed, it contemplated the recovery of contractual interest: see paragraphs 5.4.3, 6.6.33, 6.6.44(iv) and 6.7.16). It is also pertinent that judgments based on regulated agreements appear to have been excluded from the scope of the county court's power to award statutory interest in response to observations of Lord Donaldson of Lymington M.R. in *Forward Trust Ltd* v *Whymark* [1990] 2 QB 670 at 681: but that was a case based on a flat rate agreement, in which the judgment in default would include a sum for future interest not yet accrued, in contrast with a simple rate agreement of the present kind (see [2000] 1 WLR 98 at 110–111; [2000] QB 672 at 679); the logic underpinning exclusion of statutory interest in the one case would not apply, at any rate with the same force, in the other. It is understandable that when a court is exercising a statutory power to order payment by instalments it should not also be empowered to order payment of statutory interest if the instalments are duly paid, but the term is directed to the recovery of contractual and not statutory interest. I do not think that the term can be stigmatised as unfair on the ground that it violates or undermines a statutory regime enacted for the protection of consumers.

23. It is of course foreseeable that a borrower, no matter how honourable and realistic his intentions when entering into a credit agreement, may fall on hard times and find himself unable to honour his obligations. The bank's standard conditions recognise that possibility by providing for the contingency of default. The 1974 Act even more fully recognises that possibility, by providing for time orders to be made and providing that when a time order is made the terms of the underlying agreement may also be amended. These provisions are clearly framed for the relief not of the borrower who, having the means to meet his contractual obligations, chooses not to do so, but for the relief of those who cannot pay or cannot pay without more time. Properly applied, these provisions enable the undeserving borrower to be distinguished from the deserving and for the contractual obligations of the deserving to be re-drawn in terms which reasonably reflect such ability, if any, as he may then have to repay within a reasonable period. Where problems arise in practice, it appears to be because borrowers do not know of the effect of sections 129 and 136; neither the procedure for giving notice of default to the borrower nor the prescribed county court forms draw attention to them; and judgments will routinely be entered in the county court without the court considering whether to exercise its power under the sections.

24. I have no hesitation in accepting the proposition, inherent in the Director's submissions, that this situation is unacceptable. I have much greater difficulty in deciding whether the difficulties derive, as the Court of Appeal concluded, from the unfairness of the term or from the absence of procedural safeguards for the consumer at the stage of default. When the contract is made, default is a foreseeable contingency, not an expected outcome. It is not customary, even in consumer contracts, for notice to be given to the consumer of statutory reliefs open to him if he defaults. The 1974 Act does not require that notice of the effect of sections 129 and 136 be given. The evidence contains examples of clauses used by over 30 other lenders providing for the payment of interest after judgment, and none alerts the borrower to these potential grounds of relief. Regulation 4 is directed to the unfairness of a contract term, not the use which a supplier may make of a term which is in itself fair. It is readily understandable that a borrower may be disagreeably surprised if he finds that his contractual interest obligation continues to mount despite his duly paying the instalments ordered by the court, but it appears that the bank seeks to prevent that surprise by sending what is described in the evidence as a standard form of letter:

> "You need only pay the amount ordered by the Court under the terms of the judgment but you should be aware that under the terms of the agreement interest continues to accrue on your account.
> It is therefore in your interest to increase the instalment paid as soon as possible otherwise a much greater balance than the judgment debt may quickly build up."

On balance, I do not consider that the term can properly be said to cause a significant imbalance in the parties' rights and obligations under the contract to the detriment of the consumer in a manner or to an extent which is contrary to the requirement of good faith.

25. I do not think that the issues raised in this appeal raise any question on which the House requires a ruling from the European Court of Justice to enable it to give judgment and I would not accordingly order a reference to be made.

26. For the reasons I have given, and those given by each of my noble and learned friends, I would allow the bank's appeal with costs in the House and the Court of Appeal and restore the order of the judge.

27. In conclusion, I would add a footnote on sections 129 and 136 of the 1974 Act. In the course of argument the House was referred to the decision of the Court of Appeal in *Southern and District Finance Plc v Barnes and Barnes* and two related appeals reported at [1995] CCLR 62. The effect and interaction of sections 129 and 136 were there considered.

28. Of section 129 the court said (at p 68):

"When a time order is made, it should normally be made for a stipulated period on account of temporary financial difficulty. If, despite the giving of time, the debtor is unlikely to be able to resume repayment of the total indebtedness by at least the amount of the contractual instalments, no time order should be made. In such circumstances it will be more equitable to allow the regulated agreement to be enforced."

I would in general agree that time orders extending over very long periods of time are usually better avoided. But I note that the court dismissed an appeal against a judge who had rescheduled payments over a period of 15 years ("Though the judge's methods were robust and his reasoning economical, his instincts were sound and his order just": p 71), and the broad language of section 129 should be so construed as to permit the county court to make such order as seems to it just in all the circumstances.

29. Of section 136 the court said (at p 68):

"The court may include in a time order any amendment of the agreement, which it considers just to both parties, and which is a consequence of a term of the order . . ."

In the case already referred to the judge had ordered that no additional interest should be payable beyond that which had already accrued, and the Court of Appeal upheld his decision. It was right to do so: provided the amendment is a consequence of a term of the time order, the court should be ready to include in a time order any provision amending the agreement which it considers just to both parties.

LORD STEYN

My Lords,

30. This is the first occasion on which the House has had the opportunity to examine an important branch of consumer law. It is therefore appropriate to consider the framework in which the questions before the House must be considered.

31. As between the directive and the domestic implementing regulations, the former is the dominant text. Fortunately, the 1994 Regulations, and even more so the 1999 Regulations, appear to have implemented the directive in domestic law in a manner which ought not to cause serious difficulty. The purpose of the directive is twofold, viz the promotion of fair standard contract forms to improve the functioning of the European market place and the protection of consumers throughout the European Community. The directive is aimed at contracts of adhesion, viz "take it or leave it" contracts. It treats consumers as presumptively weaker parties and therefore fit for protection from abuses by stronger contracting parties. This is an objective which must throughout guide the interpretation of the directive as well as the implementing regulations. If contracting parties were able to avoid the application of the directive and regulations by exclusionary stipulations the regulatory scheme would be ineffective. The conclusion that the directive and regulations are mandatory is inescapable.

32. The directive is not an altogether harmonious text. It reflects the pragmatic compromises which were necessary to arrive at practical solutions between member states with divergent legal systems. But, despite some inelegance and untidiness in the text, the general principle that the construction must be adopted which promotes the effectiveness and practical value of the system ought to overcome difficulties. And the concepts of the directive must be given autonomous meanings so that there will be uniform application of the directive so far as is possible.

33. The directive made provision for a dual system of *ex casu* challenges and pre-emptive or collective challenges by appropriate bodies: see article 7. This system was domestically enacted in the 1994 Regulations, with the Director General of Fair Trading as the administering official to investigate and take action on complaints: see regulation 8. The 1999 Regulations extended the system of enforcement by including other bodies as qualified to undertake pre-emptive challenges. The system of pre-emptive challenges is a more effective way of preventing the continuing use of unfair terms and changing contracting practice than *ex casu* actions: see Susan Bright, "Winning the battle against unfair contract terms", (2000) 20 Legal Studies 331, 333–338. It is, however, to be noted that in a pre-emptive challenge there is not a direct *lis* between the consumer and the other contracting party. The directive and the Regulations do not always distinguish between the two situations. This point is illustrated by the emphasis in article 4.1 of the directive and regulation 4(2) on the

relevance of particular circumstances affecting a contractual relationship. The directive and the regulations must be made to work sensibly and effectively and this can only be done by taking into account the effects of contemplated or typical relationships between the contracting parties. Inevitably, the primary focus of such a pre-emptive challenge is on issues of substantive unfairness.

34. Under the Regulations, a term in a standard form contract that is unfair is not binding on the consumer. But certain provisions, sometimes called core terms, have been excepted from the regulatory regime. Regulation 3(2) so provides:

"In so far as it is in plain, intelligible language, no assessment shall be made of the fairness of any term which—(a) defines the main subject matter of the contract, or (b) concerns the adequacy of the price or remuneration, as against the goods or services sold or supplied."

Clause 8 of the contract, the only provision in dispute, is a default provision. It prescribes remedies which only become available to the lender upon the default of the consumer. For this reason the escape route of regulation 3(2) is not available to the bank. So far as the description of terms covered by regulation 3(2) as core terms is helpful at all, I would say that clause 8 of the contract is a subsidiary term. In any event, article 3(2) must be given a restrictive interpretation. Unless that is done article 3(2)(a) will enable the main purpose of the scheme to be frustrated by endless formalistic arguments as to whether a provision is a definitional or an exclusionary provision. Similarly, article 3(2)(b) dealing with "the adequacy of the price of remuneration" must be given a restrictive interpretation. After all, in a broad sense all terms of the contract are in some way related to the price or remuneration. That is not what is intended. Even price escalation clauses have been treated by the Director as subject to the fairness provision: see Susan Bright, loc. cit., at pp 345 and 349. It would be a gaping hole in the system if such clauses were not subject to the fairness requirement. For these further reasons I would reject the argument of the bank that regulation 3(2), and in particular 3(2)(b), take clause 8 outside the scope of the regulations.

35. Given these conclusions the attack on the merger principle mounted by the bank was misplaced. In any event, I am not willing to uphold criticism by the bank of the well tried and tested principle of merger. I would therefore reject the bank's submissions under this heading.

36. It is now necessary to refer to the provisions which prescribe how it should be determined whether a term is unfair. Implementing article 3(1) of the directive regulation 4(1) provides:

"'unfair term' means any term which contrary to the requirement of good faith causes a significant imbalance in the parties' rights and obligations under the contract to the detriment of the consumer."

There are three independent requirements. But the element of detriment to the consumer may not add much. But it serves to make clear that the directive is aimed at significant imbalance against the consumer, rather than the seller or supplier. The twin requirements of good faith and significant imbalance will in practice be determinative. Schedule 2 to the Regulations, which explains the concept of good faith, provides that regard must be had, amongst other things, to the extent to which the seller or supplier has dealt fairly and equitably with the consumer. It is an objective criterion. Good faith imports, as Lord Bingham has observed in his opinion, the notion of open and fair dealing: see also *Interfoto Picture Library Ltd v Stiletto Visual Programmes Ltd* [1989] QB 433. And helpfully the commentary to the 2000 edition of Principles of European Contract Law, prepared by the Commission of European Contract Law, explains that the purpose of the provision of good faith and fair dealing is "to enforce community standards of fairness and reasonableness in commercial transactions": at 113; *A fortiori* that is true of consumer transactions. Schedule 3 to the Regulations (which corresponds to the Annex to the directive) is best regarded as a check list of terms which must be regarded as potentially vulnerable. The examples given in Schedule 3 convincingly demonstrate that the argument of the bank that good faith is predominantly concerned with procedural defects in negotiating procedures cannot be sustained. Any purely procedural or even predominantly procedural interpretation of the requirement of good faith must be rejected.

37. That brings me to the element of significant imbalance. It has been pointed out by Hugh Collins that the test "of a significant imbalance of the obligations obviously directs attention to the substantive unfairness of the contract": "Good Faith in European Contract Law," (1994), 14 Oxford Journal of Legal Studies 229, 249. It is however, also right to say that there is a large area of overlap between the concepts of good faith and significant imbalance.

38. It is now necessary to turn to the application of these requirements to the facts of the present case. The point is a relatively narrow one. I agree that the starting point is that a lender ought to be able to recover interest at the contractual rate until the date of payment, and this applies both before and after judgment. On the other hand, counsel for the Director advanced a contrary argument. Adopting the test of asking what the position

of a consumer is in the contract under consideration with or without clause 8, he said that the consumer is in a significantly worse position than he would have been if there had been no such provision. Certainly, the consumer is worse off. The difficulty facing counsel, however, is that this disadvantage to the consumer appears to be the consequence not of clause 8 but of the County Courts (Interest on Judgment Debts) Order 1991. Under this Order no statutory interest is payable on a county court judgment given in proceedings to recover money due under a regulated agreement: see regulation 2. Counsel said that for policy reasons it was decided that in such a case no interest may be recovered after judgment. He said that it is not open to the House to criticise directly or indirectly this legal context. In these circumstances he submitted that it is not legitimate for a court to conclude that fairness requires that a lender must be able to insist on a stipulation designed to avoid the statutory regime under the 1991 Order. Initially I was inclined to uphold this policy argument. On reflection, however, I have been persuaded that this argument cannot prevail in circumstances where the legislature has neither expressly nor by necessary implication barred a stipulation that interest may continue to accrue after judgment until payment in full.

    39. For these reasons as well as the reasons given by Lord Bingham I agree that clause 8 is not unfair and I would also make the order which Lord Bingham proposes.

For at least three reasons, the *First National Bank* case is important: first, it offers some general guidance on the meaning of good faith; secondly, it signals that standard form dealers will not readily persuade a court that the fairness of their terms should be immune from review on the ground that any assessment will, so to speak, trespass on the main subject matter of the contract or concern the adequacy of the price or remuneration; and, thirdly, it cautions that, even if subject to review, the terms in question might survive scrutiny for their fairness. However, the second of these points needs to be read in the light of the subsequent much-publicised challenge—in *Office of Fair Trading v Abbey National Plc* (below)—to the fairness of the charges levied by retail banks for overdrafts and the like.

    Briefly, in the early years of the present century, it was commonly claimed that a number of charges made by the retail banks—for example, the charges levied where an account became overdrawn or an instruction for payment was given when there were insufficient funds in the account to cover the payment—were unfair and excessive. As the chorus of customer complaints grew, many individual litigants began proceedings against the banks and, following complaints made to it, the Office of Fair Trading (OFT) started a formal investigation into the fairness of terms relating to the banks' overdraft charges. Against the banks, it was pleaded principally (i) that the terms authorising the charges were unfair relative to the Unfair Terms in Consumer Contracts Regulations 1999 and (ii) that the charges themselves were penal (for penalties, see Ch.19 above). However, in response, the banks argued that the charges were simply part of the overall service package that they entered into with their customers; and that under Regulation 6(2) of the 1999 Regulations, subject to being in plain intelligible language, these were terms that were not to be assessed for their fairness. They were so excluded, the banks argued, because (in the language of the Regulation) they were terms that related "(a) to the definition of the main subject matter of the contract or (b) to the adequacy of the price or remuneration, as against the goods or services supplied in exchange."

    In 2007, in order to resolve the issue, and in accordance with written agreements reached between the OFT and the banks, the OFT issued proceedings in the Commercial Court seeking a declaration that Regulation 6(2) did not apply to the banks' Relevant Terms that were then current. After a 14-day hearing early in 2008, Andrew Smith J (agreeing with the OFT) held that assessment of the fairness of the Relevant Terms was not excluded by Regulation 6(2); he also held that the charges did not amount to common law penalties: see [2008] EWHC 875 (Comm). Broadly speaking, the Court of Appeal agreed with Andrew Smith J that the Relevant Terms did not fall within the exemption given by Regulation 6(2): see [2009] EWCA Civ 116. However, on final appeal, the Supreme Court unanimously ruled otherwise: the fairness of the banks' Relevant Terms was not open for assessment—or, at any rate, it was not open to review the fairness of the charges (qua prices or remuneration) as against the services supplied in exchange; the banks' package of services and charges fell within the exclusionary scope of the Regulation.

Two extracts from the *Abbey National* litigation follow. First, a long part of Andrew Smith J's extremely long judgment is extracted so that the way in which the parties sought to characterise the banks' charges can be fully appreciated. In the extract, the focus is on the following matters: (i) the interpretation of the relationship between reg.6(2)(a) [main subject matter of the contract] and 6(2)(b) [price or remuneration against goods or services supplied in exchange]; (ii) whether, for the purposes of reg.6(2)(b), the banks supply services when they consider an instruction for payment, or when they actually pay on such an instruction; (iii) the meaning of price or remuneration, and of adequacy, in reg.6(2)(b); and (iv) a trio of arguments (whole package, specific services, and specific contract) presented by the banks with a view to depicting the charges at issue in a way that would bring them within the description of reg.6(2)(b). Despite the sophisticated arguments presented by the banks, it was held that the terms relating to the charges at issue were not exempt from assessment under the Regulations. The second extract is from the Supreme Court where, as we have said, a different view was taken.

OFFICE OF FAIR TRADING v ABBEY NATIONAL PLC

High Court [2008] EWHC 875 (Comm)

MR JUSTICE ANDREW SMITH

Introduction

1. This action is about charges made by banks to their customers who have personal current accounts with them when they are requested or instructed to make a payment for which they do not hold the necessary funds in the account and which is not covered by a facility arranged with the customer. I shall refer to such requests or instructions as "Relevant Instructions", and to the charges as "Relevant Charges". I shall refer to the terms in the standard form contracts between bank and customer providing for the Relevant Charges as "Relevant Terms".

2. The Relevant Terms and Relevant Charges are being challenged on two fronts: the Office of Fair Trading (the "OFT") is investigating under the Unfair Terms in Consumer Contracts Regulations 1999 (the "1999 Regulations") the fairness of the terms under which banks make such charges, and cases have been brought by individual customers in county courts disputing charges levied by banks, many of them relying not only on the 1999 Regulations but also on common law rules about the unenforceability of penalties.

3. The claimant in these proceedings is the OFT. It is a "general enforcer" under section 213(1) of the Enterprise Act 2002, and therefore entitled under section 215(2) of the Act to apply for an enforcement order in respect of a domestic or a Community infringement (a Community infringement being an act or omission which harms the collective interests of consumers and which inter alia contravenes a listed Directive as given effect by the laws, regulations or administrative process of a state belonging to the European Economic Area), and specifically the Office of Fair Trading has a duty under the 1999 Regulations (subject to irrelevant exceptions) to consider any complaint made to it that any contract terms drawn up for general use are unfair. In March 2007 the OFT announced that it was to conduct "a formal investigation into the fairness of bank current account charges", and is considering whether to exercise its function under the 2002 Act to seek an enforcement order. It is perhaps worth emphasising that the OFT has not reached any conclusions about the fairness of the Relevant Charges or other matters that it is investigating. Mr Cavendish Elithorn, the OFT's Senior Director of Service Sectors, explained in his evidence that among the questions that the OFT is considering and wishes to continue to consider are (i) whether the Relevant Charges are sufficiently transparent and predictable for consumers; (ii) whether the Relevant Charges are too high; and (iii) whether the Relevant Charges operate fairly in relation to the individual customer (given that, as Mr. Elithorn says, the charges are borne by a minority of customers and bear no relationship to the costs of providing corresponding overdrafts but support the profitability of the current account service generally). He emphasises that the OFT is not only looking at the amount of the Relevant Charges, but at how they apply, how they are presented to the individual customer

22–015

and their impact on customers. The objection has been raised that the Relevant Charges are not subject to assessment under the 1999 Regulations.

4. These proceedings are against seven companies who, themselves or through one or more subsidiaries, operate banks and against the Nationwide Building Society, a mutual building society. I shall refer to the eight defendants simply as "the Banks". They represent, I was told, nine of the twelve members of the Cheque and Credit Clearing Company, and all operate large numbers of personal current accounts. Clydesdale, who, I understand, has the smallest share of the market, has some 2.4 million personal customers in the United Kingdom.

5. The proceedings were brought on 27 July 2007 after the OFT and seven of the Banks had made a Litigation Agreement dated 25 July 2007, to which the Financial Services Authority ("FSA") was also party, and The Royal Bank of Scotland Group Plc ("RBSG") had made a separate but similar agreement with the OFT and the FSA on 26 July 2007. The recitals to the Litigation Agreement refer to the OFT's investigation into "certain terms contained in each Bank's personal current account arrangements providing for charges to be imposed upon customers who seek to make payments for which they do not have available funds", and the proceedings brought by customers against the Banks. They go on to record the belief of the OFT and the Banks that the legal issues that have been raised in relation to the Banks' terms need to be resolved expeditiously and in a fair and orderly way, and to express concern about the scale of the litigation brought by customers. The OFT recognises the "desirability of achieving a fair and orderly resolution of the relevant issues" and agrees not to object to any request or application for a stay of other court proceedings between the Banks and their customers about the charges made by banks. I understand that, at least for the most part, the customers' litigation has not been proceeding pending the determination of issues raised in these proceedings.

6. The OFT identifies four basic categories of Relevant Charges about which it is concerned: Unpaid Item Charges; Paid Item Charges; Overdraft Excess Charges; and Guaranteed Paid Item Charges. An Unpaid Item Charge is, as the OFT pleads, "levied when the customer gives an instruction for payment or, in some cases at least, withdrawal, that the bank declines to honour because the customer does not have sufficient funds in his account" or, I would add here and in relation to other charges, an arranged facility which covers it. A Paid Item Charge is "levied when the customer gives an instruction for payment or, in some cases at least, withdrawal, for which he has insufficient funds in his account and which the bank honours". An Overdraft Excess Charge is "levied if, during a specified period (typically a day or a month) . . . an account is and/or goes overdrawn (and there is no overdraft facility), or . . . the debit balance is and/or goes above the limit on an existing overdraft facility, and in both cases irrespective of the reason why the excess has occurred". A Guaranteed Paid Item Charge refers to a charge distinct from a Paid Item Charge which some of the Banks levy when they honour "in accordance with the guarantee, a cheque issued in conjunction with a cheque guarantee card (or, in the case of some banks, a debit card payment made under a guaranteed debit payment system) for which the customer does not have sufficient funds".

7. The relief that the OFT seeks in these proceedings is directed to establishing whether the investigation falls within the ambit of the 1999 Regulations. Specifically, it seeks a declaration that

> "the Relevant Terms and Charges in Current Agreements (and to the extent relied on by the banks, in Historical Agreements) are not excluded from an assessment for fairness under the 1999 Regulations by reason of Regulation 6(2)(a) and/or (b) thereof . . ."

8. The focus of the OFT's concern is upon the Banks' current agreements, the standard form terms that the Banks now use when a customer opens an account with them and that they have introduced into their contracts with existing customers.

9. The Banks bring counterclaims in the proceedings which (i) are directed not only to current terms but also to standard form terms which they have used in the past, "historical terms" as they have been called; (ii) are directed not only to the application and effect of the 1999 Regulations but also to whether their (current and historical) terms include penalties and so to that extent are unenforceable at common law; and (iii) are concerned with the proper approach to the assessment contemplated by the 1999 Regulations of whether a term is to be regarded as unfair and in particular the reference in Regulation 5(1) to a term being "contrary to the requirement of good faith". The Banks hope that these proceedings might not only determine whether the OFT's investigation is proper but also provide guidance about the law applicable to the claims brought by individual customers . . .

331. *Is the fairness of the Relevant Terms excluded from the assessment because they "relate . . . to the adequacy of the price or remuneration, as against the goods or services supplied in exchange"?*

332. I come to the question whether no assessment of fairness of the Relevant Terms is permitted because it would "relate . . . to the adequacy of the price or remuneration, as against the goods or services supplied in exchange" under Regulation 6(2). The Banks say that Regulation 6(2)(b) applies to the Relevant Terms. (Although the pleadings refer at times also to Regulation 6(2)(a), none of the Banks argued that they could succeed in an argument based on Regulation 6(2)(a) if Regulation 6(2)(b) does not cover the Relevant Terms.)

333. The Banks put their case that the Relevant Charges are the price or remuneration, or part of the price or remuneration, for services that they supply principally in two alternative (but not mutually inconsistent) ways. First, they say that they supply to their current account customers a "bundle" or "package" of services which enables customers to manage their day-to-day finances, and this includes services whereby customers can, without making prior arrangements, request an overdraft by issuing a payment instruction which, if executed, would create or increase borrowing from the Bank, that is to say, in the terminology that I have adopted, a Relevant Instruction; and where the Bank chooses to grant such a request (or is committed to do so because a cheque guarantee card has been used or for some other reason) customers can borrow from the Bank on its standard terms. The Relevant Charges, together with other revenue in particular from interest paid by customers on borrowing and the use of credit balances in customers' accounts, are the price or remuneration for the package of services. I shall refer to this as the "whole package" argument. Secondly, the "specific services" argument is advanced: that, if the Relevant Charges are not to be regarded as part of the price or remuneration for the package of services supplied by the Banks to customers with current accounts, then they are the price or remuneration for some part of those services, that is to say for the services or a service supplied in connection with borrowing requests where no facility has been arranged in advance.

334. In response, the OFT argues that the Relevant Charges do not fall within Regulation 6(2)(b). Its main contentions include:

i)   That Regulation 6(2)(b) is directed to the main subject matter of the contract between a customer and a seller or supplier. It covers only what can properly be treated as the price or remuneration for the main subject matter of the contract, and, the OFT contends, the Relevant Charges cannot properly be said to be the price or remuneration for the main subject matter of the contract, and the Relevant Terms are not to do with the main subject matter of the contract.

ii) That in any event, even if the application of Regulation 6(2)(b) is not confined to the main subject matter of the contract, Regulation 6(2)(b) does not cover every payment which falls to be made by the consumer in a contract for goods or services but only payments that can properly be regarded as a "price or remuneration" and for which "goods or services" are "supplied in exchange".

iii) That Regulation 6(2)(b) precludes only assessment of the "adequacy" of a price or remuneration.

335. The Banks dispute both stages of the OFT's first argument. They argue that on its proper interpretation Regulation 6(2)(b) is not to do with only the main subject matter of the contract, and does not only apply where the price or remuneration is paid in exchange for the main subject matter of the contract or where the terms providing for the price or remuneration are part of the main subject matter. And the Banks also say that in fact the Relevant Charges are paid for the main subject matter of the contract between a Bank and its customer for the operation of the current account, and the Relevant Terms are part of the contract's main subject matter.

336. Two further arguments have been advanced in answer to the OFT's contentions.

i)   The first concerns whether the Relevant Terms and the Relevant Charges are to do with the main subject matter of the contract (assuming this question to arise on the proper construction of the 1999 Regulations). Mr Vos responded to the OFT's argument about this as follows: if it be right to restrict the application of Regulation 6(2)(b) as the OFT contends, the essential characteristics of a current account contract change according to whether the account is in credit or debit and this must be recognised when identifying its main subject matter.

ii) Some (but not all) of the Banks advanced what I shall call the "specific contract" argument: that when a Bank grants a customer a loan by way of unarranged overdraft, it enters into a specific contract with him in relation to that transaction (albeit a specific contract made against the background of the general contract governing their banking relationship as a whole) and the main subject matter of that specific contract is the Bank's service of providing a loan, the price for which is a Relevant Charge (or Relevant Charges). They extend this argument to cover the position when the Bank decides not to allow the customer an unarranged overdraft.

337. The OFT submits that it is for the Banks to show that the Relevant Terms fall within the exceptions from assessment for fairness under the 1999 Regulations. This seems to me correct, being in accordance with the

general principle that he who asserts must prove ("Ei qui affirmat non ei qui negat incumbit probatio": *Joseph Constantine SS Line Ltd v Imperial Smelting Corp Ltd* [1942] AC 154 at p.174 per Visc. Maugham), but my decision on this, and other questions, has not depended upon where the burden of proof lies.

Is Regulation 6(2) to be interpreted "conjunctively" or "disjunctively"?

338. I first consider the meaning and effect of Regulation 6(2), and whether it applies only where the "price or remuneration" or where the "goods or services supplied in exchange" for it are the main subject matter of the contract. The OFT submits that Regulation 6(2)(a) and 6(2)(b) are "two sides of the same coin": the former excludes from assessment the definition of the main subject matter being supplied, and the latter excludes the price or remuneration that the consumer is paying for the goods or services forming the main subject matter so defined (and, they add, even then some terms relating to the price or remuneration are open to assessment). The Banks dispute this, arguing that Regulation 6(2)(b) applies to any term that relates to the adequacy of the price (or part of the price) paid by customers for services supplied by the Banks under their agreement with their customers, whether or not they are or form part of the "main subject matter" of the contract.

339. This difference was characterised by the Banks as a choice between a "conjunctive" interpretation of the 1999 Regulations whereby Regulation 6(2)(b) is limited in its application to terms relating to the price or remuneration paid in exchange for services that fall within Regulation 6(2)(a) and a "disjunctive" interpretation whereby the two parts of the Regulation 6(2) are interpreted independently. Although these are convenient labels which I shall adopt, this distinction does not, to my mind, convey the real flavour of the OFT's argument, which is that the requirement to limit the application of Regulation 6(2)(b) is driven not by the wording of Regulation 6 but in order to recognise the purpose of the 1999 Regulations generally and the reason for the exclusions from assessment contained in Regulation 6(2) specifically.

340. The Banks submit that a disjunctive interpretation is required both by the policy and by the language and wording of the 1999 Regulations; and that a conjunctive interpretation would be impossible to apply in practice.

341. As for language and wording, I agree that Regulation 6(2)(a) and Regulation 6(2)(b) provide for two separate exemptions from assessment of fairness, and the reference to "the main subject matter" in Regulation 6(2)(a) does not on its face limit the effect of Regulation 6(2)(b). The two provisions are linked by the conjunction "or", and within Regulation 6(2)(b) the phrase "the goods and services supplied" is not qualified. This reflects the Directive in that Article 4(2) provides that "Assessment of the unfair nature of the terms shall relate neither to the definition of the main subject matter of the contract nor to the adequacy of the price or remuneration, on the one hand, as against services or goods supplied in exchange, on the other . . .". The Banks support their argument by referring to the "greylist" in schedule 2 to the 1999 Regulations. None of the terms in schedule 2 is an example of a term providing for payment for a peripheral part of the customer's purchase.

342. As for the practical application of the exception in Regulation 6(2)(b), the Banks say that it would be impossible to restrict the Regulation to the assessment of the price or remuneration for the main subject matter of the contract in those (certainly not uncommon) cases where a simple undifferentiated charge is made for a collection of goods or services, some of which are at the heart of the bargain and others of relatively minor importance.

343. I should refer to a further argument adduced in support of the disjunctive interpretation: the Banks point out that retail banking is subject to other regulatory controls: that it is regulated in respect of deposit taking under the Financial Services and Markets Act 2000; that it is subject to the jurisdiction conferred on the OFT and the Competition Commission by the Competition Act 1998 and the Enterprise Act 2002; and that the Banking Code includes a commitment by banks subscribing to it (as all eight defendant Banks do) to give customers details of any charges for the day-to-day running of the account upon opening an account (section 5.1) and to give at least 30 days' notice of any increase in the charges (section 5.3). For my part, I do not find this point compelling: I cannot accept that the particular regime for controlling competition and protecting consumers found in the United Kingdom should inform the interpretation of the Directive, which is to be given an autonomous meaning, or of the 1999 Regulations, which are to be interpreted harmoniously with the Directive.

344. However, I accept the Banks' other arguments that Regulation 6(2) is not to be given a conjunctive interpretation in as much as they demonstrate that there is no proper justification for importing the phrase "main subject matter" of the contract from Regulation 6(2)(a) and introducing it by inference into Regulation 6(2)(b). Neither the structure nor the language of Regulation 6(2) justifies that. Moreover the policy of the 1999 Regulations is not only to protect consumers but also to facilitate the establishment of the internal market and to promote competition. But it by no means follows that Regulation 6(2)(b) prohibits an assessment of any

term that relates to a payment by way of price or remuneration under a consumer contract or to its adequacy. Accordingly, while rejecting a conjunctive interpretation of the Regulation in this narrow sense, I must still consider the proper limits of the application of Regulation 6(2)(b).

The restrictive interpretation of Regulation 6(2)

345. The starting place is the speeches in the *First National Bank* case . . . [Having reviewed the speeches in *First National Bank* and the opinion of Advocate General Tizzano in *Codifis SA v Jean-Louis Fredout*, Case C–473/00, Andrew Smith J continued:]

358. The question whether a term falls within Regulation 6(2)(b) is not answered simply according to whether or not it is a default provision. It requires broader consideration of the substance of the provision and the part that the term plays in the contract, and of whether it is directly to do with a payment that is properly within the expression, "the price or remuneration". Thus it is necessary to consider both the nature of the payment and how directly the term is directed to defining the payment obligation.

Do the Banks supply "services" when they process, but do not pay upon, a Relevant Instruction?

359. Undoubtedly the Banks supply their current account customers with services. Regulation 6 proceeds on the basis that every contract to which the 1999 Regulations apply is concluded for goods or services, and there is no dispute that the 1999 Regulations do apply to the contract between each of the Banks and its current account customers.

360. It is inherent in the characteristics of a current account that the services provided by a bank to a current account customer include that of receiving money, cheques and payments by other means into the account, making payments in accordance with the customer's instructions and maintaining a running account upon which there will be a credit or debit balance. If the running account produces a debit balance, the provision by the bank of a loan on a current account is, as a matter of ordinary language, the provision of a service. This would be so whether or not the contract governing the relationship between the bank and the current account customer obliges the bank to allow the customer to borrow.

361. The Banks seek to extend this statement of the services provided on a current account. They argue that a service is provided to customers when a Bank receives a payment instruction even if it does not pay in accordance with it, in particular if it does not do so because the customer does not have sufficient funds or an adequate facility to cover it and it declines to lend in order to pay in accordance with the instruction. The argument was formulated in various ways. It was said that services are provided in these circumstances because the customer chooses to avail himself of them and they are supplied under the general umbrella of the current account contract, it being nothing to the point whether the Bank is obliged to provide the services. Another formulation was that the Bank provides "services" because, viewed at the time that the current account contract between bank and customer is made, the Bank undertakes a commitment to deal with payment instructions that it receives. It is not important which formulation is preferred, but for my part I do not think that it is a necessary characteristic of "services" within the meaning of the 1999 Regulations that the supplier contractually undertook to provide them. In the case of an estate agent, for example, the introduction of a prospective purchaser is a service even if the agent is under no contractual obligation to introduce one, or even to try to do so.

362. It is said by the Banks that they supply a service when they receive Relevant Instructions because they consider whether to make a payment, and more generally it is said that they supply a service because they deal with the instruction in accordance with standard banking procedures and, it might be, also provide additional services such as communicating to the customer the decision not to pay upon the instruction and any Relevant Charges Incurred. If (contrary to my own view) it matters whether services are provided pursuant to a contractual obligation, all of the Banks are obliged to deal with Relevant Instructions in accordance with proper banking procedures: as I have said, some but not all of the Banks expressly commit themselves to considering any Relevant Instructions that they receive before refusing payment . . .

370. There can be no fixed rule as to whether or not distinct and preliminary acts done by a seller or supplier with a view to supplying or deciding whether to supply the benefit which the consumer ultimately seeks are "services" within the meaning of the 1999 Regulations. Sometimes where the customer requests the preliminary or preparatory act (for example, an architect is engaged to produce preliminary drawings), that clearly will be a service in its own right. Equally clearly, the provision of a service might not necessarily provide the consumer with the benefit that he seeks: a doctor might fail to cure but he still provides medical services. But in these cases it is at least easy to see that something is "supplied" to the consumer. In the case of the customer giving a Relevant Instruction, the customer is seeking payment in accordance with it, not that the Bank simply considers making payment, and that is reflected in the terms of the seven Banks (other than Nationwide)

whose terms are drafted by reference to a request (or deemed request) on the part of the customer for an overdraft. In view of this and given that the customer receives no actual benefit from his Bank considering his instruction or request for payment and declining to accede to it, I am unable to accept that what the Bank does when it deals with a Relevant Instruction upon which it does not make payment is properly described as "services" and unable to accept that anything can properly be said to be "supplied" to the customer. Moreover, even if the Banks' processes of considering and processing Relevant Instructions short of paying them, or with a view to deciding whether to pay, could, in any sense, be described as services supplied to the customer, the real and essential service supplied by the Banks under their contracts with customers is that of paying upon the customer's instruction, and the Banks' procedures whereby they deal with Relevant Instructions before making payments or when they decide not to pay are ancillary to and incidental to the service of paying in accordance with the mandate.

371. I should add that it was argued by some of the Banks that when a Bank decides not to pay upon a Relevant Instruction, it provides a service, at least in some cases, by way of informing the customer of the position. The decision might involve the Bank in other procedures: for example, returning a cheque through the clearing system in accordance with the rules of the clearing house. These activities, in my view, are no more than the incidental consequences of the Bank's decision, and I am unable to regard them as services supplied to the customer. Further, on any view they are, again, ancillary or incidental activities.

372. I therefore accept the OFT's submission that if a Bank declines to pay upon a Relevant Instruction, it supplies no, or no relevant, services by way of considering, processing or otherwise dealing with it.

Do the Banks supply "services" when they pay upon a Relevant Instruction?

373. The OFT argues that when a Bank pays upon a Relevant Instruction it does not provide a "service" such as contemplated by Regulation 6(2) because the provision of overdrafts, or at least the provision of unarranged overdrafts, is not among the essential features of a personal current account. It points out, and I accept, that customers have no right to borrow by way of an unarranged overdraft; that it is not a reliable way of making payments and is expensive; that many customers never give Relevant Instructions and they represent a small proportion of the payment instructions given to banks by personal current account customers; and that unarranged overdrafts are discouraged by many of the Banks, and are not generally promoted as a feature of current accounts. The OFT also argues Relevant Instructions might well be the result of error on the part of the customer, if not improper behaviour, but here it seems to me to overstate its contention: see paragraph 60 above.

374. None of this means that a Bank does not supply its customer with services when it makes a payment in accordance with a Relevant Instruction. The OFT's argument is, to my mind, flawed because it focuses not upon what the Bank does, but upon the state of the customer's account when the Bank processes the instruction. Clearly, it is a central feature of a current account that the bank makes payments in accordance with the customer's instructions (or, as it might be said, supplies payment services). When a Bank pays upon a Relevant Instruction, it is doing just that. It is true that it is doing so in particular circumstances, but that does not change the essential character of what the Bank does. Nor is that altered because the Bank goes through additional processes before making the payment because the customer did not have available funds or facilities.

375. For similar reasons, it seems to me that the provision of an unarranged overdraft is part of the essential services supplied by a bank operating current accounts. It is an essential part of the bargain whereby a bank operates a current account that it keeps a running account of receipts into and payments from the account, and necessarily the account shows a credit or debit balance for the customer (or a nil balance). If it shows a debit balance for the customer, it of course means that the bank is allowing the customer to borrow on the account (or supplying lending services), but I am unable to accept that that in itself means that the activities of the bank have extended outside the essential services of the contract under which the current account is operated. This is so whether or not the customer's borrowing takes place without or in excess of a facility arranged in advance between bank and customer. The characterisation of what the Bank provides as an "unarranged overdraft" seems to me to define it with too great a degree of particularity for the purpose of deciding whether the Bank is supplying a service within the meaning of Regulation 6(2).

376. The point can be illustrated by an argument advanced by Mr Snowden on behalf of HSBC. If a bank operates current accounts free of charges when the credit balance is more than, say, £100, then the logic of the OFT's position would suggest that, if the bank pays upon instructions that take the balance of the account below £100 without taking the account into debit, its services are not "incidental" to those essential to a contract for a current account and so fall within the ambit of Regulation 6(2), but the position would be different if a payment takes the account into debit. This would, to my mind, be a surprising distinction.

377. I therefore reject the argument that the services of making payment upon a Relevant Instruction and of providing an unarranged overdraft are not services of a kind relevant for the purposes of Regulation 6(2) because they are incidental or ancillary to the essential bargain between the parties.

378. In view of this conclusion, the Banks do not need to rely upon the alternative argument advanced by Mr Vos that the services provided in response to a Relevant Instruction are within Regulation 6(2) because, upon proper analysis, they form part of the main subject matter of the contract. However, I shall deal with it briefly . . .

382. . . . I shall therefore not express a concluded view about Mr Vos' argument, and only say that, if I had thought that the Banks were not supplying "services" when paying upon Relevant Instructions and extending credit to customers accordingly, then I would have seen great force in the submission that the main subject matter of the contract must be determined in light of whether the account is in credit or debit and in light of whether the terms of the contract between bank and customer have been supplemented in the way explained by Professor Goode.

383. I therefore conclude that the Banks supply to current account customers services within the meaning of the 1999 Regulations when they pay in accordance with a payment instruction regardless of whether it is a Relevant Instruction and involves the Bank in carrying out additional procedures and when they operate the running account with a debit balance, that is to say, when they allow borrowing on the account, regardless of whether the borrowing is by way of an unarranged overdraft. However, this does not mean that it is irrelevant to the application of Regulation 6(2)(b) that charges are levied for carrying out payment instructions and allowing borrowing only when the instructions are Relevant Instructions and the borrowing is by way of unarranged overdraft. It is relevant to whether the Relevant Charges are covered by Regulation 6(2)(b).

The meaning of "the price or remuneration".

384. I move from consideration of what "services" are supplied by the Banks to the meaning of the phrase "the price or remuneration" in Regulation 6(2)(b)—or "the price and remuneration", as it is put in article 4 of the Directive. It is a compendious expression, and it is not helpful to analyse minutely its individual components. Just as Regulation 6 proceeds on the basis that every contract to which the 1999 Regulations apply is concluded for goods and services, so too, it seems to me, it supposes that the seller or supplier will receive a price or remuneration under it (and Regulation 6(2)(b) refers to "the" price or remuneration, not "a" price or remuneration.) While the expression "the price or remuneration" must not be interpreted so narrowly as to prevent this, it does not mean that every payment for which a consumer might be liable under the terms of his contract is a "price or remuneration" the adequacy of which is exempt from assessment.

385. The question is whether a payment falls "squarely" within Regulation 6(2) of the 1999 Regulations so that its exemption is justified by the purpose of respecting the parties' freedom of contract about the price/quality ratio as at the time when the bargain was made. The wording of the 1999 Regulations, reinforced, I think, by the connotation of the very terms "price" and "remuneration" (whether taken individually or together), confines the application of Regulation 6(2)(b) to payments that can properly be said to be payable by way of exchange. Of course, in a broad sense every contractual payment (at least in the case of contracts supported by consideration rather than those made by deed) is payable in exchange for a promise or the receipt of what the law recognises as a benefit. However, it seems to me that the 1999 Regulations contemplate something clearly recognisable as an exchange such as will typically be at the core of a consumer contract.

386. This does not mean that the payment must be in exchange for the benefit for which the consumer hoped or which was his reason for making the contract. The Banks pointed out that payments by students applying for university or, more parochially, by barristers applying for silk are payments made in consideration of the relevant bodies considering their applications and not for the success for which applicants no doubt hope. Depending upon the terms of the particular arrangements, commission to an estate agent might well be payable for the introduction of a potential purchaser although at some stage the sale falls through. The consumer, although ultimately disappointed, receives services in exchange for the payment, and I would regard these payments as falling within Regulation 6(2)(b).

387. The OFT drew a distinction between what is payable by a consumer by way of the price or remuneration and what he might pay upon a contingency or the happening of an event. The point cannot be pressed too far. A price or remuneration might be payable only contingently. Again, the estate agent example illustrates this: in a case such as *Bairstow Eves* (cit sup) the commission is payable in exchange for the introduction of a potential purchase, but payable only if a contract for purchase is made. If the only consideration that the seller or supplier receives under the contract is a promise of payment upon a contingent event, the more likely the payment will be recognisable as the price or remuneration—the typical consumer will expect to have to pay something by way of the price or remuneration under the contract. However, the Relevant Charges are not the

only "payment" that current account customers make—the essential nature of the bank/customer relationship is that of debtor and creditor, the customer either giving the bank use of his money or if he is in debit paying interest to the bank. If (as here) the seller or supplier receives other benefits under the contract, the more likely the contingent nature of payments such as the Relevant Charges will make them less recognisable as the price or remuneration and the less likely they will fall within Regulation 6(2)(b).

388. I have referred to the need for a "recognisable" exchange between the service that the customer receives and what he is to pay. This reflects a submission of the OFT that the issues that arise under Regulation 6(2) are to be considered from the point of view of the typical consumer. In the *First National Bank* case Lord Bingham (cit sup at para 20) said that, in judging the fairness of the term, it is necessary to consider the position of typical parties when the contract is made. Lord Steyn (at para 33) referred to the need to take into account "the effects of contemplated or typical relationships between the contracting parties" in order to make the Directive and the 1999 Regulations work sensibly and effectively. It is an extension of this approach to consider the position of the typical consumer when deciding whether Regulation 6(2) applies to a term (although I observe in passing that it reflects the approach of Evans-Lombe J. at first instance in the *First National Bank* case, [2000] 1 WLR 98 at p.103C–E), and it would be a narrowing of the test if the position of the typical consumer were considered to the exclusion of that of the typical seller or supplier. That said, I consider that the question whether typical parties to a transaction of the kind under consideration would recognise a payment as the price or remuneration is a useful guide as to whether a payment falls within the Regulation, and I cannot accept the submission made on behalf of RBSG that this would lead to different answers for different customers or groups of customers. As RBSG itself said and as I have already observed, the concept of an "average consumer . . . who is reasonably well informed and reasonably observant and circumspect" is a concept often used in applying and interpreting European consumer law, and to my mind it is an appropriate guide as to whether a payment is the price or remuneration within the meaning of the 1999 Regulations. Of course, it does not displace the need for the court to examine and respect the terms of the parties' contract. After all, as Lightman J. observed in *Wire TV Ltd v Cable Tel (UK) Ltd*, [1998] CLC 244 at p.258, when construing an agreement which is not a sham (and I do not consider that any of the Relevant Terms could be so described), the court recognises that the parties might have a choice as to how a contract is structured and pays appropriate respect to the structure adopted by the parties. Nevertheless, the question whether a payment is the price or remuneration depends upon the substance of the agreement between the parties and the true nature of the payment rather than upon how it is described or presented, and it would, I think, be surprising if the court felt able to conclude that a payment is the price or remuneration within Regulation 6(2)(b) even though the typical consumer would not recognise it as such when presented with the terms of the seller or supplier.

389. Against this background, I accept the submission of the OFT that a payment is likely to be the less recognisable as the price or remuneration for services supplied if it is payable only in circumstances which might well not happen and which both parties are likely to hope will not come about. I also accept that a payment is the more likely to be recognisable as the price or remuneration payable in exchange for services supplied if it can readily be understood when and what is payable.

390. The requirement that a payment be, and be recognisable as, the price or remuneration paid in exchange for services does not provide a bright-line as to what falls within Regulation 6(2). This is a question of evaluation of the facts of the particular case.

The "adequacy of the price or remuneration"

391. Regulation 6(2)(b) does not exempt all terms that relate to the price or remuneration, but only terms that relate to its "adequacy". Recognising that an exempted term has to relate directly to this, Mr Rabinowitz suggested that Regulation 6(2)(b) is directed to terms which *specify* the price, but does not cover terms that state the *method* by which the price is determined, a distinction that, I confess, I find rather elusive in its application. However, it is not necessary for the purposes of this case to decide whether terms that state the method by which the price or remuneration is determined necessarily fall outside Regulation 6(2)(b), and if so, how they are to be distinguished from terms that specify the price or remuneration. On any view the Relevant Terms deal directly with payments that the Banks claim from customers as Relevant Charges. The significance of Mr Rabinowitz's submission, to my mind, is that, first, it recognises the importance of giving effect to the reference to the "adequacy" of the price or remuneration; secondly it reflects a properly restrictive approach to interpreting the exemption from assessment under the 1999 Regulations; and thirdly, it illustrates that the precise ambit of the exemption is not susceptible of precise definition: there is no litmus test as to the application of the general principles explained in the speeches in the *First National Bank* case.

392. The Banks emphasise that it is not only terms that relate to the level of the price that are exempted

from assessment under Regulation 6(2)(b). They say that it covers all terms which bear directly upon the economic value of what is to be paid, and that includes, at least, the timing and frequency of payment. Indeed Mr Snowden, on behalf of HSBC, submitted that it "must include all terms that provide for the incidence, amount, currency, timing, frequency, and place and manner of payments because all in their interrelated way affect the burden that is placed on the consumer and the benefit to the supplier in exchange". It seems to me that this overstates the point: this formula would include provisions that (for example, the place of payment) would not typically directly impact on the economic value of what the consumer agreed to pay as at the date of the contract. It also would cover, I think, provisions such as condition 15.7 of Lloyds TSB's terms (at para 244 above), which Mr Thanki rightly recognised is not protected from assessment by Regulation 6(2): that is to say, a term providing that the Bank may take interest and charges from any account of the customer, this relating to the manner of payment. However, I accept that the expression "relate . . . to the adequacy of the price or remuneration" not only includes what relates to the amount of the price or remuneration but also covers when and in what circumstances it is payable in so far as they affect the economic value or cost of what is to be paid.

393. In the *First National Bank* case, Lord Rodger (cit sup at para 64) observed that the words corresponding to "adequacy" that are used in the French and German texts of the Directive are "adéquation" and "Angemessenheit". He said that, "Both may suggest what is in issue is the "appropriateness" of the price or remuneration as compared with the services or goods—in other words whether there is an equivalence between the services or goods and the consideration for them". The references in recital 19 to the "quality/price ratio" and the "price/ quality ratio" have similar connotations. Hence, Lord Rodger was concerned that the term "adequacy" loses some of its significance if it is understood simply to mean "the extent of the remuneration", a phrase used by Evans-Lombe J. in his first instance judgment (cit sup at p.107B–C): it requires comparison of what is paid by the consumer with what he receives.

394. This connotation of "adequacy" is reinforced in Regulation 6(2)(b) by the reference to the adequacy of the price or remuneration being assessed *as against* the goods or services supplied in exchange. The Regulation does not cover terms about charges that might be made not actually for goods or services supplied in exchange but by reference to some circumstance incidental to the exchange that is essential to the parties' bargain. For example, if a seller or supplier includes in his terms a surcharge if payment is made by cheque or by credit card, it does not seem to me that that is exempt from assessment simply because it relates to how much the consumer has to pay: it does not relate to the adequacy of what the consumer has to pay by way of price or remuneration for the goods or services supplied in exchange. Similarly, and nearer to the facts of this case, it does not seem to me that, if a supplier levies a charge or a surcharge not by reference to the actual services supplied but because of an incidental circumstance attendant upon their supply, the term imposing the charge or surcharge is covered by the Regulation. The expression "adequacy" imports reference to a relationship and the relationship here is between the Relevant Charges and the services supplied themselves.

The whole package argument

395. The first argument advanced for the Banks is that the contract between Bank and customer for the operation of a current account is one whereunder the Bank agrees to provide its customer with an overall package of services and in return the customer agrees to pay charges as and when they become payable in accordance with the contractual terms. The pricing structures adopted by the Banks, reflecting a policy of providing "free-if-in-credit" current account facilities, are, they say, simply how they have chosen to charge for the range of services supplied to customers with a current account. If they had decided, for example, upon a structure of charges whereby there was a fee for each transaction or a periodic fee for operating a current account regardless of the number of transactions during the period, the fees would surely be by way of "the price or remuneration" for "services supplied in exchange" and Regulation 6(2) would preclude any assessment of the fairness of a term reflecting their "adequacy". The position is no different, they say, where the structure of fees and charges reflects a policy of "free-if-in-credit" facilities, and fees are charged only when the account is not in credit. The Banks have simply confined their fees to specific types of transactions or to transactions carried out in particular circumstances.

396. This analysis, if accepted, by-passes a number of the OFT's arguments. First, the question whether the price or remuneration needs to be for the main services is redundant. The Relevant Charges are for all the Banks' services, whether main, subsidiary and intermediate. Secondly, there is no need to dissect the contractual dynamic of a Relevant Instruction: whether it truly is a request and whether the Banks' response accords with what is requested. That question is irrelevant, as is the question of what services, if any, the Bank supplies in response to a Relevant Instruction. Thirdly, the implication of this argument is that, if it is accepted in principle, it necessarily applies to all the Relevant Charges: there is no room to ask (for example, of the Unpaid Item

Charges) whether they are associated with anything that can really be described as services supplied by the Bank.

397. The Banks can also say with some force that this view reflects the true economics of the relationship between a Bank and the customer in a "free-if-in-credit" banking regime. The regime provides for an integrated pricing structure for the Banks' services, many of which are provided similarly to customers whether their account is in credit or in debit. The Relevant Charges are one source of revenue for the Banks under it: in addition, in particular, those customers with accounts in credit pay by lending the funds in their account to the Bank and those whose accounts are in debit pay interest. Regulation 6(2) is directed, the argument goes, to the price or remuneration for the services supplied to the customer or *part* of the price or remuneration. In these circumstances it does not matter, the Banks say, that the Relevant Charges are incurred only in particular circumstances, or when particular services are supplied by the Bank and used by the customer.

398. I am unable to accept this argument, for two (linked) reasons. First, I do not consider that the payments are made in exchange for the whole package of services supplied by the Bank when it is operating a current account. It is not a natural use of language to say that the Relevant Charges are levied or paid *in exchange* for those services supplied when an account is in credit. Secondly, I do not consider that the payments are *the price or remuneration* for those services in any natural meaning of the phrase or within the meaning of Regulation 6(2). The payments would not be so recognised by the typical customer when he opens a current account with a Bank, and they are not generally so presented by the Banks in their terms or other documentation.

399. On the contrary, the very description "free-if-in-credit" connotes that there is no price to be paid for services supplied when an account is in credit, and that a customer might pay for the Bank's services supplied if and when his account goes into debit. I do not overlook that RBSG introduced in December 2007 its leaflet, "Personal and Private Banking—A Guide to Interest and Fees", which includes its Relevant Charges under the heading "The price for your banking services" and among "the main elements of the pricing structure we use for our current accounts"; but this is not how Relevant Charges are generally presented to customers, previously RBSG's documentation did not provide this explanation, and, I have said, it is not of contractual effect.

400. Moreover, the basis of the whole package argument is that the Relevant Charges are not *the* price or remuneration for services but *part* of the price or remuneration for services. An assessment of the fairness of the Relevant Charges does not involve an assessment of the level or adequacy or appropriateness of the overall price or remuneration for the package of services supplied by the Bank, and an assessment of the fairness of the Relevant Charges as against those services, apart from being entirely beside the point, would not intrude upon the essential bargain between the parties that the Directive and the 1999 Regulations intend should be protected from assessment. The whole package argument does not engage the policy of the Directive and the 1999 Regulations for exempting the fairness of the Relevant Terms from assessment. Indeed, I am far from convinced that an assessment of part of the price or remuneration (or at least for less than what is manifestly the predominant part of the price or remuneration) for goods or services would ever be covered by Regulation 6(2)(b), but since this is not an argument advanced by the OFT, I say no more about that.

401. In my judgment the Banks' whole package argument provides no basis for concluding that the Relevant Terms fall within Regulation 6(2).

The specific services argument

402. The Banks' specific services argument is that each of the Relevant Charges is the price or remuneration in exchange for the services or a service supplied in connection with a Relevant Instruction given by the customer or by way of the Bank's response to it. Here it is necessary to consider each category of Relevant Charges separately: despite Mr Doctor's submission to the contrary, I see no reason that either all four of the OFT's categories of Relevant Charges are assessable for fairness or none is: after all, the OFT does not suggest that the adequacy of all charges or remuneration that the Banks make of their current account customers are to be, or should be, assessed for fairness.

403. For the reasons that I have already explained, I am unable to accept that the Banks supply customers with any services within the meaning of the 1999 Regulations when they refuse to pay upon Relevant Instructions, and it follows that I reject the specific services argument as far as Unpaid Item Charges are concerned. However, when payment is made, the Bank supplies payment services by way of paying in accordance with the customer's mandate and supplies lending services. The Banks submit that Paid Item Charges and Guaranteed Paid Item Charges are paid in exchange for both payment services by way of making payment in accordance with a Relevant Instruction and lending services by way of an allowing an unarranged overdraft. (They would add that they are also paid in exchange for processing the customer's Relevant Instruction, but I have rejected their argument that that in itself constitutes the supply of

services.) They submit that Overdraft Excess Charges are levied in exchange for extending an unarranged overdraft.

404. The OFT says that the Relevant Charges are not the price or remuneration in exchange for services supplied. It says that, as presented by the Banks and as perceived by the typical customer and in reality, the Relevant Charges are simply charges levied upon defined events or in defined circumstances, and they are not in reality a price or remuneration and are not payments in exchange for services. That, it argues, is clear unless one is blinded by the artificial and misleading language of the standard terms of the seven Banks (other than Nationwide) whereby the customer is said to make (or be deemed to make) a request for an unarranged overdraft, and the Bank is said to respond to it. This language does not alter the true nature of the charges.

405. I have rejected the OFT's submission that the Banks' terms are misleading as to the true nature of a Relevant Instruction and, as I have explained (see paragraph 76 above), I consider that, far from being a device, the terms reflect a proper analysis of the legal position when a customer gives a Relevant Instruction. But the OFT's argument that the Relevant Charges are not a price or remuneration in exchange for services does not depend upon its criticism of the language of the Banks' terms.

406. I am not able to accept that Paid Item Charges and the Guaranteed Paid Item Charges are the price or remuneration in exchange for services by way of the actual payment of a Relevant Instruction, or that this contention provides the essential element of exchange that is the hallmark of a price or remuneration with the meaning of the 1999 Regulations. It does not reflect how Relevant Charges are generally presented to customers, or what they are in substance. After all, the Relevant Charges are made under a contract under which the customer does not usually have to pay when payments are made upon his instructions. In reality they are not charges in exchange for services involved in making payments, but charges levied because the services are supplied in particular circumstances. While the Banks' evidence shows that additional processes are involved if the customer gives a payment instruction when he does not have funds or a facility to cover it, these are not explained in the documentation provided to customers and, even if the typical customer would suppose that this might be the case, the contract does not identify these additional processes as being provided in exchange for the charges. . . .

416. I am unable to accept the specific services argument in respect of any of the Relevant Charges.

The specific contract argument

417. I come to the specific contract argument, which was not advanced by all the Banks and was advanced with little apparent enthusiasm by those who did so. I can deal with it briefly. It is based upon the contract that arises between bank and customer when a bank provides an overdraft on a current account to which it was not contractually committed in advance. Paget's Law of Banking 13th Ed (2007) para 7.1 explains the position thus:

"[The relationship of banker to customer] consists of a general contract, which is basic to all transactions, together with special contracts which arise only as they are brought into being in relation to specific transactions or banking services. The essential distinction is between obligations which come into existence upon the creation of the banker-customer relationship and obligations which are subsequently assumed by specific agreement; or, from the standpoint of the customer, between services which a bank is obliged to provide if asked, and services which many bankers habitually do, but are not bound to, provide."

See too Lloyds Bank Plc v Voller, [2002] 2 All ER (Comm) 978.

418. Accordingly, the argument is, as I understand it, if a bank agrees to an unarranged overdraft, it makes a specific (or special) contract about it, the subject matter of which are the grant of the loan and the charges that the customer is to pay for it. The Relevant Charges are the main subject matter of such a contract. The argument is further developed, I think, that if a Bank declines to pay upon a Relevant Instruction, then similarly there is a specific contract whereunder the Bank agrees to consider the request for an overdraft and the customer agrees to pay Relevant Charges.

419. The extension of the specific contract argument can be answered shortly. The customer's request, when giving a Relevant Instruction, is for the Bank to make payment in accordance with his instructions, not that it consider doing so. If payment is refused, there is no correspondence between an offer and acceptance so as to give rise to a specific contract.

420. There is, as I see it, an equally short answer to the specific contract argument that arises when the Relevant Instruction is paid. The OFT's investigation is into the Relevant Terms in what Paget calls the "general contract" and is directed to their fairness in a general contract. If they are unfair, they are not binding upon the Banks' customers. The OFT does not seek to investigate the fairness of any special contracts (such as Paget describes) or the fairness of the Relevant Terms or any terms relating to Relevant Charges that might have

been incorporated into them. If a special or specific contract contains such terms, it is because they were in the general contract; and if the terms are not binding upon the customer as part of the general contract, they are not incorporated into any special contract so as to be binding upon the customer, and the Banks are not entitled to the Relevant Charges under specific contracts of this kind.

Conclusion about whether the fairness of the Relevant Terms is precluded from the assessment because they "relate . . . to the adequacy of the price or remuneration, as against the goods or services supplied in exchange"

121. I therefore conclude that the Relevant Terms are not exempt from assessment under the 1999 Regulations. This does not seem to me surprising. Regulation 6(2) exempts assessment of the fairness of the balance of the essential bargain between a seller or supplier and a consumer. As the Banks themselves explain, under a "free-if-in-credit" price structure the economic balance in a contract between a Bank and its current account customer is between the package of services supplied by the Bank and the total benefits to the Bank from operating the current account, not only by way of Relevant Charges but also in particular by way of the use of the funds if the account is in credit and interest if it is in debit. On no view does an assessment of the Relevant Charges (or the Relevant Terms) impinge upon the adequacy of the totality of the benefits received by the Bank in exchange for the package of services. The OFT's investigation might well involve consideration of the fairness of the structure of a "free-if-in-credit" pricing regime but that is very different from an assessment of the overall "adequacy" of the benefits to a Bank from operating it.

THE OFFICE OF FAIR TRADING v ABBEY NATIONAL PLC AND OTHERS

[2009] UKSC 6

LORD WALKER

22–016

26. The general thrust of Mr Sumption's submissions for the banks was that both the judge and the Court of Appeal had adopted an over-complicated approach to an issue which, however important both for the consumers and for the banks, is ultimately quite a short point of construction. Article 4(2) of the Directive, now transposed by Regulation 6(2) of the 1999 Regulations, is expressed in fairly simple and non-technical language, as is appropriate for a Community measure which has to be applied across a variety of national systems of contract law. It represents a compromise between consumer protection and freedom of contract. The courts below, in seeking to identify and give effect to the underlying purpose of the Directive, misread Regulation 6(2) as concerned (in paragraph (b) as well as in paragraph (a)) only with what was a "core" or "essential" part of the bargain, to which the consumer may be supposed to have consented in a meaningful sense. The courts below had overlooked that "core term", if that expression is to be used at all, must be understood as no more than shorthand for the contents of paragraphs (a) and (b). Mr Vos supplemented Mr Sumption's submissions by what he referred to as the "debit/credit argument", which focuses on the fact that customers who incur Relevant Charges will view the essence of their contract with the bank differently from those customers who never (or rarely) incur those charges.

27. Against that Mr Crow's primary submission was that the Court of Appeal had reached the right conclusion for the right reasons. The fairness of payment obligations falling within Regulation 6(2)(b) is exempt from assessment in point of "adequacy" (appropriateness) only if they form part of the essential bargain between the parties. The essential bargain constitutes only so much of the contract as the consumer can be said to have consented to freely. The banks had misunderstood the *travaux préparatoires* and drawn the wrong conclusion from them. The Court of Appeal's decision was supported by the decision of the House of Lords in *First National Bank*. The Relevant Charges were ancillary payment obligations and were not incurred in the normal performance of the contract. The typical consumer would not clearly recognise them as the price of services supplied by the banks in exchange. . . .

The meaning of Regulation 6(2)

38. After considering the judgments of Andrew Smith J and the Court of Appeal at length I am impressed, as no doubt all of us are, by the great care with which both courts have considered all the arguments and materials put before them. But I must respectfully say that I see force in Mr Sumption's criticisms of their approach as over-elaborate. The issue is a very important one, but it is essentially quite a short point, even when all the elements relevant to a purposive approach to construction are taken into account. I also respectfully think that the courts below, although cautioning themselves that "core terms" is a shorthand expression for the contents of paragraphs (a) and (b) of regulation 6(2), tended to slip into treating it as an autonomous expression which itself expressed the contents of both those paragraphs.

39. I start with the language of Article 4(2) and Regulation 6(2) (I can see no significant difference between them, although for no obvious reason Article 4(2) refers to assessing the unfair nature of a term whereas Regulation 6(2) refers to assessment of fairness of a term). Paragraphs (a) and (b) are, as I have said, concerned with the two sides of the *quid pro quo* inherent in any consumer contract. The main subject-matter may be goods or services. If it is goods, it may be a single item (a car or a dishwasher) or a multiplicity of items. If for instance a consumer orders a variety of goods from a mail-order catalogue—say clothing, blinds, kitchen utensils and toys—there is no possible basis on which the court can decide that some items are more essential to the contract than others. The main subject matter is simply consumer goods ordered from a catalogue. I think that the Court of Appeal was wrong (para 55) to dismiss the difficulties raised by the banks on this point as something that the court could decide as a question of fact in the circumstances of the particular case.

40. Similarly, a supply of services may be simple (an entertainer booked to perform for an hour at a children's party) or composite (a week's stay at a five-star hotel offering a wide variety of services). Again, there is no principled basis on which the court could decide that some services are more essential to the contract than others and again the main subject matter must be described in general terms—hotel services. The services that banks offer to their current account customers are a comparable package of services. These include the collection and payment of cheques, other money transmission services, facilities for cash distribution (mainly by ATM machines either at manned branches or elsewhere) and the provision of statements in printed or electronic form.

41. When one turns to the other part of the *quid pro quo* of a consumer contract, the price or remuneration, the difficulty of deciding which prices are essential is just the same, and Regulation 6(2)(b) contains no indication that only an "essential" price or remuneration is relevant. Any monetary price or remuneration payable under the contract would naturally fall within the language of paragraph (b) (I discount the absence of a reference to part of the price or remuneration for reasons already mentioned).

42. In the case of banking services supplied to a current account customer under the "free if in credit" regime, the principal monetary consideration received by the bank consists of interest and charges on authorised and unauthorised overdrafts, and specific charges for particular non-routine services (such as expedited or foreign money transmission services). The most important element of the consideration, however, consists of the interest forgone by customers whose current accounts are in credit, since whether their credit balance is large or small, they will be receiving a relatively low rate of interest on it (sometimes a very low rate or no interest at all). The scale of this benefit is indicated by the figure for 2006 already mentioned. Mr Sumption was wary about committing himself as to whether interest foregone constituted part of the bank's price or remuneration for the purposes of Regulation 6(2)(b). Whatever view is taken as to that, it is clear that just as banking services to current account customers can aptly be described as a package, so can the consideration that moves from the customer to the bank. Interest forgone is an important part of that package for customers whose accounts are in credit, and overdraft interest and charges are the most important element for those customers who are not in credit. Lawyers are very used to speaking of a package (or bundle) of rights and obligations, and in that sense every obligation which a consumer undertakes by a consumer contract could be seen as part of the price or remuneration received by the supplier. But non-monetary obligations undertaken by a consumer contract (for instance, to take proper care of goods on hire-purchase, or to treat material supplied for a distance-learning course as available only to the customer personally) are not part of the "price or remuneration" within the Regulation. That is the point of Lord Steyn's observation in *First National Bank*, in para 34, that "in a broad sense all terms of the contract are in some way related to the price or remuneration."

43. This House's decision in *First National Bank* shows that not every term that is in some way linked to monetary consideration falls within Regulation 6(2)(b). Paras (d), (e), (f) and (l) of the "greylist" in Schedule 2 to the 1999 Regulations are an illustration of that. But the relevant term in *First National Bank* was a default provision. Traders ought not to be able to outflank consumers by "drafting themselves" into a position where they can take advantage of a default provision. But *Bairstow Eves London Central Ltd v Smith* [2004] 2 EGLR 25 shows that the Court can and will be astute to prevent that. In *First National Bank* Lord Steyn indicated that what is now Regulation 6(2) should be construed restrictively, and Lord Bingham said that it should be limited to terms "falling squarely within it". I respectfully agree. But in my opinion the Relevant Terms and the Relevant Charges do fall squarely within Regulation 6(2)(b).

44. That conclusion is not to my mind at variance with the message to be derived from the *travaux*. It is a fairly complex message, reflecting not only a compromise between the opposing aims of consumer protection and freedom of contract, but also the contrast between consumer protection and consumer choice (the latter being more central, perhaps, to basic Community principles). This point was explored and explained in an article (not mentioned by the Court of Appeal) to which Mr Sumption referred, that is Good Faith in European

Contract Law by Professor Hugh Collins, (1994) 14 OJLS 229. Mr Sumption placed particular emphasis on the following passage:

"The history of the EC Directive on Unfair Terms in Consumer Contracts reveals the struggle between these two interpretations of the economic interests of consumers. Even at a late stage in the negotiations, the draft Directive proposed by the Commission envisaged the introduction of a general principle against substantive unfairness in consumer contracts. It invalidated terms in standard form consumer contracts which caused 'the performance of the contract to be significantly different from what the consumer could legitimately expect', or which caused 'the performance of the contract to be unduly detrimental to the consumer'. But in the battle between the advocates of consumer rights and the supporters of free competition, eventually the latter emerged victorious in the Council of Ministers. The fairness of the transaction in the sense of the price paid for the goods or services should not be subjected to review or control. This is the meaning of the obscure Article 4(2) [which is then set out]. The final reservation in this provision ['plain intelligible language'] is significant. The Directive does not require consumer contracts to be substantively fair, but it does require them to be clear. Clarity is essential for effective market competition between terms. What matters primarily for EC contract law is consumer choice, not consumer rights."

45. The Court of Appeal took account of the *travaux* and of some academic writing. It recognised as an underlying value the notion that freedom of contract should prevail where there has been meaningful negotiation between supplier and consumer, so that the latter does consent to the terms of the contract. But I respectfully think the Court went too far in interpreting the language of the Directive and the 1999 Regulations in order to meet that perceived aim. The Directive and the 1999 Regulations apply only to terms which have not been individually negotiated, and the Court departed from the natural meaning of the text in order to achieve an unnecessary duplication of the exception for individually negotiated terms.

46. I would add a postscript to this part of the discussion. A variety of expressions has been used, in the courts below and in argument (and to some extent by this House in *First National Bank*), to describe those contractual terms which are subject to review in point of fairness: ancillary, subordinate, incidental, non-core, collateral. These may all be of some assistance but it is important, in considering provisions which apply across an extraordinarily wide range of consumer contracts, to treat them with caution. I venture to repeat a paragraph from an opinion of mine (in which the other members of the Appellate Committee concurred) in *College of Estate Management v Customs & Excise Commissioners* [2005] STC 1957, para 30, an appeal raising questions of Community law about whether there is a single or multiple supply, and whether it is of goods or services, for the purposes of value added tax:

"'Ancillary' means (as Ward LJ rightly observed ([2004] STC 1471 at [39])) subservient, subordinate and ministering to something else. It was an entirely apposite term in the discussion in *British Telecommunications* (where the delivery of the car was subordinate to its sale) and in *Card Protection Plan* itself (where some peripheral parts of a package of services, and some goods of trivial value such as labels, key tabs and a medical card, were subordinate to the main package of insurance services). But there are other cases (including *Faaborg, Beynon* and the present case) in which it is inappropriate to analyse the transaction in terms of what is 'principal' and 'ancillary', and it is unhelpful to strain the natural meaning of 'ancillary' in an attempt to do so. Food is not ancillary to restaurant services; it is of central and indispensable importance to them; nevertheless there is a single supply of services (*Faaborg*). Pharmaceuticals are not ancillary to medical care which requires the use of medication; again, they are of central and indispensable importance; nevertheless there is a single supply of services (*Beynon*)."

Conversely, delivery of goods or peripheral extras may be disregarded as ancillary for the purposes of para (a) of Regulation 6(2), but the charges for them, if payable under the same contract, are part of the price for the purposes of para (b).

The application of Regulation 6(2)

47. I can state my opinion much more briefly on the second main issue in the appeal, that is the application of Regulation 6(2), properly construed, to the facts. Charges for unauthorised overdrafts are monetary consideration for the package of banking services supplied to personal current account customers. They are an important part of the banks' charging structure, amounting to over 30 per cent of their revenue stream from all personal current account customers. The facts that the charges are contingent, and that the majority of customers do not incur them, are irrelevant. On the view that I take of the construction of Regulation 6(2), the fairness of the charges would be exempt from review in point of appropriateness under Regulation 6(2)(b)

even if fewer customers paid them, and they formed a smaller part of the banks' revenue stream. Even if the Court of Appeal's interpretation had been correct, I do not see how it could have come to the conclusion that charges amounting to over 30 per cent of the revenue stream were (para 111) "not part of the core or essential bargain."

Should there be a reference under Article 234?

48. This Court, as the national court of last resort, is under an obligation to make a reference to the Court of Justice under Article 234 of the Treaty if a decision on the correct interpretation of the Directive is necessary to enable the Court to give judgment, and the point is not *acte clair*. Neither side showed any enthusiasm for a reference, because of the further delay that would be occasioned in a very large number of claims at present stayed. The Court is entitled to take the likely delay into account, although not as an overriding consideration, in deciding whether to make a reference.

49. If (as I understand to be the case) the Court is unanimous that the appeal should be allowed, then in my opinion we should treat the point as *acte clair*, and decide against making a reference. It may seem paradoxical for a court of last resort to conclude that a point is clear when it is differing from the carefully-considered judgments of the very experienced judges who have ruled on it in lower courts. But sometimes a court of last resort does conclude, without any disrespect, that the lower courts were clearly wrong, and in my respectful opinion this is such a case.

50. Even if some or all of the Court feel that the point is not *acte clair*, I would still propose that we ought not to incur the delay involved in a reference under Article 234, since a decision on the correct construction of Article 4(2) of the Directive is not essential for the determination of this appeal. The correct construction of Article 4(2) is a question of Community law, but the application of the Article, properly construed, to the facts is a question for national law. Even if the Court of Appeal was not clearly wrong on the issue of construction, it was in my respectful opinion clearly wrong in applying its construction to the facts. In other circumstances it might be regarded as rather unprincipled to take that means of avoiding an important issue of Community law, but in the special circumstances of this case I would regard it as the lesser of two evils. There is a strong public interest in resolving the matter without further delay.

Conclusion

51. For these reasons I would allow the appeal. The declaration sought by the banks in their counterclaims is inappropriate for the reasons explained by Lord Phillips at the beginning of his judgment. I would declare that the bank charges levied on personal current account customers in respect of unauthorised overdrafts (including unpaid item charges and other related charges) constitute part of the price or remuneration for the banking services provided and, in so far as the terms giving rise to the charges are in plain intelligible language, no assessment under the Unfair Terms in Consumer Contracts Regulations 1999 of the fairness of those terms may relate to their adequacy as against the services supplied.

52. If the Court allows this appeal the outcome may cause great disappointment and indeed dismay to a very large number of bank customers who feel that they have been subjected to unfairly high charges in respect of unauthorised overdrafts. But this decision is not the end of the matter, as Lord Phillips explains in his judgment. Moreover Ministers and Parliament may wish to consider the matter further. They decided, in an era of so-called "light-touch" regulation, to transpose the Directive as it stood rather than to confer the higher degree of consumer protection afforded by the national laws of some other member states. Parliament may wish to consider whether to revisit that decision.

LORD PHILLIPS

The issue

57. The agreed Statement of Facts and Issue describes the issue raised by this appeal as follows:

> "Whether an assessment of the fairness of the Relevant Terms (pursuant to which the Relevant Charges are levied) would relate to the adequacy of the price and remuneration, as against the services supplied in exchange, within the meaning of regulation 6(2)(b) of the Unfair Terms in Consumer Contracts Regulations 1999."

This does not accurately describe the issue raised by this appeal, which is very much more narrow. That issue is whether the Relevant Charges constitute "the price or remuneration, as against the services supplied in exchange" within the meaning of the Regulation. If they do not, the attack on the fairness of the terms that is open to the OFT will not be circumscribed by Regulation 6(2)(b). If they do, they will still be open to attack by the OFT on the ground that they are "unfair" as defined by Regulation 5(1), but that attack cannot be founded on an allegation that the Relevant Charges are excessive by comparison with the services which they purchase, for that is forbidden by Regulation 6(2)(b).

58. That this was indeed the issue was made clear by counsel on either side in their oral submissions. Towards the close of his reply, Mr Sumption QC said this:

"All that I can ask the courts to declare, and all that my clients have ever asked the courts to declare, is that the insufficient fund charges are included in the price within the meaning of the word "price" in [Regulation] 6 and that no assessment of the fairness of the terms imposing the IFCs may relate to their adequacy as against the service supplied."

59. Mr Crow QC for his part submitted on behalf of the OFT that even if Article 4(2) of the Directive did apply, the Relevant Terms were still subject to assessment for fairness. In that event, while it would not be open to the OFT to assess the fairness of the price by reference to the adequacy of the goods or services supplied in exchange, it would be open to the OFT to assess the fairness of the price according to other criteria.

60. This agreement between the parties reflects acceptance by the Banks in the Court of Appeal of a finding by Andrew Smith J that was contrary to one of their submissions. The Banks had submitted that a term of a contract that provided the "price or remuneration" for "goods or services supplied" was absolutely exempt from assessment for fairness by reason of Regulation 6(2). This was described as the "excluded term" construction of the Regulation. Andrew Smith J held that this was not correct. Regulation 6(2) precluded assessing a price term for fairness by reference to its adequacy as payment for the goods or services provided in exchange. It did not, however, preclude assessing a price term for fairness according to other criteria. This has been described as the "excluded assessment" construction of the Regulation.

61. Mr Sumption submitted that the difference between the "excluded term" and the "excluded assessment" constructions was "a distraction from the real issues". It is certainly a distraction from the narrow issue that the parties are now agreed is before the court. But it is only because the "excluded assessment" construction has prevailed that the issue has been narrowed from that in the Agreed Statement of Facts and Issue. Had the "excluded term" construction prevailed, a finding in favour of the Banks that the Relevant Terms were included within the meaning of the word "price" in Regulation 6(2) would have precluded any challenge to those terms on the ground of fairness. As it is, if the Banks succeed on the narrow issue, this will not close the door on the OFT's investigations and may well not resolve the myriad cases that are currently stayed in which customers have challenged Relevant Charges.

62. There is a further general point to be made. It seems likely that many of the customers who have challenged Relevant Charges have done so on the basis that they are excessive for the individual services to which they relate. They have treated the Relevant Charges as being levied in exchange for those services. Equally, one of the provisional grounds of attack advanced by the OFT has been that the Relevant Charges are out of all proportion to the cost of providing the services to which they relate. The Banks' primary case is that these attacks are founded on a misconception that the Relevant Charges are payment for the services that trigger them. According to the Banks the reality is that the Relevant Charges are simply part of the payment in exchange for a global package of services. If that is correct, it would seem to follow that the attack based on the disparity between the cost of providing the services that trigger the Relevant Charges and the amount of the Relevant Charges is based on a false premise and does not in fact involve an assessment of fairness that relates "to the adequacy of the price or remuneration, as against the goods or services supplied in exchange".

63. This was a point that was appreciated by Andrew Smith J. At paragraph 400 of his judgment he says:

"Moreover, the basis of the whole package argument is that the Relevant Charges are not *the* price or remuneration for services but *part* of the price or remuneration for services. An assessment of the fairness of the Relevant Charges does not involve an assessment of the level or adequacy or appropriateness of the overall price or remuneration for the package of services supplied by the Bank, and an assessment of the fairness of the Relevant Charges as against those services, apart from being entirely beside the point, would not intrude upon the essential bargain between the parties that the Directive and the 1999 Regulations intend should be protected from assessment. The whole package argument does not engage the policy of the Directive and the 1999 Regulations for exempting the fairness of the Relevant Terms from assessment. Indeed, I am far from convinced that an assessment of part of the price or remuneration (or at least for less than what is manifestly the predominant part of the price or remuneration) for goods or services would ever be covered by Regulation 6(2)(b), but since this is not an argument advanced by the OFT, I say no more about that."

64. Mr Crow did not submit before us that if the Relevant Charges formed part of the price paid in exchange for the package of services, they could not be included within the meaning of the word "price" in Regulation 6(2). I consider that Regulation 6(2) could apply to a complaint that the Banks' charges overall, of which the Relevant Charges are an important element, are unfair because those who pay them pay an excessive amount in exchange for the package of services in respect of which they constitute part of the payment. Thus the issue of whether or not the Relevant Charges form part of the "price or remuneration, as against the goods or services supplied in exchange" within Regulation 6(2) is not necessarily academic. No attack has yet been made, however, on the level of the Banks' charges overall. . . .

The approach to the issue

71. Early in his argument Mr Sumption said:

> "[T]here is. . .room for argument about whether the insufficient fund charges are part of the price for the package of services or just the particular service which occasions their being charged, but we will submit that it is unrealistic to say, as the judge did, that insufficient fund charges are not payable in exchange for any service at all and are, therefore, not a price at all."

72. This raises the questions by what criteria do you decide whether the charges are payment for services, if so, whether individual charges are payments for individual services or part payment for a package of services, and from whose viewpoint do you decide those questions? So far as the latter question is concerned, the choice would appear to be between the viewpoint of the customer, having regard to the facts that he would reasonably be expected to know, the viewpoint of the Banks, having regard to the more extensive knowledge held by the Banks, or no viewpoint at all, on the basis that these questions have to be answered by application of an objective test to all the material facts. There is an allied question of whether the language used to describe the obligations imposed by the terms is relevant or whether one looks simply at the nature and effect of those obligations.

73. The narrow issue raised by this appeal is only relevant as part of the wider issue that will arise if and when the Relevant Terms are challenged as being unfair. At that point the question may arise—are the terms being challenged on the ground that the Relevant Charges are excessive having regard to the services that are provided in exchange for them? The court before which the challenge is made may then have to decide whether any, and if so what, services are provided in exchange for the Relevant Charges as a stepping stone to deciding whether the challenge is one precluded by Regulation 6(2). To answer that question the court will, in my view, properly have to consider the role played by the Relevant Charges having regard to all the facts that are relevant to the operation of the contractual adventure and not just to those that are, or reasonably should be, within the knowledge of the customer. . . .

88. When the relevant facts are viewed as a whole, it seems clear that the Relevant Charges are not concealed default charges designed to discourage customers from overdrawing on their accounts without prior arrangement. Whatever may have been the position in the past, the Banks now rely on the Relevant Charges as an important part of the revenue that they generate from the current account services. If they did not receive the Relevant Charges they would not be able profitably to provide current account services to their customers in credit without making a charge to augment the value of the use of their funds.

89. For these reasons I have formed the conclusion that the Relevant Charges are, as the Banks submit, charges that they require their customers to agree to pay as part of the price or remuneration for the package of services that they agree to supply in exchange.

90. My conclusions accord with those of Lord Walker and, for the reasons that he gives as well as my own, I would allow this appeal.

LORD MANCE

97. . . . The banks' primary case is that the relevant contracts are the contracts for an overall package of banking facilities made by the banks with their customers. Andrew Smith J rejected this analysis as unnatural: payments by way of Relevant Charges could not be said to be paid in exchange for services supplied when an account is in credit; and the description "free-if-in-credit" connoted that there was no price to be paid when an account was in credit (paras. 398-9). Furthermore, if the relevant contract was taken to be the overall package, the Relevant Charges would represent no more than part of the price or remuneration, and an assessment of the fairness of such charges as against the package of services would be "beside the point" and "would not intrude upon the essential bargain" intended to be protected from assessment (para. 400).

98. There is in my opinion a flaw in this reasoning. It is not comparing like with like. Viewing the matter at the level of the banking contracts, the comparison is between, on the one hand, the package of services offered by the banks (some or all of which may or may not be used by any particular customer) and, on the other, the customer's commitment to pay such charges as may arise from whatever facilities he does use. At this level, the banks' case is that price or remuneration is or includes the customer's potential liability for charges, rather than the payments which he or she has actually to make if and when such charges are incurred. In my opinion the Court of Appeal was right in para. 97 of its judgment to identify the relevant contract as being in the first instance the banking contract for an overall package of facilities. That is the contract in which the Relevant Charges appear and were agreed.

99. Further, any challenge to the fairness of a term must be to its fairness in the context of the relevant contract in which it appears. It is "beside the point" if it is not. If, on a proper analysis, the customer's potential liability for the Relevant Charges is the or part of the "price or remuneration" in exchange for which the overall package of banking services is supplied, and it is challenged on the ground that it makes such price or remuneration disproportionate overall, then regulation 6(2)(b) excludes the challenge. If there is no challenge to the overall proportionality of the overall price or remuneration of the package, then I fail to see how a challenge to the proportionality of the Relevant Charges in relation to the cost of providing particular services in isolation can be admissible or relevant. A term which is proportionate in context cannot become disproportionate viewed out of context.

Question

22–017   In November 2014, it was reported that a couple who, having stayed overnight at a Blackpool hotel and then posted negative comments about the hotel on Trip Advisor, had been charged £100 by the hotel for so doing (see *http://www.bbc.co.uk/news/technology-30100973* [Accessed February 12, 2015]). Apparently, the hotel's booking documents included a clause that read: "Despite the fact that repeat customers and couples love our hotel, your friends and family may not. For every bad review left on any website, the group organiser will be charged a maximum of £100 per review". Local trading standards officials were investigating a possible breach of unfair trading regulations. Do you think that the clause would be assessed as unfair if it were tested under the Unfair Terms in Consumer Contracts Regulations?

B. The UCTA Test of a Fair and Reasonable Term

GEORGE MITCHELL (CHESTERHALL) LTD v FINNEY LOCK SEEDS LTD

House of Lords [1983] 2 A.C. 803; [1983] 3 W.L.R. 163; [1983] 2 All E.R. 737; [1983] 2 Lloyd's Rep. 272

22–018   In December 1973, the appellants, seed merchants, agreed to supply the respondents, farmers, with 30 lbs of Dutch winter cabbage seed for £201.60. The seed was delivered with an invoice containing a clause purporting to limit the liability of the seller, in the event of the seed not complying with the express terms of the contract to replacing defective seed or repaying the price. The seed supplied was of a different and inferior variety with result that the crop failed and had to be ploughed in. Parker J awarded the respondents £61,513.78 damages and £30,756 interest. The Court of Appeal dismissed the appeal, Oliver and Kerr LJJ, Lord Denning dissenting, on the ground (i) that the clause, on its true construction, did not apply to the breach which had occurred; and, (ii), Lord Denning concurring, that it would not be fair and reasonable to permit reliance on the clause, applying s.55(4) of the Sale of Goods Act 1979 as substituted in Sch.1 of that Act. (For the present s.55, see above, p.419) The House of Lords dismissed the appeal on ground (ii), agreeing with Lord Denning that the clause on its true construction did apply to the breach.

Lord Denning MR (in his last judgment), having reviewed the case law and the Unfair Contract Terms Act 1977 ([1983] 1 All E.R. 108, 115):

LORD DENNING MR

The effect of the changes

What is the result of all this? To my mind it heralds a revolution in our approach to exemption clauses; not only where they exclude liability altogether and also where they limit liability; not only in the specific categories in the Unfair Contract Terms Act 1977, but in other contracts too. Just as in other fields of law we have done away with the multitude of cases on "common employment," "last opportunity," "invitees" and "licensees" and so forth, so also in this field we should do away with the multitude of cases on exemption clauses. We should no longer have to go through all kinds of gymnastic contortions to get round them. We should no longer have to harass our students with the study of them. We should set about meeting a new challenge. It is presented by the test of reasonableness . . .

Fair and reasonable

There is only one case in the books so far on this point. It is *R. W. Green Ltd v Cade Bros. Farm* [1978] 1 Lloyd's Rep. 602. There Griffiths J. held that it was fair and reasonable for seed potato merchants to rely on a limitation clause which limited their liability to the contract price of the potatoes. That case was very different from the present. The terms had been evolved over 20 years. The judge said (at 607): "They are therefore not conditions imposed by the strong upon the weak; but are rather a set of trading terms upon which both sides are apparently content to do business." The judge added (at 608): "No moral blame attaches to either party; neither of them knew, nor could be expected to know, that the potatoes were infected." In that case the judge held that the clause was fair and reasonable and that the seed merchants were entitled to rely on it.

Our present case is very much on the borderline. There is this to be said in favour of the seed merchants. The price of this cabbage seed was small: £192. The damages claimed are high: £61,000. But there is this to be said on the other side. The clause was not negotiated between persons of equal bargaining power. It was inserted by the seed merchants in their invoices without any negotiation with the farmers.

To this I would add that the seed merchants rarely, if ever, invoked the clause. Their very frank director said: "The trade does not stand on the strict letter of the clause . . . Almost invariably when a customer justifiably complains, the trade pays something more than a refund." The papers contain many illustrations where the clause was not invoked and a settlement was reached.

Next, I would point out that the buyers had no opportunity at all of knowing or discovering that the seed was not cabbage seed, whereas the sellers could and should have known that it was the wrong seed altogether. The buyers were not covered by insurance against the risk. Nor could they insure. But, as to the seed merchants, the judge said ([1981] 1 Lloyd's Rep. 476 at 480):

> "I am entirely satisfied that it is possible for seedsmen to insure against this risk. I am entirely satisfied that the cost of so doing would not materially raise the price of seeds on the market. I am entirely satisfied that the protection of this clause for the purposes of protecting against the very rare case indeed, such as the present, is not reasonably required. If and in so far as it may be necessary to consider the matter, I am also satisfied that it is possible for seedsmen to test seeds before putting them on to the market."

To that I would add this further point. Such a mistake as this could not have happened without serious negligence on the part of the seed merchants themselves or their Dutch suppliers. So serious that it would not be fair to enable them to escape responsibility for it.

In all the circumstances I am of opinion that it would not be fair or reasonable to allow the seed merchants to rely on the clause to limit their liability.

I would dismiss the appeal accordingly.

In the House of Lords, Lord Diplock said that he agreed with Lord Denning and Lord Bridge; and Lords Scarman, Roskill and Brightman agreed with Lord Bridge.

LORD BRIDGE

My Lords, it seems to me, with all due deference, that the judgments of the learned trial judge and of Oliver L.J. on the common law issue come dangerously near to re-introducing by the back door the doctrine of "fundamental breach" which this House in *Securicor 1* [1980] A.C. 827, had so forcibly evicted by the front. The learned judge discusses what I may call the "peas and beans" or "chalk and cheese" cases, sc. those in which it has been held that exemption clauses do not apply where there has been a contract to sell one thing, for example, a motor car, and the seller has supplied quite another thing, for example, a bicycle. I hasten to add that the judge can in no way be criticised for adopting this approach since counsel appearing for the appellants at the trial had conceded "that if what had been delivered had been beetroot seed or carrot seed, he would not be able to rely upon the clause": [1981] 1 Lloyd's Rep. 476, 479. Different counsel appeared for the appellants in the Court of Appeal, where that concession was withdrawn.

The question of relative bargaining strength under paragraph (a) and of the opportunity to buy seeds without a limitation of the seedsman's liability under paragraph (b) were inter-related. The evidence was that a similar limitation of liability was universally embodied in the terms of trade between seedsmen and farmers and had been so for very many years. The limitation had never been negotiated between representative bodies but, on the other hand, had not been the subject of any protest by the National Farmers' Union. These factors, if considered in isolation, might have been equivocal. The decisive factor, however, appears from the evidence of four witnesses called for the appellants, two independent seedsmen, the chairman of the appellant company, and a director of a sister company (both being wholly-owned subsidiaries of the same parent). They said that it had always been their practice, unsuccessfully attempted in the instant case, to negotiate settlements of farmers' claims for damages in excess of the price of the seeds, if they thought that the claims were "genuine" and "justified." This evidence indicated a clear recognition by seedsmen in general, and the appellants in particular, that reliance on the limitation of liability imposed by the relevant condition would not be fair or reasonable.

Two further factors, if more were needed, weight the scales in favour of the respondents. The supply of autumn, instead of winter, cabbage seeds was due to the negligence of the appellants' sister company. Irrespective of its quality, the autumn variety supplied could not, according to the appellants' own evidence, be grown commercially in East Lothian. Finally, as the trial judge found, seedsmen could insure against the risk of crop failure caused by supplying the wrong variety of seeds without materially increasing the price of seeds.

My Lords, even if I felt doubts about the statutory issue, I should not, for the reasons explained earlier, think it right to interfere with the unanimous original decision of that issue by the Court of Appeal. As it is, I feel no such doubts. If I were making the original decision, I should conclude without hesitation that it would not be fair or reasonable to allow the appellants to rely on the contractual limitation of their liability.

I would dismiss the appeal.

Question

22–019   The modified s.55 of the Sale of Goods Act that applied in *Mitchell v Finney Lock* applies to contracts made between May 18, 1973 and February 1, 1978. Contracts made on or after February 1, 1978 are governed by the Unfair Contract Terms Act. Whereas under s.55 the question is whether it is fair and reasonable "to allow reliance on the term", under s.11 of the Unfair Contract Terms Act the question is whether the term was a fair and reasonable one "to be included" in the contract. In a case like *Mitchell v Finney Lock* where the contract was made after February 1, 1978 would it be possible to take into account the fact that the sellers were guilty of serious negligence? Or of anything else occurring after the contract was made?

WALKER v BOYLE

Chancery Division [1982] 1 W.L.R. 495; [1982] 1 All E.R. 634

22–020   The vendor of a house relied on her husband to conduct her affairs. He replied to a preliminary enquiry, believing his answer to be true, that there were no boundary disputes. The vendor knew there was a boundary dispute. Contracts were exchanged, using the National Conditions of Sale, condition 17(1) of which provided, "no error, mis-statement or omission in any preliminary answer . . . shall annul the sale." Dillon J held that condition 17 did not apply to misrepresentations where the true facts were within the vendor's knowledge. Alternatively, the condition was invalid under s.3 of the Misrepresentation Act 1967 and s.11(1) of the Unfair Contract Terms Act 1977. He said:

DILLON J

> It has been submitted by counsel for Mrs Boyle that as there were solicitors acting for both parties, it would be a very strong thing to say that any term of the contract which resulted is not a fair and reasonable one in the circumstances. That argument would have great force, no doubt, if the solicitors had specifically directed their minds to the problem and had evolved the clause which was under attack. In fact, however, neither solicitor directed his mind to condition 17, and they have both told me, and they are men of not inconsiderable experience as conveyancing solicitors, that they have never come across a case where any question under condition 17 has arisen. It was submitted that it was the duty of the purchaser's solicitor to advise his client, Mr Walker of the implications of condition 17 and of the other terms of the contract which Mr Walker was going to enter into, and he must be taken to have discharged that duty and satisfied himself and Mr Walker that the terms were reasonable. It is, of course, the duty of a solicitor to advise his client about any abnormal or unusual term in a contract, but I think it is perfectly normal and proper for a solicitor to use standard forms of conditions of sale such as the National Conditions of Sale. I do not think he is called on to go through the small print of those somewhat lengthy conditions with a tooth-comb every time he is advising a purchaser or to draw the purchaser's attention to every problem which on a careful reading of the conditions might in some circumstance or other conceivably arise. I cannot believe that purchasers of house property throughout the land would be overjoyed at having such lengthy explanations of the National Conditions of Sale ritually foisted on them.
>
> It has also been submitted by counsel for Mrs Boyle that the court should be very slow to hold that a common-form clause like condition 17 is not fair and reasonable. Of course it is true that there are common-form clauses which have been evolved by negotiation between trade associations, associations of merchants or associations of growers or trade unions or other such bodies concerned to protect the rights of their members, which can be regarded as representing what consensus in the trade regards as fair and reasonable. Again, the National Conditions of Sale are not the product of negotiation between such bodies and it is plain . . . that what now appears in condition 17 has come down through the ages despite very drastic limitations imposed on it by the courts. I do not think it can be said that its precarious survival until 1977 entitles it to the automatic accolade of fairness and reasonableness.

Points for reflection

In *Phillips Products Ltd v Hyland* [1987] 1 W.L.R. 659 the plaintiff hired an excavator and driver from the defendant. The contract provided that the hirer was to be responsible for all damage arising in connection with the operation of the plant by the driver. The driver drove the plant into the plaintiff's buildings and caused damage. Kenneth Jones J was not satisfied that the term was a fair and reasonable one to be included and held the defendant liable. Since the judge had not proceeded upon some erroneous principle and was not plainly and obviously wrong in his conclusion, the defendant's appeal was dismissed. In *Thompson v T Lohan (Plant Hire) and Another* [1987] 1 W.L.R. 649, the facts were similar except that the injury was to a third party, the plaintiff's husband, who was killed as a result of the driver's negligence. The plaintiff recovered damages. It was held that s.2 of the 1977 Act does not affect arrangements between the wrongdoer and others as to the sharing of the burden of compensation and that the term was effective to require the hirer to indemnify the owner. For discussion of the intricacies of these cases, see John N. Adams and Roger Brownsword, 'Double Indemnity—Contractual Indemnity Clauses Revisited' (1988) *Journal of Business Law* 146.

22–021

SMITH v ERIC S BUSH (A FIRM)

HARRIS AND ANOTHER v WYRE FOREST DISTRICT COUNCIL AND ANOTHER

House of Lords [1989] 2 All E.R. 514

22-022   In both these cases the question was whether a surveyor who was instructed by a mortgagee to value a house owed to the purchaser a duty of care in tort and whether a disclaimer of liability for negligence by or on behalf of the surveyor was effective. The House of Lords held that a surveyor who knew that the purchaser intended to buy the house and would rely on the valuation for which he had paid the mortgagee did owe such a duty. On the question of the effect of the disclaimer on the Unfair Contract Terms Act 1977:

LORD TEMPLEMAN

In *Harris v Wyre Forest DC* the Court of Appeal (Kerr, Nourse L.JJ. and Caulfield J.) accepted an argument that the 1977 Act did not apply because the council by their express disclaimer refused to obtain a valuation save on terms that the valuer would not be under any obligation to Mr and Mrs Harris to take reasonable care or exercise reasonable skill. The council did not exclude liability for negligence but excluded negligence so that the valuer and the council never came under a duty of care to Mr and Mrs Harris and could not be guilty of negligence. This construction would not give effect to the manifest intention of the 1977 Act but would emasculate the Act. The construction would provide no control over standard form exclusion clauses which individual members of the public are obliged to accept. A party to a contract or a tortfeasor could opt out of the 1977 Act by declining, in the words of Nourse L.J. to recognise "their own answerability to the plaintiff's". Caulfield J. said that the Act "can only be relevant where there is on the facts a potential liability." But no one intends to commit a tort and therefore any notice which excludes liability is a notice which excludes a potential liability. Kerr L.J. sought to confine the Act to "situations where the existence of a duty of care is not open to doubt" or where there is "an inescapable duty of care." I can find nothing in the 1977 Act or in the general law to identify or support this distinction. In the result the Court of Appeal held that the Act does not apply to "negligent misstatements where a disclaimer has prevented a duty of care from coming into existence" per Nourse L.J. My Lords, this confuses the valuer's report with the work which the valuer carries out in order to make his report. The valuer owed a duty to exercise reasonable skill and care in his inspection and valuation. If he had been careful in his work, he would not have made a "negligent misstatement" in his report.

Section 11(3) of the 1977 Act provides that, in considering whether it is fair and reasonable to allow reliance on a notice which excludes liability in tort, account must be taken of "all the circumstances obtaining when the liability arose or (but for the notice) would have arisen." Section 13(1) of the Act prevents the exclusion of any right or remedy and (to that extent) section 2 also prevents the exclusion of liability "by reference to . . . notices which exclude . . . the relevant obligation or duty." Nourse L.J. dismissed section 11(3) as "peripheral" and made no comment on section 13(1). In my opinion both these provisions support the view that the 1977 Act requires that all exclusion notices which would in common law provide a defence to an action for negligence must satisfy the requirement of reasonableness . . .

LORD GRIFFITHS

Section 11(3) provides:

"In relation to a notice (not being a notice having contractual effect), the requirement of reasonableness under this Act is that it should be fair and reasonable to allow reliance on it, having regard to all the circumstances obtaining when the liability arose or (but for the notice) would have arisen."

And section 13(1) provides:

"To the extent that this Part of this Act prevents the exclusion or restriction of any liability it also prevents—(a) making the liability or its enforcement subject to restrictive or onerous conditions; (b) excluding or restricting any right or remedy in respect of the liability, or subjecting a person to any prejudice in consequence of his pursuing any such right or remedy; (c) excluding or restricting rules of evidence or procedure; and (to that extent) sections 2 and 5 to 7 also prevent excluding or restricting liability by reference to terms and notices which exclude or restrict the relevant obligation or duty."

I read these provisions as introducing a "but for" test in relation to the notice excluding liability. They indicate that the existence of the common law duty to take reasonable care, referred to in section 1(1)(b), is to be judged by considering whether it would exist "but for" the notice excluding liability. The result of taking the notice into account when assessing the existence of a duty of care would result in removing all liability for negligent misstatements from the protection of the Act. It is permissible to have regard to the second report of the Law Commission on Exemption Clauses (Law Com. No. 69), which is the genesis of the Unfair Contract Terms Act 1977, as an aid to the construction of the Act. Paragraph 127 of that report reads:

"Our recommendations in this Part of the report are intended to apply to exclusions of liability for negligence where the liability is incurred in the course of a person's business. We consider that they should apply even in cases where the person seeking to rely on the exemption clause was under no legal obligation (such as a contractual obligation) to carry out the activity. This means that, for example, conditions attached to a licence to enter on to land, and disclaimers of liability made where information or advice is given, should be subject to control . . ."

I have no reason to think that Parliament did not intend to follow this advice and the wording of the Act is, in my opinion, apt to give effect to that intention. This view of the construction of the Act is also supported by the judgment of Slade L.J. in *Phillips Products Ltd v Hyland* [1987] 1 W.L.R. 659, when he rejected a similar argument in relation to the construction of a contractual term excluding negligence.

Finally, the question is whether the exclusion of liability contained in the disclaimer satisfies the requirement of reasonableness provided by section 2(2) of the 1977 Act. The meaning of reasonableness and the burden of proof are both dealt with in section 11(3), which provides:

"In relation to a notice (not being a notice having contractual effect), the requirement of reasonableness under this Act is that it should be fair and reasonable to allow reliance on it, having regard to all the circumstances obtaining when the liability arose or (but for the notice) would have arisen."

It is clear, then, that the burden is on the surveyor to establish that in all the circumstances it is fair and reasonable that he should be allowed to rely on his disclaimer of liability.

I believe that it is impossible to draw up an exhaustive list of the factors that must be taken into account when a judge is faced with this very difficult decision. Nevertheless, the following matters should, in my view, always be considered.

(1) Were the parties of equal bargaining power? If the court is dealing with a one-off situation between parties of equal bargaining power the requirement of reasonableness would be more easily discharged than in a case such as the present where the disclaimer is imposed on the purchaser who has no effective power to object.

(2) In the case of advice, would it have been reasonably practicable to obtain the advice from an alternative source taking into account considerations of costs and time? In the present case it is urged on behalf of the surveyor that it would have been easy for the purchaser to have obtained his own report on the condition of the house, to which the purchaser replies that he would then be required to pay twice for the same advice and that people buying at the bottom end of the market, many of whom will be young first-time buyers, are likely to be under considerable financial pressure without the money to go paying twice for the same service.

(3) How difficult is the task being undertaken for which liability is being excluded? When a very difficult or dangerous undertaking is involved there may be a high risk of failure which would certainly be a pointer towards the reasonableness of excluding liability as a condition of doing the work. A valuation, on the other hand, should present no difficulty if the work is undertaken with reasonable skill and care. It is only defects which are observable by a careful visual examination that have to be taken into account and I cannot see that it places any unreasonable burden on the valuer to require him to accept responsibility for the fairly elementary degree of skill and care involved in observing, following up and reporting on such defects. Surely it is work at the lower end of the surveyor's field of professional expertise.

(4) What are the practical consequences of the decision on the question of reasonableness? This must involve the sums of money potentially at stake and the ability of the parties to bear the loss involved, which, in its turn, raises the question of insurance. There was once a time when it was considered improper even to mention the possible existence of insurance cover in a lawsuit. But those days are long past. Everyone knows that all prudent, professional men carry insurance, and the availability and cost of insurance must be a relevant factor when considering which of two parties should be required to bear the risk of a loss. We are dealing in this case with a loss which will be limited to the value of a modest house and against which it can be expected that the surveyor will be insured. Bearing the loss will be unlikely to cause significant hardship if it has to be borne by the surveyor but it is, on the other hand, quite possible that it will be a financial catastrophe for the purchaser who may be left with a valueless house and no money to buy another. If the law in these circumstances denies the surveyor the right to exclude his liability, it may result in a few more claims but I do not think so poorly of the surveyors' profession as to believe that the floodgates will be opened. There may be some increase in surveyors' insurance premiums which will be passed on to the public, but I cannot think that it will be anything approaching the figures involved in the difference between the Abbey National's offer of a valuation without liability and a valuation with liability discussed in the speech of my noble and learned friend Lord Templeman. The result of denying a surveyor, in the circumstances of this case, the right to exclude liability will result in distributing the risk of his negligence among all house purchasers through an increase in his fees to cover insurance, rather than allowing the whole of the risk to fall on the one unfortunate purchaser.

I would not, however, wish it to be thought that I would consider it unreasonable for professional men in all circumstances to seek to exclude or limit their liability for negligence. Sometimes breathtaking sums of money may turn on professional advice against which it would be impossible for the adviser to obtain adequate insurance cover and which would ruin him if he were to be held personally liable. In these circumstances it may indeed be reasonable to give the advice on a basis of no liability or possibly of liability limited to the extent of the adviser's insurance cover.

[The House held that the disclaimers failed to satisfy the requirement of reasonableness and were ineffective.]

WATFORD ELECTRONICS LTD v SANDERSON CFL LTD

Court of Appeal [2001] EWCA Civ 317

LORD JUSTICE CHADWICK

22-023   1. This is an appeal against part of an order made on 27 July 2000 by His Honour Judge Thornton Q.C. on the hearing of preliminary issues in proceedings brought in the Technology and Construction Court. The appeal is brought with the permission of this Court (Lord Justice Simon Brown) granted on 27 October 2000.

The background facts

2. The claimant, Watford Electronics Limited (to which I shall refer as "Watford"), is a family owned business engaged in the sale of computer products, principally by mail order. It has particular expertise in the sale or supply of personal computers for educational, commercial and personal use. By 1992 the monthly turnover from its business was £1.5 million or thereabouts, derived from sales of some 8,000 catalogue items.

3. In April 1992 Watford moved to new premises in Luton. It identified a need for an integrated software system which would enable it to exercise greater control over its expanding business; in particular, over mail order sales, warehouse stock and accounts. For that purpose it entered into discussions with the defendant, Sanderson CFL Limited ("Sanderson"), a subsidiary of Sanderson Group Plc Sanderson was engaged in the supply of software products; including, in particular, a product known as "Mailbrain". Mailbrain was a marketing package for use in connection with mail order marketing; but which could be used in conjunction with another product, "Genasys", for maintaining sales, purchase and nominal ledgers and for other accounting functions.

The contractual documents

4. Negotiations took place between Mr Shiraz Jessa, then the technical director of Watford, and Mr Paul Broderick, the sales manager at Sanderson with responsibility for Mailbrain. Those negotiations, extending

over the summer of 1992, led the parties to enter into three contractual documents. Those documents, under a common reference 1078–92, were: (i) a sales contract for the supply by Sanderson of eight items of equipment at a total price of £15,508; (ii) a software licence in respect of Mailbrain and Genasys products, at an initial licence fee of £70,260 and, thereafter, at an annual licence fee of £14,231; and (iii) a software modification licence, covering certain "bespoke" modifications set out in a letter of 29 September 1992 and training, at an initial licence fee of £3,250. The software was for use with IBM compatible hardware, to be provided, I think, by Watford.

5. Each of those three documents was on a single sheet of paper. On the face of the document there was the date, 9 October 1992, a description of the equipment to be supplied or the product to be licensed (as the case might be) and the words "This contract is subject to the Terms and Conditions set out overleaf." Each document was signed, on the face, by Mr Jessa on behalf of "the Customer" and by Mr Arlidge, then the managing director of Sanderson, on behalf of "the Company". The reverse of each document contains printed terms and conditions.

6. The "Terms and Conditions of Sale", which appear on the reverse of the sales contract, contain an "entire agreement" clause in these terms:

"14 Entire Agreement
The parties agree that these terms and conditions (together with any other terms and conditions expressly incorporated in the Contract) represent the entire agreement between the parties relating to the sale and purchase of the Equipment and that no statement or representations made by either party have been relied upon by the other in agreeing to enter into the Contract."

Clause 7 of the "Terms and Conditions of Sale" is in these terms, so far as material:

"7.   Warranty and Limit of Liability"
   7.1   The Company warrants that the Equipment will perform in accordance with its specification . . ."
   7.2   The Company and the Customer agree to indemnify each other against any liability arising in respect of injury (including death) to any person or loss or damage to any property which results from the act, default or negligence of itself, its employees, agents or subcontractors."
   7.3   Neither the Company nor the Customer shall be liable to the other for any claims for indirect or consequential losses whether arising from negligence or otherwise. In no event shall the Company's liability under the Contract exceed the price paid by the Customer to the Company for the Equipment connected with any claim."

7. The "Terms and Conditions of Software Licence" which appear on the reverse of the software licence and the software modification licence contain similar provisions at clause 15 (Entire Agreement) and clause 10 (Warranty and Limit of Liability). In particular, clause 10.6 of the Terms and Conditions of Software Licence is in the same terms (save for the substitution of "Software" for "Equipment") as clause 7.3 of the Terms and Conditions of Sale.

8. The sales contract, the software licence and the software modification licence are each subject to a contemporaneous addendum to clause 7.3 or clause 10.6 (as the case may be) of the Terms and Conditions. The addendum to clause 7.3 of the Terms and Conditions of Sale is in these terms:

"In addition to Clause 7.3, Sanderson CFL Ltd commit to their best endeavours in allocating appropriate resources to the project to minimise any losses that may arise from the Contract."

The addenda to Clauses 10.6 of the Terms and Conditions of Software Licence are to the same effect.

The system fails to perform
9. The system purchased under the October 1992 contracts was brought into operation in or about February 1993. It did not perform satisfactorily. A number of meetings and visits by Sanderson representatives took place in order to identify the problems. A report was commissioned from Bull Information Systems Ltd which recommended upgrading the PC server to a Bull DPX/20. This led to two further documents, each dated 20 August 1993. One was a sales contract for the supply of the Bull mini-computer, with peripherals, at a price of £28,211. The other was a software licence, for which the price was £2,176. The August 1993 documents contained the same terms and conditions as the October 1992 documents.

10. The total paid by Watford to Sanderson for equipment and in licence fees between 1992 and 1996 amounted to £104,596. The system continued to give rise to problems and, in 1996, it was replaced by a new system from a different supplier. Watford sought redress from Sanderson.

These proceedings

11. These proceedings were commenced in 1998. The claim is put in three ways. First, it is said that Watford was induced to sign the October 1992 documents as the result of representations made by Sanderson (including, but not limited to, representations made in the Mailbrain product brochure) which were false. Second, it is said that Sanderson was in breach of terms which were to be implied in both the October 1992 documents and the August 1993 documents. These included (i) warranties in the same terms as the pre-contract representations, (ii) a term that the computer system recommended by Sanderson would be of merchantable quality and reasonable fit for the purposes for which it was supplied, (iii) a term that Sanderson would use the skill and care reasonably to be expected of experts in the performance of the contact, and (iv) a term that Sanderson would remedy any defect which became apparent within a reasonable time so as to allow Watford's business to continue without interruption. Third, it is said that Sanderson, as an expert knowing that Watford would rely upon its expertise, owed a common law duty of care to use skill and care in making its recommendations and in performing the contract induced by those recommendations. There follow allegations of the breach of the alleged contractual duties and of the alleged negligence. Put shortly, it is said that the system recommended was not capable of performing satisfactorily; that it was delivered and installed late; that it never did perform satisfactorily; and that Sanderson failed to meet Watford's complaints or to remedy the defects within a reasonable time.

12. The claim for damages for breach of contract is put under three heads: (i) a claim for loss of profits—said to be measured by a "depression of turnover"—in the amount of £4,402,694; (ii) a claim for damages arising from the increased cost of working—that is to say, from the failure to make savings in staff time and the additional costs incurred in attempting to operate the defective system—in the amount of £996,063; and (iii) a claim for the cost of mitigating the continuing losses equal to the cost of acquiring and installing alternative software in 1996, in the amount of £119,204. The whole amount of the contractual claim is a little over £5.5 million. There is an alternative claim under the Misrepresentation Act 1967 (alternatively for negligent mis-statement). The amounts claimed for misrepresentation and negligence are (i) the £104,596 paid to Sanderson for the equipment and the licence fees, and (ii) the amount of the increased costs of working (£996,063).

13. In a defence served in May 1999, Sanderson relied (amongst other matters) on the entire agreement clauses in the documents—that is to say, on clause 14 of the Terms and Conditions of Sale and clause 15 of the Terms and Conditions of Software Licence; and on the clauses excluding and limiting liability—that is to say, on clause 7.3 of the Terms and Conditions of Sale and clause 10.6 of the Terms and Conditions of Software Licence. It was said (i) that the effect of the addenda negotiated on 29 September 1992 (to which I have referred) was that the terms were no longer to be treated as standard written terms—with the consequence that the Unfair Contract Terms Act 1977 did not apply to them; alternatively, (ii) that, if the 1977 Act did apply, then the terms satisfied the requirement of reasonableness under that Act.

14. On 8 October 1999 His Honour Judge Toulmin CMG Q.C. ordered a number of issues to be tried as preliminary issues. Those issues came before His Honour Judge Thornton Q.C. for trial in February and March 2000. For the reasons given in a written judgment handed down on 27 July 2000 the judge held (so far as material in the context of this appeal) (i) that there was a single contract made between the parties, comprising the three documents signed in October 1992 as varied by the two documents signed in August 1993, and that that contract contained implied terms as to merchantability and fitness for purpose and an implied term that the services to be provided thereunder would be provided with reasonable skill and care; (ii) that the representations contained in the Mailbrain product brochure and in two letters dated 19 June and 23 September 1992 were made by Sanderson and were relied upon by Watford as an inducement to enter into the contract; (iii) that Sanderson owed a common law duty to exercise all due skill and care in giving professional advice; (iv) that, on their true construction, clauses 7.3 and 10.6 in the relevant terms and conditions were apt to exclude liability for losses claimed by Watford in excess of the total price paid for the equipment and the licences; (v) that, on their true construction, clauses 14 and 15 of the relevant terms and conditions (the entire agreement clauses) did not prevent Watford from putting forward any of its claims or from contending that representations made by Sanderson induced the contract; (vi) that both the Unfair Contract Terms Act 1977 and the Misrepresentation Act 1967 applied to the contract between Sanderson and Watford; and (vii) that clauses 7.3 and 10.6 of the relevant terms and conditions were unreasonable in their entirety under the Acts of 1967 and 1977 and could not be relied upon by Sanderson to exclude or restrict its liability to Watford or to impose a limit on any such liability.

The issue on this appeal

15. Sanderson appeals only against so much of the judge's order as gave effect to his finding under Issue 7—although referred to in the judgment as "the Eighth Issue"—that clauses 7.3 and 10.6 were unreasonable in

their entirety. It will be necessary, however, to say something in this judgment as to the true effect of clauses 14 and 15 (the entire agreement clauses) because, to my mind, the presence of those clauses in the contract colours the meaning and effect which the parties must be taken to have intended should be given to clauses 7.3 and 10.6.

[Chadwick L.J. sketched the background of UCTA and its key provisions before continuing:]

The judgment below

21. The issue for the judge—Issue 7—was posed in these terms: "Are the Defendant's written terms [contained in clauses 7.3 and 10.6] reasonable under the Unfair Contract Terms Act 1977 and the Misrepresentation Act 1967?". He answered that question in the negative. He held that the clauses "are unreasonable in their entirety . . . and cannot therefore be relied upon by the Defendant to exclude or restrict its liability to the Claimant or to impose a limit on any such liability".

22. The judge directed himself that the matters set out in schedule 2 to the 1977 Act were relevant whether or not schedule 2 was made applicable by section 11(2) of that Act. As he said, at paragraph 115 of his written judgment: "I will decide the reasonableness of the clause in question for all claims by reference to all matters including those set out in schedule 2." He addressed, first, each of the "guideline" matters set out in schedule 2—other than that in paragraph (d) which, as was common ground, could have no relevance to the contract term in relation to which the requirement of reasonableness was in issue.

23. The judge's conclusions in relation to the guideline matters may be summarised as follows:

Paragraph (a)—the strength of the bargaining positions of the parties relative to each other.

The judge held, at paragraph 120 of his written judgment, that there was no inequality of bargaining power between the parties; and, further, that neither was under any particular pressure to contract with the other. He held, at paragraph 121, that there was no inequality of bargaining skill. In particular, he found that: "Mr Jessa [for Watford] was a skilled and reliable negotiator who successfully negotiated the asking price downwards during his inevitably protracted discussions with Mr Broderick [for Sanderson]". He accepted that the market for commercially produced software packages could aptly be described as a "buyer's market", at least in the sense that prices were competitive and buyers could negotiate substantial discounts. But, at paragraph 123 of his judgment, he said this:

> "However there were other aspects of the market which would more appropriately be called a seller's market. In particular, the terms upon which Sanderson would do business were inflexible and non-negotiable. This was particularly so with the exemption clause. Mr Jessa sought to vary this but could only persuade Sanderson to offer the virtually meaningless addendum contained in the schedule which provided an obligation to use best endeavours to sort out any problem if such occurred. General evidence from Mr Broderick and from the several cases referred to at the trial where software exemption clauses were in issue suggested that it was a standard feature of this industry in the early 1990s to supply software packages on stringent standard terms exempting all or virtually all liability without providing any service or alternative service to deal with defects or breaches of terms concerned with merchantability, fitness and performance. Thus Watford could not reasonably have expected to have been able to have acquired a similar software package, if available, on better terms as to performance and as to the supplier's potential liability for non-performance."

He considered whether there were other sources of supply available to Watford. He concluded, at paragraph 126, that there were other possible mail order packages on the market but that Mailbrain was the only one which appeared to fulfil Watford's needs. He said this:

> "Sanderson did not show that such an integrated package would have been readily available elsewhere and such evidence as there was of potential rival packages suggested that no such integrated package was readily to hand."

Paragraph (b)—whether the customer received an inducement to agree the term; or had an opportunity to enter into a similar contract elsewhere without the term?

The judge held that there was no financial inducement which led Watford to accept the relevant contract term. He rejected the contention, advanced by Sanderson, that the price reduction was negotiated on the basis that Sanderson would accept a lower price if Watford would accept the term limiting liability.

Paragraph (c)—the customer's knowledge of the relevant contract term.
The judge held, at paragraph 132:

> ". . . Mr Jessa was aware of the existence of the term, only first learnt of its existence towards the end of the pre-contract discussions, attempted unsuccessfully to have it substantially amended, only succeeded in achieving a make-weight amendment and learnt from Sanderson that a term totally excluding liability was standard software industry practice."

Paragraph (e)—were the goods adapted to the special needs of the customer?
Plainly there were modifications to the system; it was the modifications which gave rise to the need for the software modification licence. But the judge thought that they were minor in relation to the standard package that was being supplied and were "an inevitable part of the process of implementing and configuring the system which Sanderson had contracted to provide and which Watford was paying for as part of the contract price".

24. The judge then addressed a number of other matters which had been canvassed before him. First, the availability of insurance; to which regard must be had under section 11(4) of the 1977 Act (in a case to which that sub-section applies). He found that Sanderson did not have any insurance cover in respect of liability for indirect and consequential losses arising from the defective performance of the Mailbrain product; but that such cover was available. He referred to the evidence of Mr Bailey, who had become Sanderson's managing director in succession, I think, to Mr Arlidge. The judge said this, at paragraph 136 of his judgment:

> "Sanderson's commercial policy at that time [1992] was to seek to maintain its exclusion of liability clause but, if a potential customer insisted on the deletion of this clause from the contract or on an amendment to cover it from an exclusion of liability clause to a limitation of liability clause, to be prepared to modify the clause in an appropriate case. In such cases, Sanderson would consider whether to obtain one-off insurance cover and would do so if Mr Bailey considered Sanderson's risk of exposure was too great. Mr Bailey referred to two contracts where an increased limit of liability had been negotiated and insurance cover had then been obtained. Mr Bailey did not explain why Sanderson had not been prepared to provide such an amendment to its exclusion of liability clause in the contracts with Watford and I infer that the reason was that Sanderson correctly assumed that Watford would be persuaded to contract without such an amendment. Mr Bailey's policy was only to contemplate an amendment if it made the difference between making a sale and not making one. I conclude, therefore, that insurance cover would have been available to Sanderson who chose not to obtain it for commercial reasons and, instead, to exclude its liability for consequential losses."

25. There was no evidence as to the availability to Watford of insurance cover against loss of profits or turnover resulting from the failure of the system which it was to purchase. The judge held that he must leave that possibility out of account. He said this, at paragraph 137:

> "Since the burden of proof in establishing the reasonableness of the exclusion clause rests with Sanderson, I conclude that I should not regard it as relevant to the potential reasonableness of the clause that it might have been possible for Watford to take out its own insurance."

26. There were two other matters which the judge thought he should leave out of account. First, he re-affirmed his view—of which he had already given an indication when considering the question of inducement to agree the term—that the fact that an overall discount was negotiated, which (as he thought) was not referable to the relevant contract term, when agreeing the contract price had no bearing on the reasonableness or unreasonableness of the term (see paragraph 139). Second, he regarded it as irrelevant that Watford's own standard terms of business contained a clause excluding liability in respect of consequential losses. The clause—clause 10 in Watford's "Terms and Conditions of Sale"—was in these terms, so far as material:

"10. Liability
  (a) The Company shall not be liable to the Customer

    (i)   . . .
    (ii) . . .
    (iii) for defects in the goods caused by fair wear and tear, abnormal conditions of storage or use or act, neglect or default of the Customer or of any third party,
    (iv) for other defects in goods or the media upon which software is supplied, unless notified to the Company within seven days of receipt of the goods or software, or where the defect would not be apparent on reasonable inspection within seven days of delivery.

(b) (i)   Where liability is accepted by the Company under paragraph (a), the Company's only obligation shall be at its option to . . . replace or repair any goods or software found to be . . . defective and/or to refund the cost thereof to the Customer, and in no event shall the Company be under any liability whatsoever and howsoever arising from any loss of profit, interruption of business or any other indirect, special or consequential losses of any type rising or alleged to have arisen out of any act or default of the Company in respect of its obligations hereunder.

   (ii)   Company's aggregate liability to the Customer hereunder or otherwise arising whether for negligence, breach of contract, misrepresentation or otherwise shall in no circumstances exceed the cost of the defective . . . goods which give rise to such liability . . .

(c)   . . .

(d)   The Company's prices are determined on the basis of the limits of liability set out in this Condition. The Customer may by written notice request the Company to agree a higher limit of liability provided insurance cover can be obtained therefor."

In declining to treat as relevant the existence of that clause in Watford's own terms of business, the judge observed that:

"Watford is a retailer of PCs, Sanderson is a supplier of tailored software systems. Those are very different businesses and, besides, Watford's exclusion clause might well be held to be unreasonable in a dispute with one of its customers."

27. The judge treated as irrelevant, also, the fact that Watford had had the opportunity to see the Mailbrain product in operation in a working environment similar to its own; and that Watford had had the benefit of a demonstration at its own premises. He held that neither the inspection nor the demonstration would have provided Watford with any opportunity to assess the risk that the system might not perform.

28. Finally, the judge referred, at paragraph 142 of his judgment, to a number of general considerations which had been advanced by Watford in support of its contention that the relevant contract term was unreasonable: (i) that the contract was for the supply of software for a particular use—so that the relevant contract term deprived Watford of any effective remedy for all possible significant breaches of contract by Sanderson; (ii) that Watford was particularly dependent on the representations made to it by Sanderson—because it was dependent on Sanderson's expertise; (iii) that the consequences of defective performance on Watford were potentially very significant; and (iv) that Sanderson had assured Watford, after having acquired some knowledge of its business, that the software system supplied would be fit for its purpose.

29. With all those factors in mind, the judge reached the conclusion that Sanderson had not established that the relevant contract term was reasonable. He expressed that conclusion in the following passage, at paragraph 144 of his judgment:

"The clause is not justified by any particularly onerous or unusual liabilities that Sanderson might encounter, nor by any difficulties in obtaining insurance nor by any particular features of either the negotiations or of the parties. Watford would have had considerable difficulties in obtaining the relevant software elsewhere without such a clause since it was a common feature of the software supply industry at that time. The effect of the clause is to deprive Watford of the opportunity of recovering any damages in circumstances in which, given the assumptions I must make about the correctness of Watford's pleaded allegations, there have been significant failures accurately to represent the features of the software and to comply with the contractual requirements as to merchantability and quality. Indeed on the basis of these assumptions, Sanderson has materially failed to perform its contract obligations. I accept the factors stressed by Watford as being ones which make it unreasonable for Sanderson to rely on the clause. It is, therefore, one which may not be relied upon in relation to any of Watford's pleaded allegations or claims."

[Having referred to the approach to be taken by an appellate court, after the guidance in the *George Mitchell* case, Chadwick LJ continued:]

The scope and effect of the relevant contract term

31. In order to decide whether the relevant contract term was a fair and reasonable one to be included having regard to the circumstances which were, or ought reasonably to have been, known to or in the contemplation of the parties when the contract was made it is necessary, as it seems to me, to determine, first, the scope and effect of that term as a matter of construction. In particular, it is necessary to identify the nature of the liability which the term is seeking to exclude or restrict. Whether or not a contract term satisfies the "requirement of

reasonableness" within the meaning of section 11 of the Unfair Contract Terms Act 1977 does not fall to be determined in isolation. It falls to be determined where a person is seeking to rely upon the term in order to exclude or restrict his liability in some context to which the earlier provisions of the 1977 Act (or the provisions of section 3 of the Misrepresentation Act 1967) apply.

32. Clause 7.3 in the Terms and Conditions of Sale and clause 10.6 in the Terms and Conditions of Software Licence each contain two sentences: (i) "Neither the Company nor the Customer shall be liable to the other for any claims for indirect or consequential losses whether arising from negligence or otherwise." (ii) "In no event shall the Company's liability under the Contract exceed the price paid by the Customer to the Company for the [Equipment/ Software] connected with any claim." It is, to my mind, plain that the reason why the clauses each contain two sentences is that each sentence is intended to have its own separate and distinct purpose. In so far as the judge held otherwise, I am satisfied that he was wrong to do so. At paragraph 145 of his judgment he said this:

> "I do not need to consider separately whether the clause could be reasonable in so far as it limits Sanderson's liability to the ceiling of recoverability imposed by the contract price. The parties accepted that the clause was either reasonable or unreasonable in full and was not one to which a blue pencilling exercise could be carried out so as to uphold it in part. In any case the very low ceiling imposed by the limitation clause is such as to render that part of the clause unreasonable for the reasons I have already provided, even if that provision stood on its own."

The need to recognise that each of the two sentences in the clause has a separate and distinct purpose—and to identify that purpose—is not to be dismissed as "a blue pencilling exercise". It is essential to a determination whether or not the relevant contract term—that is to say, the contract term which is relevant to the liability which Sanderson seeks to exclude—satisfies the requirement of reasonableness.

33. The purpose of the second sentence of the clause is, I think, clear enough. It is intended to restrict Sanderson's liability under the contract with its customer to a specified sum of money. The sum specified is the price paid by the customer for the "[Equipment/Software] connected with the claim." In that connection it is relevant to have in mind the warranties given in clauses 7.1 and 10.1 respectively. In clause 7.1 of the Terms and Conditions of Sale Sanderson warrants that "the Equipment will perform in accordance with its specification". In clause 10.1 of the Terms and Conditions of Software Licence the warranty is that "the Software (as supplied by or modified by the Company) will during normal use perform the functions detailed within the manuals supplied . . ."

34. It is relevant also, I think, to have in mind the provisions of sections 53(2) and 53(3) of the Sale of Goods Act 1979:

> "(2) The measure of damages for breach of warranty is the estimated loss directly and naturally resulting, in the ordinary course of events, from the breach of warranty.
> (3) In the case of breach of warranty of quality such loss is prima facie the difference between the value of the goods at the time of delivery to the buyer and the value they would have had if they had fulfilled the warranty."

Those provisions provide a starting point, at least in the case of any defect in the quality of the Equipment or in its failure to perform in accordance with specification. It is, I think, obvious that the attempt in the second sentence of the clause—clause 7.3 in the Terms and Conditions of Sale and clause 10.6 in the Terms and Conditions of Software Licence—to limit liability for breach of warranty to the price of the equipment or software connected with the claim is an attempt, in the context of section 53(3) of the 1979 Act, to peg the value which the goods would have had if the warranty had been fulfilled to the price paid by the buyer.

35. But, as section 53(3) of the 1979 Act makes clear, the difference in the value of the goods is only a *prima facie* measure of the damages for breach of warranty of quality. The buyer can claim loss of profits or other consequential losses where he can show that the seller knew, or ought reasonably to have had in contemplation, that a breach of the warranty would give rise to such losses—see *Hadley v Baxendale* (1854) 9 Exch 341, 354; *Victoria Laundry (Windsor) Ltd v Newman Industries* [1949] 2 KB 528, 539; *Cullinane v British "Rema" Manufacturing Co Ltd* [1954] 1 QB 292, 301. It is sufficient to identify the point by reference to a passage in the judgment of Lord Evershed, Master of the Rolls, in the last of those three cases, at page 301:

> "In the present case it is plain that to the knowledge of the defendants this machine was required to perform a particular function, and the warranty given shows what the function was that the machine was designed to perform. There is, therefore, no doubt at all that the plaintiff is entitled to rely on [the second limb of the rule in *Hadley v Baxendale*], and to claim as damages the business loss which must reasonably be supposed to have been, in the contemplation of both parties at the time when they made the contract, the probable

result of the breach. In other words, this plaintiff is not confined to the loss which might be called the natural result of having a machine which turned out to be less that the purchase he has paid for it."

36. The purpose of the first sentence of the clause is (at the least) to exclude contractual claims for indirect and consequential losses; that is to say, to exclude liability in contract for losses which could be recovered only under the second limb of the rule in *Hadley v Baxendale*. Those are losses which do not result "directly and naturally" from the breach; but which, nevertheless, were or must reasonably be supposed to have been in the contemplation of both parties at the time when the contract was made.

37. The judge took the view that the purpose of the first sentence of the clause went beyond the exclusion of contractual claims. He thought that the clause was intended to exclude claims in respect of pre-contractual misrepresentations. That he took that view appears from the answer which he gave to Issue 7. I think that he was wrong to reach that conclusion.

The effect of the entire agreement clause

38. The purpose of the first sentence of the clause must be ascertained not only in the light of the second sentence, but also in the light of the entire agreement clause. The entire agreement clause—clause 14 in the Terms and Conditions of Sale, clause 15 in the Terms and Conditions of Software Licence—is also in two parts. The second part of the clause contains an acknowledgement by the parties that "no statements or representations made by either party have been relied upon by the other in agreeing to enter into the contract".

39. The effect of an acknowledgement of non-reliance, in terms which were sufficiently similar to those in the second part of the entire agreement clause in the present case as to be indistinguishable, was considered in this Court in *E A Grimstead & Son Ltd v McGarrigan* (unreported, 27 October 1999). In a passage which was *obiter dicta*—but which followed full argument on the point—I said this (at page 32A-C of the transcript):

"In my view an acknowledgement of non-reliance . . . is capable of operating as an evidential estoppel. It is apt to prevent the party who has given the acknowledgement from asserting in subsequent litigation against the party to whom it has been given that it is not true. That seems to me to be a proper use of an acknowledgement of this nature, which, as Mr Justice Jacob pointed out in the *Thomas Witter* case [*Thomas Witter Ltd v TBP Industries Ltd* [1996] 2 All ER 573], has become a common feature of professionally drawn commercial contracts."

I went on, at page 35A–C, to say this:

"There are, as it seems to me, at least two good reasons why the courts should not refuse to give effect to an acknowledgement of non-reliance in a commercial contract between experienced parties of equal bargaining power—*a fortiori*, where those parties have the benefit of professional advice. First, it is reasonable to assume that the parties desire commercial certainty. They want to order their affairs on the basis that the bargain between them can be found within the document which they have signed. They want to avoid the uncertainty of litigation based on allegations as to the content of oral discussions at pre-contractual meetings. Second, it is reasonable to assume that the price to be paid reflects the commercial risk which each party—or, more usually, the purchaser—is willing to accept. The risk is determined, in part at least, by the warranties which the vendor is prepared to give. The tighter the warranties, the less the risk and (in principle, at least) the greater the price the vendor will require and which the purchaser will be prepared to pay. It is legitimate, and commercially desirable, that both parties should be able to measure the risk, and agree the price, on the basis of the warranties which have been given and accepted."

40. Those passages were not cited to the judge. He held that Sanderson could not rely on the acknowledgement of non-reliance contained in the second part of the entire agreement clause. He said this, at paragraph 107 of his judgment:

". . . the clause is, in substance, one that excludes liability rather than precludes liability from ever occurring. The clause states that no statement or representation has been relied on. It follows that the clause can only first bite once a statement or representation has been made that is capable of being relied on. The clause bites, therefore, on a potential misrepresentation that has been made. It is not preventing words that have been uttered from being a misrepresentation at all. Furthermore, the words that were used did, as a matter of fact, as I have found, induce the contract. Thus, this clause is one which is in substance an exclusion clause to which section 3 of the Misrepresentation Act is applicable"

I confess to some difficulty in following the reasoning in that passage. It is true that an acknowledgement of non-reliance does not purport to prevent a party from proving that a representation was made, nor that it was false. What the acknowledgement seeks to do is to prevent the person to whom the representation was made from asserting that he relied upon it. If it is to have that effect, it will be necessary—as I sought to point out in *Grimstead v McGarrigan*—for the party who seeks to set up the acknowledgement as an evidential estoppel to plead and prove that the three requirements identified by this Court in *Lowe v Lombank Ltd* [1960] 1 WLR 196 are satisfied. That may present insuperable difficulties; not least because it may be impossible for a party who has made representations which he intended should be relied upon to satisfy the court that he entered into the contract in the belief that a statement by the other party that he had not relied upon those representations was true. But the fact that, on particular facts, the acknowledgement of non-reliance may not achieve its purpose does not lead to the conclusion that the acknowledgement is "in substance an exclusion clause to which section 3 of the Misrepresentation Act is applicable". Nor does it lead to the conclusion that the entire agreement clause can be disregarded when construing the earlier limit of liability clause—clause 7.3 in the Terms and Conditions of Sale and clause 10.6 in the Terms and Conditions of Software Licence.

41. The importance of the entire agreement clause in the present context—and, in particular, the importance of the acknowledgement of non-reliance which constitutes the second part of that clause—is that the first sentence in clause 7.3 (or clause 10.6, as the case may be) has to be construed on the basis that the parties intend that their whole agreement is to be contained or incorporated in the document which they have signed and on the basis that neither party has relied on any pre-contract representation when signing that document. On that basis, there is no reason why the parties should have intended, by the words which they have used in the first sentence of the limit of liability clause, to exclude liability for negligent pre-contract misrepresentation. Liability in damages under the Misrepresentation Act 1967 can arise only where the party who has suffered the damage has relied upon the representation. Where both parties to the contract have acknowledged, in the document itself, that they have not relied upon any pre-contract representation, it would be bizarre (unless compelled to do so by the words which they have used) to attribute to them an intention to exclude a liability which they must have thought could never arise.

Was the judge's approach wrong?

42. As I have already indicated, this Court should not substitute its own view of what is fair and reasonable for that of the judge unless. satisfied that the judge proceeded upon some erroneous principle or was plainly and obviously wrong. I am satisfied that the judge fell into error in three respects; and that those errors do vitiate his conclusion.

43. The first error, in my view, lies in the judge's failure properly to identify the scope and effect of the limit of liability clause; and in the resulting failure to address the correct question or questions. For the reasons which I have sought to explain, I am satisfied that, as a matter of construction, the true scope and effect of the limit of liability clause is more restricted than the judge appreciated. The clause seeks to do two things: (i) to exclude contractual claims for indirect and consequential losses—that is to say, to exclude liability in contract for losses which could be recovered only under the second limb of the rule in *Hadley v Baxendale*—and (ii) to restrict liability for loss directly and naturally resulting, in the ordinary course of events, from breach of warranty to the price paid for the equipment (or the software, as the case may be), so avoiding an enquiry into what would have been the value of the equipment (or software) if the warranty had been fulfilled. The clause does not seek to exclude or restrict liability for pre-contract misrepresentation, whether such liability arises at common law or under statute. Liability for negligent performance plainly lies in contract and is within the scope of the clause. It has not been suggested that there could be additional, non-contractual, liability for the negligent performance of the contract.

44. The judge thought that the effect of the clause was "to deprive Watford of the opportunity to recover any damages in circumstances in which . . . there have been significant failures accurately to represent the features of the software and to comply with the contractual requirements as to merchantability and quality."—see paragraph 144 of his judgment. To ask whether a clause which has that effect is reasonable was the wrong question. It was the wrong question because the clause does not have that effect. On the basis that the purpose and effect of the limit of liability clause is as I have described, the relevant questions are: (i) was it fair and reasonable, having regard to the circumstances which were, or ought reasonably to have been in the contemplation of the parties when the contract was made, to include a term which sought to exclude contractual claims for indirect and consequential losses; and (ii) was it fair and reasonable, having regard to those circumstances, to include a term which sought to restrict loss directly and naturally resulting, in the ordinary course of things, from breach of warranty to the price paid for the equipment (or the software, as the case might be).

45. The second error, as it seems to me, was to treat the obligation added by the addenda to the contractual documents signed in October 1992 as "virtually meaningless"—see paragraph 123 of the judgment. The true position was that, in addition to the obligations under the relevant standard terms and conditions, Sanderson committed itself, by the addenda, to use best endeavours to allocate appropriate resources to the project "to minimise any losses that may arise from the contract." That obligation is superimposed on the obligations under the relevant standard terms and conditions.

46. The position can be illustrated by reference to the software licence. Clause 10.1 contains the warranty that the Software will perform the functions detailed within the manuals supplied. Clause 10.2 requires that, if the Software fails to comply with that warranty, Sanderson will modify the Software until it complies with the warranty, or will replace the Software with other Software which does comply with the warranty. It is necessary to distinguish between (i) losses suffered by Watford because the Software does not perform the functions detailed in the manuals (which, subject to the limit of liability clause, are recoverable by a claim for breach of warranty) and (ii) losses suffered by Watford because Software which does perform the functions detailed in the manuals does not, nevertheless, meet Watford's real requirements (which losses are recoverable, if at all, by a claim for negligent pre-contract statement—on the basis that Watford entered into the contract on the basis that the functions detailed in the manuals were the functions which Watford required—and which are not subject to the limit of liability clause). It is, to my mind, reasonably plain that the obligation, assumed by Sanderson under the addendum to clause 10.6, to use best endeavours to allocate appropriate resources to minimise *any losses* that may arise under the contract, is confined to losses resulting from breach of warranty; but it plainly extends to all losses arising from breach of warranty, including indirect and consequential losses. The effect of the addendum is that Sanderson cannot (as the judge thought) walk away from the contract on the basis that the only claim to which it is exposed if it fails to ensure that the Software performs the specified functions is a claim for the price paid. Unless Sanderson can show that it did use its best endeavours to allocate appropriate resources to ensure that the Software performs the specified functions, it cannot rely on the provision in clause 10.6 excluding claims for indirect or consequential losses.

47. To put the point another way, the effect of the limit of liability clause with the addendum is that Sanderson will not be liable for indirect or consequential losses suffered by Watford provided that Sanderson has done what it can to allocate appropriate resources to making the equipment and the software perform according to warranty. The safeguard which Mr Jessa obtained on behalf of Watford when the standard terms and conditions were varied by addenda signed in October 1992 was that Sanderson undertook to do its best to see that losses (including indirect or consequential losses) were kept to a minimum. If, despite Sanderson's best endeavours, indirect or consequential losses were suffered, those losses would fall on Watford. But if Sanderson had not used its best endeavours, then Watford could recover such losses (including indirect or consequential losses) as resulted from Sanderson's failure to comply with its undertaking. The judge described that safeguard as "virtually meaningless" and "a make-weight amendment" (see paragraphs 123 and 132 of his judgment). In my view, that is not an apt description of its effect.

48. The third error lies in the judge's decision to treat as "irrelevant" Watford's own standard terms of business—see paragraph 139 of his judgment. I have set out, earlier in this judgment, the material provisions in clause 10 of Watford's Terms and Conditions of Sale. They include (i) a restriction on liability, the terms of which are indistinguishable in effect from those of the first sentence of Sanderson's limit of liability clause (but which are, if anything, more explicit)—*viz.* "in no event shall the Company be under any liability whatsoever and howsoever arising from any loss of profit, interruption of business or any other indirect, special or consequential losses of any type . . ."; and (ii) a clause which explains why the restriction is there—*viz.* "The Company's prices are determined on the basis of the limits of liability set out in this Condition." The judge was correct to reject the argument that the presence of the first of those provisions in Watford's own standard conditions had the effect, in some way, of preventing Watford from asserting that the inclusion of the first sentence in Sanderson's limit of liability clause was not fair and reasonable. But the provisions cannot be dismissed as irrelevant simply because that they do not support that argument. The relevance of the provisions, to my mind, is that they show that Watford was well aware of the commercial considerations which lead a supplier to include a provision restricting liability for indirect or consequential loss; and, in particular, was well aware that a supplier would be likely to determine the price at which it was prepared to sell its products by reference (amongst other things) to its exposure to the risk of unquantifiable claims to indirect or consequential losses which might be suffered by the customer if things went wrong. In my view, Watford's obvious appreciation of the problem which the limit of liability clause was intended to meet—and its own method of dealing with that problem in the standard terms under which it supplied goods to its own customers—were very relevant to a consideration of the matter which the judge had to decide; that is to say, whether the inclusion of the limit of liability clause in Sanderson's

standard terms and conditions was fair and reasonable having regard to the circumstances which were, or ought reasonably to have been known to or in the contemplation of the parties when the contract was made.

Was the term a fair and reasonable one to be included?

49. For the reasons which I have set out, I am satisfied that this is a case in which, if this Court takes a different view from that of the judge on the question whether the inclusion of the limit of liability clause in Sanderson's standard terms and conditions was fair and reasonable having regard to the circumstances which were, or ought reasonably to have been, known to or in the contemplation of the parties when the contract was made, it is entitled to give effect to its own view. That is because I am satisfied that the judge reached his conclusion on the wrong basis.

50. I have explained why I take the view that, on a true analysis of the limit of liability clause, it comprises two distinct contract terms in relation to which it is necessary to consider whether the requirement of reasonableness is satisfied. One (to which I shall refer for convenience as "the term excluding indirect loss") is that contained in the first sentence of the clause. The other ("the term limiting direct loss") is contained in the second sentence. It is, I think, appropriate to consider, separately in relation to each term, whether the requirement of reasonableness is satisfied; although, of course, in considering whether that requirement is satisfied in relation to each term, the existence of the other term in the contract is relevant.

51. I turn, therefore, to consider whether the requirement of reasonableness is satisfied in relation to the term excluding indirect loss. It is important to keep in mind (i) that, as a matter of construction, the term does not seek to exclude loss resulting from pre-contractual statements in relation to which a claim lies (if at all) in tort or under the Misrepresentation Act 1967 and (ii) that the term is qualified by the addenda so that it does not exclude indirect or consequential loss resulting from breach of warranty unless Sanderson has used its best endeavours to ensure that the equipment and the software does comply with the warranty.

52. I accept that the court is required to have regard, in the present case, to the "guideline" matters set out in schedule 2 to the 1977 Act. There are factors, identified by the guidelines, which point to a conclusion that the term excluding indirect loss was a fair and reasonable one to include in this contract. The parties were of equal bargaining strength; the inclusion of the term was, plainly, likely to affect Sanderson's decision as to the price at which was prepared to sell its product; Watford must be taken to have appreciated that; Watford knew of the term, and must be taken to have understood what effect it was intended to have; the product was, to some extent, modified to meet the special needs of the customer. Other factors point in the opposite direction. The judge found that, although there were other mail order packages on the market, Mailbrain was the only one which appeared to fulfil Watford's needs (paragraph 126); and, further, that Watford could not reasonably have expected to have been able to have acquired a similar software package, if available, on better terms as to performance and as to the supplier's potential liability for non-performance.

53. I do not, for my part, accept that the term excluding indirect loss is a term to which section 11(4) of the 1977 Act applies. It is not, I think, properly to be regarded as a term by which a person (Sanderson) seeks to restrict liability to a specified sum of money; rather the term seeks to exclude liability for indirect or consequential loss altogether, in those circumstances in which it is intended to have effect. Nevertheless, it seems to me right to have regard, as part of the circumstances which were, or ought reasonably to have been, known to or in the contemplation of the parties when the contract was made, both to the resources which could be expected to be available to each party for the purpose of meeting indirect or consequential loss resulting from the failure of the equipment or software to perform in accordance with specification, and to the possibility that such loss could be covered by insurance.

54. It seems to me that the starting point in an enquiry whether, in the present case, the term excluding indirect loss was a fair and reasonable one to include in the contract which these parties made is to recognise (i) that there is a significant risk that a non-standard software product, "customised" to meet the particular marketing, accounting or record-keeping needs of a substantial and relatively complex business (such as that carried on by Watford), may not perform to the customer's satisfaction, (ii) that, if it does not do so, there is a significant risk that the customer may not make the profits or savings which it had hoped to make (and may incur consequential losses arising from the product's failure to perform), (iii) that those risks were, or ought reasonably to have been, known to or in the contemplation of both Sanderson and Watford at the time when the contract was made, (iv) that Sanderson was in the better position to assess the risk that the product would fail to perform but (v) that Watford was in the better position to assess the amount of the potential loss if the product failed to perform, (vi) that the risk of loss was likely to be capable of being covered by insurance, but at a cost, and (vii) that both Sanderson and Watford would have known, or ought reasonably to have known, at the time when the contract was made, that the identity of the party who was to bear the risk of loss (or to bear the cost of insurance) was a factor which would be taken into account in determining the price at which

the supplier was willing to supply the product and the price at which the customer was willing to purchase. With those considerations in mind, it is reasonable to expect that the contract will make provision for the risk of indirect or consequential loss to fall on one party or the other. In circumstances in which parties of equal bargaining power negotiate a price for the supply of product under an agreement which provides for the person on whom the risk of loss will fall, it seems to me that the court should be very cautious before reaching the conclusion that the agreement which they have reached is not a fair and reasonable one.

55. Where experienced businessmen representing substantial companies of equal bargaining power negotiate an agreement, they may be taken to have had regard to the matters known to them. They should, in my view be taken to be the best judge of the commercial fairness of the agreement which they have made; including the fairness of each of the terms in that agreement. They should be taken to be the best judge on the question whether the terms of the agreement are reasonable. The court should not assume that either is likely to commit his company to an agreement which he thinks is unfair, or which he thinks includes unreasonable terms., Unless satisfied that one party has, in effect, taken unfair advantage of the other—or that a term is so unreasonable that it cannot properly have been understood or considered—the court should not interfere.

56. In the present case the parties did negotiate as to the price. Mr Jessa, on behalf of Watford, secured substantial concessions on price from Mr Broderick. The parties negotiated, also, as to which of them should bear the risk (or the cost of insurance against the risk) of making good the loss of profits, and other indirect or consequential loss, which Watford might suffer if the product failed to perform as intended. Mr Jessa was less successful in obtaining from Mr Broderick the concession which he wanted. The most that he could get was an undertaking that Sanderson would use its best endeavours to allocate appropriate resources to ensuring that the product performed according to specification. But, for the reasons which I have sought to explain, that was worth something to Watford; and Mr Jessa decided that he would be content with what he could get. In my view it is impossible to hold, in the circumstances of the present case, that Sanderson took unfair advantage of Watford; or that Watford, through Mr Jessa, did not properly understand and consider the effect of the term excluding indirect loss.

57. It follows that I would hold that the term excluding indirect loss, applicable in the circumstances which I have described, was a fair and reasonable one to include in the contract.

58. In the light of that conclusion, the question whether the requirement of reasonableness is satisfied in relation to the term limiting direct loss can be answered shortly. Properly understood, all that the second sentence of the limit of liability clause seeks to do is to substitute a value equal to the price paid by the buyer for the goods for "the value which the goods would have had if they had fulfilled the warranty" for the purposes of the rule in section 53(3) of the Sale of Goods Act 1979 or the equivalent rule at common law. It seems to me impossible to hold that that is an unfair or unreasonable substitution to make in a case like the present.

I would allow this appeal.

There is much to be said in favour of the *Watford Electronics* (and *Photo Production*) philosophy of leaving business contractors to make their own deals. As Tuckey LJ remarked in *Granville Oil and Chemicals Ltd v Davies Turner and Co Ltd* [2003] EWCA Civ 570, at [31]:

"The 1977 Act obviously plays a very important role in protecting vulnerable consumers from the effect of draconian contract terms. But I am less enthusiastic about its intrusion into contracts between commercial parties of equal bargaining strength, who should generally be considered capable of being able to make contracts of their choosing and expect to be bound by their terms."

Even in commercial dealing, however, there are occasions when a court will judge that it would be wholly unreasonable if it did not intervene to adjust the parties' risk allocation. See, e.g., *Britvic Soft Drinks Ltd v Messer UK Ltd* [2002] EWCA Civ 548 where traces of benzene were found in carbon dioxide that was supplied for the production of fizzy drinks.

----

3. The Consumer Rights Act 2015

22–024   Part 2 of the Consumer Rights Act sweeps up the existing legislative provisions that regulate unfair terms in consumer contracts. The basic shape of Part 2 is very much as in the Unfair Terms in Consumer Contracts Regulations 1999. Section 62(4) reproduces the standard test (good faith, substantial imbalance, detriment to the consumer); Schedule 2 sets out an indicative list of terms that may be treated as unfair; and s.64(1) reworks the exclusion from assessment that gave the courts so much difficulty in the two big OFT cases (above). However, in s.62(8) of the Act we find the blacklisting approach that the Unfair Contract Terms Act employs in relation to limited classes of terms. The relevant provisions of the Act are set out below.

PART 2

UNFAIR TERMS

What contracts and notices are covered by this Part?

61 Contracts and notices covered by this Part

22–025
(1) This Part applies to a contract between a trader and a consumer.
(2) This does not include a contract of employment or apprenticeship.
(3) A contract to which this Part applies is referred to in this Part as a "consumer contract".
(4) This Part applies to a notice to the extent that it—

  (a) relates to rights or obligations as between a trader and a consumer, or
  (b) purports to exclude or restrict a trader's liability to a consumer.

(5) This does not include a notice relating to rights, obligations or liabilities as between an employer and an employee.
(6) It does not matter for the purposes of subsection (4) whether the notice is expressed to apply to a consumer, as long as it is reasonable to assume it is intended to be seen or heard by a consumer.
(7) A notice to which this Part applies is referred to in this Part as a "consumer notice".
(8) In this section "notice" includes an announcement, whether or not in writing, and any other communication or purported communication.

What are the general rules about fairness of contract terms and notices?

62 Requirement for contract terms and notices to be fair

(1) An unfair term of a consumer contract is not binding on the consumer.
(2) An unfair consumer notice is not binding on the consumer.
(3) This does not prevent the consumer from relying on the term or notice if the consumer chooses to do so.
(4) A term is unfair if, contrary to the requirement of good faith, it causes a significant imbalance in the parties' rights and obligations under the contract to the detriment of the consumer.
(5) Whether a term is fair is to be determined—
  (a) taking into account the nature of the subject matter of the contract, and
  (b) by reference to all the circumstances existing when the term was agreed and to all of the other terms of the contract or of any other contract on which it depends.
(6) A notice is unfair if, contrary to the requirement of good faith, it causes a significant imbalance in the parties' rights and obligations to the detriment of the consumer.
(7) Whether a notice is fair is to be determined—
  (a) taking into account the nature of the subject matter of the notice, and
  (b) by reference to all the circumstances existing when the rights or obligations to which it relates arose and to the terms of any contract on which it depends.
(8) This section does not affect the operation of—

(a) section 31 (exclusion of liability: goods contracts) [s.31 is set out below],
(b) section 47 (exclusion of liability: digital content contracts), [s.47 is set out below]
(c) section 56 (exclusion of liability: services contracts), [s.57 is set out below] or
(d) section 65 (exclusion of negligence liability).

63 Contract terms which may or must be regarded as unfair

(1) Part 1 of Schedule 2 contains an indicative and non-exhaustive list of terms of consumer contracts that may be regarded as unfair for the purposes of this Part.
(2) Part 1 of Schedule 2 is subject to Part 2 of that Schedule; but a term listed in Part 2 of that Schedule may nevertheless be assessed for fairness under section 62 unless section 64 or 73 applies to it.
(3) The Secretary of State may by order made by statutory instrument amend Schedule 2 so as to add, modify or remove an entry in Part 1 or Part 2 of that Schedule.
(4) An order under subsection (3) may contain transitional or transitory provision or savings.
(5) No order may be made under subsection (3) unless a draft of the statutory instrument containing it has been laid before, and approved by a resolution of, each House of Parliament.
(6) A term of a consumer contract must be regarded as unfair if it has the effect that the consumer bears the burden of proof with respect to compliance by a distance supplier or an intermediary with an obligation under any enactment or rule implementing the Distance Marketing Directive.
(7) In subsection (6)—

"the Distance Marketing Directive" means Directive 2002/65/EC of the European Parliament and of the Council of 23 September 2002 concerning the distance marketing of consumer financial services and amending Council Directive 90/619/EEC and Directives 97/7/EC and 98/27/EC;

"distance supplier" means—

(a) a supplier under a distance contract within the meaning of the Financial Services (Distance Marketing) Regulations 2004 (SI 2004/2095), or

(b) a supplier of unsolicited financial services within the meaning of regulation 15 of those regulations;

"enactment" includes an enactment contained in subordinate legislation within the meaning of the Interpretation Act 1978;

"intermediary" has the same meaning as in the Financial Services (Distance Marketing) Regulations 2004; "rule" means a rule made by the Financial Conduct Authority or the Prudential Regulation Authority under the Financial Services and Markets Act 2000 or by a designated professional body within the meaning of section 326(2) of that Act.

64 Exclusion from assessment of fairness

(1) A term of a consumer contract may not be assessed for fairness under section 62 to the extent that—
(a) it specifies the main subject matter of the contract, or
(b) the assessment is of the appropriateness of the price payable under the contract by comparison with the goods, digital content or services supplied under it.
(2) Subsection (1) excludes a term from an assessment under section 62 only if it is transparent and prominent.
(3) A term is transparent for the purposes of this Part if it is expressed in plain and intelligible language and (in the case of a written term) is legible.
(4) A term is prominent for the purposes of this section if it is brought to the consumer's attention in such a way that an average consumer would be aware of the term.
(5) In subsection (4) "average consumer" means a consumer who is reasonably well-informed, observant and circumspect.
(6) This section does not apply to a term of a contract listed in Part 1 of Schedule 2.

65 Bar on exclusion or restriction of negligence liability

(1) A trader cannot by a term of a consumer contract or by a consumer notice exclude or restrict liability for death or personal injury resulting from negligence.
(2) Where a term of a consumer contract, or a consumer notice, purports to exclude or restrict a trader's

liability for negligence, a person is not to be taken to have voluntarily accepted any risk merely because the person agreed to or knew about the term or notice.

(3) In this section "personal injury" includes any disease and any impairment of physical or mental condition.

(4) In this section "negligence" means the breach of—

    (a) any obligation to take reasonable care or exercise reasonable skill in the performance of a contract where the obligation arises from an express or implied term of the contract,

    (b) a common law duty to take reasonable care or exercise reasonable skill,

    (c) the common law duty of care imposed by the Occupiers' Liability Act 1957 or the Occupiers' Liability Act (Northern Ireland) 1957, or

    (d) the duty of reasonable care imposed by section 2(1) of the Occupiers' Liability (Scotland) Act 1960.

(5) It is immaterial for the purposes of subsection (4)—

    (a) whether a breach of duty or obligation was inadvertent or intentional,

    or

    (b) whether liability for it arises directly or vicariously.

(6) This section is subject to section 66 (which makes provision about the scope of this section).

66 Scope of section 65

(1) Section 65 does not apply to—

    (a) any contract so far as it is a contract of insurance, including a contract to pay an annuity on human life, or

    (b) any contract so far as it relates to the creation or transfer of an interest in land.

(2) Section 65 does not affect the validity of any discharge or indemnity given by a person in consideration of the receipt by that person of compensation in settlement of any claim the person has.

(3) Section 65 does not—

    (a) apply to liability which is excluded or discharged as mentioned in section 4(2)(a) (exception to liability to pay damages to relatives) of the Damages (Scotland) Act 2011, or

    (b) affect the operation of section 5 (discharge of liability to pay damages: exception for mesothelioma) of that Act.

(4) Section 65 does not apply to the liability of an occupier of premises to a person who obtains access to the premises for recreational purposes if—

    (a) the person suffers loss or damage because of the dangerous state of the premises, and

    (b) allowing the person access for those purposes is not within the purposes of the occupier's trade, business, craft or profession.

67 Effect of an unfair term on the rest of a contract

Where a term of a consumer contract is not binding on the consumer as a result of this Part, the contract continues, so far as practicable, to have effect in every other respect.

68 Requirement for transparency

(1) A trader must ensure that a written term of a consumer contract, or a consumer notice in writing, is transparent.

(2) A consumer notice is transparent for the purposes of subsection (1) if it is expressed in plain and intelligible language and it is legible.

69 Contract terms that may have different meanings

(1) If a term in a consumer contract, or a consumer notice, could have different meanings, the meaning that is most favourable to the consumer is to prevail.

(2) Subsection (1) does not apply to the construction of a term or a notice in proceedings on an application for an injunction or interdict under paragraph 3 of Schedule 3.

How are the general rules enforced?

70 Enforcement of the law on unfair contract terms

(1) Schedule 3 confers functions on the Competition and Markets Authority and other regulators in relation to the enforcement of this Part.
(2) For provision about the investigatory powers that are available to those regulators for the purposes of that Schedule, see Schedule 5.

Supplementary provisions

71 Duty of court to consider fairness of term

(1) Subsection (2) applies to proceedings before a court which relate to a term of a consumer contract.
(2) The court must consider whether the term is fair even if none of the parties to the proceedings has raised that issue or indicated that it intends to raise it.
(3) But subsection (2) does not apply unless the court considers that it has before it sufficient legal and factual material to enable it to consider the fairness of the term.

72 Application of rules to secondary contracts

(1) This section applies if a term of a contract ("the secondary contract") reduces the rights or remedies or increases the obligations of a person under another contract ("the main contract").
(2) The term is subject to the provisions of this Part that would apply to the term if it were in the main contract.
(3) It does not matter for the purposes of this section—
     (a) whether the parties to the secondary contract are the same as the parties to the main contract, or
     (b) whether the secondary contract is a consumer contract.
(4) This section does not apply if the secondary contract is a settlement of a claim arising under the main contract.

73 Disapplication of rules to mandatory terms and notices

(1) This Part does not apply to a term of a contract, or to a notice, to the extent that it reflects—
     (a) mandatory statutory or regulatory provisions, or
     (b) the provisions or principles of an international convention to which the United Kingdom or the EU is a party.
(2) In subsection (1) "mandatory statutory or regulatory provisions" includes rules which, according to law, apply between the parties on the basis that no other arrangements have been established.

74 Contracts applying law of non-EEA State

(1) If—
     (a) the law of a country or territory other than an EEA State is chosen by the parties to be applicable to a consumer contract, but
     (b) the consumer contract has a close connection with the United Kingdom, this Part applies despite that choice.
(2) For cases where the law applicable has not been chosen or the law of an EEA State is chosen, see Regulation (EC) No. 593/2008 of the European Parliament and of the Council of 17 June 2008 on the law applicable to contractual obligations.

75 Changes to other legislation

Schedule 4 (amendments consequential on this Part) has effect.

76 Interpretation of Part 2

(1) In this Part—
     "consumer contract" has the meaning given by section 61(3);
     "consumer notice" has the meaning given by section 61(7);

"transparent" is to be construed in accordance with sections 64(3) and 68(2).
(2) The following have the same meanings in this Part as they have in Part 1—
"trader" (see section 2(2));
"consumer" (see section 2(3));
"goods" (see section 2(8));
"digital content" (see section 2(9)).
(3) Section 2(4) (trader who claims an individual is not a consumer must prove it) applies in relation to this Part as it applies in relation to Part 1.

SCHEDULE 2 Section 63

CONSUMER CONTRACT TERMS WHICH MAY BE REGARDED AS UNFAIR

PART 1

LIST OF TERMS

22–026

1   A term which has the object or effect of excluding or limiting the trader's liability in the event of the death of or personal injury to the consumer resulting from an act or omission of the trader.

This does not include a term which is of no effect by virtue of section 65 (exclusion for negligence liability).

2   A term which has the object or effect of inappropriately excluding or limiting the legal rights of the consumer in relation to the trader or another party in the event of total or partial non-performance or inadequate performance by the trader of any of the contractual obligations, including the option of offsetting a debt owed to the trader against any claim which the consumer may have against the trader.

3   A term which has the object or effect of making an agreement binding on the consumer in a case where the provision of services by the trader is subject to a condition whose realisation depends on the trader's will alone.

4   A term which has the object or effect of permitting the trader to retain sums paid by the consumer where the consumer decides not to conclude or perform the contract, without providing for the consumer to receive compensation of an equivalent amount from the trader where the trader is the party cancelling the contract.

5   A term which has the object or effect of requiring that, where the consumer decides not to conclude or perform the contract, the consumer must pay the trader a disproportionately high sum in compensation or for services which have not been supplied.

6   A term which has the object or effect of requiring a consumer who fails to fulfil his obligations under the contract to pay a disproportionately high sum in compensation.

7   A term which has the object or effect of authorising the trader to dissolve the contract on a discretionary basis where the same facility is not granted to the consumer, or permitting the trader to retain the sums paid for services not yet supplied by the trader where it is the trader who dissolves the contract.

8   A term which has the object or effect of enabling the trader to terminate a contract of indeterminate duration without reasonable notice except where there are serious grounds for doing so.
This is subject to paragraphs 21 (financial services) and 24 (sale of securities, foreign currency etc).

9   A term which has the object or effect of automatically extending a contract of fixed duration where the consumer does not indicate otherwise, when the deadline fixed for the consumer to express a desire not to extend the contract is unreasonably early.

10   A term which has the object or effect of irrevocably binding the consumer to terms with which the consumer has had no real opportunity of becoming acquainted before the conclusion of the contract.

11   A term which has the object or effect of enabling the trader to alter the terms of the contract unilaterally without a valid reason which is specified in the contract.
This is subject to paragraphs 22 (financial services), 23 (contracts which last indefinitely) and 24 (sale of securities, foreign currency etc).

12   A term which has the object or effect of permitting the trader to determine the characteristics of the subject matter of the contract after the consumer has become bound by it.
This is subject to paragraph 23 (contracts which last indefinitely).

13 A term which has the object or effect of enabling the trader to alter unilaterally without a valid reason any characteristics of the goods, digital content or services to be provided.
14 A term which has the object or effect of giving the trader the discretion to decide the price payable under the contract after the consumer has become bound by it, where no price or method of determining the price is agreed when the consumer becomes bound.
This is subject to paragraphs 23 (contracts which last indefinitely), 24 (sale of securities, foreign currency etc) and 25 (price index clauses).
15 A term which has the object or effect of permitting a trader to increase the price of goods, digital content or services without giving the consumer the right to cancel the contract if the final price is too high in relation to the price agreed when the contract was concluded.
This is subject to paragraphs 24 (sale of securities, foreign currency etc) and 25 (price index clauses).
16 A term which has the object or effect of giving the trader the right to determine whether the goods, digital content or services supplied are in conformity with the contract, or giving the trader the exclusive right to interpret any term of the contract.
17 A term which has the object or effect of limiting the trader's obligation to respect commitments under-taken by the trader's agents or making the trader's commitments subject to compliance with a particular formality.
18 A term which has the object or effect of obliging the consumer to fulfil all of the consumer's obligations where the trader does not perform the trader's obligations.
19 A term which has the object or effect of allowing the trader to transfer the trader's rights and obligations under the contract, where this may reduce the guarantees for the consumer, without the consumer's agreement.
20 A term which has the object or effect of excluding or hindering the consumer's right to take legal action or exercise any other legal remedy, in particular by—
    (a) requiring the consumer to take disputes exclusively to arbitration not covered by legal provisions,
    (b) unduly restricting the evidence available to the consumer, or
    (c) imposing on the consumer a burden of proof which, according to the applicable law, should lie with another party to the contract.

31 Liability that cannot be excluded or restricted

(1) A term of a contract to supply goods is not binding on the consumer to the extent that it would exclude or restrict the trader's liability arising under any of these provisions—
    (a) section 9 (goods to be of satisfactory quality);
    (b) section 10 (goods to be fit for particular purpose);
    (c) section 11 (goods to be as described);
    (d) section 12 (other pre-contract information included in contract);
    (e) section 13 (goods to match a sample);
    (f) section 14 (goods to match a model seen or examined);
    (g) section 15 (installation as part of conformity of goods with contract);
    (h) section 16 (goods not conforming to contract if digital content does not conform);
    (i) section 17 (trader to have right to supply the goods etc);
    (j) section 28 (delivery of goods);
    (k) section 29 (passing of risk).
(2) That also means that a term of a contract to supply goods is not binding on the consumer to the extent that it would—
    (a) exclude or restrict a right or remedy in respect of a liability under a provision listed in subsection (1),
    (b) make such a right or remedy or its enforcement subject to a restrictive or onerous condition,
    (c) allow a trader to put a person at a disadvantage as a result of pursuing such a right or remedy, or
    (d) exclude or restrict rules of evidence or procedure.
(3) The reference in subsection (1) to excluding or restricting a liability also includes preventing an obligation or duty arising or limiting its extent.
(4) An agreement in writing to submit present or future differences to arbitration is not to be regarded as excluding or restricting any liability for the purposes of this section.
(5) Subsection (1)(i), and subsection (2) so far as it relates to liability under section 17, do not apply to a term of a contract for the hire of goods.

(6) But an express term of a contract for the hire of goods is not binding on the consumer to the extent that it would exclude or restrict a term that section 17 requires to be treated as included in the contract, unless it is inconsistent with that term (and see also section 62 (requirement for terms to be fair)).

(7) See Schedule 3 for provision about the enforcement of this section.

47 Liability that cannot be excluded or restricted

(1) A term of a contract to supply digital content is not binding on the consumer to the extent that it would exclude or restrict the trader's liability arising under any of these provisions—
  (a) section 34 (digital content to be of satisfactory quality),
  (b) section 35 (digital content to be fit for particular purpose),
  (c) section 36 (digital content to be as described)
  (d) section 37 (other pre-contract information included in contract), or
  (e) section 41 (trader's right to supply digital content).

(2) That also means that a term of a contract to supply digital content is not binding on the consumer to the extent that it would—
  (a) exclude or restrict a right or remedy in respect of a liability under a provision listed in subsection (1),
  (b) make such a right or remedy or its enforcement subject to a restrictive or onerous condition,
  (c) allow a trader to put a person at a disadvantage as a result of pursuing such a right or remedy, or
  (d) exclude or restrict rules of evidence or procedure.

(3) The reference in subsection (1) to excluding or restricting a liability also includes preventing an obligation or duty arising or limiting its extent.

(4) An agreement in writing to submit present or future differences to arbitration is not to be regarded as excluding or restricting any liability for the purposes of this section.

(5) See Schedule 3 for provision about the enforcement of this section.

(6) For provision limiting the ability of a trader under a contract within section 46 to exclude or restrict the trader's liability under that section, see section 62.

57 Liability that cannot be excluded or restricted

(1) A term of a contract to supply services is not binding on the consumer to the extent that it would exclude the trader's liability arising under section 49 (service to be performed with reasonable care and skill).

(2) Subject to section 50(2), a term of a contract to supply services is not binding on the consumer to the extent that it would exclude the trader's liability arising under section 50 (information about trader or service to be binding).

(3) A term of a contract to supply services is not binding on the consumer to the extent that it would restrict the trader's liability arising under any of sections 49 and 50 and, where they apply, sections 51 and 52 (reasonable price and reasonable time), if it would prevent the consumer in an appropriate case from recovering the price paid or the value of any other consideration. (If it would not prevent the consumer from doing so, Part 2 (unfair terms) may apply.)

(4) That also means that a term of a contract to supply services is not binding on the consumer to the extent that it would —
  (a) exclude or restrict a right or remedy in respect of a liability under any of sections 49 to 52,
  (b) make such a right or remedy or its enforcement subject to a restrictive or onerous condition,
  (c) allow a trader to put a person at a disadvantage as a result of pursuing such a right or remedy, or
  (d) exclude or restrict rules of evidence or procedure.

(5) The references in subsections (1) to (3) to excluding or restricting a liability also include preventing an obligation or duty arising or limiting its extent.

(6) An agreement in writing to submit present or future differences to arbitration is not to be regarded as excluding or restricting any liability for the purposes of this section.

(7) See Schedule 3 for provision about the enforcement of this section.

Further reading

Susan Bright, 'Winning the Battle against Unfair Contract Terms' (2000) 20 *Legal Studies* 331

Roger Brownsword and Geraint Howells, 'The Implementation of the EC Directive on Unfair Terms in Consumer Contracts—Some Unresolved Questions' [1995] *Journal of Business Law* 243

Roger Brownsword, Geraint Howells, and Thomas Wilhelmsson, 'Between Market and Welfare: Some Reflections on Article 3 of the EC Directive on Unfair Terms in Consumer Contracts', in Chris Willett (ed.) *Aspects of Fairness In Contract* (Blackstone Press, 1996) p.25

Mindy Chen-Wishart, 'Regulating Unfair Terms' in Louise Gullifer and Stefan Vogenauer (eds), *English and European Perspectives on Contract and Commercial Law: Essays in Honour of Hugh Beale* (Oxford: Hart, 2014) p.105

Hugh Collins, 'Good Faith in European Contract Law' (1994), 14 *Oxford Journal of Legal Studies* 229

Richard Lawson, *Exclusion Clauses and Unfair Contract Terms*, 8th edn (London: Sweet & Maxwell, 2005)

PART VI

EXCUSING CIRCUMSTANCES

23

INITIAL IMPOSSIBILITY AND MISTAKE

LEARNING OBJECTIVES

By the end of this chapter, you should:

- **be familiar with the leading cases on so-called common mistakes as to quality (of the subject matter of the contract);**
- **understand that, after *Bell v Lever Bros*, the common law will only exceptionally treat a common mistake as an excuse for non-performance (as a reason to set aside the contract);**
- **have critically reflected on the attempts made to apply an equitable doctrine of mistake in a way that qualifies the restrictive common law test;**
- **have formed a view about whether, in the *Great Peace Shipping* case, the Court of Appeal succeeded in putting the law in a more coherent and satisfactory shape.**

INTRODUCTION

This and the following chapter deal with (i) a group of cases where the principal point of law is pleaded as one of "mistake", and (ii) cases where the doctrine of "frustration" is pleaded as an excuse for non-performance. In both types of case there is a complete agreement between the parties. (Those cases of "mistake" where the parties never reach a true agreement are thought to raise a quite different problem—one of offer and acceptance—and are therefore considered in Part I of this book.) The problem in each chapter is basically the same: Does the occurrence (or non-occurrence) of some event or the existence (or non-existence) of some object destroy the obligations which would otherwise arise under the contract? The only difference is that in (i) the object or event exists (or ceases to exist) or occurs before the formation of the contract, in (ii) after its formation. Suppose, for example, that A contracts that he will sell his car to B next week. Unknown to either of them, it was destroyed five minutes ago. That is typical of the first group of problems. Where the car is destroyed five minutes later, that is typical of the second group. If the parties had agreed, "This contract shall be avoided if the car shall be destroyed now or at any time before the completion of the sale and delivery", it would be obvious that the existence of the car was a condition precedent to the existence or the performance of the contract. If, as is usually the case, the parties have not adverted to the possibility of the occurrence of such an event and the court nevertheless holds that its effect is to avoid the contract, the most obvious explanation (in the light of the traditional common law view that the court will neither make nor amend a bargain) would seem to be that this has been done by virtue of an implied condition precedent. This theory has played an important part in the development of the law but has been regarded with considerable scepticism by modern writers and judges.

In this chapter, the case-law is presented in four sections. First, there are cases on the effect of a mistake where the presumed subject-matter of the contract has been destroyed or never existed;

secondly, there are the classic common law cases (in particular, *Bell v Lever Bros*) on mistakes that simply go to the quality of the subject matter (where the common law takes a very restrictive view); thirdly, there are the modern equitable cases, starting with *Solle v Butcher*, in which there is a willingness to treat the contract as voidable (not void) for such mistakes; and, finally, there is the challenge to the equitable approach mounted in the *Great Peace Shipping* case.

1. Mistake as to the Existence of the Subject-Matter of a Contract

23–002   Where the subject-matter of a contract has ceased to exist before the contract was made, or has never existed, an implied term theory might support more than one allocation of risk. For example, the position might be that:

(i) A impliedly promised B that the thing existed (and, thus, took the risk if the thing did not exist);

(ii) A impliedly promised B that he had taken reasonable care to ascertain that the thing existed;

(iii) A and B proceeded on a common assumption, for which neither was more responsible than the other, that the thing existed and its existence was a condition precedent to the contract (hence, neither party took the risk); or

(iv) B impliedly accepted the risk that the thing did not exist.

When the thing did not exist, A would be liable for damages in (i), and, if he had not taken reasonable care, in (ii); in (iii) (and in (ii) if A had taken reasonable care) both parties would be discharged from liability—that is, the contract would be effectively void; and, in (iv), B would have to cover his own losses.

Which is the right term to imply depends on the circumstances, particularly the relative means of knowledge of the parties and whether one was relying on the other. Is there some merit in an implied term theory which admits of flexibility and permits the court to adopt the solution which most nearly fits the assumptions and intentions on which the contracting parties, as reasonable men, appear to have proceeded?

HASTIE v COUTURIER

Exchequer Chamber (1853) 9 Ex. 102; 156 E.R. 43

23–003   The plaintiffs, merchants at Smyrna, shipped a cargo of Indian corn at Salonica and sent the charter-party and bill of lading to their London agent, who employed the defendant to sell the cargo. On May 15, 1848, the defendant sold the cargo to Callender and sent him a bought note which stated that he had bought of them "1,180 quarters of Salonica Indian corn of fair average quality when shipped at 27s. per quarter, free on board, and including freight and insurance to a safe port in the United Kingdom, payment at two months from this date upon handing over shipping documents." The vessel sailed from Salonica on February 23 and met with tempestuous weather. The cargo became so heated and fermented that the vessel was obliged to put into Tunis Bay, where the cargo was found to be unfit to be carried further and sold. On May 23 Challender gave the plaintiffs notice that he repudiated the contract on the ground that at the time of the sale to him the cargo did not exist. The defendant was a del credere agent (one who guarantees the performance of their contracts by persons whom he introduces to his principal) and the plaintiffs brought an action against him to recover the price of the cargo. The question, therefore, was whether the purchaser was bound to pay for the cargo, because, if he was, the defendant was liable to make good his default. Martin B. ruled that the contract imported that, at the time of sale, the corn was in existence as such and capable of delivery, and that, as it had been sold, the plaintiffs could not recover.

The Court of Exchequer held, Pollock CB dissenting, that the true meaning of the contract was that the purchaser bought the cargo if it existed at the date of the contract; but that if it had been damaged or lost, he bought the benefit of the insurance. Parke B., delivering the judgment of the court, said: "It is very true that, when there is a sale of a specific chattel (not a contract to sell and deliver a chattel in futuro), there is an implied undertaking that it exists; and if there were nothing in this case but a bargain and sale of a certain cargo on May 15, there would be an engagement by the vendor, or a condition, that the cargo was in existence at that time; but in this case there is a great deal more." Having considered the terms of the contract, he concluded: "We think, therefore, that the true meaning of the contract was, that the purchaser bought the cargo, if it existed at the date of the contract; but if it had been damaged or lost, he bought the benefit of the insurance, but no more" (155 E.R. 1250; 8 Ex. 40).

On a bill of exceptions the judgment of the Court of Exchequer Chamber was delivered by—

COLERIDGE J

For the plaintiffs in error[1] [the defendant] it was contended, that the parties plainly contracted for the sale and purchase of goods, that the price to be paid was for goods, and that for the price the purchaser was to have the benefit of a contract to carry them and a policy of insurance; that a vendor of goods undertakes that they exist, and that they are capable of being transferred, although he may not stipulate for their condition; and that as the goods in question had been sold and delivered to other parties before the contract in question was made, there was nothing on which it could operate; and *Barr v Gibson*[2] (3 M. & W. 390) and *Strickland v Turner*[3] (7 Exch. 208) were cited.

On the other hand, it was argued that this was not a mere contract for the sale of an ascertained cargo, but that the purchaser bought the adventure, and took upon himself all risks from the shipment of the cargo. It was said that the mention of the condition of the cargo at the time of shipment was a proof of the intention of the parties that the buyer should take all risks from that time; that its condition at the time of sale, or the fact of its existence, could not then be ascertained, and therefore the purchaser must be supposed to have taken the risks; that if it had existed, however much deteriorated, the purchaser must have taken it, although the loss had been all but total, and therefore there was no reason for excluding total loss from the risk that he was to bear; that if it had ceased to exist the consideration would not fail, for the purchaser would have the shipping documents. It was further argued that the stipulation for payment, which would probably have to be made before the arrival of the cargo, indicated an intention that the purchaser was in all events to pay for it, on account of the inconvenience that would ensue, if he might have to reclaim the money back. It was not disputed that the cases of *Barr v Gibson* (3 M. & W. 390) and *Strickland v Turner* (7 Exch. 208) were well decided.

It appears to us that the contract in question was for the sale of a cargo supposed to exist, and to be capable of transfer, and that, inasmuch as it had been sold and delivered to others by the captain before the contract in question was made, the plaintiffs cannot recover in this action. With regard to the description of the cargo as "of fair average quality when shipped," we think that, if those words had not been introduced, it must have been held that the purchaser of a cargo on a voyage would take upon himself the chance of what its condition at the time of purchase might be, and that this clause was introduced for his benefit, by enabling him to object, if the fact were so, that the cargo was bad when shipped. If, in *Barr v Gibson*, there had been a stipulation that the ship, when she sailed on the voyage during which she was sold, was seaworthy, that would not have made the purchaser liable, if a total loss had occurred before the contract was entered into. It has been said, that if the loss had been all but total, if the cargo had become all but worthless, yet, if it existed in specie, the

---

[1]   i.e. the party who sued out a writ of error. Cf. Sutton and Shannon, *Personal Actions at Common Law*, Ch.8.

[2]   B paid S £4,200 for a ship then on a voyage. At the time of the sale it had been stranded and the hull was eventually sold for £10. B's action for breach of a covenant that S had power to sell failed. The ship still existed at the time of the sale; it would have been otherwise had it ceased to exist.

[3]   B bought from S an annuity on the life of X who, unknown to B and S, was already dead. It was held that B was able to recover the whole price, the consideration having totally failed.

purchaser must unquestionably have been bound, and therefore there is no reason for holding that he was not also to take the risk of a total loss. The same argument would have applied in *Strickland v Turner*. If the annuitant, at the time of the sale of the annuity, had been in extremis, and had died the next hour, the purchaser would have been bound, and could not have recovered the purchase-money, but was held to be so entitled, the annuitant having died before the sale. Again, it has been supposed that there is an inconsistency in saying that, if the cargo had sustained sea damage, constituting an average loss covered by the policy, it would pass to the purchaser so as to secure to him an indemnity, but would not pass in the event of a total loss. This seems to depend upon the same point, and not to be attended with any real difficulty.

If the contract for sale of the cargo was valid, the shipping documents would pass as accessories to it; but if, in consequence of the previous sale of the cargo, the contract failed as to the principal subject-matter of it, the shipping documents would not pass. Although we cannot find any decision in point, there is a case of *Sutherland v Pratt* (11 M. & W. 296), where this subject was mentioned. In that case, the plaintiff had bought goods on a voyage, and effected an insurance, lost or not lost. They had sustained sea damage before the sale, and the purchaser sued on the policy. The underwriters pleaded that the goods were damaged before the plaintiff had acquired any interest in them. On demurrer, it was held that the plea was bad; but the very learned counsel who argued for the plaintiff admitted, in answer to a question put by Parke B., that, if the goods had been totally lost before his contract of purchase was made, there would not have been an insurable interest, as a person cannot buy a thing that has been totally lost.

For these reasons, it appears to us that the basis of the contract in this case was the sale and purchase of goods, and that all the other terms in the bought note were dependent upon that, and that we cannot give to it the effect of a contract for goods lost or not lost. The consequence is, that the judgment of the court below must be reversed, and entered for the plaintiffs in error [the defendant] according to arrangement between the parties.

Judgment Reversed.

Questions

23-004

1. Would the buyer have been bound to pay the price if the cargo, in good order when shipped, had been damaged at the time of the sale?

2. Did the success of the action in *Strickland v Turner* imply that there was no contract or merely that any contract there may have been was not performed? Was S guilty of a breach of contract because X was dead? Would it be reasonable to impute to him a promise that X was alive? If, because of X's death, neither S nor B was under any obligation, does it not follow that the contract was void?

3. If the seller in *Barr v Gibson* had warranted that the ship was seaworthy when she sailed, would he have been able to keep the price if the ship had already (i) been stranded, (ii) become a total loss, through unseaworthiness?

COUTURIER v HASTIE

House of Lords (1856) 5 H.L.C. 673; 25 L.J.Ex. 253; 28 L.T. 240; 2 Jur.(n.s.) 1241; 10 E.R. 1065

23-005   On a writ of error to the House of Lords the judges were summoned and unanimously expressed the opinion that the judgment of the Exchequer Chamber was right and that of the Court of Exchequer wrong.

THE LORD CHANCELLOR (LORD CRANWORTH)

My Lords, that being so, I have no hesitation in advising your Lordships, and at once moving that the judgment of the court below should be affirmed. It is hardly necessary, and it has not ordinarily been usual for your Lordships to go much into the merits of a judgment which is thus unanimously affirmed by the judges who are called in to consider it, and to assist the House in forming its judgment. But I may state shortly that the whole question turns upon the construction of the contract which was entered into between the parties . . . [His Lordship then considered the construction of the contract.] The contract plainly imports that there was something which was to be sold at the time of the contract, and something to be purchased. No such thing existing, I think the Court of Exchequer Chamber has come to the only reasonable conclusion upon it, and consequently that there must be judgment given by your Lordships for the defendants in error [the defendant].

Questions

1. Did the courts in this case decide: 23–006

   (a) that there was no contract or

   (b) that there was a contract, but that it was not performed?

2. What consideration was to be supplied by the seller according to (a) the seller, (b) the buyer? Which view was accepted by the court?

3. Suppose the buyer had suffered damage (for example, through loss of a sub-contract). Does the case decide that he could not have recovered damages for the seller's failure to deliver?

LEVER BROTHERS LTD v BELL

(1931) 1 K.B. 557

Wright J said: "The simplest and oldest illustration of such a mistake [that is, 'mistake of subject-   23–007
matter, or substance, or essence, or fundamental basis'] is where the parties contracted to buy and sell a specific chattel which at the date of the contract, though both parties thought it existing, had ceased to exist: in that event, however absolute the terms of the contract, there is in law no binding contract, and this principle is now embodied in the Sale of Goods Act, 1893, s.6. The principle was applied in a sense to the sale of a cargo sold c.i.f. which had, before the date of the contract, owing to sea damage, been properly sold by the shipmaster at a port of refuge, and hence became, without the knowledge of either party, incapable of delivery, though it may be that it still existed: Couturier v Hastie."

SALE OF GOODS ACT 1979 s.6

Where there is a contract for the sale of specific goods, and the goods without the knowledge of the seller have   23–008
perished at the time when the contract is made, the contract is void.

Question

Is *Couturier v Hastie* an authority for the proposition stated by Wright J, above, or for that contained in   23–009
the Sale of Goods Act s.6?

MCRAE v THE COMMONWEALTH DISPOSALS COMMISSION

High Court of Australia, 84 C.L.R. 377; [1951] Argus L.R. 771

23-010   The defendants invited tenders for the purchase of an oil tanker described as lying on Jourmand Reef off Papua, together with its contents, which were stated to be oil. The plaintiffs made a tender of £285 which was accepted. They then incurred considerable expenditure in modifying a vessel they owned for salvage work, in purchasing equipment and engaging a crew, and on travelling expenses, etc. There was in fact no oil tanker anywhere near the latitude and longitude specified by the Commission, nor was there any place known as Jourmand Reef. The plaintiffs brought an action for (1) breach of contract, (2) deceit, and (3) negligence. Webb J gave judgment for the plaintiffs in the action for deceit. He held that *Couturier v Hastie* obliged him to hold that the contract of sale was void and the claim for breach of contract failed. The plaintiffs appealed and the defendants cross-appealed.

DIXON AND FULLAGAR JJ

The first question to be determined is whether a contract was made between the plaintiffs and the Commission. The argument that the contract was void, or, in other words, that there was no contract, was based, as has been observed, on *Couturier v Hastie*. It is true that *Couturier v Hastie* has been commonly treated in the textbooks as a case of a contract avoided by mutual mistake, and it is found cited in the company of such cases as *Gompertz v Bartlett* (1853) 2 E. & B. 849, and *Strickland v Turner* (1852) 7 Ex. 208. Section 7 of the English Sale of Goods Act, 1893, is generally regarded as expressing the effect of the case. The case has not, however, been universally regarded as resting on mistake, and Sir Frederick Pollock in his Preface to Vol. 101 of the Revised Reports, at p. vi, says "Couturier v Hastie shows how a large proportion of the cases which swell the rubric of relief against mistake in the textbooks (with or without protest from the textwriter) are really cases of construction." And in *Solle v Butcher* [below] Denning L.J. observed that the cases which it had been usual to classify under the head of "mistake" needed reconsideration since the decision of the House of Lords in *Bell v Lever Bros. Ltd* [below]. No occasion seems to have arisen for a close examination of *Couturier v Hastie*, but such an occasion does now arise.

The facts of the case were simple enough . . . [The learned judges then stated the facts of *Couturier v Hastie*.]

In considering *Couturier v Hastie* it is necessary to remember that it was, in substance, a case in which a vendor was suing for the price of goods which he was unable to deliver. If there had been nothing more in the case, it would probably never have been reported: indeed the action would probably never have been brought. But the vendor founded his claim on the provision for "payment upon handing over shipping documents." He was not called upon to prove a tender of the documents, because the defendant had "repudiated" the contract, but he was able and willing to hand them over, and his argument was, in effect, that by handing them over he would be doing all that the contract required of him. The question thus raised would seem to depend entirely on the construction of the contract, and it appears really to have been so treated throughout. [The learned judges then quoted from the judgments in *Couturier v Hastie* and Lord Atkin's reference to that case in *Bell v Lever Bros. Ltd*].

The observation of Lord Atkin in *Bell v Lever Bros. Ltd* [see below, para.23-013, n.4] seems entirely appropriate to *Couturier v Hastie*. In that case there was a failure of consideration, and the purchaser was not bound to pay the price; if he had paid it before the truth was discovered, he could have recovered it back as money had and received. The construction of the contract was the vital thing in the case because, and only because, on the construction of the contract depended the question whether the consideration had really failed, the vendor maintaining that, since he was able to hand over the shipping documents, it had not failed. The truth is that the question whether the contract was void, or the vendor excused from performance by reason of the non-existence of the supposed subject-matter, did not arise in *Couturier v Hastie*. It would have arisen if the purchaser had suffered loss through non-delivery of the corn and had sued the vendor for damages. If it had so arisen, we think that the real question would have been whether the contract was subject to an implied condition precedent that the goods were in existence. Prima facie, one would think, there would be no such implied condition precedent, the position being simply that the vendor promised that the goods were in existence. That is the real meaning of the direction of Martin B. to the jury, and so the argument for the defendant, as has already been pointed out, included the proposition that a "vendor of goods undertakes that they exist and that they are capable of being transferred, although he may not stipulate for their condition." So in *Barr v Gibson*

(1838) 3 M. & W. 390, where the contract was for the sale of a ship, Parke B. said: "And therefore the sale in this case of a ship implies a contract that the subject of transfer did exist in the character of a ship." It should be noted in this connection that in *Solle v Butcher* Denning L.J. said that the doctrine of French law, as enunciated by Pothier, is not part of English law. His Lordship was without doubt thinking of the passage quoted from Pothier in a note to the report of the argument in the House of Lords in *Couturier v Hastie*. Although we would not be prepared to assent to everything that is said by Denning L.J. in the course of this judgment, we respectfully agree with this observation. When once the common law had made up its mind that a promise supported by consideration ought to be performed, it was inevitable that the theorisings of the civilians about "mistake" should mean little or nothing to it. On the other hand, the question whether a promisor was excused from performance by existing or supervening impossibility without fault on his part was a practical every-day question of which the common law has been vividly conscious, as witness *Taylor v Caldwell* [below, Ch.24], with its innumerable (if sometimes dubious) successors. But here too the common law has generally been true to its theory of simple contract, and it has always regarded the fundamental question as being: "What did the promisor really promise?" Did he promise to perform his part at all events, or only subject to the mutually contemplated original or continued existence of a particular subject-matter? So questions of intention or "presumed intention" arise, and these must be determined in the light of the words used by the parties and reasonable inferences from all the surrounding circumstances. That the problem is fundamentally one of construction is shown clearly by *Clifford v Watts* (1870) L.R. 5 C.P. 577.

If the view so far indicated be correct, as we believe it to be, it seems clear that the case of *Couturier v Hastie* does not compel one to say that the contract in the present case was void. But, even if the view that *Couturier v Hastie* was a case of a void contract be correct, we would still think that it could not govern the present case. Denning L.J. indeed says in *Solle v Butcher*: "Neither party can rely on his own mistake to say it was a nullity from the beginning, no matter that it was a mistake which to his mind was fundamental, and no matter that the other party knew he was under a mistake. A fortiori if the other party did not know of the mistake, but shared it." But, even if this be not wholly and strictly correct, yet at least it must be true to say that a party cannot rely on mutual mistake where the mistake consists of a belief which is, on the one hand, entertained by him without any reasonable ground, and, on the other hand, deliberately induced by him in the mind of the other party . . . [The learned judge held that there was no evidence that the officials of the Commission were guilty of fraud; but that they were guilty of the grossest negligence.] Having no reasonable grounds for such a belief, they asserted by their advertisement to the world at large, and by their later specification of locality to the plaintiffs, that they had a tanker to sell. They must have known that any tenderer would rely implicitly on their assertion of the existence of a tanker, and they must have known that the plaintiffs would rely implicitly on their later assertion of the existence of a tanker in the latitude and longitude given. They took no steps to verify what they were asserting, and any "mistake" that existed was induced by their own culpable, conduct. In these circumstances it seems out of the question that they should be able to assert that no contract was concluded. It is not unfair or inaccurate to say that the only "mistake" the plaintiffs made was that they believed what the Commission told them.

The position so far, then, may be summed up as follows: It was not decided in *Couturier v Hastie* that the contract in that case was void. The question whether it was void or not did not arise. If it had arisen, as in an action by the purchaser for damages, it would have turned on the ulterior question whether the contract was subject to an implied condition precedent. Whatever might then have been held on the facts of *Couturier v Hastie*, it is impossible in this case to imply any such term. The terms of the contract and the surrounding circumstances clearly exclude any such implication. The buyers relied upon, and acted upon, the assertion of the seller that there was a tanker in existence. It is not a case in which the parties can be seen to have proceeded on the basis of a common assumption of fact so as to justify the conclusion that the correctness of the assumption was intended by both parties to be a condition precedent to the creation of contractual obligation. The officers of the Commission made an assumption, but the plaintiffs did not make an assumption in the same sense. They knew nothing except what the Commission had told them. If they had been asked, they would certainly not have said: "Of course, if there is no tanker, there is no contract." They would have said: "We shall have to go and take possession of the tanker. We simply accept the Commission's assurance that there is a tanker and the Commission's promise to give us that tanker." The only proper construction of the contract is that it included a promise by the Commission that there was a tanker in the position specified. The Commission contracted that there was a tanker there. "The sale in this case of a ship implies a contract that the subject of the transfer did exist in the character of a ship" (*Barr v Gibson*). If, on the other hand, the case of *Couturier v Hastie* and this case ought to be treated as cases raising a question of "mistake," then the Commission cannot in this case rely on any mistake as avoiding the contract, because any mistake was induced by the serious fault of their own servants, who asserted the existence of a tanker recklessly and without any reasonable ground. There was a contract, and the Commission contracted that a tanker existed in the position specified. Since there was no such tanker, there has been a breach of contract, and the plaintiffs are entitled to damages for that breach.

Before proceeding to consider the measure of damages one other matter should be briefly mentioned. The contract was made in Melbourne, and it would seem that its proper law is Victorian law. Section 11 of the Victoria Goods Act, 1928, corresponds to section 6 of the English Sale of Goods Act, 1893, and provides that "where there is a contract for the sale of specified goods, and the goods without the knowledge of the seller have perished at the time when the contract is made the contract is void." This has been generally supposed to represent the legislature's view of the effect of *Couturier v Hastie*. Whether it correctly represents the effect of the decision in that case or not, it seems clear that the section has no application to the facts of the present case. Here the goods never existed, and the seller ought to have known that they did not exist.

The conclusion that there was an enforceable contract makes it unnecessary to consider the other two causes of action . . .

McTiernan J. concurred in the conclusions of the above judgment.

Glanville Williams, Mistake and Rectification in Contract 17 M.L.R. 154

23–011   In *McRae v Commonwealth Disposals Commission*, Dixon and Fullagar J. J. analysed *Couturier v Hastie* and thought that it did not decide that the contract was void for initial impossibility, but only that the seller could not get the price. These judges left open the question whether a contract is void for initial impossibility of performance. The language of Denning L.J. in [*Rose v Pim*, above, Ch.5] seems to suggest that had it not been for the particular wording of the contract in *Couturier v Hastie* the result would have been different. But this is hard to believe, for if the subsequent destruction of specific goods frustrates an agreement for the sale of those goods, as it does under *Taylor v Caldwell* [below, para.24–003, n.1] and section 7 of the Sale of Goods Act, it is common sense that prior destruction must have a similar vitiating effect. Moreover, the common understanding of the rule in *Couturier v Hastie* is affirmed by section 6 of the Sale of Goods Act.

Questions

23–012
1. Could not s.6 be excluded by the expressed intention of the parties? Cf. s.55 of the Sale of Goods Act 1979 and the *Hansa Nord* [1976] Q.B. 44. Suppose, for example, that a seller assures a doubting buyer that the cargo is in existence in order to induce him to buy, and perhaps even puts an undertaking to that effect into the written contract. If the section can be excluded by an express term, why not by an implied one, if that appears to have been the intention of the parties?

2. Even if s.6 does lay down a rigid rule which does not yield to a contrary intention, would it not be in accordance with the principle that the consequences of both initial and subsequent impossibility—arising otherwise than through the perishing of goods—should depend upon the intention of the parties, that is, upon an implied term?

3. With reference to the views of Professor Williams (above), may it not be reasonable to impute to the owner of a ship or a theatre a promise that it exists and yet unreasonable to impute to him a promise that it will continue to exist at some future time? Cf. Atiyah, *Introduction to the Law of Contract* (4th edn), pp.198–200. Alternatively, might not a case like the *McRae* case be decided on the ground that the seller undertakes merely that he has taken reasonable steps to find out whether the ship exists? Cf. *The Moorcock* (above, Ch.16), *Esso Petroleum v Mardon* (above, Ch.15), *Liverpool City Council v Irwin* (above, Ch.16) and *The Mihalis Angelos* (above, Ch.20).

----

2. Mistakes as to Quality—the Common Law Approach

BELL v LEVER BROTHERS LTD

House of Lords [1932] A.C. 161; 101 L.J.K.B. 129; 146 L.T. 258; 48 T.L.R. 133; 76 S.J. 50, 37 Com.Cas. 98

The Lever Company, which had a controlling interest in the Niger Company, in 1923 appointed Bell **23–013** chairman, and Snelling vice-chairman, of the board of the Niger Company, at salaries of £8,000 and £6,000 a year respectively. In 1926 the arrangement was renewed to run for five years. While acting as chairman and vice-chairman Bell and Snelling, by speculating in the company's business, committed breaches of duty which would have justified the Lever Company in terminating their appointments. In 1929 the Niger Company amalgamated with another company, and the appointments of Bell and Snelling became redundant. D'Arcy Cooper, the chairman of Levers, being unaware of the breaches of duty, arranged on behalf of the Lever Company, to pay Bell £30,000 and Snelling £20,000 as compensation for terminating their services. Bell and Snelling agreed to accept these sums and they were paid. On discovering the breaches, the Lever Company and the Niger Company brought an action alleging fraudulent misrepresentation and claiming rescission of the compensation agreements and repayment of the sums paid thereunder. The jury found that if the Lever Company had been aware of the breaches of duty by the defendants, they would have terminated their agreements and dismissed them from office without compensation; and that, when entering into the compensation agreements, the defendants did not fraudulently conceal, but had not present to their minds, or did not appreciate the effect of, the breaches of duty they had committed.

Wright J and the Court of Appeal held that the compensation agreements were void as having been made under a common mistake. The defendants appealed.

Lord Blanesburgh held that, after an action based exclusively on fraud had failed, it was not open to the plaintiffs on the pleadings to raise a case of mutual mistake, implying good faith on the part of the defendants; but if it were open to the plaintiffs to raise the issue, then he agreed with Lord Atkin and Lord Thankerton.

Lord Warrington, with whom Lord Hailsham agreed, held, dissenting, that the erroneous assumption made by both parties was as fundamental to the bargain as any that could be imagined and that the contract was void.

LORD ATKIN

[having stated the facts:] Two points present themselves for decision: Was the agreement of March 19, 1929, void by reason of a mutual mistake of Mr D'Arcy Cooper and Mr Bell?

Could the agreement of March 19, 1929, be avoided by reason of the failure of Mr Bell to disclose his misconduct in regard to the cocoa dealings?

My Lords, the rules of law dealing with the effect of mistake on contract appear to be established with reasonable clearness. If mistake operates at all it operates so as to negative or in some cases to nullify consent. The parties may be mistaken in the identity of the contracting parties, or in the existence of the subject-matter of the contract at the date of the contract, or in the quality of the subject-matter of the contract. These mistakes may be by one party, or by both, and the legal effect may depend upon the class of mistake above mentioned. Thus a mistaken belief by A that he is contracting with B, whereas in fact he is contracting with C, will negative consent where it is clear that the intention of A was to contract only with B. So the agreement of A and B to purchase a specific article is void if in fact the article had perished before the date of sale. In this case, though the parties in fact were agreed about the subject-matter, yet a consent to transfer or take delivery of something not existent is deemed useless, the consent is nullified. As codified in the Sale of Goods Act the contract is expressed to be void if the seller was in ignorance of the destruction of the specific chattel. I apprehend that if the seller with knowledge that a chattel was destroyed purported to sell it to a purchaser, the latter might sue for damages for non-delivery though the former could not sue for non-acceptance, but I know of no case where a seller has so committed himself. This is a case where mutual mistake certainly and unilateral mistake by the seller of goods will prevent a contract from arising. Corresponding to mistake as to the existence of the subject-matter is mistake as to title in cases where, unknown to the parties, the buyer is already the owner of that which the seller purports to sell to him. The parties intended to effectuate a transfer of ownership: such a transfer is impossible: the stipulation is naturali ratione inutilis. This is the case of *Cooper v Phibbs*, where A agreed to take a lease of a fishery from B, though contrary to the belief of both parties at the time A was tenant for life of the fishery and B appears to have had no title at all. To such a case Lord Westbury applied the principle that if parties contract under a mutual mistake and misapprehension as to their relative and respective rights the result is that the agreement is liable to be set aside as having proceeded upon a common mistake. Applied to the context the statement is only subject to the criticism that the agreement would appear to be void rather than voidable. Applied to mistake as to rights generally it would appear to be too wide. Even where the vendor has no title, though both parties think he has, the correct view would appear to be that there is a contract: but that the vendor has either committed a breach of a stipulation as to title, or is not able to perform his contract. The contract is unenforceable by him but is not void.

Mistake as to quality of the thing contracted for raises more difficult questions. In such a case a mistake will not affect assent unless it is the mistake of both parties, and is as to the existence of some quality which makes the thing without the quality essentially different from the thing as it was believed to be. Of course, it may appear that the parties contracted that the article should possess the quality which one or other or both mistakenly believed it to possess. But in such a case there is a contract and the inquiry is a different one, being whether the contract as to quality amounts to a condition or a warranty, a different branch of law. The principles to be applied are to be found in two cases which, as far as my knowledge goes, have always been treated as authoritative expositions of the law. The first is *Kennedy v Panama Royal Mail Co* (1867) L.R. 2 Q.B. 580, 586.

In that case the plaintiff had applied for shares in the defendant company on the faith of a prospectus which stated falsely but innocently that the company had a binding contract with the Government of New Zealand for the carriage of mails. On discovering the true facts the plaintiff brought an action for the recovery of the sums he had paid on calls. The defendants brought a cross-action for further calls. Blackburn J., in delivering the judgment of the court (Cockburn C. J., Blackburn, Mellor and Shee J. J.), said: "The only remaining question is one of much greater difficulty. It was contended by Mr Mellish, on behalf of Lord Gilbert Kennedy, that the effect of the prospectus was to warrant to the intended shareholders that there really was such a contract as is there represented, and not merely to represent that the company bona fide believed it; and that the difference in substance between shares in a company with such a contract and shares in a company whose supposed contract was not binding, was a difference in substance in the nature of the thing; and that the shareholder was entitled to return the shares as soon as he discovered this, quite independently of fraud, on the ground that he had applied for one thing and got another. And, if the invalidity of the contract really made the shares he obtained different things in substance from those which he applied for, this would, we think, be good law. The case would then resemble *Gompertz v Bartlett*, 2 E. & B. 849, and *Gurney v Womersley* (1854) 4 E. & B. 133, where the person who had honestly sold what he thought a bill without recourse to him, was nevertheless held bound to return the price on its turning out that the supposed bill was a forgery in the one case, and void under the stamp laws in the other; in both cases the ground of this decision being that the thing handed over was not the thing paid for. A similar principle was acted on in *Ship's Case* (1865) 2 De G.J. & S. 544. There is, however, a very important difference between cases where a contract may be rescinded on account of fraud, and those in which it may be rescinded on the ground that there is a difference in substance between the thing bargained for and that obtained. It is enough to show that there was a fraudulent representation as to any part of that which induced the party to enter into the contract which he seeks to rescind; but where there has been an innocent misrepresentation or misapprehension, it does not authorise a rescission unless it is such as to show that there is a complete difference in substance between what was supposed to be and what was taken, so as to constitute a failure of consideration. For example, where a horse is bought under a belief that it is sound, if the purchaser was induced to buy by a fraudulent representation as to the horse's soundness, the contract may be rescinded. If it was induced by an honest misrepresentation as to its soundness, though it may be clear that both vendor and purchaser thought that they were dealing about a sound horse and were in error, yet the purchaser must pay the whole price unless there was a warranty; and even if there was a warranty, he cannot return the horse and claim back the whole price, unless there was a condition to that effect in the contract: *Street v Blay* (1831) 2 B. & Ad. 456."

The court came to the conclusion in that case that, though there was a misapprehension as to that which was a material part of the motive inducing the applicant to ask for the shares, it did not prevent the shares from being in substance those he applied for.

The next case is *Smith v Hughes* [above, Ch.5]. [His Lordship then stated the facts and quoted from the judgments in that case.]

The court ordered a new trial. It is not quite clear whether they considered that if the defendant's contention was correct, the parties were not ad idem or there was a contractual condition that the oats sold were old oats. In either case the defendant would succeed in defeating the claim.

In these cases I am inclined to think that the true analysis is that there is a contract, but that the one party is not able to supply the very thing whether goods or services that the other party contracted to take; and therefore the contract is unenforceable by the one if executory, while if executed the other can recover back money paid on the ground of failure of the consideration.[4]

We are now in a position to apply to the facts of this case the law as to mistake so far as it has been stated. It is essential on this part of the discussion to keep in mind the finding of the jury acquitting the defendants of fraudulent misrepresentation or concealment in procuring the agreements in question. Grave injustice may be done to the defendants and confusion introduced into the legal conclusion, unless it is quite clear that in considering mistake in this case no suggestion of fraud is admissible and cannot strictly be regarded by the judge who has to determine the legal issues raised. The agreement which is said to be void is the agreement contained in the letter of March 19, 1929, that Bell would retire from the Board of the Niger Company and its subsidiaries, and that in consideration of his doing so Levers would pay him as compensation for the termination of his agreements and consequent loss of office the sum of £30,000 in full satisfaction and discharge of all claims and demands of any kind against Lever Brothers, the Niger Company or its subsidiaries. The agreement, which as part of the contract was terminated, had been broken so that it could be repudiated. Is an agreement to terminate a broken contract different in kind from an agreement to terminate an unbroken contract, assuming that the breach has given the one party the right to declare the contract at an end? I feel the weight of the plaintiffs' contention that a contract immediately determinable is a different thing from a contract for an unexpired term, and that the difference in kind can be illustrated by the immense price of release from the longer contract as compared with the shorter. And I agree that an agreement to take an assignment of a lease for five years is not the same thing as to take an assignment of a lease for three years, still less a term for a few months. But, on the whole, I have come to the conclusion that it would be wrong to decide that an agreement to terminate a definite specified contract is void if it turns out that the agreement had already been broken and could have been terminated otherwise. The contract released is the identical contract in both cases, and the party paying for release gets exactly what he bargains for. It seems immaterial that he could have got the same result in another way, or that if he had known the true facts he would not have entered into the bargain. A buys B's horse; he thinks the horse is sound and he pays the price of a sound horse; he would certainly not have bought the horse if he had known, as the fact is, that the horse is unsound. If B has made no representation as to soundness and has not contracted that the horse is sound, A is bound and cannot recover back the price. A buys a picture from B; both A and B believe it to be the work of an old master, and a high price is paid. It turns out to be a modern copy. A has no remedy in the absence of representation or warranty. A agrees to take on lease or to buy from B an unfurnished dwelling-house. The house is in fact uninhabitable. A would never have entered into the bargain if he had known the fact. A has no remedy, and the position is the same whether B knew the facts or not, so long as he made no representation or gave no warranty. A buys a roadside garage business from B abutting on a public thoroughfare: unknown to A, but known to B, it has already been decided to construct a by-pass road which will divert substantially the whole of the traffic from passing A's garage. Again A has no remedy. All these cases involve hardship on A and benefit B, as most people would say, unjustly. They can be supported on the ground that it is of paramount importance that contracts should be observed, and that if parties honestly comply with the essentials of the formation of contract—for example, agree in the same terms on the same subject-matter—they are bound, and must rely on the stipulations of the contract for protection from the effect of facts unknown to them.

This brings the discussion to the alternative mode of expressing the result of a mutual mistake. It is said that in such a case as the present there is to be implied a stipulation in the contract that a condition of its efficacy is that the facts should be as understood by both parties—namely, that the contract could not be terminated till the end of the current term. The question of the existence of conditions, express or implied, is obviously one that affects not the formation of contract, but the investigation of the terms of the contract when made. A condition derives its efficacy from the consent of the parties, express or implied. They have agreed, but on what terms? One term may be that unless the facts are or are not of a particular nature, or unless an event has or has not happened, the contract is not to take effect. With regard to future facts such a condition is

---

[4]   This paragraph is the "observation" referred to in *McRae v The Commonwealth Disposals Commission* (above).

obviously contractual. Till the event occurs the parties are bound. Thus the condition (the exact terms of which need not here be investigated) that is generally accepted as underlying the principle of the frustration cases is contractual, an implied condition. Sir John Simon formulated for the assistance of your Lordships a proposition which should be recorded: "Whenever it is to be inferred from the terms of a contract or its surrounding circumstances that the consensus has been reached upon the basis of a particular contractual assumption, and that assumption is not true, the contract is avoided: that is, it is void ab initio if the assumption is of present fact and it ceases to bind if the assumption is of future fact."

I think few would demur to this statement, but its value depends upon the meaning of "a contractual assumption," and also upon the true meaning to be attached to "basis," a metaphor which may mislead. When used expressly in contracts, for instance, in policies of insurance, which state that the truth of the statements in the proposal is to be the basis of the contract of insurance, the meaning is clear. The truth of the statements is made a condition of the contract, which failing, the contract is void unless the condition is waived. The proposition does not amount to more than this: that, if the contract expressly or impliedly contains a term that a particular assumption is a condition of the contract, the contract is avoided if the assumption is not true. But we have not advanced far on the inquiry how to ascertain whether the contract does contain such a condition. Various words are to be found to define the state of things which make a condition. "In the contemplation of both parties fundamental to the continued validity of the contract," "a foundation essential to its existence," "a fundamental reason for making it," are phrases found in the important judgment of Scrutton L.J. in the present case. The first two phrases appear to me to be unexceptionable. They cover the case of a contract to serve in a particular place, the existence of which is fundamental to the service, or to procure the services of a professional vocalist, whose continued health is essential to performance. But "a fundamental reason for making a contract" may, with respect, be misleading. The reason of one party only is presumedly not intended, but in the cases I have suggested above, of the sale of a horse or of a picture, it might be said that the fundamental reason for making the contract was the belief of both parties that the horse was sound or the picture an old master, yet in neither case would the condition as I think exist. Nothing is more dangerous than to allow oneself liberty to construct for the parties contracts which they have not in terms made, by importing implications which would appear to make the contract more businesslike or more just. The implications to be made are to be no more than are "necessary" for giving business efficacy to the transaction, and it appears to me that, both as to existing facts and future facts, a condition would not be implied unless the new state of facts makes the contract something different in kind from the contract in the original state of facts. Thus, in *Krell v Henry* [below], Vaughan Williams L.J. finds that the subject of the contract was "rooms to view the procession": the postponement, therefore, made the rooms not rooms to view the procession. This also is the test finally chosen by Lord Sumner in *Bank Line v Arthur Capel & Co* [1919] A.C. 435, agreeing with Lord Dunedin in *Metropolitan Water Board v Dick Kerr* [1918] A.C. 119, 128, where, dealing with the criterion for determining the effect of interruption in "frustrating" a contract, he says: "An interruption may be so long as to destroy the identity of the work or service, when resumed, with the work or service when interrupted." We therefore get a common standard for mutual mistake, and implied conditions whether as to existing or as to future facts. Does the state of the new facts destroy the identity of the subject-matter as it was in the original state of facts? To apply the principle to the infinite combinations of facts that arise in actual experience will continue to be difficult, but if this case results in establishing order into what has been a somewhat confused and difficult branch of the law it will have served a useful purpose.

I have already stated my reasons for deciding that in the present case the identity of the subject-matter was not destroyed by the mutual mistake, if any, and need not repeat them. [His Lordship then went on to hold that the defendants owed no duty to the Lever Company to disclose the impugned transactions.]

Lord Thankerton delivered judgment to the same effect as Lord Atkin.

Points for reflection

23–014

1. As to the duty of disclosure, see above, Ch.14.

2. Was the substance of the matter that Bell was selling his right to continue in Levers' employment (a right which did not exist)? And that Levers were buying the right to terminate Bell's employment (a right which they already owned)? If so, should not the contract have been held to be void under the principles stated by Lord Atkin? If the subject-matter of the contract was Bell's

contract of service, the mistake of the parties related only to a quality of it; but, if it was Bell's right to be employed, it did not exist; and, if it was Levers' right to terminate, the case was like *Cooper v Phibbs*. How is the subject-matter best regarded? For a wonderful account of the background to the decision in *Bell v Lever Bros*, see Catharine MacMillan, 'How Temptation Led to Mistake: An Explanation of *Bell v Lever Brothers, Limited*' (2003) 119 L.Q.R. 625.

3. In the *Harvela* case, above, Ch.2, the vendors' acceptance of Sir Leonard's "referential bid" was held by Peter Gibson J to conclude a valid (though not specifically enforceable) contract. The belief of both parties that the vendors were bound to accept Sir Leonard's offer was a mistake of law which did not affect the formation of the contract. The House of Lords held that there was no such contract, following Buckley J in *Beesly v Hallwood Estates* [1960] 2 All E.R. 314 at 322. Buckley J said:

"Any transaction between two or more parties can, in my judgment, only result in a contract between them if they enter into that transaction with an intention to create binding contractual obligations or in circumstances in which such an intention must be attributed to them. The facts of the present case negative such as intention, for, as I find, these letters were written with the intention of carrying out what were thought to be existing obligations, not of creating any new obligation."

Is this explanation satisfactory? Where A and B have made a valid contract to make a contract (above, Ch.4) the second contract is certainly a good one although the intention of the parties is to carry out existing obligations, not to create new ones. The parties in *Harvela* in fact intended to create legal relations but the common assumption on which that intention was based was false. Is the principle similar to that which (in the opinion of some judges) rendered void the contract in *Cooper v Phibbs* where the parties were also making a mistake of law?

4. How would *Bell v Lever Bros* be decided under *The Principles of European Contract Law*, art.4:103, para.(1)(a)(iii) and (b), above, Ch.5?

5. In *Griffith v Brymer* (1903) 19 T.L.R. 434 Wright J held the contract void where, at 11 am on June 24, 1902, the plaintiff had entered into an oral agreement for the hire of a room to view the coronation procession on June 26, but the decision to operate on the King, which rendered the procession impossible, had been taken at about 10 am on June 24. The agreement was made on a missupposition of facts which went to the whole root of the matter: and the plaintiff was entitled to recover his £100. (What if the contract had been made at 9.00 am? Cf. *Krell v Henry* (below, Ch.24), and the *Fibrosa* case (below, Ch.24)).

6. In a well-known American case, *Sherwood v Walker* (Supreme Court of Michigan, 1887, 66 Mich. 568; 33 N.W. 919; 11 Am.St.Rep. 531), the defendants agreed to sell and the plaintiff to buy a cow, "Rose 2nd of Aberlone", for $80. The defendants believed the cow to be barren, but, before she was delivered, they discovered she was in calf. As a breeding cow she was worth $750–$1,000 and the defendants refused to deliver.

The majority of the court held that the parties contracted on the understanding and belief that she was incapable of breeding and of no use as a cow; that the mistake of both parties was "not of the mere quality of the animal, but went to the very nature of the thing", there being as much difference between them as between an ox and a cow; that "the thing sold and bought had in fact no existence" and there was "no contract to sell or sale of the cow as she actually was." The plaintiff's action of replevin failed.

Sherwood J, dissenting, held that the defendants believed the cow to be barren but that the plaintiff thought she could be made to breed; that "there was no difference between the parties, nor misapprehension, as to the substance of the thing bargained for which was a cow supposed to be barren by one party and believed not to be by the other."

Questions

23–015   1. Can *Griffith v Brymer* stand with *Bell v Lever Bros*?

2. How would an English court have decided *Sherwood v Walker* (a) if they had accepted the majority's interpretation of the facts? (b) if they had accepted Sherwood J's version?

----

3. THE MODERN EQUITABLE APPROACH

ASSOCIATED JAPANESE BANK LTD v CREDIT DU NORD SA AND ANOTHER

Queen's Bench Division (Commercial Court) [1988] 3 All E.R. 902

23–016   Bennett contracted (i) to sell to, and (ii) to lease back from, the plaintiff (AJB) four machines. The defendant (CDN) guaranteed the performance by Bennett of his obligations under the lease. Bennett was fraudulent. The machines did not exist. The plaintiff sued the defendant on the guarantee.

STEYN J

. . .held that, on a sensible construction of the guarantee against its objective setting, it was subject to an express or, if not express an implied, condition precedent that the machines existed. As the machines did not exist the guarantee was void and the action failed.

Although this was determinative of the case Steyn J. went on to consider (treating this as a different ground) whether contract was void for mistake. Discussing *Bell v Lever Bros.*, he said: Lord Atkin held:

"... a mistake will not affect assent unless it is the mistake of both parties, and is as to the existence of some quality which makes the thing without the quality essentially different from the thing as it was believed to be."

In my view none of the other passages in Lord Atkin's speech detract from that statement of the law. Lord Thankerton came to a similar conclusion. He held that common mistake "can only properly relate to something which both must necessarily have accepted in their minds as an essential and integral part of the subject-matter" (see [1932] AC 161 at 235).

That seems to me exactly the same test as Lord Atkin enunciated. Clearly, Lord Atkin did not conceive of any difference between his formulation and that of Lord Thankerton . . .

When Lord Denning M.R. referred to *Magee v Pennine Insurance Co Ltd* [below] to the views of commentators he may have had in mind comments in Cheshire and Fifoot, *Law of Contract* (6th ed., 1964), p. 196. In substance the argument was that the actual decision in *Bell v Lever Bros. Ltd*, contradicts the language of the speeches. If the test was not satisfied there, so the argument runs, it is difficult to see how it could ever be satisfied: see the latest edition of this valuable textbook for the same argument (Cheshire, Fifoot and Furmston, *Law of Contract* (11th ed., 1986), pp. 225–226). This is a point worth examining because at first glance it may seem persuasive. *Bell v Lever Bros. Ltd* was a quite exceptional case; all their Lordships were agreed that common mistake had not been pleaded and would have required an amendment in the House of Lords if it were to succeed. The speeches do not suggest that the employees were entitled to keep both the gains secretly made and the golden handshakes. The former were clearly recoverable from them. Nevertheless, the golden handshakes were very substantial. But there are indications in the speeches that the so-called "merits" were not all in favour of Lever Bros. The company was most anxious, because of a corporate merger, to terminate the two service agreements. There was apparently a doubt whether the voidability of the service agreements if revealed to the company at the time of the severance contract would have affected the company's decision. Lord Thankerton said ([1932] A.C. 161 at 236, [1931] All E.R. Rep. 1 at 37):

> ". . . I do not find sufficient material to compel the inference that the appellants, at the time of the contract, regarded the indefeasibility of the service agreements as an essential and integral element in the subject-matter of the bargain."

Lord Atkin clearly regarded it as a hard case on the facts, but concluded "on the whole" that the plea of common mistake must fail (see [1932] A.C. 161 at 223). It is noteworthy that Lord Atkin commented on the scarcity of evidence as to the subsidiaries from the boards of which the two employees resigned (see [1932] A.C. 161 at 212). Lord Blanesburgh's speech was directed to his conclusion that the amendment ought not to be allowed. He did, however, make clear that "the mistake must go to the whole consideration," and pointed to the advantages (other than the release from the service agreements) which Lever Bros. received (see [1932] A.C. 161 at 181). Lord Blanesburgh emphasised that Lever Bros. secured the future co-operation of the two employees for the carrying through of the amalgamation (see [1932] A.C. 161 at 181). And the burden, of course, rested squarely on Lever Bros. With due deference to the distinguished authors who have argued that the actual decision in *Bell v Lever Bros. Ltd* contradicts the principle enunciated in the speeches it seems to me that their analysis is altogether too simplistic, and that the actual decision was rooted in the particular facts of the case. In my judgment there is no reason to doubt the substantive reasons emerging from the speeches of the majority . . .

It is clear, of course, that in this case both parties, the creditor and the guarantor, acted on the assumption that the lease related to existing machines. If they had been informed that the machines might not exist, neither A.J.B. nor C.D.N. would for one moment have contemplated entering into the transaction. That, by itself, I accept, is not enough to sustain the plea of common law mistake. I am also satisfied that C.D.N. had reasonable grounds for believing that the machines existed. That belief was based on C.D.N.'s discussions with Mr Bennett, information supplied by National Leasing, a respectable firm of lease brokers, and the confidence created by the fact that A.J.B. were the lessors.

The real question is whether the subject matter of the guarantee (as opposed to the sale and lease) was essentially different from what it was reasonably believed to be. The real security of the guarantor was the machines. The existence of the machines, being profit-earning chattels, made it more likely that the debtor would be able to service the debt. More importantly, if the debtor defaulted and the creditor repossessed the machines, the creditor had to give credit for 97½ per cent. of the value of the machines. If the creditor sued the guarantor first, and the guarantor paid, the guarantor was entitled to be subrogated to the creditor's rights in respect of recovery against the debtor: see Goff and Jones, *Law of Restitution* (3rd ed., 1986), pp. 533–536). No doubt the guarantor relied to some extent on the creditworthiness of Mr Bennett. But I find that the prime security to which the guarantor looked was the existence of the four machines as described to both parties. For both parties the guarantee of obligations under a lease with non-existent machines was essentially different from a guarantee of a lease with four machines which both parties at the time of the contract believed to exist. The guarantee is an accessory contract. the non-existence of the subject matter of the principal contract is therefore of fundamental importance. Indeed the analogy of the classic res extincta cases, so much discussed in the authorities, is fairly close. In my judgment, the stringent test of common law mistake is satisfied; the guarantee is void ab initio.

Questions

1. Suppose that Steyn J had decided that there was no express or implied term. Would that decision have left room for any inquiry whether the contract was void for mistake? Would it not have established that the parties intended the contract to be binding in the circumstances which existed? See Smith (1994) 110 L.Q.R. pp.400, 406–409.

2. Steyn J suggests that, if Levers had known of the voidability of Bell's service agreement, it would not have affected their decision to pay him £30,000. Is this suggestion reconcilable with the finding of the jury that Levers would have exercised their right to dismiss Bell if they had known they could do so? See Smith, op. cit., pp.411–418.

3. Steyn J refers to Lord Blanesborough's point that an operative mistake must go to the whole consideration. Lord Blanesborough pointed out that £30,000 was far more than was necessary

23–017

to compensate Bell for his loss of employment. It was intended partly (i) as a recognition of outstanding services Bell had rendered to Levers and (ii) to secure his future co-operation in the amalgamation. The former was a past consideration. The latter may have been Levers' motive for their apparent generosity but can it be regarded as part of the consideration in the light of Levers' letter of March 19, 1929 which embodied the agreement with Bell: ". . . from May 1 next you will on that date retire from the boards . . . and in consideration of your doing so Lever Bros Ltd will pay you as compensation for the termination of your agreement"? Co-operation is not mentioned in the letter. Suppose Bell had failed to co-operate. Could Levers have sued him?

The Principles of European Contract Law, 1998, art.4: 102 Initial Impossibility.

23–018   A contract is not invalid merely because at the time it was concluded performance of the obligation assumed was impossible, or because a party was not entitled to dispose of the assets to which the contract relates.

SOLLE v BUTCHER

Court of Appeal [1950] 1 K.B. 671; 66 T.L.R. (Pt. 1) 448; [1949] 2 All E.R. 1107

23–019   In 1947 the plaintiff, a surveyor, and the defendant were partners in the business of estate agents. In 1931 a dwelling-house had been converted into five flats. In 1938 Flat 1 was let for three years at an annual rent of £140. In 1947 the defendant took a long lease of the building, intending to repair bomb damage and do substantial alterations. The plaintiff and the defendant discussed the rents to be charged after the work had been completed. The plaintiff told the defendant that he could charge £250 for Flat 1, both parties being satisfied that the rent of £140 in 1938 did not apply as the "standard rent." The defendant said that he relied on the plaintiff in the matter of rents. He took no steps to calculate the additions to £140 which, if that were the standard rent, would have been permitted by the Rent Act 1938 because of the improvements made to the flat. Those additions would have brought the rent up to about £250.

In September 1947 Flat 1 was let by the defendant to the plaintiff for a term of seven years at a yearly rent of £250. Once this lease was executed no notice of intention to increase the rent could be given under the Rent Restriction Acts during the contractual tenancy.

The plaintiff paid rent at £250 per year for some time and then took proceedings in the county court for a declaration that the standard rent of the flat was £140 and that he was entitled to recover from the landlord the amount overpaid since the commencement of the tenancy. The defendant contended that the flat had become a new and separate dwelling by reason of change of identity, but the county court judge found as a fact that the flat was not a new and separate dwelling. The defendant counterclaimed for rescission of the lease on the ground of mutual mistake of fact, but the county court judge rejected this claim, saying, "I find that there was no mistake of fact—possibly a mistake of law—in that both parties for some obscure reason imagined that the Rent Acts did not apply. I do not think they ever addressed their minds to the material issue of identity." He held also that the plea of estoppel was no defence against the provisions of the Rent Restriction Acts. He made an order for the recovery of the amount of the rent overpaid. The defendant appealed.

Bucknill LJ held that the lease must be set aside on the ground that both parties having, in his opinion (contrary to that of the county court judge), addressed their minds to the question whether the flat had changed its identity, the mistake which each had made was that the work done had made such a substantial alteration to the building as to make it a different flat—a common mistake of fact.

DENNING LJ

[Having held that the flat had not changed its identity and therefore the raising of the rent from £140 to £250 was invalid; and that, just as parties cannot contract out of the Rent Acts, so they cannot defeat them by any estoppel, went on:] In this plight the landlord seeks to set aside the lease. He says, with truth, that it is unfair that the tenant should have the benefit of the lease for the outstanding five years of the term at £140 a year, when the proper rent is £250 a year. If he cannot give a notice of increase now, can he not avoid the lease? The only ground on which he can avoid it is on the ground of mistake. It is quite plain that the parties were under a mistake. They thought that the flat was not tied down to a controlled rent, whereas in fact it was. In order to see whether the lease can be avoided for this mistake it is necessary to remember that mistake is of two kinds: first, mistake which renders the contract void, that is, a nullity from the beginning, which is the kind of mistake which was dealt with by the courts of common law; and, secondly, mistake which renders the contract not void, but voidable, that is, liable to be set aside on such terms as the court thinks fit, which is the kind of mistake which was dealt with by the courts of equity. Much of the difficulty which has attended this subject has arisen because, before the fusion of law and equity, the courts of common law, in order to do justice in the case in hand, extended this doctrine of mistake beyond its proper limits and held contracts to be void which were really only voidable, a process which was capable of being attended with much injustice to third persons who had bought goods or otherwise committed themselves on the faith that there was a contract. In the well-known case of *Cundy v Lindsay* [above, Ch.8], Cundy suffered such an injustice. He bought the handkerchiefs from the rogue, Blenkarn, before the Judicature Acts came into operation. Since the fusion of law and equity, there is no reason to continue this process, and it will be found that only those contracts are now held void in which the mistake was such as to prevent the formation of any contract at all.

Let me first consider mistakes which render a contract a nullity. All previous decisions on this subject must now be read in the light of *Bell v Lever Bros. Ltd* [above]. The correct interpretation of that case, to my mind, is that, once a contract has been made, that is to say, once the parties, whatever their inmost states of mind, have to all outward appearances agreed with sufficient certainty in the same terms on the same subject-matter, then the contract is good unless and until it is set aside for failure of some condition on which the existence of the contract depends, or for fraud, or on some equitable ground. Neither party can rely on his own mistake to say it was a nullity from the beginning, no matter that it was a mistake which to his mind was fundamental, and no matter that the other party knew that he was under a mistake. A fortiori, if the other party did not know of the mistake, but shared it. The cases where goods have perished at the time of sale, or belong to the buyer, are really contracts which are not void for mistake but are void by reason of an implied condition precedent, because the contract proceeded on the basic assumption that it was possible of performance.[5] So far as cases later than *Bell v Lever Bros. Ltd* are concerned, I do not think that *Sowler v Potter* [above, Ch.8] can stand with *King's Norton Metal Co Ltd v Edridge* [above, Ch.8], which shows that the doctrine of French law as enunciated by Pothier is no part of English law. Nor do I think that the contract in *Nicholson and Venn v Smith-Marriott* (1947) 177 L.T. 189[6] was void from the beginning.

Applying these principles, it is clear that here there was a contract. The parties agreed in the same terms on the subject-matter. It is true that the landlord was under a mistake which was to him fundamental: he would not for one moment have considered letting the flat for seven years if it meant that he could only charge £140 a year for it. He made the fundamental mistake of believing that the rent he could charge was not tied down to a controlled rent; but, whether it was his own mistake or a mistake common to both him and the tenant, it is not a ground for saying that the lease was from the beginning a nullity. Any other view would lead to remarkable results, for it would mean that, in the many cases where the parties mistakenly think a house is outside the Rent Restriction Acts when it is really within them, the tenancy would be a nullity, and the tenant would have to go; with the result that the tenants would not dare to seek to have their rents reduced to the permitted amounts lest they should be turned out.

Let me next consider mistakes which render a contract voidable, that is, liable to be set aside on some equitable ground. Whilst presupposing that a contract was good at law, or at any rate not void, the court of equity would often relieve a party from the consequences of his own mistake, so long as it could do so without

---

[5]   Compare this sentence with that footnoted in para.24–020.

[6]   S put up for auction table-napkins "'with the crest of Charles I and the authentic property of that monarch". B, relying on the description, bought the napkins for £787. In fact they were Georgian and worth only £105. Hallett J awarded B damages but said B might have treated the contract as void.

injustice to third parties. The court, it was said, had power to set aside the contract whenever it was of opinion that it was unconscientious for the other party to avail himself of the legal advantage which he had obtained: *Torrance v Bolton* (1872) L.R. 8 Ch. 118, 124, per James L.J.

The court had, of course, to define what it considered to be unconscientious, but in this respect equity has shown a progressive development. It is now clear that a contract will be set aside if the mistake of the one party has been induced by a material misrepresentation of the other, even though it was not fraudulent or fundamental; or if one party, knowing that the other is mistaken about the terms of an offer, or the identity of the person by whom it is made, lets him remain under his delusion and concludes a contract on the mistaken terms instead of pointing out the mistake. That is, I venture to think, the ground on which the defendant in *Smith v Hughes* [above, Ch.5] would be exempted nowadays,[7] and on which, according to the view by Blackburn J. of the facts, the contract in *Lindsay v Cundy* was voidable and not void; and on which the lease in *Sowler v Potter* was, in my opinion, voidable and not void.

A contract is also liable in equity to be set aside if the parties were under a common misapprehension either as to facts or as to their relative and respective rights, provided that the misapprehension was fundamental and that the party seeking to set it aside was not himself at fault. That principle was first applied to private rights as long ago as 1730 in *Lansdown v Lansdown* (1730) Mos. 364. There were four brothers, and the second and third of them died. The eldest brother entered on the lands of the deceased brothers, but the youngest brother claimed them. So the two rival brothers consulted a friend who was a local schoolmaster. The friend looked up a book which he then had with him called The Clerk's Remembrancer and gave it as his opinion that the lands belonged to the youngest brother. He recommended the two of them to take further advice, which at first they intended to do, but they did not do so; and, acting on the friend's opinion, the elder brother agreed to divide the estate with the younger brother, and executed deeds and bonds giving effect to the agreement. Lord Chancellor King declared that the documents were obtained by a mistake and by a misrepresentation of the law by the friend and ordered them to be given up to be cancelled. He pointed out that the maxim ignorantia juris non excusat only means that ignorance cannot be pleaded in excuse of crimes. Eighteen years later, in the time of Lord Hardwicke, the same principle was applied in *Bingham v Bingham* (1748) 1 Ves. Sen. 126.

If and in so far as those cases were compromises of disputed rights,[8] they have been subjected to justifiable criticism, but, in cases where there is no element of compromise, but only of mistaken rights, the House of Lords in 1867 in the great case of *Cooper v Phibbs* (1867) L.R. 2 HL 149, 170, affirmed the doctrine there acted on as correct. In that case an uncle had told his nephew, not intending to misrepresent anything, but being in fact in error, that he (the uncle) was entitled to a fishery; and the nephew, after the uncle's death, acting in the belief of the truth of what the uncle had told him, entered into an agreement to rent the fishery from the uncle's daughters, whereas it actually belonged to the nephew himself. The mistake there as to the title to the fishery did not render the tenancy agreement a nullity. If it had done, the contract would have been void at law from the beginning and equity would have had to follow the law. There would have been no contract to set aside and no terms to impose. The House of Lords, however, held that the mistake was only such as to make it voidable, or, in Lord Westbury's words, "liable to be set aside" on such terms as the court thought fit to impose; and it was so set aside.

The principle so established by *Cooper v Phibbs* has been repeatedly acted on: see, for instance, *Earl Beauchamp v Winn* (1873) L.R. 6 HL 223, 234, and *Huddersfield Banking Co Ltd v Lister* [1895] Ch. 273. It is in no way impaired by *Bell v Lever Bros. Ltd*, which was treated in the House of Lords as a case at law depending on whether the contract was a nullity or not. If it had been considered on equitable grounds, the result might have been different. In any case, the principle of *Cooper v Phibbs* has been fully restored by *Norwich Union Fire Insurance Society, Ltd v William H. Price, Ltd* [below].

Applying that principle to this case, the facts are that the plaintiff, the tenant, was a surveyor who was employed by the defendant, the landlord, not only to arrange finance for the purchase of the building and to negotiate with the rating authorities as to the new rateable values, but also to let the flats. He was the agent for letting, and he clearly formed the view that the building was not controlled. He told the valuation officer so. He advised the defendant what were the rents which could be charged. He read to the defendant an opinion of counsel relating to the matter, and told him that in his opinion he could charge £250 and that there was no

---

[7] The defendant was exempted if the plaintiff knew he was mistaken as to the terms of the offer, but not if he was (or appeared to be) merely mistaken as to the age of the oats.

[8] Cf. *Cook v Wright* above, Ch.10, distinguishing *Bell v Gardiner*.

previous control. He said that the flats came outside the Act and that the defendant was "clear." The defendant relied on what the plaintiff told him, and authorised the plaintiff to let at the rentals which he had suggested. The plaintiff not only let the four other flats to other people for a long period of years at the new rentals, but also took one himself for seven years at £250 a year. Now he turns round and says, quite unashamedly, that he wants to take advantage of the mistake to get the flat at £140 a year for seven years instead of the £250 a year, which is not only the rent he agreed to pay but also the fair and economic rent; and it is also the rent permitted by the Acts on compliance with the necessary formalities. If the rules of equity have become so rigid that they cannot remedy such an injustice, it is time we had a new equity, to make good the omissions of the old. But, in my view, the established rules are amply sufficient for this case.

On the defendant's evidence, which the judge preferred, I should have thought there was a good deal to be said for the view that the lease was induced by an innocent material misrepresentation by the plaintiff. It seems to me that the plaintiff was not merely expressing an opinion on the law: he was making an unambiguous statement as to private rights; and a misrepresentation as to private rights is equivalent to a misrepresentation of fact for this purpose: *MacKenzie v Royal Bank of Canada* [1934] A.C. 468. But it is unnecessary to come to a firm conclusion on this point, because, as Bucknill L.J. has said, there was clearly a common mistake, or, as I would prefer to describe it, a common misapprehension, which was fundamental and in no way due to any fault of the defendant; and *Cooper v Phibbs* affords ample authority for saying that, by reason of the common misapprehension, this lease can be set aside on such terms as the court thinks fit.

[His Lordship then held that the fact that the lease had been executed was no bar to this relief. See above, Ch.14.]

The terms will be complicated by reason of the Rent Restriction Acts, but it is not beyond the wit of man to devise them. Subject to any observations which the parties may desire to make, the terms which I suggest are these: the lease should only be set aside if the defendant is prepared to give an undertaking that he will permit the plaintiff to be a licensee of the premises pending the grant of a new lease. Then, whilst the plaintiff is a licensee, the defendant will in law be in possession of the premises, and will be able to serve on the plaintiff, as prospective tenant, a notice under section 7(4) of the Act of 1938 increasing the rent to the full permitted amount. The defendant must further be prepared to give an undertaking that he will serve such a notice within three weeks from the drawing up of the order, and that he will, if written request is made by the plaintiff, within one month of the service of the notice, grant him a new lease at the full permitted amount of rent, not, however, exceeding £250 a year, for a term expiring on September 29, 1954, subject in all other respects to the same covenants and conditions as in the rescinded lease. If there is any difference of opinion about the figures stated in the notice, that can, of course, be adjusted during the currency of the lease. If the plaintiff does not choose to accept the licence or the new lease, he must go out. He will not be entitled to the protection of the Rent Restriction Acts because, the lease being set aside, there will be no initial contractual tenancy from which a statutory tenancy can spring.

JENKINS LJ (DISSENTING)

. . . But whether the parties failed to ask themselves the right question or, having asked it, answered it wrongly, I find it impossible to hold that a mutual mistake of the character here involved affords a good ground for rescission. The defendant meant to grant and the plaintiff meant to take a lease in the terms in which the lease was actually granted of the premises which the lease as granted actually comprised. They knew all the material facts bearing upon the effect of the Rent Restriction Acts on a lease of those premises. But they mutually misapprehended the effect which, in that state of facts, those Acts would have on such a lease. That is a mistake of law of a kind which, so far as I am aware, has never yet been held to afford good ground for rescission. It is a mistake not as to the subject-matter nature, or purport of the contract entered into, nor as to any question of private right affecting the basis of the contract entered into (see *Cooper v Phibbs*), but simply a mistake as to the effect of certain public statutes on the contract made, being in all respects precisely the contract the parties intended to make.

The mistaken conclusion, to the effect that on the facts of the case (all relevant facts being known to both parties) the Rent Restriction Acts did not have the effect of making £140 the standard rent of the flat in question was, as it seems to me, equally a mistake of law whether it was due to a failure to appreciate and apply the test of identity or proceeded from an application of that test followed by an erroneous inference or opinion drawn from the facts, to the effect that the flat in question was not in substance the same dwelling-house as the flat formerly let to Howard Taylor. The application of the test, if it was indeed applied, was merely a step in the reasoning leading from the facts to the conclusion of law.

Appeal Allowed. Rescission of the Lease on the Terms Stated in the Judgment of Denning LJ.

Points for reflection

23-020   In *Norwich Union Fire Insurance Society v Price* [1934] A.C. 455, PC, the plaintiff insurance company paid to the insured the value of a cargo of lemons which the plaintiffs believed to have been damaged by a peril insured against and sold in consequence. It was ascertained later that the lemons had not been so damaged, but had been sold because they were found to be ripening. The Privy Council held that the plaintiffs could recover the sum paid by them as money paid under a mistake of fact. Lord Wright, delivering the judgment of their Lordships, said:

> "The mistake was as vital as that in *Cooper v Phibbs* (1867) L.R. 2 HL 149, 170, in respect of which Lord Westbury used these words: 'If parties contract under a mutual mistake and misapprehension as to their relative and respective rights, the result is that that agreement is liable to be set aside as having proceeded upon a common mistake.' At common law such a contract (or simulacrum of a contract) is more correctly described as void, there being in truth no intention to a contract. Their Lordships find nothing tending to contradict or overrule these established principles in *Bell v Lever Bros. Ltd.*"

Was the court concerned with the question whether a contract existed or not? Or whether a contract was voidable or not? Or neither?

Questions

23-021   1. Rescission is normally (for example, for misrepresentation) a remedy of which the injured party may avail himself without recourse to any court. But *Solle v Butcher* allows rescission only "on terms". Is this, then, a different concept of rescission from that met elsewhere?

2. How would *Solle v Butcher* be decided under *The Principles of European Contract Law* art.4:103(1)(a)(iii) and (b), above Ch.5? Could the plaintiff simply have avoided the contract without "terms"?

WILLIAM SINDALL PLC v CAMBRIDGESHIRE COUNTY COUNCIL

Court of Appeal [1994] 3 All E.R. 932

23-022   The trial judge held that the plaintiff buyer of land was entitled to rescind the contract for misrepresentation and common mistake as to the existence of a sewer. As to misrepresentation, see above, Ch.14. As to mistake:

HOFFMANN LJ

The judge found that in the absence of any actionable misrepresentations Sindall was entitled to rescind the contract for a common mistake as to the existence of a sewer. This is at first sight a startling result. As Steyn J. said in *Associated Japanese Bank (International) Ltd v Crédit du Nord SA* [above].

"Logically, before one can turn to the rules as to mistake, whether at common law or in equity, one must first determine whether the contract itself, by express or implied condition precedent or otherwise, provides who bears the risk of the relevant mistake. It is at this hurdle that many pleas of mistake will either fail or prove to have been unnecessary. Only if the contract is silent on the point is there scope for invoking mistake."

When the judge speaks of the contract allocating risk "by express or implied condition precedent or otherwise" I think he includes rules of general law applicable to the contract and which, for example, provide that, in the absence of express warranty, the law is caveat emptor. This would, in my view, allocate the risk of an unknown defect in goods to the buyer, even though it is not mentioned in the contract. Similarly, the rule in *Hill v Harris* [1965] 2 All E.R. 358, [1965] 2 Q.B. 601 that a lessor or vendor does not impliedly warrant that the premises are fit for any particular purpose means that the contract allocates the risk of the premises being unfit for such a purpose. I should say that neither in *Grist v Bailey*, [below] nor in *Laurence v Lexcourt Holdings Ltd* [below] did the judges who decided those cases at first instance advert to the question of contractual allocation of risk. I am not sure that the decisions would have been the same if they had.

In this case the contract says in express terms that it is subject to all easements other than those of which the vendor knows or has the means of knowledge. This allocates the risk of such incumbrances to the buyer and leaves no room for rescission on the grounds of mistake.

EVANS LJ

Logically, there remains the question whether the contract, notwithstanding that on its true construction it covers the situation which has arisen, and that it cannot be set aside for misrepresentation, nevertheless may be rescinded on the ground of equitable mistake, as defined by Denning L.J. in *Solle v Butcher*. It must be assumed, I think, that there is a category of mistake which is "fundamental" so as to permit the equitable remedy of rescission, which is wider than the kind of "serious and radical" mistake which means that the agreement is void and of no effect in law: see *Chitty on Contracts* (26th edn, 1989) vol 1, para 401, Treitel *The Law of Contract* (8th edn, 1991) p. 276; and Cheshire Fifoot and Furmston's *Law of Contract* (11th edn, 1986) p. 245. The difference may be that the common law rule is limited to mistakes with regard to the subject matter of the contract, whilst equity can have regard to a wider and perhaps unlimited category of "fundamental" mistake. However that may be, I am satisfied that the judge's finding in the present case was vitiated by his assumption that the presence of the sewer and of the city's easement had serious consequences for the proposed development, even if the sewer was incorporated into the public sewer that was envisaged for the development itself (Option 2A). This would not involve the loss of seven houses and three flats, as the judge appears to have thought, but, at most, of one three-bedroomed house. The additional cost of the alterations to the sewer would not have exceeded about £20,000. Given the breadth of the contract terms, in particular condition No. 14, which on its face was intended to cover precisely such a situation as this, and the relatively minor consequences of the discovery of the sewer, even if some period of delay as well as additional cost was involved, it is impossible to hold, in my judgment, that there is scope for rescission here.

Russell L.J. agreed with both judgments.

Appeal Allowed.

Points for reflection

1. *Solle v Butcher* has always been difficult to reconcile with established principles of the common law. *Smith v Hughes*, above, Ch.5, decides that there may be a contract enforceable by the seller even where the seller is aware that the buyer is making a mistake as to a (to him) fundamental quality of the goods; and, if that is right, this must, a fortiori, be so where the seller shares the mistake. If A sells to B a painting which both believe to be of small value, is the contract to be voidable if the painting turns out to be an old master? If there are degrees of "fundamentalness" (see below), this mistake is more fundamental than that in *Solle v Butcher*. But it would undermine the certainty of commercial transactions if such contracts were liable to be set aside at the discretion of the court. Hoffmann LJ's dictum, above, would exclude *Solle v Butcher* in cases of this kind. It seems obvious that an express term on the point, like that in *Sindall*, should be conclusive; but if we must also look at the "rules of general law applicable to the contract", what room, if any, does that leave for the application of the doctrine? Was not the dissent by Jenkins

23–023

LJ in *Solle v Butcher* an application of the "rules of general law applicable to the contract"? Is it likely that Lord Denning would have agreed with Hoffmann LJ? He thought (above) that "the defendant in *Smith v Hughes* would be exempted nowadays." See the discussion of *R. v Hinks*, above, Ch.2.

A second difficulty with *Solle v Butcher* is that the misapprehension must be "fundamental", yet, ex hypothesi, not so fundamental as to make the contract void, for then there would be nothing to rescind. Evans LJ, in the passage cited, appears to accept that "fundamental" may have a variable meaning; but earlier in his judgment, he questions whether "simultaneously the mistake can be fundamental yet the land not 'essentially and radically different' from what it was supposed to be . . .". Can it?

2. In *Grist v Bailey* [1967] Ch. 532 the defendant entered into a contract to sell a freehold house to the plaintiff for £850, "subject to the existing tenancy thereof." The defendant believed, and the plaintiff's agent assumed, that there was a protected tenant in occupation. The agent would not have expected to get the property with vacant possession for anything like £850. But, unknown to the defendant, the tenant and the tenant's spouse had died. It was uncertain whether their son was entitled to protection under the Act but he never claimed it and vacated the house. The value of the property with vacant possession was about £2,250. The plaintiff sued for specific performance and the defendant counterclaimed for rescission on the ground that the contract was void or voidable for mistake.

    Goff J said that the mistake in *Bell v Lever Bros* was more fundamental than any made in the present case and Lord Atkin's examples of the horse, picture and garage would apply to prevent the mistake being sufficient to avoid the agreement; but *Solle v Butcher* was binding on him. In this case there was a common mistake, namely that there was a subsisting protected tenancy, it was fundamental (£850 as against £2,250) and the defendant was not so at fault as to disentitle him to relief. The plaintiff's action was dismissed and rescission ordered.

    In *Laurence v Lexcourt Holdings Ltd* [1978] 2 All E.R. 810 plaintiffs offered to let a building for use as offices, overlooking the fact that planning permission for office use extended to part only of the building. Defendants, assuming that planning permission existed, accepted. Dillon QC dismissed a claim for specific performance because (i) the description of the premises as offices was a misrepresentation that planning permission for use as offices was available and (ii) the belief of both parties that planning permission was available was a common mistake of the same character as these in *Solle v Butcher* and *Grist v Bailey*.

Questions

23–024

1. If a case with exactly the same facts as *Bell v Lever Bros Ltd* had come before Goff J, how do you think he would have decided it? If he would have granted rescission, does it follow that *Bell v Lever Bros Ltd* was decided per incuriam?

2. Would rescission have been granted if the conveyance had been executed?

3. Recalling a famous passage in *Smith v Hughes* (above, Ch.5), would the case put by Cockburn CJ of the sale of an estate in which, unknown to the vendor, there is a mine under the surface still be decided as he thought? Cf. Professor Atiyah (1968) 2 *Ottawa Law Rev.* 337, 350.

MAGEE v PENNINE INSURANCE CO LTD

Court of Appeal [1969] 2 Q.B. 507; [1969] 2 W.L.R. 1278; [1969] 2 All E.R. 891; [1969] 2 Lloyd's Rep. 378

23–025

In 1961 the plaintiff (M) bought a car for his son to drive. He signed an insurance proposal form filled in by the seller of the car, which stated that M held a provisional licence. M had no licence. He was not dishonest but had not read what he signed. It was the basis of the contract of insurance that M's answers were true. In 1965 the car, driven by the son, was involved in an accident and completely wrecked. M claimed £600 from the insurers, the defendants, (P). P offered M £385 in settlement of his claim. M accepted. P then discovered that M had never had a licence and refused to pay. The county court judge held that M could not sue on the policy because of the misrepresentation, but that the offer and acceptance of a promise to pay £385 was a binding contract of compromise. P appealed.

LORD DENNING MR

[Having accepted, after some doubt, that there had been a contract of compromise:] But then comes the next point. Accepting that the agreement to pay £385 was an agreement of compromise. Is it vitiated by mistake? The insurance company were clearly under a mistake. They thought that the policy was good and binding. They did not know, at the time of that letter, that there had been misrepresentation in the proposal form. If Mr Magee knew of their mistake—if he knew that the policy was bad—he certainly could not take advantage of the agreement to pay £385. He would be "snapping at an offer which he knew was made under a mistake": and no man is allowed to get away with that. But I prefer to assume that Mr Magee was innocent. I think we should take it that both parties were under a common mistake. Both parties thought that the policy was good and binding. The letter of May 12, 1968, was written on the assumption that the policy was good whereas it was in truth voidable.

What is the effect in law of this common mistake? Mr Taylor said that the agreement to pay £385 was good, despite this common mistake. He relied much on *Bell v Lever Brothers Ltd* [above], and its similarity to the present case. He submitted that, in as much as the mistake there did not vitiate that contract, the mistake here should not vitiate this one. I do not propose today to go through the speeches in that case. They have given enough trouble to commentators already. I would simply say this: A common mistake, even on a most fundamental matter, does not make a contract void at law: but it makes it voidable in equity. I analysed the cases in *Solle v Butcher* [above], and I would repeat what I said there, at [1950] 1 K.B. 671, 693: "A contract is also liable in equity to be set aside if the parties were under a common misapprehension either as to facts or as to their relative and respective rights, provided that the misapprehension was fundamental and that the party seeking to set it aside was not himself at fault."

Applying that principle here, it is clear that, when the insurance company and Mr Magee made this agreement to pay £385, they were both under a common mistake which was fundamental to the whole agreement. Both thought that Mr Magee was entitled to claim under the policy of insurance, whereas he was not so entitled. That common mistake does not make the agreement to pay £385 a nullity, but it makes it liable to be set aside in equity.

This brings me to a question which has caused me much difficulty. Is this a case in which we ought to set the agreement aside in equity? I have hesitated on this point, but I cannot shut my eyes to the fact that Mr Magee had no valid claim on the insurance policy: and, if he had no claim on the policy, it is not equitable that he should have a good claim on the agreement to pay £385, seeing that it was made under a fundamental mistake. It is not fair to hold the insurance company to an agreement which they would not have dreamt of making if they had not been under a mistake. I would, therefore, uphold the appeal and give judgment for the insurance company.

WINN LJ (DISSENTING)

[Referred to the speeches of Lords Atkin and Thankerton in *Bell v Lever Bros*, (above) and continued:] For my part, I think that here there was a misapprehension as to rights, but no misapprehension whatsoever as to the subject-matter of the contract, namely, the settlement of the rights of the assured with regard to the accident that happened. The insurance company was settling his rights, if he had any. He understood them to be settling his rights; but each of them, on the assumption that the county court judge's view of the facts was right, thought his rights against the insurers were very much more valuable than in fact they were, since in reality they were worthless: the insurers could have repudiated—or avoided, that being the more accurate phrase—on the basis of the mis-statements which my Lord has narrated.

Fenton Atkinson L.J. agreed with Lord Denning.

Appeal Allowed.

Questions

23-026   1. Is *Cook v Wright*, above, Ch.10 distinguishable?

2. Should the plaintiff have been entitled to recover his premiums?

----

4. THE EQUITABLE APPROACH CHALLENGED

GREAT PEACE SHIPPING LTD v TSAVLIRIS SALVAGE (INTERNATIONAL) LTD

Court of Appeal [2002] EWCA Civ 1407

LORD PHILLIPS MR
23-027   This is the judgment of the Court

Introduction

1. In 1932 in *Bell v Lever Brothers Ltd* [1932] AC 161 Lord Atkin made a speech which he must have anticipated would be treated as the definitive exposition of the rules of law governing the effect of mistake on contract. In 1950 in *Solle v Butcher* [1950] 1 KB 671 Denning L.J. identified an equitable jurisdiction which permits the court to intervene where the parties have concluded an agreement that was binding in law under a common misapprehension of a fundamental nature as to the material facts or their respective rights. Over the last fifty years judges and jurists have wrestled with the problem of reconciling these two decisions and identifying with precision the principles that they lay down.

2. In the court below Toulson J. used this case as a vehicle to review this difficult area of jurisprudence. He reached the bold conclusion that the view of the jurisdiction of the court expressed by Denning L.J. in *Solle v Butcher* was "over-broad", by which he meant wrong. Equity neither gave a party a right to rescind a contract on grounds of common mistake nor conferred on the court a discretion to set aside a contract on such grounds.

3. Toulson J. gave permission to appeal, observing: "the appeal raises a question of general importance and the Court of Appeal might take the view that my approach to Lord Denning's principle in *Solle v Butcher* was not open to me and/or wrong".

The facts

4. We gratefully adopt, with a degree of adaptation, Toulson J.'s clear exposition of the relevant facts, as to which there is no dispute. All the times are stated by reference to British Summer Time.

5. The story concerns two vessels, the *"Cape Providence"* and the *"Great Peace"*. In September 1999 the *"Cape Providence"* was on her way from Brazil to China with a cargo of iron ore when she suffered serious structural damage in the South Indian Ocean. The defendants learned that the vessel was in difficulties and offered their salvage services, which were accepted on the terms of Lloyd's Open Form of salvage agreement. To find a tug they approached a firm of London brokers, Marint. The individuals involved at Marint were Mr Graeme Little and Mr Andrew Holder. A tug was found, but it was going to take five or six days for the tug to reach the *"Cape Providence"* from Singapore. There was serious concern that in the meantime the vessel might go down with the loss of her crew. So Mr Little was asked by the appellants' representative, Captain Lambrides, to try to find a merchant vessel in the vicinity of the *"Cape Providence"* which would be willing to assist, if necessary, with the evacuation of the crew.

6. Mr Little contacted Ocean Routes, a respected organisation which provides weather forecasting services to the shipping industry and receives reports about vessels at sea. Ocean Routes gave Mr Little the names of four vessels reported to be in the area. He was told that the *"Great Peace"*, a vessel owned by the respondents, was the nearest to the *"Cape Providence"* and should be close to a rendezvous position within about twelve hours. Mr Little noted the name of the four vessels and the estimated position of the *"Great Peace"*. Unfortunately the position which he was given was wrong.

7. At 20.30 on Friday 24 September 1999 Mr Little telephoned a contact number for the *"Great Peace's"* managers, Worlder Shipping Limited of Hong Kong. The call was answered by Mr Pierre Lee. By Hong King time it was 03.30 on Saturday 25 September.

8. Mr Lee was a businessman with no seafaring experience. He had never personally negotiated the fixture of a vessel, because his company always used brokers. But it was the middle of the night and Mr Little explained that the situation was an emergency because of the potential danger to the crew. They did not discuss the exact position of either vessel. Mr Little simply advised Mr Lee that he believed from information received from Ocean Routes that the *"Great Peace"* was the closest vessel to the *"Cape Providence"*. Mr Lee was not able to promise help there and then, because the *"Great Peace"* was under charter, carrying a cargo of soya beans from New Orleans to China, and the charterers would need to be consulted, but he asked Mr Little to send him details by fax.

9. Immediately after the conversation Mr Little faxed Mr Lee as follows:

"Further to our telcon at 22.22 hours BST 24 September, we are working on behalf of the owners of a cape size bulk carrier which has suffered serious structural damage in the southern Indian Ocean. Her position at 10.27 hours BST today was 29 40S/80 20E. She is proceeding at 5 knots on course 050 degrees direction Sunda Strait. Owners have mobilised a tug from Singapore which should reach the casualty in the next 5/6 days. We understand from Ocean Routes that your vessel *"Great Peace"* is in close proximity to the casualty and have been asked by hirers to check whether it would be possible to charter the *"Great Peace"* on a daily hire basis to escort the casualty until arrival of the tug.

We would appreciate greatly if you can check soonest with charterers whether they can agree to the request, bearing in mind that the casualty is in serious danger."

10. Shortly after midnight, Mr Lee phoned Mr Holder (who had taken over from Mr Little) and put forward an offer for the chartering of the *"Great Peace"*. During the conversation all the terms necessary for a contract were discussed. The contract was to be on the basis of a Bimco Towhire form of agreement. (This was somewhat odd because the *"Great Peace"* was a bulk carrier and was not going to be towing the *"Cape Providence"*, but the circumstances were unusual and the Bimco Towhire agreement was the form of contract with which Mr Holder was familiar). The hire was to be for a minimum of 5 days. The purpose of the charter was to be to escort and stand-by the *"Cape Providence"* for the purpose of saving life. Delivery was to be at the *"Great Peace's"* location at the time of the agreement and the hire would commence as soon as she was fixed and diverted (it being the mutual, and correct, assumption of Mr Lee and Mr Holder that there would be no practical difference between the vessel's position at the time of the agreement and at the time of deviation, since it was contemplated that there would have to be some alteration of course in order to effect a rendezvous and that the alteration of course would happen as soon as instructions could be given on the conclusion of the agreement). During the conversation Mr Holder asked Mr Lee for the position and speed of the *"Great Peace"*, and Mr Lee replied that he would check these matters with the master when he knew if the appellants were interested in the terms of the offer.

11. Captain Lambrides decided not to accept the offer at once, but at 0640 he gave instructions to Mr Holder to fix the vessel at a gross rate of US$16,500 per day (which Mr Holder knew would be acceptable to Mr Lee from their earlier conversation).

12. Mr Holder thereupon called Mr Lee. They went through and confirmed the terms of the fixture.

13. Afterwards Mr Holder sent a fax to Mr Lee thanking him for his assistance with the fixture of the *"Great Peace"* for the services of escort/stand-by to the *"Cape Providence"*; saying that he would complete the recap of the main fixture terms shortly, giving details of the *"Cape Providence's"* latest position, course and speed in order to enable the vessels to rendezvous; and concluding:

"Please instruct your master to contact the master of *"Cape Providence"* and alter course to rendezvous with the vessel as soon as possible."

14. As requested, Mr Lee faxed instructions to the master of the *"Great Peace"* to alter course towards the *"Cape Providence"*. He sent a copy of the fax to Mr Holder.

15. At 08.17 Mr Lee gave Mr Holder contact details of the *"Great Peace"*, which Mr Holder passed on to Captain Lambrides. A few minutes later, at 08.29, the master of the *"Great Peace"* sent a message to Worlder that he had contacted the *"Cape Providence"* to find her latest position and was altering course "right now".

16. Meanwhile, at 08.25, Captain Lambrides called Mr Holder to say that the vessels were 410 miles away from each other. This was not something known to Mr Holder or Mr Lee, so the likely inference is that the

master of the *"Cape Providence"* must have reported the positions of the vessels to the appellants after his conversation with the master of the *"Great Peace"*.

17. If the information previously given to Marint by Ocean Routes had been accurate, the vessels should have been only about 35 miles apart when the contract was concluded.

18. Captain Lambrides told Mr Holder that he was looking to cancel the *"Great Peace"*, but not yet, because he first wanted to know if there was a nearer available vessel which could provide assistance to the crew of the *"Cape Providence"*.

19. Mr Holder made a number of unsuccessful enquiries, about which he reported to the appellants, at 0924, recommending that the *"Great Peace"* should be allowed to continue her voyage towards the *"Cape Providence"*.

20. About the same time as that message was being sent, the *"Cape Providence"* was passed by a vessel called the *"Nordfarer"*. By chance the charterers of the *"Nordfarer"* were also the charterers of the *"Cape Providence"* and so had an interest in assisting her. At 10.10 the appellants told Mr Holder that they had contracted with the owners of the *"Nordfarer"* directly and instructed him to cancel the *"Great Peace"*.

21. At 10.25 Mr Holder told Mr Lee that the *"Great Peace"* was no longer required, i.e. she was cancelled. They discussed possible financial terms.

22. At 11.00 Mr Lee sent a fax to Mr Holder, confirming the cancellation and saying that he would do his best to persuade the owners of the *"Great Peace"* to accept 2 days' daily hire in place of the minimum 5 days due under the contract. After speaking to the appellants, Mr Holder told Mr Lee that the appellants were not prepared to pay any sum. So the respondents issued proceedings.

The contract

23. The terms of the fixture, as faxed by Mr Holder to Mr Lee, included the following:

> "1. HIRER: "TSAVLIRIS" SALVAGE: (INTERNATIONAL) LTD
>
> 2. VESSEL OWNER: WORLDER SHIPPING LTD
>
> 3. CASUALTY VESSEL: BULKCARRIER 'CAPE PROVIDENCE, 146,019 DWT/76, 324 GRT, 268 M LOA 43 M BEAM, IN LADEN CONDITION, FULL CREW ON BOARD, PLATING CONDITION/FRAME DAMAGE.
>
> 4. ESCORTING VESSEL: BULK CARRIER "GREAT PEACE" LADEN, ON VOYAGE FROM NEW ORLEANS TO CHINA VIA SINGAPORE.
>
> 5. SERVICES: ESCORT/STANDBY ONLY FOR THE PURPOSES OF SAVING OF LIFE AT SEA. "CAPE PROVIDENCE" LATEST POSITION AS OF 0720 HRS BST 25/9/99, LAT 28–20 SOUTH, LONG 082-20 EAST, HEADING 050 DEGREES, SPEED 5 KNTS, TOWARDS SUNDA STRAITS.
>
> 6. DESTINATION: DIRECTION SUNDA STRAIGHTS, WHILST AWAITING THE ARRIVAL OF TUG WHICH DEPARTED SINGAPORE 1205HRS L.T 25/09/99, ETA CASUALTY APPROX 5 DAYS.
>
> 7. DAILY HIRE: USD 16,500 PER DAY, PRO RATA INCLUDING FUEL AND LUBES FOR STANDBY/ESCORT
>
> 8. DELIVERY/ ON HIRE: TIME "GREAT PEACE" ALTERS COURSE TO RENDEZVOUS WITH "CAPE PROVIDENCE" THIS TIME TO BE ADVISED BY MASTER OF "GREAT PEACE"
>
> 9. REDELIVERY/OFF HIRE: UPON ARRIVAL OF THE TUG TO CONVOYS POSITION, TIME TO BE ADVISED BY MASTERS OF "GREAT PEACE" / "CAPE PROVIDENCE"
>
> 10. MINIMUM: 5 DAYS DUE AND EARNT UPON "GREAT PEACE" ALTERING DIRECTION, BEING USD 82,500. ANY BALANCE DUE UPON COMPLETION OF SERVICES
>
> 11. CANCELLATION FEE: MINIMUM ENGAGEMENT AS DUE.
>
> 12. CONTRACT: BIMCO TOWHIRE AGREEMENT TO APPLY
>
> A. IT IS CLEARLY UNDERSTOOD THAT THERE IS TO BE NO CLAIM FOR SALVAGE BY THE VESSEL OWNER, OR THEIR MANAGERS, OR THEIR MASTER, OFFICERS OR CREW."

The issues

24. The claimants claimed $82,500 as monies payable under the terms of the contract. Alternatively, they claimed the same sum as damages for wrongful repudiation of the contract.

25. The defendants contended that the purported contract had been concluded by reason of a fundamental mistake of fact in that both parties proceeded on the fundamental assumption that the *"Great Peace"* was "in close proximity" to the *"Cape Providence"*, when she was not. It followed either that the contract was void in law, or that the contract was voidable and the defendants were entitled to relief in equity by way of rescission.

26. In oral argument in the court below, Mr Reeder Q.C. for the defendants defined 'close proximity' as meaning sufficiently close to enable the *"Cape Providence"* to have come up with the *"Great Peace"* in the space of a few hours.

27. Toulson J. rejected the defendants' contentions and awarded the claimants the sum claimed. By this appeal the defendants reassert their defence based upon mistake.

The mistake in this case

28. A mistake can be simply defined as an erroneous belief. Mistakes have relevance in the law of contract in a number of different circumstances. They may prevent the mutuality of agreement that is necessary for the formation of a contract . . .

31. In the present case the parties were agreed as to the express terms of the contract. The defendants agreed that the *"Cape Providence"* would deviate towards the *"Great Peace"* and, on reaching her, escort her so as to be on hand to save the lives of her crew, should she founder. The contractual services would terminate when the salvage tug came up with the casualty. The mistake relied upon by the defendants is as to an assumption that they claim underlay the terms expressly agreed. This was that the *"Cape Providence"* was within a few hours sailing of the *"Great Peace"*. They contend that this mistake was fundamental in that it would take the *"Great Peace"* about 39 hours to reach a position where she could render the services which were the object of the contractual adventure.

32. Thus what we are here concerned with is an allegation of a common mistaken assumption of fact which renders the service that will be provided if the contract is performed in accordance with its terms something different from the performance that the parties contemplated. This is the type of mistake which fell to be considered in *Bell v Lever Brothers*. We shall describe it as "common mistake", although it is often alternatively described as "mutual mistake".

33. Mr Reeder for the defendants puts his case in two alternative ways. First he submits that performance of the contract in the circumstances as they turned out to be would have been fundamentally different from the performance contemplated by the parties, so much so that the effect of the mistake was to deprive the agreement of the consideration underlying it. Under common law, so he submits, the effect of such a mistake is to render the contract void. Mr Reeder draws a close analogy with the test to be applied when deciding whether a contract has been frustrated or whether there has been a fundamental breach. The foundation for this submission is *Bell v Lever Brothers*.

34. If the facts of this case do not meet that test, Mr Reeder submits that they nonetheless give rise to a right of rescission in equity. He submits that such a right arises whenever the parties contract under a common mistake as to a matter that can properly be described as "fundamental" or "material" to the agreement in question. Here he draws an analogy with the test for rescission where one party, by innocent misrepresentation, induces the other to enter into a contract—indeed that is one situation where the parties contract under a common mistake. The foundation for this submission is *Solle v Butcher*.

Bell v Lever Brothers

[Having reviewed *Bell v Lever Brothers* and the jurisprudence of common mistake at common law, the Court continued]

94. Our conclusions have marched in parallel with those of Toulson J. We admire the clarity with which he has set out his conclusions, which emphasise the importance of a careful analysis of the contract and of the rights and obligations created by it as an essential precursor to consideration of the effect of an alleged mistake. We agree with him that, on the facts of the present case, the issue in relation to common mistake turns on the question of whether the mistake as to the distance apart of the two vessels had the effect that the services that the *"Great Peace"* was in a position to provide were something essentially different from that to which the parties had agreed. We shall defer answering that question until we have considered whether principles of equity provide a second string to the defendants' bow.

Mistake in equity

95. In *Solle v Butcher* Denning L.J. held that a court has an equitable power to set aside a contract that is binding in law on the ground of common mistake. Subsequently, as Lord Denning MR, in *Magee v Pennine Insurance Co* [1969] 2 QB 507 at 514, he said of *Bell v Lever Brothers*:

"I do not propose today to go through the speeches in that case. They have given enough trouble to commentators already. I would say simply this: A common mistake, even on a most fundamental matter, does not make a contract void at law: but it makes it voidable in equity. I analysed the cases in *Solle v Butcher* [1950] 1 K.B. 671, and I would repeat what I said there, at p.693:

'A contract is also liable in equity to be set aside if the parties were under a common misapprehension either as to facts or as to their relative and respective rights, provided that the misapprehension was fundamental and that the party seeking to set it aside was not himself at fault.' "

96. Neither of the other two members of the court in *Magee v Pennine Insurance Co* cast doubt on *Bell v Lever Brothers*. Each purported to follow it, although reaching different conclusions on the facts. It is axiomatic that there is no room for rescission in equity of a contract which is void. Either Lord Denning was purporting to usurp the common law principle in *Bell v Lever Brothers* and replace it with a more flexible principle of equity, or the equitable remedy of rescission that he identified is one that operates in a situation where the mistake is not of such a nature as to avoid the contract. Decisions have, hitherto, proceeded on the basis that the latter is the true position. Thus, in *Japanese Bank v Credit du Nord* Steyn J. remarked at p.266 that it was clear that mistake in equity was not circumscribed by common law definitions. He went on to say at p.267:

"No one could fairly suggest that in this difficult area of the law there is only one correct approach or solution. But a narrow doctrine of common law mistake (as enunciated in *Bell v Lever Brothers Ltd* [1932] A.C 161), supplemented by the more flexible doctrine of mistake in equity (as developed in *Solle v Butcher* [1950] 1 K.B. 671 and later cases), seems to me to be an entirely sensible and satisfactory state of the law: see *Sheikh Bros. Ltd v Ochsner* [1957] A. C 136. And there ought to be no reason to struggle to avoid its application by artificial interpretations of *Bell v Lever Brothers Ltd*."

97. Toulson J. has taken a different view. He has concluded that it is not possible to differentiate between the test of mistake identified in *Bell v Lever Brothers* and that advanced by Lord Denning as giving rise to the equitable jurisdiction to rescind. He has examined the foundations upon which Lord Denning founded his decision in *Solle v Butcher* and found them defective. These are conclusions that we must review. If we agree with them the question will then arise of whether it was open to him, or is open to this Court, to rule that the doctrine of common mistake leaves no room for the intervention of equity . . .

126. Toulson J. described this decision by Lord Denning as one which 'sought to outflank *Bell v Lever Brothers*'. We think that this was fair comment. It was not realistic to treat the House of Lords in *Bell v Lever Brothers* as oblivious to principles of equity, nor to suggest that 'if it had been considered on equitable grounds the result might have been different'. For the reasons that we have given, we do not consider that *Cooper v Phibbs* demonstrated or established an equitable jurisdiction to grant rescission for common mistake in circumstances that fell short of those in which the common law held a contract void. Insofar as this was in doubt, the House of Lords in *Bell v Lever Brothers* delimited the ambit of operation of *Cooper v Phibbs* by holding, rightly or wrongly, that on the facts of that case the agreement in question was void at law and by holding that, on the facts in *Bell v Lever Brothers*, the mistake had not had the effect of rendering the contract void.

127. It was not correct to state that *Cooper v Phibbs*, as interpreted by Denning L.J., was 'in no way impaired by *Bell v Lever Brothers*', nor to make the inconsistent statement that the principle of *Cooper v Phibbs*, as interpreted by Denning L.J., had been 'fully restored' by *Norwich Union Fire Insurance v Price* [1934] AC 455. That was a decision of the Privy Council, on appeal from the Supreme Court of New South Wales. Insurers had paid the insured value on a cargo of lemons under a mistake, shared by the assured, that they had been destroyed by a peril insured against. In fact they had been sold in transit because they were ripening. The Privy Council allowed the insurers appeal against the refusal of the Supreme Court to allow them to recover the insurance monies on the ground that they had been paid under a mistake of fact. At pp.462–3 of their advice they observed:

"The mistake was as vital as that in *Cooper v Phibbs* in respect of which Lord Westbury used these words: 'If parties contract under a mutual mistake and misapprehension as to their relative and respective rights, the result is, that that agreement is liable to be set aside as having proceeded upon a common mistake.' At common law such a contract (or simulacrum of a contract) is more correctly described as void, there being in truth no intention to contract. Their Lordships find nothing tending to contradict or overrule these established principles in *Bell v Lever Bros Ltd*."

128. This passage reinforces the approach of the House of Lords in *Bell v Lever Brothers* of equating the test of common mistake in *Cooper v Phibbs* with one that renders a contract void at common law.

129. Nor was it accurate to state that *Cooper v Phibbs* afforded ample authority for saying that the lease could be set aside 'on such terms as the court thinks fit'. As we have demonstrated, the terms imposed by the House of Lords in *Cooper v Phibbs* were no more than necessary to give effect to the rights and interests of those involved.

130. In *Bell v Lever Brothers* the House of Lords equated the circumstances which rendered a contract void for

common mistake with those which discharged the obligations of the parties under the doctrine of frustration. Denning L.J. rightly concluded that the facts of *Solle v Butcher* did not amount to such circumstances. The equitable jurisdiction that he then asserted was a significant extension of any jurisdiction exercised up to that point and one that was not readily reconcilable with the result in *Bell v Lever Brothers*.

131. If the result in *Solle v Butcher* extended beyond any previous decision the scope of the equitable jurisdiction to rescind a contract for common mistake, the terms of Denning L.J.'s judgment left unclear the precise parameters of the jurisdiction. The mistake had to be "fundamental", but how far did this extend beyond Lord Atkin's test of a mistake "as to some quality which makes the thing without the quality essentially different from the thing as it was believed to be"? The difficulty in answering this question was one of the factors that led Toulson J. to conclude that there was no equitable jurisdiction to rescind on the ground of common mistake a contract that was valid in law. Was it open to him after half a century and is it open to this Court to find that the equitable jurisdiction that Denning L.J. identified in *Solle v Butcher* was a chimera? Principles of both equity and common law have been developed by the judges and that is not a process which ceased with the Judicature Act. Does the doctrine of precedent require, or even permit, this court to hold that the jurisdiction that Denning L.J. purported to exercise in *Solle v Butcher* does not exist because that decision was in conflict with that of the House of Lords in *Bell v Lever Brothers*?

132. That question first requires consideration of the judgment of Bucknill L.J. in *Solle v Butcher*. He did not purport to agree with the statements of principle in the judgment of Denning L.J., which he had read in draft. He simply stated that he was applying the principle in *Cooper v Phibbs* to an agreement concluded under a mistake as to a matter of fundamental importance. Nonetheless, he expressly concurred in ordering rescission on terms. At p.689, at the end of his judgment, he observed that the defendant had "established his point that the lease should be rescinded on the ground of common mistake, on a suitable undertaking being given by him as regards a new lease to the plaintiff". This was not a finding that was open to him if *Bell v Lever Brothers* had established that common mistake had no effect on a contract unless it was so significant as to render the contract void. It follows that the majority decision in *Solle v Butcher* was based on the assumption of a jurisdiction founded in equity to order rescission of a contract binding in law.

133. We turn to consider the decisions on common mistake in the years that have followed *Solle v Butcher*. [Having considered a line of decisions from *Rose v Pim* [1953] 2 QB 450 through to *Clarion Ltd v National Provident Institution* [2000] 1 WLR 1888, the Court summarised its view of the case-law applying the equitable approach]

Summary

153. A number of cases, albeit a small number, in the course of the last 50 years have purported to follow *Solle v Butcher*, yet none of them defines the test of mistake that gives rise to the equitable jurisdiction to rescind in a manner that distinguishes this from the test of a mistake that renders a contract void in law, as identified in *Bell v Lever Brothers*. This is, perhaps, not surprising, for Lord Denning, the author of the test in *Solle v Butcher*, set *Bell v Lever Brothers* at nought. It is possible to reconcile *Solle v Butcher* and *Magee v Pennine Insurance* with *Bell v Lever Brothers* only by postulating that there are two categories of mistake, one that renders a contract void at law and one that renders it voidable in equity. Although later cases have proceeded on this basis, it is not possible to identify that proposition in the judgment of any of the three Lords Justices, Denning, Bucknill or Fenton Atkinson, who participated in the majority decisions in the former two cases. Nor, over 50 years, has it proved possible to define satisfactorily two different qualities of mistake, one operating in law and one in equity.

154. In *Solle v Butcher* Denning L.J. identified the requirement of a common misapprehension that was "fundamental", and that adjective has been used to describe the mistake in those cases which have followed *Solle v Butcher*. We do not find it possible to distinguish, by a process of definition, a mistake which is "fundamental" from Lord Atkin's mistake as to quality which "makes the thing contracted for essentially different from the thing that it was believed to be".

155. A common factor in *Solle v Butcher* and the cases which have followed it can be identified. The effect of the mistake has been to make the contract a particularly bad bargain for one of the parties. Is there a principle of equity which justifies the court in rescinding a contract where a common mistake has produced this result?

"Equity is . . . a body of rules or principles which form an appendage to the general rules of law, or a gloss upon them. In origin at least, it represents the attempt of the English legal system to meet a problem which confronts all legal systems reaching a certain stage of development. In order to ensure the smooth running of society it is necessary to formulate general rules which work well enough in the majority of cases. Sooner or later, however, cases arise in which, in some unforeseen set of facts, the general rules produce substantial unfairness . . ." (*Snell's Equity*, 30th edn. Paragraph 1–03)

156. Thus the premise of equity's intrusion into the effects of the common law is that the common law rule in question is seen in the particular case to work injustice, and for some reason the common law cannot cure itself. But it is difficult to see how that can apply here. Cases of fraud and misrepresentation, and undue influence, are all catered for under other existing and uncontentious equitable rules. We are *only* concerned with the question whether relief might be given for common mistake in circumstances wider than those stipulated in *Bell v Lever Brothers*. But that, surely, is a question as to where the common law should draw the line; not whether, given the common law rule, it needs to be mitigated by application of some other doctrine. The common law has drawn the line in *Bell v Lever Brothers*. The effect of *Solle v Butcher* is not to supplement or mitigate the common law; it is to say that *Bell v Lever Brothers* was wrongly decided. . . .

160. Our conclusion is that it is impossible to reconcile *Solle v Butcher* with *Bell v Lever Brothers*. The jurisdiction asserted in the former case has not developed. It has been a fertile source of academic debate, but in practice it has given rise to a handful of cases that have merely emphasised the confusion of this area of our jurisprudence. In paragraphs 110 to 121 of his judgment, Toulson J. has demonstrated the extent of that confusion. If coherence is to be restored to this area of our law, it can only be by declaring that there is no jurisdiction to grant rescission of a contract on the ground of common mistake where that contract is valid and enforceable on ordinary principles of contract law. That is the conclusion of Toulson J. . . .

161. We can understand why the decision in *Bell v Lever Brothers Ltd* did not find favour with Lord Denning. An equitable jurisdiction to grant rescission on terms where a common fundamental mistake has induced a contract gives greater flexibility than a doctrine of common law which holds the contract void in such circumstances. Just as the Law Reform (Frustrated Contracts) Act 1943 was needed to temper the effect of the common law doctrine of frustration, so there is scope for legislation to give greater flexibility to our law of mistake than the common law allows.

The result in this case

162. We revert to the question that we left unanswered at paragraph 94. It was unquestionably a common assumption of both parties when the contract was concluded that the two vessels were in sufficiently close proximity to enable the *"Great Peace"* to carry out the service that she was engaged to perform. Was the distance between the two vessels so great as to confound that assumption and to render the contractual adventure impossible of performance? If so, the appellants would have an arguable case that the contract was void under the principle in *Bell v Lever Brothers Ltd*.

163. Toulson J. addressed this issue in the following paragraph:

"Was the *'Great Peace'* so far away from the *'Cape Providence'* at the time of the contract as to defeat the contractual purpose—or in other words to turn it into something essentially different from that for which the parties bargained? This is a question of fact and degree, but in my view the answer is no. If it had been thought really necessary, the *'Cape Providence'* could have altered course so that both vessels were heading toward each other. At a closing speed of 19 knots, it would have taken them about 22 hours to meet. A telling point is the reaction of the defendants on learning the true positions of the vessels. They did not want to cancel the agreement until they knew if they could find a nearer vessel to assist. Evidently the defendants did not regard the contract as devoid of purpose, or they would have cancelled at once."

164. Mr Reeder has attacked this paragraph on a number of grounds. He has submitted that the suggestion that the *"Cape Providence"* should have turned and steamed towards the *"Great Peace"* is unreal. We agree. The appellants were sending a tug from Singapore in an attempt to salve the *"Cape Providence"*. The *"Great Peace"* was engaged by the appellants to act as a stand-by vessel to save human life, should this prove necessary, as an ancillary aspect of the salvage service. The suggestion that the *"Cape Providence"* should have turned and steamed away from the salvage tug which was on its way towards her in order to reduce the interval before the *"Great Peace"* was in attendance is unrealistic.

165. Next Mr Reeder submitted that it was not legitimate for the Judge to have regard to the fact that the appellants did not want to cancel the agreement with the *"Great Peace"* until they knew whether they could get a nearer vessel to assist. We do not agree. This reaction was a telling indication that the fact that the vessels were considerably further apart than the appellants had believed did not mean that the services that the *"Great Peace"* was in a position to provide were essentially different from those which the parties had envisaged when the contract was concluded. The *"Great Peace"* would arrive in time to provide several days of escort service. The appellants would have wished the contract to be performed but for the adventitious arrival on the scene of a vessel prepared to perform the same services. The fact that the vessels were further apart than both parties had appreciated did not mean that it was impossible to perform the contractual adventure.

166. The parties entered into a binding contract for the hire of the *"Great Peace"*. That contract gave the appellants an express right to cancel the contract subject to the obligation to pay the 'cancellation fee' of 5 days hire. When they engaged the *"Nordfarer"* they cancelled the *"Great Peace"*. They became liable in consequence to pay the cancellation fee. There is no injustice in this result.

For the reasons that we have given, we would dismiss this appeal.

Questions

1. In para.8, in the summary of the facts, we read that "Mr Little [acting for the salvage company] simply advised Mr Lee [acting for the owners] that he believed from information received from Ocean Routes that the *Great Peace* was the closest vessel to the *Cape Providence*." How does this square with Lord Phillips MR's statement at para.162 that, "It was unquestionably a common assumption of both parties when the contract was concluded that the two vessels were in sufficiently close proximity to enable the *Great Peace* to carry out the service that she was engaged to perform"? Was the position of the *Great Peace* a material and an operative assumption made by the owners? If not, was this merely a one-sided mistake by the salvage company? If so, how would this affect the outcome of the case?

2. Might the salvage company have any recourse against Ocean Routes on whose information they relied? Compare *Customs and Excise Commissioners v Barclays Bank Plc* [2006] UKHL 28.

3. Stephen Waddams notes a certain irony in the Court of Appeal's suppression of the equitable principle by relying on the very feature (namely, the validity of the contract at common law) that gave rise to the equitable jurisdiction in the first place. As Waddams remarks: "Wherever equity intervened to set aside a contract, whether for mistake, or for unconscionability, undue influence, or misrepresentation, the contract was valid at common law (otherwise equity could not have intervened)" (Stephen Waddams, *Principle and Policy in Contract Law* (Cambridge: Cambridge University Press, 2011) p.130). What do you make of this?

23-028

Points for reflection

1. In *Brennan v Bolt Burden* [2004] EWCA Civ 1017, the Court of Appeal followed *Great Peace* in taking a tough line on the availability of common mistake as a reason for vitiating a contract. According to Maurice Kay LJ, the test is whether the mistake is such as to render the performance of the contract impossible. On the facts of *Brennan*, which involved the compromise of a claim for personal injuries, performance was still possible notwithstanding that the parties had acted on what turned out to be a mistaken assumption about the state of the law concerning the service of notice of claims and, concomitantly, time-bars. The fact that this mistaken assumption related to the state of the law rather than to some non-legal state of affairs such as the existence of goods or the location of a vessel, was not of itself a barrier to the application of the doctrine of common mistake—mistakes of law just as much as mistakes of fact are within the doctrine's (limited) remit. However, Sedley LJ suggested that there is a problem about mechanically transposing an impossibility test for operative mistakes of fact to mistakes of law. Instead, he suggested that the "equivalent question needs to be whether, had the parties appreciated that the law was what it is now known to be, there would still have been an intelligible basis for their agreement" (para.60).

23-029

2. If regimes of contract law aspire to be calculable, consistent, and in line with reasonable expectations, it is arguable that *Great Peace* scores well for calculability and consistency. However,

the obvious weakness of the decision is that it removes the flexibility that the equitable doctrine introduced to respond to cases where, in the absence of some adjustment, reasonable expectations would be frustrated. Unless *Great Peace* succeeds in deterring litigation where one party believes that it is unconscionable to proceed with the agreement as originally formed, the odds surely are that the equitable doctrine (or some surrogate) will be revived.

Further reading

P. S. Atiyah, '*Couturier v Hastie* and the Sale of Non-existent Goods' (1957) 73 LQR 340

Catharine MacMillan, 'How Temptation Led to Mistake: An Explanation of *Bell v Lever Brothers, Limited*' (2003) 119 LQR 625

Catherine MacMillan, '*Solle v Butcher* (1949)' in Charles Mitchell and Paul Mitchell (eds), *Landmark Cases in the Law of Restitution* (Oxford: Hart, 2006)

K. O. Shatwell, 'The Supposed Doctrine of Mistake in Contract: A Comedy of Errors' (1955) 33 Can. Bar Rev. 164

J.C. Smith, 'Common Law—Mistake, Frustration and Implied Terms' (1994) 110 LQR 400

24

SUBSEQUENT IMPOSSIBILITY AND FRUSTRATION

LEARNING OBJECTIVES

By the end of this chapter, you should:

- **be familiar with the leading cases on the doctrine of frustration of contract;**
- **understand that, after *Davis Contractors v Fareham UDC*, the law will only exceptionally treat an unanticipated event as an excuse for non-performance (as a reason to set aside the contract on the ground of frustration)**
- **understand how the Law Reform (Frustrated Contracts) Act 1943 modified the common law rules for the "winding up" of the contract after frustration**
- **appreciate that, in practice, commercial contracts will often include wide-ranging "force majeure" provisions that cover circumstances that might otherwise raise an issue about whether a contract is frustrated.**

INTRODUCTION

The cases in this chapter highlight the scope for a contractor to plead supervening circumstances as an excuse for non-performance. If the circumstances in question (whether the outbreak of war, industrial action, fire, flooding, shortage of materials, or the like) are expressly identified in the contract, and if they are treated as excusing conditions, then a contractor who is otherwise in breach will have an excuse built into the contract. In the absence of such express contractual provision, the contractor will have to rely on the default doctrines of the common law. Historically, the common law was slow to recognise such an excuse; and, in the modern law, although contractors might be excused under the doctrine of frustration, this is exceptional and the doctrine will not be applied simply because performance is merely inconvenient or financially onerous. In other words, in this area of contract law, the traditional principles of freedom and sanctity of contract still hold firm—even if, in practice, parties who have a cooperative trading relationship might be willing to make running adjustments where, through neither party's fault, performance has become exceptionally difficult. This is not to say that there has been no modernisation of the law. The Law Reform (Frustrated Contracts) Act 1943 does overhaul some unfair aspects of the common law. However, the reform concerns only the adjustment of the parties' positions once a contract has been frustrated; it does not affect the prior question of whether or not a contract is to be treated as having been frustrated.

24–001

This chapter is in four principal sections. First, there is the case-law determining the circumstances in which a contract is frustrated; secondly, there is the principle of "self-induced" frustration which operates to preclude a party from successfully arguing that the contract is frustrated; thirdly, there is the question of where the responsibility lies for an unexplained (arguably frustrating) event; and, finally, the effect of a contract being frustrated (including the effect of the application of the 1943 Act) is considered.

1. FRUSTRATING CIRCUMSTANCES

PARADINE v JANE

King's Bench (1647) Aleyn 26; 82 E.R. 897

24–002 In debt the plaintiff declares upon a lease for years rendering rent at the four usual feasts; and for rent behind for three years, ending at the Feast of the Annunciation, 21 Car., brings his action; the defendant pleads, that a certain German prince, by name Prince Rupert, an alien born, enemy to the King and kingdom, had invaded the realm with an hostile army of men; and with the same force did enter upon the defendant's possession, and him expelled, and held out of possession from July 19, 18 Car., till the Feast of the Annunciation, 21 Car., whereby he could not take the profits; whereupon the plaintiff demurred, and the plea was resolved insufficient.

> 1. Because the defendant hath not answered to one quarter's rent.
>
> 2. He hath not averred that the army were all aliens, which shall not be intended, and he hath his remedy against them; and Bacon cited 33 H.6.1.e. where the gaoler in bar of an escape pleaded, that alien enemies broke the prison, etc., and exception taken to it, for that he ought to shew of what countrey they were, viz., Scots, etc.
>
> 3. It was resolved, that the matter of the plea was insufficient; for though the whole army had been alien enemies, yet he ought to pay his rent. And this difference was taken, that where the law creates a duty or charge, and the party is disabled to perform it without any default in him, and hath no remedy over, there the law will excuse him. As in the case of waste, if a house be destroyed by tempest, or by enemies, the lessee is excused. Dyer 33.a. Inst.53.d.283.a.12 H.4.6. so of an escape. Co.4.84.b. 33H.6.1. So in 9E.3.16. a supersedeas was awarded to the justices, that they should not proceed in a cessavit upon a cesser during the war, but when the party by his own contract creates a duty or charge upon himself, he is bound to make it good, if he may, notwithstanding any accident by inevitable necessity, because he might have provided against it by his contract. And therefore if the lessee covenant to repair a house, though it be burnt by lightning, or thrown down by enemies, yet he ought to repair it. Dyer 33.a.E.3.6.h. Now the rent is a duty created by the parties upon the reservation, and had there been a covenant to pay it, there had been no question but the lessee must have made it good, notwithstanding the interruption by enemies, for the law would not protect him beyond his own agreement, no more then [sic] in the case of reparations; this reservation then being a covenant in law, and whereupon an action of covenant hath been maintained (as Roll said) it is all one as if there had been an actual covenant. Another reason was added, that as the lessee is to have the advantage of casual profits, so he must run the hazard of casual losses, and not lay the whole burthen of them upon his lessor; and Dyer 56.6 was cited for this purpose, that though the land be surrounded, or gained by the sea, or made barren by wildfire, yet the lessor shall have his whole rent: and judgment was given for the plaintiff.

TAYLOR v CALDWELL

Queen's Bench (1863) 3 B. & S. 826; 32 L.J.Q.B. 164; 8 L.T. 356; 11 W.R. 726; 2 Sm.L.C., 13th edn, 601; 122 E.R. 309

24–003 The plaintiffs claimed expenses, agreed at £58, necessarily incurred in preparation for a series of concerts at the defendants' Music Hall.

BLACKBURN J.

> In this case the plaintiffs and defendants had, on May 27, 1861, entered into a contract by which the defendants agreed to let the plaintiffs have the use of the Surrey Gardens and Music Hall on four days then to come, viz.,

June 17, July 15, August 5 and August 19, for the purpose of giving a series of four grand concerts, and day and night fêtes at the Gardens and Hall on those days respectively; and the plaintiffs agreed to take the Gardens and Hall on those days, and pay £100 for each day.

The parties inaccurately call this a "letting" and the money to be paid a "rent"; but the whole agreement is such as to show that the defendants were to retain the possession of the Hall and Gardens so that there was to be no demise of them, and that the contract was merely to give the plaintiffs the use of them on those days. Nothing, however, in our opinion, depends on this. The agreement then proceeds to set out various stipulations between the parties as to what each was to supply for these concerts and entertainments, and as to the manner in which they should be carried on. The effect of the whole is to show that the existence of the Music Hall in the Surrey Gardens in a state fit for a concert was essential for the fulfilment of the contract—such entertainments as the parties contemplated in their agreement could not be given without it.

After the making of the agreement, and before the first day on which a concert was to be given, the Hall was destroyed by fire. This destruction, we must take it on the evidence, was without the fault of either party, and was so complete that in consequence the concerts could not be given as intended. And the question we have to decide is whether, under these circumstances, the loss which the plaintiffs have sustained is to fall upon the defendants. The parties when framing their agreement evidently had not present to their minds the possibility of such a disaster, and have made no express stipulation with reference to it, so that the answer to the question must depend upon the general rules of law applicable to such a contract.

There seems no doubt that where there is a positive contract to do a thing, not in itself unlawful, the contractor must perform it or pay damages for not doing it, although in consequence of unforeseen accidents, the performance of his contract has become unexpectedly burthensome or even impossible. The law is so laid down in 1 Roll.Abr. 450, Condition (G), and in the note (2) to *Walton v Waterhouse* (2 Wms.Saund. 421 a, 6th ed.), and is recognised as the general rule by all the judges in the much discussed case of *Hall v Wright* (E.B. & E. 746). But this rule is only applicable when the contract is positive and absolute, and not subject to any condition either express or implied: and there are authorities which, as we think, establish the principle that where, from the nature of the contract, it appears that the parties must from the beginning have known that it could not be fulfilled unless when the time for the fulfilment of the contract arrived some particular specified thing continued to exist, so that, when entering into the contract, they must have contemplated such continuing existence as the foundation of what was to be done; there, in the absence of any express or implied warranty that the thing shall exist,[1] the contract is not to be construed as a positive contract, but as subject to an implied condition that the parties shall be excused in case, before breach, performance becomes impossible from the perishing of the thing without default of the contractor.

There seems little doubt that this implication tends to further the great object of making the legal construction such as to fulfil the intention of those who entered into the contract. For in the course of affairs men in making such contracts in general would, if it were brought to their minds, say that there should be such a condition.

Accordingly, in the civil law, such an exception is implied in every obligation of the class which they call obligatio de certo corpore. The rule is laid down in the Digest, lib. XLV., tit. 1, de verborum obligationibus, 1.33. "Si Stichus certo die dari promissus, ante diem moriatur: non tenetur promissor." The principle is more fully developed in 1.23. "Si ex legati causa, aut ex stipulatu hominem certum mihi debeas: non aliter post mortem ejus tenearis mihi, quam si per te steterit, quominus vivo eo eum mihi dares: quod ita fit, si aut interpellatus non dedisti, aut occidisti eum." The examples are of contracts respecting a slave, which was the common illustration of a certain subject used by the Roman lawyers, just as we are apt to take a horse; and no doubt the propriety, one might almost say necessity, of the implied condition is more obvious when the contract relates to a living animal, whether man or brute, than when it relates to some inanimate thing (such as in the present case a theatre) the existence of which is not so obviously precarious as that of the live animal, but the principle is adopted in the civil law as applicable to every obligation of which the subject is a certain thing. The general subject is treated of by Pothier, who in his Traité des Obligations, Partie 3, Chap. 6, Art. 3. § 668, states the result to be that the debtor corporis certi is freed from his obligation when the thing has perished, neither by his act, nor his neglect, and before he is in default, unless by some stipulation he has taken on himself the risk of the particular misfortune which has occurred.

Although the civil law is not, of itself, authority in an English court, it affords great assistance in investigating

---

[1]   Notice that Blackburn J saw no reason why a party should not promise that a thing would exist. Cf. the *McRae* case (above, Ch.23) and Professor Williams's argument (above, Ch.23).

the principles on which the law is grounded. And it seems to us that the common law authorities establish that in such a contract the same condition of the continued existence of the thing is implied by English law.

There is a class of contracts in which a person binds himself to do something which requires to be performed by him in person; and such promises, for example, promises to marry, or promises to serve for a certain time, are never in practice qualified by an express exception of the death of the party; and therefore in such cases the contract is in terms broken if the promisor dies before fulfilment. Yet it was very early determined that, if the performance is personal, the executors are not liable: *Hyde v The Dean of Windsor* (Cro.Eliz. 552, 553) See 2 Wms.Exors. 1560, 5th ed., where a very apt illustration is given. "Thus," says the learned author, "if an author undertakes to compose a work, and dies before completing it, his executors are discharged from this contract: for the undertaking is merely personal in its nature, and, by the intervention of the contractor's death, has become impossible to be performed." For this he cites a dictum of Lord Lyndhurst in *Marshall v Broadhurst* (1 Tyr. 348, 349), and a case mentioned by Patteson J. in *Wentworth v Cock* (10 A. & E. 42, 45–46). In *Hall v Wright* (E.B. & E. 746, 749) Crompton J., in his judgment, puts another case. "Where a contract depends upon personal skill, and the act of God renders it impossible, as, for instance, in the case of a painter employed to paint a picture who is struck blind, it may be that the performance might be excused."

It seems that in those cases the only ground on which the parties or their executors can be excused from the consequences of the breach of the contract is, that from the nature of the contract there is an implied condition of the continued existence of the life of the contractor, and perhaps, in the case of the painter, of his eyesight. In the instances just given, the person, the continued existence of whose life is necessary to the fulfilment of the contract, is himself the contractor, but that does not seem in itself to be necessary to the application of the principle; as is illustrated by the following example. In the ordinary form of an apprentice deed the apprentice binds himself in unqualified terms to "serve until the full end and term of seven years to be fully complete and ended," during which term it is convenated that the apprentice his master "faithfully shall serve," and the father of the apprentice in equally unqualified terms binds himself for the performance by the apprentice of all and every covenant on his part. (See the form, 2 Chitty on Pleading, 370, 7th ed., by Greening.) It is undeniable that if the apprentice dies within the seven years, the covenant of the father that he shall perform his covenant to serve for seven years is not fulfilled, yet surely it cannot be that an action would lie against the father? Yet the only reason why it would not is that he is excused because of the apprentice's death.

These are instances where the implied condition is of the life of a human being, but there are others in which the same implication is made as to the continued existence of a thing. For example, where a contract of sale is made amounting to a bargain and sale, transferring presently the property in specific chattels, which are to be delivered by the vendor at a future day; there, if the chattels, without the fault of the vendor, perish in the interval, the purchaser must pay the price and the vendor is excused from performing his contract to deliver, which has thus become impossible.

That this is the rule of the English law is established by the case of *Rugg v Minett* (11 East 210), where the article that perished before delivery was turpentine, and it was decided that the vendor was bound to refund the price of all those lots in which the property had not passed; but was entitled to retain without deduction the price of those lots in which the property had passed, though they were not delivered, and though in the conditions of sale, which are set out in the report, there was no express qualification of the promise to deliver on payment. It seems in that case rather to have been taken for granted than decided that the destruction of the thing sold before delivery excused the vendor from fulfilling his contract to deliver on payment.

This is also the rule in the civil law, and it is worth noticing that Pothier, in his celebrated Traité de Contrat de Vente (see Part 4, § 307, etc.; and Part 2, Chap. 1, Sect. 1, Art. 4, § 1), treats this as merely an example of the more general rule that every obligation de certo corpore is extinguished when the thing ceases to exist. See Blackburn on the Contract of Sale, p. 173.

The same principle seems to be involved in the decision of *Sparrow v Sowgate* (W. Jones 29), where, to an action of debt on an obligation by bail, conditioned for the payment of the debt or the render of the debtor, it was held a good plea that before any default in rendering him the principal debtor died. It is true that was the case of a bond with a condition, and a distinction is sometimes made in this respect between a condition and a contract. But this observation does not apply to *Williams v Lloyd* (W. Jones 179). In that case the count, which was in assumpsit, alleged that the plaintiff had delivered a horse to the defendant, who promised to redeliver it on request. Breach, that though requested to redeliver the horse he refused. Plea, that the horse was sick and died, and the plaintiff made the request after its death; and on demurrer it was held a good plea, as the bailee was discharged from his promise by the death of the horse without default or negligence on the part of the defendant. "Let it be admitted," say the court, "that he promised to deliver it on request, if the horse die before, that is become impossible by the act of God, so the party shall be discharged, as much as if an obligation were made conditioned to deliver the horse on request, and he died before it." And Jones, adds the report, cited 22 Ass. 41, in which it was held that a ferryman who had promised to carry a horse safe across the ferry was held chargeable for the drowning of the animal only because he had overloaded the boat, and it was agreed that notwithstanding the promise no action would have lain had there been no neglect or default on his part.

It may, we think, be safely asserted to be now English law, that in all contracts of loan of chattels or bailments if the performance of the promise of the borrower or bailee to return the things lent or bailed, becomes impossible because it has perished, this impossibility (if not arising from the fault of the borrower or bailee from some risk which he has taken upon himself) excuses the borrower or bailee from the performance of his promise to redeliver the chattel.

The great case of *Coggs v Bernard* (1 Smith's L.C. 171, 5th ed.; 2 Ld.Raym. 909) is now the leading case on the law of bailments, and Lord Holt, in that case, referred so much to the civil law that it might perhaps be thought that this principle was there derived direct from the civilians, and was not generally applicable in English law except in the case of bailments; but the case of *Williams v Lloyd* (W. Jones 179), above cited, shows that the same law had been already adopted by the English law as early as The Book of Assizes. The principle seems to us to be that, in contracts in which the performance depends on the continued existence of a given person or thing, a condition is implied that the impossibility of performance arising from the perishing of the person or thing shall excuse the performance.

In none of these cases is the promise in words other than positive, nor is there any express stipulation that the destruction of the person or thing shall excuse the performance; but that excuse is by law implied, because from the nature of the contract it is apparent that the parties contracted on the basis of the continued existence of the particular person or chattel. In the present case, looking at the whole contract, we find that the parties contracted on the basis of the continued existence of the Music Hall at the time when the concerts were to be given; that being essential to their performance.

We think, therefore, that the Music Hall having ceased to exist, without fault of either party, both parties are excused, the plaintiffs from taking the gardens and paying the money, the defendants from performing their promise to give the use of the Hall and Gardens and other things.

Problem

A grants a lease (not a licence) to B of A's music hall as from a future date. Without the fault of either party, the music hall is destroyed by fire before the date arrives. Is A discharged from his obligation to provide a music hall? Is B discharged from his obligation to pay the rent? (Cf. *Paradine v Jane* (above); *Matthey v Curling* [1922] 2 A.C. 180; *National Carriers Ltd v Panalpina Ltd* (below)).

24-004

JACKSON v UNION MARINE INSURANCE CO LTD

Exchequer Chamber (1874) L.R. 10 C.P. 125; 44 L.J.C.P. 27; 31 L.T. 789; 23 W.R. 169; 2 Asp.M.C. 435

The plaintiff, a shipowner, in November 1871 entered into a charterparty by which the ship to proceed with all possible dispatch (dangers and accidents of navigation excepted) from Liverpool to Newport, and there load a cargo of iron rails for San Francisco. The plaintiff effected an insurance on the chartered freight for the voyage. The ship sailed from Liverpool on January 2, 1872, and on the 3rd ran aground in Carnarvon Bay. She was got off on February 18 and repaired, the time necessary for the completion of the repairs extending to the end of August. On February 15 the charterers threw up the charter and chartered another ship. At the trial before Brett J the jury found that (1) the time necessary for getting the ship off and repairing her so as to be a cargo-carrying ship, was so long as to make it unreasonable for the charterers to supply the agreed cargo at the end of the time, and (2) the delay was so long as to put an end in a commercial sense to the commercial speculation entered upon by the shipowner and charterers. The question was whether the plaintiff could have maintained an action

24-005

against the charterers for not loading (for if he could, there had not been a loss of the chartered freight by any of the perils insured against). Brett J, being of opinion that there was no evidence of a loss of freight by the perils insured against, directed a verdict for the defendants. The Court of Common Pleas made an absolute rule to enter a verdict for the plaintiff, and this judgment was affirmed by the Court of Exchequer Chamber (Bramwell B, Blackburn, Mellor and Lush JJ and Amphlett B, Cleasby B dissenting).

BRAMWELL B

[Delivering the judgment of the majority], said he understood the jury to have found that "the voyage the parties contemplated had become impossible; that a voyage undertaken after the ship was sufficiently repaired would have been a different voyage, not, indeed, different as to the ports of loading and discharge, but different as a different adventure—a voyage for which at the time of the charter the plaintiff had not in intention engaged the ship, nor the charterers the cargo; a voyage as different as though it had been described as intended to be a spring voyage, while the one after the repair would be an autumn voyage." If the charterparty were read as a charter for a definite adventure there was necessarily an implied condition that the vessel should arrive at Newport in time for it. This implied stipulation was not repugnant to the express stipulation requiring all possible dispatch. The latter stipulation was not a condition precedent, the former was. Not arriving in time put an end to the contract though, as it arose from an excepted peril, it gave no cause of action. The effect of the exception clause for delay caused by perils of the sea was to excuse the shipowner, but not to give him any right. "The exception is an excuse for him who is to do the act, and operates to save him from an action and makes his non-performance not a breach of contract, but does not operate to take away the right the other party would have had, if the non-performance had been a breach of contract, to retire from the engagement: and, if one party may, so may the other."

KRELL v HENRY

Court of Appeal [1903] 2 K.B. 740; 72 L.J.K.B. 794; 89 L.T. 328

24-006   On June 17, 1902, the defendant noticed an announcement in the windows of the plaintiff's flat at 56a Pall Mall to the effect that windows to view the coronation procession were to be let. The defendant interviewed the housekeeper on the subject, when it was pointed out to him what a good view of the procession could be obtained from the premises and he agreed to take the suite for June 26 and 27, the days on which the coronation processions were to take place. On June 20 the defendant agreed in writing to pay £75 for the entire use of the rooms on the two days. The writing did not mention the procession. He paid £25 then and agreed to pay £50 on June 24. The procession did not take place owing to the serious illness of the King and the defendant declined to pay the £50. The plaintiff sued for that sum, and the defendant counterclaimed for the return of the £25 which he had paid. Darling J gave judgment for the defendant on the claim and counterclaim. The plaintiff appealed.

VAUGHAN WILLIAMS LJ

The real question in this case is the extent of the application in English law of the principle of the Roman law which has been adopted and acted on in many English decisions, and notably in the case of *Taylor v Caldwell*. That case at least makes it clear that "where, from the nature of the contract, it appears that the parties must from the beginning have known that it could not be fulfilled unless, when the time for the fulfilment of the contract arrived, some particular specified thing continued to exist, so that when entering into the contract they must have contemplated such continued existence as the foundation of what was to be done; there, in the absence of any express or implied warranty that the thing shall exist, the contract is not to be considered a positive contract, but as subject to an implied condition that the parties shall be excused in case, before breach, performance becomes impossible from the perishing of the thing without default of the contractor." Thus far it is clear that the principle of the Roman law has been introduced into the English law. The doubt in the present case arises as to how far this principle extends. The Roman law dealt with obligationes de certo corpore. Whatever may have been the limits of the Roman law, the case of *Nickoll v Ashton* [1901] 2 K.B. 126 makes it plain that the English law applies the principle not only to cases where the performance of the contract becomes impossible by the cessation of existence of the thing which is the subject-matter of the contract, but also to cases where the event which renders the contract incapable of performance is the cessation or non-existence of an express condition or state of things, going to the root of the contract, and essential to its performance. It is said, on the one side, that the specified thing, state of things, or condition the continued existence of which is necessary for the fulfilment of the contract, so that the parties entering into the contract must have contemplated the continued existence of that thing, condition, or state of things as the foundation of what was to be done under the contract, is limited to things which are either the subject-matter of the contract or a condition or state of things, present or anticipated, which is expressly mentioned in the contract. But, on the other side, it is said that the condition or state of things need not be expressly specified, but that it is sufficient if that condition or state of things clearly appears by extrinsic evidence to have been assumed by the parties to be the foundation or basis of the contract, and the event which causes the impossibility is of such a character that it cannot reasonably be supposed to have been in the contemplation of the contracting parties when the contract was made. In such a case the contracting parties will not be held bound by the general words which, though large enough to include, were not used with reference to a possibility of a particular event rendering performance of the contract impossible. I do not think that the principle of the civil law as introduced into the English law is limited to cases in which the event causing the impossibility of performance is the destruction or non-existence of some thing which is the subject-matter of the contract or of some condition or state of things expressly specified as a condition of it. I think that you first have to ascertain, not necessarily from the terms of the contract, but, if required, from necessary inferences, drawn from surrounding circumstances recognised by both contracting parties, what is the substance of the contract, and then to ask the question whether that substantial contract needs for its foundation the assumption of the existence of a particular state of things. If it does, this will limit the operation of the general words, and in such case, if the contract becomes impossible of performance by reason of the non-existence of the state of things assumed by both contracting parties as the foundation of the contract, there will be no breach of the contract thus limited. Now what are the facts of the present case? . . .

[His Lordship stated the facts.] In my judgment the use of the rooms was let and taken for the purpose of seeing the Royal procession. It was not a demise of the rooms, or even an agreement to let and take the rooms. It is a licence to use rooms for a particular purpose and none other. And in my judgment the taking place of those processions on the days proclaimed along the proclaimed route, which passed 56A Pall Mall, was regarded by both contracting parties as the foundation of the contract; and I think that it cannot reasonably be supposed to have been in the contemplation of the contracting parties, when the contract was made, that the coronation would not be held on the proclaimed days, or the processions not take place on those days along the proclaimed route; and I think that the words imposing on the defendant the obligation to accept and pay for the use of the rooms for the named days, although general and unconditional, were not used with reference to the possibility of the particular contingency which afterwards occurred. It was suggested in the course of the argument that if the occurrence, on the proclaimed days, of the coronation and the procession in this case were the foundation of the contract, and if the general words are thereby limited or qualified, so that in the event of the non-occurrence of the coronation and procession along the proclaimed route they would discharge both parties from further performance of the contract, it would follow that if a cabman was engaged to take someone to Epsom on Derby Day at a suitable enhanced price for such a journey, say £10, both parties to the contract would be discharged in the contingency of the race at Epsom for some reason becoming impossible; but I do not think this follows, for I do not think that in the cab case the happening of the race would be the foundation of the contract. No doubt the purpose of the engager would be to go to see the Derby, and the price would be proportionately high; but the cab had no special qualifications for the purpose which led to the selection of the cab for this particular occasion. Any other cab would have done as well. Moreover, I think that, under the cab contract, the hirer, even if the race went off, could have said, "Drive me to Epsom; I will pay you the agreed sum; you have nothing to do with the purpose for which I hired the cab," and that if the cabman refused he would have been guilty of a breach of contract, there being nothing to qualify his promise to drive the hirer to Epsom on a particular day. Whereas in the case of the coronation, there is not merely the purpose of the hirer to see the coronation procession, but it is the coronation procession and the relative position of the rooms which is the basis of the contract as much for the lessor as the hirer; and I think that if the King, before the coronation day and after the contract, had died, the hirer could not have insisted on having the rooms on the days named. It could not in the cab case be reasonably said that seeing the Derby race was the foundation of the contract, as it was of the licence in this case. Whereas in the present case, where the rooms were offered and taken, by reason of their peculiar suitability from the position of the rooms for a view of the coronation procession, surely the view of the coronation procession was the foundation of the contract, which is a very different thing from the purpose of the man who engaged the cab—namely, to see the race—being held to be the foundation of the contract. Each case must be judged by its own circumstances. In each case one must ask oneself, first, what, having regard to all the circumstances, was the foundation of the contract? Secondly, was the performance of the contract prevented? Thirdly, was the event which prevented the performance of the contract of such a character that it cannot reasonably be said to have been in the contemplation of the parties at the date of the contract? If all these questions are answered in the affirmative (as I think they should be in this case), I think both parties are discharged from further performance of the contract. I think that the coronation procession was the foundation of this contract, and that the non-happening of it prevented the performance of the contract; and, secondly, I think that the non-happening of the procession, to use the words of Sir James Hannen in *Baily v De Crespigny* (1869) L.R. 4 Q.B. 185, was an event "of such a character that it cannot reasonably be supposed to have been in the contemplation of the contracting parties when the contract was made, and that they are not to be held bound by general words, which, though large enough to include, were not used with reference to the possibility of the particular contingency which afterwards happened." The test seems to be whether the event which causes the impossibility was or might have been anticipated and guarded against. It seems difficult to say, in a case where both parties anticipate the happening of an event, which anticipation is the foundation of the contract, that either party must be taken to have anticipated, and ought to have guarded against, the event which prevented the performance of the contract. In both *Jackson v Union Marine Insurance Co* [above, para.24–005] and *Nickoll v Ashton* [1901] 2 K.B. 126 the parties might have anticipated as a possibility that perils of the sea might delay the ship and frustrate the commercial venture: in the former case the carriage of the goods to effect which the charterparty was entered into; in the latter case the sale of the goods which were to be shipped on the steamship which was delayed. But the court held in the former case that the basis of the contract was that the ship would arrive in time to carry out the contemplated commercial venture, and in the latter that the steamship would arrive in time for the loading of the goods the subject of the sale. I wish to observe that cases of this sort are very different from cases where a contract or warranty or representation is implied such as was implied in *The Moorcock* [above, Ch.16] and refused to be implied in *Hamlyn v Wood* [1891] 2 Q.B. 488. But *The Moorcock* is of importance in the present case as showing that whatever is the suggested implication—be it condition, as in this case, or warranty or representation—one must, in judging whether the implication ought to be made, look not only at the words of the contract but also at the surrounding facts and the knowledge of the parties of those facts. There seems to me to be ample authority for this proposition. Thus in *Jackson v Union Marine Insurance Co*, in the Common Pleas, the question whether the object of the voyage had been frustrated by the delay of the ship was left as a question of fact to the jury, although there was nothing in the charterparty defining the time within which the charterers were to supply the cargo of iron rails for San Francisco, and nothing on the face of the charterparty to indicate the importance of time in the venture; and that was a case in which, as Bramwell B. points out in his judgment at p. 148, *Taylor v Caldwell*, was a strong authority to support the conclusion arrived at in the judgment—that the ship not arriving in time for the voyage contemplated, but at such time as to frustrate the commercial venture, was not only a breach of the contract but discharged the charterer, though he had such an excuse that no action would lie. And, again, in *Harris v Dreesman* (1854) 23 L.J.Ex. 210, the vessel had to be loaded, as no particular time was mentioned, within a reasonable time; and, in judging of a reasonable time, the court approved of evidence being given that the defendants, the charterers, to the knowledge of the plaintiffs, had no control over the colliery from which both parties knew that the coal was to come; and that, although all that was said in the charterparty was that the vessel should proceed to Spital Tongue's Spout (the spout of the Spital Tongue's Colliery), and there take on board from the freighters a full and complete cargo of coals, and five tons of coke, and although there was no evidence to prove any custom in the port as to loading vessels in turn. Again it was held in *Mumford v Gething* (1859) 7 C.B.(n.s.) 305, that, in construing a written contract of service under which A was to enter the employ of B, oral evidence is admissible to show in what capacity A was to serve B. See also *Price v Mouat* (1862) 11 C.B. (n.s.) 508. The rule seems to be that which is laid down in *Taylor on Evidence*, Vol. ii, § 1082: "It may be laid down as a broad and distinct rule of law that extrinsic evidence of every material fact which will enable the court to ascertain the nature and qualities of the subject-matter of the instrument, or, in other words, to identify the persons and things to which the instrument refers, must of necessity be received." And Lord Campbell in his judgment says: "I am of opinion that, when there is a contract for the sale of a specific subject-matter, oral evidence may be received, for the purpose of showing what that subject-matter was, of every fact within the knowledge of the parties before and at the time of the contract." See per Campbell C. J., *Macdonald v Longbottom* (1859) 1 E. & E. 977, at p. 983. It seems to me that the language of Willes J. in *Lloyd v Guibert* (1865) 35 L.J.Q.B. 74, 75, points in the same direction. I myself am clearly of opinion that in this case, where we have to ask ourselves whether the object of the contract was frustrated by the non-happening of the coronation and its procession on the days proclaimed, parol evidence is admissible to show that the subject of the contract was rooms to view the coronation procession, and was so to the knowledge of both parties. When once this is established, I see no difficulty whatever in the case. It is not essential to the application of the principle of *Taylor v Caldwell* that the direct subject of the contract should perish or fail to be in existence at the date of performance of the contract. It is sufficient if a state of things or condition expressed in the contract and essential to its performance perishes or fails to be in existence at that time. In the present case the condition which fails and prevents the achievement of that which was, in the contemplation of both parties, the foundation of the contract, is not expressly mentioned either as a condition of the contract or the purpose of it; but I think for the reasons which I have given that the principle of *Taylor v Caldwell* ought to be applied. This disposes of the plaintiff's claim for £50 unpaid balance of the price agreed to be paid for the use of the rooms. The defendant at one time set up a cross-claim for the return of the £25 he paid at the date of the contract. As that claim is now withdrawn it is unnecessary to say anything about it. I have only to add that the facts of this case do not bring it within the principle laid down in *Stubbs v Holywell Ry.* (1867) L.R. 2 Ex. 311, that in the case of contracts falling directly within the rule of *Taylor v Caldwell* the subsequent impossibility does not affect rights already acquired, because the defendant had the whole of June 24 to pay the balance, and the public announcement that the coronation and processions would not take place on the proclaimed days was made early on the morning of the 24th, and no cause of action could accrue till the end of that day. I think this appeal ought to be dismissed.

Romer and Stirling L.JJ. concurred.

Questions

1. Was the plaintiff able to provide what he had promised (a) in express terms (b) in the light of the parol evidence?   **24–007**

2. The Bus Co advertises an "Excursion to Epsom on Derby Day". X buys a ticket. The Derby is cancelled. Is the contract frustrated?

3. The X University Law Society contracts to hire a coach to go to the wedding of one of their number. The wedding is cancelled. Is the contract frustrated?

Cheshire & Fifoot, Law of Contract (5th edn), p.467

In *Krell v Henry*, where it is unlikely that the cancellation of the procession occurred to the parties as a possibility, it was no doubt just and reasonable to treat the contract as discharged, but it is incompatible with the character of the hard bargainer to say that the owner of the room would have agreed to this had the proposal been put to him during the negotiations. It was a property owner's market in which the demand for suitable premises in all probability exceeded supply, and there can be little doubt that had the possibility of a cancellation have been put to the owner his reply would have been: "You must take your chance of that."   **24–008**

McElroy and Williams, "The Coronation Cases", 4 M.L.R. 241, 247

Krell v Henry was an action against the hirer of the rooms for the payment of money, and there was no impossibility, in the legal sense, in the payment of money. The defendant was held to be excused because there was a total failure of the consideration for his promise to pay . . .   **24–009**

It is thought that if the test . . . "What did he buy?" be applied to the case of *Krell v Henry* it throws much light on the true ground of the decision in the latter case. The answer in that case is that he bought "rooms to view the procession . . ."

The plaintiff's failure to provide that view, though it arose from no default of his, and therefore did not amount to a breach, was a failure going to the whole of the consideration, and this excused the defendant from his promise to pay.

HERNE BAY STEAM BOAT COMPANY v HUTTON

Court of Appeal [1903] 2 K.B. 683; 72 L.J.K.B. 879; 89 L.T. 422

24-010   It had been publicly announced that the royal naval review at Spithead would be held on June 28, 1902. The defendant wished to charter a steam boat to take paying passengers to see the review, and he entered into a contract with the plaintiffs, the owners of steamboat Cynthia, in these terms: "The Cynthia to be at Mr Hutton's disposal . . . on the morning of June 28 . . . to take out a party . . . for the purpose of viewing the naval review and for a day's cruise round the fleet; also on Sunday, June 29 for similar purposes . . . Price £250 payable, £50 down, balance before ship leaves Herne Bay."

Upon signing the agreement the defendant paid the £50 deposit. On June 25, 1902, an official announcement cancelling the review was published. The plaintiffs thereupon wired to the defendant, "What about Cynthia? She ready to start six tomorrow," but received no answer. The plaintiff then employed the ship on her ordinary sailings. On the two days in question, although the review was cancelled, the fleet remained anchored at Spithead. The plaintiffs sued for the balance of £200. The defendant alleged that it was a condition of the agreement that the naval review should take place on June 28, and that the consideration for the agreement wholly failed. The Court of Appeal (Vaughan Williams, Romer and Stirling LJJ), held, reversing Grantham J, that the plaintiffs could recover the £200 less the profits they had made by the use of the ship on the two days in question.

VAUGHAN WILLIAMS LJ

I see nothing that makes this contract differ from a case where, for instance, a person has engaged a brake to take himself and a party to Epsom to see the races there, but for some reason or other, such as the spread of an infectious disease, the races are postponed. In such a case it could not be said that he could be relieved of his bargain. So in the present case it is sufficient to say that the happening of the naval review was not the foundation of the contract.

ROMER LJ

The ship (as a ship) had nothing particular to do with the review or the fleet except as a convenient carrier of passengers to see it; and other ships suitable for carrying passengers would have done equally as well.

McElroy and Williams, "The Coronation Cases", 4 M.L.R. 241, 254

Comparing the two above cases:

24-011   It is difficult to appreciate the soundness of this distinction. It may be replied that the number of ships suitable for seeing the review which could have been in that neighbourhood at the time was not unlimited. Moreover, the same argument could be applied equally well to *Krell v Henry*. It could be said with equal truth that there was no particular fitness in the room which was let in that case. Any other room on the route of the procession would have done as well, and there must have been quite as many rooms overlooking the route of the procession as there were ships in the vicinity of Spithead capable of being hired for this particular purpose of viewing the fleet.

Sir Frederick Pollock, 20 L.Q.R. 4

24-012   In point of fact the fleet was still there, as Stirling L.J. observed, and, as the writer of these lines can bear witness, it was very well worth seeing without the review.

Question

24-013   What if the fleet had sailed away? Or if the procession had been held without the King? And, was it relevant that Hutton, unlike the hirers in *Krell v Henry*, was a businessman who hired the boat as a *commercial* venture (to take paying customers round the bay)?

BLACKBURN BOBBIN CO LTD v T W ALLEN & SONS LTD

Court of Appeal [1918] 2 K.B. 467; 87 L.J.K.B. 1085; 119 L.T. 215; 34 T.L.R. 508; 23 Com.Cas. 471

24–014

Early in 1914 the defendants, timber merchants at Hull, agreed to sell to the plaintiffs a quantity of Finland birch timber. Delivery was to commence about June or July and to continue until about November 1914. No deliveries had been made when war broke out in August 1914. Prior to the war the invariable practice was to load the timber into vessels at ports in Finland for direct sea carriage to English ports, and English timber merchants did not hold stocks of Finnish timber: but these facts were unknown to the plaintiffs. As soon as war broke out imports of timber from Finland stopped at once owing to the presence of German warships in the Baltic. The defendants alleged that the contract was dissolved by the outbreak of war. The plaintiffs claimed damages. The Court of Appeal (Pickford, Bankes and Warrington LJJ), affirming McCardie J, held that they were entitled to succeed.

PICKFORD LJ

Why should a purchaser of goods, not specific goods, be deemed to concern himself with the way in which the seller is going to fulfil his contract by providing the goods he has agreed to sell? The sellers in this case agreed to deliver the timber free on rail at Hull, and it was no concern of the buyers as to how the sellers intended to get the timber there. I can see no reason for saying—and to free the defendants from liability this would have to be said—that the continuance of the normal mode of shipping the timber from Finland was a matter which both parties contemplated as necessary for the fulfilment of the contract. To dissolve the contract the matter relied on must be something which both parties had in their minds when they entered into the contract, such for instance as the existence of the music-hall in *Taylor v Caldwell* [above] or the continuance of the vessel in readiness to perform the contract, as in *Jackson v Union Marine Insurance Co* [above]. Here there is nothing to show that the plaintiffs contemplated, and there is no reason why they should be deemed to have contemplated, that the sellers should continue to have the ordinary facilities for dispatching the timber from Finland. As I have said, that was a matter which to the plaintiffs was wholly immaterial. It was not a matter forming the basis of the contract they entered into.

Questions

1. Would it have made any difference if the goods had been specific?

    24–015

2. Can a contract for the sale of non-specific goods ever be frustrated? If so in what way? (See *Howell v Coupland* (1876) 1 QBD 258.)

NATIONAL CARRIERS LTD v PANALPINA (NORTHERN) LTD

House of Lords [1981] A.C. 675; [1981] 2 W.L.R. 45; [1981] 1 All E.R. 161

24–016

Appellants leased a warehouse from respondents for a term of 10 years from January 1, 1974 at a rent of £6,500 per annum for the first five years and £13,300 for the second five years. In May 1979 the local authority closed the street giving the only access to the warehouse because of the dangerous condition of a listed building opposite which could not be demolished without the consent of the Minister. It was contemplated that the closure would last for a year or a little longer. At the time of the case, it seemed likely to last just over 18 months, leaving the lease with three more years to run. The closure prevented the appellants from using the premises for the only purpose contemplated, that is, as a warehouse. They stopped paying rent, claiming that the lease was frustrated. Sheen J affirmed the judgment by the master for the respondents under Order 14, on the ground that the doctrine of frustration could not apply to a lease. The appellants appealed directly to the House of Lords.

LORD HAILSHAM LC

[Having reviewed the theories of frustration, and expressed his preference for the formulation by Lord Radcliffe in *Davis v Fareham* continued:] This discussion brings me to the central point at issue in this case, which, in my view, is whether or not there is anything in the nature of an executed lease which prevents the doctrine of frustration, however formulated, applying to the subsisting relationship between the parties. That the point is open in this House is clear from the difference of opinion expressed in the *Cricklewood* case [1945] A.C. 221 between Lord Russell and Lord Goddard on the one hand, who answered the question affirmatively, and Viscount Simon L.C. and Lord Wright on the other, who answered it negatively, with Lord Porter reserving his opinion until the point arose definitively for consideration. The point, though one of principle, is a narrow one. It is the difference immortalised in HMS Pinafore between "never" and "hardly ever," since both Viscount Simon L.C. and Lord Wright clearly conceded that, though they thought the doctrine applicable in principle to leases, the cases in which it could properly be applied must be extremely rare.

With the view of Viscount Simon L.C. and Lord Wright I respectfully agree. It is clear from what I have said already that, with Lord Radcliffe in the passage I have cited, I regard these cases as a sub-species of the class of case which comes so regularly before the courts, as to which of two innocent parties must bear the loss as the result of circumstances for which neither is at all to blame. Apart from Law Reform (Frustrated Contracts) Act 1943, the doctrine of frustration brings the whole contract to an end, and in the present case, apart from any adjustment under that Act and any statutory right to compensation under the closure order, the effect of frustration, had it been applicable, would have been to throw the whole burden of interruption for 20 months on the landlord, deprived as he would be of all his rent, and imposed, as he would have, on his shoulders the whole danger of destruction by fire and the burden of reletting after the interruption. As it is, with the same qualification as to possible compensation, the tenant has to pay the entire rent during the period of interruption without any part of the premises being usable at all, together with the burden (such as it may be) of the performance of the other tenant's covenants which include covenants to insure and repair. These are no light matters.

[His Lordship reviewed the authorities and continued:]

I conclude that the matter is not decided by authority and that the question is open to your Lordships to decide on principle. In my view your Lordships ought now so to decide it. Is there anything in principle which ought to prevent a lease from ever being frustrated? I think there is not. In favour of the opposite opinion, the difference in principle between real and chattel property was strongly urged. But I find it difficult to accept this, once it has been decided, as has long been the case, that time and demise charters even of the largest ships and of considerable duration can in principle be frustrated. This was sufficiently well established by 1943 to make these charters worthy of an express exception on an exception in the Law Reform (Frustrated Contracts) Act 1943, s.2(5), and since then the Suez cases have supervened. There would be something anomalous in the light of what has been going on recently in the Shatt al Arab to draw a distinction between a leased oil tank and a demise-chartered oil tanker. Other anomalies would follow if the absolute principle were to be applied to leases. Goff J. appears to have found no difficulty in applying frustration to an agreement for a lease (which creates an equitable estate in the land capable of being specifically enforced and thereby converted into a legal estate operating as from the beginning of the equitable interest): see *Rom Securities Ltd v Rogers (Holdings) Ltd* (1968) 205 Estates Gazette 427. Personally I find the absurdities postulated by Megarry and Wade (*Law of Real Property* (4th ed., 1975), p. 675) in the case of the destruction by fire of the upper flat of a tenement building (already referred to) unacceptable if the "never" doctrine were rigidly applied, and I am attracted by Professor Treitel's argument (*Law of Contract* (5th ed., 1979), p. 669) of the inequitable contrast between a contract for the provision of holiday accommodation which amounted to a licence, and thus subject to the rule in *Taylor v Caldwell*, and a similar contract amounting to a short lease. Clearly the contrast would be accentuated if Goff J.'s view be accepted as to the applicability of the doctrine to agreements for a lease (see above).

I accept of course that systems of developed land law draw a vital distinction between land, which is relatively permanent, and other types of property, which are relatively perishable. But one can overdo the contrast. Coastal erosion as well as the "vast convulsion of nature" postulated by Viscount Simon L.C. in the *Cricklewood* case [1945] 1 All E.R. 252 at 255–256, [1945] A.C. 221 at 229 can, even in this island, cause houses, gardens, even villages and their churches to fall into the North Sea, and, although the law of property in Scotland is different, as may be seen from *Tay Salmon Fisheries Co Ltd v Speedie* 1929 S.C. 593, whole estates can there, as Lord President Clyde points out (at 600), be overblown with sand for centuries and so fall subject to the rei interitus doctrine of the civil law. In *Taylor v Caldwell* (1863) 3 B. & S. 826 at 834, itself Blackburn J., after referring to the Digest (lib XLV, title 1) on the subject of "obligatio de certo corpore" on which in part he founds his new doctrine, expressly says:

"... no doubt the propriety, one might almost say the necessity, of the implied condition is more obvious when the contract relates to a living animal, whether man or brute, than when it relates to some inanimate thing (such as in the present case a theatre) the existence of which is not so obviously precarious as that of the live animal, but the principle is adopted in the Civil law as applicable to every obligation of which the subject is a certain thing."

He then refers to Pothier, Traité des Obligations (partie 3, ch. 6, Art. 3, § 668) in support of his contention.

No doubt a long lease, say for example, one for 999 years, is almost exactly identical with the freehold for this purpose, and therefore subject to the ordinary law regarding the incidence of risk (recognised as regards chattels in section 7 of the former Sale of Goods Act 1893). But there is no difference between chattels in this respect and real property except in degree. Long term speculations and investments are in general less easily frustrated than short term adventures and a lease for 999 years must be in the longer class. I find myself persuaded by the argument presented by Atkin L.J. in his dissenting judgment in *Matthey v Curling* [1922] 2 A.C. 180 at 199–200 and quoted with approval by Viscount Simon L.C. in the *Cricklewood* case [1945] A.C. 221 at 230. In that passage Atkin L.J. said:

"... it does not appear to me conclusive against the application to a lease of the doctrine of frustration that the lease, in addition to containing contractual terms, grants a term of years. Seeing that the instrument as a rule expressly provides for the lease being determined at the option of the lessor upon the happening of certain specified events, I see no logical absurdity in implying a term that it shall be determined absolutely on the happening of other events—namely, those which in an ordinary contract work a frustration."

I pause here only to observe that, in the instant case, the lease gave the lessor a contingent right of determination in case of destruction by fire or in a case of a need for the use of the premises in connection with the railways, and to point out that in the War Damage Acts the lessee was given a statutory right, albeit different in kind from the doctrine of frustration, to disclaim a current lease on the happening of other events as the result of enemy action.

In the result, I come down on the side of the "hardly ever" school of thought. No doubt the circumstances in which the doctrine can apply to leases are, to quote Viscount Simon L.C. in the *Cricklewood* case [1945] A.C. 221 at 231, "exceedingly rare." Lord Wright appears to have thought the same, whilst adhering to the view that there are cases in which frustration can apply (see [1945] 1 All E.R. 252 at 263, [1945] A.C. 221 at 241). But, as he said in the same passage: "The doctrine of frustration is modern and flexible and is not subject to being constricted by an arbitrary formula." To this school of thought I respectfully adhere. Like Lord Wright, I am struck by the fact that there appears to be no reported English case where a lease has ever been held to have been frustrated. I hope this fact will act as a suitable deterrent to the litigious, eager to make legal history by being first in this field. But I am comforted by the reflexion of the authority referred to in the Compleat Angler (Pt. i, ch. 5) on the subject of strawberries: "Doubtless God could have made a better berry, but doubtless God never did." I only append to his observation of nature the comment that it does not follow from these premises that He never will, and, if it does not follow, an assumption that He never will becomes exceedingly rash.

In the event my opinion is that the appeal should be dismissed with costs.

Lords Wilberforce, Simon of Glaisdale and Roskill delivered speeches to similar effect.

LORD RUSSELL

It is my understanding of the law that the purchaser of land, whether for a freehold or a leasehold interest, takes the risk that it may be or may turn out to be less suitable or quite unsuitable for the purpose he has in mind, unless the vendor or lessor has taken on himself by warranty or otherwise some liability in that event. A freehold purchaser cannot in that event, after completion, return the land and ask for his money back, though in an appropriate case he might be able to resist specific performance while the contract remained outstanding. So also in the case of a lease for which a premium has been paid in addition to rent, the lessee cannot require repayment of the premium and refuse to pay the rent; nor where there is no premium can he refuse to pay the covenanted rent.

Under the bargain between lessor and lessee the land for the term has passed from the lessor to the lessee, with all its advantages and disadvantages. In the instant case a disadvantage existed, or rather supervened, in that access to the building preventing its use for any purpose was blocked by administrative action which we must assume was legally permitted, and for which we were not told that any compensation could be claimed. If a principle of achieving justice be anywhere at the root of the principle of frustration, I ask myself why should justice require that a useless site be returned to the lessor rather than remain the property of the lessee? (It is not suggested that a just solution can be achieved by somehow sharing the bad luck between lessor and lessee by, for example, a reduction of rent.)

I would reserve consideration of cases of physical destruction of flying leaseholds and of the total disappearance of the site comprised in the lease into the sea so that it no longer existed in the form of a piece of terra firma and could not be the subject of re-entry or forfeiture. In that last case I would not need the intervention, of any court to say that the term of years could not outlast the disappearance of its subject matter: the site would no longer have a freeholder lessor, and the obligation to pay rent, which issues out of the land, could not survive its substitution by the waves of the North Sea.

Appeal Dismissed.

DAVIS CONTRACTORS LTD v FAREHAM URBAN DISTRICT COUNCIL

House of Lords [1956] A.C. 696; [1956] 3 W.L.R. 37; [1956] 2 All E.R. 145; 54 L.G.R. 289

24-017   In July 1946 the contractors entered into a contract with the council to build 78 houses for the sum of £92,425 within a period of eight months. They had attached to their tender, in March 1946, a letter stating that the tender was subject to adequate supplies of labour and building materials being available. No such provision was included in the written contract entered into in July. Owing to unexpected circumstances and without the fault of either party, there was a serious shortage of skilled labour and of building materials and the work took 22 months to complete, with the result that the contractors properly and unavoidably incurred additional expense, amounting to £17,651. They contended that the contract (i) was subject to adequate supplies of labour being available, by reason of the letter of March 1946; (ii) was frustrated by reason of the long delay; and that they were entitled to a sum in excess of the contract price on a quantum meruit basis. On a case stated by an arbitrator, Goddard LCJ held that the contractors could recover because the letter was incorporated into the contract; but thought that the contract was not frustrated. The Court of Appeal held that the letter was not incorporated into the contract and that the contract was not frustrated. The House of Lords (Viscount Simonds, Lords Morton, Reid, Radcliffe and Somervell) affirmed the Court of Appeal on both points.

Viscount Simonds and Lords Morton and Reid made speeches dismissing the appeal.

LORD RADCLIFFE

[Having held that the letter was not incorporated into the contract, went on:]

The theory of frustration belongs to the law of contract and it is represented by a rule which the courts will apply in certain limited circumstances for the purpose of deciding that contractual obligations, ex facie binding, are no longer enforceable against the parties. The description of the circumstances that justify the application of the rule and, consequently, the decision whether in a particular case those circumstances exist, are, I think, necessarily questions of law.

It has often been pointed out that the descriptions vary from one case of high authority to another. Even as long ago as 1918 Lord Sumner was able to offer an anthology of different tests directed to the factor of delay alone, and delay, though itself a frequent cause of the principle of frustration being invoked, is only one instance of the kind of circumstance to which the law attends (see *Bank Line Ltd v Arthur Capel & Co* [1919] A.C.

435). A full current anthology would need to be longer yet. But the variety of description is not of any importance so long as it is recognised that each is only a description and that all are intended to express the same general idea. I do not think that there has been a better expression of that general idea than the one offered by Lord Loreburn in *F.A. Tamplin Steamship Co Ltd v Anglo-Mexican Petroleum Products Co Ltd* [1916] 2 A.C. 397, 403. It is shorter to quote than to try to paraphrase it: ". . . a court can and ought to examine the contract and the circumstances in which it was made, not of course to vary, but only to explain it, in order to see whether or not from the nature of it the parties must have made their bargain on the footing that a particular thing or state of things would continue to exist. And if they must have done so, then a term to that effect will be implied, though it be not expressed in the contract . . . no court has an absolving power, but it can infer from the nature of the contract and the surrounding circumstances that a condition which is not expressed was a foundation on which the parties contracted." So expressed, the principle of frustration, the origin of which seems to lie in the development of commercial law, is seen to be a branch of a wider principle which forms part of the English law of contract as a whole. But, in my opinion, full weight ought to be given to the requirement that the parties "must have made" their bargain on the particular footing. Frustration is not to be lightly invoked as the dissolvent of a contract.

Lord Loreburn ascribes the dissolution to an implied term of the contract that was actually made. This approach is in line with the tendency of English courts to refer all the consequences of a contract to the will of those who made it. But there is something of a logical difficulty in seeing how the parties could even impliedly have provided for something which ex hypothesi they neither expected nor foresaw; and the ascription of frustration to an implied term of the contract has been criticised as obscuring the true action of the court which consists in applying an objective rule of the law of contract to the contractual obligations that the parties have imposed upon themselves. So long as each theory produces the same result as the other, as normally it does, it matters little which theory is avowed (see *British Movietonews Ltd v London and District Cinemas Ltd* [1952] A.C. 166, 184, per Viscount Simon). But it may still be of some importance to recall that, if the matter is to be approached by way of implied term, the solution of any particular case is not to be found by inquiring what the parties themselves would have agreed on had they been, as they were not, forewarned. It is not merely that no one can answer that hypothetical question: it is also that the decision must be given "irrespective of the individuals concerned, their temperaments and failings, their interest and circumstances" (*Hirji Mulji v Cheong Yue Steamship Co Ltd* [1926] A.C. 497, 510; 42 T.L.R. 359). The legal effect of frustration "does not depend on their intention or their opinions, or even knowledge, as to the event." On the contrary, it seems that when the event occurs "the meaning of the contract must be taken to be, not what the parties did intend (for they had neither thought nor intention regarding it), but that which the parties, as fair and reasonable men, would presumably have agreed upon if, having such possibility in view, they had made express provision as to their several rights and liabilities in the event of its occurrence" (*Dahl v Nelson* (1881) 6 App.Cas. 38, per Lord Watson).

By this time it might seem that the parties themselves have become so far disembodied spirits that their actual persons should be allowed to rest in peace. In their place there rises the figure of the fair and reasonable man. And the spokesman of the fair and reasonable man, who represents after all no more than the anthropomorphic conception of justice, is and must be the court itself. So perhaps it would be simpler to say at the outset that frustration occurs whenever the law recognises that without default of either party a contractual obligation has become incapable of being performed because the circumstances in which performance is called for would render it a thing radically different from that which was undertaken by the contract. Non haec in foedera veni. It was not this that I promised to do. [The formulation preferred by Lord Hailsham, above].

There is, however, no uncertainty as to the materials upon which the court must proceed. "The data for decision are, on the one hand, the terms and construction of the contract, read in the light of the then existing circumstances, and on the other hand the events which have occurred" (*Denny, Mott & Dickson Ltd v James B. Fraser & Co Ltd* [1944] A.C. 265, 274–275, per Lord Wright). In the nature of things there is often no room for any elaborate inquiry. The court must act upon a general impression of what its rule requires. It is for that reason that special importance is necessarily attached to the occurrence of any unexpected event that, as it were, changes the face of things. But, even so, it is not hardship or inconvenience or material loss itself which calls the principle of frustration into play. There must be as well such a change in the significance of the obligation that the thing undertaken would, if performed, be a different thing from that contracted for.

I am bound to say that, if this is the law, the appellants' case seems to me a long way from a case of frustration. Here is a building contract entered into by a housing authority and a big firm of contractors in all the uncertainties of the post-war world. Work was begun shortly before the formal contract was executed and continued, with impediments and minor stoppages but without actual interruption, until the 78 houses contracted for had all been built. After the work had been in progress for a time the appellants raised the claim, which they repeated more than once, that they ought to be paid a larger sum for their work than the contract allowed; but the respondents refused to admit the claim and, so far as appears, no conclusive action was taken by either side which would make the conduct of one or the other a determining element in the case.

That is not in any obvious sense a frustrated contract. But the appellants' argument, which certainly found favour with the arbitrator, is that at some stage before completion the original contract was dissolved because it became incapable of being performed according to its true significance and its place was taken by a new arrangement under which they were entitled to be paid, not the contract sum, but a fair price on quantum meruit for the work that they carried out during the 22 months that elapsed between commencement and completion. The contract, it is said, was an eight months' contract, as indeed it was. Through no fault of the parties it turned out that it took 22 months to do the work contracted for. The main reason for this was that, whereas both parties had expected that adequate supplies of labour and material would be available to allow for completion in eight months, the supplies that were in fact available were much less than adequate for the purpose. Hence, it is said, the basis or the footing of the contract was removed before the work was completed; or, slightly altering the metaphor, the footing of the contract was so changed by the circumstance that the expected supplies were not available that the contract built upon that footing became void. These are the findings which the arbitrator has recorded in his supplemental award.

In my view, these are in substance conclusions of law, and I do not think that they are good law. All that anyone, arbitrator or court, can do is to study the contract in the light of the circumstances that prevailed at the time when it was made and, having done so, to relate it to the circumstances that are said to have brought about its frustration. It may be a finding of fact that at the time of making the contract both parties anticipated that adequate supplies of labour and material would be available to enable the contract to be completed in the stipulated time. I doubt whether it is, but, even if it is, it is no more than to say that when one party stipulated for completion in eight months, and the other party undertook it, each assumed that what was promised could be satisfactorily performed. That is a statement of the obvious that could be made with regard to most contracts. I think that a good deal more than that is needed to form a "basis" for the principle of frustration.

The justice of the arbitrator's conclusion depends upon the weight to be given to the fact that this was a contract for specified work to be completed in a fixed time at a price determined by those conditions. I think that his view was that, if without default on either side the contract period was substantially extended, that circumstance itself rendered the fixed price so unfair to the contractor that he ought not to be held to his original price. I have much sympathy with the contractor, but, in my opinion, if that sort of consideration were to be sufficient to establish a case of frustration, there would be an untold range of contractual obligations rendered uncertain and, possibly, unenforceable.

Two things seem to me to prevent the application of the principle of frustration to this case. One is that the cause of the delay was not any new state of things which the parties could not reasonably be thought to have foreseen. On the contrary, the possibility of enough labour and materials not being available was before their eyes and could have been the subject of special contractual stipulation. It was not made so. The other thing is that, though timely completion was no doubt important to both sides, it is not right to treat the possibility of delay as having the same significance for each. The owner draws up his conditions in detail, specifies the time within which he requires completion, protects himself both by a penalty clause for time exceeded and by calling for the deposit of a guarantee bond and offers a certain measure of security to a contractor by his escalator clause with regard to wages and prices. In the light of these conditions the contractor makes his tender, and the tender must necessarily take into account the margin of profit that he hopes to obtain upon his adventure and in that any appropriate allowance for the obvious risks of delay. To my mind, it is useless to pretend that the contractor is not at risk if delay does occur, even serious delay. And I think it a misuse of legal terms to call in frustration to get him out of his unfortunate predicament.

Lord Somervell made a speech dismissing the appeal.

Appeal Dismissed.

Points for reflection

24–018   The closure of the Suez Canal on November 2, 1956, gave rise to a similar problem in three different cases: *Carapanayoti & Co Ltd v ET Green Ltd* [1959] 1 Q.B. 131; *Tsakiroglou & Co Ltd v Noblee Thorl* [1960] 2 Q.B. 318 and *Albert D Gaon & Co v Société Inter-Professionelle des Oléagineaux Fluides*

Alimentaires [1960] 2 Q.B. 334. By a c.i.f. contract sellers agreed to ship goods from Port Sudan to Belfast (in the first case) to Hamburg (in the second) and to a Mediterranean port (in the third). In each case the parties contemplated that the shipment would be via the Suez Canal (but did not so stipulate in the contract) and the goods had to go round the Cape, more than two and a half times as far in the first case and more than four times as far in the third. There was no evidence that the longer voyage would have caused the goods (cottonseed cake in the first case and groundnuts in the second and third) to depreciate appreciably in quality or in weight. In each case the sellers failed to deliver the goods.

In the first case, McNair J asked himself three questions and answered them all in the affirmative: (i) the availability of the canal was the basis of the contract; (ii) the closure of the canal did transmute the obligation into one of a different kind; (iii) if the officious bystander (see above) had asked: "What is to happen if the canal should be closed?" the parties, as reasonable men, would have replied: "The contract is off." He therefore held that the contract was frustrated.

In the second case Diplock J had before him a finding of fact by arbitrators that shipment via the Cape was not commercially or fundamentally different from shipment via Suez. Diplock J held that this finding was unassailable; there was evidence to support it and there was no indication that the arbitrators had misdirected themselves as to the meaning of "commercially or fundamentally different." He therefore held that the contract was not frustrated. But he emphasised that he was not saying that McNair J was wrong. This was a case in which a jury, properly directed, could have held either way.

In the third case, Ashworth J disagreed directly with McNair J. He denied that the closure of the canal transmuted the obligation into one of a different character: both before and after the closure, the thing undertaken was arranging the shipment of goods from Port Sudan to the Mediterranean. This was not rendered impossible—as, for example, a contract would be if it provided for shipment of goods from a Black Sea port to the Mediterranean and the Dardanelles were closed for an indefinite period. The mere fact that the performance of the same obligation became much more onerous was not sufficient to frustrate the contract.

The second and third cases went to the Court of Appeal and the decisions of Diplock and Ashworth JJ were affirmed. The first case was overruled: [1960] 2 Q.B. 348; [1960] 2 W.L.R. 869. The court thought that Diplock J should have felt free to review the finding of the arbitrator which involved a question of law or at least was a question of mixed fact and law (per Ormerod LJ) or was a finding of a secondary fact, namely, an inference from primary facts, and, as such, open to review (per Harman LJ). Ashworth J's view was approved. The House of Lords affirmed the decision of the Court of Appeal in the *Tsakiroglou* case: [1962] A.C. 93; [1961] 2 W.L.R. 633; [1961] 2 All E.R. 179.

Questions

1. Did McNair J ask the wrong questions or give the wrong answers?

   24–019

2. Do you think that the result in the Suez sale cases ought to have been different if either (a) there had been a stipulation in the contract that the goods were to go via the Suez Canal, or (b) the goods had been of a perishable nature and would not have survived the journey round the Cape?

OCEAN TRAMP TANKERS CORPORATION v VO SOVFRACHT, THE EUGENIA

Court of Appeal [1964] 2 Q.B.226; [1964] 2 W.L.R. 114; [1964] 1 All E.R. 161; [1963] 2 Lloyd's Rep. 231

24-020   The Eugenia was chartered for a "trip out to India via the Black Sea" from the time the vessel was delivered at Genoa. When the negotiations took place both parties realised the possibility that the Suez Canal might be closed, but the parties were unable to agree on any provision to meet this contingency. A "war clause" forbade the charterers from bringing the vessel into a dangerous zone, without the consent of the owners. The vessel, having sailed from Genoa, via Odessa, arrived at Port Said at a time when it was a "dangerous zone" and became trapped in the canal. The charterers alleged that the charter was frustrated. The owners denied this but treated the charterers' conduct as a repudiation and sued for hire during the period for which the ship was trapped.

LORD DENNING MR

[Having held that the charterer had broken the war clause by entering the Canal zone, went on:] The second question is whether the charterparty was frustrated by what took place. The arbitrator has held it was not. The judge has held that it was. Which is right? One thing that is obvious is that the charterers cannot rely on the fact that the Eugenia was trapped in the canal; for that was their own fault. They were in breach of the war clause in entering it. They cannot rely on a self-induced frustration, see *Maritime National Fish Ltd v Ocean Trawlers Ltd* [below]. But they seek to rely on the fact that the canal itself was blocked. They assert that even if the Eugenia had never gone into the canal, but had stayed outside (in which case she would not have been in breach of the war clause), nevertheless she would still have had to go round by the Cape. And that, they say, brings about a frustration, for it makes the venture fundamentally different from what they contracted for. The judge has accepted this view. He has held that on November 16, 1956, the charterparty was frustrated. The reason for taking November 16, 1956, was this: before November 16, 1956, mercantile men (even if she had stayed outside) would not have formed any conclusion as to whether the obstructions in the canal were other than temporary. There was insufficient information available to form a judgment. On November 16, 1956, mercantile men would conclude that the blockage of the southern end would last till March or April 1957; so that by that time it would be clear that the only thing to do (if the ship had never entered the canal) would be to go round the Cape. The judge said: "I hold that the adventure, involving a voyage round the Cape, is basically or fundamentally different from the adventure involving a voyage via the Suez Canal." So he held the contract frustrated. He was comforted to find in *The Massalia* [1961] 2 Q.B. 278 Pearson J. came to a similar conclusion.

I must confess that I find it difficult to apply the doctrine of frustration to a hypothetical situation, that is, to treat this vessel as if she had never entered the canal and then ask whether the charter was frustrated. The doctrine should be applied to the facts as they really are. But I will swallow this difficulty and ask myself what would be the position if the vessel had never entered the canal but stayed at Port Said. Would the contract be frustrated?

This means that once again we have had to consider the authorities on this vexed topic of frustration. But I think the position is now reasonably clear. It is simply this: if it should happen, in the course of carrying out a contract, that a fundamentally different situation arises for which the parties made no provision—so much so that it would not be just in the new situation to hold them bound to its terms—then the contract is at an end.

It was originally said that the doctrine of frustration was based on an implied term. In short, that the parties, if they had foreseen the new situation, would have said to one another: "If that happens, of course, it is all over between us." But the theory of an implied term has now been discarded by everyone, or nearly everyone, for the simple reason that it does not represent the truth.[2] The parties would not have said: "It is all over between us." They would have differed about what was to happen. Each would have sought to insert reservations or qualifications of one kind or another. Take this very case. The parties realised that the canal might become impassable. They tried to agree on a clause to provide for the contingency. But they failed to agree. So there is no room for an implied term.

It has frequently been said that the doctrine of frustration only applies when the new situation is "unforeseen"

---

[2]   Compare the sentence footnoted at para.23–019. If an implied condition is the proper explanation of the common mistake cases, why not of the frustration cases? Or has Lord Denning changed his mind?

or "unexpected" or "uncontemplated," as if that were an essential feature. But it is not so. The only thing that is essential is that the parties should have made no provision for it in their contract. The only relevance of it being "unforeseen" is this: If the parties did not foresee anything of the kind happening, you can readily infer they have made no provision for it: whereas if they did foresee it, you would expect them to make provision for it. But cases have occurred where the parties have foreseen the danger ahead, and yet made no provision for it in the contract. Such was the case in the Spanish Civil War when a ship was let on charter to the republican government. The purpose was to evacuate refugees. The parties foresaw that she might be seized by the nationalists. But they made no provision for it in their contract. Yet, when she was seized, the contract was frustrated, see *W.J. Tatem Ltd v Gamboa* [1939] 1 K.B. 132. So here the parties foresaw that the canal might become impassable: it was the very thing they feared. But they made no provision for it. So there is room for the doctrine to apply if it be a proper case for it.[3]

We are thus left with the simple test that a situation must arise which renders performance of the contract "a thing radically different from that which was undertaken by the contract," see *Davis Contractors Ltd v Fareham Urban District Council* [above] by Lord Radcliffe. To see if the doctrine applies, you have first to construe the contract and see whether the parties have themselves provided for the situation that has arisen. If they have provided for it, the contract must govern. There is no frustration. If they have not provided for it, then you have to compare the new situation with the situation for which they did provide. Then you must see how different it is. The fact that it has become more onerous or more expensive for one party than he thought is not sufficient to bring about a frustration. It must be more than merely more onerous or more expensive. It must be positively unjust to hold the parties bound. It is often difficult to draw the line. But it must be done. And it is for the courts to do it as a matter of law: see *Tsakiroglou & Co Ltd v Noblee Thorl G.m.b.H.* [1962] A.C. 93, 116, 119, by Lord Simonds and by Lord Reid.

Applying these principles to this case, I have come to the conclusion that the blockage of the canal did not bring about a "fundamentally different situation" such as to frustrate the venture. My reasons are these: (1) The venture was the whole trip from delivery at Genoa, out to the Black Sea, there load cargo, thence to India, unload cargo, and redelivery. The time for this vessel from Odessa to Vizagapatam via the Suez Canal would be 26 days, and via the Cape, 56 days. But that is not the right comparison. You have to take the whole venture from delivery at Genoa to redelivery at Madras. We were told that the time for the whole venture via the Suez Canal would be 108 days and via the Cape 138 days. The difference over the whole voyage is not so radical as to produce a frustration. (2) The cargo was iron and steel goods which would not be adversely affected by the longer voyage, and there was no special reason for early arrival. The vessel and crew were at all times fit and sufficient to proceed via the Cape. (3) The cargo was loaded on board at the time of the blockage of the canal. If the contract was frustrated, it would mean, I suppose, that the ship could throw up the charter and unload the cargo wherever she was, without any breach of contract. (4) The voyage round the Cape made no great difference except that it took a good deal longer and was more expensive for the charterers than a voyage through the canal.

The only hesitation I have had about this case is because of the views expressed by Pearson J. in *The Massalia*. That case can be distinguished because there was a sentence in the charter which read: "Captain also to telegraph to 'Maritsider Genoa' on passing Suez Canal." Pearson J. held that that meant there was actually an obligation to pass the Suez Canal, and hence the contract was frustrated by impossibility. I think he attached too much significance to the clause. I think that there, as here, there was no obligation to go through Suez Canal, but only to go by the route which was customary at the time of performance; and that there is no legitimate distinction to be drawn between that case and this. That was a voyage charter and this a time charter. That makes no difference except that the burden fell on the owners and not the charterers. Pearson J. held that the route via the Cape was fundamentally different from the route via the Suez Canal and that the charter was frustrated on that ground also. I am afraid I cannot take that view. It is important to notice also that since that case the House of Lords have held that, with goods sold c.i.f. Sudan to Hamburg, the contract of sale was not frustrated by the closure of the Suez Canal, see *Tsakiroglou & Co Ltd v Noblee Thorl G.m.b.H.* I know that a contract of affreightment is different from a contract for the sale of goods, but I should find it strange if, in the case of a ship loaded with cargo, the contract of affreightment was frustrated by the closure of the canal and the contract of sale was not frustrated. It would lead to endless complications.

I come, therefore, to the conclusion that the decision of Pearson J. in *The Massalia* was wrong and should be overruled. It is to be noticed that both in that case and in this the arbitrators held there was no frustration. I think they were right. I would allow this appeal and hold that the contract was not frustrated.

---

[3]   See the criticism in Treitel, *Law of Contract* (10th edn), p.841.

On this footing I gather there is no other point which needs to be decided.

Donovan L.J. delivered judgment allowing the appeal and Danckwerts L.J. concurred.

Appeal Allowed.

2. SELF-INDUCED FRUSTRATION

J LAURITZEN AS v WIJSMULLER BV THE "SUPER SERVANT TWO"

Court of Appeal [1990] 1 Lloyd's L. Rep. 1

24-021   On July 7, 1980 the defendants contracted to carry the plaintiffs' drilling rig (Dan King) from Japan to Rotterdam, using as the "transportation unit," Super Servant One or Super Servant Two. The defendants intended to use Super Servant Two but on January 29, 1981 it sank. The defendants had entered into contracts with other persons which they could perform only by using Super Servant One. They decided to use Super Servant One for those other contracts. Among preliminary questions for the court was (2), whether the Dan King contract was frustrated if the loss of Super Servant Two was caused (a) without the defendants' negligence or (b) by the defendants' negligence.

BINGHAM LJ

Mr Clarke for Wijsmuller submitted that the extraneous supervening event necessary to found a plea of frustration occurred when Super Servant Two sank on January 29, 1981. The Dan King contract was not, however, thereupon frustrated but remained alive until Wijsmuller decided a fortnight later that that contract could not be, or would not be, performed. There was, he submitted, factually, no break in the chain of causation between the supervening event and the non-performance of the contract. He acknowledged that *Maritime National Fish Ltd* [below] contained observations on their face inimical to his argument, but distinguished that as a decision on causation confined to its own peculiar facts and laying down no general rule. For authoritative support Mr Clarke relied on cases dealing with the application of force majeure clauses in commodity contracts, and in particular on an unreported judgment of Robert Goff J., as he then was, adopted with approval by the Court of Appeal in *Bremer Handelsgesellschaft m.b.H. v Continental Grain Co.* [1983] 1 Lloyd's Rep. 269 at p. 292:

. . . the question resolves itself into a question of causation; in my judgment, at least in a case in which a seller can (as in the present case) claim the protection of a clause which protects him where fulfilment is hindered by the excepted peril, subsequent delivery of his available stock to other customers will not be regarded as an independent cause of shortage, provided that in making such delivery the seller acted reasonably in all the circumstances of the case . . .

A similar approach was reflected in other cases, see, for example, *Intertradex S.A. v Lesieur–Tourteaux S.A.R.L.* [1977] 2 Lloyd's Rep. 146 at p. 115, per Donaldson J. as he then was; [1978] 2 Lloyd's Rep. 509 at p. 513, per Lord Denning, M.R. Reliance was also placed on passages in *The Law of Contract* (7th ed.) by Professor Treitel, which the Judge quoted in his judgment at p. 152. Thus, Mr Clarke urged, this was a case in which Wijsmuller could not perform all their contracts once Super Servant Two was lost; they acted reasonably (as we must assume) in treating the Dan King contract as one they could not perform; so the sinking had the direct result of making that contract impossible to perform.

Mr Legh-Jones answered that since the contract provided for the carriage to be performed by one or other vessel the loss of one did not render performance radically different, still less impossible. That apart, Wijsmuller's argument fell foul of the principles summarised above since (among other things) the frustration they sought to establish did not bring the contract to an end forthwith, without more and automatically and was not independent of the act or election of Wijsmuller. The force majeure cases were good law so far as they went, but it was one thing to construe and apply a consensual force majeure clause, another to determine whether the facts were such that the law should hold the contract to be discharged . . .

Had the Dan King contract provided for carriage by Super Servant Two with no alternative, and that vessel had been lost before the time for performance, then assuming no negligence by Wijsmuller (as for purposes of this question we must), I feel sure the contract would have been frustrated. The doctrine must avail a party who contracts to perform a contract of carriage with a vessel which, through no fault of his, no longer exists. But that is not this case. The Dan King contract did provide an alternative. When that contract was made one of the contracts eventually performed by Super Servant One during the period of contractual carriage of Dan King had been made, the other had not, at any rate finally. Wijsmuller have not alleged that when the Dan King contract was made either vessel was earmarked for its performance. That, no doubt, is why an option was contracted for. Had it been foreseen when the Dan King contract was made that Super Servant Two would be unavailable for performance, whether because she had been deliberately sold or accidentally sunk, Lauritzen at least would have thought it no matter since the carriage could be performed with the other. I accordingly accept Mr Legh-Jones's submission that the present case does not fall within the very limited class of cases in which the law will relieve one party from an absolute promise he has chosen to make.

But I also accept Mr Legh-Jones's submission that Wijsmuller's argument is subject to other fatal flaws. If, as was argued, the contract was frustrated when Wijsmuller made or communicated their decision on February 16, it deprives language of all meaning to describe the contract as coming to an end automatically. It was, indeed, because the contract did not come to an end automatically on January 29, that Wijsmuller needed a fortnight to review their schedules and their commercial options. I cannot, furthermore, reconcile Wijsmuller's argument with the reasoning or the decision in *Maritime National Fish Ltd* [below, para.24–022]. In that case the Privy Council declined to speculate why the charterers selected three of the five vessels to be licensed but, as I understand the case, regarded the interposition of human choice after the allegedly frustrating event as fatal to the plea of frustration. If Wijsmuller are entitled to succeed here, I cannot see why the charterers lost there. The cases on frustrating delay do not, I think, help Wijsmuller since it is actual and prospective delay (whether or not recognised as frustrating by a party at the time) which frustrates the contract, not a party's election or decision to treat the delay as frustrating. I have no doubt that force majeure clauses are, where their terms permit, to be construed and applied as in the commodity cases on which Wijsmuller relied, but it is in my view inconsistent with the doctrine of frustration as previously understood on high authority that its application should depend on any decision, however reasonable and commercial, of the party seeking to rely on it . . .

Question 2(b)

The issue between the parties was short and fundamental: what is meant by saying that a frustrating event, to be relied on, must occur without the fault or default, or without blame attaching to, the party relying on it?

Mr Clarke's answer was that a party was precluded from relying on an event only when he had acted deliberately or in breach of an actionable duty in causing it. Those conditions were not met here since it was not alleged Wijsmuller sank Super Servant Two deliberately . . .

Mr Legh-Jones argued for a less restrictive approach. He relied on what Lord Justice Griffiths, as he then was, said in *The Hannah Blumenthal*, [1982] 1 Lloyd's Rep. 582, p. 592; [1983] 1 A.C. 854 at p. 882:

"[*Denmark Productions Ltd v Boscobel Productions Ltd* [1969] 1 Q.B. 699] best illustrates what is meant by default in the context of frustration. The essence of frustration is that it is caused by some unforeseen supervening event over which the parties to the contract have no control and for which they are therefore not responsible. To say that the supervening event occurs without the default or blame or responsibility of the parties is, in the context of the doctrine of frustration, but another way of saying it is a supervening event over which they had no control. The doctrine has no application and cannot be invoked by a contracting party when the frustrating event was at all times within his control; still less can it apply in a situation in which the parties owed a contractual duty to one another to prevent the frustrating event occurring."

I do not pause to ask whether Lord Justice Griffith's opinion is formally binding upon us since in my judgment it clearly indicates the path which the law should follow. When, in *Bank Line Ltd* [1919] A.C. 435, 452, Lord Sumner made his famous observation that "Reliance cannot be placed on a self-induced frustration" he was contrasting a self-induced frustration with one arising "without blame or fault on either side." As the Judge observed—

". . . in some respects the doctrine of frustration and the concept of 'self-inducement' are simply opposite sides of the same coin."

Wijsmuller's test would, in my judgment, confine the law in a legalistic strait-jacket and distract attention from the real question, which is whether the frustrating event relied upon is truly an outside event or extraneous change of situation or whether it is an event which the party seeking to rely on it had the means and opportunity to prevent but nevertheless caused or permitted to come about. A fine test of legal duty is inappropriate; what is needed is a pragmatic judgment whether a party seeking to rely on an event as discharging him from a contractual promise was himself responsible for the occurrence of that event.

Lauritzen have pleaded in some detail the grounds on which they say that Super Servant Two was lost as a result of the carelessness of Wijsmuller, their servants or agents. If those allegations are made good to any significant extent Wijsmuller would (even if my answer to Question 2(a) is wrong) be precluded from relying on their plea of frustration.

Dillon L.J. delivered judgment to the same effect.

Points for reflection

24–022
1. *Maritime National Fish Ltd v Ocean Trawlers Ltd* [1935] A.C. 524, PC, concerned the charter of a trawler, St Cuthbert. Both parties knew that it could only be used with an otter trawl and that under Canadian law it was an offence to use an otter trawl without a licence. The charterers were operating five trawlers and applied for five licences but were granted only three and were asked to nominate the trawlers. They nominated three trawlers other than St Cuthbert and, when sued for the hire, claimed that the contract was frustrated. The Privy Council held that they were liable, any frustration having resulted from their deliberate act. They could not rely on a "self-induced frustration".

2. *The Super Servant* decision has been criticised. (i) *National Fish* is distinguishable because there it was possible for the charterer to perform all his contracts with third parties. Though the point does not appear in the Privy Council report, and Lord Wright said that it was immaterial why the charterers preferred the three trawlers selected, it appears in the decisions of the courts below in Canada that they owned the other trawlers. Unlike the owners in *Super Servant*, they were not in a position where they had to break a contract. (ii) Anson's *Law of Contract* (27th edn), p.523, puts the case of a farmer who agrees to sell 250 tons of a crop to be grown on specific land which normally yields over 500 tons to A, and 250 tons to B. If there is a poor harvest and the yield is only 250 tons neither contract would be frustrated. That is not easily reconcilable with earlier cases, notably *Howell v Coupland* (1876) 1 QBD 258; but in that case there was only one buyer and there was no question of the seller's choosing to perform another contract to his detriment.

3. On the nature of the fault required to render the frustration "self-induced", see *Thompson v Asda-MFI*, above Ch.16.

Question

24–023   A, a pianist, has undertaken to perform at a concert on June 1. What is the position if (i) on May 29 she takes an overdose of aspirin with intent to commit suicide, survives, but is disabled from performing on June 1, or (ii) on May 29 she absent-mindedly steps in front of a bus and is severely injured, or (iii) on May 29 she assaults a constable and is remanded in custody for a week?

----

3. The Responsibility to Explain

JOSEPH CONSTANTINE STEAMSHIP LINE LTD v IMPERIAL SMELTING CORPORATION LTD

House of Lords [1942] A.C. 154; 110 L.J.K.B. 433; 165 L.T. 27; 46 Com.Cas. 258; 57 T.L.R. 485; 70 Ll.L.Rep. 1; [1941] 2 All E.R. 165

The respondents chartered the appellants' steamship, Kingswood, to proceed to Port Pirie, Australia, to load a cargo. On January 3, 1937, while the ship was anchored in the roads off Port Pirie—she was due to berth on January 4 an explosion of great violence occurred which resulted in such delay that, as was admitted, the commercial object of the adventure was frustrated. The respondents claimed damages. The arbitrator found that, though various hypotheses were put forward, no one had given a satisfactory explanation of the cause of the disaster; he was not satisfied that the true cause of the explosion had as yet been suggested. The Court of Appeal held, reversing Atkinson J, that a party, prima facie guilty of a failure to perform his contract, cannot escape under the plea of frustration, unless he proves that the frustration occurred without his default; that the appellants had failed to discharge that onus; and the respondents were entitled to damages. The House of Lords (Viscount Simon LC, Viscount Maugham, Lords Russell, Wright and Porter) allowed the appeal.

24–024

LORD SIMON LC

[Having referred to the judgment of the Court of Appeal, said:] . . . if this were correct there must be many cases in which, although in truth frustration is complete and unavoidable, the defendant will be held liable because of his inability to prove a negative—in some cases, indeed, a whole series of negatives. Suppose that a vessel while on the high seas disappears completely during a storm. Can it be that the defence of frustration of the adventure depends on the owner's ability to prove that all his servants on board were navigating the ship with adequate skill and that there was no "default" which brought about the catastrophe? Suppose that a vessel in convoy is torpedoed by the enemy and sinks immediately with all hands. Does the application of the doctrine require that the owners should affirmatively prove that those on board were keeping a good look-out, were obscuring lights, were steering as directed, and so forth? There is no reported case which requires us so to hold. The doctrine on which the defence of frustration depends is nowhere so stated as to place this onus of proof on the party relying on it . . .

Every case in this branch of the law can be stated as turning on the question whether from the express terms of the particular contract a further term should be implied which, when its conditions are fulfilled, puts an end to the contract.

If the matter is regarded in this way, the question is as to the construction of a contract taking into consideration its express and implied terms. The implied term in the present case may well be—"This contract is to cease to be binding if the vessel is disabled by an overpowering disaster, provided that disaster is not brought about by the default of either party." This is very similar to an express exception of "perils of the seas," as to which it is ancient law that by an implied term of the contract the shipowner cannot rely on the exception if its operation was brought about either (a) by negligence of his servants, or (b) by his breach of the implied warranty of seaworthiness. If a ship sails and is never heard of again the shipowner can claim protection for loss of the cargo under the express exception of perils of the seas. To establish that, must he go on to prove (a) that the perils were not caused by negligence of his servants, and (b) were not caused by any unseaworthiness? I think clearly not. He proves a prima facie case of loss by sea perils, and that he is within the exception. If the cargo owner wants to defeat that plea it is for him by rejoinder to allege and prove either negligence or unseaworthiness. The judgment of the Court of Appeal in *The Glendarroch* [1894] P. 266 is plain authority for this . . .

4. Where a Contract is Frustrated

FIBROSA SPOLKA AKCYJNA v FAIRBAIRN LAWSON COMBE BARBOUR LTD

House of Lords [1943] A.C. 32; 111 L.J.K.B. 433; 167 L.T. 101; 58 T.L.R. 308; [1942] 2 All E.R. 122

21-025   On July 12, 1939, the respondents, an English company, agreed to sell, and the appellants, a Polish company, agreed to purchase machinery for £4,800 of which one-third was to be paid with the order. Delivery was to be made, within three or four months of the settlement of final details, at Gdynia, Poland. Only £1,000 was in fact paid with the order. On September 3 Britain declared war on Germany, and on September 23 Gdynia was occupied by the Germans. The appellants sued for the return of the £1,000. Tucker J and the Court of Appeal held that the contract was frustrated and that, under the principle of *Chandler v Webster*,[4] the claim must fail.

VISCOUNT SIMON LC

If we are to approach this problem anew, it must be premised that the first matter to be considered is always the terms of the particular contract. If, for example, the contract is "divisible" in the sense that a sum is to be paid over in respect of completion of a defined portion of the work, it may well be that the sum is not returnable if completion of the whole work is frustrated. If the contract itself on its true construction stipulates for a particular result which is to follow in regard to money already paid, should frustration afterwards occur, this governs the matter. The ancient and firmly established rule that freight paid in advance is not returned if the completion of the voyage is frustrated: *Byrne v Schiller*, L.R. 6 Ex. 319, should, I think, be regarded as a stipulation introduced into such contracts by custom, and not as the result of applying some abstract principle. And so, a fortiori, if there is a stipulation that the prepayment is "out and out." To take an example, not from commerce, but from sport, the cricket spectator who pays for admission to see a match cannot recover the entrance money on the ground that rain has prevented play if, expressly or by proper implication, the bargain with him is that no money will be returned. Inasmuch as the effect of frustration may be explained as arising from an implied term: see *Joseph Constantine Steamship Line Ltd v Imperial Smelting Corporation Ltd*; it is tempting to speculate whether a further term could be implied as to what was to happen, in the event of frustration, to money already paid, but, if the parties were assumed to have discussed the point when entering into the contract, they could not be supposed to have agreed on a simple formula which would be fair in all circumstances, and all that could be said is that, in the absence of such agreement, the law must decide. The question now to be determined is whether, in the absence of a term in the contract dealing with the matter, the rule which is commonly called the rule in *Chandler v Webster* should be affirmed . . .

The locus classicus for the view which has hitherto prevailed is to be found in the judgment of Collins M.R. in *Chandler v Webster*. It was not a considered judgment, but it is hardly necessary to say that I approach this pronouncement of the then Master of the Rolls with all the respect due to so distinguished a common lawyer. When his judgment is studied, however, one cannot but be impressed by the circumstance that he regarded the proposition that money in such cases could not be recovered back as flowing from the decision in *Taylor v Caldwell* [above]. *Taylor v Caldwell*, however, was not a case in which any question arose whether money could be recovered back, for there had been no payment in advance, and there is nothing in the judgment of Blackburn J., which, at any rate in terms, affirms the general proposition that "the loss lies where it falls." The application by Collins M.R. of *Taylor v Caldwell* to the actual problem with which he had to deal in *Chandler v Webster* deserves close examination. He said: "The plaintiff contends that he is entitled to recover the money

---

[4]   In *Chandler v Webster* [1904] 1 K.B. 493 CA, the defendant agreed to let to the plaintiff a room for the purpose of viewing the coronation procession of June 26, 1902, for the sum of £141 15s. payable immediately. The procession subsequently became impossible owing to the illness of the King. The plaintiff had paid £100 on account and the balance remained unpaid. The plaintiff sued to recover the £100 paid by him as on a total failure of consideration, and the defendant counterclaimed for the sum of £41 15s. The Court of Appeal (Collins MR, Romer and Matthew LJJ) held that the plaintiff's action failed and the defendant's counterclaim succeeded. The defendant's right to payment of the whole sum had accrued before the procession became impossible, and the effect of frustration was not to wipe out the contract altogether but only to release the parties from further performance.

which he has paid on the ground that there has been a total failure of consideration. He says that the condition on which he paid the money was that the procession should take place, and that, as it did not take place, there had been a total failure of consideration. That contention does no doubt raise a question of some difficulty, and one which has perplexed the courts to a considerable extent in several cases. The principle on which it has been dealt with is that which was applied in *Taylor v Caldwell*—namely, that where, from causes outside the volition of the parties, something which was the basis of, or essential to the fulfilment of, the contract has become impossible, so that, from the time when the fact of that impossibility has been ascertained, the contract can no further be performed by either party, it remains a perfectly good contract up to that point, and everything previously done in pursuance of it must be treated as rightly done, but the parties are both discharged from further performance of it. If the effect were that the contract were wiped out altogether, no doubt the result would be that money paid under it would have to be repaid as on a failure of consideration. But that is not the effect of the doctrine; it only releases the parties from further performance of the contract. Therefore the doctrine of failure of consideration does not apply."

It appears to me that the reasoning in this crucial passage is open to two criticisms: (a) The claim of a party, who has paid money under a contract, to get the money back, on the ground that the consideration for which he paid it has totally failed, is not based on any provision contained in the contract, but arises because, in the circumstances that have happened, the law gives a remedy in quasi-contract to the party who has not got that for which he bargained. It is a claim to recover money to which the defendant has no further right because in the circumstances that have happened the money must be regarded as received to the plaintif[f]'s use. It is true that the effect of frustration is that, while the contract can no further be performed, "it remains a perfectly good contract up to that point, and everything previously done in pursuance of it must be treated as rightly done," but it by no means follows that the situation existing at the moment of frustration is one which leaves the party that has paid money and has not received the stipulated consideration without any remedy. To claim the return of money paid on the ground of total failure of consideration is not to vary the terms of the contract in any way. The claim arises not because the right to be repaid is one of the stipulated conditions of the contract, but because, in the circumstances that have happened, the law gives the remedy. It is the failure to distinguish between (1) the action of assumpsit for money had and received in a case where the consideration has wholly failed, and (2) an action on the contract itself, which explains the mistake which I think has been made in applying English law to this subject-matter. Thus, in *Blakeley v Muller & Co* [1903] 2 K.B. 760n., 761n., Lord Alverstone C. J. said: "I agree that *Taylor v Caldwell* applies, but the consequence of that decision is that neither party here could have sued on the contract in respect of anything which was to be done under it after the procession had been abandoned." That is true enough, but it does not follow that because the plaintiff cannot sue "on the contract" he cannot sue dehors the contract for the recovery of a payment in *respect of which consideration has failed. In the same case, Wills J. relied on Appleby* v Myers [above, para.20–032], where a contract was made for the erection by A of machinery on the premises of B, to be paid for on completion. There was no prepayment and in the course of the work the premises were destroyed by fire. It was held that both parties were excused from further performance, and that no liability accrued on either side, but the liability referred to was liability under the contract, and the learned judge seems to have thought that no action to recover money in such circumstances as the present could be conceived of unless there was a term of the contract, express or implied, which so provided. Once it is realised that the action to recover money for a consideration that has wholly failed rests, not on a contractual bargain between the parties, but, as Lord Sumner said in *Sinclair v Brougham* [1914] A.C. 398, 452, "upon a notional or imputed promise to repay," or (if it is preferred to omit reference to a fictitious promise) upon an obligation to repay arising from the circumstances, the difficulty in the way of holding that a prepayment made under a contract which has been frustrated can be recovered back appears to me to disappear. (b) There is, no doubt, a distinction between cases in which a contract is "wiped out altogether," for example, because it is void as being illegal from the start or as being due to fraud which the innocent party has elected to treat as avoiding the contract, and cases in which intervening impossibility "only releases the parties from further performance of the contract." But does the distinction between these two classes of case justify the deduction of Collins M.R. that "the doctrine of failure of consideration does not apply" where the contract remains a perfectly good contract up to the date of frustration? This conclusion seems to be derived from the view that, if the contract remains good and valid up to the moment of frustration, money which has already been paid under it cannot be regarded as having been paid for a consideration which has wholly failed. The party that has paid the money has had the advantage, whatever it may be worth, of the promise of the other party. That is true, but it is necessary to draw a distinction. In English law, an enforceable contract may be formed by an exchange of a promise for a promise, or by the exchange of a promise for an act—I am excluding contracts under seal—and thus, in the law relating to the formation of contract, the promise to do a thing may often be the consideration, but when one is consider-ing the law of failure of consideration and of the quasi-contractual right to recover money on that ground, it is, generally speaking, not the promise which is referred to as the consideration, but the performance of the promise. The money was paid to secure performance and, if performance fails, the inducement which brought about the payment is not fulfilled.

If this were not so, there could never be any recovery of money, for failure of consideration, by the payer of the money in return for a promise of future performance, yet there are endless examples which show that money can be recovered, as for a complete failure of consideration, in cases where the promise was given but could not be fulfilled: see the notes in Bullen and Leake's *Precedents of Pleading*, (9th ed.), p. 263. In this connection the decision in *Rugg v Minett*, 11 East 210, is instructive. There the plaintiff had bought at auction a number of casks of oil. The contents of each cask were to be made up after the auction by the seller to the prescribed quantity so that the property in a cask did not pass to the plaintiff until this had been done. The plaintiff paid in advance a sum of money on account of his purchases generally, but a fire occurred after some of the casks had been filled up, while the others had not. The plaintiff's action was to recover the money he had paid as money received by the defendants to the use of the plaintiffs. The Court of King's Bench ruled that this cause of action succeeded in respect of the casks which at the time of the fire had not been filled up to the prescribed quantity. A simple illustration of the same result is an agreement to buy a horse, the price to be paid down, but the horse not to be delivered and the property not to pass until the horse had been shod. If the horse dies before the shoeing, the price can unquestionably be recovered as for a total failure of consideration, notwithstanding that the promise to deliver was given. This is the case of a contract de certo corpore where the certum corpus perishes after the contract is made, but, as Vaughan Williams L.J.'s judgment in *Krell v Henry* explained, the same doctrine applies "to cases where the event which renders the contract incapable of performance is the cessation or non-existence of an express condition or state of things, going to the root of the contract, and essential to its performance." I can see no valid reason why the right to recover prepaid money should not equally arise on frustration arising from supervening circumstances as it arises on frustration from destruction of a particular subject-matter. The conclusion is that the rule in *Chandler v Webster* is wrong, and that the appellants can recover their £1,000.

While this result obviates the harshness with which the previous view in some instances treated the party who had made a prepayment, it cannot be regarded as dealing fairly between the parties in all cases, and must sometimes have the result of leaving the recipient who has to return the money at a grave disadvantage. He may have incurred expenses in connection with the partial carrying out of the contract which are equivalent, or more than equivalent, to the money which he prudently stipulated should be prepaid, but which he now has to return for reasons which are no fault of his. He may have to repay the money, though he has executed almost the whole of the contractual work, which will be left on his hands. These results follow from the fact that the English common law does not undertake to apportion a prepaid sum in such circumstances—contrast the provision, now contained in section 40 of the Partnership Act, 1890, for apportioning a premium if a partner-ship is prematurely dissolved. It must be for the legislature to decide whether provision should be made for an equitable apportionment of prepaid moneys which have to be returned by the recipient in view of the frustra-tion of the contract in respect of which they were paid. I move that the appeal be allowed, and that judgment be entered for the appellants.

Lords Atkin, Russell, MacMillan, Wright, Roche and Porter made concurring speeches.

Appeal Allowed.

Law Reform (Frustrated Contracts) Act 1943 (As amended by Sale of Goods Act 1979)

24-026   **1.** Adjustment of rights and liabilities of parties to frustrated contracts.—

(1) Where a contract governed by English law has become impossible of performance or been otherwise frustrated, and the parties thereto have for that reason been discharged from the further performance of the contract, the following provisions of this section shall, subject to the provisions of section 2 of this Act, have effect in relation thereto.

(2) All sums paid or payable to any party in pursuance of the contract before the time when the parties were so discharged (in this Act referred to as "the time of discharge") shall, in the case of sums so paid, be recover-able from him as money received by him for the use of the party by whom the sums were paid, and in the case of sums so payable, cease to be so payable:

Provided that, if the party to whom the sums were so paid or payable incurred expenses before the time of discharge in, or for the purpose of, the performance of the contract, the court may, if it considers it just to do so having regard to all the circumstances of the case, allow him to retain or, as the case may be, recover the whole or any part of the sums so paid or payable, not being an amount in excess of the expenses so incurred.

(3) Where any party to the contract has, by reason of anything done by any other party thereto in, or for the purpose of, the performance of the contract, obtained a valuable benefit (other than a payment of money to which the last foregoing subsection applies) before the time of discharge, there shall be recoverable from him by the said other party such sum (if any), not exceeding the value of the said benefit to the party obtaining it, as the court considers just, having regard to all the circumstances of the case and, in particular—

    (a) the amount of any expenses incurred before the time of discharge by the benefited party in, or for the purpose of, the performance of the contract, including any sums paid or payable by him to any other party in pursuance of the contract and retained or recoverable by that party under the last foregoing subsection, and

    (b) the effect, in relation to the said benefit, of the circumstances giving rise to the frustration of the contract.

(4) In estimating, for the purposes of the foregoing provisions of this section, the amount of any expenses incurred by any party to the contract, the court may, without prejudice to the generality of the said provisions, include such sum as appears to be reasonable in respect of overhead expenses and in respect of any work or services performed personally by the said party.

(5) In considering whether any sum ought to be recovered or retained under the foregoing provisions of this section by any party to the contract, the court shall not take into account any sums which have, by reason of the circumstances giving rise to the frustration of the contract, become payable to that party under any contract of insurance unless there was an obligation to insure imposed by an express term of the frustrated contract or by or under any enactment.

(6) Where any person has assumed obligations under the contract in consideration of the conferring of a benefit by any other party to the contract upon any other person, whether a party to the contract or not, the court may, if in all the circumstances of the case it considers it just to do so, treat for the purposes of subsection (3) of this section any benefit so conferred as a benefit obtained by the person who has assumed the obligations as aforesaid.

2. Provision as to application of this Act.—

(1) This Act shall apply to contracts, whether made before or after the commencement of this Act, as respects which the time of discharge is on or after the first day of July, nineteen hundred and forty-three, but not to contracts as respects which the time of discharge is before the said date.

(2) This Act shall apply to contracts to which the Crown is a party in like manner as to contracts between subjects.

(3) Where any contract to which this Act applies contains any provision which, upon the true construction of the contract, is intended to have effect in the event of circumstances arising which operate, or would but for the said provision operate, to frustrate the contract, or is intended to have effect whether such circumstances arise or not, the court shall give effect to the said provision and shall only give effect to the foregoing section of this Act to such extent, if any, as appears to the court to be consistent with the said provision.

(4) Where it appears to the court that a part of any contract to which this Act applies can properly be severed from the remainder of the contract, being a part wholly performed before the time of discharge, or so performed except for the payment in respect of that part of the contract of sums which are or can be ascertained under the contract, the court shall treat that part of the contract as if it were a separate contract and had not been frustrated and shall treat the foregoing section of this Act as only applicable to the remainder of that contract.

(5) This Act shall not apply—

    (a) to any charterparty, except a time charterparty or a charterparty by way of demise, or to any contract (other than a charterparty) for the carriage of goods by sea; or

    (b) to any contract of insurance, save as is provided by subsection (5) of the foregoing section; or

    (c) to any contract to which section 7 of the Sale of Goods Act, 1979 (which avoids contracts for the sale of specific goods which perish before the risk has passed to the buyer) applies, or to any other contract for the sale, or for the sale and delivery, of specific goods, where the contract is frustrated by reason of the fact that the goods have perished.

3. Short title and interpretation.

(1) This Act may be cited as the Law Reform (Frustrated Contracts) Act, 1943.

(2) In this Act the expression "court" means, in relation to any matter, the court or arbitrator by or before whom the matter falls to be determined.

BP EXPLORATION CO (LIBYA) LTD v HUNT (NO.2)

Queen's Bench Division [1979] 1 W.L.R. 783; [1982] 1 All E.R. 925

24–027   Hunt was the owner of an oil concession in Libya. He contracted to transfer a half-share in the concession to BP, who agreed to transfer to him certain "farm-in" contributions in cash and oil and to undertake the exploration of the concession and, if oil was found, the development and production, providing all necessary finance until the field came on stream. Then, BP were to receive one half of all oil produced plus "reimbursement oil," being three eighths of Hunt's share, until they had received 125 per cent of their farm-in contributions and 50 per cent of the money spent on exploration and development before the field came on stream. Thereafter, the cost of production and development was to be borne by the two parties equally.

    BP discovered a giant oilfield and expended many millions of pounds on exploration and development. The field came on stream in January 1967. In December 1971 the Libyan government passed a law expropriating BP's interest which frustrated the contract. Hunt continued to export some oil under increasing difficulties until June 1973 when the Libyan government expropriated his interest. The government paid both parties compensation for the book value of facilities in Libya but nothing for the loss of the concession itself. The plaintiffs claimed the award of a just sum under s.1(3) of the Frustrated Contracts Act.

ROBERT GOFF J

    Said that the principle common to both s.1(2) and (3) and the fundamental principle underlying the Act, is the prevention of unjust enrichment of either party at the other's expense. Section 1(2) provided for the restitution of a net benefit but, under s.1(3), the net benefit simply provided an upper limit to the award. An award under s.1(2) is generally simply an award for the repayment of money. Under s.1(3) it has to be shown that the defendant has obtained a valuable benefit (other than a payment of money) which has to be identified and valued and forms the upper limit of the award. The court may then award a just sum, not exceeding the value of the benefit. Where the services rendered by the plaintiff have an end-product, s.1(3) shows that the value of the end-product is the benefit. Where a contract is frustrated by a fire which destroys a building on which work has been done, the award will be nil. Sometimes the services will have no end-product, as where the work is surveying or transporting goods. Then the benefit must be the value of the services. The benefit must be valued at the date of the frustration, making no allowance for "the time value of money," that is, the notional benefit derived from the fact that the defendant has had the use of the benefit for a period before the frustration. The expenses incurred by the defendant must be deducted from the value of the benefit.

    A just sum must then be assessed. The court may have regard to the consideration in the contract as evidence of the appropriate level of remuneration. If a prospector employed for a fee discovered a gold mine before the frustration a rateable part of the contract fee might provide useful evidence of the just sum. If he was to receive a stake in the concession, the just sum might be enhanced. It may be unjust to compel the defendant to pay more than the consideration, or a rateable part of it, that he has agreed to pay—though it was unnecessary to decide whether this will always be so.

    Section 2(3) should be given its natural meaning and not limited to provisions clearly intended to have effect in the event of frustration; but the fact that the contract is "entire" should not automatically preclude an award under s.1(3). Only if, upon a true construction of the contract, the plaintiff has contracted on terms that he is to receive no payment in the event which has occurred, will the fact that the contract is "entire" preclude an award.

Applying these principles, Hunt's benefits were identified as (in addition to the farm-in payments) the development of a bare concession of unknown potential into a giant oilfield in production, in which Hunt held a half-share. The benefit was to be identified as the product of the work; but it was very greatly reduced by the frustration to, broadly, the benefit of the oil Hunt obtained and benefit of the settlement with the Libyan government. Only half of that benefit should be attributed to BP's work, the other half being attributed to Hunt's own contribution, namely the concession. The court was looking at events which occurred after frustration as the best evidence of the value of Hunt's share at that time. Hunt's benefit was valued at $84,951,000.

In assessing the just sum, regard was had to the consideration which BP were to receive—the half share in the concession which they had received, and the reimbursement oil. If they had received the whole, no sum would have been awarded. In fact there remained a balance of 16,899,189 barrels and the equivalent in oil of $550,032. The just sum was valued at $35,403,146—considerably less than the benefit obtained by Hunt ($84,951,000).

Hunt argued that s.2(3) applied because clause 6 of the agreement said that he was to be under no personal liability to repay and s.9(e) of the operating agreement provided that BP's right of recovery was to be out of production. But if A advanced £100,000 to be invested in a business, the contract providing that he was to be repaid only out of the profits of the business, the contract might be frustrated the day after the advance was made. Similarly where A agreed to buy all the apples to be grown in a certain orchard and paid the price in advance, the orchard being seized by the government next day. It might have happened that the day after the field came on stream, BP but not Mr Hunt was expropriated and he might have drawn an immense fortune for years. Clause 6 and s.9 were not intended to be effective in the radically changed circumstances. The award of a just sum was not precluded by s.2(3).

Robert Goff J.'s decision was affirmed by the Court of Appeal, [1981] 1 W.L.R. 232; [1982] 1 All E.R. 978 and the House of Lords, [1983] 2 A.C. 352; [1982] 2 W.L.R. 253; [1982] 1 All E.R. 986.

Questions

What would be the effect—if any—of the Frustrated Contracts Act upon the decisions in: **24–028**

1. *Cutter v Powell*? (above, Ch.20).

2. *Sumpter v Hedges*? (above, Ch.20).

3. *Appleby v Myers*? (above, Ch.20).

4. *The Fibrosa case*? (above).

The Principles of European Contract Law, 1998

Art. 6.111 *Change of Circumstances*

(1) A party is bound to fulfil its obligations even if performance has become more onerous, whether because   **24–029** the cost of performance has increased or because the value of the performance it receives has diminished.

(2) If, however, performance of the contract becomes excessively onerous because of a change of circumstances, the parties are bound to enter into negotiations with a view to adapting the contract or terminating it, provided that:

    (a) the change of circumstances occurred after the time of conclusion of the contract,

    (b) the possibility of a change of circumstances was not one which could reasonably have been taken into account at the time of conclusion of the contract, and

    (c) the risk of the change of circumstances is not one which, according to the contract, the party affected should be required to bear.

(3) If the parties fail to reach agreement within a reasonable period, the court may:
   (a) terminate the contract at a date and on terms to be determined by the court; or
   (b) adapt the contract in order to distribute between the parties in a just and equitable manner the losses and gains from the change of circumstances.

Art. 8:108 *Excuse Due to an Impediment*

(1) A party's non-performance is excused if it proves that it is due to an impediment beyond its control and that it could not reasonably have been expected to take the impediment into account at the time of the conclusion of the contract, or to have avoided or overcome the impediment or its consequences.

(2) Where the impediment is only temporary the excuse provided by this article has effect for the period during which the impediment exists. However, if the delay amounts to a fundamental non-performance, the obligee may treat it as such.

(3) The non-performing party must ensure that notice of the impediment and of its effect on its ability to perform is received by the other party within a reasonable time after the non-performing party knew or ought to have known of these circumstances. The other party is entitled to damages for any loss resulting from the non-receipt of such notice.

Question

24-030   Would this be a better way of dealing with a fundamental change of circumstances than the common law doctrine of frustration? Does it solve the problems where performance becomes not merely excessively onerous, but impossible?

Further reading

Roger Brownsword, 'Henry's Lost Spectacle and Hutton's Lost Speculation: A Classic Riddle Solved?' (1985) 129 *Solicitors' Journal* 860

Catharine MacMillan, '*Taylor v Caldwell* (1863)' In Charles Mitchell and Paul Mitchell (eds), *Landmark Cases in the Law of Contract* (Oxford: Hart, 2008) p.167

Ewan McKendrick, 'The Regulation of Long-Term Contracts in English Law' in J. Beatson and D. Friedmann (eds), *Good Faith and Fault in Contract Law* (Oxford: Oxford University Press, 1995) p.305

Glanville Williams, *The Law Reform (Frustrated Contracts) Act 1943* (London: Stevens and Sons, 1944)

PART VII

VITIATING FACTORS

25

INCAPACITY

LEARNING OBJECTIVES

By the end of this chapter, you should:

■ be familiar with the kinds of cases where a party might be held to lack the capacity to contract;
■ understand the consequences of a finding of incapacity to contract.

INTRODUCTION

The general rule of English law is that any person is competent to bind himself to any contract he chooses to make, provided that it is not illegal or void for reasons of public policy. (See below, Ch.27). At common law there are exceptions to this rule in the case of corporations, minors, married women, mentally incompetent, and intoxicated persons. The exceptions are now greatly reduced in scope. A series of statutes from 1870 to 1949 abolished the married woman's disabilities and she now enjoys full contractual capacity. The present state of the other exceptions requires a little further explanation.

1. CORPORATIONS

A corporation created by Royal Charter has always had the same contractual capacity as an ordinary person but a company incorporated under the Companies Act could, until recently, only make such contracts as were within the scope of the objects set out in its memorandum of association. Anything beyond that was ultra vires and void.

In the leading case of *Ashbury Railway Carriage and Iron Co Ltd v Riche* (1875) L.R. 7 HL 653 the objects set out in the company's memorandum were "to make and sell, or lend on hire, railway carriages and waggons, and all kinds of railway plant, fittings, machinery and rolling stock; to carry on the business of mechanical engineers and general contractors; to purchase, lease, work and sell mines, minerals, land and buildings; to purchase and sell as merchants, timber, coal, metals, or other materials, and to buy any such materials on commission or as agents." The directors purchased a concession for making a railway in Belgium and purported to contract with Riche that he should have the construction of the line. Riche's action for breach of the alleged contract failed since the House of Lords held that the construction of a railway, as distinct from rolling stock, was ultra vires the company and that therefore the contract was void. Even if every shareholder of the company had expressed his approval of the act, it would have made no difference, for it was an act which the company had no power, in law, to do. Important changes were made by s.108 of the Companies Act 1989, substituting a new s.35 of the Companies Act 1985. Under that new section it remains the duty of the directors to observe any limitations on their powers flowing from the company's memorandum (s.35(3)) and a member of a company may bring proceedings to restrain the doing of an act in excess of those powers (s.35(2)). However, by s.35(1), it is provided that:

> "The validity of an act done by a company shall not be called into question on the ground of lack of capacity by reason of anything in the company's memorandum."

So, by applying the modern law to the *Ashbury* case, the directors committed a breach of duty by making the contract and might have been restrained by action by a member; but once the contract was made its validity could not be questioned provided that the making of the contract was "an act done by the company." In principle, it might be objected that it was not such an act because the directors had no power to make the contract. However, for some time, this objection has been covered by legislative provision and it is currently met by ss.39 and 40 of the Companies Act 2006. Thus, s.39(1) provides:

> "The validity of act done by a company shall not be called into question on the ground of lack of capacity by reason of anything in the company's constitution."

And, according to ss.40(1) and (2) of the Act:

"(1) In favour of a person dealing with a company in good faith, the power of the directors to bind the company, or authorise others to do so, is deemed to be free of any limitation under the company's constitution.

(2) For this purpose—
(a) a person "deals with" a company if he is a party to any transaction or other act to which the company is a party,
(b) a person dealing with a company—
  (i) is not bound to enquire as to any limitation on the powers of the directors to bind the company or authorise others to do so,
  (ii) is presumed to have acted in good faith unless the contrary is proved, and
  (iii) is not to be regarded as acting in bad faith by reason only of his knowing that an act is beyond the powers of the directors under the company's constitution.

An ultra vires act by the directors may now be ratified, but only by special resolution, which does not affect any liability incurred by the directors or any other person—any such relief must be agreed to separately by special resolution.

Formerly a corporation's contracts were invalid unless made under the corporate seal but, since the Corporate Bodies' Contracts Act 1960, a corporation may make contracts in the same manner as a natural person—that is the contract may be made orally unless a special rule requires a written contract—as in contracts for the sale or disposition of an interest in land—or evidence in writing—as in the case of a guarantee within s.4 of the Statute of Frauds 1677.

2. Minors

25–003   At common law persons under the age of 21 were designated "infants" and had only a limited capacity to contract. From January 1, 1970, the Family Law Reform Act 1969 reduced the age of majority to 18 and authorised the term "minor" as an alternative to "infant." "Minor" is now the preferred term. The capacity of a minor to contract is still regulated by the common law, modified by the Minors' Contracts Act 1987 which repealed a troublesome statute, the Infants Relief Act 1874.

The general principle is that a contract made by a minor with an adult is binding on the adult but not on the minor. If, after attaining his majority, he ratifies it by an act confirming the promise he made when a minor, he is bound. There need be no consideration for the act of ratification. A contract by a minor is not void and any money or property transferred by him under the contract can be recovered only if there has been a total failure of consideration. There are three exceptional cases where a minor is to some extent bound.

A. Necessaries

A minor is bound to pay for necessaries supplied to him under a contract. The Sale of Goods Act 1979 **25–004** s.3, re-enacting the Act of 1893, provides:

> ". . . where necessaries are sold and delivered to an infant (or minor) . . . he must pay a reasonable price therefor.
> 'Necessaries' in this section means goods suitable to the condition of life of such infant (or minor) . . . and to his actual requirements at the time of sale and delivery."

"Necessaries" are those things without which a person cannot reasonably exist and include food, clothing, lodging, education or training in a trade and essential services. The "condition of life" of the minor means his social status and his wealth. What is regarded as necessary for the minor residing in a stately home may be unnecessary for the resident of a council flat. Whatever the minor's status, the goods must be suitable to his actual requirements—if he already has enough fancy waistcoats, more cannot be necessary: *Nash v Inman* [1908] 2 K.B. 1 CA.

The nature of the minor's liability for necessary goods is uncertain. The fact that the Sale of Goods Act makes him liable only for goods "sold and delivered" and to pay, not any agreed price, but a reasonable price, suggests quasi-contractual liability—he must pay, not because he has contracted to do so, but because the law requires him to recompense the seller for a benefit conferred and accepted. Some dicta support this view but others treat the minor's liability as contractual. In *Roberts v Gray* [1913] K.B. 520 CA, a minor was held liable for his failure to perform a contract for a tour with the plaintiff, a noted billiards player. It was a contract for the instruction of the minor. The contract was wholly executory and the minor had received no benefit but it was held that the contract was binding on him from its formation. It may be thought that there is a distinction between necessary goods and necessary services but this is difficult to justify logically or historically. Perhaps the contract in *Roberts v Gray* belongs more properly to the category of beneficial contracts of service, below.

A contract is not binding on a minor merely because it is proved to be for the minor's benefit; but a contract which would otherwise be binding as a contract for necessaries is not so if it contains harsh and onerous terms: *Fawcett v Smethurst* (1914) 84 L.J.K.B. 473 (Atkin J).

B. Beneficial Contracts of Service

It is for the minor's benefit that he should be able to obtain employment which would be difficult if **25–005** he could not make a binding contract. The law allows him to do so, provided that the contract, taken as a whole, is manifestly for his benefit. So where a young railway porter agreed to join an insurance scheme and to forgo any claims he might have under the Employers' Liability Act, he had forfeited his rights under the Act, the contract as a whole being for his benefit: *Clements v London & North Western Railway* [1894] 2 Q.B. 482 CA. Contracts enabling a minor to pursue a career as a professional boxer and as an author have been held binding as being for their benefit; but, in *Proform Sports Management*

Ltd v Proactive Sports Management Ltd and Paul Stretford [2006] EWHC 2812 (Ch), it was held that a young footballer's (Wayne Rooney's) management and agency contract (not, it should be noted his contract with Everton FC, the football club that paid his wages) did not qualify as a binding exception.

C. Acquisition of Property with Obligations

25–006   When a minor acquires "a subject of a permanent nature . . . with certain obligations attached to it"—such as a leasehold, or shares in a company—he is bound by the obligations as long as he retains the subject. He must pay the rent or calls on the shares: *London & North Western Railway v M'Michael* (1850) 5 Ex. 114. The contract is voidable by the minor—he may repudiate it at any time during his minority or within a reasonable time thereafter. It is uncertain whether avoidance here means rescission ab initio or avoidance of only future obligations; but, whether it is retrospective or not, it seems that the minor cannot recover money which he has already paid unless there has been a total failure of consideration: *Steinberg v Scala Ltd* [1923] 2 Ch. 452 CA.

i. Restitution by a Minor

25–007   Where a minor has obtained property under a contract which is not enforceable against him, the adult party who can neither sue for the price nor get the property back may suffer an injustice. Even where the minor has lied about his age, no action in deceit will lie because this would, in effect, enable the contract to be enforced against him; and for the same reason it is improbable that the minor would be estopped from asserting his true age. The Minors' Contracts Act 1987 s.3 now affords a limited measure of redress. Where a contract made after the commencement of the Act is unenforceable against a defendant because he was a minor when it was made:

> ". . . the court may, if it is just and equitable to do so, require the defendant to transfer to the plaintiff any property acquired by the defendant under the contract or any property representing it."

This may assist the plaintiff where the property is identifiable but where the plaintiff has loaned money it will usually not be. The plaintiff will then be able to recover in equity only if he is able to prove that he loaned the money for the express purpose of enabling the minor to buy necessaries and that he in fact did so: *Lewis v Alleyne* (1888) 4 T.L.R. 560.

Section 2 of the 1987 Act provides: "Nothing in this section shall be taken to prejudice any other remedy available to the plaintiff." The plaintiff might rely on the equitable doctrine which required a fraudulent minor to return property which he had obtained by deception and which was still identifiable in his possession: *R Leslie Ltd v Shiell* [1914] 3 K.B. 607 CA; but it is not clear that there would be any advantage in doing so, since the remedy under s.1 appears to overlap the equitable remedy and does not require proof of fraud.

ii. Guarantee of a Minor's Contract

25–008   Section 3 of the 1987 Act provides that a guarantee of a minor's contract is not unenforceable against the guarantor merely because the contract made by the minor is unenforceable against him on the ground that he is a minor. The section does not apply if the contract made by the minor is unenforceable against him for some other reason, for example misrepresentation or duress by the adult party. In such a case the guarantor would not be bound.

3. Mental Incapacity

The ancient rule of the common law was that a "lunatic" could not set up his own insanity (though his **25–009** heir might) so as to avoid an obligation which he had undertaken. But by 1847 Pollock CB was able to say, in delivering the judgment of the Court of Exchequer Chamber in *Moulton v Camroux*, 2 Ex. 487, that "the rule had in modern times been relaxed, and unsoundness of mind would now be a good defence to an action upon a contract, if it could be shown that the defendant was not of the capacity to contract 'and the plaintiff knew it.'" Cf. *Imperial Loan Co v Stone* [1892] 1 Q.B. 599 CA.

The modern law is found in the Mental Capacity Act 2005. The Act, albeit not specifically focused on mental capacity with regard to the making of contracts, opens in s.1 with the following general principles:

"1 The principles

(1) The following principles apply for the purposes of this Act.

(2) A person must be assumed to have capacity unless it is established that he lacks capacity.

(3) A person is not to be treated as unable to make a decision unless all practicable steps to help him to do so have been taken without success.

(4) A person is not to be treated as unable to make a decision merely because he makes an unwise decision.

(5) An act done, or decision made, under this Act for or on behalf of a person who lacks capacity must be done, or made, in his best interests.

(6) Before the act is done, or the decision is made, regard must be had to whether the purpose for which it is needed can be as effectively achieved in a way that is less restrictive of the person's rights and freedom of action.

Having established these cautions against too hasty a judgment that a person lacks mental capacity (including, it should be noted, the inference that a person lacks capacity merely because, as s.1(4) puts it, "he makes an unwise decision"), the Act provides in s.2(1):

"For the purposes of this Act, a person lacks capacity in relation to a matter if at the material time he is unable to make a decision for himself in relation to the matter because of an impairment of, or a disturbance in the functioning of, the mind or brain."

What, for the purposes of s.2, would amount to being unable to make a decision for oneself? The answer is given by s.3(1), according to which such an inability arises where a person is unable: (a) to understand the information relevant to the decision, (b) to retain that information, (c) to use or weigh that information as part of the process of making the decision, or (d) to communicate his decision (whether by talking, using sign language or any other means). That said, there remains an exception for the provision of necessaries, s.7(1) providing that "If necessary goods or services are supplied to a person who lacks capacity to contract for the supply, he must pay a reasonable price for them" ("necessary" being defined by s.7(2) as "suitable to a person's condition in life and to his actual requirements at the time when the goods or services are supplied").

Question

25–010   Alf places an advertisement in the local newspaper saying that he is interested in buying sporting memorabilia. Bill telephones Alf to say that he has a collection of soccer shirts, that he is getting too old to have any use for them, and that he is interested in selling. Alf agrees to call round the next day. When Alf calls at Bill's house, he finds that Bill has a couple of dozen old soccer shirts, most of which are worth very little but, amongst which, there is a rare signed shirt of the 1966 England World Cup team—a shirt that Alf believes to be worth at least £1,500. Alf offers Bill £300 for the collection including the signed England shirt. Bill accepts provided that Alf pays cash. Alf does not have £300 cash to hand but agrees to return later in the day when he has had an opportunity to get to an ATM. When Alf returns with the cash, Bill's daughter, Clare, answers the door. Clare refuses to let Alf in, saying that he should be ashamed of taking advantage of Bill. Alf protests that he has a contractual right to the shirts. However, Clare claims that her father suffers from dementia, that he is unlikely to remember any supposed deal with Alf, and that he lacks the capacity to make a binding contract.

(a) What more would you need to know in order to determine whether Bill lacks the necessary mental capacity to form a contract?

(b) If Bill is judged not to have the necessary mental capacity, is it relevant whether or not Alf was aware that Bill suffered from dementia or that he was probably unable to understand that the signed England shirt was particularly valuable? (Compare *Hart v O'Connor* [1985] A.C. 1000).

----

4. Intoxicated Persons

25–011   The authorities are scanty; but in *Gore v Gibson* (1845) 13 M. & W. 621; 153 E.R. 260, it was held that a contract made by a person so intoxicated as not to know the consequences of his act is not binding on him if his condition is known to the other party. It appears, however, that such a contract is not void but merely voidable, for it was held in *Matthews v Baxter* (1873) L.R. 8 Ex. 132 that if the drunken party, upon coming to his senses, ratifies the contract, he is bound by it.

   Section 3 of the Sale of Goods Act 1979 makes the same provision for persons who are incompetent to contract by reason of "drunkenness" as for minors and the mentally incompetent. No doubt, the same rule would be applied to persons intoxicated by drugs other than alcoholic drink, either by a broad interpretation of "drunkenness", or at common law.

26

DURESS, UNDUE INFLUENCE AND UNCONSCIONABILITY

LEARNING OBJECTIVES

By the end of this chapter, you should:

- **be familiar with the leading cases on the defences of undue influence and duress;**
- **understand the circumstances in which a contract might be set aside on these grounds;**
- **have critically reflected on the relationship between undue influence and duress;**
- **understand how the concept of "illegitimate pressure" as relevant to economic duress ties in to the context of the contract and the modern notion of protecting reasonable expectations;**
- **have considered to what extent undue influence and duress might be covered by a general principle of "unconscionability".**

INTRODUCTION

It is axiomatic that contractual obligations should be *freely* and *independently* assumed. Where pressure is applied to a party, it is arguable that the resulting act of entering into a contract is not free. Similarly, where a party acts under the guidance of another (even though such guidance might be well-intended), there is a question-mark about the independence of a decision to contract that is made by the former. If there is pressure or influence of this kind, and if it is unfair or undue (whatever these terms might mean), we might recognise this as a reason for avoiding a contract. Where a party applies unfair pressure or undue influence and then takes advantage of the situation, we might characterise this as unconscionable conduct. We might also characterise it as unconscionable if one party seeks to hold another to a contract in circumstances where there is an obvious doubt about the latter's free and independent assumption of contractual responsibility.

26–001

Already, in these introductory remarks, we can sense two major difficulties. First, the key doctrinal concepts of duress (qua unfair or illegitimate pressure), undue influence, and unconscionability, seem to overlap. The question is whether we can apply them in a focused way and, in particular, whether we can stay clear about whether it is the conduct of the party applying the pressure or influence that is critical, or whether it is the response of the party to whom the pressure or influence is applied that is critical, or whether it is the disadvantageous nature of the resulting transaction that is critical, or whether all (or some) of these elements are critical. Secondly, as in any case where we are trying to draw the lines of fair dealing, we can anticipate problems about establishing precisely when pressure becomes "unfair" or "illegitimate", when influence becomes "undue", and when shabby conduct crosses the line to become "unconscionable".

In this chapter, the cases are divided into two sections: first, undue influence; and, secondly, duress. However, there is no watertight segregation of these topics, and the spectre of unconscionability may be discerned throughout the chapter.

1. Undue Influence

BARCLAYS BANK PLC v O'BRIEN AND ANOTHER

House of Lords [1994] 1 A.C. 340; [1993] 3 W.L.R. 286; [1993] 4 All E.R. 417

26–002 O'Brien (O), a shareholder in a manufacturing company, arranged with the company's bank an over-draft facility for the company of £135,000. O was to guarantee repayment and his liability to the Bank was to be secured by a second charge over the matrimonial home, jointly owned by O and his wife (W). The bank manager's instructions that O and W should be made fully aware of the effect of the security documents were not carried out. Both O and W signed the documents without reading them. When the company's indebtedness increased, the Bank brought proceedings against O and W to enforce the guarantee. W's defence was that O had (i) put undue pressure on her to sign and (ii) misrepresented that the effect of the charge was limited to £60,000 and that it would last only three weeks. The judge gave judgment for the Bank, finding that (i) O had not unduly influenced W and (ii) that O had misrepresented the effect of the charge but that the Bank was not responsible for that misrepresentation. The Court of Appeal held that the Bank was under a duty, which it had not satisfied, to take reasonable steps to ensure that W had an adequate understanding of the transaction so that it was not enforceable against her except to the extent of £60,000. The Bank appealed.

LORD BROWNE-WILKINSON

Policy considerations

The large number of cases of this type coming before the courts in recent years reflects the rapid changes in social attitudes and the distribution of wealth which have recently occurred. Wealth is now more widely spread. Moreover a high proportion of privately owned wealth is invested in the matrimonial home. Because of the recognition by society of the equality of the sexes, the majority of matrimonial homes are now in the joint names of both spouses. Therefore in order to raise finance for the business enterprises of one or other of the spouses, the jointly owned home has become a main source of security. The provision of such security requires the consent of both spouses.

In parallel with these financial developments, society's recognition of the sexes has led to a rejection of the concept that the wife is subservient to the husband in the management of the family's finances. A number of the authorities reflect an unwillingness in the court to perpetuate law based on this outmoded concept. Yet, as Scott L.J. in the Court of Appeal rightly points out, although the concept of the ignorant wife leaving all financial decisions to the husband is outmoded, the practice does not yet coincide with the ideal (see [1993], Q.B. 109 at 139). In a substantial proportion of marriages it is still the husband who has the business experience and the wife is willing to follow his advice without bringing a truly independent mind and will to bear on financial decisions. The number of recent cases in this field shows that in practice many wives are still subjected to, and yield to, undue influence by their husbands. Such wives can reasonably look to the law for some protection when their husbands have abused the trust and confidence reposed in them.

On the other hand. it is important to keep a sense of balance in approaching these cases. It is easy to allow sympathy for the wife who is threatened with the loss of her home at the suit of a rich bank to obscure an important public interest, viz the need to ensure that the wealth currently tied up in the matrimonial home does not become economically sterile. If the rights secured to wives by the law renders vulnerable loans granted on the security of matrimonial homes, institutions will be unwilling to accept such security, thereby reducing the flow of loan capital to business enterprises. It is therefore essential that a law designed to protect the vulnerable does not render the matrimonial home unacceptable as security to financial institution . . .

Undue influence

A person who has been induced to enter into a transaction by the undue influence of another (the wrongdoer) is entitled to set that transaction aside as against the wrongdoer. Such undue influence is either actual or presumed. In *Bank of Credit and Commerce International SA v Aboody* (1988) [1990] 1 Q.B. 923 at 953 the Court of Appeal helpfully adopted the following classification.

Class 1: actual undue influence. In these cases it is necessary for the claimant to prove affirmatively that the wrongdoer exerted undue influence on the complainant to enter into the particular transaction which is impugned.

Class 2: presumed undue influence. In these cases the complainant only has to show, in the first instance, that there was a relationship of trust and confidence between the complainant and the wrongdoer of such a nature that it is fair to presume that the wrongdoer abused that relationship in procuring the complainant to enter into the impugned transaction. In class 2 cases therefore there is no need to produce evidence that actual undue influence was exerted in relation to the particular transaction impugned: once a confidential relationship has been proved, the burden then shifts to the wrongdoer to prove that the complainant entered into the impugned transaction freely, for example by showing that the complainant had independent advice. Such a confidential relationship can be established in two ways, viz:

Class 2A. Certain relationships (for example solicitor and client, medical advisor and patient) as a matter of law raise the presumption that undue influence has been exercised.

Class 2B. Even if there is no relationship falling within class 2A, if the complainant proves the de facto existence of a relationship under which the complainant generally reposed trust and confidence in the wrongdoer, the existence of such relationship raises the presumption of undue influence. In a class 2B case therefore, in the absence of evidence disproving undue influence, the complainant will succeed in setting aside the impugned transaction merely by proof that the complainant reposed trust and confidence in the wrongdoer without having to prove that the wrongdoer exerted actual undue influence or otherwise abused such trust and confidence in relation to the particular transaction impugned.

As to dispositions by a wife in favour of her husband, the law for long remained in an unsettled state. In the nineteenth century some judges took the view that the relationship was such that it fell into class 2A, i.e. as a matter of law undue influence by the husband over the wife was presumed. It was not until the decisions in *Howes v Bishop* [1909] 2 K.B. 390 and *Bank of Montreal v Stuart* [1911] A.C. 120 that it was finally determined that the relationship of husband and wife did not as a matter of law raise a presumption of undue influence within class 2A.

[Lord Browne-Wilkinson examined the authorities in detail.]

Summary

I can therefore summarise my views as follows. Where one cohabitee has entered into an obligation to stand as surety for the debts of the other cohabitee and the creditor is aware that they are cohabitees: (1) the surety obligation will be valid and enforceable by the creditor unless the suretyship was procured by the undue influence, misrepresentation or other legal wrong of the principal debtor; (2) if there has been undue influence, misrepresentation or other legal wrong by the principal debtor, unless the creditor has taken reasonable steps to satisfy himself that the surety entered into the obligation freely and in knowledge of the true facts, the creditor will be unable to enforce the surety obligation because he will be fixed with constructive notice of the surety's right to set aside the transaction; (3) unless there are special exceptional circumstances, a creditor will have taken such reasonable steps to avoid being fixed with constructive notice if the creditor warns the surety (at a meeting not attended by the principal debtor) of the amount of her potential liability and of the risks involved and advises the surety to take independent legal advice.

I should make it clear that in referring to the husband's debts I include the debts of a company in which the husband (but not the wife) has a direct financial interest.

The decision of this case

Applying those principles to this case, to the knowledge of the bank Mr and Mrs O'Brien were man and wife. The bank took a surety obligation from Mrs O'Brien, secured on the matrimonial home, to secure the debts of a company in which Mr O'Brien was interested but in which Mrs O'Brien had no direct pecuniary interest. The bank should therefore have been put on inquiry as to the circumstances in which Mrs O'Brien had agreed to stand as surety for the debt of her husband. If the Burnham branch had properly carried out the instructions from Mr Tucker of the Woolwich branch, Mrs O'Brien would have been informed that she and the matrimonial home were potentially liable for the debts of a company which had an existing liability of £107,000 and which was to be afforded an overdraft facility of £135,000. If she had been told this, it would have counteracted Mr O'Brien's misrepresentation that the liability was limited to £60,000 and would last for only three weeks. In addition according to the side letter she would have been recommended to take independent legal advice.

Unfortunately Mr Tucker's instructions were not followed and to the knowledge of the bank (through the clerk at the Burnham branch) Mrs O'Brien signed the documents without any warning of the risks or any recommendation to take legal advice. In the circumstances the bank (having failed to take reasonable steps) is fixed with constructive notice of the wrongful misrepresentation made by Mr O'Brien to Mrs O'Brien. Mrs O'Brien is therefore entitled as against the bank to set aside the legal charge on the matrimonial home securing her husband's liability to the bank.

For these reasons I would dismiss the appeal with costs.

Lords Templeman, Lowry, Slynn and Woolf agreed.

Appeal Dismissed.

NATIONAL WESTMINSTER BANK PLC v MORGAN

House of Lords [1985] A.C. 686; [1985] 2 W.L.R. 588; [1985] 1 All E.R. 821

26–003   Mr Morgan's business was in financial difficulties. He was unable to meet the mortgage repayments on his home which he owned jointly with his wife. The building society obtained a possession order. Mr Morgan asked the Bank to "re-finance" the building society loan. The bank was prepared to make a loan of £14,500 to pay off the building society loan subject to the completion of a new unlimited mortgage on the house, that is, one which would cover all the husband's liabilities to the bank. The bank manager, Mr Barrow, called at the house to obtain Mrs Morgan's signature. She had no confidence in her husband's business abilities and was concerned that the document she was being asked to sign might enable him to borrow for business purposes. Mr Barrow assured her in good faith but incorrectly that the charge only secured the amount required to refinance the mortgage. It was, however, the intention of the bank to treat the charge as so limited and it at no time sought to use it for any other purpose. Mrs Morgan had no independent legal advice. The bank now claimed possession of the house from Mrs Morgan. Her defence that the charge had been obtained by undue influence was rejected by the trial judge but upheld by the Court of Appeal. The bank appealed.

LORD SCARMAN

As to the facts, I am far from being persuaded that the trial judge fell into error when he concluded that the relationship between the bank and Mrs Morgan never went beyond the normal business relationship of banker and customer. Both Lords Justices saw the relationship between the bank and Mrs Morgan as one of confidence in which she was relying on the bank manager's advice. Each recognised the personal honesty, integrity, and good faith of Mr Barrow. Each took the view that the confidentiality of the relationship was such as to impose upon him a "fiduciary duty of care." It was his duty, in their view, to ensure that Mrs Morgan had the opportunity to make an independent and informed decision; but he failed to give her any such opportunity. They, therefore, concluded that it was a case for the presumption of undue influence.

My Lords, I believe that the Lords Justices were led into a misrepresentation of the facts by their use, as is all too frequent in this branch of the law, of words and phrases such as "confidence," "confidentiality," "fiduciary duty." There are plenty of confidential relationships which do not give rise to the presumption of undue influence (a notable example is that of husband and wife, *Bank of Montreal v Stuart* [1911] A.C. 120); and there are plenty of nonconfidential relationships in which one person relies upon the advice of another for example, many contracts for the sale of goods. Nor am I persuaded that the charge, limited as it was by Mr Barrow's declaration to securing the loan to pay off the Abbey National debt and interest during the bridging period, was disadvantageous to Mrs Morgan. It meant for her the rescue of her home upon the terms sought by her—a short-term loan at a commercial rate of interest. The Court of Appeal has not, therefore, persuaded me that the judge's understanding of the facts was incorrect.

But, further, the view of the law expressed by the Court of Appeal was, as I shall endeavour to show, mistaken. Dunn L.J., at p. 90, while accepting that in all the reported cases to which the court was referred the transactions were disadvantageous to the person influenced, took the view that in cases where public policy requires the court to apply the presumption of undue influence there is no need to prove a disadvantageous transaction. Slade L.J. also clearly held that it was not necessary to prove a disadvantageous transaction where the relationship of influence was proved to exist. Basing himself on the judgment of Cotton L.J. in *Allcard v Skinner* (1887) 36 Ch.D. 145, 171, he said, at p. 92:

"Where a transaction has been entered into between two parties who stand in the relevant relationship to one another, it is still possible that the relationship and influence arising therefrom has been abused, even though the transaction is, on the face of it, one which, in commercial terms, provides reasonably equal benefits for both parties."

I can find no support for this view of the law other than the passage in Cotton L.J.'s judgment in *Allcard v Skinner*, to which Slade L.J. referred.

[Having considered the judgment of Cotton L.J. in *Allcard v Skinner*, Lord Scarman went on:] Like Dunn L.J., I know of no reported authority where the transaction set aside was not to the manifest disadvantage of the person influenced. It would not always be a gift: it can be a "hard and inequitable" agreement (*Ormes v Beadel* (1860) 2 Gif. 166, 174); or a transaction "immoderate and irrational" (*Bank of Montreal v Stuart* [1911] A.C. 120, 137) or "unconscionable" in that it was a sale at an undervalue (*Poosathurai v Kannappa Chettiar* (1919) L.R. 47 I.A. 1, 3–4). Whatever the legal character of the transaction, the authorities show that it must constitute a disadvantage sufficiently serious to require evidence to rebut the presumption that in the circumstances of the relationship between the parties it was procured by the exercise of undue influence. In my judgment, therefore, the Court of Appeal erred in law in holding that the presumption of undue influence can arise from the evidence of the relationship of the parties without also evidence that the transaction itself was wrongful in that it constituted an advantage taken of the person subjected to the influence which, failing proof to the contrary, was explicable only on the basis that undue influence had been exercised to procure it.

[Having quoted extensively from the judgment of Lindley L.J. in *Allcard v Skinner* and that of Lord Shaw in *Poosathurai v Kannappa Chesttiar* (1919) L.R. 47 Ind.App. 1 at 3, his Lordship continued:] The wrongfulness of the transaction must, therefore, be shown: it must be one in which an unfair advantage has been taken of another. The doctrine is not limited to transactions of gift. A commercial relationship can become a relationship in which one party assumes a role of dominating influence over the other. In *Poosathurai's* case, L.R. 47 I.A. 1 the Board recognised that a sale at an undervalue could be a transaction which a court could set aside as unconscionable if it was shown or could be presumed to have been procured by the exercise of undue influence. Similarly a relationship of banker and customer may become one in which the banker acquires a dominating influence. If he does and a manifestly disadvantageous transaction is proved, there would then be room for the court to presume that it resulted from the exercise of undue influence.

This brings me to *Lloyds Bank Ltd v Bundy* [1975] Q.B. 326 CA. It was, as one would expect, conceded by counsel for the respondent that the relationship between banker and customer is not one which ordinarily gives rise to a presumption of undue influence: and that in the ordinary course of banking business a banker can explain the nature of the proposed transaction without laying himself open to a charge of undue influence. This proposition has never been in doubt, though some, it would appear, have thought that the Court of Appeal held otherwise in *Lloyds Bank Ltd v Bundy*. If any such view has gained currency, let it be destroyed now once and for all time: see Lord Denning M.R. [1975] Q.B. at p. 336f, Cairns L.J. at p. 340d, and Sir Eric Sachs, at pp. 341h-342a. Your Lordships are, of course, not concerned with the interpretation put upon the facts in that case by the Court of Appeal: the present case is not a rehearing of that case. The question which the House does have to answer is: did the court in *Lloyds Bank Ltd v Bundy* accurately state the law?

Lord Denning M.R. believed that the doctrine of undue influence could be subsumed under a general principle that English courts will grant relief where there has been "inequality of bargaining power" (p. 339). He deliberately avoided reference to the will of one party being dominated or overcome by another. The majority of the court did not follow him: they based their decision on the orthodox view of the doctrine as expounded in *Allcard v Skinner*. The opinion of the Master of the Rolls, therefore, was not the ground of the court's decision, which was to be found in the view of the majority, for whom Sir Eric Sachs delivered the leading judgment.

Nor has counsel for the respondent sought to rely on Lord Denning M.R.'s general principle; and, in my view, he was right not to do so. The doctrine of undue influence has been sufficiently developed not to need the support of a principle which by its formulation in the language of the law of contract is not appropriate to cover transactions of gift where there is no bargain. The fact of an unequal bargain will, of course, be a relevant feature in some cases of undue influence. But it can never become an appropriate basis of principle of an equitable doctrine which is concerned with transactions "not to be reasonably accounted for on the ground of friendship, relationship, charity, or other ordinary motives on which ordinary men act" (Lindley L.J. in *Allcard v Skinner* at p. 185). And even in the field of contract I question whether there is any need in the modern law to erect a general principle of relief against inequality of bargaining power. Parliament has undertaken the task—and it is essentially a legislative task—of enacting such restrictions upon freedom of contract as are in its judgment necessary to relieve against the mischief: for example, the hire-purchase and consumer protection legislation of which the Supply of Goods (Implied Terms) Act 1973, Consumer Credit Act 1974, Consumer Safety Act 1978, Supply of Goods and Services Act 1982 and Insurance Companies Act 1982 are examples. I doubt whether the courts should assume the burden of formulating further restrictions.

For these reasons, I would allow the appeal. In doing so, I would wish to give a warning. There is no precisely defined law setting limits to the equitable jurisdiction of a court to relieve against undue influence. This is the world of doctrine, not of neat and tidy rules. The courts of equity have developed a body of learning enabling relief to be granted where the law has to treat the transaction as unimpeachable unless it can be held to have been procured by undue influence. It is the unimpeachability at law of a disadvantageous transaction which is the starting-point from which the court advances to consider whether the transaction is the product merely of one's own folly or of the undue influence exercised by another. A court in the exercise of this equitable jurisdiction is a court of conscience. Definition is a poor instrument when used to determine whether a transaction is or is not unconscionable: this is a question which depends upon the particular facts of the case.

Lords Keith, Roskill, Bridge and Brandon agreed.

Appeal Allowed.

Point for reflection

26–004   If there is a right to rescission for undue influence, it is subject to the condition that the rescindor make restitution of benefits received under the transaction: see *Dunbar Bank Plc v Nadeem* [1998] 3 All E.R. 876 CA where the principles of *Newbigging v Adam*, above, Ch.14, were held (obiter) to be applicable to undue influence. In the *Dunbar Bank* case, in the impugned transaction Mrs N received a share in a lease belonging to her husband, which was charged in favour of the bank. In order to rescind the transaction, she would have had to restore the beneficial interest to him; with the effect that the Dunbar Bank would have continued to have a charge over the whole property; but the husband and wife had granted a second charge to the Nat West Bank. Morritt LJ said: "One consequence of the charge on the wife's beneficial interest being voidable, as opposed to void, is that the subsequent charge, when made, was effective in respect of her beneficial interest. In my view it follows that the wife is not now in a position to restore to the husband the unencumbered benefit which she obtained from him. She is, therefore, unable to restore the benefit derived by her from the transactions she seeks to have set aside. The consequence is that the remedy of rescission is not now available to her." Nourse and Potter LJJ did not express an opinion on this matter.

CIBC MORTGAGES PLC v PITT AND ANOTHER

House of Lords [1993] 4 All E.R. 433

26–005   In 1986 Mr and Mrs Pitt's home was valued at £270,000, subject to a mortgage for £16,700. Mr Pitt (H) wanted to borrow money on the house to buy shares. Mrs Pitt (W) was unhappy about this but eventually, under pressure, agreed. H and W signed an application form for a loan by the plaintiffs of £150,000 for the stated purpose of paying off the existing mortgage and buying a holiday home. H and W signed a mortgage offer and legal charge. W received no independent advice and no one suggested to her that she should. She did not read the documents before signing them and did not know the amount being borrowed. H used the loan to speculate on the stock market. When the market crashed in October 1987 he was unable to keep up the mortgage repayments and the plaintiff applied for an order for possession of the house. W contested the application on the ground that she had been induced to sign by H's misrepresentation, fraud and duress. The judge held that H had exercised actual undue influence and that the transaction was manifestly disadvantageous to her but, since H had not acted as the plaintiff's agent and this was not a case of W standing surety for H's debt but a loan jointly to H and W, W's claim failed. The Court of Appeal dismissed W's appeal on the ground that the transaction was not manifestly disadvantageous. W appealed.

LORD BROWNE-WILKINSON

I have no doubt that the decision in *Morgan* [above, para.26–003] does not extend to cases of actual undue influence. Despite two references in Lord Scarman's speech to cases of actual undue influence, as I read his speech he was primarily concerned to establish that disadvantage had to be shown, not as a constituent element of the cause of action for undue influence, but in order to raise a presumption of undue influence within class 2. That was the only subject matter before the House of Lords in *Morgan* and the passage I have already cited was directed solely to that point. With the exception of a passing reference to *Ormes v Beadel* (1860) 2 Giff 166, 66 ER 70 all the cases referred to by Lord Scarman were cases of presumed undue influence. In the circumstances, I do not think that this House can have been intending to lay down any general principle applicable to all claims of undue influence, whether actual or presumed.

Whatever the merits of requiring a complainant to show manifest disadvantage in order to raise a class 2 presumption of undue influence, in my judgment there is no logic in imposing such a requirement where actual undue influence has been exercised and proved. Actual undue influence is a species of fraud. Like any other victim of fraud, a person who has been induced by undue influence to carry out a transaction which he did not freely and knowingly enter into is entitled to have that transaction set aside as of right. No case decided before *Morgan* was cited (nor am I aware of any) in which a transaction proved to have been obtained by actual undue influence has been upheld nor is there any case in which a court has even considered whether the transaction was, or was not, advantageous. A man guilty of fraud is no more entitled to argue that the transaction was beneficial to the person defrauded than is a man who has procured a transaction by misrepresentation. The effect of the wrongdoer's conduct is to prevent the wronged party from bringing a free will and properly informed mind to bear on the proposed transaction which accordingly must be set aside in equity as a matter of justice.

I therefore hold that a claimant who proves actual undue influence is not under the further burden of proving that the transaction induced by undue influence was manifestly disadvantageous: he is entitled as of right to have it set aside.

I should add that the exact limits of the decision in *Morgan* may have to be considered in the future. The difficulty is to establish the relationship between the law as laid down in *Morgan* and the long standing principle laid down in the abuse of confidence cases, viz the law requires those in a fiduciary position who enter into transactions with those to whom they owe fiduciary duties to establish affirmatively that the transaction was a fair one . . . The abuse of confidence principle is founded on considerations of general public policy, viz that in order to protect those to whom fiduciaries owe duties as a class from exploitation by fiduciaries as a class, the law imposes a heavy duty on fiduciaries to show the righteousness of the transactions they enter into with those to whom they owe such duties. This principle is in sharp contrast with the view of this House in *Morgan* that in cases of presumed undue influence (a) the law is not based on considerations of public policy and (b) that it is for the claimant to prove that the transaction was disadvantageous rather than for the fiduciary to prove that it was not disadvantageous. Unfortunately, the attention of this House in *Morgan* was not drawn to the abuse of confidence cases and therefore the interaction between the two principles (if indeed they are two separate principles) remains obscure: see also 48 M.L.R. 579 and *Wright v Carter* [1903] 1 Ch 27.

Notice

Even though, in my view, Mrs Pitt is entitled to set aside the transaction as against Mr Pitt, she has to establish that in some way the plaintiff is affected by the wrongdoing of Mr Pitt so as to be entitled to set aside the legal charge as against the plaintiff.

Applying the decision of this House in *O'Brien*, Mrs Pitt has established actual undue influence by Mr Pitt.

The plaintiff will not however be affected by such undue influence unless Mr Pitt was, in a real sense, acting as agent of the plaintiff in procuring Mrs Pitt's agreement or the plaintiff had actual or constructive notice of the undue influence. The judge has correctly held that Mr Pitt was not acting as agent for the plaintiff. The plaintiff had no actual notice of the undue influence. What, then, was known to the plaintiff that could put it on inquiry so as to fix it with constructive notice?

So far as the plaintiff was aware, the transaction consisted of a joint loan to the husband and wife to finance the discharge of an existing mortgage on 26 Alexander Avenue and, as to the balance, to be applied in buying a holiday home. The loan was advanced to both husband and wife jointly. There was nothing to indicate to the plaintiff that this was anything other than a normal advance to a husband and wife for their joint benefit.

Mr Price Q.C. for Mrs Pitt argued that the invalidating tendency which reflects the risk of there being class 2B undue influence was, in itself, sufficient to put the plaintiff on inquiry. I reject this submission without hesitation. It accords neither with justice nor with practical common sense. If third parties were to be fixed with constructive notice of undue influence in relation to every transaction between husband and wife, such transactions would become almost impossible. On every purchase of a home in joint names, the building society or bank financing the purchase would have to insist on meeting the wife separately from her husband, advise her as to the nature of the transaction and recommend her to take legal advice separate from that of her husband. If that were not done, the financial institution would have to run the risk of a subsequent attempt by the wife to avoid her liabilities under the mortgage on the grounds of undue influence or misrepresentation. To establish the law in that sense would not benefit the average married couple and would discourage financial institutions from making the advance.

What distinguishes the case of the joint advance from the surety case is that, in the latter, there is not only the possibility of undue influence having been exercised but also the increased risk of it having in fact been exercised because, at least on its face, the guarantee by a wife of her husband's debts is not for her financial benefit. It is the combination of these two factors that puts the creditor on inquiry.

For these reasons I agree with the Court of Appeal and would dismiss the appeal.

Lords Templeman, Lowry, Slynn and Woolf agreed.

Appeal Dismissed.

ROYAL BANK OF SCOTLAND PLC v ETRIDGE (NO.2)

House of Lords [2001] UKHL 44

LORD NICHOLLS OF BIRKENHEAD

My Lords,

26-006   5. Before your Lordships' House are appeals in eight cases. Each case arises out of a transaction in which a wife charged her interest in her home in favour of a bank as security for her husband's indebtedness or the indebtedness of a company through which he carried on business. The wife later asserted she signed the charge under the undue influence of her husband. In *Barclays Bank Plc v O'Brien* [1994] 1 AC 180 your Lordships enunciated the principles applicable in this type of case. Since then, many cases have come before the courts, testing the implications of the *O'Brien* decision in a variety of different factual situations. Seven of the present appeals are of this character. In each case the bank sought to enforce the charge signed by the wife. The bank claimed an order for possession of the matrimonial home. The wife raised a defence that the bank was on notice that her concurrence in the transaction had been procured by her husband's undue influence. The eighth appeal concerns a claim by a wife for damages from a solicitor who advised her before she entered into a guarantee obligation of this character.

Undue influence

6. The issues raised by these appeals make it necessary to go back to first principles. Undue influence is one of the grounds of relief developed by the courts of equity as a court of conscience. The objective is to ensure that the influence of one person over another is not abused. In everyday life people constantly seek to influence the decisions of others. They seek to persuade those with whom they are dealing to enter into transactions,

whether great or small. The law has set limits to the means properly employable for this purpose. To this end the common law developed a principle of duress. Originally this was narrow in its scope, restricted to the more blatant forms of physical coercion, such as personal violence.

7. Here, as elsewhere in the law, equity supplemented the common law. Equity extended the reach of the law to other unacceptable forms of persuasion. The law will investigate the manner in which the intention to enter into the transaction was secured: "how the intention was produced", in the oft repeated words of Lord Eldon L.C., from as long ago as 1807 (*Huguenin v Baseley* 14 Ves 273, 300). If the intention was produced by an unacceptable means, the law will not permit the transaction to stand. The means used is regarded as an exercise of improper or "undue" influence, and hence unacceptable, whenever the consent thus procured ought not fairly to be treated as the expression of a person's free will. It is impossible to be more precise or definitive. The circumstances in which one person acquires influence over another, and the manner in which influence may be exercised, vary too widely to permit of any more specific criterion.

8. Equity identified broadly two forms of unacceptable conduct. The first comprises overt acts of improper pressure or coercion such as unlawful threats. Today there is much overlap with the principle of duress as this principle has subsequently developed. The second form arises out of a relationship between two persons where one has acquired over another a measure of influence, or ascendancy, of which the ascendant person then takes unfair advantage. An example from the 19th century, when much of this law developed, is a case where an impoverished father prevailed upon his inexperienced children to charge their reversionary interests under their parents' marriage settlement with payment of his mortgage debts: see *Bainbrigge v Browne* (1881) 18 Ch D 188.

9. In cases of this latter nature the influence one person has over another provides scope for misuse without any specific overt acts of persuasion. The relationship between two individuals may be such that, without more, one of them is disposed to agree a course of action proposed by the other. Typically this occurs when one person places trust in another to look after his affairs and interests, and the latter betrays this trust by preferring his own interests. He abuses the influence he has acquired. In *Allcard v Skinner* (1887) 36 Ch D 145, a case well known to every law student, Lindley L.J., at p 181, described this class of cases as those in which it was the duty of one party to advise the other or to manage his property for him. In *Zamet v Hyman* [1961] 1 WLR 1442, 1444–1445 Lord Evershed M.R. referred to relationships where one party owed the other an obligation of candour and protection.

10. The law has long recognised the need to prevent abuse of influence in these "relationship" cases despite the absence of evidence of overt acts of persuasive conduct. The types of relationship, such as parent and child, in which this principle falls to be applied cannot be listed exhaustively. Relationships are infinitely various. Sir Guenter Treitel Q.C. has rightly noted that the question is whether one party has reposed sufficient trust and confidence in the other, rather than whether the relationship between the parties belongs to a particular type: see *Treitel, The Law of Contract*, 10th ed (1999), pp 380–381. For example, the relation of banker and customer will not normally meet this criterion, but exceptionally it may: see *National Westminster Bank Plc v Morgan* [1985] AC 686, 707–709.

11. Even this test is not comprehensive. The principle is not confined to cases of abuse of trust and confidence. It also includes, for instance, cases where a vulnerable person has been exploited. Indeed, there is no single touchstone for determining whether the principle is applicable. Several expressions have been used in an endeavour to encapsulate the essence: trust and confidence, reliance, dependence or vulnerability on the one hand and ascendancy, domination or control on the other. None of these descriptions is perfect. None is all embracing. Each has its proper place.

12. In *CIBC Mortgages Plc v Pitt* [1994] 1 AC 200 your Lordships' House decided that in cases of undue influence disadvantage is not a necessary ingredient of the cause of action. It is not essential that the transaction should be disadvantageous to the pressurised or influenced person, either in financial terms or in any other way. However, in the nature of things, questions of undue influence will not usually arise, and the exercise of undue influence is unlikely to occur, where the transaction is innocuous. The issue is likely to arise only when, in some respect, the transaction was disadvantageous either from the outset or as matters turned out.

Burden of proof and presumptions

13. Whether a transaction was brought about by the exercise of undue influence is a question of fact. Here, as elsewhere, the general principle is that he who asserts a wrong has been committed must prove it. The burden of proving an allegation of undue influence rests upon the person who claims to have been wronged. This is the general rule. The evidence required to discharge the burden of proof depends on the nature of the alleged undue influence, the personality of the parties, their relationship, the extent to which the transaction cannot readily be accounted for by the ordinary motives of ordinary persons in that relationship, and all the circumstances of the case.

14. Proof that the complainant placed trust and confidence in the other party in relation to the management of the complainant's financial affairs, coupled with a transaction which calls for explanation, will normally be sufficient, failing satisfactory evidence to the contrary, to discharge the burden of proof. On proof of these two matters the stage is set for the court to infer that, in the absence of a satisfactory explanation, the transaction can only have been procured by undue influence. In other words, proof of these two facts is prima facie evidence that the defendant abused the influence he acquired in the parties' relationship. He preferred his own interests. He did not behave fairly to the other. So the evidential burden then shifts to him. It is for him to produce evidence to counter the inference which otherwise should be drawn.

15. The case of *Bainbrigge v Browne*, 18 Ch D 188, already mentioned, provides a good illustration of this commonplace type of forensic exercise. Fry J. held, at p 196, that there was no direct evidence upon which he could rely as proving undue pressure by the father. But there existed circumstances "from which the court will infer pressure and undue influence." None of the children were entirely emancipated from their father's control. None seemed conversant with business. These circumstances were such as to cast the burden of proof upon the father. He had made no attempt to discharge that burden. He did not appear in court at all. So the children's claim succeeded. Again, more recently, in *National Westminster Bank Plc v Morgan* [1985] AC 686, 707, Lord Scarman noted that a relationship of banker and customer may become one in which a banker acquires a dominating influence. If he does, and a manifestly disadvantageous transaction is proved, "there would then be room" for a court to presume that it resulted from the exercise of undue influence.

16. Generations of equity lawyers have conventionally described this situation as one in which a presumption of undue influence arises. This use of the term "presumption" is descriptive of a shift in the evidential onus on a question of fact. When a plaintiff succeeds by this route he does so because he has succeeded in establishing a case of undue influence. The court has drawn appropriate inferences of fact upon a balanced consideration of the whole of the evidence at the end of a trial in which the burden of proof rested upon the plaintiff. The use, in the course of the trial, of the forensic tool of a shift in the evidential burden of proof should not be permitted to obscure the overall position. These cases are the equitable counterpart of common law cases where the principle of res ipsa loquitur is invoked. There is a rebuttable evidential presumption of undue influence.

17. The availability of this forensic tool in cases founded on abuse of influence arising from the parties' relationship has led to this type of case sometimes being labelled "presumed undue influence". This is by way of contrast with cases involving actual pressure or the like, which are labelled "actual undue influence": see *Bank of Credit and Commerce International SA v Aboody* [1990] I QB 923, 953, and *Royal Bank of Scotland Plc v Etridge (No 2)* [1998] 4 All ER 705, 711–712, paras 5–7. This usage can be a little confusing. In many cases where a plaintiff has claimed that the defendant abused the influence he acquired in a relationship of trust and confidence the plaintiff has succeeded by recourse to the rebuttable evidential presumption. But this need not be so. Such a plaintiff may succeed even where this presumption is not available to him; for instance, where the impugned transaction was not one which called for an explanation.

18. The evidential presumption discussed above is to be distinguished sharply from a different form of presumption which arises in some cases. The law has adopted a sternly protective attitude towards certain types of relationship in which one party acquires influence over another who is vulnerable and dependent and where, moreover, substantial gifts by the influenced or vulnerable person are not normally to be expected. Examples of relationships within this special class are parent and child, guardian and ward, trustee and beneficiary, solicitor and client, and medical adviser and patient. In these cases the law presumes, irrebuttably, that one party had influence over the other. The complainant need not prove he actually reposed trust and confidence in the other party. It is sufficient for him to prove the existence of the type of relationship.

19. It is now well established that husband and wife is not one of the relationships to which this latter principle applies. In *Yerkey v Jones* (1939) 63 CLR 649, 675 Dixon J. explained the reason. The Court of Chancery was not blind to the opportunities of obtaining and unfairly using influence over a wife which a husband often possesses. But there is nothing unusual or strange in a wife, from motives of affection or for other reasons, conferring substantial financial benefits on her husband. Although there is no presumption, the court will nevertheless note, as a matter of fact, the opportunities for abuse which flow from a wife's confidence in her husband. The court will take this into account with all the other evidence in the case. Where there is evidence that a husband has taken unfair advantage of his influence over his wife, or her confidence in him, "it is not difficult for the wife to establish her title to relief": see *In re Lloyds Bank Ltd, Bomze v Bomze* [1931] 1 Ch 289, at p 302, per Maugham J.

Independent advice

20. Proof that the complainant received advice from a third party before entering into the impugned transaction is one of the matters a court takes into account when weighing all the evidence. The weight, or importance, to be attached to such advice depends on all the circumstances. In the normal course, advice from a solicitor or other outside adviser can be expected to bring home to a complainant a proper understanding of what he or she is about to do. But a person may understand fully the implications of a proposed transaction, for instance, a substantial gift, and yet still be acting under the undue influence of another. Proof of outside advice does not, of itself, necessarily show that the subsequent completion of the transaction was free from the exercise of undue influence. Whether it will be proper to infer that outside advice had an emancipating effect, so that the transaction was not brought about by the exercise of undue influence, is a question of fact to be decided having regard to all the evidence in the case.

Manifest disadvantage

21. As already noted, there are two prerequisites to the evidential shift in the burden of proof from the complainant to the other party. First, that the complainant reposed trust and confidence in the other party, or the other party acquired ascendancy over the complainant. Second, that the transaction is not readily explicable by the relationship of the parties.

22. Lindley L.J. summarised this second prerequisite in the leading authority of *Allcard v Skinner*, 36 Ch D 145, where the donor parted with almost all her property. Lindley L.J. pointed out that where a gift of a small amount is made to a person standing in a confidential relationship to the donor, some proof of the exercise of the influence of the donee must be given. The mere existence of the influence is not enough. He continued, at p 185:

> "But if the gift is so large as not to be reasonably accounted for on the ground of friendship, relationship, charity, or other ordinary motives on which ordinary men act, the burden is upon the donee to support the gift."

In *Bank of Montreal v Stuart* [1911] AC 120, 137 Lord Macnaghten used the phrase "immoderate and irrational" to describe this concept.

23. The need for this second prerequisite has recently been questioned: see Nourse L.J. in *Barclays Bank Plc v Coleman* [2001] QB, 20, 30–32, one of the cases under appeal before your Lordships' House. Mr Sher Q.C. invited your Lordships to depart from the decision of the House on this point in *National Westminster Bank Plc v Morgan* [1985] AC 686.

24. My Lords, this is not an invitation I would accept. The second prerequisite, as expressed by Lindley L.J., is good sense. It is a necessary limitation upon the width of the first prerequisite. It would be absurd for the law to presume that every gift by a child to a parent, or every transaction between a client and his solicitor or between a patient and his doctor, was brought about by undue influence unless the contrary is affirmatively proved. Such a presumption would be too far-reaching. The law would out of touch with everyday life if the presumption were to apply to every Christmas or birthday gift by a child to a parent, or to an agreement whereby a client or patient agrees to be responsible for the reasonable fees of his legal or medical adviser. The law would be rightly open to ridicule, for transactions such as these are unexceptionable. They do not suggest that something may be amiss. So something more is needed before the law reverses the burden of proof, something which calls for an explanation. When that something more is present, the greater the disadvantage to the vulnerable person, the more cogent must be the explanation before the presumption will be regarded as rebutted.

25. This was the approach adopted by Lord Scarman in *National Westminster Bank Plc v Morgan* [1985] AC 686, 703–707. He cited Lindley L.J.'s observations in *Allcard v Skinner*, 36 Ch D 145, 185, which I have set out above. He noted that whatever the legal character of the transaction, it must constitute a disadvantage sufficiently serious to require evidence to rebut the presumption that in the circumstances of the parties' relationship, it was procured by the exercise of undue influence. Lord Scarman concluded, at p 704:

> "The Court of Appeal erred in law in holding that the presumption of undue influence can arise from the evidence of the relationship of the parties without also evidence that the transaction itself was wrongful in that it constituted *an advantage taken of the person subjected to the influence which, failing proof to the contrary, was explicable only on the basis that undue influence had been exercised to procure it*." (Emphasis added)

26. Lord Scarman attached the label "manifest disadvantage" to this second ingredient necessary to raise the presumption. This label has been causing difficulty. It may be apt enough when applied to straightforward transactions such as a substantial gift or a sale at an undervalue. But experience has now shown that this

expression can give rise to misunderstanding. The label is being understood and applied in a way which does not accord with the meaning intended by Lord Scarman, its originator.

27. The problem has arisen in the context of wives guaranteeing payment of their husband's business debts. In recent years judge after judge has grappled with the baffling question whether a wife's guarantee of her husband's bank overdraft, together with a charge on her share of the matrimonial home, was a transaction manifestly to her disadvantage.

28. In a narrow sense, such a transaction plainly ("manifestly") is disadvantageous to the wife. She undertakes a serious financial obligation, and in return she personally receives nothing. But that would be to take an unrealistically blinkered view of such a transaction. Unlike the relationship of solicitor and client or medical adviser and patient, in the case of husband and wife there are inherent reasons why such a transaction may well be for her benefit. Ordinarily, the fortunes of husband and wife are bound up together. If the husband's business is the source of the family income, the wife has a lively interest in doing what she can to support the business. A wife's affection and self-interest run hand-in-hand in inclining her to join with her husband in charging the matrimonial home, usually a jointly-owned asset, to obtain the financial facilities needed by the business. The finance may be needed to start a new business, or expand a promising business, or rescue an ailing business.

29. Which, then, is the correct approach to adopt in deciding whether a transaction is disadvantageous to the wife: the narrow approach, or the wider approach? The answer is neither. The answer lies in discarding a label which gives rise to this sort of ambiguity. The better approach is to adhere more directly to the test outlined by Lindley L.J. in *Allcard v Skinner*, 36 Ch D 145, and adopted by Lord Scarman in *National Westminster Bank Plc v Morgan* [1985] AC 686, in the passages I have cited.

30. I return to husband and wife cases. I do not think that, *in the ordinary course*, a guarantee of the character I have mentioned is to be regarded as a transaction which, failing proof to the contrary, is explicable only on the basis that it has been procured by the exercise of undue influence by the husband. Wives frequently enter into such transactions. There are good and sufficient reasons why they are willing to do so, despite the risks involved for them and their families. They may be enthusiastic. They may not. They may be less optimistic than their husbands about the prospects of the husbands' businesses. They may be anxious, perhaps exceedingly so. But this is a far cry from saying that such transactions as a class are to be regarded as prima facie evidence of the exercise of undue influence by husbands.

31. I have emphasised the phrase "in the ordinary course". There will be cases where a wife's signature of a guarantee or a charge of her share in the matrimonial home does call for explanation. Nothing I have said above is directed at such a case.

A cautionary note

32. I add a cautionary note, prompted by some of the first instance judgments in the cases currently being considered by the House. It concerns the general approach to be adopted by a court when considering whether a wife's guarantee of her husband's bank overdraft was procured by her husband's undue influence. Undue influence has a connotation of impropriety. In the eye of the law, undue influence means that influence has been misused. Statements or conduct by a husband which do not pass beyond the bounds of what may be expected of a reasonable husband in the circumstances should not, without more, be castigated as undue influence. Similarly, when a husband is forecasting the future of his business, and expressing his hopes or fears, a degree of hyperbole may be only natural. Courts should not too readily treat such exaggerations as misstatements.

33. Inaccurate explanations of a proposed transaction are a different matter. So are cases where a husband, in whom a wife has reposed trust and confidence for the management of their financial affairs, prefers his interests to hers and makes a choice for both of them on that footing. Such a husband abuses the influence he has. He fails to discharge the obligation of candour and fairness he owes a wife who is looking to him to make the major financial decisions.

The complainant and third parties: suretyship transactions

34. The problem considered in *O'Brien's* case and raised by the present appeals is of comparatively recent origin. It arises out of the substantial growth in home ownership over the last 30 or 40 years and, as part of that development, the great increase in the number of homes owned jointly by husbands and wives. More than two-thirds of householders in the United Kingdom now own their own homes. For most home-owning couples, their homes are their most valuable asset. They must surely be free, if they so wish, to use this asset as a means of raising money, whether for the purpose of the husband's business or for any other purpose. Their home is their property. The law should not restrict them in the use they may make of it. Bank finance is in fact by far the most important source of external capital for small businesses with fewer than ten employees. These

businesses comprise about 95 percent of all businesses in the country, responsible for nearly one-third of all employment. Finance raised by second mortgages on the principal's home is a significant source of capital for the start-up of small businesses.

35. If the freedom of home-owners to make economic use of their homes is not to be frustrated, a bank must be able to have confidence that a wife's signature of the necessary guarantee and charge will be as binding upon her as is the signature of anyone else on documents which he or she may sign. Otherwise banks will not be willing to lend money on the security of a jointly owned house or flat.

36. At the same time, the high degree of trust and confidence and emotional interdependence which normally characterises a marriage relationship provides scope for abuse. One party may take advantage of the other's vulnerability. Unhappily, such abuse does occur. Further, it is all too easy for a husband, anxious or even desperate for bank finance, to misstate the position in some particular or to mislead the wife, wittingly or unwittingly, in some other way. The law would be seriously defective if it did not recognise these realities.

37. In *O'Brien's* case this House decided where the balance should be held between these competing interests. On the one side, there is the need to protect a wife against a husband's undue influence. On the other side, there is the need for the bank to be able to have reasonable confidence in the strength of its security. Otherwise it would not provide the required money. The problem lies in finding the course best designed to protect wives in a minority of cases without unreasonably hampering the giving and taking of security. The House produced a practical solution. The House decided what are the steps a bank should take to ensure it is not affected by any claim the wife may have that her signature of the documents was procured by the undue influence or other wrong of her husband. Like every compromise, the outcome falls short of achieving in full the objectives of either of the two competing interests. In particular, the steps required of banks will not guarantee that, in future, wives will not be subjected to undue influence or misled when standing as sureties. Short of prohibiting this type of suretyship transaction altogether, there is no way of achieving that result, desirable although it is. What passes between a husband and wife in this regard in the privacy of their own home is not capable of regulation or investigation as a prelude to the wife entering into a suretyship transaction.

38. The jurisprudential route by which the House reached its conclusion in *O'Brien's* case has attracted criticism from some commentators. It has been said to involve artificiality and thereby create uncertainty in the law. I must first consider this criticism. In the ordinary course a bank which takes a guarantee security from the wife of its customer will be altogether ignorant of any undue influence the customer may have exercised in order to secure the wife's concurrence. In *O'Brien* Lord Browne-Wilkinson prayed in aid the doctrine of constructive notice. In circumstances he identified, a creditor is put on inquiry. When that is so, the creditor "will have constructive notice of the wife's rights" unless the creditor takes reasonable steps to satisfy himself that the wife's agreement to stand surety has been properly obtained: see [1994] 1 AC 180, 196.

39. Lord Browne-Wilkinson would be the first to recognise this is not a conventional use of the equitable concept of constructive notice. The traditional use of this concept concerns the circumstances in which a transferee of property who acquires a legal estate from a transferor with a defective title may nonetheless obtain a good title, that is, a better title than the transferor had. That is not the present case. The bank acquires its charge from the wife, and there is nothing wrong with her title to her share of the matrimonial home. The transferor wife is seeking to resile from the very transaction she entered into with the bank, on the ground that her apparent consent was procured by the undue influence or other misconduct, such as misrepresentation, of a third party (her husband). She is seeking to set aside her contract of guarantee and, with it, the charge she gave to the bank.

40. The traditional view of equity in this tripartite situation seems to be that a person in the position of the wife will only be relieved of her bargain if the other party to the transaction (the bank, in the present instance) was privy to the conduct which led to the wife's entry into the transaction. Knowledge is required: see *Cobbett v Brock* (1855) 20 Beav 524, 528, 531, per Sir John Romilly M.R., *Kempson v Ashbee* (1874) LR 10 Ch App 15, 21, per James L.J., and *Bainbrigge v Browne,* 18 Ch D 188, 197, per Fry J. The law imposes no obligation on one party to a transaction to check whether the other party's concurrence was obtained by undue influence. But *O'Brien* has introduced into the law the concept that, in certain circumstances, a party to a contract may lose the benefit of his contract, entered into in good faith, if he *ought* to have known that the other's concurrence had been procured by the misconduct of a third party.

41. There is a further respect in which *O'Brien* departed from conventional concepts. Traditionally, a person is *deemed* to have notice (that is, he has "constructive" notice) of a prior right when he does not actually know of it but would have learned of it had he made the requisite inquiries. A purchaser will be treated as having constructive notice of all that a reasonably prudent purchaser would have discovered. In the present type of case, the steps a bank is required to take, lest it have constructive notice that the wife's concurrence was procured improperly by her husband, do not consist of making inquiries. Rather, *O'Brien* envisages that the steps taken

by the bank will reduce, or even eliminate, the risk of the wife entering into the transaction under any misapprehension or as a result of undue influence by her husband. The steps are not concerned to discover whether the wife has been wronged by her husband in this way. The steps are concerned to minimise the risk that such a wrong may be committed.

42. These novelties do not point to the conclusion that the decision of this House in *O'Brien* is leading the law astray. Lord Browne-Wilkinson acknowledged he might be extending the law: see [1994] 1 AC 180, 197. Some development was sorely needed. The law had to find a way of giving wives a reasonable measure of protection, without adding unreasonably to the expense involved in entering into guarantee transactions of the type under consideration. The protection had to extend also to any misrepresentations made by a husband to his wife. In a situation where there is a substantial risk the husband may exercise his influence improperly regarding the provision of security for his business debts, there is an increased risk that explanations of the transaction given by him to his wife may be misleadingly incomplete or even inaccurate.

43. The route selected in *O'Brien* ought not to have an unsettling effect on established principles of contract. *O'Brien* concerned suretyship transactions. These are tripartite transactions. They involve the debtor as well as the creditor and the guarantor. The guarantor enters into the transaction at the request of the debtor. The guarantor assumes obligations. On the face of the transaction the guarantor usually receives no benefit in return, unless the guarantee is being given on a commercial basis. Leaving aside cases where the relationship between the surety and the debtor is commercial, a guarantee transaction is one-sided so far as the guarantor is concerned. The creditor knows this. Thus the decision in *O'Brien* is directed at a class of contracts which has special features of its own. That said, I must at a later stage in this speech return to the question of the wider implications of the *O'Brien* decision.

The threshold: when the bank is put on inquiry

44. In *O'Brien* the House considered the circumstances in which a bank, or other creditor, is "put on inquiry." Strictly this is a misnomer. As already noted, a bank is not required to make inquiries. But it will be convenient to use the terminology which has now become accepted in this context. The House set a low level for the threshold which must be crossed before a bank is put on inquiry. For practical reasons the level is set much lower than is required to satisfy a court that, failing contrary evidence, the court may infer that the transaction was procured by undue influence. Lord Browne-Wilkinson said ([1994] 1 AC 180, 196):

> "Therefore in my judgment a creditor in put on inquiry when a wife offers to stand surety for her husband's debts by the combination of two factors: (a) the transaction is on its face not to the financial advantage of the wife; and (b) there is a substantial risk in transactions of that kind that, in procuring the wife to act as surety, the husband has committed a legal or equitable wrong that entitles the wife to set aside the transaction."

In my view, this passage, read in context, is to be taken to mean, quite simply, that a bank is put on inquiry whenever a wife offers to stand surety for her husband's debts.

45. The Court of Appeal, comprising Stuart-Smith, Millett and Morritt L.JJ., interpreted this passage more restrictively. The threshold, the court said, is somewhat higher. Where condition (a) is satisfied, the bank is put on inquiry if, but only if, the bank is aware that the parties are cohabiting or that the particular surety places implicit trust and confidence in the principal debtor in relation to her financial affairs: see *Royal Bank of Scotland Plc v Etridge (No 2)* [1998] 4 All ER 705, 719.

46. I respectfully disagree. I do not read (a) and (b) as factual conditions which must be proved in each case before a bank is put on inquiry. I do not understand Lord Browne-Wilkinson to have been saying that, in husband and wife cases, whether the bank is put on inquiry depends on its state of knowledge of the parties' marriage, or of the degree of trust and confidence the particular wife places in her husband in relation to her financial affairs. That would leave banks in a state of considerable uncertainty in a situation where it is important they should know clearly where they stand. The test should be simple and clear and easy to apply in a wide range of circumstances. I read (a) and (b) as Lord Browne-Wilkinson's broad explanation of the reason why a creditor is put on inquiry when a wife offers to stand surety for her husband's debts. These are the two factors which, taken together, constitute the underlying rationale.

47. The position is likewise if the husband stands surety for his wife's debts. Similarly, in the case of unmarried couples, whether heterosexual or homosexual, where the bank is aware of the relationship: see Lord Browne-Wilkinson in *O'Brien's* case, at p 198. Cohabitation is not essential. The Court of Appeal rightly so decided in *Massey v Midland Bank Plc* [1995] 1 All ER 929: see Steyn L.J., at p 933.

48. As to the type of transactions where a bank is put on inquiry, the case where a wife becomes surety for her husband's debts is, in this context, a straightforward case. The bank is put on inquiry. On the other side

of the line is the case where money is being advanced, or has been advanced, to husband and wife jointly. In such a case the bank is not put on inquiry, unless the bank is aware the loan is being made for the husband's purposes, as distinct from their joint purposes. That was decided in *CIBC Mortgages Plc v Pitt* [1994] 1 AC 200.

49. Less clear cut is the case where the wife becomes surety for the debts of a company whose shares are held by her and her husband. Her shareholding may be nominal, or she may have a minority shareholding or an equal shareholding with her husband. In my view the bank is put on inquiry in such cases, even when the wife is a director or secretary of the company. Such cases cannot be equated with joint loans. The shareholding interests, and the identity of the directors, are not a reliable guide to the identity of the persons who actually have the conduct of the company's business.

The steps a bank should take

50. The principal area of controversy on these appeals concerns the steps a bank should take when it has been put on inquiry. In *O'Brien* Lord Browne-Wilkinson, at [1994] 1 AC 180, 196–197, said that a bank can reasonably be expected to take steps to bring home to the wife the risk she is running by standing as surety and to advise her to take independent advice. That test is applicable to *past* transactions. All the cases now before your Lordships' House fall into this category. For the *future* a bank satisfies these requirements if it insists that the wife attend a private meeting with a representative of the bank at which she is told of the extent of her liability as surety, warned of the risk she is running and urged to take independent legal advice. In exceptional cases the bank, to be safe, has to insist that the wife is separately advised.

51. The practice of the banks involved in the present cases, and it seems reasonable to assume this is the practice of banks generally, is not to have a private meeting with the wife. Nor do the banks themselves take any other steps to bring home to the wife the risk she is running. This has continued to be the practice since the decision in *O'Brien's* case. Banks consider they would stand to lose more than they would gain by holding a private meeting with the wife. They are, apparently, unwilling to assume the responsibility of advising the wife at such a meeting. Instead, the banking practice remains, as before, that in general the bank requires a wife to seek legal advice. The bank seeks written confirmation from a solicitor that he has explained the nature and effect of the documents to the wife.

52. Many of the difficulties which have arisen in the present cases stem from serious deficiencies, or alleged deficiencies, in the quality of the legal advice given to the wives. I say "alleged", because three of the appeals before your Lordships' House have not proceeded beyond the interlocutory stage. The banks successfully applied for summary judgment. In these cases the wife's allegations, made in affidavit form, have not been tested by cross-examination. On behalf of the wives it has been submitted that under the current practice the legal advice is often perfunctory in the extreme and, further, that everyone, including the banks, knows this. Independent legal advice is a fiction. The system is a charade. In practice it provides little or no protection for a wife who is under a misapprehension about the risks involved or who is being coerced into signing. She may not even know the present state of her husband's indebtedness.

53. My Lords, it is plainly neither desirable nor practicable that banks should be required to attempt to discover for themselves whether a wife's consent is being procured by the exercise of undue influence of her husband. This is not a step the banks should be expected to take. Nor, further, is it desirable or practicable that banks should be expected to insist on confirmation from a solicitor that the solicitor has satisfied himself that the wife's consent has not been procured by undue influence. As already noted, the circumstances in which banks are put on inquiry are extremely wide. They embrace every case where a wife is entering into a suretyship transaction in respect of her husband's debts. Many, if not most, wives would be understandably outraged by having to respond to the sort of questioning which would be appropriate before a responsible solicitor could give such a confirmation. In any event, solicitors are not equipped to carry out such an exercise in any really worthwhile way, and they will usually lack the necessary materials. Moreover, the legal costs involved, which would inevitably fall on the husband who is seeking financial assistance from the bank, would be substantial. To require such an intrusive, inconclusive and expensive exercise in every case would be an altogether disproportionate response to the need to protect those cases, presumably a small minority, where a wife is being wronged.

54. The furthest a bank can be expected to go is to take reasonable steps to satisfy itself that the wife has had brought home to her, in a meaningful way, the practical implications of the proposed transaction. This does not wholly eliminate the risk of undue influence or misrepresentation. But it does mean that a wife enters into a transaction with her eyes open so far as the basic elements of the transaction are concerned.

55. This is the point at which, in the *O'Brien* case, the House decided that the balance between the competing interests should be held. A bank may itself provide the necessary information directly to the wife. Indeed,

it is best equipped to do so. But banks are not following that course. Ought they to be obliged to do so in every case? I do not think Lord Browne-Wilkinson so stated in *O'Brien*. I do not understand him to have said that a personal meeting was the only way a bank could discharge its obligation to bring home to the wife the risks she is running. It seems to me that, provided a suitable alternative is available, banks ought not to be compelled to take this course. Their reasons for not wishing to hold a personal meeting are understandable. Commonly, when a bank seeks to enforce a security provided by a customer, it is met with a defence based on assurances alleged to have been given orally by a branch manager at an earlier stage: that the bank would continue to support the business, that the bank would not call in its loan, and so forth. Lengthy litigation ensues. Sometimes the allegations prove to be well founded, sometimes not. Banks are concerned to avoid the prospect of similar litigation which would arise in guarantee cases if they were to adopt a practice of holding a meeting with a wife at which the bank's representative would explain the proposed guarantee transaction. It is not unreasonable for the banks to prefer that this task should be undertaken by an independent legal adviser.

56. I shall return later to the steps a bank should take when it follows this course. Suffice to say, these steps, together with advice from a solicitor acting for the wife, ought to provide the substance of the protection which *O'Brien* intended a wife should have. Ordinarily it will be reasonable that a bank should be able to rely upon confirmation from a solicitor, acting for the wife, that he has advised the wife appropriately.

57. The position will be otherwise if the bank knows that the solicitor has not duly advised the wife or, I would add, if the bank knows facts from which it ought to have realised that the wife has not received the appropriate advice. In such circumstances the bank will proceed at its own risk.

[Lord Nicholls then considered questions concerning the content of the legal advice, the independence of the advisor, and any agency relationship between the adviser and the bank.]

Obtaining the solicitor's confirmation
79. I now return to the steps a bank should take when it has been put on inquiry and for its protection is looking to the fact that the wife has been advised independently by a solicitor.

(1) One of the unsatisfactory features in some of the cases is the late stage at which the wife first became involved in the transaction. In practice she had no opportunity to express a view on the identity of the solicitor who advised her. She did not even know that the purpose for which the solicitor was giving her advice was to enable him to send, on her behalf, the protective confirmation sought by the bank. Usually the solicitor acted for both husband and wife.

Since the bank is looking for its protection to legal advice given to the wife by a solicitor who, in this respect, is acting solely for her, I consider the bank should take steps to check *directly with the wife* the name of the solicitor she wishes to act for her. To this end, in future the bank should communicate directly with the wife, informing her that for its own protection it will require written confirmation from a solicitor, acting for her, to the effect that the solicitor has fully explained to her the nature of the documents and the practical implications they will have for her. She should be told that the purpose of this requirement is that thereafter she should not be able to dispute she is legally bound by the documents once she has signed them. She should be asked to nominate a solicitor whom she is willing to instruct to advise her, separately from her husband, and act for her in giving the necessary confirmation to the bank. She should be told that, if she wishes, the solicitor may be the same solicitor as is acting for her husband in the transaction. If a solicitor is already acting for the husband and the wife, she should be asked whether she would prefer that a different solicitor should act for her regarding the bank's requirement for confirmation from a solicitor.

The bank should not proceed with the transaction until it has received an appropriate response directly from the wife.

(2) Representatives of the bank are likely to have a much better picture of the husband's financial affairs than the solicitor. If the bank is not willing to undertake the task of explanation itself, the bank must provide the solicitor with the financial information he needs for this purpose. Accordingly it should become routine practice for banks, if relying on confirmation from a solicitor for their protection, to send to the solicitor the necessary financial information. What is required must depend on the facts of the case. Ordinarily this will include information on the purpose for which the proposed new facility has been requested, the current amount of the husband's indebtedness, the amount of his current overdraft facility, and the amount and terms of any new facility. If the bank's request for security arose from a written application by the husband for a facility, a copy of the application should be sent to the solicitor.

The bank will, of course, need first to obtain the consent of its customer to this circulation of confidential information. If this consent is not forthcoming the transaction will not be able to proceed.

(3) Exceptionally there may be a case where the bank believes or suspects that the wife has been misled by her husband or is not entering into the transaction of her own free will. If such a case occurs the bank must inform the wife's solicitors of the facts giving rise to its belief or suspicion.

(4) The bank should in every case obtain from the wife's solicitor a written confirmation to the effect mentioned above.

80. These steps will be applicable to future transactions. In respect of past transactions, the bank will ordinarily be regarded as having discharged its obligations if a solicitor who was acting for the wife in the transaction gave the bank confirmation to the effect that he had brought home to the wife the risks she was running by standing as surety . . .

A wider principle

82. Before turning to the particular cases I must make a general comment on the *O'Brien* principle. As noted by Professor Peter Birks Q.C., the decision in *O'Brien* has to be seen as the progenitor of a wider principle: see "The Burden on the Bank", in Restitution and Banking Law (ed Rose, 1998), at p 195. This calls for explanation. In the *O'Brien* case the House was concerned with formulating a fair and practical solution to problems occurring when a creditor obtains a security from a guarantor whose sexual relationship with the debtor gives rise to a heightened risk of undue influence. But the law does not regard sexual relationships as standing in some special category of their own so far as undue influence is concerned. Sexual relationships are no more than one type of relationship in which an individual may acquire influence over another individual. The *O'Brien* decision cannot sensibly be regarded as confined to sexual relationships, although these are likely to be its main field of application at present. What is appropriate for sexual relationships ought, in principle, to be appropriate also for other relationships where trust and confidence are likely to exist.

83. The courts have already recognised this. Further application, or development, of the *O'Brien* principle has already taken place. In *Credit Lyonnais Bank Nederland NV v Burch* [1997] 1 All ER 144 the same principle was applied where the relationship was employer and employee. Miss Burch was a junior employee in a company. She was neither a shareholder nor a director. She provided security to the bank for the company's overdraft. She entered into a guarantee of unlimited amount, and gave the bank a second charge over her flat. Nourse L.J., at p 146, said the relationship "may broadly be said to fall under [*O'Brien*]". The Court of Appeal held that the bank was put on inquiry. It knew the facts from which the existence of a relationship of trust and confidence between Miss Burch and Mr Pelosi, the owner of the company, could be inferred.

84. The crucially important question raised by this wider application of the *O'Brien* principle concerns the circumstances which will put a bank on inquiry. A bank is put on inquiry whenever a wife stands as surety for her husband's debts. It is sufficient that the bank knows of the husband-wife relationship. That bare fact is enough. The bank must then take reasonable steps to bring home to the wife the risks involved. What, then, of other relationships where there is an increased risk of undue influence, such as parent and child? Is it enough that the bank knows of the relationship? For reasons already discussed in relation to husbands and wives, a bank cannot be expected to probe the emotional relationship between two individuals, whoever they may be. Nor is it desirable that a bank should attempt this. Take the case where a father puts forward his daughter as a surety for his business overdraft. A bank should not be called upon to evaluate highly personal matters such as the degree of trust and confidence existing between the father and his daughter, with the bank put on inquiry in one case and not in another. As with wives, so with daughters, whether a bank is put on inquiry should not depend on the degree of trust and confidence the particular daughter places in her father in relation to financial matters. Moreover, as with wives, so with other relationships, the test of what puts a bank on inquiry should be simple, clear and easy to apply in widely varying circumstances. This suggests that, in the case of a father and daughter, knowledge by the bank of the relationship of father and daughter should suffice to put the bank on inquiry. When the bank knows of the relationship, it must then take reasonable steps to ensure the daughter knows what she is letting herself into.

85. The relationship of parent and child is one of the relationships where the law irrebuttably presumes the existence of trust and confidence. Rightly, this has already been rejected as the boundary of the *O'Brien* principle. *O'Brien* was a husband-wife case. The responsibilities of creditors were enunciated in a case where the law makes no presumption of the existence of trust and confidence.

86. But the law cannot stop at this point, with banks on inquiry only in cases where the debtor and guarantor have a sexual relationship or the relationship is one where the law presumes the existence of trust and confidence. That would be an arbitrary boundary, and the law has already moved beyond this, in the decision

in *Burch*. As noted earlier, the reality of life is that relationships in which undue influence can be exercised are infinitely various. They cannot be exhaustively defined. Nor is it possible to produce a comprehensive list of relationships where there is a substantial risk of the exercise of undue influence, all others being excluded from the ambit of the *O'Brien* principle. Human affairs do not lend themselves to categorisations of this sort. The older generation of a family may exercise undue influence over a younger member, as in parent-child cases such as *Bainbrigge v Browne*, 18 Ch D 188 and *Powell v Powell* [1900] 1 Ch 243. Sometimes it is the other way round, as with a nephew and his elderly aunt in *Inche Noriah v Shaik Allie Bin Omar* [1929] AC 127. An employer may take advantage of his employee, as in *Credit Lyonnais Bank Nederland NV v Burch* [1997] 1 All ER 144. But it may be the other way round, with an employee taking advantage of her employer, as happened with the secretary-companion and her elderly employer in *In re Craig, Decd* [1971] Ch 95. The list could go on.

87. These considerations point forcibly to the conclusion that there is no rational cut-off point, with certain types of relationship being susceptible to the *O'Brien* principle and others not. Further, if a bank is not to be required to evaluate the extent to which its customer has influence over a proposed guarantor, the only practical way forward is to regard banks as "put on inquiry" in every case where the relationship between the surety and the debtor is non-commercial. The creditor must always take reasonable steps to bring home to the individual guarantor the risks he is running by standing as surety. As a measure of protection, this is valuable. But, in all conscience, it is a modest burden for banks and other lenders. It is no more than is reasonably to be expected of a creditor who is taking a guarantee from an individual. If the bank or other creditor does not take these steps, it is deemed to have notice of any claim the guarantor may have that the transaction was procured by undue influence or misrepresentation on the part of the debtor.

88. Different considerations apply where the relationship between the debtor and guarantor is commercial, as where a guarantor is being paid a fee, or a company is guaranteeing the debts of another company in the same group. Those engaged in business can be regarded as capable of looking after themselves and understanding the risks involved in the giving of guarantees.

89. By the decisions of this House in *O'Brien* and the Court of Appeal in *Credit Lyonnais Bank Nederland NV v Burch* [1997] 1 All ER 144, English law has taken its first strides in the development of some such general principle. It is a workable principle. It is also simple, coherent and eminently desirable. I venture to think this is the way the law is moving, and should continue to move. Equity, it is said, is not past the age of child-bearing. In the present context the equitable concept of being "put on inquiry" is the parent of a principle of general application, a principle which imposes no more than a modest obligation on banks and other creditors. The existence of this obligation in all non-commercial cases does not go beyond the reasonable requirements of the present times. In future, banks and other creditors should regulate their affairs accordingly.

Questions

26–007
1. How should we now classify cases of undue influence?

2. Is it essential that the party who has exerted the influence has acted improperly? In *National Commercial Bank (Jamaica) Ltd v Hew* [2003] UKPC 51, at para.34, Lord Millett says that "it must be shown that the ascendant party has unfairly exploited the influence he is shown or presumed to possess over the vulnerable party." Yet, in *Pesticcio v Huet* [2004] EWCA Civ 372, at para.20, Mummery LJ says that "the basis of the court's intervention is not the commission of a dishonest or wrongful act by the defendant, but that, as a matter of public policy, the presumed influence arising from the relationship of trust and confidence should not operate to the disadvantage of the victim, if the transaction is not satisfactorily explained by ordinary motives"; and, in *Macklin v Dowsett* [2004] EWCA Civ 904, Auld LJ confirms (at [10]) that "the rationale of the doctrine of undue influence [is] the protection of the vulnerable in dealings with their property and also the lack of the need to show misconduct on the part of the transferee."

3. What is wrong with requiring proof of manifest disadvantage (to the party over whom the influence is exercised) in cases of presumed undue influence?

----

2. DURESS

WILLIAMS v BAYLEY

House of Lords (1866) L.R. 1 H.L. 200; 35 L.J.Ch. 717; 12 Jur. 875; 14 L.T. 802; 148 R.R. 396

The respondent's son gave to the appellants, bankers, promissory notes upon which he had forged the indorsements of the respondent. Both the respondent and his son had accounts with the appellants. At a meeting of all the parties at the appellants' bank, one of them said to the respondent: "If the bills are yours we are all right; if they are not, we have only one course to pursue; we cannot be parties to compounding a felony." The solicitor for the appellants said it was a serious matter and the respondent's own solicitor added, "a case of transportation for life." After further discussion as to how the son's liabilities might be met, the appellants' solicitor said that they could only look to the respondent. The respondent's solicitor refused to be a party to the respondent making himself liable for the whole amount and prepared to leave the room, when the respondent said: "What be I to do? How can I help myself? You see these men will have their money?"

26–008

The respondent then agreed to make an equitable mortgage to the appellants in consideration of the return of the promissory notes. The respondent succeeded in an action for cancellation of the agreement.

Lord Cranworth LC and Lord Chelmsford made speeches in favour of the respondent.

LORD WESTBURY

Having held that the basis of the transaction was not, as alleged by the appellants, the possible civil liability of the father for the debt but the criminal liability of the son, continued: The question, therefore, my Lords, is whether a father appealed to under such circumstances, to take upon himself an amount of civil liability with the knowledge that, unless he does so, his son will be exposed to a criminal prosecution, with the certainty of conviction, can be regarded as a free and voluntary agent? I have no hesitation in saying that no man is safe, or ought to be safe, who takes a security for the debt or a felon, from the father of a felon, under such circumstances. A contract to give security for the debt of another, which is a contract without consideration, is, above all things, a contract that should be based upon the free and voluntary agency of the individual who enters into it. But it is clear that the power of considering whether he ought to do it or not, whether it is prudent to do it or not, is altogether taken away from a father who is brought into the situation of either refusing, and leaving his son in that perilous condition, or of taking on himself the amount of that civil obligation.

I have, therefore, my Lords, in that view of the case no difficulty in saying that, as far as my opinion is concerned, the security given for the debt of the son by the father under such circumstances, was not the security of a man who acted with that freedom and power of deliberation that must, undoubtedly, be considered as necessary to validate a transaction of such a description.

My Lords, I would add to that, the great folly, nay, impropriety, of the bankers proceeding to take this security from the defenceless old man after his solicitor had left him, protesting in such an emphatic manner against the proceedings which he knew they were about to enter upon. The respondent's solicitor remained so long as a valid contract, namely, that touching the property of William Bayley, was regarded as possible. When that was impossible, and the bankers began to exert pressure on the father, the solicitor left, remonstrating with all parties against the impropriety of what they were about to do . . .

Appeal Dismissed.

BARTON v ARMSTRONG

Privy Council [1975] 2 W.L.R. 1050; [1975] 2 All E.R. 465

Armstrong, the former chairman of a company, "Landmark", threatened Barton, the managing director, with death if Landmark did not agree to pay a large sum in cash and to purchase Armstrong's

26–009

shares in Landmark. There was some evidence that Barton thought the proposed agreement was a satisfactory business arrangement both from his own point of view and that of Landmark. Barton executed a deed on behalf of Landmark carrying out the agreement. He sought a declaration that the deed was executed under duress and was void. Street J in the Supreme Court of New South Wales held that Barton, though apprehensive as to the safety of himself and his family, was not overborne by Armstrong but exercised free and independent judgment and entered into the contract for reasons of commercial necessity and that his claim failed. The Court of Appeal of New South Wales affirmed the judge's decision.

LORD CROSS

[(with whom Lord Kilbrandon and Sir Garfield Barwick agreed), having discussed the facts:] Their Lordships turn now to consider the question of law which provoked a difference of opinion in the Court of Appeal Division. It is hardly surprising that there is no direct authority on the point, for if A threatens B with death if he does not execute some document and B, who takes A's threats seriously, executes the document it can be only in the most unusual circumstances that there can be any doubt whether the threats operated to induce him to execute the document. But this is a most unusual case and the findings of fact made below do undoubtedly raise the question whether it was necessary for Barton in order to obtain relief to establish that he would not have executed the deed in question but for the threats. In answering this question in favour of Barton Jacobs J. A. relied both on a number of old common law authorities on the subject of "duress" and also—by way of analogy—on later decisions in equity with regard to the avoidance of deeds on the ground of fraud. Their Lordships do not think that the common law authorities are of any real assistance for it seems most unlikely that the authors of the statements relied on had the sort of problem which has arisen here in mind at all. On the other hand they think that the conclusion to which Jacobs J. A. came was right and that it is supported by the equity decisions. The scope of common law duress was very limited and at a comparatively early date equity began to grant relief in cases where the disposition in question had been procured by the exercise of pressure which the Chancellor considered to be illegitimate—although it did not amount to common law duress. There was a parallel development in the field of dispositions induced by fraud. At common law the only remedy available to the man defrauded was an action for deceit but equity in the same period in which it was building up the doctrine of "undue influence" came to entertain proceedings to set aside dispositions which had been obtained by fraud: see Holdsworth's *History of English Law (Vol. 38)*, p. 51. There is an obvious analogy between setting aside a disposition for duress or undue influence and setting it aside for fraud. In each case—to quote the words of Holmes J. in *Fairbanks v Snow* (1887) 13 N.E. at 598)—"the party has been subjected to an improper motive for action." Again the similarity of the effect in law of metus and dolus in connection with dispositions of property is noted by Stair in his *Institutions of the Law of Scotland* (Book IV, tit. 40, 25). Had Armstrong made a fraudulent misrepresentation to Barton for the purpose of inducing him to execute the deed of January 17, 1967, the answer to the problem which has arisen would have been clear. If it were established that Barton did not allow the representation to affect his judgment then he could not make it a ground for relief even though the representation was designed and known by Barton to be designed to affect his judgment. If on the other hand Barton relied on the misrepresentation Armstrong could not have defeated his claim to relief by showing that there were other more weighty causes which contributed to his decision to execute the deed, for in this field the court does not allow an examination into the relative importance of contributory causes. "Once make out that there has been anything like deception, and no contract resting in any degree on that foundation can stand" per Lord Cranworth L.J. in *Reynell v Spyre* (1852) 1 De G.M. & G. 660 at 708); see also the other cases referred to in Cheshire and Fifoot's *Law of Contract* (8th ed. 1972), p. 250, 251. Their Lordships think that the same rule should apply in cases of duress and that if Armstrong's threats were "a" reason for Barton's executing the deed he is entitled to relief even though he might well have entered into the contract if Armstrong had uttered no threats to induce him to do so.

[Their Lordships went on to hold that the onus was on Armstrong to prove that the threats he made contributed nothing to Barton's decision to sign; and that the proper inference was "that though it may be that Barton would have executed the documents even if Armstrong had made no threats and exerted no unlawful pressure to induce him to do so, the threats and unlawful pressure in fact contributed to his decision to sign . . . "]

Lords Wilberforce and Simon, dissenting, held that there was no justification for interfering with the findings of fact made by the courts below.

Appeal Allowed.

Questions

1. Their Lordships follow the traditional view that operative duress makes a contract merely void-able and not void. If A points a gun at B and says, "Sell me your watch for a penny—or else . . ." is there really a contract if A hands over his watch? See Lanham (1966) 29 M.L.R. 615.

2. What if, in the above problem, A's offer had been £5 for a watch which he believed to be very valuable and B, knowing the watch was worth £2, had happily accepted?

26–010

ALEC LOBB (GARAGES) LTD AND OTHERS v TOTAL OIL GB LTD

Court of Appeal [1985] 1 All E.R. 303 [1985] 1 W.L.R. 173

Alec Lobb (Garages) Ltd (the company) carried on a garage business on a site of which it owned the freehold. It was a private company and Alec Lobb and his mother were the only directors and share-holders. The company was indebted to Total and in serious financial difficulties. Mr Lobb made a proposal to Total to solve these difficulties and, after negotiation, in 1969 the company leased the site of the garage to Total for 51 years at a peppercorn rent in consideration of a premium of £35,000 paid by Total; and a sublease (the lease-back) was granted by Total to Mr and Mrs Lobb (not the company) for a term of 21 years, with a right for either party to terminate at the end of the seventh or fourteenth years, at an initial rent of £2,250. The lease-back contained an absolute prohibition on assignment and tie provisions throughout the term requiring the lessees to take all their petrol from Total and to provide a proper and efficient service at all reasonable times.

26–011

In an action commenced in 1979 the company and Mr and Mrs Lobb claimed to set aside the lease and lease-back on the grounds (inter alia) that the tie constituted an unreasonable restraint of trade. (See below, para.27–029.) The trial judge held that the tie provisions were unreasonable and void but severable from the remaining provisions. On appeal the company argued (i) that the tie provi-sions were not severable and the transaction was wholly void; and (ii) alternatively, that the trans-action ought to be set aside in equity because there was inequality of bargaining power between Total on the one hand and Mr and Mrs Lobb and the company on the other. Total cross-appealed, arguing that the lease-back was not a restraint of trade and that, even if it were it was reasonable and therefore valid.

DILLON LJ

It is logical to consider the cross-appeal first and I can deal very shortly with the second of the above argu-ments: In *Esso Petroleum Co Ltd v Harper's Garage (Stourport) Ltd* [below, Ch.27] it was held that the doctrine of restraint of trade had no applications to restraints imposed on persons who, before the transaction by which the restraints were imposed, had no right whatsoever to trade at all on the land in question. Their Lordships had in mind in particular the case where an owner of land grants a lease of the land to a person who had no previous right to occupy the land, and imposes by the lease restraints on the lessee's power to trade as he likes on the land. Such a lease would ordinarily not be regarded as an agreement in restraint of trade. In the present case however the granting of the lease-back to Mr and Mrs Lobb rather than to the company was a palpable device in an endeavour to evade the doctrine of restraint of trade. Mr and Mrs Lobb were only selected as lessees because they were the proprietors of the company previously in occupation. The court has ample power to pierce the corporate veil, recognise a continued identity of occupation and hold, as it should, that Total can be in no better position quoad restraints of trade by granting the lease-back to Mr and Mrs Lobb than if it had granted the lease-back to the company; see generally *Gilford Motor Co Ltd v Horne* [1933] Ch. 935, 961–962, and *D.H.N. Food Distributors Ltd v Tower Hamlets London Borough Council* [1976] 1 W.L.R. 852.

As for the argument that the lease-back is not an agreement in restraint of trade because the restrictions in the lease-back derive from a disposal by the company of a large part of its interest in the property, I have had considerable difficulty in understanding the argument. It is of course clear that there is no agreement in restraint of trade where a person deprives himself of all right to trade as he wishes on land by selling all his interest in that land. In the present case, however, that is not what the company did and the whole object was that trade should continue in the property. The lease and lease-back have to be taken together as two essential parts of one transaction, and in my judgment it follows from the reasoning of their Lordships in the *Esso* case that the agreement constituted by the lease and lease-back is an agreement in restraint of trade in as much as it subjects the company to a continuation for a longer period of the restraints on trading which had validly been imposed for a much shorter period before July 25, 1969 . . .

[His Lordship went on to hold that the restraint was reasonable pointing out that the consideration for the restraint, the premium of £35,000, was arrived at by a professional valuation of the 51-year lease, subject to the lease-back: that the period of 51 years was chosen because, if the term had been less than 50 years, the premium would have been taxable as income in the company's hands; that the premium for a short term could not have been enough to recapitalise the company; and that the lessees were free to break the clause at the end of seven years. He went on:]

In the circumstances of this case, and not least because at the time of the grant of the lease and lease-back the company was subject to a valid tie for a term of three to four years, I can see no real significance in the difference between a tie for five years and the term of seven years to the first break under the lease-back.

In the light of these factors the restraints on trading in the lease-back were in my judgment reasonable. Accordingly I would allow the cross-appeal.

It follows that the question of severance which is sought to be raised by the appellants' first ground of appeal does not arise. None the less, in deference to the argument and in case this dispute goes further, it may be appropriate that I should express my view . . .

[Having quoted from Lord Selborne L.C. in *Earl of Aylesford v Morris* (1873) L.R. 8 Ch.App. 484 at 490–491 his Lordship continued:]

The whole emphasis is on extortion, or undue advantage taken of weakness, an unconscientious use of the power arising out of the inequality of the parties' circumstances, and on unconscientious use of power which the court might in certain circumstances be entitled to infer from a particular—and in these days notorious—relationship unless the contract is proved to have been in fact fair, just and reasonable. Nothing leads me to suppose that the course of the development of the law over the last 100 years has been such that the emphasis on unconscionable conduct or unconscientious use of power has gone and relief will now be granted in equity in a case such as the present if there has been unequal bargaining power, even if the stronger has not used his strength unconscionably. I agree with the judgment of Browne-Wilkinson J., in *Multiservice Book-binding Ltd v Marden* [1979] Ch.84, which sets out that to establish that a term is unfair and unconscionable it is not enough to show that it is, objectively, unreasonable.

In the present case there are findings of fact by the deputy judge that the conduct of Total was not unconscionable, coercive or oppressive. There is ample evidence to support those findings and they are not challenged by the appellants. Their case is that the judge applied the wrong test; where there is unequal bargaining power, the test is, they say, whether its terms are fair, just and reasonable and it is unnecessary to consider whether the conduct of the stronger party was oppressive or unconscionable. I do not accept the appellants' proposition of law. In my judgment the findings of the judge conclude this ground of appeal against the appellants.

Inequality of bargaining power must anyhow be a relative concept. It is seldom in any negotiation that the bargaining powers of the parties are absolutely equal. Any individual wanting to borrow money from a bank, building society or other financial institution in order to pay his liabilities or buy some property he urgently wants to acquire will have virtually no bargaining power; he will have to take or leave the terms offered to him. So, with house property in a seller's market, the purchaser will not have equal bargaining power with the vendor. But Lord Denning M.R. did not envisage that any contract entered into in such circumstances would, without more, be reviewed by the courts by the objective criterion of what was reasonable: see *Lloyds Bank*

Ltd v Bundy [1975] Q.B. 326, 336. The courts would only interfere in exceptional cases where as a matter of common fairness it was not right that the strong should be allowed to push the weak to the wall. The concepts of unconscionable conduct and of the exercise by the stronger of coercive power are thus brought in and in the present case they are negatived by the deputy judge's findings.

Even if, contrary to my view just expressed, the company and Mr and Mrs Lobb had initially in 1969 a valid claim in equity to have the lease and lease-back set aside as a result of the inequality of bargaining power, that claim was, in my judgment, barred by laches well before the issue of the writ in this action.

Dunn and Waller L.JJ. delivered judgment dismissing the appeal.

Appeal Dismissed.

ATLAS EXPRESS LTD v KAFKO LTD

Queen's Bench Division [1989] Q.B. 833; [1989] 3 W.L.R. 389; [1989] 1 All E.R. 641

26–012

Kafko, a small company dealing in basketware, had secured a large contract from Woolworths and had obtained a large quantity of goods to fulfil it. They entered into a contract with Atlas, a national road carrier, to distribute the basketware to Woolworths' shops. Atlas' depot manager, Hope, had inspected a range of cartons used by Kafko and estimated that a trailer would carry a minimum of 400 and possibly as many as 600 cartons. It was on that basis that he quoted an agreed rate of £1.10 per carton. He had underestimated the size of the cartons and the first load contained only 200 which Hope said was not financially viable. After discussion but no agreement with Kafko, Hope sent an empty trailer to Kafko's premises on November 18, 1986. The driver carried a document, "Amended/Transferred Account Details," specifying a minimum charge of £440 per trailer. His instructions were that if the agreement was not signed, he was to take the trailer away unloaded. It was essential to Kafko's commercial survival that they should be able to meet delivery dates. It would have been difficult, if not impossible, to find alternative carriers to do so. A Kafko director, Armiger, signed the agreement and the deliveries were made.

TUCKER J

I find that when Mr Armiger signed that agreement he did so unwillingly and under compulsion. He believed on reasonable grounds that it would be very difficult, if not impossible, to negotiate with another contractor. He did not regard the fact that he had signed the new agreement as binding the defendants to its terms. He had no bargaining power. He did not regard it as a genuine armslength renegotiation in which he had a free and equal say and, in my judgment, that view was fully justified.

In the words of the co-director, Mr Fox, he felt that he was "over a barrel." He tried in vain to contact Mr Hope but, as he said to Mr Armiger, they really had no option but to sign. I accept the evidence of the Woolworth manager, Mr Graham, that if the defendants had told them that they could not supply the goods Woolworth would have sued them for loss of profit and would have ceased trading with them. I find that this was well known to the defendants' directors . . .

The issue which I have to determine is whether the defendants are bound by the agreement signed on their behalf on November 18, 1986. The defendants contend that they are not bound, for two reasons: first, because the agreement was signed under duress; second, because there was no consideration for it.

The first question raises an interesting point of law, that is, whether economic duress is a concept known to English law.

Economic duress must be distinguished from commercial pressure, which on any view is not sufficient to vitiate consent. The borderline between the two may in some cases be indistinct. But the authors of *Chitty on Contracts* (25th ed., 1983) and of *Goff and Jones on the Law of Restitution* (3rd ed., 1986) appear to recognise that in appropriate cases economic duress may afford a defence, and in my judgment it does. It is clear to me that in a number of English cases judges have acknowledged the existence of this concept.

Thus, in *D. & C. Builders Ltd v Rees* [above, Ch.11] Lord Denning M.R. said: "No person can insist on a settlement procured by intimidation." And in *The Siboen and the Sibotre* [1976] 1 Lloyd's Rep. 293 at 336 Kerr J.

appeared to accept that economic duress could operate in appropriate circumstances. A similar conclusion was reached by Mocatta J. in *The Atlantic Baron* [above, Ch.10].

In particular, there are passages in the judgment of Lord Scarman in *Pao On v Lau Yiu* [above, Ch.10], which clearly indicate recognition of the concept, where Lord Scarman said:

"Duress, whatever form it takes, is a coercion of the will so as to vitiate consent. Their Lordships agree with the observation of Kerr J. in *The Siboen and The Sibotre* [1976] 1 Lloyd's Rep. 293 at 336 that in a contractual situation commercial pressure is not enough. There must be present some factor 'which could in law be regarded as a coercion of his will so as to vitiate his consent.' This conception is in line with what was said in this Board's decision in *Barton v Armstrong* [above] by Lord Wilberforce and Lord Simon of Glaisdale, observations with which the majority judgment appears to be in agreement. In determining whether there was a coercion of will such that there was no true consent, it is material to enquire whether the person alleged to have been coerced did or did not protest; whether, at the time he was allegedly coerced into making the contract, he did or did not have an alternative course open to him such as an adequate legal remedy; whether he was independently advised; and whether after entering the contract he took steps to avoid it. All these matters are, as was recognised in *Maskell v Horner* [1915] 3 K.B. 106, relevant in determining whether he acted voluntarily or not. In the present case there is unanimity amongst the judges below that there was no coercion of Lau's will. In the Court of Appeal the trial judge's finding (already quoted) that Lau considered the matter thoroughly, chose to avoid litigation, and formed the opinion that the risk in giving the guarantee was more apparent than real was upheld. In short, there was commercial pressure, but no coercion. Even if this Board was disposed, which it is not, to take a different view, it would not substitute its opinion for that of the judges below on this question of fact. It is, therefore, unnecessary for the Board to embark on an enquiry into the question whether English law recognises a category of duress known as 'economic duress.' But, since the question has been fully argued in this appeal, their Lordships will indicate very briefly the view which they have formed. At common law money paid under economic compulsion could be recovered in an action for money had and received: see *Astley v Reynolds* (1731) 2 Stra. 915. The compulsion had to be such that the party was deprived of 'his freedom of exercising his will' (see 2 Stra. 915 at 916). It is doubtful, however, whether at common law any duress other than duress to the person sufficed to render a contract voidable; see *Blackstone's Commentaries* (12th ed. 1793), Vol. 1, pp. 130–131 and *Skeate v Beale* (1841) 11 Ad. & El. 983. American law (*Williston on Contracts* (3rd ed., 1970), Chap. 47) now recognises that a contract may be avoided on the ground of economic duress. The commercial pressure alleged to constitute such duress must, however, be such that the victim must have entered the contract against his will, must have had no alternative course open to him, and must have been confronted with coercive acts by the party exerting the pressure: see *Williston on Contracts*, Chapter 47, s.1603. American judges pay great attention to such evidential matters as the effectiveness of the alternative remedy available, the fact or absence of protest, the availability of independent advice, the benefit received, and the speed with which the victim sought to avoid the contract. Recently two English judges have recognised that commercial pressure may constitute duress the presence of which can render a contract voidable [Lord Scarman then referred to the judgments of Kerr and Mocatta JJ. above before continuing] Both stressed that the pressure must be such that the victim's consent to the contract was not a voluntary act on his part. In their Lordships' view, there is nothing contrary to principle in recognising economic duress as a factor which may render a contract voidable, provided always that the basis of such recognition is that it must amount to a coercion of will, which vitiates consent. It must be shown that the payment made or the contract entered into was not a voluntary act."

A further case which was not cited to me was *B & S Contracts and Design Ltd v Victor Green Publications Ltd* [1984] I.C.R. 419 at 423, where Eveleigh L.J. referred to the speech of Lord Diplock in another uncited case, *Universe Tankships Inc of Monrovia v International Transport Workers' Federation* [1983] A.C. 366 at 384:

"The rationale is that his apparent consent was induced by pressure exercised on him by that other party which the law does not regard as legitimate, with the consequence that the consent is treated in law as revocable unless approbated either expressly or by implication after the illegitimate pressure has ceased to operate on his mind."

In commenting on this Eveleigh L.J. said of the word "legitimate" ([1984] I.C.R. 419 at 423):

"For the purpose of this case it is sufficient to say that if the claimant has been influenced against his will to pay money under the threat of unlawful damage to his economic interest he will be entitled to claim that money back . . ."

Reverting to the case before me, I find that the defendants' apparent consent to the agreement was induced by pressure which was illegitimate and I find that it was not approbated. In my judgment that pressure can properly be described as economic duress, which is a concept recognised by English law, and which in the circumstances of the present case vitiates the defendants' apparent consent to the agreement.

In any event, I find that there was no consideration for the new agreement. The plaintiffs were already obliged to deliver the defendants' goods at the rates agreed under the terms of the original agreement. There was no consideration for the increased minimum charge of £440 per trailer.

Action Dismissed.

Question

What is the difference between this case and *Williams v Roffey Bros*, above, Ch.10? Does it lie in the issue of consideration or that of economic duress? Both are cases of a party who has made a bad bargain seeking additional payment. Was not the "benefit" to Kafko of having the agreement performed at least as great as that to Roffey Bros? Does the court take the side of "the little company" (Cf. Lord Denning's opening words in *D & C Builders v Rees*, above, Ch.11)?

26–013

CTN CASH AND CARRY LTD v GALLAGHER LTD

Court of Appeal [1994] 4 All E.R. 714.

The plaintiffs (C) bought cigarettes from the defendants (G) for resale in C's warehouses in six towns. G were not contractually bound to sell, each sale being a separate contract. G had arranged credit facilities for C but had an absolute discretion to withdraw these facilities. In November 1986, C ordered cigarettes to the value of £17,000 to be delivered to their Preston warehouse. By mistake, G delivered to the Burnley warehouse. C pointed out G's mistake and G agreed to arrange the carriage of the goods from Burnley to Preston but, the day before they were due to be collected, the goods were stolen. G believed, wrongly, that the goods were at C's risk and demanded payment of the price. C declined to pay until G made it clear that they would not, in future grant credit facilities unless the price was paid. C paid the price, as the lesser of the two evils. Their subsequent action to recover it on the ground of economic duress failed. They appealed.

26–014

STEYN LJ

The present dispute does not concern a protected relationship. It also does not arise in the context of dealings between a supplier and a consumer. The dispute arises out of arm's length commercial dealings between two trading companies. It is true that the defendants were the sole distributors of the popular brands of cigarettes. In a sense the defendants were in a monopoly position. The control of monopolies is, however, a matter for Parliament. Moreover, the common law does not recognise the doctrine of inequality of bargaining power in commercial dealings (see *National Westminster Bank Plc v Morgan* [1985] 1 All E.R. 821, [1985] A.C. 686). The fact that the defendants were in a monopoly position cannot therefore by itself convert what is not otherwise duress into duress.

A second characteristic of the case is that the defendants were in law entitled to refuse to enter into any future contracts with the plaintiffs for any reason whatever or for no reason at all. Such a decision not to deal with the plaintiffs would have been financially damaging to the defendants, but it would have been lawful. A fortiori, it was lawful for the defendants, for any reason or for no reason, to insist that they would no longer grant credit to the plaintiffs. The defendants' demand for payment of the invoice, coupled with the threat to withdraw credit, was neither a breach of contract nor a tort.

A third, and critically important, characteristic of the case is the fact that the defendants bona fide thought that the goods were at the risk of the plaintiffs and that the plaintiffs owed the defendants the sum in question. The defendants exerted commercial pressure on the plaintiffs in order to obtain payment of a sum which they bona fide considered due to them. The defendants' motive in threatening withdrawal of credit facilities was commercial self-interest in obtaining a sum that they considered due to them.

I also readily accept that the fact that the defendants have used lawful means does not by itself remove the case from the scope of the doctrine of economic duress. Professor Birks, in *An Introduction to the Law of Restitution* (1989) p. 177, lucidly explains:

> "Can lawful pressures also count? This is a difficult question, because, if the answer is that they can, the only viable basis for discriminating between acceptable and unacceptable pressures is not positive law but social morality. In other words, the judges must say what pressures (though lawful outside the restitutionary context) are improper as contrary to prevailing standards. That makes the judges, not the law or the legislature, the arbiters of social evaluation. On the other hand, if the answer is that lawful pressures are always exempt, those who devise outrageous but technically lawful means of compulsion must always escape restitution until the legislature declares the abuse unlawful. It is tolerably clear that, at least where they can be confident of a general consensus in favour of their evaluation, the courts are willing to apply a standard of impropriety rather than technical unlawfulness."

And there are a number of cases where English courts have accepted that a threat may be illegitimate when coupled with a demand for payment even if the threat is one of lawful action (see *Thorne v Motor Trade Association* [1937] 3 All E.R. 157 at 160–161, [1937] A.C. 797 at 806–807. *Mutual Finance Ltd v John Wetton & Sons Ltd* [1937] 2 All E.R. 657, [1937] 2 K.B. 389 and *Universe Tankships Inc of Monrovia v International Transport Workers' Federation* [1982] 2 All E.R. 67 at 76, 89, [1983] 1 A.C. 366 at 384, 401). On the other hand, *Goff and Jones Law of Restitution* (3rd ed., 1986) p. 240 observed that English courts have wisely not accepted any general principle that a threat not to contract with another except on certain terms, may amount to duress.

We are being asked to extend the categories of duress of which the law will take cognisance. That is not necessarily objectionable, but it seems to me that an extension capable of covering the present case, involving "lawful act duress" in a commercial context in pursuit of a bona fide claim, would be a radical one with far-reaching implications. It would introduce a substantial and undesirable element of uncertainty in the commercial bargaining process. Moreover, it will often enable bona fide settled accounts to be reopened when parties to commercial dealings fall out. The aim of our commercial law ought to be to encourage fair dealing between parties. But it is a mistake for the law to set its sights too highly when the critical inquiry is not whether the conduct is lawful but whether it is morally or socially unacceptable. That is the inquiry in which we are engaged. In my view there are policy considerations which militate against ruling that the defendants obtained payment of the disputed invoice by duress.

Outside the field of protected relationships, and in a purely commercial context, it might be a relatively rare case in which "lawful act duress" can be established. And it might be particularly difficult to establish duress if the defendant bona fide considered that his demand was valid. In this complex and changing branch of the law I deliberately refrain from saying "never". But as the law stands, I am satisfied that the defendants' conduct in this case did not amount to duress.

It is an unattractive result, inasmuch as the defendants are allowed to retain a sum which at the trial they became aware was not in truth due to them. But in my view the law compels the result.

For these reasons, I would dismiss the appeal.

Farquharson L.J. agreed and Nicholls V.-C. delivered a concurring judgment.

Appeal Dismissed.

Points for reflection

26–015   1. G, unlike *Atlas Express* (above), were not threatening to break any contract, but they were demanding money to which they were not entitled and reinforcing their demand with a threat. Steyn LJ thought the result "unattractive" and Nicholls VC, who was a "little troubled" by it, noted that no claim for restitution based on wrongful retention of the money had been brought. Cf. *Cook v Wright*, above, Ch.10. The withdrawal of the threat to withhold credit facilities was consideration for the payment in the present case, just as the withdrawal of the threat to sue was in *Cook v Wright*.

2. What if the plaintiffs had paid because they shared the erroneous belief of the defendants that the goods were at the plaintiffs' risk? Might the plaintiffs then have recovered under the principle of *Solle v Butcher*? The mistake was more fundamental than in *Solle*.

3. Following the decision in *CTN Cash and Carry*, we might infer that pressure applied in commercial dealings and in the lawful pursuit of self-interest will not usually be treated as illegitimate. For lawful pressure to be transformed into illegitimate pressure, it will require a context that puts hard bargaining in a different light. One such example is *Progress Bulk Carriers Ltd v Tube City IMS LLC* [2012] EWHC 273 (Comm). In this case, Progress, having contracted with Tube City for the charter of a particular vessel, repudiated the contract by chartering the vessel to a third party. Tube City, nevertheless, did not pull out of the contract and, encouraged by various assurances from Progress, entered into negotiations for the provision of a suitable substitute vessel. Eventually, Tube City found themselves driven into a corner where they had no option other than to accept a "take it or leave it" offer of a substitute vessel from Progress but on highly disadvantageous terms including waiving claims for loss or damage arising from the earlier repudiatory breach. Relying on *CTN Cash and Carry*, Progress claimed that this was simply lawful hard bargaining carried out "in the context of the state of the market and the Charterers' commercial predicament" (at para.28); against which, Tube City argued that the negotiations were coloured by the earlier repudiatory breach coupled with, in effect, Progress' bad faith in "manoeuvring [them] into a corner before producing the take it or leave it offer" (at para.28). Recognising that it will be unusual, in a commercial context, to treat lawful pressure as illegitimate pressure, Cooke J pointed out that the facts and the context were exceptional: it was Progress' "past breach, coupled with conduct since that breach, which drove the victim of the breach into a position where it had no realistic alternative but to waive its rights in respect of that breach, in order to avoid further catastrophic loss" (at para.39). Accordingly, confirming the finding made by the arbitrators, Cooke J held that Progress applied illegitimate, albeit lawful, pressure to obtain the agreement of Tube City.

4. In *DSND Subsea Ltd v Petroleum Geo-Services ASA* [2000] B.L.R. 530 at 545, Dyson J sought to clarify the requirement of improper or illegitimate pressure, saying that the factors to be taken into account include: "whether there has been an actual or threatened breach of contract; whether the person allegedly exerting the pressure has acted in good or bad faith; whether the victim had any realistic practical alternative but to submit to the pressure; whether the victim protested at the time; and whether he affirmed and sought to rely on the contract."

One of the key cases in the modern law is *R. v Attorney General for England and Wales* (below). There, pressure was applied to members of the SAS to sign confidentiality agreements whereby they undertook not to disclose information obtained while working in the military. The particular pressure was that, if members refused to sign the agreement, they would be returned back from the SAS to their original units—such a return involving a loss of reputation, reduced pay and exclusion from the social life of the regiment. Realistically, members had little alternative other than to sign, which R duly did. However, when R left the armed forces and returned to his native New Zealand, he contracted with publishers to write an account of his experience as a member of the Bravo Two Zero patrol that operated behind enemy lines during the Gulf War of 1991. Given that such a publication would violate the terms of the confidentiality agreement that R had signed, the question was whether R was bound by that agreement. The Attorney General on behalf of the Crown commenced proceedings in the High Court of New Zealand, claiming an injunction to restrain publication of the book, damages and an account of profits; in response, R argued that the pressure applied invalidated the agreement and that it did so (doctrinally speaking) either because of duress or because of undue influence.

R. v ATTORNEY GENERAL FOR ENGLAND AND WALES

Privy Council [2003] UKPC 22

LORD HOFFMANN (FOR THE PRIVY COUNCIL)

26–016   [Having outlined the background and the terms of the confidentiality agreement, Lord Hoffmann turned to the defences pleaded by R and the decisions reached by the lower courts]

12. By way of defence, R pleaded that he had signed the contract under military orders, that it had been obtained by duress or undue influence, that it was an unconscionable bargain, not supported by consideration, contrary to New Zealand public policy as a restraint of trade and upon its true construction not intended to prohibit the publication of material which was no longer confidential.

13. The judge (Salmon J.) held that R had been ordered to sign, as an exercise of the power of the Crown over members of the services. In his opinion such an order was unlawful because it was an attempt to restrict the civil rights he would ordinarily enjoy after he had left the service. He therefore found that the contract had been obtained by duress, in the form of an unlawful order combined with the threat of return to unit. He also found that the relationship between R and his superior officers gave rise to a presumption of undue influence which, in view of the unlawful nature of the order and the absence of legal advice, had not been rebutted. He rejected the claim that the contract was unconscionable, not supported by consideration, in restraint of trade or as a matter of construction inapplicable to the material proposed to be published. In the result, however, he dismissed the contractual claim.

14. The Court of Appeal disagreed with the finding that R had been given a military order to sign. He was given the choice of signing or being returned to unit; a choice which put pressure upon him but was not unlawful. It rejected the findings of duress and undue influence and supported the judge's rejection of the other defences. It therefore held that the contract was valid and that R was in breach. As a matter of discretion it refused an injunction to restrain publication but made an order for an account and an assessment of damages. There is no appeal by the Crown against the refusal of an injunction but R appeals against the orders made against him and challenges the rejection by the Court of Appeal of all the grounds upon which he alleges that the contract was invalid. Their Lordships will deal with them in turn.

Duress

15. In *Universe Tankships Inc of Monrovia v International Transport Workers Federation* [1983] 1 AC 366, 400 Lord Scarman said that there were two elements in the wrong of duress. One was pressure amounting to compulsion of the will of the victim and the second was the illegitimacy of the pressure. R says that to offer him the alternative of being returned to unit, which was regarded in the SAS as a public humiliation, was compulsion of his will. It left him no practical alternative. Their Lordships are content to assume that this was the case. But, as Lord Wilberforce and Lord Simon of Glaisdale said in *Barton v Armstrong* [1976] AC 104, 121:

"in life . . . many acts are done under pressure, sometimes overwhelming pressure, so that one can say that the actor had no choice but to act. Absence of choice in this sense does not negate consent in law: for this the pressure must be one of a kind which the law does not regard as legitimate."

16. The legitimacy of the pressure must be examined from two aspects: first, the nature of the pressure and secondly, the nature of the demand which the pressure is applied to support: see Lord Scarman in the *Universe Tankships* case, at p 401. Generally speaking, the threat of any form of unlawful action will be regarded as illegitimate. On the other hand, that fact that the threat is lawful does not necessarily make the pressure legitimate. As Lord Atkin said in *Thorne v Motor Trade Association* [1937] AC 797, 806:

"The ordinary blackmailer normally threatens to do what he has a perfect right to do—namely, communicate some compromising conduct to a person whose knowledge is likely to affect the person threatened . . . What he has to justify is not the threat, but the demand of money."

17. In this case, the threat was lawful. Although return to unit was not ordinarily used except on grounds of delinquency or unsuitability and was perceived by members of the SAS as a severe penalty, there is no doubt

that the Crown was entitled at its discretion to transfer any member of the SAS to another unit. Furthermore, the judge found, in para 123:

> "The MOD could not be criticised for its motivation in introducing the contracts. They were introduced because of the concerns about the increasing number of unauthorised disclosures by former UKSF personnel and the concern that those disclosures were threatening the security of operations and personnel and were undermining the effectiveness and employability of the UKSF. Those are legitimate concerns for the MOD to have."

18. It would follow that the MOD was reasonably entitled to regard anyone unwilling to accept the obligation of confidentiality as unsuitable for the SAS. Thus the threat was lawful and the demand supported by the threat could be justified. But the judge held that the demand was unlawful because it exceeded the powers of the Crown over a serviceman under military law. It was an attempt to restrict his freedom of expression after he had left the service and was no longer subject to military discipline.

19. The judge's reasoning was that R had signed the contract because he had been ordered to do so. The MOD could not give a serviceman an order which, as a matter of military law, he was obliged to obey after he had left the service and therefore it was an abuse of power for the MOD to try to extend the temporal reach of its orders by ordering the serviceman to sign a contract which could be enforced after he had left.

20. If R had signed the contract because as a matter of military law he had been obliged to do so, their Lordships would see much force in this reasoning. But they agree with the Court of Appeal that this was not the case. There was no order in the sense of a command which created an obligation to obey under military law. Instead, R was faced with a choice which may have constituted "overwhelming pressure" but was not an exercise by the MOD of its legal powers over him. The legitimacy of the pressure therefore falls to be examined by normal criteria and as neither of the courts in New Zealand considered either the threat to be unlawful or the demand unreasonable, it follows that the contract was not obtained by duress.

Undue influence

21. The subject of undue influence has recently been re-examined in depth by the House of Lords in *Royal Bank of Scotland Plc v Etridge (No. 2)* [2002] AC 773. Their Lordships summarise the effect of the judgments. Like duress at common law, undue influence is based upon the principle that a transaction to which consent has been obtained by unacceptable means should not be allowed to stand. Undue influence has concentrated in particular upon the unfair exploitation by one party of a relationship which gives him ascendancy or influence over the other.

22. The burden of proving that consent was obtained by unacceptable means is upon the party who alleges it. Certain relationships—parent and child, trustee and beneficiary, etc—give rise to a presumption that one party had influence over the other. That does not of course in itself involve a presumption that he unfairly exploited his influence. But if the transaction is one which cannot reasonably be explained by the relationship, that will be prima facie evidence of undue influence. Even if the relationship does not fall into one of the established categories, the evidence may show that one party did in fact have influence over the other. In such a case, the nature of the transaction may likewise give rise to a prima facie inference that it was obtained by undue influence. In the absence of contrary evidence, the court will be entitled to find that the burden of proving unfair exploitation of the relationship has been discharged.

23. The absence of independent legal advice may or may not be a relevant matter according to the circumstances. It is not necessarily an unfair exploitation of a relationship for one party to enter into a transaction with the other without ensuring that he has obtained independent legal advice. On the other hand, the transaction may be such as to give rise to an inference of undue influence even if the induced party was advised by an independent lawyer and understood the legal implications of what he was doing.

24. In the present case it is said that the military hierarchy, the strong regimental pride which R shared and his personal admiration for his commanding officer created a relationship in which the Army as an institution or the commanding officer as an individual were able to exercise influence over him. Their Lordships are content to assume that this was the case. But the question is whether the nature of the transaction was such as to give rise to an inference that it was obtained by an unfair exploitation of that relationship. Like the Court of Appeal, their Lordships do not think that the confidentiality agreement can be so described. As in the case of duress, their Lordships think that the finding that it was an agreement which anyone who wished to serve or continue serving in the SAS could reasonably have been required to sign is fatal to such a conclusion. The reason why R signed the agreement was because, at the time, he wished to continue to be a member of the SAS. If facing him with such a choice was not illegitimate for the purposes of duress, their Lordships do not think that it could have

been an unfair exploitation of a relationship which consisted in his being a member of the SAS. There seems to their Lordships to be some degree of contradiction between R's claim, in the context of duress, that he signed only because he was threatened with return to his unit and his claim, for the purposes of undue influence, that he signed because of the trust and confidence which he reposed in the Army or his commanding officer.

25. The question which has troubled their Lordships is the absence of legal advice. The only evidence that R would not have been allowed to obtain such advice was his own testimony, accepted by the judge, of what he was told by his colleague ST in London; not, perhaps, the most authoritative source. R does not say that he asked anyone at Hereford whether he could obtain advice and the commanding officer said in evidence that such a request would have presented no difficulty.

26. On this evidence the New Zealand courts made a finding that R had not been able to obtain legal advice which their Lordships of course accept. In any event they think it a matter for regret that members of SAS were not told explicitly that arrangements could be made for them to obtain legal advice. They recognise the security problems which would have had to have been overcome; R could not, for example, have consulted an outside solicitor without disclosing that he was a member of the SAS. Nevertheless, as the commanding officer said, suitable arrangements could have been made and it would have avoided suspicion and recrimination to make this known.

27. The legal question, however, is whether failing to provide an opportunity for obtaining legal advice made the transaction one in which the MOD had unfairly exploited its influence over R. Here it is important to note that R does not allege that he did not understand the implications of what he was being asked to do. The contract was in simple terms and the explanatory memorandum even plainer. He does say that he had originally thought that it would only prevent publication of matter which remained confidential. However, a moment's thought would have told him that this would not have prevented the publications to which he and other members of the SAS most objected, namely *The One That Got Away* and the film which followed. In any case, when he saw the actual contract he knew what it meant.

28. In these circumstances, their Lordships do not think that the absence of legal advice affected the fairness of the transaction. The most that R can say is that a lawyer might have advised him to reflect upon the matter and, as in fact he changed his mind within a fairly short time after signing, that might have led to his not signing at all. But that is a decision which he could have made without a lawyer's advice.

[Lord Hoffmann then rejected a number of other arguments including (i) that the agreement represented an unconscionable bargain, (ii) that it was not supported by consideration, and (iii) that there were public policy considerations that militated against the validity of the argument.]

37. As it is, their Lordships will humbly advise Her Majesty that the appeal should be dismissed. The Attorney-General does not ask for costs.

LORD SCOTT OF FOSCOTE (DISSENTING)

38. I am in general in complete and respectful agreement with the opinion of the Board which has been delivered by Lord Hoffmann. To my regret, however, I find that there is one issue in the case on which I am unable to agree. The issue is that of undue influence.

39. It is well established that the relationship between parties to a contract, coupled with the nature of the contract and, sometimes, the circumstances in which consent to it by one party was obtained by the other, may give rise to a presumption that the consent of the former was obtained by undue influence. The presumption is an evidential presumption requiring the dominant party, seeking to enforce the contract, to introduce some additional evidence to show that the consent to the contract of the subservient party was a true consent fairly obtained (see *Royal Bank of Scotland v Etridge (No 2)* [2002] 2 AC 773). The most effective way in which in most cases the presumption can be rebutted is by showing that the subservient party received independent legal advice about the contract and its implications. In the present case, it is the relationship between appellant and the Ministry of Defence, the circumstances in which the appellant signed the contract, as found by the trial judge, and the fact that he signed it without any legal advice and without any real opportunity of obtaining any, that has caused me concern.

40. *Allcard v Skinner* (1887) 36 Ch D 145 is a classic case where the relationship between donor and donee gave rise to the presumption. The donor, having gone through the grades of novice and postulant, was a nun in an order which required its members to make over their assets to the order. The donor, in obedience to this rule, made over her assets to the lady superior of her convent in trust for the order. Later, having left the order, she claimed her assets back. The court expressed the principles to be applied in terms which seem to me relevant to the present case. Cotton L.J. said:

". . . the court interferes, not on the ground that any wrongful act has in fact been committed by the donee, but on the ground of public policy, and to prevent the relations which existed between the parties and the influence arising therefrom being abused." (p 171)

Lindley L.J. said:

"In this class of cases it has been considered necessary to show that the donor had independent advice, and was removed from the influence of the donee when the gift to him was made."

And

"[The courts] have not shrunk from setting aside gifts made to persons in a position to exercise undue influence over the donors, although there has been no proof of the actual exercise of such influence; and the courts have done this on the avowed ground of the necessity of going this length in order to protect persons from the exercise of such influence under circumstances which render proof of it impossible." (p 183)

Bowen L.J. thought that the gifts had to be set aside

"unless it is shewn that the donor, at the time of making the gift, was allowed full and free opportunity for counsel and advice outside—the means of considering his or her worldly position and exercising an independent will about it." (p 190)

He went on:

"This is not a limitation placed on the action of the donor; it is a fetter placed upon the conscience of the recipient of the gift, and one which arises out of public policy and fair play." (p 190)

41. Are these principles ones that should be applied to the contract in the present case? I think they are. The appellant was not, of course, an unworldly man in a secluded religious order. He was a soldier in a highly trained and efficient fighting unit. The essence of efficiency in a military unit is obedience to orders. The Armed Services operate on a hierarchical basis. Each rank looks to the rank or ranks above for direction and, having received that direction, is expected to comply with it. It is, in my opinion, entirely artificial to draw sharp distinctions between orders from senior officers that are military orders breach of which will be an offence under military law and may attract court martial sanctions and "orders" from senior officers couched as requests or as recommendations. It has become a music-hall joke for a sergeant-major to say to the troops under him "I want three volunteers; you, you and you". The hierarchical culture of the Armed Services and the deference and obedience to senior officers, both commissioned and non-commissioned, which is part of that culture are the essential background to the circumstances in which the appellant was asked to sign the contract in the present case.

42. It is to be borne in mind that members of Her Majesty's Armed Services do not, unlike ordinary employees, enter into contracts with their employers. They are engaged and can be dismissed under the Royal Prerogative. It is their agreement to serve, not any contract, that subjects them to military discipline and military law. The Board was told by counsel for the Attorney-General that there had been no other example of members of a unit of the Armed Services being asked to enter into a contract with the Ministry of Defence.

43. This background requires, in my opinion, that any contract between a member of the Armed Forces and the Ministry of Defence be looked at very carefully to see whether the benefit conferred by it on the Ministry of Defence was a benefit that the Ministry of Defence was entitled in equity to maintain.

44. The circumstances in which the contract in the present case came to be signed by the appellant were the subject of evidence at trial and the trial judge, Salmon J., formed a number of important conclusions:

(1) The judge concluded that the appellant signed because he had been ordered to do so. An analysis of the "order" that disqualifies it from constituting a military order and regards it, no doubt correctly, merely as a recommendation or a direction is, in my opinion, of no more than marginal significance if the possibility of undue influence is being considered. What is important is how the appellant regarded it. The appellant regarded it as an order.

(2) The judge found that "the defendant was not told the terms of the contract before signing [and] was not offered any legal advice" (para 39).

(3) He found, also, that the appellant was not permitted to show the contract to a legal adviser (para 139). The weight of this finding is not diminished by evidence from the senior officer in command of the Regiment to the effect that soldiers would have been permitted to show the contract to approved legal advisers if they had asked. What is important is the perception of the appellant, and, as to that, Salmon J.'s finding stands.

In my opinion, the relationship between the appellant and his senior officers and the circumstances, as found by the judge, in which the contract came to be signed by the appellant produced a classic "relationship" case in which undue influence should be presumed. No evidence was introduced to rebut that presumption. Legal advice was not available to the appellant. As in *Allcard v Skinner*, where no suggestion of fraud or indeed any impropriety was made against the lady superior to whom the plaintiff had transferred her assets, no such suggestion has been, or could be, made against any of the appellant's senior officers who play a part in the story. It is the relationship, produced by the background to which I have referred, between a soldier and that part of the Armed Services of which he is a member, that introduces the potentially vitiating element into the contract. If the Ministry of Defence wants to impose contractual obligations on soldiers by which they will be bound when they leave the service, it must, in my opinion, at the least make available to them independent legal advice. Fairness, in my view, requires it and I think the law requires it. In this case it was not done. I would have allowed the appeal.

DANIEL v DREW

Court of Appeal [2005] EWCA Civ 507

LORD JUSTICE WARD

Introduction

26-017   1. This is an unusual family dispute. Aged aunt [Margaret Drew] alleges that her nephew [Nicholas Daniel] procured her resignation from a family trust by undue influence. On 2nd September 2004 His Hon. Judge Weeks Q.C. sitting as a deputy judge of the Chancery Division found for her and ordered that a memorandum signed by her dated 20th February 2002 and the deed of retirement made between her and her nephews dated 25th February 2002 be set aside. He gave the nephew permission to appeal.

The judge's directions as to the law

23. [The judge] said that the relevant law was not in dispute and was contained in Lord Nicholls of Birkenhead's speech in *Royal Bank of Scotland v Etridge (No. 2)* [2002] 2 A.C. 773 and he quoted from paragraphs 6 to 12 inclusive. In this part of his speech Lord Nicholls had found it "necessary to go back to first principles". He explained in paragraph 6 that:—

"Undue influence is one of the grounds of relief developed by the Courts of Equity as a court of conscience. The objective is to ensure that the influence of one party over another is not abused."

24. In paragraph 7 he explained how equity supplemented the common law which dealt narrowly with duress:—

"Equity extended the reach of the law to other unacceptable forms of persuasion. The law will investigate the manner in which the intention to enter into the transaction was secured; 'how the intention was produced'; in the oft repeated words of Lord Eldon as long ago as 1807 (*Huguenin v Baseley* 14 Ves 273, 300). If the intention was produced by an unacceptable means the law will not permit the transaction to stand. The means used is regarded as an exercise of improper or 'undue' influence and hence unacceptable, whenever the consent thus procured ought not fairly to be treated as the expression of a person's free will. It is impossible to be more precise or definite. The circumstances in which one person acquires influence over another, and the manner in which influence may be exercised, vary too widely to permit of any more specific criterion."

25. In paragraph 8 he drew the distinction between "overt acts of improper pressure or coercion such as unlawful threats" and the second form now commonly referred to as presumed undue influence which:—

"arises out of the relationship between two persons where one has acquired over another a measure of influence, or ascendancy, of which the ascendant person then takes unfair advantage."

As he explained in paragraph 9:—

"Typically this occurs when one person places trust in another to look after his affairs and interests, and the latter betrays this trust by preferring his own interests."

26. In paragraph 11 he pointed out that:

"The principle is not confined to cases of abuse of trust and confidence. It also includes, for instance, cases where a vulnerable person has been exploited. Indeed there is no single touchstone for determining whether the principle is applicable. Several expressions have been used in an endeavour to encapsulate the essence: trust and confidence, reliance, dependence or vulnerability on the one hand and ascendancy, domination or control on the other. None of these descriptions is perfect. None is all-embracing. Each has its proper place."

27. Judge Weeks, a very experienced judge, said this:

"The reference to 'exploitation of the vulnerable' in paragraph 11 was made in the context of what used to be called 'presumed undue influence'. Although this is a case, if anything, of express undue influence, I think the reference is relevant because the exploitation of the vulnerable can be regarded as an example of unacceptable conduct where the consent procured ought not fairly to be treated as an expression of a person's free will."

The judge's conclusion

28. Having asked whether Margaret's intention had been procured by unacceptable means he decided:

"Mrs Drew was, in my judgment, a vulnerable person, unversed in business, anxious to avoid confrontation and eager to comply. Nicholas Daniel was younger and according to his aunt did not show her the respect she thought he should. I have heard him give evidence. He has a keen appreciation of his own interests and scant regard for those of others. "Unscrupulous" would be too harsh a description but he is, at the very least, insensitive. Again, in my view, "aggressive" would probably be too harsh and "forceful" might be a better description of his character.

He knew that if his aunt was given the chance to talk to her son or her solicitors the transaction would not proceed as he wished. He deliberately chose not to involve them, but to take advantage of his aunt's naiveté in business matters. In my judgment the means by which her signature was procured is unacceptable. Mrs Drew's consent, obtained in the circumstances that I have described ought not fairly to be treated as an expression of her free will."

[Having rejected the appellant's submissions on the law, Ward L.J. continued]

45. It remains for me to consider whether on the facts found by the judge there was evidence of overt acts of improper pressure or coercion or persuasive conduct. I am satisfied there was an abundance of evidence to justify that finding. Not least among the many facts of this case are these:—
   i)   Nicholas told Aunt Margaret at their first meeting on 20th that she should either attend the meetings of trustees or retire and that it was not right for her to do neither.
   ii) When she said she had already retired he told her to put it in writing.
   iii) He returned later that day with the home-made memorandum for her to sign.
   iv) He returned on 25th with the deed of retirement saying:

"I reminded her she had already signed a document confirming her retirement."
   v)   He told her if she ceased to be a trustee she could not be replaced by Stephen or by any independent party.
   vi) The whole of this lengthy and distressing meeting on 25th February was capable of being viewed as coercive forcing her to do that which she did not truly desire to do.
46. The next question is whether that amounted to improper or undue influence and the unfair procurement of her consent. These factors demonstrate the impropriety of Nicholas's actions:
   i)   When Aunt Margaret said she had already resigned, Nicholas seized upon the opportunity to obtain confirmation from her there and then, knowing that what she had said was not true.
   ii) He opportunistically exploited the advantage thus presented to him of having her "cornered".
   iii) He chose not to involve her solicitors or Stephen in order "to take advantage of his Aunt's naiveté in business matters".
   iv) She was "a vulnerable person, unversed in business, anxious to avoid confrontation and eager to comply".
   v)   He on the other hand had "a keen appreciation of his own interests and scant regard for those of others."

vi) His statement that she could not be replaced as a trustee was an active, and in my view, crucial mis-representation that it was not open to her to insist on an acceptable successor as a condition of her retirement.

47. In those circumstances it is no surprise the judge should conclude that Mrs Drew's consent "ought not fairly to be treated as an expression of her free will".

48. This disposes of Mr Batstone's last complaint that the judge wrongly trespassed upon the legitimate give and take of discussion between adults and wrongly allowed Stephen's influence upon her to seek her escape from an act which upon proper analysis worked to her advantage because it brought a continuing liability as trustee to an early end. Mr Batstone seeks to bring this case within that category referred to by Lindley L.J. where the Courts of Equity repudiate any jurisdiction to set aside gifts "on the ground of the folly, imprudence or want of foresight on the part of donors". In my judgment this case falls squarely within that other category to which he referred where the court, as a court of conscience, does intervene "to protect people from being forced, tricked or misled in any way by others into parting with their property".

49. In my judgment Nicholas's actions were unconscionable and this appeal is wholly without merit. I would dismiss it.

For a further example of the courts being required to make difficult judgments about the legitimacy of pressure applied in relation to family transactions, see *Halpern v Halpern* [2007] EWCA Civ 291.

Further reading

Peter Birks and Nyuk Yin Chin, 'On the Nature of Undue Influence' in J. Beatson and D. Friedmann (eds), *Good Faith and Fault in Contract Law* (Oxford: Oxford University Press, 1995) p.57

Rick Bigwood, 'Contracts by Unfair Advantage: From Exploitation to Transactional Neglect' (2005) 25 OJLS 65

Roger Brownsword, 'Copyright Assignment, Fair Dealing, and Unconscionable Contracts' [1998] *Intellectual Property Quarterly* 311

John Phillips, 'Protecting Those in a Disadvantageous Negotiating Position: Unconscionable Bargains as a Unifying Doctrine' (2010) 45 *Wake Forest Law Review* 837

S. Smith, 'Contracting Under Pressure: A Theory of Duress' [1997] CLJ 343

Michael J. Trebilcock, *The Limits of Freedom of Contract* (Cambridge, Mass: Harvard University Press, 1993) Ch.4 ('Coercion')

S.M. Waddams, 'Unconscionability in Contracts' (1976) 39 MLR 369

27

VOID AND ILLEGAL CONTRACTS

LEARNING OBJECTIVES

By the end of this chapter, you should:

■ be familiar with the leading cases on the defence of illegality;
■ understand the circumstances in which a contract is likely to be held enforceable some element of illegality notwithstanding;
■ have critically reflected on the considerations that bear on determining whether a contract should be treated as unenforceable for reasons of illegality;
■ understand that there are limited circumstances in which a transaction will be held to be contrary to public policy.

INTRODUCTION

A contract may be complete and perfect so far as offer and acceptance, consideration, and intention to create legal relations are concerned and yet still fail because its objects are contrary to the policy of the law. This may be because they directly infringe a rule of common law or a statutory provision or because they are regarded as "contrary to public policy". This last concept is inevitably vague and imprecise and accordingly the courts are careful to assert that no new heads of public policy may now be created; but for all that, opinions as to what is injurious to the public welfare must naturally vary with shifts in social, moral and political thought down the years. Again, the consequences of a contract's falling into one of the invalidated categories vary and, for this reason, it is thought fit to distinguish offending agreements as "void" simply or "illegal". The distinction is thought to be justified and important in three main directions:

27-001

(a) void provisions may, in appropriate cases, be "severed" from the contract, so leaving unoffending undertakings fully enforceable; this does not apply to void and illegal contracts;

(b) where a contract is void, money or property which has been transferred under it may be generally recovered in a quasi-contractual or other action. Ownership does not pass under a void contract but it may do so under a contract which is illegal. Where property has been transferred under a contract which is illegal but not void, recovery is possible only in cases where the parties are not equally at fault and only by the less guilty party;

(c) collateral transactions which would themselves be tainted by an illegal contract, will be unimpaired by connection with a merely void one.

The terminology used by the courts is unhappily not uniform and some contracts are commonly described as illegal when their effects are more properly consonant with mere voidness—agreements in restraint of trade are a conspicuous example. Terminology in this connection is very varied generally—"contra bonos mores", "illegal", "void", "unenforceable", "immoral", etc., being used quite indiscriminately in the cases. Accordingly, in this chapter, some of the principal causes of voidness and illegality and their effects are offered for consideration, with statutory cases discussed first and the others classified into separate groups of void and illegal contracts respectively.

There are four principal sections in this chapter. The first section offers a general overview of the classes of contracts that fall within the ambit of this chapter; the second collects together the leading cases on the effects of illegality; the third is largely concerned with contracts and covenants that are in restraint of trade (and, as such, potentially void); and, in the final section, the question of the enforceability of pre-nuptial and post-nuptial agreements is considered.

1. THE CONTRACTS DESCRIBED

A. Cases Affected by Statute

27-002   Where a contract offends against the provisions of a statute, much depends upon the object, purpose and interpretation of the particular provision. From the middle years of the nineteenth century, a relatively coherent body of doctrine developed on the statutory invalidation of contracts in relation to gaming and wagering—these contracts being treated as "null and void" under s.18 of the Gaming Act 1845. However, in a clutch of repeals made by s.334 of the Gambling Act 2005, s.18 no longer represents the law. Rather, s.335(1) of the Gambling Act provides that the fact that a contract relates to gambling shall not prevent its enforcement. But, for the purposes of the 2005 Act, what precisely counts as "gambling"? According to s.3 of the Act:

"In this Act "gambling" means—
    (a) gaming (within the meaning of section 6),
    (b) betting (within the meaning of section 9), and
    (c) participating in a lottery (within the meaning of section 14 and subject to section 15)."
Each of these instances of gambling is then further defined in its own section. For example, s.9 defines "betting" as follows:

"(1) In this Act "betting" means making or accepting a bet on—
    (a)   the outcome of a race, competition or other event or process,
    (b)   the likelihood of anything occurring or not occurring, or
    (c)   whether anything is or is not true.

(2) A transaction that relates to the outcome of a race, competition or other event or process may be a bet within the meaning of subsection (1) despite the facts that—
    (a)   the race, competition, event or process has already occurred or been completed, and
    (b)   one party to the transaction knows the outcome.

(3) A transaction that relates to the likelihood of anything occurring or not occurring may be a bet within the meaning of subsection (1) despite the facts that—
    (a)   the thing has already occurred or failed to occur, and
    (b)   one party to the transaction knows that the thing has already occurred or failed to occur."

It should also be noted that s.335(2) makes it clear that the new enforceability of gambling transactions is "without prejudice to any rule of law preventing the enforcement of a contract on the grounds of unlawfulness (other than a rule relating specifically to gambling)." Given the complexity of some of these provisions, there might continue to be some nice points arising around whether or not a transaction is a "gambling contract" and thus enforceable other things being equal (rather than being "null and void"); and, as with the old law, the jurisprudence might continue to be guided by the object, purpose and interpretation of the legislation. Moreover, as Stephen Waddams has pointed out, although the "principle that agreements are always to be enforced would appear to demand the enforcement of bets and wagers . . . it seems very probable that modern courts, like their predecessors, would, if pressed, seek a way not to use their powers to enforce huge and random transfers of wealth on personal bets" (Stephen Waddams, *Principle and Policy in Contract Law* (Cambridge: Cambridge University Press, 2011) p.165).

Question

If, as Waddams (above) suggests, modern courts might "seek a way not to use their powers to enforce huge and random transfers of wealth on personal bets" how might they most convincingly do this? For example, how far would the idea of "unconscionability" assist a court?

27-003

B. Void Contracts

There are three main groups of such contracts—those in restraint of trade, those to oust the jurisdiction of the courts and those to the prejudice of the married state.

27-004

i. Contracts in Restraint of Trade

These agreements themselves may in turn be subdivided into three main types:

27-005

(a) agreements whereby a vendor of a business covenants with his purchaser that he will not carry on business in competition with him;

(b) agreements whereby a servant covenants with his master not to compete with the latter's business upon leaving his service;

(c) agreements whereby a group of traders contract to regulate their output, prices, etc.

Type (c) is now regulated by the Competition Act 1998.

The general rules regarding the first two types of agreement are discussed and explained in the speeches, particularly, of Lord Macnaghten in *Nordenfelt's Case* [1894] A.C. 535 and Lord Parker in *Herbert Morris & Co v Saxelby* [1916] 1 A.C. 688, and may be summed up as follows:

(1) Every covenant in restraint of trade is contrary to public policy and prima facie void: but a covenant may be upheld if

    (a) the covenantee shows that it is reasonable as between the parties to it; and
    (b) the covenantor does not show that it is unreasonable in the interests of the public.

(2) Both (a) and (b) are matters of law for the decision of the judge.

While these have been hitherto the principal categories of offending agreements, it is important to note that they are not exclusive. In particular, the agreements known as "solus" agreements, whereby garages become tied to particular suppliers of motor fuels, have in the modern era come before the courts: see *Alec Lobb (Garages) Ltd v Total Oil*, (above, Ch.26) and *Esso Petroleum v Harper's Garage* (below); it is also clear that the provisions of professional bodies for the conduct of their members may also constitute a restraint of trade which cannot be upheld as reasonable: see *Dickson v Pharmaceutical Society of Great Britain* [1967] Ch. 708; [1967] 2 All E.R. 558 CA; [1970] A.C. 403 HL; and the provisions of the Football League and Football Association concerning the transfer and retention of players were found to offend against public policy in *Eastham v Newcastle United Football Club* [1964] Ch. 413; in respect of cricket, see *Greig v Insole* [1978] 1 W.L.R. 302. In respect of restraint provisions in partnership agreements between medical practitioners, see *Peyton v Mindham* [1972] 1 W.L.R. 8; [1971] 3 All E.R. 1215 (Pennycuick VC).

In view of their relative frequency of occurrence and their importance, contracts in restraint of trade will be used to illustrate void contracts.

ii. Agreements to Oust the Jurisdiction of the Courts

27-006   That agreements to oust the jurisdiction of the courts are "illegal and void on grounds of public policy" has been already noted and a principle has been suggested to distinguish such ouster—which is ineffective—from an arrangement where there is a declared intention not to create legal relations, which is effective.

The application of that principle to a contract containing an arbitration clause is that recourse to the courts cannot be prevented. But it is possible effectively to provide that no action shall be brought until an arbitration award has been made. A clause so providing is called a *Scott v Avery* clause, after the case in which it was upheld: *Scott v Avery* (1856) 5 H.L.C. 811.

iii. Agreements Prejudicial to the Married State

27-007   Once again three main kinds of transaction are invalidated by the legal policy which protects the status of marriage:

(a)   A contract which purports to impose on one of the parties a restraint upon his liberty to marry whom he pleases. Thus, where A contracted under seal with B that he would not marry anyone other than B and would pay her £2,000 if he did so, it was held that the deed was void: *Lowe v Peers* (1768) 4 Burr. 2225. It is to be noted that, in that case, neither A nor B directly promised to marry the other: an ordinary engagement to marry with the reciprocal promises of the parties was, of course, a perfectly valid contract at common law. The action for breach of promise of marriage was abolished by s.1(1) of the Law Reform (Miscellaneous Provisions) Act 1970.

(b)   A contract under which one party is to receive a remuneration for bringing about an engagement to marry. Such a contract is generally known as a "marriage brokage" contract and is void. See *Hermann v Charlesworth* [1905] 2 K.B. 123 and R. Powell, 6 *Current Legal Problems* 254–273.

(c)   A contract which tends to encourage immorality or infidelity in a party to an existing marriage.

An agreement entered into by H and W as to possible future separation is bad because it is potentially conducive to a weakening of marital bonds: *H v W* (1857) 3 K. & J. 382. It would be a different matter in the case of an agreement for immediate separation which is, and long has been, valid.

The distinction of course is that in the latter case the marriage has already broken down when the agreement is made.

C. Illegal Contracts

Merely void contracts as just considered all bear their invalidating element, as it were, on the face of the agreement. In the illegal contracts proper, to which we now turn, the contract may be illegal ex facie or, while apparently good on its face, be vitiated by the purpose or motive behind it. This can be a matter of the greatest importance in considering the consequences and effects of an illegal contract, because the vitiating ulterior purpose may be shared by both parties or be in the contemplation of only one of them and, in this latter case, the innocent party may not always be precluded from relief (see below, s.3). Another consequence of the possible invalidation of a contract because of a motive or object not apparent upon the face of the agreement, is that questions may arise as to the manner in which the illegality comes to the attention of the court: in this connection, the reader is referred to the principles enunciated by Devlin J in *Edler v Auerbach* [1950] 1 K.B. 359.

27-008

i. Agreements to Commit an Unlawful Act

That the courts should refuse their aid in respect of contracts whose purpose is to commit an illegal act is common sense. Hence, an agreement to commit an assault or a burglary would be unenforceable, as also to publish a libel or to make a false representation. See *Brown, Jenkinson v Percy Dalton*. Instances of an arrangement seemingly valid but in substance designed to defraud will be found in *Alexander v Rayson* [1936] 1 K.B. 169 and *Miller v Karlinski* (1945) 62 T.L.R. 85.

27-009

A contract which is perfectly lawful in its inception may become unlawful through the manner in which it is performed. If A contracts to sell fertilisers to B and, in pursuance of that perfectly valid contract, delivers the goods without also delivering an invoice stating the percentage of certain chemicals therein—an omission which is an offence punishable summarily with a fine—he cannot recover the price: *Anderson v Daniel* [1924] 1 K.B. 138. This principle, however, should be considered in the light of *Marles v Philip Trant Ltd* (below) and *St John Shipping Corp v Joseph Rank Ltd* [1957] 1 Q.B. 267.

A contract is generally invalid in English law if performance of it is unlawful by the law of the country where it is to be performed. But in *Howard v Shirlstar Container Transport Ltd* [1990] 3 All E.R. 366 CA, it was held that the plaintiff could recover an agreed fee for flying the defendant's aircraft out of Nigeria although he had taken off without permission from air traffic control which was a serious statutory offence under Nigerian law. He took off because he believed on reasonable grounds that his life and that of his wireless operator were in imminent danger so long as they remained in Nigeria. Although the court said it would not be justified in departing from the judge's conclusion that the act was excusable under Nigerian criminal law, the principal ground of the decision appears to be that, even if the act was illegal, enforcement of the claim would not be an "affront to the public conscience" because it was not morally reprehensible. Staughton LJ said that it would be the same if the offence had been committed in England. The decision was doubted in *Tinsley v Milligan*, below, where the "public conscience" ground was disapproved.

The English courts will not refuse to enforce a contract governed by foreign law which is not illegal but is contrary to the public policy of that country, unless the public policy is one which also applies in England: *Lemenda Trading Co Ltd v African Middle East Petroleum Company Ltd* [1988] 1 All E.R. 513 QBD.

ii. Agreements Prejudicial to the Interest of the State

27-010   This rather vague head covers four main types of offending agreement:

Agreements with enemy aliens. An enemy alien is anyone who voluntarily resides in enemy or enemy occupied territory in time of war, and any agreement made with such a person is bad. Again, a contract made in time of peace may be abrogated if, with the advent of war, one of the parties becomes an enemy alien. This, however, is not an absolute rule: a contract will escape abrogation if its performance involves no intercourse with the enemy and is not otherwise contrary to public policy—for instance, a separation agreement between a man and his wife, who has become an enemy alien. Again, though a contract be dissolved, rights which may have accrued to either party before the invalidating event remain valid and may be enforced upon the return of peace. See *Ertel Bieber & Co v Rio Tinto Co* [1918] A.C. 260, *Arab Bank Ltd v Barclays Bank* [1954] A.C. 495 and *Bevan v Bevan* [1955] 2 Q.B. 227.

Agreements hostile to a friendly foreign state. A friendly state is, in effect, any state with which Britain is not in a state of war: any agreement which harms Britain's relations with such a state is bad and void. Examples include agreements to enable subjects of a foreign state to overthrow their government by force[1] or to smuggle liquor into a state whose constitution imposed a requirement of prohibition.[2] A striking instance of the possible width of the ban is to be seen in *Regazzoni v KC Sethia (1944) Ltd* [1958] A.C. 301, where the House of Lords refused to give effect to a contract for the export of goods to South Africa from India which infringed an Indian statute forbidding such export.

Agreements prejudicial to the administration of justice. Agreements of this type are those which aim to interfere with the due course of law, for example to suppress a prosecution, to conceal a crime, not to appear at the public examination of a bankrupt, etc. With regard to stifling prosecutions, however, it must be noted that many wrongs give rise to both civil and criminal remedies and, where the element of public wrong is subordinate to that of private injury, an agreement not to take or go on with criminal proceedings will be enforceable. Thus, for example, an agreement not to prosecute for libel or common assault would be valid; but not a similar agreement in respect of, say, a riot or obstruction of the police in the performance of their duty. The leading authority is *Keir v Leeman* (1846) 9 Q.B. 371 and reference might profitably also be made to *Jones v Merionethshire Permanent Benefit Building Society* [1892] 1 Ch. 173 and *Fisher & Co v Apollinaris Co* (1875) 10 Ch.App. 297.

Agreements prejudicial to probity in public life. Into this category fall such agreements as one to sell or procure a title of honour or public office (in which connection, see the Honours (Prevention of Abuses) Act 1925); also—and perhaps more probable in modern times—contracts for the assignment or mortgage of the salary of a holder of a public office, for the object of the salary is to enable the official to uphold the dignity of his office in a fitting manner. For the operation of this principle in relation to civil servants, see *Lucas v Lucas* [1943] P. 68 and Logan, 61 L.Q.R. 240.

----

[1]   *De Wutz v Hendricks* (1824) 2 Bing. 314.
[2]   *Foster v Driscoll* [1929] 1 K.B. 470.

iii. Contracts to Promote Sexual Immorality

Any agreement which has as its object future illicit sexual relations is bad under this head. Hence a promise to pay a monthly allowance to a mistress, even if made by deed under seal, would be void: so also a contract which, though seemingly innocent, has, to the knowledge of the parties, an immoral motive—see *Pearce v Brooks*, para.27–012. On the other hand, a promise of money, etc., in respect of past sexual immorality is not affected by the ban and consequently, if made under seal, would be enforceable: if not under seal, it would be ineffective simply on the ground that past consideration is no consideration; cf. *Beaumont v Reeve* (1846) 8 Q.B. 483.

27-011

2. EFFECTS OF ILLEGALITY

A. On Actions on the Contract

PEARCE AND ANOTHER v BROOKS

Exchequer (1866) L.R. 1 Ex. 213; 4 H. & C. 358; 35 L.J. Ex. 134; 14 L.T. 288; 20 J.P. 295; 14 W.R. 614

Declaration stating an agreement by which the plaintiffs agreed to supply the defendant with a new miniature brougham on hire, 'til the purchase-money should be paid by instalments in a period which was not to exceed 12 months; the defendant to have the option to purchase as aforesaid, and to pay £50 down; and in case the brougham should be returned before a second instalment was paid, a forfeiture of 15 guineas was to be paid in addition to the £50, and also any damage, except fair wear. Averment, that the defendant returned the brougham before a second instalment was paid, and that it was damaged. Breach, non-payment of 15 guineas, or the amount of the damage. Money counts.

27-012

Plea 3, to the first count, that at the time of making the supposed agreement, the defendant was, to the knowledge of the plaintiffs, a prostitute, and that the supposed agreement was made for the supply of a brougham to be used by her as such prostitute, and to assist her in carrying on her said immoral vocation, as the plaintiffs when they made the said agreement well knew, and in the expectation by the plaintiffs that the defendant would pay the plaintiffs the moneys to be paid by the said agreement out of her receipts as such prostitute. Issue.

The case was tried before Bramwell B at Guildhall, at the sittings after Michaelmas Term 1865. It then appeared that the plaintiffs were coachbuilders in partnership, and evidence was given which satisfied the jury that one of the partners knew that the defendant was a prostitute; but there was no direct evidence that either of the plaintiffs knew that the brougham was intended to be used for the purpose of enabling the defendant to prosecute her trade of prostitution; and there was no evidence that the plaintiffs expected to be paid out of the wages of prostitution.

The learned judge ruled that the allegation in the plea as to the mode of payment was immaterial, and he put to the jury the following questions:

1. Did the defendant hire the brougham for the purpose of her prostitution?

2. If she did, did the plaintiffs know the purpose for which it was hired?

The jury found that the carriage was used by the defendant as part of her display, to attract men; and that the plaintiffs knew it was supplied to be used for that purpose. They gave nothing for the alleged damage.

On this finding, the learned judge directed a verdict for the defendant, and gave the plaintiffs leave to move to enter a verdict for them for the 15 guineas penalty.

BRAMWELL B.

There is no doubt that the woman was a prostitute; no doubt to my mind that the plaintiffs knew it; there was cogent evidence of the fact, and the jury have so found. The only fact really in dispute is for what purpose was the brougham hired, and if for an immoral purpose, did the plaintiffs know it? At the trial I doubted whether there was evidence of this, but, for the reasons I have stated, I think the jury were entitled to infer, as they did, that it was hired for the purpose of display, that is, for the purpose of enabling the defendant to pursue her calling, and that the plaintiffs knew it.

That being made out, my difficulty was, whether, though the defendant hired the brougham for that purpose, it could be said that the plaintiffs let it for the same purpose. In one sense, it was not for the same purpose. If a man were to ask for duelling pistols, and to say: "I think I shall fight a duel tomorrow," might not the seller answer: "I do not want to know your purpose; I have nothing to do with it; that is your business: mine is to sell the pistols, and look only to the profit of trade." No doubt the act would be immoral, but I have felt a doubt whether it would be illegal; and I should still feel it, but that the authority of *Cannan v Bryce* (3 B. & A. 179) *M'Kinnell v Robinson*, (3 M. & W. 434), concludes the matter. In the latter case the plea does not say that the money was lent on the terms that the borrower should game with it; but only that it was borrowed by the defendant, and lent by the plaintiff "for the purpose of the defendant's illegally playing and gaming therewith." The case was argued by Crompton J. against the plea, and by Wightman J. in support of it; and the considered judgment of the court was delivered by Lord Abinger, who says (p. 441):

"As the plea states that the money for which the action is brought was lent for the purpose of illegally playing and gaming therewith, at the illegal game of 'Hazard,' this money cannot be recovered back, on the principle, not for the first time laid down, but fully settled in the case of *Cannan v Bryce*. This principle is that the repayment of money, lent for the express purpose of accomplishing an illegal object, cannot be enforced." This court, then, following *Cannan v Bryce*, decided that it need not be part of the bargain that the subject of the contract should be used unlawfully, but that it is enough if it is handed over for the purpose that the borrower shall so apply it. We are, then, concluded by authority on the point; and, as I have no doubt that the finding of the jury was right, the rule must be discharged."

With respect, however, to the allegation in the plea, which, as I have said, need not be proved, and which I refused to leave to the jury, I desire that it may not be supposed we are overruling anything that Lord Ellenborough has said. It is manifest that he could not have meant to lay down as a rule of law that there would be no illegality in a contract unless payment were to be made out of the proceeds of the illegal act, and that his observation was made with a different view. In the case of the hiring of a cab, which was mentioned in the argument, it would be absurd to suppose that, when both parties were doing the same thing, with the same object and purpose, it would be a lawful act in one, and unlawful in the other.

Pollock C. B., Martin and Pigott B. B. delivered concurring judgments.

Rule Discharged.

Questions

27-013
1. Could Bramwell B's seller of the pistol (above) have recovered the price? See Glanville Williams, *The Criminal Law* (2nd edn), pp.366 and following, and *National Coal Board v Gamble* [1959] 1 Q.B. 11 per Devlin J at 23.

2. Do you agree that the plaintiffs could have brought trover for the carriage? See *Taylor v Chester* (below) and *Bowmakers Ltd v Barnet Instruments Ltd* (below).

Problem

Lawrence, a landlord, lets flats (a) to Ada whom he believes to be Ben's mistress; (b) to Poppy whom he believes to be a prostitute. He is correctly informed in both cases. Does this belief debar him from recovering rent in respect of the flats?

27-014

Cf. *R. v Thomas* [1957] 1 W.L.R. 747; *Shaw v DPP* [1962] A.C. 220.

MARLES v PHILIP TRANT & SONS LTD MACKINNON, THIRD PARTY

Court of Appeal [1954] 1 Q.B. 29; [1953] 2 W.L.R. 564; 97 S.J. 189; [1953] 1 All E.R. 651

The defendants, seed merchants, bought from the third party wheat under the description of spring wheat known as Fylgia and resold part of it to the plaintiff, a farmer, under the same description. The wheat was not spring wheat and was known as Vilmorin. The farmer sued the merchants claiming damages for breach of contract and warranty, recovering judgment for £418 5s. 10d. and costs. The merchants had added the person who supplied them with the wheat as a third party, claiming from him an indemnity for the loss of what they had had to pay to the farmer and also damages. The third party took the point that since the merchants had not, in conformity with s.1 of the Seeds Act 1920, delivered to the plaintiff a statement in writing containing the prescribed particulars with respect to the seeds' variety, purity and germination, the contract of the merchants with the plaintiff was illegal and, therefore, the merchants could not recover their loss on it from the third party. The trial judge who, otherwise, would have given judgment against the third party, on the ground that it was their breach of warranty or of contract which had led to the damage, upheld the contention of the third party and gave judgment for him against the merchants. The merchants appealed and, before the Court of Appeal, the third party admitted that the merchants were entitled to recover nominal damages against the third party, but not an indemnity for their loss on their contract with the plaintiff.

27-015

Singleton LJ delivered a judgment allowing the appeal.

DENNING LJ

The first question which arises in this case is: what is the legal effect of the omission to supply the particulars prescribed under the Seeds Act? The trial judge has held that it turned the contract with the farmer, so far as the seed merchant was concerned, into an illegal contract. The judge so held on the authority of *Anderson Ltd v Daniel* [1924] 1 K.B. 138 and *B. & B. Viennese Fashions v Losane* [1952] 1 T.L.R. 750, and there are indeed some observations in those cases which warrant him taking that view. But I do not think that they are correct. There can be no doubt that the contract between the seed merchants and the farmer was not unlawful when it was made. If the farmer had repudiated it before the time for delivery arrived, the seed merchants could certainly have sued him for damages. Nor was the contract rendered unlawful simply because the seed was delivered without the prescribed particulars. If it were unlawful, the farmer himself could not have sued upon it as he has done. The truth is that it was not the contract itself which was unlawful, but only the performance of it. The seed merchants performed it in an illegal way in that they omitted to furnish the prescribed particulars. That renders the contract unenforceable by them, but it does not render the contract illegal. Atkin L.J. expressed the position with his usual accuracy in *Anderson Ltd v Daniel* when he said simply that the contract was unenforceable. I do not think that the law has ever countenanced the idea that a transaction, lawful when done, can be rendered unlawful by the doctrine of relation back: see *Elliott v Boynton* [1924] 1 Ch. 236. A transaction which is unlawful, when done, can be rendered lawful by relation back (see *Howell v Falmouth Boat Construction Co Ltd* [1951] A.C. 837) but not vice versa.

Once rid of the notion that the contract with the farmer was itself illegal, the question becomes: what is the effect of the admitted illegality in performance? It certainly prevents the seed merchants from suing the farmer for the price, but does it prevent them suing their supplier for damages? I think not. There was nothing unlawful in the contract between the seed merchants and their supplier, neither in the formation of it, nor in the performance of it. The seed merchants must therefore be entitled to damages for the breach of it. So far so good, but the difficulty comes when they seek to prove their damages. They want to be indemnified for the damages which they have been ordered to pay to the farmer. To prove those damages, they have to prove the contract with the farmer, and the circumstances under which the damages were awarded. It is said that once they begin to rely on their deliveries to the farmer, they seek aid from their own illegality; and that that is a thing which they are not allowed to do. The maxim is invoked: Ex turpi causa non oritur actio. That maxim must not, however, be carried too far . . . The omission by the seed merchants to deliver the prescribed particulars was an act of inadvertence. It was not a deliberate breach of the law. I venture to assert that there is no moral justification for the court to apply the maxim in this case. But is there any legal justification? A distinction must be drawn, I think, between an illegality which destroys the cause of action and an illegality which affects only the damages recoverable.

So far as the cause of action itself is concerned, the principle is well settled that, if the plaintiff requires any aid from an illegal transaction to establish his cause of action, then he shall not have any aid from the court. That appears in all the books from *Simpson v Bloss*, 7 Taunt. 246, down to *Berg v Sadler and Moore* [1937] 2 K.B. 158 and *J. Dennis & Co Ltd v Munn* [1949] 2 K.B. 327. In my opinion, those cases have no application to this case, because the seed merchants here can make out their cause of action perfectly well without any recourse to the illegality at all. All they need to do is to prove the contract by which the supplier agreed to supply Fylgia seed, and then show that he in fact supplied Vilmorin. That is sufficient to entitle them, by way of damages, to the estimated loss directly and naturally resulting, in the ordinary course of events, from that breach of contract: see *Cory v Thames Ironworks etc., Co* (1868) L.R. 3 Q.B. 181 and section 53(2) of the Sale of Goods Act, 1893. There was no need for them to claim the particular loss arising from the sub-contract, and so long as they refrained from claiming that loss, there could be no possible objection to the claim: see *Gordon v Chief Commissioner of Metropolitan Police* [1910] 2 K.B. 1080.

The difficulty only arises because the seed merchants claim the special loss resulting from the sub-contract. The supplier says, in effect, to the seed merchants: "I have discovered that you have been guilty of an illegality. You did not deliver the prescribed particulars to the farmers who bought from you. Therefore you cannot recover your loss." It is to be noticed that the omission to deliver the particulars does not make any practical difference in this case. Even if the seed merchants had delivered the prescribed particulars, the position would have been the same. The seed would have been described as Fylgia, and the plaintiff would have recovered his damages just the same. Nevertheless, the supplier says that he is entitled in law to be relieved of liability.

So far as this question of damages is concerned, the civil courts act on the principle that they will not lend their aid to a man so as to enable him to get a benefit from his own crime; nor will they help him to get reparation for the consequences of his own culpable criminal act. Thus, when a man committed suicide in order that the insurance moneys payable on his death might be obtained, his representatives were not allowed to recover the amount: *Beresford v Royal Insurance Co Ltd* [1937] 2 K.B. 197; [1938] A.C. 586. When a solicitor sought to be indemnified by his insurers against the consequences of his own champerty, his action failed: *Haseldine v Hosken* [1933] 1 K.B. 822. When a wholesale wine merchant bought from a manufacturer liquor which he should have known was contaminated, and resold it, without lawful excuse, to his customers, he was not allowed to recover from the manufacturers the damages which he had to pay his customers: *Askey v Golden Wine Co Ltd*, 64 T.L.R. 379; [1948] 2 All E.R. 35. In those cases the plaintiff was undoubtedly seeking to get reparation for the consequences of his own culpable crime.

But there are cases nowadays where a man can be guilty of a crime without any moral culpability at all. Thus, a man who is induced by fraud to do a criminal act will have a cause of action against the deceiver, if he himself had no knowledge of the circumstances which rendered it criminal: *Burrows v Rhodes* [1899] 1 Q.B. 816, 831. And a provision merchant who relies on a warranty by his supplier, but subsequently is convicted for selling bad food, will be able to recover any damage he suffers by reason of reselling it to his customers (*Crage v Fry* (1903) 67 J.P. 240; *Cointat v Myham & Son* [1913] 2 K.B. 220; and *Weld-Blundell v Stephens* [1919] 1 K.B. 520, 539) provided, of course, that the damages claimed are not too remote: *Simon v Pawsons & Leafs Ltd*, 38 Com.Cas. 151, 157–158. It has been held that a motorist who had to pay damages for negligence could recover an indemnity from his insurers even though the negligence was so gross as to amount to manslaughter: *Tinline v White Cross Insurance Association Ltd* [1921] 3 K.B. 327; and *James v British and General Insurance Co Ltd* [1927] 2 K.B. 311. I think that those cases were rightly decided. The right to indemnity for negligence should not depend on the chance whether a man is prosecuted, or the further chance whether he is convicted. Those cases were stronger than the present case. If public policy did not prevent recovery in those cases, it should not prevent recovery here . . .

lorry in which it was intended that the load should be carried only had a "C" licence. The defendants appealed.

PEARCE LJ

It having been proved . . . that the plaintiffs were imposed on and believed that the goods could lawfully be carried on Randall's van, are they disentitled to sue? . . . Let us assume (although I am far from satisfied on this point) that the learned judge was in error in holding that the haulage contract could have been performed by the defendants in any way they liked (that is to say, lawfully as well as unlawfully). Let us assume first that it was a contract for carriage in Randall's van only and secondly that it was not by the nature of the contract one which could be performed vicariously. It must then inevitably be carried out unlawfully if (but only if) one adds the fact that Randall's van had a "C" licence and therefore could not lawfully carry the goods in question. But that fact, though known to the defendants, was unknown to the plaintiffs.

This is not a case where the plaintiffs can assert a cause of action without relying on the contract. Mr Leonard put forward an ingenious alternative argument based on the plaintiffs' rights against the defendants as voluntary bailees of the plaintiffs' property: see *Bowmakers Ltd v Barnet Instruments Ltd* [below], so that he might claim in negligence or conversion without having any recourse to the contract or exposing to the court as part of his cause of action its alleged illegality. But I do not think that he can make good that argument. His cause of action comes from the contract, and if the contract is such that the court must refuse its aid, the plaintiffs cannot recover their damages.

If a contract is expressly or by necessary implication forbidden by statute, or if it is ex facie illegal, or if both parties know that though ex facie legal it can only be performed by illegality or is intended to be performed illegally, the law will not help the plaintiffs in any way that is a direct or indirect enforcement of rights under the contract. And for this purpose both parties are presumed to know the law.

The first question therefore, is whether this contract of carriage was forbidden by statute. The two cases on which the defendants mainly rely are *Re an Arbitration between Mahmoud and Ispahani* [above] and *J. Dennis & Co Ltd v Munn* ([1949] 2 K.B. 327). In both those cases the plaintiffs were unable to enforce their rights under contracts forbidden by statute. In the former case the statutory order said: "a person shall not . . . buy or sell . . . certain articles . . . except under and in accordance with the terms of a licence." In the latter case the statutory regulation provided: "subject to the provisions of this regulation . . . the execution . . . of any operation specified . . . shall be unlawful except in so far as authorised." In neither case could the plaintiff bring his contract within the exception that alone would have made its subject-matter lawful, namely, by showing the existence of a licence. Therefore, the core of both contracts was the mischief expressly forbidden by the statutory order and the statutory regulation respectively.

In *Mahmoud's* case the object of the order was to prevent (except under licence) a person buying and a person selling, and both parties were liable to penalties. A contract of sale between those persons was therefore expressly forbidden. In *Dennis's* case the object of the regulation was to prevent (except under licence) owners from performing building operations, and builders from carrying out the work for them. Both parties were liable to penalties and a contract between these persons for carrying out an unlawful operation would be forbidden by implication.

The case before us is somewhat different. The carriage of the plaintiffs' whisky was not as such prohibited; the statute merely regulated the means by which carriers should carry goods. Therefore this contract was not expressly forbidden by the statute.

Was it then forbidden by implication? The Road and Rail Traffic Act, 1933, s.1, says: "no person shall use a goods vehicle on a road for the carriage of goods . . . except under licence," and provides that such use shall be an offence. Did the statute thereby intend to forbid by implication all contracts whose performance must on all the facts (whether known or not) result in a contravention of that section?

The plaintiffs' part of the contract could not constitute an illegal use of the vehicle by them since they were not "using" the vehicle. If they were aware of the true facts they would, of course, be guilty of aiding and abetting the defendants, but if they acted in good faith they would not be guilty of any offence under the statute: see *Davies, Turner & Co Ltd v Brodie* ([1954] 1 W.L.R. 1364; [1954] 3 All E.R. 283) and *Carter v Mace* ([1949] 2 All E.R. 714). In this case, therefore, the plaintiffs were not committing any offence.

In *St. John Shipping Corporation v Rank* ([1957] 1 Q.B. 267; [1956] 3 All E.R. 683) Devlin J. held that the plaintiffs were entitled to recover although there had been an infringement of a statute in the performance of a contract, but in that case the contract was legal when made. Though not directly applicable to the present case, it contains an observation (with which I entirely agree) on the point which arises here. He said: "For example, a person is forbidden by statute from using an unlicensed vehicle on the highway. If one asks oneself whether there is in such an enactment an implied prohibition of all contracts for the use of unlicensed vehicles, the answer may well be that there is, and that contracts of hire would be unenforceable. But if one asks oneself whether there is an implied prohibition of contracts for the carriage of goods by unlicensed vehicles or for the repairing of unlicensed vehicles or for the garaging of unlicensed vehicles, the answer may well be different. The answer might be that collateral contracts of this sort are not within the ambit of the statute." In my judgment that distinction is valid.

The object of the Road and Rail Traffic Act 1933, was not (in this connection) to interfere with the owner of goods or his facilities for transport, but to control those who provided the transport, with a view to promoting its efficiency. Transport of goods was not made illegal but the various licence holders were prohibited from encroaching on one another's territory, the intention of the Act being to provide an orderly and comprehensive service. Penalties were provided for those licence holders who went outside the bounds of their allotted spheres. These penalties apply to those using the vehicle but not to the goods owner. Though the latter could be convicted of aiding and abetting any breach, the restrictions were not aimed at him. Thus a contract of carriage was, in the sense used by Devlin J., "collateral," and it was not impliedly forbidden by the statute.

This view is supported by common sense and convenience. If the other view were held it would have far-reaching effects. For instance, if a carrier induces me (who am in fact ignorant of any illegality) to entrust goods to him and negligently destroys them, he would only have to show that (though unknown to me) his licence had expired, or did not properly cover the transportation, or that he was uninsured, and I should then be without a remedy against him. Or, again, if I ride in a taxicab and the driver leaves me stranded in some deserted spot, he would only have to show that he was (though unknown to me) unlicensed or uninsured, and I should be without remedy. This appears to me an undesirable extension of the implications of a statute . . .

It is for the defendants to show that contracts by the owner for the carriage of goods are within the ambit of the implied prohibition of the Road and Rail Traffic Act, 1933. In my judgment they have not done so.

The next question is whether this contract, though not forbidden by statute was ex facie illegal. Must any reasonable person on hearing the terms of the contract (with presumed knowledge of the law) realise that it was illegal? There is nothing illegal in its terms. Further knowledge, namely, knowledge of the fact that Randall's van was not properly licensed, would show that it could only be performed by contravention of the statute, but that does not make the contract ex facie illegal.

However, if both parties had that knowledge the contract would be unenforceable as being a contract which to their knowledge could not be carried out without a violation of the law: see per Lord Blackburn in *Waugh v Morris* (1873) L.R. 8 Q.B. 202). But where one party is ignorant of the fact that will make the performance illegal, is it established that the innocent party cannot obtain relief against the guilty party? The case has been argued with skill and care on both sides, and yet no case has been cited to us establishing the proposition that where a contract is on the face of it legal and is not forbidden by statute, but must in fact produce illegality by reason of a circumstance known to one party only, it should be held illegal so as to debar the innocent party from relief. In the absence of such a case I do not feel compelled to so unsatisfactory a conclusion, which would injure the innocent, benefit the guilty, and put a premium on deceit. I would dismiss the appeal.

DEVLIN LJ

It is a familiar principle of law that if a contract can be performed in one of two ways, that is, legally or illegally, it is not an illegal contract, though it may be unenforceable at the suit of a party who chooses to perform it illegally. That statement of the law is meaningful if the contract is one which is by its terms open to two modes of performance; otherwise it is meaningless. Almost any contract—certainly any contract for the carriage of goods by road—can be performed illegally; any contract of carriage by road can be performed illegally simply by exceeding the appropriate speed limit. The error in the defendants' argument, I think, is that they are looking at the facts which determine their capacity to perform and not at the terms of the contract. Suppose that the contract were for a vehicle with an "A" licence, or—what is substantially the same thing—for a specified vehicle warranted as holding an "A" licence. That would not be an illegal contract for it would be a contract for the use of a licensed vehicle and not an unlicensed one. If those were the express terms of the contract, it would not be made illegal because all the carrier's vehicles, or the specified vehicle, as the case might be, had "C" licences. The most that that could show would be that the carrier might well be unable to perform his contract . . .

I think there is much to be said for the argument that in a case of this sort there is, unless the circumstances exclude it, an implied warranty that the van is properly licensed for the service for which it is required. It would be unreasonable to expect a man when he is getting into a taxicab to ask for an express warranty from the driver that his cab was licensed; the answer, if it took any intelligible form at all, would be to the effect that it would not be on the streets if it were not. The same applies to a person who delivers goods for carriage by a particular vehicle; he cannot be expected to examine the road licence to see if it is in order. But the issue of warranty was not raised in the pleadings or at the trial and so I think it is preferable to decide this case on the broad ground which Pearce L.J. has adopted and with which, for the reasons I have given, I agree.

There are many pitfalls in this branch of the law. If, for example, Mr Field had observed that the van had a "C" licence and said nothing, he might be said to have accepted a mode of performance different from that contracted for and so varied the contract and turned it into an illegal one: see *St. John Shipping Corporation v Joseph Rank Ltd* where that sort of point was considered. Or, to take another example, if a statute prohibits the sale of goods to an alien, a warranty by the buyer that he is not an alien will not save the contract. That is because the terms of the prohibition expressly forbid a sale to an alien; consequently, the question to be asked in order to see whether the contact comes within the prohibition is whether the buyer is in fact an alien, not whether he represented himself as one. *Re Mahmoud* [above] is that sort of case . . .

[Having considered *Re Mahmoud* and *Strongman v Sincock* (above), his Lordship concluded:] Apart from the pleading point, it might not matter if the last two cases were not distinguishable, since the plaintiffs could obtain damages for breach of warranty as in *Strongman v Sincock*.

Sellers L.J. concurred in the decision.

Appeal Dismissed.

Points for reflection

1. In *Ashmore, Benson, Pease & Co Ltd v A v Dawson Ltd* [1973] 2 All E.R. 856; [1973] 1 W.L.R. 828, the plaintiffs had manufactured a large piece of equipment known as a tube-bank, weighing 25 tons, and orally contracted with the defendants, a small road haulage company, for its transport from Stockton-on-Tees to Hull for £55. Nothing was said of the type of vehicle to be used but the defendants owned a small fleet of articulated lorries, the largest a "30-tonner". The plaintiffs' transport manager was present when the defendants' lorry came to take the load. When loaded, the lorry greatly exceeded the permitted weight so that the transport constituted an offence under s.64(2) of the Road Traffic Act 1960; the tube-bank should have been carried on a "low-loader" of which the defendants had none. During the journey, the lorry toppled over through an error of judgment of the driver and the tube-bank was damaged to the amount of £2,225 which the plaintiffs claimed in an action for negligence and/or breach of contract. Waller J held that the contract was lawful when made and that the defendants could not plead the illegality of their performance and gave judgment for the plaintiffs. Allowing the appeal, the Court of Appeal (Lord Denning MR, Phillimore and Scarman LJJ) held that, on the evidence, the plaintiffs' transport manager must have realised that the loading was in breach of the Road Traffic Act 1960; accordingly, despite the legality of the contract at its inception, the plaintiffs, through the manager, participated in the illegality of its performance and were thus debarred from damages.

2. In *Shaw v Groom* [1970] 2 Q.B. 504; [1970] 1 All E.R. 702 CA, to a claim by a landlord for arrears of rent, the defendant tenant pleaded, inter alia, that no rent was recoverable by the landlord in that the latter had not provided a rent book as required by the Landlord and Tenant Act 1962 s.4. Under s.4(1) of the Act, such failure on the part of a landlord constituted a criminal offence. The county court judge rejected the landlord's claim. On appeal, the Court of Appeal reversed the decision. Though failure to provide a rent book is an offence on the landlord's part, a rent book is not an essential of the contract of letting and the fact of the offence does not preclude the landlord from suing for his rent unless the relevant statute expressly or impliedly forbids it; which was not the case here. Sachs LJ said (at 526): "It seems to me appropriate, accordingly, to allow this appeal on the broad basis that, even if the provision of a rent book is an essential act as between landlords and weekly tenants, yet the legislature did not by s.4 of the 1962 Act

intend to preclude the landlord from recovering any rent due or impose any forfeiture on him beyond the prescribed penalty."

Question

27-020   A engages a builder to repair his roof; the builder uses a ladder to do the work in circumstances in which A knows the regulations to require scaffolding. When the work is complete can A refuse to pay, pleading illegality? If the work is badly done and causes damage, can A sue in contract? Cf. C. J. Hamson [1973] C.L.J. 199.

BROWN JENKINSON & CO LTD v PERCY DALTON (LONDON) LTD

Court of Appeal [1957] 2 Q.B. 621; [1957] 3 W.L.R. 403; 101 S.J. 610; [1957] 2 All E.R. 846; [1957] 2 Lloyd's Rep. 1

27-021   The defendants had a quantity of orange juice which they wished to ship to Hamburg. The plaintiffs, as agents of the owners of the vessel on which the orange juice was to be shipped, informed the defendants that the barrels containing the orange juice were old and frail and that some were leaking and that a claused bill of lading should be granted. The defendants required a clean bill of lading, and the shipowners, at the defendants' request and on a promise that the defendants would give to them an indemnity, signed bills of lading stating that the barrels were "shipped in apparent good order and condition." The defendants, pursuant to their promise, entered into an indemnity whereby they undertook unconditionally to indemnify the master and the owners of the vessel against all losses which might arise from the issue of clean bills of lading in respect of the goods. The barrels, when delivered at Hamburg, were leaking and the shipowners had to make good the loss. The plaintiffs sued the defendants under the indemnity, the benefit of which had been assigned to them. The defendants refused to pay, alleging that the contract of indemnity was illegal, because it had as its object the making by the shipowners of a fraudulent misrepresentation. It was found that the shipowners did not desire or intend that anyone should be defrauded. It appeared from the evidence that the granting of clean bills of lading against indemnities was a common practice.

Judge Block gave judgment for the plaintiffs. The defendants appealed.

MORRIS LJ

. . . On the facts as found, and indeed on the facts which are not in dispute, the position was therefore that, at the request of the defendants, the plaintiffs made a representation which they knew to be false and which they intended should be relied upon by persons who received the bill of lading, including any banker who might be concerned. In these circumstances, all the elements of the tort of deceit were present. Someone who could prove that he suffered damage by relying on the representation could sue for damages. I feel impelled to the conclusion that a promise to indemnify the plaintiffs against any loss resulting to them from making the representation is unenforceable. The claim cannot be put forward without basing it upon an unlawful transaction. The promise upon which the plaintiffs rely is in effect this: if you will make a false representation, which will deceive indorsees or bankers, we will indemnify you against any loss that may result to you. I cannot think that a court should lend its aid to enforce such a bargain.

The conclusion thus reached is one that may seem unfortunate for the plaintiffs, for I gain the impression that they did not pause to realise the significance and the implications of what they were asked to do. There was evidence that the practice of giving indemnities upon the issuing of clean bills of lading is not uncommon. That cannot in any way alter the analysis of the present transaction, but it may help to explain how the plaintiffs came to accede to the defendants' request. There may perhaps be some circumstances in which indemnities can properly be given. Thus if a shipowner thinks that he has detected some faulty condition in regard to goods to be taken on board, he may be assured by the shipper that he is entirely mistaken: if he is so persuaded by the shipper, it may be that he could honestly issue a clean bill of lading, while taking an indemnity in case it was later shown that there had in fact been some faulty condition. Each case must depend upon its circumstances. But even if it could be shown that there existed to any extent a practice of knowingly issuing clean bills when claused bills should have been issued, no validating effect for any particular transaction could in consequence result . . .

I would allow the appeal.

Pearce L.J. delivered a concurring judgment.

LORD EVERSHED MR (dissenting)

In *Alexander v Rayson* [1936] 1 K.B. 169, 182, the principle was stated by this court in the passage already recited by my brother Pearce. "It is settled law that an agreement to do an act that is illegal or immoral or contrary to public policy, or to do any act for a consideration that is illegal or immoral or contrary to public policy, is unlawful and therefore void. But it often happens that an agreement which in itself is not unlawful is made with the intention of one or both parties to make use of the subject-matter for an unlawful purpose, that is to say, a purpose that is illegal, immoral or contrary to public policy . . . In such a case any party to the agreement who had the unlawful intention is precluded from suing upon it. Ex turpi causa non oritur act."

The adjective "turpis" is thus expanded to cover the three characteristics: (1) illegal, (2) immoral and (3) contrary to public policy. The classic case of *Pearce v Brooks* [above] is the obvious instance of immorality; and when the purpose of the agreement, or the intended use of its subject-matter, is the commission of a crime or the doing of some prohibited act (for example, the infringement of the customs law), the principle is no less obviously invoked on grounds both of illegality and of public policy. The principle no doubt extends further. In *Alexander v Rayson* itself, the proved purpose of the plaintiff was to use the instruments, which he entered into with the defendant, in order to deceive and cheat (as he did) the local rating authority: and in *Berg v Sadler and Moore* [1937] 2 K.B. 158 (to take an example from the cases cited to us) the plaintiff was shown to have been engaged upon an enterprise of deliberate deception which amounted to a false pretence.

But how much further does it go? Does it cover every case in which the subject-matter of the action is shown to be part of a transaction which has involved the making by the plaintiff of a statement known to be untrue in a commercial document intended to be acted upon in the ordinary commercial course, even though it is not proved to have been acted on in fact by anyone, or (if it has been acted upon) not to have caused loss or damage to any person: and even though the plaintiff is not shown to have had at any stage in the transaction any intention that anyone should be damnified or to have been "dishonest" as that word is ordinarily understood? . . .

Thoughtless, misguided and irresponsible the plaintiffs may have been; but I am not satisfied for my part, on the evidence and what I take to have been the views of the judge, that it would be just for this court to condemn them as fraudulent and dishonest.

But even if we should conclude that the representation was made with such recklessness as to amount, in law, to the same thing as a representation made with the deliberate intention of deceiving, still I am not satisfied that it would be right to hold, or that any authority compels us to hold, that the proved circumstances were such that it would be contrary to public policy, contra bonos mores, to allow the plaintiffs to recover upon the contract of indemnity from the defendants. I have, I hope, sufficiently perused all the authorities, including those cited by my brother Morris. I have failed to find any case (apart from those involving immorality or public illegality) in which, upon the principle ex turpi causa non oritur actio, a plaintiff has been cast from the seat of judgment who has not been found personally dishonest. If there was a false statement deliberately made, it was made in accordance with a practice that was common and well known in the trade and with an intention that any consequences should be covered by their or their principals' liability to make compensation—in other words, in circumstances in which the plaintiffs, by reason of the current laxity in that respect, honestly believed would not damage anybody.

In my judgment, the result is not one which requires the court upon grounds of public policy to deny to the plaintiffs their right to sue.

Appeal Allowed.

In *ParkingEye Limited v Somerfield Stores Limited* (below), ParkingEye agreed to provide an auto-mated monitoring and control system at some of Somerfield's car parks. Payment for ParkingEye's services was to come from parking charges levied on customers who overstayed. The contract was to be for an initial period of 15 months from September 1, 2005. However, Somerfield terminated the contract in early March 2006, by which time the monitoring system had been installed at 17 stores. ParkingEye, having accepted Somerfield's termination as a repudiatory breach, claimed damages for its loss of revenue. Somerfield advanced a number of defences, one of which highlighted certain false statements (amounting at least to the tort of deceit) in the letters that ParkingEye sent to overstaying motorists. Was this an illegality that was sufficient to bar ParkingEye's claim? The Court of Appeal held that, quite clearly, it was not sufficient—indeed, that it would be disproportionate to treat ParkingEye's illegality as having such an effect.

PARKINGEYE LIMITED v SOMERFIELD STORES LIMITED

[2012] EWCA Civ 1338

SIR ROBIN JACOB

27-022   7. . . . [S]ome of the letters [ParkingEye] wrote to motorists contained falsehoods. The first letter was not so held. It perhaps might have been. For it was dressed up rather like police issued document with a chequered edging and described the amount claimed as a "penalty" when it was no more than a contractual obligation to pay. I say no more because there is no challenge to the finding that this was not a false representation. The letter claimed £75 but £37.50 if paid within 14 days.

8. The second letter called itself a ""Parking Charge Reminder". Again it was held not to contain any falsehood, despite its police style edging, the use of the word "penalty" and even the assertion, which would not have been true if the motorist who had actually overstayed had not been the owner of the vehicle as registered with the DVLA, that "as keeper, owner or hirer of the vehicle in question . . . you are responsible for the outstanding PARKING CHARGE NOTICE". There is no challenge to the Judge's finding in this regard.

9. The third letter was different. This was held to contain serious falsehoods. By this stage ParkingEye transferred the collection of money from the defaulting motorist to a company called Commercial Collection Services Ltd. This company issued the third (and in default of payment) fourth letters.

10. The third letter, sent seven days after the second if payment had not been made, was issued by "Commercial Collection Services". It was headed "Debt £75 Due to PARKING EYE (sic)". The key passages read (the emphasis is in the original):

> "I promise this isn't just another debt collector's letter. If you read it I believe that you will understand.
> My client is determined to protect the interests of their genuine customers, so they are therefore prepared to go "all the way." The cost of the issue of proceedings for what you might regard as a rather small amount is irrelevant to them, as you will understand. Customers are of paramount importance.
> As PARKING EYE have explained to you already, their objective is to deter the dishonest, the people who are not their genuine customers.
> You may choose to ignore this demand but that approach will not succeed. PARKING EYE **will issue legal proceedings** and will instruct us to prepare the documentation. The consequences of legal proceedings are, [the comma is in the original] that you would receive a Claim, and if you ignore that, a bailiff will attend your address, [comma in original] to remove goods.
> If you prefer to avoid all the hassle and the costs (which will become substantial if our client's [apostrophe in original] the means of payment are set out below and overleaf."

11. This semi-literate letter was false in a number of respects:

   i)   It said that the debt was due to ParkingEye. It was not. It was due to Somerfield.

   ii)   It talked of "their genuine customers" which suggested the letter was sent on behalf of Somerfield. It was not.

   iii)   It said "ParkingEye will issue proceedings" indicating that ParkingEye had authority to do so. It did not.

   iv)   In any event neither ParkingEye nor Somerfield actually had any settled intention of issuing legal proceedings if the money was not paid. The contract provided by Schedule 2 that if the registered keeper did not pay after a fourth letter, no further action would be taken but detailed records of non-payers and persistent offenders would be stored. If Somerfield decided to sue ParkingEye was to assist.

v) In the case of any vehicle driven by someone other than the registered keeper the recipient of the letter was not liable at all.

12. In the event of non-payment there was a fourth letter in the same crude fashion. Its most aggressive passage reads:

> "You may not have considered also the implications of a judgment being recorded against you. Such as credit becoming more expensive. **For you, with a judgment against you, interest rates could become very high, <u>if you are able to obtain credit at all</u>**."

The letter ended with: "This is your last chance."

13. The Judge not only found that the third letter contained falsehoods but that those falsehoods were deliberately made by the relevant ParkingEye executive, albeit without dishonesty. Hence the Judge found ParkingEye was guilty of the tort of deceit on those occasions when the third letter was sent on its behalf. ParkingEye does not challenge this decision. . . .

28. Illegality and the law of contract is notoriously knotty territory. Etherton LJ put it this way in the most recent case on the subject to reach this court, *Les Laboritoires Servier v Apotex Inc* [2012] EWCA Civ 593, decided after the judgment below in this case:

> "It is not necessary in order to resolve this appeal to undertake a comprehensive analysis of the decided cases. Such an exercise would in any event be complex, very lengthy and in large part unrewarding. The decisions inevitably turn on their own particular facts. The statements of law or principle they contain are not all consistent or easily reconciled. The jurisprudence in this area has been an evolving one, but its evolution has not followed a consistent pattern."

So, like Etherton LJ, I shall duck out of a comprehensive review of the cases. I would add that to my mind the facts of this case lead to its comparatively easy resolution. I do not think it is borderline, which is yet another reason for eschewing a comprehensive review.

29. The starting point for an examination of the law in this area are two Law Commission papers on the subject, the consultation paper of 2009, No. 189 and the final report of 2010 (Law Com 230) entitled "The Illegality Defence." It is the consultation paper which examines the cases in detail. Of particular relevance here is the section dealing with "Illegality under common law." One of the Law Commission's categories of this is headed "When the contract is performed in an unlawful manner" (Paras. 3.27 *et seq.*). It says:

> 3.27 In some circumstances a contract that does not require the commission of any unlawful act, and which was not entered into to facilitate an unlawful purpose is nevertheless *performed* in an unlawful way. The effect that this unlawful performance has on the parties' contractual rights is very unclear [footnote omitted].
>   3.28 At common law, historically, a distinction has been drawn between cases where the guilty party intended from the time of entering the contract unlawfully and cases where the intention to perform unlawfully was only made subsequently. . . .

30. Mr Fealy invokes the principle stated in its generality here. He says the guilty party, ParkingEye, had the intention from the outset to perform the contract unlawfully. He reinforced his submissions by reference to what Waller LJ said in *Colen v Cebrian* [2003] EWCA Civ 1676, [2004] ICR 568 at [23]:

> ". . . an analysis needs to be done as to what the party's intentions were from time to time. If the contract was unlawful at its formation or if there was an intention to perform the contract unlawfully as at the date of the contract, then the contract will be unenforceable."

31. Strong though the passage is, I do not read it as applying to any intended illegality of performance, however partial or peripheral. Indeed I do not think Waller LJ was considering a case such as the present where the intention was limited to only a partial (and minor on the facts) mode of performance, and was itself qualified in that it could be changed at any time and would be changed if the illegality had been pointed out.

32. The Law Commission itself was not prepared to accept that the law was in a straightjacket: that once it was shown illegal performance of any sort was intended at the time of the making of the contract, unenforceability would follow automatically. It said:

> 3.31 However it clearly cannot be in every case that a contract is unlawfully performed, even where this was the original intention, that the offending party loses his or her remedies. Such a proposition would result

in the widespread forfeiture of contractual remedies as a result of minor and incidental transgressions. Although there is general agreement on this point amongst academic commentators, there is surprisingly little authority [footnote omitted].

33. I would add that there is something distinctly odd about the supposed "intention from the outset" rule. Mr Fealy rightly accepted that if the relevant intention in this case (i.e. what the form of the third letter was to be) had only been formed after execution of the main contract, the rule would not apply. Instead the test would be as Waller LJ put it in *Colen* at [22]

> "whether the method of performance chosen and the degree of participation in that illegal performance is such as to "turn the contract into an illegal contract" [the phrase is that of Jenkins LJ in *B&B Viennese Fashions v Losame* [1952] 1 All ER 909 at 913."

34. I elaborate on this oddity by reference to the facts of this case. It would surely not make any rational sense for the question of whether ParkingEye had a remedy to depend on the happenstance of when the form of the letters was decided, before or after the contract was executed. Or suppose the intention was formed before the contract, but altered immediately after, so that there never was an illegal third letter? Or just one such letter before its form was changed? These considerations are, I think, linked to the Judge's reason for rejecting the illegality defence. They show or at least tend to show that the decision or agreement as to the form of letters was peripheral and something apart from the main contract.

35. It is important to emphasise that the facts in this case are different from those in any of the cases to which we were referred. For the contract here was not all-or-nothing, legal or illegal, either as regards its performance or its intended performance. That may, for instance, generally be the case in a contract of sale or one for carriage of goods. But this contract involved continuous performance over time. And its performance was never intended to be carried in a wholly illegal manner. On the contrary the performance could be carried out and was intended to be carried mainly lawfully. Indeed it was in fact largely carried out lawfully because most motorists paid on the first or second letters and never received the third, offending, letter. Moreover the Judge's finding that if the contract had carried on instead of being repudiated the letters would all have been rendered innocuous means that no part of the damages claimed would be compensation for loss of income obtained by any unlawful means.

36. There is also this factor, considered important in many of the authorities (including Waller LJ in *Colen*), that it is not necessary for ParkingEye to plead or rely upon any illegality. Of likewise importance are the facts that illegal performance was not an object of the contract nor by any means necessary for its performance.

37. Mr Fealy submitted that despite all these matters, what was crucial here was the intention at the outset to use illegal means where necessary (i.e. in the event of non-payment after the first or second letter) to induce motorists to pay. It made no difference that in most cases the motorists were in fact liable. The contemplated illegal means tainted the whole contract and public policy required that it be held unenforceable as a whole. ParkingEye's intention at the outset of the contract was so imbued with moral turpitude that the law will not assist it to enforce the contract.

38. I do not agree. Such a conclusion would be unduly sanctimonious: it would lead to the disproportionate result that Somerfield's wrongful repudiation of the contract left ParkingEye with no remedy for a lost income which would have been wholly lawful.

39. In applying the "disproportionate" test I do not think I am exercising a judicial discretion. It was settled by *Tinsley v Milligan* [1994] AC 340 that a defence of illegality point cannot be solved by applying a discretion based on public conscience. Proportionality as I see it is something rather different. It involves the assessment of how far refusal of the remedy furthers one or more of the specific policies underlying the defence of illegality. Those policies Etherton LJ identified in *Servier* (from the Law Commission report) as:

> "[66] . . . furthering the purpose of the rule which the illegal conduct has infringed; consistency; the claimant should not profit from his or her wrong; deterrence; and maintaining the integrity of the legal system."

> Etherton LJ was careful to add:

> "As the cases plainly show, this does not mean that the illegality will always apply where one of these policy rationales is relevant. It means that, if the illegality defence applies at all, it must find its justification firmly in one or more of them."

40. For the reasons I have already given, I do not think the facts of this case, considered with a sense of proportionality, involve such an invasion of any of the policy rationales as to deprive ParkingEye of its remedy. There is not a firm enough justification for that course of action.

41. I would add that I would also dismiss this appeal for the reasons given by the Judge. As I have noted, the form of the letters was too far removed from the basic operation of the contract to taint the latter.

42. For these reasons I would dismiss this appeal.

TOULSON LJ

Contract law and the doctrine of illegality

44. The fundamental reason why illegality is a difficult topic is that the doctrine is founded on public policy, and public policy not infrequently gives rise to conflicting considerations. As Lord Wright observed in *Vita Food Products Inc v Unus Shipping Co* [1939] AC 277, 293:

> "Each case has to be considered on its merits. Nor must it be forgotten that the rule by which contracts not expressly forbidden by statute or declared to be void are in proper cases nullified for disobedience to a statute is a rule of public policy only, and public policy understood in a wider sense may at times be better served by refusing to nullify a bargain save on serious and sufficient grounds."

In the present case the contract is not sought to be nullified for disobedience to a statute, but for another form of illegality. However, the broad point made by Lord Wright is no less important.

45. There is a public interest in the court not appearing to reward wrong doing or condone a breach of the law. But where, as in this case, both parties were complicit in the illegality, denial of one party's claim on that ground will be to give an unjustified benefit to the other. The rule that where both parties are equally at fault the defendant should prevail may be right in more serious cases (on the ground that the court should, in effect, wash its hands of the dispute), but may be a [disproportionately] severe response in less serious cases, especially where the parties did not appreciate that they were acting contrary to the law. There is a public interest in doing justice between the parties and, as Lord Wright said, in nullifying a bargain only on serious and sufficient grounds.

46. It is unsurprising that over several centuries the courts have never found a simple formula for resolving these policy considerations in every situation. It is wise to be wary of extracting statements from the case law which appear to lay down universal propositions and applying them in different circumstances. There are, of course, general rules but their boundaries are not always precise and the context is always important.

47. That is not to suggest that the court has a general discretion whether to disallow a claim on grounds of illegality. The courts came close to fashioning such a discretion when they developed the "public conscience test", but the House of Lords rejected that test in *Tinsley v Milligan* [1994] AC 340. At the same time Lord Goff (at page 364) lamented that the illegality rules were indiscriminate in their effect and capable of producing injustice. He urged an investigation by the Law Commission, and he subsequently encouraged the Commission to recommend that the court should be given a statutory discretion on the lines of the New Zealand Illegal Contracts Act 1970.

48. The Law Commission wrestled with the problem over the next 15 years. The subject was included in its Sixth Programme of Law Reform, (1995) LC 234, and it produced a number of consultation documents before producing its Consultative Report, (2009) LCCP 189, to which Sir Robin Jacob has referred, and its final confirmatory Report, (2010) LC 320. After much study and consultation, it concluded that a statutory scheme was not the best solution to the problems of illegality in the law of contract, because of the difficulties which close study showed that such a scheme would itself present; and it believed that the courts had the ability to develop and apply the law in a manner which was principled but moved away from the indiscriminate application of inflexible rules capable of producing injustice.

49. In its Consultative Report, (2009) LCCP No 189, the Law Commission realistically observed (paragraph 3.52) that to "expect one set of detailed and ostensibly rigid rules to cater for all circumstances that may be encountered is overly ambitious". It summarised the present state of the law follows:

> "3.53 As our overview of the present law has shown, the crude application of the general contractual illegality rules could lead to unnecessarily harsh decisions. So how have the courts successfully avoided this potential for injustice in relation to the dispute before them? This has been achieved largely by the use of two methods. The first is by the creation of the numerous exceptions to the application of the general rules. . .
>
> 3.54 The second method of avoiding harsh decisions is seen in the way in which the application of the relevant rules can be strained in order to meet the justice of the particular case. . .
>
> 3.55 Overall, the result has been a complex body of case law with technical distinctions that are difficult to justify. As one respondent to CP154 noted, illegality disputes are often adjudicated by lay arbitrators to whom the complexities and uncertainties, not to mention the contradictions, of the present law can present a formidable obstacle to its understanding, and which can therefore impede a fair resolution of the dispute."

50. The Commission commented on the public conscience test as follows:

"3.140 We agree that the public conscience test was vague. However, we believe that it was useful in suggesting that the present rules should be regarded as no more than guidance that help the court to focus its attention on particular features of the case before it. What lies behind these "rules" is a set of policies. This is why the courts are sometimes required to "bend" the rules (if possible) to give better effect to the underlying policies as they apply to the facts of the case before them. It would be preferable if the courts were to base their decisions transparently on these policies. They could then accept that existing authority helps, but only in so far as the case law illustrates the various policies to be applied.

3.141 If this approach were adopted, we consider that the illegality defence would succeed in only the most serious of cases. That is, we believe that the policy issues underlying the defence would have to be overwhelming before it would be a proportionate response to deny the claimant his or her usual contractual rights."

51. The Commission made the following provisional recommendations:

"3.142 We provisionally recommend that the courts should consider in each case whether the application of the illegality defence can be justified on the basis of the policies that underlie that defence. These include: (a) furthering the purpose of the rule which the illegal conduct has infringed; (b) consistency; (c) that the claimant should not profit from his or her own wrong; (d) deterrence; and (e) maintaining the integrity of the legal system. Against those polices must be weighed the legitimate expectation of the claimant that his or her legal rights will be protected. Ultimately a balancing exercise is called for which weighs up the application of the various policies at stake. Only when depriving the claimant of his or her rights is a proportionate response based on the relevant illegality policies, should the defence succeed. The judgment should explain the basis on which it has done so.

3.143 We also consider that it would be helpful if, rather than simply asking whether the contact is illegal—a term which itself is vague and confusing—the courts were to ask whether the particular claimant, in the circumstances which have occurred, should be denied his or her usual relief in respect of the particular claim. This focus on the particular claimant and particular claim are important. As we have suggested, one of the most important factors bearing on the case will be the closeness of the connection between the claim and the unlawful conduct. It may well be the case that it would be a proportionate response to deny the claimant relief in respect of one of the defendant's obligations, where this is closely linked to the claimant's unlawful actions, but not to any other.

3.144 We provisionally recommend that the courts should consider whether illegality is a defence to the particular claim brought by the particular claimant, rather than whether the contract is "illegal" as a whole."

52. The Law Commission's final Report was to the same effect. Over the years the Commission has explored at length the complexities of the subject and the possible ways forward. I am in no doubt about the wisdom and justice of the general approach now advocated by it. Rather than having over complex rules which are indiscriminate in theory but less so in practice, it is better and more honest that the court should look openly at the underlying policy factors and reach a balanced judgment in each case for reasons articulated by it.

53. This is not to suggest that a list of policy factors should become a complete substitute for the rules about illegality in the law of contract which the courts have developed, but rather that those rules are to be developed and applied with the degree of flexibility necessary to give proper effect to the underlying policy factors. The decision in *Les Laboratoires Servier v Apotex Inc* [2012] EWCA Civ 593 provides a good example. I would particularly endorse Etherton LJ's statement at paragraph 75 that:

". . .what is required in each case is an intensive analysis of the particular facts and of the proper application of the various policy considerations underlying the illegality principle so as to produce a just and proportionate response to the illegality. This is not the same as an unbridled discretion."

54. In some parts of the law of contract it is necessary in the interests of commercial certainty to have fixed rules, sometimes with exceptions. But in the area of illegality, experience has shown that it is better to recognise that there may be conflicting considerations and that the rules need to be developed and applied in a way which enables the court to balance them fairly.

55. This approach recognises the truth of Lord Hoffmann's statement in *Gray v Thames Trains Ltd* [2009] UKHL 33, [2009] AC 1339 at paragraph 30:

"The maxim ex turpi causa expresses not so much a principle as a policy. Furthermore, that policy is not based upon a single justification but on a group of reasons, which vary in different situations." . . .

Conclusion

75. The judge was in my view right to reject Somerfield's illegality defence. The considerations which caused him to do so were that ParkingEye had no "fixed intention" of acting unlawfully, for reasons which I have discussed, and that the illegality was incidental to part of the performance of the contract but far from central to it.

76. My reasons for agreeing with the judge can be shortly stated. If the court thought it right to do so, it could develop and apply the principle expressed in broad terms in *St John Shipping Corporation Ltd v Joseph Rank Ltd*, and repeated in cases such as *Colen v Cebrian (UK) Ltd*, so as to defeat ParkingEye's claim, but it is necessary to consider whether that would be justified by the policies underlying this branch of the law.

77. As Sir Robin Jacob has emphasised at paragraph 35, the contract was not a one-off contract, such as a contract for the sale or carriage of goods, but a contract creating a relationship that was to last for a minimum term of 15 months. The claim is for loss caused to ParkingEye by Somerfield's termination the contract after a little over 6 months. It could have been lawfully performed for the rest of the contractual term, and it would have been if Somerfield had drawn attention to the objectionable feature of pro forma letter 3 which it had previously approved. The objectionable feature of that letter was neither essential nor central to the performance of the contract as a whole.

78. If and when it belatedly dawned on Somerfield that pro forma letter 3 was objectionable in its form, the proper and just course would have been for Somerfield to have drawn this to the attention of ParkingEye and to have continued to honour the contract, provided that ParkingEye performed it in a lawful manner, as it would have done on the judge's findings. I see no justice in Somerfield having the option of either behaving in that way or, if it preferred, of repudiating the contract. This would give Somerfield a windfall reward for its own previous illegality. If Somerfield's argument is taken to its logical con[c]lusion, on appreciating that the letter was objectionable, it could have kept the point up its sleeve until ParkingEye had installed all the monitoring equipment at its car parks which it required, and then terminated the contract at whatever moment best suited its commercial interest, so enabling it to keep for itself all subsequent payments by users of the car parks who overstayed. To borrow Devlin J's phrase, that would not contribute to public morality.

79. In summary, the disallowance of ParkingEye's claim on the ground of illegality is not compelled by the authorities, and it would not be a just and proportionate response to the illegality.

Laws LJ agreed that the appeal should be dismissed.

B. On Actions for the Recovery of Property

TAYLOR v CHESTER

Queen's Bench (1869) L.R. 4 Q.B. 309; 10 B. & S. 237; 38 L.J.Q.B. 225; 21 L.T. 359; 33 J.P. 709

The judgment of the court (Mellor and Hannen JJ) was delivered by Mellor J.

27-023

MELLOR J

In this case the plaintiff declared on the bailment of the half of a £50 Bank of England note, to the defendant, to be redelivered on request, alleging a refusal by the defendant to redeliver such half-note. The second count was in detinue for the same half-note.

The defendant, after traversing the delivery and detention of the note, and to the second count denying that it was the property of the plaintiff, pleaded separately and specially to both counts, in effect, that the half-note in question had been deposited by the plaintiff with the defendant by way of pledge, to secure the repayment of money due and money then advanced by the defendant to the plaintiff and then due.

The plaintiff joined issue on the defendant's pleas, and also replied specially that the alleged debt or sum, in respect of which the defendant justified the non-delivery and detention of the half-note, was for wine and suppers, supplied by the defendant in a brothel and disorderly house kept by the defendant, for the purpose of being consumed there by the plaintiff and divers prostitutes in a debauch there, to incite them to riotous, disorderly, and immoral conduct, and for money knowingly lent for the purposes of being expended in riot and debauchery and immoral conduct.

The defendant rejoined, taking issue on the replication, and also demurred to its validity.

On the trial before me at Manchester, the case of the plaintiff was that the note had not been deposited at all with the defendant, but had been fraudulently taken and appropriated by her. The jury, however, did not adopt his view of the facts, but found that the note was deposited by way of security, as alleged by the defendant, and they further found upon the evidence that the debt was incurred and the money advanced as alleged in the plaintiff's replication to the special pleas. On these findings, the verdict was entered for the defendant, with liberty to the plaintiff to move to enter the verdict for him for £50 to be reduced to nominal damages in case the note should be returned to the plaintiff.

A rule was accordingly obtained to enter the verdict for the plaintiff, on the ground that the jury had found all the issues tendered by the plaintiff in his favour.

It was argued on the part of the defendant, in showing cause against the rule, and in support of the demurrer to the special replication of the plaintiff that, upon the finding of the jury and the facts as admitted by the demurrer, the plaintiff and defendant were in pari delicto, and that therefore upon the whole record judgment must be entered for the defendant. On the part of the plaintiff it was argued that it was the defendant who was relying on the illegal transaction as an answer to a claim of the plaintiff, founded on his ownership of the note, and his rights to recover back the same, and many startling consequences were pointed out to us as likely to result from a decision that the plaintiff could not recover. We have fully considered the case, and are satisfied that the plaintiff cannot recover under the circumstances found by the jury, and admitted on the record. The maxim that in pari delicto potior est conditio possidentis, is as thoroughly settled as any proposition of law can be. It is a maxim of law, established, not for the benefit of plaintiffs or defendants, but is founded on the principles of public policy, which will not assist a plaintiff who has paid over money or handed over property in pursuance of an illegal or immoral contract, to recover it back, "for the courts will not assist an illegal transaction in any respect": per Lord Ellenborough in *Edgar v Fowler*, 3 East 222; *Collins v Blantern*, 2 Wis. 341; Lord Mansfield in *Holman v Johnson* Cowp. at p. 343.

The true test for determining whether or not the plaintiff and the defendant were in pari delicto, is by considering whether the plaintiff could make out his case otherwise than through the medium and by the aid of the illegal transaction to which he was himself a party: *Simpson v Bloss* 7 Taunt. 246, *Fivaz v Nicholls*, 2 C.B. 501. It is to be observed that in this case the illegality is not in a collateral matter, as in the case of *Feret v Hill*, 15 C.B. 207; 23 L.J.C.P. 185, which was cited for the plaintiff; but is the direct result of the transaction upon which the deposit of the half-note took place.

Mr Herschell's argument was based upon the hypothesis that in spite of the finding of the jury, the plaintiff was entitled to recover by virtue of his property in the half-note, and that it was the defendant alone who set up an immoral transaction as the answer to the plaintiff's claim.

This argument appears to us to be founded upon an entirely erroneous view of the facts. The plaintiff, no doubt, was the owner of the note, but he pledged it by way of security for the price of meat and drink provided for, and money advanced to him by the defendant. Had the case rested there, and no pleading raised the question of illegality, a valid pledge would have been created, and a special property conferred upon the defendant in the half-note, and the plaintiff could only have recovered by showing payment or a tender of the amount due. In order to get rid of the defence arising from the plea, which set up an existing pledge on the half-note, the plaintiff had recourse to the special replication, in which he was obliged to set forth the immoral and illegal character of the contract upon which the half-note had been deposited. It was, therefore, impossible for him to recover except through the medium and by the aid of an illegal transaction to which he was himself a party. Under such circumstances, the maxim in pari delicto potior est conditio possidentis, clearly applies, and is decisive of the case.

It would appear from the case of *Scarfe v Morgan*, 4 M. & W. at pp. 281, 282, per Parke B., in delivering the judgment of the court, that, notwithstanding the illegality of the transaction itself, out of which the deposit in this case arose, the lien would exist, because the contract was executed and the special property had passed by the delivery of the half-note to the defendant, and the maxim would apply in pari delicto potior est conditio possidentis.

It is, however, sufficient in the present case to determine it on the ground that the plaintiff could not recover without showing the true character of the deposit; and that being upon an illegal consideration, to which he was himself a party, he was precluded from obtaining "the assistance of the law" to recover it back. It is not necessary to consider what might have been the effect of a tender of the amount for which the note was pledged, and there is nothing to raise any such question in this case.

The result, therefore, will be that the verdict must stand for the defendant on the issues taken on the special pleas, and for the plaintiff on the issue taken on the replication; but as upon the whole record it is manifest that the plaintiff cannot recover, judgment will be entered for the defendant.

Judgment for the Defendant.

Question

Cheshire, Fifoot and Furmston (*Law of Contract* (12th edn) p.379) cite *Taylor v Chester* for the proposition that "If . . . a seller sues for the recovery of goods sold and delivered under an illegal contract he will fail, for to justify his claim he must necessarily disclose his own iniquity." Did the plaintiff in *Taylor v Chester*, fail because he disclosed his own iniquity? Or because there was a valid and unredeemed pledge? What would have been the situation if the plaintiff had tendered the amount for which the note was pledged?

27-024

BOWMAKERS LTD v BARNET INSTRUMENTS LTD

Court of Appeal [1945] K.B. 65; 89 S.J. 22; 172 L.T. 1; 61 T.L.R. 62; [1944] 2 All E.R.

Appeal from Croom-Johnson J.

27-025

The plaintiffs, Bowmakers Ltd, sued the defendants, Barnet Instruments Ltd, to recover damages for the conversion of certain machine tools which they alleged were their property. The tools in question were the subject of three hiring agreements between the plaintiffs and the defendants, each containing an option to purchase, dated March 18, April 15 and June 16, 1944. They were described in the statement of claim as agreements Nos 1, 2 and 3. In each case the machines were originally the property of a man named Smith, who was prepared to sell them to the defendants at prices which they were willing to pay, though not at once. The goods comprised in the first agreement were originally the subject of a contract of sale between Smith and the defendants, but this contract was rescinded. Eventually it was arranged in every case, for the convenience of the defendants, that the defendants should obtain possession of the machines, not by a direct purchase from Smith, but under a hire-purchase agreement from the plaintiffs. In pursuance of this arrangement Smith sold the goods to the plaintiffs, and the plaintiffs entered into the three agreements with the defendants. The contracts between the plaintiffs and the defendants were in a familiar form. Each of them contained a provision for the monthly payment of hire and further provided that "if the hirer shall duly make the said payments and strictly observe and perform all the terms and conditions on his part herein contained then the hirer shall thereupon have the option of purchasing the said chattels for the sum of ten shillings." The defendants after making some, but by no means all the agreed payments, sold for their own advantage, and so converted to their use, all the machines except that one which was the subject of agreement 2, and this latter they also converted to their own use by refusing to deliver it up to the plaintiffs on demand. They maintained, however, that the plaintiffs had no remedy against them.

The goods comprised in agreements 1 and 2 were new machine tools and the agreements may have infringed the provisions of S.R. & O. 1940, No.1784 S.R. & O. 1940, No.1374 was infringed by agreement 3.

Croom-Johnson J held that no illegality had been proved in respect of any of the hiring agreements and, accordingly, entered judgment for the plaintiffs against the defendants for damages for conversion. The defendants appealed. The judgment of the Court of Appeal (Scott and du Parcq LJJ and Uthwatt J) was delivered by:

DU PARCQ LJ

. . . we will assume in favour of the defendants that the three hiring agreements were all, as they allege, and for the reasons which they give, affected by illegality.

The question, then, is whether in the circumstances the plaintiffs are without a remedy. So far as their claim in conversion is concerned, they are not relying on the hiring agreements at all. On the contrary, they are willing to admit for this purpose that they cannot rely on them. They simply say that the machines were their property, and this, we think, cannot be denied. We understood Mr Gallop to concede that the property had passed from Smith to the plaintiffs, and still remained in the plaintiffs at the date of the conversion. At any rate, we have no doubt that this is the legal result of the transaction and we find support for this view in the dicta of Parke B. in *Scarfe v Morgan* (1838) 4 M. & W. 270.

Why then should not the plaintiffs have what is their own? No question of the defendants' rights arises. They do not, and cannot, pretend to have had any legal right to possession of the goods at the date of the conversion. Their counsel has to rely, not on any alleged right of theirs, but on the requirements of public policy. He was entitled, and bound, to do so, although, as Lord Mansfield long ago observed, "The objection, that a contract is immoral or illegal as between plaintiff and defendant, sounds at all times very ill in the mouth of the defendant." "No court," Lord Mansfield added, "will lend its aid to a man who founds his cause of action upon an immoral or an illegal act": *Holman v Johnson* (1775) 1 Cowp. 341, 343. This principle, long firmly established, has probably even been extended since Lord Mansfield's day. Mr Gallop is, we think, right in his submission that, if the sale by Smith to the plaintiffs was illegal, then the first and second hiring agreements were tainted with the illegality, since they were brought into being to make that illegal sale possible, but, as we have said, the plaintiffs are not now relying on these agreements or on the third hiring agreement. Prima facie, a man is entitled to his own property, and it is not a general principle of our law (as was suggested) that when one man's goods have got into another's possession in consequence of some unlawful dealings between them, the true owner can never be allowed to recover those goods by an action. The necessity of such a principle to the interests and advancement of public policy is certainly not obvious. The suggestion that it exists is not, in our opinion, supported by authority. It would, indeed, be astonishing if (to take one instance) a person in the position of the defendant in *Pearce v Brooks* [above, para.27–012], supposing that she had converted the plaintiff's brougham to her own use, were to be permitted, in the supposed interests of public policy, to keep it or the proceeds of its sale for her own benefit. The principle which is, in truth, followed by the courts is that stated by Lord Mansfield, that no claim founded on an illegal contract will be enforced, and for this purpose the words "illegal contract" must now be understood in the wide sense which we have already indicated and no technical meaning must be ascribed to the words "founded on an illegal contract." The form of the pleadings is by no means conclusive. More modern illustrations of the principle on which the courts act are *Scott v Brown, Doering, McNab & Co* [1892] 2 Q.B. 724 and *Alexander v Rayson* [1936] 1 K.B. 169; but, as Lindley L.J. said in the former of the cases just cited: "Any rights which [a plaintiff] may have irrespective of his illegal contract will, of course, be recognised and enforced."

In our opinion, a man's right to possess his own chattels will as a general rule be enforced against one who, without any claim of right, is detaining them or has converted them to his own use, even though it may appear either from the pleadings, or in the course of the trial that the chattels in question came into the defendant's possession by reason of an illegal contract between himself and the plaintiff, provided that the plaintiff does not seek, and is not forced, either to found his claim on the illegal contract or to plead its illegality in order to support his claim.

Mr Gallop sought to derive assistance from the decision of the Court of Queen's Bench in *Taylor v Chester* [above]. The decision there was, however, entirely consonant with the view which we have expressed. It differed from the present case in one essential respect, since in that case the defendant had prima facie a right to possession of the half-note which the plaintiff claimed. She was holding it as a pledge to secure the payment of money which remained due. The plaintiff could only defeat her plea by showing that the money due had been lent for an immoral purpose, and this could not avail him since he was in pari delicto with her. The judgment of the court, delivered by Mellor J., makes it plain that this was the ratio of the decision. "The plaintiff," said Mellor J., "no doubt, was the owner of the note, but he pledged it by way of security for the price of meat and drink provided for, and money advanced to, him by the defendant. Had the case rested there, and no pleading raised the question of illegality, a valid pledge would have been created, and a special property conferred upon the defendant in the half-note, and the plaintiff could only have recovered by showing payment or a tender of the amount due. In order to get rid of the defence arising from the plea, which set up an existing pledge of the half-note, the plaintiff had recourse to the special replication, in which he was obliged to set forth the i[m]moral and illegal character of the contract upon which the half-note had been deposited. It was, therefore, impossible for him to recover except through the medium and by the aid of an illegal transaction to which he was himself a party. Under such circumstances, the maxim in pari delicto potior est conditio possidentis clearly applies, and is decisive of the case." The Latin maxim which Mellor J. cited must not be understood as meaning that where a transaction is vitiated by illegality the person left in possession of goods after its completion is always and of necessity entitled to keep them. Its true meaning is that, where the circumstances are such that the court will refuse to assist either party, the consequence must, in fact, follow that the party in possession will not be disturbed. As Lord Mansfield said in the case already cited, the defendant then obtains an advantage "contrary to the real justice," and, so to say, "by accident."

It must not be supposed that the general rule which we have stated is subject to no exception. Indeed, there is one obvious exception, namely, that class of cases in which the goods claimed are of such a kind that it is unlawful to deal in them at all, as for example, obscene books. No doubt, there are others, but it is unnecessary, and would we think be unwise, to seek to name them all or to forecast the decisions which would be given in a variety of circumstances which may hereafter arise. We are satisfied that no rule of law, and no considerations of public policy, compel the court to dismiss the plaintiffs' claim in the case before us, and to do so would be, in our opinion, a manifest injustice. The appeal will be dismissed, with costs.

Appeal Dismissed.

Questions

1. Do you agree with Du Parcq LJ's remark to the effect that the defendants "do not and cannot have had any legal right to possession of the goods at the date of the conversion"? Compare C.J. Hamson 10 CLJ at 251: "This is remarkable. The court has held, and rightly, that the illegal sale by Smith to the plaintiffs vested the general property of the goods in the plaintiffs. But if the sale was, despite its illegality, effective to vest the general property in the plaintiffs, the bailment by the plaintiffs to the defendants under the illegal hire-purchase agreements was and must have been equally effective to vest the special property in the defendants."   **27-026**

2. Should the owner be able to give evidence of the terms of an unlawful bailment, in order to show that the defendant (the bailee) has, by transgressing those terms, committed an act of conversion?

3. Is a bailee who sets up the bailment able to prove the performance of his obligations under the bailment, even if it be illegal, to resist an action for conversion brought by the owner/bailor?

4. Burglar A lends burglar B his jemmy. B refuses to return it. Can A sue B in conversion? Cf. *NCB v Gamble* [1959] 1 Q.B. 11 at 20, per Devlin J.

TINSLEY v MILLIGAN

House of Lords [1994] 1 A.C. 340; [1993] 3 W.L.R. 126; [1993] 3 All E.R. 65

Two women, T and M, described by the trial judge as lovers, jointly bought a house which was registered in the name of T as sole legal owner. They used the house as a lodging house in a joint business venture which provided most of their income. They agreed to register the house in the sole name of T so that M could make false claims to the Department of Social Security for benefit. After some years M told the Department what she had done and thereafter continued to draw benefit. T and M quarrelled. T moved out and brought an action, claiming possession and asserting ownership of the   **27-027** house. M counterclaimed that the house was held on trust for M and T in equal shares. T's defence to the counterclaim was based on (i) the maxim, ex turpi causa and (ii) the principle that she who comes to equity must come with clean hands. M obtained judgment on claim and counterclaim. T's appeal to the Court of Appeal was dismissed (Ralph Gibson LJ dissenting) holding that it should adopt a "flexible and pragmatic" approach to the maxim and the "clean hands" principle, asking whether enforcement would be an affront to the public conscience. Here, where both claims were tainted with illegality and it would be a disproportionate penalty to deprive M of her share her house, it would not be an affront to the public conscience. T appealed to the House of Lords.

Lord Keith, agreeing with Lord Goff, said that he would allow the appeal.

Lord Goff said that the "public conscience" test developed in a series of cases in the Court of Appeal was little different, if at all, from stating that the court has discretion to grant or refuse relief. It was very difficult to reconcile the principle of policy stated by Lord Mansfield in *Holman v Johnson* (1775) 1 Cowp. 341 at 343. Having examined the authorities, he continued:

LORD GOFF

It is sufficient for present purposes to say, with the greatest respect, that to apply the public conscience test as qualifying the principle established for nearly two hundred years as applicable in cases such as the present is, for reasons I have already stated, inconsistent with numerous authorities binding on the Court of Appeal. In expressing this opinion, I wish to stress that, as can so often happen, your Lordships have had the benefit of a far fuller citation of authority than was available to the Court of Appeal, which has revealed that (contrary to the view expressed by Nicholls L.J. [1992] Ch. 310 at 322)) the decision in *Curtis v Perry* (1802) 6 Ves 739, 31 ER 1285 was not followed by "a surprising dearth of authority, for over a century". On the contrary, there were numerous cases decided during that period, many of which I have already cited, in which the principle was recognised or applied. Nor in my opinion can it be said (as stated by Nicholls L.J. [1992] Ch. 310 at 324)) that the authorities in this line in which equity refuses its assistance can properly be regarded as examples of cases in which, in particular circumstances, the court considered that to have granted relief would have been "an affront to the public conscience", or (as suggested by Lloyd L.J. ([1992] Ch. 310 at 341)) as cases "where the equitable balance came down against the plaintiff". There is no trace of any such principle forming part of the decisions in any of the cases in question. It follows that in my opinion, on the authorities, it was not open to the majority of the Court of Appeal to dismiss the appellant's claim on the basis of the public conscience test invoked by Nicholls L.J., or indeed on the basis of the flexible approach adopted by Lloyd L.J. . . .

I recognise, of course, the hardship which the application of the present law imposes upon the respondent in this case; and I do not disguise my own unhappiness at the result. But, bearing in mind the passage from the judgment of Ralph Gibson L.J. which I have just quoted, I have to say that it is by no means self-evident that the public conscience test is preferable to the present strict rules. Certainly, I do not feel able to say that it would be appropriate for your Lordships House, in the face of a long line of unbroken authority stretching back over two hundred years, now by judicial decision to replace the principles established in those authorities by a wholly different discretionary system.

Lord Jauncey and Lord Lowry made speeches agreeing with Lord Browne-Wilkinson and dismissing the appeal.

LORD BROWNE-WILKINSON

My Lords, I agree with the speech of my noble and learned friend Lord Goff of Chieveley that the consequences of being a party to an illegal transaction cannot depend, as the majority in the Court of Appeal held, on such an imponderable factor as the extent to which the public conscience would be affronted by recognising rights created by illegal transactions. However, I have the misfortune to disagree with him as to the correct principle to be applied in a case where equitable property rights are acquired as a result of an illegal transaction. [Having reviewed the cases, his Lordship continued.]

From these authorities the following propositions emerge.

(1) Property in chattels and land can pass under a contract which is illegal and therefore would have been unenforceable as a contract.

(2) A plaintiff can at law enforce property rights so acquired provided that he does not need to rely on the illegal contract for any purpose other than providing the basis of his claim to a property right.
(3) It is irrelevant that the illegality of the underlying agreement was either pleaded or emerged in evidence: if the plaintiff has acquired legal title under the illegal contract that is enough.

I have stressed the common law rules as to the impact of illegality on the acquisition and enforcement of property rights because it is the appellant's contention that different principles apply in equity. In particular it is said that equity will not aid the respondent to assert, establish or enforce an equitable, as opposed to a legal, proprietary interest since she was a party to the fraud on the Department of Social Security. The house was put in the name of the appellant alone (instead of joint names) to facilitate the fraud. Therefore, it is said, the respondent does not come to equity with clean hands: consequently, equity will not aid her . . .

The presumption of a resulting trust is, in my view, crucial in considering the authorities. On that presumption (and on the contrary presumption of advancement) hinges the answer to the crucial question: does a plaintiff claiming under a resulting trust have to rely on the underlying illegality? Where the presumption of resulting trust applies, the plaintiff does not have to rely on the illegality. If he proves that the property is vested in the defendant alone but that the plaintiff provided part of the purchase money, or voluntarily transferred the property to the defendant, the plaintiff establishes his claim under a resulting trust unless either the contrary presumption of advancement displaces the presumption of resulting trust or the defendant leads evidence to rebut the presumption of resulting trust. Therefore, in cases where the presumption of advancement does not apply, a plaintiff can establish his equitable interest in the property without relying in any way on the underlying illegal transaction. In this case the respondent as defendant simply pleaded the common intention that the property should belong to both of them and that she contributed to the purchase price: she claimed that in consequence the property belonged to them equally. To the same effect was her evidence-in-chief. Therefore the respondent was not forced to rely on the illegality to prove her equitable interest. Only in the reply and the course of the respondent's cross-examination did such illegality emerge: it was the appellant who had to rely on that illegality.

Although the presumption of advancement does not directly arise for consideration in this case, it is important when considering the decided cases to understand its operation. On a transfer from a man to his wife, children or others to whom he stands in loco parentis, equity presumes an intention to make a gift. Therefore in such a case, unlike the case where the presumption of resulting trust applies, in order to establish any claim the plaintiff has himself to lead evidence sufficient to rebut the presumption of gift and in so doing will normally have to plead, and give evidence of, the underlying illegal purpose . . .

In my judgment the time has come to decide clearly that the rule is the same whether a plaintiff founds himself on a legal or equitable title: he is entitled to recover if he is not forced to plead or rely on the illegality, even if it emerges that the title on which he relied was acquired in the course of carrying through an illegal transaction.

As applied in the present case, that principle would operate as follows. The respondent established a resulting trust by showing that she had contributed to the purchase price of the house and that there was a common understanding between her and the appellant that they owned the house equally. She had no need to allege or prove why the house was conveyed into the name of the appellant alone, since that fact was irrelevant to her claim: it was enough to show that the house was in fact vested in the appellant alone. The illegality only emerged at all because the appellant sought to raise it. Having proved these facts, the respondent had raised a presumption of resulting trust. There was no evidence to rebut that presumption. Therefore the respondent should succeed. This is exactly the process of reasoning adopted by the Ontario Court of Appeal in *Gorog v Kiss* (1977) 78 DLR (3d) 690, which in my judgment was rightly decided.

Finally, I should mention a further point which was relied on by the appellant. It is said that, once the illegality of the transaction emerges, the court must refuse to enforce the transaction and all claims under it whether pleaded or not: see *Scott v Brown Doering McNab & Co* [1892] 2 Q.B. 724. Therefore, it is said, it does not matter whether a plaintiff relies on or gives evidence of the illegality: the court will not enforce the plaintiff's rights. In my judgment, this submission is plainly ill-founded. There are many cases where a plaintiff has succeeded, notwithstanding that the illegality of the transaction under which she acquired the property has emerged: see, for example, *Bowmakers Ltd v Barnet Instruments Ltd* [above] and *Sajan Singh v Sardara Ali* [1960] AC 167. In my judgment the court is only entitled and bound to dismiss a claim on the basis that it is founded on an illegality in those cases where the illegality is of a kind which would have provided a good defence if raised by the defendant. In a case where the plaintiff is not seeking to enforce an unlawful contract but founds his case on collateral rights acquired under the contract (such as a right of property) the court is neither bound nor entitled to reject the claim unless the illegality of necessity forms part of the plaintiff's case.

I would therefore dismiss the appeal.

Appeal Dismissed.

Points for reflection

27-028   In *Tribe v Tribe* [1995] 4 All E.R. 236 CA, the plaintiff transferred shares in a company to his son, the defendant. The transfer was expressed to be for a consideration of £78,000 which was never, and was never intended to be, paid. The purpose was to keep the shares out of the hands of the plaintiff's creditors. The creditors' claims were settled but the defendant then refused to return the shares. The plaintiff claimed that the defendant was holding the shares as a bare trustee for the plaintiff. The defendant relied on the rule that an illegal purpose could not be set up to rebut the presumption of advancement. The illegal purpose of deceiving the plaintiff's creditors, however, had never been carried out. For that reason it was held that the plaintiff was entitled to withdraw from the transaction and give evidence of the illegal purpose to rebut the presumption and to recover the shares. Nourse LJ observed that the trial judge had said that the defendant had acted "basely"; and said that "it would indeed be a cause for concern if a plaintiff who had not defrauded his creditors was prevented from recovering simply because the defendant was his son".

   Of course, the plaintiff had not covered himself with glory either—he would have defrauded his creditors if it had been necessary, and he could. Was the right judgment made between two villains? Should it be different if the creditors had been defrauded?

3. Void Contracts

A. Contracts in Restraint of Trade

KORES MANUFACTURING CO LTD v KOLOK MANUFACTURING CO LTD

Court of Appeal [1959] Ch. 108; [1958] 2 W.L.R. 858; 102 S.J. 362; [1958] 2 All E.R. 65; [1958] R.P.C. 200

27-029   Two companies agreed by letter that neither would, without the written consent of the other, employ at any time any person who had been the servant of the other company during the period of five years previous to that time. Both companies were engaged in manufacturing similar products involving chemical processes, including exceedingly dirty work, in relation to which their respective technical employees might become possessed of confidential information and trade secrets. It was contemplated at the time of the agreement that their factories would be adjoining, though this had since ceased to be the case.

   The action was brought by one company to restrain the other from employing a named former employee of the plaintiffs. Lloyd-Jacob J held the contract void as in restraint of trade. On appeal, the judgment of the Court of Appeal (Jenkins, Pearce and Ormerod LJJ) was delivered by:

JENKINS LJ

> [Having referred to and considered various authorities on restraints between master and servant:] It is true that the agreement of 1934 was between two employers, and not between employer and employee. Nevertheless, it was wholly and solely directed to preventing the employees of either contracting party, on ceasing to be employed by them, from entering the employment of the other contracting party. Apart from the question of trade secrets and confidential information, we have described the matter requiring protection as being the adequacy and stability of the plaintiffs' and defendants' respective complements of employees. That, no doubt, is an interest which employers are entitled to protect by all legitimate means, as by paying good wages and making their employment attractive. We have further described the danger against which that interest required protection as being the unimpeded secession of employees of either of the parties to that of the other

of them under the inducement of higher wages or better working conditions. But an employer has no legitimate interest in preventing an employee, after leaving his service, from entering the service of a competitor
merely on the ground that the new employer is a competitor. The danger of the adequacy and stability of his
complement of employees being impaired through employees leaving his service and entering that of a rival is
not a danger against which he is entitled to protect himself by exacting from his employees covenants that they
will not, after leaving his service enter the service of any competing concern. If in the present case the plaintiffs
had taken a covenant from each of their employees that he would not enter the service of the defendants at any
time during the five years next following the termination of his service with the plaintiffs, and the defendants
had taken from their employees covenants restraining them in similar terms from entering the employment
of the plaintiffs, we should have thought that (save possibly in very exceptional cases involving trade secrets,
confidential information and the like) all such covenants would on the face of them be bad as involving a
restraint of trade which was unreasonable as between the parties. Here the plaintiffs and the defendants
have, as it seems to us, sought to do indirectly that which they could not do directly by reciprocal undertakings
between themselves not to employ each other's former employees, entered into over the heads of their respective employees, and without their knowledge. It seems to us to be open to question whether an agreement
such as that, directed to preventing employees of the parties from doing that which they could not by individual
covenants with their respective employers validly bind themselves not to do, should be accorded any greater
validity than individual covenants by the employees themselves would possess. We prefer, however, to leave
that question open, and to found our conclusions as to the invalidity of the agreement of 1934 on the reasons
given earlier in this judgment.

Appeal Dismissed.

ESSO PETROLEUM CO LTD v HARPER'S GARAGE (STOURPORT) LTD

House of Lords [1968] A.C. 269; [1967] 2 W.L.R. 871; [1967] 1 All E.R. 699

27-030

H owned and operated two garages, Mustow Green and Corner, and had entered into solus agreements with E. The solus agreement in respect of Mustow Green garage was for a period of four years
and five months from July 1, 1963, and contained clauses providing that H should buy exclusively E's
motor fuel at their wholesale schedule prices; that sales should be made at E's retail prices (a price
maintenance provision made unenforceable by the Resale Prices Act 1964); that the garage should
be open at all reasonable hours; and that H should, if the garage were sold, get the purchaser to
enter into a similar solus agreement. In relation to Corner, E had a mortgage dated October 6, 1962,
over the premises to secure a principal sum of £7,000 lent to H and interest as well as a similar solus
agreement; the duration of this agreement was 21 years from July 1, 1962, which was also the period
over which the mortgage money was to be repayable by instalments. The mortgage contained provisions that H should buy exclusively E's motor fuels (as in the other agreement) and be open at all reasonable hours and also that the mortgage itself should not be redeemable other than in accordance
with the covenant for repayment, viz., by instalments over 21 years. From about the end of 1963 H
had sold other fuels at Mustow Green and since August 1964 at Corner. E brought actions for injunctions in respect of each garage and the suits were consolidated in the present proceedings. Mocatta
J granted an injunction. On appeal, this decision was reversed by the Court of Appeal (Denning MR,
Harman and Diplock LJJ) on the ground that the ties in the agreements were in restraint of trade and
unenforceable. E appealed to the House of Lords.

LORD REID

. . . if a contract is within the class of contracts in restraint of trade the law which applies to it is quite different
from the law which applies to contracts generally. In general unless a contract is vitiated by duress, fraud or
mistake its terms will be enforced though unreasonable or even harsh and unconscionable, but here a term
in restraint of trade will not be enforced unless it is reasonable. And in the ordinary case the court will not

remake a contract: unless in the special case where the contract is severable, it will not strike out one provision as unenforceable and enforce the rest. But here the party who has been paid for agreeing to the restraint may be unjustly enriched if the court holds the restraint to be too wide to be enforceable and is unable to adjust the consideration given by the other party.

It is much too late now to say that this rather anomalous doctrine of restraint of trade can be confined to the two classes of case to which it was originally applied. But the cases outside these two classes afford little guidance as to the circumstances in which it should be applied. In some it has been assumed that the doctrine applies and the controversy has been whether the restraint was reasonable. And in others where one might have expected the point to be taken it was not taken, perhaps because counsel thought that there was no chance of the court holding that the restraint was too wide to be reasonable.

[Having referred to various authorities, his Lordship continued:] The main argument submitted for the appellant on this matter was that restraint of trade means a personal restraint and does not apply to a restraint on the use of a particular piece of land. Otherwise, it was said, every covenant running with the land which prevents its use for all or for some trading purposes would be a covenant in restraint of trade and therefore unenforceable unless it could be shown to be reasonable and for the protection of some legitimate interest. It was said that the present agreement only prevents the sale of petrol from other suppliers on the site of the Mustow Green garage. It leaves the respondents free to trade anywhere else in any way they choose. But in many cases a trader trading at a particular place does not have the resources to enable him to begin trading elsewhere as well, and if he did he might find it difficult to find another suitable garage for sale or to get planning permission to open a new filling station on another site. As the whole doctrine of restraint of trade is based on public policy its application ought to depend less on legal niceties or theoretical possibilities than on the practical effect of a restraint in hampering that freedom which it is the policy of the law to protect.

It is true that it would be an innovation to hold that ordinary negative covenants preventing the use of a particular site for trading of all kinds or of a particular kind are within the scope of the doctrine of restraint of trade. I do not think they are. Restraint of trade appears to me to imply that a man contracts to give up some freedom which otherwise he would have had. A person buying or leasing land had no previous right to be there at all, let alone to trade there, and when he takes possession of that land subject to a negative restrictive covenant he gives up no right or freedom which he previously had. I think that the "tied house" cases might be explained in this way, apart from *Biggs v Hoddinott*,[3] where the owner of a free house had agreed to a tie in favour of a brewer who had lent him money. Restraint of trade was not pleaded. If it had been, the restraint would probably have been held to be reasonable. But there is some difficulty if a restraint in a lease not merely prevents the person who takes possession of the land under the lease from doing certain things there, but also obliges him to act in a particular way. In the present case the respondents before they made this agreement were entitled to use this land in any lawful way they chose, and by making this agreement they agreed to restrict their right by giving up their right to sell there petrol not supplied by the appellants.

In my view this agreement is within the scope of the doctrine of restraint of trade as it had been developed in English law. Not only have the respondents agreed negatively not to sell other petrol but they have agreed positively to keep this garage open for the sale of the appellants' petrol at all reasonable hours throughout the period of the tie. It was argued that this was merely regulating the respondent's trading and rather promoting than restraining his trade. But regulating a person's existing trade may be a greater restraint than prohibiting him from engaging in a new trade. And a contract to take one's whole supply from one source may be much more hampering than a contract to sell one's whole output to one buyer. I would not attempt to define the dividing line between contracts which are and contracts which are not in restraint of trade, but in my view this contract must be held to be in restraint of trade. So it is necessary to consider whether its provisions can be justified.

But before considering this question I must deal briefly with the other agreement tying the corner garage for 21 years. The rebate and other advantages to the respondents were similar to those in the mustow green agreement but in addition the appellants made a loan of £7,000 to the respondents to enable them to improve their garage and this loan was to be repaid over the 21 years of the tie. In security they took a mortgage of this garage. The agreement provided that the loan should not be paid off earlier than at the dates stipulated. But the respondents now tender the unpaid balance of the loan and they say that the appellants have no interest to refuse to accept repayment now, except in order to maintain the tie for the full 21 years. . .

---

[3]   [1898] 2 Ch. 307; 14 T.L.R. 504 CA.

The appellants argue that the fact that there is a mortgage excludes any application of the doctrine of restraint of trade. But I agree with your lordships in rejecting that argument. I am prepared to assume that, if the respondents had not offered to repay the loan so far as it is still outstanding, the appellants would have been entitled to retain the tie. But, as they have tendered repayment, I do not think that the existence of the loan and the mortgage puts the appellants in any stronger position to maintain the tie than they would have been in if the original agreements had permitted repayment at an earlier date. The appellants must show that in the circumstances when the agreement was made a tie for 21 years was justifiable . . .

The Court of Appeal held that these ties were for unreasonably long periods. They thought that, if for any reason the respondents ceased to sell the appellants' petrol, the appellants could have found other suitable outlets in the neighbourhood within two or three years. I do not think that that is the right test. In the first place there was no evidence about this and I do not think that it would be practicable to apply this test in practice. It might happen that when the respondents ceased to sell their petrol, the appellants would find such an alternative outlet in a very short time. But, looking to the fact that well over 90 per cent. Of existing filling station, are tied and that there may be great difficulty in opening a new filling station, it might take a very long time to find an alternative. Any estimate of how long it might take to find suitable alternatives for the respondents' filling stations could be little better than guesswork.

I do not think that the appellants' interest can be regarded so narrowly. They are not so much concerned with any particular outlet as with maintaining a stable system of distribution throughout the country so as to enable their business to be run efficiently and economically. In my view there is sufficient material to justify a decision that ties of less than five years were insufficient, in the circumstances of the trade when these agreements were made, to afford adequate protection to the appellants' legitimate interests. And if that is so I cannot find anything in the details of the Mustow Green agreement which would indicate that it is unreasonable. It is true that if some of the provisions were operated by the appellants in a manner which would be commercially unreasonable they might put the respondents in difficulties. But I think that a court must have regard to the fact that the appellants must act in such a way that they will be able to obtain renewals of the great majority of their very numerous ties, some of which will come to an end almost every week. If in such circumstances a garage owner chooses to rely on the commercial probity and good sense of the producer, I do not think that a court should hold his agreement unreasonable because it is legally capable of some misuse. I would therefore allow the appeal as regards the Mustow Green agreement.

But the Corner garage agreement involves much more difficulty. Taking first the legitimate interests of the appellants a new argument was submitted to your lordships that, apart from any question of security for their loan, it would be unfair to the appellants if the respondents, having used the appellants' money to build up their business, were entitled after a comparatively short time to be free to seek better terms from a competing producer. But there is no material on which I can assess the strength of this argument and I do not find myself in a position to determine whether it has any validity. A tie for 21 years stretches far beyond any period for which developments are reasonably foreseeable. Restrictions on the garage owner which might seem tolerable and reasonable in reasonably foreseeable conditions might come to have a very different effect in quite different conditions: the public interest comes in here more strongly. And, apart from a case where he gets a loan, a garage owner appears to get no greater advantage from a 21 tie than he gets from a five-year tie. So I would think that there must at least be some clearly established advantage to the producing company—something to show that a shorter period would not be adequate—before so long a period could be justified. But in this case there is no evidence to prove anything of the kind. And the other material which I have thought it right to consider does not appear to me to assist the appellant here. I would therefore dismiss the appeal as regards the Corner garage agreement.

Lords Morris of Borth-y-Gest, Hodson, Pearce and Wilberforce delivered speeches to similar effect.

Appeal Allowed in Part and Dismissed in Part.

Order of Mocatta J. Restored as to Mustow Green.

Points for reflection

In *Shell UK Ltd v Lostock Garage Ltd* [1977] 1 All E.R. 481 the solus agreement, as varied in 1966, was reasonable. The parties did not foresee in 1966, that circumstances would arise in which Shell would subsidise neighbouring garages to such an extent as to force Lostock to trade at a loss. Because of the

27-031

oil crisis, this happened in 1975. Lord Denning MR said that it is a mistake to say that a covenant in unreasonable restraint of trade is "invalid" or "void" ab initio. It is only unenforceable. He contrasted two situations: "First, when at the time of making the contract, it is seen that it may in the future operate unfairly or unreasonably, the courts will not enforce it. Secondly, when it is found afterwards to operate unreasonably or unfairly—in circumstances which were not envisaged beforehand—the courts will not enforce it." He therefore held that, so long as Shell continued to subsidise the neighbouring garages, the court should not enforce the covenant.

Ormrod and Bridge LJJ disagreed with this "novel principle". Ormrod LJ said: "It would introduce into the law an unprecedented discretion in the court to suspend for a time a term in a contract; the repercussions of this are quite unforeseeable and unmanageable. For example, it would at once alter the approach of the courts to covenants in restraint of trade generally, because, if the restraint could be temporarily suspended when it was operating oppressively, many more covenants would pass the normal test at the time they were entered into. Moreover, neither party will be able to know when a covenant is or is not enforceable, or if temporarily unenforceable, when it becomes enforceable again."

Lord Denning MR and Ormrod LJ held that it would not be just and equitable to grant Shell an injunction while they were supporting the neighbouring garages. Bridge LJ agreed in the result because Shell's breach of the term which he found to be implied, amounted to a repudiation of the contract.

And see *Alec Lobb (Garages) Ltd v Total Oil*, above, para.26–011.

A SCHROEDER MUSIC PUBLISHING CO LTD v MACAULAY

House of Lords [1974] 1 W.L.R. 1308; [1974] 3 All E.R. 616

27-032   The respondent, then young and unknown as a song-writer, entered into a contract with the appellant whereby the latter engaged his exclusive services for five years. The agreement, the appellants' standard form, provided that the respondent assigned to the appellants full copyright for the whole world in each original composition and lyric for which he, whether solely or in collaboration, was responsible at any time during the period of the agreement or at any time prior to it in so far as the respondent still owned and controlled them. The appellants agreed to pay the respondent £50 as an advance on royalties payable under the contract and to recoup the £50 therefrom. This procedure was to be repeated throughout the period of the agreement. If in that time the total of the respondent's royalties and advances equalled or exceeded £5,000, the agreement would automatically be extended for a further five years. The appellants could at any time terminate the agreement by one month's written notice but the respondent had no such reciprocal right: the appellants could further freely assign the agreement and copyright under it but the respondent could assign his rights only with the appellants' consent. The appellants were further under no obligation to publish any of the respondent's work. In the respondent's action for a declaration that the agreement was contrary to public policy, the appellants claimed that their standard form, common to agreements between song publishers and song-writers did not need justification on the ground of reasonableness. The House of Lords affirmed the decision of the Court of Appeal (Russell, Cairns LJJ, Goulding J) affirming the decision of Plowman J for the plaintiff. On the inference of the reasonableness of standard form contracts—

LORD DIPLOCK

> Standard forms of contracts are of two kinds. The first, of very ancient origin, are those which set out the terms on which mercantile transactions of common occurrence are to be carried out. Examples are bills of lading,

charter-parties, policies of insurance, contracts of sale in the commodity markets. The standard clauses in these contracts have been settled over the years by negotiation by representatives of the commercial interests involved and have been widely adopted because experience has shown that they facilitate the conduct of trade. Contracts of these kinds affect not only the actual parties to them but also others who may have a commercial interest in the transactions to which they relate, as buyers or sellers, charterers or shipowners, insurers or bankers. If fairness or reasonableness were relevant to their enforceability the fact that they are widely used by parties whose bargaining power is fairly matched would raise a strong presumption that their terms are fair and reasonable.

The same presumption, however, does not apply to the other kind of standard form of contract. This is of comparatively modern origin. It is the result of the concentration of particular kinds of business in relatively few hands. The ticket cases in the nineteenth century provide what are probably the first examples. The terms of this kind of standard form of contract have not been the subject of negotiation between the parties to it, or approved by any organisation representing the interests of the weaker party. They have been dictated by that party whose bargaining power, either exercised alone or in conjunction with others providing similar goods or services, enables him to say: "If you want these goods or services at all, these are the only terms on which they are obtainable. Take it or leave it."

To be in a position to adopt this attitude towards a party desirous of entering into a contract to obtain goods or services provides a classic instance of superior bargaining power. It is not without significance that on the evidence in the present case, music publishers in negotiating with song-writers whose success has been already established do not insist on adhering to a contract in the standard form they offered to the respondent. The fact that the appellants' bargaining power vis-à-vis the respondent was strong enough to enable them to adopt this take-it-or-leave-it attitude raises no presumption that they used it to drive an unconscionable bargain with him, but in the field of restraint of trade it calls for vigilance on the part of the court to see that they did not.

Points for reflection

The significance of *Schroeder* was underlined in *Proactive Sports Management Ltd v Wayne Rooney and others* [2011] EWCA Civ 1444. As a 17 year-old, Rooney had contracted with Proactive to manage his image rights; and, for some time, the relationship between the parties had been fine. However, as Rooney's profile became more valuable, he became dissatisfied with the terms of the contract (which tied him to Proactive for eight years) and he took on new agents. One of the questions in the ensuing litigation was whether the agreement between Rooney and Proactive was unenforceable as being in unreasonable restraint of trade. The Court of Appeal, following the trial judge, declined to accept Proactive's argument that, because Rooney remained free to play soccer, there was no restraint on his trade: the doctrine of restraint of trade was engaged and the question was whether Proactive could show the restraints to be reasonable. On the facts, it was clear that, even though (at the time) the Rooneys were content with the deal, it was oppressive. They had no independent legal advice; Proactive knew that Rooney was "hot property" (per Arden LJ at para.100); this underscored the inequality of bargaining power between the parties; and so it followed that the restraints were unreasonable.

27-033

B. SEVERANCE

In *Attwood v Lamont* [1920] 3 K.B. 571 CA Younger LJ said: "The doctrine of severance has not, I think gone further than to make it permissible in a case where the covenant is not really a single covenant but is in effect a combination of several distinct covenants. In that case and where severance can be carried out without the addition or alteration of a word, it is permissible. But in that case only."

27-034

RONBAR ENTERPRISES LTD v GREEN

Court of Appeal [1954] 1 W.L.R. 815; 98 S.J. 369; [1954] 2 All E.R. 266

27-035 By an agreement of 1951, the plaintiff company and the defendant became partners in a weekly paper of sporting and entertainment news. A clause of the agreement provided that if one partner bought the other out, "the partner whose share is purchased shall not for five years from such date directly or indirectly carry on or be engaged or interested in any business similar to or competing with the business of the partnership." The partnership was in due course determined and the clause became operative. A company was formed to publish a periodical similar to that of the plaintiff company and the defendant wrote articles for this new publication. The plaintiff company sought an injunction against the defendant in pursuance of the clause cited. Roxburgh J granted an interlocutory injunction. On appeal:

JENKINS LJ

Mr Eastham, on behalf of the defendant, argued that there had been no breach of that restrictive provision because, on its true construction, it did not extend to the rendering of services for a salary or wages as distinct from being engaged in business on one's own account. I do not agree. In my opinion the words "carry on or be engaged or interested in any business similar to or competing with the business of the partnership" are apt, particularly in view of the word "engaged" to include a case where the party subject to the restriction takes employment in a business of either of the kinds mentioned at a salary or wages, as well as a case in which he embarks on such a business on his own account or in a partnership. In my view, therefore, assuming that the covenant is valid, what has been done does prima facie amount to a breach of it.

As to its validity, that was attacked by Mr Eastham on these grounds. First, he said that if, contrary to his primary submission, it did extend to prevent the defendant working as a salaried employee, it was on that account too wide. In my view, that is not so. I do not think that it can be said that this covenant is too wide, merely because it would extend to cases of salaried employment, or employment at a wage in a business of either of the kinds mentioned.

Mr Eastham next contends that the covenant is unreasonable as being unlimited in point of area. He says that a business similar to the business of the partnership might be carried on in any part of the world, and in whatever part of the world it was carried on it would be a breach of this covenant read in accordance with its terms. In my view, that argument must almost certainly prevail unless it is possible to sever the covenant, so as to segregate the words "similar to or," and make it read "shall not . . . carry on or be engaged or interested in any business similar to the business of the partnership or any business competing with the business of the partnership," the covenant being thus treated as imposing two distinct restrictions with respect to two distinct kinds of business—that is to say, a business competing with the business of the partnership, and a business similar to the business of the partnership. . .

[Having discussed various authorities, his Lordship proceeded:] The explanation of the different conclusion reached in *Attwood v Lamont* as compared with *Goldsoll v Goldman* [1915] Ch. 292 and the *British Reinforced Concrete Case* [1921] 2 Ch. 563 appears to be that *Attwood v Lamont* was a case as between master and servant whereas the other two cases were cases as between vendor and purchaser, as is the present case. I think that it can be regarded as settled that the court takes a far stricter and less favourable view of covenants in restraint of trade entered into between master and servant than it does of similar covenants between vendor and purchaser. In the case of a covenant between vendor and purchaser, the court recognises that it is perfectly proper for the parties, in order to give efficacy to the transaction, to enter into such restrictive provisions as regards competition as are reasonably necessary to enable the purchaser to reap the benefit of that which he has bought; and restrictions of that kind are regarded as necessary, not only in the interests of the purchaser but in the interests of the vendor also, for they not only preserve the value to the purchaser of that which he buys but also enable the vendor to realise a satisfactory price. It is obvious that in many types of business the goodwill would be well-night unsaleable if it was unlawful for the vendor to enter into an adequate covenant against competition. . . . I find that what the defendant has been doing is plainly contrary to the terms of the restrictive covenant. I find further that prima facie the covenant, construed in the way that I have construed it, should not be held to be invalid.

HODSON LJ

On the question whether the covenant was unreasonably wide, Mr Hesketh conceded that, as it stood, the covenant was unreasonably wide because the words "similar to or" preceding the word "competing" would be unnecessary for the protection of the plaintiff company's interest. Recognising that position, the judge has excised those words, and thereby severed the covenant; and the question principally argued on this appeal is whether it was legitimate so to do.

I have no doubt in my own mind that it is. It is quite clear that in a "vendor and purchaser case," in so far as matters of geography are concerned—as was pointed out by this court in *Goldsoll v Goldman* which has already been cited—it is quite legitimate to deal with the area by severance.

Harman J. delivered a concurring judgment.

Appeal Dismissed.

SCORER v SEYMOUR-JONES

Court of Appeal [1966] 1 W.L.R. 1419; [1966] 3 All E.R. 347

The defendant had been employed by the plaintiff in sole charge at the Kingsbridge office of the plaintiff's estate agents' business, of which the main office was in Dartmouth. The written contract eventually concluded between them provided, inter alia, that, for three years after the termination of the contract, the defendant would not "undertake or carry on either alone or in partnership or be employed or interested directly or indirectly in any capacity whatsoever in the business of an auctioneer surveyor or estate agent or in any ancillary business carried on by (the plaintiff) at (the Kingsbridge and Dartmouth offices) within a five mile radius thereof . . .". The defendant was dismissed by the plaintiff after a few months and thereafter practised on his own account in Salcombe within five miles of Kingsbridge but outside a five miles' radius of Dartmouth. In this action by the plaintiff to enforce the covenant, the county court judge held the covenant severable to be operative only in respect of Kingsbridge and granted the plaintiff an injunction. On appeal, Sellers and Danckwerts LJJ delivered judgments dismissing the appeal.

27-036

SALMON LJ

I confess that my mind has fluctuated during the course of this appeal. It has been rightly pointed out to us on behalf of the plaintiff that this defendant behaved very badly when he was in the plaintiff's employ. Customers came to the office at Kingsbridge, of which the defendant was in charge, to sell their properties. It was his duty, at law and in common honesty, to sell those properties on behalf of his employer, the plaintiff. What he did, at any rate in one case, in breach of that duty, was to sell the property as a venture of his own and pocket the commission.

The fact, however, that he behaved improperly is really beside the point, because it cannot help to solve the only question in this case, which is: Was this covenant an unreasonable restraint of trade at the date it was written, namely, on June 2, 1964?

At one time it seemed to me that *Bowler v Lovegrove* [1921] 1 Ch. 642 went a very long way, if not the whole of the way, to getting the defendant home. The county court judge in his judgment says (rightly, I now think) that the circumstances of the instant case are quite different from the circumstances of *Bowler v Lovegrove*. He did not, however, state the respects in which the circumstances were different. Our attention has been drawn to these very important matters by Mr Crawford on behalf of the plaintiff. P.O. Lawrence J. said:

"It is true that the defendant came into personal contact with the plaintiffs' customers. But this fact loses its significance when the nature of the business carried on by the plaintiffs and the duties of the defendant in connection with such business are considered. The plaintiffs' customers with whom the defendant came into personal contact were not the ordinary recurring customers such as exist in most other businesses."

He was saying that the fact that a servant comes into personal contact with customers in the normal case might justify such a covenant but that it lost its significance in the case he was considering because the customers were not recurring customers. In the instant case, the judge has accepted the evidence which was called by the plaintiff; and there was cogent evidence on behalf of the plaintiff that he had many recurring customers. This is the fact which to my mind distinguishes the instant case from *Bowler v Lovegrove*.

When the defendant was in the Kingsbridge office he was in effect the Kingsbridge office. Every customer who came into that office dealt with him. He was in a position in which he would have every opportunity of gaining knowledge of the customers' business and influence over the customers.

[Having considered *Morris v Saxelby* [1916] 1 A.C. 688, his Lordship continued:] Mr Crawford has argued (and in my judgment he is right) that in cases such as the present a covenant such as has been suggested would be too narrow from a practical point of view to be of any use. It might be very difficult indeed for the plaintiff to know whether or not, and perhaps almost impossible to prove that, the defendant was whittling away the plaintiff's trade connection. As far as this point is concerned, it is interesting to notice that a covenant in a form such as the present was approved in the House of Lords in *Fitch v Dewes* [1921] 2 A.C. 158. That was a case of a covenant by a solicitor against his managing clerk. It was never suggested in that case by anyone, either in the Court of Appeal or the House of Lords, that the covenant was too wide because it would have been sufficient if it had merely restrained the clerk from dealing with any former client of his employers.

As far as the question as to whether this covenant is severable is concerned, I have no doubt but that it is. The defendant was restrained from carrying on the business or being engaged in the business of an estate agent or auctioneer within five miles of Kingsbridge and then, quite separately, within five miles of Dartmouth. The plaintiff does not seek to support the prohibition in respect of Dartmouth. The prohibition in respect of Kingsbridge stands quite separately and I have no difficulty in saying that the covenant is plainly severable. Equally plainly, in my view, it is not against public policy.

I agree that the appeal should be dismissed.

Appeal Dismissed.

Points for reflection

27-037   In *M & S Drapers (A Firm) v Reynolds* [1957] 1 W.L.R. 9; [1956] 3 All E.R. 814 R had been employed from March 1953 by M & S, a firm of credit drapers, bringing with him a connection of customers acquired in previous employments. In August 1955 the parties entered into a written agreement determinable by two weeks' notice on either side and providing for R a weekly wage of £10. One clause of the agreement provided, "For a period of five years following the determination of this agreement the servant shall not . . . sell or canvass or solicit orders . . . by way of the business of a credit draper from any person whose name shall have been inscribed on the books of the firm as a customer during the three years immediately preceding such determination upon whom the servant has called in the course of his duties for the firm." In 1956, R left the employment of M & S and thereafter sold goods by way of credit draper's business to persons who were on the books of M & S during the three years before he left them. M & S sought to enforce the covenant against him. The county court judge held that, although M & S might have some proprietary rights in their list of customers a restriction of five years for a man of R's position, earning a modest wage, was unreasonable and gave judgment for R. On appeal, the Court of Appeal (Hodson, Morris and Denning LJJ) dismissed the appeal. Morris LJ said, "as the judge pointed out in his judgment in his case, the customers of one credit draper can always be canvassed and are likely to be canvassed by other credit drapers. In a sphere where competition is normally free, since every householder is a potential purchaser, and where successful selling must to some extent depend upon the personal abilities of particular salesmen, and also to some extent on the quality of the goods which the salesman's employer can offer, a period of five years' banishment from particular doorsteps seems to me to be in any event of wholly unwarranted duration."

See also *T. Lucas & Co Ltd v Mitchell* [1972] 1 W.L.R. 938; *Home Countries Dairies Ltd v Skilton* [1970] 1 W.L.R. 526; [1970] 1 All E.R. 1227 CA.

GOODINSON v GOODINSON

Court of Appeal [1954] 2 Q.B. 118; [1954] 2 W.L.R. 1121; 98 S.J. 369; [1954] 2 All E.R. 255

Appeal from Judge Wrangham, sitting at Stamford County Court. **27-038**

The husband and wife having separated, on July 21, 1950, the following agreement was entered into between them: "Whereas the husband without admitting any legal liability to maintain the wife has agreed to pay a weekly sum of £2 for the maintenance and support of the wife and child of the husband and wife. Now it is hereby agreed as follows: (1) The husband will pay to the wife for her support and maintenance the sum of £1 a week and for the support and maintenance of the child of the husband and wife, namely, David Goodinson . . . the sum of £1 a week until he shall attain the age of sixteen years . . . (2) The said sum for the maintenance of the wife shall be paid by the husband during their joint lives so long as the wife shall lead a chaste life. (3) The wife will out of the said weekly sums or otherwise support and maintain herself and the said child and will indemnify the husband against all debts to be incurred by her and against all liability whatsoever in respect of the said child, and will not in any way at any time hereafter pledge the husband's credit . . . (5) The wife shall not so long as the husband shall punctually make the weekly payments agreed to be made herein, commence or prosecute any matrimonial proceedings against the husband, but upon the failure of the husband to make the said payments as and when the said payments become due, the wife shall be at full liberty at her election to pursue all and every remedy in this regard, either by enforcement of the provisions hereof or as if this agreement had not been made."

The husband having fallen into arrears in the weekly payments the wife brought the present action in the county court, claiming £200 arrears of maintenance.

For the husband it was contended that by clause 5 of the agreement the wife undertook not to commence or prosecute a petition for divorce even if the husband was guilty of adultery; and that it was therefore an illegal covenant, contra bonos mores, and the whole agreement was invalidated and unenforceable.

The county court judge found for the wife. He held that clause 5 should be read as a covenant only against taking matrimonial proceedings in respect of maintenance; that the words "in this regard," coupled with other language used in the clause, indicated that the meaning of the covenant should be so restricted; and that, therefore, the covenant was not illegal. It was clearly not enforceable and the agreement must be read as if clause 5 did not exist.

The husband appealed.

SOMERVELL LJ

. . . In *Bennett v Bennett* [the effect of which was overruled by the Maintenance Agreements Act 1957; and see now Matrimonial Causes Act 1973 s.34] it was pointed out that there are two kinds of illegality of differing effect. The first is where the illegality is criminal, or contra bonos mores, and in those cases, which I will not attempt to enumerate or further classify, such a provision, if an ingredient in a contract, will invalidate the whole, although there may be many other provisions in it. There is a second kind of illegality which has no such taint; the other terms in the contract stand if the illegal portion can be severed, the illegal portion being a provision which the court, on ground of public policy, will not enforce. The simplest and most common example of the latter class of illegality is a contract for the sale of a business which contains a provision restricting the vendor from competing in or engaging in trade for a certain period or within a certain area. There are many cases in the books where, without in any way impugning the contract of sale, some provision restricting competition has been regarded as in restraint of trade and contrary to public policy. There are many cases where not only has the main contract to purchase been left standing but part of the clause restricting competition has been allowed to stand.

That being the position, it is argued in the first place that this agreement is based on the construction of clause 5, which, it is submitted, on its true construction, is an agreement not to take matrimonial proceedings of any kind, whatever matrimonial offence may be committed by the husband. . . . I think that when the clause is read as a whole the undertaking not to prosecute any matrimonial proceedings so long as the sum is paid is restricted, as the judge held, to matrimonial proceedings in respect of the matters dealt with in the agreement. The judge put it in this way: "In my judgment the clause should be read in a limited sense, as a covenant only against taking matrimonial proceedings in respect of maintenance." He relied, quite rightly, on the words "in this regard" in the latter part of the clause. That point therefore goes. . . .

[Having discussed various authorities, his Lordship proceeded:] Of course, as regards a clause of this kind in a separation deed, it may be plain that the separation is an important ingredient which remains notwithstanding the disregard of an undertaking not to sue quoad the quantum of maintenance. But in this case it is not a separation agreement. It is sought on behalf of the husband to invoke this principle that, if the only consideration moving from one side is a covenant which the law holds to be unenforceable, then there is nothing to support the undertaking on the other side in respect of which the unenforceable covenant purported to be a consideration. Reliance is placed on the application of that principle in *Bennett v Bennett*. That was a special case in somewhat unusual circumstances and so far as this part of it is concerned it turned on the actual provisions of the agreement and equally on the circumstances in which, and the time at which, the agreement was entered into . . .

The special circumstances, I think, are emphasised by an observation of mine which is embodied in the head-note: "Any application to delete, amend, or dismiss a claim for maintenance on the ground that the husband has made provision for the wife should be left to be dealt with by the judge at the hearing of the petition, and if made to a registrar before the hearing should be adjourned." It was in those circumstances, and having regard to the terms of the agreement in that case, that we held that the unenforceable agreement was the main, though not the sole consideration for the husband's agreement as to quantum. In the present case I think that there is ample consideration to support this agreement apart from the covenant not to sue, and to enable it to be enforced as against the husband in the way in which the wife seeks to enforce it in these proceedings. First of all, clause 3, under which she agreed to support and maintain herself and the child and "indemnify the husband against all debts to be incurred by her and against all liability whatsoever in respect of the said child and will not in any way at any time hereafter pledge the husband's credit" is, of course, coextensive with the sum to be paid, subject to the time for which the agreement will subsist. Although, I think the point was not take a below, I should have thought that the undertaking by the wife to have the custody and control of the child and bring it up until it was 16 years old, in the terms of clause 4 was also a consideration.

Then there is a matter which is more directly related to clause 5. This is an agreement by the wife as to these sums as at that date and in the circumstances then existing. If she had chosen to take proceedings, say, in the following month it would not have been a complete shield but it would have been of great importance (as the passages to which I have referred point out) on the husband's side in asking the court to reject her application. It would have been the strongest possible evidence unless relevant circumstances had changed. For these reasons, therefore, I think that there is ample consideration to support this agreement . . .

Birkett L.J. concurred.

Romer L.J. gave a judgment dismissing the appeal.

Appeal Dismissed.

----

4. A CURRENT ISSUE—PRE-NUPTIAL AND POST-NUPTIAL AGREEMENTS

27-039   Prior to the decision of the Supreme Court in *Radmacher v Granatino* [2010] UKSC 42, English law held that pre-nuptial agreements were contrary to public policy and, thus, of no contractual effect. However, as the decision of the Privy Council in *MacLeod v MacLeod* (below) highlights, the courts were more comfortable with post-nuptial agreements.

The background to the dispute in *MacLeod v MacLeod* was that the parties, who were resident in the Isle of Man, had made three agreements, the first on their wedding day (but before their marriage) in 1994, a second in 1997, and the third and critical agreement in 2002 (this agreement being in a deed and clearly intended to be legally binding). The purpose of the agreement, as the parties acknowledged, was to settle fully and fairly their respective financial and proprietary rights while they remained married and in the event of their divorce or the death of Mr MacLeod. In the following year, Mr MacLeod issued divorce proceedings. By the time that the case reached the Privy Council, the sole issue was whether the housing needs of Mrs MacLeod and her children should be catered for by a lump sum (as ordered by the Manx judge) or by a trust fund (as proposed by Mr MacLeod). It was argued for Mr MacLeod that the terms of the 2002 agreement lent support to his proposed provision for Mrs MacLeod and the children. Stated simply, the question for the Privy Council was as to the validity and effect of the 2002 agreement.

MACLEOD v MACLEOD

Privy Council [2008] UKPC 64

BARONESS HALE

[Having rehearsed the factual background and the proceedings leading to the appeal, Baroness Hale continued:]   **27-040**

The validity and effect of separation and maintenance agreements
19. At common law, husband and wife had a duty to live together. This could originally be enforced by the husband by self help and by either party by a decree of restitution of conjugal rights. The Ecclesiastical Courts looked upon agreements to live separate and apart as contrary to public policy and void but the common law courts would enforce them. Equity took longer to decide upon its approach. According to Lord Atkin in *Hyman v Hyman* [1925] AC 601, at p 625, Lord Eldon "doubted but enforced them: cf *St John v St John* (1803) 11 Ves 525, 529 and *Bateman v Countess of Ross* (1813) 1 Dow 235". This was confirmed in *Jones v Waite* (1842) 9 Clark & F 101; 4 Man & G 1104 and in *Wilson v Wilson* (1848) 1 H of L Cas 538. There Lord Cottenham concluded that the authorities in the House of Lords were against the husband, who wished to resile from the articles of separation agreed between himself, his wife and his wife's trustees, and a decree of specific performance was upheld. *Wilson* was regarded as binding on this point in *Hunt v Hunt* (1862) 4 de GF & J 221 As Lord Atkin commented in *Hyman v Hyman* [1929] AC 601, at p625–626:

> "Full effect has therefore to be given in all Courts to these contracts as to all other contracts. It seems not out of place to make this obvious reflection, for a perusal of some of the cases in the matrimonial Courts seems to suggest that at times they are still looked at askance, and enforced grudgingly. But there is no caste in contracts. Agreements for separation are formed, construed and dissolved and to be enforced on precisely the same principles as any respectable commercial agreements, of whose nature indeed they sometimes partake. As in other contracts stipulations will not be enforced which are illegal either as being opposed to positive law or public policy. But this is a common attribute of all contracts, though we may recognize that the subject-matter of separation agreements may bring them more than others into relation with questions of public policy."

In *Westmeath v Westmeath* (1830) 1 Dow & Cl 519, however, a distinction was drawn between an agreement providing for the consequences of an existing separation and an agreement providing for the consequences of a future separation. The latter were null and void. That same principle was applied to agreements made before marriage which provided for the financial consequences of a future separation, in *Cocksedge v Cocksedge* (1844) 14 Sim 244, *Cartwright v Cartwright* (1853) 3 de GM & G 982, and *H v W* (1857) 3 K & J 382. It was applied to a pre-nuptial agreement to live apart re-signed immediately after marriage in *Brodie v Brodie* [1917] P 271.
20. A different aspect of public policy in relation to separation agreements arose in *Hyman v Hyman* [1929] AC 601. The husband and wife had married in 1914. A deed of separation was executed in 1919 when the husband was living with another woman. He covenanted to pay two lump sums to the wife immediately and £20 per week for the rest of her life. She agreed not to institute any proceedings to compel him to pay more than that. The husband paid the sums due under the agreement. In 1923, wives were given the same right as husbands had had since the institution of judicial divorce in 1857 to obtain a divorce on the sole ground of their husbands' adultery. The wife duly obtained such a divorce and filed an application for permanent maintenance

under the powers available to the court on granting a divorce. The husband objected that she had contracted not to do so. But his objection failed. Lord Hailsham L.C. held, at p 614, that:

". . . the power of the Court to make provision for a wife on the dissolution of her marriage is a necessary incident of the power to decree such a dissolution, conferred not merely in the interests of the wife, but of the public, and that the wife cannot by her own covenant preclude herself from invoking the jurisdiction of the Court or preclude the Court from the exercise of that jurisdiction."

Lord Atkin made the same point, at p 629:

"In my opinion the statutory powers of the Court . . . were granted partly in the public interest to provide a substitute for this husband's duty of maintenance and to prevent the wife from being thrown upon the public for support. If this be true, the powers of the Court in this respect cannot be restricted by the private agreement of the parties. 'Quilibet potest renunciare juri pro se introducto.' "

21. That same principle was later held to apply to other statutory powers to award maintenance in the High Court and in the magistrates' courts: see *Morton v Morton* [1942] 1 All ER 273; *Tulip v Tulip* [1951] P 378; *Dowell v Dowell* [1952] 2 All ER 141. The wife's undertaking not to apply for maintenance was also held to be no answer to a claim by the National Assistance Board against her husband as "liable relative": *National Assistance Board v Parkes* [1955] 2 QB 506. This placed the wife in a difficulty if her promise not to go to court was the main consideration given for the husband's promise to pay and could not be severed: see *Bennett v Bennett* [1952] 1 KB 249.

22. Separation and maintenance agreements were considered by the *Royal Commission on Marriage and Divorce 1951–1955, Report*, 1956, Cmd 9678, at pp 192–195. The decision in *Bennett* was one criticism of the existing law; but another was that the husband might be strictly bound by the terms of a maintenance agreement whereas the wife could always go to court and ask for more. The Commission recommended that the wife should be bound by her covenant not to apply to the court for maintenance for herself unless there was a change in the circumstances and that the husband should also be able to go to court to ask for a variation if their circumstances changed. An undertaking not to apply to court for maintenance for the children would remain contrary to public policy.

23. In the event, the provision made by Parliament in the Maintenance Agreements Act 1957 was slightly different. The Law Commission recommended further changes in its Report on Financial Provision in Matrimonial Proceedings, 1969, Law Com No 25, paras 94 to 96. These were implemented in the Matrimonial Proceedings and Property Act 1970 and consolidated as sections 34 to 36 of the Matrimonial Causes Act 1973. The equivalent provision is contained in sections 49 to 51 of the Manx Matrimonial Proceedings Act 2003, the most important parts of which for present purposes are as follows:

"49 Validity of maintenance agreements

> (1) If a maintenance agreement includes a provision purporting to restrict any right to apply to a court for an order containing financial arrangements, then—
>   (a) that provision shall be void; but
>   (b) any other financial arrangements contained in the agreement shall not thereby be rendered void or unenforceable and shall, unless they are void or unenforceable for any other reason (and subject to sections 50 and 51), be binding on the parties to the agreement.
> (2) In this section and in sections 50 and 51—

'maintenance agreement' means any agreement in writing made at any time between the parties to a marriage, being—

> (a) an agreement containing financial arrangements, whether made during the continuance or after the dissolution or annulment of the marriage; or
> (b) a separation agreement which contains no financial arrangements in a case where no other agreement in writing between the same parties contains such arrangements;

'financial arrangements' means provisions governing the rights and liabilities towards one another, when living separately, of the parties to a marriage (including a marriage which has been dissolved or annulled) in respect of the making or securing of payments or the disposition or use of any property, including such rights and liabilities with respect to the maintenance or education of any child, whether or not a child of the family.

50 Alteration of agreements by court during lives of parties

(1) Where a maintenance agreement is for the time being subsisting and each of the parties to the agreement is for the time being either domiciled or resident in the Island, then, subject to subsection (4), either party may apply to the Court or to a court of summary jurisdiction for an order under this section.

(2) The Court may make an order under this section if it is satisfied either—

(a) that by reason of a change in the circumstances in the light of which any financial arrangements contained in the agreement were made or, as the case may be, financial arrangements were omitted from it (including a change foreseen by the parties when making the agreement), the agreement should be altered so as to make different or, as the case may be so as to contain, financial arrangements; or

(b) that the agreement does not contain proper financial arrangements with respect to any child of the family.

(3) The order which that court (subject to subsection (4), (5) and (6)) may make under this section is an order making such alterations in the agreement—

(i) by varying or revoking any financial arrangements contained in it; or

(ii) by inserting in it financial arrangements for the benefit of one of the parties to the agreement or of a child of the family,

as appear to the court to be just having regard to all the circumstances, including, if relevant, the matters mentioned in section 32(4); and the agreement shall have effect afterwards as if any alteration made by the order had been made by agreement between the parties and for valuable consideration.

. . .

(9) For the avoidance of doubt, it is hereby declared that nothing in this section or in section 49 affects—

(a) any power of a court before which any proceedings between the parties to a maintenance agreement are brought under any other enactment (including a provision of this Part) to make an order containing financial arrangements, or

(b) any right of either party to apply for such an order in such proceedings."

24. It will be seen that this retains the rule in *Hyman v Hyman*, reverses the effect of *Bennett v Bennett*, in that the agreement is still valid and enforceable even if the only or main consideration is the invalid promise not to go to court, and provides a power of variation. Section 51 of the 2003 Act (section 36 of the 1973 Act) provides a similar power of variation after the death of one of the parties.

The effect of separation and maintenance agreements in divorce and other matrimonial proceedings

25. In *Hyman v Hyman*, their Lordships took pains to stress that it might well turn out that the maintenance agreed in the separation deed was reasonable. Lord Hailsham, at p 609, regarded the existence of the deed and its terms as "most relevant factors for consideration by the Court in reaching a decision". The leading English case on the weight to be given to such agreements in subsequent divorce proceedings is *Edgar v Edgar* [1980] 1 WLR 1410. The facts are remarkably similar to the facts of this case, save that the separation deed was made when the marriage had already broken down and the wife was saying that she wanted a divorce. It provided for the wife to have a substantial house into which to move with the four children and periodical payments for herself and each of the children. She agreed not to ask for any capital or lump sum order on divorce. Ormrod L.J. considered that the agreement should be taken into account as part of the conduct of the parties. As to its weight, he said this, at p 1417:

"To decide what weight should be given, in order to reach a just result, to a prior agreement not to claim a lump sum, regard must be had to the conduct of both parties leading up to the prior agreement, and to their subsequent conduct in consequence of it. It is not necessary in this connection to think in formal legal terms, such as misrepresentation or estoppel; *all* the circumstances as they affect each of two human beings must be considered in the complex relationship of marriage. So, the circumstances surrounding the making of the agreement are relevant. Undue pressure by one side, exploitation of a dominant position to secure an unreasonable advantage, inadequate knowledge, possibly bad legal advice, an important change of circumstances, unforeseen or overlooked at the time of making the agreement, are all relevant to the question of justice between the parties. Important too is the general proposition that, formal agreements, properly and fairly arrived at with competent legal advice, should not be displaced unless there are good and substantial grounds for concluding that an injustice will be done by holding the parties to the terms of their agreement. There may well be other considerations which affect the justice of this case; the above list is not intended to be an exclusive catalogue."

He also referred, at p 1418, to the following two propositions of the trial judge:

"(4) Providing that there is equality stated-above, the mere fact that the wife would have done better by going to the court, would not generally be a ground for giving her more as, in addition to its duty under section 25, the court had a duty also to uphold agreements which do not offend public policy.
(5) If the court, on the evidence, takes the view that having regard to the disparity of bargaining power, it would be unjust not to exercise its powers under section 23 (having regard to the considerations under section 25), it should exercise such powers even if no fraud, misrepresentation or duress is established which, at common law, would entitle a wife to avoid the deed."

He commented as follows, at p 1418:

"I agree with these propositions, subject to two reservations. First, as to proposition (4), I am not sure that it is helpful to speak of the court having 'a duty' to uphold agreements, although I understand the sense in which the word was used. Secondly, the reference to 'disparity of bargaining power' in proposition (5) is incomplete. It is derived from a phrase taken from *Brockwell v Brockwell* [(unreported) November 5, 1975, Court of Appeal (Civil Division) Transcript No 468 of 1975] and for which I must accept ultimate responsibility. I used it as a shorthand way of describing a situation with which all experienced practitioners are familiar, where one spouse takes an unfair advantage of the other in the throes of marital breakdown, a time when emotional pressures are high, and judgment apt to be clouded. It is unfortunate, because Eastham J. has based his decision solely on this notion of disparity of bargaining power as such, and not on the use, if any, made of it by the husband. The wife, herself, in her affidavit in support of her application, gave as her reasons for disregarding the advice of her counsel and solicitors and entering into the covenant not to claim a lump sum, the fact that she felt overpowered by her husband's enormous wealth and position, coupled with her fears of losing the children. There can be no doubt that in this case, as in so many, there is a disparity of bargaining power. The crucial question, however, for present purposes is not whether the husband had a superior bargaining power, but whether he exploited it in a way which was unfair to the wife, so as to induce her to act to her disadvantage."

Oliver L.J. agreeing, made the following comment, at pp 1420–1421:

"If, however the judge meant that the court must engage in an exercise of dissecting the contract and weighing the relative advantages and bargaining position on each side in order to ascertain whether there is some precise or approximate equilibrium, then I respectfully disagree. Men and women of full age, education and understanding, acting with competent advice available to them, must be assumed to know and appreciate what they are doing and their actual respective bargaining strengths will in fact depend in every case upon a subjective evaluation of their motives for doing it. One may, of course, find that some unfair advantage has been taken of a judgment impaired by emotion, or that one party is motivated by fear induced by some conduct of the other or by some misapprehension of a factual or legal position, but in the absence of some such consideration as that—and these are examples only—the mere strength of one party's desire for a particular result or the mere fact that one party has greater wealth than the other cannot, I think, affect the weight to be attributed to a freely negotiated bargain."

He later summed up his position in rather stronger terms than those used by Ormrod L.J., at p 1424:

"the court must, I think, start from the position that a solemn and freely negotiated bargain by which a party defines her own requirements ought to be adhered to unless some clear and compelling reason, such as, for instance, a drastic change of circumstances, is shown to the contrary."

26. In *Edgar*, of course, there had been a valid and enforceable separation deed. The same principles are, however, also applied to agreements to compromise a claim for ancillary relief, although it has been held that such agreements do not give rise to a contract enforceable in law and are not specifically enforceable: see *Xydhias v Xydhias* [1999] 2 All ER 386, 394. Unlike other court orders made by consent, a consent order in ancillary relief proceedings derives its authority from the court order and not from the preceding agreement: see *de Lasala v de Lasala* [1980] AC 546. A recent example of converting a freely negotiated agreement to compromise divorce proceedings into an order of the court is *X v X (Y and Z intervening)* [2002] 1 FLR 508. The

Edgar principles have also been said to apply to a post-nuptial agreement made when the marriage was in great difficulties in *NA v MA* [2006] EWHC 2900 (Fam), [2007] 1 FLR 1760 (although in that case the agreement was set aside by the judge for undue influence).

27. Rather more variable have been the views expressed as to the relevance of ante-nuptial agreements, which are, in the current state of the law, not valid and enforceable as ordinary contracts. In *F v F (ancillary relief: substantial assets)* [1995] 2 FLR 45, Thorpe J. expressed the view that very limited weight should be attached to ante-nuptial contracts made in Germany between a couple who were both German. Nevertheless, there are several cases in which they have been held relevant to the choice of forum in divorce proceedings: see, for example, *N v N (foreign divorce: financial relief)* [1997] 1 FLR 900, *S v S (divorce: staying proceedings)* [1997] 2 FLR 100, *C v C (divorce: stay of English proceedings)* [2001] 1 FLR 624, *Ella v Ella* [2007] EWCA Civ 99, [2007] 2 FLR 35. And there are other cases in which they have been held relevant to an ancillary relief claim but in rather less positive terms than *Edgar*. In *M v M (Pre-nuptial agreement)* [2002] 1 FLR 654, for example, Connell J. said this, at para 44:

"The pre-nuptial agreement in my view is relevant as tending to guide the court to a more modest award than might have been made without it. I reject outright the suggestion that it should dictate the wife's entitlement; but I bear it in mind nevertheless."

A similar but even more cautious approach was adopted in *K v K (ancillary relief: pre-nuptial agreement)* [2003] 1 FLR 120, which unusually concerned a pre-nuptial agreement made in this country. Recently, in *NG v KR* [2008] EWHC 1532 (Fam), at paras 118 and 119, Baron J. commented:

"This review shows that, over the years, Judges have become increasingly minded to look at the precise terms of agreements and will seek to implement their terms provided the circumstances reveal that the agreement is fair . . . Upon divorce, when a party is seeking quantification of a claim for financial relief, it is the Court that determines the result after applying the Act. The Court grants the award and formulates the order with the parties' agreement being but one factor in the process and perhaps, in the right case, it being the most compelling factor."

28. An example of the "right case" is *Crossley v Crossley* [2007] EWCA Civ 1491, where the Court of Appeal upheld an order for the wife to show cause why the terms of an ante-nuptial agreement should not be implemented without further ado (an order of the type made in *Dean v Dean* [1978] Fam 161). But Thorpe L.J. observed, at para 15, that:

"All these cases are fact-dependent and this is a quite exceptional case on its facts, but if ever there is to be a paradigm case in which the court will look to the prenuptial agreement as not simply one of the peripheral factors in the case but as a factor of magnetic importance, it seem to me that this is just such a case."

Discussion

29. Mr Martin Pointer Q.C., on behalf of the husband, has understandably drawn our attention to the *obiter dicta* of Hoffmann L.J. in *Pounds v Pounds* [1994] 1 WLR 1535, 1550–1551:

"The result of the decision of this court in *Edgar v Edgar* [1980] 1 WLR 1410 and the cases which have followed it is that we have, as it seems to me, the worst of both worlds. The agreement may be held to be binding, but whether it will be can be determined only after litigation and may involve, as in this case, examining the quality of the advice which was given to the party who wishes to resile. It is then understandably a matter for surprise and resentment on the part of the other party that one should be able to repudiate an agreement on account of the inadequacy of one's own legal advisers, over whom the other party had no control and of whose advice he had no knowledge."

Either of the alternatives, that such agreements were always binding or that they were never so, might in his view be better.

30. Mr Pointer argues that all agreements, whether ante- or post-nuptial, should be valid and binding. He accepts that the rule of public policy laid down in *Hyman v Hyman* and confirmed in section 49(1)(a) of the 2003 Act (section 34(1)(a) of the 1973 Act) means that such agreements cannot oust the jurisdiction of the court to make orders containing financial arrangements. But he argues that such agreements should be "presumptively dispositive" of claims to such an order.

31. The Board takes the view that it is not open to them to reverse the long standing rule that ante-nuptial agreements are contrary to public policy and thus not valid or binding in the contractual sense. The Board has

been referred to the position in other parts of the common law world. It is clear that they all adopted the rule established in the 19th century cases. It is also clear that most of them have changed that rule, and provided for ante-nuptial agreements to be valid in certain circumstances. But with the exception of certain of the United States of America, including Florida, this has been done by legislation rather than judicial decision. There is an enormous difference in principle and in practice between an agreement providing for a present state of affairs which has developed between a married couple and an agreement made before the parties have committed themselves to the rights and responsibilities of the married state purporting to govern what may happen in an uncertain and unhoped for future. Hence where legislation does provide for such agreements to be valid, it gives careful thought to the necessary safeguards.

32. An illustration of some of the difficult policy questions involved in such legislation can be found in the response of all the Judges of the Family Division to the proposals in the Government's 1998 Green Paper, *Supporting Families: a consultation document*, published in [1999] Fam Law 159, at 162. They expressed their "unanimous lack of enthusiasm for the pre-nuptial agreement"; they pointed out that there would have to be full financial disclosure and separate legal advice for each side; they presumed that state-funded legal advice would in principle be available; that "it is the emotional moment when legal advice is easily brushed aside"; and that in their view the advent of a child, necessarily not a party to the agreement, "should deprive the nuptial agreement of much if not all of its effect".

33. It is said that calls for the legislative recognition of ante-nuptial agreements appear to have increased with the development of more egalitarian principles of financial and property adjustment on divorce, following the decisions of the House of Lords in *White v White* [2001] 1 AC 596 and *Miller v Miller, McFarlane v McFarlane* [2006] UKHL 24, [2006] 2 AC 618. If such calls are motivated by a perception that equality within marriage is wrong in principle, the more logical solution would be to examine the principles applicable to ascertaining the fair result of a claim for ancillary relief, rather than the pre-marital attempt to predict what the fair result will be long before the event. If such calls are motivated by a fear that people who feel threatened by what might happen in the event of divorce will not get married at all, there is a need for serious research and consideration of the extent of and reasons for the reduction in marriage rates over recent decades. It certainly cannot be demonstrated that the lack of enforceable ante-nuptial agreements in this country is depressing the marriage rate here as compared with other countries where such agreements can be made.

34. The Board notes that the Law Commission for England and Wales, in their 10th programme of Law Reform, have declined to embark upon a review of the principles governing ancillary relief on divorce. But they have announced their intention to examine the status and enforceability of agreements made between spouses and civil partners (or those contemplating marriage or civil partnership) concerning their property and finances: see 2008, Law Com No 311, para 2.17.

35. In the Board's view the difficult issue of the validity and effect of ante-nuptial agreements is more appropriate to legislative rather than judicial development. It is worth noting, for example, that in the Florida case of *Posner v Posner*, where such agreements were recognised, attention was drawn to the statutory powers of the courts to vary such agreements. The Board is inclined to share the view expressed by Baron J. in *NG v KR* [2008] EWHC 1532 (Fam), at para 130, that the variation power in section 50 of the 2003 Act (section 35 of the 1973 Act) does not apply to agreements made between people who are not yet parties to a marriage. Yet it would clearly be unfair to render such agreements enforceable if, unlike post-nuptial agreements, they could not be varied.

36. Post-nuptial agreements, however, are very different from pre-nuptial agreements. The couple are now married. They have undertaken towards one another the obligations and responsibilities of the married state. A pre-nuptial agreement is no longer the price which one party may extract for his or her willingness to marry. There is nothing to stop a couple entering into contractual financial arrangements governing their life together, as this couple did as part of their 2002 agreement. There is a presumption that the parties do not intend to create legal relations: see *Balfour v Balfour* [1919] 2 KB 571. There may also be occasional problems in identifying consideration for the financial promises made (now is not the time to enter into debate about whether domestic services constitute good consideration for such promises). But both of these are readily soluble by executing a deed, as was done here.

37. There is also nothing to stop a married couple from entering into a separation agreement, which will then be governed by sections 49 to 51 of the 2003 Act (sections 34 to 36 of the 1973 Act). As already noted, section 49 applies to "any agreement in writing made at any time between the parties to a marriage". There is nothing to limit this to people who are already separated or on the point of separating. It is limited to agreements containing "financial arrangements" or to separation agreements which contain no financial arrangements. And "financial arrangements" are limited to those governing their rights and liabilities towards one another

when living separately. But section 49(1)(b) provides that such financial arrangements shall be binding "unless they are void or unenforceable for any other reason".

38. Leaving aside the usual contractual reasons, such as misrepresentation or undue influence, the only other such reason might be the old rule that agreements providing for a future separation are contrary to public policy. But the reasons given for that rule were founded on the enforceable duty of husband and wife to live together. This meant that there should be no inducement to either of them to live apart: see, for example, *H v W* (1857) 3 K & J 382, 386. There is no longer an enforceable duty upon husband and wife to live together. The husband's right to use self-help to keep his wife at home has gone. He can now be guilty of the offences of kidnapping and false imprisonment if he tries to do so: see *R v Reid* [1973] QB 299. The decree of restitution of conjugal rights, disobedience to which did for a while involve penal sanctions, has not since the abolition of those sanctions been used to force the couple to live together: see *Nanda v Nanda* [1968] P 351. It was abolished by the Matrimonial Proceedings and Property Act 1970, at the same time as the Law Reform (Miscellaneous Provisions) Act 1970 abolished all the common law actions against third parties who interfered between husband and wife.

39. Hence the reasoning which led to the rule has now disappeared. It is now time for the rule itself to disappear. It has long been of uncertain scope, as some provisions which contemplate future marital separation have been upheld: see, for example, *Duchess of Marlborough v Duke of Marlborough* [1901] 1 Ch 165. This means that sections 49 to 51 of the 2003 Act (sections 34 to 36 of the 1973 Act) can apply to such agreements in just the same way as they do to any other. In particular, they can be varied in either of the circumstances provided for in section 50(2). The first is that there has been a change in the circumstances in the light of which any financial arrangements were made or omitted; following the amendment proposed by the Law Commission in 1969, this now includes a change which the parties had actually foreseen when making the agreement. The second is that the agreement does not contain proper financial arrangements with respect to any child of the family.

40. In the Board's view, therefore, the 2002 agreement was a valid and enforceable agreement, not only with respect to the arrangements made for the time when the parties were together, but also with respect to the arrangements made for them to live separately. However, the latter arrangements were subject to the court's powers of variation and the provisions which purported to oust the jurisdiction of the court, whether on divorce or during the marriage, were void. The existence of such powers does not deprive such agreements of their utility. Countless wives and mothers benefited from such agreements at a time when it was difficult for them to take their husbands to court to ask for maintenance. Enforcing an existing agreement still has many attractions over going to court for discretionary relief.

41. The question remains of the weight to be given to such an agreement if an application is made to the court for ancillary relief. In *Edgar v Edgar*, the solution might have been more obvious if mention had been made of the statutory provisions relating to the validity and variation of maintenance agreements. One would expect these to be the starting point. Parliament had laid down the circumstances in which a valid and binding agreement relating to arrangements for the couple's property and finances, not only while the marriage still existed but also after it had been dissolved or annulled, could be varied by the court. At the same time, Parliament had preserved the parties' rights to go to court for an order containing financial arrangements. It would be odd if Parliament had intended the approach to such agreements in an ancillary relief claim to be different from, and less generous than, the approach to a variation application. The same principles should be the starting point in both. In other words, the court is looking for a change in the circumstances in the light of which the financial arrangements were made, the sort of change which would make those arrangements manifestly unjust, or for a failure to make proper provision for any child of the family. On top of that, of course, even if there is no change in the circumstances, it is contrary to public policy to cast onto the public purse an obligation which ought properly to be shouldered within the family.

42. The Board would also agree that the circumstances in which the agreement was made may be relevant in an ancillary relief claim. They would, with respect, endorse the oft-cited passage from the judgment of Ormrod L.J. in *Edgar v Edgar*, at p 1417, in preference to the passages from the judgment of Oliver L.J., both quoted above at paragraph 25. In particular the Board endorses the observation that "it is not necessary in this connection to think in formal legal terms, such as mispresentation or estoppel". Family relationships are not like straightforward commercial relationships. They are often characterised by inequality of bargaining power, but the inequalities may be different in relation to different issues. The husband may be in the stronger position financially but the wife may be in the stronger position in relation to the children and to the home in which they live. One may care more about getting or preserving as much money as possible, while the other may care more about the living arrangements for the children. One may want to get out of the relationship as quickly as

possible, while the other may be in no hurry to separate or divorce. All of these may shift over time. We must assume that each party to a properly negotiated agreement is a grown up and able to look after him- or herself. At the same time we must be alive to the risk of unfair exploitation of superior strength. But the mere fact that the agreement is not what a court would have done cannot be enough to have it set aside.

Is there a case for variation of the 2002 agreement?

43. The Deputy Deemster clearly found that there was nothing about the circumstances in which the agreement was made to cast doubt upon its validity or the weight which it should be given by the court. The wife may have been under pressure, but not from her husband: "any pressure which the wife felt was occasioned in the main at least by her own circumstances, by the life which she, over 20 years her husband's junior, was choosing to follow" (para 38). The agreement was negotiated over a long period with every eventuality in mind. It was concluded just over a year before the couple finally separated. They foresaw that separation while hoping against hope that it would not happen. If anything, the change which took place was one which might be thought to favour the husband, in that the agreement contemplated that the wife might become the primary carer for the children, whereas the eventual order was for equally shared care. There was a change in the circumstances at the time of the agreement in that the couple did separate. But that was fully contemplated and provided for at the time, which was not long beforehand. There was not such a change in their circumstances as should lead a court to vary the financial arrangements made for the wife.

44. The agreement did not contain, or even purport to contain, proper financial arrangements for the children. Clearly the court had to intervene to provide for them. The general view taken in English law is that children are entitled to a suitable home, to an upbringing, and to an education which is appropriate to their family's circumstances and standard of living. But they are not entitled to long term provision into adulthood unless they have some special need: see *Lilford (Lord) v Glynn* [1979] 1 WLR 78. It is agreed that Dove's Hill is not a suitable home for the children while they are living with their mother. They need something better. The only question is whether the Deputy Deemster was right to provide for such a home by way of a lump sum for the mother, without any obligation upon her to spend it for that purpose, or whether he should have acceded to the father's proposal for a trust.

45. Any appeal court should be very slow to interfere with the exercise of discretion by a trial judge who has seen the parties in person and heard all the evidence: see *Piglowska v Piglowski* [1999] 1 WLR 1360, at p 1372. The Deputy Deemster had clearly got the measure of this family. But the Board has reached the conclusion that he went wrong in principle. The only principled basis for interfering with this particular agreement was in order to make proper provision for the children. However lacking in generosity the provision made for the wife, and of course it was much less than she could have expected had there been no agreement, there was no basis for interfering with it. Rightly or wrongly, the law has taken the view that provision for children is to give them the best possible start in life, rather than to endow them for ever. It has also taken the view that, while the needs of the caring parent can be taken into account as part of the children's needs, the object of providing for the children is not to provide for her. While the ante-nuptial agreement did not make adequate provision for her as a mother, the 2002 agreement did so. The effect of the Deputy Deemster's order was to make further provision for her rather than to make proper provision for the children.

46. Accordingly the Board will humbly advise Her Majesty that this appeal should be allowed and the matter remitted to the High Court for an appropriate trust deed to be drafted if it cannot be agreed. It would, of course, be appropriate for the mother to be a beneficiary of the trust while it subsists. It is fervently to be hoped that the parties can agree both this and the monthly support for the children without further costly contested litigation between them. The parties are invited to make submissions on costs within 14 days.

Further reading

S Smith, 'Reconstructing Restraint of Trade' (1995) 15 OJLS 565

APPENDIX

MISREPRESENTATION ACT 1967

Removal of certain bars to rescission for innocent misrepresentation

1. Where a person has entered into a contract after a misrepresentation has been made to him, and—

(a)   the misrepresentation has become a term of the contract; or

(b)   the contract has been performed;

or both, then, if otherwise he would be entitled to rescind the contract without alleging fraud, he shall be so entitled, subject to the provisions of this Act, notwithstanding the matters mentioned in paragraphs (a) and (b) of this section.

Damages for misrepresentation

2.—(1) Where a person has entered into a contract after a misrepresentation has been made to him by another party thereto and as a result thereof he has suffered loss, then, if the person making the misrepresentation would be liable to damages in respect thereof had the misrepresentation been made fraudulently, that person shall be so liable notwithstanding that the misrepresentation was not made fraudulently, unless he proves that he had reasonable ground to believe and did believe up to the time the contract was made the facts represented were true.

(2) Where a person has entered into a contract after a misrepresentation has been made to him otherwise than fraudulently, and he would be entitled, by reason of the misrepresentation, to rescind the contract, then, if it is claimed, in any proceedings arising out of the contract, that the contract ought to be or has been rescinded, the court or arbitrator may declare the contract subsisting and award damages in lieu of rescission, if of opinion that it would be equitable to do so, having regard to the nature of the misrepresentation and the loss that would be caused by it if the contract were upheld, as well as to the loss that rescission would cause to the other party.

(3) Damages may be awarded against a person under subsection (2) of this section whether or not he is liable to damages under subsection (1) thereof, but where he is so liable any award under the said subsection (2) shall be taken into account in assessing his liability under the said subsection (1).

Avoidance of provision excluding liability for misrepresentation

3. If a contract contains a term which would exclude or restrict—

(a)   any liability to which a party to a contract may be subject by reason of any misrepresentation made by him before the contract was made; or

(b)   any remedy available to another party to the contract by reason of such a misrepresentation, that term shall be of no effect except in so far as it satisfies the requirement of reasonableness as stated in section 11(1) of the Unfair Contract Terms Act 1977; and it is for those claiming that the term satisfies that requirement to show that it does.[1]

4. [. . .][2]

Saving for past transactions

5. Nothing in this Act shall apply in relation to any misrepresentation or contract of sale which is made before the commencement of this Act.

Short title, commencement and extent

6.—(1) This Act may be cited as the Misrepresentation Act 1967.

(2) This Act shall come into operation at the expiration of the period of one month beginning with the date on which it is passed.

(3) This Act [. . .][3] does not extend to Scotland.

(4) This Act does not extend to Northern Ireland.

---

[1]   s.3 substituted by Contract Terms Act 1997 (c.50) s.8(1).
[2]   Repealed by Sale of Goods Act 1979 (c.54) ss.62, 63, Sch.3.
[3]   Words repealed by Sale of Goods Act 1979 (c.54) ss.62, 63, Sch.3.

UNFAIR CONTRACT TERMS ACT 1977

Scope of Part I

1.—(1) For the purposes of this Part of this Act, "negligence" means the breach—

(a)   of any obligation, arising from the express or implied terms of a contract, to take reasonable care or exercise reasonable skill in the performance of the contract;

(b)   of any common law duty to take reasonable care or exercise reasonable skill (but not any stricter duty);

(c)   of the common duty of care imposed by the Occupiers' Liability Act 1957 or the Occupiers' Liability Act (Northern Ireland) 1957.

(2) This Part of this Act is subject to Part III; and in relation to contracts, the operation of sections 2 to 4 and 7 is subject to the exceptions made by Schedule 1.

(3) In the case of both contract and tort, sections 2 to 7 apply (except where the contrary is stated in section 6(4)) only to business liability, that is liability for breach of obligations or duties arising—

(a)   from things done or to be done by a person in the course of a business (whether his own business or another's); or

(b)   from the occupation of premises used for business purposes of the occupier;

and references to liability are to be read accordingly [but liability of an occupier of premises for breach of an obligation or duty towards a person obtaining access to the premises for recreational or educational purposes, being liability for loss or damage suffered by reason of the dangerous state of the premises, is not a business liability of the occupier unless granting that person such access for the purposes concerned falls within the business purposes of the occupier].[1]

(4) In relation to any breach of duty or obligation, it is immaterial for any purpose of this Part of this Act whether the breach was inadvertent or intentional, or whether liability for it arises directly or vicariously.

Negligence liability

2.—(1) A person cannot by reference to any contract term or to a notice given to persons generally or to particular persons exclude or restrict his liability for death or personal injury resulting from negligence.

(2) In the case of other loss or damage, a person cannot so exclude or restrict his liability for negligence except in so far as the term or notice satisfies the requirement of reasonableness.

(3) Where a contract term or notice purports to exclude or restrict liability for negligence a person's agreement to or awareness of it is not of itself to be taken as indicating his voluntary acceptance of any risk.

Liability arising in contract

3.—(1) This section applies as between contracting parties where one of them deals as consumer or on the other's written standard terms of business.

(2) As against that party, the other cannot by reference to any contract term—

---

[1] Words inserted by Occupiers' Liability Act 1984 (c.3), s.2 and by the Occupiers' Liability (Northern Ireland) Order 1987 SI 1987/1280 (N.I. 15), art.4

(a)   when himself in breach of contract, exclude or restrict any liability of his in respect of the breach; or

(b)   claim to be entitled—

(i)   to render a contractual performance substantially different from that which was reasonably expected of him, or

(ii)   in respect of the whole or any part of his contractual obligation, to render no performance at all,

except in so far as (in any of the cases mentioned above in this subsection) the contract term satisfies the requirement of reasonableness.

Unreasonable indemnity clauses

4.—(1) A person dealing as consumer cannot by reference to any contract term be made to indemnify another person (whether a party to the contract or not) in respect of liability that may be incurred by the other for negligence or breach of contract, except in so far as the contract term satisfies the requirement of reasonableness.

(2) This section applies whether the liability in question—

(a)   is directly that of the person to be indemnified or is incurred by him vicariously;

(b)   is to the person dealing as consumer or to someone else.

"Guarantee" of consumer goods

5.—(1) In the case of goods of a type ordinarily supplied for private use or consumption, where loss or damage—

(a)   arises from the goods proving defective while in consumer use; and

(b)   results from the negligence of a person concerned in the manufacture or distribution of the goods,

liability for the loss or damage cannot be excluded or restricted by reference to any contract term or notice contained in or operating by reference to a guarantee of the goods.

(2) For these purposes—

(a)   goods are to be regarded as "in consumer use" when a person is using them, or has them in his possession for use, otherwise than exclusively for the purposes of a business; and

(b)   anything in writing is a guarantee if it contains or purports to contain some promise or assurance (however worded or presented) that defects will be made good by complete or partial replacement, or by repair, monetary compensation or otherwise.

(3) This section does not apply as between the parties to a contract under or in pursuance of which possession or ownership of the goods passed.

Sale and hire-purchase

6.—(1) Liability for breach of the obligations arising from—

(a)   [section 12 of the Sale of Goods Act 1979][2] (seller's implied undertakings as to title, etc.);

(b)   section 8 of the Supply of Goods (Implied Terms) Act 1973 (the corresponding thing in relation to hire-purchase),

cannot be excluded or restricted by reference to any contract term.

(2) As against a person dealing as consumer, liability for breach of the obligations arising from—

(a)   [section 13, 14 or 15 of the 1979 Act][3] (seller's implied undertakings as to conformity of goods with description or sample, or as to their quality or fitness for a particular purpose);

(b)   section 9, 10 or 11 of the 1973 Act (the corresponding things in relation to hire-purchase),

cannot be excluded or restricted by reference to any contract term.

(3) As against a person dealing otherwise than as consumer, the liability specified in subsection (2) above can be excluded or restricted by reference to a contract term, but only in so far as the term satisfies the requirement of reasonableness.

(4) The liabilities referred to in this section are not only the business liabilities defined by section 1(3), but include those arising under any contract of sale of goods or hire-purchase agreement.

Miscellaneous contracts under which goods pass

7.—(1) Where the possession or ownership of goods passes under or in pursuance of a contract not governed by the law of sale of goods or hire-purchase, subsections (2) to (4) below apply as regards the effect (if any) to be given to contract terms excluding or restricting liability for breach of obligation arising by implication of law from the nature of the contract.

(2) As against a person dealing as consumer, liability in respect of the goods' correspondence with description or sample, or their quality or fitness for any particular purpose, cannot be excluded or restricted by reference to any such term.

(3) As against a person dealing otherwise than as consumer, that liability can be excluded or restricted by reference to such a term, but only in so far as the term satisfies the requirement of reasonableness.

(3A) Liability for breach of the obligations arising under section 2 of the Supply of Goods and Services Act 1982 (implied terms about title etc. in certain contracts for the transfer of the property in goods) cannot be excluded or restricted by reference to any such term.

(4) Liability in respect of—

(a)   the right to transfer ownership of the goods, or give possession; or

(b)   the assurance of quiet possession to a person taking goods in pursuance of the contract,

cannot (in a case to which subsection (3A) above does not apply) be excluded or restricted by reference to any such term except in so far as the term satisfies the requirement of reasonableness.

[. . .][4]

8. [. . .][5]

---

[2] Words substituted by Sale of Goods Act 1979 (c.54) ss.62, 63, Sch.2 para.19(a).
[3] Words substituted by Sale of Goods Act 1979 (c.54) ss.62, 63, Sch.2 para.19(b).
[4] Repealed by SI 2005/871 (Regulatory Reform (Trading Stamps) Order) Sch.1 para.1.
[5] Substitutes new s.3 in Misrepresentation Act 1967 (c.7) and Misrepresentation Act (Northern Ireland) 1967 (c.14).

Effect of breach

9.—(1) Where for reliance upon it a contract term has to satisfy the requirement of reasonableness, it may be found to do so and be given effect accordingly notwithstanding that the contract has been terminated either by breach or by a party electing to treat it as repudiated.

(2) Where on a breach the contract is nevertheless affirmed by a party entitled to treat it as repudiated, this does not of itself exclude the requirement of reasonableness in relation to any contract term.

Evasion by means of secondary contract

10. A person is not bound by any contract term prejudicing or taking away rights of his which arise under, or in connection with the performance of, another contract, so far as those rights extend to the enforcement of another's liability which this Part of this Act prevents that other from excluding or restricting.

The "reasonableness" test

11.—(1) In relation to a contract term, the requirement of reasonableness for the purposes of this Part of this Act, section 3 of the Misrepresentation Act 1967 and section 3 of the Misrepresentation Act (Northern Ireland) 1967 is that the term shall have been a fair and reasonable one to be included having regard to the circumstances which were, or ought reasonably to have been, known to or in the contemplation of the parties when the contract was made.

(2) In determining for the purposes of section 6 or 7 above whether a contract term satisfies the requirement of reasonableness, regard shall be had in particular to the matters specified in Schedule 2 to this Act; but this subsection does not prevent the court or arbitrator from holding, in accordance with any rule of law, that a term which purports to exclude or restrict any relevant liability is not a term of the contract.

(3) In relation to a notice (not being a notice having contractual effect), the requirement of reasonableness under this Act is that it should be fair and reasonable to allow reliance on it, having regard to all the circumstances obtaining when the liability arose or (but for the notice) would have arisen.

(4) Where by reference to a contract term or notice a person seeks to restrict liability to a specified sum of money, and the question arises (under this or any other Act) whether the term or notice satisfies the requirement of reasonableness, regard shall be had in particular (but without prejudice to subsection (2) above in the case of contract terms) to—

(a)   the resources which he could expect to be available to him for the purpose of meeting the liability should it arise; and

(b)   how far it was open to him to cover himself by insurance.

(5) It is for those claiming that a contract term or notice satisfies the requirement of reasonableness to show that it does.

"Dealing as consumer"

12.—(1) A party to a contract "deals as consumer" in relation to another party if—

(a)   he neither makes the contract in the course of a business nor holds himself out as doing so; and

(b)   the other party does make the contract in the course of a business; and

(c)   in the case of a contract governed by the law of sale of goods or hire-purchase, or by section 7 of this Act, the goods passing under or in pursuance of the contract are of a type ordinarily supplied for private use or consumption.

(1A) But if the first party mentioned in subsection (1) is an individual paragraph (c) of that subsection must be ignored.

(2) But the buyer is not in any circumstances to be regarded as dealing as consumer—

(a)   if he is an individual and the goods are second hand goods sold at public auction at which individuals have the opportunity of attending the sale in person;

(b)   if he is not an individual and the goods are sold by auction or by competitive tender.[6]

(3) Subject to this, it is for those claiming that a party does not deal as consumer to show that he does not.

Varieties of exemption clause

13.—(1) To the extent that this Part of this Act prevents the exclusion or restriction of any liability it also prevents—

(a)   making the liability or its enforcement subject to restrictive or onerous conditions;

(b)   excluding or restricting any right or remedy in respect of the liability, or subjecting a person to any prejudice in consequence of his pursuing any such right or remedy;

(c)   excluding or restricting rules of evidence or procedure;

and (to that extent) sections 2 and 5 to 7 also prevent excluding or restricting liability by reference to terms and notices which exclude or restrict the relevant obligation or duty.

(2) But an agreement in writing to submit present or future differences to arbitration is not to be treated under this Part of this Act as excluding or restricting any liability.

Interpretation of Part I

14. In this Part of this Act—

"business" includes a profession and the activities of any government department or local or public authority;

"goods" has the same meaning as in the Sale of Goods Act 1893;

"hire-purchase agreement" has the same meaning as in the Consumer Credit Act 1974;

"negligence" has the meaning given by section 1(1);

"notice" includes an announcement, whether or not in writing, and any other communication or pretended communication; and

"personal injury" includes any disease and any impairment of physical or mental condition.

Scope of Part II

15.—(1) This Part of this Act [. . .],[7] is subject to Part III of this Act and does not affect the validity of any discharge or indemnity given by a person in consideration of the receipt by him of compensation in settlement of any claim which he has.

---

6   Substituted by SI 2002/3045 (Sale and Supply of Goods to Consumers Regulations) reg.14 (3).
7   Words repealed by Law Reform (Miscellaneous Provisions) (Scotland) Act 1990 (c.40) ss.68(2)(6), 74(2), Sch.9.

(2) Subject to subsection (3) below, sections 16 to 18 of this Act apply to any contract only to the extent that the contract—

(a)   relates to the transfer of the ownership or possession of goods from one person to another (with or without work having been done on them);

(b)   constitutes a contract of service or apprenticeship;

(c)   relates to services of whatever kind, including (without prejudice to the foregoing generality) carriage, deposit and pledge, care and custody, mandate, agency, loan and services relating to the use of land;

(d)   relates to the liability of an occupier of land to persons entering upon or using that land;

(e)   relates to a grant of any right or permission to enter upon or use land not amounting to an estate or interest in the land.

(3) Notwithstanding anything in subsection (2) above, section 16 to 18—

(a)   do not apply to any contract to the extent that the contract—

(i)   is a contract of insurance (including a contract to pay an annuity on human life);
(ii)   relates to the formation, constitution or dissolution of any body corporate or unincorporated association or partnership;

(b)   apply to—

a contract of marine salvage or towage;

a charter party of a ship or hovercraft;

a contract for the carriage of goods by ship or hovercraft; or,

a contract to which subsection (4) below relates,

only to the extent that—

(i)   both parties deal or hold themselves out as dealing in the course of a business (and then only in so far as the contract purports to exclude or restrict liability for breach of duty in respect of death or personal injury); or

(ii)   the contract is a consumer contract (and then only in favour of the consumer).

(4) This subsection relates to a contract in pursuance of which goods are carried by ship or hovercraft and which either—

(a)   specifies ship or hovercraft as the means of carriage over part of the journey to be covered; or

(b)   makes no provision as to the means of carriage and does not exclude ship or hovercraft as that means, in so far as the contract operates for and in relation to the carriage of the goods by that means.

Liability for breach of duty

16.—(1) [Subject to subsection (1A) below,][8] where a term of a contract [, or a provision of a notice given to persons generally or to particular persons,][9] purports to exclude or restrict liability for breach of duty arising in the course of any business or from the occupation of any premises used for business purposes of the occupier, that term [or provision][10]—

    (a)   shall be void in any case where such exclusion or restriction is in respect of death or personal injury;

    (b)   shall, in any other case, have no effect if it was not fair and reasonable to incorporate the term in the contract [or, as the case may be, if it is not fair and reasonable to allow reliance on the provision][11].

[(1A) Nothing in paragraph (b) of subsection (1) above shall be taken as implying that a provision of a notice has effect in circumstances where, apart from that paragraph, it would not have effect.][12]

(2) Subsection (1)(a) above does not affect the validity of any discharge and indemnity given by a person, on or in connection with an award to him of compensation for pneumoconiosis attributable to employment in the coal industry, in respect of any further claim arising from his contracting that disease.

(3) Where under subsection (1) above a term of a contract[or a provision of a notice][13] is void or has no effect, the fact that a person agreed to, or was aware of, the term[or provision][14] shall not of itself be sufficient evidence that he knowingly and voluntarily assumed any risk.

Control of unreasonable exemptions in consumer or standard form contracts

17.—(1) Any term of a contract which is a consumer contract or a standard form contract shall have no effect for the purpose of enabling a party to the contract—

    (a)   who is in breach of a contractual obligation, to exclude or restrict any liability of his to the consumer or customer in respect of the breach;

    (b)   in respect of a contractual obligation, to render no performance, or to render a performance substantially different from that which the consumer or customer reasonably expected from the contract;

if it was not fair and reasonable to incorporate the term in the contract.

(2) In this section "customer" means a party to a standard form contract who deals on the basis of written standard terms of business of the other party to the contract who himself deals in the course of a business.

---

[8] Words inserted by Law Reform (Miscellaneous Provisions) (Scotland) Act 1990 (c.40) s.68(3),(6).
[9] Words inserted by Law Reform (Miscellaneous Provisions) (Scotland) Act 1990 (c.40) s.68(3),(6).
[10] Words inserted by Law Reform (Miscellaneous Provisions) (Scotland) Act 1990 (c.40) s.68(3),(6).
[11] Words inserted by Law Reform (Miscellaneous Provisions) (Scotland) Act 1990 (c.40) s.68(3),(6).
[12] s.16(1A) inserted by Law Reform (Miscellaneous Provisions) (Scotland) Act 1990 (c.40) s.68(3)(b),(6).
[13] Words inserted by Law Reform (Miscellaneous Provisions) (Scotland) Act 1990 (c.40) s.68(3)(c),(6).
[14] Words inserted by Law Reform (Miscellaneous Provisions) (Scotland) Act 1990 (c.40) s.68(3)(c),(6).

Unreasonable indemnity clauses in consumer contracts

18.—(1) Any term of a contract which is a consumer contract shall have no effect for the purpose of making the consumer indemnify another person (whether a party to the contract or not) in respect of liability which that other person may incur as a result of breach of duty or breach of contract, if it was not fair and reasonable to incorporate the term in the contract.

(2) In this section "liability" means liability arising in the course of any business or from the occupation of any premises used for business purposes of the occupier.

"Guarantee" of consumer goods

19.—(1) This section applies to a guarantee—

(a)   in relation to goods which are of a type ordinarily supplied for private use or consumption; and

(b)   which is not a guarantee given by one party to the other party to a contract under or in pursuance of which the ownership or possession of the goods to which the guarantee relates is transferred.

(2) A term of a guarantee to which this section applies shall be void in so far as it purports to exclude or restrict liability for loss or damage (including death or personal injury)—

(a)   arising from the goods proving defective while—

(i)   in use otherwise than exclusively for the purposes of a business; or
(ii)   in the possession of a person for such use; and

(b)   resulting from the breach of duty of a person concerned in the manufacture or distribution of the goods.

(3) For the purposes of this section, any document is a guarantee if it contains or purports to contain some promise or assurance (however worded or presented) that defects will be made good by complete or partial replacement, or by repair, monetary compensation otherwise.

Obligations implied by law in sale and hire-purchase contracts

20.—(1) Any term of a contract which purports to exclude or restrict liability for breach of the obligations arising from—

(a)   section 12 of the Sale of Goods Act [1979][15] (seller's implied undertakings as to title etc.);

(b)   section 8 of the Supply of Goods (Implied Terms) Act 1973 (implied terms as to title in hire-purchase agreements),

shall be void.

(2) Any term of a contract which purports to exclude or restrict liability for breach of the obligations arising from—

(a)   section 13, 14 or 15 of the said Act of [1979][16] (seller's implied undertakings as to conformity of goods with description or sample, or as to their quality or fitness for a particular purpose);

---

[15] Word substituted Sale of Goods Act 1979 (c.54) ss.62, 63, Sch.2 para.21.
[16] Word substituted by Sale of Goods Act 1979 (c.54) ss.62, 63, Sch.2 para.21.

(b) section 9, 10 or 11 of the said Act of 1973 (the corresponding provisions in relation to hire-purchase),

shall—

(i) in the case of a consumer contract, be void against the consumer;

(ii) in any other case, have no effect if it was not fair and reasonable to incorporate the term in the contract.

Obligations implied by law in other contracts for the supply of goods

21.—(1) Any term of a contract to which this section applies purporting to exclude or restrict liability for breach of an obligation—

(a) such as is referred to in subsection (3)(a) below—

(i) in the case of a consumer contract, shall be void against the consumer, and

(ii) in any other case, shall have no effect if it was not fair and reasonable to incorporate the term in the contract;

(b) such as is referred to in subsection (3)(b) below, shall have no effect if it was not fair and reasonable to incorporate the term in the contract.

(2) This section applies to any contract to the extent that it relates to any such matter as is referred to in section 15(2)(a) of this Act, but does not apply to—

(a) a contract of sale of goods or a hire-purchase agreement; or

(b) a charter party of a ship or hovercraft unless it is a consumer contract (and then only in favour of the consumer).

(3) An obligation referred to in this subsection is an obligation incurred under a contract in the course of a business and arising by implication of law from the nature of the contract which relates—

(a) to the correspondence of goods with description or sample, or to the quality or fitness of goods for any particular purpose; or

(b) to any right to transfer ownership or possession of goods, or to the enjoyment of quiet possession of goods.

(3A) Notwithstanding anything in the foregoing provisions of this section, any term of a contract which purports to exclude or restrict liability for breach of the obligations arising under section 11B of the Supply of Goods and Services Act 1982 (implied terms about title, freedom from encumbrances and quiet possession in certain contracts for the transfer of property in goods) shall be void.

[. . .][17]

Consequence of breach

22. For the avoidance of doubt, where any provision of this Part of this Act requires that the incorporation of a term in a contract must be fair and reasonable for that term to have effect—

---

[17] Repealed by SI 2005/871 (Regulatory Reform (Trading Stamps) Order) Sch.1 para.1.

(a)   if that requirement is satisfied, the term may be given effect to notwithstanding that the contract has been terminated in consequence of breach of that contract;

(b)   for the term to be given effect to, that requirement must be satisfied even where a party who is entitled to rescind the contract elects not to rescind it.

Evasion by means of secondary contract

23. Any term of any contract shall be void which purports to exclude or restrict, or has the effect of excluding or restricting—

(a)   the exercise, by a party to any other contract, of any right or remedy which arises in respect of that other contract in consequence of breach of duty, or of obligation, liability for which could not by virtue of the provisions of this Part of this Act be excluded or restricted by a term of that other contract;

(b)   the application of the provisions of this Part of this Act in respect of that or any other contract.

The "reasonableness" test

24.—(1) In determining for the purposes of this Part of this Act whether it was fair and reasonable to incorporate a term in a contract, regard shall be had only to the circumstances which were, or ought reasonably to have been, known to or in the contemplation of the parties to the contract at the time the contract was made.

(2) In determining for the purposes of section 20 or 21 of this Act whether it was fair and reasonable to incorporate a term in a contract, regard shall be had in particular to the matters specified in Schedule 2 to this Act; but this subsection shall not prevent a court or arbiter from holding, in accordance with any rule of law, that a term which purports to exclude or restrict any relevant liability is not a term of the contract.

[(2A) In determining for the purposes of this Part of this Act whether it is fair and reasonable to allow reliance on a provision of a notice (not being a notice having contractual effect), regard shall be had to all the circumstances obtaining when the liability arose of (but for the provision) would have arisen.][18]

(3) Where a term in a contract [or a provision of a notice][19] purports to restrict liability to a specified sum of money, and the question arises for the purposes of this Part of this Act whether it was fair and reasonable to incorporate the term in the contract [or whether it is fair and reasonable to allow reliance on the provision],[20] then, without prejudice to subsection (2) above [in the case of a term in a contract],[21] regard shall be had in particular to—

(a)   the resources which the party seeking to rely on that term [or provision][22] could expect to be available to him for the purpose of meeting the liability should it arise;

(b)   how far it was open to that party to cover himself by insurance.

(4) The onus of proving that it was fair and reasonable to incorporate a term in a contract [or that it is fair and reasonable to allow reliance on a provision of a notice][23] shall lie on the party so contending.

---

[18] s.24(2A) inserted by Law Reform (Miscellaneous Provisions) (Scotland) Act 1990 (c.40) s.68(4)(a), (6).
[19] Words inserted by Law Reform (Miscellaneous Provisions) (Scotland) Act 1990 (c.40) s.68(4)(b), (6).
[20] Words inserted by Law Reform (Miscellaneous Provisions) (Scotland) Act 1990 (c.40) s.68(4)(b), (6).
[21] Words inserted by Law Reform (Miscellaneous Provisions) (Scotland) Act 1990 (c.40) s.68(4)(b), (6).
[22] Words inserted by Law Reform (Miscellaneous Provisions) (Scotland) Act 1990 (c.40) s.68(4)(b), (6).
[23] Words inserted by Law Reform (Miscellaneous Provisions) (Scotland) Act 1990 (c.40) s.68(4)(c), (6).

Interpretation of Part II

25.—(1) In this Part of this Act—

"breach of duty" means the breach—

(a)   of any obligation, arising from the express or implied terms of a contract, to take reasonable care or exercise reasonable skill in the performance of the contract;

(b)   of any common law duty to take reasonable care or exercise reasonable skill;

(c)   of the duty of reasonable care imposed by section 2(1) of the Occupiers' Liability (Scotland) Act 1960;

"business" includes a profession and the activities of any government department or local or public authority;
"consumer" has the meaning assigned to that expression in the definition in this section of "consumer contract";
"consumer contract" means subject to subsections (1A) and (1B) below a contract in which—

(a)   one party to the contract deals, and the other party to the contract ("the consumer") does not deal or hold himself out as dealing, in the course of a business, and

(b)   in the case of a contract such as is mentioned in section 15(2)(a) of this Act, the goods are of a type ordinarily supplied for private use or consumption;

and for the purposes of this Part of this Act the onus of proving that a contract is not to be regarded as a consumer contract shall lie on the party so contending;

"goods" has the same meaning as in the Sale of Goods Act 1979;

"hire-purchase agreement" has the same meaning as in section 189(1) of the Consumer Credit Act 1974;

"notice" includes an announcement, whether or not in writing, and any other communication or pretended communication;

"personal injury" includes any disease and any impairment of physical or mental condition.

[(1A) Where the consumer is an individual, paragraph (b) in the definition of "consumer contract" in subsection (1) must be disregarded.
(1B) The expression of "consumer contract" does not include a contract in which—

(a)   the buyer is an individual and the goods are second hand goods sold by public auction at which individuals have the opportunity of attending in person; or

(b)   the buyer is not an individual and the goods are sold by auction or competitive tender.][24]

(2) In relation to any breach of duty or obligation, it is immaterial for any purpose of this Part of this Act whether the act or omission giving rise to that breach was inadvertent or intentional, or whether liability for it arises directly or vicariously.

---

[24] Added by SI 2002/3045 (Sale and Supply of Goods to Consumers Regulations) reg.14(4)(b).

(3) In this Part of this Act, any reference to excluding or restricting any liability includes—

(a)   making the liability or its enforcement subject to any restrictive or onerous conditions;

(b)   excluding or restricting any right or remedy in respect of the liability, or subjecting a person to any prejudice in consequence of his pursuing any such right or remedy;

(c)   excluding or restricting any rule of evidence or procedure;

but does not include an agreement to submit any question to arbitration.

(5) In sections 15 and 16 and 19 to 21 of this Act, any reference to excluding or restricting liability for breach of an obligation or duty shall include a reference to excluding or restricting the obligation or duty itself.

International supply contracts

26.—(1) The limits imposed by this Act on the extent to which a person may exclude or restrict liability by reference to a contract term do not apply to liability arising under such a contract as is described in subsection (3) below.

(2) The terms of such a contract are not subject to any requirement of reasonableness under section 3 or 4: and nothing in Part II of this Act shall require the incorporation of the terms of such a contract to be fair and reasonable for them to have effect.

(3) Subject to subsection (4), that description of contract is one whose characteristics are the following—

(a)   either it is a contract of sale of goods or it is one under or in pursuance of which the possession or ownership of goods passes; and

(b)   it is made by parties whose places of business (or, if they have none, habitual residences) are in the territories of different States (the Channel Islands and the Isle of Man being treated for this purpose as different States from the United Kingdom).

(4) A contract falls within subsection (3) above only if either—

(a)   the goods in question are, at the time of the conclusion of the contract, in the course of carriage, or will be carried, from the territory of one State to the territory of another; or

(b)   the acts constituting the offer and acceptance have been done in the territories of different States; or

(c)   the contract provides for the goods to be delivered to the territory of a State other than that within whose territory those acts were done.

Choice of law clauses

27.—(1) Where the [law applicable to]25 a contract is the law of any part of the United Kingdom only by choice of the parties (and apart from that choice would be the law of some country outside the United Kingdom) sections 2 to 7 and 16 to 21 of this Act do not operate as part [of the law applicable to the contract].26

---

25 Words substituted by Contracts (Applicable Law) Act 1990 (c.36) s.5, Sch.4 para.4.
26 Words substituted by Contracts (Applicable Law) Act 1990 (c.36) s.5, Sch.4 para.4.

(2) This Act has effect notwithstanding any contract term which applies or purports to apply the law of some country outside the United Kingdom, where (either or both)—

(a)   the term appears to the court, or arbitrator or arbiter to have been imposed wholly or mainly for the purpose of enabling the party imposing it to evade the operation of this Act; or

(b)   in the making of the contract one of the parties dealt as consumer, and he was then habitually resident in the United Kingdom, and the essential steps necessary for the making of the contract were taken there, whether by him or by others on his behalf.

(3) In the application of subsection (2) above to Scotland, for paragraph (b) there shall be substituted—

"(b) the contract is a consumer contract as defined in Part II of this Act, and the consumer at the date when the contract was made was habitually resident in the United Kingdom, and the essential steps necessary for the making of the contract were taken there, whether by him or by others on his behalf.".

Temporary provision for sea carriage of passengers

28.—(1) This section applies to a contract for carriage by sea of a passenger or of a passenger and his luggage where the provisions of the Athens Convention (with or without modification) do not have, in relation to the contract, the force of law in the United Kingdom.

(2) In a case where—

(a)   the contract is not made in the United Kingdom, and

(b)   neither the place of departure nor the place of destination under it is in the United Kingdom,

a person is not precluded by this Act from excluding or restricting liability for loss or damage, being loss or damage for which the provisions of the Convention would, if they had the force of law in relation to the contract, impose liability on him.

(3) In any other case, a person is not precluded by this Act from excluding or restricting liability for that loss or damage—

(a)   in so far as the exclusion or restriction would have been effective in that case had the provisions of the Convention had the force of law in relation to the contract; or

(b)   in such circumstances and to such extent as may be prescribed, by reference to a prescribed term of the contract.

(4) For the purposes of subsection (3)(a), the values which shall be taken to be the official values in the United Kingdom of the amounts (expressed in gold francs) by reference to which liability under the provisions of the Convention is limited shall be such amounts in sterling as the Secretary of State may from time to time by order made by statutory instrument specify.

(5) In this section—

(a)   the references to excluding or restricting liability include doing any of those things in relation to the liability which are mentioned in section 13 or section 25(3) and (5); and

(b)   "the Athens Convention" means the Athens Convention relating to the Carriage of Passengers and their Luggage by Sea, 1974; and

(c)   "prescribed" means prescribed by the Secretary of State by regulations made by statutory instrument;

and a statutory instrument containing the regulations shall be subject to annulment in pursuance of a resolution of either House of Parliament.[27]

Saving for other relevant legislation

29.—(1) Nothing in this Act removes or restricts the effect of, or prevents reliance upon, any contractual provision which—

(a)   is authorised or required by the express terms or necessary implication of an enactment; or

(b)   being made with a view to compliance with an international agreement to which the United Kingdom is a party, does not operate more restrictively than is contemplated by the agreement.

(2) A contract term is to be taken—

(a)   for the purposes of Part I of this Act, as satisfying the requirement of reasonableness; and

(b)   for those of Part II, to have been fair and reasonable to incorporate,

if it is incorporated or approved by, or incorporated pursuant to a decision or ruling of, a competent authority acting in the exercise of any statutory jurisdiction or function and is not a term in a contract to which the competent authority is itself a party.

(3) In this section—

"competent authority" means any court, arbitrator or arbiter, government department or public authority;

"enactment" means any legislation (including subordinate legislation) of the United Kingdom or Northern Ireland and any instrument having effect by virtue of such legislation; and

"statutory" means conferred by an enactment.[28]

30. [. . .][29]

Commencement; amendments; repeals

31.—(1) This Act comes into force on 1st February 1978.

(2) Nothing in this Act applies to contracts made before the date on which it comes into force; but subject to this, it applies to liability for any loss or damage which is suffered on or after that date.

(3) [. . .][30]

(4) [. . .][31]

---

[27] Power to modify s.28 conferred by Merchant Shipping Act 1979 (c.39) s.16(3).
[28] s.29(1) modified by Telecommunications Act 1984 (c.12) s.109, Sch.5 para.12(7).
[29] Repealed by Consumer Safety Act 1978 (c.38) s.10(1), Sch.3.
[30] Provides for amendment of enactments specified in Sch.3.
[31] Repeals enactments specified in Sch.4.

Citation and extent
32.—(1) This Act may be cited as the Unfair Contract Terms Act 1977.
(2) Part I of this Act extends to England and Wales and to Northern Ireland; but it does not extend to Scotland.
(3) Part II of this Act extends to Scotland only.
(4) This Part of this Act extends to the whole of the United Kingdom.

SCHEDULE 1

SCOPE OF SECTIONS 2 TO 4 AND 7

1. Sections 2 to 4 of this Act do not extend to—

    (a)   any contract of insurance (including a contract to pay an annuity on human life);

    (b)   any contract so far as it relates to the creation or transfer of an interest in land, or to the termination of such an interest, whether by extinction, merger, surrender, forfeiture or otherwise;

    (c)   any contract so far as it relates to the creation or transfer of a right or interest in any patent, trade mark, copyright [or design right],[32] registered design, technical or commercial information or other intellectual property, or relates to the termination of any such right or interest;[33]

    (d)   any contract so far as it relates—

        (i)   to the formation or dissolution of a company (which means any body corporate or unincorporated association and includes a partnership), or
        (ii)   to its constitution or the rights or obligations of its corporators or members;

    (e)   any contract so far as it relates to the creation or transfer of securities or of any right or interest in securities.

2. Section 2(1) extends to—

    (a)   any contract of marine salvage or towage;

    (b)   any charterparty of a ship or hovercraft; and

    (c)   any contract for the carriage of goods by ship or hovercraft;

but subject to this sections 2 to 4 and 7 do not extend to any such contract except in favour of a person dealing as consumer.

3. Where goods are carried by ship or hovercraft in pursuance of a contract which either—

    (a)   specifies that as the means of carriage over part of the journey to be covered, or

    (b)   makes no provision as to the means of carriage and does not exclude that means,

---

[32] Words inserted by Copyright, Designs and Patents Act 1988 (c.48) s.303(1), Sch.7 para.24.
[33] para.1(c) extended by Patents, Designs and Marks Act 1986 (c.39) ss.2(3), 4(7), Sch.2 para.1(2)(f), SI 1987/1497 reg.9(2), Sch.2.

then sections 2(2), 3 and 4 do not, except in favour of a person dealing as consumer, extend to the contract as it operates for and in relation to the carriage of the goods by that means.

4. Section 2(1) and (2) do not extend to a contract of employment, except in favour of the employee.

5. Section 2(1) does not affect the validity of any discharge and indemnity given by a person, on or in connection with an award to him of compensation for pneumoconiosis attributable to employment in the coal industry, in respect of any further claim arising from his contracting that disease.

SCHEDULE 2
GUIDELINES FOR APPLICATION OF REASONABLENESS TEST

1. The matters to which regard is to be had in particular for the purposes of sections 6(3), 7(3) and (4), 20 and 21 are any of the following which appear to be relevant—

(a)   the strength of the bargaining positions of the parties relative to each other, taking into account (among other things) alternative means by which the customer's requirements could have been met;

(b)   whether the customer received an inducement to agree to the term, or in accepting it had an opportunity of entering into a similar contract with other persons, but without having to accept a similar term;

(c)   whether the customer knew or ought reasonably to have known of the existence and extent of the term (having regard, among other things, to any custom of the trade and any previous course of dealing between the parties);

(d)   where the term excludes or restricts any relevant liability if some condition is not complied with, whether it was reasonable at the time of the contract to expect that compliance with that condition would by practicable;

(e)   whether the goods were manufactured, processed or adapted to the special order of the customer.

UNFAIR TERMS IN CONSUMER CONTRACTS REGULATIONS 1999

(SI 1999/2083)

Citation and commencement

1. These Regulations may be cited as the Unfair Terms in Consumer Contracts Regulations 1999 and shall come into force on 1st October 1999.

Revocation

2. The Unfair Terms in Consumer Contracts Regulations 1994 are hereby revoked.

Interpretation

3.—(1) In these Regulations—

"the Community" means the European Community;

"consumer" means any natural person who, in contracts covered by these Regulations, is acting for purposes which are outside his trade, business or profession;

"court" in relation to England and Wales and Northern Ireland means a county court or the High Court, and in relation to Scotland, the Sheriff or the Court of Session;

"Director" means the Director General of Fair Trading;

"EEA Agreement" means the Agreement on the European Economic Area signed at Oporto on 2nd May 1992 as adjusted by the protocol signed at Brussels on 17th March 1993;[1]

"Member State" means a State which is a contracting party to the EEA Agreement;

"notified" means notified in writing;

"qualifying body" means a person specified in Schedule 1;

"seller or supplier" means any natural or legal person who, in contracts covered by these Regulations, is acting for purposes relating to his trade, business or profession, whether publicly owned or privately owned;

"unfair terms" means the contractual terms referred to in regulation 5.

[(1A) The references—

  (a)   in regulation 4(1) to a seller or a supplier, and

  (b)   in regulation 8(1) to a seller or supplier,

include references to a distance supplier and to an intermediary.
  (1B) In paragraph (1A) and regulation 5(6)—

"distance supplier" means—

  (a)   a supplier under a distance contract within the meaning of the Financial Services (Distance Marketing) Regulations 2004, or

---

[1] Protocol 47 and certain Annexes to the EEA Agreement were amended by Decision No.7/94 of the EEA Joint Committee which came into force on July 1, 1994 ([1994] O.J. L160/1). Council Directive 93/13/EEC was added to Annex XIX to the Agreement by Annex 17 to the said Decision No.7/94.

(b)   a supplier of unsolicited financial services within regulation 15 of those Regulations; and

"intermediary" has the same meaning as in those Regulations.]²

(2) In the application of these Regulations to Scotland for references to an "injunction" or an "interim injunction" there shall be substituted references to an "interdict" or "interim interdict" respectively.

Terms to which these Regulations apply

4.—(1) These Regulations apply in relation to unfair terms in contracts concluded between a seller or a supplier and a consumer.

(2) These Regulations do not apply to contractual terms which reflect—

(a)   mandatory statutory or regulatory provisions (including such provisions under the law of any Member State or in Community legislation having effect in the United Kingdom without further enactment);

(b)   the provisions or principles of international conventions to which the Member States or the Community are party.

Unfair Terms

5.—(1) A contractual term which has not been individually negotiated shall be regarded as unfair if, contrary to the requirement of good faith, it causes a significant imbalance in the parties' rights and obligations arising under the contract, to the detriment of the consumer.

(2) A term shall always be regarded as not having been individually negotiated where it has been drafted in advance and the consumer has therefore not been able to influence the substance of the term.

(3) Notwithstanding that a specific term or certain aspects of it in a contract has been individually negotiated, these Regulations shall apply to the rest of a contract if an overall assessment of it indicates that it is a pre-formulated standard contract.

(4) It shall be for any seller or supplier who claims that a term was individually negotiated to show that it was.

(5) Schedule 2 to these Regulations contains an indicative and non-exhaustive list of the terms which may be regarded as unfair.

[(6) Any contractual term providing that a consumer bears the burden of proof in respect of showing whether a distance supplier or an intermediary complied with any or all of the obligations placed upon him resulting from the Directive and any rule or enactment implementing it shall always be regarded as unfair.

(7) In paragraph (6)—

"the Directive" means Directive 2002/65/EC of the European Parliament and of the Council of 23 September 2002 concerning the distance marketing of consumer financial services and amending Council Directive 90/619/EEC and Directives 97/7/EC and 98/27/EC; and

"rule" means a rule made by the Financial Services Authority under the Financial Services and Markets Act 2000 or by a designated professional body within the meaning of section 326(2) of that Act.]³

---

² Added by SI 2004/2095 (Financial Services (Distance Marketing) Regulations) reg.24(2).
³ Added by SI 2004/2095 (Financial Services (Distance Marketing) Regulations) reg.24(3).

Assessment of unfair terms

6.—(1) Without prejudice to regulation 12, the unfairness of a contractual term shall be assessed, taking into account the nature of the goods or services for which the contract was concluded and by referring, at the time of conclusion of the contract, to all the circumstances attending the conclusion of the contract and to all the other terms of the contract or of another contract on which it is dependent.

(2) In so far as it is in plain intelligible language, the assessment of fairness of a term shall not relate—

(a)   to the definition of the main subject matter of the contract, or

(b)   to the adequacy of the price or remuneration, as against the goods or services supplied in exchange.

Written contracts

7.—(1) A seller or supplier shall ensure that any written term of a contract is expressed in plain, intelligible language.

(2) If there is doubt about the meaning of a written term, the interpretation which is most favourable to the consumer shall prevail but this rule shall not apply in proceedings brought under regulation 12.

Effect of unfair term

8.—(1) An unfair term in a contract concluded with a consumer by a seller or supplier shall not be binding on the consumer.

(2) The contract shall continue to bind the parties if it is capable of continuing in existence without the unfair term.

Choice of law clauses

9. These Regulations shall apply notwithstanding any contract term which applies or purports to apply the law of a non-Member State, if the contract has a close connection with the territory of the Member States.

Complaints—consideration by Director

10.—(1) It shall be the duty of the Director to consider any complaint made to him that any contract term drawn up for general use is unfair, unless—

(a)   the complaint appears to the Director to be frivolous or vexatious; or

(b)   a qualifying body has notified the Director that it agrees to consider the complaint.

(2) The Director shall give reasons for his decision to apply or not to apply, as the case may be, for an injunction under regulation 12 in relation to any complaint which these Regulations require him to consider.

(3) In deciding whether or not to apply for an injunction in respect of a term which the Director considers to be unfair, he may, if he considers it appropriate to do so, have regard to any undertakings given to him by or on behalf of any person as to the continued use of such a term in contracts concluded with consumers.

Complaints—consideration by qualifying bodies

11.—(1) If a qualifying body specified in Part One of Schedule 1 notifies the Director that it agrees to consider a complaint that any contract term drawn up for general use is unfair, it shall be under a duty to consider that complaint.

(2) Regulation 10(2) and (3) shall apply to a qualifying body which is under a duty to consider a complaint as they apply to the Director.

Injunctions to prevent continued use of unfair terms

12.—(1) The Director or, subject to paragraph (2), any qualifying body may apply for an injunction (including an interim injunction) against any person appearing to the Director or that body to be using, or recommending use of, an unfair term drawn up for general use in contracts concluded with consumers.

(2) A qualifying body may apply for an injunction only where—

(a)   it has notified the Director of its intention to apply at least fourteen days before the date on which the application is made, beginning with the date on which the notification was given; or

(b)   the Director consents to the application being made within a shorter period.

(3) The court on an application under this regulation may grant an injunction on such terms as it thinks fit.

(4) An injunction may relate not only to use of a particular contract term drawn up for general use but to any similar term, or a term having like effect, used or recommended for use by any person.

Powers of the Director and qualifying bodies to obtain documents and information

13.—(1) The Director may exercise the power conferred by this regulation for the purpose of—

(a)   facilitating his consideration of a complaint that a contract term drawn up for general use is unfair; or

(b)   ascertaining whether a person has complied with an undertaking or court order as to the continued use, or recommendation for use, of a term in contracts concluded with consumers.

(2) A qualifying body specified in Part One of Schedule 1 may exercise the power conferred by this regulation for the purpose of—

(a)   facilitating its consideration of a complaint that a contract term drawn up for general use is unfair; or

(b)   ascertaining whether a person has complied with—

(i)   an undertaking given to it or to the court following an application by that body, or
(ii)   a court order made on an application by that body,

as to the continued use, or recommendation for use, of a term in contracts concluded with consumers.

(3) The Director may require any person to supply to him, and a qualifying body specified in Part One of Schedule 1 may require any person to supply to it—

(a)   a copy of any document which that person has used or recommended for use, at the time the notice referred to in paragraph (4) below is given, as a pre-formulated standard contract in dealings with consumers;

(b)   information about the use, or recommendation for use, by that person of that document or any other such document in dealings with consumers.

(4) The power conferred by this regulation is to be exercised by a notice in writing which may—

(a)   specify the way in which and the time within which it is to be complied with; and

(b)   be varied or revoked by a subsequent notice.

(5) Nothing in this regulation compels a person to supply any document or information which he would be entitled to refuse to produce or give in civil proceedings before the court.

(6) If a person makes default in complying with a notice under this regulation, the court may, on the application of the Director or of the qualifying body, make such order as the court thinks fit for requiring the default to be made good, and any such order may provide that all the costs or expenses of and incidental to the application shall be borne by the person in default or by any officers of a company or other association who are responsible for its default.

Notification of undertakings and orders to Director

14. A qualifying body shall notify the Director—

(a)   of any undertaking given to it by or on behalf of any person as to the continued use of a term which that body considers to be unfair in contracts concluded with consumers;

(b)   of the outcome of any application made by it under regulation 12, and of the terms of any undertaking given to, or order made by, the court;

(c)   of the outcome of any application made by it to enforce a previous order of the court.

Publication, information and advice

15.—(1) The Director shall arrange for the publication in such form and manner as he considers appropriate, of—

(a)   details of any undertaking or order notified to him under regulation 14;

(b)   details of any undertaking given to him by or on behalf of any person as to the continued use of a term which the Director considers to be unfair in contracts concluded with consumers;

(c)   details of any application made by him under regulation 12, and of the terms of any undertaking given to, or order made by, the court;

(d)   details of any application made by the Director to enforce a previous order of the court.

(2) The Director shall inform any person on request whether a particular term to which these Regulations apply has been—

(a)   the subject of an undertaking given to the Director or notified to him by a qualifying body; or

(b)   the subject of an order of the court made upon application by him or notified to him by a qualifying body;

and shall give that person details of the undertaking or a copy of the order, as the case may be, together with a copy of any amendments which the person giving the undertaking has agreed to make to the term in question.

(3) The Director may arrange for the dissemination in such form and manner as he considers appropriate of such information and advice concerning the operation of these Regulations as may appear to him to be expedient to give to the public and to all persons likely to be affected by these Regulations.

The functions of the Financial Services Authority

16. The functions of the Financial Services Authority under these Regulations shall be treated as functions of the Financial Services Authority under the [Financial Services and Markets Act 2000].[4]

SCHEDULE 1

PART I

QUALIFYING BODIES

[1. The Information Commissioner.][5]

[2. The Gas and Electricity Markets Authority.][6]

[3. The Director General of Electricity Supply for Northern Ireland.][7]

[4. The Director General of Gas for Northern Ireland.][8]

5. [The Office of Communications][9]

6. [The Water Services Regulation Authority].[10]

[7. The Rail Regulator.][11]

[8. Every weights and measures authority in Great Britain.][12]

---

[4] Words substituted by SI 2001/3649 (Financial Services and Markets Act 2000 (Consequential Amendments and Repeals) Order), Pt 9 art.583.
[5] Words substituted by SI 2001/1186 (Unfair Terms in Consumer Contracts (Amendment) Regulations) reg.2(b).
[6] Words substituted by SI 2001/1186 (Unfair Terms in Consumer Contracts (Amendment) Regulations) reg.2(b).
[7] Words substituted by SI 2001/1186 (Unfair Terms in Consumer Contracts (Amendment) Regulations) reg.2(b).
[8] Words substituted by SI 2001/1186 (Unfair Terms in Consumer Contracts (Amendment) Regulations) reg.2(b).
[9] Words substituted by SI 2003/3182 (Communications Act 2003 (Consequential Amendments No.2) Order), art.2(2).
[10] Entry substituted by SI 2006/523 (Unfair Terms in Consumer Contracts (Amendment) and Water Act 2003 (Transitional Provision) Regulations) reg.2(2).
[11] Words substituted by SI 2001/1186 (Unfair Terms in Consumer Contracts (Amendment) Regulations) reg.2(b).
[12] Words substituted by SI 2001/1186 (Unfair Terms in Consumer Contracts (Amendment) Regulations) reg.2(b).

[9. The Department of Enterprise, Trade and Investment in Northern Ireland.][13]

[10. The Financial Services Authority.][14]

11. Consumers' Association.

SCHEDULE 2
INDICATIVE AND NON-EXHAUSTIVE LIST OF TERMS WHICH MAY BE REGARDED AS UNFAIR

1. Terms which have the object or effect of—

(a)   excluding or limiting the legal liability of a seller or supplier in the event of the death of a consumer or personal injury to the latter resulting from an act or omission of that seller or supplier;

(b)   inappropriately excluding or limiting the legal rights of the consumer vis-a-vis the seller or supplier or another party in the event of total or partial non-performance or inadequate performance by the seller or supplier of any of the contractual obligations, including the option of offsetting a debt owed to the seller or supplier against any claim which the consumer may have against him;

(c)   making an agreement binding on the consumer whereas provision of services by the seller or supplier is subject to a condition whose realisation depends on his own will alone;

(d)   permitting the seller or supplier to retain sums paid by the consumer where the latter decides not to conclude or perform the contract, without providing for the consumer to receive compensation of an equivalent amount from the seller or supplier where the latter is the party cancelling the contract;

(e)   requiring any consumer who fails to fulfil his obligation to pay a disproportionately high sum in compensation;

(f)   authorising the seller or supplier to dissolve the contract on a discretionary basis where the same facility is not granted to the consumer, or permitting the seller or supplier to retain the sums paid for services not yet supplied by him where it is the seller or supplier himself who dissolves the contract;

(g)   enabling the seller or supplier to terminate a contract of indeterminate duration without reasonable notice except where there are serious grounds for doing so;

(h)   automatically extending a contract of fixed duration where the consumer does not indicate otherwise, when the deadline fixed for the consumer to express his desire not to extend the contract is unreasonably early;

(i)   irrevocably binding the consumer to terms with which he had no real opportunity of becoming acquainted before the conclusion of the contract;

(j)   enabling the seller or supplier to alter the terms of the contract unilaterally without a valid reason which is specified in the contract;

---

[13] Words substituted by SI 2001/1186 (Unfair Terms in Consumer Contracts (Amendment) Regulations) reg.2(b).
[14] Words substituted by SI 2001/1186 (Unfair Terms in Consumer Contracts (Amendment) Regulations) reg.2(b).

(k)   enabling the seller or supplier to alter unilaterally without a valid reason any characteristics of the product or service to be provided;

(l)   providing for the price of goods to be determined at the time of delivery or allowing a seller of goods or supplier of services to increase their price without in both cases giving the consumer the corresponding right to cancel the contract if the final price is too high in relation to the price agreed when the contract was concluded;

(m)   giving the seller or supplier the right to determine whether the goods or services supplied are in conformity with the contract, or giving him the exclusive right to interpret any term of the contract;

(n)   limiting the seller's or supplier's obligation to respect commitments undertaken by his agents or making his commitments subject to compliance with a particular formality;

(o)   obliging the consumer to fulfil all his obligations where the seller or supplier does not perform his,

(p)   giving the seller or supplier the possibility of transferring his rights and obligations under the contract, where this may serve to reduce the guarantees for the consumer, without the latter's agreement;

(q)   excluding or hindering the consumer's right to take legal action or exercise any other legal remedy, particularly by requiring the consumer to take disputes exclusively to arbitration not covered by legal provisions, unduly restricting the evidence available to him or imposing on him a burden of proof which, according to the applicable law, should lie with another party to the contract.

Scope of paragraphs 1(g), (j) and (l)

2. (a)   Paragraph 1(g) is without hindrance to terms by which a supplier of financial services reserves the right to terminate unilaterally a contract of indeterminate duration without notice where there is a valid reason, provided that the supplier is required to inform the other contracting party or parties thereof immediately.

(b)   Paragraph 1(j) is without hindrance to terms under which a supplier of financial services reserves the right to alter the rate of interest payable by the consumer or due to the latter, or the amount of other charges for financial services without notice where there is a valid reason, provided that the supplier is required to inform the other contracting party or parties thereof at the earliest opportunity and that the latter are free to dissolve the contract immediately.

Paragraph 1(j) is also without hindrance to terms under which a seller or supplier reserves the right to alter unilaterally the conditions of a contract of indeterminate duration, provided that he is required to inform the consumer with reasonable notice and that the consumer is free to dissolve the contract.

(c)   Paragraphs 1(g), (j) and (l) do not apply to:

—   transactions in transferable securities, financial instruments and other products or services where the price is linked to fluctuations in a stock exchange quotation or index or a financial market rate that the seller or supplier does not control;

—   contracts for the purchase or sale of foreign currency, traveller's cheques or international money orders denominated in foreign currency;

(d)   Paragraph 1(l) is without hindrance to price indexation clauses, where lawful, provided that the method by which prices vary is explicitly described.

EXPLANATORY NOTE

These Regulations revoke and replace the Unfair Terms in Consumer Contracts Regulations 1994 (SI 1994/3159) which came into force on July 1, 1995.

Those Regulations implemented Council Directive 93/13/EEC on unfair terms in consumer contracts ([1993] O.J. L95/29). Regulations 3 to 9 of these Regulations re-enact regs 2 to 7 of the 1994 Regulations with modifications to reflect more closely the wording of the Directive.

The Regulations apply, with certain exceptions, to unfair terms in contracts concluded between a consumer and a seller or supplier (reg.4). The Regulations provide that an unfair term is one which has not been individually negotiated and which, contrary to the requirement of good faith, causes a significant imbalance in the parties' rights and obligations under the contract to the detriment of the consumer (reg.5). Schedule 2 contains an indicative list of terms which may be regarded as unfair.

The assessment of unfairness will take into account all the circumstances attending the conclusion of the contract. However, the assessment is not to relate to the definition of the main subject matter of the contract or the adequacy of the price or remuneration as against the goods or services supplied in exchange as long as the terms concerned are in plain, intelligible language (reg.6). Unfair contract terms are not binding on the consumer (reg.8).

The Regulations maintain the obligation on the Director General of Fair Trading (contained in the 1994 Regulations) to consider any complaint made to him about the fairness of any contract term drawn up for general use. He may, if he considers it appropriate to do so, seek an injunction to prevent the continued use of that term or of a term having like effect (regs 10 and 12).

The Regulations provide for the first time that a qualifying body named in Sch.1 (statutory regulators, trading standards departments and Consumers' Association) may also apply for an injunction to prevent the continued use of an unfair contract term provided it has notified the Director General of its intention at least 14 days before the application is made (unless the Director General consents to a shorter period) (reg.12). A qualifying body named in Pt One of Sch.1 (public bodies) shall be under a duty to consider a complaint if it has told the Director General that it will do so (reg.11).

The Regulations provide a new power for the Director General and the public qualifying bodies to require traders to produce copies of their standard contracts, and give information about their use, in order to facilitate investigation of complaints and ensure compliance with undertakings or court orders (reg.13).

Qualifying bodies must notify the Director General of undertakings given to them about the continued use of an unfair term and of the outcome of any court proceedings (reg.14). The Director General is given the power to arrange for the publication of this information in such form and manner as he considers appropriate and to offer information and advice about the operation of these Regulations (reg.15). In addition the Director General will supply enquirers about particular standard terms with details of any relevant undertakings and court orders.

A Regulatory Impact Assessment of the costs and benefits which will result from these Regulations has been prepared by the Department of Trade and Industry and is available from Consumer Affairs Directorate, Department of Trade and Industry, Room 407, 1 Victoria Street, London SWIH 0ET (Telephone 0171 215 0341). Copies have been placed in the libraries of both Houses of Parliament.

INDEX

This index has been prepared using Sweet and Maxwell's Legal Taxonomy. Main index entries conform to keywords provided by the Legal Taxonomy except where references to specific documents or non-standard terms (denoted by quotation marks) have been included. These keywords provide a means of identifying similar concepts in other Sweet & Maxwell publications and online services to which keywords from the Legal Taxonomy have been applied. Readers may find some minor differences between terms used in the text and those which appear in the index. Suggestions to *sweetandmaxwell.taxonomy@thomson.com.*

In my opinion, therefore, the loss suffered by the seed merchants was due to the breach of contract by the supplier; and they are entitled to recover it notwithstanding their omission to deliver the particulars.

I agree with my Lord that the appeal should be allowed.

Hodson L.J. dissented, holding that there was no escape from the consequences of the decision in *Anderson v Daniel*.

Appeal Allowed.

STRONGMAN (1945) LTD v SINCOCK

Court of Appeal [1955] 2 Q.B. 525; [1955] 3 W.L.R. 360; 99 S.J. 540; [1955] 3 All E.R. 90

Sincock, an architect owner, contracted with Strongman (1945) Ltd, builders, to supply materials and to carry out work at his premises and promised orally that he would obtain all the licences necessary at that date under reg.56a of the Defence (General) Regulations 1939. Work considerably in excess of the licences granted was carried out. In an arbitration on a claim by the builders for the balance of the price over the licensed amount of work and materials, or alternatively damages for a similar amount for breach of a warranty that Sincock would obtain the licences, the official referee, the arbitrator, found that the warranty alleged was established and held that, though the plaintiffs were precluded from recovering under the contract, which was illegal, they were entitled to the same sums by way of damages for breach of the warranty. Sincock appealed.

27-016

DENNING LJ

Let me say first that the builders cannot sue here on the contract to do the work, which was done in 1948 and 1949. At the time it was unlawful under Defence Regulation 56a for the work to be done without a proper licence. Licences were only in force to the amount of £2,150. When work was done to the value of over £6,000 the builders and the architect were all guilty of an offence for which they might have been prosecuted. Under many decisions in this court it has been held that a builder doing work without a licence cannot recover under the contract.

The builders seek to overcome this objection by saying that there was a warranty, or (putting it more accurately) a promise by the architect that he would get supplementary licences, or that if he failed to get them he would stop the work. The builders say that on the faith of that promise they did the work, and as the promise was broken they can recover damages in respect of it. . . . Applying the test which Lord Moulton laid down in *Heilbut, Symons & Co v Buckleton* [above, Ch.15] the assurance given by the architect amounted to a collateral contract by which the architect promised that he would get any necessary supplementary licences or, if he could not get them, that he would stop the work.

The second question is whether the builders can recover in law on this collateral promise. The promise itself was not illegal, but it is said that damages cannot be recovered for the breach of it. It is said that, if damages could be recovered, it would be an easy way of getting round the law about illegality. This does not alarm me at all. It is, of course, a settled principle that a man cannot recover for the consequences of his own unlawful act, but this has always been confined to cases where the doer of the act knows it to be unlawful or is himself in some way morally culpable. It does not apply when he is an entirely innocent party. Take a case where a master sends out his servant to drive a lorry, and the servant has an accident and injures a third person on the road. It then turns out that the master had not taken out a proper insurance policy to cover them. Both master and servant are guilty of an offence under the Road Traffic Act, 1930, but, nevertheless, the servant, if sued for damages can claim an indemnity against the master. The reason is because the master impliedly promises that he will not ask the servant to do anything unlawful. The master having broken that promise, the servant can recover against him, although the servant was himself guilty of the criminal act of driving without being insured.

[Having considered *Gregory v Ford* [1951] 1 All E.R 121, *Road Transport & General Insurance Co Ltd v Irwin & Adams* (unreported) and *Burrows v Rhodes* [1899] 1 Q.B. 816, his Lordship proceeded:] I think the law is that, although a man may have been guilty of an offence which is absolutely prohibited so that he is answerable in a criminal court, nevertheless if he has been led to commit that offence by the representation or by the promise of another, then in those circumstances he can recover damages for fraud if there is fraud, or for breach of promise or warranty if he prove such to have been given, provided always that he himself has not been guilty of culpable negligence on his part disabling him from that remedy. . . . On the findings of the official referee, the plaintiffs were entirely innocent people who were led into this unfortunate illegality by the representation of the architect, amounting to a collateral contract, that he would get the licences. That contract not having been fulfilled, I see no objection in point of law to the plaintiffs recovering the damages, and I think that the appeal should be dismissed.

BIRKETT LJ

Mr Dingle Foot suggested that if this method of suing on a warranty could be successfully raised the whole purpose of the regulation would be defeated. The position with regard to that is that, on the law as stated by Denning L.J., while it is perfectly plain that it is impossible to sue on a contract for the reasons given, where the particular facts of any one case do permit the finding that a collateral contract in fact existed, I can see no special reason on the special facts of that case why that particular cause of action should not succeed, even if it does mean that it puts one virtually in the same position as one would be in if one were able to sue on the contract.

Romer L.J. delivered a concurring judgment.

Appeal Dismissed.

Question

27-017   In *Re Mahmoud and Ispahani* [1921] 2 K.B. 716 a sale of linseed oil without a licence was prohibited by the Seed, Oils and Fats Order 1919. The plaintiff, who had a licence to sell linseed oil, asked the defendant whether he had a licence under the Order and the defendant replied that he did; in fact he did not. Relying on the representation, the plaintiff sold linseed oil to the defendant. The defendant subsequently refused to accept delivery of the oil and, in an action by the plaintiff for damages for non-acceptance, pleaded the illegality of the contract on the ground that he did not himself have a licence. The Court of Appeal, reversing Rowlatt J, held that the defence succeeded. Do you think that, in similar circumstances now, *Strongman v Sincock* would be of assistance to the plaintiff? Cf. *Mohamed v Alaga & Co* [1998] 2 All E.R. 720 Ch D.

ARCHBOLDS (FREIGHTAGE) LTD v S SPANGLETT LTD

Court of Appeal [1961] 1 Q.B. 374; [1961] 2 W.L.R. 170; 105 S.J. 149; [1961] 1 All E.R. 417

27-018   In March 1957 Archbolds employed the defendants for reward to carry a third party's goods, a load of whisky, by road from Leeds to London. The agreement was made through the defendants' lorry driver, Randall, and Field, the plaintiffs' traffic manager at their Leeds office. The Road and Rail Traffic Act 1933, provides that no person shall use a vehicle for the carriage of goods unless he holds an "A" or a "C" licence; the former entitles him to carry the goods of others for reward; the latter allows him only to carry his own goods and not those of others. The vehicle in which the load of whisky was carried had only a "C" and not an "A" licence, a fact which the defendants knew but the plaintiffs neither knew nor ought to have known. During the journey from Leeds to London, the load was lost through the negligence of Randall. Archbolds claimed for the loss and the defendants contended that the contract was illegal, being prohibited under the Road and Rail Traffic Act 1933, since the vehicle used for carriage had only a "C" licence. Slade J gave judgment for the plaintiffs; he held that the plaintiffs were deceived into letting the defendants carry the load to London and that they did not know that the